About the author

Steve Keen is professor of economics and finance at the University of Western Sydney. Steve predicted the financial crisis as long ago as December 2005, and warned back in 1995 that a period of apparent stability could merely be 'the calm before the storm'. His leading role as one of the tiny minority of economists to both foresee the crisis and warn of it was recognized by his peers when he received the Revere Award from the *Real-World Economics Review* for being the economist who most cogently warned of the crisis, and whose work is most likely to prevent future crises.

DEBUNKING ECONOMICS – REVISED AND EXPANDED EDITION

THE NAKED EMPEROR DETHRONED?

Steve Keen

Zed Books

LONDON | NEW YORK

Debunking Economics – Revised and Expanded Edition: The Naked Emperor Dethroned? was first published in 2011 by Zed Books Ltd, 7 Cynthia Street, London N1 9JF, UK and Room 400, 175 Fifth Avenue, New York, NY 10010, USA

The first edition of *Debunking Economics* was first published in the United Kingdom and the United States of America in 2001 by Zed Books Ltd, and in Australia by Pluto Press Australia Ltd.

www.zedbooks.co.uk
www.debunkingeconomics.com
www.debtdeflation.com

Set in Monotype Plantin and FontFont Kievit by Ewan Smith, London
Index: ed.emery@thefreeuniversity.net
Cover designed by Rogue Four Design
Printed and bound in the United States of America

Distributed in the USA exclusively by Palgrave Macmillan, a division of St Martin's Press, LLC, 175 Fifth Avenue, New York, NY 10010, USA

A catalogue record for this book is available from the British Library
Library of Congress Cataloging in Publication Data available

ISBN 978 1 84813 993 0 hb
ISBN 978 1 84813 992 3 pb

CONTENTS

TABLES, FIGURES AND BOXES

WHERE ARE THE DIAGRAMS?

The potential audience for this book has grown enormously in the last decade, since the 'Great Recession' made many more people doubt what conventional economists claim, and also since I am now much better known, given my public warnings that the crisis they didn't see coming was imminent.

One thing I didn't want to do was to scare a large part of that potential audience off with a multitude of diagrams. The MEGO effect of mathematics ('My Eyes Glaze Over') applies to a lesser degree with diagrams – what is intended as a book for the public gets interpreted as a textbook, and gets shelved at the back of the bookshop where very few would-be readers venture. So even more so than for the first edition, I've attempted to explain all the flaws in a superficially mathematical and diagram-dominated discipline without using mathematics or graphs.

But I know that the diagrams are useful to those who aren't put off by them, so they still exist – in fact there are many more of them – and they're accessible in three different ways from the Debunking Economics website: http://debunkingeconomics.com/figures/.

- you can view the figures directly on the website;
- download a free PDF (this is also available on the publisher's website: www.zedbooks.co.uk/debunking_economics) or use the Scan2Read code below;

- order a print copy, which will give you a physical book with the same layout quality as this book. There are two options: monochrome or a more expensive color version.

References to these additional figures are given throughout the book in the outside margin (**§1**, etc.).

PREFACE TO THE SECOND EDITION

Debunking Economics was far from the first book to argue that neoclassical economics was fundamentally unsound. If cogent criticism alone could have brought this pseudo-science down, it would have fallen as long ago as 1898, when Thorstein Veblen penned 'Why is economics not an evolutionary science?' (Veblen 1898). Yet in 1999, when I began writing *Debunking Economics*, neoclassical economics was more dominant than it had ever been.

My reason for adding to this litany of thus far unsuccessful attempts to cause a long-overdue scientific revolution in economics was the belief that a prerequisite for success was just around the corner. As I noted in my concluding chapter, I felt that a serious economic crisis was approaching, and that when this crisis hit, fundamental change in economic theory would be possible:

> I am not wishing an economic crisis upon the modern world – instead, I think one has been well and truly put in train by the cumulative processes described in chapters 10 and 11 [on finance]. If that crisis eventuates – one which neoclassical economic theory argues is not possible – then economics will once again come under close and critical scrutiny. (*Debunking Economics*, 1st edn, p. 312)

When I finished *Debunking Economics*, I hoped to be able to start work on a book with the working title of *Finance and Economic Breakdown*, which would have provided a comprehensive theory of the forces that would cause this crisis. Instead, the reaction from neoclassical economists to Chapter 4 of *Debunking Economics* – 'Size does matter', on the neoclassical model of competition – was so vehement that I spent much of the next four years developing the arguments in that chapter in response to their attacks.

Finally, in December 2005, I returned to writing *Finance and Economic Breakdown* (for Edward Elgar Publishers). Almost immediately, unforeseen circumstances intervened once more, when I was asked to be an expert witness in a predatory lending case. One look at the exponential growth in the debt-to-GDP ratios for Australia and the USA convinced me that a truly huge crisis was imminent.

I decided that raising the public alarm was more important than writing an academic treatise on the topic, so I reluctantly delayed the book once more and turned to the media and the Internet instead. I published a monthly report on debt, starting in November 2006 (Keen 2006), became sufficiently well known in the media to be described as a 'media tart' by some Australian critics, established the blog Debtwatch (www.debtdeflation. com/blogs), which now has over 10,000 registered users and attracts about 50,000 unique readers each month (with about 25,000 of those being Australian, and most of the rest coming from America and the UK), and in what passed for spare time, worked to complete a model of debt deflation to inform my public comments.

The economic crisis began with a vengeance in September 2007. Unemployment in the USA doubled in the next year, while a 5 percent rate of inflation rapidly gave way to 2 percent deflation.

The complete failure of neoclassical economics to anticipate the crisis also meant, as I expected, that economic theory and economists are under public attack as never before. Their defense has been to argue that 'no one could have seen this coming.' They have taken refuge in the phrase that this crisis was a 'Black Swan,' using Nassim Taleb's phrase completely out of context (Taleb 2007), and ignoring the fact that I and many other non-neoclassical economists did in fact see this coming.

I therefore decided that, for both positive and negative reasons, a new edition of *Debunking Economics* was needed.

The negative reason is that there is no better time to attack a fallacious theory than after it has made a spectacularly wrong prediction. By arguing that the macroeconomy had entered a permanent 'Great Moderation' (the phrase Ben Bernanke popularized to describe the apparent reduction in economic volatility and falls in unemployment and inflation between 1975 and 2007), neoclassical economics couldn't have been more wrong about the immediate economic future. Now is the time to show that, not only was this crisis eminently foreseeable, but also neoclassical economists were about the only ones who were ill equipped to see it coming. The main positive reason is that, with the public and policymakers much more amenable to alternative ways of thinking about economics, now is the time to provide a brief and accessible look at an alternative, realistic model of the economy.

There have also been some important developments in economics since the first edition – notably the growth of econophysics, and the concession by finance academics that the Efficient Markets Hypothesis has been empirically disproven (Fama and French 2004).

Several new chapters have been added on the dynamics of debt-based money, and the continuing economic crisis – currently called the Great Recession in America (and the 'Global Financial Crisis' in my home country, Australia), but which I fully expect to be renamed the Second Great Depression by future economic historians. These new chapters 'break the mold' for the rest of the book, in that they are not critiques of the neoclassical theory of financial instability and economic crises – because there simply is no such theory. Instead they set out, in an introductory way, the non-neoclassical theories of debt deflation and endogenous money that I have played a role in developing (Keen 2008, 2009a, 2009b, 2010), and the model of financial instability that I will cover in detail in *Finance and Economic Breakdown*.

I have also edited a number of chapters where there have been significant theoretical developments since the first edition. By far the most important development here has been a substantial deepening of the critique of the theory of the firm in 'Size does matter.' There is also substantially more information on why the theory of demand is false in 'The calculus of hedonism' and 'The price of everything and the value of nothing,' and a record of the recanting of the Efficient Markets Hypothesis by its major advocates Fama and French in the addendum to 'The price is not right.'

Lastly, a book that was in its first incarnation almost exclusively about microeconomics now covers microeconomics and macroeconomics in roughly equal measure.

The one glaring omission is the absence of any discussion of international trade theory. The reason for this is that, while the flaws in the theory of comparative advantage are, to me, both huge and obvious, a detailed critique of the mathematical logic has not yet been done, and nor is there a viable alternative. That is a task that I may tackle after *Finance and Economic Breakdown* is completed, but not before.

Looking back

The reception of the first edition was both gratifying and predictable. The gratifying side was the public reception: sales far exceeded the norm for this class of book, it continued to sell well a decade after it was first published, and the critical response from the public was almost universally positive.

The predictable side was the reaction from neoclassical economists. They disparaged the book in much the way they have treated all critics – as Keynes once remarked, he expected his work to be treated as being both 'quite wrong and nothing new.' My critique received the same treatment, and as well neoclassicals were incensed by my critique of the theory of the firm.

Their rejoinders to that critique led me to develop it far beyond the version first published in 2001, and in ways that I thought would be very difficult to convey without mathematics, but which in fact I found quite easy to explain in the addendum to 'Size does matter.' However, for a detailed treatment mathematics is still necessary, so for those who can cope with the odd – or rather frequent! – equation, the most accessible papers are in the journals (Keen 2003, 2004; Keen and Standish 2006, 2010) and book chapters (Keen 2005, 2009a). The paper in the free online journal *The Real-World Economic Review* is the most easily accessed of these (www.paecon. net/PAEReview/issue53/KeenStandish53.pdf), while my chapter in the book *A Handbook for Heterodox Economics Education* (edited by Jack Reardon and published by Routledge), 'A pluralist approach to microeconomics,' covers the critique of the Marshallian model of the firm in a manner that should be useful to academics and schoolteachers.

Looking forward

I knew when I wrote the first edition of *Debunking Economics* that its real aim – the elimination of neoclassical economics and its replacement by an empirically based, dynamic approach to economics – could not be achieved until a serious economic crisis called into question the Panglossian view of market economies that neoclassical economics promulgates. That crisis is well and truly with us, and the public has turned on economists as I had hoped it would. Unfortunately, the economics profession is also reacting as I expected – by pretending that nothing is wrong.

As I write these words I have just returned from the 2011 American Economic Association (AEA) annual conference, where close to 10,000 mainly US and overwhelmingly neoclassical economists meet every year to present and hear 'the latest' in the profession. Though there were quite a few sessions devoted to the Great Recession and what its implications are for economic theory (mainly organized by non-neoclassical associations within the AEA, such as the Union for Radical Political Economics), the majority of the profession continues to believe, as Ben Bernanke put it some months beforehand, that 'the recent financial crisis was more a failure of economic engineering and economic management than of what I have called economic science' (Bernanke 2010).

Bernanke's belief could not be farther from the truth: as a means to understand the behavior of a complex market economy, the so-called science of economics is a melange of myths that make the ancient Ptolemaic earth-centric view of the solar system look positively sophisticated in comparison. What his opinion reveals is his inability to think about the economy in any way other than the neoclassical one in which he has been trained – an inability he shares with most of his colleagues.

If we leave the development of economics to economists themselves, then it is highly likely that the intellectual revolution that economics desperately needs will never occur – after all, they resisted change so successfully after the Great Depression that the version of neoclassical economics that reigns today is far more extreme than that which Keynes railed against seven decades ago. I concluded the first edition with the observation that economics is too important to leave to the economists. That remains the case today.

If change is going to come, it will be from the young, who have not yet been indoctrinated into a neoclassical way of thinking, and from those from other professions like physics, engineering and biology, who will be emboldened by the crisis to step onto the turf of economics and take the field over from the economists. It is to those real engines of change in economics that this book is dedicated.

PREFACE TO THE FIRST EDITION

In the preface to the *General Theory*, Keynes commented that its writing had involved a long process of escape from 'habitual modes of thought and expression.' He implored his audience of professional economists to likewise escape the confines of conventional economic thought, and observed that 'The ideas which are here expressed so laboriously are extremely simple and should be obvious. The difficulty lies, not in the new ideas, but in escaping from the old ones, which ramify, for those brought up as most of us have been, into every corner of our minds' (Keynes 1936).

This statement was unfortunately prophetic. Keynes's own escape was incomplete, and the residue of traditional thought the *General Theory* contained obscured many of its most innovative aspects. Faced with a melange of the new and unfamiliar with the old and familiar, the bulk of his audience found it easier to interpret his new ideas as no more than embellishments to the old. The Keynesian Revolution died, slowly but surely, as economists reconstructed the 'habitual modes of thought and expression' around the inconvenient intrusions Keynes had made into economic dogma. Economics failed to make the escape which Keynes had implored it to do, and as time went on, 'modern' economics began to resemble more and more closely the 'old ideas' which Keynes had hoped economics would abandon.

I was initially educated in this resurgent tradition – known as the Keynesian-Neoclassical synthesis – some thirty years ago. The catalyst for my escape from this dogma was extremely simple: my first-year microeconomics lecturer pointed out a simple but glaring flaw in the application of conventional theory.

The economic theory of markets argues that combinations of any sort, whether by workers into unions or manufacturers into monopolies, reduce social welfare. The theory therefore leads to the conclusion that the world would be better off without monopolies and unions. If we were rid of both, then the economic theory of income distribution argues that, effectively, people's incomes would be determined solely by their contribution to society. The world would be both efficient and fair.

But what if you have both monopolies and unions? Will getting rid of just one make the world a better place?

The answer is categorically no. If you abolish just unions, then according to 'conservative' economic theory, workers will be exploited: they will get substantially less than their contribution to society (equally, if you abolish just monopolies, then workers will exploit companies). If you have one, then you are better off having the other too, and a single step towards the economist's nirvana takes you not closer to heaven but towards hell.[1]

I was struck by how fragile the outwardly impregnable theory of economics was. What seemed self-evident at a superficial level – that social welfare would rise if unions or monopolies were abolished – became problematic, and even contradictory, at a deeper level.

Had I come across that fragility in my Honors or postgraduate education, which is when students of economics normally learn of such things, I would quite possibly have been willing to gloss over it, as most economists do. Instead, because I learnt it 'out of sequence,' I was immediately suspicious of the simplistic statements of economic principle. If the pivotal concepts of competition and income distribution could be so easily overturned, what else was rotten in the House of Economics?

That skepticism initiated a gradual process of discovery, which made me realize that what I had initially thought was an education in economics was in fact little better than an indoctrination. More than a decade before I became an undergraduate, a major theoretical battle had broken out over the validity of economic theory. Yet none of this turned up in the standard undergraduate or honors curriculum – unless it was raised by some dissident instructor. There were also entire schools of thought which were antithetical to conventional economics, which again were ignored unless there was a dissident on the staff.

Thirty years after starting my skeptic's intellectual tour, I am completely free of the 'habitual modes of thought and expression' which so troubled Keynes. There are many non-orthodox economists like me, who are all trying to contribute to a new, deeper approach to economics.

But still the world's universities churn out economists who believe, for example, that the world would be a better place if we could just get rid of unions, or monopolies.

Worse still, over the last thirty years, politicians and bureaucrats the world over have come to regard economic theory as the sole source of wisdom about the manner in which a modern society should be governed. The world has been remade in the economist's image.

This ascendancy of economic theory has not made the world a better place. Instead, it has made an already troubled society worse: more unequal, more unstable, and less 'efficient.'

Why has economics persisted with a theory which has been comprehensively shown to be unsound? Why, despite the destructive impact of economic policies, does economics continue to be the toolkit which politicians and bureaucrats apply to almost all social and economic issues?

1 This is actually an application of the 'theory of the second best' (Lancaster and Lipsey 1956). Briefly, Lancaster and Lipsey showed that any single step towards what economics describes as the ideal situation could reduce welfare, if more than one step was required to move from the present situation to the ideal.

The answer lies in the way economics is taught in the world's universities.

When I became an academic economist, I realized that very few of my colleagues had any knowledge of the turbulent streams in economics. Most were simply dismissive of any attempt to criticize orthodox thinking, and equally dismissive of any of their peers who showed tendencies towards unconventional thought.

This was not because these conventional economists were anti-intellectual – far from it. Even though conventional economics is flawed, it still takes intellectual muscle to master its principles – as you will soon discover. Yet still economists refused to consider any criticisms of economic theory, even when they emanated from other economists, and met rigorous intellectual standards.

Nor were they ill intentioned – most of them sincerely believed that, if only people followed the principles of economic theory, the world would be a better place. For a group of people who espoused a philosophy of individualistic hedonism, they were remarkably altruistic in their commitment to what they saw as the common good. Yet the policies they promoted often seem to non-economists to damage the fabric of human society, rather than to enhance it.

They also rejected out of hand any suggestion that they were ideologically motivated. They were scientists, not political activists. They recommended market solutions, not because they were personally pro-capitalist, but because economic theory proved that the market was the best mechanism by which to determine economic issues. Yet virtually everything they recommended at least appeared to favor rich over poor, capitalist over worker, privileged over dispossessed.

I came to the conclusion that the reason they displayed such anti-intellectual, apparently socially destructive, and apparently ideological behavior lay deeper than any superficial personal pathologies. Instead, the way in which they had been educated had given them the behavioral traits of zealots rather than of dispassionate intellectuals.

As anyone who has tried to banter with an advocate of some esoteric religion knows, there is no point trying to debate fundamental beliefs with a zealot. After many similar experiences with economists, I abandoned any delusion that I might be able to persuade committed economists to see reason (though there has been the odd exception to this rule). Instead, I prefer to spend my time developing an alternative approach to economics, while persuading others not to fall for the superficially persuasive but fundamentally flawed arguments of conventional theory.

Hence this book, which is aimed at a broader audience than Keynes's target of his fellow economists. Instead, my primary target market is those people who feel that they have been effectively silenced by economists. One of the many reasons why economists have succeeded in taking over social policy is that they have claimed the high intellectual ground against anyone who opposed their recommendations. The object of this book is to show that this claim is spurious.

Though I am the sole author, and thus responsible for all its errors and omissions, I cannot claim sole credit for what is good in it. In particular, I owe an enormous debt to the pioneers of critical thinking in economics.

Pre-eminent amongst these is Piero Sraffa – a name which is known to almost no non-economists, and very few economists. There are many others whose names turn up in subsequent pages – Blatt, Garengani, Goodwin, Kalecki, Kaldor, Keynes, Minsky, Veblen, to name a few. But none has had quite the impact of Sraffa.

I owe a more personal debt to those few teachers who were, as I am now, dissidents in a sea of believers. Pre-eminent here is Frank Stilwell – the first-year lecturer who, many years ago, introduced me to the first of many flaws in conventional economics. I also gratefully acknowledge the influence which Ted Wheelwright's panoptic knowledge of the many currents in economic thought had upon my intellectual development. My colleagues in HETSA, the History of Economic Thought Society of Australia, have also enriched my appreciation of the many 'roads not taken' by mainstream economics.

Colleagues around the world have provided feedback on the arguments presented here. None can be held liable for what follows, but all influenced it, either directly, in debate, or by providing a forum in which heterodox views could flourish. My thanks go to Trond Andresen, George Argyrous, Tony Aspromorgous, Joanne Averill, Aldo Balardini, Bill Barnett, James Dick, Marchessa Dy, Geoff Fishburn, John Gelles, Ric Holt, Julio Huato, Alan Isaac, James Juniper, Gert Kohler, John Legge, Jerry Levy, Henry Liu, Basil Moore, Marc-Andre Pigeon, Clifford Poirot, Jason Potts, Barkley Rosser, Gunnar Tomasson, Sean Toohey, Robert Vienneau, Graham White, and Karl Widerquist, for reading and commenting upon drafts of this book. I would especially like to thank Karl Widerquist for detailed suggestions on content and the flow of arguments, John Legge for assistance with the proofs of some propositions, Alan Isaac for providing a testing foil to many propositions in the early chapters, and Geoff Fishburn for many years of intelligent and critical discussion of economic theory.

Joyce Hitchings provided valuable feedback on how to make the book's arguments and counter-arguments more accessible to readers with no prior training in economics.

I have also received great encouragement and feedback from my publishers Tony Moore of Pluto Press, and Robert Molteno of Zed Books. My editor, Michael Wall, did a sterling job of making the final product more concise and accessible than the original manuscript.

Sabbatical leave granted by the University of Western Sydney gave me the time away from the everyday demands of an academic life needed to complete a book. The Jerome Levy Institute of Bard College, New York, and the Norwegian University of Science and Technology in Trondheim, Norway, kindly accommodated me while the finishing touches were applied to the manuscript.

And so to battle.

1 | PREDICTING THE 'UNPREDICTABLE'

A major motivation for writing the first edition of this book was my feeling in 2000 that a serious economic crisis was imminent, and that it was therefore an apt time to explain to the wider, non-academic community how economic theory was not merely inherently flawed, but had helped cause the calamity I expected. At the time, I thought that the bursting of the DotCom Bubble would mark the beginning of the crisis – though I was cautious in saying so, because my work in modeling Minsky's Financial Instability Hypothesis (Keen 1995) had confirmed one aspect of his theory, the capacity of government spending to prevent a debt crisis that would have occurred in a pure credit economy.

Statements that a crisis *may* occur were edited out of this edition, because the crisis has occurred – after the Subprime Bubble, which was in the background during the DotCom Bubble, finally burst as well.[1] But these pre-crisis statements remain important, because they indicate that, without the blinkers that neoclassical economic theory puts over the eyes of economists, the crisis now known as the Great Recession was not an unpredictable 'Black Swan' event, but an almost blindingly obvious certainty. The only question mark was over when it would occur, not if.

This brief chapter therefore provides excerpts from the first edition on the likelihood of a crisis as seen from the vantage point of non-neoclassical economics – and in particular, Minsky's 'Financial Instability Hypothesis' – in 2000 and early 2001. I hope these pre-crisis observations persuade you to reject the 'Nobody could have seen this coming' smokescreen. Rather than being a 'Black Swan', the Great Recession was a 'White Swan' made invisible to neoclassical economists because their theory makes them ignore the key factors that caused it: debt, disequilibrium, and time.

The destabilizing effect of neoclassical economics

The belief that a capitalist economy is inherently stabilizing is also one for which inhabitants of market economies may pay dearly in the future. As they were initially during the Great Depression, economists today may be the main force preventing the introduction of countervailing measures to any future economic slump. Economics may make our recessions deeper, longer and more intractable, when the public is entitled to expect economics to have precisely the opposite effect.

---

1 Though somewhat later than I had anticipated, since the continued growth of the Subprime Bubble (and Federal Reserve interventions) had papered over the DotCom downturn.

Fortunately for economists, the macroeconomy – at least in the United States – appeared to be functioning fairly well at the end of the year 2000. It is thus possible for economists to believe and preach almost anything, because they can bask in the entirely coincidental fact that the macroeconomy appears healthy.

However, this accidental success may not last long if the pressures which have been clearly growing in the financial side of the economy finally erupt (Keen 2001a: 213).

Possibility of debt deflation in the USA

If a crisis does occur after the Internet Bubble finally bursts, then it could occur in a milieu of low inflation (unless oil price pressures lead to an inflationary spiral). Firms are likely to react to this crisis by dropping their margins in an attempt to move stock, or to hang on to market share at the expense of their competitors. This behavior could well turn low inflation into deflation.

The possibility therefore exists that America could once again be afflicted with a debt deflation – though its severity could be attenuated by the inevitable increase in government spending that such a crisis would trigger. America could well join Japan on the list of the global economy's 'walking wounded' – mired in a debt-induced recession, with static or falling prices and a seemingly intractable burden of private debt (ibid.: 254).

The likelihood of a Japanese outcome for America after the crash

Only time will tell whether the bursting of the Internet Bubble will lead to as dire an outcome as the Great Depression. Certainly, on many indicators, the 1990s bubble has left its septuagenarian relative in the shade. The price to earnings ratio peaked at over one and a half times the level set in 1929, the private and corporate debt to output ratio is possibly three times what it was prior to the Great Crash, and prices, though rising in some sectors, are generally quiescent. On all these fronts, Fisher's debt-deflation theory of great depressions seems a feasible outcome.

On the other hand, Minsky argued that 'Big Government' could stabilize an unstable economy, by providing firms with cash flow from which their debt commitments could be financed despite a collapse in private spending. Certainly, the US government of 2000 is 'big' when compared to its 1920s counterpart, and its automatic and policy interventions will probably attenuate any economic crash to something far milder than the Great Depression. What appears more likely for post-Internet America is a drawn-out recession like that experienced by Japan since its Bubble Economy collapsed in 1990 (ibid.: 256–7).

The impact of the Maastricht Treaty on Europe during a crisis

Macroeconomics is economic policy par excellence, but economic theory itself has virtually reached the position that there should be no macroeconomic policy. The clearest evidence of this is the Maastricht Treaty, which made restricting budget deficits to no more than 3 percent of GDP a condition for membership of the European Union. While some fudging has been allowed to make membership possible in the first place, when an economic crisis eventually strikes, Europe's governments may be compelled to impose austerity upon economies which will be in desperate need of a stimulus (ibid.: 212–13).

The Efficient Markets Hypothesis encouraging debt-financed speculation

[According to the Efficient Markets Hypothesis] The trading profile of the stock market should therefore be like that of an almost extinct volcano. Instead, even back in the 1960s when this [Sharpe] paper was written, the stock market behaved like a very active volcano. It has become even more so since, and in 1987 it did a reasonable, though short-lived, impression of Krakatau. In 2000, we saw 25 percent movements in a week. October 2000 lived up to the justified reputation of that month during bull markets; heaven only knows how severe the volatility will be when the bubble finally bursts (ibid.: 232).

What can I say? By promulgating the efficient markets hypothesis, which is predicated on each investor having the foresight of Nostradamus, economic theory has encouraged the world to play a dangerous game of stock market speculation. When that game comes unstuck, America in particular will most likely find itself as badly hobbled by debt as Japan has been for the past decade. This speculative flame may have ignited anyway, but there is little doubt that economists have played the role of petrol throwers rather than firemen. When crisis strikes, conventional economists will be the last people on the planet who can be expected to provide sage advice on how to return to prosperity – unless, as often happens in such circumstances, they drop their theoretical dogmas in favor of common sense.

When the Great Crash of 1929 led to the Great Depression of the 1930s, many of the erstwhile heroes of the finance sector found themselves in the dock. It is unlikely that any particular economists will find themselves so arraigned, but there is little doubt that economic theory has been complicit in encouraging America's investing public to once again delude itself into a crisis (ibid.: 256).

Deregulation and crisis

Deregulation of the financial sector was not the sole cause of the financial instability of the past twenty years. But it has certainly contributed to its severity, by removing some of the limited constraints to cyclical behavior which exist in a regulated system.

These deregulations were mooted as 'reforms' by their proponents, but they were in reality retrograde steps, which have set our financial system up for a real crisis. I can only hope that, if the crisis is serious enough, then genuine reform to the finance sector will be contemplated. Reform, of course, cannot make capitalism stable; but it can remove the elements of our corporate system which contribute most strongly to instability.

The major institutional culprit has to be the finance sector itself, and in particular the elements of the stock market which lead to it behaving more like a casino than a place of reasoned calculation [...]

Surely, when the Internet Bubble really bursts, it will be time to admit that one fundamental excess of the market as currently organized is its ability to allow sky-high valuations to develop (ibid.: 255–6).

The history of crises causing – and not causing – paradigm shifts in economics

This is far from the first book to attack the validity of economics, and it is unlikely to be the last. As Kirman commented, economic theory has seen off many attacks, not because it has been strong enough to withstand them, but because it has been strong enough to ignore them.

Part of that strength has come from the irrelevance of economics. You don't need an accurate theory of economics to build an economy in the same sense that you need an accurate theory of propulsion to build a rocket. The market economy began its evolution long before the term 'economics' was ever coined, and it will doubtless continue to evolve regardless of whether the dominant economic theory is valid. Therefore, so long as the economy itself has some underlying strength, it is a moot point as to whether any challenge to economic orthodoxy will succeed.

However, while to some extent irrelevant, economics is not 'mostly harmless'. The false confidence it has engendered in the stability of the market economy has encouraged policy-makers to dismantle some of the institutions which initially evolved to try to keep its instability within limits. 'Economic reform,' undertaken in the belief that it will make society function better, has instead made modern capitalism a poorer social system: more unequal, more fragile, more unstable. And in some instances, as in Russia, a naive faith in economic theory has led to outcomes which, had they been inflicted by weapons rather than by policy, would have led their perpetrators to the International Court of Justice.

But even such a large-scale failure as Russia seems to have little impact upon the development of economic theory. For economics to change, it appears that things have to 'go wrong' on a global scale, in ways which the prevailing theory believed was impossible. There have been two such periods this century.

The first and most severe was the Great Depression, and in that calamity, Keynes turned economic theory upside down. However, Keynes's insights were rapidly emasculated, as Chapter 9 showed. 'Keynesian economics' became dominant, but it certainly was not the economics of Keynes.

The second was the 'stagflationary crisis' – the coincidence of low growth, rising unemployment and high inflation during the 1970s. That crisis led to the final overthrow of the emasculated creature that Keynesian economics had become, and its replacement by an economic orthodoxy which was even more virile than that against which Keynes had railed.

One step forward and two steps back – with the first step backwards being taken when the economy was doing well, in the aftermath of the Depression and WWII and hence when the ramblings of economists could comfortably be ignored.

That historical record is both comforting and disturbing. Change is possible in economics, but normally only when the fabric of society itself seems threatened; and change without crisis can involve the forgetting of recent advances.

It is possible, therefore, that economic theory may continue to function mainly as a surrogate ideology for the market economy, right up until the day, in some distant future, when society evolves into something so profoundly different that it no longer warrants the moniker 'capitalism.'

I hope, however, that events follow a different chain. I am not wishing an economic crisis upon the modern world – instead, I think one has been well and truly put in train by the cumulative processes described in chapters 10 and 11. If that crisis eventuates – one which neoclassical economic theory argues is not possible – then economics will once again come under close and critical scrutiny (ibid.: 311–12).

Public reactions to the failure of neoclassical economics

This time, the chances are much better that something new and indigestibly different from the prevailing wisdom will emanate from the crisis. As this book has shown, critical economists are much more aware of the flaws in conventional economics than they were during Keynes's day, non-orthodox analysis is much more fully developed, and advances in many other fields of science are there for the taking, if economics can be persuaded – by force of circumstance – to abandon its obsession with equilibrium.

The first factor should mean that the lines will be much more clearly drawn between the old orthodoxy and the new. The latter two should mean that the techniques of the old orthodoxy will look passé, rather than stimulating, to a new generation of economists schooled in complexity and evolutionary theory.

But ultimately, schooling is both the answer and the problem. If a new economics is to evolve, then it must do so in an extremely hostile environment – the academic journals and academic departments of Economics and Finance, where neoclassic orthodoxy has for so long held sway.[2] The nurturing of a new way of thinking about economics could largely be left in the hands of those who have shown themselves incapable of escaping from a nineteenth-century perspective.

There are two possible palliatives against that danger. The first is the development, by non-orthodox economists, of a vibrant alternative approach to analyzing the economy which is founded in realism, rather than idealism. Such a development would show that there is an alternative to thinking about the economy in a neoclassical way, and offer future students of economics a new and hopefully exciting research program to which they can contribute.

The second is an informed and vigilant public. If you have struggled to the end of this book, then you now have a very strong grasp on the problems in conventional economic thought, and the need for alternative approaches to economics. Depending on your situation, you can use this knowledge as a lever in all sorts of ways.

If you are or you advise a person in authority in the private or public sectors, you should know now not to take the advice of economists on faith. They have received far

2 There will be resistance aplenty too from government departments, and the bureaucracies of central banks, where promotion has come to those who have held the economic faith.

too easy a ride as the accepted vessels of economic knowledge. Ask a few enquiring questions, and see whether those vessels ring hollow. When the time comes to appoint advisers on economic matters, quiz the applicants for their breadth of appreciation of alternative ways to 'think economically,' and look for the heterodox thinker rather than just the econometric technician.

If you are a parent with a child who is about to undertake an economics or business degree, then you're in a position to pressure potential schools to take a pluralist approach to education in economics. A quick glance through course structure booklets and subject outlines should be enough to confirm what approach they take at present.

If you are a student now? Well, your position is somewhat compromised: you have to pass exams, after all! I hope that, after reading this book, you will be better equipped to do that. But you are also equipped to 'disturb the equilibrium' of both your fellow students and your teachers, if they are themselves ignorant of the issues raised in this book.

You have a voice, which has been perhaps been quiescent on matters economic because you have in the past deferred to the authority of the economist. There is no reason to remain quiet.

I commented at the beginning of this book that economics was too important to leave to the economists. I end on the same note (ibid.: 312–13).

Postscript 2011

As these excerpts emphasize, the never-ending crisis in which the USA and much of the OECD is now ensnared was no 'Black Swan.' Its inevitability was obvious to anyone who paid attention to the level of debt-financed speculation taking place, and considered what would happen to the economy when the debt-driven party came to an end. The fact that the vast majority of economists pay no attention at all to these issues is why they were taken by surprise.

It may astonish non-economists to learn that conventionally trained economists ignore the role of credit and private debt in the economy – and frankly, it is astonishing. But it is the truth. Even today, only a handful of the most rebellious of mainstream 'neoclassical' economists – people like Joe Stiglitz and Paul Krugman – pay any attention to the role of private debt in the economy, and even they do so from the perspective of an economic theory in which money and debt play no intrinsic role. An economic theory that ignores the role of money and debt in a market economy cannot possibly make sense of the complex, monetary, credit-based economy in which we live. Yet that is the theory that has dominated economics for the last half-century. If the market economy is to have a future, this widely believed but inherently delusional model has to be jettisoned.

2 | NO MORE MR NICE GUY

Why economics must undergo a long-overdue intellectual revolution

A decade ago, economics appeared triumphant. Though the spiritually inclined might have railed at its materialistic way of looking at the world, it nonetheless appeared that the materialistic road to riches was working. After decades of stagnation, significant sections of the developing world were in fact developing; a long-running boom in the USA had continued with only the slightest hiccup after the Nasdaq crash in April 2000; and in the USA and many other advanced nations, both inflation and unemployment were trending down in a process that leading economists christened 'The Great Moderation.'

It seemed that, after the turmoil of the period from the late 1960s till the recession of the early 1990s, economists had finally worked out how to deliver economic nirvana. To do so, they rejected many of the concepts that had been introduced into economics by the 'Keynesian Revolution' in the 1930s.

The resulting theory of economics was called Neoclassical Economics, to distinguish it from the 'Keynesian Economics' it had overthrown (though in a confusing twist, the major subgroup within neoclassical economics called itself 'New Keynesian').[1] In many ways, it was a return to the approach to economics that had been dominant prior to Keynes, and for that reason it was often referred to as 'the Neoclassical Counter-Revolution.'

At a practical level, neoclassical economics advocated reducing government intervention in the economy and letting markets – especially finance markets – decide economic outcomes unimpeded by politicians, bureaucrats or regulations. Counter-cyclical government budget policy – running deficits during downturns and surpluses during booms – gave way to trying to run surpluses all the time, to reduce the size of the government sector. The only policy tool in favor was manipulation of the interest rate – by a politically independent central bank which itself was controlled by neoclassical economists – with the objective of controlling the rate of inflation.

At a deep theoretical level, neoclassical economics replaced many tools that Keynes and his supporters had developed to analyze the economy as a whole ('macroeconomics') with their own tools. Unlike the analytic tools

---

1 The other sub-group calls itself 'New Classical.' As I explain in Chapter 10, neither of these subgroups bears any resemblance to either Keynes or the Classical School of economic thought. But their battle – publicized in the press as a battle between 'Keynesians' and the rest – has confused many members of the public into believing that the dominant school of thought in economics at the time of the crisis was 'Keynesian economics.' Nothing could be farther from the truth – if Krugman, Woodford and other self-described 'New Keynesians' are Keynesian, then because I can say 'quack,' I am a duck.

of Keynesian macroeconomics, the new neoclassical macroeconomics toolset was derived directly from microeconomics – the theory of how the individual agents in the economy behave.

Purge

Not all academic economists joined in this overthrow of the previous Keynesian orthodoxy. Many fought against it, though ultimately to no avail, and academic economics eventually divided into roughly six camps: the dominant neoclassical school that represented perhaps 85 percent of the profession, and several small rumps called Post-Keynesian, Institutional, Evolutionary, Austrian and Marxian economics.

An outsider might have expected this situation to lead to vigorous debates within the academy. In fact, what eventually evolved was a mixture of both hostility and indifference. Neoclassical economists didn't pay any attention to what these rumps said, but they also gave up on early attempts to eliminate them. Try as they might, they could never get rid of the dissidents completely, for two main reasons.

First, some, like myself, had always been opposed to neoclassical economics, and were hard to remove because of impediments like academic tenure. Secondly, others would begin as neoclassical economists, but then undergo some personal epiphany that would lead them to abandon this approach and swap horses to one of the dissident streams.

So, though neoclassical economists dominated almost all academic economic departments, they were also forced to tolerate the odd critic within. But it was hardly peaceful coexistence.

In teaching, core courses on microeconomics, macroeconomics and finance were purged of non-neoclassical ideas. The odd non-neoclassical course continued as an option to give dissenters something to do, but generally, non-neoclassical staff filled out most of their teaching time giving tutorials in subjects that taught neoclassical ideas with which they fundamentally disagreed. They toed the line in tuition and marking – though they would occasionally grumble about it, to encourage dissent in students who seemed more critical than the run of the mill.

In research, the purge was more complete, because neoclassical editors and referees could exclude the dissidents from the journals they edited. Up until the early 1970s, non-neoclassical authors were regularly published in the prestigious journals of the profession – for example, a major debate over the theories of production and distribution between neoclassical and non-neoclassical economists, known as the 'Cambridge Controversies,' largely occurred in the *American Economic Review* (*AER*), the *Economic Journal* (*EJ*), and the *Quarterly Journal of Economics* (*QJE*) – witness Joan Robinson's papers (Robinson 1971a, 1971b, 1972, 1975), including one entitled 'The second crisis of economic theory' in the *AER*. However, by the mid-1980s, these, their companion major journals the *Journal of Political Economy*, the *Journal of Economic Theory* and many other minor journals had become bastions of neoclassical thought. Papers that did not use neoclassical concepts were routinely rejected – frequently without even being refereed.

Non-neoclassical economists in general gave up on these citadels of orthodoxy, and instead established their own journals in which they communicated with each other, and vigorously criticized neoclassical theory. The *Journal of Post Keynesian Economics* (*JPKE*), founded in 1978 by Sidney Weintraub and Paul Davidson, was the first dedicated to non-neoclassical economics, and many others were subsequently established.

In public policy, as in the most prestigious journals, neoclassical economics reigned supreme. Few dissidents were ever appointed to positions of public influence,[2] and most bureaucratic positions were filled by graduates from the better colleges who – because of the purging of non-neoclassical ideas from the core curriculum – generally didn't even know that any other way of thinking about economics was possible. To them, neoclassical economics *was* economics.

Triumph

This purge within academia was aided and abetted by developments in the economy itself. Inflation, which had been as low as 1 percent in the early 1960s, began to rise in a series of cycles to a peak of 15 percent in 1980. Unemployment, which had in the past gone down when inflation went up, began to rise as well in the 1970s – in apparent contradiction of Keynesian doctrine.

As a result, the media and the public were clamoring for change, supporting the efforts of leading neoclassicals like Milton Friedman to overthrow their Keynesian overlords in the academy. The public policy focus shifted from the Keynesian emphasis upon keeping unemployment low – and tolerating higher inflation as a side effect – to keeping inflation low, in the belief that this would allow the private sector to 'do its thing' and achieve full employment.

The initial results were mixed – inflation plunged as Fed chairman Volcker pushed the cash rate[3] to 20 percent, but unemployment exploded to its post-war peak of almost 11 percent in 1983. But that painful crisis proved to be the worst under neoclassical management of economic policy. The next recession in the early 1990s had a peak unemployment rate of less than 8 percent. The one after that in 2003 had a peak unemployment rate of 6.3 percent.

Inflation had also come down, and fluctuated in a band between 1 and 4 percent, with occasional spikes up to 6 percent – far below the tumultuous

---

2 Bill White, the research director at the Bank of International Settlements, was a notable exception here since he was a proponent of the non-neoclassical 'Financial Instability Hypothesis.'

3 The rate of interest the Federal Reserve charges when it loans to a commercial bank.

level of the period from 1965 to 1985, when the *average* had been over 6 percent. Neoclassical economists enshrined the objective of keeping inflation low in the rules they set for central banks, which instructed them to manipulate the rate of interest to keep inflation in a narrow band between 1 and 3 percent.

Looking back on how neoclassical economics had remodeled both economic theory and economic policy, the current US Federal Reserve chairman Ben Bernanke saw two decades of achievement. Writing in 2004, he asserted that there had been:

> not only significant improvements in economic growth and productivity but also a marked reduction in economic volatility, both in the United States and abroad, a phenomenon that has been dubbed 'the Great Moderation.'
>
> Recessions have become less frequent and milder, and quarter-to-quarter volatility in output and employment has declined significantly as well.
>
> The sources of the Great Moderation remain somewhat controversial, but as I have argued elsewhere, there is evidence for the view that improved control of inflation has contributed in important measure to *this welcome change in the economy*. (Bernanke 2004b; emphasis added)

The chief economist of the OECD, Jean-Philippe Cotis, was equally sanguine about the immediate economic prospects in late May of 2007:

> In its Economic Outlook last Autumn, the OECD took the view that the US slowdown was not heralding a period of worldwide economic weakness, unlike, for instance, in 2001. Rather, a 'smooth' rebalancing was to be expected, with Europe taking over the baton from the United States in driving OECD growth.
>
> Recent developments have broadly confirmed this prognosis. Indeed, *the current economic situation is in many ways better than what we have experienced in years*. Against that background, we have stuck to the rebalancing scenario. *Our central forecast remains indeed quite benign:* a soft landing in the United States, a strong and sustained recovery in Europe, a solid trajectory in Japan and buoyant activity in China and India. In line with recent trends, sustained growth in OECD economies would be underpinned by strong job creation and falling unemployment. (Cotis 2007: 7; emphases added)

§1   Then, in late 2007, the 'Great Moderation' came to an abrupt end.

Crisis

Suddenly, everything that neoclassical economics said couldn't happen, happened all at once: asset markets were in free-fall, century-old bastions of finance like Lehman Brothers fell like flies, and the defining characteristics of the Great Moderation evaporated: unemployment skyrocketed, and mild inflation gave way to deflation.

Confronted by a complete disconnect between what they believed and what was happening, economists reacted in a very human way: they panicked. Suddenly, they threw their neoclassical policy rules out the window, and began to behave like 'Keynesian' economists on steroids. Having eschewed government intervention, budget deficits, and boosting government-created money for decades, at their command the government was everywhere. Budget deficits hit levels that dwarfed anything that old-fashioned Keynesians had ever run in the 1950s and 1960s, and government money flowed like water over the Niagara Falls. Ben Bernanke, as Federal Reserve chairman, literally doubled the level of government-created money in the US economy in five months, when the previous doubling had taken thirteen years. A long decay in the ratio of government-created money to the level of economic activity, from 15 percent of GDP in 1945 to a low of 5 percent in 1980, and 6 percent when the crisis began, was eliminated in less than a year as Bernanke's 'Quantitative Easing 1' saw the ratio rocket back to 15 percent by 2010. §2

The tenor of these times is well captured in Hank Paulson's *On the Brink*:

> 'We need to buy hundreds of billions of assets,' I said. I knew better than to utter the word trillion. That would have caused cardiac arrest. 'We need an announcement tonight to calm the market, and legislation next week,' I said.
>
> What would happen if we didn't get the authorities we sought, I was asked.
>
> 'May God help us all,' I replied. (Paulson 2010: 261)

As they threw their once-cherished neoclassical economic principles out the window, and ran about in panic like a coop full of Chicken Littles, the overwhelming refrain from the public was 'Why didn't you see this coming? And if you're experts on the economy and you were in control of it, why did the crisis happen in the first place?' The first question was famously put directly to academic economists by the Queen of England at the prestigious London School of Economics:

> During a briefing by academics at the London School of Economics on the turmoil on the international markets the Queen asked: 'Why did nobody notice it?'
>
> Professor Luis Garicano, director of research at the London School of Economics' management department, had explained the origins and effects of the credit crisis when she opened the £71 million New Academic Building.
>
> The Queen, who studiously avoids controversy and never gives away her opinions, then described the turbulence on the markets as 'awful'. (Pierce 2008)

The answer these economists later gave the Queen[4] was a popular refrain for a profession that, after decades of dominating economic and social policy around the world, suddenly found itself under concerted attack, with

4 See media.ft.com/cms/3e3b6ca8-7a08-11de-b86f-00144feabdc0.pdf.

its opinions openly derided. It wasn't their fault, because 'No One Could Have Seen This Coming': though the risks to individual positions could be calculated, no one could have foreseen the risk to the system as a whole:

> the difficulty was seeing the risk to the system as a whole rather than to any specific financial instrument or loan. Risk calculations were most often confined to slices of financial activity, using some of the best mathematical minds in our country and abroad. But they frequently lost sight of the bigger picture. (Besley and Hennessy 2009: 1)

Balderdash. Though the precise timing of the crisis was impossible to pick, a systemic crisis was both inevitable and, to astute observers in the mid-2000s, likely to occur in the very near future. That is why I and a handful of other unconventional economists went public in the years leading up to the crisis, warning whenever and however we could that a serious economic calamity was imminent.

'No one saw this coming'

In a paper with the mocking title of '"No one saw this coming": understanding financial crisis through accounting models'[5] (Bezemer 2009, 2010, 2011), Dutch academic Dirk Bezemer trawled through academic and media reports looking for any people who had warned of the crisis before it happened, and who met the following exacting criteria:

Only analysts were included who:

- provided some account of how they arrived at their conclusions.
- went beyond predicting a real estate crisis, also making the link to real-sector recessionary implications, including an analytical account of those links.
- the actual prediction must have been made by the analyst and available in the public domain, rather than being asserted by others.
- the prediction had to have some timing attached to it. (Bezemer 2009: 7)

Bezemer came up with twelve names: myself and Dean Baker, Wynne Godley, Fred Harrison, Michael Hudson, Eric Janszen, Jakob Brøchner Madsen and Jens Kjaer Sørensen, Kurt Richebächer, Nouriel Roubini, Peter Schiff, and Robert Shiller.

He also identified four common aspects of our work:

1 a concern with financial assets as distinct from real-sector assets,
2 with the credit flows that finance both forms of wealth,
3 with the debt growth accompanying growth in financial wealth, and
4 with the accounting relation between the financial and real economy. (Ibid.: 8)

5 mpra.ub.uni-muenchen.de/15892/1/MPRA_paper_15892.pdf.

TABLE 2.1 Anticipations of the housing crisis and recession

Analyst	Country	Capacity	Forecast
Dean Baker	USA	Co-director, Center for Economic and Policy Research	… plunging housing investment will likely push the economy into recession (2006)
Wynne Godley	USA	Distinguished Scholar, Levy Economics Institute of Bard College	The small slowdown in the rate at which US household debt levels are rising resulting from the house price decline will immediately lead to a … growth recession … before 2010 (2006); [will] start to rise significantly and does not come down again (2007)
Fred Harrison	UK	Economic commentator	The next property market tipping point is due at end of 2007 or early 2008 … only way prices can be brought back to affordable levels is a slump or recession (2005)
Michael Hudson	USA	Professor, University of Missouri	Debt deflation will shrink the economy, drive down real wages, and push our debt-ridden economy into Japan-style stagnation or worse (2006)
Eric Janszen	USA	Investor and iTulip commentator	The US will enter a recession within years (2006); stock markets are likely to begin in 2008 to experience a 'Deflation Bear Market' (2007)
Stephen Keen	Australia	Associate Professor, University of Western Sydney	Long before we manage to reverse the current rise in debt, the economy will be in a recession. On current data, we may already be in one (2006)
Jakob Brøchner Madsen and Jens Kjaer Sørensen	Denmark	Professor and graduate student, Copenhagen University	We are seeing large bubbles and if they bust, there is no backup. The outlook is very bad (2005); The bursting of this housing bubble will have a severe impact on the world economy and may even result in a recession (2006)
Kurt Richebächer	USA	Private consultant and investment newsletter writer	The new housing bubble – together with the bond and stock bubbles – will invariably implode in the foreseeable future, plunging the US Economy into a protracted, deep recession (2001); recession and bear market in asset prices are inevitable for the US economy … All remaining questions pertain solely to speed, depth and duration of the economy's downturn (2006)
Nouriel Roubini	USA	Professor, New York University	Real home prices are likely to fall at least 30% over the next three years; itself this house price slump is enough to trigger a US recession (2006)
Peter Schiff	USA	Stockbroker, investment adviser and commentator	The United States economy is like the Titanic … I see a real financial crisis coming for the United States (2006); will be an economic collapse (2007)
Robert Shiller	USA	Professor, Yale University	There is significant risk of a very bad period, with rising default and foreclosures, serious trouble in financial markets, and a possible recession sooner than most of us expected (2006)

If you have never studied economics before, this list may surprise you: don't *all* economists consider these obviously important economic issues?

As you will learn in this book, the answer is no. Neoclassical economic theory ignores all these aspects of reality – even when, on the surface, they might appear to include them. Bezemer gives the example of the OECD's 'small global forecasting' model, which makes forecasts for the global economy that are then disaggregated to generate predictions for individual countries – it was the source of Cotis's statement 'Our central forecast remains indeed quite benign' in the September 2007 *OECD Economic Outlook*.

This OECD model apparently includes monetary and financial variables. However, these are not taken from data, but are instead derived from theoretical assumptions about the relationship between 'real' variables – such as 'the gap between actual output and potential output' – and financial variables. As Bezemer notes, the OECD's model lacks *all* of the features that dominated the economy in the lead-up to the crisis: 'There are no credit flows, asset prices or increasing net worth driving a borrowing boom, nor interest payment indicating growing debt burdens, and no balance sheet stock and flow variables that would reflect all this' (ibid.: 19).

How come? Because standard 'neoclassical' economic theory assumes that the financial system is rather like lubricating oil in an engine – it enables the engine to work smoothly, but has no driving effect. Neoclassical economists therefore believe that they can ignore the financial system in economic analysis, and focus on the 'real' exchanges going on behind the 'veil of money.'

They also assume that the real economy is, in effect, a miracle engine that always returns to a state of steady growth, and never generates any undesirable side effects – rather like a pure hydrogen engine that, once you take your foot off the accelerator or brake, always returns to a steady 3,000 revs per minute, and simply pumps pure water into the atmosphere.[6]

To continue the analogy, the common perspective in the approaches taken by the economists Bezemer identified is that we see finance as more akin to petrol than oil. Without it, the 'real economy' engine revs not at 3,000 rpm, but zero, while the exhaust fumes contain not merely water, but large quantities of pollutants as well.

As the financial crisis made starkly evident, neoclassical economists were profoundly wrong: the issues they ignored were vital to understanding how a market economy operates, and their deliberate failure to monitor the dynamics of private debt was the reason why they did not see this crisis coming – and why they are the last ones who are likely to work out how to end it.

---

6 If you're a neoclassical economist, you're probably offended by this statement and regard it as a parody; if you're a professional from another discipline – say, engineering – who has not had any previous exposure to economic theory, you probably regard this as hyperbole. In either case, I'd suggest that you hold judgment until you finish this book.

Consequently, neoclassical economics, far from being the font of economic wisdom, is actually the biggest impediment to understanding how the economy actually works – and why, periodically, it has serious breakdowns. If we are ever to have an economic theory that actually describes the economy, let alone one that helps us manage it, neoclassical economics has to go.

Revisionism

Yet this is not how neoclassical economists themselves have reacted to the crisis. Bernanke, whose appointment as chairman of the US Federal Reserve occurred largely because he was regarded by his fellow neoclassical economists as *the* academic expert on the Great Depression, has argued that there is no need to overhaul economic theory as a result of the crisis. Distinguishing between what he termed 'economic science, economic engineering and economic management,' he argued that:

> the recent financial crisis was more a failure of economic engineering and economic management than of what I have called economic science [...]
>
> Shortcomings of [...] economic science [...] were for the most part less central to the crisis; indeed, although the great majority of economists did not foresee the near-collapse of the financial system, economic analysis has proven and will continue to prove critical in understanding the crisis, in developing policies to contain it, and in designing longer-term solutions to prevent its recurrence. (Bernanke 2010: 3)

However, Bernanke's primary argument in defense of neoclassical economics is simply silly, because he defends modern economic theory by pointing to the work of theorists that most neoclassical economists would never have heard of: 'The fact that dependence on unstable short-term funding could lead to runs is hardly news to economists; it has been a central issue in monetary economics since Henry Thornton and Walter Bagehot wrote about the question in the 19th century' (ibid.: 6).

This might give non-economists the impression that the works of Thornton and Bagehot are routinely studied by today's economists – or that today's neoclassical economic toolkit is based, among other pillars, on such historically informed sources. However, a significant aspect of the Neoclassical Counter-Revolution was the abolition of courses on economic history and the history of economic thought, in which the works of Thornton and Bagehot would have occasionally featured.

Today, only rebel, non-neoclassical economists – or a central banker with a personal interest in monetary history like Bernanke – is likely to have read Thornton, Bagehot, or any analysis of any financial crises prior to this one. Core neoclassical courses on microeconomics and macroeconomics are devoid of any discussion of financial crises, let alone pre-twentieth-century analysis of them, while even specialist 'Money and Banking' courses teach neoclassical models of money and banking, rather than historical or pre-neoclassical analysis.[7]

One of the few textbook writers who has been trying – largely without success – to broaden the economic curriculum reacted similarly to Bernanke's paper.

> I find this justification very strange. In my view, the fact that Thornton and Bagehot provided useful insights into macroeconomic policy problems is an indictment of fundamental macroeconomic science as currently conceived. If it were fundamental science, it would be taught somewhere – ideally in the core macro courses. That doesn't happen. The core macroeconomic courses teach DSGE ['Dynamic Stochastic General Equilibrium'] modeling almost exclusively.
>
> Not only are the writings of Thornton or Bagehot missing, the writings of Keynes, Minsky, Hicks, Clower, Leijonhufvud, Gurley, Davidson, Goodhardt, Clower, or even Friedman, to mention just a few of those whose writings could also have contributed to a better understanding of the crisis, are missing as well. Most students who have graduated in the past twenty years would never have even heard of half of them, let alone read them.
>
> *If nobody reads them, and their ideas aren't part of the material that students study or learn, how can Bernanke consider them part of modern economic science?* (Colander 2011: 4–5; emphasis added)

In other words, defending modern economics by pointing to the work of pre-neoclassical economists is rather like rebutting criticisms of modern art by extolling the virtues of Leonardo Da Vinci. It is a fob-off, rather than a serious response to criticism.

Bernanke comes closer to engaging with reality when he admits that mainstream neoclassical models failed to predict the crisis: 'Standard macroeconomic models, such as the workhorse new-Keynesian model, did not predict the crisis, nor did they incorporate very easily the effects of financial instability' (Bernanke 2010: 16–17).

But rather than seeing this as a weakness that necessitated revision, Bernanke defended these models on the basis that they are appropriate for non-crisis times:

> Do these failures of standard macroeconomic models mean that they are irrelevant or at least significantly flawed? I think the answer is a qualified no. Economic models are useful only in the context for which they are designed. *Most of the time, including during recessions, serious financial instability is not an issue. The standard models were designed for these non-crisis periods, and they have proven quite useful in that context.* Notably, they were part of the intellectual

---

7 The 'Money and Banking' course at Bernanke's alma mater, where he gave this speech, is a case in point. See www.anababus.net/teach/syllabusECO342.pdf.

framework that helped deliver low inflation and macroeconomic stability in most industrial countries during the two decades that began in the mid-1980s. (Ibid.: 17; emphasis added)

The sheer naivety of this argument caused me pause when writing this chapter. How does one even begin to respond to such a blasé perspective on the role of economic theory, especially when expressed by someone of such reputed knowledge, and in a position of such responsibility, who surely should know better?

There are many tacks I could have taken. The defense of having models for good times would be valid only if there were also models for bad times – but neoclassical economics has no such models. The quaint belief that the conditions prior to the crisis – the so-called Great Moderation – had no connection with the events that followed shows that he has no idea as to what caused the Great Recession.

Ultimately, the most apposite critique of Bernanke's defense of the indefensible is to compare his position with that of the post-Keynesian economist Hyman Minsky. Minsky argued that, since crises like the Great Depression have occurred, a crucial test for the validity of an economic theory is that it must be able to generate a depression as one of its possible states:

Can 'It' – a Great Depression – happen again? And if 'It' can happen, why didn't 'It' occur in the years since World War II? These are questions that naturally follow from both the historical record and the comparative success of the past thirty-five years. To answer these questions it is necessary to have an economic theory which makes great depressions one of the possible states in which our type of capitalist economy can find itself. (Minsky 1982: 5)

On this basis, Minsky rejected neoclassical economics for the very reason that Bernanke defends it above: in its core models, a depression is an impossibility. Therefore, the neoclassical model is an inadequate basis for modeling and understanding capitalism:

The abstract model of the neoclassical synthesis cannot generate instability. When the neoclassical synthesis is constructed, capital assets, financing arrangements that center around banks and money creation, constraints imposed by liabilities, and the problems associated with knowledge about uncertain futures are all assumed away. For economists and policy-makers to do better we have to abandon the neoclassical synthesis. (Ibid.: 5)

Clearly, Bernanke shows no such inclination. Even in the aftermath of a financial crisis that took him and the vast majority of neoclassical economists completely by surprise, and which terrified them as much as it bewildered the public, Bernanke and his many neoclassical colleagues still cling to their belief in an economic theory that asserts that events like this could never happen.

Ignorance

A major reason for Bernanke's inability to accept that the core of neo-classical economics is 'irrelevant or at least significantly flawed' is that, in common with so many of his neoclassical peers, he innately believes that the neoclassical model of the economy is essentially correct – so much so that even the financial crisis could not shake his faith in it.

This faith emanates from the seductive nature of the neoclassical vision. It portrays capitalism as a perfect system, in which the market ensures that everything is 'just right.' It is a world in which meritocracy rules, rather than power and privilege as under previous social systems. This vision of a society operating perfectly without a central despotic authority is seductive – so seductive that neoclassical economists *want* it to be true.

This faith is maintained by a paradoxical, transcendental truth: *neoclassical economists don't understand neoclassical economics*. Their belief that it is a coherent, comprehensive theory of how a market economy operates is based on a profound ignorance of the actual foundations of the theory.[8]

In one sense, their ignorance is utterly justified, because they are behaving in the same way that professionals do in genuine sciences like physics. Most physicists don't check what Einstein actually wrote on the Theory of Relativity, because they are confident that Einstein got it right, and that their textbooks accurately communicate Einstein's core ideas. Similarly, most economists don't check to see whether core concepts like 'supply and demand microeconomics' or 'representative agent macroeconomics' are properly derived from well-grounded foundations, because they simply assume that if they're taught by the textbooks, then there must be original research that confirms their validity.

In fact, the exact opposite is the case: *the original research confirms that all these concepts are false.* Virtually every concept that is taught as gospel in the textbooks has been proved to be unsound in the original literature.

If they actually appreciated what the foundations were – and how utterly flawed they really are – then neoclassical economists would run a mile from their beliefs, and feel compelled to look for alternatives. But they have no knowledge of the actual state of neoclassical economics because their education shields them from it, right from their very first exposure to economic theory (for the rest of the book, if I say 'economics' without qualification, I will normally mean 'neoclassical economics,' unless otherwise noted).

8 An interesting instance of this is the observation by Mark Thoma on the Economist's View blog on 'What's wrong with modern macroeconomics: comments' (economistsview.typepad.com/economist-sview/2009/11/whats-wrong-with-modern-macroeconomics-comments.html), which shows that he was unaware of significant papers that show the foundations of neoclassical theory are unsound – research I discuss in the next chapter: 'One thing I learned from it is that I need to read the old papers by Sonnenschein (1972), Mantel (1974), and Debreu (1974) since these papers appear to undermine representative agent models. According to this work, you cannot learn anything about the uniqueness of an equilibrium, whether an equilibrium is stable, or how agents arrive at equilibrium by looking at individual behavior (more precisely, there is no simple relationship between individual behavior and the properties of aggregated variables – someone added the axiom of revealed preference doesn't even survive aggregating two heterogeneous agents).'

Educated into ignorance

If the real world were accurately described by economic textbooks, there would not now be a financial crisis – and nor would there ever have been one in the past either: the Great Depression would not have happened. The economy would instead be either in equilibrium, or rapidly returning to it, with full employment, low inflation, and sensibly priced assets.

Of course, the real world is nothing like that. Instead, it has been permanently in disequilibrium, and in near-turmoil, ever since the financial crisis began in 2007. So the textbooks are wrong. But there is a bizarre irony in this disconnect between reality and economic textbooks. *If those same textbooks gave an accurate rendition of the underlying theory, they would describe an economy that generated cycles, was in disequilibrium all the time, and was prone to breakdown.*

This is not because the theory itself envisages a turbulent, cyclical world – far from it. The underlying neoclassical vision of the market economy is of permanent equilibrium, just as the textbooks portray it. However, there are preconditions for that state of equilibrium to apply, and deep economic research has established that none of them holds.

These preconditions arise from the neoclassical practice of analyzing the economy from the point of view of individual 'agents,' where those agents can be consumers, firms, workers, or investors. Generally speaking, though the description of the individual itself can be criticized as stylized and barren, this analysis is internally consistent: if you accept the model's assumptions, then the conclusions about *individual* behavior flow logically from them.

However, to be a theory of economics rather than one of individual psychology, this model of the individual must be aggregated to derive a model of a market, where many individual consumers and sellers interact, or an entire economy where multiple markets interact with each other. The analysis of the individual must be aggregated somehow, to derive a theory of the aggregate entity called 'The Market' or 'The Economy.'

In literally every case, the attempt to move from the analysis of the individual to the aggregate failed – in the sense that results that were easily derived for the isolated individual could not be derived for the aggregate. But this failure to derive a coherent model of aggregate economic behavior was suppressed from the economics textbooks. Students were therefore taught a theory of how markets and economies behave which was strictly true only for isolated individuals, and was false for markets and economies themselves.

As I explain in the next chapter, this applies to the simplest and in many ways most fundamental concept in neoclassical economics – the 'downward-sloping demand curve' that is one half of its iconic 'supply and demand' analysis of markets. The theory proves that an individual's demand curve is downward-sloping – i.e. that an individual will buy more units of a commodity if its price falls – but the attempt to prove that the market demand curve also sloped downwards failed. However, textbooks writers are either truly ignorant of this failure, or delude themselves about the failure, or deliberately obfuscate it.

For example, the latest edition of Samuelson's textbook (whose first edition in 1948 set the neoclassical standard for economic instruction ever since) asserts that to derive a market demand curve, all you have to do is add together individual demand curves, and the resulting market demand curve will behave just like the individual demand curves from which it was derived: 'The market demand curve is found by adding together the quantities demanded by all individuals at each price. Does the market demand curve obey the law of downward-sloping demand? It certainly does' (Samuelson and Nordhaus 2010: 48).

That statement is provably false. The true situation is honestly stated in a leading research book, the *Handbook of Mathematical Economics*: 'market demand functions need not satisfy in any way the classical restrictions which characterize consumer demand functions [...] The utility hypothesis tells us nothing about market demand unless it is augmented by additional requirements' (Shafer and Sonnenschein 1982: 671).

As I explain in the next chapter, the 'additional requirements' needed to ensure that a market demand curve slopes downwards are patently absurd. The realistic conclusion therefore is that market demand curves should have any shape *except* the one that is drawn in the textbooks, and standard 'supply and demand' analysis becomes impossible.

However, economics students don't get to learn about this or any other aggregation failure. As the extract from Samuelson and Nordhaus illustrates, neoclassical textbooks present a sanitized, uncritical rendition of conventional economic theory, either ignoring problems with aggregation, or directly contradicting the results of advanced research. The courses in which these textbooks are used do little to counter this mendacious presentation. Students might learn, for example, that 'externalities' reduce the efficiency of the market mechanism. However, they will not learn that the 'proof' that markets are efficient is itself flawed.

Since this textbook rendition of economics is also profoundly boring, many students do no more than an introductory course in economics, and instead go on to careers in accountancy, finance or management – in which, nonetheless, many continue to harbor the simplistic notions they were taught many years earlier.

The minority which continues on to further academic training is taught the complicated techniques of neoclassical economic analysis, with little to no discussion of whether these techniques are actually intellectually valid. The enormous critical literature is simply left out of advanced courses, while glaring logical shortcomings are glossed over with specious assumptions. However, most students accept these assumptions because their training leaves them both insufficiently literate and insufficiently numerate.

Modern-day economics students are insufficiently literate because economic education eschews the study of the history of economic thought. Even a passing acquaintance with this literature exposes the reader to critical perspectives on conventional economic theory – but students today receive no such exposure. They are insufficiently numerate because the material which establishes the intellectual weaknesses of economics is complex. Understanding this literature in its raw form requires an appreciation of some quite difficult areas of mathematics – concepts which require up to two years of undergraduate mathematical training to understand.

Curiously, though economists like to intimidate other social scientists with the mathematical rigor of their discipline, most economists do *not* have this level of mathematical education.

Instead, most economists learn their mathematics by attending courses in mathematics given by other economists. The argument for this approach – the partially sighted leading the partially sighted – is that generalist mathematics courses don't teach the concepts needed to understand mathematical economics (or the economic version of statistics, known as econometrics). This is quite often true. However, this has the side effect that economics has produced its own peculiar versions of mathematics and statistics, and has persevered with mathematical methods which professional mathematicians have long ago transcended. This dated version of mathematics shields students from new developments in mathematics that, incidentally, undermine much of economic theory.

One example of this is the way economists have reacted to 'chaos theory' (discussed in Chapter 9). Most economists think that chaos theory has had little or no impact – which is generally true in economics, but not at all true in most other sciences. This is partially because, to understand chaos theory, you have to understand an area of mathematics known as 'ordinary differential equations.'[9] Yet this topic is taught in very few courses on mathematical economics – and where it is taught, it is not covered in sufficient depth. Students may learn some of the basic techniques for handling what are known as 'second-order linear differential equations,' but chaos and complexity begin to manifest themselves only in 'third order nonlinear differential equations.'[10]

Economics students therefore graduate from master's and PhD programs with an uncritical and unjustified belief that the foundations of economic analysis are sound, no appreciation of the intellectual history of their discipline, and an approach to mathematics which hobbles both their critical understanding of economics, and their ability to appreciate the latest advances in mathematics and other sciences.

9 It is also because complexity theory tends to be incompatible with neoclassical economics, since a common property of complex systems is that they have unstable equilibria: see Chapter 9.

10 Nonlinear 'difference' equations also generate chaos, but economics courses normally cover only linear difference equations.

A minority of these ill-informed students themselves go on to be academic economists, and then repeat the process. Ignorance is perpetuated.

The attempt to conduct a critical dialogue within the profession of academic economics has therefore failed, not because neoclassical economics has no flaws, but because – figuratively speaking – neoclassical economists have no ears. As Bernanke's reaction shows, even the global financial crisis wasn't enough to make them listen.

So then, 'No More Mr Nice Guy.' If economists can't be trusted to follow the Queensberry Rules of intellectual debate, then we critics have to step out of the boxing ring and into the streets.

Does economics matter?

Economists have been justly criticized for failing to anticipate the financial crisis, but if that had been their only failing, they would be no different to weather forecasters who failed to warn of a destructive storm. They could be at fault for failing to give the warning, but you couldn't blame them for the storm itself. Economics, on the other hand, has direct responsibility for the economic storm we are currently experiencing. This is not to say that capitalism is inherently stable – far from it. But the beliefs and actions of economists made this economic crisis far worse than it would have been without their interventions.

First, the naive theories they developed, especially in finance, encouraged reckless behavior in finance by their ex-students. More than a generation of business students were unleashed on the world who believed – or at least paid lip-service to – the fallacies that finance markets always price financial assets correctly, and that debt was good.

Secondly, economists also developed many of the tools of the financial trade that Warren Buffett so aptly described as 'weapons of financial mass destruction.' Options pricing models, 'value at risk' formulas and the like were all based on neoclassical economics, and many were developed by academic economists – some of whom received the Nobel Prize in Economics for their inventions.

Thirdly, probably their greatest negative contribution to human history was that, as regulators, they allowed the excesses of the finance sector to go on for perhaps two decades longer than would have occurred without their 'rescues.'

Here, pride of place goes to the central bankers – especially Alan Greenspan. In Chapter 12, I make the case that were it not for the extreme rescue efforts he initiated in 1987, the stock market crash of that year would have precipitated a serious recession, but one far milder than that we are now experiencing. Instead, that rescue and the many others in the crises that followed – the Savings and Loans crisis, the Long Term Capital Management crisis, and finally the DotCom crisis – encouraged the speculative excesses of Wall Street to continue. The ultimate result was the subprime crisis, the fallout from which was so big that a further rescue was impossible.

The key indicator here – and the key reason that I and the others Bezemer identified as having predicted the crisis could tell that one was coming – is the ratio of private debt to national income (known as GDP, which stands for 'gross domestic product'). Every time the US Fed (and its counterparts in the rest of the OECD) rescued the financial sector from its latest folly, that sector continued doing what it is best at: creating debt.

If the Fed hadn't intervened in 1987, this process of escalating debt would probably have ended there, and America would have begun the painful but necessary process of deleveraging from a debt-to-GDP level of 160 percent – about 10 percent below the 175 percent level that precipitated the Great Depression – and in a milieu of moderate inflation.

Instead, rescued by the Fed, the financial sector lived to lend another day, and went through the veritable nine lives of the cat before the excesses of the Subprime Bubble brought Wall Street to its knees. By then, however, the debt ratio had risen to almost 300 percent of GDP – 1.7 times the 1930s level, and even 1.25 times the peak level of 235 percent of GDP achieved in 1932, when rampant deflation and plunging output drove the debt ratio higher even as Americans drastically reduced the nominal level of debt. §3

By delaying the day of reckoning, neoclassical economists thus turned what could have been a 'run of the mill' financial crisis and recession into possibly the greatest capitalism will ever experience. The jury won't be in on the scale of 'The Great Recession' for several decades, but I expect that history will judge it to be more severe than the Great Depression – probably not in the depths of the downturn, but almost certainly in its duration and apparent intractability. It could not have got this bad without the assistance afforded by neoclassical economics.

Revolt

Bernanke's refusal to countenance that neoclassical economics could be flawed is indicative of the profession as a whole. The vast majority of neoclassical economists have sailed through the financial crisis and the Great Recession with their belief in neoclassical economics intact. If left to their own devices, economists will continue teaching that the economy is fundamentally stable, despite the abounding evidence that they are wrong.

The public could still afford to ignore economics if the discipline had the ability to correct its own excesses. But it does not. Despite its record at forecasting, despite the evidence that economic theories are not consistent, and despite the Great Recession that they have no choice but to admit they failed to foresee, the intellectual discipline of economics shows no tendency to reform itself. Instead, unsound theories continue to be taught to students as if they were incontrovertible. Economics cannot be trusted to reform its own house. Therefore, just as politics is too important to leave to the politicians, economics is too important to leave to the economists. The revolt against neoclassical economics has to go beyond the academic profession itself.

But it seems to make sense ...

One of the great difficulties in convincing believers that neoclassical economics fundamentally misunderstands capitalism is that, at a superficial and individual level, it seems to make so much sense. This is one reason for the success of the plethora of books like *The Undercover Economist* (Harford 2005) and *Freakonomics* (Levitt and Dubner 2009) that apply economic thinking to everyday and individual issues: at an individual level, the basic economic concepts of utility-maximizing and profit-maximizing behavior seem sound.

As I explain later, there are flaws with these ideas even at the individual level, but by and large they have more than a grain of wisdom at this level. Since they seem to make sense of the personal dilemmas we face, it is fairly easy to believe that they make sense at the level of society as well.

The reason this does not follow is that most economic phenomena at the social level – the level of markets and whole economies rather than individual consumers and producers – are 'emergent phenomena': they occur because of our interactions with each other – which neoclassical economics cannot describe – rather than because of our individual natures, which neoclassical economics seems to describe rather well.

The concept of emergent properties is a complex one, and I don't expect you to accept this argument right away; but as it happens, neoclassical economic theory provides an excellent example of an emergent phenomenon which I cover in Chapter 3 (and at the beginning of Chapter 10). Once you've read that, I think you'll understand why the fact that neoclassical economics seems sensible at the individual level has no bearing on whether it can make sense of capitalism itself.

Sincerity is no defense

Much – well, pretty much all – of what I have to say about neoclassical economics will be offensive to neoclassical economists.[11] Since this edition is far more likely than its predecessor to actually be read by some neoclassical economists, let me say now that I mean no personal offense. Pardon the cliché, but some of my best friends are neoclassical economists, and I've never for a second doubted the sincerity of most neoclassical economists. Though many in the public believe that neoclassical economists say what they say for personal gain, or to curry favor with the powers that be, the vast majority of neoclassical economists that I have met, or whose work I have read, are undoubtedly sincere in the belief that their work is intended

---

11 By way of balance, I also know that some of what I say about Marxism will be offensive to Marxist economists.

to improve society as a whole, and not merely the situation of the powerful within it.

Unfortunately, as I learnt long ago, sincerity is no defense. A schoolteacher of mine put it this way in a discussion my class was having about politics, when one student defended a particular politician with the statement 'Well, at least he's sincere!'

The class nodded sagely: yes, whatever we individually thought of this politician, we all had to concede that he was sincere. Our teacher, who normally let class discussions proceed unmonitored, suddenly piped up from the back of the room. 'Don't overrate sincerity,' he said. 'The most sincere person you'll ever meet is the maniac chasing you down the street with an ax, trying to chop your head off!'

I never did find out what personal experience led to that epiphany for Brother Gerard, but I've had many opportunities to reflect on its wisdom since: the most dangerous people on the planet are those who sincerely believe something that is false.

So while there is a mass of criticism of neoclassical economics – and of neoclassical economists for believing in it – I mean no offense to neoclassical economists as people. But as would-be scientists, their beliefs should not be provably false, as most of neoclassical economics is.

Debunking economics: a user's guide

Who is this book for? Interest in economics as an intellectual pursuit for its own sake has waned significantly over the last thirty years, and I have often heard academic economists lament this fact – especially since falling student enrollments have undermined their job security.

I am not at all amazed by this drop in interest: it is a predictable side effect of the very philosophy of life which neoclassical economists espouse.[12] They have told all and sundry that the world would be a better place if we all focused upon our own self-interest, and let the market take care of the common good. Why, then, is it surprising that students have swallowed this spiel, and decided to study subjects which more clearly lead to a well-paid job – business management, human resources, computing, etc. – rather than to study economics?

In its first incarnation in 2000, this book was directed at this audience, which economists once derided, and whose absence they now lament: people who are interested in 'the common good.' Its message, that the economic mantra ('individuals should pursue their own interests and leave society's overall interests to the market') is wrong, is not new. Many books have made the same point in the past. What is new about this book is that it makes that point using economic theory itself.

12 Curiously, academic neoclassical economists don't follow this philosophy themselves: they really believe that they are promoting the common good by developing and teaching neoclassical economics.

In this second edition, I have an additional audience in mind: the professional economist who is honest enough to consider that perhaps the failure of the economics profession at large to anticipate the biggest economic event of the last seventy years could be due to deficiencies in the underlying theory itself. There will, I expect, be only a handful of such readers (and on current form, Ben Bernanke and Paul Krugman won't be among them), but if so they will be stunned at how much critical economic literature was omitted in their original education in economics. This book provides a compendium of that literature.[13]

I can guarantee that mainstream economists will hate the irreverent tone of this book. Nonetheless, I'd ask them to persevere with open – but skeptical – minds. I hope that exposure to the many published critiques of economics might explain to them why a theory which they accepted too uncritically was so manifestly unable to explain how a market economy actually behaves.

This book should also be useful to budding students of economics, in at least two ways. First, unless they are lucky enough to attend one of the few universities where pluralism rules, they are about to submit to an education in economics that is in reality an indoctrination. This book covers the issues which should form part of an education in economics, but which are omitted by the vast majority of textbooks.

Secondly, they should find that the explanations of economic theory in this book make it easier to pass exams in economics. I have found that one of the main barriers which new students face in learning economics sufficiently well to be able to pass exams in it is that they can't reconcile the theory with their own 'gut feelings' about economic issues. Once students realize that they should trust their gut feelings, and treat economic theory as irrelevant to the real economy, then suddenly it becomes much easier to pass exams. Just treat economics like a game of chess, play the games the exam questions require of you, and you'll pass easily (just don't mention the inconsistencies in the rules!).

If you are already a somewhat uncomfortable student of economics, but you lack confidence because you are surrounded by peers who can't understand your disquiet, then this book should allay your fears. Normally, the journey from troubled student to informed critic is a difficult and lonely one. I hope to make that journey far less difficult, and less lonely. I hope it also gives you the confidence to confront your teachers if, while an economic crisis continues to rage about them in the real world, they continue teaching theories that argue that such things can't happen.

Similarly, I hope that professional critical economists will find this book a useful introductory compendium to those many critiques of economic

13 In the first edition, since my target audience didn't have access to academic journals, I decided to make references to academic papers uncluttered by not giving page references. Since I am now catering for an audience that does have access to those journals, all new references in this edition have page references for quotations.

theory that are currently scattered through dozens of books and hundreds of journal articles. While the arguments are not presented with the rigor of those formal critiques, the book provides an accessible and understandable introduction to that important and neglected literature. The curious student can be told to use this book as a guide before delving into the more difficult, formal literature.

Because it explains and debunks economic theory from first principles, this book will also be of use to anyone whose career makes them reliant upon the advice of economists. Hopefully it will encourage such people to look more widely for advice in future.

What's in this book? This book has been primarily written for people who are inclined to be critical of economics, but who are intimidated by its apparently impressive intellectual arsenal. I start from the premise that, though you might be familiar with the conclusions of economic theory, you are unfamiliar with how those conclusions were derived. You therefore don't have to have studied economics previously to be able to read this book.

I have also eschewed the use of mathematical formulas.[14] Though I frequently use mathematics in my own research, I'm well aware of the impact that mathematical symbols have on the intelligent lay reader (a Norwegian colleague calls it the MEGO effect: 'My Eyes Glaze Over.') Instead, where some mathematical concept is needed to understand a critique, I present it, as well as is possible, in verbal (and sometimes tabular) form.

Despite the absence of mathematics, this book will still require significant intellectual exertion by the reader. The arguments of economic theory are superficially appealing, as Veblen long ago observed. To understand why they are nonetheless flawed requires thought at a deeper level than just that of surface appearances. I have attempted to make both economic theory and the flaws behind it relatively easy to comprehend, but there will be times when the difficulty of the material defeats my abilities as an expositor.

This problem is amplified by the fact that this book is effectively two books in one.

First, it provides a detailed exposition of the conventional theory, and takes none of the short cuts followed by the vast majority of conventional economic texts. As I noted above, one reason why economic instruction takes short cuts is because the foundations of conventional economics are not only difficult to grasp, but also profoundly boring. Economics should be an exciting, stimulating intellectual challenge, but conventional economics almost goes out of its way to be mundane. Unfortunately, I have to explain conventional economics in detail in order to be able to discuss the critiques

14 Except in one footnote, where the equation concerns meteorology rather than economics, and can easily be skipped. Occasionally, when some proposition in the text is best stated in mathematical form, I have used words rather than mathematical symbols.

of this theory. There are thus sections of this book which are inherently tedious – despite my attempts to lighten the discourse. This applies especially to the chapters on the neoclassical theories of consumption (Chapter 3) and production (Chapter 4).

Secondly, this book provides a detailed debunking of conventional theory. This is, I hope, rather more interesting than conventional theory itself – though nowhere near as interesting as an exposition of a truly relevant economics would be. But it is quite possible that the exposition of conventional theory which precedes each debunking may persuade you that the conventional economic argument makes sense. Your mind will therefore be tossed first one way and then the other, as you first grind through understanding the foundations of conventional economics, and then attempt to comprehend profound but subtle critiques of the superficially convincing conventional logic.

So, especially if you have never read a book on economic theory, you will undoubtedly find some sections very difficult. You may therefore find it easier to treat this book as a reference work, by reading Part 1 (Chapters 3–6) carefully, and then turning to the rest when you have some specific economic issue to explore. Alternatively, you can read the chapters in Parts 2 (Chapters 7–12) and 3 (Chapters 13–18) before you attempt the earlier, foundation ones. This is possible because in these later chapters I 'cut economics some slack,' and accept concepts which have in fact been debunked in the earlier chapters. After you've considered the failings of economics in these more interesting applied areas, you could then turn to the flaws in its foundations.

Whichever way you approach it, this book will be a difficult read. But if you are currently a skeptic of economics, and you wish to develop a deeper understanding of why you should be skeptical, I believe the effort will be worth it.

Not left versus right but right versus wrong One possible interpretation of this book – certainly one I expect to get from many economists – is that it is just a left-wing diatribe against rational economics. This common response to intellectual criticism – categorize it and then dismiss it out of hand – is one of the great sources of weakness in economics, and indeed much political debate.

It is probably true that the majority of those who criticize conventional economic theory are closer to the left than the right end of the political spectrum – though there are many profoundly right-wing critics of conventional economics. Only those occupying the middle of the political spectrum tend to espouse and implement conventional economics.

However, the critiques in this book are not based on politics, but on logic. No political position – left, right or middle – should be based on foundations which can easily be shown to be illogical. Yet much of conventional economic theory is illogical. Those who occupy the center stage of modern politics should find a firmer foundation for their politics than an illogical economic theory.

The same comment, of course, applies to those at the left-wing end of the political spectrum, who base their support for radical social change on conventional Marxian economics. As I argue in Chapter 17, conventional Marxism is as replete with logical errors as is neoclassical economics, even though Marx himself provides a far better foundation for economic analysis than did Walras or Marshall.

Escher without the panache One thing which sets economics apart from other social sciences, and which makes it hard for non-economists to understand economics, is the extent to which its arguments are presented in the form of diagrams. Even leading economists, who develop their theories using mathematics, will often imagine their models in diagrammatic form.

These diagrams represent models which are supposed to be simplified but nonetheless accurate renditions of aspects of the real-world phenomena of production, distribution, exchange, consumption, and so on. When an economist talks of the economy behaving in a particular fashion, what he really means is that a model of the economy – and normally a graphical model – has those characteristics.

To learn economics, then, one has to learn how to read diagrams and interpret the models they represent. This applies to critics as much as believers, but the very act of learning the diagrams tends to separate one from the other. Most critical thinkers find the process tedious, and drop out of university courses in economics. Most of those who stay become seduced by the diagrams and models, to the point where they have a hard time distinguishing their models from reality.

The critical thinkers, who could not cope with the diagrammatic representation of economic reality, were fundamentally correct: economic reality cannot be shoehorned into diagrams. Consequently, these diagrams often contain outright fallacies, conveniently disguised by smooth but technically impossible lines and curves.

In other words, rather than being accurate renditions of the economy, the standard economic diagrams are rather like Escher drawings, in which the rules of perspective are used to render scenes which appear genuine – but which are clearly impossible in the real, three-dimensional world.

Whereas Escher amused and inspired with his endless staircases, eternal waterfalls and the like, economists believe that their models give meaningful insights into the real world. But they could only do so if the Escher-like assumptions economists make could apply in reality – if, metaphorically speaking, water could flow uphill. Since it cannot, economic models are dangerously misleading when used to determine real-world policy.

Obviously, therefore, I do not wish to encourage you to 'think diagram-matically,' since this mode of thought has helped to confuse economics rather than to inform it. However, to be able to understand where economics has gone wrong, you need to see what has led it astray. I have attempted to explain economic theory without diagrams, but it is still probable that to be able to fully comprehend the fallacies in neoclassical economics, you will need to learn how to read diagrams – though not, I hope, to believe them (see 'Where are the diagrams?', p. ix).

Blow by blow In most chapters, I take a key facet of economics, and first state the theory as it is believed by its adherents. I then point out the flaws in this superficially appealing theory – flaws that have been established by economists and, in most instances, published in economic journals. As I show, the effect of each flaw is normally to invalidate the theoretical point completely, yet in virtually every case, economics continues on as if the critique had never been made.

Economics is a moving target, and the outer edges of the theory sometimes bear little resemblance to what is taught at undergraduate level. Except in the case of macroeconomics, I concentrate upon the fare served up to undergraduates, rather than the rarefied extremities of new research – mainly because this is the level at which most economists operate, but also because much of the work done at the theoretical 'cutting edge' takes as sound the foundations learnt during undergraduate days. However, for some topics – notably macroeconomics – the difference between undergraduate and postgraduate economics is so extreme that I cover both topics.

The Great Recession has resulted in a much-expanded treatment of macroeconomics, and also two new chapters that 'break the mold' of the rest of the book by being expositions of my own approach to economics.

Chapter by chapter The book commences with two introductory chapters – which hopefully you have just read!:

- Chapter 1 ('Predicting the "unpredictable"') shows that the 'unpredictable' Great Recession was easily foreseeable almost a decade before it occurred.
- Chapter 2 ('No more Mr Nice Guy') gives an overview of the book.

Part 1, 'Foundations,' considers issues which form part of a standard education in economics – the theories of demand, supply, and income distribution – and shows that these concepts have very rickety foundations. It has four chapters:

- Chapter 3 ('The calculus of hedonism') reveals that economics has failed to derive a coherent theory of consumer demand from its premise that people are no more than self-interested hedonists. As a result, economic theory can't justify a crucial and seemingly innocuous element of its analysis of markets – that demand for a product will fall smoothly as its price rises. Far from being innocuous, this failure cripples neoclassical theory, but neoclassical economists have both ignored this failure, and responded to it in ways that make a mockery of their claims to being scientific.

- Chapter 4 ('Size does matter') shows that the economic theory of 'the firm' is logically inconsistent. When the inconsistencies are removed, two of the central mantras of neoclassical economics – that 'price is set by supply and demand' and 'equating marginal cost and marginal revenue maximizes profits' are shown to be false. Economic theory also cannot distinguish between competitive firms and monopolies, despite its manifest preference for small competitive firms over large ones.
- Chapter 5 ('The price of everything and the value of nothing') argues that the theory of supply is also flawed, because the conditions which are needed to make the theory work are unlikely to apply in practice. The concept of diminishing marginal returns, which is essential to the theory, is unlikely to apply in practice, 'supply curves' are likely to be flat, or even downward-sloping, and the dynamic nature of actual economies means that the neoclassical rule for maximizing profit is even more incorrect than it was shown to be in the previous chapter.
- Chapter 6 ('To each according to his contribution') looks at the theory of the labor market. The theory essentially argues that wages in a market economy reflect workers' contributions to production. Flaws in the underlying theory imply that wages are not in fact based on merit, and that measures which economists argue would reduce unemployment may in fact increase it.

Part 2, 'Complexities,' considers issues which should be part of an education in economics, but which are either omitted entirely or trivialized in standard economics degrees. It has five chapters:

- Chapter 7 ('The holy war over capital') complements Chapter 5 by showing that the theory of capital is logically inconsistent. Profit does not reflect capital's contribution to output, and changing the price of capital relative to labor may have 'perverse' impacts on demand for these 'factors of production.'
- Chapter 8 ('There is madness in their method') examines methodology and finds that, contrary to what economists tell their students, assumptions do matter. What's more, the argument that they don't is actually a smokescreen for neoclassical economists – and especially journal editors, since they routinely reject papers that don't make the assumptions they insist upon.
- Chapter 9 ('Let's do the Time Warp again') discusses the validity of applying static (timeless) analysis to economics when the economy is

clearly dynamic itself. The chapter argues that static economic analysis is invalid when applied to a dynamic economy, so that economic policy derived from static economic reasoning is likely to harm rather than help an actual economy.

- Chapter 10 ('Why they didn't see it coming') tracks the development of macroeconomics into its current sorry state, and argues that what has been derided as 'Keynesian' macroeconomics was in fact a travesty of Keynes's views. It explains the otherwise bizarre fact that the people who had the least inkling that a serious economic crisis was imminent in 2007 were the world's most respected economists, while only rebels and outsiders like myself raised the alarm.

- Chapter 11 ('The price is not right') deals with the economic theory of asset markets, known as the 'Efficient Markets Hypothesis'. It argues that the conditions needed to ensure what economists call market efficiency – which include that investors have identical, accurate expectations of the future, and equal access to unlimited credit – cannot possibly apply in the real world. Finance markets cannot be efficient, and finance and debt do affect the real economy.

- Chapter 12 ('Misunderstanding the Great Depression and the Great Recession') returns to macroeconomics, and considers the dominant neoclassical explanation of the Great Depression – that it was all the fault of the Federal Reserve. The great irony of today's crisis is that the person most responsible for promoting this view is himself now chairman of the Federal Reserve.

Part 3, 'Alternatives,' considers alternative approaches to economics. It has six chapters:

- Chapter 13 ('Why I did see "It" coming') outlines Hyman Minsky's 'Financial Instability Hypothesis,' and my nonlinear and monetary models of it, which were the reason I anticipated this crisis, and why I went public with my warnings in late 2005.

- Chapter 14 ('A monetary model of capitalism') shows how a strictly monetary model of capitalism can be built remarkably simply, once all the factors that neoclassical theory ignores are incorporated: time and disequilibrium, and the institutional and social structure of capitalism.

- Chapter 15 ('Why stock markets crash') presents four non-equilibrium approaches to the analysis of asset markets, all of which indicate that finance destabilizes the real economy.

- Chapter 16 ('Don't shoot me, I'm only the piano') examines the role of mathematics in economic theory. It argues that mathematics itself is not to blame for the state of economics today, but instead that bad and inappropriate mathematics by economists has resulted in them persisting with an inappropriate static equilibrium analysis of the economy. The dynamic, non-equilibrium social system that is a market economy should be analyzed with dynamic, non-equilibrium tools.

- Chapter 17 ('Nothing to lose but their minds') dissects Marxian economics, arguing that this potential alternative to conventional economics is seriously flawed. However, much of the problem stems from an inadequate understanding of Marx by not just his critics, but also his alleged friends.
- Finally, Chapter 18 ('There are alternatives') briefly presents several alternative schools in economics, and shows that viable if somewhat underdeveloped alternative ways to 'think economically' already exist.

There's even more on the Web This book does not begin and end with the chapters just mentioned. It is also intimately linked to one of my two websites, www.debunkingeconomics.com (my other website, www.debtdeflation.com, currently supports my blog on the financial crisis and ultimately will be the online companion to my next book, *Finance and Economic Breakdown*).

The website complements the book in several ways. First, sections of the argument have been placed on the Web. These are technically necessary, but somewhat tedious, and therefore could distract attention from key issues. These web entries are noted in the text with a comment like 'I've skipped explaining a concept called XX. Check the link More/XX if you want the full version,' which indicates both what has been placed on the Web, and where it is located.

Secondly, more lengthy discussion of some topics has been placed on the Web. For instance, the failure of the conventional theory of market demand means that alternative approaches must be developed. These, and additional critiques of conventional theory, are on the website and referred to under the heading 'But wait, there's more.' The locations of these additional discussions are given by comments like 'These and other issues are discussed on the Web. Follow the links to More/Hedonism.' These sections raise many issues which should be of interest to those critical of conventional economics.

Thirdly, while there are no mathematical formulas used in this book, the logic underlying many of the critiques is mathematical. The mathematically inclined reader can check the original logic by consulting the website. These links are indicated by a parenthetical statement such as '(follow the link Maths/Size/PC_eq_M for the maths).'

Fourthly, some related topics are not covered in the book. One obvious omission is the theory of international trade. The major reason for this omission is that, while sound critiques of international trade theory exist, what I regard as the most obvious and telling critique has not yet been formally developed (I outline this on the website at the link More/Trade, as well as discussing the formal critiques that have been published). Another reason is that the theory of international trade also depends on many basic concepts that are thoroughly debunked in this book.

Passing judgment on modern economics This book can be thought of as a critical report card on economics at the beginning of the third millennium. Economic theory, as we know it today, was born in the late nineteenth century in the work of Jevons, Walras, Menger and (somewhat later) Marshall. I have a reasonably high regard for these founders of what has become mainstream economics. They were pioneers in a new way of thinking, and yet, in contrast to their modern disciples, they were often aware of possible limitations of the theory they were trying to construct. They expected their heirs to extend the boundaries of economic analysis, and they expected economics to develop from the precocious but hobbled child to which they gave birth into a vibrant and flexible adult.

Instead, economics today is ridden with internal inconsistencies: an economic model will start with some key proposition, and then contradict that proposition at a later stage. For example, the theory of consumer demand begins with the proposition that each consumer is unique, but then reaches a logical impasse which it sidesteps by assuming that all consumers are identical.

This raises an important general point about scientific theories. Any theory will have some starting point, which can be chosen in any of a number of ways. Newtonian physics, for example, began with the starting point that any object subject to a force (in a vacuum) will accelerate; Einsteinian physics began with the starting point that the speed of light (also in a vacuum) sets an absolute speed limit for any material object.

Clearly the starting point of a theory can be challenged, but the basis of such a critique is normally what we might term 'external consistency.' That is, since the theory is supposed to describe some objective reality, it must be possible to show significant consistency between the predictions of the theory and that objective reality.

Here the degree of proof often comes down to some statistical measure of accuracy. Using the example of physics again, it is obvious that, at the speeds which humans could impart to a physical body during the nineteenth century, the Newtonian vision was extremely accurate.

Internal consistency, on the other hand, requires that everything within the theory must legitimately follow from its starting point. Here, statistical accuracy is not good enough: the fit of the theory with the starting point from which it is derived must be exact. If a theory at some point requires a condition which contradicts its starting point, or any other aspect of itself, then the theory is internally inconsistent and therefore invalid. It is possible to criticize much of economics on the basis that 'reality isn't like that' – and this is occasionally done in the subsequent chapters. However, in general I take two allegedly related aspects of economic theory – the theory of individual consumption and the theory of the market demand curve, for example – and show that to get from one to the other, a clearly contradictory condition must be imposed.

A theory cannot survive with such contradictions – or rather, it should not. They are clear signals that something is fundamentally wrong with the starting position of the theory itself, and that real progress involves radically revising or even abandoning that starting point. Even some of the most committed economists have conceded that, if economics is to become less of a religion and more of a science, then the foundations of economics should be torn down and replaced. However, if left to its own devices, there is little doubt that the profession of academic economics would continue to build an apparently grand edifice upon rotten foundations.

The founding fathers of modern economics would, I expect, be surprised to find that a manner of thinking they thought would be transitional has instead become ossified as the only way one can do economics and be respectable. They would, I hope, be horrified to find that the limitations of economic theory have been soundly established, and that most 'respectable' economists nevertheless transgress these limits without conscience, and often without knowledge.

Respectability be damned. Like the populace watching the parade of the emperor, respectability has led us to kowtow to a monarch in fine cloth, when an unindoctrinated child can see that the emperor has no clothes. It's time to expose the nakedness of neoclassical economics.

PART 1 | FOUNDATIONS

THE LOGICAL FLAWS IN THE KEY CONCEPTS OF CONVENTIONAL ECONOMICS

The belief that price and quantity are jointly determined by the interaction of supply and demand is perhaps the most central tenet of conventional economics. In Alfred Marshall's words, supply and demand are like the two blades of a pair of scissors: both are needed to do the job, and it's impossible to say that one or the other determines anything on its own. Demand for a commodity falls as its price rises, supply rises as price rises, and the intersection of the two curves determines both the quantity sold and the price.

This argument still forms the core of modern instruction in economics, and much of economic policy is directed at allowing these twin determinants to act freely and unfettered, so that economic efficiency can be at its maximum. But both mainstream and dissident economists have shown that the real world is not nearly so straightforward as Marshall's famous analogy. The next four chapters show that the 'blades of supply and demand' cannot work in the way economists believe.

3 | THE CALCULUS OF HEDONISM

Why the market demand curve is not downward-sloping

Maggie Thatcher's famous epithet that 'There is no such thing as society' succinctly expresses the neoclassical theory that the best social outcomes result from all individuals looking after their own self-interest: if individuals consider only their own well-being, the market will ensure that the welfare of all is maximized. This hedonistic, individualistic approach to analyzing society is a source of much of the popular opposition to economics. Surely, say the critics, people are more than just self-interested hedonists, and society is more than just the sum of the individuals in it?

Neoclassical economists will concede that their model does abstract from some of the subtler aspects of humanity and society. However, they assert that treating individuals as self-interested hedonists captures the essence of their economic behavior, while the collective economic behavior of society can be derived by summing the behavior of this self-interested multitude. The belief that the economic aspect of society is substantially more than the sum of its parts, they say, is misguided.

This is not true. Though mainstream economics began by assuming that this hedonistic, individualistic approach to analyzing consumer demand was intellectually sound, it ended up proving that it was not. The critics were right: society is more than the sum of its individual members, and a society's behavior cannot be modeled by simply adding up the behaviors of all the individuals in it. To see why the critics have been vindicated by economists, and yet economists still pretend that they won the argument, we have to take a trip down memory lane to late eighteenth-century England.

The kernel

Adam Smith's famous metaphor that a self-motivated individual is led by an 'invisible hand' to promote society's welfare asserts that self-centered behavior by individuals necessarily leads to the highest possible level of welfare for society as a whole. Modern economic theory has attempted, unsuccessfully, to prove this assertion. The attempted proof had several components, and in this chapter we check out the component which models how consumers decide which commodities to purchase.

According to economic theory, each consumer attempts to get the highest level of satisfaction he can from his income, and he does this by picking the combination of commodities he can afford which gives him the greatest personal pleasure. The economic model of how each individual does this is intellectually watertight.[1]

However, economists encountered fundamental difficulties in moving from the analysis of a solitary individual to the analysis of society, because they had to 'add up' the pleasure which consuming commodities gave to different individuals. Personal satisfaction is clearly a subjective thing, and there is no objective means by which one person's satisfaction can be added to another's. Any two people get different levels of satisfaction from consuming, for example, an extra banana, so that a change in the distribution of income which effectively took a banana from one person and gave it to another could result in a different level of social well-being.

Economists were therefore unable to prove their assertion, unless they could somehow show that altering the distribution of income did not alter social welfare. They worked out that two conditions were necessary for this to be true: (a) that all people have to have the same tastes; (b) that each person's tastes remain the same as his income changes, so that every additional dollar of income was spent exactly the same way as all previous dollars – for example, 20 cents per dollar on pizza, 10 cents per dollar on bananas, 40 cents per dollar on housing, etc.

The first assumption in fact amounts to assuming that there is only one person in society (or that society consists of a multitude of identical drones) – since how else could 'everybody' have the same tastes? The second amounts to assuming that there is only one commodity – since otherwise spending patterns would necessarily change as income rose. These 'assumptions' clearly contradict the case economists were trying to prove, since they are necessarily violated in the real world – in fact, they are really a 'proof by contradiction' that Adam Smith's invisible hand doesn't work. Sadly, however, this is not how most economists have interpreted these results.

When conditions (a) and (b) are violated, as they must be in the real world, then several important concepts which are important to economists collapse. The key casualty here is the vision of demand for any product falling as its price rises. Economists can prove that 'the demand curve slopes downward in price' for a single individual and a single commodity. But in a society consisting of many different individuals with many different commodities, the 'market demand curve' can have any shape at all – so that sometimes demand will rise as a commodity's price rises, contradicting the 'Law of Demand.' An essential building block of the economic analysis of markets, the market demand curve, therefore does not have the characteristics needed for economic theory to be internally consistent.

The roadmap

The chapter opens with an outline of Jeremy Bentham's philosophy of utilitarianism, which is the philosophical foundation for the economic analysis

1 However it is also also empirically impossible, as I discuss in the addendum.

of individual behavior. The conventional economic analysis is outlined. The chapter's punchline is that economic theory cannot derive a coherent analysis of market demand from its watertight but ponderous analysis of individual behavior. In addenda, I show that this analysis is only a toy model anyway – it can't apply to actual human behavior, and experimentally, it has been a failure.

Pleasure and pain

The true father of the proposition that people are motivated solely by self-interest is not Adam Smith, as is often believed, but his contemporary, Jeremy Bentham. With his philosophy of 'utilitarianism,' Bentham explained human behavior as the product of innate drives to seek pleasure and avoid pain. Bentham's cardinal proposition was that

> Nature has placed mankind under the governance of two sovereign masters, pain and pleasure. It is for them alone to point out what we ought to do, as well as to determine what we shall do. On the one hand the standard of right and wrong, on the other the chain of causes and effects, are fastened to their throne. They govern us in all that we do, in all we say, in all we think; every effort we can make to throw off our subjection, will serve but to demonstrate and confirm it. In a word a man may pretend to abjure their empire; but in reality he will remain subject to it all the while. (Bentham 1948 [1780])

Thus Bentham saw the pursuit of pleasure and the avoidance of pain as the underlying causes of everything done by humans, and phenomena such as a sense of right and wrong as merely the surface manifestations of this deeper power. You may do what you do superficially because you believe it to be right, but fundamentally you do it because it is the best strategy to gain pleasure and avoid pain. Similarly, when you refrain from other actions because you say they are immoral, you in reality mean that, for you, they lead to more pain than pleasure.

Today, economists similarly believe that they are modeling the deepest determinants of individual behavior, while their critics are merely operating at the level of surface phenomena. Behind apparent altruism, behind apparent selfless behavior, behind religious commitment, lies self-interested individualism.

Bentham called his philosophy the 'principle of utility' (ibid.), and he applied it to the community as well as the individual. Like his Tory disciple Maggie Thatcher some two centuries later, Bentham reduced society to a sum of individuals:

> The community is a fictitious body, composed of the individual persons who are considered as constituting as it were its members. The interests of the community then is, what? – the sum of the interests of the several members who compose it. It is in vain to talk of the interest of the community, without understanding what is in the interest of the individual. (Ibid.)

The interests of the community are therefore simply the sum of the interests of the individuals who comprise it, and Bentham perceived no difficulty in performing this summation: 'An action then may be said to be conformable to the principle of utility when the tendency it has to augment the happiness of the community is greater than any it has to diminish it' (ibid.).

This last statement implies measurement, and Bentham was quite confident that individual pleasure and pain could be objectively measured, and in turn summed to divine the best course of collective action for that collection of individuals called society.[2] Bentham's attempts at such measurement look quaint indeed from a modern perspective, but from this quaint beginning economics has erected its complex mathematical model of human behavior. Economists use this model to explain everything from individual behavior, to market demand, to the representation of the interests of the entire community. However, as we shall shortly see, economists have shown that the model's validity terminates at the level of the single, solitary individual.

Flaws in the glass

In most chapters, the critique of conventional theory has been developed by critics of neoclassical economics, and neoclassical economists are unaware of it because, in general, they cope with criticism by ignoring it.

This isn't the case with this first critique because, ironically, it was an 'own goal': the people who proved that the theory was flawed were themselves leading neoclassical economists, who were hoping to prove that it was watertight.

It is not. While economics can provide a coherent analysis of the individual in its own terms, it is unable to extrapolate this to an analysis of the market.

Since this critique was developed by neoclassical economists themselves, many mainstream academic economists are aware of it, but they either pretend or truly believe that this failure can be managed with a couple of additional assumptions. Yet, as you'll see shortly, the assumptions themselves are so absurd that only someone with a grossly distorted sense of logic could accept them. That twisted logic is acquired in the course of a standard education in economics.

This 'education' begins with students being taught conclusions which would apply if the theory had no logical flaws. Students normally accept that these conclusions have been soundly derived from the basic economic propositions of individual behavior, and they are in no position to believe otherwise, since the basic building blocks of this analysis are not taught at the introductory level because they are 'too hard.' This abbreviated induction is sufficiently boring to dissuade the majority of business students from pursuing further economics, and they graduate in some other discipline. However, a minority find the game intriguing, and continue on to another year.

---

2 Most of Bentham's endeavors in this regard related to devising a scale of punishments that he regarded as just sufficient to discourage the commission of crime.

In later undergraduate years, they finally encounter indifference curves and the derivation of the individual demand curve. The mildly relevant 'Engel curves' and the complete chimera of the 'Giffen good' are explored as apparent applications of the theory. Market demand curves, and sometimes the basic concepts of 'general equilibrium' (the conditions under which many markets will simultaneously be in equilibrium), are discussed – again, without considering whether the step from the individual to the aggregate is valid.

Most economics graduates seek employment in the private sector, and parts of the public sector, where they normally champion the neoclassical perspective. However, a minority of this minority pursues further study, to seek employment as academic economists – and in search of education rather than remuneration, since academic salaries are far lower than private and even public sector ones. Once they have embarked upon this road to ordination as an economist, most students are fully inculcated in the neoclassical way of thinking.

Finally, in honors, master's or PhD courses, they study the full exposition given below, and finally learn that the aggregation of individual demand is valid only under patently absurd conditions. However, by this time the indoctrination into the neoclassical mindset is so complete that most of them cannot see the absurdity. Instead, they accept these conditions as no more than simple devices to sidestep pesky but minor problems, so that 'rational' economic analysis can be undertaken.

It would be easy to accede to a simplistic conspiracy theory to explain why economic education takes such a convoluted route on this issue. However, I believe the explanation is both more mundane and more profound.

At the mundane level, the proposition that individual behavior is motivated by utility maximization, the concept of a downward-sloping demand curve, and the vision of society as simply an aggregate of individuals are easier to grasp than the many qualifications which must be applied to keep these notions intact. Academic economists therefore instruct their students in the easy bits first, leaving the difficult grist for higher-level courses.

At the profound level, it reflects the extent to which economists are so committed to their preferred methodology that they ignore or trivialize points at which their analysis has fundamental weaknesses. Were economics truly worthy of the moniker 'social science' these failures would be reason to abandon the methodology and search for something sounder.

Whatever the reasons, this lazy pedagogy trifurcates economics students into three camps. The vast majority study a minimum of economics in a business degree, and graduate unaware of any flaws in the glass. Members of the second, much smaller group go on to professional academic careers, and treat the flaws as marks of a fine crystal, rather than clear evidence of a broken vessel. The third, a handful, become critics within the profession, who aspire to build more realistic theories and, sometimes, try to make the second group see the cracks in their beloved but broken goblet. These sentiments may appear extreme now, but I doubt that they will appear so by the time you have read this chapter.

Now pour yourself a strong cup of coffee – or any other appropriate stimulant. The next few sections are crucial to understanding both economic theory and its weaknesses, but they can't help but be boring.

'The sum of the interests'

Bentham's statement that 'The community is a fictitious body [...] The interests of the community then is [sic] the sum of the interests of the several members who compose it' is no more than an assertion. To turn this into a theory, economists had to achieve two tasks: to express Bentham's analysis mathematically, and to establish mathematically that it was possible to derive social utility by aggregating individual utility.

One century after Bentham, the founders of neoclassical economics accomplished the first task with relative ease. Over time, the representation of these concepts matured from simple but flawed notions to arcane but watertight models of individual behavior.

The individual consumer as represented by economic theory In keeping with the notion that beneath all individual actions lie the motivations of pleasure-seeking and pain avoidance, early attempts to use utility theory to explain behavior – by which economists meant almost exclusively the consumption of commodities[3] – postulated that each unit consumed of any commodity yielded a certain number of underlying units of satisfaction, called 'utils.' Additional units of a given commodity resulted in a smaller number of additional utils. The picture is as shown in Table 3.1.

TABLE 3.1 'Utils' and change in utils from consuming bananas

Bananas	Utils	Change in utils
1	8	8
2	15	7
3	19	4
4	20	1

For example, one unit of a commodity – say, a banana – yields 8 'utils' of satisfaction to the consumer. Two bananas yield 15 utils, so that the second

---

3 Jevons, one of the three co-founders of neoclassical economics, was justly skeptical that mathematics could treat all behavior. He argued that 'economy does not treat of all human motives. There are motives nearly always present with us, arising from conscience, compassion, or from some moral or religious source, which economy cannot and does not pretend to treat. These will remain to us as outstanding and disturbing forces; they must be treated, if at all, by other appropriate branches of knowledge' (Jevons 1866). However, subsequent economists have applied this theory to all behavior, including interpersonal relations.

banana has contributed seven additional utils to the consumer's satisfaction: one less than the first banana, but still a positive quantity. Three bananas yields

§4 19 utils, so that the change in utils from consuming the third banana is 4 utils.

This concept, that a consumer always derives positive utility from consuming something, but that the rate of increase in utility drops as more units of the commodity are consumed, is the key concept in the economic analysis of human behavior. The change in total utility is known as 'marginal utility,' and the essential belief that this falls as the level of consumption rises is known as the 'law of diminishing marginal utility.' This 'law' asserts that marginal utility is always positive, but always falling: more is always better, but each additional unit consumed gives less satisfaction than previous units.

Obviously, utility is derived from consuming more than just one commodity. Economists assume that the law of diminishing marginal utility applies across *all* commodities, so that additional units of any commodity give the consumer positive but falling amounts of utility. This is shown in Table 3.2, where the first commodity is bananas, and the second, biscuits. Each number in the table shows how many utils the consumer garnered from each combination of bananas and biscuits. Graphically, this yields a set of 3D bars, with the bars getting ever higher as more biscuits and bananas are consumed.

TABLE 3.2 Utils arising from the consumption of two commodities

		BISCUITS			
		0	1	2	3
BANANAS	0	0	8	13	14
	1	9	13	15	18
	2	15	19	24	25
	3	18	25	30	31

§5 However, this representation is already clumsy. For a start, while it is possible to show the absolute number of utils given by any combination of bananas and biscuits, it is a cumbersome way to show the change in the number of utils caused by going from any one combination of biscuits and bananas to any other. Since marginal utility is a key concept, this was a major technical failing of this approach. It is also impossible to provide a geometric picture for more than two commodities.

However, there is another, more obvious shortcoming. By postulating an objective measure of utility, it mooted an apparently impossible degree of precision and objectivity in the measurement of something so intrinsically subjective as personal satisfaction. As a result, the 'cardinal' concept of objectively measurable utility gave way to an 'ordinal'[4] notion, where all that

---

4 Cardinal refers to the ability to attach a precise quantity, whereas ordinal refers to the ability to rank things in size order, without necessarily being able to ascribe a numeric value to each.

could be said is that one combination of commodities gave more or less satisfaction than another combination.[5]

§6

Metaphorically, this treated utility as a mountain, and the consumer as a mountain-climber whose objective was to get as high up this mountain as possible. The mountain itself was a peculiar one: first, it started at 'sea level' – zero consumption gave you zero utility – and then rose sharply because the first units consumed give you the highest 'marginal utility'; and secondly, it went on for ever – the more you consumed, the higher you got. The 'utility mountain' would get flatter as you consumed more, but it would never become completely flat since more consumption always increased your utility.[6]

The final abstraction en route to the modern theory was to drop this '3D' perspective – since the actual 'height' couldn't be specified numerically anyway – and to instead link points of equal 'utility height' into curves, just as contours on a geographic map indicate locations of equal height, or isobars on a weather chart indicate regions of equal pressure.[7]

§7

This representation enabled a conceptual advance which basically gave birth to modern consumer theory – however, as we shall see later, it also introduced an insurmountable intellectual dilemma. Since consumers were presumed to be motivated by the utility they gained from consumption, and points of equal utility height gave them the same satisfaction, then a consumer should be 'indifferent' between any two points on any given curve, since they both represent the same height, or degree of utility. These contours were therefore christened 'indifference curves.'

§8

Since indifference curves were supposed to represent the innate preferences of a rational utility-maximizing consumer, economists turned their minds to what properties these curves could have if the consumer could be said to exhibit truly rational behavior – as neoclassical economists perceived it. In 1948, Paul Samuelson codified these into four principles:

- Completeness: If presented with a choice between two different combinations of goods, a consumer can decide which he prefers (or can decide that he gets the same degree of satisfaction from them, in which case he is said to be indifferent between them).
- Transitivity: If combination A is preferred to combination B, and B to C, then A is preferred to C.

5 As I point out later, the mathematician John von Neumann developed a way that a cardinal measure of utility could be derived, but this was ignored by neoclassical economists (Von Neumann and Morgenstern 1953: 17–29).

6 At its base (where, using my 'bananas and biscuits' example, zero bananas and zero biscuits were consumed), its height was zero. Then as you walked in the bananas direction only (eating bananas but no biscuits), the mountain rose, but at an ever-diminishing rate – it was its steepest at its base, because the very first units consumed gave the greatest 'marginal utility.' The same thing applied in the biscuits direction, while there was some path in the combined 'biscuits and bananas' direction that was the steepest of all to begin with.

7 The Wikipedia entry on contours explains how isobars are derived, and actually mentions indifference curves as an example of them in economics: en.wikipedia.org/wiki/Contour_line.

- Non-satiation: More is always preferred to less. If combination A has as many of all but one commodity as B, and more of that one than B, then A is necessarily preferred to B.
- Convexity: The marginal utility a consumer gets from each commodity falls with additional units, so that indifference curves are convex in shape (shaped like a 'slippery dip').

This meant that indifference curves had a very specific shape: they had to look like a slippery dip that was steepest at its start, and always sloped downwards: the more of a good was consumed, the flatter the curve became, but it never became completely horizontal. And there were a multitude of such curves stacked on top of each other, with each higher one representing a higher degree of utility than the ones below. Economists then used these curves to derive the consumer's demand curve.

§9

Deriving the individual demand curve

Obviously, since utility rises as more is consumed, the consumer would eat an infinite number of bananas and biscuits (yes, I know this is absurd) if not constrained by some other factors. The constraints are the consumer's income, and the prices of bananas and biscuits, so the next step in the economic saga is to notionally combine indifference curves with a consumer's income and prices to determine what a consumer will buy.

In terms of the 'utility mountain' analogy, this amounts to slicing the base of the mountain at an angle, where the slope of the slice represents the prices of biscuits and bananas, and cutting the mountain off at a distance that represents the consumer's income. There is now an obvious peak to the mountain, representing the highest point that the consumer can climb to.

In the '2D' model that economists actually use, the consumer's income is shown by a straight line which connects the quantity of bananas he could buy if he spent all his income on bananas, and the quantity of biscuits he could buy if he spent all his income on biscuits. If the consumer's income was $500, and biscuits cost 10 cents each, then he could purchase 5,000 biscuits; if bananas cost $1 each, then he could purchase 500 bananas. The budget line then connects these two points in a straight line – so that another

§10

feasible combination is 4,000 biscuits and 100 bananas.

According to economists, a rational consumer would purchase the combination of biscuits and bananas which maximized his utility. This combination occurs where the budget line just touches a single indifference curve – in the 3D analogy, it's reaching the edge of the cliff at its highest point. If the consumer purchased any other feasible combination of biscuits and bananas using his income, then he would be forgoing some utility, which would be 'irrational.'[8]

8 Economists assume that consumers spend all their income. They treat savings, in effect, as a form of consumption – only what is 'consumed' are goods in the future.

Have you started to fall asleep yet? Sorry, but as I warned, this stuff is boring. But have some more coffee and stay tuned; after a few more introductory bits, things start to get interesting.

The impact of changing prices on consumer demand

At this point, we have presented only the economic explanation of how a consumer will determine the consumption of any one bundle of commodities, given a fixed income and fixed prices. But what interests economists is what they call a 'demand curve,' which shows how demand for a commodity changes as its price changes, *while the consumer's income remains constant.*

This last condition is crucial – and as we'll see shortly, it is where the whole enterprise comes unstuck. Economists are trying here to separate how a consumer's behavior changes when prices change, from how behavior changes when incomes change. To do this, they have to assume that a change in prices won't change the consumer's income. This is OK if we're considering an isolated consumer who makes a living from, say, producing clothing: changing the price of bananas will have precious little impact on the income he makes from producing clothing.

If we consider a lower price for bananas, then the number of bananas the consumer can buy rises. If at the same time his income and the price of biscuits remain constant, then the budget line moves farther out on the bananas axis, but remains in the same spot on the biscuits axis. In the 3D analogy, this is like cutting a slice through the utility mountain at a different angle. The maximum point in the biscuits direction remains the same, but the maximum point in the bananas direction rises, and the overall hill is larger too – the consumer's maximum utility has risen because he can buy more. §11

Economic theory then repeats this process numerous times – each time considering the same income and same price for biscuits, but a lower and lower price for bananas. Each time, there will be a new combination of biscuits and bananas that the consumer will buy, and the combination of the prices and quantities of bananas purchased is the consumer's demand curve for bananas. We finally have a demand curve, which *normally* slopes downwards as economists predicted. But it doesn't have to – there is still one wrinkle left. This is because, when the price of one good falls, and your income remains fixed, it's possible to increase the consumption of *all* goods – not just the one that has become cheaper.

It is even possible that your consumption of the good that has become cheaper could actually fall as its price falls, if it is so undesirable that you consume it simply because you are poor. Economists call such commodities 'Giffen Goods,' and their favorite alleged example is potatoes during the potato famine in Ireland in the nineteenth century. They argue that as the price of potatoes rose during the famine, the Irish could no longer afford to buy more palatable goods like pork, so their consumption of potatoes actually rose as the famine continued and the price of potatoes also rose.

§12

How's that coffee cup going? Empty? Then it's time you got a refill! There are two more tedious sections to come before the punchline that makes this banal trudge worthwhile.

Income and substitution effects and the 'Law of Demand'

The fact that a fall in price actually lets you consume more of everything can mean that it's possible for the demand curve for a given good to slope upwards at some points – to show the consumer consuming *less* as its price falls (and therefore more of it as its price rises!). This anomaly occurs because when the price of a commodity falls, the consumer's real income in effect increases.

This can be seen in our bananas and biscuits example: if the price of bananas falls while income and all other prices remain constant, then the consumer can buy more bananas without reducing his purchases of any other commodities. Therefore he is materially better off, even though his income hasn't changed.

This in turn can lead to perverse effects if one item in his shopping basket is relatively undesirable compared to more expensive alternatives – say, instant coffee rather than freshly ground beans – and it plays a large role in his budget. If the price of this commodity falls, it is possible the consumer could respond to the effective increase in income by consuming *less* of this product, even though it has become cheaper.

The increase in overall well-being due to the price of a commodity falling is known as the 'income effect.' It can lead you to consume more of the product, or it can lead you to consume less – it depends on the commodity. The pure impact of a fall in price for a commodity is known as the 'substitution effect.' So long as we are dealing with 'goods' – things which increase the consumer's utility – then the substitution effect is always going to be in the opposite direction to the change in price.

For this reason, economists say that the substitution effect is always negative. They don't mean that substitution is a bad thing, but that price and quantity move in opposite directions: if price falls, consumption rises. The income effect can be negative too – so that you consume *more* of a good as the *fall* in its price effectively increases your real income. But it can also be positive: you can consume *less* of a good when the *fall* in its price effectively increases your real income.

The always negative substitution effect is the phenomenon economists are trying to isolate with the demand curve, to establish what they call the 'Law of Demand' – that demand always increases when price falls. This 'law' is an essential element of the neoclassical model of how prices are set, which says that in competitive markets, supply will equal demand at the equilibrium price. For this model to work, it's vital that there is only one price at which that happens, so it's vital for the model that demand always increases as price falls (and similarly that supply always rises as price rises).

However the income effect can get in the way.

Economists thus found it necessary to search for a way to divide the impact of any change in price into the income effect and the substitution effect. If the income effect could be subtracted from a price change, this would leave the substitution effect as the pure impact on consumption of a change in relative prices. The problem is, though, that neither the 'income effect' nor the 'substitution effect' is directly observable: all we actually see is a consumer's purchases changing as the price of a commodity changes.

Economists dreamt up a way of at least notionally subtracting the income effect from a price change, using indifference curves. The clue is that, with income fixed and price falling, the lower price lets a consumer enjoy a higher effective standard of living – which in their model was manifested by the consumer reaching a higher indifference curve.

Since, to an economist, the real object of individual behavior is utility maximization, and since any point on a single indifference curve generates the same utility as any other point, then in utility terms the consumer's 'psychic income' is constant along this curve.

The substitution effect of a price fall could thus be isolated by 'holding the consumer's utility constant' by keeping him to the same indifference curve, and rotating the budget constraint to reflect the new relative price regime. This amounts to reducing the consumer's income until such time as he can achieve the same level of satisfaction as before, but with a different combination of biscuits and bananas. Then the budget constraint is moved out to restore the consumer's income to its actual level and, *voilà*, we have separated the impact of a price change into the substitution and income effects.

§13

The demand curve derived from neutralizing the income effect is known as the 'Hicksian compensated demand curve,' after both the person who first dreamed it up (the English economist John Hicks) and the procedure used. It finally establishes the 'Law of Demand' for a single, isolated consumer: the demand for a commodity will rise if its price falls.

The dissident Australian economist Ted Wheelwright once described this hypothesized activity as 'tobogganing up and down your indifference curves until you disappear up your own abscissa,' and it's easy to see why.

Nonetheless, the end result is that desired by economists: increasing a product's price will reduce a consumer's demand for that product: an individual's demand curve slopes downwards. The 'Law of Demand' holds for a single consumer. There will be the odd commodity where a positive income effect outweighs the negative substitution effect, but these can be regarded as 'the exceptions that prove the rule' and safely ignored.

OK, take one more swig of coffee for the final tedious bit of detail – how economists consider the impact of changes in income on demand.

How rising income affects demand

As with all other issues, economic theory uses indifference curves to handle this topic. The relevant commodity is placed on the horizontal axis, all other commodities on the vertical, and the budget constraint is 'moved out' (see Figure 14). This represents an increase in income with relative prices held constant – unlike a pivot, which represents a change in relative prices with income held constant. Economists say that the resulting plot – known as an 'Engel curve' – shows a consumer maximizing his utility as his income rises.

One point that is essential to the approaching critique is that Engel curves can take almost any shape at all. The shapes show how demand for a given commodity changes as a function of income, and four broad classes of commodities result: necessities or 'inferior goods,' which take up a diminishing share of spending as income grows; 'Giffen goods,' whose actual consumption declines as income rises; luxuries or 'superior goods,' whose consumption takes up an increasing share of income as it increases; and 'neutral' or 'homothetic' goods, where their consumption remains a constant proportion of income as income rises.

Necessities include such things as, for example, toilet paper. Your purchases of toilet paper will fall as a percentage of your total spending as you get wealthier (though you may buy more expensive paper). Some products that are substitutes for better-quality products when you are very poor – baked beans, perhaps – will disappear altogether from your consumption as you get wealthier, and economists refer to these as Giffen goods. Luxuries range from, for example, tourism to original works of art. Spending on holidays rises as income rises, and artworks are definitely the province of the rich.

I can't provide an example of a 'neutral good,' because strictly speaking, there are none. Spending on such a commodity would constitute the same percentage of income as a person rose from abject poverty to unimaginable wealth, and there is simply no commodity which occupies the same proportion of a homeless person's expenditure as it does of a billionaire's. But economists nonetheless have termed a word for someone whose preferences look like this: they call this pattern of consumption 'homothetic' (I call it 'neutral' in Figure 14d).

§14

Strictly speaking, no one could have homothetic preferences, and society in general would not display 'homothetic preferences' either: as income rose, the pattern of consumption of both individuals and society would change. Poor individuals and societies spend most of their money on staples (such as rice) while rich individuals and societies spend most of theirs on discretionary items (like the latest high-tech gadgets).

It may seem like explaining the obvious to say this, but the point is crucial to the approaching critique: as you age and as your income (hopefully) rises, your consumption pattern will change, as will the consumption pattern of a society as it gets richer. Thus any consumer is going to have lots of necessities and luxuries in his consumption, but no 'homothetic' goods.

Two is a crowd

The 'Law of Demand' has thus been proved – but only for a single consumer. Is it possible to generalize it so that it applies at the level of the market as well? In a nutshell, the answer is no. In the first of the many 'aggregation fallacies' that plague neoclassical economics, what applies when one consumer is isolated from all others does not apply when there is more than one consumer: what is true of Robinson Crusoe, so to speak, is not true of the society consisting of Robinson Crusoe and Man Friday.

With Crusoe alone on his island, the distribution of income doesn't matter. But when Man Friday turns up, the distribution of income does matter, in ways that completely undermine everything involved in deriving an individual's demand curve.

One condition for deriving an individual's 'Hicksian compensated' demand curve for bananas was that changing the price of bananas didn't *directly* alter that individual's income.[9] That condition fails when you move from a one-person, two-commodity model to a two-person, two-commodity world – let alone anything more complicated – because changing the price of bananas (relative to biscuits) will alter the incomes of both individuals.

Unless they're clones of each other, one individual will earn more than the other from selling bananas – so an increase in the price of bananas makes the banana producer – let's call him Crusoe – richer, while making Friday poorer. This means that Crusoe is capable of buying more biscuits when the price of bananas rises. It's no longer possible to change the price of bananas while keeping constant the number of biscuits that the consumer can buy.

The complications don't stop there. Since the theory of the supply curve – which we'll encounter in the next two chapters – assumes that an increase in demand will drive up the price, the budget 'line' can't be a line: *it must be a curve*. In the isolated consumer example, not only did we assume that changing prices didn't alter the consumer's income, we also assumed that the consumer's purchases didn't affect the market price. This assumption is also invalid once we consider more than one consumer, which we must do to construct a market demand curve.

When Friday purchases the first banana, he pays a low price; the second banana costs more to produce (because of 'diminishing marginal productivity,' which we encounter in the next two chapters), so as well as his income changing, the price for bananas rises as his consumption of them rises. Each additional banana that Friday buys will therefore be more expensive than the

---

9 This is different to indirectly altering the consumer's effective income via a change in prices.

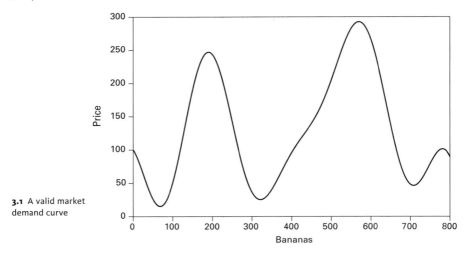

3.1 A valid market demand curve

previous one. The budget *curve* might start at the same point as the 'line' did (with an isolated consumer) when consumption is zero, but it must slope more steeply than the line as the consumer's consumption rises above zero.

The situation is no better when we consider the demand that Crusoe has for the bananas he produces himself: his income rises as price rises, increasing his income, and his demand for bananas still drives the cost up – because according to the theory of the supply curve, the cost of production rises owing to falling productivity as output rises. There is no way to know which effect will dominate.

What was a straightforward exercise when each consumer was considered in isolation is therefore an unholy mess when we consider more than one individual, which we must do to derive a market demand curve. You can still derive points of tangency between these moving budget curves and the fixed indifference curves for each individual, and thus derive an individual demand curve, but it will no longer necessarily obey the 'Law' of Demand – and you can no longer easily separate the income and substitution effects either, since you cannot control incomes independently of prices anymore.

Finally, the market demand curve that is produced by summing these now poorly behaved individual demand curves will conflate these wildly varying influences: increasing price will favor the producer (thus increasing his demand) while disadvantaging the consumer (thus decreasing his demand); rising income for the luxury-good producer will increase his income while decreasing that of the necessity producer. As the sum of these tendencies, the market demand curve will thus occasionally show demand rising as price falls, but it will also occasionally show demand falling as price falls. It will truly be a curve, because, as the neoclassical economists who first considered this issue proved (Gorman 1953), *it can take any shape at all* – except one that doubles back on itself.

Crucially, it can disobey the so-called 'Law of Demand': the quantity demanded can rise as the price rises. This has nothing to do with snob value, or price signaling quality, or any of the behavioral wrinkles that critics often throw at the assumptions that neoclassical economists make. The wavy demand curve shown in Figure 3.1 can be generated by ordinary, everyday commodities as soon as you move beyond the isolated individual.

This result – known as the 'Sonnenschein-Mantel-Debreu [SMD] conditions' – proves that the 'Law' of Demand does not apply to a market demand curve. If the market demand curve can have any shape at all, then there can be two or more possible demand levels for any given price, even if all consumers are rational utility maximizers who individually obey the Law of Demand. If only neoclassical economists had stated the result that honestly and accurately when it was first derived almost sixty years ago, economics today might be very different.

Instead, because the result was found by neoclassical economists who wished to prove the opposite of what they had in fact discovered, the result has been buried by a degree of obfuscation and evasion that makes the average corporate cover-up look tame by comparison.

Cut off at Pythagoras' pass

This result was first derived by neoclassical economists who had posed the question 'under what conditions will the market demand curve have the same properties as the individual demand curve?', and they were hardly pleased with their discovery. Though technically the analysis was a 'tour de force' – the sort of technical prowess that wins you awed respect from your peers – practically they clearly wished that they had proved the opposite result: that, despite the conundrums in moving from an isolated individual to multiple consumers, the Law of Demand still held.

They found themselves in the same situation as the ancient Pythagorean mathematicians, who believed that all numbers could be expressed as the ratio of two integers. The discovery that this was not the case 'destroyed with one stroke the belief that everything could be expressed in integers, on which the whole Pythagorean philosophy up to then had been based' (Von Kurt 1945: 260).

Today, we're all familiar with the fact that if you draw two lines at right angles that are precisely one inch long, and draw a line between them, that line's length will be the square root of two inches long, which is an irrational number – a number that can't be expressed as the ratio of two integers. The fact that combining two rational numbers according to the laws of geometry generates an irrational number is now common knowledge. Neither mathematics nor the world has collapsed as a result – in fact both mathematics and the world are far richer for this discovery and the many that followed on from it.

However, the initial reaction of Pythagorean mathematicians to this discovery was brutal: they allegedly drowned Hippasus of Metapontum, who was the first to discover that irrational numbers existed. But to their credit, they subsequently embraced the existence of irrational numbers, and mathematics developed dramatically as a result.

Economists could have reacted intelligently to their discovery too. They had proved that if you take two consumers whose individual demand curves obey the Law of Demand, and add them together to get a market demand curve, that curve does not necessarily obey the Law of Demand. So adding two or more 'rational' consumers together generates an 'irrational' market. Therefore, market analysis has to transcend the simple rules that seemed to work for isolated consumers, just as mathematicians had to transcend the rules that apply when mathematical operations on rational numbers return only rational numbers.

Such a reaction by economists could have led to a far richer vision of economics than the simplistic one in which the Law of Demand applies, and in which all markets are assumed to be in equilibrium. Unfortunately, the way that they did react made the irate Pythagoreans who drowned Hippasus look like amateurs. Rather than drowning the discoverer of the result, neoclassical economists drowned the result itself.

Having proved that in general the 'Law of Demand' did not apply at the level of the market, they looked for the conditions under which it would apply, *and then assumed that those conditions applied to all markets*. It's as if Pythagoreans, on discovering that the square root of two was an irrational number, forbade for evermore the drawing of equal-sided right-angled triangles.

The Pythagorean analogy continues to apply here, because the conditions that were needed to 'ensure' that the Law of Demand applied at the market level are in fact a 'proof by contradiction' that it can't apply. Proof by contradiction is a venerable mathematical technique, and it can be used to establish that the square root of two is an irrational number. Not knowing the answer to a question – 'Is the square root of two a rational number?' – you assume that the answer is 'Yes,' and then follow through the logic of your assumption. If you generate a contradiction, you then know that the correct answer is 'No: the square root of two is not a rational number.'[10]

The two 'conditions' that economists found were necessary to guarantee that the 'Law of Demand' applied to the market demand curve were:

a) that all Engel curves are straight lines; and
b) that the Engel curves of all consumers are parallel to each other.

The first condition means that all commodities have to be neither luxuries

---

10 Hippasus apparently used the geometry of pentagrams to prove the existence of irrational numbers. The proof by contradiction that the square root of two is irrational, though mathematical, is very easy to understand. See footnote 1, page 404.

nor necessities nor inferior goods, but 'neutral' or 'homothetic.' Therefore your ratios in which you consume different goods would have to remain fixed regardless of your income: if on an income of $100 a week, you spent $10 on pizza, then on an income of $100,000 a week you would have to spend $10,000 on pizza.

§15

Clearly this is nonsense: as incomes rise, your consumption pattern would alter. There is only one situation in which this wouldn't apply: if there was only one commodity to consume. That is the real meaning of condition (a): there is only one commodity.

Condition (b) is just as absurd. For all consumers to have parallel Engel curves, all consumers have to have identical tastes. Clearly this is also nonsense: different consumers are identifiable by the very fact that they do have different tastes.

Even saying that the Engel curves of different consumers are parallel to each other is an obfuscation – it implies that two consumers could have parallel *but different* Engel curves, just as two lines that are parallel to each other but separated by an inch are clearly different lines. However, as anyone who has studied geometry at school knows, parallel lines that pass through the same point *are the same line*. Since a consumer with zero income consumes zero goods in neoclassical theory,[11] all Engel curves pass through the point 'zero bananas, zero biscuits' when income is zero. Therefore condition (b) really is that 'the Engel curves of all consumers are identical.'

There is only one situation in which this could apply: if there was only one consumer.

That is the real meaning of these two conditions: *the Law of Demand will apply if*, and only if, *there is only one commodity and only one consumer*. But in such a situation, the very idea of a 'Law of Demand' makes no sense. The whole purpose of the Law of Demand is to explain how relative prices are set, but if there is just one commodity and one consumer, then there can be no relative prices. We have a contradiction: we start from assuming that the Law of Demand applies, and then find that for this to be true, there can be only one commodity and one consumer – a situation in which the Law of Demand has no meaning.

These conditions are thus a proof by contradiction that the Law of Demand does not apply to the market demand curve: market demand does not necessarily increase when price falls, even if individual demand does.

This discovery is thus akin to the Pythagorean discovery of irrational numbers: adding together 'rational' consumers can result in an 'irrational' market. This discovery should have had an equally revolutionary – and ultimately beneficial – impact upon economic theory. The simple parables of intersecting demand and supply curves would have had to give way to a more

11 They ignore the role of credit in the economy, an issue that looms very large in my later critique of macroeconomics.

complicated but necessarily more realistic theory, in which prices would not be in equilibrium and the distribution of income would alter as prices alter.

If only.

Drowning the result

The economist who first discovered this result – the Hippasus of neo-classical economics – was William Gorman. As noted earlier, Hippasus was (allegedly) drowned for his trouble. Gorman, on the other hand, drowned his own result. He proved the result in the context of working out whether there was an economy-wide equivalent to an individual's indifference curves: 'we will show that there is just one community indifference locus through each point *if, and only if*, the Engel curves for different individuals at the same prices are parallel straight lines' (Gorman 1953: 63; emphasis added).

He then concluded, believe it or not, that these conditions were 'intuitively reasonable': 'The necessary and sufficient condition quoted above is intuitively reasonable. It says, in effect, that an extra unit of purchasing power should be spent in the same way no matter to whom it is given' (ibid.: 64).

'*Intuitively reasonable*'? As I frequently say to my own students, I couldn't make this stuff up! Far from being either intuitive or reasonable, Gorman's rationalization is a denial of one of the fundamental issues that most non-economists think economists must understand: the distribution of income. If the distribution of income changes, then surely the consumption pattern of society will change. I regard Gorman's statement here as the economic equivalent of the remark attributed to Marie Antoinette on being told that the peasants had no bread: 'Let them eat cake.'[12]

Gorman's original result, though published in a leading journal, was not noticed by economists in general – possibly because he was a precursor of the extremely mathematical economist who became commonplace after the 1970s but was a rarity in the 1950s. Only a handful of economists would have been capable of reading his paper back then. Consequently the result was later rediscovered by a number of economists – hence its convoluted name as the 'Sonnenschein-Mantel-Debreu conditions.'

These economists were far less sanguine than Gorman about the 'conditions' needed for the Law of Demand to apply to a market demand curve. However, they still failed to make the logical leap to realize that they had disproved a core belief of neoclassical economics, and their statements of the result were, if anything, even more obtuse than was Gorman's: 'Can an arbitrary continuous function [...] be an excess demand function for some commodity in a general equilibrium economy? [...] we prove that every polynomial [...] is an excess demand function for a specified commodity

---

12 The remark may well be apocryphal – see en.wikipedia.org/wiki/Let_them_eat_cake; but the sentiment of the wealthy disregarding the fate of the poor certainly played a major role in ushering in the French Revolution.

in some *n* commodity economy [...] every continuous real-valued function is approximately an excess demand function' (Sonnenschein 1972: 549–50).

Translating this into English, a polynomial is a function consisting of constants and powers of some variable. The most well-known polynomials are the equation for a straight line, which is a polynomial of order one, and a parabola (a polynomial of order two). Any smooth curvy line that doesn't cross over itself can be fitted by a polynomial of sufficiently high order, so what Sonnenschein is saying here is that a demand curve can take any shape at all, except one that intersects with itself.[13] Therefore the 'Law of Demand' does *not* apply to the market demand curve. His joint summary of this result with Shafer for the encyclopedic *Handbook of Mathematical Economics* (Arrow et al. 1981–93) was more aware of the absurdity of the conditions, but still didn't connect the dots to comprehend that the conditions were a proof by contradiction that the Law of Demand is false:

> First, when preferences are homothetic and the distribution of income (value of wealth) is independent of prices, then the market demand function (market excess demand function) has all the properties of a consumer demand function [...]
>
> Second, with general (in particular non-homothetic) preferences, even if the distribution of income is fixed, market demand functions need not satisfy in any way the classical restrictions which characterize consumer demand functions [...]
>
> The importance of the above results is clear: strong restrictions are needed in order to justify the hypothesis that a market demand function has the characteristics of a consumer demand function. Only in special cases can an economy be expected to act as an 'idealized consumer.' The utility hypothesis tells us nothing about market demand unless it is augmented by additional requirements. (Shafer and Sonnenschein 1993)

As opaque as those statements might be, if they had been clearly passed on to economics students, the realization that the simple parables of supply and demand had to be replaced by something more sophisticated could have developed.

If only.

Don't tell the children

We now confront what will become a common theme in this book: the mendacious nature of economic textbooks. In the hands of economics textbook writers, the opaque but accurate statements of the SMD conditions above either disappear completely, or are portrayed in such a way that their significance will be perceived only by hypercritical students – like yours truly when I suffered through these courses while doing my Master's.

13 Or returns two values for one input.

For many years, the leading text for Honors, Master's and PhD programs was Hal Varian's *Microeconomic Analysis* (Varian 1992). Varian 'summarized' this research so opaquely that it's no surprise that most PhD students – including those who later went on to write the next generation of undergraduate textbooks – didn't grasp how profoundly it challenged the foundations of neoclassical theory.

Varian started with the vaguest possible statement of the result: 'Unfortunately [...] The aggregate demand function will in general possess no interesting properties [...] Hence, the theory of the consumer places no restrictions on aggregate behavior in general.'

The statement 'no interesting properties' could imply to the average student that the market demand curve didn't differ in any substantive way from the individual demand curve – the exact opposite of the theoretical result. The next sentence was more honest, but rather than admitting outright that this meant that the 'Law of Demand' didn't apply at the market level, he immediately reassured students that there was a way to get around this problem, which was to: 'Suppose that all individual consumers' indirect utility functions take the Gorman form [... where] the marginal propensity to consume good j *is independent of the level of income of any consumer and also constant across consumers* [...] This demand function can in fact be *generated* by a representative consumer' (ibid.: 153–4; emphases added. Curiously the innocuous word 'generated' in this edition replaced the more loaded word 'rationalized' in the 1984 edition.)

Finally, when discussing aggregate demand, he made a vague and reassuring reference to more technical work: 'it is sometimes convenient to think of the aggregate demand as the demand of some "representative consumer" [...] The conditions under which this can be done are rather stringent, but a discussion of this issue is beyond the scope of this book [...]' (Varian 1984: 268).

It's little wonder that PhD students didn't realize that these conditions, rather than merely being 'rather stringent,' undermined the very foundations of neoclassical economics. They then went on to build 'representative agent' models of the macroeconomy in which the entire economy is modeled as a single consumer, believing that these models have been shown to be valid. In fact, the exact opposite is the case.

The modern replacement for Varian is Andreu Mas-Colell's hyper-mathematical – but utterly non-empirical – *Microeconomic Theory* (Mas-Colell, Whinston et al. 1995). At one level, this text is much more honest about the impact of the SMD conditions than was Varian's. In a section accurately described as 'Anything goes: the Sonnenschein-Mantel-Debreu Theorem,' Mas-Colell concludes that a market demand curve can have any shape at all, even when derived from consumers whose individual demand curves are downward-sloping:

Can [... an arbitrary function] coincide with the excess demand function of an economy for every p [price ...] Of course [... the arbitrary function] must be continuous, it must be homogeneous of degree zero, and it must satisfy Walras' law. But for any [arbitrary function] satisfying these three conditions, it turns out that the answer is, again, 'yes.' (Ibid.: 602)

But still, the import of this result is buried in what appear to the student to be difficult problems in mathematics, rather than a fundamental reason to abandon supply and demand analysis. Earlier, when considering whether a market demand curve can be derived, Mas-Colell begins with the question: 'When can we compute meaningful measures of aggregate welfare using [...] the welfare measurement techniques [...] for individual consumers? (ibid.: 116).

He then proves that this can be done when there is 'a fictional individual whose utility maximization problem when facing society's budget set would generate the economy's aggregate demand function' (ibid.: 116). However, for this to be possible, there must also exist a 'social welfare function' which: 'accurately expresses society's judgments on how individual utilities have to be compared to produce an ordering of possible social outcomes. We also assume that social welfare functions are increasing, concave, and whenever convenient, differentiable' (ibid.: 117).

This is already a case of assuming what you wish to prove – any form of social conflict is assumed away – but it's still not sufficient to generate the result Mas-Colell wants to arrive at. The problem is that the actual distribution of wealth and income in society will determine 'how individual utilities are compared' in the economy, and there is no guarantee that this will correspond to this 'social welfare function.'

The next step in his 'logic' should make the truly logical – and the true believers in economic freedom – recoil in horror, but it is in fact typical of the sorts of assumptions that neoclassical economists routinely make to try to keep their vision of a perfectly functioning market economy together. To ensure that the actual distribution of wealth and income matches the social welfare function, *Mas-Colell assumes the existence of a benevolent dictator who redistributes wealth and income prior to commerce taking place*: 'Let us now hypothesize that there is a process, *a benevolent central authority* perhaps, *that*, for any given prices p and aggregate wealth function w, *redistributes wealth in order to maximize social welfare*' (ibid.: 117; emphases added).

So free market capitalism will maximize social welfare *if, and only if, there is a benevolent dictator who redistributes wealth prior to trade*??? Why don't students in courses on advanced microeconomics simply walk out at this point?

I surmise that there are three main reasons, the first of which is banal. Mas-Colell's book is huge – just short of 1,000 pages – and lecturers would cherry-pick the sections they teach. I doubt that most students are exposed to this statement by their instructors, and few are likely to read parts that aren't required reading for pleasure alone.

Secondly, the entire text is presented as difficult exercises in applied mathematics. Students are probably so consumed with deriving the required answers that they gloss over English-language statements of these assumptions which make it blatantly obvious how insane they are.

Thirdly, by the time students get to this level – normally in PhD programs – they are so locked into the neoclassical 'assumptions don't matter' mindset that I discuss in Chapter 8 that they don't even worry if an assumption is insane.

From this bizarre point on, Mas-Colell, like Varian before him, encourages students to build models of the macroeconomy in which all agents have 'the Gorman form' of utility function – i.e. models of the macroeconomy in which there is one commodity and one consumer – so that students believe that the entire economy can be modeled as a single representative agent. Mas-Colell cautions that this involves a special assumption, but that caution is probably lost in the mist that envelops the mind of a budding neoclassical economist:

> If there is a normative representative consumer, the preferences of this consumer have welfare significance and the aggregate demand function can be used to make welfare judgments by means of the techniques [used for individual consumers]. In doing so however, *it should never be forgotten that a given wealth distribution rule* [imposed by the 'benevolent central authority'] *is being adhered to and that the 'level of wealth' should always be understood as the 'optimally distributed level of wealth.'* (Ibid.: 118; emphasis added)

These high-level texts, though, are at least honest that there is a problem in aggregating from the individual consumer to the market demand curve. Undergraduate students instead are reassured that there is no problem. Paul Samuelson's iconic undergraduate textbook makes the following didactic statement about how a market demand curve is derived, and whether it obeys the 'Law of Demand,' which flatly contradicts the SMD results:

> The market demand curve is found by adding together the quantities demanded by all individuals at each price. *Does the market demand curve obey the law of downward-sloping demand? It certainly does.*
>
> If prices drop, for example, the lower prices attract new customers through the substitution effect. In addition, a price reduction will induce extra purchases of goods by existing consumers through both the income and the substitution effects. Conversely, a rise in the price of a good will cause some of us to buy less. (Samuelson and Nordhaus 2010: 48; emphasis added)

The leading undergraduate textbook today, by Gregory Mankiw, is equally misleading. It also implies that all that is needed to derive a market demand curve is to horizontally sum individual demand curves: 'The table in Figure 2 shows the demand schedules for ice cream for the two individuals in this market – Catherine and Nicholas [...] The market demand at each price is the sum of the two individual demands [...] Notice that we sum the individual demand curves horizontally to obtain the market demand curve [...]' (Mankiw 2008: 68).

Other undergraduate textbooks either ignore the issue completely, or make similarly false statements. Who, then, can blame undergraduate economics students for believing that all is well with the underlying theory? The blame instead lies with textbook writers, and the question this raises is, *do they know they are at fault?* Did they knowingly conceal this advanced result from their students, or were they themselves ignorant of it?

Samuelson was certainly aware of Gorman's result, though he may not have followed the subsequent work of Sonnenschein and others because he believed he had proved that the Law of Demand *does* apply to the market demand curve (Samuelson 1956). And so he had – but using an assumption which shows how utterly unrealistic even the most famous of neoclassical economists can be. He began quite sensibly, by noting that it was absurd to model an entire country as a single utility-maximizing individual:

> What defense do we make when challenged on the use of community indifference curves for a country or group of individuals? I suppose one of the following:
>
> (a) We may claim that our country is inhabited by Robinson Crusoe alone and claim only to show how trade between such single person countries is determined. This is admittedly not very realistic.
>
> (b) In order to give the appearance of being more realistic, we may claim that our country is inhabited by a number of identical individuals with identical tastes; they must also have identical initial endowments of goods if this artifice of examining what happens to the representative individual's indifference curves is to give us a true description of the resulting market equilibrium. This case, too, is not very realistic, though it may seem a slight improvement over Robinson Crusoe [...]. (Ibid.: 3)

He then noted that most shopping is done by families, and since these consist of separate individuals, it is impossible even to construct a 'family indifference curve,' so that consumption by a family will also violate the foundations of the Law of Demand (the so-called Axioms of Revealed Preference, which are discussed in the addendum to this chapter).

However, he next surmised that *if, within the family, optimal transfers of income are undertaken,* then a family indifference curve *can* be constructed which has all the properties of an individual indifference curve.

> Since blood is thicker than water, the preferences of the different members are interrelated by what might be called a 'consensus' or 'social welfare function' which takes into account the deservingness or ethical worths of

the consumption levels of each of the members. The family acts as if it were maximizing their joint welfare function [...] *Income must always be reallocated among the members of our family society so as to keep the 'marginal social significance of every dollar' equal.* (Ibid.: 10–11; emphasis added)

Finally, he hypothesized that if the entire nation behaves like one big happy family, and optimally reallocates income between its members prior to consumption, then society will also have 'well-behaved' indifference curves that obey the 'Law of Demand':

The same argument will apply to all of society *if optimal reallocations of income can be assumed to keep the ethical worth of each person's marginal dollar equal.* By means of Hicks's composite commodity theorem and by other considerations, a rigorous proof is given that the newly defined social or community indifference contours have the regularity properties of ordinary individual preference contours (nonintersection, convexity to the origin, etc.). (Ibid.: 21; emphasis added)

Words fail me. Samuelson had 'proved' that social indifference curves exist – and therefore that market demand curves behave just like individual ones – by assuming that in a capitalist society, incomes are continuously adjusted so that an ethical distribution of income is achieved. *Did he even live in the United States?*[14] Yet on this basis, he confidently flourishes to his students that the market demand curve 'certainly does [...] obey the law of downward-sloping demand.'

Samuelson's reason for perpetuating a falsehood is thus similar to Gorman's, who was capable of holding the equally delusional view that the proposition that 'an extra unit of purchasing power should be spent in the same way no matter to whom it is given' is 'intuitively reasonable.' So Samuelson, in a bizarre way, 'knew' what he was doing.

But in general I expect that the reason that undergraduate textbooks (written by lesser lights than Samuelson and Gorman) are so misleading is that *the authors themselves are unaware of this critical literature.*

This may seem bizarre: surely textbook writers must know the economic literature thoroughly in order to write a textbook in the first place? And haven't they done Master's and PhD courses, where they would at least have to read Varian or Mas-Colell on this topic?

Maybe. However, as I've pointed out above, the advanced textbooks present this result in such an obtuse way that it would be possible for a Mankiw to read this material, pass exams on it, and never even contemplate its true import. He might remember the 'Gorman form' limitation that had to be imposed to make aggregation possible, but he would probably

14 Mas-Colell's assumption of a 'benevolent central authority' that 'redistributes wealth in order to maximize social welfare' is probably derived from this ridiculous paper by Samuelson, since he references it as a paper 'For further discussion' (Mas-Colell, Whinston et al. 1995: 118).

regard this as just too difficult to teach to undergraduates. Undergraduate economic textbooks themselves have been 'dumbed down' so much in the last thirty years that even indifference curves – an essential element in this farce – are no longer taught in first-year courses. So the basics needed to even explain why there might be a problem are no longer part of the introductory pedagogy. Also, I expect that the Mankiws of the economics profession haven't read the original papers by Sonnenschein, Mantel and so on – and as I've noted, in a way they can't be criticized for this. Academics are accustomed to not having to read the original literature in their discipline, because they rely on their textbooks to accurately portray the key results of fundamental research. This belief is justified in physics – where even introductory texts point out that quantum mechanics and relativity can't be reconciled – but it is a false belief in economics.

Finally, in stark contrast to how a true science develops, this entire literature was developed not to explain an empirically observed phenomenon, but to examine the logical coherence of an utterly abstract, non-empirical model of consumer behavior. Downward-sloping demand curves were therefore not an empirical regularity for which a theory was needed, but a belief that economists had about the nature of demand that the vast majority of them took for granted. Most of them continue to hold this belief, unaware that mathematically erudite economists have shown that it is false. Since the underlying discipline is non-empirical, there is no disconnect between theory and reality that might warn them that something is wrong with the theory.

Worse still, the rationalization of a 'representative consumer' permeates modern economics – it has even taken over macroeconomic analysis, so that economists model an entire economy as if there is only one person in it (which they describe by the more general term of 'representative agent'). Many academic economists doubtless believe that the representative agent has been shown to be a valid abstraction. Yet far from being valid, it is in fact a fudge, devised to get around the failure to prove that society can be reduced to the sum of its constituent individuals.

Following the madding crowd

There are many other reasons why economists did not recoil from the patent absurdities outlined above, and search for a sounder approach to economic theory than Bentham's individualistic calculus.

One is that economics has been wedded to the vision of society as simply a sum of utility-maximizing individuals since the inception of neoclassical economics in the 1870s. When the proof came, one century later, that this vision was internally inconsistent, the commitment to the vision was too strong to break. Better to search for special conditions which could let the theory survive – however ludicrous they might be – than to admit failure.

A second reason is that the peculiar language and mathematics used to derive these results makes it difficult to see just how absurd the assumptions needed to sustain the aggregation process are. It sounds much more highbrow to say that 'preferences are assumed to be homothetic and affine in income' than it does to say 'we assume all consumers are identical and never change their spending habits as their incomes increase.'

A third reason, perhaps the key one, is the division of mainstream economists into effective 'castes,' with only a tiny but exalted subset of the profession undertaking the detailed mathematical work needed to discover the weaknesses in the theory. The vast majority of economists believe that this high caste, the mathematical economists, did their work properly, and proved that the theory is internally consistent. The caste has indeed done its work properly, but it has proved precisely the opposite: that the theory is consistent only under the most restrictive and specious of assumptions.

However, rather than taking the next logical step, and acknowledging that the foundations of economics are unsound and must therefore be changed, most mathematical economists are so wedded to this way of thinking, and so ignorant of the real world, that they instead invent some fudge to disguise the gaping hole they have uncovered in the theory.

The majority of economists, blithely unaware of this state of affairs, then accept this fudge by the Brahmins of the profession as faithfully as devout Hindus accept the cleansing properties of the Ganges river. As a result, the fudge then turns up in more mundane areas of economics, such as 'macroeconomics' (discussed in Chapter 10), where economists today analyze the economy as if it consisted solely of a single representative agent.

Consequently, these supposedly more practical theories can provide zip guidance in the serious business of managing a market economy. You would do as well to consult a Ouija board as an economist who rigorously follows economic theory when giving advice.

The Sonnenschein-Mantel-Debreu result is one of many that have effectively split the caste of mathematical economists into two sects. One pretends that business as usual can continue, despite the presence of this (and many other) fallacies in the creed. The other is dabbling in alternative religions – such as complexity theory, or evolutionary economics.

Sadly, the uninformed majority of the profession believes that the first sect is the bearer of the true religion, and that the members of the second sect have betrayed the faith. A more accurate analogy is that the dabblers in alternative religions are experiencing the first flushes of adolescence, while the majority of the profession remains mired in infancy. Clearly, the Benthamite ambition to portray society as simply an aggregate of its individual members is a failure. The whole is more than the sum of the parts.

The neoclassical rejoinder The great irony of this particular critique of economics is that it was constructed by its supporters. There is, as a result, no articulate rejoinder. Instead there are rationalizations, such as the 'representative agent' – which, as in Varian (1984), are often openly described as such.

If a defence were to be given of this practice, it would probably be what Samuelson termed 'the F-twist': that the assumptions of a theory don't matter; instead all that counts is how accurately a theory predicts reality. This popular but clearly invalid methodological defense is debunked in Chapter 8.

So what?

It might seem strange to make such a song and dance about whether market demand curves slope downwards. While economic theory clearly fails to prove that market demand falls smoothly as price rises, there are some sound reasons why demand might generally be a negative function of price. For example, a rise in the price of a commodity can force poorer consumers to substitute some cheaper alternative – or go without. So why does it matter that economists can't prove this?

First, it matters because economists had hoped to prove that a market economy necessarily maximizes social welfare. The SMD conditions establish that there is no measure of social welfare that is independent of the existing distribution of income, and that the distribution of income is not based solely on merit – it also reflects consumption patterns as well, since a change in consumption will alter the distribution of income.

Secondly, if we take the SMD conditions seriously, economic theory cannot rule out demand curves with a shape like that of Figure 3.1 (see page 52). Aesthetics aside, one of the many problems which such a curve presents for economic theory is that the resulting marginal revenue curve (defined on page 79) is even more volatile, and it can intersect the marginal cost curve (which we confront in the next chapter) in more than one place. This possibility undermines one of the key articles of the neoclassical faith, that 'everything happens in equilibrium.' If there are multiple points of intersection between marginal cost and marginal revenue, there will be multiple points where 'everything happens.' How then can you determine which will prevail in practice, let alone decide whether any one equilibrium is better or worse than any other?

These dilemmas flow from what appeared at the time to be a conceptual advance – dropping the fiction that utility could be measured in units akin to those we use to gauge weight, etc. While this was indeed more realistic, its interaction with two other aspects of economic theory made it impossible to aggregate the utility of two or more individuals.   §16

The culprits are the highly subjective nature of the concept of utility, and the belief that the price system determines income distribution. Since a change in relative prices will change the distribution of income, it therefore changes who consumes what, and hence the 'sum' of the subjective utility of all individuals. Since utility is subjective,[15] there is no way to determine whether one distribution of income generates more or less aggregate utility than any other.

Economists originally used this aspect of their theory to argue against social reformers who wished to redistribute income from the rich to the poor. They argued that such a redistribution might actually reduce social welfare by taking a unit of a commodity from a rich person who derived a great deal of utility out of it, and giving it to a poor person who derived very little utility from it.

It is ironic that this ancient defense of inequality ultimately backfires on economics, by making it impossible to construct a market demand curve which is independent of the distribution of income. If the market demand curve depends upon the distribution of income, if a change in prices will alter the distribution of income, and if this does not result in a single equilibrium between marginal revenue and marginal cost, then economics cannot defend any one distribution of income over any other. A redistribution of income that favors the poor over the rich cannot be formally opposed by economic theory – in fact, economic theory requires such a redistribution before it can even derive a market demand curve!

Finally, this failure rehabilitates the approach of classical economics to analyzing the economy. Classical economists such as Smith, Ricardo and Marx divided society into social classes, and considered how different policies might favor one social class over another. The notion of class has been expunged from economics by the concept of the indifference curve and its 'one size fits all' treatment of everyone from the poorest Somali to the richest American. Yet because the preferences of different individuals cannot be meaningfully aggregated, this concept is invalid for the analysis of anything more than an isolated individual.

But the conditions under which aggregation is valid – when tastes are identical and unaffected by changes in income – are at least reasonable as first approximations when the analysis splits society into different social classes. It is not too unreasonable to lump all workers, all landlords, and all capitalists together, as Smith, Ricardo and Marx used to do. Incomes within a class vary substantially less than incomes between classes, and tastes are far more likely to be common within classes than between them. A model with both Robinson Crusoe and Friday is at least slightly more reasonable than a model with Robinson Crusoe alone.

Leading mathematical economists have made very similar musings to this. Alan Kirman made one of the strongest such statements in his provocatively titled paper 'The intrinsic limits of modern economic theory: the emperor

---

15 Say gives a typical statement (reproduced on the Web at Hedonism/Say) of this approach to utility, which denies the ability of anyone to judge or measure the utility any other individual garners from a particular commodity.

has no clothes.'[16] After discussing these and other theoretical failures of neoclassical economics, Kirman concluded that

> If we are to progress further we may well be forced to theories in terms of groups who have collectively coherent behavior. Thus demand and expenditure functions if they are to be set against reality must be defined at some reasonably high level of aggregation. The idea that we should start at the level of the isolated individual is one which we may well have to abandon. (Kirman 1989: 138)

In the end, then, the one benefit of neoclassical economics may be to have established why classical economists were correct to reason in terms of social class in the first place.

Addendum: an anti-empirical theory

There is one striking empirical fact about this whole literature, and that is that there is not one single empirical fact in it. The entire neoclassical theory of consumer behavior has been derived in 'armchair philosopher' mode, with an economist constructing a model of a hypothetical rational consumer in his head, and then deriving rules about how that hypothetical consumer must behave.

The aim of this armchair theorizing was to derive a watertight proof of market rationality from an underlying set of principles of rational individual behavior. The fact that this endeavor failed – that rational individual behavior can lead to an 'irrational' market – therefore means that the entire endeavor has been a waste of time. But many economists cling to this 'utility-maximizing' vision of how consumers behave because it seems so intuitively reasonable to them as a description of individual behavior.

Fittingly, this armchair theory has been proved to be empirically false by an experimental study. The experiment, by the German economist Reinhard Sippel, attempted to test the 'Axioms of Revealed Preference' that were developed by Paul Samuelson (Samuelson 1938a, 1938b) – one of the truly dominant figures in the development of neoclassical economics – as a way to derive a theory of consumer behavior in which utility did not need to be explicitly considered. Though this was not Samuelson's main intention, it also incidentally allowed the theory of utility maximizing behavior to be tested.

Samuelson defined a 'rational consumer' on the basis of how that consumer would behave when confronted with choices between bundles of goods, and he devised four rules to distinguish rational behavior from irrational: Completeness, Transitivity, Non-satiation and Convexity.

---

16 Kirman's paper is an eloquent and well-argued instance of the phenomenon that those who have constructed the 'high theory' of economics are far less confident about its relevance than more ordinary economists.

- *Completeness* meant that a rational consumer was able to compare different bundles of commodities – shopping trolleys containing different selections of goods from a supermarket – and decide which bundle he preferred. There were three possible outcomes: given a choice between the selection of goods in shopping trolley A and shopping trolley B, a rational consumer should be able to say that (a) he preferred trolley A to trolley B; (b) that he preferred B to A; or (c) that he was indifferent between the two.
- *Transitivity* meant that if the consumer said he preferred trolley A to trolley B, and he also preferred trolley B to trolley C, then he necessarily had to prefer trolley A to trolley C.
- *Non-satiation* means that more is preferred to less. So if trolley B has the same contents as trolley A plus one additional chocolate bar, trolley B must be preferred to trolley A.
- Finally, the most complex property was *Convexity*, which is a mathematical expression of the concept of diminishing marginal utility. It argues that if you have two very different shopping trolleys, A and B, then any linear combination of the contents of these two trolleys should be preferred to the trolleys themselves. For example, imagine that trolley A contains ten chocolate bars and nothing else, while trolley B contains ten packs of chips and nothing else. Ten other shopping trolleys could be constructed by swapping one chocolate bar for one pack of chips, each of which would be more desirable than trolleys A and B.

These rules sound reasonable to most people when first explained to them – like many concepts in neoclassical economics, they are superficially appealing – but Sippel's experiment concluded that, if obeying these rules makes one rational, then the vast majority of us are irrational.

Sippel tested the theory in a very systematic way. He gave his student subjects a set of eight commodities from which to choose (see Table 3.3), a budget line, and a set of relative prices. This was repeated ten times, with each of the ten different price and budget line combinations being designed to test various aspects of Revealed Preference. Subjects were given as much time as they liked to make their choices, and after the ten tests, they got to consume one of the bundles they had selected.

I expect that Sippel conducted the experiment in order to confirm the theory. I would not be surprised to find that his intention was to use the results to derive 'indifference curves' for each of his subjects, and thus confirm that economic theory accurately described their behavior. But the results were a surprise: eleven of his twelve subjects failed the test of rationality! He repeated it with a larger group of thirty – to find that twenty-two of these were also 'irrational' according to Samuelson's definition of rational behavior.

Sippel then tried to rescue the theory in a number of ways, none of which worked. One of the most ingenious methods was to hypothesize that real-

TABLE 3.3 The commodities in Sippel's 'Revealed Preference' experiment

Good	Max. amount (if all budget spent on one good)
Video clips	30–60 minutes
Computer games	27.5–60 minutes
Magazines	30–60 minutes
Coca-Cola	400ml–2 liters
Orange juice	400ml–2 liters
Coffee	600ml–2 liters
Candy	400gm–2 kilos
Pretzels, peanuts	600gm–2 kilos

world consumers can't as easily distinguish the utility they get from different bundles of goods, by assuming that indifference curves were 'thicker' than the thin lines drawn in neoclassical textbooks. This did indeed reduce the number of violations of the 'Axioms of Revealed Preference'; but it also had the undesirable impact that it made random choice – simply choosing what to consume by rolling dice – appear more rational than the consumption decisions of his students!

To his great credit, Sippel concluded with an understated but accurate reflection on the implications of his experiment for economic theory:

> We conclude that the evidence for the utility maximization hypothesis is at best mixed. While there are subjects who appear to be optimizing, the majority of them do not. The high power of our test might explain why our conclusions differ from those of other studies where optimizing behavior was found to be an almost universal principle applying to humans and non-humans as well. In contrast to this, we would like to stress the diversity of individual behavior and call the universality of the maximizing principle into question [...]
>
> We find a considerable number of violations of the revealed preference axioms, which contradicts the neoclassical theory of the consumer maximizing utility subject to a given budget constraint. We should therefore pay closer attention to the limits of this theory as a description of how people actually behave, i.e. as a positive theory of consumer behavior. Recognizing these limits, we economists should perhaps be a little more modest in our 'imperialist ambitions' of explaining non-market behavior by economic principles. (Sippel 1997: 1442–3)

Sippel did not speculate as to what his subjects were actually doing if they weren't in fact maximizing their utility, but it is fairly easy to show that these subjects were behaving rationally in the face of a real-world phenomenon of which armchair economic theorists are blithely unaware: the 'curse of dimensionality.'

Rational behavior and the curse of dimensionality

The neoclassical definition of rational behavior argues that a rational person, when confronted with a set of options, will attempt to choose the best option available. It appeared to Sippel that this was exactly what his subjects were doing:

> A closer look at the actual demand data corroborates the view that the subjects did not choose randomly. Every subject showed a marked preference for some of the goods while other goods were not chosen at all, even at low prices. Some subjects' demand was quite price inelastic, whereas others substituted cheaper goods for their more expensive counterparts, e.g. Coke for orange juice, sometimes to the extent that they always switched from one to the other, depending upon which was cheaper in the particular situation. There can be no doubt that the subjects tried to select a combination of goods that came as close as possible to what they really liked to consume given the respective budget constraints. (Ibid.: 1439)

However, despite this intention to choose the best option, they failed to do so rationally according to Samuelson's rules. So what's at fault – human behavior, or the neoclassical model of rationality?

The latter, of course. It is a 'toy' model that looks OK on paper, but fails completely when one takes even a tiny step into the real world – as Sippel's experiment did.

Let's look at what his subjects were being asked to do more closely. Sippel gave them a choice between eight different commodities, and let them choose any amount of them that they could afford with their budget. How many different 'shopping trolleys' could this mean they were looking at – each containing a different combination of goods?

Unfortunately, the answer is 'an infinite number of shopping trolleys,' so let's simplify it and imagine that students considered their choices in discrete units – say 5-minute segments for the videos and computer games (30 minutes, 35 minutes, and so on out to 60 minutes), 250ml units of drinks (400ml, 650ml, out to 2 liters), and 250 gram units of sweets (400 grams, 650 grams, out to 2 kilos). This means roughly eight different quantities for each of the eight goods. How many different shopping trolleys does that give us?

The answer will probably surprise you: *you could fill over 16.7 million shopping trolleys with different combinations of these eight goods.* Sixty-four would contain varying amounts of only one good – from 30 to 60 minutes of video, from 400 grams to 2 kilos of candy. The other 16.7 million-plus would have varying combinations of all the goods available.

This is a consequence of the real-world phenomenon that computer scientists have dubbed 'the curse of dimensionality.' The standard neoclassical 'toy' model of consumption shows you choosing between two different commodities. Most of these drawings don't show quantities on their axes, but if the quantities being considered were between zero and ten units of each good, then there would be 121 different combinations you could choose: zero units of both ([0,0]), ten units of both ([10,10]), and another 119 combinations in addition to that ([0,1], [1,0] right out to [10,9] and [9,10]).

The general rule for choices involving many commodities is that the number of different combinations equals one plus the number of units that you could buy of each commodity,[17] raised to the power of the number of commodities you are considering. In the simple two-commodity case, this results in 11-squared choices – or 121. Your budget might allow you to rule out 90 percent of these, leaving just 10 or so choices to consider.

In Sippel's experiment, however, this resulted in 8 raised to the power of 8 – or in longhand 8 by 8 by 8 by 8 by 8 by 8 by 8 by 8, which equals 16.7 million.[18] Many of these 16.7 million combinations would be ruled out by the budget – the trolley containing the maximum amount of each item is clearly unattainable, as are many others. But even if the budget ruled out 99.99 percent of the options – for being either too expensive or too cheap compared to the budget – there would still be over 1,600 different shopping trolleys that Sippel's subjects had to choose between every time.

The neoclassical definition of rationality requires that, when confronted with this amount of choice, the consumer's choices are consistent every time. So if you choose trolley number 1355 on one occasion when trolley 563 was also feasible, and on a second occasion you reversed your choice, then according to neoclassical theory, you are 'irrational.'

Nonsense. The real irrationality lies in imagining that any sentient being could make the number of comparisons needed to choose the optimal combination in finite time. The weakness in the neoclassical vision of reality starts with the very first principle of 'Completeness': it is simply impossible to hold in your head – or any other data storage device – a complete set of preferences for the bewildering array of combinations one can form from the myriad range of commodities that confront the average Western shopper. With this principle being impossible, any sane person's shopping behavior will certainly also violate the neoclassical rules of Transitivity and Convexity (and probably Non-satiation as well). But it will be because the neoclassical principles themselves are irrational, not because the shopper is.

Consider, for example, your regular visit to a supermarket. The typical supermarket has between 10,000 and 50,000 items, but let's segment them into just 100 different groups. How many different shopping trolleys could

---

17 The 'plus one' rule covers the case of buying no units of one commodity. This isn't an issue in my discrete interpretation of Sippel's experiment.

18 If this sounds extraordinary to you, consider that 10 multiplied by itself 8 times is equal to 100 million.

you fill if you limited your decision to simply whether to buy or not buy one item from each group?

You would be able to fill two to the power of one hundred shopping trolleys with different combinations of these goods: that's 1,267,650,600,22 8,229,401,496,703,205,376 trolleys in total, or in words over 1,000 million trillion trillion shopping trolleys. If you could work out the utility you gained from each trolley at a rate of 10 trillion trolleys per second, it would take you 100 billion years to locate the optimal one.

Obviously you don't do that when you go shopping. Instead, what you do is use a range of commonplace heuristics to reduce the overwhelming array of choices you face to something manageable that you can complete in less than an hour. You partition your choices into a few basic groups, rather than looking at every separate product; and within the groups you use habit to guide your purchases – if you normally have muesli for breakfast, you ignore cornflakes. Truly rational behavior is therefore not choosing the best option, but *reducing the number of options you consider so that you can make a satisfactory decision in finite time.*

This is a commonplace observation in computer science, which unlike economics has built its knowledge of how decisions are made from experimentation and experience. What are sometimes called the 'Laws of Computational Theory' put front and center – in a rather paradoxical way – the fact that most real-world problems have so many potential solutions that an optimum cannot be found:

1 You cannot compute nearly all the things you want to compute.
2 The things you can compute are too expensive to compute. (Ballard 2000: 6)

The first law reflects research by Turing which established that most logical problems cannot be solved by a computer program. The second states that for the minority of problems that can be solved, the 'Curse of Dimensionality' means that an optimum solution cannot be found in finite time, no matter how much computing power is thrown at it. Computer scientists are much more informed than economists about the capacity of any reasoning system to solve even the simplest problems, and they are much more cautious as a result.

Economists should respect their greater knowledge, and accept that individual behavior will be 'satisficing' in nature rather than optimizing, as the behavioral economist Herbert Simon put it (Simon 1996).

Conclusion

There are of course reasonable grounds to expect that, for many commodities, demand will rise as price falls. One, given by the marketer and statistician Andrew Ehrenberg, was that consumers allocated a fairly constant percentage of their spending to different classes of commodities (shelter, food, clothing, etc.) and a fall in the price of any item within a class resulted in an increase in the purchases of it, though very little change in the aggregate amount spent on that class of commodities overall (Ehrenberg 1975: 275–9).

This empirical reality cannot, however, rescue the neoclassical theory of consumer behavior from its result that market demand curves derived from consumers having 'rational' preferences (as neoclassical theory defines them) can have any shape at all. As I note later, this is an example of what is known in complexity theory as 'Emergent Behavior' – that the behavior of the sum of a set of isolated individuals cannot be deduced from the behavior of any of them in isolation.

This could imply that the best research strategy to develop economics is to abandon the model of rational behavior – as neoclassical economics defines it – and adopt the behavioral perspective of satisficing or bounded rationality instead.

I am more inclined to take Alan Kirman's lead here: that the failure of the endeavor to derive market rationality from individual rationality implies that the whole agenda of trying to derive systemic economic laws from the analysis of the isolated individual – known as 'methodological individualism' – is a waste of time. Instead, as Kirman put it, 'If we are to progress further we may well be forced to theories in terms of groups who have collectively coherent behavior' (Kirman 1989: 138). This implies that the old classical economics focus on social classes as the ideal level of analysis was correct – even if many of the conclusions derived from that in the 1800s were false.

That is the approach I take to macroeconomic modeling – as you will see in Chapters 13 and 14. I am inclined to leave studies of satisficing behavior to the psychologists.

So one half of the iconic 'supply and demand' model is unsound: what about the other half, the supply curve?

4 | SIZE DOES MATTER

Why there is no supply curve

The image of one downward-sloping line intersecting with another upward-sloping one to determine an equilibrium is so iconic to neoclassical economics that a renowned wit once described it as the 'Totem' of economics. In a wonderful satire entitled 'Life among the Econ,' Swedish economist Axel Leijonhufvud imagined himself as an anthropologist investigating academic economists, whom he portrayed as a tribe living in the cold and arid Arctic: 'The Econ tribe occupies a vast territory in the far North. Their land appears bleak and dismal to the outsider, and travelling through it makes for rough sledding; but the Econ, through a long period of adaptation, have learned to wrest a living of sorts from it' (Leijonhufvud 1973: 327).

The Econ, he noted, were xenophobic towards the neighboring PolScis and the Sociogs tribes, obsessed with the building of 'modls,' and sharply divided into castes, the most numerous of which were the Micro and the Macro. The castes distinguished themselves from each other using Totems that were, to the outsider, remarkably similar. The 'Totem of the Micro' was a pair of lines labeled 'S' and 'D,' while (when Leijonhufvud wrote the paper in 1973) the totem of the Macro was a pair of intersecting lines labeled 'IS' and 'LM':

The Totems are easily drawn, but deriving them logically from the underlying theory is another matter altogether. As we saw in the previous chapter, a demand curve derived in accordance with the underlying theory can have any shape at all – it will more often look like a snake in a hurry than the simple downward-sloping line drawn here.

The supply curve suffers an even worse fate: it doesn't exist.

Economists attempt to derive the supply curve from their theory of how profit-maximizing firms decide how much output to produce. One essential

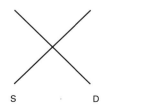

4.1 Leijonhufvud's 'Totems' of the Econ tribe

step in this derivation is that firms must produce so that the price they are paid for their output equals what is known as the 'marginal cost' of production – the additional expense incurred in producing one more unit of output. Unless this condition is met, a supply curve cannot be drawn.

This explains the extreme hostility that neoclassical economists have towards monopolies. It's not only because they can abuse the power that being a monopoly can confer: it's also because, according to neoclassical theory, a monopoly will set its price above the marginal cost of production. If monopolies were the rule, then there could be no supply curve, and standard neoclassical microeconomic analysis would be impossible.

Conversely, neoclassical economists love the market structure they call 'perfect competition,' because it guarantees that profit-maximizing behavior will cause firms to produce an output at which marginal cost equals price.

Only it won't. The manner in which neoclassical economics derives the result that profit-maximizing behavior by competitive firms means that they will produce where marginal cost equals price commits one of the simplest mathematical mistakes possible: it confuses a very small quantity – an 'infinitesimal,' as mathematicians describe it – with zero.

When that error is corrected, it is easily shown that a competitive market will also set price above marginal cost, and therefore a supply curve that is independent of the demand curve can't be drawn. The other half of the 'Totem of the Micro' disappears.

The kernel

Try this party trick: convince someone that the world is flat, starting from the premise that it is a sphere.

The argument is simple. If you take a small enough segment of the world – say, the two feet your victim is standing on – then the curvature of that segment is so small that it is, to all intents and purposes, flat. Then consider the segment you're standing on – it is also so small that it is effectively flat.

Next, consider the angle between the two segments: it too will be so small that it is effectively zero. So these two small segments are effectively flat.

Finally, extrapolate your argument from these two tiny segments and the angle between them up to the level of the entire globe. If you consider the segment your victim occupies and the segment behind him, that pair is also effectively flat. Keep on going, and the entire world is flat.

The fallacy in the argument, clearly, is that while it will do as an approximation to treat your immediate surroundings as effectively flat, it will not do to ignore those imperceptible but non-zero angles if you move from the scale of one or two segments to the entire globe.

Yet this fallacy lies at the heart of the economic preference for small, competitive firms over large monopolistic ones. At crucial stages of the economic argument, an imperceptibly small quantity is treated as zero, and then all these zeros are added up to yield zero at the scale of an entire market. This is intellectually and mathematically unsound. When the correct position is imposed – that something which is extremely small is nonetheless not zero – the economic argument against monopolies and in favor of small competitive firms collapses.

Oh, and if your party trick convinces your victim? Then he is either stoned, or an economist.

Prelude: the War over Perfect Competition

Most of this book explains flaws in neoclassical economic theory that have been known for decades, but have been ignored by neoclassical economists. When I first wrote *Debunking Economics*, I thought that the argument presented in this chapter was a new critique.

As I found out shortly after the book was published in 2001, it wasn't: the same key point had been made forty-four years earlier, and not by a critic of neoclassical economics but by one of the most strident defenders, George Stigler. In his paper 'Perfect competition, historically contemplated' (Stigler 1957: 8, n. 31), Stigler applied one of the most basic rules of mathematics, the 'Chain Rule,' to show that the slope of the demand curve facing the competitive firm was exactly the same as the slope of the market demand curve – see Figure 4.2.

If you haven't yet studied economics, then the importance of that result won't yet be obvious to you. But if you have, this should shock you: a central tenet of your introductory 'education' in economics is obviously false, and has been known to be so since at least 1957.

Stigler's mathematics deconstructed the demand curve for the individual firm into two components:

- the slope of the market demand curve; multiplied by
- how much market output changes given a change in the output of a single firm.

Neoclassical theory assumes that the slope of the market demand curve

THE JOURNAL OF

POLITICAL ECONOMY

Volume LXV   FEBRUARY 1957   Number 1

PERFECT COMPETITION, HISTORICALLY CONTEMPLATED

GEORGE J. STIGLER

$$\frac{d\,(p\,q_i)}{d\,q_i} = p + q_i\,\frac{d\,p}{d\,Q}\,\frac{d\,Q}{d\,q_i},$$

where Q is total sales, and $dQ/dq_i = 1$. Letting

4.2 Stigler's proof that the horizontal firm demand curve is a fallacy is negative: a fall in price will cause demand to increase. So the demand curve for the individual firm can only be zero if the second component is zero: the amount that industry output changes given a change in output by a single firm.

However, Stigler very correctly stated that this second component is not zero, but instead equals one. In the basic 'Marshallian' theory of the firm that is taught to undergraduates, individual firms are assumed not to react strategically to what other firms do or might do. Therefore if one firm changes its output by ten units, there is no instantaneous reaction to this by the other firms, so that industry output also changes by ten units (though it might alter afterwards as other firms adjust to the new market price). The ratio of the change in industry output to the change in output by a single firm is therefore 1.

As a consequence, *the slope of the demand curve for the individual competitive firm equals the slope of the market demand curve.* Far from the individual firm's demand curve being horizontal, it has the same negative slope as the market demand curve.

I was stunned. This had been known for over four decades, and yet economic textbooks everywhere continued to mouth the fallacy that the individual competitive firm had a horizontal demand curve?

Even by the standards of mendacity that I had come to expect of economic textbooks, this surprised me. Most critiques of neoclassical theory involve complicated concepts – like the critique of the 'Law of Demand' outlined in the previous chapter, or the disputes over the nature of capital in Chapter 7. Frequently, when I have criticized textbooks for not discussing these issues, I have been hit with the rejoinder that this material is just too complicated for undergraduates to understand: better leave it for more advanced courses.[1] But this error in the theory is so simple that it can be explained in a few lines of English (and one line of calculus).

Neoclassical economists ignored most of this book, but vigorously attacked this chapter. As I responded to their attacks, the critique grew in depth and complexity. Attempts to get it into neoclassical journals failed, but it was published in a range of non-neoclassical outlets, including the journal of interdisciplinary physics *Physica A* (Keen and Standish 2006), *A Guide to What's Wrong with Economics* (Keen and Fullbrook 2004), the *Handbook of Pluralist Economics Education* (Keen 2009a), and the *Real-World Economics Review* (Keen and Standish 2010).[2]

Though nothing in that war with neoclassical economists challenged the accuracy of the case I first made in 2000, I have made extensive changes to

---

1 In fact, the advanced courses also ignore these more difficult critiques, which means that students who do them, if anything, are even more ignorant than undergraduates.

2 This last paper – 'Debunking the theory of the firm – a chronology' – is freely downloadable from www. paecon.net/PAEReview/issue53/KeenStandish53.pdf.

this chapter to focus on the key challenge it makes to neoclassical orthodoxy: that a 'supply curve' cannot be drawn. I have also added new material, including the key advance over the case made in 2000: a proof that the alleged profit-maximizing formula ('set marginal cost and marginal revenue equal to maximize profits') does not maximize profits. I derive another formula that does maximize profits, given the assumptions of neoclassical theory.

The roadmap

In this chapter I outline the neoclassical analysis of monopolies on the one hand, and 'perfect competition' on the other, and point out that the sole difference between them is that a monopolist is shown to face falling marginal revenue, whereas the competitive firm faces constant marginal revenue which is equal to the market price. From this proposition alone flows the crucial result, for the neoclassical approach to economics, that a supply curve can be derived that is independent of the demand curve.

I then show that this proposition leads to logical fallacies: a quantity that economists assume is zero actually has to be minus one; firms that are allegedly profit maximizers must produce more than the amount which maximizes profits; zero amounts at the individual level must somehow aggregate to negative amounts at the aggregate.

A careful analysis of what is implied by this proposition that marginal revenue equals price for competitive firms shows that it is based on a simple mathematical error. Once this is corrected, it is obvious that a competitive market with profit-maximizing firms that faces the same cost conditions as a monopoly will produce the same amount at the same price.

It follows that the amount supplied by a competitive industry is not determined by the aggregate marginal cost curve alone, but instead depends on conditions of demand as well, as with a monopoly. A supply curve that is independent of the demand curve therefore cannot be derived.

Economic perfection

Pejorative expressions abound in economics, despite its claim to be a value-free science, and 'perfect competition' is possibly the most value-laden of all. To economists, however, the word 'perfect' has a very precise meaning: it is a market in which the competitively set price equals the marginal cost of production.

This is 'perfect' because, according to economic theory, it achieves the maximum possible gap between community welfare and the cost of providing it. Community welfare is maximized when the gap between total benefit to society from consuming a given product and the total cost of providing that benefit is as big as it can be. Given the shape that economists assume that these benefits and costs take – the benefit of consumption rising but at a decreasing rate, the cost of production rising at an increasing rate – the gap between the two is highest when the rate of change of total benefit equals the rate of change of total cost.

The demand curve (which we deconstructed in the last chapter) represents the rate of change of the total benefit, while the supply curve represents the rate of change of total cost. Therefore the benefit to society is maximized where these two rates of change – one rising, the other falling – are equal.

Producers are trying to maximize the benefit to them – their profits – not society's benefits. These two interests – consumers aiming to get the maximum benefit out of consumption, producers trying to get the maximum profit out of production – only coincide if the price equals the change in revenue that producers get from selling an extra unit, which economists call 'marginal revenue.' This is because the price – the amount that consumers are willing to pay – tells you the 'marginal utility' they get from the last item consumed. Only if this also equals the 'marginal revenue' that the producer gets from selling this very last unit of output will the benefits to society also equal the individual gain for the producer who sells it. This can only occur if the 'marginal revenue' for producing this last item sold equals its price.

Only perfect competition guarantees this outcome, because, economists believe, only then does marginal revenue always equal price.

Perfect competition is also 'perfect' because a supply curve exists if, and only if, price equals marginal cost. Without perfect competition, though a marginal cost curve can still be drawn, this will not be the supply curve, and as we shall see, the amount supplied to the market will be less than the amount that will maximize social welfare.

This concept of economic perfection relies upon downward-sloping market demand curves, which we already know is invalid. However, even if we accept, for the sake of argument, that the market demand curve is smoothly downward sloping and represents community welfare, the neoclassical argument for the superiority of the perfectly competitive market over the monopoly firm is still internally flawed. To establish this, we'll first consider the market form least favored by economics: monopoly.[3]

Monopoly

A monopoly has the entire market demand curve to itself. If the market demand curve is smoothly downward sloping, the price at which its output can be sold decreases as the quantity it tries to sell increases. In this chapter I'll work with a hypothetical example in which the market price is assumed to start at $1,000 for the first unit sold, and then to drop by five cents for every additional unit (see Table 4.1).

---

3 Economists are likely to deflect these critiques by arguing that the theory has moved well beyond the simplistic models taught to undergraduates. However, at the very least economists should stop teaching these models. Secondly, economists still see the model of perfect competition as describing the ideal economy. This chapter argues that this ideal is in fact a farce.

TABLE 4.1 Demand schedule for a hypothetical monopoly

Quantity	Price	Total revenue	Marginal revenue
1	1,000	1,000	1,000.00
2	999.95	1,999.90	999.90
3	999.90	2,999.70	999.80
10	999.55	9,995.50	999.10
11	999.50	10,994.50	999.00
2,001	900.00	1,800,900	800.00
2,002	899.95	1,801,700	799.90
4,001	800.00	3,200,800	600.00
6,001	700.00	4,200,700	400.00
8,001	600.00	4,800,600	200.00
10,001	500.00	5,000,500	0.00
12,001	400.00	4,800,400	−200.00
14,001	300.00	4,200,300	−400.00
16,001	200.00	3,200,200	−600.00
18,001	100.00	1,800,100	−800.00
20,000	0.05	1,000	−999.90

This may seem silly if you've never read an economics textbook before – why not simply use some real data on a real firm instead? – and you are right! The reason, as I explain in Chapter 5, is that *there are no such data*: the revenue and costs of real firms are nothing like those assumed by neoclassical economists. As a result, they always use made-up number in their examples. To critique their theory, I have to do the same. So here we go ...

Since the firm can sell one unit of output for $1,000.00, its total revenue is $1,000.00, and its 'marginal revenue' – the change in total revenue from zero dollars for zero units sold, to $1,000.00 for one unit sold – is also $1,000.00. So price equals marginal revenue at this level; but as soon as another unit is sold, price and marginal revenue diverge. Two units can only be sold if the firm drops the price for all units by 5 cents, so the market price becomes $999.95, the total revenue is $1,999.90, and the marginal revenue for the firm – the change in revenue from selling one unit to selling two – is $999.90.[4]

The interests of the firm therefore diverge from those of society, since the marginal benefit to it (the marginal revenue) is less than the marginal benefit to society as a whole (the price).

The price consumers are willing to pay drops smoothly as the quantity supplied rises, so that for an output of 10 units, the sale price has to drop to $999.55 per unit. The total revenue for selling 10 units is $9,995.50. If 11 units were to be sold, the monopolist would have to drop the price per

4 Astute readers would already see a problem here with the model of perfect competition.

unit by 5 cents, to $999.50 each. Total revenue would be $10,994.50 (eleven times $999.50), and marginal revenue would be $999.00.

The same process continues indefinitely, so that if output were 2,001 units, then sale price would have to drop to $900. Total revenue would be $1,800,900, and marginal revenue – the amount of additional revenue added by selling the 2,002nd unit – would be $800.00.

Eventually, the point is reached at which any further increase in output requires a price cut which reduces, rather than increases, total revenue. In this example, this occurs at an output of 10,001 units, where the sale price is $500. The sale of the 10,001st unit adds nothing to total revenue, and any increase in sales past this point actually reduces total revenue – marginal revenue has become negative.

That covers the revenue side of the analysis. The picture is completed by the analysis of costs, which I'll cover extensively in Chapter 5. Briefly, the firm has two types of costs: fixed costs, which apply no matter what the level of output is, and variable costs, which depend directly on how many units are produced.

Fixed costs are just that – fixed – so that the fixed cost *per unit of output* will fall as output rises. One fixed cost is the design of a product, and if this was, say, $10 million, then that component of the fixed costs per unit would be $1 million per unit when output was 10 units, and $1 per unit when output was 10 million units.

Variable costs depend on how many units are produced. One obvious variable cost is labor, and clearly you will need more labor to produce 10 million units than to produce 10. Neoclassical economics also assumes that, eventually, the productivity of the variable inputs such as labor will fall as output rises (we explore this assumption in Chapter 5). Therefore the variable costs to produce the 10 millionth unit will be much higher than those for the 10th unit. In my example, fixed costs are $10,000, and variable costs are defined by an equation in which they start at just over $15 each, fall for a while but then ultimately rise (see Table 4.2).[5]

Variable costs fall for a while because the firm experiences 'rising marginal productivity' as the ratio of the variable factors of production to fixed factors approaches the ideal level. This means that, for a while, the additional cost involved in producing the next unit of output falls. In my example, while it cost an additional $15 to go from producing zero units of output to producing one unit, it cost only an additional $8.80 to go from producing 2,001 units to 2,002 units.

This change in the cost of production resulting from producing one more unit is a very important concept in neoclassical economics, called the

5 These numbers come from a mathematical function (a cubic – of the form a+bx+cx2+dx3 – to be precise), whereas most neoclassical textbooks, if they use numerical examples at all (most don't, and simply use drawings instead), simply 'pluck them out of the air.'

TABLE 4.2 Costs for a hypothetical monopoly

Quantity	Fixed cost	Total cost	Marginal cost
1	1,000,000	1,000,015	15.00
2	1,000,000	1,000,030	15.00
3	1,000,000	1,000,045	14.99
10	1,000,000	1,000,150	14.96
11	1,000,000	1,000,165	14.95
2,001	1,000,000	1,022,419	8.80
2,002	1,000,000	1,022,428	8.80
4,001	1,000,000	1,042,433	13.41
6,001	1,000,000	1,086,464	33.62
8,001	1,000,000	1,190,514	74.23
10,001	1,000,000	1,400,190	140.05
12,001	1,000,000	1,770,696	235.86
14,001	1,000,000	2,366,836	366.48
16,001	1,000,000	3,263,017	536.70
18,001	1,000,000	4,543,241	751.32
20,000	1,000,000	6,300,100	1,015.01

'marginal cost of production.' As you can see from this example, marginal cost depends only on the change in variable costs – since fixed costs are the same no matter what level of output you produce – and it changes only because of changes in productivity that in turn reflect how many variable inputs are being used (workers) relative to the fixed inputs (machines).

Common sense, and earlier theories of economics like Ricardo's theory of rent, might consider that maybe the productivity of the individual inputs changes. Ricardo, for example, assumed that the cost of producing food rose as population rose because farmers started off using the most productive land, and had to use less fertile land as population increased. Common sense might suggest that as a firm demands more workers, it affects the wage at which workers can be hired, thus driving its costs per worker higher.

But neoclassical economists rule both these effects out, by assuming first that all inputs are homogeneous, and secondly that, while the monopoly has its own market to itself, it is a small player in the labor market and can hire as many workers as it likes at the going wage. The only source of changes in marginal cost that they allow arises from changing the ratio of variable inputs to the fixed inputs.

Consider a road construction firm, whose fixed costs include a number of jackhammers – say 100 of them. At a very low level of production, it will have only one worker and 100 jackhammers, so the worker will be very inefficient (*please read the footnote here*).[6] However, as the number of workers

6 If this example seems silly to you – surely you would only use workers and machines in the ideal ratio,

rises the firm will approach the ideal ratio of one worker per jackhammer, at which point maximum efficiency will be reached. But once the firm hits the ideal ratio, additional workers will add to output at a diminishing rate. Marginal productivity will fall, and therefore marginal costs will rise.

Table 4.3 combines the revenue information from Table 4.1 with the cost information from Table 4.2, and indicates the role of marginal revenue and marginal cost in identifying the point of maximum profit. For a while, each additional unit sold adds much more to revenue than it causes the total cost of production to rise: marginal revenue exceeds marginal cost, and therefore the final column in the table, which shows marginal revenue minus cost, is positive. But once marginal revenue and marginal cost are equal, profit is maximized.

The precise point at which this occurs lies between 8,973 and 8,974 units in this table, but the firm can't sell a fraction of a unit, so it will produce the lower amount of 8,973 units, at which the marginal cost is $102.77 and its profit will be $3,671,679.

The second column tells us that the market is willing to pay a price of $551.40 per unit if total supply is 8,973 units – so the sale price is $448.63 higher than the marginal cost of production (and $409.19 above the average cost).[7] Thus to maximize its profits, the firm produces where marginal cost equals marginal revenue, and sells the output at a much higher price.

As well as substantially exceeding the average cost of production, the market price exceeds the marginal cost of producing the last unit sold. This means, in economic welfare terms, that the marginal benefit of the last unit sold exceeds the marginal cost of producing it. Society would therefore benefit from an increased level of production, since additional units of output would increase social welfare. But the monopolist has no incentive to produce more: in fact producing any more would reduce his profits. Therefore, according to economists, monopolies reduce social welfare.

Crucially for the way neoclassical economists prefer to model the economy, §17 a supply curve can't be derived for a monopoly. Instead, if monopolies were the rule, then three curves – price, marginal revenue, and marginal cost – would be needed for a complete 'Totem of the Micro.' The intersection of the marginal revenue curve with the marginal cost curve would determine the amount the firm produced, and the market price would then depend on

---

so if you have just one worker, he works one jackhammer while the other ninety-nine are left idle? – then congratulations, you're right! The whole idea that firms vary the ratio of fixed to variable factors as economists assume they do is a nonsense that we tackle in the next chapter.

7 Average fixed costs start off very high – in this example, at $10,000 per unit for the first unit produced – and fall uniformly from then on. Variable costs per unit may fall for a while too as productivity rises, but eventually they start increasing as output rises, and marginal productivity falls. The combination of falling fixed costs per unit of output, and rising variable costs, means that average costs are 'u-shaped': they fall while the firm experiences rising marginal productivity, flatten out as diminishing marginal productivity kicks in, and finally rise when marginal productivity has diminished so much that each additional unit costs more to produce than the average to date.

TABLE 4.3 Sales and costs determine the level of output that maximizes profit

Quantity	Price	Total revenue	Total cost	Profit	Average cost	Marginal revenue	Marginal cost	Marginal revenue minus marginal cost
1	1,000	1,000	1,000,015	-999,015	1,000,015	1,000	15	985
2	999.95	2,000	1,000,030	-998,030	500,015	999.90	15.00	984.90
3	999.90	3,000	1,000,045	-997,045	333,348	999.80	14.99	984.81
10	999.55	9,996	1,000,150	-990,154	100,015	999.10	14.96	984.14
11	999.50	10,995	1,000,165	-989,170	90,924	999.00	14.95	984.05
8,973	551.40	4,947,712	1,276,033	3,671,679	142.21	102.80	102.77	0.03
8,974	551.35	4,947,815	1,276,136	3,671,679	142.20	102.70	102.80	-0.10
10,001	500.00	5,000,500	1,400,190	3,600,310	140.01	0.00	140.05	-140.05
13,456	327.25	4,403,476	2,177,950	2,225,526	161.86	-345.50	327.16	-672.66
13,457	327.20	4,403,130	2,178,277	2,224,853	161.87	-345.60	327.23	-672.83
14,001	300.00	4,200,300	2,366,836	1,833,464	169.05	-400.00	366.48	-766.48
16,001	200.00	3,200,200	3,263,017	-62,817	204	-600.00	536.70	-1,136.70
18,001	100.00	1,800,100	4,543,241	-2,743,141	252	-800.00	751.32	-1,551.32
20,000	0.05	1,000	6,300,100	-6,299,100	315	-999.90	1,015.01	-2,014.90

this quantity. In place of the simple mantra that 'prices are set by supply and demand,' the minimum statement of the 'Creed of the Micro' would be 'price is set by the demand curve, given the quantity set by marginal cost and marginal revenue.'

It's no wonder, then, that, despite all the criticisms leveled at it, neoclassical economists cling to the model of the 'perfect' competitive market. In a competitive market, since marginal revenue equals price, profit-maximizing behavior leads to an output level at which price equals marginal cost. This is the embodiment of Smith's 'invisible hand' metaphor about the capacity of market economy to reconcile private interest and public virtue, and that is the real message of the 'Totem of the Micro.'[8]

Perfect competition

The main distinguishing feature of the perfectly competitive market is the number of firms in it. Whereas a monopoly has just one firm – which therefore has the entire market demand curve to itself – a perfectly competitive market has many little firms, each competing for a tiny slice of total demand.

In the standard 'Marshallian' model that economists teach in undergraduate courses, these firms are assumed to be profit maximizers who behave in an 'atomistic' way: they neither know of, nor react in any way to, what other firms do or may hypothetically do – they simply respond to the market price.[9] In addition, it is assumed that entry into and exit from a competitive industry is 'free,' or more accurately, not subject to any barriers. Therefore firms outside the industry can move in at any time to take advantage of any above-normal profits if they exist.[10]

All firms are assumed to produce a product that is homogeneous from the consumers' point of view, so that there is no brand loyalty. All firms are therefore 'price-takers': they cannot influence the market price, but instead must take price as given.

At the market level, demand is still a negative function of price. Therefore, total market revenue will initially be a rising and then a falling function

---

8 In fact, on the two occasions that Smith used this phrase, it was in relation to income distribution, and whether local producers would ship production offshore, not how the market mechanism operated. But the metaphor had a compelling impact on the development of economic theory about the market.

9 There are two other models, known as the Cournot-Nash and Bertrand models, in which firms do react to what they think other firms will do, which also reach the outcome that price equals marginal cost. Though they don't make the same mathematical error as the Marshallian model does, they have other problems that we discuss in Keen and Standish (2010). In a third edition of *Debunking Economics*, I might add an addendum on this – since I'm sure it will be the refuge of those who wish to cling to the neoclassical model – but I've left it out of this edition to avoid boring the rest of my audience to death.

10 This assumption is inconsistent with the assumption of a 'short run,' during which some factor of production cannot be changed, which is essential to get the phenomenon of diminishing marginal productivity, which in turn generates a rising marginal cost (see Chapter 4). Firms already inside the industry are assumed to be unable to alter their capital equipment at all, but in the same time period firms not currently in the industry can build a factory and move in on the market? Hello? This logic is about as watertight as the script of the average TV soap opera. However, this assumption plays no part in the standard mathematical model of perfect competition, which focuses simply on the impact of the number of firms currently in the industry.

of price, and marginal revenue at the market level will be less than price (because to increase overall sales, the average price must fall).

However, economists argue that for each price-taking firm, marginal revenue and price are identical. The argument is that since they are each so small, no single firm can influence the market price. As a result, if any firm increases its price above the market equilibrium price, it will lose all its customers; while if any firm decreases its price below the market equilibrium, it will suddenly be swamped by all customers for that commodity. Therefore, the firm effectively sees a horizontal demand curve (set by the intersection of supply and demand at the level of the market).[11]

Given the assumption that they can sell as much as they like at the price set by the market, then as profit maximizers they will produce until the marginal cost of producing this amount equals the marginal revenue from doing so. Since price is a constant for them, marginal revenue equals price, so they produce at the point where marginal cost equals price. In a 100-firm industry whose costs are identical to the monopoly I discussed previously, this results in the representative firm producing about 135 units.[12] This then results in a profit of $22,255.26 for the firm, or $2,225,526 dollars for the industry in total.

§18   Since the total revenue for a perfectly competitive firm is simply a constant price times the number of units it sells, increasing its sales has no effect on its price, so its marginal revenue is constant. This in turn is why a supply curve can be derived for perfect competition, but not for monopoly.

The amount a monopolist will supply depends both on the firm's marginal cost function, and the market's demand function. Since both are needed to determine supply, and since many different demand curves can be drawn through the same point – each with a different slope and therefore different marginal revenue implications – it is impossible to derive a curve which shows how much a monopolist will supply at each price level (all you can do is consider specific examples of hypothetical demand curves, as I did to generate Table 1).

However, for the perfectly competitive firm, since price equals marginal revenue, the amount the firm will produce corresponds in every case to its marginal cost curve. The supply curve of a single firm in a perfectly competitive market is thus its marginal cost curve.

§19   The supply curve for a perfectly competitive industry is constructed simply by adding up the amounts that each firm is willing to supply at a given price. This amounts to summing up their marginal cost curves, so that the supply curve for the industry represents the marginal cost of producing

---

11 If this argument doesn't convince you, good – because this is the point at which the economic argument starts to take on that 'flat earth' feeling.

12 There is no specification of time in the standard neoclassical model, so this could be, for example, 135 units per minute.

output. Since demand equals supply in equilibrium, the marginal benefit for the last unit consumed equals its marginal cost of production, and social utility is maximized. This results in both a higher level of output and a lower price than would occur if the industry were a monopoly.

§20

Checking our sums

This argument normally convinces economics students, and it explains much of the hostility economists in general have towards monopolies, or any market in which firms have some market power by virtue of their size. This 'social radicalism' is unusual for a profession which is normally perceived as socially conservative. It is also curiously at odds with the real world, where it's fairly obvious that industries have a clear tendency to end up being dominated by a few large firms – why fight the real world?

Economists argue that their opposition to large firms, and their allegedly uncharacteristic radicalism on this issue, is based on sound analysis. But is it? Let's check, after first seeing how moving from a monopoly to a perfectly competitive industry would benefit society in my example.

Table 4.4 adds up the costs and revenues of all the competitive firms, to show the aggregate outcome for a competitive industry with 100 firms. Note that the output of this industry (in the rows shown in italic) is higher than the monopoly's output – roughly 13,456 units, versus 8,973 – and its price is lower – roughly $327.25 per unit, versus $551.40 for the monopoly.

Economists therefore put forward three reasons to prefer a competitive industry to a monopoly:

- the competitive industry produces where marginal cost equals price, thus maximizing social welfare;
- it produces a higher level of output than a monopoly; and
- it sells this higher output at a lower price.

However, the key reason why neoclassical economists themselves prefer perfect competition to monopoly is that perfect competition is the only market structure in which price and quantity are set by the intersection of the supply curve and the demand curve.

§21

Well, that's the theory. Now we will consider a subtle but profound set of problems which invalidate this entire analysis.

Calculus 101 for economists: infinitesmals ain't zero

Throughout the economic analysis of perfect competition, the assumption is made that the perfectly competitive firm is so small, relative to the overall market, that its impact on the market can be treated as zero. As I intimated earlier in this chapter, this kind of logic is OK when you are dealing with local approximations – such as whether you can regard the ground on which you stand as either flat or curved – but it will not do when those local

TABLE 4.4 Cost and revenue for a 'perfectly competitive' industry identical in scale to hypothetical monopoly

Quantity	Price	Total revenue	Total cost	Profit	Average cost	Marginal cost	Price minus marginal cost
1	1,000	1,000	1,000,015	−999,015	1,000,015	15	985
2	999.95	2,000	1,000,030	−998,030	500,015	15.00	984.95
3	999.90	3,000	1,000,045	−997,045	333,348	14.99	984.91
10	999.55	9,996	1,000,150	−990,154	100,015	14.96	984.59
11	999.50	10,995	1,000,165	−989,170	90,924	14.95	984.55
8,973	551.40	4,947,712	1,276,033	3,671,679	142.21	102.77	448.63
8,974	551.35	4,947,815	1,276,136	3,671,679	142.20	102.80	448.55
10,001	500.00	5,000,500	1,400,190	3,600,310	140.01	140.05	359.95
13,456	327.25	4,403,476	2,177,950	2,225,526	161.86	327.16	0.09
13,457	327.20	4,403,130	2,178,277	2,224,853	161.87	327.23	−0.03
14,001	300.00	4,200,300	2,366,836	1,833,464	169.05	366.48	−66.48
16,001	200.00	3,200,200	3,263,017	−62,817	204	536.70	−336.70
18,001	100.00	1,800,100	4,543,241	−2,743,141	252	751.32	−651.32
20,000	0.05	1,000	6,300,100	−6,299,100	315	1,015.01	−1,014.96

approximations are aggregated together. When we insist that infinitesimally small amounts are not in fact zero, the apparently watertight logic behind the comparison of monopoly and perfect competition falls apart.

Too small to matter? An essential part of the argument for perfect competition is that each firm is so small that it can't affect the market price – which it therefore takes as given. Consequently the demand curve, as perceived by each firm, is effectively horizontal at the market price. The firms are also so small that they do not react to any changes in behavior by other firms: in the language of economic theory, their 'conjectural variation' – how much all other firms change their output in response to a change in output by one firm – is zero.

These two assumptions are alleged to mean that the slope of the individual firm's demand curve is zero: both the firm's price and the market price do not change when a single firm changes its output. However, they also mean that, if a single firm increases its output by one unit, then total industry output should also increase by one unit – since other firms won't react to the change in output by a single firm.

However, there is a problem: these two assumptions are inconsistent.

If the market demand curve is downward sloping, then an increase in total market output must mean a fall in the market price – regardless of how small a fall it might be. Since the theory assumes that other firms don't react to an increase in production by one firm, total market output must increase. Since the market demand curve is downward sloping, and supply has increased – the supply curve has shifted outwards – market price must fall.

Therefore market price *does* change because of the actions of a single firm. The only way market price could not react would be if all other firms reduced their output by as much as the single firm increased it: then the market supply curve would not shift, and the price would remain constant. But the theory assumes that firms don't react to each other's behavior.

So the market price will be affected by the actions of a single firm, in which case the demand curve facing a single firm will be downward sloping – however slight the slope may be.

Putting this critique another way, the economic argument is that if you break a large downward-sloping line (the market demand curve) into lots of very small lines (the demand curves perceived by each firm), then you will have a huge number of perfectly flat lines. Then if you add all these perfectly flat lines together again, you will get one downward-sloping line.

This is mathematically impossible. If you add up a huge number of flat lines, you will get one very long flat line. If you break one downward-sloping line into many small lines, you will have many downward-sloping lines. The economic concept of perfect competition is based on a mathematical error of confusing a very small quantity with zero.

The market matters: marginal revenue is marginal revenue A second problem with this economic model is the nature of the marginal revenue function. Economists unconsciously reason as if the marginal revenue curve at the market level is a function of the number of firms that produce the industry's output: it exists if there is only one firm, but if there are a large number of firms, it disappears. They then show that a monopoly sets its price where marginal revenue equals marginal cost, which is consistent with their theory. However, they show a competitive industry setting price where the supply curve and the demand curve intersect, with no pesky marginal revenue curve getting in the way.

Unfortunately, marginal revenue exists independently of the number of firms in the industry. If the market demand curve is downward sloping, then so is the market marginal revenue curve, and they diverge right from the very first unit sold (as you can see in the example I give on page 80).

So if a competitive industry did result in output being set by the intersection of the demand curve and the supply curve, then at the collective level the competitive industry must be producing where marginal cost *exceeds* marginal revenue. Rather than maximizing profits, as economists argue firms do, the additional output – that produced past the point where marginal revenue equals marginal cost at the industry level – must be produced at a loss. This paradox means that the individual firm and the market level aspects of the model of perfect competition are inconsistent.

Creative accounting For the assertion that perfect competition results in a higher level of output at a lower price than monopoly to be correct, then in the aggregate, the individually rational profit-maximizing behavior of perfectly competitive firms must lead to a collectively irrational outcome. This would be OK if the theory actually admitted this – as do the theories of Cournot and Bertrand competition[13] – but the Marshallian model taught to undergraduates claims instead that equating marginal cost and marginal revenue maximizes profits for the competitive firm.

According to the theory, the monopoly firm produces only to the point at which marginal cost equals marginal revenue, because this output maximizes its profit. Each perfectly competitive firm likewise produces to a point at which its marginal cost equals its marginal revenue, and for the same reason – because this level of output maximizes its profit.

But at the market level, competitive firms produce to a point at which the collective marginal cost exceeds marginal revenue. The perfectly competitive *industry* produces where marginal cost equals price but exceeds marginal

13 The Cournot and Bertrand theories erroneously argue that the level that maximizes firms' profits is identified by the firms behaving collusively, like a pseudo-monopoly. Instead, in Keen and Standish (2010), we show that the so-called collusive output level is simply the level the firms would produce if they behaved as simple profit maximizers.

revenue; yet all firms in it are supposed to be producing where marginal cost equals marginal revenue.

The monopoly sets price where marginal revenue equals marginal cost, while the competitive industry sets price where the supply curve (which is the sum of all the individual firms' marginal cost curves) intersects the demand curve: this is supposed to be the result of setting marginal cost equal to marginal revenue at the firm level, which means each firm makes the maximum profit that it can. Yet at the aggregate level, while the monopoly has produced where profit is maximized, the competitive firms have produced beyond this point, so that the industry's output past the point of monopoly output has been produced at a loss – which is why the profit level for the competitive firm is lower than that for the monopoly, even though all its firms are supposed to be profit maximizers.

Where did this loss come from? It certainly can't be seen in the standard graph economists draw for perfect competition, which shows the individual competitive firm making profits all the way out to the last item produced.

Instead, this 'loss out of nowhere' is hidden in the detail that economists lose by treating infinitesimally small quantities as zeros. If perfectly competitive firms were to produce where marginal cost equals price, then they would be producing part of their output *past* the point at which marginal revenue equals marginal cost. They would therefore make a loss on these additional units of output.

As I argued above, the demand curve for a single firm cannot be horizontal – it must slope downwards, because if it doesn't, then the market demand curve has to be horizontal. Therefore, marginal revenue will be less than price for the individual firm. However, by arguing that an infinitesimal segment of the market demand is effectively horizontal, economists have treated this loss as zero. Summing zero losses over all firms means zero losses in the aggregate. But this is not consistent with their vision of the output and price levels of the perfectly competitive industry.

The higher level of output must mean losses are incurred by the industry, relative to the profit-maximizing level chosen by the monopoly. Losses at the market level must mean losses at the individual firm level – yet these are presumed to be zero by economic analysis, because it erroneously assumes that the perfectly competitive firm faces a horizontal demand curve.

Perfect competition equals monopoly The above critique raises an interesting question: what will the price and output of a perfectly competitive industry be, if we drop the invalid assumption that the output of a single firm has no effect on the market price? The answer is: the price and output levels of a competitive industry will be exactly the same as for the monopolist (if the aggregate marginal cost curve of the competitive firms is identical to the marginal cost of the monopoly, which economic theory assumes it is).

Economic explanations of price-setting in a competitive market normally start from the level of the market, where they show that the intersection of supply and demand sets both price and quantity. They then argue that the price set by this intersection of supply and demand is taken as given by each competitive firm, so that the supply curve for the individual firm is its marginal cost curve. Then they notionally add all these marginal cost curves up, to get the supply curve for the industry – and its point of intersection with the demand curve determines the market price.

But there is a 'chicken and egg' problem here. Which comes first – price being set by the intersection of supply and demand, or individual firms equating marginal cost to price? And why should a level of output which involves making a loss on part of output (the part past where market marginal revenue equals marginal cost) determine where each individual firm perceives price as being set?

Economists have been bewitched by their own totem. They draw a downward-sloping market demand curve, and an upward-sloping supply curve, and assume that price and quantity must be set by the intersection of the two curves. But the 'supply curve' is really only the aggregate of the marginal cost curves of all the competitive firms. It isn't a supply curve unless they can prove that, whatever the market demand curve looks like, the industry will supply the quantity given by the intersection of the demand curve and the aggregate marginal cost curve.

This isn't the case in their own model of monopoly. The intersection of marginal cost and marginal revenue determines the quantity produced, while the price charged is set by the price the demand curve gives for that quantity: price and quantity are *not* determined by the intersection of the demand curve and the marginal cost curve.

Economists claim that price and quantity are set by the intersection of the demand curve and the aggregate marginal cost curve in the case of perfect competition, but their 'proof' relies on the erroneous proposition that the demand curve perceived by each individual firm is, you guessed it, horizontal.

Once this spurious proposition is removed, the price that the competitive firm takes as given is the price determined by the intersection of the market demand curve and the aggregate marginal cost curve – which is precisely the same price as a monopoly would charge. To argue otherwise is to argue for either irrational behavior at the level of the individual firm – so that part of output is produced at a loss – or that, somehow, individually rational behavior (maximizing profit) leads to collectively irrational behavior – so that profit-maximizing behavior by each individual firm leads to the industry somehow producing part of its output at a loss. However, the essence of the neoclassical vision is that individually rational behavior leads to collectively rational behavior.

Therefore, the price that the perfectly competitive firm will take as given when it adjusts its output is not a market price set by equating price to marginal cost, but a market price set by equating marginal revenue to marginal cost. The quantity produced at this price will be equivalent, when summed, to the output of a single monopolist. On the grounds of properly amended economic theory, monopoly and perfect competition are identical.

Returns to scale and the durability of perfect competition

To date I have accepted the assumption that a monopoly has no scale advantages over a perfectly competitive firm, so that it is possible to sum the cost functions of numerous small firms and come up with aggregate costs similar to those of a large firm.

In general, this assumption of scale-invariant costs will be invalid. If we are simply considering the costs of producing a homogeneous product, then it is likely that a very large firm will have scale advantages over a very small one. In the vernacular of economics, large firms benefit from returns to scale.

Returns to scale occur when the cost of production rises less rapidly than the output as the scale of production increases. A simple example is in farming, where farms need to be separated from each other by fences. The amount of fencing required depends on the perimeter of the farm. If we consider a square block of land, fencing will depend on the length of the four sides of the square. Cost is thus the cost of fencing per mile, times four times the length of a side. But the area enclosed by the fence depends on the length of a side squared. The output of a farm is related to its area, so that output is a function of the length of a side squared. Doubling the perimeter of a farm thus doubles its fencing costs, but increases its output fourfold.

As a result, large farms have a scale advantage over smaller farms. A farm with a square mile of land requires four miles of perimeter fencing to each square mile, while a farm with four square miles of land requires eight miles of perimeter fencing – or just two miles of perimeter fencing to each square mile of land.

The same concept applies in numerous ways. For a substantial range of §22
output, a large blast furnace will be more cost effective than a smaller one, a large ship than a smaller one, a large car factory than a smaller one.

If large firms have cost advantages over small ones, then given open competition, the large firms will drive the small ones out of business (though marketing and debt problems will limit the process, as Sraffa notes). Hence increasing returns to scale mean that the perfectly competitive market is unstable: it will, in time, break down to a situation of either oligopoly (several large firms) or monopoly (one large firm).

Economists have been well aware of this dilemma since Marshall at the end of the nineteenth century, and the fiction that has been invented to cope with it is the concept of the long run average cost curve.[14] The curve is 'u-shaped,' which asserts that there is some ideal scale of output at which the cost of production is minimized. In the long run, all inputs can be varied, so this shape is supposed to represent increasing returns to scale up to the point of minimum cost, beyond which decreasing returns to scale start to occur, so that the cost of production rises.

A competitive industry is supposed to converge to this ideal scale of output over time, in which case its many extremely big firms are safe from the predations of any much larger firm, since such a competitor would necessarily have higher costs.

This defence is specious on several counts.

First, the question of whether perfect competition can exist in a particular industry becomes an empirical one: what is the ideal scale of output, and how many firms could then occupy a particular industry at a particular time?

For some industries, the answer might well be 'very many' – the ever popular wheat farm comes to mind. However, for some other industries, the answer might well be 'very few.' It seems, for example, that the worldwide market for large intercontinental passenger airplanes can support at most three firms.

The argument that, 'in the long run,' this industry could be perfectly competitive because it could grow big enough to support hundreds or thousands of competitors is ludicrous. By the time the world was large enough to support hundreds of Boeings and Airbuses, it is highly likely that some entirely different form of transport would have superseded the airplane.

Secondly, the long run supply curve is actually constructed under the assumption of constant technology: in other words, it is not really a concept in time at all. The scale economies are supposedly there all the time, ready to be exploited.

If so, then unless an industry is already big enough to support the enormous number of firms surmised by the model of perfect competition – all operating at the ideal scale – large firms can immediately out-compete small firms. In other words, the only way competitive firms can survive is if the industry is already so large that it can support an enormous number of firms of the ideal scale.

The theoretical response of economists to this dilemma has been to presume constant returns to scale. With constant returns, 'size does not matter': a small firm will be just as cost efficient as a large one.

Unfortunately, size does matter. Economies of scale are an important part of the reason that most industries are dominated by a small number of

---

14 Sraffa's paper 'The law of returns under competitive conditions' (Sraffa 1926) critiqued a forerunner to this idea: that economies of scale could be external to the firm, but internal to the industry. This would mean that as an industry expanded, all firms benefited from lower costs, but none benefited any more than any other. Sraffa argued that few, if any, economies of scale would fit in this category: instead most would be internal to a firm, and thus advantage the big firm more than the small.

very large firms. We do need an adequate analysis of how such an industry functions, but neoclassical economics does not provide it.

Addendum: the war over perfect competition

As noted, my plan to start work on *Finance and Economic Breakdown* (a book-length treatment of Minsky's 'Financial Instability Hypothesis') when I finished *Debunking Economics* was derailed for the next four years as I found myself embroiled in disputes with neoclassical economists – via email, in web forums, in public and in referee comments on my papers – about this argument. The end result was a substantial strengthening of the critique, the most important component of which was a proof that *equating marginal cost and marginal revenue does not maximize profits.*

I developed this proof after realizing that the key result in this chapter – that the demand curve for a competitive firm cannot be horizontal – was discovered by the neoclassical economist George Stigler over half a century ago. Why, I wondered, did he nonetheless continue to subscribe to and defend neoclassical theory?

Apart from the usual psychological explanation – that when you've committed yourself to a particular belief system and made your reputation in it, it is extraordinarily hard to accept that it might be false – there is a technical reason in the same paper. Though he proved that the individual firm's demand curve had the same negative slope as the market demand curve, Stigler also proved that, *if firms produced where marginal cost equaled marginal revenue,* then the more firms there were in an industry, the closer industry output would be to where price equaled marginal cost.

> It is intuitively plausible that with infinite numbers all monopoly power (and indeterminacy) will vanish [...] But a simple demonstration, in case of sellers of equal size, would amount only to showing that Marginal revenue = Price + Price/Number of sellers [times] Market elasticity, and that this last term goes to zero as the number of sellers increases indefinitely. (Stigler 1957: 8)

Stigler thus believed that he had neutralized his finding in the same paper. Yes, the conventional neoclassical belief that the individual competitive firm faces a horizontal demand curve is false, but if there are a large number of firms in an industry, then marginal revenue for the individual firm will be very close to the market price. Therefore the collective effect is the same: price will be set where supply equals demand. The key result of competition is restored.

From this point on, the standard failings of neoclassical research and pedagogy took over. Only a minority of economists read the paper; textbooks continued to teach the concept that Stigler had disproved; and the minority of economists who were aware of Stigler's paper defended the failure to take his result seriously because, in the end, the outcome was alleged to be the same: supply will equal demand in a competitive market.

I instead saw a logical error: Stigler's proof that marginal revenue for the individual firm would converge to market price as the number of firms increased was correct, *if* those firms all set marginal revenue equal to marginal price. But all the problems that I had identified in this chapter still remained: in particular, producing where supply equaled demand required 'profit-maximizing' firms to actually make losses on all goods sold past the point at which industry-level marginal revenue equaled marginal cost.

There was only one explanation: *equating marginal cost and marginal revenue couldn't be profit-maximizing behavior.*

I followed the logic forward and proved that the true profit-maximizing formula was quite different. If competitive firms did actually profit-maximize, they would produce an output much lower than the level where marginal cost equaled marginal revenue. The market outcome was that a competitive industry would produce the same amount as a monopoly, and market price would exceed marginal cost.

Equating marginal cost and marginal revenue does not maximize profits

The logic is fairly simple to follow if you imagine that you are running a competitive firm, and ask yourself this question: 'Is my level of output the *only* factor that can affect my profits?' The answer is, of course not: your profit depends not just on how much you produce, but also how much all the other firms in the industry produce. This is true even if you can't control what other firms do, and even if you don't try to react to what you think they might do. You work in a multi-firm industry, and the actions of all other firms impinge upon your own profits.

However, the neoclassical 'profit-maximizing' formula implies that your output is the only factor determining your profits: it uses simple calculus to advise you to produce where the change in your profits *relative to your own output* is zero. What you really need to do – if you're going to try to use calculus to work out what to do – is to work out where the change in your profits *relative to total industry output* is zero.

Intuitively, this is likely to mean that the actual amount you produce – which is something you can control – should be *less* than the amount the neoclassical formula recommends. This is because it's highly likely that the impact on your profit of changes in output by other firms – which you can't control – will be negative: if other firms increase their output, your profit is likely to fall. So when you work out the impact that changes in output by other firms has on your profits, the sign of this change is likely to be negative.

Therefore, to find the point at which your profit is at a maximum with respect to total industry output, you're likely to want the sign for the impact of *your* changes in output on *your* profit to be positive. This will mean that your output level will be less than the level at which your marginal cost equals your marginal revenue.

The best way to solve this problem precisely is to work out when what is known as the 'total differential' of the firm's profit is equal to zero (to avoid using symbolic terms like 'n' for the number of firms in the industry, I'll work with a hypothetical industry with 1,000 firms in it, but the logic applies independently of the number of firms in the industry).

The profit of your firm will be its revenue – which will equal your firm's output times the market price – minus costs. What we have to do is work out how these two aspects of profit are influenced by the changes in output by *all* the firms in the industry, including your own.

Using a calculus procedure known as the Product Rule, the change in the revenue side of this calculation can be broken down into two bits:

- *your* output, times how much a given firm's change in output changes market price; plus
- market price, times how much a given firm's change in output causes *you* to alter your own output.

Thanks to Stigler's accurate calculus from 1957, we know that we can substitute the slope of the market demand curve for 'how much a given firm's change in output changes market price,' so the first term in the change in revenue calculation becomes your firm's output, times the slope of the market demand curve. With 1,000 firms in the industry, we get 1,000 copies of this term, which is your firm's output, multiplied by the slope of the market demand curve.

The second term in the change in revenue is the market price, times the amount that *your* output changes owing to a change in output by a given firm. Since we're working with the Marshallian model, which assumes that firms don't react strategically to what other firms do, then 999 times out of 1,000 this term will be the market price times zero. But once, it will be how much *your output* changes, given a change in *your output*. The ratio of the change in your output to the change in your output is one, so once – and only once – this calculation will return the market price.

Finally, we have to consider the cost side of the calculation: this will be how much your total costs change, given a change in output by a given firm. As with the last calculation for revenue, 999 times out of 1,000 this will be zero – because your costs don't change when the output of another firm changes. But once, and only once, it will be how much your total costs change, given a change in your output. This is your firm's marginal cost.

That gives you three terms, and when the output level you choose causes the sum of these three to be zero, you have identified the output level for your firm that will maximize your profits. These three terms are:

- the market price (a positive number);
- plus the slope of the market demand curve multiplied by *1,000 times* your

output (a negative number, since the slope of the market demand curve is negative);

- minus your marginal cost.

The difference between this formula and the neoclassical formula is subtle and the size of an elephant at the same time. The neoclassical formula tells you that you maximize your profits when these three terms are equal:

- the market price;
- plus the slope of the market demand curve multiplied by your output;
- minus your marginal cost.

Whoops! The neoclassical formula has erroneously omitted 999 times your output times the slope of the market demand curve – a very large negative term (since the slope of the market demand curve is negative). It therefore takes a larger marginal cost to reduce the whole neoclassical expression to zero, which you can only achieve by producing a higher output. All of this additional output will be sold at a loss: the increase in revenue you get from selling those additional units will be less than the increase in costs the additional production causes.

The neoclassical formula is thus categorically wrong about the level of output by the individual firm that will maximize its profits – except in the one case of a monopoly, where the two formulas coincide.

If competitive firms are truly profit maximizers, then they will produce substantially less output each than neoclassical theory says they will (roughly half as much), and the sum of this output will – if they face identical costs of production – be the same as would be produced by a monopoly.

It could be argued that the accurate formula derived above requires the firm to know something that it can't possibly know – which is how many firms there are in the industry. In fact, this is less of a problem than it seems, because it's possible to reorganize this formula into a form in which the number of firms in the industry isn't that important.[15] But a more important point is that in reality firms don't 'do calculus.' They are far more likely to work out the answer to this and other questions by trial and error.

Calculus schmalculus

What firms would actually do is work out the ideal amount to produce to maximize profits by choosing some output level at random, and then vary this amount to see what happens to their profits. If a firm's profit rose, then it would continue altering its output in the same direction; but if its profit fell, then it would reverse direction.

15 The revised formula, in this 1,000-firm example, is that the firm should make the gap between its marginal revenue and marginal cost equal to 999/1000th of the gap between market price and its marginal cost. The number of firms can be safely ignored and the output level chosen will still be approximately right, whereas the neoclassical formula remains precisely wrong.

Unfortunately we can't test this using empirical data, because, as I argue later, the assumptions of the neoclassical model (a falling demand curve, a rising supply curve, and a static setting in which to maximize profits) don't even come close to describing reality. But one can today create an artificial market using a computer model that does fit the neoclassical assumptions, and then see what happens.

The next few graphs show the results of this simulation:

- firms choose an initial output level at random;
- the initial market price is determined by the sum of these randomly chosen outputs;
- each firm then chooses a random amount to vary its output by, and changes its initial output by this amount;
- a new market price is calculated;
- if a firm's profit has risen as a result of the change in output, it continues changing its output in the same direction;
- otherwise it reverses direction.

At the extremes considered here, of a monopoly and a 100-firm industry, neoclassical theory is correct for a monopoly, but very wrong for the 100-firm industry. It predicts that such an industry will produce effectively where marginal cost equals price – where the 'supply curve' intersects the demand curve – but in practice the 100-firm industry produces an output that is almost the same as the monopoly's.

Neoclassical theory also predicts that industry output will converge to the §23 competitive ideal as the number of firms in the industry rises. Simulations with between 1 and 100 firms in the industry show no pattern, though in general the output level is well below that predicted by neoclassical theory – but close to the prediction of my equation (see Figure 4.3).

This market outcome is not caused by collusion, but is simply the result §24 of profit-maximizing behavior. Firms also follow very different paths in their output, even though the basic 'strategy' is the same for each firm: vary output and try to find the output level that generates the largest profit.

Firms have very different outcomes with respect to profit as well, though §25 in general most make far more profit from this 'suck it and see' algorithm than they would make if they followed the neoclassical formula.

Many different outcomes are possible with different assumptions – in particular, the introduction of some irrationality by firms (continuing to increase output when the last increase in output reduced profit, for example), or a greater dispersal in the size of the changes in output by firms causes the aggregate result to move in the direction of the neoclassical formula (Keen and Standish 2010: 69–74). But the neoclassical proposition that strictly rational behavior leads to a competitive industry producing where individual marginal revenue equals marginal cost is strictly false.

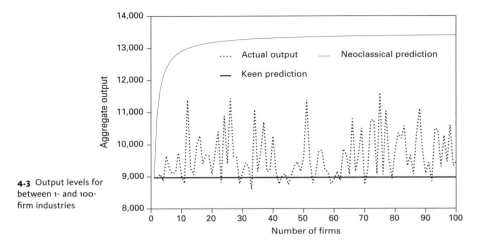

4.3 Output levels for between 1- and 100-firm industries

Dialogue with the deaf

There are other theories of competition (the Cournot-Nash and Bertrand models of game-theoretic behavior, where firms do react strategically to what other firms might do), where a 'perfectly competitive' outcome can occur from non-profit-maximizing behavior. But the standard Marshallian model of the firm is categorically false: the demand curve for a competitive firm is not horizontal, equating marginal cost and marginal revenue does not maximize profits, and a competitive industry will produce the same amount of output as a monopoly and sell it for the same price. The 'Marshallian' model of the competitive firm is dead.

Or it should be. Instead, given the resistance of neoclassical economics to criticism, this false model is likely to live on for decades. Though this critique has been published in a range of journals – including one edited by physicists, whose mathematical capabilities far exceed those of economists – I have been unable to get it published in neoclassical economics journals. The odds that this critique will ever be recognized by economics textbooks writers are therefore effectively zero.

Every manner of excuse has been offered to avoid confronting these uncomfortable but mathematically unimpeachable results. The most remarkable excuses came from referees for the *Economic Journal* and the *Journal of Economics Education*.[16]

A referee for the former journal admitted that this result was significant, but argued that it did not matter because, he alleged, the conventional theory assumed that firms attempted to maximize their profits *while assuming that the output of other firms was fixed*. This alleged assumption cannot be found in any textbook on perfect competition, and amounts to an assumption of

---

16 The then editor of the *Journal of Economics Education*, Bill Becker, was himself keen to have the paper published, and submitted it to eminent referees to try to improve its chances of being accepted.

irrational behavior on behalf of firms: 'Needless to say, this result is worthy of publication on *Economic Journal* if it is correct. However, after reading the paper, I am not convinced that this is the case. On the contrary I think the result is due to authors' confusion about an individual firm's rationality: maximizing its profit given others' outputs fixed [...]' (Referee, *Economic Journal*).

Though neoclassical economics has always insisted that it is a mathematically based theory, a referee for the *Journal of Economics Education* refused to consider that one of the most basic procedures in calculus – the Chain Rule – could be applied in microeconomics: 'Stigler's many attempts to save neoclassical theory have always caused more problems than they have solved. His version of the chain rule is contrary to the partial equilibrium method and thus is irrelevant' (Referee, *Journal of Economics Education*).

These and many other frankly irrational responses by editors and referees for other neoclassical journals emphasize a frequent refrain in this book, that neoclassical economics is far more a belief system than it is a science.

So what?

The main consequence of this critique for neoclassical economics is that it removes one of the two essential pillars of their approach to modeling the economy. Unless perfect competition rules, there is no supply curve.

This fact goes a long way to explaining why neoclassical economists cling to using a notion that is so unrealistic, and so unlike any industry in the real world: because without it, their preferred method of modeling becomes impossible.

Economics has championed the notion that the best guarantee of social welfare is competition, and perfect competition has always been its ideal. The critiques in this chapter show that economic theory has no grounds whatsoever for preferring perfect competition over monopoly. Both fail the economist's test of welfare, that marginal cost should be equated to price.

Worse, the goal of setting marginal cost equal to price is as elusive and unattainable as the Holy Grail. For this to apply at the market level, part of the output of firms must be produced at a loss. The social welfare ideal thus requires individual irrationality. This would not be a problem for some schools of economics, but it is for the neoclassical school, which has always argued that the pursuit of individual self-interest would lead to the best, most rational outcome for all of society.

Economics can therefore no longer wave its preferred totem, but must instead only derive supply as a point determined by intersection of the marginal cost and marginal revenue curves.

Worse still, once we integrate this result with the fact that the demand curve can have any shape at all, the entire 'Totem of the Micro' has to be discarded. Instead of two simple intersecting lines, we have at least two squiggly lines for the demand side – marginal revenue and price, both of which will be curves – an aggregate marginal cost curve, and lots of lines joining the many intersections of the marginal revenue curve with the marginal cost curve to the price curve. The real Totem of the Micro is not the one shown at the beginning of this chapter, but a couple of strands of noodles wrapped around a chopstick, with lots of toothpicks thrown on top.[17]

There is thus very little left of conventional economic theory. The last two chapters leave very little of the 'Totem of the Micro' standing: in place of the simple intersecting supply and demand curve of conventional neoclassical belief, we have wavy intersecting lines. But even this is too generous to the neoclassical model, because – as Sraffa pointed out almost ninety years ago – there is no empirical justification for the one neoclassical microeconomics concept that we have not yet critiqued: the rising marginal cost curve.

17 In addition, to compare competitive firms to monopolies at all scales of output, then – for reasons outlined in Chapter 5 – the marginal cost curve must be drawn horizontally.

5 | THE PRICE OF EVERYTHING AND THE VALUE OF NOTHING

Why most products cost less to produce as output rises

We have already seen that both the demand and supply aspects of conventional economic analysis are unsound: first, market demand curves don't obey the 'Law' of Demand, and can have any shape at all. Secondly, a supply curve doesn't exist.

But surely, on the supply side, it makes sense that, to elicit a larger supply of a commodity, a higher price must be offered?

There is, in fact, an alternative proposition, which held sway in economics for its first century. This was the argument of the classical school of economics that price was set by the cost of production, while the level of demand determined output.[1] When this proposition is put in the same static form as economics uses to describe a commodity market, it translates as a horizontal (or even a falling) supply curve, so that the market price doesn't change as the quantity produced rises (and it can actually fall). This chapter shows that, though the modern neoclassical position is superficially more appealing and apparently more sophisticated, there are logical problems with it which mean that the classical position is a more accurate description of reality.

The kernel

One of the peculiar aspects of modern Western society is that the majority of the population has no direct experience of how the commodities it consumes are produced. Only a small and decreasing minority is directly involved in production, and only a minority of that minority has direct knowledge of how factories are designed and managed. In contrast to consumption, the conditions under which commodities are produced are a mystery to most people, and the economic analysis of production appears to illuminate that mystery.

Neoclassical theory argues that, in the 'short run,' productivity falls as output rises, so that higher levels of output result in higher prices. The 'marginal cost curve' therefore slopes upwards, and a higher price has to be offered to entice firms to produce a higher output.

Though this sounds intuitively plausible, when this theory was put to those who do know how factories are designed and managed, they rejected it as

---

1 Smith and Ricardo allowed exceptions to this rule; neoclassical economics in effect made these exceptions the rule.

'the product of the itching imaginations of uninformed and inexperienced arm-chair theorizers' (Lee 1998: 73, citing Tucker).

How could something which seems so reasonable to the inexperienced be so absurd according to those 'in the know'? The answer in part lies in the assumptions economists make about production. Though these seem sound to the uninitiated, two key assumptions are in fact contradictory: if one applies for a given industry, then the other one almost certainly does not. When one applies, supply and demand become interdependent; when the other does, the marginal cost curve is likely to be horizontal.

Economic theory also doesn't apply in the 'real world' because engineers purposely design factories to avoid the problems that economists believe force production costs to rise. Factories are built with significant excess capacity, and are also designed to work at high efficiency right from low to full capacity. Only products that can't be produced in factories (such as oil) are likely to have costs of production that behave the way economists expect.

The outcome is that costs of production are normally either constant or falling for the vast majority of manufactured goods, so that average and even marginal cost curves are normally either flat or downward sloping. This causes manufacturers no difficulties, but it makes life impossible for neoclassical economists, since most of neoclassical theory depends on supply curves sloping upwards.

The roadmap

In this chapter I outline the neoclassical analysis of production, which concludes that productivity will fall as output rises, leading to rising costs of production. This in turn leads to a need for the market price to rise if producers are to supply more, which economists represent as a 'supply curve' that slopes upward in price.

Next I detail Sraffa's argument that two crucial assumptions of this analysis – that supply and demand are independent, and that at least one input to production can't be varied in the short run – are mutually exclusive. A number of potential neoclassical rejoinders to this argument are considered and dismissed.

The outline of the neoclassical model of production below will probably convince you that the theory makes sense, but as with the corresponding section in Chapter 3, it is almost certain to bore you senseless. It is also unavoidably laden with jargon, and less accessible than Chapter 3 since few of us have any experience of production to the same depth as we have experience of consumption. So go back to the coffee pot, pour yourself a strong one, and read on.

Diminishing productivity causes rising price

The neoclassical theory of production argues that capacity constraints play the key role in determining prices, with the cost of production – and therefore prices – rising as producers try to squeeze more and more output out of a fixed number of machines, in what they call 'the short run.' The short run is a period of time long enough to change variable inputs – such as labor – but not long enough to change fixed inputs – such as machines – or for new entrants to come into the industry.

The argument has several stages: stage one puts the proposition that productivity falls as output rises; stage two takes the declining productivity argument and rephrases it as rising costs; and stage three determines the point of maximum profitability by identifying where the gap between revenue and costs is greatest.

Stage one: productivity falls as output rises Neoclassical theory asserts that the supply curve slopes upward because productivity falls as output rises. This falling productivity translates into a rising price. There is thus a direct link between what economists call 'marginal productivity' – the amount produced by the last worker – and 'marginal cost' – the cost of producing the last unit.

Table 5.1 shows an example of production as neoclassicals imagine it. This mythical firm has fixed costs of $250,000, and pays its workers a wage of $1,000.[2] It can sell as many units as it can produce at the market price of $4. To produce output at all, the firm must hire workers: with no workers, output is zero. The first worker enables the firm to produce 52 units of output. This is shown in the first row of the table: the labor input is one unit, and total output is 52 units.

The marginal product of this worker – the difference between production without him (zero) and production with – is 52 units. The marginal cost of the output is the worker's wage – $1,000 – divided by the number of units produced – 52 – which yields a marginal cost of $19.20.

The average fixed costs of output at this point are enormous – $250,000 divided by just 52, or $4,807 per unit. The average total cost is $251,000 divided by 52, or $4,827 per unit – which implies a loss of $4,823 per unit sold, if this were the chosen level of production.

At this stage, production benefits from economies of scale. Just one worker had to perform all tasks, whereas a second worker allows them to divide up the jobs between them, so that each specializes to at least that extent. With specialization, the productivity of both workers rises. The same process continues with the ninth and tenth workers, so that the marginal product of the ninth – the amount he adds to output over and above the amount produced by eight workers – is 83.6 units. Similarly, the marginal product of the tenth worker is 87.5 units.

---

2 Money is simply a measuring stick in this analysis, and the monetary unit could as easily be pigs as dollars.

TABLE 5.1 Input and output data for a hypothetical firm

Labor	Output	Wage bill	Total cost	Marginal product	Marginal cost	Average variable cost	Average fixed cost	Average total cost	Total revenue	Profit
1	52	1,000	251,000	52.0	19.2	19	4,808	4,827	208	-250,792
9	611	9,000	259,000	83.6	12.0	15	409	424	2,443	-256,557
10	698	10,000	260,000	87.5	11.4	14	358	372	2,793	-257,207
100	23,333	100,000	350,000	398.5	2.5	4	11	15	93,333	-256,667
276	131,111	276,000	526,000	772.5	1.3	2	2	4	524,444	-1,556
277	131,885	277,000	527,000	773.7	1.3	2	2	4	527,539	539
400	233,333	400,000	650,000	850.0	1.2	2	1	3	933,333	283,333
500	316,667	500,000	750,000	800.5	1.2	2	1	2	1,266,667	516,667
700	443,333	700,000	950,000	401.5	2.5	2	1	2	1,773,333	823,333
725	452,370	725,000	975,000	323.5	3.1	2	1	2	1,809,479	834,479
730	453,938	730,000	980,000	307.1	3.3	2	1	2	1,815,753	835,753
735	455,424	735,000	985,000	290.5	3.4	2	1	2	1,821,698	836,698
740	456,827	740,000	990,000	273.7	3.7	2	1	2	1,827,307	837,307
745	458,144	745,000	995,000	256.6	3.9	2	1	2	1,832,576	837,576
746	458,397	746,000	996,000	253.1	4.0	2	1	2	1,833,588	837,588
747	458,647	747,000	997,000	249.7	4.0	2	1	2	1,834,587	837,587
748	458,893	748,000	998,000	246.2	4.1	2	1	2	1,835,572	837,572
800	466,667	800,000	1,050,000	52.0	19.2	2	1	2	1,866,667	816,667

If the firm actually produced this number of units, it would lose $257,207 dollars – more than its fixed costs. However, the process of rising marginal productivity – and therefore falling marginal cost – comes to the rescue as output rises. By the 100th worker, the firm is still making a loss, but the loss is falling because its marginal cost has fallen below the sale price. The 100th worker adds 398.5 units to output, at a marginal cost of $1,000 divided by 398.5, or just $2.50 a unit. This is less than the sale price of $4 a unit, so the firm is making a profit on the increase in output – but only enough to reduce its losses at this stage, rather than to put it into the black.

Black ink arrives with the 277th worker, who brings in $3,090 profit – the proceeds of selling the 772.5 additional units the worker produces at the sale price of $4 a unit – for the cost of his wage of $1,000.

This process of rising marginal productivity continues right up to the 400th worker hired. By this stage, marginal cost has fallen dramatically. The 400th worker adds 850 units to output, so that the marginal cost of his output is the wage of $1,000 divided by 850, or $1.18 (rounded up to $1.2 in the table). Average fixed costs, which were enormous at a tiny level of output, are relatively trivial at the output level of 233,333 units: they are down to just over a dollar.

From this point on, productivity of each new worker ceases to rise. Each new worker adds less to output than his predecessor. The rationale for this is that the ratio of workers – the 'variable factor of production' – to machinery – the 'fixed factor of production' – has exceeded some optimal level. Now each extra worker still adds output, but a diminishing rate. In economic parlance, we have reached the region where diminishing marginal productivity applies. Since marginal product is now falling, marginal cost will start to rise.

But profit continues to rise, because though each additional worker adds less output and therefore brings in less revenue, the revenue from the additional units still exceeds the cost of hiring the worker. In economic parlance, marginal revenue exceeds marginal cost.

We can see this with the 500th worker, who adds 800.5 units to output. The marginal cost of his output is the wage ($1,000) divided by 800.5, or $1.25 (rounded down in the table). This is higher than the minimum level of $1.18 reached with the 500th worker. But the additional units this worker produces can all be sold at $4, so the firm still makes a profit out of employing the 500th worker.

The same principle still applies for the 600th worker, and the 700th. Productivity has dropped sharply now, so that this worker adds only 401.5 units to output, for a marginal cost of $2.50. But this is still less than the amount the additional output can be sold for, so the firm makes a profit out of this worker.

This process of rising profit comes to an end with the 747th worker, whose additional product – 249.7 units – can only be sold for $998.8, versus the cost of his wage of $1,000. From this point on, any additional workers cost more to employ than the amount of additional output they produce can be sold for.

The firm should therefore employ 746 workers, and maximize its profit at $837,588. At this point, the marginal cost of production equals the marginal revenue from sale, and profit is maximized.

The 800th adds 52 units, for a now soaring marginal cost of $19.20. By the time we get to the 812th worker, workers are – metaphorically speaking – falling over each other on the factory floor, and this worker adds a mere 3.3 units to output, for a marginal cost of $300. The next worker actually reduces output.

§26–31

From minnow to market The exposition above simply describes the situation for a single firm. To derive the market supply curve, we have to aggregate the supply curves of a multitude of producers – just as to complete the derivation of the market demand curve, the demand curves of a multitude of consumers had to be added together.[3] Since each individual firm's marginal cost curve is upward sloping, the market supply curve is also upward sloping.

§32

Things don't add up

There is no doubt that the economic analysis of production has great superficial appeal – sufficient to explain much of the fealty which neoclassical economists swear to their vision of the market. But at a deeper level, the argument is fundamentally flawed – as Piero Sraffa first pointed out in 1926.

The crux of Sraffa's critique was that 'the law of diminishing marginal returns' will not apply in general in an industrial economy. Instead, Sraffa argues that the common position would be constant marginal returns, and therefore horizontal (rather than rising) marginal costs.

Sraffa's argument constitutes a fundamental critique of economic theory, since, as I've just explained, diminishing marginal returns determine everything in the economic theory of production: the output function determines marginal product, which in turn determines marginal cost. With diminishing marginal productivity, the marginal cost of production eventually rises to equal marginal revenue. Since firms seek to maximize profit, and since this equality of (rising) marginal cost to marginal revenue gives you maximum profit, this determines the level of output.

If instead constant returns are the norm, then the output function instead is a straight line through the origin, just like the total revenue line – though with a different slope. If (as a factory owner would hope) the slope of revenue is greater than the slope of the cost curve, then after a firm had met its fixed costs, it would make a profit from every unit sold: the more units it sold, the greater its profit would be.

---

3 As we'll see shortly, this generates just as many problems as aggregation of demand curves did.

In terms of the model of perfect competition, there would be no limit to the amount a competitive firm would wish to produce, so that neoclassical theory could not explain how firms (in a competitive industry) decided how much to produce. In fact, according to the conventional model, each firm would want to produce an infinite amount.

§33

This is so patently impossible *within the uncorrected neoclassical model* that, when told of Sraffa's critique, most neoclassicals simply dismiss it out of hand: if Sraffa was right, then why don't firms produce an infinite amount of goods? Since they don't, Sraffa must be wrong.

This knee-jerk response to Sraffa's critique brings to mind the joke that an economist is someone who, when shown that something works in practice, comments, 'Ah, but does it work in theory?' Sraffa instead put the opposite case: sure, the neoclassical model of production works in theory, if you accept its assumptions. But can the conditions that the model assumes actually apply in practice? If they can't, then regardless of how watertight the theory might be given its assumptions, it will be irrelevant in practice. It therefore should not be used as the theory of production, because above all else, such a theory must be realistic.

Sraffa's argument focused upon the neoclassical assumptions that there were 'factors of production' which were fixed in the short run, and that supply and demand were independent of each other. He argued that these two assumptions could not be fulfilled simultaneously.

In circumstances where it was valid to say that some factor of production was fixed in the short run, supply and demand would not be independent, so that every point on the supply curve would be associated with a different demand curve. On the other hand, in circumstances where supply and demand could justifiably be treated as independent, then in general it would be impossible for any factor of production to be fixed. Hence the marginal costs of production would be constant.

Sraffa began by noting that the preceding classical school of economics also had a 'law of diminishing marginal returns.' However, for the classical school, it was not part of price theory, but part of the theory of income distribution. Its application was largely restricted to the explanation of rent.

The classical argument was that farming would first be done on the best land available, and only when this land was fully utilized would land of a lesser quality be used. Thus, as population grew, progressively poorer land would be brought into use. This poorer land would produce a lower yield per acre than the better land. Diminishing marginal returns therefore applied, but they occurred because the quality of land used fell – not because of any relationship between 'fixed' and 'variable' factors of production.

Sraffa argued that the neoclassical theory of diminishing marginal productivity was based on an inappropriate application of this concept in the context of their model of a competitive economy, where the model assumed that all firms were so small relative to the market that they could not influence the price for their commodity, and that factors of production were homogeneous. In the neoclassical model, therefore, falling quality of inputs couldn't explain diminishing marginal productivity. Instead, productivity could only fall because the ratio of 'variable factors of production' to fixed factors exceeded some optimal level.

The question then arises of when is it valid to regard a given factor of production – say, land – as fixed. Sraffa said that this was a valid assumption when industries were defined very broadly, but this then contradicted the assumption that demand and supply are independent.

Sraffa's broad arrow If we take the broadest possible definition of an industry – say, agriculture – then it is valid to treat factors it uses heavily (such as land) as fixed. Since additional land can only be obtained by converting land from other uses (such as manufacturing or tourism), it is clearly difficult to increase that factor in the short run. The 'agriculture industry' will therefore suffer from diminishing returns, as predicted.

However, such a broadly defined industry is so big that changes in its output must affect other industries. In particular, an attempt to increase agricultural output will affect the price of the chief variable input – labor – as it takes workers away from other industries (and it will also affect the price of the 'fixed' input).

This might appear to strengthen the case for diminishing returns – since inputs are becoming more expensive as well as less productive. However, it also undermines two other crucial parts of the model: the assumption that demand for and supply of a commodity are independent, and the proposition that one market can be studied in isolation from all other markets.

Instead, if increasing the supply of agriculture changes the relative prices of land and labor, then it will also change the distribution of income. As we saw in Chapter 2, changing the distribution of income changes the demand curve. There will therefore be a different demand curve for every different position along the supply curve for agriculture. This makes it impossible to draw independent demand and supply curves that intersect in just one place. As Sraffa expressed it:

> If in the production of a particular commodity a considerable part of a factor is employed, the total amount of which is fixed or can be increased only at a more than proportional cost, a small increase in the production of the commodity will necessitate a more intense utilization of that factor, and this will affect in the same manner the cost of the commodity in question and the cost of the other commodities into the production of which that factor enters; and since commodities into the production of which a common special factor enters are frequently, to a certain extent, substitutes for one

another the modification in their price will not be without appreciable effects upon demand in the industry concerned. (Sraffa 1926: 539)

These non-negligible impacts upon demand mean that the demand curve for this 'industry' will shift with every movement along its supply curve. It is therefore not legitimate to draw independent demand and supply curves, since factors that alter supply will also alter demand. Supply and demand will therefore intersect in multiple locations, and it is impossible to say which price or quantity will prevail.

Thus while diminishing returns do exist when industries are broadly defined, no industry can be considered in isolation from all others, as supply and demand curve analysis requires.

§34

As you can see, Sraffa's argument here was a precursor of the Sonnenschein-Mantel-Debreu conditions that undermine the neoclassical mode of the market demand curve, analyzed from the point of view of the producer rather than the consumer. This allows an upward-sloping supply curve to be drawn, but makes it impossible to derive an independent demand curve.

Sraffa's next argument leaves the demand curve intact, but undermines the concept of a rising supply curve.

Sraffa's narrow arrow When we use a more realistic, narrow definition of an industry – say, wheat rather than agriculture – Sraffa argues that, in general, diminishing returns are unlikely to exist. This is because the assumption that supply and demand are independent is now reasonable, but the assumption that some factor of production is fixed is not.

While neoclassical theory assumes that production occurs in a period of time during which it is impossible to vary one factor of production, Sraffa argues that in the real world, firms and industries will normally be able to vary all factors of production fairly easily.[4] This is because these additional inputs can be taken from other industries, or garnered from stocks of under-utilized resources. That is, if there is an increased demand for wheat, then rather than farming a given quantity of land more intensively, farmers will instead convert some land from another crop – say, barley – to wheat. Or they will convert some of their own land which is currently lying fallow to wheat production. Or farmers who currently grow a different crop will convert to wheat. As Sraffa expressed it:

> If we next take an industry which employs only a small part of the 'constant factor' (which appears more appropriate for the study of the particular equilibrium of a single industry), we find that a (small) increase in its production is generally met much more by drawing 'marginal doses' of the constant

---

4 Significant fixtures like factory buildings are an exception here, though machinery within the factory is not. Kornai's observations about the spare capacity in production, which I note later, supplement Sraffa's critique on this point.

factor from other industries than by intensifying its own utilization of it; thus the increase in cost will be practically negligible. (Ibid.: 539)

This means that, rather than the ratio of variable to 'fixed' outputs rising as the level of output rises, all inputs will be variable, the ratio of one input to another will remain constant, and productivity will remain constant as output rises. This results in constant costs as output rises, which means a constant level of productivity. Output will therefore be a linear function of the inputs: increase inputs by 20 percent, and output will rise by the same amount.

Since the shapes of the total, average and marginal cost curves are entirely a product of the shape of the output curve, a straight-line output curve results in constant marginal costs, and falling average costs.

With this cost structure, the main problem facing the firm is reaching its 'break-even point,' where the difference between the sale price and the constant variable costs of production just equal its fixed costs. From that point on, all sales add to profit. The firm's objective is thus to get as much of the market for itself as it can. This, of course, is not compatible with the neoclassical model of perfect competition.

Irrational managers Sraffa's broad and narrow critiques accept that, if a firm's output was actually constrained by a fixed resource, then its output would at first rise at an accelerating rate, as the productivity of additional variable inputs rose; then the rate of growth of output would reach a peak as the maximum level of productivity was reached, after which output would still rise, but at a diminishing rate. Finally, when even more variable inputs were added, total output would actually start to fall. In the vernacular of economics, the firm would at first experience increasing marginal productivity, then diminishing marginal productivity, and finally negative marginal productivity.

However, Sraffa disputes even this proposition. He instead argues that a firm is likely to produce at maximum productivity right up until the point at which diminishing marginal productivity sets in. Any other pattern, he argues, shows that the firm is behaving irrationally.

His argument is probably best illustrated with an analogy. Imagine that you have a franchise to supply ice creams to a football stadium, and that the franchise lets you determine where patrons are seated. If you have a small crowd one night – say, one quarter of capacity – would you spread the patrons evenly over the whole stadium, so that each patron was surrounded by several empty seats?

Of course not! This arrangement would simply force your staff to walk farther to make a sale. Instead, you'd leave much of the ground empty, thus minimizing the work your staff had to do to sell the ice creams. There's no sense in using every last inch of your 'fixed resource' (the stadium) if demand is less than capacity.

Sraffa argued that the same logic applied to a farm, or to a factory. If a variable input displays increasing marginal returns at some scale of output, then the sensible thing for the farmer or factory owner to do is leave some of the fixed resource idle, and work the variable input to maximum efficiency on part only of the fixed resource.

To give a numerical example, consider a wheat farm of 100 hectares, where one worker per hectare produces an output of 1 bushel per hectare, 2 workers per hectare produces 3 bushels, 3 per hectare produces 6 bushels, 4 per hectare produces 10 bushels, and 5 workers per hectare produces 12 bushels.

According to economists, if a farmer had 100 workers, he would spread them out 1 per hectare to produce 100 bushels of wheat. But, according to Sraffa, the farmer would instead leave 75 hectares of the farm idle, and work 25 hectares with the 100 workers to produce an output of 250 bushels. The farmer who behaves as Sraffa predicts comes out 150 bushels ahead of any farmer who behaves as economists expect.

Similarly, economic theory implies that a farmer with 200 workers would spread them over the farm's 100 hectares, to produce an output of 300 bushels. But Sraffa says that a sensible farmer would instead leave 50 hectares fallow, work the other 50 at 4 workers per hectare, and produce an output of 500 bushels. One again, a 'Sraffian' farmer is ahead of an 'economic' one, this time by 200 bushels.

The same pattern continues right up until the point at which 400 workers are employed, when finally diminishing marginal productivity sets in. A farm will produce more output by using less than all of the fixed input, up until this point.

§35

This might seem a minor point, but as usual with Sraffa, there is a sting in the tail. If marginal cost is constant, then average cost must be *greater* than marginal cost, so that any firm which sets price equal to marginal cost is going to make a loss. The neoclassical theory of price-setting can therefore only apply when demand is such that all firms are producing well beyond the point of maximum efficiency. The theory therefore depends on both labor and capital normally being fully employed.

So is full employment – not just of labor, but of other resources as well – the norm in a market economy? If all you read was neoclassical economic theory, you'd believe so – right from the standard textbook definition of economics as 'the study of the allocation of limited resources to unlimited wants.'

Of course, there is recorded unemployment of labor, but neoclassical economists (at least those of the 'freshwater' variety – see pp. 255–66) attribute that to the labor–leisure choice that households make: those who are recorded as unemployed are really deciding that at the wage rates that are on offer, they'd prefer not to work. But surely firms use their capital efficiently, so that it – the 'fixed resource' – is fully employed?

5.1 Capacity utilization over time in the USA

Even a cursory look at the economic data shows that this is not so. Even during the boom years of the 1960s, at least 10 percent of the USA's industrial capacity lay idle; even during subsequent booms, capacity utilization rarely reached 85 percent; and capacity utilization has rarely exceeded 80 percent since 2000, and fell below 70 percent in the depths of the Great Recession (see Figure 5.1).

This situation may seem bizarre from a neoclassical point of view – and there is a trend towards lower utilization over time that could indicate a secular problem – but it makes eminent sense from a very realistic perspective on both capitalism and socialism put forward by the Hungarian economist Janos Kornai.

Resource-constrained versus demand-constrained economies

Kornai's analysis was developed to try to explain why the socialist economies of eastern Europe had tended to stagnate (though with superficially full employment), while those of the capitalist West had generally been vibrant (though they were subject to periodic recessions). He noted that the defining feature of socialist economies was *shortage*: 'In understanding the problems of a socialist economy, the problem of shortage plays a role similar to the problem of unemployment in the description of capitalism' (Kornai 1979: 801).

Seeing this as an inherent problem of socialism – and one that did not appear to afflict capitalism – Kornai built an analysis of both social systems, starting from the perspective of the constraints that affect the operations of firms:

The question is the following: what are the constraints limiting efforts at increasing production? [...] Constraints are divided into three large groups:

1 Resource constraints: The use of real inputs by production activities cannot exceed the volume of available resources. These are constraints of a physical or technical nature [...]

2 Demand constraints: Sale of the product cannot exceed the buyer's demand at given prices.

3 Budget constraints: Financial expenses of the firm cannot exceed the amount of its initial money stock and of its proceeds from sales. (Credit will be treated later.)[5]

Which of the three constraints is effective is a defining characteristic of the social system [...] (Ibid.: 803)

Kornai concluded that 'With the classical capitalist firm it is usually the demand constraint that is binding, while with the traditional socialist firm it is the resource constraint' (Kornai 1990: 27).

This meant there were unemployed resources in a capitalist economy – of both capital and labor – but this also was a major reason for the relative dynamism of capitalist economies compared to socialist ones. Facing competition from rivals, insufficient demand to absorb the industry's potential output, and an uncertain future, the capitalist firm was under pressure to innovate to secure as much as possible of the industry's demand for itself. This innovation drove growth, and growth added yet another reason for excess capacity: a new factory had to be built with more capacity than needed for existing demand, otherwise it would already be obsolete.

Therefore most factories have plenty of 'fixed resources' lying idle – for very good reasons – and output can easily be expanded by hiring more workers and putting them to work with these idle 'fixed resources.' An increase in demand is thus met by an expansion of both employment of labor and the level of capital utilization – and this phenomenon is also clearly evident in the data.   §36

Kornai's empirically grounded analysis thus supports Sraffa's reasoning: diminishing marginal productivity is, in general, a figment of the imaginations of neoclassical economists. For most firms, an increase in production simply means an increased use of both labor and currently available machinery: productivity remains much the same, and may even increase as full capacity is approached – and surveys of industrialists, which I discuss later in this chapter, confirm this.

Summing up Sraffa

Sraffa's critiques mean that the economic theory of production can apply in only the tiny minority of cases that fall between the two circumstances he

---

5 Kornai used this last constraint to develop the concept of 'Hard and soft budget constraints.' This has great relevance to the position of banks during the Great Recession (see Kornai, Maskin et al. 2003: 1123–6; Kornai 1986), but is less relevant here.

outlines, and only when those industries are operating beyond their optimum efficiency. Then such industries will not violate the assumed independence of supply and demand, but they will still have a relatively 'fixed' factor of production and will also experience rising marginal cost. Sraffa concludes that only a tiny minority of industries are likely to fit all these limitations: those that use the greater part of some input to production, where that input itself is not important to the rest of the economy. The majority of industries are instead likely to be better represented by the classical theory, which saw prices as being determined exclusively by costs, while demand set the quantity sold. As Sraffa put it:

> Reduced within such restricted limits, the supply schedule with variable costs cannot claim to be a general conception applicable to normal industries; it can prove a useful instrument only in regard to such exceptional industries as can reasonably satisfy its conditions. In normal cases the cost of production of commodities produced competitively must be regarded as constant in respect of small variation in the quantity produced. And so, as a simple way of approaching the problem of competitive value, the old and now obsolete theory which makes it dependent on the cost of production alone appears to hold its ground as the best available. (Sraffa 1926)

§37

If not rising marginal cost, what?

Sraffa's argument dismisses the neoclassical proposition that rising costs and constant (or falling) marginal revenue determines the output from a single firm, or a single industry. This raises the question that if increasing costs don't constrain a firm's output, what does?

Sraffa's argument is simple. The output of a single firm is constrained by all those factors that are familiar to ordinary businessmen, but which are abstracted from economic theory. These are, in particular, rising marketing and financing costs, both of which are ultimately a product of the difficulty of encouraging consumers to buy your output rather than a rival's. These in turn are a product of the fact that, in reality, products are not homogeneous, and consumers do have preferences for one firm's output over another's. Sraffa mocked the economic belief that the limit to a firm's output is set by rising costs, and emphasized the importance of finance and marketing in constraining a single firm's size:

> Business men, who regard themselves as being subject to competitive conditions, would consider absurd the assertion that the limit to their production is to be found in the internal conditions of production in their firm, which do not permit of the production of a greater quantity without an increase in cost. The chief obstacle against which they have to contend when they want gradually to increase their production does not lie in the cost of production

– which, indeed, generally favors them in that direction – but in the difficulty of selling the larger quantity of goods without reducing the price, or without having to face increased marketing expenses. (Ibid.)

Economics assumes this real-world answer away by assuming that products are homogeneous, consumers are indifferent between the outputs of different firms and decide their purchases solely on the basis of price, that there are no transportation costs, etc. In such a world, no one needs marketing, because consumers already know everything, and only price (which consumers already know) distinguishes one firm's output from another. But Sraffa says that these postulates are the exception to the rule which applies in reality.

In most industries, products are heterogeneous, consumers do not know everything, and they consider other aspects of a product apart from price. Even where products are homogeneous, transportation costs can act to give a single firm an effective local monopoly. As a result, even the concept of a competitive market – in which all firms are price-takers – is itself suspect. Instead, most firms will to varying degrees act like monopolists – who, according to neoclassical theory, face a downward-sloping demand curve.

Each firm has a product that may fit within some broad category – such as, for example, passenger cars – but which is qualitatively distinguished from its rivals in a fashion that matters to a particular subset of buyers. The firm attempts to manipulate the demand for its product, but faces prohibitive costs in any attempt to completely eliminate their competitors and thus take over the entire industry. Not only must the firm persuade a different niche market to buy its product – to convince Porsche buyers to buy Volvos, for example – it must also convince investors and banks that the expense of building a factory big enough to produce for both market niches is worth the risk. Therefore, with the difficulty of marketing beyond your product's niche goes the problem of raising finance:

> The limited credit of many firms, which does not permit any one of them to obtain more than a limited amount of capital at the current rate of interest, is often a direct consequence of its being known that a given firm is unable to increase its sales outside its own particular market without incurring heavy marketing expenses. (Ibid.)

Economic theory also can't be saved by simply adding marketing costs to the cost of production, and thus generating a rising marginal cost curve. As Sraffa pointed out, there are at least three flaws with this. First, it is a distortion of the truth – marketing is not a cost of production, but a cost of distribution. Secondly, it is inconsistent with the underlying economic premise that marginal cost rises because of diminishing marginal productivity. Thirdly, it is implausible in the context of the economic theory of the firm.

There is no point in 'saving' the concept of a rising marginal cost curve by introducing marketing costs, since this requires acknowledging that one firm's product differs from another. If products differ from one firm to another, then products are no longer homogeneous, which is an essential assumption of the theory of perfect competition. It is far more legitimate to treat marketing as a cost of distribution, whose object is to alter the demand faced by an individual firm.

Sraffa's critique strengthens the case made in the preceding chapters. Rather than firms producing at the point where marginal cost equals marginal revenue, the marginal revenue of the final unit sold will normally be substantially greater than the marginal cost of producing it, and output will be constrained, not by marginal cost, but by the cost and difficulty of expanding sales at the expense of sales by competitors.[6]

Sraffa's alternative However, Sraffa was not satisfied with this revised picture, which is still dominated by intersecting marginal revenue and marginal cost curves. He instead expressed a preference for a more realistic model, which focused upon those issues that are most relevant to actual businesses.

The firm faces falling average costs as its large fixed costs are amortized over a larger volume of sales, and as its variable costs either remain constant or fall with higher output.[7] It will have a target level of output which it tries to exceed, and a target markup which it tries to maintain. The size of the firm is constrained by the size of its niche within the given market, and the difficulty of raising finance for a much larger scale of operation.

§38 The margin between costs of production and target sale price will be set by the degree of product differentiation within the industry, competitive pressures and general market conditions. Each firm will endeavor to sell as much output as it can, but the level of output will be constrained by the size of the firm's market niche and the marketing efforts of rivals.

So what?

To the non-economist, Sraffa's conclusions might still look like fairly minor points. The supply curve should be horizontal rather than upward sloping; the output of an individual firm isn't set by the intersection of marginal revenue and marginal cost; and marketing and finance issues, rather than cost of production issues, determine the maximum scale of a firm's output. This is a big deal?

Strange as it may seem, yes, this is a very big deal. If marginal returns are constant rather than falling, then the neoclassical explanation of everything

---

6 Marketing expenses cannot be added in to 'rescue' the doctrine, since the true purpose of marketing is to alter the firm's demand curve, and this only makes sense if firms produce differentiated products – something the theory of perfect competition explicitly rules out.

7 The 'cost curve' for any one firm or industry is the product of interactions between all industries, an issue that is ignored in the neoclassical treatment of a single market. This issue is discussed in Chapter 6.

collapses. Not only can economic theory no longer explain how much a firm produces, it can explain nothing else either.

Take, for example, the economic theory of employment and wage determination (discussed in more detail in Chapter 6). The theory asserts that the real wage is equivalent to the marginal product of labor. The argument goes that each employer takes the wage level as given, since with competitive markets no employer can affect the price of his inputs. An employer will employ an additional worker if the amount the worker adds to output – the worker's marginal product – exceeds the real wage. The employer stops employing workers once the marginal product of the last one employed has fallen to the same level as the real wage.

This explains the economic predilection for blaming everything on wages being too high – neoclassical economics can be summed up, as Galbraith once remarked, in the twin propositions that the poor don't work hard enough because they're paid too much, and the rich don't work hard enough because they're not paid enough (Galbraith 1997). The output of the firm is subject to diminishing marginal returns, and thus marginal product falls as output increases. The real wage is unaffected by the output level of the firm. The firm will keep on hiring workers until the marginal product of the last worker equals the real wage.

Since the rational employer stops at that point, the real wage – which the employer takes as given – determines how many workers this firm employs. Since employment in turn determines output, the real wage determines the level of output. If society desires a higher level of employment and output, then the only way to get it is to reduce the real wage (and the logical limit of this argument is that output will reach its maximum when the real wage equals zero). The real wage in turn is determined by the willingness of **§39** workers to work – to forgo leisure for income – so that ultimately the level of employment is determined by workers alone.

If in fact the output-to-employment relationship is relatively constant, then the neoclassical explanation for employment and output determination collapses. With a flat production function, the marginal product of labor will be constant, and it will never intersect the real wage. The output of the firm then can't be explained by the cost of employing labor, and neoclassical **§40** economics simply explains nothing: neither the level of employment, nor output, nor, ultimately, what determines the real wage.

Sraffa's critique is thus a fundamental one: if his argument is accepted then the entire edifice of economics collapses.

Clearly, no such thing has happened: economics has continued on as if Sraffa's article was never even published. One might hope that this is because there is some fundamental flaw in Sraffa's argument, or because there is some deeper truth that neoclassical economics discovered to justify preserving the old model with a new explanation. Sadly, neither is the case.

The neoclassical rejoinder

Sraffa's paper evoked several responses from the economic heavyweights of the time. However, these focused upon another aspect of the paper, his critique of the notion of external economies of scale in the long run. Sraffa's primary argument, that the concept of diminishing marginal returns in the short run is invalid, was ignored – so much so that in 1927, 1928 and 1930, Pigou, Robbins and Harrod respectively set out the theory of short-run price determination by rising marginal cost in complete confidence of its validity, and without any reference to Sraffa's paper. Few, if any, conventional economists have since referred to Sraffa's paper.

There are many possible reasons for this complete neglect of a serious challenge to economic orthodoxy. The simplest explanation is that the argument was ignored because its implications, if accepted, were too destructive of conventional economics for neoclassical economists to contemplate. As Chapter 7 argues, this is a not uncommon initial response in all sciences – the key difference with economic 'science' being that this can also be the final response. However, it must be acknowledged that even Keynes – who was, like Sraffa, critical of the mainstream – failed to realize the import of Sraffa's arguments.

The situation has not improved with time. Sraffa's paper is today cited only by critics of economic orthodoxy, while the textbooks teach the theory of rising marginal cost without reference to Sraffa's counter-arguments. It is therefore difficult to put forward a neoclassical response to Sraffa. However, many economists put forward the following arguments when they are informed of Sraffa's paper.

The first is that Sraffa has completely failed to understand the concept of the short run. Neoclassical economics defines three concepts of time: the market period, during which no factor of production can be varied, so that supply is fixed and only price can vary; the short run, during which at least one factor of production cannot be varied, so that output can be varied but only at the cost of diminishing returns; and the long run, during which all inputs can be varied. Since production takes place during the short run, the remainder of the theory follows logically. Diminishing marginal returns will apply, marginal cost will rise, price and quantity will be jointly determined by supply and demand, and the entire edifice of the theory of production and distribution remains intact.

The second is that Sraffa misunderstands the nature of production in a capitalist economy. Since there is enormous pressure to be competitive, no firm can survive long with excess capacity. Therefore competition will drive all firms towards full capacity, and in this realm diminishing returns will apply.

Time and the short run

As Chapter 9 points out, time – or rather, the absence of time in its analysis – is one of the fundamental weaknesses of conventional economics. It is therefore somewhat ironic that economists defend their theory from attack by appealing to the importance of time. However, far from helping to defend economic theory from criticism, the proper analysis of time highlights a critical weakness.

A firm's revenue and costs clearly vary over time, as well as varying as the firm changes its level of output at any one point in time. The economic rule that (in the context of diminishing returns) 'profit is maximized where marginal cost equals marginal revenue' is derived by 'holding time constant' and thus describing revenue and cost as simply a function of the quantity produced. The gap between revenue and cost is widest where marginal cost equals marginal revenue.

But in fact this rule applies only 'when time stands still' – which time never does. Not even an economist can make time stand still (though some victims of economics lectures might dispute that!). Similarly, the rule tells you how to maximize profit with respect to quantity, but real businessmen are more interested in maximizing profit over both time and output.

It is possible to consider profit as a function of both time and quantity, as opposed to the economic approach of dividing time into artificial segments, by explicitly acknowledging that profit is a function of both time and quantity (which the firm can vary at any point in time, and that will also change – and hopefully grow – over time).[8] Profit therefore depends both on the amount a firm produces, and the historical time during which it produces.

Using a rule of mathematics, we can then decompose the change in profit into the contribution due to the progress of time, and the contribution due to changes in quantity (which will also change over time). This results in the formula:

Change in profit equals change in profit due to change in time multiplied by the change in time, plus change in profit due to change in quantity multiplied by the change in quantity.

This formula tells us how big a change in profit will be, so if a firm wants to maximize its profit, it wants this number to be as big as possible.

Change in profit due to change in quantity is the same thing as 'marginal revenue minus marginal cost.' Neoclassical theory argues that profit is maximized when marginal revenue equals marginal cost – which we already know is a fallacy – but if you followed the neoclassical profit maximization rule here, you would deliberately set this quantity to zero. Since you get zero when you multiply any number by zero, following this rule sets the second

8 Economics ignores the issue of ecological sustainability, though clearly it must be considered by a reformed economics.

half of the formula (change in profit due to change in quantity multiplied by the change in quantity) to zero.

Therefore, economic theory tells us that the change in profit will be maximized when we eliminate the contribution that changes in quantity make to changes in profit. Change in profit is thus reduced simply to the first half of the formula, where changes due to time alone determine the change in profit. But economic theory has given us no advice about how to make change in profit due to change in time as big as possible.

What's going on? Suddenly, advice that previously seemed sensible (before we considered Sraffa's critique of the notion of a fixed factor of production) looks obviously absurd. Clearly something is wrong: but what?

An analogy might help you interpret it. Imagine you have a formula which describes how much fuel your car uses at any given speed, and you want to work out the most economical speed at which to drive. What you need to do is to work out the lowest rate at which to consume petrol per unit of distance traveled per second. If instead you first work out the most economical speed at which to travel, the answer to this first question will be zero miles per hour – because at this speed you consume the lowest possible amount of petrol per unit of time, zero. This is an accurate but useless answer, since you're not interested in staying put. If you want to work out the speed that minimizes petrol consumed but still gets you to your destination, you have to handle both problems simultaneously.

The neoclassical theory of the firm ignores time, in the same way that the wrong answer to the 'most economical speed at which to travel' question ignores distance. But time is an essential aspect of economic behavior, in the same sense that distance is an essential aspect of travel. The neoclassical policy for profit maximization is thus false twice: first, it ignores the impact of other firms in an industry on your profit, as the previous chapter showed; then it ignores time. It is thus a kindred spirit to the advice that the cheapest way to get from point A to point B is to travel at zero miles per hour.

There is also an economic way of interpreting this apparent paradox: that advice which appears sound when you ignore (or compartmentalize) time becomes absurd when you take time into account. This is that, by ignoring time in its analysis of the firm, economic theory ignores some of the most important issues facing a firm. Its 'static' emphasis upon maximizing profit 'now' ignores the fact that, to survive, a firm must also grow over time. To grow it must invest and develop new products, and this takes energy and resources. If instead it devotes all its resources to maximizing profit now, then it will not have any energy or resources left to devote to investment and new product development.

If we try to interpret economic theory in the context of historical time, then what the theory is attempting to do is work out the ideal level of output of a product for all time. But in the real world there is no such level of output. The appropriate number of motor cars to produce in 1900 was quite different from the appropriate number to produce in 2000.

This is how something that once looked so right (before Sraffa's critique of the concept of a fixed factor of production) looks so absurd now. The formula discussed above explicitly takes time into account, and is therefore dynamic, while the economic theory of the firm is static: it ignores time, and is therefore only relevant in a world in which time does not matter. But time clearly does matter in our world, and what is right in a static setting is wrong in a dynamic one.

Let's go back to that formula, which is true by definition, and see what it tells us to do.

If the firm's output is growing over time, then the term change in quantity will be positive. Setting marginal revenue equal to marginal cost means multiplying this positive number by zero – which results in a smaller increase in profit than if marginal revenue exceeds marginal cost. With rising sales, you will get a higher profit if 'change in profit due to change in quantity' is also positive, which requires that marginal revenue be greater than marginal cost. Thus a careful consideration of time argues that a firm should ensure that its marginal revenue is greater than its marginal cost.

This is the position which Sraffa argued actually applies in reality, so that the proper consideration of time strengthens Sraffa's critique, rather than weakening it. It also strengthens the point I made in the previous chapter that the neoclassical 'short-run profit maximization' formula is false; it's false in the long run too.

This is one of the many instances of the phenomenon I mentioned in Chapter 1, that advice derived from static reasoning, which ignores time, is often categorically opposed to advice derived from dynamic analysis, which takes time into account. Since the economy is fundamentally dynamic, static analysis is therefore normally dangerously wrong. I explore these issues in more depth in Chapter 8.

The flaws in economic reasoning pointed out in this chapter and Chapter 4 have a very direct impact on public policy in the area of the pricing of public services. Because economists believe that competitive industries set price equal to marginal cost, economists normally pressure public utilities to price their services at 'marginal cost.' Since the marginal costs of production are normally constant and well below the average costs, this policy will normally result in public utilities making a loss. This is likely to mean that public utilities are not able to finance the investment they need in order to maintain the quality of services over time. This dilemma in turn interacts with the pressure that economists also apply to privatize public assets, and to let individuals 'opt out' of the public provision of essential services. The end result, as Galbraith so eloquently put it, is 'private affluence and public squalor.'

TABLE 5.2 Cost drawings for the survey by Eiteman and Guthrie (1952: 834–5)

Illustration	Explanation	Chosen by
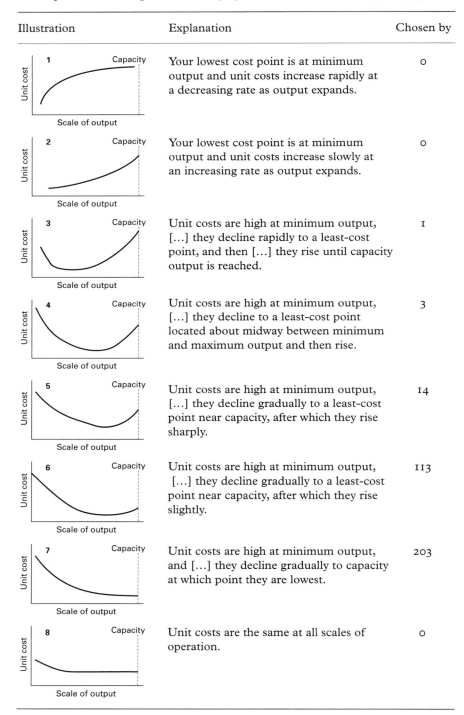	Your lowest cost point is at minimum output and unit costs increase rapidly at a decreasing rate as output expands.	0
	Your lowest cost point is at minimum output and unit costs increase slowly at an increasing rate as output expands.	0
	Unit costs are high at minimum output, [...] they decline rapidly to a least-cost point, and then [...] they rise until capacity output is reached.	1
	Unit costs are high at minimum output, [...] they decline to a least-cost point located about midway between minimum and maximum output and then rise.	3
	Unit costs are high at minimum output, [...] they decline gradually to a least-cost point near capacity, after which they rise sharply.	14
	Unit costs are high at minimum output, [...] they decline gradually to a least-cost point near capacity, after which they rise slightly.	113
	Unit costs are high at minimum output, and [...] they decline gradually to capacity at which point they are lowest.	203
	Unit costs are the same at all scales of operation.	0

Ironically, economic theory also makes economists essentially 'anti-capitalist,' in that they deride real businesses for pricing by a markup on cost, when theory tells them that prices should be set at the much lower level of marginal cost. Industrialists who have to cope with these attitudes in their dealings with government-employed economists are often among the greatest closet anti-economists of all. Maybe it's time for them to come out of the closet.

Competition and capacity The argument that competition would drive all firms to use their fixed capital at full capacity does look convincing at first glance, but deeper thought reaches precisely the opposite conclusion. A firm with no spare capacity has no flexibility to take advantage of sudden, unexpected changes in the market, and it also has to consider building a new factory as soon as its output grows. Excess capacity is essential for survival in a market economy.

Wrong in fact as well as theory

Sraffa's critique was entirely based upon an appeal to logic; a defence which might appear to be open to economic theory was, of course, that the facts supported them rather than Sraffa. However, over 150 empirical studies have been conducted into what the costs of actual firms really are, and with rare unanimity, every last one of them has found that the vast majority of firms report that they have very large fixed costs, and either constant or falling marginal costs, so that average costs of production fall as output rises.

One of the most interesting such studies showed factory managers eight drawings of the shape of cost curves, only three of which bore any resemblance to the standard drawings in neoclassical textbooks (see Table 5.2).

When asked to choose which drawings most closely resembled the relationship between cost and output levels in their factories, only one of the 334 companies chose curve 3, the one that looks most like the curve drawn in virtually every neoclassical microeconomics textbook – for example, this one in Figure 5.2 from Varian's *Microeconomic Analysis* (Varian 1992: 68) – while another seventeen chose curves that looked something like it.

Ninety-five percent of the managers chose drawings that did not conform to the standard textbook model, but instead illustrated either constant or falling marginal costs (Eiteman and Guthrie 1952: 837).

Predictably, neoclassical economists ignored this empirical research – and in fact the purpose of one of the most famous papers in economics, Milton Friedman's 'as if' paper on methodology (discussed in Chapter 8), was to encourage economists to ignore these empirical results.[9]

---

9 Friedman argued that the result that businessmen do not make their decisions on the basis of marginal cost and marginal revenue was 'largely irrelevant' (Friedman 1953: 15).

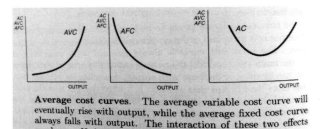

Average cost curves. The average variable cost curve will eventually rise with output, while the average fixed cost curve always falls with output. The interaction of these two effects produces a U-shaped average cost curve.

5.2 Varian's drawing of cost curves in his 'advanced' micro-economics textbook

This practice of ignoring empirical research continues today, even though the most recent researcher to rediscover these results was not a critic of neoclassical economics, but one-time vice-president of the American Economic Association and vice-chairman of the Federal Reserve, Alan Blinder (Blinder 1982, 1998). Blinder surveyed 200 medium-to-large US firms, which collectively accounted for 7.6 percent of America's GDP, and he put his results with beguiling honesty:

> *The overwhelmingly bad news here (for economic theory) is that, apparently, only 11 percent of GDP is produced under conditions of rising marginal cost* [...]
> Firms report having very high fixed costs – roughly 40 percent of total costs on average. And many more companies state that they have falling, rather than rising, marginal cost curves. While there are reasons to wonder whether respondents interpreted these questions about costs correctly, *their answers paint an image of the cost structure of the typical firm that is very different from the one immortalized in textbooks.* (Blinder 1998: 102, 105; emphases added)

The neoclassical model of the u-shaped average cost curve and rising marginal cost is thus wrong in theory and wrong in fact. That it is still taught as gospel to students of economics at all levels of instruction, and believed by the vast majority of neoclassical economists, is one of the best pieces of evidence of how truly unscientific economics is.

TABLE 5.3 Empirical research on the nature of cost curves (summarizing Table 4 in Eiteman and Guthrie 1952: 838)

	By firms	By products
Supports MC=MR	18	62
Contradicts MC=MR	316	1,020
Percent supporting MC=MR	5.4	5.7

A totem in tatters

While the neoclassical model of why production costs rise with output is thus fallacious, it is still feasible that, in some instances, price will rise as output rises. Feasible 'real-world' reasons for this include the inflexibility of supply in some markets across some timeframes (something economics attempts to deal with by its concept of the market period, as opposed to the short-run theory debunked in this chapter), firms exploiting high demand to set higher margins, and, in some circumstances, wage demands rising during periods of high employment.[10] But the neoclassical attempt to link higher prices directly to declining productivity is a failure.

This of itself would not be catastrophic, were it not for the extent to which diminishing marginal productivity permeates neoclassical economics. It is a foundation stone which, when it is withdrawn, brings down virtually everything else with it. Sraffa's critique thus provides one more illustration of the remarkable fragility of this outwardly confident social theory we call economics. Economics is not the emperor of the social sciences, but the Humpty Dumpty.

Just as with Humpty Dumpty after his fall, it is impossible to reconstruct the totemic supply and demand diagram after the criticisms outlined in this and the preceding chapters. First, the Sonnenschein-Mantel-Debreu conditions show that 'diminishing marginal utility,' which in theory applies at the individual level and means that individual demand curves slope downwards, doesn't survive aggregation to the market level – so that a market demand curve can have any shape at all (apart from doubling back on itself, or intersecting itself). Secondly, the marginal revenue curve derived from this demand curve will be even more unstable. Thirdly, equating marginal revenue and marginal cost isn't profit-maximizing. Finally, diminishing marginal productivity is a theoretical and empirical fallacy, so that for most factories, marginal cost is either constant or falling.

Taken together, these critiques eliminate the 'Totem of the Micro' completely. Virtually every concept in neoclassical microeconomics depends on diminishing marginal productivity for firms on the one hand, and diminishing marginal utility for the community on the other. If both these foundations are unsound, then almost nothing else remains standing. Without diminishing marginal productivity, neoclassical economists cannot explain how a firm decides how much to produce. This alone invalidates their analysis of market structures and income distribution. Without a community utility map, everything from the analysis of optimum output levels to the theory of international trade collapses.

Yet still they teach the standard mantra to their students, and still they apply the same simplistic logic to many other areas of economics.

10 Though empirical work suggests that, in practice, there is little sign of any negative relationship between the quantity sold and the price – and hence little evidence of a 'demand curve' (Lee 1996).

In the chapters to come, we will temporarily 'forget' the criticisms of these fundamental building blocks, and examine the validity of neoclassical theory as it is applied to specific issues. As you will see, even if we allow, for the sake of argument, that demand falls smoothly as price rises, that production is subject to diminishing marginal returns, and that demand and supply set prices, the neoclassical theories of the distribution of income, the behavior of the macroeconomy, and the role of finance are all intellectually unsound.

6 | TO EACH ACCORDING TO HIS CONTRIBUTION

Why productivity doesn't determine wages

One of the most striking aspects of the late twentieth century was the increase in the gap between the poorest worker and the richest. While many bemoaned this increase in inequality, economists counseled that the growing gap merely reflected the rising productivity of the highly paid.

The basis for this advice is the proposition that a person's income is determined by his contribution to production – or more precisely, by the marginal productivity of the 'factor of production' to which he contributes. Wages and profits – or 'factor incomes,' as economists prefer to call them – reflect respectively the marginal product of labor and of capital. The argument that highly paid workers – merchant bankers, managers of major corporations, stock and money market traders, financial commentators, etc. – deserve the high wages they receive compared to the less highly paid – nuclear physicists, rocket scientists, university professors, schoolteachers, social workers, nurses, factory workers, etc. – is simply an extension of this argument to cover subgroups of workers. Members of the former group, we are told, are simply more productive than members of the latter, hence their higher salaries.

I'll defer discussion of the proposition that profits reflect the marginal productivity of capital until the next chapter. Here we'll consider the argument that wages equal the marginal product of labor.

Once again, the argument relies heavily on concepts we have already dismissed: that productivity per worker falls as more workers are hired; that demand curves are necessarily downward sloping; that price measures marginal benefit to society; and that individual supply curves slope upwards and can easily be aggregated. Even allowing these invalid assumptions, the economic analysis of the labor market is still flawed.

The kernel

Economists prefer to treat everything, including labor, as a simple commodity, subject to the same 'laws of supply and demand' as the simple apple. Yet their own analysis of labor shows that it is fundamentally different. In all other markets, demand decisions are made by consumers and supply decisions by producers. But in the labor market, supply decisions are made by *consumers* (households supplying labor), whereas labor demand decisions are made by *producers* (firms hiring labor). Thus the conventional economic

analysis of markets, which is suspect enough on its own terms, is highly unlikely to apply in this most crucial of markets. As a result, wages are highly
unlikely to reflect workers' contributions to production, as economists argue.

The roadmap

In this chapter, I outline the economic analysis of labor supply, and the
normal economic argument in favor of letting the market decide both wages
and the level of employment.

I show that irregularities in the supply of labor – when compared to a
normal commodity – are easily derived from this analysis, yet economists
unjustifiably assume that labor supply will be an upward-sloping function of
the wage. However, these labor market irregularities can make the supply of
labor 'backward-bending,' so that reducing wages could actually cause the
supply of labor to rise rather than fall.

Though economists normally oppose unions, there are economic arguments
in favor of a cartel when sellers (such as workers selling their labor) face a
buyer with market power. The opposition economists normally present to
unions, to interventionist labor market policies, and to attempts to reduce
income inequality are thus shown to be unjustified, even on the grounds of
standard economic logic.

Labor demand and supply: an inverted commodity

The economic theory that a person's income reflects his contribution
to society relies on being able to treat labor as no different from other
commodities, so that a higher wage is needed to elicit a higher supply of
labor, and reducing the wage will reduce supply. In fact, economic theory
supports no such conclusion. Even economists can't escape the fact that, as
commodities go, labor is something out of the ordinary.

The demand for ordinary commodities is determined by consumer incomes
and tastes, while supply is determined by the costs of production. However,
unlike other commodities, no one actually 'consumes' labor: instead, firms
hire workers so that they can produce other commodities for sale. Secondly,
unlike all other commodities, labor is not produced for profit – there are
no 'labor factories' turning out workers according to demand, and labor
supply certainly can't be said to be subject to the law of diminishing returns
(whatever parents might think!).

These two peculiarities mean that, in an inversion of the usual situation,
the demand for labor is determined by producers, while the supply of labor
is determined by consumers. Demand reflects firms' decisions to hire workers
to produce output for sale; supply reflects workers' decisions about how long
to work, on the basis of their preferences for income on the one hand and
leisure time on the other.

If economists are to argue that the labor market is to behave like all other markets, then these peculiarities must not complicate the usual totemic duet of a downward-sloping demand curve and an upward-sloping supply curve. Unfortunately for economists, they do.

Marginal workers

According to economic theory, a firm's labor-hiring decision is determined simply by the impact that each additional worker has on the firm's bottom line. If hiring an additional worker will add to the firm's profit, he is hired; if not, the firm stops hiring.

With a perfectly competitive labor market, the firm can hire as many workers as it wishes to at the going wage. However, since one input (capital) is fixed in the short run, output is subject to diminishing returns: each additional worker hired adds a lesser amount to output than his predecessor. Diminishing marginal productivity therefore rules the hiring roost.

For each firm, the wage is a constant (set by the labor market in which each firm is an infinitesimally small actor). The amount each worker adds to profits, however, is variable. The firm keeps hiring workers up until the point at which the wage equals the amount for which the last worker's additional output can be sold.

If the industry itself is perfectly competitive, the additional units can be sold without the firm having to reduce its price (yes, I know that's been debunked already; but let's pretend otherwise). In general, the revenue the firm gains by hiring its last employee is equal to the price for which it sells its output, multiplied by the marginal product of the last worker. The firm's demand for labor is therefore the marginal physical product of labor multiplied by the price of the output.   §41

A disaggregated picture of this is used to explain why some workers get much higher wages than others. They – or rather the class of workers to which they belong – have a higher marginal revenue product than more poorly paid workers. Income disparities are the product of differential contributions to society, and though sociologists may bemoan it, both the rich and the poor deserve what they get.

Aggregate demand

The demand curves for individual firms are aggregated to form this industry's demand curve for labor, which itself will be a small part of the economy-wide demand curve for labor (since workers can generate many different kinds of output). The real wage is set by the point of intersection of this aggregate demand for labor curve – labor's aggregate marginal revenue product curve – with the aggregate supply curve.

Aggregate supply, in turn, is simply the sum of the supply decisions of individual workers. According to economists, a worker's decision about how much labor to supply is made the same way he decides how much to consume.

Indifferent workers

Individual labor supply is determined by the individual's choice between work and leisure. Work is a 'bad' in Bentham's calculus: work is a 'pain' while leisure is a 'pleasure.' Therefore the pain of work must be compensated for by the pleasure of the wage, to make up for the sacrifice of leisure required to earn the wage.

This choice is represented, as always, by indifference curves where potential income is one of the goods, and potential leisure time is the other. The indifference map represents a consumer's preferences between leisure and income, while the budget line represents the hourly wage rate: the higher the wage, the steeper the budget line.

This model has one peculiarity when compared to that applied to normal commodities. With standard commodities, the budget line can be drawn anywhere, so long as it reflects the relative price of the commodities in its slope, and the consumer's income. But with labor, one end of the budget line is fixed at twenty-four hours, since that's the maximum amount of leisure anyone can have in a day. For this reason, all that the budget line can do in this model is pivot about the twenty-four-hour mark, with the slope representing the hourly wage. The distance from zero to the twenty-four-hour mark represents the maximum possible leisure of twenty-four hours a day.

§ 42 and 43

As with the consumption of bananas and biscuits, the amount of leisure and income that a consumer will 'consume' is worked out by varying the wage, and seeing what combination of leisure and work the consumer chooses. This generates an individual labor *supply* curve – not a demand curve – from this worker.

The individual supply curve is then summed with that of all other workers to produce the market supply curve. We are back in the familiar economic territory of a downward-sloping demand curve and an upward-sloping supply curve intersecting to determine an equilibrium price: the average wage. The 'Totem of the Micro' is once again held aloft.

This argument, which strictly speaking applies to labor in the aggregate, is extended by analogy to a disaggregated level in order to explain why some workers get much higher wages than others.

§ 44

At a policy level, this model is used to emphasize the futility of minimum wage legislation, demand management policies, and any other attempts to interfere with the free working of the market mechanism in this most political of markets. If a government attempts to improve workers' incomes by legislating a minimum wage, then this will result in unemployment, because it will increase the number of hours workers are willing to work, while reducing the demand from employers because the wage will now exceed the marginal product of labor. The gap between the increased hours offered and the reduced hours demand represents involuntary unemployment at this artificially high wage level.

Demand management measures – trying to boost aggregate demand to increase employment – will also fail, because they can't alter the marginal physical product of labor, which can only be done by raising the productivity of labor on the supply side. Attempts to increase aggregate demand will thus merely cause inflation, without increasing the real returns to firms. §45

The essential message is that 'you can't beat the market.' Whatever society may think is a fair wage level, or a socially desirable level of unemployment, ultimately the market will decide both income distribution and the rate of unemployment. Moreover, both these market outcomes will be fair: they will reflect individual productivity on the one hand, and the labor–leisure preferences of individuals on the other. §46

Problems

There are at least six serious problems with this meritocratic view of income distribution and employment determination:

- the supply curve for labor can 'slope backwards' – so that a fall in wages can cause an increase in the supply of labor;
- when workers face organized or very powerful employers, neoclassical theory shows that workers won't get fair wages unless they also organize;
- Sraffa's observations about aggregation, noted in Chapter 3, indicate that it is inappropriate to apply standard supply and demand analysis to the labor market;
- the basic vision of workers freely choosing between work and leisure is flawed;
- this analysis excludes one important class from consideration – bankers – and unnecessarily shows the income distribution game between workers and capitalists as a zero-sum game. In reality, there are (at least) three players in the social class game, and it's possible for capitalists and workers to be on the same side in it – as they are now during the Great Recession; and
- most ironically, to maintain the pretense that market demand curves obey the Law of Demand, neoclassical theory had to assume that income was redistributed by 'a benevolent central authority' (Mas-Colell et al. 1995: 117) prior to exchange taking place.

Backward-bending supply curves

Neoclassical economists blithely draw upward-sloping individual and aggregate labor supply curves, but in fact it is quite easy to derive individual labor supply curves that slope downwards – meaning that workers supply *less* labor as the wage rises.

The logic is easy to follow: a higher wage rate means that the same total wage income can be earned by working *fewer* hours. This can result in an

§47 individual labor supply curve that has a 'perverse' shape: less labor is supplied as the wage rises. Economists normally get around anomalies like this by dividing the impact of a higher price into its income and substitution effects – where this time the price of labor is the hourly wage. The substitution effect necessarily means that you'll provide more labor, since each hour of leisure that you forgo gives you a higher return. It's the income effect which stuffs things up – the fact that with a higher wage you can manage to get both a higher income and work fewer hours.

This ruse works when you're considering normal commodities: you simply notionally alter a consumer's income – this was the basis of the 'Hicksian compensated demand curve' that played a role in the proof of the Law of Demand for an individual consumer in Chapter 2. However, this is no use when considering labor supply, because while it's quite easy to notionally add or subtract income from a consumer – thus varying uniformly the amount of both biscuits and bananas that he can consume – it's not possible to add or subtract hours from a day: you can't magically give a worker twenty-eight hours in a day, or take away four.

As a result, it makes no sense to separate the impact of an increase in the wage rate into its substitution effect and income effect: the fact that the substitution effect will always result in an increase in hours worked is irrelevant, since everyone will always have twenty-four hours to allocate between work and leisure.

§48 Since an increase in wages will make workers better off, individual workers are just as likely to work fewer hours as more when the wage rate increases. Individual labor supply curves are just as likely then to slope backwards – showing falling supply as wages rise – as they are to slope forwards.

§49 At the aggregate level, a labor supply curve derived by summing many such individual supply curves could have any shape at all. There could be multiple intersections of the supply curve with the demand curve (accepting, for the moment, that a downward-sloping demand curve is valid). There may be more than one equilibrium wage rate, and who is to say which one is valid? There is therefore no basis on which the aggregate amount of labor that workers wish to supply can be unambiguously related to the wage offered. Economic theory thus fails to prove that employment is determined by supply and demand, and reinforces the real-world observation that involuntary unemployment can exist: that the employment offered by firms can be less than the labor offered by workers, and that reducing the wage won't necessarily reduce the gap.

This imperfection in the theory – the possibility of backward-bending labor supply curves – is sometimes pointed out to students of economics, but then glossed over with the assumption that, in general, labor supply curves will be upward sloping. But there is no theoretical – or empirical – justification for this assumption.

This strong assumption would be of little consequence if economists didn't derive such strong conclusions from their model of the labor market. Declarations that minimum wage legislation is ineffective and causes unemployment, or that demand management policies can't alter the rate of unemployment, are hardly insignificant pronouncements. Their truth is dependent in part on the supply curve for labor being upward sloping.

For example, if the aggregate demand and supply curves for labor both §50 slope downwards, then the 'equilibrium' of the two could be unstable: falling supply could be met by falling demand, resulting in runaway unemployment. Putting a floor to this process via a minimum wage could actually make the labor market stable and decrease unemployment.

Didactic policy positions should be based upon robust intellectual or empirical foundations, rather than the flimsy substrate of mere fancy. Neoclassical economists are quite prone to dismissing alternative perspectives on labor market policy on this very basis – that they lack any theoretical or empirical foundations. Yet their own policy positions on the labor market are based as much on wishful thinking as on wisdom.

Monopoly and monopsony

The conclusion that workers receive the value of their marginal contribution to output depends upon the assumption that both the product market and the labor market are perfectly competitive. The notion of perfect competition has already been debunked, but even if it were intellectually sound, it is clearly a dubious thing to assume for an overall economy.

If we instead accept that in practice both product and labor markets will not be perfectly competitive, then economic theory predicts that workers will not, in general, receive the value of their marginal contribution to production. In this more general case, economic theory concedes that workers' incomes are determined not only by their contribution to production, but also by the relative bargaining power of workers and employers.

Let's first consider the case in which the product market is not perfectly competitive: workers are being hired by firms that have to reduce their average selling price to increase output. In this case, the price received per unit falls as output increases. Marginal revenue is thus less than price, and the worker's marginal revenue product is the product of marginal revenue and marginal productivity.

One ironic consequence of this analysis – given how vehemently anti-union most neoclassical economists are – is that neoclassical theory can be shown to favor the existence of trade unions. Without trade unions, the labor supply will be competitive and will therefore be 'exploited,' because the wage will be less than the price for which the marginal worker's output can be sold. With a trade union acting as a single seller of labor, however, the price charged for each additional worker will rise as more workers are hired. This situation – known as a monopsony or single seller – means that the marginal cost of supply lies above the supply curve.

With a monopoly seller of labor confronting non-competitive purchasers of labor, the wage is indeterminate. It will lie between the minimum set by the marginal revenue product of labor (which means that firms are exploiting workers), and the maximum set by the rising marginal cost of workers (which means that workers are exploiting firms). The final position will be determined by the relative bargaining power of the two groups, which cannot be determined by the market.

Thus while economists normally portray unions as bad because they restrict competition in the labor market, this may be a preferable situation to leaving competitive workers to be exploited by less than perfectly competitive hirers of labor.

Sraffa's observations on aggregation

You will remember from Chapter 5 that Sraffa had two criticisms of economic demand and supply analysis: one for a broad definition of an industry, the other for a narrow definition. The labor market is clearly a broadly defined industry, and Sraffa's first critique is therefore relevant to it.

The critique was that, with a broad definition of an industry, it is not feasible to draw independent demand and supply curves, since any change in supply will have income distributional effects which will in turn alter demand.

This is clearly the case when the supply curve refers to the entire labor force. Remember that the aggregate demand curve, in this market, is supposed to represent the aggregate marginal revenue product for labor. This in turn is a product of physical labor productivity on the one hand, and the price for which output produced by that labor is sold.

If an increase in supply requires an increase in the price of labor – if, in other words, the supply curve for labor is upward sloping – then this is clearly going to alter income distribution, the demand for commodities, and hence their prices. This means that a different 'demand curve' for labor will apply at every different point along a labor supply curve.

This means that multiple equilibria will exist, none of which can be said to be more fundamental than any other. It is also quite feasible that 'perverse' outcomes will apply: that, for example, a higher wage could be associated with a higher level of employment rather than a lower one (this dilemma is explored in detail in Chapter 7, in the context of the demand for capital).

§51 The economist's ubiquitous tool of supply and demand analysis is therefore particularly unsuited to analyzing this crucial market.

Freedom and labor

The vision of a worker deciding how many hours to work on the basis of his preferences between income and leisure, and offering more labor as the wage rises, is, like so much else of economic theory, superficially appealing. But, again like so much else in economics, it implicitly raises a question which undermines the superficial appeal. In this case, the question is 'how can one enjoy leisure time without income?'

If there is a positive relationship between the wage rate and hours worked, then as the wage rate falls, so too will the number of hours worked. As a result, income – the product of the hourly wage times the number of hours worked – falls even faster. So according to economists, a fall in the wage rate should mean that workers will substantially reduce their incomes, and simultaneously devote more time to 'leisure activities.'

In reality, the only 'leisure activity' which one can devote more time to with less income is sleeping (just ask a homeless person). Most leisure activities are just that – active – and cost money. The only way that workers could behave as economics fantasizes is if they have alternative sources of income.

This in effect is the economic vision of a worker: someone who has alternative means to generate income at his disposal, and has to be enticed by the wage to undertake wage labor for an employer over the alternative of working for himself.

For that choice to be a reality, workers need something else: capital, his own means of production.

Some workers are so endowed. Some farmers can be enticed into working as farm laborers if the wage is high enough, and if it's not, then they can work their own land. Some office workers have the alternative of working for a wage, or operating as independent consultants out of their home offices. Some 'wage slaves' can make the transition from employee to employer by an innovative idea, hard work, good luck, skill or good timing – or fraud.

But the majority do not have that choice – or rather don't have it to the degree that they could avoid bankruptcy or starvation by turning to self-employment. For this majority, work is not an option but – in the absence of a very generous social security system – a necessity. Rather than smoothly choosing between work and leisure, in a completely free market system they face the choice of either working or starving. In a market economy attenuated by the welfare state, this choice is less stark, but still present.

A three-horse race

This point will become clearer in later chapters, when I outline the monetary approach to economics that I take, in which bankers are treated as a separate social class to capitalists. The précis for now is that bankers' incomes depend on the level of debt, and if a Ponzi scheme develops, then the level of debt can escalate dramatically. This then transfers income from *both workers and capitalists* to bankers, and to the detriment of society in general since it also normally results in a lower level of real investment.

This issue might seem arcane now, but it has serious implications during a financial crisis, such as the one we are currently in. Neoclassical efforts to get out of such a crisis – once they've gotten over the shock of one actually happening, and revert to form after behaving like 'born-again Keynesians' when the crisis begins – invariably argue that wages have to fall to end the crisis, because high employment clearly indicates that wages are too high.

In fact, policies based on this notion actually make a debt deflation worse, because they drive down the general price level and actually increase the debt burden on society. What is really needed is not lower wages, but lower debt levels – and paradoxically that can be achieved by *increasing* wages. A boost to money wages during a depression can cause inflation far more effectively than 'printing money,' and this inflation can reduce the real debt burden.

If such a policy is ever proposed, you can bet your bottom dollar that the main opposition to it will come from neoclassical economists – and their advice, as always, will be wrong.

'A benevolent central authority'

I've saved the unkindest cut of all for last: even though neoclassical economists are normally vehement opponents of the redistribution of income by the state – everything, they normally argue, should be decided by the market – their own theory of demand and supply only works if, and only if, a 'benevolent central authority' (Mas-Colell et al. 1995: 117) redistributes income in order to 'keep the ethical worth of each person's marginal dollar equal' (Samuelson 1956: 21).

This nonsensical condition is yet another 'proof by contradiction' that neoclassical economics is unsound. Starting from the assumption that the market economy maximizes social welfare, it concludes that this is possible only if, prior to the market operating, a dictatorship redistributes wealth so that everyone in society is happy with the resulting distribution.

This is, of course, absurd. Rather than using neoclassical economics to justify dictatorships, that neoclassical theory literally needs a dictatorship to make its model work is a reason to abandon neoclassical theory. The fact that neoclassical economists not only cling to their theory but argue against income redistribution in policy debates also shows how little they understand their own theory.

Normally this happens because the analysis that establishes bizarre results like this is only in the journal literature that most neoclassical economists don't read – in this case, Samuelson's 1956 paper 'Social indifference curves.' However, here I have to thank Andreu Mas-Colell and colleagues for putting this nonsense in their market-dominating PhD textbook *Microeconomic Theory*, which makes it impossible for neoclassical economists to hide behind their ignorance of their own literature. This section is worth reiterating here, even though I previously cited some of it in Chapter 3:

For it to be correct to treat aggregate demand as we did individual demand [...] there must be a positive representative consumer. However, although this is a necessary condition for the property of the aggregate demand that we seek, it is not sufficient. We also need to be able to assign welfare significance to this fictional individual's demand function. This will lead to the definition of a normative representative consumer. To do so, however, we first have to be more specific about what we mean by the term social welfare. We accomplish this by introducing the concept of a social welfare function [...]

The idea behind a social welfare function is that it accurately expresses society's judgments on how individual utilities have to be compared to produce an ordering of possible social outcomes [...] *Let us now hypothesize that there is a process, a benevolent central authority perhaps, that [...] redistributes wealth in order to maximize social welfare [...]* this indirect utility function provides a positive representative consumer for the aggregate demand function [...]

If there is a normative representative consumer, the preferences of this consumer have welfare significance and the aggregate demand function can be used to make welfare judgments [...] In doing so however, *it should never be forgotten that a given wealth distribution rule is being adhered to and that the 'level of wealth' should always be understood as the 'optimally distributed level of wealth.'* (Mas-Colell et al. 1995: 116–18; emphases added)

Ahem; please, stop snoring – that was important! In the turgid and boring prose of a neoclassical textbook – and one which has been used in the training of virtually every American PhD student since the late 1990s – you've just been told that neoclassical economics has to assume the existence of a dictator (benevolent of course!).

Most neoclassical economists don't realize this – if they did, they would, I hope, abandon the neoclassical approach as a waste of time. But instead it's likely they don't even read this section of their 1,000-page instruction manual, let alone realize the import of what it says at this point.

I hope you do, however. Certainly, this conundrum makes anything neoclassical economists have to say about the distribution of income irrelevant.

So what?

Few issues provide better examples of the negative impact of economic theory on society than the distribution of income. Economists are forever opposing 'market interventions' which might raise the wages of the poor, while defending astronomical salary levels for top executives on the basis that if the market is willing to pay them that much, they must be worth it. In fact, the inequality which is so much a characteristic of modern society reflects power rather than justice. This is one of the many instances where unsound economic theory makes economists the champions of policies which, if anything, undermine the economic foundations of modern society.

Economics should accept that labor is unlike any other commodity, and develop an analysis suited to its peculiarities, rather than attempt to warp this most personal of markets to fit the conventional cloth of supply and demand.

Keynes did just that in the General Theory. But mainstream economics after Keynes pulled away from this innovation on the basis that Keynes's argument 'did not have good microeconomic foundations.' As this and the preceding three chapters have shown, conventional microeconomic theory itself has unsound foundations. And things get even worse when we turn our attention to problems with the other 'factor of production,' capital.

PART 2 | COMPLEXITIES

ISSUES OMITTED FROM STANDARD COURSES
THAT SHOULD BE PART OF AN EDUCATION IN
ECONOMICS

Why the productivity of capital doesn't determine profits

The economist Dharma Kumar is said to have once remarked that 'Time is a device to stop everything from happening at once, and space is a device to stop everything from happening in Cambridge.'

Nevertheless, a lot did happen at Cambridge during the 1960s and 1970s, where 'Cambridge' refers to both Cambridge, Massachusetts, USA, and Cambridge, England. The former is home to the Massachusetts Institute of Technology (better known by its initials MIT); the latter is the home of the famous University of Cambridge. MIT was the bastion for the leading true believers in economics, while the University of Cambridge housed an important group of heretics.

For twenty years, these two Cambridges waged a theoretical 'Holy War' over the foundations of neoclassical economics. The first shot was fired by the heretics, and after initial surprise the true believers responded strongly and confidently. Yet after several exchanges, the leading bishop of the true believers had conceded that the heretics were substantially correct. Summing up the conflict in 1966, Paul Samuelson observed that the heretics 'merit our gratitude' for pointing out that the simple homilies of economic theory are not in general true. He concluded that 'If all this causes headaches for those nostalgic for the old time parables of neoclassical writing, we must remind ourselves that scholars are not born to live an easy existence. We must respect, and appraise, the facts of life' (Samuelson 1966: 583).

One might hope that such a definitive capitulation by as significant an economist as Paul Samuelson would have signaled a major change in the evolution of economics. Unfortunately, this was not to be. While many of the bishops have conceded that economics needs drastic revision, its priests preach on in a new millennium, largely unaware that they lost the holy war thirty years earlier.

The kernel

The term 'capital' has two quite different meanings in economics: a sum of money, and a collection of machinery. Economists assume that they can use the two terms interchangeably, and use the money value of machines as a proxy for the amount of machinery used in production. They prefer to abstract from the complexity that there are many different types of machines, many of which (such as, for example, blast furnaces) are solely suited to producing one particular commodity, and instead work with the generic term 'capital' – as if there is some ubiquitous productive substance which is just as suited to turning out sheep as it is to producing steel. For the economic theories of production and distribution to work, the behavior of this hypothetical generic substance must be little different from the behavior of the actual real world of many different machines.

However, a careful analysis of production as a system by which commodities are produced by combining other commodities and labor shows that the money value of machinery cannot be used as a proxy for the amount of machinery used in production. As a result, the economic theory of how commodities are produced is wrong, and the theory's argument that profit is a reward for capital's contribution to production is also wrong. This reinforces the observations made in Chapter 6, that the distribution of income is not the result of impersonal market forces, but instead reflects the relative power of different social classes.

The roadmap

This quite difficult chapter begins with an outline of the economic theory of the production of commodities by 'factors of production,' with its assumption that all machinery can be lumped into the aggregate called 'capital' and measured by the money value placed upon those machines. Then Sraffa's 'abstraction-free' analysis of production is outlined. It is shown that, rather than the rate of profit depending upon the amount of capital, as neoclassical economists argue, the measured amount of capital in fact depends upon the rate of profit.

Measuring capital

Though the war began in earnest only in 1960, the possibility of conflict was first flagged by Piero Sraffa in his 1926 paper 'The law of returns under competitive conditions' (discussed in Chapter 5). In passing, Sraffa observed that an essential aspect of the economic theory of production was the assumption that the interdependence of industries could be ignored. The problem was that this assumption was invalid when changes in one industry's output affected the costs of many other industries, which in turn determined the costs facing the first industry. As Sraffa put it,

> the assumption becomes illegitimate, when a variation in the quantity produced by the industry under consideration sets up a force which acts directly, not merely upon its own costs, but also upon the costs of other industries; in such a case the conditions of the 'particular equilibrium' which it was intended to isolate are upset, and it is no longer possible, without contradiction, to neglect collateral effects. (Sraffa 1926)

Sraffa spent the better part of the next thirty-five years turning this

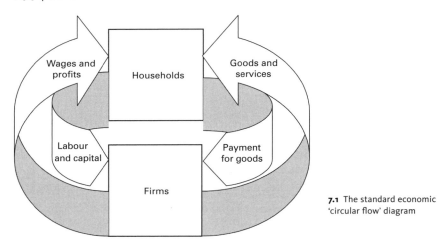

7.1 The standard economic 'circular flow' diagram

observation into a rigorous theoretical argument. The product was a book with the bland but descriptive title of *The Production of Commodities by Means of Commodities* (Sraffa 1960), and the rather more revealing but still oracular subtitle of 'Prelude to a critique of economic theory.' Essentially, Sraffa provided the techniques needed to highlight fundamental internal inconsistencies in the economic theory of production.

This theory argues that commodities – everything from cornflakes to steel mills – are produced by 'factors of production.' These are normally reduced to just labor on the one hand, and capital on the other. This concept is normally embodied in a 'circular flow diagram' like that of Figure 7.1, which shows factors of production 'flowing' from households to the factory sector, and goods flowing from the factory sector to households.

For this flow to be truly circular, households must transform goods into factors of production, while factories must transform factors of production into goods. The factories-to-households half of the circle is reasonable: factories can transform capital and labor inputs into goods. To complete the circle, households must transform the goods they receive from factories into factors of production – labor and capital.

The proposition that households convert goods into labor is unproblematic. However, the questionable proposition is that households also convert goods into capital. This raises a vital question: what is capital, in the context of this diagram? Is it machinery, etc., or is it financial instruments? If it is the former, then this raises the question of where these machines are produced. The model implies that households take goods produced by firms and internally convert them into machines, which are then sold to firms by households. Clearly this is nonsense, since in this case 'households' must also be factories. Therefore, the flow of capital from households to firms must be a financial flow.

However, economic theory treats this financial flow as directly contributing to production: the 'capital' from households to firms generates a profit flow back from firms to households, where that profit reflects the marginal productivity of capital.

One way this would be possible is if financial instruments directly produced output (in combination with labor) – which clearly they don't.

There is only one other solution, which is to acknowledge that the model is not complete. Factories actually produce capital machines, and this is left out of the diagram. The flow of capital from households to firms is therefore a financial flow, but hopefully there is a direct and unequivocal relationship between the measurement of capital in financial terms and its physical productivity.

A standard 'education' in economics simply ignores these complexities, and explains profit just as it explains wages: the payment to capital represents its marginal productivity. The argument goes that a profit-maximizing firm will §52 hire capital up to the point at which its marginal contribution to output just equals the cost of hiring it. The cost of hiring it is the rate of interest, while its marginal contribution is the rate of profit. The two are equal in equilibrium, so the demand curve for capital slopes downwards – just like all other demand curves – reflecting rising demand for capital as the cost of capital falls.

The sum of all the individual demand for capital curves gives the market §53 demand curve for capital, while the supply curve – the willingness of households to supply capital – rises as the rate of interest increases. The point of intersection of this downward-sloping demand curve with the upward-sloping supply curve yields the equilibrium rate of profit.

This argument should already be looking somewhat suspect to you, after the previous chapters. For instance, production is supposed to occur in the short run, when at least one factor of production can't be varied. That notion appears at least arguably OK when capital is the fixed factor – though we've shown it to be invalid even there. But it makes no apparent sense to imagine that machinery is now variable while labor is fixed. Surely machinery should be the least flexible factor of production – so that if it can be varied, then everything else can be varied too?

The arguments put by Sraffa against the concept of diminishing marginal productivity can also be applied here in a simple and devastating critique, which was first put formally by Bhaduri in 1969. As with the labor market, the 'capital market' is a broadly defined 'industry': there would be thousands of products being lumped together into the general rubric of 'capital,' and there is no industry which does not use some 'capital' as an input. This raises Sraffa's argument in Chapter 5, that a change in the price of such an input would affect numerous industries, and therefore alter the distribution of income. This is a similar point to that made earlier for the labor market, but it can now be put in a more explicit form.[1]

---

1 While this case is most easily made with equations, I'll stick to words here.

If we notionally divide all people into either workers or capitalists, then total income will be the sum of wages and profits. Profits in turn are the product of the rate of profit, times the amount of capital hired. Applying this at the level of the single firm, this gives us the relationship that:

Income equals
(a) the wage rate multiplied by the number of employees plus
(b) the rate of profit multiplied by the stock of capital

If we now consider changes in output (which we have to do to derive the marginal product of capital), then a rule of mathematics tells us that the changes in output have to equal the changes in wages and profits. Another rule of mathematics lets us decompose the change in profits into two bits: the rate of profit times the change in capital, and capital times the change in the rate of profit.[2] This yields the relationship that:

Change in income equals
a) change in the wages bill (which we leave aggregated), plus
b) change in profit (which we disaggregate)

Disaggregating changes in profit leads to the statement that:

Change in income equals
a) change in the wages bill, plus
b) the rate of profit multiplied by the change in capital, plus
c) the amount of capital multiplied by the change in the rate of profit

At the level of the individual firm, economists assume that (a) and (c) are zero: a change in the firm's level of output caused solely by hiring more capital has no impact on either the real wage or the rate of profit. Thus the relationship can be reduced to:

Change in income equals
a) change in wages [zero], plus
b) the rate of profit multiplied by the change in capital [one[3]], plus
c) capital multiplied by the change in the rate of profit [zero]

Canceling out the terms we know are zero or one yields the desired relationship:

Change in output due to a change in capital (marginal product) equals the rate of profit

However, while this is a reasonable approximation at the level of the individual firm, it is not true at the level of the overall economy. There, any

---

2 The same case can be made with respect to the change in the wages bill, but I focus just on profit times capital to keep the argument simple.

3 The ratio of a change in capital to a change in capital is 1.

change in capital will definitely have implications for the wage rate, and for the rate of profit. Therefore the aggregate relationship is

Change in output due to a change in capital (marginal product) equals
a) change in wages due to change in capital [non-zero], plus
b) the rate of profit, plus
c) the amount of capital multiplied by the change in the rate of profit due to the change in capital [non-zero]

The rate of profit will therefore not equal the marginal product of capital unless (a) and (c) exactly cancel each other out.[4] Thus at the aggregate level, the desired relationship – the rate of profit equals the marginal product of capital – will not hold true. This proves Sraffa's assertion that, when a broadly defined industry is considered, changes in its conditions of supply and demand will affect the distribution of income.

A change in the capital input will change output, but it also changes the wage, and the rate of profit. These changes alter the distribution of income between workers and capitalists, and will therefore alter the pattern of demand. Exactly the same argument applies to wages, so that in general a person's income will not be equal to their marginal contribution to output. As a result, the distribution of income is neither meritocratic nor determined by the market. The distribution of income is to some significant degree determined independently of marginal productivity and the impartial blades of supply and demand.

This adds what mathematicians call an additional 'degree of freedom' to the model of the economy. To be able to work out prices, it is first necessary to know the distribution of income; and there will be a different pattern of prices for every different division of the economic cake between workers and capitalists. There is therefore nothing sacrosanct about the prices that apply in the economy, and equally nothing sacrosanct about the distribution of income. It reflects the relative power of different groups in society – though it is also constrained by limits set by the productive system, as we will soon discuss.

This contradicts economic theory, which says that the distribution of income is uniquely determined by the market (via the mechanisms discussed in these two chapters), and therefore there's nothing that policy-makers can or should do to alter it.[5] Instead, rather than prices determining the distribution of income as economists allege, the distribution of income determines prices. Within limits, the distribution of income is something which is determined, not by market mechanisms, but by relative political power.

4 This will apply only when the capital-to-labour ratio is the same in all industries – which is effectively the same as saying there is only one industry.
5 Of course, this argument has already been eliminated by the 'benevolent central authority' assumption derived from the Sonnenschein-Mantel-Debreu conditions.

Bhaduri's critique still accepts the assumption that it is possible to define a factor of production called capital. However, as I intimated above, the machinery aspect of the term 'capital' covers too great a multitude of things to be easily reduced to one homogeneous substance. It includes machines and the buildings that house them; trucks, ships and planes; oil wells, steel works and power stations. Each of these items itself consists of numerous other sub-assemblies which are themselves commodities. A truck contains an engine, which contains valves, springs and cables, the manufacture of which requires inputs from other types of capital, and so on.

The only thing that such disparate commodities obviously have in common is a price, and this is how economists would prefer to aggregate capital. But the price of a piece of capital should depend on the rate of profit, and the rate of profit will vary as prices change: there is an impossible circularity in this method of aggregation.

This problem was explicitly considered by Sraffa in his 1960 magnum opus. His purpose was to provide a firm foundation upon which a critique of the economic theory of production and income distribution could be built. He built his argument up stage by stage, with great care taken at each stage to make sure that the analysis was sound.

This meticulous method uncovered a number of paradoxes that invalidated the simplistic beliefs economists held about the relationship between productivity and income. Just as the peculiar conditions of 'production' of labor complicate the argument that the wage equals the marginal product of labor, so do the more conventional conditions of the production of capital disturb the argument that profit represents the marginal productivity of capital.

Note: the next section is possibly the most difficult part of this entire book. If you're satisfied with the debunking above, then you can skip this section for now and move to the next chapter. But I do recommend reading this section at some stage.

The whole box and dice

Sraffa's technique was to eschew the initial aggregation of capital, and to say, in place of 'factors of production produce goods,' that 'goods produce goods' – in concert with labor. Sraffa then used this 'assumption-free' model of production to show that the economic theories of price and of income distribution were invalid.

The essential point in his analysis was that capital does not exist as an easily definable entity, yet such an existence is necessary for the simple parable that profit represents the marginal productivity of capital to be true. He made this point by constructing a series of models that directly confronted the true complexity of a system of commodity production.

Sraffa built his models up very carefully, from a simple model with very little real-world realism to a more complex model which, with one exception, was a fairly realistic rendition of a market system of production.

The exception was that Sraffa considered an economy in equilibrium, when a real-world economy is certain not to be in equilibrium. However, Sraffa's purpose was to critique economics on its own terms, and since economics assumes equilibrium, Sraffa made the same assumption. He took it to its logical conclusion, considering an economy which was not only in equilibrium now, but had been in equilibrium for the indefinite past.

Model one: production with no surplus His first model was one in which the economy was just able to reproduce itself, and in which there was no 'fixed capital' – instead, all inputs were 'circulating capital' which are used up in each round of production.

In this economy, the output of each industry was just sufficient to supply the demand for its output by itself and the other industries. Labor was not explicitly treated, but it was feasible to envisage that part of the inputs to an industry represented workers receiving a subsistence wage. Sraffa's example is shown in Table 7.1.

In this hypothetical economy, combining 240 quarters of wheat, 12 tons of iron and 18 pigs in a production process results in an output of 450 quarters of wheat. Similarly, 90 quarters of wheat, 6 tons of iron and 12 pigs are used to produce 21 tons of iron; and 120 quarters of wheat, 3 tons of iron and 30 pigs are used to produce 60 pigs.

The total output of each sector just equals the amount of its output used to produce both its own output and that of all other sectors. Thus the total demand for wheat as an input is 450 quarters: 240 in wheat production, 90 in iron and 120 in pig production.

Sraffa posed the question of what would determine prices in this hypothetical economy, and the answer was not 'demand and supply,' but 'the conditions of production': each sector's price had to enable it to just purchase its inputs. Specifying this for the wheat industry, this meant that 240 times the price of wheat, plus 12 times the price of iron, plus 18 times the price of pigs, had to just equal 450 times the price of wheat.

Similar equations applied for iron and pigs, and with three equations (the price equations for each sector) and three unknowns (the prices), there

TABLE 7.1 Sraffa's hypothetical subsistence economy

Industries	Wheat input (qrs)	Iron input (tons)	Pig input (pigs)	Total outputs
Wheat	240	12	18	450 qrs
Iron	90	6	12	21 tons
Pigs	120	3	30	60 pigs
Total inputs	450	21	60	

was one unique set of prices which made it possible for the economy to reproduce.[6]

Neoclassical economists might have endeavored to find this set of prices by considering the demand curves for wheat, pigs and iron, and the supply curves for wheat, pigs and iron, and solving these to find the set of relative prices that equated supply and demand in each industry. However, in this context this would have been overkill: the only prices that work for this economy are those that enable each sector to buy its inputs.

Model two: production with a surplus The next step towards realism was to consider an economy which produced a surplus: where at least one sector produced more of its output than was used up to produce itself and all other commodities. This step closer to a real market economy raises the issue of profits – which weren't an issue in the first model. For this economy to be in equilibrium, the rate of profit has to be the same across all sectors – even if only one sector produced a physical surplus. Otherwise, capitalists in sectors with a low rate of profit would be tempted to move to sectors with a high rate of profit, and the economy would not be in equilibrium. Sraffa used a two-sector example, as shown in Table 7.2.

TABLE 7.2 Production with a surplus

Industries	Wheat input	Iron input	Total output
Wheat	280	12	575
Iron	120	8	20
Total inputs	400	20	

This economy uses 280 quarters of wheat and 12 tons of iron to produce 575 quarters of wheat; another 120 quarters of wheat and 8 tons of iron are used to produce 20 tons of iron. 175 bushels of wheat are produced over and above the 400 used in production, whereas the entire 20 tons of iron are used up in producing wheat and iron.

For a uniform rate of profit r to apply, the prices in this economy must be such that the 'money' value of inputs, multiplied by $(1+r)$, must equal the money value of its outputs. For this example economy, the price ratio is 15 bushels of wheat for 1 ton of iron, and the uniform rate of profit is 25 percent.

Model three: production with a surplus and explicit labor The economy above had to have labor in it, since nothing can be produced without labor.[7]

---

6 The rule in this example is that 10 quarters of wheat had to exchange for 1 ton of iron, or 2 pigs. These are relative price ratios in which commodities exchange – rather than absolute prices in terms of money.

7 At least, not until a 'von Neumann machine' – a machine that can both produce output and reproduce itself – is invented.

However, this was not explicitly shown. The next model added further realism by showing that output was produced by combining both commodities and labor in a production process.

This introduces the wage as an additional unknown, and establishes the first element in Sraffa's critique of the economic theory of income distribution: rather than prices determining the distribution of income, the distribution of income between wages and profits must be known before prices can be calculated.[8]

Sraffa then shows that there is an appropriate measuring stick (the 'standard commodity') which reveals a simple, linear relationship between the wage w, the actual rate of profit r, and the maximum feasible rate of profit for a given economy, R.[9] The wage w falls linearly as the rate of profit r rises towards its maximum value R.

The example economy in Table 7.2 has a maximum rate of profit of 25 percent, and results in the wage/profit function shown in Figure 4. If the wage w is .8 – which means that workers' wages represent 80 percent of the surplus output of this economy – then the corresponding rate of profit r is 5 percent. This is shown numerically in Table 7.3.

TABLE 7.3 Relationship between maximum and actual rate of profit and the wage share of surplus

Maximum R Wage (% of surplus)	25% Profit rate
0	25
10	23
20	20
30	18
40	15
50	13
60	10
70	8
80	5
90	3
100	0

What this table says is that if workers, for example, get a zero wage, then all of the surplus goes to the capitalists, who then make a profit of 25 percent. If, however, workers get 10 percent of the surplus as their wage,

8 This is often all economists know of Sraffa's critique, and they dismiss it immediately by saying that it wrongly ignores the issue of marginal productivity. In fact, there is much more to Sraffa's critique, and Bhaduri's critique establishes the invalidity of the assertion that the rate of profit equals the marginal productivity of capital.

9 When output is measured in terms of a 'standard commodity,' and when the wage is normalized so that when the rate of profit r is zero, the wage w equals 1.

then the rate of profit falls to 23 percent (rounded up). The same linear process continues right out to the point at which workers get 100 percent of the surplus, at which point capitalists get nothing and therefore have a

§54 rate of profit of zero.

Clearly, this analysis is reasonably realistic, and therefore, one might think, rather innocuous. However, this apparently innocuous step sets up the *coup de grâce* for the economic theory of income distribution.

The punchline: capital behaving badly

The key concept in the neoclassical theory of income distribution is that factors get paid in accordance with their marginal contribution to output in the context of diminishing marginal returns. This means that as the supply of a factor increases, its return should fall.

The difficulty is, as alluded to earlier, that it is not easy to see how one can add units of capital together. Workers can be aggregated by adding up the number of hours they work – after notionally standardizing for different levels of productivity by multiplying the hours of skilled labor by some amount to reflect higher productivity. Land can be aggregated by adding up acres – and again by adjusting numerically for varying degrees of fertility.

But machines have no apparent common property apart from price. This is in fact how economic theory aggregates capital, but this involves an obvious circularity, because the price of a machine reflects the profit expected from it, yet the rate of profit is the ratio of profit to price.

Sraffa proposed an ingenious and logically sound method of aggregation: to reduce capital to dated inputs of labor. The previous linear relationship between the wage and the rate of profit was an essential element in this analysis.

All items of capital are produced by other items of capital and labor. When an economy has been in equilibrium for the indefinite past, it is thus possible to regard the value of a machine as being equal to the value of the machines used to produce it, plus the value of the labor involved, times a rate of profit to reflect the passage of time. If we notionally treat the period of production as a year, then if the equilibrium rate of profit is 5 percent, 1.05 times the value of the inputs last year should equal the value of the machine this year.

The same argument applies to all the machines and labor inputs used to produce the inputs, and to all the machines and labor that produced them, and so on.

If we repeat this process, and each time reduce machinery inputs to the machinery and labor used to produce them, then we get a set of labor terms and a declining – *but never zero* – residual of machinery inputs. Each labor input is multiplied both by the wage, and by one plus the rate of profit raised to a power which reflects how many years ago the input was made.

If, for example, we are considering a machine manufactured eleven pro-

TABLE 7.4 The impact of the rate of profit on the measurement of capital

Profit rate (%)	Years								
	0	1	2	3	4	5	10	20	25
0	1	1	1	1	1	1	1	1	1
1	0.96	0.97	0.98	0.99	1.00	1.01	1.06	1.17	1.23
2	0.92	0.94	0.96	0.98	1.00	1.02	1.12	1.37	1.51
3	0.88	0.91	0.93	0.96	0.99	1.02	1.18	1.59	1.84
4	0.84	0.87	0.91	0.94	0.98	1.02	1.24	1.84	2.24
5	0.80	0.84	0.88	0.93	0.97	1.02	1.30	2.12	2.71
10	0.60	0.66	0.73	0.80	0.88	0.97	1.56	4.04	6.50
20	0.20	0.24	0.29	0.35	0.41	0.50	1.24	7.67	19.08
21	0.16	0.19	0.23	0.28	0.34	0.41	1.08	7.24	18.78
22	0.12	0.15	0.18	0.22	0.27	0.32	0.88	6.40	17.31
23	0.08	0.10	0.12	0.15	0.18	0.23	0.63	5.03	14.15
24	0.04	0.05	0.06	0.08	0.09	0.12	0.34	2.95	8.66
25	0.00	0.00	0.00	0.00	0.00	0.00	0.00	0.00	0.00

duction periods ago, then this term will be the amount of direct labor bestowed in producing all the relevant components in the twelfth year, times the wage, plus the capital input, all raised to the twelfth power. It is therefore possible to substitute an expression in terms of labor for the capital inputs used up in producing a given commodity.[10]

We can now approximately[11] express the value of a machine in terms of the sum of the value of the labor inputs used to produce it. Each element in this sum consists of a physical quantity of labor, multiplied by two terms: one representing the wage, and another representing the impact of accumulated profit over time.

The former term is a negative function of the rate of profit (as in Table 7.3 on page 151); the latter is as a positive function of the rate of profit, raised to a power. The former will fall in size as the rate of profit rises; the latter will rise, and it will also rise more for inputs made a long time ago.

This combination of opposing effects – one term that falls as r falls, the other that rises as r falls – evokes the possibility that one effect can prevail for a time, only to be overwhelmed by the opposite effect at a higher rate of profit. Therefore, the individual terms that interact to determine the value of an item of capital can rise for a while as the rate of profit rises, only to fall as the rate of profit rises still further.

This can be illustrated using Sraffa's example economy where the maxi-

---

10 This correspondence is not exact, but it can be made accurate to any level short of 100 percent by continuing the process of reduction for long enough.

11 Approximately because of the irreducible commodity residue left from the reduction process.

mum rate of profit was 25 percent, and considering a machine which was made using one unit of labor as an input at some time in the past.

If the rate of profit was zero, then no matter how many years ago that machine was made, if a machine cost one (standard commodity) unit to make, its measured value would still be 1, as shown by the first row of Table 7.4. If the rate of profit was instead 1 percent, then the measured value of that machine falls to 0.96, if it is used today – reflecting the lower value of labor in terms of Sraffa's measuring stick.

The value of the machine rises a bit if it was made two years ago, because its value is calculated to be 0.96 times 1 plus the rate of profit. This is 0.96 times 1.01, or roughly 0.97. This larger amount, though, is still less than 1, which would have been its value if the rate of profit had been zero. The same applies if the machine was used two periods ago, in which case its calculated value would be 0.98 – or 0.96, multiplied by 1.01 squared.

However, if the machine was produced five years ago, then its value in terms of the standard commodity rises to 1.01. This is because, while one part of the overall term has fallen to 0.96, the other has risen to 1.01 multiplied by itself five times – which roughly equals 1.05 – and 1.05 times 0.96 gives us 1.01.

The same effect applies across the row of the table, showing that as the rate of profit rises, the measured value of this capital input rises. The second term, 1.06, is 0.96 times 1.05 raised to the 10th; the third, 0.96 times 1.05 raised to the 15th; and so on.

The measured value of the machine therefore falls because of a higher rate of profit, but then rises if it was used many years ago. And the table has even more complications.

Notice that as we go down the table – so that the rate of profit increases – the value of a machine input today falls smoothly. However, the value of a machine applied five years ago rises for a while, but then falls. This accurate picture is a lot more complicated than economists assumed it to be, and these complications rule out the simple correspondence economists believed existed between the 'amount' of capital and the rate of profit.

The complications arise because the two different effects in Sraffa's accurate measure of capital don't cancel each other out. The first is the value of a wage unit, given the rate of profit r. On the first row, that is 1 (reflecting a zero rate of profit); on the second, 0.96 (at a 1 percent rate of profit); the third, 0.92 (at a 2 percent profit rate); and so on. But the second effect is $1+r$, raised to a power of 5, reflecting how many years ago the input was made. On the first row, that term is 1 – because the rate of profit is zero – and 1 times 1 is 1. On the second row, it is 0.96 times 1.05, which is 1.01 raised to the fifth power. This is roughly 1.01, so the measured value of the machine has risen. On the third row, it has risen further to 1.02 – which is 0.92 times 1.1, which is 1.02 raised to the 5th. On the fourth, it is roughly the same – 0.88 times 1.16, which is 1.03 raised to the 5th.

But by the time we get to a 10 percent rate of profit, the value goes down to 0.97: here we have 0.6 times 1.61, which is 1.10 raised to the 10th. The impact of the falling value of the first term now outweighs the impact of the rising value of the second. By the time we get to a rate of profit of 20 percent, the value of this machine (in terms of the standard commodity) has fallen to just 0.5, having been as high as 1.02 at lower rates of profit.

So the measured value of a machine rises and then falls as the rate of profit rises, and also rises and then falls as the time at which the machine was used to produce a commodity becomes farther in the past.

This is not exactly how economists think about capital as a factor of production. They had hoped that the rate of profit would fall smoothly as the amount of capital used in production rose, so that capital, like labor, would manifest diminishing marginal productivity. But Sraffa instead showed that not only was there no uniform relationship between the rate of profit and the amount of capital, but also the direction of causation was the opposite of what economists wanted. Rather than the rate of profit depending on the 'amount' of capital, the measured amount of capital actually depended on the rate of profit. This makes it impossible to argue that the rate of profit is determined by the marginal productivity of capital, and so this second leg of the economic theory of income distribution collapses.

Not only that, but the perverse relationship that exists between the measurement of capital and the rate of profit is going to cause perverse effects in production. A rising rate of profit might for a while make one method of producing a commodity cheaper than alternatives, but then at a still higher rate of profit, it might make it more expensive.

Sraffa provides one illustration of this by comparing the price of two commodities which start out equal when the rate of profit is zero, and where one becomes more expensive than the other as the rate of profit rises, only to have the other become more expensive as the rate of profit rises farther still. One product has relatively more 'direct labor' applied to its production in the recent past, while the other has more direct labor applied in the far distant past. Sraffa likens the latter to wine produced by being aged in a barrel; the former could be regarded as producing wine of identical quality using advanced chemical processes.[12] The latter process would be regarded as 'capital intensive,' since so much machinery is used directly in its production, while the former would be called perhaps 'time intensive' (or labor intensive if you imagine the barrels being tended over the years by cellar masters).

At a zero rate of profit, the cost of each barrel of wine equals simply the sum of the wages paid to produce the wine – and for both methods of production to exist in equilibrium, the cost of the two techniques must be identical.

As the rate of profit rises from zero to a moderate uniform rate, the far

12 I'm enough of a wine buff to realize that this example is practically impossible, but it will do as an illustration.

distant application of labor needed to produce the barrel has comparatively little impact, so that the wine produced using modern technology is more expensive. In this range of the rate of profit, production using modern technology would cease, since it would be uncompetitive with wine produced using the aging process.

However, as the rate of profit becomes higher still, the effect of compounding the rate of profit on the making of the cask becomes enormous, so that the aged wine becomes more expensive than its mass-produced cousin. Mass production would take over again – we would switch back to the apparently more 'capital intensive' means of production.

Finally, when the rate of profit reaches its maximum value and wages fall to zero, the cost of wine falls to simply the cost of the irreducible commodity components (the original grapes, etc.), and the price of the two types of wine could again coincide.

Subsequent economists used Sraffa's building blocks to illustrate that a method of production could start out superior to all others at a zero profit rate, become less profitable than some other methods at a higher rate, only to once again become the most profitable at a higher rate still.

This phenomenon of 'reswitching' destroyed the simple proposition that the rate of return on capital represented the marginal product of capital. If a particular production technique had lost primacy to others at one rate of profit, then it could not regain that primacy at a higher rate of profit still, unless for a period it benefited from increasing marginal product. But if marginal product could alternately rise and fall, then there was no necessity that the market for capital should be well behaved. Demand curves could slope up as well as down, supply curves down as well as up, and no unique equilibrium position could be defined.

The causes of this apparent paradox are that the concept of capital as a homogeneous substance is an illusion, and that what is capital intensive depends on the rate of profit. If the rate of profit is low, then the labor embodied in an ancient wine barrel is of little consequence, and the process of aging wine may well appear to be labor intensive. But if the rate of profit is high, then compounding of this high rate of profit makes that ancient wine barrel of great value – and the process could be described as capital intensive. Rather than the rate of profit depending on the quantity of capital, the quantity of capital (in terms of its value measured in embodied labor value) depends upon the rate of profit.

The intricate and interdependent processes of production thus generate many opportunities for factor returns to move one way and then the other as factor intensities rise. There is therefore no consistent relationship between factor productivity and factor incomes. Instead, the distribution of income between wages and profits is largely independent of the system of production. The distribution of income is a social phenomenon.

Economists fought against this conclusion, but every apparent victory was shown to be invalid. Ironically, the rebuttals to economic rejoinders often showed that the only conditions under which the economic position could hold would be if the ratio of capital to output was the same in all industries. This is the same condition needed to make Marx's labor theory of value hold, yet the neoclassical revolution which gave us modern economic theory was supposedly free of the nonsense conditions needed by its Marxian rival.

So what?

Just as Chapter 6 showed that the wage can't be explained as the marginal product of labor, this chapter has established that economic theory cannot justify the existing rate of profit as somehow reflecting the marginal productivity of capital. Instead, the rate of profit reflects relative power in our society, as well as the technical capabilities of factories and the success or otherwise of recent waves of investment. It is clearly possible for the rate of profit to be 'too high' or 'too low,' but conventional economics is of no use in establishing either level.

Ignorance is bliss

Of course, the average economist would never tell you that economic theory had suffered such a devastating blow. This is because the average young economist doesn't even know that this intellectual bout took place – the concepts in this debate don't make it onto the curriculum for either undergraduate or postgraduate students. Older economists cannot avoid some knowledge of the war, but they either erroneously believe that their camp won, or they dismiss the issue completely.

Today, economic theory continues to use exactly the same concepts which Sraffa's critique showed to be completely invalid – capital as an amorphous mass that can be costlessly moved from producing any commodity to any other, whose return reflects its marginal productivity, and which can be aggregated by adding up its price times quantity.

There are few better signs of the intellectual bankruptcy of economics than this.

However, this madness is often justified by an appeal to a methodological precept that the absurdity of a theory's assumptions is irrelevant – all that matters is that the theory's predictions accord with reality. We now turn to consider this popular but false defense of economics.

Why assumptions do matter, and why economics is so different from the true sciences

Economics would have us believe that it is a science, fully able to stand tall beside the more conventional physical sciences and mathematics.

After the preceding chapters, you should be inclined to reject that belief. Surely, whatever 'science' is, one might hope that it is undertaken with more impartiality, regard for the facts and logical consistency than economics has displayed.

However, the critiques of conventional economics which form the substance of this book were devised by critical economists (and sometimes, inadvertently, by conventional economists themselves) and some of these critiques have been acknowledged as valid by some conventional economists. There is also a small but robust minority working on other approaches to economic analysis, as you'll find in Chapter 18. There are thus some systematic and logical aspects to what economists in general do, which could qualify as scientific behavior.

The position I now favor is that economics is a pre-science, rather like astronomy before Copernicus, Brahe and Galileo. I still hold out hope of better behavior in the future, but given the travesties of logic and anti-empiricism that have been committed in its name, it would be an insult to the other sciences to give economics even a tentative membership of that field.[1]

Before better behavior can take widespread root, economics will have to wean itself from a methodological myth. This is the proposition, first put by Milton Friedman, that a theory cannot be judged by its assumptions, but only by the accuracy of its predictions.

Leaving aside the question of whether economics has ever accurately predicted anything, the argument that 'the more significant the theory, the more unrealistic [are] the assumptions' is simply bad philosophy.

The kernel

Have you heard the joke about the chemist, the physicist and the economist who get wrecked on a desert isle, with a huge supply of canned baked beans as their only food? The chemist says that he can start a fire using the neighboring palm trees, and calculate the temperature at which a can will

---

1 I have hardened my opinion on this front since the first edition, when I was willing to describe economics as a science, though a rather 'pathological' one.

explode. The physicist says that she can work out the trajectory of each of the baked beans, so that they can be collected and eaten. The economist says, 'Hang on, guys, you're doing it the hard way. Let's assume we have a can opener.'[2]

That assumption is not too different from the type of assumption that economists routinely make, and yet they defend themselves on the apparently convincing grounds that the assumptions don't matter – a theory can be evaluated only on the basis of the accuracy of its predictions.

This methodological defense is invalid, because it confuses 'negligibility' assumptions, which argue that some minor details can be ignored, with 'domain' assumptions, which determine the range of applicability of a given theory. Assumptions also do matter to economists, in that they genuinely believe that their theories describe reality, and they reject economic argument that is not based upon their preferred set of assumptions.

The roadmap

In this chapter I outline the paper in which Friedman introduced the notion that 'assumptions don't matter.' Following Musgrave, I classify assumptions under three headings: negligibility assumptions, domain assumptions, and heuristic assumptions. Friedman's paradoxical statement that 'the more significant the theory, the more unrealistic the assumptions' is only partially true of the first class of assumptions, and manifestly untrue of the latter two classes. Finally, I detail the many ways in which assumptions do matter to economists.

A paradoxical proposition

There would be few if any academic economists who have not had a lecture disturbed by some recalcitrant student, interjecting that the assumptions of the model being discussed are unrealistic. Fortunately, there is a simple weapon at hand: an appeal to the authority of Milton Friedman that a theory can't be judged by its assumptions, but only by how well its predictions accord with reality.

In fact, Friedman's case went farther: he argued that unrealistic assumptions were the hallmark of good theory. In what Paul Samuelson later dubbed 'the F-twist,' Friedman argued that

> Truly important and significant hypotheses will be found to have 'assumptions' that are wildly inaccurate descriptive representations of reality, and, in general, the more significant the theory, the more unrealistic the assumptions (in this sense). The reason is simple. A hypothesis is important if it 'explains' much by little, that is, if it abstracts the common and crucial elements from

2 I first heard this joke in a public debate between my then professor of economics and a physicist. I now appreciate the irony that physicists are turning their attention to economics – and in general being horrified by neoclassical economic theory.

the mass of complex and detailed circumstances surrounding the phenomena to be explained and permits valid predictions on the basis of them alone. To be important, therefore, a hypothesis must be descriptively false in its assumptions; it takes account of, and accounts for, none of the many other attendant circumstances, since its very success shows them to be irrelevant for the phenomena to be explained.

To put this point less paradoxically, the relevant question to ask about the 'assumptions' of a theory is not whether they are descriptively 'realistic,' for they never are, but whether they are sufficiently good approximations for the purpose in hand. And this question can be answered only by seeing whether the theory works, which means whether it yields sufficiently accurate predictions. (Friedman 1953)

The proposition that a theory is not regarded as a description of reality, but merely as a way of predicting the future, is known as 'instrumentalism.' This position is superficially appealing, and sufficiently persuasive to quieten the average interjector. It appears scientific, in that most scientists would admit that their theories can never exactly describe reality. It also implies a healthy dose of theoretical agnosticism, in that the economist is purportedly detached from his theory, and is only really interested in 'the facts.'

However, despite its superficial appeal, instrumentalism suffers from several flaws, which were clearly set out by the philosopher Alan Musgrave in 1981. Musgrave argued that there were three classes of assumptions, and that Friedman's dictum was only partially true in the least important of them.

Negligibility assumptions Negligibility assumptions state that some aspect of reality has little or no effect on the phenomenon under investigation. Friedman's paper made heavy use of the example of a ball being dropped near the earth, which fell very nearly 'as if' it had been dropped in a vacuum. In this instance it was valid to assume that the ball was falling in a vacuum, since air resistance has negligible impact on the ball's fall. However, the same was obviously not true of a feather dropped under the same circumstances.

Friedman argued that though it was unrealistic to say 'assume the ball was dropped in a vacuum,' the theory of gravity had great explanatory power: it explained much (the acceleration of bodies in free fall close to the earth) with very little (a gravitational constant and simple calculus). This theory should be dropped in favor of another only if a rival is at least as accurate and equally acceptable on other grounds, or 'when there exists a theory that is known to yield better predictions but only at a greater cost' (Friedman 1953).

Musgrave argued that many of Friedman's musings were reasonable in this domain, but that even here his 'dialectical' proposition that 'the more significant the theory, the more unrealistic the assumptions' is overblown.

In fact, it is possible to rephrase these 'unrealistic' statements as 'realistic' ones: for example, it is realistic to say that air resistance is negligible for dense bodies falling from rest over short distances. As Musgrave put it, these assumptions:

> are not necessarily 'descriptively false,' for they do not assert that present factors are absent but rather that they are 'irrelevant for the phenomena to be explained' [...] Galileo's assumption that air-resistance was negligible for the phenomena he investigated was a true statement about reality, and an important part of the explanation Galileo gave of those phenomena. (Musgrave 1981)

However, negligibility assumptions are the minnows of the assumptions family. Far more important are domain assumptions, and it is these to which rightly troubled students often object.

Domain assumptions A domain assumption specifies the conditions under which a particular theory will apply. If those conditions do not apply, then neither does the theory.

An economic example of this is the assumption that risk can be used as a proxy for uncertainty – an assumption that permeates the conventional theories of macroeconomics and finance, which we will investigate in Chapters 10 and 11.

Risk applies to situations in which the regularity of past events is a reliable guide to the course of future events. Gambling gives us many such examples: if a tossed coin is seen to land showing heads roughly half the time, then you can reliably bet that there will be a 50:50 chance of heads in the future. If anyone bet you that heads would in future come up only 40 percent of the time, it would be sensible to take the bet. A risky event will have a probability associated with it, and a variance of outcomes around those probabilities, which can be reliably estimated using the techniques of statistics.

Uncertainty applies when the past provides no reliable guide to future events. Though the fact that we cannot predict the future is the essence of the human condition, the very nebulousness of uncertainty means that many people – and certainly the vast majority of economists – have difficulty grasping the concept. As a result, they act as if the quantifiable concept of risk can be safely substituted for unquantifiable uncertainty.

A somewhat intimate example might illustrate the fallacy of identifying uncertainty with risk.[3] Imagine that you are very attracted to a particular individual, and that you know this person has gone out with 20 percent of those who have asked him or her out in the past. Does this mean that you have a 20 percent chance of being lucky if you 'pop the question'?

Of course not. Each instance of attraction between two people is a unique

3 I am grateful to my student Marchessa Dy for suggesting this very evocative analogy.

event, and the past behavior of the object of your desires provides no guide as to how your advances will be received. How he or she will react cannot be reduced to some statistical prediction based on past apparent regularities. From your perspective, their reaction is truly uncertain – and this uncertainty is at the root of much of the angst that romantic attraction generates.

A similar observation can be made about each new business investment. Even if similar investments have been made in the past, the economic environment of a new investment differs from those which have gone before. Past trends therefore cannot be confidently extrapolated to predict future performance – but this procedure is the essential assumption behind using statistics to calculate risk.

The assumption that risk can be used as a proxy for uncertainty when evaluating investments is therefore unrealistic. A theory that makes such an assumption is quite clearly not better than an alternative one which does not – quite the opposite in fact. This assumption says that the domain of relevance of the theory is a world in which the future is simply subject to chance.

Since there is no such world, the domain of applicability of theories which make such an unrealistic assumption is 'nowhere.' Yet assumptions of this type abound in economic theory (especially, it must be said, in the work of Milton Friedman).

Such an assumption should be made only if it fits into Musgrave's third class, the heuristic assumption.

Heuristic assumptions A heuristic assumption is one which is known to be false, but which is made as a first step towards a more general theory. Musgrave gives the example of Newton's assumption that the solar system consisted only of the sun and the earth. This gave rise to the theory that planets would follow elliptical orbits (which is a reasonable medium-term guide to actual planetary orbits in our solar system).

The next major step came with Poincaré in 1899, when he tried to develop a formula describing planetary motion in a system with more than one planet. His proof that there was no such formula – and that the actual orbits would interact in wildly unpredictable ways – ushered in what is now known as 'chaos theory' or 'complexity theory' (though it lay dormant for sixty-eight years until modern computers allowed its accidental rediscovery).

The modern theory of planetary behavior now recognizes that the stable orbits of our solar system can only have evolved – over an enormous period of time – from far less stable orbits, which must have led to collisions between proto-planets. It is now accepted that the moon, for example, was the product of a collision between another proto-planet and the early earth.

Collisions are not possible in a single-planet solar system – the kind of system that Newton assumed to derive his initial theory. Though that heuristic assumption was a major step in the development of the scientific mode of thinking about astronomy, dropping it led to a better theory, not a worse one.

When heuristic assumptions are made consciously by a theorist in the course of developing a theory, they are normally explicitly described as such. For instance, when developing the theory of relativity, Einstein at one point stated that the distance covered by a person walking from one side to the other of a moving train is equal to the sum of the distance covered by the train, and the width of the carriage. However, he continued that 'We shall see later that this result cannot be maintained; in other words, the law that we have just written down does not hold in reality. For the time being, however, we shall assume its correctness' (Einstein 1961 [1916]). When Einstein dropped this heuristic assumption, the theory of relativity was the result.

The greater realism at the heart of Einstein's theory transformed our understanding of reality, and dramatically expanded the physical and intellectual capabilities of our species. Yet if we accept Friedman's methodology, then we would have to argue that Einstein's theory was poorer than Newton's because it was more realistic.

In general, then, and contrary to Friedman, abandoning a factually false heuristic assumption will normally lead to a better theory – not a worse one.

Judging the assumptions Theories can therefore be evaluated by their assumptions to some extent, if one has an intelligent taxonomy of assumptions. A theory may well draw power from 'unrealistic' assumptions if those assumptions assert, rightly, that some factors are unimportant in determining the phenomena under investigation. But it will be hobbled if those assumptions specify the domain of the theory, and real-world phenomena are outside that domain.

These assumptions may be justified if they are merely heuristic devices used to simplify the process of deriving a more general theory – but only if that more general theory is in fact derived. Economists often imply, when they fob off some critical student, that the unrealistic assumptions in introductory economics courses are dropped in more advanced theory – which portrays these assumptions as heuristic tools. In fact, as preceding chapters have illustrated, the assumptions used in more advanced theory are often more unrealistic than those presented in introductory lectures.

Scientific realism versus instrumentalism Musgrave also points out that most scientists reject an instrumental view of science in favor of 'scientific realism' – the belief that scientific theories should not merely predict reality but should, in some sense, represent it.

Ironically, this is actually the belief that most economists have about economic theory. Friedman's instrumentalism is little more than a smokescreen behind which to hide when one wishes to quell a budding class rebellion.

It is often evident to the student objector that, though professing that the assumptions don't matter, his teachers continue to use the same small class of assumptions over and over again: rational utility-maximizing individuals, profit-maximizing firms, and a plethora of ancillary assumptions built on these foundations.

These assumptions are used because economists believe that these assumptions do capture essential elements of reality, and regard any theory which does not use these building blocks as 'unrealistic.' This belief is most clearly seen in the manner in which the 'bibles' of economics, its academic journals, filter out papers that do not make this core set of assumptions.

Assumptions do matter – to economists The proposition that assumptions don't matter implies that economists would be quite willing to accept a theory which assumed irrational behavior if the model generated results which accorded with observation. It also implies that the development of economic theory would be driven primarily by the desire to produce theories that provide a closer fit to observed data.

Both these implications are strongly at variance with reality.

As any non-orthodox economist knows, it is almost impossible to have an article accepted into one of the mainstream academic economic journals unless it has the full panoply of economic assumptions: rational behavior (according to the economic definition of rational!), markets that are always in equilibrium, risk as an acceptable proxy for uncertainty, and so on. When it comes to safeguarding the channels of academic advancement, little else matters apart from preserving the set of assumptions that defines economic orthodoxy.

Similarly, the development of economic theory over time has been propelled by the desire to make every aspect of it conform to the preferred economic model. Macroeconomics, when it first began, bore little resemblance to microeconomics. Fifty years later, macroeconomics is effectively a branch of microeconomics. As I outline in Chapter 10, a major factor behind this tribal coup was the belief that, regardless of its predictive validity, macroeconomics was unsound because its assumptions did not accord with those of microeconomics. It was therefore extensively revised, especially during the 1970s and 1980s, so that macroeconomic theory was more consistent with microeconomic assumptions. Far from assumptions not mattering to economists, assumptions in fact drove the development of economic theory.

Assumptions and logic Assumptions matter in a more profound sense because, as this book shows, assumptions can be logically incoherent. For example, as discussed in Chapter 4, the economic model of the firm is internally contradictory. A theory that contains logically inconsistent assumptions will be a bad theory – and, as this book shows, economics is replete with logical inconsistencies.

This is a science? The behavior of economists hardly fits the stereotype of scientists as dispassionate seekers of truth. But their behavior does fit modern, sociological theories of how scientists behave.[4]

Briefly, these theories argue that each 'science' is as much a society as it is an intellectual discipline. A collection of scholars in a science will share a perspective on what defines their discipline, and what constitutes scientific behavior. This shared mindset includes core beliefs, which cannot be challenged without threatening your membership of the group (and hence your status as a scientist), ancillary beliefs which are somewhat malleable, a set of analytic techniques, and as yet unsolved problems to which these techniques should be applied. The core beliefs are known as the 'hard core' – since they cannot be altered without rejecting, in some crucial sense, the very foundations of the science. The ancillary beliefs are known as the 'protective belt,' since their function is to protect the core beliefs from attack.

The scholars expect that their beliefs and techniques will be able to solve the outstanding problems, thus increasing the explanatory power of their science. If they fail, then the first response is to adjust the ancillary beliefs rather than the core propositions. Only when the problem proves both intractable and crucial is there any possibility that core beliefs will be abandoned, leading to the formation of a new school of thought – or the ascendancy of an existing rival school. While a school of thought is expanding the range of phenomena it can explain using its core beliefs – by experiments that confirm its predictions, or extensions of its theories to novel areas – then it is said to be a 'progressive' scientific research program which manifests a 'positive heuristic.' If, instead, experimental results contradict its predictions, and its theories are adjusted to rationalize these failures, then it is said to be 'degenerative' with a 'negative heuristic.'

It is possible for more than one such collection of scholars to exist in a science at any one time, so it makes sense to speak of schools of thought within a science. Each school of thought will compete with the others, emphasizing their weaknesses and its own strengths.

Clearly this sociological description of a science fits the historical record of economics. At the beginning of the third millennium, there are at least five schools of thought. The neoclassical school is clearly dominant, but there are several other competing schools – in particular, the post-Keynesian, Austrian, and evolutionary schools of economics. Each is developing its own approach to explaining similar phenomena, and there is clearly a rivalry between the

---

4 The analysis below is a brief summary of Imre Lakatos's concept of competing 'scientific research programs.' The philosophy of science is today dominated by more 'postmodernist' concepts. I will leave exploration of these newer strands to the interested reader to pursue.

minority schools and neoclassical economics – the other schools criticize neoclassical economics while it largely ignores its rivals.

However, it might be thought that this provides a fairly demeaning perspective on science itself. Surely this behavior is aberrant, and true sciences are beyond this petty bickering? No, strange as it may seem, a similar picture can be painted even of the queen of sciences, physics.

Quantum uncertainty? In order to comprehend some of the bizarre results of experimental particle physics, most physicists argue that matter is in some sense 'probabilistic,' and that the observer fundamentally affects reality. If an observer tries to 'tie down' one aspect of a particle – say, its location – then some other aspect becomes fundamentally unknowable. Physicists say that an elementary particle is always in a 'superposition' of both states, and testing for one leads to the other state resolving itself in a completely random way. The act of observing a particle thus directly – but unpredictably – alters its state. This is not because of any statistical properties of large numbers of electrons, but because randomness is an inherent feature of fundamental particles.

Two crucial aspects of this 'Copenhagen school' interpretation of quantum reality are (a) that particles can be treated as 'wave functions' in what is known as the wave–particle duality, so that a fundamental particle can be completely represented by its wave function; and (b) that there are two sets of physical laws, one which applies when there is no observer ('superposition') and one which exists when there is an observer.

The most famous popular representation of what this means, when put in terms of everyday objects, is 'Schrodinger's cat.' This is a thought experiment in which a box contains a cat, a radioactive element, and a vial of poison. If the radioactive element emits a particle, the vial opens and the cat dies. If it doesn't, the cat lives.

What state is the cat in before an experimenter opens the lid to see whether it is alive or dead? In the Copenhagen school interpretation, the cat is in a superposition of being both alive and dead. The act of the observer opening the box resolves the cat into one or other state.

But this is not the only way to make sense of the experimental data. A rival interpretation, established by David Bohm, provides a completely deterministic interpretation, with none of the 'quantum uncertainty' of the Copenhagen school. It can explain the same experimental results as can the Copenhagen school – and some which it can't explain – without resorting to the apparently metaphysical position that the observer somehow affects reality at the quantum level. In Bohm's theory, Schrodinger's cat is either alive and well if the radioactive element hasn't emitted a particle, or dead if it has, independent of the human observer who eventually opens the box to check.

How have physicists reacted to this coexistence of two rival explanations of reality? As the physicist David Albert sees it, in much the same way that economists have reacted to alternative schools of thought – by refusing to take them seriously. It is worth citing Albert at some length to show that, quite possibly, scientists in other disciplines are no different from economists when it comes to their reaction to intellectual challenges to accepted dogma:

> Despite all the rather spectacular advantages of Bohm's theory, an almost universal refusal even to consider it, and an almost universal allegiance to the standard formulation of quantum mechanics, has persisted in physics, astonishingly, throughout most of the past 40 years. Many researchers have perennially dismissed Bohm's theory on the grounds that it granted a privileged mathematical role to particles. The complaint was that this assignment would ruin the symmetry between position and momentum, as if ruining that symmetry amounted to a more serious affront to scientific reason than the radical undermining, in the Copenhagen formulation, of the very idea of an objective reality. Others dismissed Bohm's theory because it made no empirical predictions (no obvious ones, that is) that differed from those of the standard interpretation – as if the fact that those two formulations had much in common on that score somehow transparently favored one of them over the other. Still others cited 'proofs' in the literature that no deterministic replacement for quantum mechanics of the kind that Bohm had already accomplished was even possible. (Albert 1994)

After the above was published in the first edition, several physicists contacted me and put forward criticisms of Bohm's theory. However, the relevance of his theory in the context of this chapter was the alleged behavior of physicists in rejecting this alternative perspective in the manner described by Albert.

At this sociological level, therefore, economics appears to have some similarities to the conventional sciences – though the extent to which alternative perspectives are suppressed in economics is far greater than in physics.

A degenerate scientific research program There was a time when the neoclassical school of economics was clearly progressive, while its main rival was clearly degenerate. When the neoclassical school coalesced in the 1870s in the works of Jevons, Menger and Walras, the preceding classical school was in crisis. The classical school always had a difficulty in explaining the relationship between what it called value and prices; yet it insisted that value was in some way fundamental to the determination of price. This problem was accentuated by the work of the final member of the classical school, Karl Marx (the subject of Chapter 17).

At the same time, the neoclassical school was expanding its core belief that human behavior was driven by the desire to maximize utility. This had developed from a guiding principle, in Bentham's hands, to a coherent theory of consumer and producer behavior in the hands of Jevons, and to an explanation for the overall coordination of a market economy in Walras. At the turn of the nineteenth century, neoclassical economists were confident that their science could continue expanding its explanation of the economy. It was clearly then a progressive scientific research program.

Though the majority of economists still believe that this is the case today, there are manifest signs that this is no longer true. Instead, the theory today is degenerate: rather than expanding the range of phenomena it can explain, the leading edge of the theory is dominated by adjusting the protective belt of ancillary beliefs to defend the hard-core beliefs from attack. For example, the Sonnenschein-Mantel-Debreu conditions (discussed in Chapter 3) are a way of maintaining the hard-core belief that individual behavior is driven by utility maximization, despite the proof that individual preferences cannot be aggregated. A similar interpretation could be given of responses of neoclassical economics to the many logical problems documented in this book.

But the problems with economics go beyond just this, since if economics were as fully a science as astronomy, eventually its litany of failures would lead to at least a general acknowledgment of crisis.

The incredible inertness of economics What makes economics different from and inferior to other sciences is the irrational tenacity with which it holds to its core beliefs in the face of either contrary factual evidence or theoretical critiques that establish fundamental inconsistencies in its intellectual apparatus.

The discovery, for example, that firms believe they experience constant or falling marginal costs (Eiteman and Guthrie 1952), and generally set prices by placing a markup on average cost, led not to the abandonment of the economic theory of price-setting, but to a welter of papers arguing that in a competitive market, the effect of markup pricing was the same as if firms did consciously equate marginal cost to marginal revenue (Langlois 1989). On the same note, Sraffa's theoretical argument that diminishing marginal returns were unlikely to occur in practice was ignored.

As a result, students at the beginning of the twenty-first century are receiving much the same instruction about how firms set prices as did their counterparts at the end of the nineteenth century.

Physical sciences hold on to their core beliefs with some tenacity, but nowhere near this much – even Albert's paper goes on to observe that 'serious students of the foundations of quantum mechanics rarely defend the standard formulation anymore' (Albert 1994). As a result, revolutions in physical sciences – where one dominant paradigm is replaced by another – occur much more frequently than they do in economics. Often, these revolutions outpace the popular understanding of a science.

Astronomy provides an example of this. I expect that most lay people think that the dominant theory of how the universe came into being is the

'Big Bang.' In this theory, the universe originated in a 'quantum singularity' some 12–15 billion years ago. This explosion kick-started matter and time, leading to the immense universe we observe today. Back in the 1950s, this theory won out against its rival, that the universe had always been in a 'steady state' of expansion.

The Big Bang was indeed the dominant theory for some time – until it was pointed out that, according to calculations from quantum mechanics, the Big Bang would have resulted in a universe consisting of a mere handful of elementary particles.

A rival theory then developed which argued that, for a substantial period of time, the laws of physics of the current universe did not apply. Matter, for example, could move much faster than the speed of light. This 'inflationary universe' theory has subsequently been embellished to predict that there are many universes – as opposed to the one universe postulated by the Big Bang.

The shifts from the Big Bang paradigm to the inflationary universe, to 'multiverses,' are big ones conceptually. The first envisages a single finite universe, while the last muses that ours may be only one of many universes, each with different 'fundamental' physical laws. But the science of astronomy made this move over a period of about twenty years, and it continues to undergo development today. Now even the inflationary/multiverse theory is under challenge, as measurements imply that the rate of expansion of the universe is actually increasing with time.[5]

Economics, in contrast, has had only one acknowledged revolutionary episode in the last century – the Keynesian revolution during the 1930s. Yet at the end of the twentieth century, the dominant school of thought in economics retains nothing from that revolution, and is in fact a direct descendant of pre-Keynesian neoclassical economics.

Think of the many revolutions in our understanding of the physical world which have occurred in the twentieth century: from Newtonian to Einsteinian physics; from Mendelian genetics to DNA and the human genome; from determinism to chaos theory. Any scientist from the nineteenth century would be bewildered by what is commonplace today in his discipline – save an economist.

Why is economics so resistant to change? Is it because everything economists believed at the end of the nineteenth century was correct? Hardly, as this book shows. Instead, to understand the incredible inertness of economics, we have to consider an essential difference between social sciences in general and the physical sciences, and the thorny topic of ideology.

My kingdom for an experiment In the nineteenth century, scientists and philosophers of science generally believed that what distinguished the social

5 This reference to physics is now seriously dated, since this empirical observation has now been cor- roborated – see the Wikipedia item on the 'Accelerating Universe' for a brief discussion.

sciences from the physical sciences was that the latter could undertake experiments to test their theories, whereas the former could not. In the twentieth century, Popper instead argued that the distinction between a science – like physics – and a non-science – like astrology – was not that one could undertake experiments and the other could not, but that one made falsifiable statements, while the other did not. Popper's distinction between science and non-science wasn't completely relevant to the 'experiments versus no experiments' distinction, but it did tend to play down the importance of experimentation in deciding what was and what was not a science.

The history of economics implies that Popper's distinction does not give sufficient attention to whether or not a falsifiable statement can in fact be experimentally falsified. For example, Milton Friedman is famous as the father of the now defunct sub-branch of economics known as monetarism. One falsifiable statement he made was that inflation is caused by the government increasing the money supply more rapidly than the economy is going.

This implied that, to reduce inflation, all the government had to do was to increase the money supply more slowly than the economy was growing. This was the basis of the economic policies of Margaret Thatcher, yet eventually this approach was abandoned. One reason why was that the government was never able to meet its targets for the rate of growth of the money supply – it might aim to increase it by, say, 6 percent, only to see it grow by 11 percent. Also, the relationship between the three crucial variables in Friedman's theory – the rate of inflation, the rate of growth of the economy, and the rate of growth of the money supply – was never as watertight in practice as it appeared to be in his theory.

You could thus argue that Friedman's statement – that inflation is caused by the government expanding the money supply faster than the rate of growth of the economy – had been falsified. Did this lead Milton and his supporters to abandon his theory? Of course not: monetarists instead argued that all sorts of attenuating features disturbed the results.

In other words, because the monetarist experiment in Great Britain wasn't a controlled experiment, monetarist economists could refuse to accept that their theory had been falsified.

The same observation can be made about Marxist economists, and their attitude toward the data on Marx's theory that the rate of profit would tend to fall, or the inevitability of socialism, and so on. In other words, this isn't just a disease of the political right, but an endemic problem in economics: without the ability to undertake controlled experiments, statements which could be falsified will be unfalsifiable in practice. Economists of all persuasions are therefore liable to hang on to beliefs that they argue are scientific, but which in the end are ideological.

The experience of another social science, psychology, provides some support for the argument that the ability to undertake experiments is crucial to scientific progress. For much of the twentieth century, psychology was dominated by the 'behaviorist' school. This school argued that an organism's behavior had to be understood as a response to an external stimulus: it was 'unscientific' to postulate any unobservable mental processes of the organism which mediated between the stimulus and the response. To this school, complex behavior – such as playing a piano – had to be understood as a chain of stimuli and responses. However, experiments showed that

> even average pianists move their hands too quickly for the tactile information to pass along the sensory nerves to the central nervous system and for the command to move the hands to be sent down the motor nerves [...] Therefore, the behaviorist hypothesis that each new action is a response to an external stimulus is implausible. (Bond 2000)

This and several other experimental falsifications of behaviorism led to its demise, and replacement by cognitive psychology, which accepts that 'there are cognitive processes that determine our behavior which we, as psychologists, must explain, even if they are not directly observable' (ibid.). Thus psychology, with the help of experiments, was able to undergo a revolution from one dominant school to another – while economics continues to be dominated by the same school (which, ironically, has a very behaviorist view of human behavior). Unless it develops a means to undertake experiments to test rival theories, economics may be unable to break from the grip of ideology.

Equilibrium and an invisible ideology Economics as a discipline arose at a time when English society was in the final stages of removing the controls of the feudal system from its mercantile/capitalist economy. In this climate, economic theory had a definite (and beneficial) political role: it provided a counter to the religious ideology that once supported the feudal order, and which still influenced how people thought about society. In the feudal system the preordained hierarchy of king, lord, servant and serf was justified on the basis of the 'divine right of kings.' The king was God's representative on earth, and the social structure which flowed down from him was a reflection of God's wishes.

This structure was nothing if not ordered, but this order imposed severe restrictions on the now dominant classes of merchants and industrialists. At virtually every step, merchants were met with government controls and tariffs. When they railed against these imposts, the reply came back that they were needed to ensure social order.

Economic theory – then rightly called political economy – provided the merchants with a crucial ideological rejoinder. A system of government was not needed to ensure order: instead, social order would arise naturally in a market system in which each individual followed his own self-interest.

Smith's phrase 'the invisible hand' came along rather late in the process, but the notion played a key role in the political and social transformations of the late eighteenth and early nineteenth centuries.

An essential aspect of this market social order was equilibrium.

From the outset, economists presumed that the market system would achieve equilibrium. Indeed, the achievement of equilibrium was often touted as an advantage of the free market over any system where prices were set by fiat. Equilibrium was therefore an essential notion of the economic defense of capitalism: the equilibrium of the capitalist market would replace the legislative order of the now defunct feudal hierarchy.

More importantly, whereas the feudal order endowed only the well born with welfare, the equilibrium of the market would guarantee the best possible welfare for all members of society. The level of individual welfare would reflect the individual's contribution to society: people would enjoy the lifestyle they deserved, rather than the lifestyle into which they had been born.

If, instead of equilibrium, economists had promised that capitalism would deliver chaos; if, instead of meritocracy, economists had said that the market would concentrate inequality, then economists could have hindered rather than helped the transition to capitalism (though they more likely would have been ignored).

By the middle of the nineteenth century, the transition to capitalism was complete: what was left of feudalism was a mere vestige. But rather than the promised equilibrium, nineteenth-century capitalism was racked by cycles and enormous disparities of wealth. A major depression occurred roughly every twenty years, workers' conditions would improve and then rapidly deteriorate, prices rise and then fall, banks expand and then collapse. New 'robber barons' replaced the barons of old. It appeared that, while promising a meritocratic equilibrium, capitalism had instead delivered unbalanced chaos. A new political challenge arose: that of socialism.

Once again, economics rose to the challenge, and once again equilibrium was a central tenet. This time the defense was mounted by what we today call neoclassical economics, since classical economics had been turned into a weapon against capitalism by the last great classical economist, Karl Marx.

In contrast to the hand-waving of Smith, the neoclassical economists of the late nineteenth century provided a substantive mathematical analysis of how equilibrium could be achieved by an idealized market economy, and how this equilibrium could be fair to all. However, unlike the earlier classical championing of capitalism, this technical edifice provided very little in the way of libertarian slogans for the battle against the ideology of socialism. Instead of arming capitalism's defenders with rhetoric to deploy against socialists, it gave birth to the academic discipline of economics.

Capitalism eventually transcended the challenge of socialism, with little real assistance from economic theory. But while the economics had little impact upon capitalism, the need to defend capitalism had a profound impact upon the nature of economic theory. The defensive imperative, and the role of equilibrium in that defense, cemented equilibrium's role as a core belief of economic theory.

At the beginning of the third millennium, there is no competing social system against which capitalism must prove its superiority. Feudalism is long dead, and those socialist societies which remain are either socialist in name only, or bit players on the world stage.

Today, most economists imperiously dismiss the notion that ideology plays any part in their thinking. The profession has in fact devised the term 'positive economics' to signify economic theory without any value judgments, while describing economics with value judgments as 'normative economics' – and the positive is exalted far above the normative.

Yet ideology innately lurks within 'positive economics' in the form of the core belief in equilibrium.[6] As previous chapters have shown, economic theory has contorted itself to ensure that it reaches the conclusion that a market economy will achieve equilibrium.[7] The defense of this core belief is what has made economics so resistant to change, since virtually every challenge to economic theory has called upon it to abandon the concept of equilibrium. It has refused to do so, and thus each challenge – Sraffa's critique, the calamity of the Great Depression, Keynes's challenge, the modern science of complexity – has been repulsed, ignored, or belittled.

This core belief explains why economists tend to be extreme conservatives on major policy debates, while simultaneously believing that they are non-ideological, and motivated by knowledge rather than bias.

If you believe that a free market system will naturally tend towards equilibrium – and also that equilibrium embodies the highest possible welfare for the highest number – then, *ipso facto*, any system other than a complete free market will produce disequilibrium and reduce welfare. You will therefore oppose minimum wage legislation and social security payments – because they will lead to disequilibrium in the labor market. You will oppose price controls – because they will cause disequilibrium in product markets. You will argue for private provision of services – such as education, health, welfare, perhaps even police – because governments, untrammeled by the discipline of supply and demand, will either under- or oversupply the market (and charge too much or too little for the service).

In fact, the only policies you will support are ones that make the real world conform more closely to your economic model. Thus you may support anti-monopoly laws – because your theory tells you that monopolies are bad.

6 Ironically, Austrian economics, an alternative school of thought that is very closely related to neoclassical economics, differs by singing the praises of capitalism as a disequilibrium system (see Chapter 18).

7 Equilibrium in turn has been endowed with essential welfare properties, with a 'Pareto optimal equilibrium' being a situation in which no one can be made any better off without making someone else worse off.

You may support anti-union laws, because your theory asserts that collective bargaining will distort labor market outcomes.

And you will do all this without being ideological.

Really?

Yes, really – in that most economists genuinely believe that their policy positions are informed by scientific knowledge, rather than by personal bias or religious-style dogma. Economists are truly sincere in their belief that their policy recommendations will make the world a better place for everyone in it – so sincere, in fact, that they often act against their own self-interest.

For example, there is little doubt that an effective academic union could increase the wages paid to academic economists. If economists were truly self-motivated – if they behaved like the entirely self-interested rational economic man of their models – they would do well to support academic unions, since the negative impacts they predict unions to have would fall on other individuals (fee-paying students and unemployed academics). But instead, one often finds that economists are the least unionized of academics, and they frequently argue against actions that, according to their theories, could conceivably benefit the minority of academics at the expense of the greater community. However ideological economists may appear to their critics, in their hearts they are sincerely non-partisan – and, ironically, altruistic.

But non-partisan in self-belief does not mean non-partisan in reality. With equilibrium both encapsulating and obscuring so many ideological issues in economics, the slavish devotion to the concept forces economists into politically reactionary and intellectually contradictory positions.

Of course, if economists were right that equilibrium embodies the best possible outcome for the greatest number, then their apparently ideological policy positions would be justified – if the economy always headed back to equilibrium when disturbed from its nirvana. In the next chapter, we'll put aside the critiques which establish that the building blocks of equilibrium are invalid, and instead ask whether economic equilibrium, as defined by economic theory, is in fact stable.

9 | LET'S DO THE TIME WARP AGAIN

Why economics must finally treat time seriously

Forget everything you know about riding a bicycle, and imagine that someone who purports to be a 'bicycle guru' has convinced you that there are two steps to learning how to ride a bike. In step 1, you master balancing on a stationary bike. In step 2, you master riding a moving bike, applying the skills acquired at step 1.

After several difficult months at step 1, you would know that to remain upright, you must keep your center of gravity directly above the point of contact between your wheels and the road.

Step 2 arrives. Applying the lessons in stage 1, you keep your bike at a perfect 90 degrees to the ground, balance against the uneven pressure of your legs, get up some speed and you're away.

So far, so good. But what if you want to change direction? The handlebars appear to provide the only means of turning, so you rotate them in the direction you wish to go – and fall flat on your face.

What went wrong with this apparently logical advice? 'Elementary, my dear Watson': the gyroscopic force which keeps you upright when a bike is moving simply doesn't exist when it is stationary. Manipulating this force is what enables you to turn a moving bike, and the lessons learnt in the static art of balancing a stationary bike are irrelevant to the dynamic art of actually riding one.[1]

Replace the bicycle with the economy, and the point still stands: the procedures which apply in a static economy are irrelevant to a dynamic, changing one; the forces which apply in a static economy simply don't exist in a dynamic one.[2] Lessons learnt from managing an economy in which processes of change either don't occur, or in which changes occur instantly, are irrelevant to an economy in which change does occur, and takes time to occur.

---

1 If you have ever taught a child to ride a bike, you would know that this lesson is the most difficult one to grasp – that a moving bike balances itself, without the need for training wheels or other props which would keep it upright when it was stationary.

2 This analogy is apt in more ways than one. The art of balancing a stationary bike requires great skill, and anyone who has mastered it is likely to 'show it off' at every opportunity, regardless of how impractical it might be. Similarly, economists who have mastered the difficult mental gymnastics involved in equilibrium analysis take every opportunity to parade their prowess – regardless of how irrelevant this skill might be to the art of managing a real economy.

The kernel

Neoclassical economic models in general ignore processes which take time to occur, and instead assume that everything occurs in equilibrium. For this to be allowable, the equilibrium of the dynamic processes of a market economy must be stable, yet it has been known for over forty years now that those processes are unstable: that a small divergence from equilibrium will *not* set up forces which return the system to equilibrium. The dynamic path of the economy therefore cannot be ignored, and yet most economists remain almost criminally unaware of the issues involved in analyzing dynamic, time-varying systems.

The roadmap

In this chapter I detail the roots of the economic propensity to ignore time, and to instead focus on what happens in equilibrium. Then I point out that economic research in the 1950s and 1960s established that the equilibrium of a market economy was unstable, so that the economy could never be in equilibrium. A brief discussion of chaos theory outlines the type of analysis which economists should undertake, but do not.

Cobwebs of the mind

Economic processes clearly take time, and yet economists don't consider time in analyzing demand, supply, or any of their other key variables. For example, the quantity demanded of a commodity and the quantity supplied are both treated as functions of price, and the outcome is an equilibrium quantity. To illustrate what they believe will happen if the demand for a commodity rises, neoclassical economists compare one equilibrium with another, using what they call comparative statics. The time path from one equilibrium to another is ignored.

§ 55

But what if the initial market price happens not to be the equilibrium price? Then demand and supply will be out of balance: if price exceeds the equilibrium, demand will be too low and supply too high. For equilibrium to be restored, this disequilibrium must set off dynamic processes in supply and demand which cause them both to converge on the equilibrium price. This dynamic process of adjustment will obviously take time. However, in general, economists simply assume that, after a disturbance, the market will settle down to equilibrium. They ignore the short-term disequilibrium jostling, in the belief that it is just a short-term sideshow to the long-run main game of achieving equilibrium.

A similar belief permeates even some of the alternative schools of economics. The dynamic process is ignored because it is believed to be a short-term, transitory phenomenon, and attention is focused on the long-term, allegedly enduring phenomenon of equilibrium. As a result, time itself, the change in variables over time, and disequilibrium situations are all ignored. Even econometric programs which attempt to forecast the future value of macro-economic variables such as output and employment assume that the current levels are equilibrium values, and they predict what the future equilibrium values will be.

Economics has invented numerous intellectual devices to enable itself to ignore time, and focus upon the equilibrium situations rather than consider the processes of change over time in an economy. One of these devices is one to which many budding students of economics initially object: the 'all other things being equal,' or '*ceteris paribus*' assumption that nothing changes outside the single market being considered. This assumption lies behind the analysis of supply and demand in a single market, which we've already debunked in Chapters 3 to 5.

Such troubled students are reassured that at higher levels of analysis, this 'partial equilibrium' assumption is dropped for the more realistic proposition that all things are interrelated. However, rather than this more general analysis being more realistic, dynamic, and allowing for disequilibrium as well as equilibrium, it is in fact 'general *equilibrium*': a model of how all aspects of an economy can be in equilibrium simultaneously.

Budding economists who object to the assumption of *ceteris paribus* would walk away in disgust if they were immediately told of the assumptions needed to sustain the concept of general equilibrium. However, their fears assuaged by the promise of more realistic notions to come, they continue up the path of economic inculcation. By the time they confront general equilibrium in graduate education, they treat these assumptions and the analysis which goes with them as challenging intellectual puzzles, rather than as the asinine propositions they truly are. Normally, these students work at less rarefied levels of economic theory, and confidently presume that the leading lights of the profession will generalize the assumptions and solve the remaining puzzles.

As is so often the case with neoclassical economics, the leading lights have done their job very well, but they have not delivered the goods expected of them by the troops. Instead, they have proved that, in general, general equilibrium is unattainable. Even economic models will not achieve general equilibrium, let alone the real economies that general equilibrium once purported to model. General equilibrium is at one and the same time the crowning achievement of economic theory and its greatest failure.

General equilibrium

In the late nineteenth century, three economists in different countries independently gave birth to the neoclassical school of thought: Jevons in England, Menger in Austria, and Walras in France. Today, Walras is the most exalted of these, because his model of general equilibrium set the mold by which economics has since been crafted.

Groping towards equilibrium According to neoclassical theory, equilibrium occurs in a particular market when demand at a given price equals supply at the same price. For equilibrium to occur in all markets simultaneously, the price in every market has to be such that demand and supply are equal in all markets. However, a change of price in one market will affect consumer demand in all other markets. This implies that a move towards equilibrium by one market could cause some or all others to move away from equilibrium. Clearly it is possible that this 'dance of many markets' might never settle down to equilibrium.

This will be especially so if trades actually occur at disequilibrium prices – as in practice they must, since who could ever know when one real-world market was in equilibrium, let alone all of them simultaneously? A disequilibrium trade will mean that the people on the winning side of the bargain – sellers if the price is higher than equilibrium – will gain real income at the expense of the losers, compared to the alleged standard of equilibrium. This shift in income distribution will then affect all other markets, making the dance of many markets even more chaotic.

Walras provided a simple initial abstraction to sidestep this dilemma: he assumed that no trades take place until equilibrium is achieved in all markets. Having satisfied himself that, in the absence of trade, the jiggling of prices up and down would eventually converge to equilibrium, he extended the same faith to a system with production and exchange at disequilibrium prices.

Walras envisaged the market as being a huge, and very unusual, auction. The audience for this auction includes all the owners of the goods for sale, who are simultaneously the buyers for all the goods on sale. At a normal auction, the quantity of each commodity offered for sale is fixed. In Walras's auction, the total amount of each commodity is fixed, but sellers will offer anywhere from none to all of this for sale, depending on the price offered. The quantity offered rises as the price rises, and vice versa, with any amount not sold being taken back home by the seller for his/her own consumption (there are no stocks; everything is either sold or consumed by the producer).

The most peculiar features of Walras's auction market are that, rather than selling each commodity one at a time, the 'auctioneer' attempts to sell all goods at once; and rather than treating each commodity independently, this auctioneer refuses to accept any price for a commodity until supply equals demand for all commodities. In Walras's words:

> First, let us imagine a market in which only consumer goods and services are bought and sold [...] Once the prices or the ratios of exchange of all these goods and services have been cried at random in terms of one of them selected as numeraire, each party to the exchange will offer at these prices those goods or services of which he thinks he has relatively too much, and he will demand those articles of which he thinks he has relatively too little

for his consumption during a certain period of time. The quantities of each thing effectively demanded and offered having been determined in this way, the prices of those things for which the demand exceeds the offer will rise, and the prices of those things of which the offer exceeds the demand will fall. New prices now having been cried, each party to the exchange will offer and demand new quantities. And again prices will rise or fall until the demand and the offer of each good and each service are equal. Then the prices will be current equilibrium prices and exchange will effectively take place. (Walras 1954 [1874])

This is clearly not the way markets work in the real world.[3] Nonetheless, this mythical construct became the way in which economics attempted to model the behavior of real-world markets.

Walras's auctioneer starts the market process by taking an initial stab at prices. These arbitrarily chosen prices are almost certainly not going to equate demand and supply for each and every commodity – instead, for some commodities, demand will exceed supply, while for others supply will exceed demand. The auctioneer then refuses to allow any sale to take place, and instead adjusts prices – increasing the price of those commodities where demand exceeded supply, and decreasing the price where demand was less than supply. This then results in a second set of prices, which are also highly unlikely to balance demand and supply for all commodities; so another round of price adjustments will take place, and another, and another.

Walras called this iterative process of trying to find a set of prices which equates supply to demand for all commodities '*tatonnement*' – which literally translates as 'groping.' He believed that this process would eventually converge to an equilibrium set of prices, where supply and demand are balanced in all markets (so long as trade at disequilibrium prices can be prevented).

This was not necessarily the case, since adjusting one price so that supply and demand are balanced for one commodity could well push demand and supply farther apart for all other commodities. However, Walras thought that convergence would win out because the direct effects on demand – of increasing the price of a commodity where demand exceeds supply, which directly reduces demand – would outweigh the indirect effects of changes in demand for other commodities. In his words:

This will appear probable if we remember that the change from p'b to p''b, which reduced the above inequality to an equality, exerted a direct influence that was invariably in the direction of equality at least so far as the demand for (B) was concerned; while the [consequent] changes from p'c to p''c, p'd to p''d, which moved the foregoing inequality farther away from equality, exerted indirect influences, some in the direction of equality and some in

3 Only the gold market in London even approaches this structure, and even that is a market at which only one commodity is traded, rather than 'all commodities' (O'Hara 1995).

the opposite direction, at least so far as the demand for (B) was concerned, so that up to a certain point they cancelled each other out. Hence, the new system of prices (p"b, p"c, p"d) is closer to equilibrium than the old system of prices (p'b, p'c, p'd); and it is only necessary to continue this process along the same lines for the system to move closer and closer to equilibrium. (Ibid.)

'Generalizing' Walras Walras's ruse, of an auctioneer who stopped any trades taking place until such time as demand equaled supply in all markets, was clearly artificial. However, it enabled economists to make use of the well-known and relatively simple techniques for solving simultaneous linear equations.

The alternative was to describe the dynamics of a multi-commodity economy, in which trades could occur at non-equilibrium prices in anywhere from a minimum of two to potentially all markets. At a technical level, modeling non-equilibrium phenomena would have involved nonlinear difference or differential equations. In the nineteenth century, the methodology for them was much less developed than it is now, and they are inherently more difficult to work with than simultaneous linear equations.

Walras's auctioneer was therefore arguably a justifiable abstraction at a time when, as Jevons put it, it would have been 'absurd to attempt the more difficult question when the more easy one is yet so imperfectly within our power' (Jevons 1888: ch. 4, para. 25).

But it suggests an obvious, dynamic, research agenda: why not see what happens when the artifact of no non-equilibrium trades is dispensed with? Why not generalize Walras's general equilibrium by removing the reliance upon the concept of equilibrium itself? Why not generalize Walras by dropping the fiction that everything happens at equilibrium?

This potential path was, for economics, the path not chosen.

Instead, the neoclassical 'Holy Grail' became to formalize Walras's concept of equilibrium: to prove that general equilibrium existed, and that it was the optimum position for society.

Unfortunately, reality had to be seriously distorted to 'prove' that general equilibrium could be attained. But, for the reasons given in Chapter 8, economists would rather sacrifice generality than sacrifice the concept of equilibrium.

The pinnacle of this warping of reality came with the publication in 1959 of Gerard Debreu's *Theory of Value*, which the respected historian of economic thought Mark Blaug has described as 'probably the most arid and pointless book in the entire literature of economics' (Blaug 1998). Yet this 'arid and pointless' tome set the mold for economics for the next forty years – and won for its author the Nobel Prize for economics.

'The formal identity of uncertainty with certainty'

Walras's vision of the market, though highly abstract, had some concept of process to it. Buyers and sellers would haggle, under the guidance of the auctioneer, until an equilibrium set of prices was devised. Exchange would then take place, and those prices would also determine production plans for the next period. There is at least some primitive notion of time in this series of sequential equilibria.

No such claim can be made for Debreu's vision of general equilibrium. In this model, there is only one market – if indeed there is a market at all – at which all commodities are exchanged, for all times from now to eternity. Everyone in this 'market' makes all their sales and purchases for all of time in one instant. Initially everything from now till eternity is known with certainty, and when uncertainty is introduced, it is swiftly made formally equivalent to certainty. A few choice extracts give a clearer picture of Debreu's total divorce from reality:

> For any economic agent a complete action plan (*made now for the whole future*), or more briefly an action, is a specification for each commodity of the quantity that he will make available or that will be made available to him, i.e., a complete listing of the quantities of his inputs and of his outputs.
>
> For a producer, say the *jth* one, a production plan (made now for the whole future) is a specification of the quantities of all his inputs and all his outputs. *The certainty assumption implies that he knows now what input-output combinations will be possible in the future* (although he may not know the details of technical processes which will make them possible).
>
> As in the case of a producer, the role of a consumer is to choose a complete consumption plan. His role is to choose (and carry out) a consumption plan made now for the whole future, i.e., a specification of the quantities of all his inputs and all his outputs.
>
> The analysis is extended in this chapter to the case where uncertain events determine the consumption sets, the production sets, and the resources of the economy. A contract for the transfer of a commodity now specifies, in addition to its physical properties, its location and its date, an event on the occurrence of which the transfer is conditional. *This new definition of a commodity allows one to obtain a theory of uncertainty free from any probability concept and formally identical with the theory of certainty developed in the preceding chapters.* (Debreu 1959; emphases added)

I can provide no better judgment of the impact this brazenly irrelevant theory had on economics than that given by Blaug:

> Unfortunately this paper soon became a model of what economists ought to aim for as modern scientists. In the process, few readers realized that Arrow and Debreu had in fact abandoned the vision that had originally motivated

Walras. For Walras, general equilibrium theory was an abstract but nevertheless realistic description of the functioning of a capitalist economy. He was
therefore more concerned to show that markets will clear automatically via
price adjustments in response to positive or negative excess demand – a
property that he labeled 'tatonnement' – than to prove that a unique set of
prices and quantities is capable of clearing all markets simultaneously.

By the time we got to Arrow and Debreu, however, general equilibrium
theory had ceased to make any descriptive claim about actual economic
systems and had become a purely formal apparatus about a quasi economy.
It had become a perfect example of what Ronald Coase has called 'black-
board economics,' a model that can be written down on blackboards using
economic terms like 'prices,' 'quantities,' 'factors of production,' and so on,
but that nevertheless is clearly and even scandalously unrepresentative of any
recognizable economic system. (Blaug 1998)

A hobbled general It is almost superfluous to describe the core assumptions of
Debreu's model as unrealistic: a single point in time at which all production
and exchange for all time is determined; a set of commodities – including
those which will be invented and produced in the distant future – which is
known to all consumers; producers who know all the inputs that will ever be
needed to produce their commodities; even a vision of 'uncertainty' in which
the possible states of the future are already known, so that certainty and
uncertainty are formally identical. Yet even with these breathtaking dismissals
of essential elements of the real world, Debreu's model was rapidly shown to
need additional restrictive assumptions – the Sonnenschein-Mantel-Debreu
conditions discussed in Chapter 3. Rather than consumers being able to
have any utility function consistent with what economists decreed as rational,
additional restrictions had to be imposed which, as one economist observed,
came 'very close to simply assuming that the consumers in the aggregate
have identical tastes and income' (Diewert 1977: 361).

This was not the end of the restrictions. As Blaug observes above, Walras
hoped to show that the process of *tatonnement* would lead, eventually, to
equilibrium being achieved, and that the same outcome would follow even
if disequilibrium trading occurred. In mathematical terms, he hoped to
show that general equilibrium was stable: that if the system diverged from
equilibrium, it would return to it, and that if the process of *tatonnement* began
with disequilibrium prices, it would eventually converge on the equilibrium
prices. Debreu abandoned this aspect of Walras's endeavor, and focused solely
on proving the existence of general equilibrium, rather than its stability. But
stability cannot be ignored, and mathematicians have shown that, under fairly
general conditions, general equilibrium is unstable.

Positive prices and negative stability Walras's assumption that the direct effects of the price change would outweigh the indirect effects – so that the process of *tatonnement* would converge on the set of equilibrium prices – was reasonable, given the state of mathematics at the time. However, mathematical theorems worked out in the twentieth century established that, in general, this assumption is wrong.

These theorems established that the conditions which ensure that an economy can experience stable growth simultaneously guarantee that Walras's *tatonnement* process is unstable (Blatt 1983). Therefore if the auctioneer's first stab at prices is only a tiny bit different from the set of prices which would put all markets in equilibrium, his next stab – derived by increasing prices for goods where demand exceeded supply, and vice versa – will be farther away from the equilibrium set of prices. The process of *tatonnement* will never converge to the equilibrium set of prices, so if equilibrium is a prerequisite for trade, trade will never take place.

These theorems[4] are too complex to be conveyed accurately by either words or figures, but in keeping with the objectives of this book, I'll attempt an explanation. If you don't want to twist your mind around the mathematical concepts involved, then please skip to the following heading ('A transitional methodology?').

The 'general equilibrium problem' is to find a set of prices which result in the amount consumers demand of each and every product equaling the amount supplied. Prices obviously have to be positive, as do the quantities demanded and the quantities produced.[5]

Before commodities can be demanded, they must be produced, and the means of production are simply other commodities. If the economy is going to last indefinitely, the system of production must be able to generate growth.

This can be described by a set of equations in which the prices are the variables, and the quantities required to produce each commodity are the coefficients. A single equation adds up the cost of inputs needed to produce a given commodity at a given price. There will be as many equations as there are commodities to produce.

It is then possible to separate the prices into a column of numbers called a vector, and the quantities into a square of numbers called a matrix – where, as noted earlier, every element is either a positive number or zero. The properties of this matrix can then be analyzed mathematically, and its mathematical properties can be used to answer economic questions.

This matrix is known as a Leontief input-output matrix, after the Russian economist who first developed this method of analysis. The first row of such a matrix effectively says that 'α units of commodity α combined with β units of

---

4 The main theorem is the Perron-Frobenius theorem on the eigenvalues of a positive matrix. See en.wikipedia.org/wiki/Perron%E2%80%93Frobenius_theorem for an explanation.

5 Debreu used a notation that allowed for negative prices and negative quantities. However, this was a convenience only, and has no impact on the analysis in this section.

commodity β and ζ units of commodity ζ will produce 1 unit of commodity α.' It is the simplest method of describing a system of production, in that it implies that there is one and only one best way to make each commodity: no substitution of one technology for another is allowed.

While this is a much simpler model of production than economists like to work with, it turns out that the properties of this very simple system determine whether the equilibrium of any more general model is stable. If this simple system can't guarantee stability, then no more complex system is going to either (this is a general property of dynamic models: the stability of the system very close to its equilibrium is determined by its 'linear' parts, and Leontief's matrix is the linear component of any more complex model of production).

There are two stability conditions in the simple Leontief system: the quantities produced each year have to enable the system to reproduce itself (this won't happen if, for example, the required inputs of iron for year 10 exceed the output of iron in year 9); and the prices must be feasible (the iron-producing sector can't depend on the price of some required input to producing iron being negative, for example).

It turns out that the first stability condition is governed by a characteristic of the input-output matrix, whereas the second stability condition is governed by the same characteristic of the inverse of that matrix. As with simple constants, a matrix and its inverse have, to some extent, opposite properties. Thus if you have a constant a which is less than 1, then a squared will be much less than 1, a cubed even more so, and higher powers of a will eventually converge to zero. However, the inverse of a, $1/a$, will be greater than 1, and powers of $1/a$ will blow out to infinity. If the stability of some system depends upon both a and the inverse of a being less than 1, then no number can fulfill both requirements, and the system is going to be unstable.

Since economic models are supposed to concern themselves with real economies, which can and do change in size, the general conclusion is that a real economy will never be in a state of general equilibrium. If economics is to have any relevance to the real world – if economics is even to be internally consistent – then it must be formulated in a way which does not assume equilibrium. Time, and dynamic analysis, must finally make an appearance in economic analysis.

A transitional methodology?

The founding fathers of economics had no problem accepting such a conclusion. In fact, to them, static analysis was merely a stop-gap measure, a transitional methodology which would be superseded by dynamic analysis as economics reached maturity. Jevons, for example, argued that 'If we wished to have a complete solution we should have to treat it as a problem of dynamics.' But he instead pioneered static analysis because 'it would surely be absurd to attempt the more difficult question when the more easy one is yet so imperfectly within our power' (Jevons 1888).

Similarly, and at more length, Marshall noted that

> The Mecca of the economist lies in economic biology rather than in economic dynamics. But biological conceptions are more complex than those of mechanics; a volume on Foundations must therefore give a relatively large place to mechanical analogies; and frequent use is made of the term 'equilibrium,' which suggests something of statical analogy. This fact, combined with the predominant attention paid in the present volume to the normal conditions of life in the modern age, has suggested the notion that its central idea is 'statical,' rather than 'dynamical.' But in fact it is concerned throughout with the forces that cause movement: and its key-note is that of dynamics, rather than statics. (Marshall 1920 [1890]: Preface, para. 19)

At the end of the nineteenth century, J. B. Clark, the economist who developed the marginal productivity theory of income distribution (critiqued in Chapter 5), looked forward to the twentieth century as the period during which economic dynamics would supplant economic statics:

> A point on which opinions differ is the capacity of the pure theory of Political Economy for progress. There seems to be a growing impression that, as a mere statement of principles, this science will fairly soon be complete. It is with this view that I take issue. The great coming development of economic theory is to take place, I venture to assert, through the statement and solution of dynamic problems. (Clark 1898)

In this paper, Clark gave many good reasons why economics should be analyzed using dynamics rather than statics. Foremost among these was that 'A static state is imaginary. All actual societies are dynamic; and those that we have principally to study are highly so. Heroically theoretical is the study that creates, in the imagination, a static society' (ibid.).

One century later, economic dynamics has indeed been developed – but not by the school to which J. B. Clark belonged. Instead, neoclassical economics still by and large ignores the issue of time. Students are often told that dynamics is important, but they are taught nothing but statics. A typical undergraduate macroeconomics textbook, for example, states that 'the examination of the process of moving from one equilibrium to another is important and is known as dynamic analysis.' However, it then continues that 'Throughout this book we will assume that the economic system is stable and most of the analysis will be conducted in the comparative static mode' (Taslim and Chowdhury 1995).

The leading textbook used today to teach graduate students makes a similar claim – that while other disciplines use dynamics, economists model processes as if they occur in equilibrium because economists are good at identifying equilibrium! Two-thirds through his voluminous 1,000-page tome, Mas-Colell, the current doyen of neoclassical instruction, writes:

> We have, so far, carried out an extensive analysis of equilibrium equations. A characteristic feature that distinguishes economics from other scientific fields is that, for us, the equations of equilibrium constitute the center of our discipline. Other sciences, such as physics or even ecology, put comparatively more emphasis on the determination of dynamic laws of change. In contrast, up to now, we have hardly mentioned dynamics.
>
> The reason, informally speaking, is that economists are good (or so we hope) at recognizing a state of equilibrium but poor at predicting how an economy in disequilibrium will evolve.
>
> Certainly there are intuitive dynamic principles: if demand is larger than supply, then the price will increase, if price is larger than marginal cost then production will expand, if industry profits are positive and there are no barriers to entry, then new firms will enter and so on. The difficulty is in translating these informal principles into precise dynamic laws. (Mas-Colell et al. 1995: 620)

This is nonsense, and to give Mas-Colell his due I think he realizes it here. Economists model in equilibrium, not because they are 'good (or so we hope) at recognizing a state of equilibrium,' but simply because they can't get the results they want in dynamic analysis and have therefore not made the leap from static to dynamic modeling that has occurred in all other disciplines.

Mas-Colell admits this when he discusses the attempts to generalize Walras's *tatonnement* process to a disequilibrium one. While he argues that a two-commodity exchange economy is stable,[6] he admits that this result does not generalize to three or more commodities: 'Unfortunately, as soon as [there are more than two goods] neither the local conclusions nor the global conclusions of the two-commodity case generalize' (ibid.: 622).

This may be unfortunate, but the correct reaction to it is to abandon static analysis and work in disequilibrium. This, clearly, is not what neoclassical economists have done – and unfortunately, economists of many other persuasions also use static analysis because they believe that equilibrium is the enduring state of the economy, while dynamics merely captures the transient moments between different equilibria. For example, a Sraffian economist defended static methodology in economics by arguing that '"static" analysis does not "ignore" time. To the contrary, that analysis allows enough time for changes in prime costs, markups, etc., to have their full effects' (Steedman 1992).

6 My discussion of the instability of general equilibrium above was with respect to a production economy, where the nature of the input-output matrix makes stability impossible. There is no input–output matrix in an exchange-only economy because there is no production!

As this chapter shows, this confidence that 'the end point of a dynamic process is the state of static equilibrium' is false. Equally false was the belief of the founding fathers of economics, that dynamic analysis 'does not invalidate the conclusions of a static theory' (Clark 1898). But even if they were right, even if dynamic forces did lead, eventually, to static outcomes, it would still be invalid to model the economy using static techniques. Keynes put the case best in 1923, when he made his oft-quoted but rarely appreciated observation that 'in the long run we are all dead.' The full statement gives a rather better picture of his intent: 'But this long run is a misleading guide to current affairs. In the long run we are all dead. Economists set themselves too easy, too useless a task if in tempestuous seasons they can only tell us that when the storm is long past the ocean is flat again' (Keynes 1971 [1923]).

Keynes was right: it is not valid to ignore the transient state of the economy. As Fisher later observed in very similar terms, equilibrium conditions in the absence of disturbances are irrelevant, because disturbances will always occur. Whether equilibrium is stable or not, disequilibrium will be the state in which we live:

We may tentatively assume that, ordinarily and within wide limits, all, or almost all, economic variables tend, in a general way, toward a stable equilibrium [...]

It follows that, unless some outside force intervenes, any 'free' oscillations about equilibrium must tend progressively to grow smaller and smaller, just as a rocking chair set in motion tends to stop.

But the exact equilibrium thus sought is seldom reached and never long maintained. New disturbances are, humanly speaking, sure to occur, so that, in actual fact, any variable is almost always above or below the ideal equilibrium [...]

Theoretically there may be – in fact, at most times there must be – over- or under-production, over- or under-consumption, over- or under-spending, over- or under-saving, over- or under-investment, and over or under everything else. It is as absurd to assume that, for any long period of time, the variables in the economic organization, or any part of them, will 'stay put,' in perfect equilibrium, as to assume that the Atlantic Ocean can ever be without a wave. (Fisher 1933: 339)

We also live in a changing – and normally growing – economy. Surely we should be concerned, not with absolute levels of variables, but with their rates of change? Should not demand and supply analysis, for instance, be in terms of the rate of change of demand, and the rate of change of supply? Should not the outcome of supply and demand analysis be the rate of change of price and quantity over time, rather than static levels? Should not macroeconomics concern itself with the rate of change of output and employment, rather than their absolute levels?

Of course they should. As Keynes also once remarked, 'equilibrium is blither.' So why, fifty years after Keynes, are economists still blithering? Why do economists persist in modeling the economy with static tools when dynamic ones exist; why do they treat as stationary entities which are forever changing?

There are many reasons, but the main one, as outlined in the previous chapter, is the extent to which the core ideological beliefs of neoclassical economics are bound up in the concept of equilibrium. As a by-product of this, economists are driven to maintain the concept of equilibrium in all manner of topics where dynamic, non-equilibrium analysis would not only be more relevant, but frankly would even be easier. This obsession with equilibrium has imposed enormous costs on economics.

First, unreal assumptions are needed to maintain conditions under which there will be a unique, 'optimal' equilibrium. These assumptions are often justified by an appeal to Friedman's methodological 'assumptions don't matter' argument, but as Chapter 8 pointed out, this notion is easily debunked. However, most economists take it as an article of faith, with insidious results. If you believe you can use unreality to model reality, then eventually your grip on reality itself can become tenuous – as Debreu's bizarre model of general equilibrium indicates.

Secondly, as shown in this chapter, even the unreal assumptions of general equilibrium theory are insufficient to save it from irrelevance, since even the model of general equilibrium has been shown to be unstable, so that no modeled or real economy could ever be in a state of equilibrium. Many of those who pioneered general equilibrium analysis are grudgingly conceding that these results require economics to radically alter direction. But they are also quite aware that lesser economists are, as Alan Kirman put it, 'not even concerned over the sea-worthiness of the vessel in which they are sailing' (Kirman 1989).

Thirdly, the emphasis on modeling everything as an equilibrium phenomenon has isolated economics from most if not all other sciences, where dynamic analysis – and in particular evolutionary analysis – is now dominant. Economists are now virtually the only 'scientists' who attempt to model a real-world system using static, equilibrium tools. As a result of this isolation, economists have been shielded from developments in mathematics and other sciences which have revolutionized how scientists perceive the world.

This isolation is to some extent fortuitous, because if economists really knew what is common knowledge in other sciences, then they would finally have to abandon their obsession with equilibrium, and economics as outlined in this book would cease to exist. Most modern-day economists believe, as did the founding fathers of economics, that dynamic analysis would simply 'fill in the dots' between the static snapshots, thus replacing a series of still photographs with a moving picture. In fact, modern research in mathematics, physics, biology and many other disciplines has shown that dynamic analysis normally leads to results which contradict those of static analysis.

In the long run, we are all in the short run

Equilibrium can be the long-run destination of the economy only if it is stable – if any divergence sets up forces which will return the economy to equilibrium. Even after the proofs of the instability of general equilibrium, most economists believe that this is a non sequitur: surely, the equilibrium of any real-world system must be stable, since if it were unstable, wouldn't it break down? John Hicks articulated this view when he criticized one of the earliest dynamic models developed by an economist. He commented that Harrod (1939)

> welcomes the instability of his system, because he believes it to be an expla-
> nation of the tendency to fluctuation which exists in the real world. I think,
> as I shall proceed to show, that something of this sort may well have much
> to do with the tendency to fluctuation. But mathematical instability does not
> in itself elucidate fluctuation. A mathematically unstable system does not
> fluctuate; it just breaks down. The unstable position is one in which it will
> not tend to remain. (Hicks 1949)

The modern discipline known colloquially as chaos theory has established that this belief, though still widespread among economists today, is quite simply wrong. The equilibrium of a real-world system can be unstable without the system itself breaking down.

The first and best illustration of this occurred, not in economics, but in meteorology. I'll give a brief exposition of this model, because it illustrates several ways in which the conventional economic understanding of dynamics is profoundly wrong. But first, we need a brief technical interlude to explain the difference between the mathematical methods used in static analysis and those used in dynamics (you can skip to 'The weather and the butterfly' if you'd like to avoid mathspeak).

Straight lines and curved paths What static analysis means in technical terms is that the equations most neoclassical economists (and many non-orthodox economists) use in their mathematical models are 'algebraic' rather than 'differential.'

Algebraic equations are simply larger and more complicated versions of the equations we all did at school in geometry, when we were asked to work out the intersection of two lines. Given two equations for Y in terms of X, with different slopes and Y intercepts, we worked out the only X point where the two formulas gave the same Y point. Continuing with the geometry analogy, most of the equations used by economists use only straight lines, rather than more complicated shapes like parabolas, etc. Algebraic techniques with

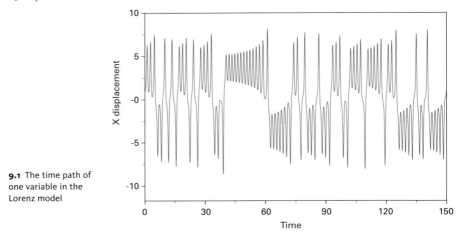

9.1 The time path of one variable in the Lorenz model

these equations scale indefinitely – you can have equations with hundreds of 'straight lines' and still get unique solutions.

Differential equations, on the other hand, are more complicated descendants of the technique of differentiation, which you might have learnt if you did calculus at school or college. Rather than being expressed in terms of X and Y, these equations are expressed in terms of the rate of change of X and the rate of change of Y. While school calculus dealt only with 'the rate of change of Y with respect to X,' differential equations typically are in terms of 'the rate of change of Y with respect to Y itself, other variables, and time.'

Most differential equation models also involve curved relationships between variables, rather than straight lines. A straight line is in fact the simplest type of relationship which can exist between two variables (other than that of no relationship at all). Straight-line relationships in differential equation models with unstable equilibria lead to ultimately absurd outcomes, such as negative prices, or cycles which approach infinite amplitude as time goes on. Nonlinear relationships, however, result in bounded behavior: the forces which repel the system when it is very close to equilibrium are eventually overwhelmed by attractive forces when the system is substantially distant from the equilibrium.

Unlike linear algebraic equations, nonlinear differential equations don't scale well. Only a very few simple nonlinear differential equations can be solved – the vast majority can't be solved at all. Once there are more than two variables in a system of nonlinear differential equations, there is in fact no analytic solution. Such systems must be simulated to see what is actually going on.

The weather and the butterfly In 1963, the meteorologist E. N. Lorenz devised a simple mathematical model of turbulent flow in a weather cell, using a simplified version of a well-known mathematical model of turbulent

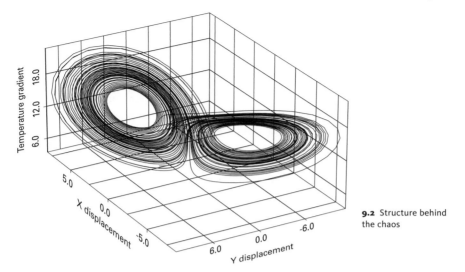

9.2 Structure behind the chaos

flow. His model had just three equations, with three variables and three constants. The first (x) equation described the intensity of convective motion, the second (y) the temperature difference between ascending and descending columns of air, and the third (z) described the divergence from linearity of the temperature gradient across the weather cell.[7]

It would be hard to think of a simpler set of three equations, and yet the behavior they generated was unbelievably complex. Figure 9.1 shows the time path of the east–west fluid displacement.

The y and z patterns were equally complex. Even more mysteriously, a tiny difference in the initial x, y or z values led, very quickly, to a totally different time path. It had been thought in the past that a tiny difference in any initial measurement would mean only a tiny error in predicting the future behavior of a variable. However, in this model, a tiny difference initially has no apparent effect, but then abruptly leads to a totally different outcome.   §56

Finally, though the pattern for any one variable appeared erratic, behind this apparent randomness lay a beautiful structure which is visible when the three variables are plotted on the one graph. Figure 9.2 shows the 'butterfly' behind the superficial chaos.

Detailed analysis of this system reveals that it has not one equilibrium, but three. *More importantly, all three equilibria are unstable*. A slight divergence from any equilibrium causes the system moving to move away from it very rapidly. A tiny divergence from one equilibrium point leads to the system instantly being propelled from that equilibrium. It then approaches another,

7 The actual equations were: 'the rate of change of x with respect to time equals the constant a multiplied by (y–z); the rate of change of y with respect to time equals x multiplied by (b–z) minus y; the rate of change of z with respect to time equals (x multiplied by y) minus (c multiplied by z).'

only to be flung off to a third. It orbits that equilibrium, only to be eventually repelled from it. Finally, it approaches and then is repelled from the second §57 equilibrium back towards the first.

There are at least four lessons for economics in this model.

First, a system with unstable equilibria doesn't have to 'break down.' Instead, such a system can display complex cyclical behavior rather like that we see in real-world weather – and, more to the point, in real-world economies.

Secondly, if the equilibria of a model are unstable, then neither the initial nor the final position of the model will be equilibrium positions. The economic belief that dynamic analysis simply plots the movement between one equilibrium and another is therefore wrong. Instead, even simple dynamic models will display 'far from equilibrium' behavior. As a result, rather than equilibrium being where the action is, equilibrium tells you where the model will never be.

Thirdly, extrapolating from models to the real world, actual economic variables are likely to always be in disequilibrium – even in the absence of external shocks (or 'exogenous' shocks, as economists prefer to call them), which is the usual economic explanation for cycles – and the conditions which economists have 'proved' apply at equilibrium will therefore be irrelevant in actual economies. In this sense, equilibrium truly is, as Keynes put it, 'blither.' Static economic analysis therefore can't be used as a simplified proxy for dynamic analysis: the two types of analysis will lead to completely different interpretations of reality. In all such cases, the static approach will be completely wrong and the dynamic approach will be at least partially right.

Finally, even as simple a system as Lorenz's, with just three variables and three constants, can display incredibly complex dynamics because the interactions between variables are nonlinear (if you check the equations in note 7, you will see terms like 'x times y'). As noted earlier, nonlinear relationships in differential equation models can lead to complex but bounded behavior.

From meteorology to economics

There are many models in economics which have properties akin to those of Lorenz's weather model – very few of which have been developed by neoclassical economists. Most were instead developed by economists who belong to alternative schools, in particular complexity theorists and evolutionary economists. One of the best-known such models, Goodwin's model of cyclical growth, put in mathematical form a model first suggested by Marx.

Marx argued that – in a highly simplified economy consisting of just capitalists and workers – there would be cycles in employment and income shares. In Marx's words:

A rise in the price of labor, as a consequence of accumulation of capital [... means that] accumulation slackens in consequence of the rise in the price of labor, because the stimulus of gain is blunted. The rate of accumulation lessens; but with its lessening, the primary cause of that lessening vanishes, i.e., the disproportion between capital and exploitable labor-power.

The mechanism of the process of capitalist production removes the very obstacles that it temporarily creates. The price of labor falls again to a level corresponding with the needs of the self-expansion of capital, whether the level be below, the same as, or above the one which was normal before the rise of wages took place [...]

To put it mathematically: the rate of accumulation is the independent, not the dependent, variable; the rate of wages, the dependent, not the independent, variable. (Marx 1867: ch. 25, section 1)[8]

In point form, the model is as follows:

- A high rate of growth of output led to a high level of employment.
- The high level of employment encouraged workers to demand large wage rises, which reduced profits.
- The reduced level of profits caused investment to decline, and growth to slow.
- The slower rate of growth led to increasing unemployment, which in turn led to workers accepting lower wages.
- Eventually the fall in workers' share of output restored profit to levels at which investment would resume, leading to a higher rate of growth and higher employment levels.
- This in time led to high wage demands once more, thus completing the cycle.

This cycle can also be stated in terms of causal relationships between key economic variables – the amount of capital, the level of output, and so on – which shows that the process Marx describes was based on an accurate view of the overall structure of the economy, and also an accurate deduction that this would lead to cycles in income distribution and employment, rather than either equilibrium or breakdown:

1 The amount of physical capital determines the amount of output.
2 Output determines employment.
3 The rate of employment determines the *rate of change* of wages (the 'Phillips Curve' relationship I discuss in the addendum to this chapter).
4 Wages times employment determines the wage bill, and when this is subtracted from output, profit is determined.
5 Profit determines the level of investment.
6 Investment determines the rate of change of capital – and this closes the causal loop of the model.

8 I use chapter and section references for Marx, rather than page numbers, since his work is now freely accessible via the Internet from the site www.marxists.org/archive/marx/.

In mathematical form, this model reduces to two equations which are easily stated verbally:

- The rate of change of workers' share of output equals workers' wage demands minus the rate of productivity growth.
- The rate of change of employment equals the rate of growth of output, minus population growth and technological change.[9]

This mathematical model generates the cycle envisaged by Marx. Rather than converging to equilibrium values, workers' share of output and the rate of employment both cycle indefinitely.

§58

When wages share and employment are plotted against each other, the result is a closed loop. This is a far less complex structure than Lorenz's model, but it has one thing in common with it: *the model does not converge to its equilibrium* (which lies in the center of the loop), *but orbits around it indefinitely*.

§59

It is also easily extended to capture more aspects of the real world, and when this is done, dynamic patterns as rich as those in Lorenz's model appear – as I detail in Chapters 13 and 14.

Real-world phenomena therefore simply cannot be modeled using 'comparative statics' or equilibrium – unless we are willing to believe that cyclones are caused by something 'exogenous' to the weather, and stock market bubbles are caused by something outside the economy. Complexity theory has established that such phenomena can be modeled dynamically, so that abandoning static equilibrium analysis does not mean abandoning the ability to say meaningful things about the economy.

Instead, what has to be abandoned is the economic obsession with achieving some socially optimal outcome. As noted in this and the previous chapter, economists have conflated the concept of equilibrium with the vision of an 'economic utopia' in which no one could be made better off without making someone else worse off. But a free market economy could never remain in an optimal position, because economic equilibria are unstable. The real question is whether we can control such an unstable system – whether we can constrain its instability within acceptable bounds.

This question was once at the heart of what is known as macroeconomics – the study of the entire economy and the attempt to control it using government fiscal and monetary policy. Unfortunately, as we shall see in the next chapter, neoclassical economists have emasculated this once virile area of analysis. As they did so, they ignored possibly the most important lesson to flow from the advances in dynamic analysis since Lorenz: the realization that complex systems have what are known as 'emergent behaviors' which mean

---

9 The two equations are linked, because workers' wage demands depend on the rate of employment, while investment – which determines the rate of growth – depends on income distribution (a higher workers' share means lower profits, and hence lower investment).

that they cannot be understood by studying their constituent parts alone. This reality invalidates a key aspect of modern neoclassical macroeconomics: the attempt to derive models of the macroeconomy from microeconomic models of the behavior of individuals. A discussion of emergent behavior properly belongs in this chapter, but its neglect by neoclassical economists – and the practice of its opposite philosophy, 'reductionism' – has been so essential to the neoclassical ruination of macroeconomics that I have delayed a discussion of it until the next chapter.

Before I move on, there is one other topic that also belongs in this chapter, rather than the next on macroeconomics, where it would normally be discussed in a conventional textbook: the 'Phillips Curve.' This is an alleged relationship between the level of unemployment and the rate of inflation that, though it is hotly disputed within economics, nonetheless plays a role in virtually every theory of macroeconomics, from Marx's at one extreme to neoclassical economics at the other.

It belongs in this chapter on dynamics, because the real objective of the person after whom it was named – the New Zealand-born engineer-turned-economist A. W. ('Bill') Phillips – was to persuade economists to abandon their static methods and embrace dynamic analysis. This is precisely what I am attempting to do now, so Phillips's work – including the 'Phillips Curve' – deserves to be discussed here as a valiant but unsuccessful previous attempt to shake economists out of their static straitjackets.

Addendum: Misunderstanding Bill Phillips, wages and 'the Phillips Curve'

Bill Phillips the man was undoubtedly one of the most dynamic human beings of all time. Compared to that of Phillips, the lives of most economists – even non-neoclassical ones – are as pale as the theories that neoclassical economists have concocted about the world. He left school at fifteen, worked as a crocodile hunter and gold miner in Australia, learnt engineering by correspondence, was awarded an MBE for his role in the defence of Singapore in 1942, and, as a prisoner of war, made a miniaturized radio from components he stole from the camp commander's radiogram. Despite the effects of malnutrition and abuse in the camp, within five years of the war finishing – and while still an undergraduate student of economics – he had his first paper published in a leading journal (Phillips 1950). The paper described an analog computer dynamic simulation model of the economy (MONIAC) that he constructed at a cost of £400, just three years after the first digital computer (ENIAC) had been constructed at a cost of US$500,000 (Leeson 1994, 2000).

MONIAC put into mechanical-hydraulic form the principles of dynamics that Phillips had learnt as an engineer, and it was this approach which he tried to communicate to economists, on the sound basis that their preferred methodology of comparative statics was inappropriate for economic modeling:

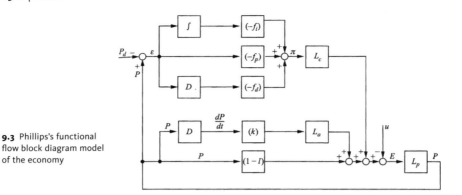

9.3 Phillips's functional flow block diagram model of the economy

RECOMMENDATIONS for stabilizing aggregate production and employment have usually been derived from the analysis of multiplier models, using the method of comparative statics. This type of analysis does not provide a very firm basis for policy recommendations, for two reasons.

First, the time path of income, production and employment during the process of adjustment is not revealed. It is quite possible that certain types of policy may give rise to undesired fluctuations, or even cause a previously stable system to become unstable, although the final equilibrium position as shown by a static analysis appears to be quite satisfactory.

Second, the effects of variations in prices and interest rates cannot be dealt with adequately with the simple multiplier models which usually form the basis of the analysis. (Phillips 1954: 290)

Phillips instead proposed that economists should build dynamic models of the economy – models in which time was embraced rather than ignored via the device of comparative statics – and his underlying method here was the functional flow block diagram. This had been devised by engineers in the 1920s as a way to visually represent dynamic processes, which previously had been shown as either differential equations, or transformations of these equations into other mathematical forms.[10] Phillips drew such a diagrammatic representation of a simple dynamic economic model (ibid.: Fig. 10, p. 306; see Figure 9.3), with symbols to indicate operations like time lags, differentiation and integration with respect to time, addition and subtraction, etc. The model recast the standard comparative-static, multiplier-accelerator models of the time into dynamic form.

This model was only the starting point of a project to develop a complete dynamic model of the economy, in which the feedback effects and disequilibrium dynamics that were ignored by the conventional 'Keynesian' models of the time could be fully accounted for.

10 For more details, see the Wikipedia entries en.wikipedia.org/wiki/Functional_flow_block_diagram, en.wikipedia.org/wiki/Transfer_function, http://en.wikipedia.org/wiki/State_space_(controls) and en.wikipedia.org/wiki/Systems_engineering.

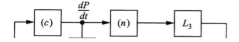

9.4 The component of Phillips's Figure 12 including the role of expectations in price setting

In particular, Phillips extended his model to consider the impact of expectations upon prices. Given how much his work has been falsely denigrated by neoclassical economists for ignoring the role of expectations in economics, this aspect of his model deserves attention prior to considering the Phillips Curve itself:

> Demand is also likely to be influenced by the rate at which prices are changing [...] this influence on demand being greater, the greater the rate of change of prices [...] *The direction of this change in demand will depend on expectations about future price changes.* If changing prices induce expectations of further changes in the same direction, as will probably be the case after fairly rapid and prolonged movements, demand will change in the same direction as the changing prices [...]
>
> *If, on the other hand, there is confidence that any movement of prices away from the level ruling in the recent past will soon be reversed, demand is likely to change in the opposite direction to the changing prices* [...]. (Ibid.: 311; emphases added)

Phillips didn't merely talk about expectations: he extended his model to incorporate them – see Figure 9.4.

As part of this project, Phillips also hypothesized that there was a nonlinear relationship between 'the level of production and the rate of change of factor prices [labor and capital]' (ibid.: 308), and he sketched a hypothetical curve for this relationship – see Figure 9.5.

The role of this relationship in his dynamic model was to limit the rate at which prices would fall when unemployment was high, in line with 'the greater rigidity of factor prices in the downward than in the upward direction' (ibid.: 308). In a dynamic model itself, this does not lead to a stable trade-off between inflation and unemployment – which is the way

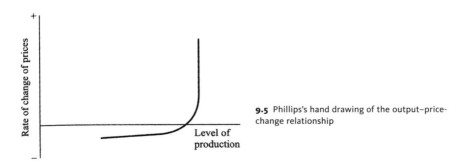

9.5 Phillips's hand drawing of the output–price-change relationship

9.6 A modern flow-chart simulation program generating cycles, not equilibrium

his empirically derived curve was subsequently interpreted – but rather limits the volatility of the cycles that occur compared to what a linear relationship would yield.

This was hard for Phillips to convey in his day, because then functional flow block diagrams were merely means to describe a dynamic model – they didn't let you simulate the model itself. But today, numerous computer programs enable these diagrams to be turned into active simulations. There is also an enormous analytic framework for analyzing stability and incomplete information supporting these programs: engineers have progressed dramatically in their capacity to model dynamic processes, while economics has if anything gone backwards.

Figure 9.6 illustrates both these modern simulation tools, and this difference between a linear and a nonlinear 'Phillips Curve' in Goodwin's growth cycle model. One of these programs (Vissim) turns the six-step verbal description of Marx's cycle model directly into a numerical simulation, using a linear 'Phillips Curve.' This model cycles as Marx expected, but it has extreme, high-frequency cycles in both employment and wages share.

Embedded in the diagram is an otherwise identical model, which has a nonlinear Phillips Curve with the shape like that envisaged by Phillips. This has smaller, more realistic cycles and these have a lower frequency as well, closer to the actual frequency of the business cycle.

What this model doesn't have – and this is a very important point – is

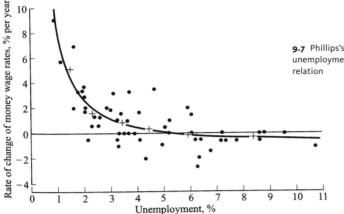

9.7 Phillips's empirically derived unemployment–money-wage-change relation

an equilibrium 'trade-off' between inflation (proxied here by the rate of change of wages) and unemployment. Instead the model economy is inherently cyclical, and Phillips's overall research agenda was to devise policy measures – inspired by engineering control theory – that might attenuate the severity of the cycles.

Had Phillips stuck with just a sketch of his hypothesized nonlinear relationship between the level of production and factor prices, it is possible that he would be known today only for these attempts to develop dynamic economic analysis – and possibly relatively unknown too, given how other pioneers of dynamics like Richard Goodwin (Goodwin 1986, 1990) and John Blatt (Blatt 1983) have been treated. Instead, he made the fateful decision to see whether he could find such a relationship in the UK data on unemployment and the rate of change of money wages.

This decision led to him being immortalized for work that he later told a colleague 'was just done in a weekend' while 'his best work was largely ignored – his early control work' (Leeson 1994: 613).

To do his statistical analysis, Phillips assembled annual data for the UK from 1861 until 1957 from a range of sources. He then used the subset from 1861 till the outbreak of World War I to derive a nonlinear function that appeared to fit the data very tightly (see Figure 9.7). When he fitted the post-WWI data to this curve, the 'out of sample' data also had a relatively close fit to his equation (except for some deviations which he explained as due to negotiated inflation-wage deals between unions and employers, and the impact of World War II on forcing up agricultural prices in Britain).

He then summarized his results in the following accurate but poorly considered statement:

Ignoring years in which import prices rise rapidly enough to initiate a wage-price spiral, which seem to occur very rarely except as a result of war, and assuming an increase in productivity of 2 per cent per year, it seems from the relation fitted to the data that if *aggregate demand were kept at a value which would maintain a stable level of product prices the associated level of unemployment would be a little under 2 per cent.*

If, as is sometimes recommended, *demand were kept at a value which would maintain stable wage rates the associated level of unemployment would be about 5 per cent.* (Phillips 1954: 299; emphases added)

To actually achieve the preconditions that Phillips set out here – keeping aggregate demand 'at a value which would maintain a stable level of product prices' or 'at a value which would maintain stable wage rates' – would have required a whole host of control mechanisms to be added, even to Phillips's model of the economy, let alone the real economy itself. As the Goodwin model indicates, a dynamic model of the economy will have endogenous tendencies to cyclical behavior, and these in turn are merely a caricature of the cyclical nature of evolutionary change in a capitalist economy.

Developing these control mechanisms was, as noted, Phillips's main research agenda, but the economics profession at large, and politicians as well, latched on to this statement as if it provided a simple menu by which the economy could be controlled. If you wanted stable prices (in the UK), just set unemployment to 2 percent; if you wanted stable money wages instead, set unemployment to 5 percent; and pick off any other combination you like along the Phillips Curve as well.

This simplistic, static 'trade-off' interpretation of Phillips's empirically derived curve rapidly came to be seen as the embodiment of Keynesian economics, and since the 1960s data also fitted the curve very well, initially this appeared to strengthen 'Keynesian' economics.

But in the late 1960s, the apparent 'trade-off' began to break down, with higher and higher levels of both inflation and unemployment. Since the belief that there was a trade-off had become equivalent in the public debate to Keynesian economics, the apparent breakdown of this relationship led to a loss of confidence in 'Keynesian' economics – and this was egged on by Milton Friedman as he campaigned to restore neoclassical economics to the position of primacy it had occupied prior to the Great Depression.

Phillips's empirical research recurs throughout the development of macroeconomics, as I am about to recount in the next chapter – as Robert Leeson observed: 'For over a third of a century, applied macroeconomics has, to a large extent, proceeded from the starting point of the trade-off interpretation of the work of A. W. H. "Bill" Phillips. It is hardly an exaggeration to say that any student destitute of the geometry of the Phillips curve would have difficulty passing an undergraduate macroeconomics examination' (Leeson 1997: 155).

However, even his empirical research has been distorted, since it has focused on just one of the factors that Phillips surmised would affect the rate of change of money wages – the level of employment. Phillips in fact put forward three causal factors:

When the demand for a commodity or service is high relatively to the supply of it we expect the price to rise, the rate of rise being greater the greater the excess demand. Conversely when the demand is low relatively to the supply we expect the price to fall, the rate of fall being greater the greater the deficiency of demand. It seems plausible that this principle should operate as one of the factors determining the rate of change of money wage rates, which are the price of labor services.

When the demand for labor is high and there are very few unemployed we should expect employers to bid wage rates up quite rapidly, each firm and each industry being continually tempted to offer a little above the prevailing rates to attract the most suitable labor from other firms and industries. On the other hand it appears that workers are reluctant to offer their services at less than the prevailing rates when the demand for labor is low and unemployment is high so that wage rates fall only very slowly. The relation between unemployment and the rate of change of wage rates is therefore likely to be highly non-linear.

Phillips then added that the *rate of change* of employment would affect the rate of change of money wages:

It seems possible that a second factor influencing the rate of change of money wage rates might be the rate of change of the demand for labor, and so of unemployment. Thus in a year of rising business activity, with the demand for labor increasing and the percentage unemployment decreasing, employers will be bidding more vigorously for the services of labor than they would be in a year during which the average percentage unemployment was the same but the demand for labor was not increasing. Conversely in a year of falling business activity, with the demand for labor decreasing and the percentage unemployment increasing, employers will be less inclined to grant wage increases, and workers will be in a weaker position to press for them, than they would be in a year during which the average percentage unemployment was the same but the demand for labor was not decreasing.

Thirdly, he considered that there could be a feedback between the rate of inflation and the rate of change of money wages – though he tended to discount this except in times of war: 'A third factor which may affect the rate of change of money wage rates is the rate of change of retail prices, operating through cost of living adjustments in wage rates' (Phillips 1954: 283).

In subsequent work, Phillips went farther still, and considered that attempts to control the economy that relied upon the historically observed relationship could change the relationship itself: 'In my view it cannot be too strongly stated that in attempting to control economic fluctuations we do not have two separate problems of estimating the system and controlling it, we have a single problem of jointly controlling and learning about the system, that is, a problem of learning control or adaptive control' (Phillips 1968: 164; Leeson 1994: 612, n. 13).

Phillips didn't consider the other two causal relationships in his empirical work because, at the time he did it, and with the computing resources available to him (a hand-operated electronic desk calculator), quite simply, it was impossible to do so. But today it is quite feasible to model all three causal factors, and adaptive learning as well, in a modern dynamic model of the kind that Phillips had hoped to develop.

Unfortunately, Phillips's noble intentions resulted in a backfire: far from helping wean economists off their dependency on static methods, the misinterpretation of his simple empirical research allowed the rebirth of neoclassical economics and its equilibrium methodology – and ultimately, the reduction of macroeconomics to applied microeconomics.

Why the world's leading macroeconomists were the last ones capable of realizing that a major economic crisis was imminent

Proverbs become proverbs because they succinctly state a profound truth, and no proverb better describes the state of neoclassical macroeconomics before the Great Recession than 'Pride goes before the fall.' The full proverb puts it even better: 'Pride goes before Destruction, and a Haughty Spirit before a Fall.' Before the 'Great Recession' (as the sudden economic downturn that began in 2007 is known in America), a popular '*topic du jour*' in the leading macroeconomic journals of the world (which are dominated by neoclassical economists) was explaining 'The Great Moderation' – the apparent decline in both the levels and volatility of unemployment and inflation since 1990. It was a trend they expected to see continue, and they were largely self-congratulatory as to why it had come about: it was a product of their successful management of the economy.

Few were more prominent in promulgating this view than Federal Reserve chairman Ben Bernanke. In 2004, while a member of the board of governors of the Reserve,[1] Bernanke gave a speech with precisely that title, in which he observed that:

> One of the most striking features of the economic landscape over the past
> twenty years or so has been a substantial decline in macroeconomic volatility
> [...] the variability of quarterly growth in real output [...] has declined
> by half since the mid-1980s, while the variability of quarterly inflation has
> declined by about two thirds. Several writers on the topic have dubbed this
> remarkable decline in the variability of both output and inflation 'the Great
> Moderation.' (Bernanke 2004b)

He nominated three possible causes of this phenomenon: 'structural change, improved macroeconomic policies, and good luck.' While he conceded that a definitive selection could not be made between the three factors, he argued that 'improved monetary policy' deserved more credit than it had received to date:

> improved monetary policy has likely made an important contribution
> not only to the reduced volatility of inflation (which is not particularly
> controversial) but to the reduced volatility of output as well. Moreover,

---

1 He became Fed chairman in February 2006, having briefly served as chairman of the President's Council of Economic Advisers before that.

because a change in the monetary policy regime has pervasive effects, I have suggested that some of the effects of improved monetary policies may have been misidentified as exogenous changes in economic structure or in the distribution of economic shocks. This conclusion on my part makes me optimistic for the future, because I am confident that monetary policy-makers will not forget the lessons of the 1970s. (Ibid.)

Equally confident that neoclassical economics had delivered a better world was Nobel laureate Robert Lucas, who is one of the key architects of modern neoclassical macroeconomics. In his Presidential Address to the American Economic Association in 2003, he went even farther in his optimism than Bernanke, to assert that macroeconomic theory had made another depression impossible:

> Macroeconomics was born as a distinct field in the 1940's, as a part of the intellectual response to the Great Depression. The term then referred to the body of knowledge and expertise that we hoped would prevent the recurrence of that economic disaster. My thesis in this lecture is that macroeconomics in this original sense has succeeded: *Its central problem of depression prevention has been solved, for all practical purposes, and has in fact been solved for many decades.* (Lucas 2003: 1; emphasis added)

They had no idea of what was about to happen. And fundamentally, they had no one but themselves to blame for their ignorance.

The kernel

Macroeconomics, the study of the behavior of the entire economy, was once an area of economic research independent from microeconomics, the study of individual markets. However, working with a cavalier ignorance of the many flaws in microeconomics, economists reshaped macroeconomics, not to increase its relevance to the economy, but to make it a branch of microeconomics. Today, macroeconomics is based on propositions which have been shown to be untenable in the preceding chapters. This process of decay was set in train first by Keynes's incomplete escape from conventional theory at the time he wrote *The General Theory of Employment, Interest and Money*, and accelerated by Hicks's dubious interpretation of Keynes as a marginalist.

From Hicks's IS-LM (investment and savings–liquidity and money) model on, the road was cleared for the novelty in macroeconomics to be eliminated, and for the key conclusion of pre-Keynesian economics – that a market economy could not experience a depression – to be restored, just in time for the next depression to occur.

The roadmap

This is a complicated chapter, and not merely because the subject matter itself is difficult. An additional complication comes from the way in which the version of neoclassical theory taught to undergraduates is very different to that taught to students in PhD programs.

Undergraduate courses teach what is known as the IS-LM (and/or AS-AD, aggregate supply–aggregate demand) model of macroeconomics, which is presented as a précis of Keynes's theory, but in reality was devised by Keynes's contemporary and intellectual rival John Hicks. PhD students, on the other hand, learn a class of models that goes by the grandiose – and utterly misleading – name of 'dynamic stochastic general equilibrium' (DSGE) models.

Both IS-LM and DSGE models are derived from the microeconomic concepts that I have shown are fallacious in the preceding chapters. They differ only in how extreme their reliance is on microeconomic theory, and on the presumption that everything happens in equilibrium. But they are also very different models, and therefore they have to be discussed independently, so in some ways there are two chapters in this one.

I precede these mini-chapters with a discussion of the fallacy they have in common: the belief that macroeconomics can and should be derived from microeconomic theory.

Then in the first mini-chapter I outline Keynes's critique of 'Say's Law,' the argument that 'supply creates its own demand,' and embellish it by comparing it to Marx's critique of the same proposition. I next argue that a key concept in all of neoclassical economics, 'Walras's Law,' is simply Say's Law in a more formal guise, and that it is false in a credit-driven economy. Keynes's and Marx's critiques of the conventional economics of their day are therefore still applicable to modern economics. Hicks's reinterpretation of Keynes as a 'marginalist' is debunked. Finally I detail Hicks's late realization that his interpretation of Keynes was untenable once uncertainty was taken into account as a key determinant of the level of investment.

In the second mini-chapter I cover the manner in which the DSGE approach to neoclassical macroeconomics overthrew the IS-LM model, and show that the key motivations for this were the desire to reduce macroeconomics to applied microeconomics, and to prove that there was a natural rate of unemployment that could not be altered by government policy. The inevitable intrusion of realism into this story led to the dominance of what is called the 'New Keynesian' faction of neoclassical macroeconomists. Neoclassical economists were confident that they had finally managed to reconcile Walras with Keynes, and this confidence made them optimistic about the economic future.

Then the Great Recession hit.

Macroeconomics and the reductionist fallacy

Humanity made great progress in understanding reality by ignoring the overwhelming complexity of the universe, and focusing on small components of it in isolation from each other. Compare, for example, the ancient vision of the physical world of consisting of four elemental factors, earth, water, air and fire, to our understanding of the periodic table and the quantum mechanical factors beneath that today. We would not have got from the ancient view of the world to the modern without ignoring the overall complexity of the universe and focusing on individual components of it, in isolation from all others.

The success of this approach – known as 'reductionism' – once led to the belief that there was a hierarchical ranking of sciences, in which more complex areas were merely simplified manifestations of the underlying fundamental determinants. For example, the biological processes in living organisms were thought to be merely a surface manifestation of the underlying chemical processes, and they in turn were just surface manifestations of the quantum mechanics that ruled chemical interactions. This attitude, known as 'strong reductionism,' argued that, ultimately, all sciences could be reduced to physics.

This belief was best put by the man who first showed its true limits, Henri Poincaré:

> This conception was not without grandeur; it was seductive, and many among us have not finally renounced it; they know that one will attain the ultimate elements of things only by patiently disentangling the complicated skein that our senses give us; that it is necessary to advance step by step, neglecting no intermediary; that our fathers were wrong in wishing to skip stations; but they believe that when one shall have arrived at these ultimate elements, there again will be found the majestic simplicity of celestial mechanics. (Poincaré 1956 [1905]: 166)

In turn, strong reductionism implied that all large-scale systems could be understood by working up from the small-scale. In the case of economics, this implied that the behavior of the macroeconomy should be derived directly from microeconomics, and this belief indeed dominated the development of macroeconomic theory from shortly after the publication of Keynes's *General Theory*. Today, neoclassical macroeconomics truly is applied microeconomics.

In the physical sciences, a very different development occurred. Poincaré showed that there were limits to reductionism in 1899, when he proved that, while a gravitational system with two celestial bodies (one sun and one planet) was utterly predictable, it was impossible to predict the behavior of a solar system with more than one planet. Reductionism still dominated the physical sciences for another seventy years, however, until these limits became apparent with the advent of the computer.

Before the computer, reductionism had a natural ally in the inability of researchers to analyze nonlinear relationships between variables. Strong reductionism implies that the behavior of any complex system can be entirely understood by considering the behavior of its constituents, and then summing their effects: 'the whole is the sum of the parts.' This belief was consistent with the limitations of linear algebra, which was relatively easy to do before computers.

Then the number-crunching power of computers enabled researchers to consider systems with nonlinear relations between variables – as with Lorenz's model of the weather, where two of the three variables are multiplied by each other in two of the three equations – and they consistently observed a remarkable result: in systems where variables interact in nonlinear ways, 'the whole is *more than* the sum of its parts,' and behaviors will occur at the aggregate level that cannot be found at the level of the system's elementary components. This phenomenon, the occurrence of behaviors at the aggregate level that could not be explained by behaviors at the component level, was christened 'emergent properties.'

Scientists then reconsidered the role of reductionism. It still had its place, but they were now aware of the fallacy in the belief that the best way to understand any systems was from the bottom up. In a paper tellingly entitled 'More is different,' the Physics Nobel laureate Philip Anderson called this fallacy 'constructionism.' It had two manifestations. First, even if a reductionist vision of a particular system was correct, the belief that the best way to understand the system was to construct it from its constituent parts was false:

> The main fallacy in this kind of thinking is that the reductionist hypothesis does not by any means imply a 'constructionist' one: The ability to reduce everything to simple fundamental laws does not imply the ability to start from those laws and reconstruct the universe. In fact, the more the elementary particle physicists tell us about the nature of the fundamental laws the less relevance they seem to have to the very real problems of the rest of science, much less to those of society. (Anderson 1972: 393)

The second was that larger systems turned out to have behaviors which were unique to their scale: *scale itself resulted in new behaviors which could not be deduced from the behavior of isolated components of a system*:

> The behavior of large and complex aggregates of elementary particles, it turns out, is not to be understood in terms of a simple extrapolation of the properties of a few particles. Instead, at each level of complexity entirely new properties appear, and the understanding of the new behaviors requires research which I think is as fundamental in its nature as any other. (Ibid.: 393)

Anderson was willing to entertain the proposition that there was a hierarchy to science, so that: 'one may array the sciences roughly linearly in a hierarchy, according to the idea: "The elementary entities of science X obey the laws of science Y"' (Table 10.1).

But he rejected the idea that any science in the X column could simply be treated as the applied version of the relevant science in the Y column: 'But this hierarchy does not imply that science X is "just applied Y." At each

TABLE 10.1 Anderson's ranking of sciences

X	Y
Solid state or many-body physics	Elementary particle physics
Chemistry	Many-body physics
Molecular biology	Chemistry
Cell biology	Molecular biology
...	...
Psychology	Physiology
Social sciences	Psychology

stage entirely new laws, concepts, and generalizations are necessary, requiring inspiration and creativity to just as great a degree as in the previous one. Psychology is not applied biology, nor is biology applied chemistry' (ibid.: 393).

The physical sciences embraced this discovery of emergent behavior, and what was first dubbed 'chaos theory' (Li and Yorke 1975) and is now known as 'complexity theory' (May and Oster 1976) is a fertile aspect of research in fields as diverse as physics and biology.

Among neoclassical economists, however, the reductionist fallacy held sway, and this is nowhere more evident than in the deliberate reduction of macroeconomics to applied microeconomics *in the confident but false belief that this was possible.*

Ironically, despite its adherence to strong reductionism, neoclassical economics provides one of the best examples of emergent phenomena ever: the 'Sonnenschein-Mantel-Debreu conditions' that were discussed in Chapter 3. This research proved that a market demand curve derived from the preferences of individual consumers who in isolation obeyed the Law of Demand – i.e. they had 'downward-sloping demand curves' – will not itself obey the Law of Demand: a market demand curve can have any shape at all.[2]

This is emergence par excellence: a behavior which, under the assumptions of revealed preference, is provably absent from individual consumers – demand curves that can rise as well as fall when price increases – can occur at the level of single markets in a multiple-consumer, multiple-commodity economy.

The correct inference from that research is that, not only is macroeconomics not applied microeconomics, but even microeconomics itself can't be based on a simple extrapolation from the alleged behavior of individual consumers and firms. Thus, even within microeconomics, the study of markets cannot be reduced to the analysis of individual behaviors, while under no circumstances can macroeconomics be derived from microeconomics.

2 More strictly, a market demand curve can have any shape that can be described by a polynomial equation. This rules out a curve that returns two or more prices for the same quantity, but allows curves that return the same price for many different quantities.

However, with some honorable exceptions (Kirman 1989, 1992), neoclassical economists resiled from this discovery of emergent properties within economics. The result was misinterpreted, and buried in poor pedagogy, so that three generations of post-WWII neoclassical economists continued to believe in the reductionist fallacy.

In this, they continued the behavior of their pre-WWII forebears. Ever since Adam Smith's *Wealth of Nations*, the dominant tendency in economics has been to analyze the economy from the perspective of the behavior of individual rational agents, and to derive from this the inference that, so long as prices are flexible, there can be no macroeconomic problems. Thinkers who took a different perspective, such as Malthus in his debates with Ricardo, or Marx and other critics, were driven to the periphery of economics.

In the language of the nineteenth century, the mainstream economists of that time argued that there could be no 'general glut': while individual markets might have more supply than demand, in the aggregate there had to be other markets where there was more demand than supply. Therefore, while there could be problems in individual markets, the entire economy should always be in balance, because a deficiency in one market would be matched by an excess in another. All that would be required to correct the imbalance would be to let the market mechanism work, so that the price of the good with excess demand would rise while the one with excess supply would fall. Macroeconomics, as we call it today, was seen as unnecessary.

Prior to the 1870s, this belief that there could be no macroeconomic problem involved a strange mishmash of ideas, because the classical school of thought that dominated economics 'proved' the absence of macroeconomic problems by borrowing arguments from Jean Baptiste Say, who was effectively an early neoclassical. After the 1870s, there was no such disconnect, as the neoclassical revolution led by Menger, Walras and Marshall swept away the old classical school. Economists continued to be confident that there could never be a general glut, and this macroeconomic belief was now derived from a consistent microeconomic theory.

Then the Great Depression began. As unemployment relentlessly climbed to 25 percent of the American workforce, and fascism broke out in Europe, neoclassical economists of the day were in disarray. Into this breach stepped Keynes. With the publication of *The General Theory of Employment, Interest and Money* in 1936, Keynes effectively invented macroeconomics as a separate sub-discipline within economics.

From that point on, neoclassical economists attempted to undermine it.

Say, Walras, and the self-equilibrating economy …

The *General Theory* was conceived and published during capitalism's greatest slump, the Great Depression, when America's output fell by 30 percent in four years, stock prices fell by 90 percent, commodity prices fell by almost

10 percent a year in its first two years, and unemployment remained above 15 percent for a decade.

Prior to then, mainstream economists did not believe there were any intractable macroeconomic problems. Individual markets might be out of equilibrium at any one time – and this could include the market for labor or the market for money – but the overall economy, the sum of all those individual markets, was bound to be balanced.

The basis for this confidence was the widespread belief, among economists, in what Keynes termed Say's Law. As Keynes described it, this was the proposition that 'supply creates its own demand' (Keynes 1936). Some economists dispute Keynes's rendition of Say's Law (Kates 1998), and I concur that in several ways Keynes obscured what Say actually meant. So it is appropriate to turn to the horse's mouth for a definition:

> Every producer asks for money in exchange for his products, only for the purpose of employing that money again immediately in the purchase of another product; for we do not consume money, and it is not sought after in ordinary cases to conceal it: thus, when a producer desires to exchange his product for money, he may be considered as already asking for the merchandise which he proposes to buy with this money. It is thus that the producers, though they have all of them the air of demanding money for their goods, do in reality demand merchandise for their merchandise. (Say 1967 [1821])

Say's core proposition is that overall balance is assured because, to quote Steve Kates, the strongest modern-day proponent of Say's Law: '[t]he sale of goods and services to the market is the source of the income from which purchases are financed' (Kates 1998).

This, according to the 'classical' economists from whom Keynes hoped to distinguish himself,[3] meant that there could never be a slump due to an overall deficiency in demand. Instead, slumps, when they occurred, were due to sectoral imbalances.

If the demand for one market – such as labor – was too low relative to supply, this was because demand exceeded supply in one or more other markets. The solution was for sellers in the market suffering from excess supply – workers – to accept a lower price for their commodity.

Money was also treated as a commodity in the pre-Keynesian model, and it was possible that, at some point in time, many people would want to hold money and very few would want goods. There could then be a serious slump, as producers of goods found that people did not want to part with their money. Physical commodity markets and the labor market could then be in excess supply – with unsold goods and unemployed workers – but

---

3 Keynes lumped what we today term neoclassical economists with those we today call the classical economists. While they are distinctly different schools of thought, Keynes was correct to group them together on this issue, since they concurred that a general deficiency of aggregate demand was impossible.

this would be because of the excess demand for money, and not because of any overall deficiency of aggregate demand. In the aggregate, demand and supply would be in balance.

Keynes's attempt to refute this notion was, to put it kindly, rather confusing, and on this basis alone I can to some extent understand the inability of many neoclassical economists to comprehend his theory. I reproduce Keynes's argument in its entirety in the next quote, and if you don't comprehend it completely on a first reading, don't worry – in fact, I'd worry if you did comprehend it! After you've waded through this, I'll provide a far clearer explanation that Keynes was aware of at the time he wrote the *General Theory*, but which – probably for political reasons – he chose not to use.

OK: take a good swig of coffee, a deep breath, and read on:

This theory can be summed up in the following propositions:

1 In a given situation of technique, resources and costs, income (both money-income and real income) depends on the volume of employment N.

2 The relationship between the community's income and what it can be expected to spend on consumption, designated by D_1, will depend on the psychological characteristic of the community, which we shall call its propensity to consume. That is to say, consumption will depend on the level of aggregate income and, therefore, on the level of employment N, except when there is some change in the propensity to consume.

3 The amount of labor N which the entrepreneurs decide to employ depends on the sum (D) of two quantities, namely D_1, the amount which the community is expected to spend on consumption, and D_2, the amount which it is expected to devote to new investment. D is what we have called above the effective demand.

4 Since $D_1 + D_2 = D = f(N)$, where f is the aggregate supply function, and since, as we have seen in (2) above, D_1 is a function of N, which we may write $c(N)$, depending on the propensity to consume, it follows that $f(N) - c(N) = D_2$.

5 Hence the volume of employment in equilibrium depends on (i) the aggregate supply function, (ii) the propensity to consume, and (iii) the volume of investment, D_2. This is the essence of the *General Theory of Employment*.

6 For every value of N there is a corresponding marginal productivity of labor in the wage-goods industries; and it is this which determines the real wage. (5) is, therefore, subject to the condition that N cannot exceed the value which reduces the real wage to equality with the marginal disutility of labor. This means that not all changes in D are compatible with our temporary assumption that money-wages are constant. Thus it will be essential to a full statement of our theory to dispense with this assumption.

7   On the classical theory, according to which $D = f(N)$ for all values of N, the volume of employment is in neutral equilibrium for all values of N less than its maximum value; so that the forces of competition between entrepreneurs may be expected to push it to this maximum value. Only at this point, on the classical theory, can there be stable equilibrium.

8   When employment increases, D_1 will increase, but not by so much as D; since when our income increases our consumption increases also, but not by so much. The key to our practical problem is to be found in this psychological law. For it follows from this that the greater the volume of employment the greater will be the gap between the aggregate supply price (Z) of the corresponding output and the sum (D_1) which the entrepreneurs can expect to get back out of the expenditure of consumers. Hence, if there is no change in the propensity to consume, employment cannot increase, unless at the same time D_2 is increasing so as to fill the increasing gap between Z and D_1. Thus – except on the special assumptions of the classical theory according to which there is some force in operation which, when employment increases, always causes D_2 to increase sufficiently to fill the widening gap between Z and D_1 – the economic system may find itself in stable equilibrium with N at a level below full employment, namely at the level given by the intersection of the aggregate demand function with the aggregate supply function. (Keynes 1936: 28–9; emphasis added)

You got that? Oh, come on, pull the other one! It's far more likely that your head is still spinning after reading that extract, and the same applied to the handful of leading neoclassical economists who read Keynes, and tried to work out how he could argue that aggregate demand could be deficient.

It's a tragedy that what Keynes himself described as 'the essence of the General Theory of Employment' was expressed in such a convoluted and turgid fashion – especially given his capacity for brilliant prose. It is therefore not altogether amazing that neoclassical economists believed that Keynes either misunderstood what they believed was the true concept at the heart of Say's Law, or that he intended to refute the clearly incorrect belief that overall balance meant that there could never be involuntary unemployment – whereas Say's Law allowed for involuntary unemployment as a by-product of sectoral imbalances.

The upshot is that the essence of Say's Law lives on in modern economics, though it now goes under the more respectable name of 'Walras's Law' (or, in some circles, 'Say's Principle'). Its modern definition is that 'the sum of all notional excess demands is zero,' and this proposition is accepted as valid – indeed as irrefutable – by modern-day economists.

However, I argue that this is precisely the concept which Keynes intended to refute, and that he was right to do so.

Say no more? The modern attempt to reconcile Keynes with Say and Walras (Leijonhufvud 1968; Clower and Leijonhufvud 1973)[4] starts from the proposition that, on the average, agents in a market economy are neither thieves (who want to take more than they give) nor philanthropists (who want to give more than they get). Therefore the normal agent will intend to have balanced supplies and demands: the value of what he wishes to sell will equal the value of what he wishes to buy, so that 'the sum of his notional excess demands is zero.'

The excess demand for any single product by a single agent can be positive – so that the agent wishes to be a net buyer of that product – or negative – so that the agent wishes to be a net seller. However, in sum, his excess demands will be zero.

This balance at the level of the individual agent necessarily carries over to the aggregate of all agents: if the intended excess demands of each individual agent sum to zero, then the intended excess demands of all agents sum to zero.

However, this identity of aggregate supply and aggregate demand at the overall market level doesn't necessarily translate to identity at the level of each individual market. In particular, as noted earlier, it is possible for excess demand for money to be positive – in which case commodity markets would be 'glutted.' Excess demand for labor can also be negative – the supply of workers can exceed the demand for them – so that there will be involuntarily unemployed workers (and also a notional excess demand for the products that the unemployed workers intended to buy).

These two circumstances are both explanations of a depression. The former would involve a 'rising price' for money – or in other words 'deflation' as the money price of all other commodities fell. The latter would involve a falling price for labor – falling wages. However, both these forces would make a depression a temporary phenomenon. As Dixon puts it:

> [F]ollowers of Walras would say that involuntary unemployment cannot
> persist in a market economy with flexible wages and prices. They would
> argue that if the commodities market has excess demand then the prices of
> commodities will tend to rise and this will tend to reduce the level of excess
> demand in that market. In the labor market, where there is excess supply,
> they would assert that money wages will tend to fall. The joint effect of the
> rising price together with a falling money wage is that the real wage will tend
> to drop thus reducing (and eventually removing entirely) the excess supply
> in the labor market.

> As a consequence of the above, many would see the pronouncements of
> Keynes that the economy could find itself with an excess supply of labor
> and yet, in all (other) respects be in 'equilibrium,' as being in conflict with

---

4 Surprisingly few books give this argument in full, given the extent to which it is a core belief in economics. Two that do are Baird (1981: ch. 3) and Crouch (1972: ch. 6).

Walras' Law and therefore wrong or 'bad' in theory and so inadmissible. (Dixon 2000b)

Keynes's critique Let's now simplify Keynes's argument from that pivotal passage to see whether it's consistent with the way in which neoclassical economists later interpreted it. Keynes divided all output into two classes: consumption and investment. If the economy was in equilibrium, then Say's Law would argue that excess demand for consumption goods would be zero, and likewise for investment goods.

Keynes then imagined what would happen if demand for consumption goods fell, so that excess demand for consumption goods was negative (supply exceeded demand).[5] Say's Law would argue that demand for investment goods would rise to compensate: notional excess demand for investment goods would be positive.

However, as Keynes argued extensively throughout the *General Theory*, demand for investment goods is driven by expectations of profit, and these in turn depend heavily upon expected sales to consumers. A fall in consumer demand now could lead entrepreneurs to expect lower sales in the future – since in an uncertain environment 'the facts of the existing situation enter, in a sense disproportionately, into the formation of our long-term expectations; our usual practice being to take the existing situation and to project it into the future' (Keynes 1936: 148).

Dampened expectations would therefore lead entrepreneurs to reduce their demand for investment goods in response to a reduced demand for consumer goods. Thus a situation of negative excess demand for consumer goods could lead to a state of negative excess demand for investment goods too – a general slump.

This clearly contradicts Walras's Law. Since economists regard Walras's Law as irrefutable, this led some economists to ridicule Keynes's argument, and others to attempt to find how Keynes's argument could be reconciled with Walras's Law. The most widely accepted reconciliation was achieved by Robert Clower and Axel Leijonhufvud.

Say's Principle Clower and Leijonhufvud asserted that Keynes and Walras *were* compatible, because Walras's Law applied effectively only in equilibrium. Out of equilibrium, then, though the sum of *notional* excess demands was still zero, the sum of *effective* demands could be negative.

For example, if there was negative excess demand in the labor market – so that some workers were involuntarily unemployed – then it didn't help that these unemployed workers wanted to buy commodities. Without employment,

---

5 His actual procedure was to argue that, when employment increased, demand for consumer goods would increase by less than the increase in employment, and that equilibrium would be achieved only if investment demand automatically took up the slack. This confusing argument is equivalent to the simpler case set out here.

their notional demands remained just that. Though they might want to buy commodities, without a wage their notional demand had no impact upon actual sales of commodities. Actual negative excess demand for labor might therefore not be balanced by actual positive excess demand for commodities, so that overall, the sum of excess demand could be negative. Keynes was vindicated as a disequilibrium theorist.[6] Keynes and Walras were reconciled.

But were they? Prior to the publication of the *General Theory*, Keynes indicated that he rejected the very basis of Walras's Law – the proposition that the sum of notional excess demands is zero – when he praised the author of what he had once described as an 'obsolete economic textbook which I know to be not only scientifically erroneous but without interest for the modern world' (Keynes 1925): Karl Marx.

The circuit of capital Marx's critique of Say's Law went to the heart of Walras's Law (and Say's Law). Marx rejected Say's initial proposition that '[e]very producer asks for money in exchange for his products, only for the purpose of employing that money again immediately in the purchase of another product' (Say 1967 [1821]). Instead, Marx pointed out that this notion asserted that no one in a market economy wished to accumulate wealth. If there was never any difference between the value of commodities someone desired to sell and buy on the market, then no one would ever desire to accumulate wealth. But an essential feature of capitalism is the existence of a group of agents with precisely that intention.

Believers in Say's Principle or Walras's Law might find these agents rather bizarre, since in their terms these agents are 'thieves,' who wish to take more than they give. However, far from being bizarre, these agents are an essential part of a market economy. They are known as capitalists. Far from their behavior being aberrant in a market economy, it is in fact the essence of capitalism – and according to Marx, they do this without being thieves.

Whereas both Say's Law and Walras's Law assert that people simply desire to consume commodities, Marx asserted that an essential aspect of capitalism is the desire to accumulate. He derided Say's belief that the ultimate objective of every agent in a market economy was simply consumption – which is still generally accepted by economists today, as well as the economists of Marx's time – as an ideologically convenient but misleading fiction which obscures the actual dynamics of capitalism:

> It must never be forgotten, that in capitalist production what matters is
> not the immediate use-value but the exchange-value, and, in particular,
> the expansion of surplus-value. This is the driving motive of capitalist
> production, and it is a pretty conception that – in order to reason away the

---

6 As Milgate observed, 'Received opinion, that Keynes's General Theory is a contribution to "disequilibrium" analysis, was stamped indelibly upon the collective consciousness of the economics profession at an early date – by critics and converts alike' (Milgate 1987).

contradictions of capitalist production – abstracts from its very basis and depicts it as a production aiming at the direct satisfaction of the consumption of the producers. (Marx 1968 [1861]: ch. 17, section 6)

Capitalists are clearly fundamental to capitalism, and their behavior directly contradicts the Walras's and Say's Law presumption that every agent's intended excess demand is zero. As Marx put it:

> The capitalist throws less value in the form of money into the circulation than he draws out of it [...] Since he functions [...] as an industrial capitalist, his supply of commodity-value is always greater than his demand for it. If his supply and demand in this respect covered each other it would mean that his capital had not produced any surplus-value [...] His aim is not to equalize his supply and demand, but to make the inequality between them [...] as great as possible. (Marx 1885: ch. 4, section 'The meeting of demand and supply')

The dilemma for Marx was to explain how this inequality could be achieved without 'robbing' other participants in the market, and without violating the principle that commodities were bought and sold at fair values. His solution points out the fallacy underlying the economist's superficially appealing arguments in Say's Law, Walras's Law, and Say's Principle.

This was that the market process had to include a production stage where the quantity and value of output exceeded the value of inputs – in Marx's terms and in Sraffa's (discussed in Chapter 6), a surplus is produced. The capitalist pays a fair price for his raw materials, and a fair wage to his employees. They are then combined in a production process which generates commodities for sale where the physical quantity of commodities and their monetary value exceed the quantity and value of inputs. The commodities are then sold for more than the cost of the raw materials and workers' wages, yielding a profit. The profit allows the capitalist to fulfill his desire to accumulate wealth, without robbing any other market participants, and without having to buy commodities below their value and sell them above it.[7]

Say's Law and Walras's Law, on the other hand, begin from the abstraction of an exchange-only economy: an economy in which goods exist at the outset, but where no production takes place (production is shoehorned into the analysis at a later point, but unsatisfactorily, as I outline below). The market simply enables the exchange of pre-existing goods. In such an economy, surplus in Marx's sense would be impossible. Equally, if one agent desired to and did accumulate wealth, that would necessarily involve theft in the Say's Principle sense. However, this condition does not hold when we move from the fiction of an exchange-only economy to the reality of a production and exchange economy. With production, it is possible for agents to desire to accumulate wealth without therefore aspiring to be thieves.

7 I explain how Marx derived this result in Chapter 17.

Marx formalized this analysis in terms of two 'circuits,' the 'Circuit of Commodities' and the 'Circuit of Capital.'

In the Circuit of Commodities, people come to market with commodities, which they exchange for money in order to buy other commodities. Marx stylized this as C – M – C:

Commodity→Money→Commodity

Though Marx discussed various ways in which this circuit could fail – owing primarily to delays between the sale of one commodity and the purchase of the next – generally speaking it obeys Walras's Law. Each 'agent' desires to convert commodities of a given value into different commodities of equivalent value.

However, in the Circuit of Capital, people came to market with money, with the intention of turning this money into more money. These agents buy commodities – specifically, labor and raw materials – with money, put these to work in a factory to produce other commodities, and then sell these commodities for (hopefully) more money, thus making a profit. Marx stylized this as M – C – M+:

Money→Commodity→More money

The complete circuit, and the one which emphasizes the fallacy behind Walras's Law, was M – C(L, MP) ... P ... C+c – M+m:

Money→Labor and means of production ... Production ... Different commodities, of greater value than paid for the labor and means of production→Sale of commodities to generate more money

This circuit specifically violates Say's Principle and Walras's Law. Rather than simply wanting to exchange one set of commodities for another of equivalent value, the agents in this circuit wish to complete it with more wealth than they started with. If we focus upon the commodity stages of this circuit, then, as Marx says, these agents wish to supply more than they demand, and to accumulate the difference as profit which adds to their wealth. Their supply is the commodities they produce for sale. Their demand is the inputs to production they purchase – the labor and raw materials. In Say's Principle's terms, the sum of these, their excess demand, is negative. When the two circuits are added together, the sum of all excess demands in a capitalist economy is likewise negative (prior to the introduction of credit, which we consider below).

This explanation of why Say's Law and Walras's Law don't apply to a market economy is far clearer than Keynes's, and the great pity is that Keynes didn't use it in the *General Theory*, because it was in his 1933 draft. In this draft, Keynes observes that Marx made the 'pregnant observation' that:

[T]he nature of production in the actual world is not C – M – C', i.e. of exchanging commodity (or effort) for money in order to obtain another commodity (or effort). That may be the standpoint of the private consumer. But it is not the attitude of business, which is a case of M – C – M', i.e., of parting with money for commodity (or effort) in order to obtain more money. (Dillard 1984: 424, citing Keynes's Collected Works, vol. 29, p. 81)

Keynes continued in a footnote that this vision of capitalism as having two circuits, one of which was motivated solely by the desire to accumulate wealth, in turn implied the likelihood of periodic crises when expectations of profit were not met:

> Marx, however, was approaching the intermediate truth when he added that the continuous excess of M' [over M] would be inevitably interrupted by a series of crises, gradually increasing in intensity, or entrepreneur bankruptcy and underemployment, during which, presumably M must be in excess. My own argument, if it is accepted, should at least serve to effect a reconciliation between the followers of Marx and those of Major Douglas, leaving the classical economics still high and dry in the belief that M and M' are always equal. (Ibid.: 424, citing Keynes's Collected Works, vol. 29, p. 82n.)

Unfortunately, Keynes later substituted his own convoluted reasoning for Marx's, I expect for two reasons. First, his argument was an attempt to put Marx's logic into the Marshallian framework in which Keynes was educated; secondly, he probably made a political judgment, at a time when Stalin's power was rising and communism had great political appeal, not to acknowledge the 'father of communism' in his critique of conventional economics.

Had Marx's clear logic been brought to center stage by Keynes, it is feasible that the 'neoclassical counter-revolution' initiated by Hicks might not have even commenced, because the fact that Keynes rejected Walras's Law, and his sound reasons for doing so, would have been so much clearer. So although Keynes's decision can be understood in the context of his times, with the benefit of hindsight, it was a serious mistake. Keynes's obscure and confusing argument allowed economists to continue believing that Walras's Law was an irrefutable truth. Only those working outside the neoclassical mainstream realized otherwise.

Credit and the fallacy of Walras's Law

Minsky, like Keynes before him, also omitted any reference to Marx in his own work, but his reasons for doing so are far easier to accept: given that he was an American academic during the McCarthyist period, any acknowledgment of Marx would have seriously impeded his academic career, if not ended it altogether.[8] However, he was strongly influenced by Marx's analysis, and

---

8 For those of you for whom McCarthyism is ancient history, see en.wikipedia.org/wiki/McCarthyism. Though McCarthy was out of the picture by the late 1950s, the influence of that period continued for many years.

took Marx's logic one step farther. He pointed out that since there is a buyer for every seller, and since accounting demands that expenditure must equal receipts, and yet growth also occurs over time, *then credit and debt must make up the gap.* Credit and debt are therefore fundamental to capitalism:

> If income is to grow, the financial markets, where the various plans to save and invest are reconciled, must generate an aggregate demand that, aside from brief intervals, is ever rising. For real aggregate demand to be increasing, […] it is necessary that current spending plans, summed over all sectors, be greater than current received income and that some market technique exist by which aggregate spending in excess of aggregate anticipated income can be financed. *It follows that over a period during which economic growth takes place, at least some sectors finance a part of their spending by emitting debt or selling assets.* (Minsky 1982 [1963]: 6; emphasis added)

Minsky's insight here points out the pivotal blind spot in thinking which leads neoclassical and Austrian economists to believe respectively in Walras's Law and Say's Law: *they fail to consider the role of credit in a capitalist economy.*

Say, banker, can you spare a dime? Say's Law and Walras's Law envisage a world in which commodities are purchased only from the proceeds of selling other commodities, and in which commodities are the only things that are bought and sold. As Kates put it:

> According to the law of markets [Say's Law], aggregate demand was a conception unnecessary for a proper understanding of the cyclical behavior of economies. There were, of course, purchases and sales, and one could add together in some way everything bought during a period of time and describe this as aggregate demand […] [but] demand was not thought of as independent of supply. Instead, demand was constituted by supply; one could not demand without first having produced. Or to be more precise, demand in aggregate was made up of supplies in aggregate. (Kates 2003: 73–4)

In contrast to the position put by Kates, the world in which we live is one in which goods are purchased using both the proceeds of selling other goods and credit, while what is bought and sold includes existing assets as well as newly produced goods.

Aggregate demand is therefore aggregate supply *plus the change in debt,* while aggregate demand is expended on both commodities and assets (shares and property).[9] This guarantees the overall accounting balance that is an

---

9 I have found that many people find this confusing on the basis that, if debt has financed a purchase, wouldn't that already be recorded in GDP? There are two reasons why this is not the case. First, part of spending is on pre-existing assets – which are not a component of GDP. Secondly, in our demand-driven economy, the demand comes first – before the supply – and demand can be sourced either from previously earned income, or an increase in debt – where this debt reflects an increase in the money supply by the private banking system, as I explain in Chapters 12 and 14. The debt-financed demand for commodities does

integral part of both Say's Law and Walras's Law, but it includes both the role of credit and the role of asset sales in a capitalist economy, which both of those 'laws' omit. Those 'laws' are thus relevant only to a world of either pure exchange or simple commodity production – the world that Marx characterizes as C→M→C – but are not relevant to the (normally) growing capitalist world in which we actually live.

The Say's Law/Walras's Law fallacy of ignoring the role of credit is the foundation of the neoclassical (and Austrian) argument that 'general gluts' and depressions are impossible, and that all crises are really sectoral imbalances which can be corrected by price adjustments alone. Once this fallacy is removed, depressions or 'general gluts' (and general booms) are possible, and the contraction of credit plays a key role in them. But credit which is not backed by existing goods is also an essential feature of an expanding economy as well, as Schumpeter explains more clearly than either Minsky or Marx.

Schumpeter focused upon the role of entrepreneurs in capitalism, and made the point that an entrepreneur is someone with an idea but not necessarily the finance needed to put that idea into motion.[10] The entrepreneur therefore must borrow money to be able to purchase the goods and labor needed to turn his idea into a final product. This money, borrowed from a bank, adds to the demand for existing goods and services generated by the sale of those existing goods and services.

> The fundamental notion that the essence of economic development consists in a different employment of existing services of labor and land leads us to the statement that the carrying out of new combinations takes place through the withdrawal of services of labor and land from their previous employments [...] this again leads us to two heresies: first to the heresy that money, and then to the second heresy that also other means of payment, perform an essential function, hence that processes in terms of means of payment are not merely reflexes of processes in terms of goods. In every possible strain, with rare unanimity, even with impatience and moral and intellectual indignation, a very long line of theorists have assured us of the opposite [...]
>
> *From this it follows, therefore, that in real life total credit must be greater than it could be if there were only fully covered credit.* The credit structure projects not only beyond the existing gold basis, but also beyond the existing commodity basis. (Schumpeter 1934: 95, 101; emphasis added)

This Marx-Schumpeter-Minsky perspective thus integrates production, exchange and credit as holistic aspects of a capitalist economy, and therefore

---

later generate production of more commodities, and this turns up in GDP – but the debt precedes the supply. This relationship is thus best thought of in 'continuous time' terms: aggregate demand at a point in time equals income at that time, plus the change in debt at that time. Aggregate supply (and the sale of existing assets) follows slightly later.

10 Sometimes they do, of course, but in order to clarify his argument Schumpeter considers the case where an entrepreneur does not have pre-existing money and must therefore borrow to finance his venture.

as essential elements of any theory of capitalism. Neoclassical economics, in contrast, can only analyze an exchange or simple commodity production economy in which money is simply a means to make barter easier.

Say's Principle, which insists that the sum of all notional excess demands is zero, is a model of a capitalist economy without production and, most importantly, without capitalists.

Walrasian rejoinders?

There are a number of objections which economists could make to this Marx-Schumpeter-Minsky model of a monetary production economy.

First, Marx's circuits clearly cover not one market, but two: one when the capitalist buys his inputs, the other when he sells his outputs. Since these are two distinct markets in time, there is no reason, even under Walras's Law, why demands in one should equal supplies in the other. However, in each market, Walras's Law will apply.

Secondly, it is incorrect to conflate the exchange process with the production process. It is quite possible that agents could purchase inputs to production in one market, then combine them in production, produce a larger value of commodities and subsequently bring those commodities to sale at a subsequent market.

Thirdly, Marx's notion of a surplus implies that there are some commodities which can be purchased and, through production, turned into a larger value of commodities. This implies a 'free lunch.' If such a possibility ever existed, it would have long ago been 'arbitraged' away by the price of these commodities rising, or the price of the outputs falling.

Fourthly, Marx neglects the concept of a rate of time discount. Though some agents may appear to want to accumulate over time, if we discount future incomes to reflect the fact that the commodities that income will enable you to buy will be consumed in the future, then overall these agents are simply maintaining their level of satisfaction over time.

Taking the first and second hypothetical objections together, one of the strengths of Marx's approach is that his model covers a process through time, rather than merely considering an instant in time. In reality, at the aggregate level, exchange and production occur simultaneously. Factories are continuously producing commodities, sales rooms continually moving recently produced stock, workers are being paid wages, and spending them on consumer goods. Marx's circuits analysis captures the organic nature of the production and exchange processes of a market economy, whereas the neoclassical approach artificially separates these into distinct stages.

This organic approach therefore enables Marx to consider the economy as a dynamic process, in which growth is an integral aspect of a capitalist economy. As part of this process, there are some agents who are continually accumulating wealth (when economic conditions are favorable), and others who are continually simply maintaining their level of economic well-being (though they can also gain in wealth if real wages are increasing, and if the wage exceeds subsistence).

Walras's Law, on the other hand, is best suited to the economic irrelevance of an exchange-only economy, or a production economy in which growth does not occur (which Marx called simple commodity production). If production and growth do occur, then they take place outside the market, when ironically the market is the main intellectual focus of neoclassical economics. Conventional economics is thus a theory which suits a static economy – and which can only be adapted to a dynamic economy with great difficulty, if at all – when what is needed are theories to analyze dynamic economies. Marx's 'through time' model of circuits is thus better suited to the analysis of a market economy than the 'moment in time' model of Walras's Law.

Marx's model of capitalist expectations is also far more valid than Walras's. A capitalist might well have his purchases and supplies balanced in any one market, as Walras's Law requires. However, purchases in this period are undertaken with the intention of selling a greater quantity in the next market. Marx's notion of the circuit of capital thus provides a link between one 'market period' and the next, which Walras's Law does not.

Since Say's Law and Walras's Law are in fact founded upon the hypothesized state of mind of each market participant at one instant in time, and since at any instant in time we can presume that a capitalist will desire to accumulate, then the very starting point of Say's/Walras's Law is invalid. In a capitalist economy, the sum of the intended excess demands at any one point in time will be negative, not zero. Marx's circuit thus more accurately states the intention of capitalists by its focus on the growth in wealth over time, than does Walras's Law's dynamically irrelevant and factually incorrect instantaneous static snapshot.

The arbitrage argument highlights the difference between neoclassical theory and Marx's theory of value,[11] which I discuss in more detail in Chapter 17 (where, I had better point out, I reject the 'labor theory of value' which conventional Marxists regard as integral to Marx's analysis). Neoclassical theory basically argues that the average rate of profit is driven down to the marginal productivity of capital, so that profit simply reflects the contribution which capital makes to output. This rate of profit is then called 'normal profit,' treated as a cost of production, and notionally set as the zero mark. Only profit above this level, called super-normal profit, is formally acknowledged in the theory, and in the pervasive theory of perfectly competitive equilibrium, super-normal profit is zero, so that profit fails to appear as a variable in economic theory.

The notion that profit is determined by the marginal product of capital

11 Marx's theory of value is normally regarded as the labor theory of value, which is criticized in Chapter 13. I argue that his theory of value is something quite different.

was debunked in Chapter 7. Marx's theory of value, on the other hand, sees profit as a surplus of sales over the cost of production, allows for a positive rate of profit, and makes the rate of profit an integral part of the theory of production and exchange.

The time discount argument, that people are simply maintaining their level of satisfaction over time, has problems on at least two fronts. First, it is very hard to believe, for example, that Warren Buffett would feel that his level of wealth in 2011 was equivalent to his wealth in 1970. Successful capitalists would clearly feel that they have gained in wealth over time – and unsuccessful capitalists would definitely know that they have lost or at least failed to gain. Secondly, all this argument does is move the zero position when calculating whether someone is accumulating, staying the same, or losing out. If the normal rate of time discount is, say, 2 percent, then anyone who is accumulating wealth at more than 2 percent per annum is increasing their wealth – the sum of their time-discounted excess demands is negative.

So what?

The Walrasian argument that the sum of all excess demands is zero provides an apparent center of gravity for the economy. Rather like a seesaw, if one sector of the economy is down, then another sector is necessarily up. Furthermore, economists postulate that there are countervailing forces at work: a 'down' sector will have the price of its output driven down, thus increasing demand and restoring balance, and vice versa for an 'up' sector. The seesaw will ultimately return to balance.

A negative sum for aggregate excess demand – and the requirement that this be made up for by borrowing money from banks – moves that center of gravity. Instead of the economy behaving like a seesaw where the pivot is carefully placed at the center of gravity, it behaves like one where the pivot is instead off-center, and can move abruptly one way or the other. A down sector is not necessarily offset by an up sector, so that, contrary to Walras's Law, the entire economy can remain down – or up – for an indefinite period.

In particular, a general slump is feasible. As Keynes argued, a decline in spending on consumption by consumers could lead investors to also reduce their demand for investment goods, so that the economy could remain in a situation of inadequate excess demand.

The key destabilizing force is investment. As both Keynes and Marx emphasize, investment is undertaken not for its own sake, but to yield a profit. If expectations of profit evaporate, then so too will investment spending, and the economy will be thrown into a general slump. Equally, if expectations of profit become too euphoric, investment can be overdone, and the economy can be thrown into an unsustainable boom – in that the profits expected by the investors will not be realized, and the boom will give way to bust. The non-Say's/Walras's Law vision of the economy shared by Marx, Schumpeter, Keynes and Minsky thus accords with the manifest instability of the macroeconomy, whereas Walras's Law asserts that, despite appearances to the contrary, the macroeconomy really is stable.

At the same time, this potential for instability is also a necessary aspect of the potential for growth. Instability, in and of itself, is not a bad thing, but in fact is fundamental to any dynamic, growing system. To extend the seesaw analogy, the fact that the real-world economic seesaw is not in equilibrium means that the only way to stop it tipping over is to keep the seesaw itself moving in the direction of its imbalance.[12] The neoclassical obsession with equilibrium is therefore a hindrance to understanding the forces that enable the economy to grow, when growth has always been a fundamental aspect of capitalism.[13]

Unfortunately, this perspective on Keynes's *General Theory* was buried beneath economists' mistaken belief that Walras's Law was incontrovertible. By forging a reconciliation between Keynes and Walras, the resulting 'Keynesian economics' was not Keynes's economics at all. It is little wonder that this Keynesian 'straw man' was so easily deconstructed by its conservative critics.

Say no more! Though Keynes unintentionally obscured Marx's critique of Say's Law, he also provided an eloquent explanation of why this shallow, simplistic notion held, and continues to hold, such a strong grip upon the minds of economists:

> That it reached conclusions quite different from what the ordinary unin-
> structed person would expect, added, I suppose, to its intellectual prestige.
> That its teaching, translated into practice, was austere and often unpalatable,
> lent it virtue. That it was adapted to carry a vast and consistent logical
> superstructure, gave it beauty. That it could explain much social injustice
> and apparent cruelty as an inevitable incident in the scheme of progress,
> and the attempt to change such things as likely on the whole to do more
> harm than good, commended it to authority. That it afforded a measure of
> justification to the free activities of the individual capitalist, attracted to it
> the support of the dominant social force behind authority. (Keynes 1936)

However, Keynes continued, this contrariness had, by the time of the Great Depression, led to a diminution of economics in the eyes of the public:

---

12 There is an interesting parallel in research into producing robots that can walk. The first attempts designed a robot that always kept its center of gravity directly above the foot in contact with the ground – resulting in a robot that was always in gravitational equilibrium, but which could walk only in straight lines with five seconds between steps. To enable fluid motion, the researchers found they had to put the center of gravity in continuous disequilibrium: then it could walk as naturally as we humans do. See world.honda.com/ASIMO/history/eo.html and world.honda.com/ASIMO/technology/walking_o2.html for details.

13 Whether this growth can be sustained indefinitely is another matter altogether that I do not address in this book. On that front I regard *The Limits to Growth* (Meadows, Randers et al. 1972) as the definitive reference.

But although the doctrine itself has remained unquestioned by orthodox economists up to a late date, its signal failure for purposes of scientific prediction has greatly impaired, in the course of time, the prestige of its practitioners. For professional economists, after Malthus, were apparently unmoved by the lack of correspondence between the results of their theory and the facts of observation – a discrepancy which the ordinary man has not failed to observe, with the result of his growing unwillingness to accord to economists that measure of respect which he gives to other groups of scientists whose theoretical results are confirmed by observation when they are applied to the facts. (Ibid.)

Despite Marx's and Keynes's critiques, Say's Law and Walras's Law lived on, and still dominate economic thinking today. The attempts by well-meaning economists like Clower and Leijonhufvud to reconcile Keynes with Walras's Law thus robbed Keynes of a vital component of his argument, making 'Keynesian economics' a severely emasculated version of Keynes's thought. But this was far from the only way in which Keynesian economics became a travesty of Keynes's original vision.

Hamlet without the prince

Rather as the Bible is for many Christians, the *General Theory* is the essential economics reference which few economists have ever read – including the vast majority of those who call themselves Keynesian economists.

There are many reasons for this.

One is that the *General Theory* is a difficult book. There are at least two roots to this difficulty. The good root is that Keynes was so much more insightful than most other economists that the concepts in the *General Theory* are difficult for more ordinary mortals to grasp; the bad root is that, as Keynes himself acknowledged, the book was replete with concepts from the very school of economics which he was hoping to overthrow. As cited previously, in the Preface Keynes observed that

The composition of this book has been for the author a long struggle of escape, and so must the reading of it be for most readers if the author's assault upon them is to be successful – a struggle of escape from habitual modes of thought and expression. The ideas which are here expressed so laboriously are extremely simple and should be obvious. The difficulty lies, not in the new ideas, but in escaping from the old ones, which ramify, for those brought up as most of us have been, into every corner of our minds. (Ibid.: xxiii)

The second and most important reason is this transcendental truth: neoclassical economists don't believe that macroeconomics should exist. The attitude of strong reductionism is so strong in neoclassical economics that the very existence of macroeconomics as an independent field of research within economics was an affront to them. Neoclassical economists could read the *General Theory* and find it incomprehensible, because the concepts they expect – utility-maximizing consumers, profit-maximizing producers, equilibrium and so on – are not the foundations of Keynes's thought.[14]

A final reason for not reading it is laziness: it is much easier to read the 'Reader's Digest' version given in a textbook than it is to slog through the unabridged original. As a result, many economists were inclined to rely upon summaries, rather than reading the original. Keynes obliged by providing his own summary, of just fifteen pages, in 1937.

Keynes and uncertainty The key concept in Keynes's summary was the impact of expectations upon investment, when those expectations were about what might happen in an uncertain future.

Investment is undertaken to augment wealth, and yet the outcome of any investment depends upon economic circumstances in the relatively distant future. Since the future cannot be known, investment is necessarily undertaken on the basis of expectations formed under uncertainty. Keynes was at pains to distinguish the concept of uncertainty from the simpler concept of risk.

Risk occurs when some future event can only be one of a number of already known alternatives, and when there is a known history of previous outcomes which enables us to assign a reliable and definite probability to each possible outcome. A dice roll is an example of risk. The dice can land only on one of six sides, and therefore only one of six numbers will turn up. If they are fair dice, each number has a 1 in 6 chance of turning up. The theory of probability can then be used to help predict the chances of various patterns of numbers occurring in future rolls of the dice.

Uncertainty is fundamentally different, and it has proved to be a difficult concept for economists before and after Keynes to grasp. Keynes gave several examples. Neither roulette, nor life expectancy, nor even the weather qualified. Instead, uncertainty referred to such things as the chance that war might break out (this was in 1937, not long before Chamberlain's 'peace in our time' deal with Hitler), the rate of interest twenty years in the future, or when some invention would become obsolete. I gave a more positive and I hope evocative example of uncertainty in Chapter 8 on page 161.

Probability theory cannot be used to help guide us in these circumstances because there is no prior history to go on, and because the outcomes are not constrained to any known finite set of possibilities. As Keynes put it, 'About these matters there is no scientific basis on which to form any calculable probability whatever. We simply do not know' (Keynes 1937: 214).

14 Though because Keynes hadn't completely escaped from the neoclassical way of thinking, those concepts do occasionally occur in the *General Theory*, in a very muddled way – as the lengthy quote from the *General Theory* illustrates.

Faced with this uncertainty, and yet compelled to act in spite of it, we develop conventions to help us cope. In marked contrast to his clumsy critique of Say's Law in the *General Theory*, Keynes, in explaining these conventions, was at his eloquent best:

> How do we manage in such circumstances to behave in a manner which saves our faces as rational, economic men? We have devised for the purpose a variety of techniques, of which much the most important are the three following:
>
> 1 We assume that the present is a much more serviceable guide to the future than a candid examination of past experience would show it to have been hitherto. In other words we largely ignore the prospect of future changes about the actual character of which we know nothing.
> 2 We assume that the existing state of opinion as expressed in prices and the character of existing output is based on a correct summing up of future prospects, so that we can accept it as such unless and until some-thing new and relevant comes into the picture.
> 3 Knowing that our own individual judgment is worthless, we endeavor to fall back on the judgment of the rest of the world which is perhaps better informed. That is, we endeavor to conform with the behavior of the majority or the average. The psychology of a society of individuals each of whom is endeavoring to copy the others leads to what we may strictly term a conventional judgment. (Ibid.: 214)

Keynes notes that expectations formed in this manner are certain to be disappointed, but there is no other way in which to form them. Expecta-tions are therefore bound to be fragile, since future circumstances almost inevitably turn out to be different from what we expected. This volatility in expectations will mean sudden shifts in investor (and speculator) sentiment, which will suddenly change the values placed on assets, to the detriment of anyone whose assets are held in non-liquid form.

As a consequence, money plays an essential role in a market economy because of its instant liquidity. The extent to which we desire to hold our wealth in the form of non-income-earning money, rather than income-earning but illiquid assets, 'is a barometer of the degree of our distrust of our own calculations and conventions concerning the future' (ibid.: 216).

This 'liquidity preference,' Keynes argued, determines the rate of interest: the less we trust our fragile expectations of the future, the higher the rate of interest has to be to entice us to sacrifice unprofitable but safe cash for potentially profitable but volatile assets.

In assets themselves investors face two broad alternatives: lending money at the prevailing rate of interest (effectively purchasing bonds), or buying shares which confer part-ownership of capital assets. Both these activities are effectively 'placement,' as Blatt (1983) put it, rather than investment proper, however, which is the building of new capital assets (Boyd and Blatt 1988).[15]

New capital assets are produced not for their own sake, but in expectation of profits, and profits will come in the form of capital gain if their market prices (the result of placement activity) exceed their costs of construction. Physical investment is, therefore, also extremely volatile because 'it depends on two sets of judgments about the future, neither of which rests on an adequate or secure foundation – on the propensity to hoard [the flip side of liquidity preference] and on opinions of the future yield of capital-assets' (Keynes 1937: 218). These two factors, which play a key role in determining how much investment takes place, are likely to feed upon and destabilize each other: if we become more pessimistic about the future prospects of investments, we are likely to want to hoard more, not less.

Having explained why expectations are so important in economic practice and economic theory, why uncertainty makes expectations so fragile and volatile, and how these factors affect the rate of interest and the level of investment, Keynes returned once more to an attack on Say's Law. He divided expenditure into consumption – which is relatively stable – and investment – which is highly volatile – and emphasized that investment is the key determinant of the level and rate of change of output (and hence employment). His theory was, therefore, a theory 'of why output and employment are so liable to fluctuation' (ibid.: 221). In contrast to the unintelligible summary in the *General Theory* itself, Keynes gave a relatively pithy summary in which expectations, investment and uncertainty had pivotal roles:

> The theory can be summed up by saying that, given the psychology of the public, the level of output and employment as a whole depends on the amount of investment. I put it in this way, not because this is the only factor on which aggregate output depends, but because it is usual in a complex system to regard as the causa causans that factor which is most prone to sudden and wide fluctuation.
>
> More comprehensively, aggregate output depends on the propensity to hoard, on the policy of the monetary authority as it affects the quantity of money, on the state of confidence concerning the prospective yield of capital-assets, on the propensity to spend and on the social factors which influence the level of the money-wage. But of these several factors it is those which determine the rate of investment which are most unreliable, since it is they which are influenced by our views of the future about which we know so little. (Ibid.: 221; emphasis added)

Keynes peppered this paper with observations about how conventional economics ignored the issue of uncertainty, and how expectations are formed

---

15 Blatt also provides an excellent mathematical treatment of investment under uncertainty – see Chapters 12 and 13 respectively of Blatt (1983) and Boyd and Blatt (1988).

under uncertainty, by simply assuming the problem away: 'I accuse the classical economic theory of being itself one of these pretty, polite techniques which tries to deal with the present by abstracting from the fact that we know very little about the future' (ibid.: 215).

Finally, in a departure from the *General Theory* of just a year earlier, Keynes criticized the concept of the 'marginal efficiency of capital' – the ratio of the yield of newly produced capital assets to their price. Whereas he used this concept extensively in the *General Theory*, here he argued that it is indeterminate, since the price of capital assets is so volatile, and there will be a different 'marginal efficiency of capital' for every different level of asset prices. Rather than being a determinant of investment, the 'marginal efficiency of capital' might simply be a by-product of the level of investment and current expectations.

These are all difficult concepts, especially for economists who were bred in the neoclassical tradition in which 'at any given time facts and expectations were assumed to be given in a definite and calculable form; and risks, of which, though admitted, not much notice was taken, were supposed to be capable of an exact actuarial computation' (ibid.: 213).

But if Keynes had truly unleashed a revolution in economic thought, then economists should have attempted to get their minds around these difficult concepts, and fought to escape from the 'habitual modes of thought and expression' which had gripped them prior to the calamity of the Great Depression.

Did economists do so? Some did, but the majority did not – and for that reason the profession bifurcated into two camps: a minority which swore fealty to Keynes's revolutionary vision (who generally call themselves 'post-Keynesian'), and a majority which paid lip-service to some of Keynes's words, but which rapidly fell back into old, familiar ways. These economists ignored Keynes's *General Theory*, and even his pithy summary, instead clutching at another alleged summary by one J. R. Hicks.

Slimming Keynes down to size: the IS-LM model Hicks's 'Mr. Keynes and the Classics' purported to be a book review of the *General Theory*. Hicks began by disputing that neoclassical economists held quite the views Keynes alleged that they held, and therefore tried to construct a more typical classical theory 'in a form similar to that in which Mr. Keynes sets out his own theory [...] Thus I assume that I am dealing with a short period in which the quantity of physical equipment of all kinds available can be taken as fixed' (Hicks 1937: 148).

Was this really the manner in which Keynes set out his own theory? Not according to Keynes, who criticized 'the classics' (by which he meant what we today call neoclassical economists) for working with a model in which 'the amount of factors employed was given' (Keynes 1937: 212). Nonetheless,

Hicks continued. He summarized the 'typical Classical theory' in three equations, which argued that:

- the amount of money determined total output (output was some constant times the money stock);
- the rate of interest determined the level of investment; and
- the rate of interest determined the level of savings (and savings equaled investment).[16]

The first equation determines total output and total employment,[17] while the second two simply determine how much of output is devoted to investment, and how much to current consumption. If the savings rate increases, then so does investment. Increasing money wages 'will necessarily diminish employment and raise real wages' (Hicks 1937), while the obverse policy – cutting money wages – will necessarily increase employment and reduce the real wage. Decreasing the money supply directly decreases income and employment, and is the main explanation for economic downturns (an argument which Milton Friedman later revived).

Clearly, Keynes's theory was substantially different from this. But how did Hicks summarize Keynes? In three more equations, where:

- the demand for money depends upon the rate of interest (in place of the 'classical' fixed relationship between money and output);
- investment is a function of the rate of interest; and
- savings is a function of income.

Hello? What happened to uncertainty, expectations, liquidity preference determining the rate of interest, speculative capital asset prices, and so on? They are nowhere to be seen. Sometime later, Hyman Minsky commented that 'Keynes without uncertainty is rather like Hamlet without the Prince' (Minsky 1975: 75), but this is what Hicks served up as Keynes. Even the *Reader's Digest* would draw the line at this level of abridging, but this was not the end of Hicks's rephrasing of Keynes's Shakespearean sonnets into schoolyard doggerel.

He next argued that 'Keynes's' first equation omitted the impact of income on demand for money. This was the traditional 'transactions demand for money' argument that some level of money was needed to finance everyday transactions, so that an increase in income would generate an increase in the demand for money. To be truly general, said Hicks, the 'general theory' should include the impact of income on the demand for money, as well as the impact of the rate of interest.

16 Hicks also had savings depending upon the level of output, but output was already determined by the first equation and therefore 'we do not need to bother about inserting Income here unless we choose' (Hicks 1937).

17 Total employment is the sum of the number of workers needed to produce investment output and the number needed to produce consumption output, so if labour productivities differ between the two sectors then the breakdown has to be known before total employment is determined.

Keynes had omitted discussion of the transactions demand for money because this demand was relatively stable, and therefore less important than the more important demand set by liquidity preference. But Hicks believed that 'however much stress we lay upon the "speculative motive," the "transactions motive" must always come in as well' (Hicks 1937: 153). So he proposed a revised set of equations in which the demand for money depends upon two variables – the rate of interest and the level of income – though not, as Keynes had it, on 'the degree of our distrust of our own calculations and conventions concerning the future' (Keynes 1937: 216).

With this revision, Keynes, who was at such pains to distinguish himself from his predecessors – primarily though not exclusively on the basis of the importance he attached to uncertainty and expectations – is pushed back into the camp from which he desired to escape. As Hicks put it: 'With this revision, Mr. Keynes takes a big step back to Marshallian orthodoxy, and his theory becomes hard to distinguish from the revised and qualified Marshallian theories, which, as we have seen, are not new. Is there really any difference between them, or is the whole thing a sham fight? Let us have recourse to a diagram' (Hicks 1937: 153).

Hicks's diagram explains why his rendition of Keynes was so readily accepted by economists, while Keynes's own summary was ignored (see Figure 10.1). It was the old familiar totem of two intersecting curves, though now relabeled to reflect its somewhat different derivation: in place of 'S' and 'D' for supply and demand, we now had 'IS' and 'LM.' The 'Totem of the Micro,' as Leijonhufvud satirized the supply and demand diagrams of Marshallian microeconomics, now had a bigger sibling for macroeconomics – though it was not derived in a way that microeconomists would accept, nor did it reach conclusions about the macro economy with which they would agree, as we shall see later.

The downward-sloping curve, the equivalent of the microeconomic demand curve, was derived from the investment and savings relations in Hicks's model. The upward-sloping curve, the equivalent of the microeconomic supply curve,

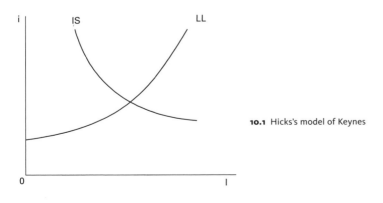

10.1 Hicks's model of Keynes

was derived from the money demand relation (on the assumption that the money supply was controlled by the monetary authorities, and was therefore determined outside the model).

The IS curve showed all those combinations of the rate of interest (i) and the level of income (I) which yielded equilibrium in the goods market. The LL curve (which economists today call the LM curve) showed all those combinations of the rate of interest and the level of income which gave equilibrium in the money market.

§ 60 and 61

Here, at last, in comparison to the strange concepts of Keynes, economists were back on familiar ground. As Hicks put it:

> Income and the rate of interest are now determined together at P, the point
> of intersection of the curves LL and IS. They are determined together;
> just as price and output are determined together in the modern theory of
> demand and supply. Indeed, Mr. Keynes's innovation is closely parallel, in
> this respect, to the innovation of the marginalists. (Ibid.)

One problem with this 'general theory,' however, was that many of Keynes's conclusions could not be derived from it – something which would not have surprised Keynes a great deal, since this model omitted his key concepts of uncertainty and expectations. But Hicks had an apparent dilemma:

> But if this is the real 'General Theory,' how does Mr. Keynes come to
> make his remarks about an increase in the inducement to invest not raising
> the rate of interest? It would appear from our diagram that a rise in the
> marginal-efficiency-of-capital schedule must raise the curve IS; and, there-
> fore, although it will raise income and employment, it will also raise the rate
> of interest. (Ibid.: 154)

To Keynes, the reason why an increased desire to invest would not neces-sarily raise the rate of interest is because the latter was determined by liquidity preference, which 'is a barometer of the degree of our distrust of our own calculations and conventions concerning the future.' In a depressed economy, an increase in investment could well reduce the 'degree of distrust,' leading to a fall in the rate of interest rather than a rise. But with Hicks's picture of Keynes shorn of uncertainty, conventions and expectations, there were no such mechanisms to draw upon. Fortunately, Hicks's model provided a simple and far more conventional solution: simply bend the curves:

> This brings us to what, from many points of view, is the most important
> thing in Mr. Keynes's book. It is not only possible to show that a given
> supply of money determines a certain relation between Income and inter-
> est (which we have expressed by the curve LL); it is also possible to say
> something about the shape of the curve. It will probably tend to be nearly
> horizontal on the left, and nearly vertical on the right. This is because there

is (1) some minimum below which the rate of interest is unlikely to go, and (though Mr. Keynes does not stress this) there is (2) a maximum to the level of income which can possibly be financed with a given amount of money. If we like we can think of the curve as approaching these limits asymptotically. (Ibid.)

This 'liquidity trap' enabled Hicks to provide an explanation for the Great Depression, and simultaneously reconcile Keynes with 'the Classics.' Keynes was consigned to one end of the LM curve, where the liquidity trap applied, and 'the Classics' to the other, where full employment was the rule (see Figure 4). In the 'classical' range of the LM curve, conventional economics reigned supreme: there was a maximal, full employment level of income, where any attempts to increase output would simply cause a rising interest rate (or inflation, in extensions of the IS-LM model). In the 'Keynesian' region, monetary policy (which moved the LM curve) was ineffective, because the LM curve was effectively horizontal, but fiscal policy (which moved the IS curve) could generate greater output – and hence employment – without increasing interest rates. A higher level of government expenditure could shift the IS curve to the right, thus moving the point of intersection of the IS and LM curves to the right and raising the equilibrium level of output. §62

Hicks put the position pithily. In the 'Keynesian region' of his model, a depression can ensue because traditional monetary policy is ineffective – but Keynes's prescription of fiscal policy can save the day: 'So the General Theory of Employment is the economics of Depression' (ibid.: 155).

Hicks next proposed that, for reasons of mathematical elegance rather than economic relevance, all three variables (demand for money, investment and savings) should be made functions of both income and the rate of interest (though not uncertainty or expectations):

> In order to elucidate the relation between Mr. Keynes and the 'Classics,' we have invented a little apparatus. It does not appear that we have exhausted the uses of that apparatus, so let us conclude by giving it a little run on its own.
>
> With that apparatus at our disposal, we are no longer obliged to make certain simplifications which Mr. Keynes makes in his exposition. We can reinsert the missing i in the third equation, and allow for any possible effect of the rate of interest upon saving; and, what is much more important, we can call in question the sole dependence of investment upon the rate of interest, which looks rather suspicious in the second equation. Mathematical elegance would suggest that we ought to have I and i in all three equations, if the theory is to be really General. (Ibid.: 156)

Economists, having been threatened by Keynes with the need to completely retrain themselves, could now engage in their favorite game of tobogganing up and down one curve, moving another to the left or right, just as they did in microeconomics. It is little wonder that this Hicksian IS-LM model was adopted as the basis for 'Keynesian' economics, and equally little wonder that, many years later, macroeconomics was converted to a subset of microeconomics.

The true origins of IS-LM Though 'cutting-edge' economic analysis has left Hicks's model behind, most macroeconomists still think in IS-LM terms, and this model is still the common fodder served up to undergraduate students as Keynesian economics. It therefore still has pedagogic and disciplinary relevance. So the question arises: from where did this model emanate? It clearly was not derived from Keynes's *General Theory*, apart from the adoption of some of Keynes's terminology. The mystery of its origins was finally solved by one Sir John Hicks – an older, be-nighted and somewhat wiser J. R. Hicks.

ISLM: an apology Hicks's detective work was published in a paper entitled 'IS-LM: an explanation,'[18] but in many ways it was an apology. Published in the non-orthodox *Journal of Post Keynesian Economics* in 1980, the paper's opening sentence was: 'The IS-LM diagram, which is widely, though not universally, accepted as a convenient synopsis of Keynesian theory, is a thing for which I cannot deny that I have some responsibility' (Hicks 1981: 141).

Even after this rueful opening, Hicks clung to a very Walrasian vision of Keynes, and elsewhere he described the IS-LM diagram as 'a product of my Walrasianism' (Hicks 1979: 990). But he conceded that his rendition had erroneously omitted any discussion of uncertainty or expectations. His explanation as to how he could have missed so fundamental an aspect of Keynes's thought was that, shortly before the *General Theory* was published, he had published a paper which, he believed, had strong similarities to Keynes's argument (Hicks 1935).[19] What he then published as a review of Keynes was actually a restatement of his own model, using some of Keynes's terminology.

Hicks saw two key problems in cross-dressing as Keynes. The first was that his model was 'a flexprice model [...] while in Keynes's the level of money wages (at least) was exogenously determined' (Hicks 1981: 141);[20] the second 'more fundamental' problem was that Hicks's model used a period of a single week, while Keynes used 'a "short-period," a term with

18 Another paper in a mainstream journal makes some similar concessions (Hicks 1979).

19 Only Hicks could see similarities between Keynes's work and this bizarre model of a one-commodity economy (bread) which had a market in which prices were set on one day (Monday) that then applied for the remainder of the week, and in which there was no model of how the bakery that made the bread was actually manufactured.

20 This is false, as a simple check of the table of contents of the *General Theory* can confirm: Chapter 19 is entitled 'Changes in money-wages.' In it, Keynes concludes that flexible wages would not eliminate the prospect of deficient aggregate demand.

connotations derived from Marshall; we shall not go far wrong if we think of it as a year' (Hicks 1980).

Discussing the second problem, Hicks argued that the difference in period length had a drastic impact upon the relevance of expectations. With a time period of just a week, it is not unreasonable to keep expectations constant – and therefore to ignore them. But keeping expectations constant over a year in an IS-LM model does not make sense, because 'for the purpose of generating an LM curve, which is to represent liquidity preference, it will not do without amendment. For there is no sense in liquidity, unless expectations are uncertain' (Hicks 1981: 152).

This was precisely the point Keynes himself made, in ironic form, in 1937:

> Money [...] is a store of wealth. So we are told, without a smile on the face.
> But in the world of the classical economy, what an insane use to which to
> put it! For it is a recognized characteristic of money as a store of wealth that
> it is barren; whereas practically every other form of storing wealth yields
> some interest or profit. Why should anyone outside a lunatic asylum wish to
> use money as a store of wealth?
>
> Because, partly on reasonable and partly on instinctive grounds, our
> desire to hold money as a store of wealth is a barometer of the degree of
> our distrust of our own calculations and conventions concerning the future
> [...] The possession of actual money lulls our disquietude; and the premium
> which we require to make us part with money is the measure of the degree
> of our disquietude. (Keynes 1937: 215–16)

Thus, without uncertain expectations, there is no sense in liquidity preference, and Hicks cannot justify the LM half of his IS-LM model. But with uncertain expectations, there is no sense in equilibrium analysis either, since equilibrium can be maintained only if expectations are continually being fulfilled. Hicks concluded that the equilibrium/constant expectations framework of the IS-LM model was theoretically unsound, and practically irrelevant to the problems of the macroeconomy:

> I accordingly conclude that the only way in which IS-LM analysis usefully
> survives – as anything more than a classroom gadget, to be superseded,
> later on, by something better – is in application to a particular kind of
> causal analysis, where the use of equilibrium methods, even a drastic use of
> equilibrium methods, is not inappropriate [...]
>
> When one turns to questions of policy, looking towards the future instead
> of the past, the use of equilibrium methods is still more suspect. For one
> cannot prescribe policy without considering at least the possibility that policy
> may be changed. There can be no change of policy if everything is to go on
> as expected – if the economy is to remain in what (however approximately)
> may be regarded as its existing equilibrium. (Hicks 1981)

There is one more, crucial weakness in Hicks's model that he touched upon but did not consider properly, and which would invalidate his model even if an LM curve could be derived: his use of 'Walras's Law' to reduce the number of markets in the model from three to two: 'Keynes had three elements in his theory: the marginal efficiency of capital, the consumption function, and liquidity preference. The market for goods, the market for bonds, and the market for money [...]' (ibid.: 142).

He then explained that he dropped the second of these markets by applying Walras's Law: 'One did not have to bother about the market for "loanable funds," since it appeared, on the Walras analogy, that if these two "markets" were in equilibrium, the third must be also. So I concluded that the intersection of IS and LM determined the equilibrium of the system as a whole' (ibid.: 142).

Next he noted that there was in fact one other market that should be part of the model: the labor market – which was, of course, an integral part of Keynes's analysis in the *General Theory* itself: 'In strictness, we now need four markets, since labor and goods will have to be distinguished [...]' (ibid.: 142–3).

He went on to argue that its omission was justified, but here his neoclassical fixation with equilibrium analysis led him astray, because – ignoring for the moment that Walras's Law is false in a capitalist economy – Walras's Law allows you to drop one market only when all other markets are in equilibrium.[21] In the IS-LM model, this applies only where the two curves cross: where the combination of GDP and the interest rate is such that both the goods market (the IS curve) and the money market (the LM curve) are in equilibrium. Then, in a three-market model – goods, money, and labor – if the money and goods markets are in equilibrium, then so too must be the labor market.

However, if the combination of the interest rate and the GDP are such that one of these two markets is out of equilibrium, then so too must be the labor market. Therefore only in equilibrium can the labor market be ignored. At any other location, the labor market must also be considered – and therefore the IS-LM model is incomplete. Everywhere except at the point of intersection of IS and LM, it needs to be the IS-LM-'LSLD' model (where 'LS' and 'LD' refer to labor supply and labor demand respectively).

Furthermore, since at anywhere except the intersection of IS and LM at least one of those two markets is in disequilibrium, the third, ignored 'LSLD' market must also be in disequilibrium: wages must be higher (or lower) than the level that will clear the labor market. Therefore price-setting in this market – and the other one that is in disequilibrium – must be a dynamic, disequilibrium process, not a simple calculation of the equilibrium

---

21 Walras's Law is invalid in a growing economy, as I explained earlier. This section considers when it can't be applied to eliminate one market from the analysis even in the no-growth realm to which it does apply.

wage. Even Hicks's emasculated version of Keynes's macroeconomics must employ dynamic, disequilibrium analysis, in contrast to the comparative static mode in which the IS-LM model is normally applied.

This IS-LM model is thus invalid, even on its own terms, if it is pushed anywhere beyond working out what rate of interest and GDP combination represent equilibrium in the economy. To be used as a model of economic dynamics, it must become a three-equation model, and these must all be disequilibrium equations. This is not how IS-LM is taught, or used.[22]

But in its heyday, the IS-LM model gave economists something they had never really had previously: a framework on which to build models that were not merely drawings, or symbolic equations, but numerical equations that they could use to predict the future course of the economy.

The age of large-scale econometric models

Hicks's model and the later development of the 'Aggregate Supply-Aggregate Demand' model set off the heyday of attempts by economists to turn these models into numerical simulations of the economy, using the newly developed tool of the computer.

With a careful choice of parameter values, these models could generate a reasonable fit between the inputs ('exogenous variables') and the variables like future output and employment levels ('endogenous variables'). If a model's fit to the data wasn't too good, it could be improved by fine-tuning the parameters, or adding more variables, and as a result most of these models 'grew like Topsy.' One of the earliest such model, developed by Lawrence Klein (Klein 1950; Renfro 2009), had just six equations; eventually models with thousands of equations were developed – and many are still in use.

There were five aspects of these models that made them easy to simulate, but which also made them fundamentally unsuited for economic analysis.

First, the models were frequently linear – variables in the equations were multiplied by constants, and added together to produce predictions for other variables – in contrast to the nonlinear models outlined in Chapter 9, so they couldn't develop interactions between variables that caused cyclical behavior, let alone complex behavior as in Lorenz's weather model.

Secondly, even when nonlinearities existed – when employment was divided by population to calculate an employment rate, for example, or when logarithms of variables were used rather than the raw variables – the model was solved as if these nonlinearities did not affect the system's tendency towards equilibrium (McCullough and Renfro 2000). Simulations therefore worked out what the equilibrium of the model would be, and their predictions had

---

22 Many neoclassical macroeconomic models to this day are based on IS-LM and have time-based equations – including one for the price level – in them that appear superficially dynamic. However, most of these models are solved by assuming that the price level (and everything else) converges to a long-run equilibrium over the medium term, which is a travesty of proper dynamic modeling.

the economy converging to this point over time (see, for example, Renfro 2009: 46).[23]

Thirdly, the models effectively assumed that the economy's dynamics involved movements from one equilibrium position to another, with movement being caused by 'exogenous shocks' – events external to the economy (such as damaging floods or unexpected bountiful harvests). This continued the convention in econometrics of seeing fluctuations in the economy having non-economic causes: 'The majority of the economic oscillations which we encounter [...] seem to be explained by the fact that certain exterior impulses hit the economic system and thereby initiate more or less regular oscillations' (Frisch 1933: 171 [1]).[24] Even though this argument was made during the Great Depression, where no 'external impulse' could be blamed for the crisis, and when economists like Schumpeter, Keynes and Fisher were arguing that cycles and possibly breakdowns were endemic to capitalism, this belief became the standard view in numerical simulations of the economy.[25]

Fourthly, they were based on a neoclassical vision of the economy, and therefore omitted the credit and debt variables that we now know are crucial to macroeconomics.

Finally, they omitted any consideration of how expectations are formed under pervasive uncertainty, a key aspect of Keynes's vision of the macroeconomy that was lacking in the parent IS-LM model.

There were therefore many good grounds on which these models could have been criticized. However, the one focused on by economists was something entirely different: they objected to these numerical models simply because, as with Hicks's stylized IS-LM model from which they were derived, they argued that there could be involuntary unemployment, and that the level of unemployment could be affected by government demand-management policies – conclusions which neoclassical economists mistakenly believed contradicted neoclassical microeconomics.

23 Mathematicians and system dynamics practitioners would find the first of these references very strange. It gives a detailed discussion of how to solve a nonlinear model where the solution involves approximating a matrix inversion – which can only derive the equilibrium for a model – yet makes no mention of standard numerical techniques for simulating systems of differential equations (like the Runge-Kutta or Levenberg-Marquardt methods), which can return the actual time path of a model rather than simply its equilibrium. It's as if economists live in a parallel universe where techniques that are commonplace in real sciences haven't been invented yet.

24 The number in square brackets refers to the page numbers of the online reprint of Frisch's paper, available at www.frisch.uio.no/Frisch_Website/PPIP.pdf.

25 As so often happens in economics, the 'founding father' responsible for this view also contemplated the alternative possibility, that fluctuations were endogenous to the economy, as Schumpeter argued at the time. However, since this was more difficult to model, he left it for others to do later: 'The idea of erratic shocks represents one very essential aspect of the impulse problem in economic cycle analysis, but probably it does not contain the whole explanation [...] In mathematical language one could perhaps say that one introduces here the idea of an auto-maintained oscillation [...] It would be possible to put the functioning of this whole instrument into equations under more or less simplified assumptions about the construction and functioning of the valve, etc. I even think this will be a useful task for a further analysis of economic oscillations, but I do not intend to take up this mathematical formulation here.' (Frisch 1933: 33–5). Unfortunately, his successors stuck with his easier-to-model exogenous shocks analogy, leaving his sensible suggestion to model endogenous fluctuations to wither on the vine.

From IS-LM to the representative agent

Hicks's critical epiphany about the IS-LM model came far too late to stop the revisionist juggernaut he had set in motion by reinterpreting Keynes as a Walrasian back in 1937. His recantation in 1981 was generally ignored by economists, who – if they were aware of it at all – would have been more inclined to put his views down to approaching senility than to any blinding logical revelation. In any case, the gradual demolition of IS-LM by economists was substantially advanced by 1980.

This demolition began back in the 1950s with the 'strong reductionist' critique that Hicks's 'Keynesian' model did not have good microeconomic foundations, by which neoclassical economists meant that it was not possible to derive results that IS-LM could generate – such as the economy settling into a less than full-employment equilibrium – from standard microeconomics.

Of course, in making this critique they were profoundly ignorant of the aggregation errors in the theory itself that I have outlined in preceding chapters. Properly understood, it is possible to derive results like involuntary unemployment from a neoclassical model. A properly derived market demand curve can have any shape at all (Chapter 3), leading to a market marginal revenue curve that would therefore intersect the constant or falling marginal cost curve (Chapters 4 and 5) in its market in multiple locations. Complexities in distribution and production covered in Chapters 6 and 7 would complicate the outcome even further, while price-setting would have to be done in dynamic disequilibrium, raising the specter of nonlinear dynamics and chaos (Chapter 9).

A macroeconomic model derived properly from neoclassical foundations would probably be more chaotic than the real world itself, even without introducing the complications the neoclassical model omits by improperly excluding money and debt from its analysis.[26]

However, all this was unknown to the neoclassicals, who continually chipped away at the IS-LM model and its cousin the AS-AD model ('Aggregate Supply-Aggregate Demand'), and even to the many defenders of these models. Non-orthodox economists, who were aware of these issues, watched on in bemused horror as a model that was already a bastardization of Keynes's analysis[27] was further emasculated over time. The extent to which this was an agenda driven by ignorance rather than wisdom can be seen in the memoir of Nobel laureate Robert Lucas, one of the key actors in this process, when he delivered the keynote address to the 2003 History of Political Economy conference.

He began by asserting stridently that he was once a Keynesian:

26 There's at least one PhD in producing such a simulation model – I hope some brave student takes that task on one day (brave because it would be a difficult task that would make him highly unpopular with neoclassical economists).

27 Joan Robinson, who played a leading role in the Cambridge controversies outlined in Chapter 8, coined the term 'Bastard Keynesianism' to describe the neoclassical interpretation of Keynes (Robinson 1981).

My credentials? Was I a Keynesian myself? Absolutely. And does my Chicago training disqualify me for that? No, not at all [...] Our Keynesian credentials, if we wanted to claim them, were as good as could be obtained in any graduate school in the country in 1963.

Then he continued:

I thought when I was trying to prepare some notes for this talk that people attending the conference might be arguing about Axel Leijonhufvud's thesis that IS-LM was a distortion of Keynes, but I didn't really hear any of this in the discussions this afternoon. So I'm going to think about IS-LM and Keynesian economics as being synonyms.

I remember when Leijonhufvud's book came out and I asked my colleague Gary Becker if he thought Hicks had got the *General Theory* right with his IS-LM diagram. Gary said, 'Well, I don't know, but I hope he did, because if it wasn't for Hicks I never would have made any sense out of that damn book.' That's kind of the way I feel, too, so I'm hoping Hicks got it right. (Lucas 2004: 13–14; emphases added)

This was over twenty years after Hicks himself said that he had got it wrong! And Lucas had the hide to call himself a Keynesian, when he admits that 'if it wasn't for Hicks,' both he and fellow Nobel laureate Gary Becker 'never would have made any sense out of that damn book'? This is one reason I bridle when I hear the comment that 'Keynesian economics has failed'; what most self-described Keynesians in economics mean by the word 'Keynesian' is the economics of Hicks and Samuelson, not Keynes.

Starting from the false belief that Hicks had accurately summarized Keynes, Lucas then conformed to the unfortunate rule within economics, that poor scholarship is built upon poor scholarship. He played a crucial role in undermining IS-LM analysis itself in the early 1970s, first with the development of 'rational expectations macroeconomics' and then with what became known as 'the Lucas critique' – an attack on using numerical macroeconomic models as a guide to policy. These developments led to the final overthrow of any aspect of Hicksian, let alone 'Keynesian,' thought from mainstream macroeconomics. In the ultimate fulfillment of the program of strong reductionism, macroeconomics was reduced to no more than applied microeconomics – and based on the premise that all the concepts that I have shown to be false in the preceding chapters were instead true.

Lucas's assault on IS-LM[28] With Hicks's IS-LM model accepted as providing a mathematical expression of Keynes, Lucas (Lucas 1972) focused on models that economists had constructed using Hicks's model as a foundation, which

---

28 Lucas was far from the only exponent of this microeconomic takeover of macroeconomics – others who made a significant contribution to the microeconomic hatchet job on macroeconomics include Muth, Wallace, Kydland, Prescott, Sargent, Rapping, and latterly Smets and Woodford.

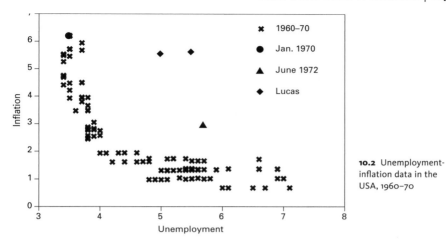

10.2 Unemployment-inflation data in the USA, 1960–70

concluded that macroeconomic policy could alter the level of economic activity. He began by conceding that most economists believed that the 'Phillips Curve' accurately described the 'trade-off' society faced between inflation and unemployment. He also conceded that the statistical evidence certainly showed a negative relationship between inflation and unemployment: when: 'It is an observed fact that, in U.S. time series, inflation rates and unemployment are negatively correlated' (ibid.: 50).

The 'Phillips Curve trade-off' interpretation of these statistics turned an empirical regularity into a guide for policy. Since the statistics implied that unemployment and inflation moved in opposite directions, it seemed that the government could choose the level of employment it wanted by manipulating aggregate demand (so long as it was willing to tolerate the inflation rate that went with it). This 'rule of thumb' policy conclusion was also consistent with the results of the large-scale econometric models derived from Hicks's IS-LM model.

However, Lucas put himself in the skeptics' camp, and argued instead in favor of what he called the 'Natural Rate Hypothesis,' that there was no such trade-off – instead, that the economy had a natural rate of employment towards which it tended, and any attempt to increase employment above this rate would simply increase the rate of inflation, without altering employment. He defined the 'Natural Rate Hypothesis' as: 'the hypothesis that different time paths of the general price level will be associated with time paths of real output that do not differ on average' (ibid.: 50).

This, in a convoluted way, asserted the pre-Great Depression neoclassical belief that the economy tended toward an equilibrium in which relative prices were stable, and any attempt to increase the number of people employed would simply cause inflation. Lucas's problem, in asserting this belief, was the evidence. He presented this paper before the 'stagflation' of the 1970s, when inflation and unemployment both rose at the same time, and the evidence of the period from 1960 to 1970 showed a clear trade-off between inflation and unemployment – see Figure 10.2.

Though the inflation-unemployment data at the precise date at which he spoke had a much higher unemployment level than had been experienced at a comparable rate of inflation in the 1960s, shortly after he spoke (in October 1970) the inflation rate plunged in an apparent lagged response to the rise in unemployment during the 1969–70 recession.

§63

How then to justify skepticism about what seemed an obvious reality? He argued that the 'Phillips Curve' was simply an artifact of how 'agents form and respond to price and wage expectations,' and that attempting to exploit this curve for policy reasons would destroy the apparent trade-off, because agents would change their expectations: 'The main source of this skepticism is the notion that the observed Phillips curve results from the way agents form and respond to price and wage expectations, and that attempts to move along the curve to increase output may be frustrated by changes in expectations that shift the curve' (ibid.: 50).

Lucas thus accepted the empirical evidence of the negative relationship between inflation and unemployment – in that a higher level of inflation was statistically correlated with a lower level of unemployment. However, he argued that this could not be used as a policy tool, alleging that attempts to drive unemployment down by driving inflation up would simply result in higher inflation at the same rate of unemployment.

This was not an entirely new argument – Friedman had made a similar assertion two years earlier (Friedman 1968), using what became known as 'Adaptive Expectations' (Friedman 1971: 331). But Milton's model wasn't good enough for Lucas – though not for the reasons you might expect.

Helicopter Milton Ben Bernanke copped the nickname 'Helicopter Ben' for his observation that a deflation could always be reversed by the government 'printing money':

> the U.S. government has a technology, called a printing press, that allows it to produce as many U.S. dollars as it wishes at essentially no cost. By increasing the number of U.S. dollars in circulation under a fiat (that is, paper) money system, a government should always be able to generate increased nominal spending and inflation [...] and sufficient injections of money will ultimately always reverse a deflation. (Bernanke 2002a)

However, the 'Helicopter' part of the nickname alluded not to work by Bernanke, but by his intellectual mentor Milton Friedman, who, more than any other neoclassical, was responsible for the overthrow of the IS-LM model and its replacement by a resurgent neoclassical orthodoxy.

In any sane discipline, Friedman's starting point for his dismantling of the then Keynesian orthodoxy would have been good enough reason to ignore him completely – if not recommend he see a psychiatrist. A key aspect of the neoclassical model is the proposition known as 'money neutrality': that the nominal quantity of money has no effect on the real performance of the macroeconomy, apart from causing inflation. Friedman reasserted that belief, but also clearly stated the condition required for it to operate in reality. The condition was that, if the quantity of money in circulation increased by some factor, then all nominal quantities including the level of debts was also increased by the same factor:

> It is a commonplace of monetary theory that nothing is so unimportant as the quantity of money expressed in terms of the nominal monetary unit – dollars, or pounds, or pesos. Let the unit of account be changed from dollars to cents; that will multiply the quantity of money by 100, but have no other effect. Similarly, *let the number of dollars in existence be multiplied by 100; that, too, will have no other essential effect, provided that all other nominal magnitudes (prices of goods and services, and quantities of other assets and liabilities that are expressed in nominal terms) are also multiplied by 100.* (Friedman 1969: 1; emphases added)

This condition is so clearly not fulfilled in reality that the opposite conclusion therefore applies: since the value of assets and liabilities is not adjusted when inflation occurs, therefore the nominal quantity of money in circulation is important. However, Friedman, who had already given us the 'assumptions don't matter' methodological madness, continued straight on as if it didn't matter that this condition was not fulfilled in reality.

Friedman's next counterfactual assertion was that, left to its own devices, a free market economy with no growth and a constant stock of money would settle into an equilibrium in which supply equaled demand in all markets, and all resources including labor were fully employed (where full employment was defined as supply equaling demand at the equilibrium real wage):[29] 'Let us suppose that these conditions have been in existence long enough for the society to have reached a state of equilibrium. Relative prices are determined by the solution of a system of Walrasian equations' (ibid.: 3).

He then considered what would happen to money prices in such a situation if there was a sudden increase in the money supply: 'Let us suppose now that one day a helicopter flies over this community and drops an additional $1,000 in bills from the sky, which is, of course, hastily collected by members of the community. Let us suppose further that everyone is convinced that this is a unique event which will never be repeated' (ibid.: 4–5).

If you are gobsmacked by this absurd vision of how money is created –

---

29 Of course, an economy without growth hasn't existed, but Friedman extended this belief in the economy tending to full-employment equilibrium over to his model with growth, and he had the same views about the actual economy.

dropped from the air like manna from heaven – brace yourself: ideas even more absurd that this are about to come your way.

Friedman's 'helicopter' is of course a parable for the behavior of a central bank (which is not a market actor) that injects money into the system – as Bernanke has himself done twice already, though during the Great Recession rather than when the economy was in 'a state of equilibrium.'[30] But it is a parable which takes for granted that the money supply is completely under the Fed's control – that it is 'exogenous' in the parlance of economics. In contrast, the empirically derived 'endogenous' theory of money I'll outline in Chapter 14 argues that the money supply is largely outside the Fed's control.

However, with his simplistic model of money creation, Friedman decided that the consequence of doubling the money supply would be that nominal prices would ultimately double. Relative prices and real output would be unaffected in the long run, but – in an important qualification compared to Lucas's later analysis – Friedman conceded that in the interim there could be disturbances to relative prices and the levels of output and employment:

> It is much harder to say anything about the transition. To begin with, some producers may be slow to adjust their prices and may let themselves be induced to produce more for the market at the expense of non-market uses of resources. Others may try to make spending exceed receipts by taking a vacation from production for the market. Hence, measured income at initial nominal prices may either rise or fall during the transition. Similarly, some prices may adjust more rapidly than others, so relative prices and quantities may be affected. There might be overshooting and, as a result, a cyclical adjustment pattern [...]. (Ibid.: 6)

Friedman then extended this 'one-off' thought experiment to a theory of inflation by assuming that this 'helicopter drop' of money becomes a continuous process:

> Let us now complicate our example by supposing that the dropping of money, instead of being a unique, miraculous event, becomes a continuous process, *which, perhaps after a lag, becomes fully anticipated by everyone*. Money rains down from heaven at a rate which produces a steady increase in the quantity of money, let us say, of 10 per cent per year. (Ibid.: 8; emphasis added)

The highlighted phrase in the preceding quote is what Friedman later called 'Adaptive Expectations': people form expectations of what will happen in the future based on experience of what has happened in the recent past. He also considered that there could be disturbances in the short term in this new situation of a permanent 10 percent per annum increase in the

---

30 Now you know where the 'Helicopter Ben' moniker that is applied to Ben Bernanke actually comes from! I would regard this as unfair to Bernanke, were it not for his fawning speech at Friedman's ninetieth birthday, noted later.

money supply: 'If individuals did not respond instantaneously, or if there were frictions, the situation would be different during a transitory period. The state of affairs just described would emerge finally when individuals succeeded in restoring and maintaining initial real balances' (ibid.: 10).

However, in the long run, these disturbances dissipate and the economy settles into a long-run equilibrium where all 'real magnitudes' (relative prices, output, employment) are the same as before, but the absolute price level is rising at 10 percent per annum. This occurs not because markets are in disequilibrium with demand exceeding supply, causing prices to rise, but because of the expectations all agents have formed that prices always rise by 10 percent per annum. It is thus expectations which cause prices to rise, rather than disequilibrium: 'One natural question to ask about this final situation is, "What raises the price level, if at all points markets are cleared and real magnitudes are stable?" The answer is, "Because everyone confidently anticipates that prices will rise"' (ibid.).

This was the basis for Friedman's argument against Keynesian demand-management policies, which attempted to exploit the apparent negative relationship between unemployment and the rate of inflation: though a higher rate of growth of the money supply could in the transition cause employment to rise, ultimately the economy would return to its equilibrium level of employment, but at a higher rate of inflation. This was characterized as the 'short-run Phillips Curve' 'moving outwards' – the temporary trade-off between higher inflation and lower unemployment in the transition involved higher and higher levels of inflation for the same level of unemployment – while the 'long-run Phillips curve' was vertical at the long-run equilibrium level of unemployment.

Though Friedman's model was highly simplistic, his vigorous promotion of his 'monetarist' theories just preceded the outbreak of stagflation during the 1970s, giving an apparent vindication of his position. There did indeed seem to be an outward movement of the negative relationship between unemployment and inflation, while there appeared to be a 'long-run' rate of unemployment the economy kept tending towards, at about a 6 percent rate of unemployment compared to the level of below 4 percent that had been achieved in the 1960s.

§64

Friedman's monetarism thus defeated Keynesian demand management both inside the academic profession, and in public policy, with central banks trying to limit the growth of the money supply in order to reduce the inflation rate.[31] The period of 'stagflation' – rising unemployment and rising

---

31 While inflation did ultimately fall, the policy was nowhere near as easy to implement as Friedman's analysis implied – the Federal Reserve almost always failed to achieve its targets for money growth by large margins, the relationship between monetary aggregated and inflation was far weaker than Friedman implied, and unemployment grew far more than monetarists expected it would. Central banks ultimately abandoned money growth targeting, and moved instead to the 'Taylor Rule' approach of targeting short-term interest rates. See Desai (1981) and Kaldor (1982) for critiques of the monetarist period.

inflation – thus sounded the death-knell for 'Keynesian' economics within the academic profession. However, monetarism's defeat of 'Keynesian' theory wasn't enough for Lucas, since monetarism still implied that the government could alter the level of employment.

'Improving' on Friedman The problem with monetarism, as Lucas saw it, was Friedman's admission that in the short run, a boost to the money supply could have real effects. Lucas began by stating the paradox – for a neoclassical economist – that in neoclassical theory there should be *no* relationship between inflation and employment: changes in aggregate demand caused by changes in the money supply should simply alter the price level while leaving supply unchanged:

> It is natural (to an economist) to view the cyclical correlation between real output and prices as arising from a volatile aggregate demand schedule that traces out a relatively stable, upward-sloping supply curve. This point of departure leads to something of a paradox, *since the absence of money illusion on the part of firms and consumers appears to imply a vertical aggregate supply schedule*, which in turn implies that aggregate demand fluctuations of a purely nominal nature should lead to price fluctuations only. (Lucas 1972: 51; emphasis added)

Lucas's comment about 'money illusion' shows that, though he criticized Friedman, it was because Friedman was not neoclassical enough for him – Friedman's macroeconomics was not sufficiently based upon neoclassical microeconomic theory. Since microeconomics predicted that changing all prices and incomes wouldn't affect the output decision of a single consumer, macroeconomics had to conclude that the aggregate rate of unemployment couldn't be altered by monetary means:

> On the contrary, as soon as Phelps and others made the first serious attempts to rationalize the apparent trade-off in modern theoretical terms, the zero-degree homogeneity of demand and supply functions was re-discovered in this new context (as Friedman predicted it would be) and re-named the 'natural rate hypothesis.' (Lucas 1976: 19)

After discussing models used to explain the perceived inflation–unemployment trade-off based on adaptive expectations, Lucas observed that under Adaptive Expectations, it was possible that actual inflation (which was driven by the actual rate of growth of the money supply at a given time) might differ from expected inflation (which was based on people's experience of past inflation that adjusted 'after a lag' to the current rate of inflation). This in turn would mean that, if actual inflation exceeded expected inflation, then there could be 'unlimited real output gains from a well-chosen inflationary policy. Even a once-and-for-all price increase, while yielding no output expansion in the limit, will induce increased output over the (infinity of) transition periods. Moreover, a sustained inflation will yield a permanently increased level of output' (Lucas 1972: 53).

But herein lay a dilemma: Lucas's logic had revealed that the only way to conclude that there was a natural rate of employment was to assume that expected inflation always equaled actual inflation, which in turn means assuming that people can accurately predict the future.

Obviously Lucas couldn't assume this.

Well, obviously, if he wasn't a neoclassical economist! Because that's precisely what he did assume. His way of stating this was obtuse, but none-theless unmistakable:

> In the preceding section, the hypothesis of adaptive expectations was rejected as a component of the natural rate hypothesis on the grounds that, under some policy [the gap between actual and expected inflation] is non-zero. If the impossibility of a non-zero value [...] is taken as an essential feature of the natural rate theory, *one is led simply to adding the assumption that [the gap between actual and expected inflation] is zero as an additional axiom* [...]. (Ibid.: 54; emphasis added)

Such an 'axiom' is transparently nonsense – something that might have led a sensible person to stop at this point. But instead Lucas immediately moved on to an equivalent way of stating this 'axiom' that wasn't so obvi-ously absurd: 'or to assume that expectations are rational in the sense of Muth' (ibid.).

Thus neoclassical macroeconomics began its descent into madness which, thirty-five years later, left it utterly unprepared for the economic collapse of the Great Recession.

Expectations and rationality Decades before, when the Great Depression also forced economists to consider reality rather than their largely verbal models of equilibrium, Keynes made a similar point to Lucas's, that expectations about the future affect decisions today, and he pilloried the neoclassical theorists of his day for ignoring this.

Keynes welded the role of expectations in economics with uncertainty about the future, and considered how people still manage to make decisions despite uncertainty. Thirty-five years later, Lucas reintroduced expectations into macroeconomics, but with the assumption that people could accurately predict the future and thus eliminate uncertainty – an even more absurd position than that of his pre-Great Depression predecessors, whom Keynes merely accused of 'abstracting from the fact that we know very little about the future.'

It is one of the greatest abuses of language committed by neoclassical economists that a proposition which in any other discipline would be deemed

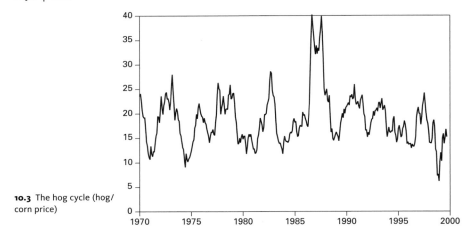

10.3 The hog cycle (hog/corn price)

as insane – that on average, people's expectations about the future are accurate – goes under the name of 'rational expectations' in economics. That the idea could even be countenanced shows the extent to which neo-classical economics is driven by a teleological desire to prove that capitalism is fundamentally stable, rather than by a desire to understand the empirical record of the actual economy.

The paper that initially developed the concept of 'rational expectations' (Muth 1961) applied it to microeconomics, to develop a critique of a simplified theory of price cycles in agricultural markets known as 'the Cobweb model.' Agricultural products like pork were subject to irregular cycles in prices – see Figure 10.3 – and one explanation that microeconomists developed was that time lags in production generated the cycles.

The Cobweb cycle model argued that suppliers would take prices one season as a guide to how many hogs to breed in the next season. When prices were high, many hogs would be raised the subsequent season, which would cause prices to crash the season after; while when prices were low, few hogs would be raised the next season, which would cause prices to rise. Prices thus fluctuated in disequilibrium over time, overshooting and undershooting the equilibrium price.

The Cobweb assumed the existence of standard Marshallian supply and demand curves – something we have debunked in Chapters 3–5 – and also had a hard time explaining the lengthy cycles that could occur, which were measured in multiples of the breeding cycle itself.[32] Seizing on the latter weakness, Muth proposed that farmers' price expectations were not simply that last year's prices would be next year's, but that they would be to some degree informed by experience – a sensible observation in itself. However, he extrapolated from this to the following hypothesis: 'I should like to suggest that expectations, since they are informed predictions of future events,

32 See www.ukagriculture.com/production_cycles/pigs_production_cycle.cfm.

are essentially the same as the predictions of the relevant economic theory' (ibid.: 316).

That is, he assumed that farmers formed their expectations of next year's price by assuming that it would be the equilibrium price as given by the Marshallian model of supply and demand, and that these expectations were correct – they were what would happen because the model itself was accurate: 'The hypothesis can be rephrased a little more precisely as follows: that expectations of firms (or, more generally, the subjective probability distribution of outcomes) tend to be distributed, for the same information set, about the prediction of the theory (or the "objective" probability distributions of outcomes)' (ibid.).

Not only did Muth believe that the predictions of the theory were that price would equal marginal cost in equilibrium (erroneously, as we saw in Chapter 4), he also assumed that the producers had implicit knowledge of the market's supply and demand functions, and would form their expectations accordingly and therefore correctly anticipate the future.

Muth's rationality was thus rationality on steroids – not only did people know of and behave in their own best interests, they also knew how the system in which they were bit players actually behaved. This is not mere utility-maximizing rationality with respect to one's own interests (something I showed was computationally impossible in Chapter 3), but 'meta-rationality' – knowledge of how the entire system in which we are embedded works which is so good that the average expectation of the future will be correct.

This is the opposite of the realistic concept of uncertainty that Keynes had tried, unsuccessfully, to introduce into economic theory. Muth introduced expectations into his model in a manner that neutralized uncertainty.

Though there were some nuances later in the article which made it somewhat less unrealistic – including that expectations might 'consistently over- or under-discount the effect of current events' (ibid.: 321), the impact of inventories, speculators and so on[33] – the impact of this 'rational expectations hypothesis' on the model of price fluctuations in an agricultural market was that the expected market price was the equilibrium price, and all fluctuations about this price were caused by random shocks.

This is a familiar tune in neoclassical economics: whenever an attempt to incorporate a more realistic vision of how the economy functions results in a need to think in a disequilibrium way, economists dream up ways of relegitimizing equilibrium analysis once more. This is accepted within neoclassical economics itself, even if it involves doing severe damage to realism – as the assumption that the future can be (on average) accurately predicted surely does – and even if it involves an obvious contradiction of other parts of neoclassical economics.

---

33 None of these made it through to the version of rational expectations that was incorporated into models of the macroeconomy.

Muth committed such a contradiction when he put forward as a justification for assuming rational expectations at the market level the proposition that: 'Information is scarce, and the economic system generally does not waste it' (ibid.: 316).

Leaving aside the very concept of information about the future, this assertion within neoclassical economic theory leads to the conclusion that expectations should be less than rational.

If information is scarce, then it should have a price, and a rational agent should purchase information (about the future ...) up until the point at which the marginal cost of this information equals the marginal benefit from acquiring it. This would necessarily occur before enough information (about the future ...) was purchased to allow completely rational expectations (about the future ...) to be formed, so that actual expectations should be less than fully 'rational.'

No such limit occurred to Muth, however, let alone to Lucas, who appropriated this concept from the model of a single market to apply it at the level of the entire economy.

The macroeconomics of Nostradamus The argument that producers in a given market have at least some idea of how that market works, and can therefore produce slightly informed predictions of what next season's price might be, given this season's outcome, is not entirely unreasonable. But the argument that agents in a macroeconomy can know how the macroeconomy works and therefore correctly anticipate the future course of macroeconomic variables like inflation is simply absurd.

However, this absurdity was in fact a necessity for neoclassical economics. If it were to maintain the belief that the economy was fundamentally stable, then expectations of the future had to be either ignored or tamed.

In Keynes's day, as he himself noted, neoclassical economics did the former. After Keynes, expectations were again ignored in Hicks's development of the IS-LM model, and then the numerical forecasting models derived from it. Then, in one of the greatest travesties in the history of economic thought, Muth and Lucas could claim that they were introducing expectations into economic theory, because they were clearly unaware of Keynes's earlier insistence on the importance of expectations in the context of uncertainty about the future.

However, here they were constrained by the dilemma that Keynes observed afflicted his neoclassical contemporaries, when he noted that they attempted 'to deal with the present by abstracting from the fact that we know very little about the future' (Keynes 1937: 215). Neoclassical economics could only maintain its belief that the economy was in equilibrium if actions today, taken on the basis of how conditions were expected to be in the future, were correct. So the choice that neoclassical economics faced was between ignoring the future, or pretending that it could be accurately foreseen.

Keynes's contemporaries chose the former route; Lucas and modern neoclassicals instead embraced the latter – and had the hide to call such a view 'rational.' In reality, 'rational expectations' was a device, not to introduce expectations into economic modeling, but to keep time and uncertainty about the future out of it. In place of dealing with the present 'by abstracting from the fact that we know very little about the future,' rational expectations deals with the present 'by pretending that we can predict the future.'

Microeconomic macroeconomics The concept that agents in a complex system like the macroeconomy can accurately predict its future should have been rejected on first sight. Not only does it ignore uncertainty, even prediction of what a model itself will do in the future is only possible if the model is 'ergodic' – meaning that the past history of the model is a reliable guide to its future behavior.

The complex dynamic models we considered in Chapter 9, such as Lorenz's model of atmospheric turbulence, are non-ergodic.[34] The past history of a complex model is not a reliable guide to its future behavior, because where the model will evolve to is dependent on where it starts from – the so-called 'Butterfly Effect' applies. Two situations with differences in initial conditions that are too small to be distinguished from each other will have drastically different outcomes in the future: they will be similar for a short while (which is why weather forecasting is accurate only about a week in advance) but then diverge completely.

Only if models of the economy are not of this class are 'rational expectations' possible even within the model. The easiest way to make rational expectations work within a model is to make it linear – and this is what Muth did in his first model:

> For purposes of analysis, we shall use a specialized form of the hypothesis. In particular, we assume:
>
> 1. The random disturbances are normally distributed.
> 2. Certainty equivalents exist for the variables to be predicted.
> 3. The equations of the system, including the expectations formulas, are linear.
>
> These assumptions are not quite so strong as may appear at first because any one of them virtually implies the other two. (Muth 1961: 317)

Though some subsequent 'rational expectations' models used in macroeconomics had nonlinearities, they continued to make Muth's second

---

34 'Ergodic' is a frequently misunderstood term, especially within economics. It is properly defined by the Wiktionary (en.wiktionary.org/wiki/ergodic), and the Wikipedia entry on Ergodic Theory (en.wikipedia.org/wiki/Ergodic_theory) makes the important point that 'For the special class of ergodic systems, the time average is the same for almost all initial points: statistically speaking, the system that evolves for a long time "forgets" its initial state.' This is not the case for complex or chaotic models, which show 'sensitive dependence on initial conditions' (see en.wikipedia.org/wiki/Butterfly_effect and en.wikipedia.org/wiki/Chaos_theory).

assumption – that the 'exogenous shocks,' which are the only explanation these models have for cyclical behavior, are 'normally distributed' – and as Muth observes, this is effectively the same as having a linear model.

However, 'rational expectations' makes no sense in non-ergodic models: any predictions made from within such a model about the model's future behavior would be wrong (let alone predictions made about the economy the model is alleged to simulate). Crucially, the errors made by agents within that model would not be 'normally distributed' – they would not be neatly distributed around the model's mean as in the classic 'Bell Curve.' Instead the distribution would be 'chaotic,' with lots of what Nassim Taleb labeled 'Black Swan events' (Taleb 2007). It would be futile to have 'rational expectations' in such a model, because these would be misleading guides to the model's future. The model's future would be uncertain, and the best thing any agent in such a model could do would be to project forward its current trajectory, while also expecting that expectation to be wrong.

What applies to a model applies in extremis to the real world, and parallels Keynes's observations about how people in a market economy actually behave: they apply conventions, the most common of which is to extrapolate forward current conditions, even though 'candid examination of past experience' (Keynes 1937: 214) would show that these conditions did not persist.

Keynes remarked that superficially this might appear irrational, but there is no better course of action when the future is uncertain. One of Keynes's observations, highlighted in the next quote, directly contradicts the key assumption of rational expectations, which is that on average people's expectations about the future will be correct:

> It *would be foolish, in forming our expectations, to attach great weight to matters which are very uncertain. It is reasonable, therefore, to be guided to a considerable degree by the facts about which we feel somewhat confident, even though they may be less decisively relevant to the issue than other facts about which our knowledge is vague and scanty.*
>
> For this reason the facts of the existing situation enter, in a sense disproportionately, into the formation of our long-term expectations; our usual practice being to take the existing situation and to project it into the future [...]
>
> The essence of this convention [...] lies in assuming that the existing state of affairs will continue indefinitely, except in so far as we have specific reasons to expect a change. This does not mean that we really believe that the existing state of affairs will continue indefinitely. We know from extensive experience that this is most unlikely. The actual results of an investment over a long term of years very seldom agree with the initial expectation.
>
> *Nor can we rationalize our behavior by arguing that to a man in a state of ignorance errors in either direction are equally probable, so that there remains a mean actuarial expectation based on equi-probabilities. For it can easily be*

shown that the assumption of arithmetically equal probabilities based on a state of ignorance leads to absurdities.

We are assuming, in effect, that the existing market valuation, however arrived at, is uniquely correct in relation to our existing knowledge of the facts which will influence the yield of the investment, and that it will only change in proportion to changes in this knowledge; though, philosophically speaking, it cannot be uniquely correct, since our existing knowledge does not provide a sufficient basis for a calculated mathematical expectation [...]

In abnormal times in particular, when the hypothesis of an indefinite continuance of the existing state of affairs is less plausible than usual even though there are no express grounds to anticipate a definite change, *the market will be subject to waves of optimistic and pessimistic sentiment, which are unreasoning and yet in a sense legitimate where no solid basis exists for a reasonable calculation.* (Keynes 1936: 148, 152, 154; emphasis added)

The concept of rational expectations should therefore have died at birth, but because it let neoclassical economists return to their pre-Keynesian practice of arguing that the economy was self-regulating and always either in or tending toward equilibrium, rational expectations was instead embraced. Lucas and his colleagues Thomas Sargent, Neil Wallace, Edward Prescott, Leonard Rapping, and several others produced a series of papers that developed models of the macroeconomy that extrapolated directly from the alleged behavior of a single utility-maximizing and profit-maximizing agent who was endowed, via 'rational expectations,' with the capacity to accurately predict the future.

One of these predictions was that increasing the money supply would cause inflation. In a model without 'rational expectations,' if the government increased the money supply in order to reduce unemployment, there would be a lag between when the money supply was increased, and when the inflation actually occurred. In the meantime, the increased money supply would have the impact desired by the government, of increasing economic activity – and hence reducing unemployment. This was Friedman's adaptive expectations, leading to the undesirable result – from the point of view of neoclassical economists – that the government could reduce the unemployment rate below equilibrium via a policy of permanent accelerating inflation.

The twist of adding expectations into the model, when expectations were identical to the prediction of the model, was that inflation would occur instantly, rather than with a lag. This is because, since everyone expects an increased money supply to cause inflation, everyone instantly puts their prices up as soon as the money supply rises. The lag between an increase in the money supply and an increase in prices is eliminated, and with it disappears any temporary impact of the money supply on unemployment. In one of the pivotal papers in this literature, Sargent and Wallace put it this way:

The public knows the monetary authority's feedback rule and takes this into account in forming its expectations [... therefore] unanticipated movements in the money supply cause movements in [output], but anticipated movements do not [...]

[R]emoving the assumption that the authority can systematically trick the public eliminates the implication that there is an exploitable tradeoff between inflation and unemployment in any sense pertinent for making policy. *The assumption that the public's expectations are 'rational' and so equal to objective mathematical expectations accomplishes precisely this.*

In this system, there is no sense in which the authority has the option to conduct countercyclical policy. To exploit the Phillips Curve, it must somehow trick the public. But by virtue of the assumption that expectations are rational, there is no feedback rule that the authority can employ and expect to be able systematically to fool the public. This means that *the authority cannot expect to exploit the Phillips Curve even for one period.* Thus, combining the natural rate hypothesis with the assumption that expectations are rational transforms the former from a curiosity with perhaps remote policy implications into an hypothesis with immediate and drastic implications about the feasibility of pursuing countercyclical policy. (Sargent and Wallace 1976: 173, 176, 177–8; emphases added)

Not surprisingly, this doctrine was termed the 'policy ineffectiveness proposition.' If anything that was consciously done by policymakers to manipulate the economy led instantly to countervailing behavior by people in the economy, then nothing the government could do would alter the rate of unemployment. Instead, all the government could do was cause inflation.

This doctrine also provided a basis on which to attack the strongest edifices of macroeconomics at the time, the large-scale numerical simulations of the economy derived from Hicks's IS-LM model.

The Lucas critique These numerical simulations had two roles: providing a means to organize economic statistics from the past, and providing a means to forecast what might happen to the economy if a new government policy were implemented. Lucas's critique focused on this second role, by arguing that the parameters in the models' equations reflected the expectations that agents in the economy had under past policies. A new policy would evince new reactions from agents within the economy, thus altering the parameters and rendering projected economic outcomes based on them invalid. As Lucas put it:

The thesis of this essay is that [...] the 'theory of economic policy' [...] is in need of major revision. More particularly, I shall argue that the features which lead to success in short-term forecasting are unrelated to quantitative policy evaluation, that the major econometric models are (well) designed to perform the former task only, and that simulations using these models can, in principle, provide no useful information as to the actual consequences of alternative economic policies. (Lucas 1976: 19–20)

Leaving aside the absurdity of using this critique to justify the assumption of rational expectations, Lucas's general point was valid: one of the many things that an economic model should incorporate is the possibility that the behavior of the economy could alter in response to a change in government policy.

However, it is a wild extrapolation to then argue that the change would be sufficient to completely neutralize the policy, as rational expectations exponents contended. It is also committing the fallacy of strong reductionism to believe that this justifies overthrowing explicitly macroeconomic models and replacing them with ones in which macroeconomics is directly extrapolated from microeconomics.

The applicability of the Lucas critique to the existing IS-LM-based macroeconomic modeling tradition was also a matter of degree, as Gordon argued at the same conference:

> While I am prepared to grant the validity of the proposition that the mechanical extrapolation of a model with fixed parameters cannot provide useful information on the effects of all policy changes, on the other hand the effects of some policy changes can be determined if parameter shifts are allowed and are either (a) estimated from the response of parameters to policy changes within the sample period or (b) are deduced from a priori theoretical consideration. (Gordon 1976: 47)

However, Lucas and the Rational Expectations Mafia[35] weren't interested in nuances: their objective was the elimination of macroeconomics as a separate discipline, and the replacement of IS-LM-based macroeconomic models with models that extrapolated the neoclassical microeconomics to an analysis of the entire economy. Manifestos to this effect are spread throughout the economic literature.

The microeconomic manifesto The belief that macroeconomics should be applied microeconomics was an article of faith for neoclassical economists, and this faith was radiantly on display at Lucas's keynote speech to the History of Political Economy conference in the year in which he became president of the American Economic Association. In this memoir, he reiterated the view that macroeconomics had to be based on Walrasian microeconomics:

> I think Patinkin was absolutely right to try and use general equilibrium

35 I can think of no more apt term to describe the group that led the campaign to make macroeconomics a branch of neoclassical microeconomics. Certainly the neoclassical attitude to researchers who refused to use 'rational expectations' in their models approached the old Mafia cliché of 'an offer you can't refuse': 'assume rational expectations, or your paper won't get published in a leading journal.'

theory to think about macroeconomic problems. Patinkin and I are both Walrasians, whatever that means. I don't see how anybody can not be.

I also held on to Patinkin's ambition somehow, that the theory ought to be microeconomically founded, unified with price theory. I think this was a very common view [...] Nobody was satisfied with IS-LM as the end of macroeconomic theorizing. The idea was we were going to tie it together with microeconomics and that was the job of our generation. Or to continue doing that. That wasn't an anti-Keynesian view. You can see the same ambition in Klein's work or Modigliani's. (Lucas 2004: 16, 20)

Today, macroeconomic textbooks start from the presumption that macroeconomics must have microeconomic foundations. Ljungqvist and Sargent's 2004 text gives a typical justification for this:

This book is about micro foundations for macroeconomics. [There are] two possible justifications for putting microfoundations underneath macroeconomic models. The first is aesthetic and pre-empirical: models with micro foundations are by construction coherent and explicit. And because they contain descriptions of agents' purposes, they allow us to analyze policy interventions using standard methods of welfare economics. Lucas [...] gives a distinct second reason: a model with micro foundations broadens the sources of empirical evidence that can be used to assign numerical values to the model's parameters [...] We don't think that the clock will soon be turned back to a time when macroeconomics was done without micro foundations. (Ljungqvist and Sargent 2004: xxvi–xxvii)

The problem for early would-be neoclassical macroeconomists was that, strictly speaking, there was no microeconomic model of macroeconomics when they began their campaign. So they developed a neoclassical macro model from the foundation of the neoclassical growth model developed by Nobel laureate Robert Solow (Solow 1956) and Trevor Swan (Swan 2002). They interpreted the equilibrium growth path of the economy as being determined by the consumption and leisure preferences of a representative consumer, and explained deviations from equilibrium – which the rest of us know as the business cycle – by unpredictable 'shocks' to technology and consumer preferences.

This resulted in a model of the macroeconomy as consisting of a single consumer, who lives for ever, consuming the output of the economy, which is a single good produced in a single firm, which he owns and in which he is the only employee, which pays him both profits equivalent to the marginal product of capital and a wage equivalent to the marginal product of labor, to which he decides how much labor to supply by solving a utility function that maximizes his utility over an infinite time horizon, which he rationally expects and therefore correctly predicts. The economy would always be in equilibrium except for the impact of unexpected 'technology shocks' that change the firm's productive capabilities (or his consumption preferences) and thus temporarily cause the single capitalist/worker/consumer to alter his working hours. Any reduction in working hours is a voluntary act, so the representative agent is never involuntarily unemployed, he's just taking more leisure. And there are no banks, no debt, and indeed no money in this model.

You think I'm joking? I wish I was. Here's Robert Solow's own summary of these models – initially called 'real business cycle' models, though over time they morphed into what are now called 'Dynamic Stochastic General Equilibrium' models:

> The prototypical real-business-cycle model goes like this. There is a single, immortal household – a representative consumer – that earns wages from supplying labor. It also owns the single price-taking firm, so the household receives the net income of the firm. The household takes the present and future wage rates and present and future dividends as given, and formulates an optimal infinite-horizon consumption-saving (and possibly labor-saving) plan [...] The firm looks at the same prices, and maximizes current profit by employing labor, renting capital and producing and selling output [...] (Solow 2001: 23)

> In the ordinary way, an equilibrium is a sequence of inter-temporal prices and wage rates that makes the decisions of household and firm consistent with each other. This is nothing but the neoclassical growth model [...]

> The theory actually imagines that the model economy is disturbed from time to time by unforeseeable shocks to the technology and the household's tastes [...] There is thus nothing pathological or remediable about observed fluctuations. Unforeseeable disturbances are by definition unforeseen; after one of them has happened, the economy is already making optimal adjustments, given its technology and the inter-temporal preferences of its single inhabitant or identical inhabitants. There is no role for macroeconomic policy in this world [...] the best it [the government] can do is to perform its necessary functions in the most regular, predictable way, so as not to add unnecessary variance to the environment. (Ibid.: 23–4)

If you get the feeling that Solow – a neoclassical economist par excellence and, as noted, the author of the growth model from which real business cycle models were derived – is not happy with the microeconomic takeover of macroeconomics, you'd be right. Though microeconomics masquerading as macroeconomics took over PhD programs across the USA, and it is all the current crop of neoclassicals really knows, there has always been opposition to this approach to macroeconomics from within the neoclassical school itself. Solow's own reactions are the most notable, since Solow's growth model is acknowledged by Finn Kydland and Edward Prescott, the originators of these models, as its fountainhead (Kydland and Prescott 1991: 167–8).

Solow's reaction to the fact that his growth model was used as the basis of modern neoclassical macroeconomics was one of bewilderment:

> The puzzle I want to discuss – at least it seems to me to be a puzzle, though part of the puzzle is why it does not seem to be a puzzle to many of my younger colleagues – is this. More than forty years ago, I [...] worked out [...] neoclassical growth theory [...] [I]t was clear from the beginning what I thought it did not apply to, namely short-run fluctuations in aggregate output and employment [...] the business cycle [...]
>
> [N]ow [...] if you pick up an article today with the words 'business cycle' in the title, there is a fairly high probability that its basic theoretical orientation will be what is called 'real business cycle theory' and the underlying model will be [...] a slightly dressed up version of the neoclasssical growth model. The question I want to circle around is: how did that happen? (Solow 2001: 19)

Solow inadvertently provided one answer to his own question when he discussed the preceding IS-LM model:

> For a while the dominant framework for thinking about the short run was roughly 'Keynesian.' I use that label for convenience; *I have absolutely no interest in 'what Keynes really meant.'* To be more specific, the framework I mean is what is sometimes called 'American Keynesianism' as taught to many thousands of students by Paul Samuelson's textbook and a long line of followers. (Ibid.: 21)

How bizarre! Solow is decrying that poor scholarship led to his growth cycle model being used for a purpose for which it was not designed, and yet he is blasé about whether or not the models of the economy he helped develop, and which he labels Keynesian (albeit with the qualifier 'American'), have anything to do with Keynes's ideas.

The old saying 'As ye sow, so shall ye reap' applies here. The poor scholarship that let American economists delude themselves into believing that they were Keynesians, when in fact they were extending models originated by – and later disowned by – John Hicks, now let them use Solow's growth model as a foundation for models of the business cycle, even though Solow himself disowned the enterprise on two very valid grounds.

The first is that the limitations of IS-LM modeling pointed out in the Lucas critique did not justify modeling the entire macroeconomy as a single representative agent. Unlike many neoclassicals, Solow was aware that the Sonnenschein-Mantel-Debreu conditions discussed in Chapter 3 invalidate attempts to model the entire economy by extrapolating from microeconomic theory about the behavior of individual consumers:

> the main argument for this modeling strategy has been a more aesthetic

one: its virtue is said to be that it is compatible with general equilibrium theory, and thus it is superior to ad hoc descriptive models that are not related to 'deep' structural parameters. The preferred nickname for this class of models is 'DSGE' (dynamic stochastic general equilibrium). I think that this argument is fundamentally misconceived [...] *The cover story about 'microfoundations' can in no way justify recourse to the narrow representative-agent construct* [...]

He also supplied a simple analogy as to why the valid criticism of IS-LM models – that they don't consider that economic agents may change their behavior when government policies change – does not justify the strong reductionist approach of reducing macroeconomics to applied micro-economics:

> The nature of the sleight-of-hand involved here can be made plain by an analogy. I tell you that I eat nothing but cabbage. You ask me why, and I reply portentously: I am a vegetarian! But vegetarianism is reason for a meatless diet; it cannot justify my extreme and unappetizing choice. Even in growth theory (let alone in short-run macroeconomics), reasonable 'micro-foundations' do not demand implausibility; indeed, they should exclude implausibility. (Solow 2007: 8; emphasis added)

Solow's second point is a practical one: the standard fare of macroeconomics – booms and slumps, inflation and deflation, unemployment rising as people are sacked during recessions – cannot occur in pure DSGE models. They are therefore a particularly useless foundation from which to analyze such phenomena. In a paper tellingly entitled 'Dumb and dumber in macroeconomics,' Solow observed that, though 'The original impulse to look for better or more explicit micro foundations was probably reasonable [...]'

> What emerged was not a good idea. The preferred model has a single representative consumer optimizing over infinite time with perfect foresight or rational expectations, in an environment that realizes the resulting plans more or less flawlessly through perfectly competitive forward-looking markets for goods and labor, and perfectly flexible prices and wages.
>
> *How could anyone expect a sensible short-to-medium-run macroeconomics to come out of that set-up?* My impression is that this approach (which seems now to be the mainstream, and certainly dominates the journals, if not the workaday world of macroeconomics) has had no empirical success; but that is not the point here. *I start from the presumption that we want macroeconomics to account for the occasional aggregative pathologies that beset modern capitalist economies, like recessions, intervals of stagnation, inflation, 'stagflation,' not to mention negative pathologies like unusually good times. A model that rules out pathologies by definition is unlikely to help.* (Solow 2003: 1; emphases added)

In typical neoclassical fashion, Solow's legitimate complaints about 'micro-foundations-based representative agent macroeconomics' have been ignored. The accepted wisdom within neoclassical economics remains that macro models had to have 'good microeconomic foundations,' and the only dispute, prior to the Great Recession, was over what constituted good foundations. This led to a bifurcation within neoclassical macroeconomics into two camps, one of which preferred to model the entire economy as a single agent existing in a perfectly competitive general equilibrium, the other of which modeled the economy as one (and occasionally more than one) agent existing in a state of imperfectly competitive general equilibrium.

It was a sham dichotomy, because they both shared the vision that, if the neoclassical fantasy of perfect competition applied, there would be no macroeconomic problems. They differed only on whether they believed that the neoclassical fantasy could be assumed to apply in reality or not. As the end of the first decade of the twenty-first century approached, they had largely reached a rapprochement. And then the Great Recession crushed both their visions.

Much ado about almost nothing: freshwater versus saltwater macroeconomics
Nobel laureate Paul Krugman popularized the monikers 'freshwater' and 'saltwater' economists for these two approaches to economics, and makes much of their differences (Krugman 2009a, 2009b). But the reality is that what they share is far more important than their slight differences, because they are both neoclassical theories in which macroeconomic problems arise only if there are microeconomic 'imperfections,' and they both believe that a perfectly competitive economy with flexible prices is the definition of perfection.

As I explained in Chapters 3–5 of this book, this vision even of their own model is fundamentally wrong. Demand curves derived from aggregating the individual demand of 'perfectly rational' consumers could have any shape at all. Competitive firms would not produce where marginal cost equals price, but where marginal revenue equals demand, and set price above this level. Market demand curves would intersect with the marginal revenue curves of the industry's suppliers in multiple locations, making the very notion of an equilibrium price in a single market problematic. Incorporating the issues covered in subsequent chapters results in even more of a mess. Not even microeconomic analysis can be based on neoclassical microeconomics – let alone the analysis of an entire economy.

Both saltwater and freshwater economists were therefore up Strong Reductionism Creek without a paddle when the Great Recession hit. I would prefer to leave them there, but since their squabbling and mea culpas dominate even today's debate about where macroeconomics should go from now, I have to detail how they got there in the first place, and why they remain lost in an irrelevant intellectual tributary of their own making when the real world is drowning in the flood of the Great Recession.

From Keynes to freshwater macroeconomics Both freshwater and saltwater macroeconomics had their genesis in the pre-Keynesian belief that all dilemmas at the level of the overall economy must instead be signs of malfunctioning in particular markets – and normally the labor market. As Coddington noted in the very early days of the neoclassical revolt against Keynesian macroeconomics, Keynes's neoclassical predecessors – whom he labeled 'Classical' – had precisely the same view, and it was based on a reductionist vision of how economics should be done:

> Keynes attacked a body of theory that he designated 'Classical.' [... and] called into question the method of analysis by which this system was constructed [...] this method consisted of analyzing markets on the basis of the choices made by individual traders [...] This method of analysis [...] I will refer to as 'reductionism,' on the grounds that the central idea is the reduction of market phenomena to (stylized) individual choices. (Coddington 1976: 1258)

This pre-Keynesian vision was reconstructed by neoclassical macroeconomists after Keynes. Their starting point was the key implication of 'The predominant theory of markets, namely the Walrasian or Arrow Debreu model of general competitive equilibrium,' which was

> that unemployment never appears and that economic policy never has universally good effects. First, it postulates that the supply and demand by price-taking agents equilibrates in the market for any commodity, including labor. Hence, no unemployment occurs. Second, Walrasian equilibria are efficient, as anticipated by Adam Smith's 'invisible hand' [...] Thus, either economic policy has no effects or it hurts some group of citizens. (Silvestre 1993: 105)

This pre-Keynesian attitude was reborn with the development of what Coddington termed 'Reconstituted Reductionism,' because believers in neoclassical economics could give Keynes's work any intellectual credence only if it were seen as a statement of what would happen out of equilibrium, since in general equilibrium, Walras's Law would apply and there could be no macroeconomic problems. As Robert Clower put it, Keynes either had such a hypothesis 'at the back of his mind, or most of the *General Theory* is theoretical nonsense' (Clower 1969: 290).

As I've explained above, Walras's Law itself is a theoretical nonsense that ignores the role of credit in a market economy. However, the belief that Walras's Law was a universal truth, and that any deviation from its fundamental result – that macroeconomic crises were in fact manifestations of disequilibrium in individual markets – must be a fallacy was shared by both sides of the neoclassical saltwater/freshwater divide. Coddington correctly noted that both saltwater and freshwater economists assumed that economics had to be conducted from a reductionist perspective.

> the claim that equilibrium theorizing must be abandoned in order to accommodate Keynesian ideas postulates that theorizing must be carried out in accordance with the reductionist program. (Coddington 1976: 1269)

> To ask this question, one needs a construction in which prices adjust less than instantaneously to economic circumstances, so that at any point in time the prices may be effectively providing incentives to act, but the information they reflect will not be appropriate for the equilibrium that is being approached. (Ibid.: 1270)

Saltwater economists were willing to abandon equilibrium (or at least perfectly competitive equilibrium) but still believed they had to reason in a reductionist way. Freshwater economists clung to modeling the economy as if it were always in equilibrium, which gave rise to the problem for them of the historical fact that unemployment occurred – or, in their terms, that economic statistics reported that, on occasions, lots of people were not working. But according to their theory, if all markets including labor were in equilibrium apart from the impact of unexpected shocks, unemployment in general could not exist. How, then, to interpret past instances when high levels of unemployment were recorded – like, for example, the Great Depression?

Their interpretation, in a nutshell, was that the Great Depression was an extended holiday: something happened that caused workers to decide to work less, and this increase in leisure was recorded by the statistical agencies as an increase in unemployment. This something was a change in government policy that made it rational for workers to voluntarily reduce their working hours in order to maximize their lifetime utility.

You think I'm joking? Consider these statements by the doyen of the freshwater or 'New Classical' faction of neoclassical macroeconomists, Nobel laureate Edward Prescott:

> the key to defining and explaining the Great Depression is the behavior of *market hours worked per adult* [...] there must have been a fundamental change in labor market institutions and industrial policies that lowered steady-state, or normal, market hours [...]

> [T]he economy is continually hit by shocks, and what economists observe in business cycles is the effects of past and current shocks. A bust occurs if a number of negative shocks are bunched in time. A boom occurs if a number of positive shocks are bunched in time. Business cycles are, in the language of Slutzky, the 'sum of random causes.'

The fundamental difference between the Great Depression and business cycles is that market hours did not return to normal during the Great Depression. Rather, market hours fell and stayed low. In the 1930s, labor market institutions and industrial policy actions changed normal market hours. I think these institutions and actions are what caused the Great Depression [...]

From the perspective of growth theory, the Great Depression is a great decline in steady-state market hours. I think this great decline was the unintended consequence of labor market institutions and industrial policies designed to improve the performance of the economy. Exactly what changes in market institutions and industrial policies gave rise to the large decline in normal market hours is not clear [...]

The Marxian view is that capitalistic economies are inherently unstable and that excessive accumulation of capital will lead to increasingly severe economic crises. Growth theory, which has proved to be empirically successful, says this is not true. *The capitalistic economy is stable, and absent some change in technology or the rules of the economic game, the economy converges to a constant growth path with the standard of living doubling every 40 years.* In the 1930s, there was an important change in the rules of the economic game. This change lowered the steady-state market hours. The Keynesians had it all wrong. *In the Great Depression, employment was not low because investment was low. Employment and investment were low because labor market institutions and industrial policies changed in a way that lowered normal employment.* (Prescott 1999: 1–3; emphases added)

Prescott's culprit for these changes, predictably, is the government: 'government policies that affect TFP [total factor productivity] and hours per working-age person are the crucial determinants of the great depressions of the 20th century [...]' (Kehoe and Prescott 2002: 1).

The reason that Prescott and his fellow freshwater economists were led to such a frankly crazy interpretation of the Great Depression is that their model allowed no other alternative.

As a reminder, their model, in a nutshell, is the following. There is a single consumer, endowed with rational expectations, who aims to maximize his utility from consumption and leisure over the infinite future. His income emanates from the profits of the single firm in the economy, of which he is the sole owner, and in which he is the sole worker, where the profits he receives are the marginal product of capital times the amount of capital employed by the firm, and his wages are the marginal product of labor times the hours he works in the firm. The output of the firm determines consumption and investment output today, and today's investment (minus depreciation) determines tomorrow's capital stock. The single consumer/capitalist/worker decides how much of current output to devote to investment, and how many hours to work, so that the discounted expected future value of his consumption plus leisure plan is maximized. Technology enables expanding production over time, with productivity growing at a constant rate but subject to random shocks, and these shocks cause the equilibrium levels of labor and investment chosen by the consumer/capitalist/worker to alter – but the choices made are always equilibrium choices.

With that bizarre vision of a market economy, while standard business cycle fluctuations in employment can be explained as a rational response by workers to work less today – because productivity has increased owing to a series of positive technology shocks – the only explanation for the sustained decline in employment that occurs during a depression is that it is a rational response by the household sector to a change in government policy to take more leisure.

The saltwater–freshwater dialectic Saltwater neoclassicals like Krugman, Stiglitz and so on can at least be congratulated for being realistic enough to reject this extreme Panglossian view of how the economy operates. But the dilemma for them is that the freshwater vision is more faithful to the underlying neoclassical vision of the economy that they share with the freshwaters.

Herein lies the dialectic that has defined the development of neoclassical macroeconomics over time, between theoretical purity on the one hand and reality on the other. To a neoclassical, theoretical purity involves reducing everything to the Walrasian vision of a perfectly equilibrating economy – in which case no macroeconomic crises can occur (since price movements will rapidly eliminate any macro imbalances caused by disequilibria in individual markets). Reality introduces the vexing counterpoint that recessions do occur, and persist for an inordinate period of time, and that it simply beggars belief that the dole queues of the 1930s – and the massive unemployment of the Great Recession – are manifestations of workers voluntarily taking more leisure.

This in turn leads to a dialectical division of labor within neoclassical economics. Ideologues who are most committed to the vision of the free market as the perfect system were the first to respond to any challenge to this vision – thus firstly Friedman, then Lucas, Prescott and the other freshwater economists led the revolt against IS-LM Keynesianism, and the Real Business Cycle/DSGE approach to economics evolved.

Then the liberals or comparative realists within neoclassical economics – Stiglitz, Krugman, Woodford and the like – reacted to the unrealism that the extreme purity approach embodies, though at the same time they took this perspective as the proper point from which to commence macroeconomic modeling. So they embellished the purist model with deviations from microeconomic perfection, and generated a model that can more closely emulate the economic data on which they focus – predominantly the rates of real economic growth, employment and inflation. This became known as the 'New Keynesian' or saltwater approach to economics, in contrast to the 'New Classical' or freshwater approach: start from precisely the same vision of a macroeconomy that would be in perfect equilibrium with no involuntary unemployment if all consumers were homogeneous, markets were perfect and prices adjusted instantly to any shocks; then add in maybe two types of agents, imperfect competition and other deviations from perfection to generate inflation and involuntary unemployment.

The founding editor of the American Economic Association's specialist macroeconomics journal, Olivier Blanchard (Blanchard 2008, 2009) described the basic or 'toy' saltwater/New Keynesian' model as starting from the freshwater/New Classical model without capital, to which it added two 'imperfections': monopolistic competition and inflation caused expectations of future inflation plus a gap between what output actually is and the higher level that neoclassical theory says it would be if there were no 'imperfections.'[36] It then added monetary policy conducted by a central bank using the Taylor Rule,[37] with which it attempts to control inflation by setting the real interest rate on the basis of the rate of inflation and the output gap.

This results in a model that can be expressed in three equations – one for consumption or aggregate demand as a function of the real interest rate and (rationally) expected future output, another for inflation, and a third for the central bank's interest-rate-setting policy. Blanchard stated that the model was

> simple, analytically convenient, and has largely replaced the IS-LM model as the basic model of fluctuations in graduate courses (although not yet in undergraduate textbooks). Similar to the IS-LM model, it reduces a complex reality to a few simple equations. Unlike the IS-LM model, it is formally, rather than informally, derived from optimization by firms and consumers. (Blanchard 2009: 214–15)

The weaknesses in the model[38] are addressed by adding yet more microeconomic imperfections. These include adding the reality that the labor market is not homogeneous to explain involuntary unemployment – 'One striking (and unpleasant) characteristic of the basic NK model is that there is no unemployment!' (ibid.: 216) – and using the concept of asymmetric information to explain problems in credit markets. This saltwater approach necessarily achieved a better fit to the data than the extreme neoclassical vision of the freshwater faction, but for reasons that are hardly exemplary, as Solow observed:

36 This is based on the belief that output would be higher (and prices lower) under competition than under monopoly, which I showed to be false in Chapter 4.

37 A rule of thumb that asserts that the central bank can control inflation by increasing real interest rates roughly twice as much as any increase in inflation. See Box 10.1.

38 He noted that 'the first two equations of the model are patently false [...] The aggregate demand equation ignores the existence of investment, and relies on an intertemporal substitution effect in response to the interest rate, which is hard to detect in the data on consumers. The inflation equation implies a purely forward-looking behavior of inflation, which again appears strongly at odds with the data' (Blanchard 2009: 215).

The simpler sort of RBC model that I have been using for expository purposes has had little or no empirical success, even with a very undemanding notion of 'empirical success.' As a result, some of the freer spirits in the RBC school have begun to loosen up the basic framework by allowing for 'imperfections' in the labor market, and even in the capital market [...]

The model then sounds better and fits the data better. *This is not surprising: these imperfections were chosen by intelligent economists to make the models work better* [...] (Solow 2001: 26; emphasis added)

Nonetheless, the better apparent fit to the data from models engineered to do so by the saltwaters meant that, over time, and despite the vigorous protests of the freshwaters, the 'New Keynesian' approach became the dominant one within neoclassical macroeconomics. It appeared to neoclassicals that macroeconomics was converging on a 'New Keynesian consensus,' and Blanchard claimed so in 2008:

there has been enormous progress and substantial convergence. For a while – too long a while – the field looked like a battlefield. Researchers split in different directions, mostly ignoring each other, or else engaging in bitter fights and controversies. Over time however, largely because facts have a way of not going away, a largely shared vision both of fluctuations and of methodology has emerged. Not everything is fine. Like all revolutions, this one has come with the destruction of some knowledge, and it suffers from extremism, herding, and fashion. But none of this is deadly. The state of macro is good [...]

Facts have a way of eventually forcing irrelevant theory out (one wishes it happened faster), and good theory also has a way of eventually forcing bad theory out. The new tools developed by the new-classicals came to dominate. The facts emphasized by the new-Keynesians forced imperfections back in the benchmark model. A largely common vision has emerged. (Blanchard 2009: 210)

Given the time lags involved in academic publishing, this unfortunate paper, which was first completed in August 2008 (Blanchard 2008) (eight months *after* the start of the Great Recession, according to the National Bureau of Economic Research), was published in an academic journal in May 2009, by which time the world as neoclassical economists thought they knew it had come to an end. Forces their models completely ignored finally overwhelmed the economy, and took their vision of the economy with it.

Conclusion

Though I can argue about logical fallacies till the cows come home, this is no substitute for an empirical proof that neoclassical economics is wrong. This was provided in spectacular fashion by the Great Recession. Not only

Box 10.1 The Taylor Rule

The Taylor Rule was first devised by John Taylor as a reasonable empirical approximation to the way the Federal Reserve had in fact set nominal interest rates (Taylor 1993: 202). He noted that the Fed had increased the cash rate by 1.5 percent for every percent that inflation exceeded the Fed's target inflation rate, and reduced the cash rate by 0.5 percent for every percent that real GDP was below the average for the previous decade. When New Keynesian economists incorporated this in their model, they introduced the neoclassical concept of an 'equilibrium' real rate of interest (which is unobservable), so that if actual inflation and the rate of growth were equal to their target levels, the cash rate should be equal to the inflation rate plus this unobservable 'equilibrium' rate.

After the crisis hit, Taylor himself blamed it on the Fed deviating from his rule:

> Why did the Great Moderation end? In my view, the answer is simple. The Great Moderation ended because of a 'Great Deviation,' in which economic policy deviated from what was working well during the Great Moderation. Compared with the Great Moderation, policy became more interventionist, less rules-based, and less predictable. When policy deviated from what was working well, economic performance deteriorated. And lo and behold, we had the Great Recession. (Taylor 2007: 166)

There is some merit in Taylor's argument – certainly the low rates in that period encouraged the growth of Ponzi behavior in the finance sector. But his neoclassical analysis ignores the dynamics of private debt, which, as I show in Chapters 12 and 13, explain both the 'Great Moderation' and the 'Great Recession.' Taylor's Rule was more of a statistical coincidence in this period than a reason for the stability prior to the recession.

The Rule also evidently gave Taylor no inkling that a crisis was imminent, since as late as 10 September 2007, he concluded a speech on his Rule with the following statement:

> Of course, we live in a fluid economic world, and we do not know how long these explanations or predictions will last. I have no doubt that in the future – and maybe the not so distant future – a bright economist – maybe one right in this room – will show that some of the explanations discussed here are misleading, or simply wrong. *But in the meantime, this is really a lot of fun.* (Ibid.: 15; emphasis added)

was this not predicted by neoclassical models – according to them, such an event could not even happen.

The economic crash of the Great Recession was accompanied by the crash of both the stock market and the housing market, and predictably the neoclassical theory of finance – known as the Efficient Markets Hypothesis – also argued that asset market crashes couldn't happen. In the next chapter, we'll take a diversion to the world of asset markets before returning to the key empirical fact that neoclassical economists were the last people on the planet to see the Great Recession coming.

Postscript: intellectual miasma or corporate corruption?

The extent to which economic theory ignored crucial issues like the distribution of wealth and the role of power in society leads many to extend a conspiracy theory explanation of how economics got into this state. Surely, they argue, economic theory says what the wealthy want to hear?

I instead lay the focus upon the teleological vision to which economists have been committed ever since Adam Smith first coined the phrase 'an invisible hand' as an analogy to the workings of a market economy. The vision of a world so perfectly coordinated that no superior power is needed to direct it, and no individual power sufficient to corrupt it, has seduced the minds of many young students of economics. I should know, because I was one; had the Internet been around when I was a student, someone somewhere would have posted an essay I wrote while in my first year as an undergraduate, calling for the abolition of both unions and monopolies. No corporation paid me a cent to write that paper (though now, if it could be found, I would happily pay a corporation to hide it!).

What enabled me to break away from that delusional analysis was what Australians call 'a good bullshit detector.' At a certain point, the fact that the assumptions needed to sustain the vision of the Invisible Hand were simply absurd led me to break away, and to become the critic I am today.

However, the corporate largesse interpretation of why neoclassical economics has prospered does come into play in explaining why neoclassical economics became so dominant. Many of the leading lights of US academic economics have lived in the revolving door between academia, government and big business, and in particular big finance. The fact that their theories, while effectively orthogonal to the real world, nonetheless provided a smokescreen behind which an unprecedented concentration of wealth and economic power took place, make these theories useful to wealthy financiers, even though they are useless – and in fact outright harmful – to capitalism itself.

The fact that both government and corporate funding has helped the development of these theories, while non-orthodox economists like me have had to labor without research grants to assist them, is one reason why the nonsense that is neoclassical economics is so well developed, while its potential rivals are so grossly underdeveloped.

The corporate dollar may also have played a role in enabling neoclassical economists to continue believing arrant nonsense as they developed their theories. So while I don't explain neoclassical theory on the basis of it serving the interests of the elite, the fact that it does – even though it is counterproductive for the economy itself – and that the corporate and particularly financial elite fund those who develop it surely has played a role.

On this note, the website LittleSis (http://littlesis.org/) is well worth consulting. It documents the links between business and government figures in the USA, and leading neoclassical economists like Larry Summers feature prominently (see http://blog.littlesis.org/2011/01/10/evidence-of-an-american-plutocracy-the-larry-summers-story/).

11 | THE PRICE IS NOT RIGHT

Why finance markets can get the price of assets so badly wrong

In the first edition of this book, this chapter began with the following paragraphs:

The Internet stock market boom was[1] the biggest speculative bubble in world history.

Other manias have involved more ridiculously overvalued assets, or more preposterous objects of speculation – such as the tulip craze in 17th century Holland, the South Sea Bubble and Mississippi Bubble of the 18th century, or Japan's 1980s Bubble Economy speculation over Tokyo real estate. But no other bubble – not even the 'Roaring Twenties' boom prior to the Great Depression – has involved so many people, speculating so much money, in so short a time, to such ridiculous valuations.

But of course, an economist wouldn't tell you that. Instead, economists have assured the world that the stock market's valuations reflect the true future prospects of companies. The most famous – and fatuous – such assurance is given in Dow 36,000, which its authors were defending even when the Dow had officially entered a correction from its all-time high of March 2000, and the Nasdaq was firmly in bear market territory (*Time*, 22 May 2000: 92–93). The mammoth valuations, argued Hassett and Glassman, were simply the product of investors reassessing the risk premiums attached to stocks, having realized that over the long term, stocks were no riskier than bonds.

Economists were similarly reassuring back in 1929, with the most famous such utterance being Irving Fisher's comment that:

Stock prices have reached what looks like a permanently high plateau. I do not feel that there will soon, if ever, be a fifty or sixty point break below present levels, such as Mr. Babson has predicted. I expect to see the stock market a good deal higher than it is today within a few months. (Irving Fisher, *New York Times*, 15 October 1929)

This was published less than two weeks before 'Black Monday,' 28 October 1929, when the Dow Jones Industrial Average closed 12.8% below its previous level, and fell another 11.7% the following day. In just 15 days of

---

1 The first draft of this chapter, completed in March 2000, began with the sentence 'The Internet stock market boom is the biggest speculative bubble in world history.' This was before the Nasdaq crash of 4 April 2000 – when, as luck would have it, I was actually in New York on holiday, and, as one then could, observed the action on a tour of the NYSE (and later in Times Square on the giant Nasdaq screen). For the publication itself, 'is' became 'was,' since the book was sent to the typesetters in November 2000, when the Nasdaq was down 50 percent from its peak, and the bubble was clearly over.

wild gyrations from the day of Fisher's comments, the market fell over 120
points (from a level of about 350): twice as far as even Fisher's bearish rival
Babson had predicted, and twice as much as Fisher had believed would ever
be possible. Three years later, the stock market indices had fallen 90%, and
many a once-rich speculator was bankrupt. Investors who trusted economists
back then lost their shirts. Trusting souls who accept economic assurances
that markets are efficient are unlikely to fare any better this time when the
Bull gives way to the Bear.

At the time, I thought that the DotCom Bubble would be the last of the
big asset bubbles. I couldn't envisage then that any other asset market could
ever be more overvalued. I couldn't imagine that any more preposterous object
of speculation could emerge than the plethora of 'DotCom' companies with
negative cash flows and over-the-top valuations that lit up the Super Bowl
in 2000, and had burnt their investors' money into oblivion months later.

Silly me: I had obviously underestimated the inventiveness of Wall Street.
Even as the Nasdaq crashed and burnt, Wall Street had found an even
more ridiculous way to entice the public into debt: the fantasy that money
could be made by lending money to people with a history of not repaying
debt. The Subprime Bubble was born. By the time it burst, the academic
sub-discipline of Finance was finally starting to concede that its model of
how asset markets operate was seriously wrong. But by then, it was too late.

The kernel

'There's glory for you!'

'I don't know what you mean by "glory,"' Alice said.

Humpty Dumpty smiled contemptuously. 'Of course you don't – till I tell
you. I meant "there's a nice knock-down argument for you!"'

'But "glory" doesn't mean "a nice knock-down argument,"' Alice
objected.

'When I use a word,' Humpty Dumpty said in rather a scornful tone, 'it
means just what I choose it to mean – neither more nor less.'

All sciences invent their own language, just as Lewis Carroll's famous
egghead invented his own meanings for words. Many sciences harness words
which are in are common usage, but give them a quite different technical
meaning. But no other science plays so fast and loose with the English
language as economics.

Physics, for example, calls the fundamental constituents of matter 'strings.'
This isn't particularly confusing, since it's obvious that physicists don't believe
that a length of yarn is the basic unit of matter.

However, when economists call stock markets 'efficient,' the usage is
nowhere near as clear cut. A colloquial meaning of efficient is 'does things
quickly with a minimum of waste,' and it's clear that this meaning can apply

to modern, computerized, Internet-accessible bourses. Thus it often seems reasonable to the public that economists describe finance markets as 'efficient.'

However, when economists say that the stock market is efficient, they mean that they believe that stock markets accurately price stocks on the basis of their unknown future earnings. That meaning shifts 'efficient' from something which is obvious to something which is a debatable proposition. But that's not the end of the story, because to 'prove' that markets are efficient in this sense, economists make three bizarre assumptions:

- that all investors have identical expectations about the future prospects of all companies;
- that these identical expectations are correct; and
- that all investors have equal access to unlimited credit.

Clearly, the only way these assumptions could hold would be if each and every stock market investor were God. Since in reality the stock market is inhabited by mere mortals, there is no way that the stock market can be efficient in the way that economists define the term. Yet economists assert that stock markets are 'efficient,' and dismiss criticism of these assumptions with the proposition that you can't judge a theory by its assumptions. As Chapter 7 showed, this defense is bunk.

In a way, it's fitting that Lewis Carroll put those words in Humpty Dumpty's mouth, rather than equally appropriate vessels such as the Mad Hatter, or the Red Queen. Humpty Dumpty, after all, had a great fall …

The roadmap

The chapter begins by considering the development over time of the prevailing attitude to finance, starting with the medieval prohibition against the lending of money at interest, and culminating in economists treating the lending of money as no different from any other commodity exchange. The main economist responsible for the economic theory of lending was Irving Fisher, who, as just mentioned, effectively went bankrupt during the depression by following his own theories. However, he subsequently developed a quite different theory, which argued that excessive debt and falling prices could cause depressions. After outlining this theory, I consider the modern theory of finance known as the 'efficient markets hypothesis.' The validity of the assumptions needed to buttress this theory is assessed in the light of the logic outlined in Chapter 7. Since these are domain assumptions, the theory is inapplicable in the real world, so that markets cannot possibly be 'efficient' as economists define the term.

Fisher on finance: from reassuring oracle to ignored Cassandra

Irving Fisher was one of the many victims of the Great Crash of 1929, losing a fortune worth over $100 million in today's dollars, and being reduced to penury.[2] But his greater loss, in many ways, was one of prestige. Before this infamous utterance, he was easily America's most respected and famous economist, renowned for developing a theory of money that explained the valuation of financial assets. After it, he was a pariah.

This was a great pity, because in the depths of the Great Depression, he developed an explanation of how financial speculation could lead to economic collapse. However, this new theory – which rejected many of the assumptions of his previous model of finance – was ignored. Instead, Fisher's pre-Great Depression theory of finance continued as the economic theory of how asset prices are determined.

Decades later, Fisher's 'Debt Deflation Theory of Great Depressions' was rediscovered by the non-orthodox economist Hyman Minsky, while at much the same time Fisher's pre-Great Depression theory was formalized into the efficient markets hypothesis. Fisher thus has the dubious distinction of fathering both the conventional theory of finance – which, like his 1929 self, reassures finance markets that they are rational – and an unconventional theory which argues that speculative bubbles can cause economic depressions.

Pre-Depression Fisher: the time value of money In 1930 Fisher published *The Theory of Interest*, which asserted that the interest rate 'expresses a price in the exchange between present and future goods' (Fisher 1930).[3] This argument was a simple extension of the economic theory of prices to the puzzle of how interest rates are set, but it has an even older genealogy: it was first argued by Jeremy Bentham, the true father of modern neoclassical economics, when in 1787 he wrote 'In defence of usury.'

Never a lender nor a borrower be … Today, usury means lending money at an exorbitant rate of interest; in antiquity, it meant lending money at any rate of interest at all. However, the medieval objection was not to the rate of interest itself, but to the lender's desire to profit from a venture without sharing in its risks. A usurious contract was one in which the lender was guaranteed a positive return, regardless of whether the borrower's venture succeeded or failed: 'The primary test for usury was whether or not the lender had contracted to lend at interest without assuming a share of the risk inherent to the transaction. If the lender could collect interest regardless of the debtor's fortunes he was a usurer' (Jones 1989).

As trade came to play a larger role in society, the prohibitions against usury were weakened, and the legal definition was modified to match today's

2 Though he avoided bankruptcy thanks to loans from his wealthy sister-in-law (they were never repaid, and she forgave them in her will; Barber 1997), and selling his house to Yale in return for life tenancy.

3 Fisher's theory was first published in another work in 1907; *The Theory of Interest* restated this theory in a form which Fisher hoped would be more accessible than was the 1907 book.

colloquial meaning.[4] By Bentham's time, the legal definition referred to a rate of interest greater than 5 percent.

Adam Smith supported this legal limit. Smith argued that the complete prohibition, 'like all others of the same kind, is said to have produced no effect, and probably rather increased than diminished the evil of usury' (Smith 1838 [1776]). However, Smith supported the concept of a legal limit to the rate of interest set just above the going market rate,[5] because such a limit actually improved the allocation of the country's credit. The advantage of a legal limit, according to Smith, was that when set properly it excluded only loans to 'prodigals and projectors,' thus making more of the country's capital available for loan to industrious people:

> The legal rate [...] ought not to be much above the lowest market rate. If the legal rate of interest in Great Britain, for example, was fixed so high as eight or ten per cent, the greater part of the money which was to be lent would be lent to prodigals and projectors, who alone would be willing to give this high interest [...] A great part of the capital of the country would thus be kept out of the hands which were most likely to make a profitable and advantageous use of it, and thrown into those which were most likely to waste and destroy it. Where the legal rate of interest, on the contrary, is fixed but a very little above the lowest market rate, sober people are universally preferred, as borrowers, to prodigals and projectors. The person who lends money gets nearly as much interest from the former as he dares to take from the latter, and his money is much safer in the hands of the one set of people than in those of the other. A great part of the capital of the country is thus thrown into the hands in which it is most likely to be employed with advantage. (Ibid.)

In defence of usury Bentham's rejoinder to Smith's arguments may well have set the standard for fanciful and specious reasoning to which modern economics has since aspired.

Smith referred to two classes of borrowers who could be expected to accede to rates of interest substantially above the lowest market rate: 'prodigals and projectors.' The former are individuals who would waste the money on conspicuous consumption; the latter are those who promote ill-conceived schemes to the public, which result in inappropriate investment. Smith's case in favor of a legal ceiling to the rate of interest thus had both a 'micro-economic' and a 'macroeconomic' aspect.

Macroeconomics was Smith's key concern: encouraging 'prodigals and

---

4 Muslim societies continue with the traditional definition, and therefore prohibit – with varying degrees of effectiveness – any loan contract in which the lender does not share in the risk of the project.

5 'In a country, such as Great Britain, where money is lent to government at three per cent and to private people upon a good security at four and four and a half, the present legal rate, five per cent, is perhaps as proper as any' (Smith 1838 [1776]: Book II, ch. 4).

projectors' would result in 'a great part of the capital of the country' being thrown into the hands of 'those which were most likely to waste and destroy it.' The ceiling, by removing the incentive to lend to such borrowers, would result in a higher overall quality of investment, and thus higher growth.

Bentham's riposte ignored macroeconomics. Instead, it began from the microeconomic and libertarian presumption that 'no man of ripe years and of sound mind, acting freely, and with his eyes open, ought to be hindered, with a view to his advantage, from making such bargain, in the way of obtaining money, as he thinks fit' (Bentham 1787).

He initially conceded that the restraint of prodigal behavior may give grounds for setting a ceiling to the rate of interest, only to then argue that in practice a prodigal would not be charged an exorbitant rate of interest. He began with the proposition that 'no man [...] ever thinks of borrowing money to spend, so long as he has ready money of his own, or effects which he can turn into ready money without loss.' Secondly, the exceptions to the above rule who have the requisite collateral can get a loan at the usual rate. Thirdly, those who do not have security will only be lent to by those who like them, and these friendly persons will naturally offer them the standard rate: 'Persons who either feel, or find reasons for pretending to feel, a friendship for the borrower, can not take of him more than the ordinary rate of interest: persons who have no such motive for lending him, will not lend him at all' (ibid.).

If Bentham were to be believed, the friendly bank manager of the 1950s had many a precursor in eighteenth-century Britain, while the rapacious Shylock perished with Shakespeare in the seventeenth.

A bit of empirical research would have revealed that, though rates of interest had fallen dramatically as finance became institutionalized, there was no shortage of lenders willing to hand prodigals ready cash at high rates of interest, in return for ownership of their assets should they go bankrupt. But Bentham's more important sleight of mind was to ignore the macroeconomic argument that the legislative ceiling to the rate of interest improved the overall quality of investment by favoring 'sober people' over 'prodigals and projectors.'

The historical record favored Smith. The seventeenth, eighteenth and nineteenth centuries are awash with examples of projectors promoting fantastic schemes to a gullible public. The most famous have entered the folklore of society: the Tulip Mania, the South Sea Bubble, the Mississippi Land Scheme (Mackay 1841). What has not sunk in so deeply is that the financial panics that occurred when these bubbles burst frequently ruined whole countries.[6]

However, the tide of social change and the development of economic theory favored Bentham. The statutes setting maximum rates were eventually

---

6 The best record of the famous early panics is in Charles Mackay's *Extraordinary Popular Delusions and the Madness of Crowds*. The chronicler of our day is Charles P. Kindleberger.

repealed, the concept of usury itself came to be regarded as one of those quaint preoccupations of a more religious age, and modern economics extended Bentham's concept that 'putting money out at interest, is exchanging present money for future' (Bentham 1787). Of course, the magnificent edifice economists built upon Bentham's morsel assumed that everything happened in equilibrium.

The time value of goods In keeping with the economic belief that the economy is fundamentally a barter system, in which money is merely a lubricant, Fisher restated Bentham's concept in terms of goods, rather than money: the rate of interest 'expresses a price in the exchange between present and future goods' (Fisher 1930).

Fisher's model had three components: the subjective preferences of different individuals between consuming more now by borrowing, or consuming more in the future by forgoing consumption now and lending instead; the objective possibilities for investment; and a market which reconciled the two.

From the subjective perspective, a lender of money is someone who, compared to the prevailing rate of interest, has a low time preference for present over future goods. Someone who would be willing to forgo $100 worth of consumption today in return for $103 worth of consumption next year has a rate of time preference of 3 percent. If the prevailing interest rate is in fact 6 percent, then by lending out $100 today, this person enables himself to consume $106 worth of commodities next year, and has clearly made a personal gain. This person will therefore be a lender when the interest rate is 6 percent.

Conversely, a borrower is someone who has a high time preference for present goods over future goods. Someone who would require $110 next year in order to be tempted to forgo consuming $100 today would decide that, at a rate of interest of 6 percent, it was worth his while to borrow. That way, he can finance $100 worth of consumption today, at a cost of only $106 worth of consumption next year. This person will be a borrower at an interest rate of 6 percent.

The act of borrowing is thus a means by which those with a high preference for present goods acquire the funds they need now, at the expense of some of their later income.

Individual preferences themselves depend in part upon the income flow that an individual anticipates, so that a wealthy individual, or someone who expects income to fall in the future, is likely to be a lender, whereas a poor individual, or one who expects income to rise in the future, is likely to be a borrower.

At a very low rate of interest, even people who have a very low time preference are unlikely to lend money, since the return from lending would be below their rate of time preference. At a very high rate of interest, even those who have a high time preference are likely to be lenders instead, since the high rate of interest would exceed their rate of time preference. This relationship between the rate of interest and the supply of funds gives us an upward-sloping supply curve for money.

The objective perspective reflects the possibilities for profitable investment. At a high rate of interest, only a small number of investment projects will be expected to turn a profit, and therefore investment will be low. At a low rate of interest, almost all projects are likely to turn a profit over financing costs, so the demand for money will be very high. This relationship between the interest rate and the demand for money gives us a downward-sloping demand curve for money.

The market mechanism brings these two forces into harmony by yielding the equilibrium rate of interest.

§65

Economics, it appears, is back in familiar territory. But there are some special, time-based nuances to the credit market. In the goods market, transactions occur immediately: one bundle of goods today is exchanged for another bundle of goods today. However, in the credit market, the 'purchaser' (the company offering an investment opportunity) takes immediate delivery of the loan, but repays principal and interest in installments over time. Ancillary assumptions were therefore required to stretch the standard static vision of the market to the time-based creature that credit really is. These additional assumptions, in Fisher's words, were: '(A) The market must be cleared – and cleared with respect to every interval of time. (B) The debts must be paid' (ibid.).

Fisher saw nothing wrong with these ancillary assumptions, until he and countless others personally violated them during the Great Depression.

Fisher during the Crash: 'don't panic'

To his credit, Fisher's response to the Great Depression was worthy of Keynes's apocryphal statement that 'when the facts prove me wrong, I change my mind.' But at first Fisher clung to his pre-Crash optimism that the American economy was fundamentally sound, that a wave of invention had introduced a new era of higher productivity, that the new medium of radio would revolutionize business. It all sounds so familiar today …

A new era … Fisher's comments to a bankers' forum on 'Black Wednesday' – 23 October, when stocks fell by an unprecedented 6.3 percent in one day – confirm the old adage that 'the more things change, the more they remain the same.' Every factor that Fisher then thought justified the stock market's bull run has its counterpart today: it was 'a new era,' a wave of invention (read 'the Internet') justified high valuations, stable prices reduced the uncertainty of share ownership, stocks were better long-term investments than bonds, investment trusts (read 'mutual funds') enabled much more intelligent stock selection, a debt-financed consumer boom was natural when a great increase in income was rationally anticipated.

Fisher first recounted the ways in which the 1929 stock market boom was remarkable. Shares had doubled in value since 1926, and any investor who had 'followed the herd' and bought and sold shares simply on the basis of their popularity would have increased his wealth tenfold in those three years. Stock prices had risen so much that dividend yields were below bond yields. Brokers' loans – effectively margin call lending – were at their highest level in history. All these observations supported the notion that the market 'seems too high and to warrant a major bear movement' (Fisher 1929).

However, he then gave four reasons why the 1929 valuations were sensible: changed expectations of future earnings, reinvestment of dividends, a change in risk premiums, and a change in the way in which future income is discounted.

He supported the first argument with the statement that

> We are now applying science and invention to industry as we never applied it before. *We are living in a new era,* and it is of the utmost importance for every businessman and every banker to understand this new era and its implications [...] All the resources of modern scientific chemistry, metallurgy, electricity, are being utilized – for what? To make big incomes for the people of the United States in the future, to add to the dividends of corporations which are handling these new inventions, and necessarily, therefore, to raise the prices of stocks which represent shares in these new inventions. (Ibid.; emphasis added)

This wave of invention, with its return in years yet to come, meant that it was quite natural for the ratio of share price to historic earnings to rise. In fact, these new firms should be expected to make losses as they established their new inventions: 'In the airline industry very little attention is paid to the earnings today, because the price of the stock is purely a speculation on the far bigger returns that are expected in the future. Any new invention [...] at first does not give any profit [...]' (ibid.).

Low inflation also played a role in high stock valuations, since a stable price level gives 'an immense impulse towards prosperity' (ibid.).

The second factor, the reinvestment of dividends, was a positive force since firms that did this – rather than handing dividends back to investors – were able to grow more rapidly. Hence 'many of the stocks which sell the highest on the stock exchange and which have had the most spectacular rise are not paying any dividends' (ibid.).

The third reason, a change in the way the public estimates risk, occurred because Edgar Smith's influential book *Common Stocks as Long Term Investments* had shown that over the longer term stocks outperformed bonds. As a result, '[t]here has been almost a stampede towards stocks, and away from bonds' (ibid.; in the late 1990s, Hassett and Glassman's *Dow 36,000* and its ilk spread the same delusion).

This movement had led to the establishment of the new profession of investment counseling, and then the new institution of investment trusts, which 'can afford to make studies of stocks which the individual investor could not study' (ibid.). As well as diversifying and spreading risk, these institutions enabled stocks to be scientifically selected. This explained why 'our stock market is highly selective today,' and as a result Fisher wasn't troubled by the fact that: 'Half of the stocks during the last year have fallen in spite of the fact that the average as shown by the index numbers had risen. The leaders are becoming fewer and fewer, and those stocks that are leading have a greater and greater scarcity value' (ibid.).

Fisher conceded that rank speculation played some role in the market, but he blamed this 'lunatic fringe' more for the crash in stock prices than for its run-up over the preceding four years: 'There is a certain lunatic fringe in the stock market, and there always will be whenever there is any successful bear movement going on [...] they will put the stocks up above what they should be and, when frightened, [...] will immediately want to sell out' (ibid.).

This speculative fringe ranked fifteenth out of Fisher's fifteen determinants of the level of stock prices, though he was not so confident of his ranking after the market's 6 percent fall on Black Wednesday. Nonetheless, he still argued that 'the other fourteen causes are far more important than this one cause itself.' He acknowledged that most speculation took place with borrowed money – a theme that would later become his *bête noire*. But he argued that most of this money had been borrowed to finance consumption today – rather than just rank speculation – because consumers were simply cashing in on rationally anticipated future increases in income:

> To a certain extent it is normal that during an era such as we are now pass-ing through, where the income of the people of the United States is bound to increase faster perhaps than ever before in its history, and it has during the last few years increased amazingly, that we should try to cash in on future income in advance of its occurring, exactly on the principle that when a young man knows he has been given unexpectedly a large bequest, and that it will be in his hands inside a year, he will borrow against it in advance. In other words, there ought to be a big demand for loans at a high rate of interest during a period of great increase in income. (Ibid.)

He concluded with an expectation that the market's 12 percent fall in the preceding eight days was an aberration:

> Great prosperity at present and greater prosperity in view in the future [...] rather than speculation [...] explain the high stock markets, and when it is finally rid of the lunatic fringe, the stock market will never go back to 50 per

cent of its present level [...] We shall not see very much further, if any, recession in the stock market, but rather [...] a resumption of the bull market, not as rapidly as it has been in the past, but still a bull rather than a bear movement. (Ibid.)

Fisher after the Crash: the debt-deflation hypothesis Fisher was, of course, profoundly wrong, and at great personal cost to himself. The market receded 90 percent from its peak, and the index did not regain its 1929 level for a quarter of a century.[7] As the Crash persisted, the slump deepened into the Great Depression, with, at its nadir, over 25 percent of America's workers unemployed. Fisher's personal fortune evaporated, and his perspective on the American financial system shifted from one of confidence to one of alarm.

He eventually developed a radically different analysis of finance, one in which his ancillary assumptions in *The Theory of Interest* – that 'the market must be cleared, and cleared with respect to every interval of time' and that 'The debts must be paid' – were systematically violated. Now he acknowledged that the market was never in equilibrium, and that debts could fail to be repaid, not just individually but en masse. Static reasoning gave way to an analysis of the dynamic forces which could have caused the Great Depression.

Whereas he had previously assumed that the economy was always in equilibrium, now he appreciated that even if the real economy actually momentarily reached equilibrium, this state would be short lived since 'new disturbances are, humanly speaking, sure to occur, so that, in actual fact, any variable is almost always above or below the ideal equilibrium' (Fisher 1933).

Equilibrium was also likely to be precarious. Whereas beforehand he had simply taken it for granted that equilibrium was stable, now he realized that equilibrium, 'though stable, is so delicately poised that, after departure from it beyond certain limits, instability ensues.' A slight movement away from equilibrium could set in train forces that would drive the economy even farther away, rather than returning it to balance.

While any of a multitude of factors could, according to Fisher, push the system away from equilibrium, the crucial ingredient needed to turn this limited instability into a catastrophic collapse was an excessive level of debt, where 'the breaking of many debtors constitutes a "crash," after which there is no coming back to the original equilibrium.'

He ventured the opinion that the 'two dominant factors' that cause depressions are 'over-indebtedness to start with and deflation following soon after.' Though other factors are important, debt – the entry into a contractual obligation to repay principal with interest – and a falling price level are crucial:

---

7 Of course, many of the high-flying companies of 1929 were no longer in the index in 1955, so that anyone who held on to their 1929 share portfolio took far more than twenty-five years to get their money back, and most of the shares they held were worthless.

Thus over-investment and over-speculation are often important; but they would have far less serious results were they not conducted with borrowed money. That is, over-indebtedness may lend importance to over-investment or to over-speculation. The same is true as to over-confidence. I fancy that over-confidence seldom does any great harm except when, as, and if, it beguiles its victims into debt. (Ibid.)

The final sentence in this quote is rather poignant, since Fisher himself was a classic instance of someone whom overconfidence had beguiled into debt.[8]

Overconfidence leads investors to overestimate the prospective gain from investment, or to underestimate the risks, and thus commit themselves to an unsustainable level of debt. In either case, the investor commits funds well beyond the level which returns an optimum gain. Such overconfidence is an inevitability in the real world because, as noted above, all real-world variables are bound to be either above or below their ideal equilibrium values.

A chain reaction then ensues that can tip the economy into depression. It begins with distress selling, at severely reduced prices, driven by the need to cover debt repayments. Falling prices means that the real burden of debt actually rises, even as nominal debt is reduced, and the repayment of debts also reduces the money supply. These effects cause further bankruptcies, reducing profits, investment, output and employment. Pessimism rises, causing those with money to hoard it, which further reduces business activity. The falling price level also has the perverse effect that the real rate of interest rises even though nominal rates have fallen, and this drastically reduces investment.

Fisher's theory was thus an alternative explanation of the Great Depression to both Keynes's rejection of Say's Law and Hicks's 'liquidity trap' (discussed in Chapter 9). But though the chain reaction argument is plausible, Fisher provided no formal proof for it – in contrast to his previous emphasis upon formal mathematical reasoning. Partly for this reason, his thesis was received poorly by the economics profession, and his insights were swamped by the rapid adoption of Hicks's IS-LM analysis after the publication of Keynes's *General Theory*.[9]

After the Great Depression, economists continued to cite his pre-Crash work on finance, while his debt-deflation theory was largely ignored.[10] As a result, the antipathy he saw between the formal concept of equilibrium and the actual performance of asset markets was also ignored. Equilibrium once

---

8 Barber notes that after Fisher came into great wealth when his filing invention was taken over by the Remington Rand Corporation, he was 'eager to add to his portfolio of common stocks and placed himself in some exposed positions in order to do so. At this time, his confidence in the soundness of the American economy was complete' (Barber 1997).

9 Barber observed that among the other reasons was the fact that 'In the 1930s, his insistence on the urgency of "quick fix" solutions generated frictions between Fisher and other professional economists' (ibid.).

10 Almost 90 percent of the over 1,200 citations of Fisher in academic journals from 1956 were references to his pre-Great Depression works (Feher 1999).

again became the defining feature of the economic analysis of finance. This process reached its zenith with the development of what is known as the 'efficient markets hypothesis.'

The efficient markets hypothesis

Non-economists often surmise that the term 'efficient' refers to the speed at which operations take place on the stock market, and/or the cost per transaction. Since the former has risen and the latter fallen dramatically with computers, the proposition that the stock market is efficient appears sensible. Market efficiency is often alleged to mean that 'investors are assumed to make efficient use of all available information,' which also seems quite reasonable.

However, the economic concept of efficiency means something quite different from the normal parlance. In the case of the stock market, it means at least four things:

- that the collective expectations of stock market investors are accurate predictions of the future prospects of companies;
- that share prices fully reflect all information pertinent to the future prospects of traded companies;
- that changes in share prices are entirely due to changes in information relevant to future prospects, where that information arrives in an unpredictable and random fashion; and
- that therefore stock prices 'follow a random walk,' so that past movements in prices give no information about what future movements will be – just as past rolls of dice can't be used to predict what the next roll will be.

These propositions are a collage of the assumptions and conclusions of the 'efficient markets hypothesis' (EMH) and the 'capital assets pricing model' (CAPM), which were formal extensions to Fisher's (pre-Depression) time value of money theories. Like the Fisher theories of old, these new theories were microeconomic in nature, and presumed that finance markets are continually in equilibrium. There were several economists who developed this sophisticated equilibrium analysis of finance. In what follows I will focus on the work of W. F. Sharpe.

Risk and return It seems reasonable, a priori, to argue that an asset that gives a high return is likely to be riskier than one that gives a lower return. If an investor wants complete safety, then he can invest in government bonds. If a higher rate of return is desired, then he can invest in corporate bonds, or shares. The former hold the risk of default, while the latter can rise or fall unpredictably in price, and do not have a guaranteed income flow. Therefore there is a 'trade-off' between return and risk: a higher return can be earned, but only at the cost of a higher level of risk.

§66

Sharpe provided an explanation for this in terms of the theory of individual behavior discussed in Chapter 3. Once again, we find ourselves tobogganing up and down indifference curves.

The individual rational investor Sharpe began by assuming that 'an individual views the outcome of any investment in probabilistic terms; he is willing to act on the basis of [...] expected value and standard deviation' (Sharpe 1964: 427–8). An investor gets greater utility from a higher return than a lower one, and lower utility from an asset with a high standard deviation than a lower one. This assumption enabled Sharpe to plot an investor's preferences in terms of indifference curves, with the two 'goods' being risk and return.

However, there was one twist compared to standard indifference curve analysis as outlined in Chapter 3. Risk is a 'bad,' not a 'good' – and a consumer maximizes his utility by experiencing as little risk as possible. So the most desirable investment is one that gives a very high return with very little risk. Consequently, rather than being drawn to show that more of both goods is better, these indifference curves are drawn to show that more return and less risk is better.

With standard goods, the consumer prefers more of both, so the desirable direction to move in on the indifference map is up and to the right – which means you feel better as you get more of both commodities. But with return and risk as the 'goods,' the desirable direction is more return and less risk. Sharpe drew expected return on the horizontal axis and risk on the vertical, so the most desirable direction was to the right – which gave you more return – and down – which gave you less risk. The highest utility comes from the highest return and the *lowest* risk.

That takes care of the consumer's preferences. To complete the analysis, a budget line is needed as well – and here again there was a twist compared to the analysis of consumption. Rather than the budget line being the investor's income, the budget 'line' was the spectrum of investments that an investor could make. Each individual investment was a share in some company,[11] and all the information about them was reduced to their expected returns and the standard deviation of their expected returns. These could have any pattern at all – some investments would have a very high expected return and low variability, others a low expected return and high variability, and so on. Each company could then be described by a point on the graph of return versus risk, where the horizontal position was the return and the vertical position was the risk.

This resulted in a 'cloud' of possible investments that were potentially available to investors, where the most desirable investments were those with high return – the farther out along the horizontal axis, the better – and low risk – the lower down on the vertical axis, the better.

11 Strictly speaking, this was supposed to be anything in which one could invest, but practically the theory was applied as if the investments were restricted to shares.

With this picture of investor behavior, Sharpe showed that the only invest-ments that are rational for this investor are those that fall on the edge of the cloud of possible investments, which he labels the 'investment opportunity curve' or IOC (ibid.: 429). These investments give the highest return and the lowest risk possible. Any other combination that is not on the edge of the cloud can be topped by one farther out that has both a higher return and a lower risk.[12]

If this were the end of the matter, then the investor would choose the particular combination that coincided with their preferred risk–return trade-

§67 off, and that would be that.

However, it's possible to combine share-market investments with a bond that has much lower volatility, and Sharpe assumed the existence of a bond that paid a very low return, but had no risk. Sharpe linked bond and share investments with one further assumption: *that the investor could borrow as much as he wanted at the riskless rate of interest*. This assumption meant that, in Sharpe's model, an investor could invest some money in the riskless (but low-return) bond, and some money in risky (but higher-return) shares to create an investment portfolio.

This portfolio was represented by a straight line linking the riskless bond with a selection of shares (where the only selection that made sense was one that was on the Investment Opportunity Curve, and tangential to a line drawn through the riskless bond). Sharpe called this line the 'capital market

§68 line' or CML (ibid.: 425).

With borrowing, the investor's risk–return preferences no longer deter-mined which shares he bought; instead, they determined where he sat on the CML.

An ultra-conservative investor would just buy the riskless bond and nothing else: that would put him on the horizontal axis (where risk is zero) but only a short distance out along the horizontal axis – which means only a very low return. Someone who was happy with the market return – the return on an investment in shares alone – would buy only shares. Someone who wanted a *higher* return than shares provided could do so by borrowing money at the riskless rate and buying shares with this borrowed money as well as their own (in the real world, this is called buying shares on margin).

All together now? At this stage, Sharpe encountered a problem. As well as every investor having a different set of indifference curves between risk and return, each would also have a different opinion about the return and risk that would be associated with each possible investment. Thus investor C might think that investment F – say the Internet company Yahoo – was

---

12 Since diversification reduces risk, all investments along this edge must be portfolios rather than individual shares. This concept is important in Sharpe's analysis of the valuation of a single investment, which I don't consider in this summary.

likely to yield a low return at high risk, while investor A might expect that Yahoo will give high returns with little variation.

In other words, each investor would perceive a different 'cloud' of investment opportunities. The edge of the cloud of investment opportunities, the IOC, would be different for every investor, in terms of both location and the investments in it.

Equally, lenders may charge a different rate of interest to every borrower, so that the location P would differ between individuals. They might also restrict credit to some (or all) investors, so that the length of the line between each investor's P would differ – rather than being infinitely long, as Sharpe assumed. It might not even be a line, but could well be a curve, with lenders charging a higher rate of interest as borrowers committed themselves to more and more debt.

In other words, as with every neoclassical theorem, Sharpe encountered an aggregation problem in going from the isolated individual to the level of society. And, like every neoclassical economist, he took the time-honored approach of assuming the problem away. He assumed (a) that all investors could borrow or lend as much as they liked at the same rate, and (b) that investors all agreed on the expected prospects for each and every investment.

Sharpe admitted that these were extreme assumptions, but he justified them by an appeal to the methodological authority of 'assumptions don't matter' Milton Friedman. In Sharpe's words:

> In order to derive conditions for equilibrium in the capital market we invoke two assumptions. First, we assume a common pure rate of interest, with all investors able to borrow or lend funds on equal terms. Second, we assume homogeneity of investor expectations: investors are assumed to agree on the prospects of various investments – the expected values, standard deviations and correlation coefficients described in Part II. *Needless to say, these are highly restrictive and undoubtedly unrealistic assumptions.* However, since the proper test of a theory is not the realism of its assumptions but the acceptability of its implications, and since these assumptions imply equilibrium conditions which form a major part of classical financial doctrine, it is far from clear that this formulation should be rejected – especially in view of the dearth of alternative models leading to similar results. (Ibid.; emphasis added)

Though Sharpe doesn't explicitly say this, he also assumes that investor expectations are accurate: that the returns investors expect firms to achieve will actually happen.

With these handy assumptions under his belt, the problem was greatly simplified. The riskless asset was the same for all investors. The IOC was the same for all investors. Therefore all investors would want to invest in some combination of the riskless asset and the same share portfolio. All that differed were investor risk–return preferences.

Some would borrow money to move farther 'northeast' (towards a higher return with higher risk) than the point at which their indifference map was tangential to the IOC. Others would lend money to move 'southwest' from the point of tangency between their indifference map and the IOC, thus getting a lower return and a lower risk.

Since all investors will attempt to buy the same portfolio, and no investors will attempt to buy any other investment, the market mechanism kicks in. This one portfolio rises in price, while all other investments fall in price. This process of repricing investments alters their returns, and flattens the edge of the IOC.

§69

The final step in Sharpe's argument relates the return on any single share to the overall market return, with a relation known these days as the share's 'beta.'[13] What this means in practice is that the efficient markets hypothesis asserts that the more volatile a share's returns are, the higher will be its expected yield. There is a trade-off between risk and return.

Sharpe's paper formed the core of the EMH. Others added ancillary elements – such as the argument that how a firm is internally financed has no impact on its value, that dividends are irrelevant to a share's value, and so on. If this set of theories were correct, then the propositions cited earlier would be true: the collective expectations of investors will be an accurate prediction of the future prospects of companies; share prices will fully reflect all information pertinent to the future prospects of traded companies.[14] Changes in share prices will be entirely due to changes in information relevant to future prospects; and prices will 'follow a random walk,' so that past movements in prices give no information about what future movements will be.

Reservations The outline above covers the theory as it is usually presented to undergraduates (and victims of MBA programs), and as it was believed by its adherents among stockbrokers and speculators (of whom there are now almost none). But Sharpe was aware that it was unsatisfactory, mainly because of side effects from the assumptions that investors are in complete agreement about the future prospects of traded companies, and that all investors can borrow or lend as much as they want at the riskless rate of interest.

One obvious side effect of the first assumption is that, once equilibrium is reached, trade on the stock exchange should cease. Thereafter, any trading should merely be the result of the random arrival of new information, or the temporary disturbance of equilibrium via the floating of some new security. The trading profile of the stock market should therefore be like that of an almost extinct volcano.

13 In words, this formula asserts that the expected return on a share will equal the risk-free rate (P), plus 'beta' times the difference between the overall market return and the risk-free rate. Beta itself is a measure of the ratio of the variability of a given share's return to the variability of the market index, and the degree of correlation between the share's return and the market index return.

14 There are three variations on this, known as the weak, semi-strong and strong forms of the EMH.

Instead, even back in the 1960s when this paper was written, the stock market behaved like a very active volcano in terms of both price volatility and the volume of trades. It has become even more so since, and in 1987 it did a reasonable, though short-lived, impression of Krakatoa.

The second assumption implies that anyone could borrow sufficient money to purchase all the shares in, say, Microsoft, and pay no more than the riskless rate of interest to do it. This implies a degree of liquidity that is simply impossible in the real world.

Sharpe very honestly discussed both the reality of these assumptions, and the implications of dropping them. He readily conceded that 'even the most casual empiricism' suggests that the assumption of complete agreement is false: 'People often hold passionately to beliefs that are far from universal. The seller of a share of IBM stock may be convinced that it is worth considerably less than the sales price. The buyer may be convinced that it is worth considerably more' (Sharpe 1970). If this assumption is dropped, then in place of the single 'security market line,' and a spectrum of efficient investments which is the same for all investors, there is a different security market line for each investor. The clean simplicity of the EMH collapses.

The assumption that we can all borrow (or lend) as much as we like at the riskless rate of interest is just as unrealistic as the assumption that all investors agree. Sharpe concedes that the theory collapses once one accepts the reality that the borrowing rate normally exceeds the lending rate, that investors are credit rationed, and that the borrowing rate tends to rise as the amount being borrowed increases:

> The consequence of accommodating such aspects of reality are likely to be disastrous in terms of the usefulness of the resulting theory [...] The capital market line no longer exists. Instead, there is a capital market curve – linear over some ranges, perhaps, but becoming flatter as [risk] increases over other ranges. Moreover, there is no single optimal combination of risky securities; the preferred combination depends upon the investors' preferences [...]
> The demise of the capital market line is followed immediately by that of the security market line. The theory is in a shambles. (Ibid.)

But in the end, faced with a choice between an unrealistic theory and no theory at all, Sharpe opts for theory. His comfort in this choice continues to be Milton Friedman's methodological escape route that the unrealism of assumptions 'is not important in itself. More relevant, the implications are not wildly inconsistent with observed behavior' (ibid.).

But as discussed in Chapter 9, this argument that assumptions don't matter is valid only if they are negligibility assumptions (which dismiss features of the real world which are irrelevant or immaterial to the system being modeled) or heuristic assumptions (which are used to simplify argument en route to a more general theory, where the assumptions are dropped).

Do Sharpe's assumptions qualify under either of those headings? Clearly not. They are not negligibility assumptions – if they were, then dropping them would not leave the theory 'in a shambles.' They are not heuristic assumptions since, as Sharpe concedes, once they are dropped the theory collapses, and he had no alternative to offer.

Instead, they are domain assumptions (factors that are required to make the theory valid, and in the absence of which the theory is invalid), and therefore the theory is valid only in a world in which those assumptions apply.

That is clearly not our world. The EMH cannot apply in a world in which investors differ in their expectations, in which the future is uncertain, and in which borrowing is rationed. It should have been taken seriously only had Sharpe or its other developers succeeded in using it as a stepping stone to a theory which took account of uncertainty, diverse expectations, and credit rationing. Since they did not do so, the EMH should never have been given any credibility – yet instead it became an article of faith for academics in finance, and a common belief in the commercial world of finance.

Sharpe deserves commendation for honestly discussing the impact on his theory of relaxing his assumptions – unfortunately, the same can't be said for the textbook writers who promulgated his views. However, the problems he saw with his theory are just the tip of the iceberg. There are so many others that it is difficult to think of a theory that could less accurately describe how stock markets behave.

Efficient or prophetic market? Figure 11.1 illustrates the process which the EMH alleges investors use to determine the value of capital assets. Investors objectively consider information about the investment opportunities offered by different companies, and data about world economic prospects. Information

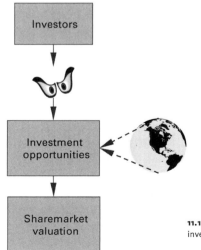

11.1 How the EMH imagines that investors behave

that affects the future prospects of investments arrives randomly, generating random movements in the expected future prospects of firms. Investors' rational appraisal of this information leads to an efficient valuation of shares on the basis of expected return and risk, with price variations being caused by the random arrival of new information pertinent to share prices.

This is a one-way process: there is no feedback from share market valuations to investor perceptions, and most importantly, investors are uninterested in what other investors are doing. This, of course, follows naturally from the assumption that all investors agree about the valuations of all companies: why bother checking what your neighbor thinks when you know he thinks exactly what you do (and any difference between his behavior and yours simply reflects his different risk–return preferences)?

To put it mildly, there are serious problems with this theory of stock market behavior. For starters, the EMH makes no distinction between investors' expectations of the future and the future which actually occurs. In essence, the EMH presumes that investors' expectations will be fulfilled: that returns will actually turn out to be what investors expected them to be. In effect, every stock market investor is assumed to be Nostradamus. What economists describe as 'efficient' actually requires that investors be prophetic.

As soon as you allow that investors can disagree, then this economic notion of 'efficient expectations' also collapses. If investors disagree about the future prospects of companies, then inevitably the future is not going to turn out as most – or perhaps even any – investors expect.

This divergence between expectations and outcomes will set up disequilibrium dynamics in the stock market – precisely the sort of behavior that the EMH cannot model, because it is above all a theory of market equilibrium. If investors influence each other's expectations, this is likely to lead to periods when the market is dominated by pessimistic and optimistic sentiment, and there will be cycles in the market as it shifts from one dominant sentiment to the other.

The efficient markets hypothesis was used to berate market participants for believing that such phenomena as 'bull' and 'bear' markets actually existed: there was always only the efficient market. But even a slight concession to reality indicates that bull and bear phases will be part and parcel of a real-world stock market.

Risks ain't risks Sharpe's measure of risk was standard deviation, a statistical measure of how much the values thrown up by some process vary. If values are fairly evenly distributed around an average, then roughly two-thirds of all outcomes will be one standard deviation either side of the average.

For example, tests of IQ often have an average of 100 and a standard deviation of 16. This means that two-thirds of the population will score between 84 and 116 on an IQ test.

There are at least two problems with applying this concept to investment:

- Is variability really what an investor means by risk?
- To actually work out a standard deviation, you need some process that has thrown up lots of historical data with a pattern which can be expected to continue recurring in the future.

Consider two investments: Steady has an average return of 3 percent, and a standard deviation of 3 percent; Shaky has an average return of 9 percent, and a standard deviation of 6 percent. Which one is 'riskier'?

According to Sharpe's criterion, Shaky is riskier: its standard deviation is twice as big as Steady's. However, according to any sane investor, Steady would be riskier – since there's a much higher chance of getting a negative return from Steady than there is from Shaky. In other words, what an investor really worries about is not so much variability as downside risk. Standard deviation is a very poor proxy for this, even if a standard deviation can be meaningfully calculated in the first place.

This brings us to the second problem. Standard deviation can be used as a measure of variability for things such as the expected outcome of a dice roll, the age at which someone will die, even a golfer's possible scores. However, even here there are differences in how reliable a guide historical averages and standard deviations can be to future outcomes. So long as the dice are well designed, a roll is going to have a one in six chance of turning up a 2 for a considerable time – until, for example, repeated rolls erode its edges. The historical averages for death, however, have changed dramatically in the West even during one lifetime, and major changes (for better or worse, depending on whether genetic engineering or global ecological problems come out on top during the twenty-first century) can be expected in the future. And if an eighteen-year-old golfer had an average of 70 and a standard deviation of 5 now, would you rely on those numbers as a guide to his performance in thirty years' time?

In other words, for measures like standard deviation to be reliable, past outcomes must remain a reliable guide to future outcomes. This is not going to be the case for an investment, because the future performance of a company depends upon future economic circumstances, future inventions, the actions of future competitors, all things to which the past provides no reliable guide beyond a very short time horizon. Investment, and stock market speculation, are, in other words, subject not to risk, but to uncertainty.

We have already discussed the implications of uncertainty for economic analysis. For stock market investors, uncertainty means that the expected yield of an investment over the medium- to long-term future simply can't be known:

> Our knowledge of the factors which will govern the yield of an investment some years hence is usually very slight and often negligible. If we speak

frankly, we have to admit that our basis of knowledge for estimating the yield
ten years hence of a railway, a copper mine, a textile factory, the goodwill
of a patent medicine, an Atlantic liner, a building in the City of London,
amounts to little and sometimes to nothing; or even five years hence. In fact,
those who seriously attempt to make any such estimate are often so much in
the minority that their behavior does not govern the market. (Keynes 1936)

Uncertainty, not risk, is the main factor standing between investors and
an accurate knowledge of the future prospects of companies. As a result,
the expected yield of an investment, the other variable in the EMH model
of investor behavior, simply can't be known.

'The dark forces of time and ignorance ...' The efficient markets hypothesis
argues that investors try to maximize their utility, where the only determinants
of that utility are expected returns on the one hand, and risk on the other.

This kind of analysis has been soundly applied to interpret gambling. A
gambler playing a game of blackjack faces known payoffs, and the known
probabilities of drawing any given card. A good gambler is someone who
intelligently applies these well-known regularities to decide how much to bet,
when to hold, and when to risk another flip of the card.

This is an invalid concept to apply to an investor's behavior, since the game
played in the casino of the stock market is subject to uncertainty, not risk.

Nonetheless, investors still need to form some expectations of the future if
they are going to act at all. These will be based partly on factors they currently
know – such as prevailing economic conditions – and partly on factors they
can't know. In practice, they rely mainly upon the knowable factors simply
because they are knowable: investors therefore extrapolate current trends
into the indefinite future. As Keynes puts it:

It would be foolish, in forming our expectations, to attach great weight to
matters which are very uncertain. It is reasonable, therefore, to be guided to
a considerable degree by the facts about which we feel somewhat confident,
even though they may be less decisively relevant to the issue than other facts
about which our knowledge is vague and scanty. For this reason the facts of
the existing situation enter, in a sense disproportionately, into the formation
of our long-term expectations; our usual practice being to take the existing
situation and to project it into the future, modified only to the extent that we
have more or less definite reasons for expecting a change. (Ibid.)

This is clearly an unreliable practice, but in an uncertain world there is
simply no other way to act. It is something that we must do in order not to
be paralyzed into inaction, but it is something that, at a deep level, we are
aware is untrustworthy. As a result, our forecasts of the future are tempered
by an additional factor, the degree of confidence we have that these forecasts

will be at least approximately correct. The more significant the degree of change expected, the more fragile that confidence will be.

The share market's valuations therefore reflect both collective forecasts, and the confidence with which these forecasts are made. In tranquil times these valuations will be relatively stable, but

> [i]n abnormal times in particular, when the hypothesis of an indefinite continuance of the existing state of affairs is less plausible than usual even though there are no express grounds to anticipate a definite change, the market will be subject to waves of optimistic and pessimistic sentiment, which are unreasoning and yet in a sense legitimate where no solid basis exists for a reasonable calculation. (Ibid.)

Therefore, in this uncertain world, the stock market will be ruled not by dispassionate analysis, but by euphoria, fear, uncertainty and doubt. It will be a place, not of analytic rationality, but of emotion.

The madness of the third degree Keynes once described himself as a speculator who had lost two fortunes and made three. His assessment of the behavior of stock market speculators was thus that of a well-informed insider. Keynes described the stock market as a game of 'Musical Chairs [...] a pastime in which he is victor [...] who secures a chair for himself when the music stops. These games can be played with zest and enjoyment, though all the players know that [...] when the music stops some of the players will find themselves unseated' (ibid.).

The essence of this game is not to work out what particular shares are likely to be worth, but to work out what the majority of other players are likely to think the market will think they are worth, since 'it is not sensible to pay 25 for an investment of which you believe the prospective yield to justify a value of 30, if you also believe that the market will value it at 20 three months hence' (ibid.). In one of the most evocative analogies ever used by an economist, Keynes compared investing in shares to

> those newspaper competitions in which the competitors have to pick out the six prettiest faces from a hundred photographs, the prize being awarded to the competitor whose choice most nearly corresponds to the average preferences of the competitors as a whole; so that each competitor has to pick, not those faces which he himself finds prettiest, but those which he thinks likeliest to catch the fancy of the other competitors, all of whom are looking at the problem from the same point of view. It is not a case of choosing those which, to the best of one's judgment, are really the prettiest, nor even those which average opinion genuinely thinks the prettiest. We have reached the third degree where we devote our intelligences to anticipating what average opinion expects the average opinion to be. (Ibid.)

Though this may seem to be a description of the behavior of amateur investors in Internet chat rooms, Keynes insists that it is also the modus operandi of professional stock managers. First, because the future is uncertain, the kind of long-term forecasting which the EMH assumes is the norm is effectively impossible. It is far easier to anticipate 'changes in the conventional basis of valuation a short time ahead of the general public' (ibid.).

Secondly, the boards that employ such professional stock managers discipline their behavior to make them conform to the norm. Any manager who is truly trying to anticipate future economic trends is bound to make recommendations that are wildly at variance with what is popular in the market, and this behavior will appear eccentric and ill informed in comparison to the current market favorites. Imagine, for example, what would have happened to a funds manager who in mid-2000 advised the fund to sell all its shares in Yahoo, or Amazon, and spend the proceeds buying, for example, bonds.

As Keynes eloquently put it, 'Worldly wisdom teaches that it is better for reputation to fail conventionally than to succeed unconventionally.' Unconventional managers are thus weeded out, leaving behind only those who swim with the crowd.

Thirdly, the long-term investor has to ignore the prospect of quick short-term capital gains, and this runs counter to human nature's desire for quick results.

Finally, a long-term investor can't afford to be highly geared, since the results of being wrong will be expensive and the accumulated financing cost over the long run will be great. Speculators, on the other hand, are attracted to gearing by the allure of large immediate gains now, at a cost of only minor short-term interest charges (especially when the prevailing aura of confidence during a bull market leads them to discount the possibility of large losses).

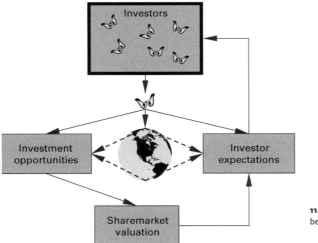

11.2 How speculators actually behave

Thus, according to Keynes, rather than looking dispassionately at invest-ment prospects and world economic conditions, the main thing share market investors do is look furtively and emotionally at each other, to attempt to predict how the majority will value particular companies in the immediate future.

This behavior is pictured in Figure 11.2. Though investors do still keep an eye on individual investments and world conditions, and the world does throw in surprising events from time to time, in the main investors analyze the investment community itself.

As a result, there is a feedback from current share valuations to investors' behavior via the impact that present valuations have on investor expectations. A rising market will tend to encourage investors to believe that the market will continue rising; a falling market will maintain the sentiment of the bears. Such a market can find itself a long way from equilibrium as self-reinforcing waves of sentiment sweep through investors. These waves can just as easily break – though long after any rational calculation might suggest that they should – when it becomes clear that the wave has carried valuations far past a level which is sustainable by corporate earnings.

Addendum: Fama overboard

Eugene Fama and his collaborator Kenneth French played a key role in promoting the efficient markets hypothesis, right from Fama's first major paper while still a PhD student, in which he stated that: 'For the purposes of most investors the efficient markets model seems a good first (and second) approximation to reality. In short, the evidence in support of the efficient markets model is extensive, and (somewhat uniquely in economics) contradic-tory evidence is sparse' (Fama 1970: 416).

Since then, Fama has become almost synonymous with the efficient markets hypothesis – he, rather than Sharpe, is the author referred to as the origina-tor of the hypothesis in most textbooks on finance. So it's rather significant that, in a major survey article published in 2004, he and French effectively disowned the theory:

> The attraction of the CAPM is that it offers powerful and intuitively pleasing predictions about how to measure risk and the relation between expected return and risk. Unfortunately, the empirical record of the model is poor – poor enough to invalidate the way it is used in applications. The CAPM's empirical problems may reflect theoretical failings, the result of many simplifying assumptions [...]
>
> In the end, we argue that whether the model's problems reflect weak-nesses in the theory or in its empirical implementation, *the failure of the CAPM in empirical tests implies that most applications of the model are invalid.* (Fama and French 2004: 25; emphasis added)

Their reasons for reaching this conclusion mirror many of the points covered in Chapter 15 on the alternative 'Fractal Markets Hypothesis' and 'Inefficient Markets Hypothesis' (which I wrote in 2000, four years before Fama and French's paper was published): empirical research shows that the actual behavior of the market strongly contradicts the predictions of the EMH. Specifically:

- share market returns are not at all related to the so-called 'betas';
- much higher returns and lower volatility can be gained by selecting under-valued stocks (ones whose share market value is substantially below their book value); and
- far from there being a trade-off between risk and return, it is possible to select a portfolio that has both high return and low volatility, by avoiding the so-called 'growth stocks' that are popular with market participants.

In considering why the data so strongly contradicted the theory, Fama admitted two points that I labored to make in this chapter: that the theory assumes that all agents have the same expectations about the future *and that those expectations are correct*. Though they put this in a very awkward way, this is unmistakably what they said in this paragraph:

> Sharpe (1964) and Lintner […] add two key assumptions to the Markowitz model to identify a portfolio that must be mean-variance-efficient. The first assumption is *complete agreement*: given market clearing asset prices at *t-1*, investors agree on the joint distribution of asset returns from *t-1* to *t*. *And this distribution is the true one* – that is, it is the distribution from which the returns we use to test the model are drawn. (Ibid.: 26; emphasis added)

A whole generation of economists has thus been taught a theory about finance that assumes that people can predict the future – without that being admitted in the textbook treatments to which they have been exposed, where instead euphemisms such as 'investors make use of all available information' hide the absurd assumptions at the core of the theory.

So wrong it's almost right

The critiques above raise one curious question: how could a theory which was so obviously wrong nonetheless generate predictions about stock market behavior that, at a superficial level, looked roughly right?

One of the key predictions of the EMH is that 'you can't beat the market': in a perfect capital market, price fluctuations simply reflect the random arrival of new information, and yesterday's price trends are as relevant to tomorrow's as the last roll of the dice is to the next.

On the other hand, if the market is as 'imperfect' as argued above, and trends therefore exist, surely it should be possible for the intelligent investor to profit from these trends? If so, wouldn't this eventually lead to all opportunities for profit being sought out, thus removing the trends and, hey presto, making the market efficient? Not necessarily, for two reasons: a factor discussed briefly in Chapter 8: 'chaos,' and the institutional structure of the market, which Keynes detailed in the *General Theory*.

We'll consider these issues in detail in Chapters 13–14, when I finally leave behind the surreal world of neoclassical economics and consider alternative theories that actually try to be realistic about how a complex monetary economy operates. But first, we have to consider the ultimate denouement of neoclassical economics: its utter failure to anticipate the biggest economic event since the Great Depression.

As this and the previous chapter have pointed out, neoclassical economists of the 1920s also failed to see the Great Depression coming, so their failure to anticipate this crisis was par for the course. Then, their failure led to the temporary overthrow of neoclassical economics by Keynes, but as detailed in Chapter 10, neoclassical economists led a successful counter-revolution that not only eliminated Keynes's ideas from economics, but also set Keynes up to be blamed for this crisis – since the most prominent neoclassical economists of the early twenty-first century called themselves 'New Keynesians.'

In the 1920s, the most prominent neoclassical economist was Irving Fisher, and his failure to see the crisis coming destroyed his public reputation.[15] But though Fisher could be criticized for not foreseeing the Great Depression, he could not be blamed for causing it. He was, after all, merely an observer.

This time round, the most prominent neoclassical was Milton Friedman's acolyte Ben Bernanke. Whereas Fisher had merely been an observer, when the Great Recession hit, Bernanke was chairman of the organization charged with ensuring that such calamities don't happen: the Federal Reserve. And he had gotten the job because neoclassical economists believed that, out of all of them, he knew best why the Great Depression occurred, and he was therefore the best man to make sure that 'It' could never happen again.

How wrong they were.

15 As I have explained, however, to Fisher's credit, his failure led to an epiphany that resulted in him renouncing neoclassical thinking, and making a major contribution to the alternative approach to economics that Minsky later developed into the Financial Instability Hypothesis.

12 | MISUNDERSTANDING THE GREAT DEPRESSION AND THE GREAT RECESSION

Bernanke's *Essays on the Great Depression* (Bernanke 2000) is near the top of my stack of books that indicate how poorly neoclassical economists understand capitalism. Most of the others are books of pure theory, such as Debreu's *Theory of Value* (Debreu 1959), or textbooks like Varian's *Microeconomic Analysis* (Varian 1992). Bernanke's distinguished itself by being empirical: he was, he claimed, searching the data to locate the causes of the Great Depression, since:

> To understand the Great Depression is the Holy Grail of macroeconomics. Not only did the Depression give birth to macroeconomics as a distinct field of study, but also – to an extent that is not always fully appreciated – the experience of the 1930s continues to influence macroeconomists' beliefs, policy recommendations, and research agendas. And, practicalities aside, finding an explanation for the worldwide economic collapse of the 1930s remains a fascinating intellectual challenge. (Bernanke 2000: 5)

However, what Bernanke was actually doing was searching for an explanation *that was consistent with neoclassical theory*. Statements to this effect abound throughout the *Essays*, and they highlight the profound difficulty he faced – since according to neoclassical theory, events like the Great Depression should not occur. This disconnection between reality and neoclassical theory had at least the following manifestations that Bernanke admitted to in his *Essays*:

- Monetary variables affect inflation, but are not supposed to affect real variables – money is supposed to be 'neutral':

> Of course, the conclusion that monetary shocks were an important source of the Depression raises a central question in macroeconomics, which is *why nominal shocks should have real effects* (p. 7)

> the gold standard theory leaves unsolved the corresponding 'aggregate supply puzzle,' namely, why were the observed worldwide declines in nominal aggregate demand associated with such deep and persistent contractions in real output and employment? Or, in the language of contemporary macroeconomics, *how can we explain what appears to be a massive and very long-lived instance of monetary nonneutrality*? (p. 277)

- A prolonged macro downturn is inconsistent with rational micro behavior:

  my theory [...] does have the virtues that, first, it seems capable of explaining the unusual length and depth of the Depression; and, second, it can do this without assuming markedly irrational behavior by private economic agents. *Since the reconciliation of the obvious inefficiency of the Depression with the postulate of rational private behavior remains a leading unsolved puzzle of macroeconomics, these two virtues alone provide motivation for serious consideration of this theory* (p. 42; emphasis added)

- Rational behavior by agents should lead to all prices – including money wages – adjusting rapidly to a monetary shock, so that its impact should be transient:

  slow nominal-wage adjustment (in the face of massive unemployment) is *especially difficult to reconcile with the postulate of economic rationality.* We cannot claim to understand the Depression until we can provide a rationale for this paradoxical behavior of wages (p. 7)

- Rapid adjustment of prices should bring the economy back to equilibrium:

  the failure of nominal wages (and, similarly, prices) to adjust seems *inconsistent with the postulate of economic rationality* (p. 32; emphasis added)

Bernanke began well when he stated that the causes of the Great Depression had to lie in a collapse in aggregate demand – though even here he manifested a neoclassical bias of expecting capitalism to rapidly return to equilibrium after any disturbance:

Because the Depression was characterized by sharp declines in both output and prices, the premise of this essay is that declines in aggregate demand were the dominant factor in the onset of the Depression.

This starting point leads naturally to two questions: First, what caused the worldwide collapse in aggregate demand in the late 1920s and early 1930s (the 'aggregate demand puzzle')? Second, why did the Depression last so long? In particular, why didn't the 'normal' stabilizing mechanisms of the economy, such as the adjustment of wages and prices to changes in demand, limit the real economic impact of the fall in aggregate demand (the 'aggregate supply puzzle'). (Ibid.: ix)

However, from this point on, his neoclassical priors excluded both salient data and rival intellectual perspectives on the data. His treatment of Hyman Minsky's 'Financial Instability Hypothesis' – which is outlined in Chapter 13 – is particularly reprehensible. In the entire volume, there is a single, utterly dismissive reference to Minsky:

Hyman Minsky (1977) and Charles Kindleberger [...] have in several places argued for the inherent instability of the financial system but in doing so have had to depart from the assumption of rational economic behavior. [A footnote adds:] I do not deny the possible importance of irrationality in economic life; however it seems that the best research strategy is to push the rationality postulate as far as it will go. (Ibid.: 43)

As we shall see, this is a parody of Minsky's hypothesis. He devoted slightly more space to Irving Fisher and his debt-deflation theory, but what he presented was likewise a parody of Fisher's views, rather than a serious consideration of them:

> The idea of debt-deflation goes back to Irving Fisher (1933). Fisher envisioned a dynamic process in which falling asset and commodity prices created pressure on nominal debtors, forcing them into distress sales of assets, which in turn led to further price declines and financial difficulties. His diagnosis led him to urge President Roosevelt to subordinate exchange-rate considerations to the need for reflation, advice that (ultimately) FDR followed.
>
> Fisher's idea was less influential in academic circles, though, because of the counterargument that debt-deflation represented no more than a redistribution from one group (debtors) to another (creditors). Absent implausibly large differences in marginal spending propensities among the groups, it was suggested, pure redistributions should have no significant macro-economic effects [...] (Ibid.: 24)[1]

There are many grounds on which this is a misrepresentation of Fisher,[2] but the key fallacy is the proposition that debt has no macroeconomic effects. From Bernanke's neoclassical perspective, debt merely involves the transfer of spending power from the saver to the borrower, while deflation merely increases the amount transferred, in debt servicing and repayment, from the borrower back to the saver. Therefore, unless borrowers and savers have very different propensities to consume, this transfer should have no impact on aggregate demand.

The contrast with the theoretical case that Marx, Schumpeter, Keynes and Minsky made about debt and aggregate demand (see pages 217–19) could not be more stark – and in the next chapter I'll make the empirical case that

---

1 Bernanke went on to rephrase debt deflation using several concepts from neoclassical microeconomics – including information asymmetry, the impairment of banks' role as adjudicators of the quality of debtors, and so on. He also ultimately developed a cumbersome neoclassical explanation for nominal wage rigidity which gave debt a role, arguing that 'nonindexation of financial contracts, and the associated debt-deflation, might in some way have been a source of the slow adjustment of wages and other prices' (Bernanke 2000: 32–3). By 'nonindexation,' he meant the fact that debts are not adjusted because of inflation. This is one of many instances of Bernanke criticizing real-world practices because they don't conform to neoclassical theory. In fact, the only country ever to put neoclassical theory on debts into practice was Iceland – with disastrous consequences when its credit bubble burst.

2 For a start, Fisher's process began with over-indebtedness, and falling asset prices were one of the consequences of this.

a collapse in debt-financed demand was *the* cause of both the Great Depression and the Great Recession. Bernanke's neoclassical goggles rendered him incapable of comprehending the best explanations of the Great Depression, and led him to ignore the one data set that overwhelmingly explained the fall in aggregate demand and the collapse in employment.

The three reasons he ultimately provided for the Great Depression were (a) that it was caused by the then Federal Reserve's mismanagement of the money supply between 1928 and 1931; (b) that the slow adjustment of money wages to the fall in aggregate demand is what made it last so long; and (c) that the gold standard transmitted the collapse internationally. His conclusion on the first point was emphatic: 'there is now overwhelming evidence that the main factor depressing aggregate demand was a worldwide contraction in world money supplies. This monetary collapse was itself the result of a poorly managed and technically flawed international monetary system (the gold standard, as reconstituted after World War I)' (ibid.: ix).

He was also emphatic about his 'smoking gun': the Great Depression was triggered by the Federal Reserve's reduction of the US base money supply between June 1928 and June 1931:

> The monetary data for the United States are quite remarkable, and tend to underscore the stinging critique of the Fed's policy choices by Friedman and Schwartz [...] the United States is the only country in which the discretionary component of policy was arguably significantly destabilizing [...] the ratio of monetary base to international reserves [...] fell consistently in the United States from [...] 1928:II [...] through the second quarter of 1931. As a result, U.S. nominal money growth was precisely zero between 1928:IV and 1929:IV, despite both gold inflows and an increase in the money multiplier.
>
> The year 1930 was even worse in this respect: between 1929:IV and 1930:IV, nominal money in the United States fell by almost 6 [percent], even as the U.S. gold stock increased by 8 [percent] over the same period. The proximate cause of this decline in M_1 was continued contraction in the ratio of base to reserves, which reinforced rather than offset declines in the money multiplier. This tightening seems clearly inconsistent with the gold standard's 'rules of the game,' and locates much of the blame for the early (pre-1931) slowdown in world monetary aggregates with the Federal Reserve. (Ibid.: 153)

There are four problems with Bernanke's argument, in addition to the fundamental one of ignoring the role of debt in macroeconomics. First, as far as smoking guns go, this is a pop-gun, not a Colt .45. Secondly, it has fired at other times since World War II (once in nominal terms, and many times when adjusted for inflation) without causing anything remotely like the Great Depression. Thirdly, a close look at the data shows that the correlations between changes in the rate of growth of the money supply[3] and unemployment conflict with Bernanke's argument that mismanagement of the monetary base was the *causa causans* of the Great Depression. Fourthly, the only other time that it has led to a Great Depression-like event was when Bernanke himself was chairman of the Federal Reserve.

Between March 1928 and May 1929, base money fell at an average rate of just over 1 percent per annum in nominal terms, and a maximum rate of minus 1.8 percent.[4] It fell at the same rate between 1948 and 1950, and coincided with a garden-variety recession, rather than a prolonged slump: unemployment peaked at 7.9 percent and rapidly returned to boom levels of under 3 percent. So the pop-gun has fired twice in nominal terms, and only once did it 'cause' a Great Depression.

It could also be argued, from a neoclassical perspective, that the Fed's reduction in base money in the lead-up to the Great Depression was merely a response to the rate of inflation, which had turned negative in mid-1924. Neoclassical theory emphasizes money's role as a means to facilitate transactions, and a falling price level implies a need for less money. On this point Milton Friedman, whom Bernanke cited as a critic of the Federal Reserve for letting base money fall by 1 percent per annum, argued elsewhere that social welfare would be maximized if the money supply actually fell by 10 percent per year.[5]

§70

When the inflation-adjusted rate of change of base money is considered, there were numerous other periods when base money fell as fast as in 1928/29, without leading to a depression-scale event. The average inflation-adjusted rate of growth of M_0 in mid-1928 to mid-1929 was minus 0.5 percent, and

---

3 There are numerous measures of the money supply, with varying definitions of each in different countries. The normal definitions start with currency; then the 'Monetary Base' or M0, which is currency plus the reserve accounts of private banks at the central bank; next is M1, which is currency plus check accounts but *does not include* reserve accounts; then M2, which includes M1 plus savings accounts, small (under $100,000) time deposits and individual money market deposit accounts, and finally M3 – which the US Federal Reserve no longer measures, but which is still tracked by Shadowstats – which includes M2 plus large time deposits and all money market funds.

4 It then grew at up to 2.2 percent per annum until October 1929 (the month of the stock market crash) and then turned sharply negative, falling at a rate of up to 6 percent per annum by October 1930. However, here it is quite likely that the Fed was being swamped by events, rather than being in control, as even Bernanke concedes was the case by 1931: 'As in the case of the United States, then, the story of the world monetary contraction can be summarized as "self-inflicted wounds" for the period through early 1931, and "forces beyond our control" for the two years that followed' (Bernanke 2000: 156).

5 'When prices are stable, one component of the cost [of holding money balances] is zero – namely, the annual cost – but the other component is not – namely, the cost of abstinence. This suggests that, perhaps, just as inflation produces a welfare loss, *deflation may produce a welfare gain.* Suppose therefore that we substitute a furnace for the helicopter. Let us introduce a government which imposes a tax on all individuals and burns up the proceeds, engaging in no other functions. *Let the tax be altered continuously to yield an amount that will produce a steady decline in the quantity of money at the rate of, say, 10 per cent a year*' (Friedman 1969: 16; emphases added). Friedman went on to recommend a lower rate of deflation of 5 percent for expediency reasons ('The rough estimates of the preceding section indicate that that would require for the U.S. a decline in prices at the rate of at least 5 percent per year, and perhaps decidedly more' – p. 46), but even this implied a rate of reduction of the money supply of 2 percent per annum – the same rate that he criticized the Fed for maintaining in the late 1920s.

even in 1930 M_0 fell by a maximum of 2.2 percent per annum in real terms. There were six occasions in the post-World War II period when the real rate of decline of M_0 was greater than this without causing a depression-like event[6] (though there were recessions on all but one occasion). Why did the pop-gun fire then, but emit no smoke?

The reason is, of course, that the pop-gun wasn't really the guilty culprit in the crime of the Great Depression, and Friedman and Bernanke's focus upon it merely diverted attention from the real culprit in this investigation: the economy itself. Capitalism was on trial because of the Great Depression, and the verdict could well have been attempted suicide – which is the last verdict that neoclassical economists could stomach, because they are wedded to the belief that capitalism is inherently stable. They cannot bring themselves to consider the alternative perspective that capitalism is inherently unstable, and that the financial sector causes its most severe breakdowns.

To neoclassicals like Friedman and Bernanke, it was better to blame one of the nurses for incompetence, than to admit that capitalism is a manic-depressive social system that periodically attempts to take its own life. It was better to blame the Fed for not administering its M_0 medicine properly, than to admit that the financial system's proclivity to create too much debt

§71   causes capitalism's periodic breakdowns.

It is therefore a delicious if socially painful irony that the only other time that the pop-gun fired and a depression-like event *did* follow was when the chairman of the Federal Reserve was one Ben S. Bernanke.

Bernanke began as chairman on 1 February 2006, and between October 2007 and July 2008, the change in M_0 was an inflation-adjusted *minus* 3 percent – one percent lower than its steepest rate of decline in 1930–33. The rate of change of M_0 had trended down in nominal terms ever since 2002, when the Greenspan Fed had embarked on some quantitative easing to stimulate the economy during the recession of 2001. Then, M_0 growth had turned from minus 2 percent nominal (and minus 6 percent real) at the end of 2000 to plus 11 percent nominal (and 8 percent real) by July 2001. From there it fell steadily to 1 percent nominal – and minus 3 percent real – by the start of 2008.

§72   Whatever way you look at it, this makes a mockery of the conclusion to Bernanke's fawning speech at Milton Friedman's ninetieth birthday party in November 2002: 'Let me end my talk by abusing slightly my status as an official representative of the Federal Reserve. I would like to say to Milton and Anna: Regarding the Great Depression. You're right, we did it. We're very sorry. But thanks to you, we won't do it again' (Bernanke 2002b).

Either Bernanke forgot what he learnt from Friedman and his own research once in office – since Friedman *and Bernanke's* criticism of the 1920s Fed

---

6   These were June 1946 till January 1949, June 1950 till December 1951, 1957/58, June 1974 till June 1975, 1979–82 and December 2000 till January 2001.

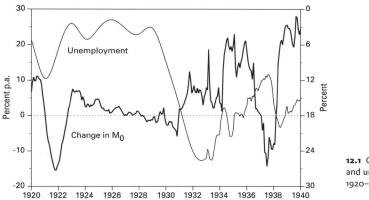

12.1 Change in M_0 and unemployment, 1920–40

was that it let the growth rate of M_0 drop too low *before* the crisis – or the advice itself was irrelevant. The latter is of course the case. As I argue in the next chapter, the key to preventing depressions is to prevent an explosion in the ratio of private debt to GDP, so that debt-financed demand cannot reach a level from which its collapse will trigger a depression. Far from explaining what caused the Great Depression, Friedman and Bernanke's simplistic perspective diverted attention from the real culprit – the expansion of private debt by the banking sector – and ignored the enormous growth of debt that occurred while the central bank was under the thrall of neoclassical economics.

The relative irrelevance of changes in base money as a cause of changes in unemployment, let alone a cause of serious economic breakdown, can be gauged by looking at the correlation between the growth of M_0 and the rate of unemployment over the period from 1920 till 1940 – across both the boom of the Roaring Twenties and the collapse of the Great Depression (see Figure 12.1). If too slow a rate of growth of M_0 can trigger a depression, as Bernanke asserts, then surely there should be a *negative* correlation between the change in M_0 and the rate of unemployment: unemployment should fall when the rate of change of M_0 is high, and rise when it is low.

The correlation has the right sign for the period from 1920 till 1930 (minus 0.22 for changes in nominal M_0 and minus 0.19 after inflation) but the wrong one for the period from 1930 till 1940 (plus 0.28 for nominal M_0 and 0.54 after inflation), and it is positive for the entire period 1920–40 (plus 0.44 for nominal change to M_0, and 0.61 for the inflation-adjusted rate of change). Therefore unemployment *increased* when the rate of growth of M_0 increased, and fell when it fell. Lagging the data on the basis that changes in M_0 should precede changes in unemployment doesn't help either – the correlation remains positive.

On the other hand, the correlation of changes in M_1 to unemployment is negative as expected over both the whole period (minus 0.47 for nominal change and minus 0.21 for inflation-adjusted change) and the sub-periods of the Roaring Twenties (minus .31 for nominal M_1 and 0.79 for inflation-adjusted) and the Great Depression (minus 0.62 for nominal and 0.31 for real). So any causal link relates more to private-bank-driven changes in M_1 than to central-bank-driven changes in M_0.

§73

There are only two interpretations of this, neither of which supports the case that Bernanke made against the 1920s Fed.

The first is that, far from changes in M_0 driving unemployment, *the unemployment rate drives changes in M_0.* The Fed largely ignored the level of unemployment when it was low (during the 1920s), but went into panic policy mode when it exploded during the Great Depression. It therefore increased the level of M_0 when unemployment rose, and decreased it when unemployment seemed to be falling. The causation between changes in M_0 and unemployment is therefore the reverse of the one Bernanke sought to prove.

§74

The second is that other factors are far more important in determining the rate of unemployment – and by extension, causing Great Depressions as well – than the Fed's quantitative monetary policy. Two hints that the private financial system was the culprit are given by the negative relationship between changes in M_1 and unemployment, and by the fact that the relationship of M_0 to M_1 shifted dramatically when the Great Depression hit.

§75

Before the Great Depression, there was a positive relationship between changes in M_0 and changes in M_1, and changes in M_0 appeared to lead changes in M_1 by about one to two months. This is the direction of causation expected by the conventional model of money creation – the 'Money Multiplier' – which argues that commercial banks need reserves in order to be able to lend (though the magnitude is lower than might be expected).

§76

After the Great Depression, this relationship broke down completely, and changes in M_1 appeared to lead changes in M_0 by up to fifteen months. This contradicts the conventional theory – a point I elaborate upon shortly.

So Bernanke's analysis of what caused the Great Depression is erroneous, and to make matters worse, he didn't even follow his own advice prior to the Great Recession when chairman of the Federal Reserve. But he certainly took his own analysis seriously *after* the Great Recession began – increasing M_0 as never before in an attempt to turn deflation into inflation.

After the Great Recession: Bernanke to the rescue?

Bernanke foreshadowed that he might do this in a speech for which he gained the nickname 'Helicopter Ben' in 2002. With the unfortunate title of 'Deflation: making sure "It" doesn't happen here,' it proved to be remarkably unprescient in terms of the economic future, since the US did slip into deflation. But the speech accurately signaled what he did do, once what he had hoped to avoid actually occurred:

Like gold, U.S. dollars have value only to the extent that they are strictly limited in supply. But the U.S. government has a technology, called a printing press (or, today, its electronic equivalent), that allows it to produce as many U.S. dollars as it wishes at essentially no cost. By increasing the number of U.S. dollars in circulation [...] the U.S. government can also reduce the value of a dollar in terms of goods and services, which is equivalent to raising the prices in dollars of those goods and services. We conclude that, under a paper-money system, a determined government can always generate higher spending and hence positive inflation [...]

Normally, money is injected into the economy through asset purchases by the Federal Reserve. To stimulate aggregate spending when short-term interest rates have reached zero, the Fed must expand the scale of its asset purchases or, possibly, expand the menu of assets that it buys. Alternatively, the Fed could find other ways of injecting money into the system – for example, by making low-interest-rate loans to banks or cooperating with the fiscal authorities. Each method of adding money to the economy has advantages and drawbacks, both technical and economic. One important concern in practice is that calibrating the economic effects of nonstandard means of injecting money may be difficult, given our relative lack of experience with such policies. Thus, as I have stressed already, prevention of deflation remains preferable to having to cure it. If we do fall into deflation, however, we can take comfort that the logic of the printing press example must assert itself, and sufficient injections of money will ultimately always reverse a deflation. (Bernanke 2002a)

In late 2008, Bernanke turned on the printing presses as never before, doubling base money in a mere five months, when the previous doubling had taken thirteen years. §77

In inflation-adjusted terms, he expanded M_0 at a rate of over 100 percent a year, when its average annual rate of growth for the preceding five decades was 2.3 percent. By the time Bernanke finally took his foot off the M_0 accelerator one and a half years later, base money had jumped from $850 billion to $2.15 trillion (see Figure 12.2).

There is little doubt that this massive, unprecedented injection of base money did help reverse the deflation that commenced very suddenly in 2008, when inflation fell from plus 5.6 percent in mid-2008 to minus 2.1 percent a year later – the sharpest fall in inflation in post-World War II history. But I expect Bernanke was underwhelmed by the magnitude of the change: inflation rose from minus 2.1 percent to a peak of 2.7 percent, and it rapidly fell back to a rate of just 1 percent. That is very little inflationary bang for a large amount of bucks.

According to the conventional model of money creation – known as the 'Money Multiplier' – this large an injection of government money into the

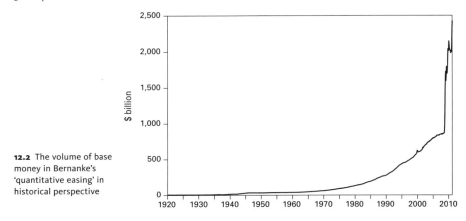

12.2 The volume of base money in Bernanke's 'quantitative easing' in historical perspective

reserve accounts of private banks should have resulted in a far larger sum of bank-created money being added to the economy – as much as $10 trillion. This amplification of Bernanke's $1.3 trillion injection should have rapidly revived the economy – according to neoclassical theory. This is precisely what President Obama, speaking no doubt on the advice of his economists, predicted when he explained the strategy they had advised him to follow, twelve weeks after he took office:

> And although there are a lot of Americans who understandably think that government money would be better spent going directly to families and businesses instead of banks – 'where's our bailout?' they ask – the truth is that a dollar of capital in a bank can actually result in eight or ten dollars of loans to families and businesses, *a multiplier effect* that can ultimately lead to a faster pace of economic growth. (Obama 2009: 3; emphasis added)

Only that isn't what happened. The dramatic increase in bank reserves spurred only a tiny increase in money in circulation: the 110 percent growth rate of M_0 resulted in only a 20 percent rate of growth of M_1.

§78

The difference in growth rates was so great that there is now *less* money in check accounts and currency in circulation than there is money in the reserve accounts of the commercial banks.

§79

The 'eight or ten dollars of loans to families and businesses' from each extra 'dollar of capital in a bank' simply didn't happen. What went wrong?

The mythical Money Multiplier

Few concepts are more deserving than the 'Money Multiplier' of Henry Mencken's aphorism that 'Explanations exist; they have existed for all time; there is always a well-known solution to every human problem – neat, plausible, and wrong.'[7]

In this model, money is created in a two-stage process. First, the govern-

7 See en.wikiquote.org/wiki/H._L._Mencken.

ment creates 'fiat' money, say by printing dollar bills and giving them to an individual. The individual then deposits the dollar bills in his bank account. Secondly, the bank keeps a fraction of the deposit as a reserve, and lends out the rest to a borrower. That borrower then deposits this loaned money in another bank account, and the process repeats.

Let's say that the amount created by the government is $100, the fraction the banks keep as a reserve (known as the 'Reserve Requirement' and set by the government or central bank) is 10 percent, and it takes banks a week to go from getting a new deposit to making a loan. The process starts with the $100 created by the government. One week later, the first bank has created another $90 by lending 90 percent of that money to a borrower. A week later, a second bank creates another $81 – by keeping $9 of the new deposit in reserve and lending out the other $81. The process keeps on going so that, after many weeks, there will be $1,000 created, consisting of the initial printing of $100 by the government, and $900 in credit money created by the banking system – which is matched by $900 in additional debt. There will be $900 of credit money in circulation, facilitating trade, while another $100 of cash will be held by the banks in reserve (see Table 12.1).

TABLE 12.1 The alleged Money Multiplier process ($)

Week	Loans	Deposits	Cash kept by bank	Sum of loans	Sum of cash
0	0	100	10	0	10
1	90	90	9	90	19
2	81	81	8	171	27
3	73	73	7	244	34
4	66	66	7	310	41
5	59	59	6	369	47
6	53	53	5	422	52
7	48	48	5	470	57
8	43	43	4	513	61
9	39	39	4	551	65
10	35	35	3	586	69
Total after 10 weeks	686.19	586.19	68.62	586.19	68.62
Final totals	1,000	900	100	900	100

In this simple illustration, all the notes remain in the banks' vaults, while all commerce is undertaken by people electronically transferring the sums in their deposit accounts. Of course, we all keep some notes in our pockets as well for small transactions, so there's less credit created than the example implies, but the model can be modified to take account of this.

This process is also known as 'Fractional Reserve Banking,' and it's the process that Obama, on the advice of his economists, relied upon to rapidly bring the Great Recession to an end. Its failure to work was superficially due to some issues that Bernanke was well aware of,[8] but the fundamental reason why it failed is that, as a model of how money is actually created, it is 'neat, plausible, and wrong.'

The fallacies in the model were first identified by practical experience, and then empirical research.

In the late 1970s, when Friedman's monetarism dominated economic debate and the Federal Reserve Board under Volcker attempted to control inflation by controlling the rate of growth of the money supply, the actual rate normally exceeded the maximum target that the Board set (Lindsey, Orphanides et al. 2005: 213). Falling below the target range could be explained by the model, but consistently exceeding it was hard to reconcile with the model itself.

§80

Empirical research initiated by Basil Moore (Moore 1979, 1983, 1988a, 1997, 2001) and later independently corroborated by numerous researchers, including Kydland and Prescott (1990), confirmed a simple operational observation about how banks actually operate made in the very early days of the monetarist controversy, by the then senior vice-president of the New York Federal Reserve, Alan Holmes.

The 'Money Multiplier' model assumes that banks need excess reserves before they can make loans. The model process is that first deposits are made, creating excess reserves, and then these excess reserves allow loans to be made, which create more deposits. Each new loan reduces the level of excess reserves, and the process stops when this excess has fallen to zero.

But in reality, Holmes pointed out, banks create loans first, which simultaneously creates deposits. If the level of loans and deposits then means that banks have insufficient reserves, then they get them afterwards – and they have a two-week period in which to do so.[9] In contrast to the Money Multiplier fantasy of bank managers who are unable to lend until they receive more deposits, the real-world practicality of banking was that the time delay between deposits and reserves meant that the direction of causation flowed, not from reserves to loans, but from loans to reserves.

8 The minimum fraction that banks can hold is mandated by law, but banks can hold more than this, weakening the multiplier; and the public can decide to hang on to its cash during a financial crisis, which further weakens it. Bernanke considered both these factors in his analysis of why the Great Depression was so prolonged: 'In fractional-reserve banking systems, the quantity of inside money (M1) is a multiple of the quantity of outside money (the monetary base) [...] the money multiplier depends on the public's preferred ratio of currency to deposits and the ratio of bank reserves to deposits [...] sharp variations in the money multiplier [...] were typically associated with banking panics, or at least problems in the banking system, during the Depression era. For example, the money multiplier in the United States began to decline precipitously following the "first banking crisis" identified by Friedman and Schwartz, in December 1930, and fell more or less continuously until the final banking crisis in March 1933, when it stabilized. Therefore, below we interpret changes in national money stocks arising from changes in the money multiplier as being caused primarily by problems in the domestic banking system' (Bernanke 2000: 125–6).

9 '[T]he reserves required to be maintained by the banking system are predetermined by the level of deposits existing two weeks earlier' (Holmes 1969: 73).

Banks, which have the reserves needed to back the loans they have previously made, extend new loans, *which create new deposits simultaneously*. If this then generates a need for new reserves, and the Federal Reserve refuses to supply them, then it would force banks to recall old or newly issued loans, and cause a 'credit crunch.'

The Federal Reserve is therefore under great pressure to provide those reserves. It has some discretion about how to provide them, but unless it is willing to cause serious financial ructions to commerce on an almost weekly basis, it has no discretion about whether those reserves should be provided.

Holmes summed up the monetarist objective of controlling inflation by controlling the growth of base money – and by inference the Money Multiplier model itself – as suffering from 'a naive assumption':

> that the banking system only expands loans after the [Federal Reserve] System (or market factors) have put reserves in the banking system. *In the real world, banks extend credit, creating deposits in the process, and look for the reserves later.* The question then becomes one of whether and how the Federal Reserve will accommodate the demand for reserves. In the very short run, the Federal Reserve has little or no choice about accommodating that demand; over time, its influence can obviously be felt. (Holmes 1969: 73; emphasis added)

With causation actually running from bank lending and the deposits it creates to reserve creation, the changes in credit money should therefore precede changes in fiat money. This is the opposite of what is implied by the 'Money Multiplier' model (since in it government money – base money or M_0 – has to be created before credit money – M_1, M_2 and M_3 – can be created), and it is precisely what Kydland and Prescott found in their empirical analysis of the timing of economic variables:

> There is no evidence that either the monetary base or M_1 leads the cycle, although some economists still believe this monetary myth. Both the monetary base and M_1 series are generally procyclical and, if anything, the monetary base lags the cycle slightly [...] The difference in the behavior of M_1 and M_2 suggests that the difference of these aggregates (M_2 minus M_1) should be considered [...] The difference of M_2–M_1 leads the cycle by even more than M_2, with the lead being about three quarters [...] (Kydland and Prescott 1990: 4)

Well before Kydland and Prescott reached this statistical conclusion, the post-Keynesian economist Basil Moore pointed out the implication of the actual money creation process for macroeconomic theory. When macroeconomic models actually considered the role of money, they treated the money supply as an exogenous variable under the direct control of the government – this is an essential feature of Hicks's IS-LM model, for instance. But since credit money is created before and causes changes in government money, the money supply must instead be endogenous. The 'Money Multiplier' model of money creation was therefore a fallacy:

> This traditional view of the bank money creation process relies on the bank reserves–multiplier relation. The Fed is posited to be able to affect the quantity of bank deposits, and thereby the money stock, by determining the nominal amount of the reserve base or by changing the reserve multiplier [...]
>
> There is now mounting evidence that the traditional characterization of the money supply process, which views changes in an exogenously controlled reserve aggregate as 'causing' changes in some money stock aggregate, is fundamentally mistaken. Although there is a reasonably stable relationship between the high-powered base and the money stock, and between the money stock and aggregate money income, the causal relationship implied is exactly the reverse of the traditional view. (Moore 1983: 538)

It is possible to interpret this reverse causation as representing 'a lack of moral fiber' by central bankers – accommodating banks' loan-creation rather than regulating it in the interests of the economy – but Moore pointed out that the provision of reserves by central banks to match loan-creation by banks merely mirrored the standard behavior of banks with respect to their business clients. Businesses need credit in order to be able to meet their costs of production prior to receiving sales receipts, and this is the fundamental beneficial role of banks in a capitalist economy:

> In modern economies production costs are normally incurred and paid prior to the receipt of sales proceeds. Such costs represent a working capital investment by the firm, for which it must necessarily obtain finance. Whenever wage or raw materials price increases raise current production costs, unchanged production flows will require additional working capital finance. In the absence of instantaneous replacement cost pricing, firms must finance their increased working capital needs by increasing their borrowings from their banks or by running down their liquid assets. (Ibid.: 545)

Banks therefore accommodate the need that businesses have for credit via additional lending – and if they did not, ordinary commerce would be subject to Lehman Brothers-style credit crunches on a daily basis. The Federal Reserve then accommodates the need for reserves that the additional lending implies – otherwise the Fed would cause a credit crunch: 'Once deposits have been created by an act of lending, the central bank must somehow ensure that the required reserves are available at the settlement date. Otherwise the banks, no matter how hard they scramble for funds, could not in the aggregate meet their reserve requirements' (ibid.: 544).

Consequently, attempts to use the 'Money Multiplier' as a control mechanism – either to restrict credit growth as during the monetarist period of the

12.3 The empirical 'Money Multiplier', 1920–40

late 1970s, or to cause a boom in lending during the Great Recession – are bound to fail. It is not a control mechanism at all, but a simple measure of the ratio between the private banking system's creation of credit money and the government's creation of fiat money. This can vary dramatically over time: growing when the private banks are expanding credit rapidly and the government tries – largely vainly – to restrain the growth in money; collapsing when private banks and borrowers retreat from debt in a financial crisis, and the government tries – again, largely vainly – to drive the rate of growth of money up.

This is something that Bernanke should have known from his own research on the Great Depression. Then, the 'Money Multiplier' rose from under 6 in the early 1920s to over 9 in 1930, only to plunge to below 4.5 by 1940 (see Figure 12.3).

Perhaps he did remember this lesson of history, since his increase in base money was far greater than that of his predecessors. He may well have put such a massive influx of money into the system simply because he feared that little or no additional credit money would be forthcoming as a result. Better then to flood the economy with fiat money and hope that that alone would cause the desired boost to aggregate demand.

We will have to await his memoirs to know, but even if so, he (and Obama's other neoclassical economic advisors) made the wrong choice by putting this injection of fiat money into the reserve accounts of the banks, rather than giving it to the public – as Obama considered in his 'where's our bailout?' counterpoint in his April 2009 speech.

The money drove up the unused reserves of the banking sector as never before (from \$20 billion before the crisis to over \$1 trillion after it) and the 'Money Multipliers' – which in reality are no more than the ratios of the three measures of the broad money supply, M_3, M_2 and M_1, to base money – collapsed as never before. The M_3 ratio fell from over 16 to under 8, and has continued to fall to below 7 since then; the M_2 ratio – the one most comparable to the M_1 ratio back in the 1920s–1940s – fell from 9 to below 4, while most embarrassingly of all, the M_1 ratio fell below 1, hit as low as 0.78, and is still below 0.9 two years after Bernanke's fiat money injection.

Some 'multiplier effect.' Obama was sold a pup by his neoclassical advisors. The huge injection of fiat money would have been far more effective had it been given to the public, who at least would have spent it into circulation.

§81

Don't mention the data

As this book details, neoclassical economics is awash with examples of its internal contradictions being ignored by its believers, so in one sense their practice of pretending that the Money Multiplier determines the amount of money in the economy is just another example of neoclassical economists believing in something that doesn't exist. However, the Money Multiplier is different in at least two ways. First, many neoclassical economists *know* that it doesn't exist, and secondly, its non-existence is empirically obvious. So rather than ignoring the problem because they are unaware of it, or of its ramifications – as with the Sonnenschein-Mantel-Debreu conditions – they ignore it simply because it is inconvenient to acknowledge it.

Admitting that the Money Multiplier doesn't exist is inconvenient because, if so, then the supply of money is not exogenous – set by the government – but endogenous – determined by the workings of a market economy. This in turn means that this endogenous process affects real economic variables such as the level of investment, the level of employment and the level of output, when it has always been a tenet of neoclassical theory that 'money doesn't matter.' So acknowledging the empirically bleedingly obvious fact that the Money Multiplier is a myth also means letting go of another favorite neoclassical myth, that the dynamics of money can safely be ignored in economic analysis. Consequently, clear evidence that the Money Multiplier is a myth has been ignored even by the neoclassical economists who know otherwise.

One of the clearest instances of this is the difference between the very emphatic conclusion that Kydland and Prescott reached about the importance of credit, and their subsequent theoretical work. In their conclusion to their empirical paper, they made a clear case for the need to develop a theory of endogenous credit:

> The fact that the transaction component of real cash balances (M_1) moves contemporaneously with the cycle while the much larger nontransaction component (M_2) leads the cycle suggests that credit arrangements could play a significant role in future business cycle theory. *Introducing money and credit into growth theory in a way that accounts for the cyclical behavior of monetary as well as real aggregates is an important open problem in economics.* (Kydland and Prescott 1990: 15; emphasis added)

However, they have done nothing since to develop such a theory. Instead, they have continued to champion the 'Real Business Cycle Theory' that they developed prior to this empirical research, and Carpenter and Demiralp note that Kydland continues 'to refer to the very narrow money multiplier and accord it a principal role in the transmission of monetary policy' (Carpenter and Demiralp 2010: 2, commenting on Freeman and Kydland 2000).

This charade of continuing to believe in a concept whose non-existence was an empirical fact could be maintained for as long as the Money Multiplier didn't have any real-world significance. Unfortunately, the 'bailout the banks' strategy that Obama was advised to follow by Bernanke depended crucially on the Money Multiplier working to turn the huge increase in reserves into an even larger increase in private sector lending. It was an abject failure: excess reserves increased by a factor of 50, but private sector lending fell, as did credit money.

§82

A recent paper by Federal Reserve associate director Seth Carpenter entitled 'Money, reserves, and the transmission of monetary policy: does the Money Multiplier exist?' (Carpenter and Demiralp 2010) finally acknowledges this:

> Since 2008, the Federal Reserve has supplied an enormous quantity of reserve balances relative to historical levels as a result of a set of non-traditional policy actions. These actions were taken to stabilize short-term funding markets and to provide additional monetary policy stimulus at a time when the federal funds rate was at its effective lower bound.
>
> The question arises whether or not this unprecedented rise in reserve balances ought to lead to a sharp rise in money and lending. *The results in this paper suggest that the quantity of reserve balances itself is not likely to trigger a rapid increase in lending [...] the narrow, textbook money multiplier does not appear to be a useful means of assessing the implications of monetary policy for future money growth or bank lending.* (Ibid.: 29; emphasis added)

This acknowledgment of reality is good to see, but – compared both to the data and the empirically oriented work of the rival 'post-Keynesian' school of thought – it is thirty years and one economic crisis too late. It also post-dates the effective abolition of the Reserve Requirement – an essential component of the 'Money Multiplier' model – by about two decades.

Since 1991, the publicly reported Reserve Requirement has been effectively applicable only to household bank accounts, which are a tiny fraction of the aggregate deposits of the banking system (see Table 12 in O'Brien 2007: 52). As Carpenter and Demiralp note, today reserve requirements 'are assessed on only about one-tenth of M_2':

> Casual empirical evidence points away from a standard money multiplier and away from a story in which monetary policy has a direct effect on broader monetary aggregates. The explanation lies in the institutional structure in the United States, especially after 1990.

First, there is no direct link between reserves and money – as defined as M_2. Following a change in required reserves ratios in the early 1990s, reserve requirements are assessed on only about one-tenth of M_2.

Second, there is no direct link between money – defined as M_2 – and bank lending. Banks have access to non-deposit funding (and such liabilities would also not be reservable), so the narrow bank lending channel breaks down in theory. Notably, large time deposits, a liability that banks are able to manage more directly to fund loans, are not reservable and not included in M_2. Banks' ability to issue managed liabilities increased substantially in the period after 1990, following the developments and increased liquidity in the markets for bank liabilities.

Furthermore, the removal of interest rate ceilings through Regulation Q significantly improved the ability of banks to generate non-reservable liabilities by offering competitive rates on large time deposits. Additionally, money market mutual funds account for about one-fifth of M_2, but are not on bank balance sheets, and thus they cannot be used to fund lending. These facts imply that the tight link suggested by the multiplier between reserves and money and bank lending does not exist. (Carpenter and Demiralp 2010: 4–5)

The effective freedom of banks to decide how much money they will keep in reserve – and thus not use as a source of income – versus the amount they will lend, effectively leaves the private banks free to create as much credit as they wish. This is a freedom they have exploited with gusto, as I detail in the next chapter.

After the Great Recession II: neoclassical responses

One would hope that the complete failure of neoclassical models to anticipate the Great Recession might lead to some soul-searching by neoclassical economists: was there not something fundamentally wrong in their modeling that they could be blindsided by such a huge event?

Unfortunately, they are so wedded to their vision of the economy that even an event like the Great Recession can't shake them. Their near-universal reaction has been that it was simply an extreme event – like a sequence of a dozen coin-tosses that all resulted in 'heads,' which is a feasible though very rare outcome.[10] Though such a thing is possible, when it will happen can't be predicted.

In saying this, they of course ignored the public warnings from myself and others, as documented by Bezemer (Bezemer 2009, 2010, 2011), despite the fact that those warnings were made, not merely in non-mainstream academic publications, but in the media as well. Here I can't resist quoting the governor of my own country's central bank, Glenn Stevens: 'I do not know anyone who predicted this course of events. This should give us cause to reflect on

---

10 Such a sequence has a 1 in 4,000 chance of occurring.

how hard a job it is to make genuinely useful forecasts. What we have seen is truly a "tail" outcome – the kind of outcome that the routine forecasting process never predicts. But it has occurred, it has implications, and so we must act on it' (Stevens 2008).

That speech, made in Sydney in December 2008, ignored not only the well-known warnings in the USA by Peter Schiff and Nouriel Roubini, but my own in Australia since December 2005. These had included appearances on the leading current affairs programs *60 Minutes* (60 Minutes 2008) and *The 7.30 Report* (7.30 Report 2007).

Central bankers like Stevens and Bernanke had to live in a cocoon not to know of such warnings, and neoclassical economics provides the silk of this cocoon, because it refuses to consider any analysis of economics that does not make neoclassical assumptions. Since those who predicted the crisis did so – as they had to – using non-neoclassical tools, to Bernanke and his brethren around the world, those warnings did not exist.

Unfortunately, the Great Recession does exist, and neoclassical economists have been forced to consider it. Their responses have taken two forms: tweaking the 'exogenous shocks' to their models until the models generate results that look like the Great Recession; and adding additional tweaks to the core neoclassical model that at least to some degree incorporate the effects of debt. Both approaches completely miss the real causes of this crisis.

It's just a jolt to the left …

As of February 2011, there were two neoclassical papers that attempted to comprehend the Great Recession using New Keynesian models which, of course, had completely failed to anticipate it (McKibbin and Stoeckel 2009; Ireland 2011). Since the underlying theory generates tranquil equilibrium growth rather than crises, the authors instead looked for a plausible set of exogenous shocks that, if simulated in their models, generate something that resembled the Great Recession. These shocks remain unspecified, however, beyond stating that they emanate from 'households,' or 'technology.' *Neither even considered modifying their models to include the role of private debt.*[11]

Ireland started promisingly, with the thought that perhaps the underlying theory itself should be challenged: 'Indeed, the Great Recession's extreme severity makes it tempting to argue that new theories are required to fully explain it' (Ireland 2011: 31).

However, the apostate road was quickly abandoned, with the assertion that 'it would be premature to abandon existing models just yet.' One ground given for persevering with neoclassical models displayed the standard neoclassical ignorance of dynamic modeling, by asserting that: 'Attempts to explain movements in one set of endogenous variables, like GDP and employment,

11 The word 'debt' doesn't even appear in the Ireland paper, and while McKibbin and Stoeckel's model does incorporate borrowing, it plays no role in their analysis.

by direct appeal to movements in another, like asset market valuations or interest rates, sometimes make for decent journalism but rarely produce satisfactory economic insights' (ibid.: 32).

Having dismissed the need for a change of approach, he went in search of 'shocks' that might explain why the economy so suddenly and for so long diverged from its equilibrium, with the objective of showing that the Great Recession was really no different to 'the two previous downturns in 1990–91 and 2001': 'this paper asks whether, in terms of its macro-economics, the Great Recession of 2007–09 really stands apart from what came before [...]' (ibid.).

Using his small-scale 'New Keynesian' model, Ireland concluded that unspecified 'adverse shocks' to the household's consumption preferences and the firm's technology caused all three recessions: 'the Great Recession began in late 2007 and early 2008 with a series of adverse preference and technology shocks in roughly the same mix and of roughly the same magnitude as those that hit the United States at the onset of the previous two recessions [...]'. What made this recession different, however, was that the shocks went on for longer, and got bigger over time: 'The string of adverse preference and technology shocks continued, however, throughout 2008 and into 2009. Moreover, these shocks grew larger in magnitude, adding substantially not just to the length but also to the severity of the great recession [...]' (ibid.: 48).

Ireland stated his positive conclusions for the New Keynesian approach halfway through the paper, claiming that his results: 'speak to the continued relevance of the New Keynesian model, perhaps not as providing the very last word on but certainly for offering up useful insights into both macroeconomic analysis and monetary policy evaluation' (ibid.: 33).

This is laughable, given both the author's methodology, and manifest ignorance of the fallacies in neoclassical thought – as evidenced by the manner in which he measured the gap between output during the recessions and the ideal level of output. He envisages a 'benevolent social planner,' who can derive a 'social welfare function' that reconciles all social conflict over the distribution of income, reproducing – I am sure without knowing the source – Samuelson's bizarre vision of capitalism as one big happy family:

> it is helpful to define a welfare-theoretic measure of the output gap, based on a comparison between the level of output that prevails in equilibrium and *the level of output chosen by a benevolent social planner* who can overcome the frictions associated with monetary trade and sluggish nominal price adjustment. *Such a planner chooses* the efficient level of output and the efficient amounts of labor to allocate to [...] production [...] *to maximize a social welfare function reflecting the same preference orderings over consumption and leisure embedded into the representative household's utility function.* (Ibid.: 38; emphases added)

McKibbin and Stoekel use a larger scale with six household-firm agents – one for each of six economic sectors (energy, mining, agriculture, manufacturing durables, manufacturing non-durables, and services) – and fifteen countries as well. As a New Keynesian model it allows for various 'imperfections,' and tellingly they remark that without 'short-run nominal wage rigidity' and a stylized but trivial role for money ('Money is introduced into the model through a restriction that households require money to purchase goods'), the model would simply predict that full-employment equilibrium would apply at all times:

> The model also allows for short-run nominal wage rigidity (by different degrees in different countries) and therefore allows for significant periods of unemployment depending on the labor-market institutions in each country. *This assumption, when taken together with the explicit role for money, is what gives the model its 'macroeconomic' characteristics.* (Here again the model's assumptions differ from the standard market-clearing assumption in most CGE models.) [...]
>
> Although *it is assumed that market forces eventually drive the world economy to neoclassical steady-state growth equilibrium,* unemployment does emerge for long periods owing to wage stickiness, to an extent that differs between countries owing to differences in labor-market institutions. (McKibbin and Stoeckel 2009: 584; emphases added)

As with Ireland, they manipulate the shocks applied to their model until its short-run deviations from the steady state mimic what occurred during the Great Recession, and as with Ireland, one shock is not enough – three have to be used:

1   the bursting of the housing bubble, causing a reallocation of capital and a loss of household wealth and drop in consumption;
2   a sharp rise in the equity risk premium (the risk premium of equities over bonds), causing the cost of capital to rise, private investment to fall, and demand for durable goods to collapse;
3   a reappraisal of risk by households, causing them to discount their future labor income and increase savings and decrease consumption. (Ibid.: 587)

Not even this was enough to replicate the data: they also needed to assume that two of these 'shocks' – the risk tolerances of business and households – changed their magnitudes over the course of the crisis. A previous paper had found that 'a temporary shock to risk premia, as seems to have happened in hindsight, does not generate the large observed real effects,' so they instead considered an extreme shock, followed by an attenuation of it later: 'The question is then, what would happen if business and households initially assumed the worst – that is, a long lasting permanent rise in risk premia – but unexpectedly revised their views on risk to that of a temporary scenario 1 year later whereby things are expected to return to "normal"?' (ibid.: 582).

The procedure adopted in both these papers amplifies Solow's acerbic observation that 'New Keynesian' models fit the data better than 'New Classical' ones do, simply because the modelers add 'imperfections [...] chosen by intelligent economists to make the models work better [...]' (Solow 2001: 26). Now, to cope with the Great Recession – whose characteristics cannot be fitted even by the base New Keynesian model – the modeler also adds shocks that make the imperfections fit the data better, and even manipulates the shocks themselves until the model's output finally appears to match reality.

This is not science, but evasion. Adding tweaks to a deficient model – now including adding variable shocks – to avoid confronting the reality that the model itself has failed, is the behavior of a 'degenerative scientific research program,' to use Lakatos's phrase.

Krugman's paper should have been better than these, in that at least he admits that one key component of reality that has been omitted in neoclassical economics – the role of private debt – needs to be incorporated to explain the Great Recession.

'Like a dog walking on its hind legs': Krugman's Minsky model

While Krugman's 'Debt, deleveraging, and the liquidity trap: a Fisher-Minsky-Koo approach' (Krugman and Eggertsson 2010) deserves some praise as the first neoclassical attempt to model Minsky after decades of ignoring him, the paper itself embodies everything that is bad in neoclassical economics.

This reflects poorly, not so much on Krugman – who has done the best he can with the neoclassical toolset to model what he thinks Minsky said – but on the toolset itself, which is so inappropriate for understanding the economy in which we actually live.

Attempts to increase the realism of the neoclassical model follow a mold that is as predictable as sunrise – but nowhere near as beautiful. The author takes the core model – which cannot generate the real-world phenomenon under discussion – and then adds some twist to the basic assumptions which, hey presto, generate the phenomenon in some highly stylized way. The mathematics (or geometry) of the twist is explicated, policy conclusions (if any) are then drawn, and the paper ends.

The flaw with this game is the very starting point, and since Minsky put it best, I'll use his words to explain it:

> Can 'It' – a Great Depression – happen again? And if 'It' can happen, why didn't 'It' occur in the years since World War II? These are questions that naturally follow from both the historical record and the comparative success of the past thirty-five years. *To answer these questions it is necessary to have an economic theory which makes great depressions one of the possible states in which our type of capitalist economy can find itself.* (Minsky 1982: xii; emphasis added)

The flaw in the neoclassical game is that it never achieves Minsky's final objective, because the 'twist' that the author adds to the basic assumptions of the neoclassical model are never incorporated into its core. The basic theory therefore remains one in which the key phenomenon under investigation – in this case, the crucial one Minsky highlights of how depressions come about – cannot happen. With the core theory unaltered, the performance is rather like that of a dog that learns how to walk on its hind legs on command, but which will revert to four-legged locomotion when the performance is over.[12]

Krugman himself is unlikely to stop walking on two legs – he enjoys standing out in the crowd of neoclassical quadrupeds – but the pack will return to form once this crisis ultimately gives way to tranquility.

However, one way in which Krugman doesn't stand out from the pack is how he treats rival schools of thought in economics: he ignores them.

The scholarship of ignorance and the ignorance of scholarship Krugman's paper cites nineteen works,[13] three of which are non-neoclassical – Fisher's classic 1933 'debt deflation' paper, Minsky's last book, *Stabilizing an Unstable Economy* (Minsky 1986), and Richard Koo's *The Holy Grail of Macroeconomics: Lessons from Japan's Great Recession* (Koo 2009). The other sixteen include one empirical study (McKinsey Global Institute 2010) and fifteen neoclassical papers written between 1989 (Bernanke and Gertler 1989) and 2010 (Woodford 2010) – five of which are papers by Krugman or his co-author.

Was this the best he could have done? Hardly! For starters, the one Minsky reference he used was, in my opinion, Minsky's worst book – and I'm speaking as someone in a position to know. Anyone wanting to get a handle on the Financial Instability Hypothesis from Minsky himself would be far better advised to read the essays in *Can 'It' Happen Again?* (Minsky 1982 [1963]), or his original book *John Maynard Keynes* (Minsky 1975) – which, despite its title, is not a biography, but the first full statement of his hypothesis.[14]

Krugman's ignorance of Minsky prior to the crisis was par for the course among neoclassical authors, since they only read papers published in what they call the leading journals – such as the *American Economic Review* – which routinely reject non-neoclassical papers without even refereeing them.[15] Almost all academic papers on or by Minsky have been published in non-mainstream journals – the *American Economic Review* (*AER*), for example,

---

12 Samuel Johnson's aphorism, that something is 'like a dog's walking on his hind legs. It is not done well; but you are surprised to find it done at all,' is one of those phrases that was offensive in its origins – since Johnson used it to deride the idea of women preaching – but utterly apt in its usage today.

13 An update in February 2011 made no changes to the paper apart from adding an additional eleven works, only one of which – a 1975 paper by James Tobin – could even remotely be described as non-neoclassical.

14 I actually posted a comment to this effect on Krugman's blog when he announced that he had decided to read Minsky and had purchased this book.

15 A paper based on the model that I described in this chapter (Keen 2011) was rejected unrefereed by both the *AER* and the specialist *AER: Macroeconomics*, before being accepted by the *Journal of Economic Behavior and Organization*.

has published a grand total of two papers on or by Minsky, one in 1957 (Minsky 1957) and the other in 1971 (Minsky 1971). If the *AER* and the other so-called leading journals were all you consulted as you walked up and down the library aisles, you wouldn't even know that Minsky existed – and most neoclassicals didn't know of him until after 2007.

Before the 'Great Recession' too, you might have been justified in ignoring the other journals – such as the *Journal of Post Keynesian Economics*, the *Journal of Economic Issues*, the *Review of Political Economy* (let alone the *Nebraska Journal of Economics and Business*, where several of Hyman's key papers were published) because these were 'obviously' inferior journals, where papers not good enough to make it into the *AER*, the *Economic Journal, Econometrica* and so on were finally published.

But after the Great Recession, when the authors who foresaw the crisis came almost exclusively from the non-neoclassical world (Bezemer 2009, 2010, 2011), and whose papers were published almost exclusively in the non-mainstream journals, neoclassical economists like Krugman should have eaten humble pie and consulted the journals they once ignored.

That might have been difficult once: which journals would you look in, if all you knew was that the good stuff – the models that actually predicted what happened – *hadn't* been published in the journals you normally consulted? But today, with the Internet, that's not a problem. Academic economists have as their bibliographic version of Google the online service Econlit (www.aeaweb.org/econlit/index.php), and there it's impossible to do even a cursory search on Minsky and not find literally hundreds of papers on or by him. For example, a search on the keywords 'Minsky' and 'model' turned up 106 references (including three by yours truly – Keen 1995, 1996, 2001b).

Twenty-seven of these are available in linked full text (one of which is also by yours truly; Keen 1995), so that you can download them direct to your computer from within Econlit, while others can be located by searching through other online sources, without having to trundle off to a physical library to get them. To not have any references at all from this rich literature is simply poor scholarship. Were Krugman a student of mine, he'd have failed this part of his essay.

So in attempting to model a debt crisis in a capitalist economy, Krugman has used as his guide Fisher's pivotal paper, Minsky's worst book, and about ten neoclassical references written by someone other than himself and his co-author. How did he fare?

Mishandling an 'omitted variable' One thing I can compliment Krugman for is honesty about the state of neoclassical macroeconomic modeling before the Great Recession. His paper opens with the observation that 'If there is a single word that appears most frequently in discussions of the economic problems now afflicting both the United States and Europe, that word is surely "debt"' (Krugman and Eggertsson 2010: 1), and then admits that private debt played no role in neoclassical macroeconomic models before the crisis:

> Given both the prominence of debt in popular discussion of our current economic difficulties and the long tradition of invoking debt as a key factor in major economic contractions, one might have expected debt to be at the heart of most mainstream macroeconomic models – especially the analysis of monetary and fiscal policy. Perhaps somewhat surprisingly, however, it is quite common to abstract altogether from this feature of the economy. Even economists trying to analyze the problems of monetary and fiscal policy at the zero lower bound – and yes, that includes the authors – have often adopted representative-agent models in which everyone is alike, and in which the shock that pushes the economy into a situation in which even a zero interest rate isn't low enough takes the form of a shift in everyone's preferences. (Ibid.: 2)

This, along with the unnecessary insistence on equilibrium modeling, is the key weakness in neoclassical economics: if you omit so crucial a variable as debt from your analysis of a market economy, there is precious little else you will get right. So Krugman has taken at least one step in the right direction.

However, from this mea culpa, it's all downhill, because he made no fundamental shift from a neoclassical approach; all he did was modify his base 'New Keynesian' model to incorporate debt as he perceived it. On this front, he fell into the same trap that ensnared Bernanke, of being incapable of conceiving that aggregate debt can have a macroeconomic impact: 'Ignoring the foreign component, or looking at the world as a whole, the overall level of debt makes no difference to aggregate net worth – one person's liability is another person's asset' (ibid.: 3).

This one sentence established that Krugman failed to comprehend Minsky, who realized – as did Schumpeter and Marx before him – that growing debt in fact boosts aggregate demand:

> If income is to grow, the financial markets [...] must generate an aggregate demand that, aside from brief intervals, is ever rising. For real aggregate de-mand to be increasing [...] it is necessary that current spending plans, summed over all sectors, be greater than current received income [...] It follows that over a period during which economic growth takes place, at least some sectors finance a part of their spending by emitting debt or selling assets. (Minsky 1982: 6)

Krugman also has no understanding of the endogeneity of credit money – that banks create an increase in spending power by simultaneously creating money and debt. Lacking any appreciation of how money is created in a credit-based economy, Krugman instead sees lending as simply a transfer of spending power from one agent to another: *neither banks nor money exist in the model he built.*

Instead, rather than modeling the economy as a single representative agent, he modeled it as consisting of two agents, one of whom was impatient while the other was patient. Debt was simply a transfer of spending power from the patient agent to the impatient one, and therefore the debt itself had no macroeconomic impact – it simply transferred spending power from the patient agent to the impatient one. The only way this could have a macroeconomic impact was if the 'impatient' agent was somehow constrained in ways that the patient agent was not, and that's exactly how Krugman concocted a macroeconomic story out of this neoclassical microeconomic fantasy: 'In what follows, we begin by setting out a flexible-price endowment model in which "impatient" agents borrow from "patient" agents [where what is borrowed is not money, but "risk-free bonds denominated in the consumption good" (p. 5)], but are subject to a debt limit.'

To then generate a crisis, Krugman had to introduce an ad hoc and unexplained change to this debt limit: 'If this debt limit is, *for some reason,* suddenly reduced, the impatient agents are forced to cut spending; if the required deleveraging is large enough, the result can easily be to push the economy up against the zero lower bound. If debt takes the form of nominal obligations, Fisherian debt deflation magnifies the effect of the initial shock' (Krugman and Eggertsson 2010: 3; emphasis added)

He then generalized this with 'a sticky-price model in which the deleveraging shock affects output instead of, or as well as, prices' (ibid.), brought in nominal prices *without money* by imagining 'that there is a nominal government debt traded in zero supply [...] We need not explicitly introduce the money supply' (ibid.: 9), modeled production – yes, the preceding analysis was of a no-production economy in which agents simply trade existing 'endowments' of goods distributed like manna from heaven – under imperfect competition (ibid.: 11), added a central bank that sets the interest rate (in an economy without money) by following a Taylor Rule, and on it went.

The mathematics was complicated, and real brain power was exerted to develop the argument – just as, obviously, it takes real brain power for a poodle to learn how to walk on its hind legs. But it was the wrong mathematics: it compared two equilibria separated by time, whereas truly dynamic analysis considers change over time regardless of whether equilibrium applies or not. And it was wasted brain power, because the initial premise – that aggregate debt has no macroeconomic effects – was false.

Krugman at least acknowledged the former problem – that the dynamics are crude: 'The major limitation of this analysis, as we see it, is its reliance on strategically crude dynamics. To simplify the analysis, we think of all the action as taking place within a single, aggregated short run, with debt paid down to sustainable levels and prices returned to full ex ante flexibility by the time the next period begins' (ibid.: 23).

But even here, I doubt that he would consider genuine dynamic modeling without the clumsy neoclassical device of assuming that all economic processes involve movements from one equilibrium to another. Certainly this paper remained true to the perspective he gave in 1996 when speaking to the European Association for Evolutionary Political Economy: 'I like to think that I am more open-minded about alternative approaches to economics than most, but *I am basically a maximization-and-equilibrium kind of guy. Indeed, I am quite fanatical about defending the relevance of standard economic models* in many situations [...].' He described himself as an 'evolution groupie' to this audience, but then made the telling observation that:

> Most economists who try to apply evolutionary concepts start from some deep dissatisfaction with economics as it is. I won't say that I am entirely happy with the state of economics. But let us be honest: I have done very well within the world of conventional economics. I have pushed the envelope, but not broken it, and have received very widespread acceptance for my ideas. What this means is that I may have more sympathy for standard economics than most of you. My criticisms are those of someone who loves the field and has seen that affection repaid.

Krugman's observations on methodology in this speech also highlight why he was incapable of truly comprehending Minsky – because he starts from the premise that neoclassical economics itself has proved to be false, that macroeconomics must be based on individual behavior: 'Economics is about what individuals do: not classes, not "correlations of forces," but individual actors. This is not to deny the relevance of higher levels of analysis, but they must be grounded in individual behavior. *Methodological individualism is of the essence*' (Krugman 1996; emphases added)

No it's not: methodological individualism is one of the key flaws in neoclassical macroeconomics, as the SMD conditions establish. Economic processes have to be modeled at a higher level of aggregation, as Kirman argued (Kirman 1989: 138) and Minsky, in practice, did.

So while Krugman reached some policy conclusions with which I concur – such as arguing against government austerity programs during a debt-deflationary crisis – his analysis is proof for the prosecution that even 'cutting-edge' neoclassical economics, by continuing to ignore the role of aggregate debt in macroeconomic dynamics, is part of the problem of the Great Recession, not part of its solution.

Conclusion: neat, plausible, and wrong

Mencken's aphorism suits not merely the Money Multiplier, but the whole of neoclassical economics: 'neat, plausible, and wrong.' If we are to avoid another Great Depression – more bleakly, if we are to get out of the one we are still in – then neoclassical economics has to be consigned to the dustbin of intellectual history. But that by itself is not enough: we need a replacement theory that does not make the many methodological mistakes that have made neoclassical economics such a singularly misleading and dangerous guide to the management of a capitalist economy.

The manner in which neoclassical economists have dealt with the crisis also makes a mockery of the basis on which neoclassical macroeconomics was based: its criticism of the preceding IS-LM 'Keynesian' models that they were based on many 'ad hoc' parameters – as Solow observed, 'the main argument for this modeling strategy has been a more aesthetic one: its virtue is said to be that it is compatible with general equilibrium theory, and thus it is superior to ad hoc descriptive models that are not related to "deep" structural parameters' (Solow 2007: 8). However, to cope with the Great Recession, neoclassical economists are now introducing ad hoc changes to these '"deep" structural parameters' – in order to explain why risk is suddenly re-evaluated and so on – and even introducing 'ad hoc' shocks. Neoclassical attempts to reproduce the crisis therefore fail the Lucas Critique which gave birth to this approach in the first place.

A complete, ready-made replacement does not exist. But there are alternative ways of thinking about economics that provide a good foundation on which an empirically grounded, non-ideological theory of economics can be built. I now turn to these alternatives, starting with the perspective that enabled me to be one of the very few economists who saw the Great Recession coming.

PART 3 | ALTERNATIVES

DIFFERENT WAYS TO THINK ABOUT ECONOMICS

I was certainly not the only economist to expect that a serious economic crisis was imminent before the Great Recession began.

The post-Keynesian and Austrian schools of thought explicitly consider credit and money in their models of the economy, and many economists in these schools expected a crisis – the former group because of their familiarity with Hyman Minsky's Financial Instability Hypothesis, and the latter because of their familiarity with Hayek's argument about the impact of interest rates being held too low by government policy. However, the vast majority of these did not go public with their warnings.

Bezemer identified twelve individuals including myself who did publicly warn of the approaching crisis (Bezemer 2009, 2010, 2011), and a poll conducted by the *Real-World Economics Review* to decide who should win the inaugural Revere Award for Economics[1] resulted in an additional eighty-four individuals being nominated (Fullbrook 2010).

What distinguished me (and the late Wynne Godley) from the rest of these prescient and voluble few is that I had developed a mathematical model of how this crisis might come about. That model put into dynamic, disequilibrium form the economic vision of the late Hyman Minsky, which was in turn built on the insights of the great non-neoclassical thinkers Marx, Schumpeter, Fisher and Keynes. Minsky's strength was to weave these individually powerful and cohesive but incomplete analyses into one coherent tapestry that explained capitalism's greatest weakness: its proclivity to experience not merely economic cycles, but also occasional depressions that challenged the viability of capitalism itself.

The Financial Instability Hypothesis

Minsky's starting point was that, since the Great Depression had occurred, and since similar if smaller crises were a recurrent feature of the nineteenth century, before 'Big Government' became the norm in market economies, an economic model had to be able to generate a depression as one of its possible outcomes: 'Can "It" – a Great Depression – happen again? And

---

1 The Revere Award recognized 'the three economists who first and most clearly anticipated and gave public warning of the Global Financial Collapse and whose work is most likely to prevent another GFC in the future.' More than 2,500 people – mainly economists – cast votes for a maximum of three out of the ninety-six candidates. I was the eventual winner with 1,152 of the 5,062 votes cast; Nouriel Roubini came second with 566 votes and Dean Baker third with 495 votes. See rwer.wordpress.com/2010/05/13/keen-roubini-and-baker-win-revere-award-for-economics-2/ for full details.

if "It" can happen, why didn't "It" occur in the years since World War II? These are questions that naturally follow from both the historical record and the comparative success of the past thirty-five years. *To answer these questions it is necessary to have an economic theory which makes great depressions one of the possible states in which our type of capitalist economy can find itself'* (Minsky 1982: 5; emphasis added).

For this reason, Minsky explicitly rejected neoclassical economics:

> The abstract model of the neoclassical synthesis cannot generate instability. When the neoclassical synthesis is constructed, capital assets, financing arrangements that center around banks and money creation, constraints imposed by liabilities, and the problems associated with knowledge about uncertain futures are all assumed away. For economists and policy-makers to do better we have to abandon the neoclassical synthesis. (Ibid.: xiii)

In place of the non-monetary, equilibrium-fixated, uncertainty-free, institutionally barren and hyper-rational individual-based reductionist neoclassical model, Minsky's vision of capitalism was strictly monetary, inherently cyclical, embedded in time with a fundamentally unknowable future, institution-rich and holistic, and considered the interactions of its four defining social entities: industrial capitalists, bankers, workers and the government.

I published my first paper on Minsky's hypothesis in 1995 (Keen 1995), and the following summary of Minsky's verbal model of a financially driven business cycle is reproduced from that paper.[2] I provide it verbatim here since its conclusion – written in 1993, long before neoclassical economists began to congratulate themselves about the 'Great Moderation' – shows that the calamity the world economy fell into in 2007/08 was not an unpredictable 'Black Swan' event, but something that was entirely foreseeable *with the right economic theory*:

> Minsky's analysis of a financial cycle begins at a time when the economy is doing well (the rate of economic growth equals or exceeds that needed to reduce unemployment), but firms are conservative in their portfolio management (debt to equity ratios are low and profit to interest cover is high), and this conservatism is shared by banks, who are only willing to fund cash-flow shortfalls or low-risk investments. The cause of this high and universally practiced risk aversion is the memory of a not too distant system-wide financial failure, when many investment projects foundered, many firms could not finance their borrowings, and many banks had to write off bad debts. Because of this recent experience, both sides of the borrowing relationship prefer extremely conservative estimates of prospective cash flows: their risk premiums are very high.

2 From Steve Keen (1995), 'Finance and economic breakdown: modeling Minsky's "Financial Instability Hypothesis"', *Journal of Post Keynesian Economics*, 17(4): 607–35. Copyright © 1995 by M. E. Sharpe, Inc. Used by permission.

However, the combination of a growing economy and conservatively financed investment means that most projects succeed. Two things gradually become evident to managers and bankers: 'Existing debts are easily validated and units that were heavily in debt prospered: it pays to lever' (Minsky 1982, p. 65). As a result, both managers and bankers come to regard the previously accepted risk premium as excessive. Investment projects are evaluated using less conservative estimates of prospective cash flows, so that with these rising expectations go rising investment and asset prices. The general decline in risk aversion thus sets off both growth in investment and exponential growth in the price level of assets, which is the foundation of both the boom and its eventual collapse.

More external finance is needed to fund the increased level of investment and the speculative purchase of assets, and these external funds are forthcoming because the banking sector shares the increased optimism of investors (Minsky 1980, p. 121). The accepted debt to equity ratio rises, liquidity decreases, and the growth of credit accelerates.

This marks the beginning of what Minsky calls 'the euphoric economy' (Minsky 1982, pp. 120–124), where both lenders and borrowers believe that the future is assured, and therefore that most investments will succeed. Asset prices are revalued upward as previous valuations are perceived to be based on mistakenly conservative grounds. Highly liquid, low-yielding financial instruments are devalued, leading to a rise in the interest rates offered by them as their purveyors fight to retain market share.

Financial institutions now accept liability structures for both themselves and their customers 'that, in a more sober expectational climate, they would have rejected' (Minsky 1980, p. 123). The liquidity of firms is simultaneously reduced by the rise in debt to equity ratios, making firms more susceptible to increased interest rates. The general decrease in liquidity and the rise in interest paid on highly liquid instruments triggers a market-based increase in the interest rate, even without any attempt by monetary authorities to control the boom. However, the increased cost of credit does little to temper the boom, since anticipated yields from speculative investments normally far exceed prevailing interest rates, leading to a decline in the elasticity of demand for credit with respect to interest rates.

The condition of euphoria also permits the development of an important actor in Minsky's drama, the Ponzi financier (Minsky 1982, pp. 70, 115 [...]). These capitalists profit by trading assets on a rising market, and incur significant debt in the process. The servicing costs for Ponzi debtors exceed the cash flows of the businesses they own, but the capital appreciation they anticipate far exceeds the interest bill. They therefore play an important role in pushing up the market interest rate, and an equally important role in increasing the fragility of the system to a reversal in the growth of asset values.

Rising interest rates and increasing debt to equity ratios eventually affect the viability of many business activities, reducing the interest rate cover, turning projects that were originally conservatively funded into speculative ones, and making ones that were speculative 'Ponzi.' Such businesses will find themselves having to sell assets to finance their debt servicing – and this entry of new sellers into the market for assets pricks the exponential growth of asset prices. With the price boom checked, Ponzi financiers now find themselves with assets that can no longer be traded at a profit, and levels of debt that cannot be serviced from the cash flows of the businesses they now control. Banks that financed these assets purchases now find that their leading customers can no longer pay their debts – and this realization leads initially to a further bank-driven increase in interest rates. Liquidity is suddenly much more highly prized; holders of illiquid assets attempt to sell them in return for liquidity. The asset market becomes flooded and the euphoria becomes a panic, the boom becomes a slump.

As the boom collapses, the fundamental problem facing the economy is one of excessive divergence between the debts incurred to purchase assets, and the cash flows generated by them – with those cash flows depending upon both the level of investment and the rate of inflation.

The level of investment has collapsed in the aftermath of the boom, leaving only two forces that can bring asset prices and cash flows back into harmony: asset price deflation, or current price inflation. This dilemma is the foundation of Minsky's iconoclastic perception of the role of inflation, and his explanation for the stagflation of the 1970s and early 1980s.

Minsky argues that if the rate of inflation is high at the time of the crisis, then though the collapse of the boom causes investment to slump and economic growth to falter, rising cash flows rapidly enable the repayment of debt incurred during the boom. The economy can thus emerge from the crisis with diminished growth and high inflation, but few bankruptcies and a sustained decrease in liquidity. Thus, though this course involves the twin 'bads' of inflation and initially low growth, it is a self-correcting mechanism in that a prolonged slump is avoided.

However, the conditions are soon reestablished for the cycle to repeat itself, and the avoidance of a true calamity is likely to lead to a secular decrease in liquidity preference.

If the rate of inflation is low at the time of the crisis, then cash flows will remain inadequate relative to the debt structures in place. Firms whose interest bills exceed their cash flows will be forced to undertake extreme measures: they will have to sell assets, attempt to increase their cash flows (at the expense of their competitors) by cutting their margins, or go bankrupt. In contrast to the inflationary course, all three classes of action tend to further depress the current price level, thus at least partially exacerbating the original imbalance. The asset price deflation route is, therefore, not self-correcting but rather self-reinforcing, and is Minsky's explanation of a depression.

The above sketch basically describes Minsky's perception of an economy in the absence of a government sector. With big government, the picture changes in two ways, because of fiscal deficits and Reserve Bank interventions. With a developed social security system, the collapse in cash flows that occurs when a boom becomes a panic will be at least partly ameliorated by a rise in government spending – the classic 'automatic stabilizers,' though this time seen in a more monetary light. The collapse in credit can also be tempered or even reversed by rapid action by the Reserve Bank to increase liquidity. With both these forces operating in all Western economies since World War II, Minsky expected the conventional cycle to be marked by 'chronic and … accelerating inflation' (Minsky 1982, p. 85). However, by the end of the 1980s, the cost pressures that coincided with the slump of the early 1970s had long since been eliminated, by fifteen years of high unemployment and the diminution of OPEC's cartel power. The crisis of the late 1980s thus occurred in a milieu of low inflation, raising the specter of a debt deflation. (Keen 1995: 611–14)

I added the following qualification about the capacity for government action to attenuate the severity of a debt deflation – while not addressing its underlying causes – to my précis of Minsky in the first edition of *Debunking Economics*:

If a crisis does occur after the Internet Bubble finally bursts, then it could occur in a milieu of low inflation (unless oil price pressures lead to an inflationary spiral). Firms are likely to react to this crisis by dropping their margins in an attempt to move stock, or to hang on to market share at the expense of their competitors. This behavior could well turn low inflation into deflation.

The possibility therefore exists that America could once again be afflicted with a debt deflation – though its severity could be attenuated by the inevitable increase in government spending that such a crisis would trigger. America could well join Japan on the list of the global economy's 'walking wounded' – mired in a debt-induced recession, with static or falling prices and a seemingly intractable burden of private debt. (Keen 2001a: 254)

That a crisis might occur, and even that government action might attenuate it, was something that one could anticipate with Minsky's verbal economic theory. But a market economy is a complex system – the most complex social system that has ever existed – and its very complexity means that feedback effects might occur that are simply impossible to predict with a verbal model alone. For that reason, in my PhD I decided to attempt what Minsky had not succeeded in doing: to provide a mathematical model that did justice to the compelling verbal description he gave of debt deflation.

Modeling Minsky

Minsky did develop a mathematical model of a financially driven business cycle in his PhD, which resulted in the one paper he ever had published in a mainstream economic journal, the *American Economic Review* (Minsky 1957).[3] But the model was unsatisfactory for a number of reasons, and he subsequently abandoned it to stick with predominantly verbal reasoning.

Minsky's failure to develop a satisfactory mathematical model was partly due to bad timing: the 1950s pre-dated the development of complexity theory, which made trying to build a model of his hypothesis virtually impossible. Minsky simply added a financial dimension to the dominant linear trade cycle model of the day, which was a particularly unsuitable foundation for his hypothesis.[4] In 1993, well after complexity theory had developed, I built my initial Minsky model using the far more suitable foundation of the cyclical growth model developed by the non-neoclassical economist Richard Goodwin (Goodwin 1967).

Goodwin's model considered the level of investment and the distribution of income in a simple two-class model of capitalism. A high initial wage and high rate of employment meant that wages absorbed most of output, so that profit was low – and therefore investment was low. The low rate of investment meant that the capital stock grew slowly (or fell because of depreciation), leading to a low rate of growth of output (or even falling output) and hence a growing unemployment rate – since population growth would then exceed the rate of economic growth.

The rising unemployment rate reduced workers' bargaining power, leading to stagnant or falling wages – which increased capitalists' profit share. They then increased investment, leading to a boom that drove the employment rate up, which strengthened the bargaining power of workers. Wages then rose and, because employment was high, wages absorbed most of output – which is where the cycle began.[5]

This was a classic dynamic model of 'circular causation' that is very common in biological modeling, but sadly a rarity in economics because of the neoclassical obsession with equilibrium. It also had a startling characteristic compared to the standard fare in economics: it was inherently cyclical. Given an arbitrary starting point, the model generated regular cycles in both the distribution of income and the employment rate. There was no tendency

---

3 Minsky made it into the *AER* on one other occasion, but only as a discussant of another paper at its annual conference.

4 The base model he used, known as the Hicks-Hansen-Samuelson multiplier-accelerator model, also derived its cycles from the economic error of equating an expression for actual savings with one for desired investment. See Keen (2000: 88–92).

5 This verbal model of perpetual cycles in employment and income distribution was first developed by Marx, and published in Section 1 of Chapter 25 of Volume 1 of *Capital* (Marx 1867). Marx finished his verbal model with the statement 'To put it mathematically: the rate of accumulation is the independent, not the dependent, variable; the rate of wages, the dependent, not the independent, variable,' and it is believed that his attempt to learn calculus late in his life was motivated by the desire to express this model in mathematical form (Marx 1983 [1881]).

toward equilibrium, but no tendency to breakdown either: the same cycle
§83 repeated for ever.

Economists were falsely of the opinion that this was impossible. As John
Hicks (remember him?) put it: 'A mathematically unstable system does not
fluctuate; it just breaks down. The unstable position is one in which it will
not tend to remain' (Hicks 1949).

As is so often the case, Hicks was right in particular and wrong in
general. If they were unstable, then dynamic versions of the linear models
that he and most neoclassical economists worked with would indeed break
down – by returning impossible values for variables, such as negative prices
or infinite levels of output. But Goodwin's model was inherently nonlinear,
because two variables in the system – the wage rate and the level of employment – had to be multiplied together to work out wages and hence profits.
As I explained in Chapter 9, nonlinear models can have persistent cycles
without breaking down.

The professor of applied mathematics turned non-orthodox economist
John Blatt observed that Goodwin's model was the best of the many dynamic
economic models he had reviewed, and suggested that it would provide
an excellent foundation for modeling financial dynamics in capitalism. In
stark contrast to the neoclassical obsession with equilibrium, one of Blatt's
criticisms of Goodwin's basic model was that its equilibrium was not unstable:

> Of course, the model is far from perfect. In particular, we feel that the
> existence of an equilibrium which is not unstable (it is neutral) is a flaw in
> this model [...] The first flaw can be remedied in several ways [...] [such
> as] introduction of a financial sector, including money and credit as well as
> some index of business confidence. Either or both of these changes is likely
> to make the equilibrium point locally unstable, as is desirable [...] But, while
> it is obvious that much work remains to be done, we have no doubt that the
> Goodwin model is the most promising of all the 'schematic models' of the
> trade cycle and well deserves further investigation. (Blatt 1983: 210–11)

I took up Blatt's suggestion in my PhD, by adding Keynes's model of
how capitalists form conventions to cope with uncertainty, and Minsky's
emphasis upon the role of debt in financing investment plans during a boom.

Of Keynes's three conventions to cope with uncertainty, the most important
was the tendency to project forward current conditions: 'We assume that
the present is a much more serviceable guide to the future than a candid
examination of past experience would show it to have been hitherto' (Keynes
1937: 214).

A simple way to capture this in a mathematical model was to argue that
capitalists would invest very little when the rate of profit today was very low,
and invest a lot when the rate of profit was high. This was easily captured

by replacing Goodwin's simple but unrealistic assumption that capitalists invested *all* their profits with a nonlinear relationship that meant investment would be less than profits when the rate of profit was low, and more than profits when the rate of profit was high.

Minsky improved upon Keynes by incorporating the insights of Schumpeter and Fisher on the essential role of debt in a capitalist economy: when capitalists' desire to invest exceeded retained earnings – as they would do during a boom – then capitalists would borrow to finance the additional investment. I introduced this with a simple differential equation that said the rate of change of debt equaled investment minus profits.[6]

My first Minsky model This added one additional dynamic to Goodwin's model: the rate of change of debt, which rose when investment exceeded profits and fell when profits exceeded investment. During a boom, capitalists borrow to finance investment, and this drives up the debt-to-output ratio. During a slump, capitalists invest less than profits, and this reduces the debt-to-output ratio. The change in the debt ratio then affects the rate of profit, since profits are now equal to output, minus wages, minus interest on outstanding debt.

This simple extension to Goodwin's model dramatically altered its behavior. Goodwin's basic model generated fixed cycles indefinitely; this extended system could generate several different outcomes, ranging from a convergence to equilibrium values for income distribution, the employment rate and the debt-to-output ratio; cycles in all three variables of varying magnitudes over time; or a blowout in the debt-to-GDP ratio: a debt-induced depression.

The model also had three fascinating and, as it turned out, prescient characteristics.

First, even though capitalists were the only borrowers in this simple model, the debt repayment burden actually fell on workers: the wages share of output fell as the debt level rose, while the profit share fluctuated around an equilibrium value.

Secondly, if the model did head toward a debt-induced breakdown, the debt-to-output ratio ratcheted up over time: debt would rise during a boom, reach a peak and then fall during a slump, but a new boom would begin §84 before the debt-to-output ratio had dropped to its original value.

Thirdly, the breakdown was preceded by a period of reduced volatility: fluctuations in employment and output would start off very large and then fall – the model generated a 'Great Moderation' *before* one appeared in the empirical record. But slowly, as the debt ratio rose even higher, the volatility

---

6 Fama and French give empirical support for this equation, which is rather ironic given their role in promoting the empirically invalid CAPM model of finance: 'These correlations confirm the impression that debt plays a key role in accommodating year-by-year variation in investment' (Fama and French 1999: 1954). In a draft version, they stated this even more clearly: 'Debt seems to be the residual variable in financing decisions. Investment increases debt, and higher earnings tend to reduce debt.'

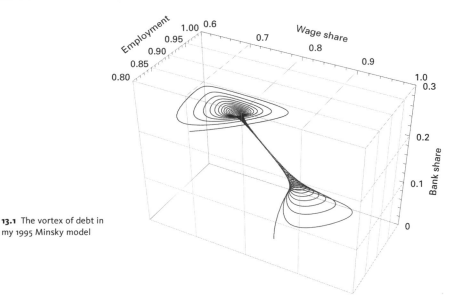

13.1 The vortex of debt in my 1995 Minsky model

started to rise again, until there was one last extreme cycle in which the debt level went so high that debt repayments overwhelmed the capacity of capitalists to pay.

The economy then went into a death spiral as the level of debt overwhelmed the capacity of capitalists to service that debt. A 'Great Moderation' gave way to a 'Great Recession' – see Figure 13.1.

When I first completed this model in April 1992, the 'Great Moderation' had yet to begin, but the peculiar dynamics of the model struck me as remarkable. This led me to finish my first published paper on this model with a flourish that, at the time, seemed grandiose, but which ultimately proved to be prophetic:

> From the perspective of economic theory and policy, this vision of a capitalist economy with finance requires us to go beyond that habit of mind which Keynes described so well, the excessive reliance on the (stable) recent past as a guide to the future. *The chaotic dynamics explored in this paper should warn us against accepting a period of relative tranquility in a capitalist economy as anything other than a lull before the storm.* (Keen 1995: 634; emphasis added)

However, Minsky had also noted that government spending could stabilize an unstable economy. In that same paper I modeled this possibility by introducing government spending as an effective subsidy to capitalists that grew as unemployment rose and fell as it subsided – though workers receive unemployment benefits, the unemployed spend everything they get on consumption, so that corporations are the ultimate recipients of government welfare. Similarly, I modeled government taxation of business as rising as profits rose, and falling when profits fell.

As well as adding a fourth 'system state' to the model – the level of net government spending as a proportion of output – this modified the definition of profit. It was now output, minus wages, minus interest payments on debt, minus taxes plus the government subsidy.

In the model, the presence of government spending acted as a counter-weight to the private sector's tendency to accumulate debt: a rising subsidy and falling taxes during a slump gave business additional cash flows with which to repay debt during a slump, while rising taxes and a falling subsidy during a boom attenuated the private sector's tendency to accumulate debt.

The result was a system which was inherently cyclical, but in which the cycles stayed within manageable bounds: there was no systemic breakdown, as there had been in the pure private sector model. It was a pure limit cycle of the kind Blatt thought should be generated by a realistic model (Blatt 1983: 211). §85

Reality, I expected, lay somewhat between these two extremes of a private sector en route to a debt-induced breakdown, and a cyclical system kept within bounds by the 'automatic stabilizers' of government spending and taxation. The government sector modeled in this paper 'held the line' against rising unemployment, whereas in the real world governments had retreated from trying to restrain rising unemployment. I also knew that Ponzi-style behavior had become more dominant in the real world over time – something that I had not modeled explicitly, since in my model all borrowing led to productive investment. Also, though the models considered the role of private debt, they were only implicitly monetary, and I could not capture the impact of inflation or deflation upon the economy.

So there were ways in which I did not expect the real world to match my models. I resolved to extend them over time – to make them explicitly monetary, to model governments that gradually reduced their role as fiscal stabilizers, to incorporate borrowing for purely speculative reasons and so on – but in the immediate aftermath I was distracted from this agenda by the ferocious reaction that neoclassical economists had to the chapter 'Size does matter' in the first edition of *Debunking Economics*. That dispute consumed my research energies in the four years from 2001 till 2005.

Finally in December 2005, I attempted to leave this argument behind and at long last write the book-length treatment of Minsky's hypothesis that I had first committed to do in 1998.[7] When I checked the ratio of private debt to GDP for the first time in over a decade, I quickly realized that a crisis would strike long before my technical book on how such crises came about would be ready.

---

7 I signed a contract that year with Edward Elgar Publishers to deliver a book entitled *Finance and Economic Breakdown* in 2002. That long-overdue book will hopefully be available in 2013.

Reality check, December 2005

The last thing I expected was that the real world would be in worse shape than my models implied, but that's what appeared to be the case in December 2005. While drafting an expert witness report on debt in a predatory lending case, I scribbled – before I had checked the data – that 'Debt to GDP ratios have been rising exponentially.' I expected that I'd need to attenuate that statement once I checked the data – the ratio would have been rising, I thought, though not at an exponential rate.

I vividly remember my stunned reaction when I first plotted the data, at about 1 a.m. on 22 December in Perth, Western Australia. Australia's private debt to GDP level had increased more than fivefold since the mid-1960s, and the rate of increase was clearly exponential – and it had a burst super-bubble in the 1980s, similar to the cyclical fluctuations in the debt-to-income ratio generated by my Minsky model.

§86

I quickly downloaded the US Flow of Funds data to see whether Australia was unique. Obviously, it wasn't – see Figure 13.2. This was, as I expected, a global phenomenon. The US debt ratio was slightly less obviously exponential, but had increased even more than the Australian, and over a longer time period. Similar data could be found for most OECD nations, and especially the Anglo-Saxon countries.

Such an exponential rise in the debt ratio had to break, and when it did the global economy would be thrust into a downturn that would surely be more severe than those of the mid-1970s and early 1990s – the last times that the bursting of speculative bubbles had caused serious recessions. There was even the prospect that this would be an 'It' break: a debt-induced downturn so severe that the outcome would be not merely a recession, but a depression.

Someone had to raise the alarm, and I realized that, at least in Australia, I was probably that somebody. I once again put *Finance and Economic Breakdown* on the backburner, and devoted myself to warning the general public

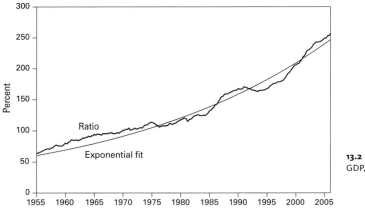

13.2 US private debt to GDP, 1955–2005

and policy-makers of the impending economic crisis. I began with media interviews, progressed to sending out a 'Debtwatch' report on debt coinciding with the Reserve Bank of Australia's monthly meetings from November 2006 (Keen 2006),[8] and in March 2007 I established the Debtwatch blog (www.debtdeflation.com/blogs).

Raising the alarm was not enough. I also had to dramatically improve my empirical understanding of the role of debt in a capitalist economy, and extend my Minsky model to cover the issues that I clearly had not paid sufficient attention to in 1995: the impact of Ponzi finance, and the active role of the financial sector in financial crises.

The empirical dynamics of debt

The key insight about the role of debt in a capitalist society was provided by Schumpeter: in a growing economy, the increase in debt funds more economic activity than could be funded by the sale of existing goods and services alone: 'in real life total credit must be greater than it could be if there were only fully covered credit. The credit structure projects not only beyond the existing gold basis, but also beyond the existing commodity basis' (Schumpeter 1934: 95, 101).

Aggregate demand in a credit-driven economy is therefore equal to income (GDP) *plus the change in debt.* This makes aggregate demand far more volatile than it would be if income alone was its source, because while GDP (and the level of accumulated debt) changes relatively slowly, the change in debt can be sudden and extreme. In addition, if debt levels are already high relative to GDP, then the change in the level of debt can have a substantial impact on demand.

A numeric example illustrates this process (see Table 13.1). Consider an economy with a GDP of $1,000 billion that is growing at 10 percent per annum, where this is half due to inflation and half due to real growth, and which has a debt level of $1,250 billion that is growing at 20 percent per annum. Aggregate demand will therefore be $1,250 billion: $1,000 billion from GDP, and $250 billion from the increase in debt (which will rise from $1,250 billion to $1,500 billion over the course of the year).

Imagine that the following year, GDP continues to grow at the same 10 percent rate, but debt growth slows down from 20 percent per annum to 10 percent (the debt-to-GDP ratio will therefore stabilize at 150 percent). Demand from income will be $1,100 billion – 10 percent higher than the previous year – while demand from additional debt will be $150 billion (10 percent of the $1,500 billion level at the start of the year).

Aggregate demand in this second year will thus be $1,250 billion – exactly

---

8 This and later reports are downloadable from www.debtdeflation.com/blogs/pre-blog-debtwatch-reports/. I ceased writing the monthly report in April 2009, in order to devote more time to fundamental research. The blog posts, however, continued.

TABLE 13.1 A hypothetical example of the impact of decelerating debt on aggregate demand

Year	0	1
Real growth	5%	5%
Inflation	5%	5%
Nominal GDP	$1,000	$1,100
Nominal debt	$1,250	$1,500
Debt growth rate	20%	10%
Growth in debt	$250	$150
Nominal aggregate demand	$1,250	$1,250
Change in nominal demand ($)	N/A	0
Change in nominal demand (%)	N/A	0
Real aggregate demand	$1,250	$1,187.5
Change in real demand	N/A	–5.0%

the same as the year before. However, since inflation is running at 5 percent, this will mean a fall in real output of about 5 percent – a serious recession. So just a slowdown in the rate of growth of debt can be enough to trigger a recession. An absolute fall in debt isn't needed to cause problems, though it certainly will make things worse still.

Schumpeter ignored the role of asset markets in the economy, so that in his model the increase in debt financed investment (and the sale of goods financed consumption). Therefore in his model, aggregate demand equals aggregate supply, but part of aggregate demand is debt-financed. In this example, demand financed by the sale of goods and services purchased $1,000 billion of consumer goods, while $250 billion of investment goods were bought on credit. Twenty percent of aggregate demand therefore came from rising debt.

Two consequences follow from this, of which Schumpeter was fully cognizant.

First, the expansion of credit must come, not from someone's savings being transferred to another person via a loan – which is the conventional model of how banks operate – but by the banking sector creating new money and credit 'out of nothing':

[I]n so far as credit cannot be given out of the results of past enterprise [...] it can only consist of credit means of payment created ad hoc, which can be backed neither by money in the strict sense nor by products already in existence [...]

It provides us with the connection between lending and credit means of payment, and leads us to what I regard as the nature of the credit phenomenon [...] credit is essentially the creation of purchasing power for the purpose of transferring it to the entrepreneur, but not simply the transfer of existing purchasing power. (Ibid.: 106–7)

The banking sector therefore must have the capacity to create purchasing power – an issue I return to in the next chapter.

Secondly, the numerical example given here involves an unsustainable rate of growth of debt in the first year, so that there has to be a slowdown in the rate of growth of debt, which will cause a recession. However, the increased debt also helps create productive capacity for the economy, which can later be used to service the debt. There is thus a limit to the severity of cycles that can result: though excessive debt growth will cause a boom, and the inevitable slowdown in the growth of debt will cause a slump, the economy's capacity to produce is expanded by the growth of debt. Serious adjustments might be needed – falling prices, debt write-offs as some firms go bankrupt, and so on – but ultimately the economy will be able to reduce debt to manageable levels again, and growth will resume once more.

Minsky extended Schumpeter by considering Ponzi finance as well – lending to finance the speculative purchase of existing assets. Now, as well as aggregate demand being both income plus the change in debt, aggregate supply is both the output of new goods and services *and the net turnover of existing assets*. This breaches the virtuous cycle that Schumpeter saw between rising debt and a rising capacity to service that debt, because the money borrowed to buy assets adds to society's debt level without increasing its productive capacity. Thus when a slump follows a debt-fuelled boom, it is possible that debt servicing will exceed the economy's available cash flows – leading to not merely a recession, but a depression.

This Minskian process has been playing out in America ever since the mid-1960s when Minsky first developed his Financial Instability Hypothesis. Minsky himself identified 1966 as the time at which America made the transition from a productive to a Ponzi economy: 'A close examination of experience since World War II shows that the era quite naturally falls into two parts. The first part, which ran for almost twenty years (1948–1966), was an era of largely tranquil progress. This was followed by an era of increasing turbulence, which has continued until today' (Minsky 1982: xiii).

Minsky's judgment was based largely on his financial interpretation of the US business cycle from that point on:

The first serious break in the apparently tranquil progress was the credit crunch of 1966. Then, for the first time in the postwar era, the Federal Reserve intervened as a lender of last resort to refinance institutions – in this case banks – which were experiencing losses in an effort to meet liquidity requirements. The credit crunch was followed by a 'growth' recession, but the expansion of the Vietnam War promptly led to a large federal deficit which facilitated a recovery from the growth recession.

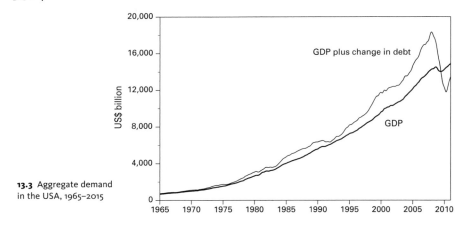

13.3 Aggregate demand in the USA, 1965–2015

The 1966 episode was characterized by four elements: (1) a disturbance in financial markets that led to lender-of-last-resort intervention by the monetary authorities; (2) a recession (a growth recession in 1966); (3) a sizable increase in the federal deficit; and (4) a recovery followed by an acceleration of inflation that set the stage for the next disturbance. The same four elements can be found in the turbulence of 1969–70, 1974–75, 1980, and 1981. (Ibid.: xiv–xv)

Empirically, the late 1960s also marked the point at which the accumulated debt of the private sector exceeded 100 percent of GDP. From that point on, the dynamics of debt began to dominate macroeconomic performance in the USA – first generating a false prosperity, and then a calamitous collapse when the great debt bubble finally burst (see Figure 13.3).

TABLE 13.2 The actual impact of decelerating debt on aggregate demand

Year	2007/08	2008/09
Real growth	2.3%	−2.7%
Inflation	4.3%	0%
Nominal GDP	$14.29 tn	$14.19 tn
Nominal debt	$40.6 tn	$42.1 tn
Debt growth rate	28.1%	10.7%
Growth in debt	$4 tn	$1.52 tn
Nominal aggregate demand	$18.3 tn	$15.7 tn
Change in nominal demand ($)	N/A	−$2.6 tn
Change in nominal demand (%)	N/A	−14.2%
Real aggregate demand	$18.3 tn	$15.7 tn
Change in real demand[1]		−14.2%

Note: 1 The change in real demand was the same as the change in nominal demand since inflation was effectively zero in 2009

For the first time since the Great Depression, the aggregate level of private debt began to fall in January 2009. But the economic downturn began well before, when the rate of growth of debt slowed from its peak level, just as the numerical example illustrates.

§87

The debt bubble went out with a bang: the increase in private sector debt in 2008, the final year of the bubble, was a truly stupendous $4 trillion, which boosted aggregate demand from GDP alone by over 28 percent. A year later, debt was growing by 'only' $1.5 trillion, with the result that aggregate demand slipped from its peak level of US$18.3 trillion in 2008 to $15.7 trillion at the beginning of 2009. Though GDP had fallen slightly over calendar year 2009 – from $14.3 trillion to $14.2 trillion – by far the biggest hit to the USA's solar plexus came simply from a slowdown in the rate of growth of debt. Though real GDP fell by a mere 2.7 percent, aggregate demand fell by a massive 14.2 percent – see Table 13.2.

The year 2008 thus brought to a close a period of literally half a century in which private debt had always been growing, and thus adding to aggregate demand. This of itself was not inherently a problem: as both Schumpeter and Minsky argued, rising debt is necessary to finance entrepreneurial activity and to enable the economy to grow. The problem for America, and most of the OECD, was that this increase in debt was rising relative to GDP – indicating that what was being funded was not good, Schumpeterian innovation, but bad Ponzi-finance speculation. The annual increase in debt, which had hovered around 5 percent of GDP in the 1950s and 1960s, rose in a series of peaks and troughs to the 28 percent peak of 2008, from where it plunged to a maximum rate of decline of over 18 percent in early 2010 – see Figure 13.4.

The $2.6 trillion drop in aggregate demand hit America's asset markets hard. Though the Dow Jones rallied towards the end of the year, it closed 34 percent down – a bone-crushing decline in the apparent wealth of America's stockholders (see Figure 13.5).

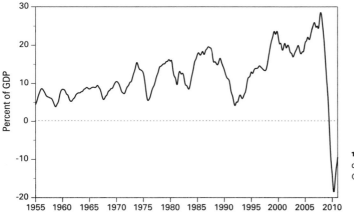

13.4 The change in debt collapses as the Great Recession begins

13.5 The Dow Jones nosedives

January 2007 to December 2008

The long bubble in the housing market – which neoclassical economists like Ben Bernanke had strenuously denied was a bubble – burst under the weight of sheer fraud involved in subprime lending, well before the debt bubble propelling it started to slow.[9] It continued its decline relentlessly in 2008/09, with house prices falling another 19 percent (in real terms) on top of the 10 percent decline from their peak in March 2006 – see Figure 13.6.

Unemployment rose from 4.4 percent at the beginning of 2007 to 5.5 percent at its end, and then to 7.6 percent as 2009 began. Here the hand of debt was clearly visible, for the simple reason that, since the change in debt is a major component of aggregate demand, and aggregate demand determines employment, *unemployment rises if the rate of change of debt falls* (and vice versa). As the level of debt has risen relative to GDP, the ebb and flow of unemployment has fallen more and more under the sway of changes §88 in the level of private debt.

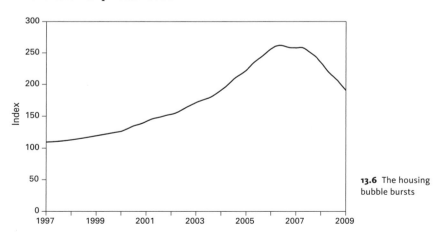

13.6 The housing bubble bursts

9 The authority here is Bill Black of the University of Missouri Kansas City, who as a public servant played a major role in enforcing the law against fraudsters in the aftermath to the Savings and Loans fiasco. See Black (2005a, 2005b); Galbraith and Black (2009).

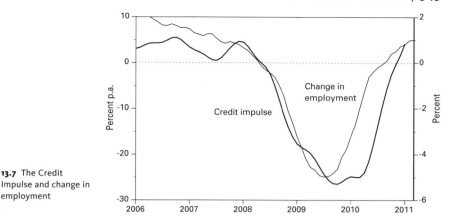

13.7 The Credit Impulse and change in employment

The dominance of debt has been obvious, not only in the collapse into the Great Recession, but even in the apparent recovery from it in late 2010 and early 2011 (a recovery that I believe will prove temporary, and which is also exaggerated by unreliable government statistics). Here an apparent paradox emerges: because aggregate demand is the sum of GDP plus the change in debt, the rate of change of aggregate demand can be boosted by *a slowdown in the rate at which debt is falling*.

The logic here is a simple extrapolation from the observation that the level of aggregate demand is the sum of GDP[10] plus the change in debt: given this, the *change* in aggregate demand is equal to the change in GDP plus the *acceleration* of debt. Therefore the factor that determines debt's impact upon the rate of economic growth – and hence the change in the rate of unemployment – is not the rate of change of debt, but *the rate of change of its rate of change*.

Biggs, Mayer and Pick, who first made this observation, noted that it had a seemingly counter-intuitive outcome that the economy can receive a boost from credit, even if the aggregate level of debt is falling, so long as the rate of that fall decreases: 'the flow of credit and GDP can increase even while the stock of credit is falling' (Biggs, Mayer et al. 2010: 5). They measured the impact of the acceleration of credit on changes in aggregate demand using the ratio of the acceleration of debt to GDP (which they termed 'the Credit Impulse'; ibid.: 3), and this measure clearly illustrated their apparently bizarre conclusion that the slight recovery in late 2010 was driven in large measure by a slowdown in the rate of deceleration of credit – see Figure 13.7.[11]

There are thus three factors that need to be considered to understand the impact of debt on a capitalist economy: the level of debt, the rate of

10 When I use GDP in this context I am referring to GDP as estimated by the income measure, not the production measure.

11 The federal government's fiscal stimulus also played a major role – a topic I will consider in more detail in my next book.

Box 13.1 Definitions of unemployment

The official definition of unemployment has been reworked numerous times, in ways that reduce the recorded number, so much so that the published levels drastically understate the actual level. The official OECD definition (see stats.oecd.org/glossary/detail.asp?ID=2791) requires that those recorded as unemployed must be both available for work and actively looking for work in the reference period, which excludes those who have become discouraged by the sheer unavailability of employment opportunities during a major recession, but many OECD countries have further tailored the definition to reduce the recorded numbers.

The Australian government's definition is typical here: in addition to the OECD requirements, it also records as employed people who 'worked *for one hour* for pay, profit, commission or payment in kind in a job or business, or on a farm; or worked *for one hour or more without pay* in a family business or on a farm' (McLennan 1996: 47). To regard someone who has worked only one hour in a week as employed is simply absurd – at least fifteen hours of work at the minimum wage are needed to be paid even the equivalent of unemployment benefits.

Similar distortions apply in other countries. The USA, for example, ceases counting someone as unemployed if they have been out of work for more than a year – a change in definition introduced in 1994 (see en.wikipedia.org/wiki/Unemployment#United_States_Bureau_of_Labor_Statistics and en. wikipedia.org/wiki/Current_Population_Survey#Employment_classification for more details). Abuses of statistics like this have prompted private citizens to record what official statistics ignore. The opinion-polling organization Roy Morgan

---

change of debt, and its rate of acceleration – all measured with respect to the level of GDP.

The first factor indicates the aggregate burden that debt imposes upon society. Since the level of debt is a stock, while the level of GDP is a flow (of income per year), the ratio tells us how many years of income it would take to reduce debt to zero. Of course, a target of zero debt is neither feasible nor desirable – as explained earlier, some debt is necessary to support entrepreneurial innovation. But the ratio indicates how debt-encumbered an economy has become, and the larger it is, the longer it will take to get back to any desired lower level.

It also provides the best measure of the burden the financial sector imposes upon the economy, since the net cost of the financial sector is the level of

Research (www.roymorgan.com.au/) now publishes its own survey of Australian unemployment, which it puts at 7.9 percent versus the recorded figure of 5.5 percent (the not-seasonally-adjusted figure as of January 2011).

Shadowstats (www.shadowstats.com/alternate_data/unemployment-charts) maintains an alternative measure for the USA that includes long-term discouraged workers. This is now more than twice as high as the official US measure: at the time of writing (February 2011), the official U-3 measure was 9.0 percent, while the Shadowstats measure was 22.2 percent.

This, plus changes in the structure of employment, make comparisons with past economic crises like the Great Depression very difficult. John Williams, the founder of Shadowstats, estimates that his measure of unemployment would have shown that 34–35 percent of the workforce was unemployed during the Great Depression – versus the 25 percent actually recorded back then, since the proportion of the population working on farms was much higher in the 1930s than now (27 percent then versus 2 percent now). The workers who were underemployed on farms – but nonetheless fed – reduced the numbers officially recorded as unemployed back then.

Given these problems, I regard the US's U-6 measure of unemployment today – which includes those who have been unemployed for two years or less – as more comparable to the Great Depression figures than its U-3 measure, which omits those who have been unemployed for a year or more. On that basis, one in six Americans are out of work today, versus the peak rate of one in four during the Great Depression. The current crisis, though it is called the Great Recession, is therefore really a depression too.

debt (multiplied by the inflation-adjusted gap between the rate of interest on loans and that on deposits – a gap that has been relatively constant, though the nominal and real rates of interest themselves have been very volatile).

The second factor indicates how much aggregate demand is being generated by rising debt – or reduced by falling debt. When the economy is growing, so too will credit, and again this is not a bad thing when that debt finances investment. The danger arises when the rate of growth of debt becomes a substantial determinant of overall demand – as it has in the Ponzi economy the USA has become. A large debt-financed contribution to aggregate demand will almost certainly have a large component of Ponzi finance behind it, and such an increase necessarily requires a decline in debt-financed spending in the near future, which will usher in a recession.

The third factor is the best leading indicator of whether employment and the economy are likely to grow in the near future. The Credit Impulse leads both changes in GDP and changes in employment, with the lead (in the USA) being about two months to employment and four months to GDP.

§89

The Credit Impulse is also the key financial source of capitalism's inherently cyclical nature. To maintain a stable rate of employment, the rate of growth of aggregate demand has to equal the rate of growth of employment and labor productivity, which are both relatively stable. But since the rate of growth of aggregate demand depends on the rate of growth of GDP and the *acceleration* of debt, a stable rate of growth of aggregate demand requires a constant acceleration of debt.

The only level at which this is possible is zero. Just as maintaining a constant *positive* rate of acceleration while driving a car is impossible – since otherwise the car would ultimately be travelling faster than the speed of light – a constant positive rate of acceleration of debt can't be maintained, because this would mean that debt would ultimately be infinitely larger than GDP. Since in the real world it is impossible for the acceleration of debt to always be zero, the economy will therefore necessarily have cycles driven by the expansion and contraction of credit.

These three factors – the level of debt, its rate of change, and its acceleration – interact in complex ways that are best explained by an analogy to driving in which the debt-to-GDP ratio is like the distance back to your starting point, its rate of change relative to GDP is like the speed of the car, and the Credit Impulse is like the car's acceleration or deceleration.

A low ratio of debt to GDP is like having taken a short drive – say, from Los Angeles to Phoenix (a distance of 370 miles). It's easy to get back to LA at any time, and the return journey is not something one has to plan all that much for. A high ratio is like a drive from LA to New York: it's a huge distance (2,800 miles), and the drive back – which corresponds to reducing the debt to GDP ratio – will take a long time.

The rate of change of debt (with respect to GDP) is like your speed of travel – the faster you drive, the sooner you'll get there – but there's a twist. On the way out, increasing debt makes the journey more pleasant – the additional spending increases aggregate demand – and this experience is what fooled neoclassical economists, who ignore the role of debt in macroeconomics, into believing that the economy was experiencing a 'Great Moderation.' But rising debt increases the distance you have to travel backwards when you want to reduce debt, which is what the USA is now doing. So rising debt feels great on the outward drive from LA east (increasing debt), but lousy when you want to head home again (and reduce debt).

The Credit Impulse is like acceleration – it's a measure of the g-forces, so to speak, generated by either rapid acceleration or rapid deceleration. Acceleration in the debt level felt great on the way up: it was the real source of the booms in the Ponzi economy that the USA has become. Equally, acceleration in the opposite direction – in effect going backwards at an accelerating speed – is terrifying: as the rate of decline in debt increases, the fall in aggregate demand increases and unemployment explodes.

The interactions of the level of debt, rate of growth of debt and the Credit Impulse are akin to those between distance, speed and acceleration as well – and here I'll limit my analogy to the last few years, when America went from increasing debt – the drive from LA to New York – and then abruptly changed direction into deleveraging.

The reversal of direction necessarily involves your acceleration changing from zero or positive to negative, and it feels dreadful: imagine the feeling of slamming on the brakes, putting the car in reverse, and then driving backwards at an accelerating speed.

At some point, however, you will reach the maximum reverse speed of the car, and at that point the terrifying feeling of driving backwards more rapidly will give way to merely the unpleasant feeling of driving backwards at high speed. If you then start driving backwards less rapidly, you will actually feel a positive acceleration – *even though you are still driving backwards.* However, if you keep slowing down your reverse speed, then at some point you will reverse direction, and start heading back towards New York again. You can't maintain positive acceleration indefinitely without at some point changing from a negative to a positive velocity, and thus resuming your journey towards a place that you were initially trying to leave.

We can now get a handle on why this recession has been so extreme compared to its post-World War II predecessors, and why I believe that the crisis has many years to run.

First, all three debt indicators reached levels that are unprecedented in the post-World War II period. The debt-to-GDP ratio, which began the post-war period at barely 50 percent, increased by a factor of 6 in the subsequent five decades to reach a peak of 298 percent of GDP in early 2009.

Secondly, while private debt itself grew at a relatively constant if volatile 10 percent per annum between 1955 and 2008, the debt-financed proportion of aggregate demand rose from 5 percent in the 1950s to 28 percent in 2008. §90

This occurred because the rate of growth of nominal debt was about 3 percent higher than that of nominal GDP from 1945 till 2008. The impact of rising debt on aggregate demand therefore doubled every twenty-three years.[12]

It then plunged to minus 19 percent in early 2010 – an unprecedented event in post-World War II economic history. This debt level is still falling, though the rate of fall has slowed in recent times, from a peak rate of minus 19 percent of GDP in early 2010 to minus 12 percent in September 2010 (the last date at which debt data were available at the time of writing).

12 A variable that is growing at 1 percent per annum will double in roughly seventy years, so a 3 percent rate of growth means that it will double roughly every twenty-three years.

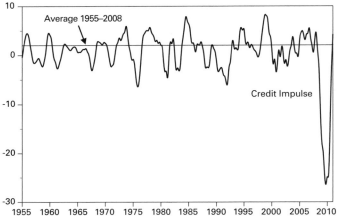

13.8 The biggest collapse in the Credit Impulse ever recorded

§91   Thirdly, the Credit Impulse averaged plus 1.2 percent from 1955 till 2008, and then hit at an unprecedented minus 27 percent in 2009 at the depths of the downturn. It is now returning toward zero – which in part reflects its inevitable return toward zero as deleveraging becomes entrenched.[13] This puts far less drag on aggregate demand, but also removes the 'turbo boost' that a positive Credit Impulse gave to growth in the previous half-century. The Credit Impulse will also tend to be negative while deleveraging continues, just as it tended to be positive when rising debt was boosting aggregate demand. This means the economy will have a tendency toward recessions rather than booms until the debt-to-GDP ratio stabilizes at some future date.

The interaction of these three factors will determine the economic future of the United States (and many other OECD nations, which are in a similar predicament).

The Credit Impulse, as the most volatile factor, will set the immediate economic environment. While it remains negative, the rate at which the USA is deleveraging accelerates, so it therefore had to rise again at some stage – as it has since mid-2009. This will accelerate aggregate demand, but it can't lead to a sustained rise in aggregate demand without causing the debt-to-GDP ratio to rise. That is extremely unlikely to happen, since even after the deleveraging of the last two years, the aggregate level of private debt is 100 percent of GDP higher than it was at the start of the Great Depression.

These dynamics of debt were the key cause of both the Great Moderation and the Great Recession, yet they were completely ignored by neoclassical economists because of their fallacious belief that changes in private debt have no macroeconomic effects (Bernanke 2000: 24). Therefore, far from

13 It also partly reflects the impact of misguided neoclassically inspired government policies that are trying to return to 'business as usual' by encouraging private credit growth – an issue I will consider in much more detail in my next book.

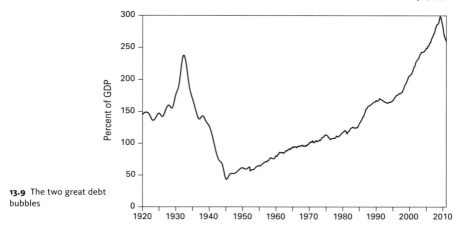

13.9 The two great debt bubbles

making sure that 'It' won't happen again, as Bernanke asserted in 2002, by ignoring and in fact abetting the rise in private debt, neoclassical economists have allowed the conditions for another Great Depression to develop. Worse, a comparison of today's debt data to those from 1920–40 shows that the debt-deflationary forces that have been unleashed in the Great Recession are far larger than those that caused the Great Depression – see Figure 13.9.

Debt deflation then and now

Comparing the 1920s–1940s to now – the Roaring Twenties and the Great Recession to the 'Noughty Nineties'[14] and the Great Recession – is feasible, but complicated both by differences in the economic circumstances at the time, and differences in the quality of the statistics.

A major complication is the extreme volatility in economic performance over the 1920s – no one was writing about 'the Great Moderation' back then. The decade began and ended with a depression, and recorded output fluctuated wildly. The average increase in nominal GDP over 1921–29 was 4.5 percent, but it fluctuated wildly from –2 to +13 percent, with a standard deviation of 4.4 percent. In contrast, the Noughty Nineties recorded a higher rate of nominal growth of 5.3 percent, and this was very stable, ranging between 2.6 and 6.6 percent with a standard deviation of only 1.4 percent.

§92

However, as well as being a decade of stock market speculation, the 1920s also saw serious Schumpeterian investment and 'creative destruction.' It was the decade of the Charleston and *The Great Gatsby*, but it was the decade of the production line, technological innovation in manufacturing and transportation, and the continuing transformation of American employment from agriculture to industry. The average rate of real economic growth was

14 I expect that history will judge the period from 1997 to 2009 as one continuous Ponzi scheme with two phases: the Internet Bubble and the Subprime Bubble. A term will be needed to describe the period, and this is my nomination for it.

therefore higher in the 1920s than in the period from 1999 to 2009 – though
§93 disentangling this from the gyrations in the price level is extremely difficult.

For example, the nominal rate of growth in 1922/23 was 13 percent, but
the 'real' rate was an even higher 20 percent. This impossible level reflected
the simultaneous recovery from deflation of over 10 percent to inflation of
3 percent, and unemployment falling – and hence output rising – from 12
percent to 2.5 percent as the economy recovered from the depression of
§94 January 1920 to June 1921.

Overall, the rate of unemployment is the best means to compare the two
periods, but here we run into the distortions caused by politically motivated
redefinitions of the unemployment rate since the late 1970s (see Box 13.1).
The U-3 measure for 1999–2009 averages 5 percent, only marginally higher
than the average of 4.7 percent for 1920–29; but the U-6 measure for
1999–2009 averages 8.8 percent, and I regard this as a fairer comparison
§95 of the two periods.

The upshot of all this is that the Roaring Twenties saw more real growth
than the Noughty Nineties, and this masked the importance of debt at the
time. But categorically, the fundamental cause of both the Great Depression
and the Great Recession was the bursting of a debt-financed speculative bubble that had fueled the false but seductive prosperity of the previous decade.

The Great Depression remains the greatest economic crisis that capitalism
has ever experienced, but on every debt metric, the forces that caused the
Great Recession are bigger.[15] Private debt rose 50 percent over the 1920s,
from $106 billion (yes, billion) in 1920 to $161 billion by 1930; it rose from
§96 $17 trillion to $42 trillion between 1999 and 2009 – a 140 percent increase.

In inflation-adjusted terms, the increase was very similar – a 72 percent
increase over the Roaring Twenties versus an 85 percent increase from 1999
to 2009. Remarkably, the real level of debt grew at almost precisely the same
rate for the first eight years in both periods – a rate of about 7 percent per
year. This chimes with one implication of the monetary model of capitalism
I outline in the next chapter: banks increase their profits by increasing debt,
and they therefore have an incentive to increase debt as fast as is possible.
The easiest way to do this is to fund Ponzi schemes, which were the hallmark
§97 of both the Roaring Twenties and the 'Noughty Nineties.'

Though the rate of growth of debt was similar, the level of debt compared
to GDP is far higher now than in the 1930s. The debt-to-GDP ratio was
175 percent when the Great Depression began; it is over 100 percent higher
today, and hit 298 percent before it began to reverse in 2009. The degree

---

15 Comparing the two periods is feasible, though changes in statistical standards complicate matters.
On the negative side, debt data from the 1920s (derived from the US Census) are annual, whereas those data
are quarterly today, so the date of changes can't be pinpointed as well for the 1920s–1940s as for today. On
the positive side, the measure of unemployment was far less distorted back then than it is today, after all the
politically motivated massaging of definitions that has occurred since the mid-1970s to understate the level of
unemployment in the OECD, and especially in the USA.

of deleveraging needed to eliminate the Ponzi overhang is therefore much higher today than it was in 1930.

Rising debt fueled the Roaring Twenties, just as rising debt fueled the false prosperity of the Internet and Subprime Bubbles in the 'Noughty Nineties.' Since the rate of real economic growth was higher back in the 1920s than today, the debt ratio itself remained roughly constant prior to the bursting of the Ponzi Scheme in the 1920s; however, debt grew as rapidly in real terms in the 1920s as it did in the noughties, and the collapse of debt in real terms when the crisis hit was also remarkably similar.

But from there they diverge, because the second scourge of the 1930s – deflation – has yet to occur in a sustained manner during the Great Recession. Consequently, while the real burden of debt rose during the early 1930s even as the nominal level of debt was falling, so far the Great Recession has involved falling debt in both real and nominal terms.

One possible reason for the marked difference in inflationary dynamics between the two periods is the composition of private debt. In the 1920s, the vast bulk of the debt was owed by business. Business debt was three times that of household debt, and four times that of the financial sector. Therefore, when the Roaring Twenties boom collapsed as debt-financing fell, businesses were the ones in serious financial difficulties. As Fisher surmised, individual businesses responded by cutting their markups to try to entice customers into their stores and not their competitors', leading to a general fall in the price level that actually increased the debt-to-GDP ratio, even as nominal debt levels fell.

Today the ranking is reversed in the insolvency stakes: the financial sector carried the highest level of debt leading into the Great Recession – virtually 125 percent of GDP, five times the level of debt it had in 1930. Households come second now, with a debt level of almost 100 percent of GDP, two and a half times the level they had in 1930. The business sector carried a modest debt level of 80 percent of GDP, when compared to its 1930s level of 110 percent – though even this is more than twice its debt level during the 'Golden Age' of the 1950s and 1960s.

This composition difference may have implications for how the debt-deflationary dynamics of the Great Recession will play out. The prospects of a 1930s-style deflationary collapse are low, since businesses do not face the direct pressure of insolvency that they faced back then. However, their retail customers, the consumer sector, have never been this debt-encumbered, and it is far harder for households to reduce debt than it is for businesses: to put it colloquially, businesses can get out of debt by going bankrupt, ceasing investment, and sacking the workers. Bankruptcy is far more painful for individuals than companies; it is much harder to stop consuming than it is to stop investing, and households can't 'sack the kids.'

This implies a far less severe tendency to deflation, but a more intractable

§98

§99

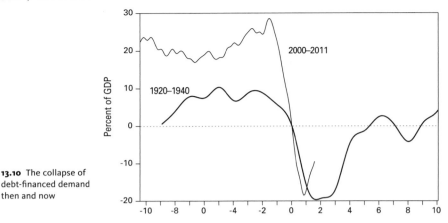

13.10 The collapse of debt-financed demand then and now

§100   one at the same time since consumer demand will remain muted while debt levels remain high.

Finally, though the Roaring Twenties became a reference period for frivolous speculation in popular culture, they have nothing on the Noughty Nineties. Debt-financed spending never exceeded 10 percent of GDP in the 1920s. In the noughties, it rarely fell below 20 percent of GDP. The popular culture of the twenty-first century may ignore the Roaring Twenties and see the Noughty Nineties as the hallmark of delusional economic behavior.

Given this much higher level of debt-financed speculation, the plunge into negative territory was far faster in 2008/09 than it was in 1929–31 – but the reversal of direction has also been far more sudden. The change in debt went from adding 28 percent of GDP to aggregate demand in 2008 to subtracting 19 percent from it in 2010, but the rate of decline turned around merely a year after the crisis began, compared to the three years that elapsed before the debt-financed contribution started to rise from the depths in the 1930s (see Figure 13.10) (a large part of this may be the product of the huge intervention by both the federal government and the Federal Reserve).

The Credit Impulse was also far more dramatic in the noughties than in the twenties: it was higher during the boom, and plunged far more rapidly and deeply during the slump. The Credit Impulse took four years to go from its positive peak of 2.5 percent before the Great Depression to –16 percent in 1931. It began from the much higher level of 5 percent in late 2007 and fell to a staggering –26 percent in late 2009 – a plunge of over 30 percent in just two years versus an 18 percent fall over four years in the

§101   Great Recession.

The collapse in debt-financed aggregate demand was the key factor behind both the Great Depression and the Great Recession. Though debt-financed demand played less of a role in the 1920s than it did in the noughties, the collapse in the Great Depression was as deep as today's, and far more prolonged, which caused unemployment to hit the unprecedented level of 25 percent in 1932. When the Credit Impulse finally rose again in 1933, so did employment, and unemployment fell to just over 11 percent in mid-1937 – leading to hopes that the depression was finally over.

However, debt-financed demand turned negative once again in 1938, and unemployment rose with it to 20 percent. Only with the onset of the war with Japan did unemployment fall back to the average experienced during the 1920s.

§102

The same pattern has played out during the Great Moderation and Great Recession. When debt-financed demand collapsed, unemployment exploded to 10 percent on the U-3 measure, and 17 percent on the more comparable U-6 measure. Just as significantly, the unemployment rate stabilized when the decline in debt-financed demand turned around. Though the huge fiscal and monetary stimulus packages also played a role, changes in debt-financed demand dominate economic performance.

One statistical indicator of the importance of debt dynamics in causing both the Great Depression and the Great Recession and the booms that preceded them is the correlation coefficient between changes in debt and the level of unemployment. Over the whole period from 1921 till 1940, the correlation coefficient was minus 0.83, while over the period from 1990 till 2011, it was minus 0.91 (versus the maximum value it could have taken of minus one). A correlation of that scale, over time periods of that length, when economic circumstances varied from bust to boom and back again, is staggering.

§103

The Credit Impulse confirms the dominant role of private debt. The correlation between the Credit Impulse and the rate of change of unemployment was minus 0.53 in 1922–40, and minus 0.75 between 1990 and 2011.

§104 and 105

Changes in the rate of change of credit also lead changes in unemployment. When the Credit Impulse is lagged by four months, the correlation rises to minus 0.85.

§106

This correlation is, if anything, even more staggering than that between debt-financed demand and the level of unemployment. The correlation between change in unemployment and the Credit Impulse is one between a rate of change and *the rate of change of a rate of change*. There are so many other factors buffeting the economy in addition to debt that finding any correlation between a first-order and second-order effect is remarkable, let alone one so large, and spanning such different economic circumstances – from the recession of the early 1990s, through the 'Great Moderation,' into the Great Recession and even the apparent beginnings of a recovery from it.

Fighting the Great Recession

The global economy won't return to sustained growth until debt levels are substantially reduced. With debt at its current level, the general tendency of the private sector will be to delever, so that the change in credit will deduct from economic growth rather than contributing to it. Any short-term boost to demand from the Credit Impulse – such as that occurring in early 2011 – will ultimately dissipate, since if it were sustained then ultimately debt levels would have to rise again. Since the household sector in particular is debt-saturated, credit growth will hit a debt ceiling and give way to deleveraging again. The US economy in particular is likely to be trapped in a never-ending sequence of 'double dips,' just as Japan has been for the last two decades.

There is a simple, but confrontational, way to stop this process: a unilateral write-off of debt.

This policy – which occurred regularly in ancient societies, where it was known as a Jubilee (Hudson 2000: 347) – goes strongly against the grain of a modern capitalist society, where paying your debts is seen as a social obligation. But the ancient and biblical practice addressed a weakness in those societies – the tendency for debtors to become hopelessly indebted given the enormous interest rates that were common then:

> Mesopotamian economic thought c. 2000 BC rested on a more realistic mathematical foundation than does today's orthodoxy. At least the Babylonians appear to have recognized that over time the debt overhead came to exceed the ability to pay, culminating in a concentration of property ownership in the hands of creditors. While debts grew exponentially, the economy grew less rapidly. The earning capacity of Babylonian rural producers hardly could be reconciled with creditor claims mounting up at the typical 33.333 percent rate of interest for agricultural loans, or even at the commercial 20 percent rate. Such charges were unsustainable for economies as a whole. (Ibid.: 348)

It would be foolish to deny that we have a similar weakness in modern capitalist society: our tendency to be sucked into Ponzi schemes by a banking sector that profits from rising debt.

As I explain in the next chapter, when lending is undertaken for investment or consumption, debt tends not to get out of hand. But when borrowing is undertaken to speculate on asset prices, debt tends to grow more rapidly than income. This growth causes a false boom while it is happening, but results in a collapse once debt growth terminates – as it has done now.

Though borrowers can be blamed for having euphoric expectations of unsustainable capital gains, in reality the real blame for Ponzi schemes lies with their financiers – the banks and the finance sector in general – rather than the borrowers. That was blindingly obvious during the Subprime Bubble in the USA, where many firms willfully wrote loans when they knew – or should have known – that borrowers could not repay them.

Such loans should not be honored. But that is what we are doing now, by maintaining the debt and expecting that debtors should repay debts that should never have been issued in the first place.

The consequences of our current behavior are twofold. First, the economy will be encumbered by a debt burden that should never have been generated, and will limp along for a decade or more, as has Japan. Secondly, the financial sector will continue to believe that 'the Greenspan Put' will absolve them from the consequences of irresponsible lending.

A debt jubilee would address both those consequences. First, debt repayments that are hobbling consumer spending and industrial investment would be abolished; secondly, this would impose the pain of bankruptcy and capital loss on the financial sector – a pain it has avoided in general thus far through all the rescues since Greenspan's first back in 1987.

Needless to say, this would not be an easy policy to implement.

Its biggest hurdle would be political: it is obvious that the major political force in the USA today – and much of the OECD – is the financial sector itself. Since widespread debt abolition would bankrupt much of this sector, and eliminate individual fortunes (those that have not already been salted away), it will be opposed ferociously by that sector.

The same was the case – though on a smaller scale than today – during the Great Depression. It took a Ferdinand Pecora (Perino 2010) to turn the tide against the bankers then, and a Franklin Roosevelt (Roosevelt 1933) to convert that tide into political power – and policies that included debt moratoria.

The recent Financial Crisis Inquiry Commission (Financial Crisis Inquiry Commission 2011) was a farce compared to Pecora's work, and Obama's administration to date has focused more on returning the financial sector to its old ways than on bringing it to account.

The policy would also need to re-establish the practice of banking providing working capital and investment funds for industrial capitalism. This should be the primary role of banking, but it virtually died out as the financial sector became more and more an engine for speculation, so that most companies today raise their funds on the commercial paper market.[16] A debt jubilee would bankrupt many banks, and put them into receivership; though it would be painful, the receivers could also be required to re-establish this key but neglected banking practice.

It would also be necessary to compensate to some extent those not in debt as well – though they would also benefit from the sudden increase in spending power that such a policy would cause.

Such a policy would have to be accompanied by institutional reforms to finance that prevented a travesty like the Subprime Bubble from recurring; I discuss some possible reforms at the end of Chapter 14. It would also be far from a panacea for America's woes on its own, since it would also expose the

---

16 This is why the bankruptcy of Lehman Brothers was so disastrous: they had largely cornered the market for commercial paper, and when they went bankrupt this market collapsed – meaning that many ordinary firms could not pay their workers or suppliers.

extent to which the gutting of American industry in the last three decades has been disguised by the growth of the financial sector on the back of the Ponzi schemes of the stock and housing markets. The finance sector would shrink dramatically, and unlike in the 1930s, there would not be potential factory jobs awaiting unemployed financial advisors.

A debt jubilee, and the reforms I suggest in Chapter 14, is politically improbable now. But the alternative I believe is a decade or more of economic stagnation. At some stage we are going to have to accept the wisdom in Michael Hudson's simple phrase that 'Debts that can't be repaid, won't be repaid.'

Conclusion

The data on debt confirm the conclusions that can be reached from assessing the logical coherence – or lack of it – in neoclassical theory: every methodological choice neoclassical economics made was wrong. The belief that economics can be reduced to microeconomics is false; money and credit cannot be ignored, capitalism cannot be modeled as a single 'representative agent,' finance destabilizes the economy, and the economy is permanently in disequilibrium.

If we are to develop an economics that is relevant to capitalism, then it must be a strictly monetary, dynamic theory in which finance plays a fundamentally destabilizing role. In the next chapter, I show how such an economic theory can be developed, by building on the work of both the great non-neoclassical economists and recent empirical work by economists from the 'post-Keynesian' school of thought.

14 | A MONETARY MODEL OF CAPITALISM

Many of the foundations on which neoclassical macroeconomics is built arose from persevering with methodological choices that the nineteenth-century founding fathers of neoclassicism made out of expediency rather than preference. They assumed that all economic processes occurred in equilibrium, so that they could model the economy using comparative statics rather than using more difficult dynamic differential equations; they avoided thinking about money and modeled the simpler process of barter instead; they ignored uncertainty about the future and, as Keynes put it, tried to 'deal with the present by abstracting from the fact that we know very little about the future' (Keynes 1937: 215) and so on.

Though these choices made it easy to concoct simple parables about supply and demand, they actually made mathematical modeling of the economy harder, not easier. The absurdities that later neoclassicals added – from the fallacy of the horizontal demand curve to the intellectual travesty of the 'representative agent' – were products of clinging to these simple parables, despite the deep research that contradicted them.

Economists trained on these methods are now scrambling to make ad hoc modifications to the core neoclassical parable to produce hybrid models that mimic the real-world phenomenon of the Great Recession – which, according to the parables, cannot occur.[1] Though such models will superficially ape reality, they will do so for the reasons that Solow gave, that the addition of various 'imperfections' results in a model that 'sounds better and fits the data better' simply because 'these imperfections were chosen by intelligent economists to make the models work better [...]' (Solow 2001: 26).

This is the difficult road to relevance – take a theoretical framework in which the real-world phenomenon you are trying to describe cannot happen, and tinker with it until something resembling reality emerges. It will not last. Once the global economy emerges from this crisis, if this approach still dominates economics, then within decades these 'imperfections' will go the way of the dodo. Economists will return to the core parable, and the crisis we are now in will be seen as the result of bad Federal Reserve policy,[2] rather than a manifestation of capitalism's innate instability – amplified by a finance sector that is almost designed to generate Ponzi schemes.

1 Discussed in Chapter 10.
2 The nominated policy failing this time would probably be the alleged deviation from the Taylor Rule after 2001 – the case Taylor himself is already making (see Box 10.1, page 267).

We have to do better than that. We have to start with foundations from which the phenomena of reality emerge naturally by constructing monetary models of capitalism built on the melded visions of Marx, Schumpeter, Keynes and Minsky.

Methodological precepts

An essential first step towards a meaningful macroeconomics is to acknowledge the one profound lesson from the failure of the neoclassical experiment: that strong reductionism is a fallacy. Macroeconomic phenomena – and even phenomena within one market – are emergent properties of the dynamic, disequilibrium interactions of individuals and social groups in a rich institutional environment, constrained by the physical, temporal and environmental realities of production. These phenomena will not be predictable from the behavior of isolated individuals. Instead, macroeconomics is a self-contained field of analysis, and it must be reconstructed as such. The reductionist route must be abandoned.

There are basically two routes by which models of a new 'emergent phenomena' macroeconomics could be built: the 'bottoms-up' approach that has always dominated economics, but modified in the light of the modern knowledge of complex systems; or the 'tops-down' approach that typified the work of Marx, Schumpeter, Keynes and Minsky, in which the economy is described at the level of aggregates – evolutionary change, social classes, aggregate production, aggregate debt levels and so on.

The former approach takes the macroeconomic phenomena as given, and attempts to build computer-based multi-agent models in which those macroeconomic phenomena arise as emergent properties of the models. The latter works at the level of aggregates, and puts the verbal models of the great non-neoclassical thinkers into the form of dynamic equations.

Most economists who are trying to build macroeconomic models that transcend the neoclassical dead end are taking the former approach (Barr, Tassier et al. 2008; Seppecher 2010).[3] This approach is worthwhile, though there are inherent difficulties in it that I discuss briefly later. I have taken the latter approach of trying to put the Marx-Schumpeter-Keynes-Minsky vision directly into mathematical form.

Doing this turned out to be far easier than I expected, once I made money the starting point of my analysis of capitalism.

Endogenous money

One of the many issues on which Keynes failed to convince his fellow economists was the importance of money in modeling the economy. One reason for this was that money's explicit role in the *General Theory* itself was restricted largely to the impact of expectations about an uncertain future,

3 Seppecher's Java-based model is accessible at p.seppecher.free.fr/jamel/.

and the difference between real and nominal wages. Keynes acknowledged that money did not feature heavily in his technical analysis, and that he saw a substantial continuity between monetary analysis and the Marshallian model of supply and demand:

> whilst it is found that money enters into the economic scheme in an essential and peculiar manner, *technical monetary detail falls into the background.* A monetary economy, we shall find, is essentially one in which changing views about the future are capable of influencing the quantity of employment and not merely its direction. But *our method* of analyzing the economic behavior of the present under the influence of changing ideas about the future is one which *depends on the interaction of supply and demand, and is in this way linked up with our fundamental theory of value.* We are thus led to a more general theory, which includes the classical theory with which we are familiar, as a special case. (Keynes 1936: xxii–xxiii; emphases added)

It is therefore difficult to attack neoclassical 'supply and demand'-oriented models of money as misrepresentations of Keynes. Nonetheless, the post-Keynesian school of thought has made the fundamental importance of money a byword of its analysis. An essential aspect of this has been the empirically based analysis of how money is created (detailed in the previous chapter), which contradicts the conventional fractional reserve banking, 'Money Multiplier' model of money formation.

Having empirically eliminated one model of money creation, another was needed – but the initial attempts to create one were clumsy. Rather than the 'vertical money supply curve' of Hicks's IS-LM model, some post-Keynesian economists proposed a 'horizontal money supply curve' in which banks simply passively supplied whatever quantity of credit money firms wanted, at the prevailing interest rate. This model, known as 'Horizontalism' (Moore 1988b), led to a lengthy dispute within post-Keynesian economics over whether the money supply curve was horizontal, or sloped upwards (Dow 1997).

This dispute put the empirically accurate findings of post-Keynesian researchers into the same methodological straitjacket that neoclassical economics itself employed: the equilibrium analysis of intersecting supply and demand curves. Though this was hardly the intention of the originators of endogenous money analysis, it effectively made monetary analysis an extension of supply and demand analysis.

Participants in this debate were aware of the limitations of this approach – as Sheila Dow observed, '[T]he limitations of a diagrammatic representation of a non-deterministic organic process become very clear. This framework is being offered here as an aid to thought, but it can only cope with one phase of the process, not with the feedbacks' (ibid.: 74). But one of the great ironies of economics is that, because critics of neoclassical economics were themselves trained by neoclassical economists, most critics weren't trained in suitable alternative modeling methods, such as differential equations or multi-agent simulation.

For real analytic progress to be made, a watertight basis for Keynes's assertion that money 'enters into the economic scheme in an essential and peculiar manner' was required, as well as a methodological approach that captured the feedback effects that diagrams and equilibrium analysis could not.

The former was supplied by the 'Monetary Circuit' school in Europe, and specifically the Italian economist Augusto Graziani. Graziani argued that, if money is treated as just another commodity subject to the 'laws' of supply and demand, then the economy is effectively still a barter system: all that has happened is that one more commodity has been added to the mix, or singled out as the commodity through which all barter must occur. This is quantitative change, not qualitative, and yet something qualitative must change if a monetary economy is to be distinguished from a barter system.

Graziani's brilliant insight was that, for a monetary economy to be clearly distinguished from a barter economy, *the monetary economy could not use a commodity as money.* Therefore money had to be a non-commodity – something that was intrinsically worthless, and which could not be simply produced as commodities themselves can: 'a commodity money is by definition a kind of money that any producer can produce for himself. But an economy using as money a commodity coming out of a regular process of production, cannot be distinguished from a barter economy' (Graziani 1989: 3). This then led to a simple but profound principle: 'A true monetary economy must therefore be using a token money, which is nowadays a paper currency' (ibid.: 3).

The fact that a monetary economy uses a token – something that is intrinsically worthless – as a means of exchange implies two further key conditions 'In order for money to exist':

b) money has to be accepted as a means of final settlement of the transaction (otherwise it would be credit and not money);

c) money must not grant privileges of seigniorage to any agent making a payment. (Ibid.: 3)

From this Graziani derived the insight that 'any monetary payment must therefore be a triangular transaction, involving at least three agents, the payer, the payee, and the bank':

The only way to satisfy those three conditions is to have payments made by means of *promises of a third agent*, the typical third agent being nowadays a bank [...] Once the payment is made, no debt and credit relationships are left between the two agents. But one of them is now a creditor of the bank, while the second is a debtor of the same bank. (Ibid.: 3; all emphases in original)

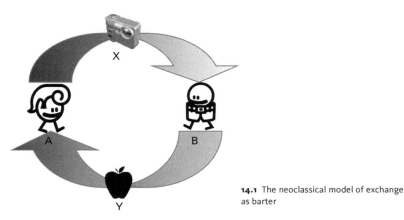

14.1 The neoclassical model of exchange as barter

This perspective clearly delineates a monetary vision of capitalism from the neoclassical barter paradigm. As shown in Figure 14.1, in the neoclassical world, transactions are two-sided, two-commodity, barter exchanges: person *A* gives person *B* one unit of commodity *X* in return for some number of units of commodity *Y*. Calling one of these 'the money commodity' does not alter the essentially barter personality of the transaction.

But in our monetary world, transactions are three-sided, single-commodity, financial exchanges, as portrayed in Figure 14.2: person *B* instructs bank *Z* to debit *Y* units of currency from *B*'s account, and credit *A*'s account with the same amount, in return for which person *A* gives person *B* one unit of commodity *X*.

Banks are thus an essential component of capitalism, and are inherently different to industrial firms. Firms produce goods (and services) for sale by

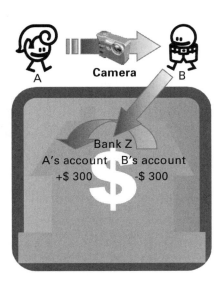

14.2 The nature of exchange in the real world

combining labor and other commodities in a production process that takes both time and effort. Banks generate and honor promises to pay that are used by third parties to facilitate the sale of goods.[4] Therefore firms and banks must be clearly distinguished in any model of capitalism: 'Since in a monetary economy money payments necessarily go through a third agent, the third agent being one that specializes in the activity of producing means of payment (in modern times a bank), *banks and firms must be considered as two distinct kinds of agents* [...] In any model of a monetary economy, *banks and firms cannot be aggregated into one single sector*' (ibid.: 4; emphasis in original).

This simple but profound perspective on what is the essence of a monetary capitalist economy yielded two essential requirements for a model of capitalism:

- all transactions involve transfer of funds between bank accounts;
- the minimum number of classes[5] in a model of capitalism is three: capitalists, workers and bankers.

It also implied that the best structure for modeling the financial side of capitalism is a double-entry system of bank accounts. This led me to develop a means to derive dynamic monetary models of capitalism from a system of double-entry bookkeeping accounts (Keen 2008, 2009b, 2010, 2011), and a remarkable amount of the Marx-Schumpeter-Keynes-Minsky perspective on capitalism arose naturally out of this approach.

I'll outline the simplest possible version of this model before expanding it to provide a monetary version of the Minsky model outlined in Chapter 13.

A 'pure credit' economy

Our modern monetary economy is a system of such complexity that it makes the outrageous contraptions of Rube Goldberg, Heath Robinson and Bruce Petty appear trite by comparison: the Bank of International Settlements, central banks, commercial banks; merchant banks, hedge funds, superannuation funds, building societies; fiat money, credit money, multiple measures of money (base money, M_0, M_1, M_2, M_3, broad money); reserve ratios, Taylor Rules, Basel Rules ...

Many of these components were instituted to try to control bank lending

---

4 And they incur essentially no costs in doing so – the cost of 'producing' a dollar is much less than a dollar. This is the source of Graziani's third stricture that the system can't enable banks to exploit this opportunity for seigniorage.

5 Economists normally say 'agents' here rather than classes – given the microeconomic focus of neoclassical modeling, and the pejorative association that class was given by nineteenth-century politics. I use the term classes because social classes are an objective reality in capitalism, and because the SMD conditions, as Alan Kirman put it, suggest that 'If we are to progress further we may well be forced to theorise in terms of groups who have collectively coherent behaviour [...] Thus demand and expenditure functions if they are to be set against reality must be defined at some reasonably high level of aggregation. The idea that we should start at the level of the isolated individual is one which we may well have to abandon' (Kirman 1989: 138).

after the catastrophe of the Great Depression; many others were responses by the financial system to evade the intentions of these controls. To my cynical eye, the evasive maneuvers of the financial system have been far more effective than the regulatory structures themselves, and in essence our financial system approximates the behavior of the almost completely unregulated private banks of the 'free banking' period in the nineteenth century.

For that reason, my base monetary model is a pure credit economy with no government or central bank, in which the private bank prints its own paper notes, and where transactions involve transferring paper notes from the accounts of the buyers to that of the sellers. There are three classes – workers, capitalists and bankers – and, in the simplest possible model with no Ponzi lending behavior, firms are the only borrowers, and they borrow in order to be able pay the wages needed to hire workers.

§107

Five accounts are needed to describe the basic monetary flows in this system:

1   a vault, in which the bank stores its notes prior to lending;
2   a 'bank safe,' into and out of which interest payments are made;
3   deposit accounts for firms, into which money lent by the banks is put and through which all the firm sector's transactions occur;
4   deposit accounts for workers, into which their wages are paid; and
5   a loan register, which is *not* an account as such, but a ledger that records the amounts that have been lent by the banks to firms, and on which loan interest is charged.

The basic monetary operations that occur in this simple model are:[6]

1   the banking sector makes loans to the firm sector;
2   the banks charge interest on outstanding loans;
3   firms pay the interest;
4   firms hire workers;
5   workers and bankers consume the output of the firms; and
6   firms repay their loans.

These operations are shown in Table 14.1, which (based on the standard accounting practice of showing 'assets minus liabilities equals equity') shows the economy from the point of view of the banks, with the banking sector's assets on the left-hand side of the ledger and its liabilities and residual equity on the right-hand side.[7]

Actual transfers of money are shown in normal text, while operations

---

6   To register as a bank, and therefore to be able to print its own notes, 'free banking' banks still had to meet various regulatory requirements, and normally also purchase government bonds of an equivalent value to their initial printing of notes. In what follows, I'm taking these operations as given, and focusing just on the banking operations that followed incorporation.

7   My thanks to Peter Humphreys from the School of Accounting at UWS for advice on how to lay out this table in accordance with standard banking practice.

TABLE 14.1 A pure credit economy with paper money

| | Bank assets | | Bank liabilities plus equity | | |
| | | | Liabilities (deposits) | | Equity |
Operation	Vault	Loan ledger	Firms	Workers	Safe
Lend money	− Lend money		+ Lend money		
Record loans		− Lend money			
Charge interest		+ Charge interest			
Pay interest			− Charge interest		+ Charge interest
Record payment		− Charge interest			
Deposit interest			+ Deposit interest		− Deposit interest
Hire workers			− Wages	+ Wages	
Bankers consume			+ Bankers' consumption		− Bankers' consumption
Workers consume			+ Workers' consumption	− Workers' consumption	
Loan repayment	+ Loan repayment		− Loan repayment		
Record repayment		− Loan repayment			

that are not money transfers but accounting operations – such as the bank recording that interest due on loans has been paid – are shown in italics.

Since all the entries in this table indicate flows into and out of accounts (or additions and subtractions from the loan ledger), a remarkable thing is possible: a dynamic model of this monetary model can be derived just by 'adding up' the entries in the columns, as in Table 14.2.

TABLE 14.2 The dynamics of a pure credit economy with no growth

Rate of change of:	Equals:
Vault	– Lend money + Repay loans
Loan ledger	+ Loan money – Repay loans
Firm deposits	+ Loan money – Charge interest + Deposit interest – Wages + Bankers' consumption + Workers' consumption – Repay loans
Worker deposits	+ Wages – Workers' consumption
Safe	+ Charge interest – Deposit interest – Bankers' consumption

This model can be simulated if we put values on these flows. Some of these are obvious: the interest charged, for example, will equal the rate of interest on loans times the amount currently recorded on the loan ledger; interest paid is the rate of interest on deposits times the amount currently in the firms' deposit accounts.[8]

Others – lending from the vault, payment of wages, consumption by workers and bankers and loan repayment – will in the real world depend on a whole host of factors, but to model the simplest possible system, I relate them here to the balances in these other accounts, and use constants rather than variables simply to see whether the model is viable: obviously, if it's impossible to find a set of constants that makes this model viable, then no set of variables is likely to do it either.

Thus lending from the vault is modeled occurring at some constant rate times the amount of money in the vault; the flow of wages is some constant times the balance in firms' deposit accounts; workers' and bankers' consumption depend on the balances in the workers' deposit accounts and the safe respectively; while the flow of loan repayments is some constant times the amount of loans outstanding.

The constants (known as 'time constants' in dynamic modeling)[9] used tell

8 I have ignored interest on workers' deposit accounts simply to make the table less cluttered. They are included in my more technical description of this model in the paper 'Solving the paradox of monetary profits' (Keen 2010), which is downloadable from www.economics-ejournal.org/economics/journalarticles/2010-31.

9 See en.wikipedia.org/wiki/Time_constant for an exposition. These are normally expressed as fractions of a year – so that the assumption that workers turn their accounts over twenty-six times a year means that the time constant for workers' consumption is 1/26 – but to simplify the exposition I'm expressing them in times per year instead.

us how many times in a year the given account will turn over – so a value of ½, for example, indicates that the balance in the relevant account will be turned over every two years. One obvious value here is that for workers' consumption: since workers' wages are paid on a weekly basis, and most of workers' incomes is expended on consumption, the constant for workers' consumption will be 26 – indicating that the balance in the workers' accounts turns over twenty-six times a year. For the sake of illustration, I use ½ for lending money (so that the vault turns over every two years), 3 for wages, 1 for bankers' consumption, 26 for workers' consumption, 1/10 for loan repayment, and I set the rate of interest on loans to 5 percent and the rate of interest on deposits to 2 percent.

If the model starts with $100 million initially in the vault and no money in any other account, then after ten years, the amount in the vault falls to $16.9 million, with $83.1 million in outstanding loans, $2.7 million in the safe, $72.1 million in firm deposit accounts, and $8.3 million in the workers' deposit accounts – see Figure 14.3.[10] It is also possible to calculate the annual wages bill and bank earnings. The annual wages bill is the time constant for wage payments times the balance in the firms' deposit account, which is three times $72.1 million or $216.3 million, while bank gross earnings are the rate of interest on loans times the outstanding loan balance (5 percent times $83.1 million or $4.16 million) minus the rate of interest on deposits times the firms' deposit balance (2 percent times $72 million or $1.44 million), for a net bankers' income of $2.7 million per annum.

Capitalists' income isn't as obvious in this simple model, and to explain it properly will require incorporating production and pricing as well. But we can imply what profits are by realizing that net annual income in this simple model equals the sum of wages plus profits – the income of bankers cancels out and adds nothing to aggregate income (see Table 14.3).

TABLE 14.3 Net incomes

Class	Net Income components	Amounts
Workers	Wages	216.3
Capitalists	Profits minus Loan interest plus Deposit interest	$72.1 - 4.16 + 1.44$
Bankers	Loan interest minus Deposit interest	$4.16 - 1.44$
Total income	Wages plus Profits	288.4

Since wages represent part of the net surplus generated in production, profits must represent the remainder. If workers' wages represent, say, 75

10 This point was disputed by early Circuitist literature, but this was an error of logic due to a confusion of stocks with flows (for a detailed exposition on this point, see Keen 2010: 10–12).

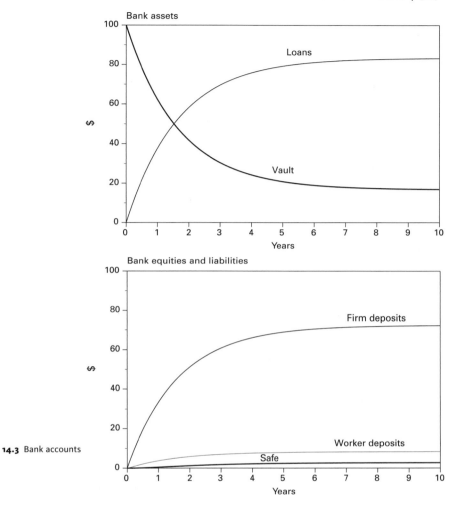

14.3 Bank accounts

percent of net income, then profits represent 25 percent – so in this numerical example they equal $72.1 million.[11]

Annual income in this example is thus $288.4 million – almost three times the amount of money in the model, and precisely four times the amount of money in firms' deposit accounts. How can this be? Marx's insight into why Say's Law is invalid in a capitalist economy holds the key. Remember that Say's Law holds under simple commodity production (*Commodity→Money→Commodity*), but not in capitalism, because that also has the circuit *Money→Commodity→More Money*. Marx also pointed out that this 'Circuit of Capital' takes time: it involves getting money in the first place, using it to hire workers and buy inputs, combine them in a production

---

11 It is just a coincidence that this equals the equilibrium amount in the firms' deposit accounts – a different wage/profit share would return a different profit level.

process, ship the finished goods and finally sell them to customers. There is thus a time lag between outlaying M and earning $M+$, which Marx called the 'period of turnover.' This can be significantly shorter than a year, though it's highly unlikely to be as short as the example Marx himself gave: 'Let the period of turnover be 5 weeks, the working period 4 weeks [...] In a year of 50 weeks [...] Capital I of £2,000, constantly employed in the working period, is therefore turned over 12½ times. 12½ times 2,000 makes £25,000' (Marx 1885: ch. 16).

Expressed as a fraction of a year, Marx's example gives a value of 1/12.5 for the period of turnover – and in general, the smaller the number, the faster a given amount of money turns over, and the more profit (and wages) that can be generated. Marx's numerical example was extreme, but the basic insight is correct, that a given sum of money can finance several times as much turnover in a given year.

The period of turnover can also be derived for our example, using the facts that the value of the time constant for wages is 3, and 75 percent of national income goes to workers as wages. Total income – wages plus profits – is thus four times the amount of money in the firms' deposit accounts. The turnover period is therefore one year divided by 4: it takes three months, in this toy economy, to go from M to $M+$.

Though the turnover period is an unfamiliar concept, it's related to the well-known if less well-defined concept of the velocity of money. The turnover period tells us how often the money in firms' deposit accounts turns over; the velocity of money in this model is the value of wages plus profits (GDP, which is $288.4 million in this example) divided by either the total money supply ($100 million) or the money in active circulation, which is the sum of the amounts in the deposit accounts plus the safe ($83.1 million). Measured the former way, the velocity of money is 2.88; measured the latter way, it's 3.47.

This is an incredibly simple system, but even at this point it can give us some insights into why Bernanke's QE1 was far less effective than he had hoped – and why it would have been far more effective if the money had been given to the debtors rather than to the banks.

A credit crunch

The crisis of 2007 was not merely a credit crunch (where the problem is liquidity) but the end point in the process of Ponzi lending that made much of the US economy insolvent. However, the credit-crunch aspect of this crisis can be simulated in this model by halving the rate at which the bank lends from the vault, and doubling the speed at which firms try to repay their debts. The time constant for bank lending therefore drops from ½ to ¼ – so that the amount in the vault turns over every four years rather than every two – while that for repaying debts goes from 1/10 to 1/5 – so that loans are repaid every five years rather than every ten.

The credit crunch has a drastic impact upon both bank account balances and incomes. The level of loans drops from over $83 million to under $56 million, while the amount in the vault – and therefore inactive – rises from $16.9 million to $44.1 million.

§108

All incomes drop substantially as well: wages drop from $216 million to $145 million per year, profits drop from $72 million to $48.5 million, and bank income drops from $2.7 million to $1.8 million – a 32.8 percent drop.

Now let's consider what would happen if an injection of $10 million was made one year after the crunch began, into either the vault, or into the deposit accounts of the firms. The former approximates what Bernanke did in his attempt to exploit the mythical 'Money Multiplier,' the latter approximates what might have happened if the bailout had gone to debtors rather than to the banks – and this is also very similar to what was in fact done in Australia, where the Rudd government effectively gave every Australian with a pulse $1,000 to spend.[12]

The results are intriguing, complex even though the model itself is simple, and the reverse of what Obama was told would happen by his neoclassical advisors.

Whose bailout works best?

The bank bailout injects $10 million into the vault over a one-year period; the firm and worker bailouts inject the same amount of money over the same period of time into the deposit accounts of the firms or workers.

If you believed that the most important thing was to get lending going again after a credit crunch, then the bank bailout wins hands down: neither the firm nor the worker bailouts affect the level of loans at all, which remain on the depressed credit-crunch trajectory, while the bank bailout leads to loans falling less steeply, so that ten years after the crunch, they are $5.5 million higher than they would have been without the bailout.

§109

However, if you believed that the most important thing was to restore economic activity, then the bank bailout is the least effective way to do this!

Profits and wages do rise because of the bank bailout, but the rise in income is far greater when the firms or workers receive the bailout than when the banks do.[13] The increase in incomes is immediate and large in the case of the firms' bailout, versus gradual and modest for the bank bailout.

§110

The only people that do better if the bailout goes to the bankers ... are the bankers. Not only do they do better under their bailout than if nothing is done, they do worse if the bailout goes to firms or workers than if there

---

12 A cash handout of $960 was sent to every Australian over eighteen who had a tax return for the previous year.

13 There is only a transient difference between the firm and worker bailouts on this front, while the bailout is being made. Workers' consumption is higher for the duration of the bailout if they receive the money – since they spend almost all of what they receive – but their incomes are slightly lower than when the firms get the bailout.

is no bailout at all! The reason is that the firm (or worker) bailout increases the deposit accounts of the banks while leaving their loans unaffected. Their payment of interest to the rest of the economy therefore increases, while their receipts of interest payments remain the same.

§111

This is a very basic and incomplete model, and much more needs to be added to it before any definitive implications could be drawn about the impact of a government bailout during a credit crunch.[14] But the differences between this simple dynamic model, and the even simpler but false Money Multiplier model that lay behind Obama's decision to bail out the banks rather than the public, tempt me to write what Obama *could* have said, if his advisers were not neoclassical economists:

> And although the banks have argued that government money would be more effective if it were given to them to lend, rather than going directly to families and businesses– 'where's our bailout?' they ask – the truth is that an additional dollar of capital in a bank will dribble out slowly through the choked arteries of our sclerotic financial system, while that same dollar, if given to families and businesses, will enter circulation rapidly, a process that will cause a faster pace of economic growth.

But that's enough of fantasy. Let's bring this model up to date in terms of how money is created endogenously today, and extend it to include production, prices and growth.

A modern credit crunch

The model we've just considered has a fixed amount of money in it, and since it's a paper-money system, the banks would need to print more notes if they wanted to expand the money supply. However, the majority of banking transactions have always involved the buyer writing a check drawn on an account in a bank, rather than handing over paper notes in return for goods – and today's innovation of electronic transfer banking has taken this one step farther. The fact that these promises by banks to pay are accepted as money in their own right is what makes it possible for banks to expand the money supply simply by creating a new loan. The new loan creates a debt between the borrower and the bank, and it also creates additional spending power.

It's this capacity to create money 'out of nothing' which state policies like Reserve Requirements and Basel Rules attempted to control, but the empirical evidence shown in the last chapter shows that these control mechanisms have failed: the banks create as much new money as they can get away with, because, fundamentally, banks profit by creating debt.

---

14 However, a more complete model is as likely to amplify these basic results as it is to attenuate them. For example, the injection of fiat money puts the banking sector's assets and liabilities out of balance, when an essential aspect of banking practice is that they are balanced. The firms bailout could thus force the banks to lend more rapidly to bring their assets back into line with their liabilities, thus amplifying the boost from the fiat money injection.

TABLE 14.4 A growing pure credit economy with electronic money

	Bank assets		Bank liabilities plus equity		
			Liabilities (deposits)		Equity
Operation	Vault	Loan ledger	Firms	Workers	Safe
Lend money	− Lend money		+ Lend money		
Record loans		− Lend money			
Charge interest		+ Charge interest			
Pay interest			− Charge interest		+ Charge interest
Record payment		− Charge interest			
Deposit interest			+ Deposit interest		− Deposit interest
Hire workers			− Wages	+ Wages	
Bankers consume			+ Bankers' consumption		− Bankers' consumption
Workers consume			+ Workers' consumption	− Workers' consumption	
Loan repayment	+ Loan repayment		− Loan repayment		
Record repayment		− Loan repayment			
Lend new money			+ New loan		
Record new loan		+ New loan			

We can model this endogenous creation of both debt and new money (in a check-account or electronic-money banking system) by adding two new rows to the table – one in which the firms' deposit accounts are credited with new money, the second in which the new debt the firms have to the banks is recorded on the loan ledger (see Table 14.4).

This extension helps explain why banks are so willing to create debt, and discourage its repayment: the source of bank profits is interest on outstanding debt, and the more debt that is out there, the more they make. The amount of outstanding debt will rise if existing money is turned over more rapidly, if new money is created more rapidly, and if debts are repaid *more slowly*. Banks therefore have an innate desire to create as much debt as possible – which is why it is unwise to leave the level of debt creation up to the financial sector. As the Great Recession shows, they will be willing to create as much debt as they can, and if they can persuade borrowers to take it on – which is easy to do when banks finance a Ponzi scheme – then the economy will ultimately face a debt crisis where the banks' willingness to lend suddenly evaporates.

§112

The extension also provides the means to link this purely monetary model to the cyclical Minsky model I outlined in the previous chapter, in a manner that is consistent with the argument that aggregate demand is the sum of income *plus the change in debt*.

In the model above, we were in a 'Say's Law' world in which aggregate demand equaled aggregate supply, and there was no change in debt. However, we now consider firms that wish to invest, and which are willing to take on new debt to finance it – which also causes new money to be created. Aggregate demand is now income plus the change in debt, where incomes finance consumption, and the change in debt finances investment. The new loans thus provide the money needed to finance the investment that was an integral part of the Minsky model.

For simplicity, I assume that new money is created at a constant rate relative to the current level of debt (which halves when the credit crunch strikes); in the full Minsky model, this is a function of the rate of profit.

To link the two models, one more component is needed: a formula that describes how prices are set. For obvious reasons, this doesn't involve working out where 'marginal cost equals marginal revenue.' However, the equation I use is based on the proposition that prices will tend to converge to a level that equates the monetary value of demand and the monetary value of supply. At the same time, the equation conforms to the empirical research into how firms set prices (see Chapter 4) – that they involve a markup on the wage cost per unit of output – which is the theory of price-setting used by post-Keynesian economists (Lee 1998; Downward 1999).[15]

15 The equation is derived in Keen (2010: 17–19). The basic idea is as follows. The monetary value of demand equals wages plus profits, and as explained above this equals the money in the firms' deposit accounts, divided by the turnover period. The monetary value of supply is the price level times output, and output is labor times average labor productivity. The number of workers employed in turn equals the monetary value

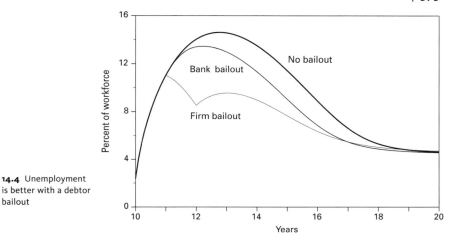

14.4 Unemployment is better with a debtor bailout

We also need an explanation of how wages are set, and this raises the vexed issue of 'the Phillips Curve.' As explained earlier, a properly specified Phillips Curve should have three factors in determining money wages – the employment rate, its rate of change, and a feedback from inflation – but for simplicity here I'll just use the first factor (all three are used later in my monetary Minsky model).

The results of this model amplify the case made in the money-only, no-growth model. The firms' bailout works better on every front, on every metric – except one (any guesses which one?).

Loans recover more rapidly when the firms are bailed out rather than the banks.   §113

The rate of unemployment is turned around almost instantly with the firm bailout, and never reaches the extreme levels that apply with the bailout going to the banks (see Figure 14.4).

Both profits and wages are higher if the firms get the bailout money rather than the banks.   §114

The only losers from the bailout going to the firms rather than to the banks are ... the banks (did you guess right?). Once again, not only do they do worse if the firms get the bailout rather than them, they do worse under the firms' bailout than they do from no policy intervention at all.   §115

This is still a very simple model, and much more needs to be done to complete it – from replacing time constants with variables (which I do in the Minsky model to come), through to properly modeling government finances as well as those of private banks (which I haven't yet done). But again it

---

of wages divided by the wage rate. In this simple model, the monetary value of wages also depends on the balance in the firms' deposit accounts: it's equal to the amount in the firms' deposit accounts, divided by the turnover period, and multiplied by the share of surplus that goes to workers. Some cancelation yields the result that, in equilibrium, the price level will equal the wage level, divided by labor productivity and multiplied by the inverse of workers' share of surplus. A dynamic equation has prices converging to this level over time.

reaches results that are the opposite of the neoclassical 'Money Multiplier' model that Obama, acting on the advice of his neoclassical advisors, actually followed. Given the poor response of the economy to the stimulus and QE1, I think it's reasonable to argue that it's time Obama – and politicians in general – looked elsewhere for their economic advice.

From tranquility to breakdown

To a neoclassical economist, the most striking aspect of the Great Recession was the speed with which apparent tranquility gave way to sudden breakdown. With notable, noble exceptions like Nouriel Roubini, Robert Shiller, Joe Stiglitz and Paul Krugman, economists paid little attention to the obvious Bonfire of the Vanities taking place in asset markets, so in a sense they didn't see the warning signs, which were obvious to many others, that this would all end in tears.

My model, in contrast, is one in which the Great Moderation and the Great Recession are merely different phases in the same process of debt-financed speculation, which causes a period of initial volatility to give way to damped oscillations as rising debt transfers income from workers to bankers, and then total breakdown occurs when debt reaches a level at which capitalists become insolvent.

The fixed parameters used in the previous models are replaced by functions where the rates of money creation and relending and debt repayment depend on the rate of profit, and where the rate of change of wages depends on the level of employment, its rate of change, and the rate of inflation. The link between the monetary and physical models is the creation of new money, which finances investment.

The model generates as sudden a turnaround in output as any neoclassical

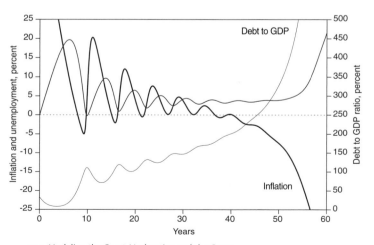

14.5 Modeling the Great Moderation and the Great Recession – inflation, unemployment and debt

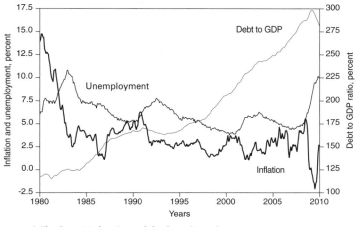

14.6 The Great Moderation and the Great Recession –
actual inflation, unemployment and debt

model hit by 'exogenous shocks,' but unlike in those models there is continuity between the Great Moderation and the Great Recession.

§116

The model's numbers and the magnitude of its crash are hypothetical,[16] and the main question is whether its qualitative behavior matches that of the US economy – which it clearly does. A period of extreme cycles in unemployment and inflation is followed by diminishing cycles which, if they were the only economic indicators one focused upon, would imply that a 'Great Moderation' was occurring. But the third factor ignored by neoclassical economics – the ratio of debt to GDP – rises in a series of cycles until it takes off exponentially (see Figure 14.5).

The qualitative similarity of this pattern to the actual US data (prior to the massive intervention by both the government and the Federal Reserve) is striking – see Figure 14.6. As in my 1995 model, though capitalists are the ones who actually take on debt, in practice the workers pay for it via a fall in their share of national income.

§117
and 118

This strictly monetary model generates one aspect of Minsky's hypothesis that my 1995 model could not: the 'deflation' part of the process of debt deflation. Debt rises in a series of booms and busts as in my 1995 paper, but as well the rate of inflation falls in a cyclical manner until it becomes accelerating deflation.

This generates the phenomenon observed in the early years of the Great Depression: the debt-to-GDP ratio continues to rise, even though nominal debt is falling (see Figure 14.7).

The model dynamic is more extreme than the data because the model

---

16 Fitting a nonlinear model to data is something mathematicians describe as a 'non-trival' exercise – which in lay-speak is something that takes eons to do and requires supercomputer processing power. I will do this for my next book with a far more complex model than the one shown here.

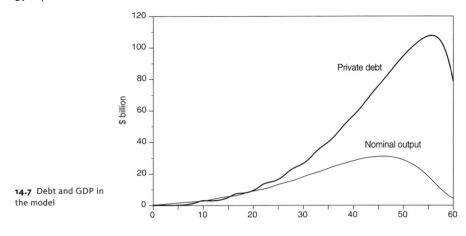

14.7 Debt and GDP in the model

doesn't yet include the impact of bankruptcy – which reduces debt during a depression. But again, the qualitative similarity between the model and the empirical data is striking – see Figure 14.8.

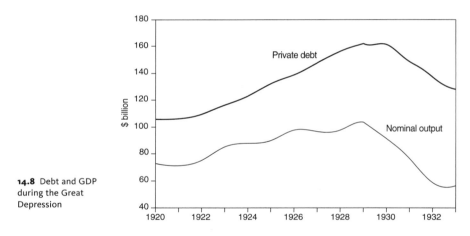

14.8 Debt and GDP during the Great Depression

Making monetary modeling accessible: QED

I originally developed the models in this chapter using differential equations, and I found it very difficult to extend them, or explain them to other economists who weren't familiar with this approach to mathematics. Then a chance challenge to the accuracy of my models – Scott Fullwiler asserted that there must be errors in my models from the point of view of double-entry bookkeeping – inspired me to see whether I could in fact explain my models using double-entry bookkeeping.

Not only did that prove possible, it also transpired that a double-entry bookkeeping layout of financial flows could be used to generate the models in the first place.

This overcame a major problem that I had with using system dynamics programs like Vissim (www.vissim.com) and Simulink (www.mathworks.com/products/simulink/) to build models of the financial sector. While these technologies were brilliant for designing engineering products like cars, computers and airplanes, they were poorly suited to modeling financial flows.

These programs use 'wires' to link one variable to another, and this is fine for physical processes where, for example, a wire from the fuel injector module to the cylinder module indicates a flow of gas from one point to another, and only one such link exists per cylinder. However, in a model of financial flows, the same term could turn up as often as three times in one diagram: once for the source account for some monetary transfer, once for its destination, and once to record it on a ledger. This resulted in almost incomprehensible models, and made 'wiring up' such a model extremely tedious.

I now use my double-entry bookkeeping methodology to develop models like the one in this chapter, and a simulation tool has also been developed for me to showcase this method. It's free, fairly easy to use, and you can both simulate the models I've shown in this chapter and build your own using it.

It's called QED – which stands for Quesnay Economic Dynamics – and can be downloaded from my blog at www.debtdeflation.com/blogs/qed/.

Conclusion

There are many aspects of this model of which I am critical. For example, it doesn't distinguish borrowing for investment from borrowing for speculation, the government sector isn't incorporated, and many factors that are variable in reality (such as interest rates and the markup that sets prices) are constants in the model. But these missing aspects can be easily introduced into later extensions of the model – a topic that I will take up in my next book, *Finance and Economic Breakdown* – without needing to make the absurd assumptions that neoclassical economics makes when it tries to combine more realism with the fantasy that everything happens in equilibrium.

It is also possible – indeed it is essential – to make this theory one not merely of macroeconomics, but of finance as well. In counterpoint to the false neoclassical dichotomy between macroeconomics and finance on the basis of the counterfactual proposition that debt has no macroeconomic effects, a valid economic theory has to explain the behavior of both the macroeconomy and the financial markets. Such a coherent theory has not yet been developed. However, there are several realistic models of the behavior of financial markets themselves, which we'll now consider.

The Efficient Markets Hypothesis says that the stock market's volatility is due to the random arrival of new information that affects the equilibrium value of shares. Allegedly, if it were not for the arrival of new information from outside the market, the market itself would be quiescent.

However, there are alternative explanations that attribute most (though not all) of the market's volatility to its own internal dynamics. Remarkably, these two explanations can predict statistical outcomes for share market prices that are almost indistinguishable from each other.

The kernel

If financial markets aren't efficient, then what are they? According to Behavioral Finance, they are markets where agents make systematically irrational choices, thus resulting in both inefficiency and trading opportunities for the more rational. According to the Fractal Markets Hypothesis, they are highly unstable dynamic systems that generate stock prices which appear random, but behind which lie deterministic patterns. According to the Inefficient Markets Hypothesis, they are systems which overreact to good news and bad, leading to excessive asset price volatility which inhibits the performance of the real economy. According to the burgeoning field of Econophysics, they are akin to nuclear reactors or tectonic plates, where interdependent interactions between speculators can occasionally give rise to runaway processes like nuclear reactions or earthquakes.

All these non-neoclassical theories support the argument that unless finance markets are institutionally tamed, capitalism will remain subject to potentially catastrophic breakdown caused by the finance sector.

The roadmap

In this chapter I outline four different but consistent non-equilibrium theories of finance – 'Behavioral Finance,' the 'Fractal Markets Hypothesis,' the 'Inefficient Markets Hypothesis,' and 'Econophysics.' The chapter concludes with two proposals to institutionally limit the capacity of the finance sector to entice us into debt.

Behavioral finance

Given the failure of the Efficient Markets Hypothesis (EMH), which is predicated on the belief that investors are 'rational' as neoclassical economists define the word, it is little wonder that the most popular response to the failure of the EMH has been to argue instead that investors are in fact irrational – or rather that their behavior deviates from pure rationality in systematic ways. This is then used as part of the explanation as to why the stock market is not efficient – as the Efficient Markets Hypothesis defined the word – so that asset prices deviate from their fundamental values in systematic ways.

As you can imagine, I have rather more sympathy for this approach – which is known as Behavioral Finance – than I do for the EMH. But there are several aspects of this approach that make me rather less enthusiastic than you might expect. I'll detail these before I move on to the legitimate contributions that Behavioral Finance has made to understanding the behavior of finance markets.

What is rational? The development of Behavioral Finance was motivated by the results of experiments in which people were presented with gambles where their decisions consistently violated the accepted definition of rational behavior under conditions of risk, which is known as 'expected utility theory.' Under this theory, a rational person is expected to choose an option that maximizes their expected return – and expected return is simply the sum of the returns for each outcome, multiplied by the odds of that outcome actually happening.

For example, say you were asked whether you'd be willing to take the following 'heads or tails' bet:

Heads: You win $150
Tails: You lose $100

Most people say 'no thanks!' to that gamble – and according to expected utility theory, they're being irrational. Why? Because the 'expected value' of that gamble is greater than zero: a 50 percent chance of $150 is worth $75, while a 50 percent chance of minus $100 is worth minus $50. The sum is plus $25, so that a person who turns the gamble down is walking away from a positive expected value.

Do you think it's irrational to turn that gamble down? I hope not! There's at least one good reason to quite sensibly decline it.[1]

This is that, if you take it, you don't get the 'expected value': you get *either* $150 *or* minus $100. Though you can know the odds of a particular random event like a coin toss, those odds are *almost* irrelevant to any given outcome.[2] Whether the coin will come down heads or tails in any given throw is an

1 A subscriber to my blog pointed out another reason: accepting the gamble involves wagering money that has taken you time and effort to earn, against the possibility of a chance gain. Most people sensibly value the effort they've put into earning something more highly than what they might get from a gamble.

2 I say 'almost' because the degree of uncertainty drops as the probability rises. If you were spinning a roulette wheel, and only one of its thirty-eight slots would lose you money, there's far less uncertainty about the outcome of any one spin than there is with a coin toss.

uncertain event, not a risky one. The measurement of risk is meaningful only when the gamble is repeated multiple times.

This is easily illustrated by modifying the bet above so that if you chose it, you have to play it 100 times. Think carefully now: would you still turn it down?

I hope not, because the odds are extremely good that out of 100 coin tosses, you'll get more than 40 heads, and 40 is the breakeven point. There is only a 1 percent chance that you'd get fewer than 40 heads and therefore lose money. If you get the most common outcome of 50 heads (which occurs 8 percent of the time), you'll make $2,500, while your odds of making between zero (from 40 heads) and $5,000 (from 60 heads) are better than 19 out of 20.

In other words, you get the expected value if, and only if, you repeat the gamble numerous times. But the expected value is irrelevant to the outcome of any individual coin toss.

The concept of expected value is thus not a good arbiter for rational behavior in the way it is normally presented in Behavioral Economics and Finance experiments – why, then, is it used?

If you've read this far into this book, you won't be surprised to learn that it's because economists have misread the foundation research on this topic by the mathematician John von Neumann, and his economist collaborator Oskar Morgenstern, *The Theory of Games and Economic Behavior* (Von Neumann and Morgenstern 1953).

Misunderstanding von Neumann John von Neumann was one of the greatest intellects of all time, a child prodigy who went on to make numerous pivotal contributions to a vast range of fields in mathematics, physics, and computer science. He was a polymath at a time when it was far more difficult to make contributions across a range of fields than it had been in earlier centuries. One of the fields he dabbled in was economics.

His collaboration with Oskar Morgenstern resulted in whole fields of economic theory being developed by later researchers – including Game Theory, much of neoclassical finance theory, and ultimately Behavioral Economics – but one key thing he actually wanted to achieve never happened: *he wanted to eliminate indifference curves and immeasurable utility from economics.* He regarded these concepts as a sign of the immaturity of economic theory – primarily because it was so lacking in sound empirical data. His observations on this front are sadly even more relevant today:

> In some branches of economics the most fruitful work may be that of
> careful, patient description; indeed, this may be by far the largest domain
> for the present and for some time to come [...] the empirical background
> of economic science is definitely inadequate. Our knowledge of the relevant

facts of economics is incomparably smaller than that commanded in physics at the time when the mathematization of that subject was achieved. Indeed, the decisive break which came in physics in the seventeenth century, specifically in the field of mechanics, was only possible because of previous developments in astronomy. It was backed by several millennia of systematic, scientific, astronomical observation, culminating in an observer of unparalleled caliber, Tycho de Brahe. Nothing of this sort has occurred in economic science. It would have been absurd in physics to expect Kepler and Newton without Tycho – and there is no reason to hope for an easier development in economics. (Ibid.: 2, 4)

Von Neumann was particularly disparaging about the role that the concept of immeasurable utility took in economic theory. You'll remember from Chapter 1 that early economists imagined that there was a measurable unit of utility they called the 'util,' but that this idea of measurable or 'cardinal' utility gave way to the concept of 'ordinal' utility – in which the satisfaction gained from different bundles of commodities could be ranked, but not measured – because measurement of individual subjective utility was deemed impossible.

Von Neumann disagreed, and proved that in situations in which it was possible to define indifference curves, it was also possible to calculate numerical values for utility by using gambles.

His idea was to set an arbitrary starting point for utility – for example, to define that, for a given individual, one banana was worth one 'util' – and then present that individual with a gamble where the options were either one banana, or a gamble between zero bananas and two bananas with a variable probability. The probability at which the consumer is willing to accept the gamble then lets you derive a numerical estimate of the utility of two bananas. As von Neumann and Morgenstern put it:

> The above technique permits a direct determination of the ratio q of the utility of possessing 1 unit of a certain good to the utility of possessing 2 units of the same good. The individual must be given the choice of obtaining 1 unit with certainty or of playing the chance to get two units with the probability α or nothing with the probability $1-\alpha$ ...; if he cannot state a preference then $\alpha=q$. (Ibid.: 18–19, n. 3)

For example, if you were willing to accept a gamble that gave you either 2 bananas or zero when the odds of getting 2 bananas was 6 out of 10, then the ratio of the utility of 1 banana to the utility of 2 bananas for this consumer was 0.6. A bit of algebraic manipulation shows that this consumer gets 1.67 utils of utility from consuming two bananas, compared to 1 util from one banana. A hypothetical example of using this procedure to provide a numerical measure of utility is shown in Table 15.1.

TABLE 15.1 Von Neumann's procedure for working out a numerical value for utility
Consumer: Joan Cheng

| Number of bananas | | | | |
Certain	Gamble	Accepted odds (%)	Utility	Marginal utility
0			0.00	
1	0 or 2	60	1.00	1.00
2	0 or 3	78	1.67	0.67
3	0 or 4	92	2.14	0.47
4	0 or 5	97	2.32	0.19
5	0 or 6	99	2.39	0.07

An essential element of this procedure was that it had to be repeatable, and for obvious reasons. If it were done just once, and the experimental subject was hungry, then he might be unwilling to take the risk of starving that the gamble implied, if the outcome were that he had to forgo the banana he already had.

Von Neumann was emphatic about this: to make sense, his procedure had to be applied to *repeatable experiments only*:

> Probability has often been visualized as a subjective concept more or less in the nature of an estimation. Since we propose to use it in constructing an individual, numerical estimation of utility, the above view of probability would not serve our purpose. The simplest procedure is, therefore, to *insist upon the alternative, perfectly well founded interpretation of probability as frequency in long runs*. (Ibid: 19; emphasis added)

Unfortunately, both neoclassical and behavioral economists ignored this caveat, and applied the axioms that von Neumann and Morgenstern developed to situations of one-off gambles, in which the *objective risk* that would apply in a repeated experiment was replaced by the *subjective uncertainty* of a single outcome. Neoclassical economists combined the concept of expected utility with their ordinal, 'indifference curve' theory of consumer choice to develop the Capital Assets Pricing Model, despite the fact that von Neumann was adamant that he wanted to replace the concept of indifference curves with his concept of cardinal utility:

> we hope we have shown that the treatment by indifference curves implies either too much or too little: if the preferences of the individual are not at all comparable, then the indifference curves do not exist. If the individual's preferences are all comparable, then we can even obtain a (uniquely defined) numerical utility which renders the indifference curves superfluous. (Ibid.: 19–20)

Behavioral economists, on the other hand, developed all sorts of 'paradoxes of irrational behavior' from how people's behavior in experiments violated von Neumann's 'Axioms of Expected Utility' – but all of these paradoxes evaporate when the correct, objective, 'frequency in long runs' version of probability is used.

The four axioms were Completeness, Transitivity, Independence and Continuity:[3]

Completeness: A subject can always decide whether he prefers one combination to another, or is indifferent between them.

Transitivity: Choices are consistent so that if shopping trolley A is preferred to trolley B, and B to C, then A is preferred to C.

Independence: Adding two gambles together doesn't change the rankings that apply when the gambles are undertaken separately. And

Continuity: If A is preferred to B and B to C, then there must be some combination of the best (A) and worst (C) option that is as desirable as the middle option (B).

One alleged instance of a violation of these axioms is the famous 'Allais Paradox,' named after the French economist Maurice Allais. The violations definitely occur when a single experiment is all that is conducted, but would disappear if the experiment were repeated multiple times, as von Neumann intended.

Allais compared two experiments, the first of which is shown in Table 15.2:

TABLE 15.2 The Allais 'Paradox': Experiment 1

Option 1A		Option 1B	
Winnings	Odds	Winnings	Odds
$1 million	100%	$1 million	89%
		Nothing	1%
		$5 million	10%

The expected value of Option 1B is higher than that of 1A: 1B is worth $1.39 million (0.89 times $1 million plus 0.1 times $5 million, or $890,000 plus $500,000), so according to expected utility theory, a rational person should choose option A over option B. But in practice, most people choose

---

3 These are obviously very similar to those used by Samuelson to derive the concept of revealed preference, but one interesting difference is that von Neumann was aware that at least the first of these was doubtful in practice. However, he argued that, if this were true, then it undermined both his approach and indifference curves:

'We have conceded that one may doubt whether a person can always decide which of two alternatives – with the utilities u, v – he prefers. But, whatever the merits of this doubt are, this possibility – i.e. the completeness of the system of (individual) preferences – must be assumed even for the purposes of the "indifference curve method." But if this property of u≷v is assumed, then our use of the much less questionable [probabilistic method] yields the numerical utilities too!' (von Neumann and Morgenstern 1953: 28–9).

A – presumably because people prefer a sure thing of a million dollars against even the slightest chance of walking away with nothing.

Rather than calling this behavior irrational, behavioral economists say that this shows 'risk-averse' behavior.

The second experiment is shown in Table 15.3:

TABLE 15.3 The Allais 'Paradox' Part 2: Experiment 2

Option 2A		Option 2B	
Winnings	Odds	Winnings	Odds
Nothing	89%	Nothing	90%
$1 million	11%	$5 million	10%

Here the expected value of Option B is higher than that of A: B is worth $500,000 whereas A is worth $110,000. And here, most people in fact choose option B rather than option A. So in this experiment, most people are consistent with expected utility theory, whereas in the first experiment, most people are inconsistent.

Much was then made of this alleged inconsistency. It was said that it displayed people switching from risk-averse to risk-seeking behavior, that it was provably inconsistent with the Independence Axiom, and so on – the Wikipedia entry on the Allais Paradox gives quite a reasonable summary.

However, these 'inconsistencies' disappear when one uses the 'frequency in long runs' approach that von Neumann *insisted* upon – see his words above. Imagine now that you are offered the chance of repeating Experiment 1 a thousand times. The person who picked option A would certainly walk away a billionaire, but anyone who chooses B will probably walk away about $400 million richer. Ditto with Experiment 2: Option A would see you probably end up with $100 million, while your wealth via option B would be of the order of half a billion. Only Option B makes any sense in both experiments now – it would clearly be a sign of poor reasoning to choose A instead.

The 'Allais Paradox' is thus not a paradox at all, but a typical case of economists misreading their own literature. I have a similar attitude to all other 'paradoxes' in the behavioral economics literature.

However, this doesn't mean that this entire literature is a waste of time, because the exercises do point out the difference between an uncertain outcome and a risky one – and it is clearly the uncertain outcome which is relevant to people's behavior in stock markets. Uncertainty introduces an asymmetry into people's reactions to losses and gains, and this results in a multitude of ways in which people's behavior deviates from the predictions of the Efficient Markets Hypothesis – which, in their own peculiar way, are similar to the predictions of this misreading of von Neumann.

Many of these behaviors are also clearly counterproductive in the context of stock market gambling, and in turn they make it highly likely that market prices will deviate substantially from 'innate value.' These effects also form part of the Inefficient Markets Hypothesis, so I'll delay discussion of them until then.

The inherent instability of stock markets

The Efficient Markets Hypothesis explains the price fluctuations that characterize financial markets as rational reactions by the markets to the random arrival of new information affecting the future prospects of companies. The three different approaches to finance outlined in this chapter all argue that these price fluctuations are due to the markets' own internal dynamics. These are two fundamentally different explanations for the same phenomenon: one based on exogenous shocks – the random arrival of external economic news – the other on internal dynamics – today's market prices being a reaction to yesterday's. How can two such different explanations account for the same data?

An analogy might help here. Some animal populations – for example, lemmings – are known to fluctuate wildly from year to year. There could be two explanations: the environment in which lemmings live could be so volatile that it causes extreme variations in population from one year to the next, and without this environmental volatility, lemming numbers could be constant. Or, the environment could be relatively stable, but the population dynamics of lemmings could be so volatile that they cause huge fluctuations in numbers from year to year.

§ 119
and 120

It turns out that it's very difficult to know which process is generating a given set, just from the numbers themselves: an unstable dynamic process can generate numbers which are very difficult to distinguish from a set of random numbers – unless you have a very large data set. The Efficient Markets Hypothesis claimed that the movements in stock prices would be random, and at least initially this contention did seem to be supported by the data from a small sample (between 1950 and 1966). But stock market data actually support a far different contention: that the stock market is inherently unstable.

The Efficient Markets Hypothesis was also developed before the scientific world became reacquainted with the concept of chaos,[4] and it fitted neatly with the economic predilection to see everything in terms of equilibrium. It also meant that economists working in finance theory could avail themselves of all the mathematical and statistical tools devised by mathematicians and scientists to study random processes.

4 Chaos was first 'discovered' by Henri Poincaré in 1899, when he tried to find a solution to the 'many body problem' – the problem of gravitational attraction between a star and more than just one planet – and instead proved that there was no analytic solution; instead, the bodies would follow complex aperiodic paths (i.e. cycles occur which never exactly repeat themselves, unlike conventional cyclical functions like sine waves, etc.), which were later labelled 'chaotic.'

This was an intellectual bonanza – though it simultaneously meant that stock market speculators had to be told that, sadly, there was no bonanza for them hidden in the daily data of the stock exchange. Technical analysts, those looking for trends and waves within waves, were wasting their time.

However, as time went on, more and more data turned up which were not consistent with the EMH. As I detail in the next section, this led to something of a 'siege mentality' by supporters of the EMH, as they fought to defend their theory from attack. But it also inspired other researchers to develop alternative theories of stock market movements.

The Fractal Markets Hypothesis

The Fractal Markets Hypothesis is primarily a statistical interpretation of stock market prices, rather than a model of how the stock market, or investors in it, actually behave. Its main point is that stock market prices do not follow the random walk predicted by the EMH,[5] but conform to a much more complex pattern called a fractal. As a result, the statistical tools used by the EMH, which were designed to model random processes, will give systematically misleading predictions about stock market prices.

The archetypal set of random numbers is known as the 'normal' distribution, and its mathematical properties are very well known. A normal distribution with an average value of zero and a standard deviation of 1 will throw up a number greater than 1 15 percent of the time, a number greater than 2 just over 2 percent of the time, and a number greater than 3 only once every 750 times, and so on. The chance of a 'far from average' event occurring diminishes rapidly and smoothly the farther the event is from the average.

The standard deviation of daily movements on the Dow Jones Industrial Average is roughly 1 percent. If stock market prices were generated by a normal process, then extreme movements – say a fall of more than 5 percent in just one day – would be vanishingly rare. The odds of any such event having occurred even once during the twentieth century would be just over 1 in a 100.

In fact, there were over sixty such daily downward movements (and over fifty daily upward movements of 5 percent or more) during the twentieth century.

The fact that extreme movements occurred roughly 10,000 times more often than for a random process is fairly strong evidence that the process is not random at all (and there's lots more evidence besides this morsel).

A fractal set of numbers, on the other hand, is a far more pernicious beast. Specifically, it is much more likely to generate extreme events than a normal distribution, and one large movement is likely to be followed by another large movement – another feature of stock markets which the EMH

5 More complex data distributions are predicted by some more elaborate versions of the EMH, but the normal distribution is still the overall yardstick.

finds very difficult to explain.[6] A fractal pattern also displays 'self-similarity': the data pattern looks the same regardless of whether you are looking at a short data period – such as one day, or a week – or longer periods, such as a year or even a century.

The basic idea behind a fractal is that each number in the series is a simple but nonlinear function of previous numbers in the series. This differs from a true 'random number generator' such as dice, where the next number is independent of all previous numbers – rolling a 6 now doesn't change the odds of rolling a 6 on your next throw, they will still be 1 in 6.

Applying this to the stock market, it is quite possible that each price movement is a complex function of previous price movements.

This might seem to imply that, if the fractal markets hypothesis is correct, it should be easy to make money out of the stock market – in which case the hypothesis would be invalid, since it isn't easy to profit as a trader. However, there is another key aspect of fractal systems which comes into play here, which is known as 'sensitive dependence on initial conditions.'

Even if you knew precisely the 'system' which generated the Dow Jones Industrial Average, you could never know the precise value of the index because of rounding error. Let's say your initial measure of its value was out by 1/10th of a percent – rather than being, say, 10396.5, it was actually 10396.6.

One day (or iteration) later, your model would be wrong by (say) 1 percent; one day later by 10 percent; and a day after that, it would be completely useless as a means of predicting the following day's value. This is because any measurement errors you make in specifying the initial conditions of a fractal model grow exponentially with time, whereas for a random model the errors normally grow linearly (and can even fall with time for a stable system). As Ott puts this dilemma: 'The exponential sensitivity of chaotic solutions means that, as time goes on, small errors in the solution can grow very rapidly (i.e., exponentially). Hence, after some time, effects such as noise and computer roundoff can totally change the solution from what it would be in the absence of these effects' (Ott 1993).

Ott gives the example of a chaotic function called the Henon Map being simulated on a computer which is accurate to fifteen decimal places: the smallest difference it can record between two numbers is 0.000000000000001. He shows that if your initial measurement of the system was out by precisely this much, then after forty-five iterations of the model, your estimate of where the system is would be completely wrong. Attempting to overcome this problem by more computing power is futile: 'Suppose that we wish to predict to a longer time, say, twice as long. Then we must improve our accuracy by a tremendous amount, namely 14 orders of magnitude! In any practical

---

6 There are a number of econometric analyses that attempt to account for this. As Peters comments, they capture some of the local statistical features, but fail to capture the overall characteristics (Peters 1994).

situation, this is likely to be impossible. Thus, the relatively modest goal of an improvement of prediction time by a factor of two is not feasible' (ibid.).

Applying this to the stock market, it is possible to hold two apparently contradictory attitudes simultaneously: the market is driven largely by endogenous processes in which previous price movements determine future price movements; and it is impossible – or very difficult – to predict which way the market will move, and by how much.

Much of the Fractal Markets Hypothesis is directed at critiquing the notion that price movements in the stock market are random – as I noted earlier, it is primarily a way to characterize the properties of the statistics the market throws up, rather than a theory of how the market actually behaves. However, it makes one important behavioral observation that runs directly counter to the EMH's assumptions about investors.

This is that the market will be stable when it allows investors with different time horizons to trade smoothly. As a result, heterogeneity – the fact that all investors are not the same – is a vital part of this theory. As Peters puts it:

> Take a typical day trader who has an investment horizon of five minutes and is currently long in the market. The average five-minute price change in 1992 was –0.000284 per cent [it was a 'bear' market], with a standard deviation of 0.05976 per cent. If, for technical reasons, a six standard deviation drop occurred for a five minute horizon, or 0.359 per cent, our day trader could be wiped out if the fall continued. However, an institutional investor – a pension fund, for example – with a weekly trading horizon, would probably consider that drop a buying opportunity because weekly returns over the past ten years have averaged 0.22 per cent with a standard deviation of 2.37 per cent. In addition, the technical drop has not changed the outlook of the weekly trader, who looks at either longer technical or fundamental information. Thus the day trader's six-sigma [standard deviation] event is a 0.15-sigma event to the weekly trader, or no big deal. The weekly trader steps in, buys, and creates liquidity. This liquidity in turn stabilizes the market. (Peters 1994)

The Fractal Markets Hypothesis thus explains the stability of the market by the realistic assumption that traders differ in their time horizons. It also alleges that instability is likely to occur if all investors suddenly switch to the same time horizon.

The Fractal Markets Hypothesis is thus more consistent with stock market data, more robust, and completely untainted by any assumption that the market is in, or tends toward, equilibrium. But it still doesn't provide an answer to what is actually generating the data: what is the system behind the fractal? To answer that question, we have to return to the kind of institutional analysis that Keynes provided in 1936. Two such analyses have been provided: by Robert Haugen in the 'Inefficient Markets Hypothesis,' and Hyman Minsky in the 'Financial Instability Hypothesis,' as discussed in Chapter 13.

The Inefficient Markets Hypothesis

After a long career as an academic finance economist, Bob Haugen presents the diametrically opposite case from the Efficient Markets Hypothesis with gusto in three short books: *The Beast on Wall Street*, *The New Finance*, and *The Inefficient Stock Market*. Anyone who is or is thinking of speculating in the market – or is suffering from having done so – should read all three. Amid an extensive catalogue of data that contradicts the Efficient Markets Hypothesis, Haugen presents the alternative case for 'a noisy stock market that overreacts to past records of success and failure on the part of business firms, and prices with great imprecision' (Haugen 1999b).[7]

Though Haugen makes no reference to Keynes, the reasons he gives for the market behaving in this way echo the arguments Keynes made back in 1936 – that in the real world of uncertainty, few if any stock market speculators trade on the basis of new information. Instead, they trade on the basis of how they think other market participants will, on average, expect the market to react to news. Unlike the efficient market hypothesis, this 'news' can include the most recent movements of stock prices themselves.

In fact, in today's stock market, the major news will always be the most recent movements in stock prices, rather than 'real' news from the economy.

Haugen argues that there are three sources of volatility: event-driven, error-driven, and price-driven (the Efficient Markets Hypothesis models only the first, on the belief that the other two can't exist in the equilibrium of an efficient market). The second results from the market overreacting to news, then over-adjusting itself once the initial mistake has become obvious.

The third is the phenomenon of the market reacting to its own volatility, building price movements upon price movements, in the same way that neighborhood dogs can sometimes keep yelping almost indefinitely after one of them has started. Haugen argues that this endogenous instability accounts for over three-quarters of all volatility.

He also argues that the market's endogenous instability has a severe and deleterious impact on the functioning of a modern capitalist economy.

First, if the stock market has any role at all in directing investment funds, then its valuations will direct them very badly. Price-driven volatility will lead to some companies which will in the long term turn out to be worthless being given massive funding – which will then be wasted – while potentially worthy ventures will be starved of funds. According to Haugen, the managers of a firm that has been seriously overvalued by the market over-invest: 'Consumers get what they don't want.' On the other hand, an undervalued firm 'would invest to produce a product that consumers really want, if it could raise capital at a fair price, but in this market, it

---

7 Haugen is effectively a proponent of 'behavioral finance,' which has been gaining acceptance in applied and academic finance in recent years, though its adherents are still a minority compared to supporters of the Efficient Markets Hypothesis.

can't' (Haugen 1999a). Overall, by providing too much money to ventures which, in the long run, are going to turn out not to be all that profitable, while providing too little money to those which, in the long run, will be worthwhile, the market causes the economy to grow less rapidly and less smoothly than it could.

Secondly, Haugen argues that, as well as causing investment to be badly apportioned, the stock market's endogenous volatility reduces the overall level of investment. Over the long term, the risk-free real rate of return has averaged about 1 percent, whereas the risk premium for investing in stocks has averaged about 6 percent. This means that investors have required a return of about 7 percent on their investments – with the result that investments which predict a lower expected rate of return don't get funded.

Haugen argues that investors require this higher return to compensate them for the risk of investing on the market, yet most of this risk results from the endogenous instability of the market itself. Since his statistical research indicates that price-driven volatility accounts for almost 95 percent of all volatility, he argues that this risk premium would be substantially lower – perhaps as low as just 0.4 percent, versus the 6 percent it has been historically (ibid.). If the risk premium could be reduced to this level, then the rate of investment would be substantially higher: 'Price-driven volatility has greatly inhibited investment spending over the years. Ultimately, it has acted, and acts, as a serious drag on economic growth' (ibid.).

At the individual level, Haugen argues that the market's tendencies to overreact to news, and to be consumed with endogenous instability in prices, provide opportunities for non-institutional investors to profit from the market. However, at the macroeconomic level, Haugen believes, as did Keynes, that the economy would benefit if the market were restrained. His recommendation, again very similar to Keynes's, is to reduce the length of the trading day, or to limit trading to just one computer-assisted auction per day. He hopes that this would eliminate the phenomenon of price volatility driven by the market reacting to its own every move.

Econophysics

Broadly speaking, Econophysics is the application of the analytic techniques of modern physics to the social sciences. This is rather ironic, since the founders of neoclassical economics themselves aped what they thought were the methods of physicists in the nineteenth century.

What Walras and others attempted to mimic then was physics before it had developed a number of key innovations, including not merely quantum mechanics but the concept of entropy, which introduced the notion of irreversible change into physics. Mirowski coined the term 'proto-energetics' to describe the type of physics on which neoclassical economic theory modeled itself:

From now on I shall need a term that will serve to identify a type of physical theory that includes the law of conservation of energy and the bulk of rational mechanics, but excludes the entropy concept and most post-1860 developments in physics. This collection of analytical artifices is more an historical than a systematic subset of physics: it includes the formalisms of vector fields, but excludes Maxwell's equations, or even Kelvin's mechanical models of light.

Since this resembles the content of the energetics movement, I trust it will not do the phenomena too much violence to call it 'proto-energetics.' Classical thermodynamics diverges from proto-energetics in one very critical aspect: Thermodynamic processes only change in one direction. In proto-energetics, time is isotropic, which means that no physical laws would be violated if the system ran backward or forward in time. (Mirowski 1989: 63)

Since then, physics has evolved rapidly, while economics has developed rather as can the language of a group of migrants who, separated from their home country, hang on to terms that have become obsolete in the original language.

The new incursion of physics into economics is being led by physicists themselves, and motivated partly by the innate curiosity that physicists like Cheng Zhang had about economic issues, and partly by the fact that 'we'd run out of things to do in physics.'[8] Though called Econophysics, a more accurate term for this school of thought at present would be 'Finaphysics' – since the vast bulk of its research has concerned the behavior of financial markets, rather than the broader economy.

This orientation reflects the inherently empirical nature of physics, and the fact that its analytic techniques have been developed to process enormous amounts of data generated by non-equilibrium experiments in physics. Economics does not generate a sufficient volume of data, but financial markets do in abundance, with the price and volume data of financial transactions; as Joe McCauley put it, 'the concentration is on financial markets because that is where one finds the very best data for a careful empirical analysis' (McCauley 2004: xi).

Given that it is a relatively new field, there are numerous explanations of the volatility of financial markets within Econophysics – including Power Law models of stock market movements (Gabaix, Gopikrishnan et al. 2006), Didier Sornette's earthquake-based analysis (Sornette 2003), Joe McCauley's empirically derived Fokker-Planck model (McCauley 2004), and Mandelbrot's fractal geometry (Mandelbrot and Hudson 2004) – and it would require another book to detail them all.

A unifying theme is that the behavior of financial markets is driven by

8   A remark that Yi-Cheng Zhang made in response to a question from Paul Ormerod as to how Econophysics came about, during a dinner at the first Econophysics conference in Bali in 2002.

the interactions of numerous market participants with each other, and these generate a highly unstable and therefore relatively unpredictable time series in financial data themselves. These characteristics resemble the behavior of fissile materials in a nuclear reactor, or tectonic plates in an earthquake zone, physical processes for which physicists have developed an enormous arsenal of mathematical analytic techniques in the last century. Econophysics is essentially the application of these techniques to financial data.

This Econophysics explanation of the unpredictability of finance markets is thus diametrically opposed to the explanation that neoclassical economics has given of precisely the same phenomenon – the difficulty of predicting the market – and Econophysicists react with incredulity to the simplistic 'random disturbances to an equilibrium process' explanation that neoclassical economists provide:

> Three states of matter – solid, liquid, and gas – have long been known. An analogous distinction between three states of randomness – mild, slow and wild – arises from the mathematics of fractal geometry. Conventional finance theory assumes that variation of prices can be modeled by random processes that, in effect, follow the simplest 'mild' pattern, as if each uptick or downtick were determined by the toss of a coin. What fractals show [...] is that by that standard, real prices 'misbehave' very badly. A more accurate, multifractal model of wild price variation paves the way for a new, more reliable type of financial theory. (Mandelbrot and Hudson 2004: v)

> Economists teach that markets can be described by equilibrium. Econo-physicists teach that markets are very far from equilibrium and are dynamically complex [...] equilibrium is never a good approximation [...] market equilibrium does not and cannot occur [...] (McCauley 2004: 185)

> Uncertainties and variabilities are the key words to describe the ever-changing environments around us. Stasis and equilibrium are illusions, whereas dynamics and out-of-equilibrium are the rule. The quest for balance and constancy will always be unsuccessful. (Sornette 2003: xv)

I'll single out Didier Sornette's work here, not because it will necessarily be 'the' approach of Econophysics, but because he is making a direct challenge to one tenet of conventional finance: that the market cannot be predicted. Using his model that the behavior of stock markets follows the 'log-periodic' pattern of earthquakes, he has made predictions about future stock market crashes that can be verified after the predicted crashes have (or have not) occurred: 'The Financial Crisis Observatory (FCO) is a scientific platform aimed at testing and quantifying rigorously, in a systematic way and on a large scale, the hypothesis that financial markets exhibit a degree of inefficiency and a potential for predictability, especially during regimes when bubbles develop' (Sornette 2011).

The result of the FCO can be tracked at the website www.er.ethz.ch/fco. The voluminous literature of the Econophysics movement can be tracked from its website unifr.ch/econophysics.

Conclusion: progress versus ossification

There are thus numerous vigorous alternatives to the failed paradigm of neoclassical finance – but students of economics are unlikely ever to learn of them, if all they do is study the textbooks of neoclassical finance courses. Despite the manifest failures of the Efficient Markets Hypothesis, and the recanting of it by the very same economists who developed it in the first place (Fama and French 2004), and the numerous stock market booms and crashes of the past quarter-century that could not have happened if the EMH were correct, textbooks continue to teach that finance markets are 'efficient,' in the bastardized way that economists use the term. This extract from a brand-new 2011 text – published seven years after the developers of the EMH concluded that 'the failure of the CAPM in empirical tests implies that most applications of the model are invalid' (ibid.: 25) – is typical:

> A financial market is informationally efficient if prices reflect all available information [...] there are likely to be noise traders [...] who trade on information unrelated to the true value of shares. If the information they trade on is random, they will tend to cancel each other out, leading to efficient market prices. However, it is likely that they trade on similar information, so that noise trading will lead to either an undervaluation or an overvaluation [...] it would pay arbitragers to take an offsetting position [...] This process will cause share prices to stay close to their true values [...]
>
> Academic studies usually conclude that the share market is efficient. (Valentine, Ford et al. 2011: 245–7)

The unwillingness – and possibly even the inability – of neoclassical economists to admit that their paradigm has failed means that, if change is left to them alone, it will not occur.

Reforming finance?

The results of the non-neoclassical theories of stock market behavior surveyed in this chapter emphasize one point: asset markets perform their alleged role of the allocation of investment capital very poorly.[9] In this they echo Keynes's dictum during capitalism's last major crisis, that speculation should not be allowed to dominate capital formation and allocation:

> Speculators may do no harm as bubbles on a steady stream of enterprise. But the position is serious when enterprise becomes the bubble on a whirlpool of speculation. *When the capital development of a country becomes a*

9 I will cover these approaches to finance in more detail in my next book, *Finance and Economic Breakdown.*

by-product of the activities of a casino, the job is likely to be ill-done. The measure
of success attained by Wall Street, regarded as an institution of which the
proper social purpose is to direct new investment into the most profitable
channels in terms of future yield, cannot be claimed as one of the outstanding triumphs of laissez-faire capitalism – which is not surprising, if I am
right in thinking that the best brains of Wall Street have been in fact directed
towards a different object. (Keynes 1936: 159; emphasis added)

Though deregulation of the financial sector was far from the sole cause of
the financial crisis that began in 2007, removing the fetters from the financial
sector resulted in a crisis that was more extreme than it would have been
had the previous regulations been kept in place. The USA's 'shadow banking'
sector could not have invented and sold nearly so many 'weapons of financial
mass destruction' as it did – to use Warren Buffett's evocative phrase – had
Glass-Steagall not been abolished during Bill Clinton's term, for example.

I expect that history will judge that signing that bill into law was a far
more reckless act than anything Clinton did with Monica Lewinsky. The
comments of the handful of senators who opposed its repeal back in 1999
make interesting reading today:

> 'I think we will look back in 10 years' time and say we should not have
> done this but we did because we forgot the lessons of the past, and that that
> which is true in the 1930's is true in 2010,' said Senator Byron L. Dorgan,
> Democrat of North Dakota. 'I wasn't around during the 1930's or the debate
> over Glass-Steagall. But I was here in the early 1980's when it was decided to
> allow the expansion of savings and loans. We have now decided in the name
> of modernization to forget the lessons of the past, of safety and of soundness.'
>
> Senator Paul Wellstone, Democrat of Minnesota, said that Congress had
> 'seemed determined to unlearn the lessons from our past mistakes.'
>
> 'Scores of banks failed in the Great Depression as a result of unsound
> banking practices, and their failure only deepened the crisis,' Mr. Wellstone
> said. 'Glass-Steagall was intended to protect our financial system by insulat-
> ing commercial banking from other forms of risk. It was one of several
> stabilizers designed to keep a similar tragedy from recurring. Now Congress
> is about to repeal that economic stabilizer without putting any comparable
> safeguard in its place.' (Labaton 1999)

In contrast, the beliefs of those who campaigned to end the Act have the
ring of delusion:

> 'The world changes, and we have to change with it,' said Senator Phil
> Gramm of Texas, who wrote the law that will bear his name along with the
> two other main Republican sponsors, Representative Jim Leach of Iowa and
> Representative Thomas J. Bliley Jr. of Virginia. 'We have a new century com-
> ing, and we have an opportunity to dominate that century the same way we

dominated this century. Glass-Steagall, in the midst of the Great Depression, came at a time when the thinking was that the government was the answer. In this era of economic prosperity, we have decided that freedom is the answer.' (Ibid.: 2)

Far from strengthening America, the financial follies that followed the repeal of Glass-Steagall have left it crippled at the start of the twenty-first century, and facing an economic eclipse by China. Far from reducing the role of the government in the US economy, the collapse of the Subprime Bubble has resulted in the government taking a larger role in the economy than it did even during the Great Depression.

Back in 2000, in the first edition of this book, I sided with the opponents of deregulation, noting that though they were 'mooted as "reforms" by their proponents, [...] they were in reality retrograde steps, which have set our financial system up for a real crisis' (Keen 2001a: 255). That real crisis duly arrived eight years after the repeal of Glass-Steagall.

However, blocking the abolition of Glass-Steagall wouldn't have prevented the crisis, since its underlying cause was a debt bubble that had already driven the USA to the brink of Great Depression debt levels by 1989. Deregulation simply allowed the debt bubble to continue growing for another two decades, from the 170 percent of GDP level it reached as the 1990s recession began, and the 200 percent level it was at when Glass-Steagall was abolished, to the 300 percent of GDP peak hit ten years later in 2009.

I also wrote in 2000 that 'I can only hope that, if the crisis is serious enough, then genuine reform to the finance sector will be contemplated' (ibid.: 256), but the first and second response of government to this crisis has been to try to restore the 'business as usual' that applied prior to the crisis.

This is to be expected. Politicians, as Keynes observed long ago, are just as beholden to the ideas of neoclassical economics as are professional economists: 'Practical men, who believe themselves to be quite exempt from any intellectual influences, are usually the slaves of some defunct economist. Madmen in authority, who hear voices in the air, are distilling their frenzy from some academic scribbler of a few years back' (Keynes 1936: 383).

It takes time before a real reformer comes along and challenges, not merely the belief systems that gave rise to mistakes like the abolition of Glass-Steagall, but the beneficiaries of those belief systems as well. We await a politician who is willing to not merely try to resuscitate the financial sector but to challenge it, as Roosevelt was during the Great Depression.

[A] host of unemployed citizens face the grim problem of existence, and an equally great number toil with little return. Only a foolish optimist can deny the dark realities of the moment.

Yet our distress comes from no failure of substance [...] Plenty is at our doorstep, but a generous use of it languishes in the very sight of the supply.

Primarily this is because the rulers of the exchange of mankind's goods have failed, through their own stubbornness and their own incompetence, have admitted their failure, and abdicated. Practices of the unscrupulous money changers stand indicted in the court of public opinion, rejected by the hearts and minds of men.

True they have tried, but their efforts have been cast in the pattern of an outworn tradition. *Faced by failure of credit they have proposed only the lending of more money. Stripped of the lure of profit by which to induce our people to follow their false leadership, they have resorted to exhortations, pleading tearfully for restored confidence.* They know only the rules of a generation of self-seekers. They have no vision, and when there is no vision the people perish.

The money changers have fled from their high seats in the temple of our civilization. We may now restore that temple to the ancient truths. The measure of the restoration lies in the extent to which we apply social values more noble than mere monetary profit. (Roosevelt 1933; emphasis added)

The reforms enacted in Roosevelt's era clearly worked, but as subsequent history has indicated, the problem with real reforms of our financial system is that, if successful, they will be abolished. The era of financial tranquility they usher in will be misinterpreted – particularly if economists continue to believe in the fantasy world of neoclassical economics – as inherent to capitalism, and not merely the product of regulations that inhibit the financial system's innate tendency to create too much debt.

Politicians who did not live through the crisis that caused these regulations to be enacted will then weaken these regulations over time, and we will be back in a crisis again.

Fundamentally, reforms of the financial sector fail because they try to constrain the sector's innate desire to create debt. They will work for a while in the aftermath to a crisis like the Great Depression or the Great Recession, where the carnage wreaked by a financial crisis is so great that the sector behaves prudently for a while. However, the incentives to create debt are so great for this sector that, over time, a debt-driven culture will replace prudence.

Institutional control of finance is also flawed, for reasons that should be obvious from our current crisis: 'regulatory capture.' Not only are regulators slower to move than the organizations they are intended to control, they often become advocates rather than monitors of those organizations. There is little doubt that Greenspan's actions in rescuing the financial sector from itself after numerous crises, in championing the development of financial assets now universally regarded as toxic, and in restricting the development of new regulations to control new financial instruments, turned a potentially garden-variety would-be depression in 1987 into the near-death experience of the Great Recession. The regulators, by delaying the inevitable for two decades, have made this crisis more intractable than it would have been without them.[10]

Reforms also fail because they do not recognize that the financial system has what Kornai called a 'soft budget constraint' (Kornai, Maskin et al. 2003).[11] A bank is not constrained in its lending by its reserves, but by the willingness of borrowers to take on additional debt (see Holmes 1969; Moore 1979). It therefore faces a 'soft budget constraint': to expand its operations, all it has to do is to persuade borrowers (firms and households) to borrow more money, and its income will grow – as will the level of debt.

This growth in bank income and debt is in turn dependent on the willingness of borrowers to incur debt. If this is based solely on their income, then the 'hard budget constraint' that households and firms face will put a limit on the amount of debt they will take on.

If, however, a Ponzi scheme develops in some asset class – so that people are willing to borrow money in the expectation of future capital gain – then the amount of borrowing will no longer be constrained by incomes. While capital gains are made, the borrowers also operate with a soft budget constraint: any deficiency of revenue over costs can be covered by selling an asset whose price has been inflated by the increase in leverage.

Initially banks – after they have forgotten the previous crisis – will be willing to fund this process, since it increases their incomes. But inevitably a crisis will result because the borrowing is adding to debt levels without increasing the capacity of the economy to service those debts. Though individuals can operate with a soft budget constraint while the price bubble lasts, the entire economy is stuck with the hard budget constraint that, in the long run, the debt must be serviced from income.[12]

If we are to prevent this process playing out yet again in the future, then we need to prevent the formation of Ponzi schemes in the first place. Unfortunately, the way that financial assets are currently defined contains the seeds of not one Ponzi scheme but two.

Because shares currently have an indefinite lifespan, it is quite possible for someone to assert, as Henry Blodget did about Amazon in 1998, that a given company's shares will go from $1 to $400 in a matter of a year (Blodget 2010). Faced with those hypothetical gains, ordinarily sane people are liable to succumb to the euphoria that produces them and be willing to borrow to speculate.

---

10 The fact that unemployment to date has not reached Great Depression heights – owing in part to the under-reporting of unemployment in official statistics, as noted earlier – should be no comfort until this crisis is over and unemployment has returned to pre-crisis levels. Since the level of private debt is still enormous – 260 percent of GDP as of December 2010, 90 percent higher than the pre-Great Depression level – it is likely that this crisis has many years to run.

11 I am going somewhat beyond Kornai's logic in this paper, but in the spirit of his concepts of hard and soft budget constraints.

12 Debt that adds to the economy's productive capacity can expand this constraint over time, but Ponzi lending inflates asset prices without increasing the quantity or productivity of assets.

Because there is no effective limit to the debt that can be secured against a property, property prices reflect the leverage that people are willing to incur to buy them. When houses are bought as residences, that isn't a problem. But when they are bought as speculative assets, then again people's willingness to borrow can become unhinged from their incomes.

We therefore need not merely reforms, but changes to the incentives that encourage people into debt – because so long as those incentives exist, we can be sure that at some point the financial sector will find a way to entice the public into debt, leading to yet another financial crisis.

I have two simple proposals to achieve this objective. Neither of them has any chance of being implemented immediately, but there is some prospect that they might be considered more seriously if, as I expect, this crisis causes a prolonged slump for America that resembles Japan's two 'Lost Decades' since its bubble economy collapsed in the early 1990s. They are:

1 Jubilee shares: To redefine shares so that, if purchased from a company directly, they last for ever (as all shares do now), but once these shares are sold by the original owner, they last another fifty years before they expire; and
2 Property Income Limited Leverage: To limit the debt that can be secured against a property to ten times the annual rental of that property.

Jubilee shares Ninety-nine percent of all trading on the stock market involves speculators selling pre-existing shares to other speculators. Valuations are ostensibly based on the net present value of expected future dividend flows, but in reality based on the 'Greater Fool' principle, where rising debt funds the Greater Fool. Anticipated capital gain is the real basis of valuation, and the overwhelming source of that capital gain is not increased productivity, but increased leverage. This trading adds zip to the productive capacity of society, while promoting bubbles in stock prices as leverage drives up prices, encouraging more leverage, leading to a crash after price-to-earnings ratios reach levels even the Greater Fool regards as ridiculous. When the share market crashes, prices fall but the debt that drove prices up remains.

If instead shares on the secondary market lasted only fifty years, then even the Greater Fool couldn't be enticed to buy them with borrowed money – since their terminal value would be zero. Instead a buyer would purchase a share on the secondary market only in order to secure a flow of dividends for fifty years (or less). One of the two great sources of rising unproductive debt would be eliminated.

This reform would dramatically tilt the balance in favor of the raising of capital via primary share issues, force valuations to be based on prospective earnings rather than capital gain, and make leveraged speculation on the value of shares on the secondary market much less attractive.

Jubilee shares could be introduced very easily, if the political will existed – something that is still years away in practice. All existing shares could be grandfathered on one date, so that they were all ordinary shares; but as soon as they were sold, they'd become Jubilee shares with an expiry date of fifty years from the date of first sale.

Property Income Limited Leverage Obviously some debt is needed to purchase a house, since the cost of building a new house far exceeds the average wage. But debt past a certain level drives not house construction, but house price bubbles: as soon as house prices start to rise because banks offer more leverage to home buyers, a positive feedback loop develops between house prices and leverage, and we end up where Australia and Canada are now, and where America was before the Subprime Bubble burst: with house prices out of reach of ordinary wage earners, and leverage at ridiculous levels so that 95 percent or more of the purchase price represents debt rather than owner equity.

Property Income Limited Leverage ('the *PILL*') would break the positive feedback loop that currently exists between leverage and property prices. With this reform, all would-be purchasers would be on equal footing with respect to their level of debt-financed spending, and the only way to trump another buyer would be to put more non-debt-financed money into purchasing a property.

This doesn't happen under our current system because the amount ex-tended to a borrower is allegedly based on his/her income. During a period of economic tranquility that is initiated after a serious economic crisis has occurred and is finally over – like the 1950s after the Great Depression and World War II – banks set a responsible level for leverage, such as the requirement that borrowers provide 30 percent of the purchase price, so that the loan-to-valuation ratio was limited to 70 percent. But as economic tranquility continues, banks, which make money by extending debt, find that an easy way to extend more debt is to relax their lending standards, and push the loan-to-valuation ratio (LVR) to, say, 75 percent.

Borrowers are happy to let this happen, for two reasons: borrowers with lower income who take on higher debt can trump other buyers with higher incomes but lower debt in bidding on a house they desire; and the increase in debt drives up the price of houses on sale, making the sellers richer and leading all current buyers to believe that their notional wealth has also risen.

Ultimately, you get the runaway process that we saw in the USA, where leverage rises to 95 percent, 99 percent, and even beyond – to the ridiculous level of 120 percent, as it did with Liar Loans at the peak of the subprime frenzy. Then it all ends in tears when prices have been driven so high that new borrowers can no longer be enticed into the market – since the cost of servicing that debt can't be met out of their incomes – and as existing borrowers are forced into bankruptcy by impossible repayment schedules. The housing market is then flooded by distressed sales, and the bubble bursts. The high house prices collapse, but as with shares, the debt used to purchase them remains.

If we instead based the level of debt on the income-generating capacity of the property being purchased, rather than on the income of the buyer, then we would forge a link between asset prices and incomes that is currently easily punctured by rising debt. It would still be possible – indeed necessary – to buy a property for more than ten times its annual rental. But then the excess of the price over the loan would be genuinely the savings of the buyer, and an increase in the price of a house would mean a fall in leverage, rather than an increase in leverage as now. There would be a negative feedback loop between house prices and leverage. That hopefully would stop house price bubbles developing in the first place, and take dwellings out of the realm of speculation back into the realm of housing, where they belong.

Conclusion

As the above 'bubble on a whirlpool of speculation' quote from Keynes indicates, this is not the first time that the conventional theory of finance has been attacked. What is unique about these most recent critiques is that the contribution from physicists in particular turns one of the alleged strengths of neoclassical economics against it: mathematics.

In the past, neoclassical economists have disparaged their critics with the assertion that they object to neoclassical theory because they don't understand mathematics. This time, however, they are under attack, not merely from critics who eschew the use of mathematics, but from those to whom mathematical thinking is second nature.

The impact of this power inversion can be seen in the physicist Joe McCauley's observations about the need to reform economics education:

> The real problem with my proposal for the future of economics departments is that current economics and finance students typically do not know enough mathematics to understand (a) what econophysicists are doing, or (b) to evaluate the neo-classical model (known in the trade as 'The Citadel') critically enough to see, as Alan Kirman put it, that 'No amount of attention to the walls will prevent The Citadel from being empty.'
>
> I therefore suggest that the economists revise their curriculum and require that the following topics be taught: calculus through the advanced level, ordinary differential equations (including advanced), partial differential equations (including Green functions), classical mechanics through modern nonlinear dynamics, statistical physics, stochastic processes (including solving Smoluchowski–Fokker–Planck equations), computer programming (C, Pascal, etc.) and, for complexity, cell biology.

Time for such classes can be obtained in part by eliminating micro- and macro-economics classes from the curriculum. The students will then face a much harder curriculum, and those who survive will come out ahead. So might society as a whole. (McCauley 2006: 607–8)

This amplifies a point that, as a critic of economics with a reasonable grounding in mathematics myself, has long set me apart from most other critics: neoclassical economics is not bad because it is mathematical per se, but because it is bad mathematics.

Why mathematics is not the problem

Many critics of economics have laid the blame for its manifest failures at the feet of mathematics. Mathematics, they claim, has led to an excessive formalism in economics, which has obscured the inherently social nature of the subject.

While it is undeniable that an inordinate love of mathematical formalism has contributed to some of the intellectual excesses in economics, generally this reaction is as erroneous as blaming the piano for the discordant notes of a bad piano player. If anything should be shot, it is the pianist, not the piano.

Though mathematics has definite limitations, properly used it is a logical tool that should illuminate, rather than obscure. Economists have obscured reality using mathematics because they have practiced mathematics badly, and because they have not realized the limits of mathematics.

The kernel

If you divided the world's population into those who dislike mathematics, those who like it, and those who were indifferent, I suspect that 95 percent would be in the first camp, 5 percent in the second, and 0 percent in the third. Neoclassical economists come almost exclusively from the 'like it' camp, and therefore their arguments are almost always expressed in mathematical form. Most critics of economics come from the 'dislike it' camp, and frequently criticism of mathematics per se forms part of their criticism of economics.

Call me weird: I'm a critic of neoclassical economics who likes mathematics. But I am not alone. There are numerous mathematically inclined critics of neoclassical economics, and in many ways this book was written to convey their critiques to a non-mathematical audience. Not only is it possible to simultaneously like mathematics and dislike mainstream economics, but a sound knowledge of mathematics makes you an even more confirmed opponent – because much of the mathematics in conventional economic theory is unsound.

At one level, it is unsound because conditions that economists assume contradict other conditions needed for their models, so that the theory is built on a mathematical error. For example, as shown in Chapter 4, one crucial assumption in the neoclassical argument in favor of small competitive firms over monopolies violates one of the most basic rules of calculus, the Chain Rule.

At a second level, it employs the wrong mathematical tools to analyze the dynamic processes that characterize a market economy – employing complicated comparative static equilibrium analysis when dynamic systems analysis is not only more appropriate but frankly easier.

At a third and more profound level, conventional economics is mathematically unsound because it has not learnt the lesson which true mathematicians have learnt in the last century: that there are limits to mathematical logic.

The roadmap

In this chapter I argue that conventional economics has abused mathematics in two main ways: by practicing bad mathematics, and by not acknowledging the limitations of mathematics. Many economic theorems result in logical contradictions which economists fail to recognize as such, and many other theorems are derived by falsely assuming that different quantities are in fact equal. Modern mathematics has also realized that there are limits to mathematical logic, but economists have evaded this realization by effectively but unintentionally isolating themselves from mainstream mathematical science.

Bad mathematics

In a classic instance of 'those who live by the sword die by the sword,' the school of economics that prides itself on being mathematical is subject to the indictment that its mathematics is erroneous. There are numerous theorems in economics that rely upon mathematically fallacious propositions. There are basically four ways in which this manifests itself in economic theory:

- logical contradiction, where the theory is allegedly 'saved' by an assumption which in fact contradicts what the theory purports to show;
- omitted variables, where an essential aspect of reality must be ignored to derive the mathematical results that economists wish to prove;
- false equalities, where two things that are not quite equal are treated as if they are equal; and
- unexplored conditions, where some relation is presumed without exploring what conditions are needed to make this relation feasible.

Logical contradiction The case outlined in Chapter 2 – the failed attempt to aggregate individual preferences to form community preferences with the same properties – is an excellent example of logical contradiction.

The economic theory of consumer behavior begins with the proposition that it is possible to aggregate individual demand curves to derive a market demand curve that has the same characteristics as an individual's demand curve. Economists have proved that this is possible only when the Sonnenschein-Mantel-Debreu conditions apply: (a) that all consumers have the same preference map; and (b) that preferences do not change with income.

Condition (a) effectively means that there is only one consumer. Condition (b) effectively means that there is only one commodity. Aggregation is therefore strictly possible if there is only one consumer and only one commodity.

Clearly this is not aggregation at all.

A good mathematician would recognize this as proof by contradiction (Franklin and Daoud 1988). This is a clever technique whereby, to prove a statement, you assume its opposite and then show a contradiction. Therefore the statement is true.

For example, consider the problem that confronted Pythagoras and friends when they tried to work out the length of the hypotenuse of a right-angled triangle whose other sides were both one unit long. According to Pythagoras's theorem that 'the square of the length of the hypotenuse is equal to the sum of the squares of the other sides,' this meant that the length of the hypotenuse was the square root of 2.

These Ancient Greeks initially believed that all numbers were 'rational,' which meant that any number could be expressed as the fraction of two integers: thus 1.5, for example, is the integer 3 divided by the integer 2. But they could never accurately measure the value of the square root of 2 in terms of the ratio of two integers: every more accurate measurement led to a different fraction.

The reason that they couldn't find the 'right' two integers is that the square root of 2 is an irrational number: it can't be defined as the ratio of two integers.

This can be proved quite easily using proof by contradiction. You start with the opposite assumption – that it is possible to express the square root of 2 as a ratio of two integers. You then work on from this point, to show this leads to a contradiction. Therefore you show that the square root of 2 is irrational.[1]

The proofs which led to the Sonnenschein-Mantel-Debreu conditions can easily be described in the same fashion. You wish to prove that it is *not* possible to aggregate individual preferences to derive community preferences which display the same characteristics as individual preferences.

You start with the opposite assumption – that it is possible to aggregate the preferences of two or more different consumers over two or more different commodities to market demand curves that have the same characteristics as individual demand curves. You then show that this is possible only if

---

1 This proof is very easy to understand, even if you don't think you're good at mathematics. If you assume that the square root of 2 is the ratio of two integers, then you can label these two as yet unknown integers *a* and *b*, and know that they have no common factors. Starting from the assumption that the square root of 2 equals *a* divided by *b*, you get rid of the square root by squaring both sides, so that *a* squared divided by *b* squared equals 2. This now tells you that *a* squared equals 2 times *b* squared, which is only possible if *a* is an even number – since if you square an odd number, you get another odd number. This now means that *a* has to equal two times some other number – call this *c*. Since *a* squared equals 2 times *b* squared, and *a* equal 2 times *c*, it also follows that 4 times *c* squared equals 2 times *b* squared. Divide both sides by 2 and you now find that *b* squared equals 2 times *c* squared. This means that *b* is also an even number – but this means that *a* and *b* have the common factor of 2. This contradicts your assumption that they have no common factors. Therefore the square root of 2 can't be the ratio of two integers, and it is therefore irrational.

there is only one individual and only one commodity. This contradicts your starting assumption that there are multiple different consumers and different commodities. Therefore you have proved, by contradiction, that it is not possible to aggregate individual preferences to derive market demand curves that obey the 'Law' of Demand.

The trouble is that economists were hoping that they could prove that it was possible to aggregate. In this sense, they were in the same situation as the ancient Pythagoreans, who were trying to prove that all numbers were rational – they were not at all pleased to find that they were wrong.

At least the Pythagoreans relented: they abandoned the belief that all numbers were rational, and accepted that there were numbers which could not be described as the ratio of two integers. Mathematics thus absorbed the existence of irrational numbers, and went on from there to many other discoveries.

Economists, on the other hand, have been unwilling to abandon their concept of rationality. Faced with an equivalent discovery – that society cannot be understood as the sum of the rational individuals within it – economics has instead enshrined these and similar logical contradictions as 'intuitively reasonable' (Gorman 1953) abstractions that are needed to forge a link between individual and collective utility.

This is bad mathematics. It has led to bad economics, which has avoided the more complex but richer visions of the economy that flow from coming to terms with the myriad contradictions of the simplistic notions underlying neoclassical economics.

Omitted variables

Bad mathematics also shows up in such hallowed economic concepts as maximizing profit by equating marginal cost and marginal revenue. As is shown in Chapter 4, this mantra of the everyday economist is false even on its own terms, but it is doubly so if we ignore time. Once time is rightly included in the analysis, then it is mathematically evident that, to maximize profits over time, a firm should ensure that its marginal revenue exceeds its marginal cost.

Many critics of conventional economics have previously argued that time is the most crucial variable left out of economic analysis, but most of these critics have then eschewed mathematics itself as a result. However, good mathematical economics incorporates time as an essential aspect of reality, and results in a type of economic analysis that is profoundly different from conventional neoclassical economics.

Time is not the only vital factor omitted by neoclassical economists, of course. Other notable examples include uncertainty, and the formation of expectations under uncertainty, and, most importantly of all, given the debt-induced crisis we are now in, money and debt. The basis of this is the so-called 'money illusion,' which is drummed into new economics students in their first year – ordinarily when most are too naive about the world to see the fallacy behind it[2] – resulting in macroeconomic models that ignore the role of money and debt in our fundamentally credit-driven market economies.

False equalities

One popular but erroneous step in conventional economic argument is to assert that something that is extremely small can be treated as zero. This is especially so when economists then pretend to 'aggregate up' from the individual firm to derive a result that applies at the aggregate level. What results is not mathematical analysis, but a mathematical sleight of hand – the intellectual equivalent of a magician's trick.

The model of perfect competition illustrates this nicely. The argument starts with the market having a downward-sloping demand curve and an upward-sloping supply curve. Step one of the trick is to omit showing the downward-sloping marginal revenue curve, which must be there if the market demand curve slopes downward, and which is distinctly different from, and steeper than, the demand curve. Step two is to break the market demand curve into lots of tiny bits, each of which must also slope downwards if the whole curve slopes downwards, but to persuade the audience that the slope of each of these little lines is so flat that they can be treated as horizontal. Hence for the individual firm, the demand curve and the marginal revenue curve are identical. The final stage of the trick is to return to the market level by adding up all the individual firm's marginal cost curves, and to show that price is set by the intersection of the demand curve and the supply curve. The troublesome market marginal revenue curve has been made to disappear, and the trick is complete.

The special irony of this piece of magic is that the magician doesn't realize that a trick is being pulled. Economists are so used to presuming that an infinitesimal amount is equivalent to zero that they don't even realize they are breaching one of the fundamental rules of mathematics.

Unexplored conditions

There are numerous examples of this phenomenon. The comparison of monopoly to perfect competition presumes that the supply curve for the competitive industry is equivalent to the marginal cost curve for the monopoly. However, this is possible only if the two 'curves' are the same horizontal straight line (Keen and Standish 2010: 89–91). The theory of the labor market presumes that the supply curve of labor is upward sloping; Chapter 5 showed that this is not a necessary outcome of the neoclassical theory of labor supply. The analysis of production requires that the money value of

---

2 This is that for changing all incomes and prices by the same factor to have no effect, 'all other nominal magnitudes [including] assets and liabilities that are expressed in nominal terms' (Friedman 1969: 1) have to be altered by the same factor as well – and even this ignores the fact that debt amortization makes the effect of interest rates nonlinear.

capital is an adequate measure of the amount of capital; Chapter 6 showed that it is not, once we acknowledge that machines are produced by other machines and labor.

That these (and doubtless many other) logical conundrums exist indicates that economists do not explore the logical foundations of their beliefs. This in itself is not necessarily unscientific; as discussed in Chapter 7, it is a standard practice that scientists in a given school within a science do not challenge what Lakatos describes as the 'hard core' of their beliefs. But it is a sign of how fragile the neoclassical hard core is that so many elements of it can be shown so easily to be internally inconsistent.

It is also unscientific that, when such logical flaws are either pointed out by critics (as with Sraffa's critique in Chapter 6) or discovered by believers (as with the Sonnenschein-Mantel-Debreu conditions in Chapter 2), neoclassical theory adopts 'ancillary assumptions' which are clearly absurd (such as the 'machines as putty' notions which were put forward during the debate with Sraffa and his supporters, or the SMD conditions used to save the theory of consumption, which amount to assuming that all consumers have identical, income-independent tastes). This, to Lakatos, is the sign of a degenerative scientific research program which is preoccupied with adjusting its ancillary beliefs to defend its hard core, whereas a truly progressive program would be expanding the range of real-world phenomena which its theory explains. The school of economics which gives pride of place to the word 'rational' hardly displays rational behavior when its core beliefs are challenged. I expect that the new logical conundrums pointed out in this book will generate further displays of irrational behavior by conventional economists.[3]

Mathematics is therefore not the reason why conventional economics is so bad. Instead, bad economics is supported by bad mathematical practice. But this is only half of the story about how economics has abused mathematics. Economics has also accidentally inoculated itself against many of the advances of modern mathematics. One essential aspect of modern mathematics that economics has not realized is that mathematics today has a humility that economics lacks, because mathematicians have proved that mathematics has limits.

The limits to mathematics

Economics remains perhaps the only area of applied mathematics that still believes in Laplace's dictum that, with an accurate enough model of

3 One example of this is the paper by Caplan (2000) which attempts to explain findings which show that experimental subjects do not conform to the neoclassical definition of rational. Rather than accepting that the neoclassical definition of rationality may be flawed, Caplan proposes that irrationality may be a 'good,' which people 'consume' like any other, and then represents a rationality–irrationality trade-off using indifference curves. This one article is not the final word on the neoclassical response to such findings. But I expect it to be far more readily adopted by the profession than any acknowledgment that the 'curse of dimensionality' makes rational behavior as economists define it simply impossible in the real world.

the universe and accurate enough measurement today, the future course of the universe could be predicted.

For mathematicians, that dictum was dashed in 1899 by Poincaré's proof of the existence of chaos. Poincaré showed that not only was it impossible to derive a formula which could predict the future course of a dynamic model with three or more elements to it, but even any numerical approximation to this system would rapidly lose accuracy. The future could be predicted only if the present was known to infinite accuracy, and this was clearly impossible.

Today, mathematicians are quite comfortable with the proposition that most mathematical problems cannot be explicitly solved in a manner which yields the kind of didactic statements which economics makes as a matter of course – such as 'perfect competition gives superior welfare outcomes to monopoly,' 'free trade is superior to protection,' and so on. Such definitive pronouncements are generally only possible when the problem is essentially the same as working out where two straight lines intersect. This class of models is known as algebraic.

Some algebraic equations are rather difficult to solve because there is no standard formula to apply. But there are standard formulas available to solve systems of algebraic equations where all the equations are 'straight lines.' This is the type of mathematics which economic theory generally tries to apply to economic problems.

However, this body of mathematics is an appropriate model of only a tiny subset of real-world systems – and that subset does not include true economic analysis.[4]

The more appropriate starting point for mathematical models of the economy is dynamic equations, in which the relationships between variables cannot be reduced to straight lines. These are known in mathematics as nonlinear differential equations. The vast majority of these cannot be solved, and once three or more such equations interact, they are impossible to solve.

Table 16.1 summarizes the situation. Economic theory attempts to analyze the economy using techniques appropriate to the upper left-hand part of Table 16.1 (with italic text), when in fact the appropriate methods are those in the lower right-hand part (with cells shaded gray).

Other developments, such as Gödel's proof that a mathematical system cannot be self-contained – so that it must take some axioms on faith – and the proof that there were some mathematical problems which could not be solved, added to this realization by mathematicians and physicists that mathematics and science had innate limits. As a result, in place of Laplace's grand conceit, there is a humility to modern mathematics. The future cannot be known, mathematics cannot solve every problem, some things may not be knowable.

---

4 Though this branch of mathematics provides many tools which enable mathematicians to characterize the behavior of more complex and realistic models of the real world – including such things as differential equation models of the economy.

TABLE 16.1 The solvability of mathematical models (adapted from Costanza 1993)

	Linear			Non-linear		
Equations	One	Several	Many	One	Several	Many
Algebraic	*Trivial*	*Easy*	*Possible*	Very difficult	Very difficult	Impossible
Ordinary differential	Easy	Difficult	Essentially impossible	Very difficult	Impossible	
Partial differential	Difficult	Essentially impossible	Impossible			

But these epiphanies passed economists by: they continue to believe in a clockwork universe, in which a proper specification of the conditions of today could enable you to predict the future for all time. Nowhere is this vanity more obvious than in the school's defining works, Walras's *Elements of Pure Economics* and Debreu's *Theory of Value*.

Walras's arrogance towards those economists who would not practice mathematics is still the typical attitude today held by economists towards those who criticize their use of mathematics:

> As for those economists who do not know any mathematics, who do not even know what is meant by mathematics and yet have taken the stand that mathematics cannot possibly serve to elucidate economic principles, let them go their way repeating that 'human liberty will never allow itself to be cast into equations' or that 'mathematics ignores frictions which are everything in social science' and other equally forceful and flowery phrases. They can never prevent the theory of the determination of prices under free competition from becoming a mathematical theory. Hence, they will always have to face the alternative either of steering clear of this discipline and consequently elaborating a theory of applied economics without recourse to a theory of pure economics or of tackling the problems of pure economics without the necessary equipment, thus producing not only very bad pure economics but also very bad mathematics. (Walras 1954 [1874])

As this book has shown, it is neoclassical economists who have been guilty of very bad mathematics. But just as important is the fact that they do not appreciate the limits to mathematics.

At least Walras could be forgiven for not being aware of Poincaré's theorem of 1899 – though he had sought out Poincaré in a forlorn attempt to garner support for his mathematization of economics. Debreu's opus pre-dated the rediscovery of chaos by Lorenz, but that he could even conceive of modeling the economy as a system in which all production and exchange decisions were 'made now for the whole future,' and in which the theory of uncertainty was 'free from any probability concept and formally identical with the theory of certainty,' betrayed a profound lack of appreciation of the mathematics of his day (not to mention the real world).

The modern manifestation of this ignorance of the limits of mathematics is a widespread – though not universal – failure by economists to appreciate the importance of nonlinear analysis and chaos theory. If I had a cent for every time I heard an economist comment that 'chaos theory hasn't amounted to much' – well, I wouldn't be wealthy, but I could afford an expensive meal or two.

Chaos theory has 'not amounted to much' in economics because its central tenets are antithetical to the economic obsession with equilibrium. In other sciences, chaos theory, complexity analysis and their close cousin evolutionary theory have had profound impacts. It shows how isolated economics has become from the scientific mainstream of the late twentieth and early twenty-first century that such ignorant views could be commonplace.

The recurring nightmare of straight lines

Virtually every critique detailed in this book has led to the result that some relationship between phenomena that economics argued was curved had to instead be a straight line.

The economic theory of consumer behavior argued that a person's consumption of a commodity could change in any direction as his income rose: if it was a luxury, consumption would rise relative to other commodities; if a necessity, consumption could fall. Instead, the Sonnenschein-Mantel-Debreu conditions show that if the theory is to aggregate from the individual to the market demand curve, Engel curves must be straight lines.

The economic theory of production argues that output is subject to diminishing marginal returns, so that as the variable input rises, output rises less than proportionately – the relationship is curved. Sraffa's critique shows that, in general, output should rise proportionately: the relationship should be a straight line.

The economic theory of competition argues that perfect competition is superior to monopoly. But the only conditions under which the comparison is watertight involve a straight-line relationship between inputs and outputs – not the curved relationship asserted by the concept of diminishing marginal productivity.

Why do straight lines haunt economic theory, when it is forced to be logical?

The answer to this dilemma has a lot to do with one of the basic notions of economics, the belief that society is no more than the sum of its parts. This asserts that to work out the whole, all you have to do is add the parts up. This requires that the interactions between the parts are either zero or negligible. The only interaction that one variable can have with another is the one neoclassical economists want to use, simple addition: your utility plus my utility equals social utility; your output plus my output equals industry output; and so on.

This categorically rules out interactions where one variable is multiplied by another (where both are likely to be large numbers). One obvious such interaction occurs in working out a firm's revenue. A firm's revenue equals the number of units it sells, times the sale price. Economics argues that the quantity a firm will sell is a function of price – to invoke a higher supply from the firm, the price has to rise to offset the effect of diminishing marginal productivity.

If both the price and the quantity are treated as variables, then the firm's revenue is equal to one variable (price) times another (quantity). This can't be allowed if economists are to treat society as no more than the sum of its parts, so economists assume that the price a competitive firm faces is a constant. Then the firm's revenue equals a constant (price) times a variable (quantity).

However, neoclassicals then want it both ways: they want price for the entire industry to be a variable, but price for the individual firm to be a constant, without the firms interacting in any way. This just can't happen mathematically – as discussed in Chapter 4. So if they force this situation by making an invalid assumption, it inevitably means that something else that they want to treat as a variable has to instead be treated as a constant. Hence the recurrent nightmare of a straight line.

The future of mathematics in economics

There is little doubt that the close identification of neoclassical economics with mathematical analysis has given mathematics a bad name among critical economists, and members of the ordinary public who are critical of economics.

This is likely to lead to a backlash against mathematics in economics, if the discipline ever rids itself of its dominance by neoclassical economics. This would be a great pity, since, as I hope this book has shown, properly used, mathematical reasoning debunks unsound economics. Furthermore, with its limitations fully appreciated, it and computer simulations can assist in the construction of sound alternative analyses. But if mathematics is avoided for its own sake, in reaction to how economics embraced it for its own sake, then the development of a meaningful economics will be stymied.

I now turn to some of the alternatives to conventional economics that do exist – warts and all. We begin with the most radical alternative – Marxian economics. You may, if you have typecast me as 'left-wing,' expect me to praise Marxian analysis. If so, you are in for a surprise.

Why most Marxists are irrelevant, but most of Marx is not

Marxian economics is clearly one of the alternatives to the neoclassical way of 'thinking economically,' and by rights I should be discussing it in the next chapter, which looks at alternatives to conventional economics. However, in an illustration of the fact that conservative economists do not have a monopoly on unsound analysis, Marxian economics, as conventionally understood, is hobbled by a logical conundrum as significant as any of those afflicting neoclassical economics.

This conundrum has split non-orthodox economists into two broad camps. One tiny group continues to work within what they see as the Marxian tradition, and spends most of its time trying to solve this conundrum. The vast majority largely ignore Marx and Marxian economics, and instead develop the schools of thought discussed in the next chapter.

I find this ironic, since if Marx's philosophy is properly understood, the conundrum disappears, and Marx provides an excellent basis from which to analyze capitalism – though bereft of the revolutionary message that makes Marx both so appealing to his current followers, and anathema to so many others.

The kernel

One defining belief in conventional Marxian economics is that labor is the only source of profit: while machines are necessary for production, labor alone generates profit for the capitalist. This proposition is a key part of the radical appeal of Marxism, since it argues that capitalist profit is based upon exploitation of the worker.

Marxists argue that labor is the only source of profit because it is the only commodity where one can distinguish between 'commodity' and 'commodity-power.' When any other commodity is sold, the purchaser takes it lock, stock and barrel. But with labor, the capitalist 'purchaser' does not own the worker. Instead, he pays a subsistence wage, which can be represented by a bundle of commodities; this is the cost of production of the ability to work, which Marxists describe as the commodity 'labor-power.' The capitalist then puts the laborer to work for the length of the working day, during which time the worker produces a different bundle of commodities that is worth more than his subsistence wage. The difference between the output of labor and the cost of maintaining labor-power is the source of profit.

Since no such distinction can be made for machinery, the capitalist 'gets what he paid for' and no more when he buys a machine, whereas with labor, he gets more than he paid for. Therefore machines transfer their value only to the product.

This proposition has been shown to lead to severe logical problems, so the vast majority of critical economists have in practice abandoned Marx's logic. However, a minority of economists continue to swear allegiance to what they perceive as Marx's method, and continue to strive to invent ways in which the proposition that labor is the only source of profit can be maintained.

The critiques which have been made of this notion on mathematical grounds are cogent, but have been challenged by Marxian economists on philosophical or methodological grounds.

However, there are philosophical reasons why the proposition that labor is the only source of profit are invalid, and these reasons were first discovered by Marx himself. Unfortunately, Marx failed to properly understand his own logic, and instead preserved a theory that he had in fact shown to be erroneous.

Once Marx's logic is properly applied, his economics becomes a powerful means of analyzing a market economy – though not one which argues that capitalism must necessarily give way to socialism. Unfortunately, given the ideological role of Marxism today, I expect that Marxian economists will continue to cling to an interpretation of Marx that argues for capitalism's ultimate demise.

The roadmap

In this chapter I explain the classical economics concept of 'value,' and the manner in which Marx developed this into the labor theory of value. I illustrate the logical problems with the proposition that labor is the only source of value. I then outline Marx's brilliant philosophical analysis of the commodity, and show that this analysis contradicts the labor theory of value by arguing that all inputs to production are potential sources of value.

Marxian economics and the economics of Marx

If a nineteenth-century capitalist Machiavelli had wished to cripple the socialist intelligentsia of the twentieth century, he could have invented no more cogent weapon than the labor theory of value. Yet this theory was the invention, not of a defender of capitalism, but of its greatest critic: Karl Marx.

Marx used the labor theory of value to argue that capitalism harbored an internal contradiction, which would eventually lead to its downfall and replacement by socialism. However, Marx's logic in support of the labor theory of value had an internal contradiction that would invalidate Marx's critique of capitalism if it could not be resolved. Consequently, solving this enigma became the 'Holy Grail' for Marxist economists. Whereas nineteenth-century revolutionaries spent their time attempting to overthrow capitalism, twentieth-century revolutionaries spent theirs attempting to save the labor theory of value. Capitalism itself had no reason to fear them.

Despite valiant efforts, Marxist economists failed in their quest – and they achieved little else. As a result, while Marx's thought still has considerable influence upon philosophers, historians, sociologists and left-wing political activists, at the beginning of the twenty-first century, Marx and Marxists are largely ignored by other economists.[1] Most non-orthodox economists would acknowledge that Marx made major contributions to economic thought, but it seems that overall Samuelson was right: Marx was a 'minor Post-Ricardian' – someone who took classical economics slightly farther than had David Ricardo, but who ultimately led it into a dead end.

This conclusion is false. Properly understood, Marx's theory of value liberates classical economics from its dependence on the labor theory of value, and makes it the basis for a deep and critical understanding of capitalism. But in a truly Machiavellian irony, the main factor obscuring this richer appreciation of Marx is the slavish devotion of Marxist economists to the labor theory of value.

To see why Marx's theory of value is not the labor theory of value, we have to first delve into the minds of the great classical economists Adam Smith and David Ricardo.

Value – a prelude

The proposition that something is the source of value raises two questions: what is 'value' anyway, and why should any one thing be the source of it?

A generic definition of value – one which encompasses the several schools of thought in economics which have used the term – is that value is the innate worth of a commodity, which determines the normal ('equilibrium') ratio at which two commodities exchange. One essential corollary of this concept is that value is unrelated to the subjective valuation which purchasers put upon a product. In what follows, I'll use 'value' in this specific sense, not in any of its more colloquial senses.

The classical economists also used the terms 'value in use' (or 'use-value') and 'value in exchange' (or 'exchange-value') to distinguish between two fundamental aspects of a commodity: its usefulness, and the effort involved in producing it. Value in use was an essential aspect of a commodity – why buy something which is useless? – but to the classical economists, it played no role in determining price.

Their concept of usefulness was also objective, focusing upon the commodity's actual function rather than how it affected the user's feelings of well-being. The use-value of a chair was not how comfortable it made you feel, but that you could sit in it.

---

1 Though economists from several other schools of thought still pay great attention to Marx's original writings on economics, and see Marx as the father of many important concepts in economic analysis.

In contrast, the neoclassical school argues that value, like beauty, is 'in the eye of the beholder' – that utility is subjective, and that the price, even in equilibrium, has to reflect the subjective value put upon the product by both the buyer and the seller. Neoclassical economics argues that the equilibrium ratio at which two products exchange is determined by the ratio of their marginal utilities to their marginal costs.

As we have seen in Chapters 3 and 4, there are serious problems with the economic theory of pricing. But it has some appeal in comparison to the classical approach, since it seems reasonable to say that price should be determined both by the innate worth of a product, however that is defined, and by the buyer's subjective valuation of it.

The general classical reply to this concept was that, sure, in the short run and out of equilibrium, that would be true. But the classical school was more interested in 'long run' prices, and in the prices of things which could easily be reproduced.

In the long run, price would be determined by the value of the product, and not by the subjective valuations of the buyer or seller. For this reason, the classical school tended to distinguish between price and value, and to use the former when they were talking about day-to-day sales, which could be at prices which were above or below long-run values.

As well as having some influence out of equilibrium, subjective utility was the only factor that could determine the value of rare objects. As Ricardo put it:

> There are some commodities, the value of which is determined by their scarcity alone. No labor can increase the quantity of such goods, and therefore their value cannot be lowered by an increased supply. Some rare statues and pictures, scarce books and coins, wines of a peculiar quality, which can be made only from grapes grown on a particular soil, of which there is a very limited quantity, are all of this description. Their value is wholly independent of the quantity of labor originally necessary to produce them, and varies with the varying wealth and inclinations of those who are desirous to possess them. (Ricardo 1817)

Thus where scarcity was the rule, and the objects sold could not easily be reproduced, price was determined by the seller's and buyer's subjective utilities. But this minority of products was ignored by the classical economists.

Marx gave an additional explanation of why, in a developed capitalist economy, the subjective valuations of both buyer and seller would be irrelevant to the price at which commodities exchanged.

This was the historical argument that, way back in time, humans lived in small and relatively isolated communities, and exchange between them was initially a rare and isolated event. At this stage, the objects being exchanged would be items that one community could produce but the other could not.

As a result, one community would have no idea how much effort had gone into making the product, and the only basis for deciding how to exchange one product for another was the subjective valuation that each party put upon the products. As Marx put it:

> The exchange of commodities, therefore, first begins on the boundaries of such communities, at their points of contact with other similar communities, or with members of the latter. So soon, however, as products once become commodities in the external relations of a community, they also, by reaction, become so in its internal intercourse. The proportions in which they are exchangeable are at first quite a matter of chance. What makes them exchangeable is the mutual desire of their owners to alienate them. Meantime the need for foreign objects of utility gradually establishes itself. The constant repetition of exchange makes it a normal social act. In the course of time, therefore, some portion at least of the products of labor must be produced with a special view to exchange. From that moment the distinction becomes firmly established between the utility of an object for the purposes of consumption, and its utility for the purposes of exchange. Its use-value becomes distinguished from its exchange-value. On the other hand, the quantitative proportion in which the articles are exchangeable, becomes dependent on their production itself. (Marx 1867)

The most famous example of two products being exchanged on the basis of the perceived utility rather than their underlying value is the alleged exchange of the island of Manhattan for a bunch of beads.[2] This price would never have been set if trade between the Dutch and the Indians had been a long-established practice, or if the Indians knew how little work it took to produce the beads.

In an advanced capitalist nation, factories churn out mass quantities of products specifically for exchange – the seller has no interest in the products his factory produces. The sale price reflects the cost of production, and the subjective utility of the buyer and seller are irrelevant to the price.[3]

There is thus at least a prima facie plausibility to the argument that value alone determines the equilibrium ratio at which commodities are exchanged. The problem comes with the second question: what is the source of value?

Physiocrats

The first economists to systematically consider this question[4] answered that the source of all value was land.

---

2 This story may or may not be apocryphal. Check the website thebeadsite.com/FRO-MANG.html for one perspective, and www.crazyhorse.org/ for another.

3 Sraffa's critique of the concept of an upward-sloping demand curve, and the critiques of the market demand curve covered earlier, also undermine the neoclassical position and support the classical view.

4 The subject was a bone of contention from the time of Aristotle on. However, predecessors to the physiocrats were quite unsystematic about the determination of value and price.

The argument, in a nutshell, was that land existed before man did. Therefore man – or more specifically, man's labor – could not be the source of value. Instead, value came from the land as it absorbed the energy falling on it from the sun. Man's labor simply took the naturally generated wealth of the land and changed it into a different form. Land generated a surplus, or net product, and this enabled both growth and discretionary spending to occur.

Manufacturing, on the other hand, was 'sterile': it simply took whatever value the land had given, and transformed it into different commodities of an equivalent value. No formal proof was given of this latter proposition, beyond an appeal to observation:

> Maxims of Economic Government. I: Industrial work does not increase wealth. Agricultural work compensates for the costs involved, pays for the manual labor employed in cultivation, provides gains for the husbandmen, and, in addition, produces the revenue of landed property. Those who buy industrial goods pay the costs, the manual labor, and the gain accruing to the merchants; but these goods do not produce any revenue over and above this. Thus all the expenses involved in making industrial goods are simply drawn from the revenue of landed property – no increase of wealth occurs in the production of industrial goods, since the value of these goods increases only by the cost of the subsistence which the workers consume. (Quesnay, cited in Meek 1972)

Since land determined the value of commodities, and the price paid for something was normally equivalent to its value, the ratio between the prices of two commodities should be equivalent to the ratios of the land needed to produce them.

Smith (and Ricardo)

The physiocratic answer to the source of value reflected the school's origins in overwhelmingly rural France. Adam Smith, a son of Scotland and neighbor to the 'nation of shopkeepers,' was strongly influenced by the physiocrats. But in *The Wealth of Nations* (which was published in the year in which the first steam engine was installed) Smith argued that labor was the source of value. In Smith's words: 'The annual labor of every nation is the fund which originally supplies it with all the necessaries and conveniences of life which it annually consumes, and which consist always either in the immediate produce of that labor, or in what is purchased with that produce from other nations' (Smith 1838 [1776]).

The growth of wealth was due to the division of labor, which increased because the expansion of industry allowed each job to be divided into ever smaller specialized sub-tasks. This allowed what we would today call economies of scale: an increase in the size of the market allowed each firm to make work more specialized, thus lowering production costs (his most famous example of this was of a pin factory; this passage, which is better known than it is read, is reproduced on the web at Marx/More).[5]

Smith therefore had an explanation for the enormous growth in output which occurred during the Industrial Revolution. However, he had a dilemma: for reasons discussed below, Smith knew that, though labor was the source of value, it could not possibly determine price. Yet value was supposed to determine the ratio at which two commodities exchanged.

The dilemma arose because two commodities could exchange only on the basis of the amount of direct labor involved in their manufacture if only labor was required for their production. Smith gave the example of exchange in a primitive hunting society:

> In that early and rude state of society which precedes both the accumula-tion of stock and the appropriation of land, the proportion between the quantities of labor necessary for acquiring different objects seems to be the only circumstance which can afford any rule for exchanging them for one another. If among a nation of hunters, for example, it usually costs twice the labor to kill a beaver which it does to kill a deer, one beaver should naturally exchange for or be worth two deer. (Ibid.)

However, once there had been an 'accumulation of stock' – once a market economy had evolved – then paying for the labor alone was not sufficient; the price had also to cover profit:

> As soon as stock has accumulated in the hands of particular persons, some of them will naturally employ it in setting to work industrious people, whom they will supply with materials and subsistence, in order to make a profit by the sale of their work, or by what their labor adds to the value of the materials. In exchanging the complete manufacture either for money, for labor, or for other goods, over and above what may be sufficient to pay the price of the materials, and the wages of the workmen, something must be given for the profits of the undertaker of the work who hazards his stock in this adventure. (Ibid.)

So Smith was forced to concede that the price had to be high enough to pay for not just the hours of labor involved in making something, but also a profit. For example, if the deer hunter was an employee of a deer-hunting firm, then the price of the deer had to cover the hunter's labor, and also a profit margin for the firm.

The problem became more complicated still when land was involved. Now the price had to cover labor, profit, and rent. Smith's statement of this reveals that this 'father of economics' was rather more cynical and critical

---

5 This means that as output rose, costs of production fell. Smith was thus thinking in terms of a 'downward-sloping supply curve' – at least in the medium to long term – in contrast to the upward-sloping supply curve that is so central to economics today, which was debunked in Chapter 5.

of market relations than some of his descendants: 'As soon as the land of any country has all become private property, the landlords, like all other men, love to reap where they never sowed, and demand a rent even for its natural produce' (ibid.).

In the end, Smith was reduced to an 'adding up' theory of prices: the price of a commodity represented in part payment for labor, in part payment for profit, and in part payment for rent. There was therefore no strict relationship between value and price.

Ricardo Though he paid homage to his predecessor, Ricardo was, to say the least, critical of Smith's treatment of the relationship between value and price. He began his *Principles of Political Economy and Taxation* (Ricardo 1817) with an emphatic statement of the belief he shared with Smith, that labor was the determinant of the value of a commodity: 'The value of a commodity, or the quantity of any other commodity for which it will exchange, depends on the relative quantity of labor which is necessary for its production' (ibid.). However, he was much more aware than Smith of the need for precise definitions, and of the difficulties in going from value to price.

Smith had used two measures of the amount of labor contained in a product: 'labor embodied' and 'labor commanded.' Labor embodied was the amount of direct labor time it actually took to make a commodity. Labor commanded, on the other hand, was the amount of labor-time you could buy using that commodity.

If, for example, it took one day for a laborer to make a chair, then the chair embodied one day's labor. However, that chair could well sell for an amount equivalent to two days' wages – with the difference accounted for by profit and rent. The chair would therefore command two days' labor.

Ricardo argued that the former measure was far less volatile than the latter. He believed, in common with most classical economists, that workers received a subsistence wage. Since this would always be equivalent to a fairly basic set of commodities – so much food, clothing, and rental accommodation – it would not change much from one year to the next. The latter measure, however, reflected the profit earned by selling the worker's output, and this would vary enormously over the trade cycle.

His solution for the value/price dilemma was that the price of a commodity included not just direct labor, but also the labor involved in producing any tools. Ricardo took up Smith's deer and beaver example and elaborated upon it. Even in Smith's example, some equipment had to be used to kill the game, and variations in the amount of time it took to make the equipment would affect the ratio in which deer and beavers were exchanged:

> Even in that early state to which Adam Smith refers, some capital, though possibly made and accumulated by the hunter himself, would be necessary

to enable him to kill his game. Without some weapon, neither the beaver nor the deer could be destroyed, and therefore the value of these animals would be regulated, not solely by the time and labor necessary to their destruction, but also by the time and labor necessary for providing the hunter's capital, the weapon, by the aid of which their destruction was effected.

Suppose the weapon necessary to kill the beaver was constructed with much more labor than that necessary to kill the deer, on account of the greater difficulty of approaching near to the former animal, and the consequent necessity of its being more true to its mark; one beaver would naturally be of more value than two deer, and precisely for this reason, that more labor would, on the whole, be necessary to its destruction. (Ibid.)

Thus the price of any commodity reflected the labor which had been involved in creating it, and the labor involved in creating any means of production used up in its manufacture. Ricardo gave many numerical examples in which the labor involved in producing the means of production simply reappeared in the product, whereas direct labor added additional value over and above its means of subsistence – because of the difference between labor embodied (which equaled a subsistence wage) and labor commanded (which included a profit for the capitalist).[6]

However, Smith and Ricardo were both vague and inconsistent on key aspects of the theory of value.

Though he generally argued that labor was the source of value, on several occasions Smith counted the work of farm animals as labor.[7] Though he failed to account for the role of machinery in the creation of value, he also argued that machines could produce more value than it took to produce them – which would mean that machinery (and animals) would be a source of value, in addition to labor: 'The expense which is properly laid out upon a fixed capital of any kind, is always repaid with great profit, and increases the annual produce by a much greater value than that of the support which such improvements require' (Smith 1838 [1776]).

Ricardo more consistently implied that a machine added no more value to output than it lost in depreciation, but he also occasionally lapsed into completely ignoring the contribution of machinery to value.[8]

Marx's labor theory of value

Where his forebears implied and were vague, Marx stated and was emphatic: labor was the only source of value, in the sense that it could

---

6 All these examples were hypothetical, of course: Ricardo did not go out and measure the labor involved in producing the means of production in any industry, and then present his findings.

7 'Not only his labouring servants, but his labouring cattle, are productive labourers' (Smith 1838 [1776]).

8 'By the invention of machinery [...] a million of men may produce double, or treble the amount of riches, [...] but they will on no account add anything to value' (Ricardo 1817). Marx commented that 'This is quite wrong. The value of the product of a million men does not depend solely on their labor but also on the value of the capital with which they work' (Marx 1968 [1861]: Part II, p. 538).

add 'more value than it has itself' (Marx 1867). Marx called this difference between the value embodied in a worker and the value the worker added to production 'surplus value,' and saw it as the sole source of profit.

He was critical of Ricardo for not providing an explanation of why this difference existed – in Ricardo's terms, for not having a systematic explanation of why labor embodied differed from labor commanded. As Marx put it:

> Ricardo starts out from the actual fact of capitalist production. The value of labor is smaller than the value of the product which it creates – The excess of the value of the product over the value of the wages is the surplus-value – For him, it is a fact, that the value of the product is greater than the value of the wages. How this fact arises, remains unclear. The total working-day is greater than that part of the working-day which is required for the production of wages. Why? That does not emerge. (Marx 1968 [1861]: Part II)

The best that Ricardo could offer, Marx claimed, was that:

> [t]he value of labor is therefore determined by the means of subsistence which, in a given society, are traditionally necessary for the maintenance and reproduction of the laborers.
>
> But why? By what law is the value of labor determined in this way?
>
> Ricardo has in fact no answer, other than – the law of supply and demand – He determines value here, in one of the basic propositions of the whole system, by demand and supply – as Say notes with malicious pleasure. (Ibid.)

Similarly, Marx rejected Smith's musings on the productivity of machinery, and concurred with Ricardo that a machine only added as much value to output as it lost through depreciation:

> The maximum loss of value that they can suffer in the process, is plainly limited by the amount of the original value with which they came into the process, or in other words, by the labor-time necessary for their production. Therefore, the means of production can never add more value to the product than they themselves possess independently of the process in which they assist. However useful a given kind of raw material, or a machine, or other means of production may be, though it may cost £150, or, say 500 days' labor, yet it cannot, under any circumstances, add to the value of the product more than £150. (Marx 1867)

Marx likewise concurred with Ricardo's definition of value, cited above, that it 'depends on the relative quantity of labor which is necessary for its production.' Value in turn determined the price at which commodities exchanged, with commodities of an equivalent value – commodities containing an equivalent quantity of labor[9] – exchanging for the same price (in equilibrium).

---

9 Marx qualified this as 'socially necessary labor-time,' to take account of the possibility of out-of-equilibrium situations in which more labor-time might be lavished on a product than could be recouped by its sale.

This exchange of equivalents nonetheless still had to enable capitalists to make a profit, and Marx was disparaging of any explanation of profits which was based on 'buying cheap and selling dear':

> To explain, therefore, the general nature of profits, you must start from the theorem that, on the average, commodities are sold at their real values, and that profits are derived by selling them at their values, that is, in proportion to the quantity of labor realized in them. If you cannot explain profit upon this supposition, you cannot explain it at all. (Marx 1847)

Marx gave two explanations for the origin of surplus value. One was a 'negative' proof, by a process of elimination based on the unique characteristics of labor. The other was a 'positive' proof, based on a general theory of commodities. Most Marxist economists are aware of only the negative proof.

The origin of surplus value (I)

This was that labor was a unique commodity, in that what was sold was not actually the worker himself (which would of course be slavery), but his capacity to work, which Marx called labor-power. The value (or cost of production) of labor-power was the means of subsistence, since that is what it took to reproduce labor-power. It might take, say, six hours of labor to produce the goods which are needed to keep a worker alive for one day.

However, what the capitalist actually received from the worker, in return for paying for his labor-power, was not the worker's capacity to work (labor-power), but actual work itself. If the working day was twelve hours long (as it was in Marx's day), then the worker worked for twelve hours – twice as long as it actually took to produce his value. The additional six hours of work was surplus labor, which accrued to the capitalist and was the basis of profit. As Marx put it:

> The laborer receives means of subsistence in exchange for his labor-power; the capitalist receives, in exchange for his means of subsistence, labor, the productive activity of the laborer, the creative force by which the worker not only replaces what he consumes, but also gives to the accumulated labor a greater value than it previously possessed. (Ibid.)

This difference between labor and labor-power was unique to labor: there was no other commodity where 'commodity' and 'commodity-power' could be distinguished. Therefore other commodities used up in production simply transferred their value to the product, whereas labor was the source of additional value. Surplus value, when successfully converted into money by the sale of commodities produced by the worker, was in turn the source of profit.

The labor theory of value and the demise of capitalism This direct causal relationship between surplus value and profit meant there was also a direct causal relationship between what Marx called the rate of surplus-value and the rate of profit.

The rate of surplus value was the ratio of the surplus labor-time performed by a worker to the time needed to reproduce the value of labor-power. In our example above, this ratio is 1 to 1, or 100 percent: six hours of surplus labor to six hours of what Marx called necessary labor.

Marx defined the rate of profit as the ratio of surplus (which he denoted by the symbol s) to the sum of the inputs needed to generate the surplus. Two types of inputs were needed: necessary labor, and the means of production (depreciation of fixed capital plus raw materials, intermediate goods, etc.). Marx called necessary labor variable capital (for which he used the symbol v), because it could increase value, and he called the means of production used up constant capital (for which he used the symbol c), because it could not increase value.

Taking the example of weaving which Marx used extensively, during one working day a weaver might use 1,000 yards of yarn and wear out one spindle. The yarn might have taken twelve hours of (direct and indirect) labor to make, and the spindle the same. Thus the sum of the direct labor-time of the worker, plus the labor-time embodied in the yarn and the spindle, is thirty-six hours: twelve hours' labor by the weaver, twelve for the yarn, and twelve for the spindle. The ratio of the surplus to $c + v$ is 6:30 for a rate of profit of 20 percent.

Marx assumed that the rate of surplus value – the ratio of s to v – was constant, both across industries and across time.[10] Simultaneously, he argued that the competitive forces of capitalism would lead to capitalists replacing direct labor with machinery, so that for any given production process, c would get bigger with time. With s/v constant, this would decrease the ratio of s to the sum of c and v, thus reducing the rate of profit.

Capitalists would thus find that, regardless of their best efforts, the rate of profit was falling.[11] Capitalists would respond to this by trying to drive down the wage rate, which would lead to revolt by the politically aware working class, thus leading to a socialist revolution.[12]

Well, it was a nice theory. The problem was that, even if you accepted the premise that labor was the only source of value, the theory still had major logical problems. Chief among these was what became known as the transformation problem.

---

10 There is no reason why the rate of surplus value should be constant over time in practice, and Joan Robinson used this as the basis of her critique of Marxian economics. She argued that an increase in c could cause a rise in s/v, the rate of surplus value, so that the rate of profit would not fall over time.

11 There were several counter-tendencies that could attenuate this, but ultimately Marx thought the tendency of the rate of profit to fall would prevail.

12 This is an extremely brief outline of a much more complicated argument. Its purpose is not to provide a detailed exposition of Marx's theory of revolution, but to prepare the ground for critiques of the labor theory of value.

The transformation problem The transformation problem arises from the fact that capitalists are motivated not by the rate of surplus value, but by the rate of profit. If the rate of surplus value is constant across industries, and labor is the only source of surplus, then industries with a higher than average ratio of labor to capital should have a higher rate of profit. Yet if a capitalist economy is competitive, this situation cannot apply in equilibrium, because higher rates of profit in labor-intensive industries should lead to firms moving out of capital-intensive industries into labor-intensive ones, in search of a higher rate of profit.

Marx was not an equilibrium theorist, but this problem was serious because his description of equilibrium was inconsistent. Somehow, he had to reconcile a constant rate of surplus value across industries with at least a tendency towards uniform rates of profit.

Marx's solution was to argue that capitalism was effectively a joint enterprise, so that capitalists earned a profit which was proportional to their investment, regardless of whether they invested in a labor-intensive or capital-intensive industry:

> Thus, although in selling their commodities the capitalists of the various spheres of production recover the value of the capital consumed in their production, they do not secure the surplus-value, and consequently the profit, created in their own sphere by the production of these commodities – So far as profits are concerned, the various capitalists are just so many stockholders in a stock company in which the shares of profit are uniformly divided per 100. (Marx 1894)

He provided a numerical example (ibid.) that purported to show that this was feasible. He first provided a table (Table 17.1) showing the production of surplus value by a number of industries with differing ratios of variable to constant capital (in modern terms, varying labor-to-capital ratios).

In this 'value' table, a higher ratio of labor to capital is associated with a higher rate of profit. Thus 'labor-intensive' industry III, with a labor-to-capital ratio of 2:3, earns the highest 'value' rate of profit of 40 percent, while 'capital-intensive' industry V, with a 1:20 ratio, makes a 'value' rate of profit of just 5 percent.

Then Marx provided a second table in which the same industries earned a uniform rate of profit, now in terms of price rather than value. In contrast to Table 17.1, now all industries earned the same rate of profit.

The numbers in this example appeared feasible. The sums are consistent: the sum of all prices in Table 17.2 equals the sum of the value created in Table 17.1; the sum of surplus value in Table 17.1 equals the sum of the differences between input costs (500) and the price of output in Table 17.2 (610). But this apparent consistency masks numerous internal inconsistencies. The best proof of this was provided by the Sraffian economist Ian

TABLE 17.1 Marx's unadjusted value creation table, with the rate of profit dependent upon the variable-to-constant ratio in each sector

Capitals	Constant capital	Variable capital	Rate of surplus value (%)	Surplus value	Product	Rate of profit (%)
I	80	20	100	20	120	20
II	70	30	100	30	130	30
III	60	40	100	40	140	40
IV	85	15	100	15	115	15
V	95	5	100	5	105	5
Sum	390	110	100	110	610	22

TABLE 17.2 Marx's profit distribution table, with the rate of profit now uniform across sectors

Capitals	Constant capital	Variable capital	Surplus value	Price	Rate of profit	Deviation
I	80	20	22	122	22%	2%
II	70	30	22	122	22%	−8%
III	60	40	22	122	22%	−18%
IV	85	15	22	122	22%	7%
V	95	5	22	122	22%	17%
Sum	390	110	110	610	22%	

Steedman (this next section is unavoidably technical, and can be skipped at first reading).

Marxist economics after Sraffa

We have already seen in Chapter 6 the damage Sraffa's crucible did to the economic theory of price determination and income distribution. In an illustration of the comparatively non-ideological nature of Sraffian analysis, Steedman showed that Sraffa's method could equally well critique Marxian economics.

The basis of Sraffa's system is the acknowledgment that commodities are produced using other commodities and labor. Unlike conventional economics – which has invented the fictional abstraction of 'factors of production' – Marx's system is consistent with Sraffa's 'production of commodities by means of commodities' analysis (indeed, Marx's economics was a major inspiration for Sraffa).

Steedman began with an illustrative numerical model of an economy with just three commodities: iron, corn and gold. Iron and labor were needed to produce all three commodities, but neither gold nor corn was needed to produce anything.[13] Table 17.3 shows the quantities of inputs and outputs in Steedman's hypothetical economy.

TABLE 17.3 Steedman's hypothetical economy

Industries	Inputs		Outputs		
	Iron	Labour	Iron	Gold	Corn
Iron	28	56	56		
Gold	16	16		48	
Corn	12	8			8
Totals	56	80	56	48	8

The numbers in this table represent arbitrary units: the iron units could be tons, the labor units hours, gold units ounces, and corn units bushels – and any other set of arbitrary units would do as well. However, since each input is measured in a completely different unit, the numbers add up only down the columns: they don't add across the rows.

To analyze the labor theory of value, Steedman first had to convert these into the 'labor-value' units which Marx used. For simplicity, he set the labor-value of one unit ('hour') of labor at 1. Converted into value terms, Table 17.4 then says that it takes 28 times whatever the 'labor-value' of a ton of iron

13 This is clearly unrealistic, but the logic is the same even if we incorporate the reality that corn would be needed to produce corn. Steedman's example just made the numerical algebra easier to follow. He then continued his argument using symbolic linear algebra, to establish the generality of his analysis.

is, plus 56, to produce 56 times whatever the 'labor-value' of a ton of iron is. A bit of simple algebra shows that one ton of iron has a labor-value of 2.

TABLE 17.4 Steedman's physical table in Marx's value terms

	c	v	s	Totals
Iron	56	14	42	112
Gold	32	4	12	48
Corn	24	2	6	32
Totals	112	20	60	192

Similar calculations show that the labor-value of an ounce of gold is 1, and the labor-value of a bushel of corn is 4.

The next stage in the analysis is to work out the value of the commodity labor-power. It might appear that this has already been done – didn't he set this equal to 1? No, because this represents the total amount of labor performed, and in Marx's theory, workers get paid less than this. They get paid, not for their contribution to output, but for the commodity labor-power, whose value is equal to the means of subsistence.

Steedman assumed that it took five bushels of corn to reproduce the labor used in this hypothetical economy. Therefore the total value of labor-power in the entire economy was equal to the labor-value of five bushels of wheat. Since a bushel of wheat has a labor-value of 4, this means that the value of labor-power across the whole economy was 20 (and therefore, one unit of labor had a labor-value of 1/4). The difference between this amount and the total labor performed – 80 hours of labor, which we have set to equal 80 units of labor-value – is surplus value. So v, in Marx's scheme, is 20, while s is 60, for a rate of surplus value of 300 percent.

These numbers now allow the physical input data in Table 31 to be converted into Marx's labor-value terms. Since Marx assumed that the rate of surplus value was the same across all industries, ¼ of the labor input in each industry represents v, while ¾ represents s. Taking the iron industry, of the 56 labor-value units of direct labor, 14 represent v and 42 represent s. Since Table 17.5 is now in consistent units (everything is measured in labor-value units), the table adds up both horizontally and vertically.

With this table constructed, we can now calculate the average rate of profit in Marx's terms – which is the ratio of total s to the sum of c and v, or 60/132 (this factors to 5/11, and is equal to a rate of profit of 455Ú11 percent). In equilibrium, this rate of profit will apply across all industries, since otherwise capitalists would be shifting their resources from one sector to another. Steedman then multiplied the input values by 1 plus this uniform rate of profit to yield Marx's 'transformation' of values into prices.

TABLE 17.5 Steedman's prices table in Marx's terms

| | | Inputs | | | | | |
	c	v	Total	Profit rate	Markup (%)	Total price	Per unit price
Iron price of production	56	14	70	45	31.82	101.82	1.82
Gold price of production	32	4	36	45	16.36	52.36	1.09
Corn price of production	24	2	26	45	11.82	37.82	4.73
	112	20	132		60	192	

So far, so good. Just as with Marx's table, the sum of values equals the sum of prices, and the sum of profits equals the sum of surplus values. However, all is not as well as it seems.

Table 17.5 tells us that the price of the total output of the iron industry is 101.82 (let's call this dollars, even though in these models the price simply means the ratios in which commodities exchange). If we divide this by the physical output of 56 tons of iron, then this means the price per ton is $1.82. If the iron industry pays this price for its iron inputs in the next period, it will pay out $50.91. To hire the workers it needs, it has to buy sufficient corn: the amount works out to 3.5 bushels (this is the total amount of corn consumed by all workers – 5 bushels – multiplied by the fraction of the total workforce employed in the iron industry). This costs $16.55. The iron industry's total outlays are thus $67.46, and yet (if Marx's equilibrium price calculations are accurate), it can sell its output for $101.82, for a profit of $34.36. But this is $2.55 more than the profit in the previous period.

Clearly there is an inconsistency – or rather, at least one. The simplest is that Marx converted the output into price terms, but didn't convert the inputs. However, it's worse than this: even if you amend this error, you get nonsense results: what is supposed to be an equilibrium (and therefore stationary) turns out not to be stationary at all.

Steedman then shows that you don't have to 'transform' physical quantities into values, and values into prices: you can instead derive prices directly from the physical data and the equilibrium assumption of a uniform rate of profit. The basis of this is that, in equilibrium, the prices have to enable each sector to just pay for its inputs and make the average rate of profit. Thus for the iron industry, the price of its 28 tons of iron inputs, plus the price of its 56 hours of labor, plus the standard markup, must just equal the price of its 56 tons of iron output. There are two similar equations for corn and gold, and one final relation linking the wage to the cost of the subsistence amount of corn. If the gold price is notionally set to $1, this yields the average rate of profit, wage, and prices of iron and corn (in terms of gold) shown in Table 17.6.

TABLE 17.6 Profit rate and prices calculated directly from output/wage data

Variable	Value; price in terms of gold
Rate of profit	52%
Iron price of production	1.71
Gold price of production	1
Corn price of production	4.3

Things don't look so good for Marx's tables now. First, the rate of profit and prices worked out directly from the data (in Table 17.6) differ from those derived by taking Marx's route through the concept of value (in Table 17.5). Worse, whereas Marx's numbers aren't consistent – they are supposed to describe an equilibrium situation, but don't – the numbers derived directly from the data are consistent.

Take iron, for example. The iron sector pays $1.71 per ton for its 28 tons of inputs, for a total of $47.88. It buys 3.5 bushels of wheat for $4.3 a bushel, for an outlay of $15.05. Total expenses of production are therefore $62.93. It then marks this up by the rate of profit to a total of $95.65. Except for the effect of rounding error, this equals the price of iron ($1.71) times the output (56 tons).[14]

Steedman concluded that, far from value determining prices, prices could not be accurately derived from values. Instead, prices could be worked out directly from the physical production data, and knowledge of the real wage: value calculations were both superfluous and misleading. He concluded that

> [t]here is no problem of transforming values into prices, etc., to be solved. The 'transformation problem' is a 'non-problem,' a spurious problem which can only be thought to arise and to have significance when one is under the misapprehension that the rate of profit must be determined in terms of labor quantities. Once it is seen that there is no such necessity, the 'problem' simply evaporates. (Steedman 1977)

Though he did not put his conclusion in this way, Steedman was essentially saying that Marx cannot be right that labor is the only source of surplus. We are better off to forget the whole question of 'where does the surplus come from?' and instead simply accept that it exists, and analyze capitalism on that basis.

14 If I had worked with exact numbers rather than rounded them to two decimal places, the two calculations would have corresponded exactly. The value calculations, on the other hand, differ systematically, and by far more than can be attributed to rounding error.

The inconsistencies Steedman establishes[15] undermined Marx's sequence of claims that labor is the only source of value, that value is the only source of profits, and that value determines price. Marx could also provide no reason why capitalism, possible the most internally competitive social system ever, should ultimately behave so cooperatively, with capitalists sharing in total social profit as 'just so many stockholders in a stock company in which the shares of profit are uniformly divided per 100.'

Thus, though Marx used the labor theory of value to both attack capitalism and predict its downfall, the theory did not even seem to provide a consistent model of capitalism itself – let alone a 'scientific' explanation of why capitalism would wilt and socialism blossom. It appeared that the great revolutionary challenger to capitalism had promised a bang, but delivered a whimper.

The Marxist response This was no great disappointment to his conservative critics, who happily pointed out the flaws in Marx's logic, and turned to developing economics as we know it today. But devoted Marxists tried valiantly to resurrect Marx's program of 'scientific socialism' by showing that, somehow, at some deep level, Marx's theory of value was internally consistent.

Many years before Steedman turned Sraffa's blowtorch onto Marx's economics, leading Marxist economists had applauded Sraffa's methodical critique of neoclassical economics. However, some of them could also see that Sraffa's dispassionate analysis posed serious problems for the labor theory of value. One of the most thoughtful of such responses came from Ronald Meek in his scholarly *Studies in the Labor Theory of Value*. In a section headed 'From values to prices: was Marx's journey really necessary?,' Ronald Meek asked:

> Why did he think that anything had to be 'transformed' in order to arrive at the equilibrium prices characteristic of competitive capitalism? And if something did have to be 'transformed' in order to arrive at them, why did it have to be these mysterious, non-observable, Volume I 'values'? Personally, although I am no longer at all religious about such matters, I find myself leaning much more towards the 'neo-Ricardians' than towards their critics. I think that it is useful to talk in terms of a broad Ricardo-Marx-Sraffa tradition or stream of thought, in which the question of the relation between the social surplus and the rate of profit has always been (and still is) a central theme. (Meek 1972)

In other words, Meek was prepared to abandon the emphasis upon value, and instead develop Marx's analysis of capitalism – minus the insistence that labor is the only source of value, and that value determines profit and prices. Many other scholars followed Meek's lead, and abandoned strict Marxist economics, with its insistence upon value analysis.

15 Similar arguments had been made before, as early as at the end of the nineteenth century. Steedman simply provided the most comprehensive and definitive critique.

However, a minority has persisted, and continue to argue that, somehow, value is an essential part of Marxist analysis. This minority's response to Steedman's critique is best summarized in the title of a paper by Anwar Shaikh: 'Neo-Ricardian economics: a wealth of algebra, a poverty of theory' (Shaikh 1982).

The implication is that, somehow, Marx's philosophy sidesteps the mathematical problems highlighted by Steedman, or it points out a step in the mathematical chain which Steedman missed. To date, no Marxist has been able to put forward an explanation of this rejoinder, which has commanded assent from the majority of Marxists: there are almost as many competing ways to try to avoid Steedman's critique as there are Marxist economists. However, they all assent that there is something in Marx's philosophy which counteracts Steedman's mathematical attack.

Over one century after Marx's flawed solution to the transformation problem was first published, and almost a quarter of a century after Steedman's devastating critique, they are still at it. The latest attempts argue that, since Marx's theory was actually dynamic rather than static, the transformation problem should be solvable in a dynamic model.

Nice try, guys, but you really shouldn't bother. The labor theory of value is internally inconsistent, and perhaps even more flawed than conventional economic theory itself. And far from philosophy saving the labor theory of value from mathematical criticism, philosophy provides further compelling reasons for its rejection. One convincing proof of this was given by the Indian economist Arun Bose.

Arun Bose: Marx's 'capital axioms'

Bose was well aware of the criticism leveled at Steedman that his argument, while mathematically impeccable, was somehow philosophically lacking. Though he disparagingly referred to this as 'a theological tendency to go so strictly by what Marx said as to adhere to the rule: "where logic contradicts Marx's words, go by his words"' (Bose 1980), Bose nonetheless tried to avoid this judgment by looking for textual support in Marx. He called his interpretation of Marx the 'capital theory' approach, and argued that: 'as far as logic goes, there are "two Marxes," the Marx of the "labor value" approach, and the Marx of the "capital theory" approach,' and that the 'second Marx' should be supported in preference to the first (in scientific discussion) (ibid.).[16]

Bose, unlike Steedman, accepted the Marxian position that the concept of value was somehow essential. However, what he argued was that, if value was in some sense the essence of a commodity, then that essence could not be reduced solely to labor. Therefore labor alone was not the essence of value:

---

16 I dispute Bose's reading of Marx on this subject, but find the logic in his 'essence of value' analysis impeccable.

instead, both labor and commodities were the essence of value. As Bose put it: 'labor is never the only or the main "source of value" in any system which is defined as capitalist on the basis of a reasonable set of axioms. Labor is not, immediately or ultimately, the only or main source of price, surplus or profit. Labor and commodities are the two sources of wealth, value, price, of surplus value and profit' (ibid.). His logic used a concept we saw earlier in Chapter 6: the reduction of commodity inputs to dated labor.[17]

The manufacture of any commodity requires direct labor, machinery, intermediate goods, and raw materials. All the non-labor inputs had to have been produced at some time in the past: even unprocessed raw materials had to have been previously either mined or harvested. They in turn were made using some direct labor, and other commodity inputs (machinery, intermediate goods, raw materials). These again can be reduced to even earlier dated labor, and other commodity inputs.[18]

This process can go on indefinitely, with each step further reducing the commodity content. But no matter how far back you go, you can never eliminate this commodity residue. If you could, then there would be some commodities that can be created with absolutely no commodity inputs – or in other words, by magic.[19] Therefore if value is the essence of a commodity, then that essence consists of both labor and commodities – it cannot be derived solely from labor.

Bose's conclusion probably helped sway some more Marxists to abandon the faith. But generally, his argument was simply not acknowledged by Marxist economists. A similar fate has to date befallen the next argument, which establishes that the labor theory of value is inconsistent, not just with mathematical logic, or with any reductionist notion of the commodity, but with Marx's own philosophy.

The origin of surplus value (II)

As noted earlier, most Marxists believe that Marx reached the conclusion that labor was the source of value by a 'negative' proof, which eliminated any other possible contenders. This was true up until 1857, when he developed an alternative, and far superior, 'positive' proof. To understand this proof, we have to delve into Marx's 'dialectical' philosophy.[20]

17 He also employed a set of axioms from which his conclusions were derived.

18 At each step in the reduction, one period's capital inputs are reduced to the previous period's direct labor and capital inputs, marked up by the equilibrium rate of profit.

19 Services such as a massage, which might appear to be a commodity-free good, involve commodities directly (massage bench, oil), and if even these are forgone (an oil-free massage while lying on bare ground), they involve it indirectly through the need for the masseur to eat to stay alive. The commodity 'massage' could therefore not be reproduced in the absence of commodity inputs, such as food.

20 Marx's philosophy was derived from Hegel's, with Marx arguing that he replaced Hegel's idealism with realism. Dialectics is popularly known as the trio of thesis-antithesis-synthesis, and though this concept is popularly associated with both Hegel and Marx, it in fact derives from another, lesser-known philosopher, Fichte. For an intelligent discussion of dialectical philosophy in general, and Marx's application of it in particular, see Wilde (1989).

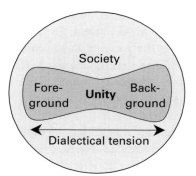

17.1 A graphical representation of Marx's dialectics

In brief, dialectics is a philosophy of change. It begins from the proposition that any entity exists in a social environment (see Figure 17.1). The environment will emphasize some aspect of the entity, and necessarily places less emphasis upon all other aspects of the entity. However, the entity cannot exist without both the foreground aspects (the features the environment emphasizes) and background aspects (the ones it neglects). This sets up a tension within the entity, and possibly between the entity and the environment. This tension can transform the nature of the entity, and even the environment itself.

Marx first applied this logic to the concept of the commodity in 1857. He reasoned that the commodity was the unity of use-value and exchange-value. In a capitalist economy, the exchange-value of a commodity is brought to the foreground[21] while its use-value is pushed into the background. What this means in practice is that the use-value of a commodity is irrelevant to its price: its price is instead determined by its exchange-value. Yet the commodity can't exist without its use-value (something useless can't be a commodity), so that a dynamic tension is set up between use-value and exchange-value in capitalism.

Prior to this realization, Marx had concurred with Smith and Ricardo that use-value was irrelevant to economics. After it, the concept of use-value, in unison with exchange-value, became a unifying concept for his whole analysis of capitalism.

Marx's first exploration of this concept occurred when he was working on the 'rough draft' of *Capital* in 1857: 'Is not value to be conceived as the unity of use-value and exchange-value? In and for itself, is value as such the general form, in opposition to use-value and exchange-value as particular forms of it? Does this have significance in economics?' (Marx 1857).[22]

21 In a different type of economy, use-value could well be brought to the foreground: commodities could be produced for the ruling elite at ostentatious expense, without regard to their cost of production. I well remember seeing a backscratcher in the Forbidden Palace in Beijing, made out of jade, gold, diamonds, emeralds and rubies.

22 This 'discovery' of the application of dialectical philosophy to economics occurred after Marx happened to re-read Hegel while he was drafting the *Grundrisse* (Oakley 1983; Mandel 1971).

The manner in which he first puts the proposition, as questions to himself rather than didactic statements, and especially his comment 'Does this have significance in economics?', shows how novel the concept was to him. From this point on, Marx exclusively used this positive methodology, based on a general axiomatic analysis of the commodity, to explain the source of surplus value. Since this point is appreciated by so few Marxists, it is worth citing several of Marx's many pronouncements on this issue.

I noted earlier that Marx mocked Ricardo for not having an explanation of why labor embodied differed from labor commanded. He notes that Smith fell for the fallacy that, under capitalism, a worker should be paid his full product. He continues:

> Ricardo, by contrast, avoids this fallacy, but how? 'The value of labor, and the quantity of commodities which a specific quantity of labor can buy, are not identical.' Why not? 'Because the worker's product is not = to the worker's pay.' I.e. the identity does not exist, because a difference exists – Value of labor is not identical with wages of labor. Because they are different. Therefore they are not identical. This is a strange logic. There is basically no reason for this other than it is not so in practice. (Ibid.)

Marx then contrasts his easy ability to derive the source of surplus value with Ricardo's struggles to do the same: 'What the capitalist acquires through exchange is labor capacity; this is the exchange value which he pays for. Living labor is the use-value which this exchange value has for him, and out of this use-value springs the surplus value and the suspension of exchange as such' (ibid.).

There are many similar such statements, many of which were written in documents which were either not intended for publication or were never formally completed by Marx. But even in the most well-known passage where Marx derives the source of surplus value, in *Capital* I, this positive derivation takes precedence over the negative proof.

Marx began *Capital* by clearing intellectual cobwebs en route to uncovering the source of surplus, criticizing explanations based upon unequal exchange or increasing utility through exchange. He then restated the classical axiom that exchange involves the transfer of equivalents, and the conclusion that therefore exchange of itself cannot provide the answer. Yet at the same time circulation based on the exchange of equivalents must be the starting point from which the source of surplus value is deduced. Marx put the dilemma superbly:

> The conversion of money into capital has to be explained on the basis of the laws that regulate the exchange of commodities, in such a way that the starting point is the exchange of equivalents. Our friend, Moneybags, who as yet is only an embryo capitalist, must buy his commodities at their

value, must sell them at their value, and yet at the end of the process must withdraw more value from circulation than he threw into it at starting. His development into a full-grown capitalist must take place, both within the sphere of circulation and without it. These are the conditions of the problem. (Marx 1867)

He began the solution of this dilemma with a direct and powerful application of the dialectic of the commodity. If the exchange-value of the commodity cannot be the source of surplus, then the dialectical opposite of value, use-value, is the only possible source:

The change of value that occurs in the case of money intended to be converted into capital must take place in the commodity bought by the first act, M-C, but not in its value, for equivalents are exchanged, and the commodity is paid for at its full value. We are, therefore, forced to the conclusion that the change originates in the use-value, as such, of the commodity, i.e. its consumption. In order to be able to extract value from the consumption of a commodity, our friend, Moneybags, must be so lucky as to find, within the sphere of circulation, in the market, a commodity, whose use-value possesses the peculiar property of being a source of value. (Ibid.)

Marx then used the quantitative difference between the exchange-value of labor-power and its use-value to uncover the source of surplus value in the transaction between worker and capitalist:

The past labor that is embodied in the labor power, and the living labor that it can call into action; the daily cost of maintaining it, and its daily expenditure in work, are two totally different things. The former determines the exchange-value of the labor power, the latter is its use-value. The fact that half a [working] day's labor is necessary to keep the laborer alive during 24 hours, does not in any way prevent him from working a whole day. Therefore, the value of labor power, and the value which that labor power creates in the labor process, are two entirely different magnitudes; and this difference of the two values was what the capitalist had in view, when he was purchasing the labor power. What really influenced him was the specific use-value which this commodity possesses of being a source not only of value, but of more value than it has itself. This is the special service that the capitalist expects from labor power, and in this transaction he acts in accordance with the 'eternal laws' of the exchange of commodities. The seller of labor power, like the seller of any other commodity, realizes its exchange-value, and parts with its use-value. (Ibid.)

The one way in which Marx's 'negative' derivation survived was in the claim that labor-power was the only commodity with the property of being 'a source not only of value, but of more value than it has itself.' In *Capital*

I, Marx appeared to successfully reach the conclusion that the means of production could not be a source of surplus value. However, he did so by contradicting a basic premise of his 'positive' proof, that the use-value and the exchange-value of a commodity are unrelated. Properly applied, his 'positive proof' contradicts the negative one by showing that all inputs to production are potential sources of surplus-value.

'Guilty of this or that inconsistency because of this or that compromise' In the course of his attempt to preserve the labor theory of value proposition that labor-power is the only source of surplus value, Marx advanced three propositions which fundamentally contravene his general approach to commodities: that, in the case of the means of production, the purchaser makes use of their exchange-value, not their use-value; that their use-value cannot exceed their exchange-value; and that the use-value of commodity inputs to production somehow reappears in the use-value of the commodities they help create.

Marx began with the simple assertion that the means of production can transfer no more than their exchange-value to the product. He next attempted to forge an equality between the exchange-value and the use-value of the means of production, by equating the depreciation of a machine to its productive capacity.

> Value exists only in articles of utility. If therefore an article loses its utility, it also loses its value. The reason why means of production do not lose their value, at the same time that they lose their use-value, is this: they lose in the labor process the original form of their use-value, only to assume in the product the form of a new use-value. Hence it follows that in the labor process the means of production transfer their value to the product only so far as along with their use-value they lose also their exchange-value. They give up to the product that value alone which they themselves lose as means of production. (Ibid.)

Don't worry if you found that paragraph hard to understand: it is replete with erroneous and ambiguous propositions. First, the two final sentences, which appear to link the transfer of value by the machine to its depreciation, are incorrect (see below). Secondly, the statement that the use-value of a machine reappears in the use-value of the product equates the use-value of the machine to the utility enjoyed by the 'consumers' who purchase the goods the machine produces. But the use-value of a machine is specific to the capitalist purchaser of the machine only. By arguing that the use-value of the machine reappears in the product, Marx is in fact contemplating the existence of abstract utility, with the 'usefulness' of the machinery being transmuted into the 'usefulness' of the commodities it produces. If anything, this is neoclassical economics, not Marx.

The ambiguous statement concerns the transfer of value by the means of production. Which of their two 'values' do machines transfer, their exchange-value or their use-value? If Marx meant that they transfer their use-value, then this sentence would be correct in terms of his analysis of commodities. But later he makes it clear that by this expression he meant that the means of production transfer not their use-value (which is the case with a worker) but their exchange-value. In the clearest illustration of the flaw in his logic, he states that over the life of a machine, 'its use-value has been completely consumed, and therefore its exchange-value completely transferred to the product' (ibid.: 197). This amounts to the assertion that in the case of machinery and raw materials, what is consumed by the purchaser is not their use-value, as with all other commodities, but their exchange-value.

This ambiguity reappears as Marx discusses the example of a machine which lasts only six days. He first states the correct proposition that the machine transfers its use-value to the product, but then equates this to its exchange-value. He says that if a machine lasts six days '[t]hen, on the average, it loses each day one sixth of its use-value, and therefore parts with one-sixth of its value to the daily product.' Initially he draws the correct if poorly stated inference that 'means of production never transfer more value to the product than they themselves lose during the labor-process by the destruction of their own use-value.' However, the ambiguity between exchange-value and use-value is strong, and his conclusion takes the incorrect fork. Stating his conclusion rather more succinctly than his reasoning, he says:

> The maximum loss of value that they [machines] can suffer in the process, is plainly limited by the amount of the original value with which they came into the process, or in other words, by the labor-time necessary for their production. However useful a given kind of raw material, or a machine, or other means of production may be, though it may cost £150 – yet it cannot, under any circumstances, add to the value of the product more than £150. (Ibid.)

Essentially, Marx reached the result that the means of production cannot generate surplus value by confusing depreciation, or the loss of value by a machine, with value creation. The truisms that the maximum amount of value that a machine can lose is its exchange-value, and that a machine's exchange-value will fall to zero only when its use-value has been completely exhausted, were combined to conclude that the value a machine adds in production is equivalent to the exchange-value it loses in depreciation. With the value added by a machine equated to value lost, no net value is transferred to the product, and therefore only labor can be a source of surplus value.

While the argument may appear plausible, in reality it involves a confusion of two distinct attributes of a machine: its cost (exchange-value) and its usefulness (use-value). From a Marxist perspective, depreciation is the writing-off of the original exchange-value of a machine over its productive life. Consequently, the maximum depreciation that a machine can suffer is its exchange-value. As it wears out, both its residual value and its usefulness will diminish, and both will terminate at the same time. However, it does not follow that the usefulness (the value-creating capacity) of the machine is equal to its cost (its depreciation). Though a capitalist will 'write off' the latter completely only when the former has been extinguished, the two aspects are nonetheless completely different and unrelated. There is no reason why the value lost by the machine should be equivalent to the value added.

An analogy with labor highlights the fallacy involved in equating these two magnitudes. If workers receive a subsistence wage, and if the working day exhausts the capacity to labor, then it could be argued that in a day a worker 'depreciates' by an amount equivalent to the subsistence wage – the exchange-value of labor-power. However, this depreciation is not the limit of the amount of value that can be added by a worker in a day's labor – the use-value of labor. Value added is unrelated to and greater than value lost; if it were not, there could be no surplus.

But don't take my word for it. Take Marx's.

The origin of surplus value (III)

As noted above, Marx first developed his dialectical analysis of the commodity while working on the rough draft of *Capital*. He was initially so enthused with this approach that he explored it freely, with almost no regard for how it meshed with his previous analysis. While doing this, he made a statement that correctly applied this new logic and directly contradicted the old, by stating that a machine could add more value than it lost through depreciation.

Table 1 is typical of Marx's standard numerical examples of value productivity. In that table, surplus value is directly proportional to labor-power ('variable capital'), and the value of the total product is the sum of the value of the means of production, plus variable capital, plus surplus value. In this analysis, the contribution of non-labor inputs to the value of output is exactly equal to their depreciation. However, when referring to a similar table shortly after developing his use-value/exchange-value analysis, Marx comments: 'It also has to be postulated (which was not done above) that the use-value of the machine significantly [*sic*] greater than its value; i.e. that its devaluation in the service of production is not proportional to its increasing effect on production' (Marx 1857).

There then follows the example shown in Table 17.7.

Both firms employ the same amount of variable capital – four days' labor which is paid 40 'thalers' (a unit in the German currency of the time), the value of the labor-power purchased. However, the first firm ('Capital 1'), with older capital, produces surplus value of just 10, while the second, with

TABLE 17.7 Marx's example where the use-value of machinery exceeds its depreciation

Production	Paper	Press	Working days	Wage bill	Surplus	Output	Rate SV (%)	Profit (%)
Capital 1	30	30	4	40	10	30	25.0	10.0
Capital 2	100	60	4	40	13.33	100	33.3	6.7

newer capital, produces a surplus of 13.33. The 3.33 difference in the surplus they generate is attributable to the difference in their machinery, and the fact that 'the use-value of the machine significantly greater than its value; i.e. – its devaluation in the service of production is not proportional to its increasing effect on production.'[23]

Marx without the labor theory of value

Marx's dialectical analysis thus contradicts a central tenet of the labor theory of value, that labor is the only source of surplus value. Having reached the conclusion above, Marx suddenly found himself trapped, as he had argued (in his PhD thesis) that Hegel was, in a compromise with his own principles. The principle of the dialectical analysis of the commodity was powerful, and the conclusions that followed logically from it inescapable: the labor theory of value could be true only if the use-value of a machine was exactly equal to its exchange-value, and yet a basic tenet of this analysis was that use-value and exchange-value are incommensurable.[24]

If Marx had followed his newfound logic, the labor theory of value would have been history. But with the labor theory of value gone, so too would be the tendency for the rate of profit to fall, and with it the inevitability of socialism.

The tendency for the rate of profit to fall was predicated upon the propositions that (a), over time, the capital-to-labor ratio would rise, and that (b), this would cause the rate of profit to fall. But (b) was dependent upon labor being the only source of surplus value, so that a rising capital-to-labor ratio would mean a falling rate of profit. If surplus could instead be garnered from any input to production, not just labor, then an increase in the capital-to-labor ratio would have no necessary implications for the rate of profit: it could fall, rise, or stay the same.

23 Marx's discussion of this example still attributed the increased surplus-value to labor; however, the source of this difference was not any difference in the rate of surplus value with respect to labor employed, but to the postulate that the machine's use-value exceeded its exchange-value.

24 'Exchange-value and use-value [are] intrinsically incommensurable magnitudes' (Marx 1867). Notice that Marx describes use-value as a magnitude in this circumstance. Outside production, when commodities are purchased to be consumed rather than being used to produce other commodities, their use-value will be qualitative, and therefore incommensurable with their exchange-values.

With no necessity for the rate of profit to fall, there was similarly no necessity for capitalism to give way to socialism. Yet Marx had prided himself upon being the 'scientific socialist,' the one who in contrast to 'utopian socialists,' who merely dreamed of a better world, would prove why socialism had to come about. Now he finds that his new logical tool, which is evidently so superior to his old, challenges the basis of his argument for the inevitability of socialism.

It is little wonder that Marx then tried to find a way to make his new logic appear consistent with the old. By the time of *Capital*, he had convinced himself that the two were consistent: that the new positive methodology concurred with the old on the issue of the value productivity of machinery. Marx succumbed to the same flaw that (in his PhD thesis) he once noted in Hegel:

> It is conceivable that a philosopher should be guilty of this or that inconsistency because of this or that compromise; he may himself be conscious of it. But what he is not conscious of is that in the last analysis this apparent compromise is made possible by the deficiency of his principles or an inadequate grasp of them. So if a philosopher really has compromised it is the job of his followers to use the inner core of his thought to illuminate his own superficial expression of it. In this way, what is a progress in conscience is also a progress in knowledge. This does not involve putting the conscience of the philosopher under suspicion, but rather construing the essential characteristics of his views, giving them a definite form and meaning, and thus at the same time going beyond them. (Karl Marx, 1839: notes to his doctoral dissertation, reprinted in McLellan 1971)

So Marx succeeded in compromising his theory in a way which hid 'the deficiency of his principles or an inadequate grasp of them.' But 'success' came at a cost. The new logic, of which Marx was so proud, was ignored by his successors. In part, Marx contributed to this by the obfuscation he undertook to make his positive method appear consistent with the old negative one. But I can't detract from the impressive contribution 'Marxists' themselves have made to the misinterpretation of Marx.

The misinterpretation of Marx

Though much of this occurred after his death, Marx had one taste of how his theories would be misinterpreted by friend and foe alike. He wrote a caustic commentary on the German economist Adolph Wagner's gross misinterpretation of his arguments in *Capital*, yet ironically, Wagner's hostile misinterpretation became the accepted interpretation of Marx by his followers after his death.

Wagner argued that Marx had completely misunderstood the notion of use-value, and that use-value played no part in Marx's analysis. Marx acerbically commented that:

Rodbertus had written a letter to him – where he, Rodbertus, explains why 'there is only one kind of value,' use value – Wagner says: 'This is completely correct, and necessitates an alteration in the customary illogical "division" of 'value' into use-value and exchange-value' – and this same Wagner places me among the people according to whom 'use-value' is to be completely 'dismissed' 'from science.' (Marx 1971 [1879])

Marx then made an emphatic statement of the role that use-value played in his economics:

> All this is 'driveling.' Only an obscurantist, who has not understood a word of *Capital*, can conclude: Because Marx, in a note to the first edition of *Capital*, overthrows all the German professorial twaddle on 'use-value' in general, and refers readers who want to know something about actual use-value to 'commercial guides,' – therefore, use-value does not play any role in his work. The obscurantist has overlooked that my analysis of the commodity does not stop at the dual mode in which the commodity is presented, [but] presses forward [so] that surplus value itself is derived from a 'specific' use-value of labor-power which belongs to it exclusively etc. etc., that hence with me use-value plays an important role completely different than [it did] in previous [political] economy. (Ibid.)

Marx's protestations were to no avail. Despite such a strident statement that use-value was an essential component of his analytic method, and despite the fact that this document was available to and read by early twentieth-century Marxists, use-value and the 'positive' methodology of which it was an integral part were expunged from mainstream Marxism. Paul Sweezy stated in his influential *The Theory of Capitalist Development* that

> 'Every commodity,' Marx wrote, 'has a twofold aspect, that of use-value and exchange-value.' Use-value is an expression of a certain relation between the consumer and the object consumed. Political economy, on the other hand, is a social science of the relations between people. It follows that 'use-value as such lies outside the sphere of investigation of political economy.' (Sweezy 1942, citing Marx 1859)

Yet ironically, the statement Sweezy used to support the notion that use-value plays no role in Marx's analysis was the very one referred to by Marx (in the reference to the 'first edition of *Capital*,' by which he meant the 1859 work *A Contribution to the Critique of Political Economy*), when he labeled Wagner an 'obscurantist.' In Marx's own words, therefore, twentieth-century Marxism has completely misunderstood the philosophical core of Marx's analysis of capitalism.

A poverty of philosophy Bose's critique and Marx's dialectic of the commodity establish that philosophy can't save the labor theory of value from

Steedman's critique. Philosophical analysis strengthens Steedman's case that the labor theory of value is logically flawed.

Instead, mathematics and Marx's philosophy confirm that surplus value – and hence profit – can be generated from any input to production. There is no one source of surplus: Adam Smith's apparently vague musings that animals and machines both contribute to the creation of new value were correct.

Whither Marxism?

Marxist economics is analytically far stronger once it is shorn of the labor theory of value. The use-value/exchange-value methodology, which was applied above only to the question of the source of surplus value, has application to a huge range of issues on which labor theory of value Marxism is either silent or pedestrian (see Groll 1980 and Keen 1993a, 1993b and 2000 for a discussion of some of these). Marxism becomes the pinnacle of classical economics, rather than its dead end.

However, I am as pessimistic about the chances of this 'new, improved Marxism' being adopted by today's Marxists as I am about the chances of neoclassical economists abandoning the concept of equilibrium.

Their resistance, as with neoclassical economists to the critiques outlined in this book, is due in large part to ideology.

The advantage Marxists have over economists is that at least they are upfront about having an ideology. Marxists are as consciously committed to the belief that capitalism should give way to a socialism as economists are to the often unconscious belief that, if only we could rid ourselves of government intervention in the market, we would currently reside in the best of all possible worlds.

The tendency for the rate of profit to fall is crucial to this belief in the inevitability of socialism, and it is one of the many concepts that evaporate once the labor theory of value is expunged. Marxist economists are likely to continue to cling to the labor theory of value, to hang on to the faith, in preference to embracing logic.

If my pessimism is well founded, then Marxist economics will continue its self-absorbed and impossible quest for a solution to the transformation problem, and will remain irrelevant to the future development of economics.

However, labor theory of value Marxism will continue to be the ideology of choice of the left, particularly in the Third World. The argument that labor is the only source of profit, and that capitalism is thus based upon the exploitation of the worker, is a simple, compelling analysis to the downtrodden in our obscenely unequal world. A specter may no longer be haunting Europe, but Marxism will continue to be the banner of the dispossessed for many a year to come.

However, if non-neoclassical and non-Marxist economists can ignore the hullabaloo generated by the remaining band of adherents to the labor theory of value, and instead extract from Marx his rich philosophical foundation for the analysis of capitalism, then Marx's dialectical theory of value may yet play a role in the reform of economic theory. At present, however, the various non-neoclassical schools of thought have no coherent theory of value as an alternative to the neoclassical school's flawed subjective theory of value. But even though they lack the central organizing concept of a theory of value, these alternative schools of thought contain the promise of an economic theory that may actually be relevant to the analysis and management of a capitalist economy.

18 | THERE ARE ALTERNATIVES[1]

Why there is still hope for a better economics

Maggie Thatcher's second-best-known comment, in defence of following monetarist economic policies, was 'There is NO alternative.' A similar attitude pervades economics: if not neoclassical economics, then what?

In fact, there are many alternative schools of thought within economics. In addition to Marxian economics, the main alternatives are:

- Austrian economics, which shares many of the features of neoclassical economics, save a slavish devotion to the concept of equilibrium.
- Post-Keynesian economics, which is highly critical of neoclassical economics, emphasizes the fundamental importance of uncertainty, and bases itself upon the theories of Keynes and Kalecki.
- Sraffian economics, based on Sraffa's concept of the production of commodities by means of commodities.
- Complexity theory and Econophysics, which apply concepts from nonlinear dynamics, chaos theory and physics to economic issues. And
- Evolutionary economics, which treats the economy as an evolving system along the lines of Darwin's theory of evolution.

None of these is at present strong enough or complete enough to declare itself a contender for the title of 'the' economic theory of the twenty-first century. However, they all have strengths in areas where neoclassical economics is fundamentally flawed, and there is also a substantial degree of overlap and cross-fertilization between schools. It is possible that this century could finally see the development of a dominant economic theory which actually has some relevance to the dynamics of a modern capitalist economy.

I would probably be regarded as partisan to the post-Keynesian approach. However, I can see varying degrees of merit in all five schools of thought, and I can imagine that a twenty-first-century economics could be a melange of all five.

In this chapter I give a very brief overview of each school, emphasizing the ways in which they are superior to neoclassical economics, but also noting when they share its weaknesses, or have problems of their own. This will necessarily be an inadequate survey – doing a proper survey would

---

1 This is a necessarily brief and personally opinionated survey of five very complex schools of thought. Readers who wish to delve deeper should consult the references given in this chapter. I have also omitted separate discussion of a notable school of economic thought, institutional economics, because I expect it to be subsumed under evolutionary economics.

necessitate another book. But as I commented earlier, it is essential to at least outline the alternatives, to debunk the myth that there is no alternative.

Austrian economics

The Austrian school (so called because its main early protagonists – Menger, Hayek and von Mises – were Austrian, though it is now mainly an American tradition) is a close relative of mainstream economics. It developed at much the same time, shared the same intellectual parents, and is comfortable with virtually every aspect of neoclassical economics save one: its obsession with equilibrium. This one divergence results in a theory which is markedly different from its dominant but wayward cousin.

Strengths Far from arguing that capitalism is the best social system because of the conditions which pertain in equilibrium, Austrian economists argue that capitalism is the best social system because of how it responds to disequilibrium.

The Austrians make the sensible observation that equilibrium is an intellectual abstraction which is unlikely ever to occur in the real world. All real-world economic situations will thus be disequilibrium ones, some of which enable entrepreneurs to make above-normal profits. By seeking out these profit opportunities, entrepreneurs make capitalism a dynamic, adaptive social system.

The Austrians therefore have an evolutionary perspective on capitalism, and argue that capitalism is evolutionarily superior to other social systems, such as feudalism and socialism.

The Austrians emphasize the importance of uncertainty in analyzing capitalism, whereas neoclassical economists, as we have seen, either ignore uncertainty, or trivialize it by equating it to probabilistic risk. This again gives Austrians an ideological reason to prefer capitalism to any other social system, since they argue that the disaggregated nature of capitalist society makes it more adaptable to uncertainty than other, more centralized systems.

The entrepreneur is the key actor in the Austrian vision of capitalism. It is the entrepreneur who attempts to profit from disequilibrium situations, thus innovating and adding to the diversity and strength of the capitalist system. The entrepreneurs are those who boldly act in the face of uncertainty, and though many will fail, some will succeed – thus strengthening the economic system via an evolutionary process.

The Austrians thus demonstrate that the economic fixation with equilibrium is unnecessary: it is possible to be an ideological supporter of capitalism even if you believe that equilibrium is irrelevant.

However, as a near-relative of neoclassical economics, this school shares a number of its disabilities.

Weaknesses First, the Austrians accept the economic argument that production is characterized by diminishing returns. As a corollary of this, they also accept the marginal productivity theory of income distribution – though they temper this by arguing that disequilibrium allows for entrepreneurs to make supernormal profits.

As was shown in Chapters 3, 5 and 6, these economic notions are fundamentally unsound. To the extent that Austrian economics relies upon these same concepts, it is also unsound.

A simple illustration of this arises from the Austrian theory of production. The economic model argues that an increase in the quantity of a factor of production – such as capital – will decrease its marginal product, and thus reduce its income.

The Austrians instead argue that a cheapening of capital – via a fall in the rate of interest – will lead to a more 'roundabout' approach to production, meaning that less direct labor and more indirect capital will be applied to its production.

Sraffa's critique of the neoclassical theory of production, detailed in Chapter 6, is equally applicable to this Austrian theory. By providing a way to measure capital inputs in terms of wage units, Sraffa showed that the economic concept of a quantity of capital was dependent on the rate of profit: the same logic shows that it is impossible to define one way of producing a commodity as 'more roundabout' than another independently of the rate of profit.

Consider two ways of making wine: process A, which involves the application of 1 wage unit now, 8 units last year, and 1 unit 8 years earlier; and process B, which involves 1 unit now and 1 unit 20 years ago. At a low rate of profit, process A might be more roundabout than process B; at a higher rate of profit, the order could reverse; and it could reverse again for a higher rate of profit. Therefore, the Austrian notion of roundaboutness is as internally inconsistent as the neoclassical concept of the marginal productivity of capital.

Secondly, even more so than conventional economics, Austrian economics has a faith in the self-adjusting properties of the capitalist economy, with Say's Law providing much of that confidence. As was argued in Chapter 9, Say's Law is invalid in a production economy with growth.

Thirdly, while it is in general an evolutionary approach to economics, at least one branch of Austrian economics, associated with Murray Rothbard, has a quite non-evolutionary attitude towards both the existence of the state and the role of money. The market economy may have evolved, but it seems the state was simply imposed from outside as an alien artifact upon our landscape. This is certainly one way to consider the growth of the welfare state; but an equally tenable argument is that the welfare state evolved as a response to the failures of the pure market system during the Great Depression.

Similarly, while they believe that the money supply should be determined endogenously – by either handing over money creation to private banks, or by returning to the gold standard – they argue that the current system of state money means that the money supply is entirely exogenous, and under the control of the state authorities. They then attribute much of the cyclical behavior of the economy to government meddling with the money supply and the rate of interest.

The post-Keynesian school, on the other hand, argues that though it may appear that the state controls the money supply, the complex chain of causation in the finance sector actually works backwards. Rather than the state directly controlling the money supply via its control over the issue of new currency and the extent to which it lets banks leverage their holdings of currency, private banks and other credit-generating institutions largely force the state's hand. Thus the money supply is largely endogenously determined by the market economy, rather than imposed upon it exogenously by the state.

The empirical record certainly supports post-Keynesians rather than Austrians on this point. Statistical evidence about the leads and lags between the state-determined component of money supply and broad credit shows that the latter 'leads' the former (Kydland and Prescott 1990). If the Austrians were correct, state money creation would instead precede private credit creation.

Maggie Thatcher's embrace of monetarism also provides an evocative counter-example. Despite her toughness, and her adherence to Milton Friedman's mantra that controlling the money supply would control inflation, even Thatcher's England was forced to abandon monetary targeting – setting some goal for the rate of growth of the money supply in order to force down the rate of inflation – because it could never meet the targets. If the 'Iron Lady' couldn't control the money supply, then no one could: evidence enough that the post-Keynesians are closer to the mark than the Austrians.

This non-evolutionary weakness in Austrian economics is a sign of a wider problem. The philosopher Chris Sciabarra, a specialist on the Austrian school and Ayn Rand, identifies an inconsistency between Hayek's notion of 'spontaneous order' – which corresponds to evolutionary development – and 'designed order' – where change is imposed from outside the market by the state. While such a distinction makes for good polemic writing against state intervention, it ignores the extent to which the state's own behavior might be reactive to the market, and thus, to some extent, also a form of spontaneous order. As Sciabarra puts it:

> There are more fundamental problems with Hayek's social theory. By positing such a sharp distinction between spontaneous order and designed order, Hayek has not provided us with any explanation of the emergence of those institutions which are agents of constructivism [designed order]. To what extent is the state itself a spontaneous, emergent product of social evolution?

To what extent does the state define the parameters of the extended order which Hayek celebrates? What are the actual interrelationships between the spontaneous order of the market and the designed institutions of the state? The reader of Hayek's works will strain to find developed answers to any of these important questions. (Sciabarra 1995)

Finally, though Austrians eschew equilibrium analysis, and regard it as an unattainable state, their preference for capitalism as a social system is partly dependent on the belief that it will remain close to equilibrium. If, instead, capitalism is endogenously unstable, then it may remain substantially distant from equilibrium situations all the time. This weakens Austrian economics, to the extent that its support for capitalism emanates from conditions which are assumed to apply in equilibrium.

The Austrian scorecard Overall, I regard the Austrian school as too close to its neoclassical cousin to make a major contribution to a reformed economics. However, it does have some contributions to make, and for ideological reasons it is likely to be far stronger in the future – regardless of what I or other non-orthodox economists might think of it.

The Austrian emphasis upon innovation, and the role of the entrepreneur, are valid concepts which capture the way in which a market economy adapts. This aspect of capitalism is to some extent underrated by the other non-neoclassical schools, except for evolutionary economics. This aspect of Austrian thought could be valuable to a reformed twenty-first-century economics.

However, it is far more likely that the 'pure and simple' Rothbardian stream of Austrian economics will play a large role in twenty-first-century economics. This is because the Rothbardian approach provides an alternative way to ideologically support a capitalist economy as the best possible social system, whereas all other non-orthodox schools are to some degree critical of the concept of unfettered capitalism. If neoclassical economics becomes untenable for any reason, the Austrians are well placed to provide an alternative religion for believers in the primacy of the market over all other forms of social organization.

The one barrier which stands in the way of today's neoclassical economist transmuting into tomorrow's Austrian is the Austrian insistence that there is little, if any, role for mathematics in economic analysis. Because the Austrians believe that all real-world data are generated in a situation of disequilibrium, and because they take seriously the aggregation problems noted in Chapters 2 and 4, Austrians deny that mathematical aggregate analysis has any validity. Faced with a choice between ideology and their beloved equilibrium mathematics, most economists would probably prefer to keep the mathematics. The one way out for neoclassicals would be to embrace the Austrian celebration of capitalism as a dynamic, disequilibrium system, and then model this using chaos and complexity theory. But this leads to the dilemma that such models almost always display 'far from equilibrium' behavior, which undermines the validity of beliefs about capitalism and welfare that depend on the economy not straying too far from equilibrium.

Post-Keynesian economics

This school of thought developed in reaction to the 'bastardization' of Keynes's economics in the so-called Keynesian–neoclassical synthesis. Regarding themselves as the true carriers of Keynes's message, they emphasized the importance of uncertainty in economic analysis, and the profound difference between the monetary economy in which we live, and the barter economy which neoclassical economics regards as an adequate proxy for the real world. As Arestis et al. (1999) put it, the main unifying themes in post-Keynesian economics are 'a concern for history, uncertainty, distributional issues, and the importance of political and economic institutions in determining the level of activity in an economy.'

Strengths The emphasis upon uncertainty as a fundamental aspect of the real world – one which cannot be approximated by risk – makes the post-Keynesian approach to economics far more realistic than the neoclassical.

Realism, in fact, is a central methodological emphasis of this school. Though there is no agreed post-Keynesian methodology to rival the hedonistic calculus of the neoclassicals, post-Keynesians are united by their belief that an economic model has to be realistic.

One essential aspect of this is the insistence that a monetary economy is fundamentally different from one in which commodities simply exchange against other commodities. The issues of credit creation, the nature of money, the role of debt, etc., are far more pressing to post-Keynesians than they are to neoclassicals.

Macroeconomics is also a far more important concern. In fact, post-Keynesians reverse the neoclassical pecking order, to argue that whatever microeconomics is developed must be consistent with the observed behavior of the macroeconomy. A microeconomic model which is inconsistent with such things as business cycles, sustained unemployment, commonplace excess capacity, and the importance of credit is to post-Keynesians an invalid model.

Their preferred model of the firm emphasizes monopoly and quasi-monopoly power, decreasing costs of production with increased scale, markup pricing, the competitive need to sustain excess capacity, and the link between macroeconomic conditions and the firm's investment decisions.

Post-Keynesians are also not hung up on the need to show whether capitalism is a better or worse social system than any other. They are relatively agnostic on the question of what might constitute a better society.

This comparative independence from ideology means that post-Keynesians do not feel compelled, as neoclassicals do, to show that capitalism generates the best welfare outcome for the majority of the people. They are therefore much more comfortable with acknowledging the existence of social class in their models – something which leading neoclassical economists admit they might have to consider, given the failure of their individualistic approach to explain human behavior.

Weaknesses One of this school's great strengths is also a weakness. Unlike the neoclassical or Marxian schools, they do not have a 'theory of value' – they have nothing to compare to the theory of utility maximization, or even the labor theory of value.

This is certainly a strength when one considers how these theories of value have led these rival schools up intellectual garden paths. However, at the same time it means that post-Keynesians lack a methodological consistency: they are more united by what they oppose than by what they have in common – though there are many common threads.

This lack of a theory of value makes it difficult for post-Keynesians to explain why their approach is superior to fledgling students of economics, who have yet to confront any of the intellectual conundrums which afflict neoclassical economics (and they also have difficulty communicating with radical students who are attracted to Marxism). One must normally become disenchanted with mainstream or Marxian economics before one can become a post-Keynesian. That is perhaps too tortuous a path to rely upon, if this school ever hopes to gain the ascendancy in economics.

A final problem is that, despite their rejection of neoclassical economics, they tend to also use static logic in their analysis – even though their building blocks might be, for instance, markup pricing rather than 'marginal cost equals marginal revenue.' This lack of appreciation of how different dynamic analysis is from static is not universal among post-Keynesian authors, but it is widespread enough to be a problem. However, it must be said that younger members of the post-Keynesian school are much more comfortable with dynamic analysis than are some of its older members.

The post-Keynesian scorecard Despite the lack of an agreed methodological foundation, the post-Keynesians are easily the most coherent alternative school of economic thought today. They are also likely to gain substantial credence in the event of a financial crisis, given their explicitly monetary approach to economics.

Sraffian economics

No prizes for guessing which economist provided the major inspiration to this particular group of economists. Sraffa's *Production of Commodities* by *Means of Commodities* became the icon for these economists. As well as applying it to critique other schools – notably neoclassical economics and Marxism – they attempted to turn it into a means to analyze the real economy.

Strengths There is no doubt that Sraffa's analysis constituted the most detailed and careful analysis of the mechanics of production in the history of economics. Not for him any simple abstractions, such as the neoclassicals' 'factors of production,' or even Marx's 'industry sectors': his model analyzed the interrelations of production at the level of the individual commodity.

This study turned up many subtleties that escaped other schools of economics: the dependence of the 'quantity of capital' on the profit rate, rather than vice versa, the phenomenon of reswitching, etc. No other school of economics matches the Sraffians on this insistence of assumption-free rigor. Well, almost assumption-free rigor.

Weaknesses The one assumption Sraffians do make is that the economy can be analyzed using static tools. As a result, even though the proper treatment of time was an essential component of Sraffa's critique of neoclassical economics, modern Sraffian economics makes no use of time or dynamics. Ian Steedman gave the pithiest explanation of why Sraffians analysis ignores dynamics. It is because '"static" analysis does not "ignore" time. To the contrary, that analysis allows enough time for changes in prime costs, markups, etc., to have their full effects' (Steedman 1992).

This proposition can be true only if the long-run position of an economy is an equilibrium one: if, in other words, the economy has just one equilibrium, and it is stable. As Chapter 9 showed, this is highly unlikely to be the case. A market economy is likely to have multiple equilibria, and they are all likely to be unstable. The Sraffian position is thus ignorant of modern dynamic analysis.

Sraffians also have one other flaw: they pay too little attention to Piero Sraffa.

Some post-Keynesians are fond of pointing out how pedantic Sraffa was, and therefore how important was the subtitle to his magnum opus. Sitting beneath the title of *The Production of Commodities by Means of Commodities* was the caveat 'Prelude to a critique of economic theory.'

In other words, these economists argue that Sraffa's method was intended solely to provide a means to critique other economic theories: it was never meant to provide a basis for an economic theory in itself.

Sraffa's 1926 paper provides support for this position. When discussing how the firm should be modeled, Sraffa put great stress upon the issues of importance to 'business men': the necessity and expense of marketing a non-homogeneous product to a market of non-homogeneous consumers, the cost and dangers of credit as a major force limiting firm size, etc. The concepts Sraffa discusses here can be considered only with extreme difficulty in the framework of his 1960 book (check the web link Alternatives/Sraffa for a relevant extract from Sraffa's 1926 paper).

The Sraffian scorecard Though the Sraffian school was fairly influential up until 2000, there have been few developments in it since, certainly in comparison to the growth in post-Keynesian economics since that date.

Complexity theory and Econophysics

Complexity theory is not so much a school of thought in economics as a group of economists who apply what is popularly known as 'chaos theory' to economic issues. Since the first edition of this book, there has also been an enormous growth in the number of physicists taking an active interest in economics and finance, and this new school of 'Econophysics' has largely subsumed the complexity theory approach.

The concept of chaos itself was first discovered in 1899 by the French mathematician Henri Poincaré. However, knowledge of it languished until the mid-1960s because it could not be fully explored until after the invention of computers. Chaotic models of necessity cannot be understood simply by writing down the equations which represent them: instead, they must be simulated, and their properties analyzed numerically. This was simply not possible before the advent of computers.

An essential aspect of complexity is the existence of nonlinear relationships between elements of a system, and the apparent ability of complex systems to 'self-organize.' The Lorenz model, noted in Chapter 8, has both these attributes: the nonlinear relations between displacement and temperature lead to behavior which on the surface is 'chaotic,' but behind which lies the beautiful organizing force of Lorenz's 'strange attractor.' Complexity theorists argue that the economy demonstrates similar attributes, and these are what give rise to the cycles which are a self-evident aspect of real-world economies.

Econophysics substantially adds to the contribution made by the early proponents of complexity in economics – such as Richard Goodwin (Goodwin 1990, 1991), Benoit Mandelbrot (Mandelbrot 1971, 2005), Hans-Walter Lorenz (Lorenz 1987a, 1987b, 1989), Paul Ormerod (Ormerod 1997, 2001, 2004); Ormerod and Heineike (2009), Carl Chiarella (Chiarella and Flaschel 2000, Chiarella, Dieci et al. 2002, Chiarella et al. 2003) and myself, among many others – by bringing both the techniques and the empirical mindset of physicists to bear upon economic data.

Over the last century, physicists have developed a vast array of techniques to interpret the equally vast range of physical processes encountered in everything from fluid dynamics to the behavior of subatomic particles. Their approach has been fundamentally empirical, and devoid of any a priori assumption that physical processes occur in equilibrium – and the concept of equilibrium itself is far more richly specified.

These techniques have enabled Econophysicists to make substantial progress in understanding how finance markets in particular actually operate, with a range of models that accurately capture the 'fat tails' that bedevil asset price data and lie well outside the predictive capacity of neoclassically inspired models.

Strengths It is extremely difficult to work in complexity theory and not understand dynamics. Though some neoclassical dabblers occasionally attempt to use equilibrium thinking in so-called chaotic models, in the main practitioners in this camp are extremely well versed in dynamics.

They are also normally very competent in mathematics; far more so, not only than other alternative schools of economics, but also than most neoclassicals. Many complexity theorists in economics started out doing PhDs in physics, biology, or mathematics itself, and later delve into economics out of curiosity.

This alone has meant that complexity theorists have had a significant impact upon the profession. While they rarely indulge in direct attacks upon neoclassical economics per se, neoclassical economists are aware that they are quite capable of doing so if provoked. This technical superiority over neoclassical economists has taken the mathematical 'big stick' out of the hands of neoclassicals. This has been taken to another level by Econophysicists, whose training in mathematics and computing is far more rigorous and extensive than that undertaken by economists.

Weaknesses Though many complexity economists are inclined to a post-Keynesian perspective on economics, in general they lack a full appreciation of the history of economic thought. For this reason, they will often generate models which combine incompatible streams in economics. Concepts such as IS-LM and rational expectations often crop up in complexity or Econophysics models of the economy, with the authors rarely being aware of the origins of these 'tools.'

While Econophysics has developed a very rich and empirically based analysis of financial markets to date, and their statistical analysis here – involving concepts like Power Law distributions and Tsallis-statistics – is far more accurate than neoclassical models, success here has led to neglect of the 'econo' part of the developing discipline's name: at present it could more accurately be called 'Finaphysics' than 'Econophysics.'

Econophysicists also occasionally succumb to the temptation to introduce one of the strongest weapons in their arsenal, which I believe has no place in economics: 'conservation laws.' These apply where some fundamental aspect of a system – such as, for example, the amount of mass and energy in the universe – is not altered by the physical processes that apply to it, though its distribution and nature may alter. This condition that 'the change in the amount of X equals zero' has been the source of many of the greatest advances in physics, including the derivation of the theory of relativity.

No such equivalent concepts exist in economics, which is more akin to biology than physics in this respect: biological populations fluctuate, and there is no law requiring the mass of biological entities to remain constant, for example. Consequently economics belongs to the class of dynamical systems known as 'dissipative,' rather than 'conservative.'

A concern that conservation laws were being introduced into areas where they did not belong – for example, the analysis of money (Patriarca, Chakraborti et al. 2004; Ding, Xi et al. 2006) or the distribution of wealth – led me to contribute to a paper that was critical of recent developments in Econophysics (Gallegati, Keen et al. 2006). However, over time I expect developments like these to dissipate, given the innately empirical focus of physicists.

The complexity scorecard Complexity theory and Econophysics are among the 'glamour' areas of science in general today, and this affects economics, even given its relative isolation from the scientific mainstream. The techniques which complexity modelers in economics employ are thus 'refertilizing' economics with concepts from other disciplines. The economic fixation upon equilibrium appears quaint to these mathematically literate economists, and this alone may significantly undermine the hold which static thinking has on economics.

If statics were to die, then inevitably so too would neoclassical economics, since its way of thinking is unsustainable in dynamics. So Econophysics may be a harbinger of real change in economics, after sixty years of effective ossification.

Evolutionary economics

Evolutionary economics draws its inspiration from the theory of evolution. In this, it has much in common with the majority of physical sciences, which in recent years have started to apply the concept of evolution – so much so that it has been proposed that Darwinism is the 'universal' basis of science (Nightingale 2000).[2]

In all sciences, the basic building blocks of the evolutionary way of thinking are diversity, the environment, and adaptation. Diversity gives a range of possible 'solutions' to the challenges thrown up by the environment. The environment interacts with these diverse forms to favor some over others –

2 Though evolutionary theorists themselves now argue that Darwin's vision of the evolutionary process, in which 'nature did not make jumps,' is flawed, and that therefore Darwinism is an inappropriate label for modern evolutionary theory (Schwartz 2000).

and the environment itself may be altered by feedback between it and these newly emergent species (Levins and Lewontin 1986). Adaptation occurs at the systemic level through the differential survival of some of these diverse forms: while some die out, others prosper, and thus their characteristics are passed on more strongly to subsequent generations.

The economic equivalents of diversity are the heterogeneity of consumers, and the variety of commodities; the equivalents of adaptation are new product development, and the consequent endogenous alteration of consumer tastes; the equivalent of the environment is the economy itself, which is endogenously created by the actions of myriad individuals, social groups and corporations.

Strengths It is undeniable that the economy is an evolutionary system – with the one embellishment that change in economics is often purposeful, as opposed to the random nature of variation in the environment (though of course, purposive change can fail to achieve its intended ends).[3] This self-evident fact was the basis for Thorstein Veblen's query, over a century ago, of 'Why is economics not an evolutionary science?'

Manifestly it should be, and this alone should be a major factor in the rise of evolutionary thinking in economics.

Weaknesses One problem with evolutionary systems is that, effectively, every-thing can change. Economists, on the other hand, have been wedded to the notion of '*ceteris paribus*' ('all other things remaining equal') as a way of being able to impose some order on the apparent chaos of the market.

Ceteris paribus is of course an illusion, but the illusion often seems prefer-able to reality when it appears that fully acknowledging reality forces one to abandon structure.

This, of course, is not correct: evolutionary modeling still has structure, as shown by the advances made in genetics and many other areas where evolutionary thinking rules. However, economists are thrown back upon analogy here, since in economic systems there is no comparable entity to the gene, nor to the processes of biological interaction.

The difficulty evolutionary economists face is developing analytic tools which are consistent with evolution, and yet which still enable meaning-ful statements to be made about economic issues. Generally these have to include computer simulation, but unfortunately economists receive no training in computer programming. Fortunately, many students arrive at university with these skills already, and programming tools for evolutionary modeling – such as NetLogo (ccl.northwestern.edu/netlogo/) and Repast (repast.sourceforge.net/) – are far more accessible than their predecessors of even a decade ago.

3 And, ironically, some evolutionary theorists are now arguing that biological evolution may in some ways be purposive (McFadden 2001).

The evolutionary scorecard Evolutionary economics is still in its infancy, and a lot of its time is spent defining basic philosophical concepts at one extreme, and developing computer-based evolutionary economic models at the other. If it can coalesce into a coherent school of thought with effective analytic tools, then it could at last make economics what, one century ago, Veblen knew it should be: an evolutionary science.

W(h)ither economics?

We are now well into the economic crisis that I anticipated in the first edition of this book in 2000, and which I (and a handful of other non-neoclassical economists) had actively warned of since late 2005. The public backlash against neoclassical economics that I expected this would cause has also occurred, with one-time supporters like *The Times* of London's economic columnist Anatole Kaletsky now openly attacking it:

> These are just a few examples of the creative thinking that has started again in economics after 20 years of stagnation. But the academic establishment, discredited though it is by the present crisis, will fight hard against new ideas. The outcome of this battle does not just matter to academic econo-mists. Without a better understanding of economics, financial crises will keep recurring and faith in capitalism and free markets will surely erode. Changes in regulation are not sufficient after this financial crisis – it is time for a revolution in economic thought. (Kaletsky 2009)

Now that the need for 'a revolution in economic thought' is more widely acknowledged, the question is, how to achieve it?

I have no faith in the capacity of academic economics to reform itself. The historic record on this front is evidence enough: Keynes's challenge was assimilated and emasculated within a year of it being made by Hicks's IS-LM misinterpretation, and within thirty years all semblance of the change Keynes wished to cause had been eliminated. The misinterpretation of Fisher's debt-deflation hypothesis dismembered the one other substantive challenge to the neoclassical equilibrium, non-monetary mindset. Conse-quently, the neoclassical orthodoxy that dominated academic economics prior to this crisis was even more extreme, virulent and intolerant of alternative approaches than that which Keynes and Fisher tried to challenge during the Great Depression.

Though there have been some signs of contrition and realization that the core of neoclassical economics may not be the perfect jewel they once believed it was, the overwhelming reaction of neoclassical economists to this crisis has been to maintain business as usual. I attended the 2011 American Economic Association meeting in Denver this year, at which there was a session on 'the 50th Anniversary of Rational Expectations.' What should have been a wake was in fact a celebration, and when one of its proponents was asked what economics would be like in fifty years, he was adamant that 'rational expectations' would still be at the heart of macroeconomic modeling.

Not if I can help it. If that fate does eventuate, then there will be another financial crisis right around the corner, and another rebel will have to try to bring about real change where I – and my colleagues in reform Edward Fullbrook, Paul Ormerod, Michael Hudson and many others – will have failed.

Change, if it is to come now rather than later, will have to be driven by outside influences: by journalists and influential commentators like Kaletsky who now realize how barren the neoclassical approach is; by a public far better informed via the Internet about the weaknesses of conventional economic thinking than was the public of the 1930s; by intellectuals from other disciplines who have long questioned the merits of neoclassical theory and can no longer be rebuffed when the global economy wallows in a crisis that neoclassical economics completely failed to anticipate; and by new students who, again via the Internet, now know that there are other ways to think about economics.

There are some encouraging signs today, though only time will tell if these lead to the change that economics desperately needs:

- The PAECON ('Protest against Autistic ECONomics') movement that began in France with the rebellion of a group of young economics students has since spawned an international movement, with both a network that unites the many academic opponents of neoclassical economics (www. paecon.net/PAEmovementindex1.htm), a publicly accessible journal, the *Real-World Economics Review* (www.paecon.net/PAEReview/), and an active blog (rwer.wordpress.com/).
- George Soros has put some of his substantial wealth behind the Institute for New Economic Thinking (INET, ineteconomics.org/), in an effort to redress the effective exclusion of non-neoclassical researchers from official funding channels like, to be parochial, the Australian Research Council (which, to be personal, has turned down my applications for funding to develop models of debt deflation nine times since 1996).
- The 'blogosphere,' a phenomenon that has arisen since the first edition of *Debunking Economics* was published, now allows a plethora of commentators to take pot-shots at conventional thinking on economics. I list my favorites (in no particular order) below; while I don't agree with everything published by these commentators, I agree with a lot, and they are doing serious good in letting people know that economics need serious reform:

  - Yves Smith at *Naked Capitalism*: www.nakedcapitalism.com/
  - David Hirst at *Planet Wall Street* (website currently not available)
  - Dan Denning at www.dailyreckoning.com.au/author/dan/
  - Max Keiser at *The Keiser Report*: maxkeiser.com/

- Mish Shedlock at *MISH'S Global Economic Trend Analysis*: global economicanalysis.blogspot.com/
- Chris Martenson: www.chrismartenson.com/
- Doug Noland at *The PrudentBear*: www.prudentbear.com/index.php/ commentary/creditbubblebulletin
- Harry Dent at www.hsdent.com/
- Edward Harrison at *Credit Writedowns*: www.creditwritedowns.com/
- *Zero Hedge*: www.zerohedge.com/
- *The Automatic Earth*: theautomaticearth.blogspot.com/
- *The Levy Institute*'s program: www.levyinstitute.org/ and its blog *The Multiplier Effect*: www.multiplier-effect.org/
- The University of Missouri Kansas City Economics Department's blog *New Economic Perspectives*: neweconomicperspectives.blogspot.com/
- The *Institute for New Economic Thinking*'s (ineteconomics.org/) blog *The Money View*: ineteconomics.org/blog
- Bill Mitchell's *Billy Blog*: bilbo.economicoutlook.net/blog/
- Michael Hudson – one of the Bezemer 12 who foresaw and warned of the 2007 financial crisis, and a leading contributor to the academic literature on the origins on money – at michael-hudson.com/
- And my own *Steve Keen's Debtwatch*: www.debtdeflation.com/blogs/

Much more than this is needed, however.

Within universities, I would like to see other departments start to offer courses on economics using their methodologies, rather than that of neoclassical economics. Here I believe it is possible to use the ideology of neoclassical economics against it. Neoclassical economists are vehement opponents of monopolies, and yet in the past economics departments have jealously and destructively protected their monopoly on the word 'economics.' However, the empirical failure of neoclassical economics in predicting the Great Recession, and the paucity of alternative approaches within economics departments, is a good reason to remove this monopoly from them. I would be especially pleased to see engineering departments start to offer courses on a Systems Engineering Approach to Economics.

New students of economics can also do their bit. Don't let lecturers get away with teaching the same old stuff during the Great Recession that they taught before. Challenge them about why they exclude money and debt from their macro models, why they pretend to model dynamic processes using comparative statics, and so on. Make a nuisance of yourself – and organize with your fellow students to get a voice in designing the curriculum. This is how I began on my path thirty-eight years ago, and it is even more necessary now than it was then – and fortunately, there are much better resources to guide you about what an alternative curriculum should include.

Go beyond the standard curriculum too, to learn the skills you will need to be a twenty-first-century economist, rather than a not-yet-extinct fossil from the nineteenth century. Do basic courses in mathematics (calculus, algebra and differential equations), computer programming, history and sociology, rather than the additional fare neoclassical economists prescribe. If you're really lucky, and you have an engineering department that teaches system dynamics (see en.wikipedia.org/wiki/System_dynamics), do those courses. Download and become familiar with programs like QED (www.debtdefla-tion.com/blogs/qed/), Vensim (vensim.com/), NetLogo, and build your own dynamic models, working from the leads I've given in this book.

Ultimately, I have faith in humanity's ultimate capacity to develop a realistic theoretical perspective on how a complex monetary market economy functions, and to leave behind the neat, plausible and wrong creation that is neoclassical economics.

Whether my faith on this front proves justified or delusional is not up to me, but to you.

BIBLIOGRAPHY

60 Minutes (2008) 'Chat: Professor Steve Keen,' sixtyminutes.ninemsn.com.au/webchats/643288/chat-professor-steve-keen.

7.30 Report (2007) 'Web extra: extended interview with Assoc. Prof. Steve Keen,' www.abc.net.au/7.30/content/2007/s2006034.htm.

Albert, D. Z. (1992) *Quantum Mechanics and Experience*, Cambridge, MA: Harvard University Press.

— (1994) 'Bohm's alternative to quantum mechanics,' *Scientific American*, 270(5): 32–9.

American Review of Political Economy (2011), www.arpejournal.com, forthcoming.

Anderson, P. W. (1972) 'More is different,' *Science*, 177(4047): 393–6.

Arestis, P., S. P. Dunn and M. Sawyer (1999) 'Post Keynesian economics and its critics,' *Journal of Post Keynesian Economics*, 21: 527–49.

Arrow, K. J., M. D. Intriligator et al. (1982) *Handbook of Mathematical Economics*, Amsterdam: Elsevier.

Baird, W. C. (1981) *Elements of Macroeconomics*, New York: West St Paul.

Ballard, D. H. (2000) *An Introduction to Natural Computation*, Cambridge, MA: MIT Press.

Barber, W. J. (ed.) (1997) *The Works of Irving Fisher*, London: Pickering and Chatto.

Barbier, E. B. (ed.) (1993) *Economics and Ecology*, London: Chapman & Hall.

Barnett, W. (1999) 'A single-blind controlled competition among tests for nonlinearity and chaos,' *Journal of Econometrics*, 82: 157–92.

Barnett, W. A. (1979) 'Theoretical foundations for the Rotterdam model,' *Review of Economic Studies*, 46: 109–30.

Barnett, W. A., C. Chiarella, S. Keen, R. Marks and H. Schnabl (eds) (2000) *Commerce, Complexity and Evolution*, New York: Cambridge University Press.

Barr, J. M., T. Tassier et al. (2008) 'Symposium on agent-based computational economics: introduction,' *Eastern Economic Journal*, 34(4): 421–2.

Battalio, R. C., J. H. Kagel, R. C. Winkler, E. B. Fisher, R. L. Bassmann and L. Krasner (1977) 'A test of consumer demand theory using observations of individual consumer purchases,' *Western Economic Journal*, 11: 411–28.

Bell, D. and I. Kristol (1981) *The Crisis in Economic Theory*, New York: Basic Books.

Bentham, J. (1787) *In Defence of Usury*, socserv2.socsci.mcmaster.ca:80/~econ/ugcm/3ll3/bentham/usury.

— (1948 [1780]) *The Principles of Morals and Legislation*, New York: Hafner Press.

Bernanke, B. S. (2000) *Essays on the Great Depression*, Princeton, NJ: Princeton University Press.

— (2002a) *Deflation: Making Sure 'It' Doesn't Happen Here*, Washington, DC: Federal Reserve Board.

— (2002b) 'Remarks by Governor Ben S. Bernanke at the Conference to Honor Milton Friedman,' *Conference to Honor Milton Friedman*, Chicago, IL: University of Chicago.

— (2004a) 'Panel discussion: what have we learned since October 1979?' *Conference on Reflections on Monetary Policy 25 Years after October 1979*, St Louis, MI: Federal Reserve Bank of St Louis.

— (2004b) 'The Great Moderation: remarks by Governor Ben S. Bernanke at the meetings of the Eastern Economic Association, Washington, DC, February 20, 2004,' *Eastern Economic Association*, Washington, DC: Federal Reserve Board.

— (2010) 'On the implications of the financial crisis for economics,' *Conference Co-sponsored by the Center for Economic Policy Studies and the Bendheim Center for Finance, Princeton University*, Princeton, NJ: US Federal Reserve.

Bernanke, B. S. and M. Gertler (1989) 'Agency costs, net worth and business fluctuations,' *American Economic Review*, 79: 14–31.

Besley, T. and P. Hennessy (2009) *Letter to Her Majesty the Queen about the 'The Global Financial Crisis – Why Didn't Anybody Notice?'* London: London School of Economics.

Bezemer, D. J. (2009) *'No One Saw This Coming': Understanding Financial Crisis through Accounting Models*, Groningen: Faculty of Economics, University of Groningen.

— (2010) 'Understanding financial crisis through accounting models,' *Accounting, Organizations and Society*, 35(7): 676–88.

— (2011) 'The credit crisis and recession as a paradigm test,' *Journal of Economic Issues*, 45: 1–18.

Bhaduri, A. (1969) 'On the significance of recent

controversies in capital theory: a Marxian view,' *Economic Journal*, 79: 532–9.

Bharadwaj, K. and B. Schefold (eds) (1990) *Essays on Pierro Sraffa: Critical Perspectives on the Revival of Classical Theory*, London: Unwin Hyman.

Biggs, M., T. Mayer et al. (2010) 'Credit and economic recovery: demystifying phoenix miracles,' SSRN eLibrary.

Bishop, R. L. (1948) 'Cost discontinuities, declining costs and marginal analysis,' *American Economic Review*, 38: 607–17.

Black, W. K. (2005a) '"Control frauds" as financial super-predators: how "pathogens" make financial markets inefficient,' *Journal of Socio-Economics*, 34(6): 734–55.

— (2005b) *The Best Way to Rob a Bank Is to Own One: How Corporate Executives and Politicians Looted the S&L Industry*, Austin: University of Texas Press.

Blanchard, O. J. (2008) 'The state of macro,' SSRN eLibrary.

— (2009) 'The state of macro,' *Annual Review of Economics*, 1(1): 209–28.

Blatt, J. M. (1983) *Dynamic Economic Systems: A post-Keynesian approach*, Armonk, NY: M. E. Sharpe.

Blaug, M. (1998) 'Disturbing currents in modern economics,' *Challenge!*, 41(3): 11–34.

Blinder, A. S. (1982) 'Inventories and sticky prices: more on the microfoundations of macroeconomics,' *American Economic Review*, 72(3): 334–48.

— (1998) *Asking about Prices: A new approach to understanding price stickiness*, New York: Russell Sage Foundation.

Blodget, H. (2010) '10 Years after NASDAQ 5000,' finance.yahoo.com/tech-ticker/article/440898/10-Years-After-NASDAQ-5000,-Henry-Blodget-Reflects.

Böhm-Bawerk, E. (1949 [1896]) *Karl Marx and the Close of His System*, ed. P. Sweezy, New York: Orion Editions.

Bond, N. W. (2000) 'Psychology: a science of many faces,' in N. W. Bond and K. M. McConkey (eds), *An Introduction to Psychological Science*, Sydney: McGraw-Hill.

Bose, A. (1980) *Marx on Exploitation and Inequality*, Delhi: Oxford University Press.

Bowles, H. and S. Gintis (1993) 'The revenge of Homo Economicus: contested exchange and the revival of political economy,' *Journal of Economic Perspectives*, 7(1): 83–102.

Boyd, I. and J. M. Blatt (1988) *Investment Confidence and Business Cycles*, Berlin: Springer.

Braun, M. (1993) *Differential Equations and Their Applications*, New York: Springer-Verlag.

Caldwell, B. (ed.) (1984) *Appraisal and Criticism in Economics: A Book of Readings*, London: Allen & Unwin.

Caldwell, B. J. and S. Boehm (eds) (1992) *Austrian Economics: Tensions and New Directions*, Boston, MA: Kluwer Academic.

Caplan, B. (2000) 'Rational irrationality: a framework for the neoclassical-behavioral debate,' *Eastern Economic Journal*, 26: 191–212.

Carpenter, S. B. and S. Demiralp (2010) *Money, Reserves, and the Transmission of Monetary Policy: Does the Money Multiplier Exist?*, Finance and Economics Discussion Series, Washington, DC: Federal Reserve Board.

Carter, J. R. and M. D. Irons (1991) 'Are economists different, and if so, why?' *Journal of Economic Perspectives*, 5(2): 171–7.

Chiarella, C. et al. (2003) 'Asset price dynamics among heterogeneous interacting agents,' *Computational Economics*, 22(2/3): 213–23.

Chiarella, C. and P. Flaschel (2000) *The Dynamics of Keynesian Monetary Growth*, Cambridge: Cambridge University Press.

Chiarella, C., R. Dieci et al. (2002) 'Speculative behaviour and complex asset price dynamics: a global analysis,' *Journal of Economic Behavior and Organization*, 49(2): 173–97.

Chipman, J. S. (1974) 'Homothetic preferences and aggregation,' *Journal of Economic Theory*, 8: 26–38.

Clapham, J. H. (1922a) 'Of empty economic boxes,' *Economic Journal*, 32: 303–14.

— (1922b) 'The economic boxes – a rejoinder,' *Economic Journal*, 32: 560–3.

Clark, J. B. (1898) 'The future of economic theory,' *Quarterly Journal of Economics*, 13: 1–14.

Clower, R. W. (1969) 'The Keynesian counter-revolution: a theoretical appraisal,' in R. W. Clower, *Monetary Theory*, Harmondsworth: Penguin.

Clower, R. W. and A. Leijonhufvud (1973) 'Say's Principle, what it means and doesn't mean: Part I,' *Intermountain Economic Review*, 4(2): 1–16.

Coddington, A. (1976) 'Keynesian economics: the search for first principles,' *Journal of Economic Literature*, 14(4): 1258–73.

Colander, D. (2011) 'Is the fundamental science of macroeconomics sound?' American Economic Association Annual Conference, Denver, CO.

Costanza, R. (1993) 'Ecological economic systems analysis: order and chaos,' in E. B. Barbier, *Economics and Ecology*, London: Chapman & Hall, pp. 29–45.

Cotis, J.-P. (2007) 'Editorial: achieving further rebalancing,' *OECD Economic Outlook*, 2007/1: 7–10.

Crouch, R. (1972) *Macroeconomics*, New York: Harcourt Brace Jovanovich.

Debreu, G. (1959) *Theory of Value: An Axiomatic Analysis of Economic Equilibrium*, New Haven, CT: Yale University Press.

— (1970) 'Economies with a finite set of equilibria,' *Econometrica*, 38: 387–92.

— (1974) 'Excess demand functions,' *Journal of Mathematical Economics*, 1: 15–21.

Desai, M. (1981) *Testing Monetarism*, London: Frances Pinter.

Dierker, E. (1972) 'Two remarks on the number of equilibria of an economy,' *Econometrica*, 40: 951–3.

Diewert, W. E. (1977) 'Generalized Slutsky conditions for aggregate consumer demand functions,' *Journal of Economic Theory*, 15(2): 353–62.

Dillard, D. (1984) 'Keynes and Marx: a centennial appraisal,' *Journal of Post Keynesian Economics*, 6(3): 421–32.

Ding, N., N. Xi et al. (2006) 'The economic mobility in money transfer models,' *Physica A: Statistical Mechanics and Its Applications*, 367: 415–24.

Dixon, R. (2000a) *A Formal Proof of Walras' Law*, www.ecom.unimelb.edu.au/ ecowww/rdixon/ walproof.html.

— (2000b) *Walras' Law and Macroeconomics*, www.ecom.unimelb.edu.au/ecowww/rdixon/ wlaw.html.

Dow, S. C. (1997) 'Endogenous money,' in G. C. Harcourt and P. A. Riach (eds), *A 'Second Edition' of the General Theory*, London: Routledge, pp. 61–78.

Downward, P. (1999) *Pricing Theory in Post Keynesian Economics: A realist approach*, Cheltenham: Edward Elgar.

Downward, P. and P. Reynolds (1999) 'The contemporary relevance of Post-Keynesian economics: editors' introduction,' *Economic Issues*, 4: 1–6.

Dumenil, G. and D. Levy (1985) 'The classicals and the neo-classicals: a rejoinder to Frank Hahn,' *Cambridge Journal of Economics*, 9: 327–45.

Earl, P. E. (1995) *Microeconomics for Business and Marketing*, Cheltenham: Edward Elgar.

Ehrenberg, A. S. C. (1975) *Data Reduction: Analysing and interpreting statistical data*, London: Wiley.

Einstein, A. (1961 [1916]) *Relativity: The Special and the General Theory*, New York: Random House.

Eiteman, W. J. (1947) 'Factors determining the location of the least cost point,' *American Economic Review*, 37: 910–18.

— (1948) 'The least cost point, capacity and marginal analysis: a rejoinder,' *American Economic Review*, 38: 899–904.

Eiteman, W. J. and G. E. Guthrie (1952) 'The shape of the average cost curve,' *American Economic Review*, 42(5): 832–8.

Fama, E. F. (1970) 'Efficient capital markets: a review of theory and empirical work,' *Journal of Finance*, 25(2): 383–417.

Fama, E. F. and K. R. French (1999) 'The corporate cost of capital and the return on corporate investment,' *Journal of Finance*, 54(6): 1939–67.

— (2004) 'The Capital Asset Pricing Model: theory and evidence,' *Journal of Economic Perspectives*, 18(3): 25–46.

Feher, D. C. (1999) *Debt Deflation: The Birth of a Concept and Its Development over Time*, Unpublished honors thesis, University of Western Sydney.

Financial Crisis Inquiry Commission (2011) *The Financial Crisis Inquiry Report: Final Report of the National Commission on the Causes of the Financial and Economic Crisis in the United States*.

Fisher, I. (1929) 'Transcript of an address of Professor Irving Fisher,' in W. J. Barber (ed.) (1997), *The Works of Irving Fisher*, vol. 10, London: Pickering and Chatto.

— (1930) *The Theory of Interest*, New York: Macmillan, reprinted in W. J. Barber (ed.) (1997), *The Works of Irving Fisher*, vol. 3, London: Pickering and Chatto.

— (1932) *Booms and Depressions: Some First Principles*, reprinted in W. J. Barber (ed.), *The Works of Irving Fisher*, vol. 10, London: Pickering and Chatto.

— (1933) 'The debt-deflation theory of great depressions,' *Econometrica*, 1: 337–55.

Frank, R. H., T. Gilovich and D. T. Regan (1993) 'Does studying economics inhibit cooperation?' *Journal of Economic Perspectives*, 7(2): 159–71.

— (1996) 'Do economists make bad citizens?' *Journal of Economic Perspectives*, 10(1): 187–92.

Franklin, J. and A. Daoud (1988) *Introduction to Proofs in Mathematics*, New York: Prentice-Hall.

Freeman, A. and G. Carchedi (1996) *Marx and Non-Equilibrium Economics*, Cheltenham: Edward Elgar.

Freeman, S. and F. E. Kydland (2000) 'Monetary aggregates and output,' *American Economic Review*, 90(5): 1125–35.

Friedman, M. (1953) 'The methodology of positive economics,' reprinted in B. Caldwell (ed.) (1984), *Appraisal and Criticism in Economics: A Book of Readings*, London: Allen & Unwin.

— (1968) 'The role of monetary policy,' *American Economic Review*, 58(1): 1–17.

— (1969) 'The optimum quantity of money,' in *The Optimum Quantity of Money and Other Essays*, Chicago, IL: Macmillan, pp. 1–50.

— (1971) 'A monetary theory of nominal income,' *Journal of Political Economy*, 79(2): 323–37.

Frisch, R. (1933) 'Propagation problems and impulse problems in dynamic economics,' in *Economic Essays in Honour of Gustav Cassel*, London: George Allen & Unwin Ltd.

Fullbrook, E. (2010) 'Keen, Roubini and Baker win Revere Award for Economics,' *Real-World Economics Review* blog, New York.

Gabaix, X., P. Gopikrishnan et al. (2006) 'Institutional investors and stock market volatility,' *Quarterly Journal of Economics*, 121(2): 461–504.

Galbraith, J. K. (1997) *The Socially Concerned Today: The First Honorary Keith Davey Lecture*, Toronto: University of Toronto Press.

Galbraith, J. K. and W. K. Black (2009) 'Trust but verify,' in K. van den Heuvel (ed.), *Meltdown: How Greed and Corruption Shattered Our Financial System and How We Can Recover*, New York: Nation Books, pp. 244–7.

Gallegati, M., S. Keen et al. (2006) 'Worrying trends in econophysics,' *Physica A: Statistical Mechanics and Its Applications*, 370(1): 1–6.

Glassman, J. K. and K. A. Hassett (1999) *DOW 36,000: The New Strategy for Profiting from the Coming Rise in the Stock Market*, New York: Times Business.

Goodwin, R. (1967) 'A growth cycle,' in C. H. Feinstein (ed.), *Socialism, Capitalism and Economic Growth*, Cambridge: Cambridge University Press, pp. 54–8.

Goodwin, R. M. (1986) 'The economy as an evolutionary pulsator,' *Journal of Economic Behavior and Organization*, 7(4): 341–9.

— (1990) *Chaotic Economic Dynamics*, Oxford: Oxford University Press.

— (1991) 'New results in non-linear economic dynamics,' *Economic Systems Research*, 3(4): 426–7.

Gordon, R. J. (1976) 'Can econometric policy evaluations be salvaged? – a comment,' *Carnegie-Rochester Conference Series on Public Policy*, pp. 47–61.

Gorman, W. M. (1953) 'Community preference fields,' *Econometrica*, 21(1): 63–80.

Graziani, A. (1989) 'The theory of the monetary circuit,' *Thames Papers in Political Economy*, Spring, pp. 1–26.

Groll, S. (1980) 'The active role of "use value" in Marx's economics,' *History of Political Economy*, 12(3): 336–71.

Hahn, F. (1982) 'The neo-Ricardians,' *Cambridge Journal of Economics*, 6: 353–74.

Haines, W. W. (1948) 'Capacity production and the least cost point,' *American Economic Review*, 38: 617–24.

Harcourt, G. (1982) *The Social Science Imperialists*, ed. P. Kerr, London: Routledge & Kegan Paul.

Harford, T. (2005) *The Undercover Economist*, London: Oxford University Press.

Harrod, R. (1939) 'An essay in dynamic theory,' *Economic Journal*, 49: 14–33.

Haugen, R. A. (1999a) *The Beast on Wall Street*, New Jersey: Prentice-Hall.

— (1999b) *The New Finance*, New Jersey: Prentice-Hall.

— (1999c) *The Inefficient Stock Market*, New Jersey: Prentice-Hall.

Henwood, D. (1997) *Wall Street*, New York: Verso.

Hicks, J. R. (1935) 'Wages and interest: the dynamic problem,' *Economic Journal*, 45(179): 456–68.

— (1937) 'Mr. Keynes and the "Classics": a suggested interpretation,' *Econometrica*, 5(2): 147–59.

— (1949) 'Mr. Harrod's dynamic theory,' *Economica*, 16(62): 106–21.

— (1979) 'On Coddington's interpretation: a reply,' *Journal of Economic Literature*, 17(3): 989–95.

— (1980) 'IS-LM: an explanation,' *Journal of Post Keynesian Economics*, 3(2): 139–54.

Hirshleifer, J. (1993) 'The dark side of the force,' *Economic Inquiry*, 32: 1–10.

Hodgson, G. (1991) *After Marx and Sraffa*, New York: St Martin's Press.

Hodgson, G. M. (1998) *The Foundations of Evolutionary Economics*, Cheltenham: Edward Elgar.

— (1999) *Evolution and Institutions: On Evolutionary Economics and the Evolution of Economics*, Cheltenham: Edward Elgar.

Hodgson, G. M., W. J. Samuels and M. R. Tool (eds) (1994) *The Elgar Companion to Institutional and Evolutionary Economics*, Aldershot: Edward Elgar.

Hogan, C. J., R. P. Kirshner and N. B. Suntzeff (1999) 'Surveying space–time with supernovae,' *Scientific American*, 280(1): 28–33.

Holmes, A. R. (1969) 'Operational constraints on the stabilization of money supply growth,' in F. E. Morris (ed.), *Controlling Monetary Aggregates*, Nantucket Island, MA: Federal Reserve Bank of Boston, pp. 65–77.

Hudson, M. (2000) 'The mathematical economics of compound interest: a 4,000-year overview,' *Journal of Economic Studies*, 27(4/5): 344–63.

Institute of Chartered Financial Analysts (eds) (1991) *The Founders of Modern Finance: Their Prize-winning Concepts and 1990 Nobel Lectures*, Charlottesville, VA: Institute of Chartered Financial Analysts.

Ireland, P. N. (2011) 'A new Keynesian perspective on the Great Recession,' *Journal of Money, Credit and Banking*, 43(1): 31–54.

Jevons, W. S. (1866) 'Brief account of a general mathematical theory of political economy,' *Journal of the Royal Statistical Society, London*, 29: 282–7, www.marxists.org/reference/subject/economics/jevons/mathem.htm.

— (1888) *The Theory of Political Economy*, Internet: Library of Economics and Liberty, www.

econlib.org/library/YPDBooks/Jevons/jvnPE4. html.

Jones, N. L. (1989) *God and the Moneylenders*, Oxford: Basil Blackwell.

Jorgenson, D. W. (1960) 'A dual stability theorem,' *Econometrica*, 28: 892–9.

— (1961) 'Stability of a dynamic input-output system,' *Review of Economic Studies*, 28: 105–16.

— (1963) 'Stability of a dynamic input-output system: a reply,' *Review of Economic Studies*, 30: 148–9.

Kaldor, N. (1982) *The Scourge of Monetarism*, Oxford: Oxford University Press.

Kaletsky, A. (2009) 'Now is the time for a revolution in economic thought,' *The Times*, London, 9 February.

Kariya, T. (1993) *Quantitative Methods for Portfolio Analysis: MTV Model Approach*, Dordrecht: Kluwer Academic Publishers.

Kates, S. (1998) *Say's Law and the Keynesian Revolution*, Cheltenham: Edward Elgar.

— (2003) 'Economic management and the Keynesian revolution: the policy consequences of the disappearance of Say's Law,' in *Two Hundred Years of Say's Law*, Cheltenham: Edward Elgar.

Keen, S. (1993a) 'Use-value, exchange-value, and the demise of Marx's labor theory of value,' *Journal of the History of Economic Thought*, 15: 107–21.

— (1993b) 'The misinterpretation of Marx's theory of value,' *Journal of the History of Economic Thought*, 15: 282–300.

— (1995) 'Finance and economic breakdown: modeling Minsky's "Financial Instability Hypothesis,"' *Journal of Post Keynesian Economics*, 17(4): 607–35.

— (1996) 'The chaos of finance: the chaotic and Marxian foundations of Minsky's "Financial Instability Hypothesis,"' *Economies et Sociétés*, 30(2/3): 55–82.

— (1998) 'Answers (and questions) for Sraffians (and Kaleckians),' *Review of Political Economy*, 10: 73–87.

— (2000) 'The nonlinear dynamics of debt-deflation,' in W. A. Barnett, C. Chiarella, S. Keen, R. Marks and H. Schnabl (eds), *Commerce, Complexity and Evolution*, New York: Cambridge University Press.

— (2001a) *Debunking Economics: The naked emperor of the social sciences*, Annandale, Sydney/London: Pluto Press Australia/Zed Books.

— (2001b) 'Minsky's thesis: Keynesian or Marxian?' in R. Bellofiore and P. Ferri (eds), *The Economic Legacy of Hyman Minsky*, vol. 1: *Financial Keynesianism and Market Instability*, Cheltenham: Edward Elgar, pp. 106–20.

— (2003) 'Standing on the toes of pygmies: why econophysics must be careful of the economic foundations on which it builds,' *Physica A: Statistical Mechanics and Its Applications*, 324(1/2): 108–16.

— (2004) 'Deregulator: Judgment Day for microeconomics,' *Utilities Policy*, 12: 109–25.

— (2005) 'Why economics must abandon its theory of the firm,' in M. Salzano and A. Kirman (eds), *Economics: Complex Windows*, New Economic Windows series, Milan and New York: Springer, pp. 65–88.

— (2006) Steve Keen's Monthly Debt Report, 'The recession we can't avoid?' *Steve Keen's Debtwatch*, Sydney, 1: 21, November.

— (2008) 'Keynes's "revolving fund of finance" and transactions in the circuit,' in R. Wray and M. Forstater (eds), *Keynes and Macroeconomics after 70 Years*, Cheltenham: Edward Elgar, pp. 259–78.

— (2009a) 'A pluralist approach to microeconomics,' in J. Reardon (ed.), *The Handbook of Pluralist Economics Education*, London: Routledge, pp. 120–49.

— (2009b) 'The dynamics of the monetary circuit,' in S. Rossi and J.-F. Ponsot (eds), *The Political Economy of Monetary Circuits: Tradition and Change*, London: Palgrave Macmillan, pp. 161–87.

— (2010) 'Solving the paradox of monetary profits,' *Economics: The Open-Access, Open Assessment E-Journal*, 4(2010-31).

— (2011) 'A monetary Minsky model of the Great Moderation and the Great Recession,' *Journal of Economic Behavior and Organization*, forthcoming.

Keen, S. and E. Fullbrook (2004) 'Improbable, incorrect or impossible? The persuasive but flawed mathematics of microeconomics,' in *A Guide to What's Wrong with Economics*, London: Anthem Press, pp. 209–22.

Keen, S. and R. Standish (2006) 'Profit maximization, industry structure, and competition: a critique of neoclassical theory,' *Physica A: Statistical Mechanics and Its Applications*, 370(1): 81–5.

— (2010) 'Debunking the theory of the firm – a chronology,' *Real-World Economics Review*, 54(54): 56–94.

Kehoe, T. J. and E. C. Prescott (2002) 'Great Depressions of the 20th century,' *Review of Economic Dynamics*, 5(1): 1–18.

Keynes, J. M. (1925) *Essays in Persuasion*, London: Macmillan for the Royal Economic Society.

— (1936) *The General Theory of Employment, Interest and Money*, London: Macmillan.

— (1937) 'The General Theory of Employment,' *Quarterly Journal of Economics*, 51(2): 209–23.

— (1971 [1923]) 'A tract on monetary reform,' in

The Collected Works of John Maynard Keynes, vol. IV, London: Macmillan.

— (1972 [1925]) 'A short view of Russia', in J. M. Keynes, *Essays in Persuasion*, Cambridge: Cambridge University Press.

Kirman, A. (1989) 'The intrinsic limits of modern economic theory: the emperor has no clothes,' *Economic Journal*, 99(395): 126–39.

Kirman, A. P. (1992) 'Whom or what does the representative individual represent?' *Journal of Economic Perspectives*, 6(2): 117–36.

Kirzner, I. M. (1996) *Essays on Capital and Interest*, Cheltenham: Edward Elgar.

Klein, L. R. (1950) *Economic Fluctuations in the United States 1921–1941*, New York: John Wiley & Sons.

Klein, P. A. (1994) 'The reassessment of institutionalist mainstream relations,' *Journal of Economic Issues*, 28: 197–207.

Koo, R. (2009) *The Holy Grail of Macroeconomics: Lessons from Japan's Great Recession*, New York: John Wiley & Sons.

Kornai, J. (1979) 'Resource-constrained versus demand-constrained systems,' *Econometrica*, 47(4): 801–19.

— (1986) 'The soft budget constraint,' *Kyklos*, 39(1): 3–30.

— (1990) *Economics of Shortage*, Amsterdam: North-Holland.

Kornai, J., E. Maskin et al. (2003) 'Understanding the soft budget constraint,' *Journal of Economic Literature*, 41(4): 1095–136.

Kregel, J. A. (1983) 'Post-Keynesian theory: an overview,' *Journal of Economic Education*, 14(4): 32–43.

Kreps, D. M. (1990) *A Course in Microeconomic Theory*, Princeton, NJ: Princeton University Press.

Krugman, P. (1996) 'What economists can learn from evolutionary theorists,' web.mit.edu/krugman/www/evolute.html.

— (2009a) 'A Dark Age of macroeconomics (wonkish),' in *The Conscience of a Liberal*, New York: New York Times.

— (2009b) 'How did economists get it so wrong?' in *The Conscience of a Liberal*, New York: New York Times.

Krugman, P. and G. B. Eggertsson (2010) *Debt, Deleveraging, and the Liquidity Trap: A Fisher-Minsky-Koo approach*, 2nd draft 14 February 2011, New York: Federal Reserve Bank of New York and Princeton University, www.princeton.edu/~pkrugman/debt_deleveraging_ge_pk.pdf.

Kuhn, T. (1962) *The Structure of Scientific Revolutions*, Chicago, IL: University of Chicago Press.

Kydland, F. E. and E. C. Prescott (1990) 'Business cycles: real facts and a monetary myth,' *Federal Reserve Bank of Minneapolis Quarterly Review*, 14(2): 3–18.

— (1991) 'The econometrics of the general equilibrium approach to business cycles,' *Scandinavian Journal of Economics*, 93(2): 161–78.

Labaton, S. (1999) 'Congress passes wide-ranging bill easing bank laws,' *New York Times*, 5 November, p. 2.

Lakatos, I. (1978) *The Methodology of Scientific Research Programs*, ed. J. Worrall and G. Currie, New York: Cambridge University Press.

Lancaster, K. and R. G. Lipsey (1956) 'The general theory of the second best,' *Review of Economic Studies*, 24: 11–32, reprinted in K. Lancaster (1996), *Trade, Markets and Welfare*, Cheltenham: Edward Elgar.

Langlois, C. (1989) 'Markup pricing versus marginalism: a controversy revisited,' *Journal of Post Keynesian Economics*, 12: 127–51.

Lavoie, M. (1994) 'A Post Keynesian approach to consumer choice,' *Journal of Post Keynesian Economics*, 16: 539–62.

Lee, F. (1996) 'Pricing and the business enterprise,' in C. W. Whalen (ed.), *Political Economy for the 21st century*, Armonk, NY: M. E. Sharpe.

— (1998) *Post Keynesian Price Theory*, Cambridge: Cambridge University Press.

Leeson, R. (1991) 'The validity of the expectations-augmented Phillips curve model,' *Economic Papers*, 10: 92–6.

— (1994) 'A. W. H. Phillips M.B.E. (Military Division),' *Economic Journal*, 104(424): 605–18.

— (1997) 'The trade-off interpretation of Phillips's Dynamic Stabilization Exercise,' *Economica*, 64(253): 155–71.

— (1998) 'The origins of Keynesian discomfiture,' *Journal of Post Keynesian Economics*, 20: 597–619.

— (2000) *A. W. H. Phillips: Collected works in contemporary perspective*, Cambridge, New York and Melbourne: Cambridge University Press.

Leijonhufvud, A. (1968) *On Keynesian Economics and the Economics of Keynes: A Study in Monetary Theory*, New York: Oxford University Press.

— (1973) 'Life among the Econ,' *Western Economic Journal*, 11(3): 327–37, republished in C. P. Clotfelter (ed.) (1996), *On the Third Hand: Humor in the Dismal Science*, Ann Arbor: University of Michigan Press, pp. 24–35.

— (1986) 'What would Keynes have thought of rational expectations?' in J. L. Butkiewicz, K. J. Koford and J. B. Miller (eds), *Keynes' Economic Legacy: Contemporary Economic Theories*, New York: Praeger, pp. 25–52.

— (1991 [1967]) 'Keynes and the Keynesians: a suggested interpretation,' in E. Phelps (ed.),

Recent Developments in Macroeconomics, Aldershot: Edward Elgar.

Levins, R. and R. C. Lewontin (1986) *The Dialectical Biologist*, London: Harvard University Press.

Levitt, S. D. and S. J. Dubner (2009) *Freakonomics: A Rogue Economist Explores the Hidden Side of Everything*, New York: Harper Perennial.

Li, T.-Y. and J. A. Yorke (1975) 'Period three implies chaos,' *American Mathematical Monthly*, 82(10): 985–92.

Lindsey, D. E., A. Orphanides et al. (2005) 'The reform of October 1979: how it happened and why,' *Federal Reserve Bank of St Louis Review*, 87(2): 187–235.

Littlefield, S. (ed.) (1990) *Austrian Economics*, Aldershot: Edward Elgar.

Ljungqvist, L. and T. J. Sargent (2004) *Recursive Macroeconomic Theory*, 2nd edn, Cambridge, MA: MIT Press.

Lorenz, H.-W. (1987a) 'Goodwin's nonlinear accelerator and chaotic motion,' *Zeitschrift fur Nationalokonomie* [Journal of Economics], 47(4): 413–18.

— (1987b) 'Strange attractors in a multisector business cycle model,' *Journal of Economic Behavior and Organization*, 8(3): 397–411.

— (1989) *Nonlinear Dynamical Economics and Chaotic Motion (Lecture Notes in Economics and Mathematical Systems)*, Berlin: Springer.

Lucas, R. E., Jr (1972) 'Econometric testing of the Natural Rate Hypothesis,' *The Econometrics of Price Determination Conference, October 30–31 1970*, Washington, DC: Board of Governors of the Federal Reserve System and Social Science Research Council, pp. 50–9.

— (1976) 'Econometric policy evaluation: a critique,' *Carnegie-Rochester Conference Series on Public Policy*, 1: 19–46.

— (2003) 'Macroeconomic priorities,' *American Economic Review*, 93(1): 1–14.

— (2004) 'Keynote address to the 2003 HOPE Conference: my Keynesian education,' *History of Political Economy*, 36: 12–24.

Mackay, C. (1841) *Extraordinary Popular Delusions and the Madness of Crowds*, New York: Crown Trade Paperbacks, www.litrix.com/madraven/madneo01.htm.

Mandel, E. (1971) *The Formation of the Economic Thought of Karl Marx*, London: NLB.

Mandelbrot, B. (1971) 'Linear regression with non-normal error terms: a comment,' *Review of Economics and Statistics*, 53(2): 205–6.

— (2005) 'The inescapable need for fractal tools in finance,' *Annals of Finance*, 1(2): 193–5.

Mandelbrot, B. B. and R. L. Hudson (2004) *The (Mis)behaviour of Markets: A fractal view of risk, ruin and reward*, London: Profile.

Mankiw, N. G. (2008) *Principles of Microeconomics, 5E*, Boston, MA: South-Western College Publishers.

Mantel, R. R. (1974) 'On the characterisation of aggregate excess demand,' *Journal of Economic Theory*, 7: 348–53.

— (1976) 'Homothetic preferences and community excess demand functions,' *Journal of Economic Theory*, 12: 197–201.

Marks, R. (2000) 'Evolved perception and the validation of simulation models,' in W. A. Barnett, C. Chiarella, S. Keen, R. Marks and H. Schnabl (eds), *Commerce, Complexity and Evolution*, New York: Cambridge University Press.

Marshall, A. (1920 [1890]) *Principles of Economics*, Internet: Library of Economics and Liberty, www.econlib.org/library/Marshall/marPo.html.

Martin, S. (2000) *Advanced Industrial Economics*, Oxford: Basil Blackwell.

Marwell, G. and R. Ames (1981) 'Economists free-ride, does anyone else?' *Journal of Public Economics*, 15(3): 295–310.

Marx, K. (1847) *Wage Labor and Capital*, Moscow: Progress Press.

— (1857) *Grundrisse*, Harmondsworth: Penguin.

— (1859) *A Contribution to the Critique of Political Economy*, Moscow: Progress Press.

— (1867) *Capital*, vol. 1, Moscow: Progress Press.

— (1885) *Capital*, vol. 2, Moscow: Progress Press.

— (1894) *Capital*, vol. 3, Moscow: Progress Press.

— (1951 [1865]) 'Wages, price and profit,' in Marx-Engels-Lenin Institute (ed.), *Marx-Engels Selected Works*, vol. I, Moscow: Foreign Languages Publishing House.

— (1968 [1861]) *Theories of Surplus Value*, Parts I, II and III, Moscow: Progress Press.

— (1971 [1879]) 'Marginal notes on A. Wagner,' in D. McLennan (ed.), *Karl Marx: Early Texts*, Oxford: Basil Blackwell.

— (1983 [1881]) *Marx's Mathematical Manuscripts*, London, New Park Publications.

Mas-Colell, A. (1977) 'On the equilibrium price set of an exchange economy,' *Journal of Mathematical Economics*, 4: 117–26.

— (1986) 'Notes on price and quantity tatonnement dynamics,' in H. F. Sonnenschein (ed.), *Lecture Notes in Economics and Mathematical Systems*, Berlin: Springer-Verlag.

Mas-Colell, A., M. D. Whinston et al. (1995) *Microeconomic Theory*, New York: Oxford University Press.

May, R. M. and G. F. Oster (1976) 'Bifurcations and dynamic complexity in simple ecological models,' *American Naturalist*, 110(974): 573–99.

McCauley, J. (2004) *Dynamics of Markets: Econophysics and Finance*, Cambridge: Cambridge University Press.

— (2006) 'Response to "Worrying trends in econophysics,"' *Physica A*, 371: 601–9.

McCullough, B. D. and C. G. Renfro (2000) 'Some numerical aspects of nonlinear estimation,' *Journal of Economic and Social Measurement*, 26(1): 63–77.

McDonough, T. and J. Eisenhauer (1995) 'Sir Robert Giffen and the great potato famine: a discussion of the role of a legend in neo-classical economics,' *Journal of Economic Issues*, 29: 747–59.

McFadden, D., A. Mas-Colell and R. R. Mantel (1974) 'A characterisation of community excess demand functions,' *Journal of Economic Theory*, 9: 361–74.

McFadden, J. (2001) *Quantum Evolution: How Physics' Weirdest Theory Explains Life's Biggest Mystery*, New York: W. W. Norton.

McKibbin, W. J. and A. Stoeckel (2009) 'Modelling the global financial crisis,' *Oxford Review of Economic Policy*, 25(4): 581–607.

McKinsey Global Institute (2010) *Debt and Deleveraging: The Global Credit Bubble and Its Economic Consequences*, http://www.mckinsey.com/mgi/publications/books/.

McLellan, D. (1971) *Karl Marx: Early Texts*, Oxford: Blackwell.

McLennan, W. (1996) *Standards for Labour Force Statistics*, Australian Bureau of Statistics, Canberra: Australian Government Publishing Service.

McManus, M., (1963) 'Notes on Jorgenson's model,' *Review of Economic Studies*, 30: 141–7.

Meadows, D. H., J. Randers et al. (1972) *The Limits to Growth*, New York: Signet.

Means, G. C. (1972) 'The administered-price thesis reconsidered,' *American Economic Review*, 62: 292–306.

Meek, R. (1972) *The Economics of Physiocracy*, London: George Allen & Unwin.

Milgate, M. (1987) 'Keynes's General Theory,' in J. Eatwell, M. Milgate and P. Newman (eds), *The New Palgrave: A Dictionary of Economics*, London: Macmillan.

Minsky, H. (1957) 'Monetary systems and accelerator models,' *American Economic Review*, 67: 859–83.

— (1970) 'Financial instability revisited: the economics of disaster,' reprinted in H. Minsky (1982 [1963]), *Can 'It' Happen Again?: Essays on instability and finance*, Armonk, NY: M. E. Sharpe, pp. 117–61.

— (1971) 'The allocation of social risk: discussion,' *American Economic Review*, 61(2): 389–90.

— (1975) *John Maynard Keynes*, New York: Columbia University Press.

— (1977) 'The financial instability hypothesis: an interpretation of Keynes and an alternative to "standard" theory,' *Nebraska Journal of Economics and Business*, reprinted in H. Minsky (1982 [1963]), *Can 'It' Happen Again?: Essays on instability and finance*, Armonk, NY: M. E. Sharpe, pp. 59–70.

— (1980) 'Capitalist financial processes and the instability of capitalism,' *Journal of Economic Issues*, 14, reprinted in H. Minsky (1982 [1963]), *Can 'It' Happen Again?: Essays on instability and finance*, Armonk, NY: M. E. Sharpe, pp. 71–89.

— (1982) *Inflation, Recession and Economic Policy*, Brighton: Wheatsheaf.

— (1982 [1963]) *Can 'It' Happen Again?: Essays on instability and finance*, Armonk, NY: M. E. Sharpe.

— (1986) *Stabilizing an Unstable Economy*, Twentieth Century Fund Report series, New Haven, CT and London: Yale University Press.

Mirowski, P. (1984) 'Physics and the "marginalist revolution,"' *Cambridge Journal of Economics*, 8: 361–79.

— (1989) *More Heat than Light: Economics as social physics: Physics as nature's economics*, Cambridge: Cambridge University Press.

Mohun, S. (1994) *Debates in Value Theory*, New York: St Martin's Press.

Moore, B. J. (1979) 'The endogenous money stock,' *Journal of Post Keynesian Economics*, 2(1): 49–70.

— (1983) 'Unpacking the Post Keynesian black box: bank lending and the money supply,' *Journal of Post Keynesian Economics*, 5(4): 537–56.

— (1988a) 'The endogenous money supply,' *Journal of Post Keynesian Economics*, 10(3): 372–85.

— (1988b) *Horizontalists and Verticalists: The Macroeconomics of Credit Money*, Cambridge: Cambridge University Press.

— (1997) 'Reconciliation of the supply and demand for endogenous money,' *Journal of Post Keynesian Economics*, 19(3): 423–8.

— (2001) 'Some reflections on endogenous money,' in L.-P. Rochon and M. Vernengo (eds), *Credit, Interest Rates and the Open Economy: Essays on horizontalism*, Cheltenham: Edward Elgar, pp. 11–30.

Musgrave, A. (1981) '"Unreal assumptions" in economic theory: the untwisted,' *Kyklos*, 34: 377–87, reprinted in B. Caldwell (1984), *Appraisal and Criticism in Economics: A Book of Readings*, London: Allen & Unwin.

Muth, J. F. (1961) 'Rational expectations and the theory of price movements,' *Econometrica*, 29(3): 315–35.

Nightingale, J. (2000) 'Universal Darwinism and social research: the case of economics,' in W. A. Barnett, C. Chiarella, S. Keen, R. Marks and H. Schnabl (eds), *Commerce, Complexity and Evolution*, New York: Cambridge University Press.

Nikaido, H. (1996) *Prices, Cycles and Growth*, Cambridge, MA: MIT Press.

Oakley, A. (1983) *The Making of Marx's Critical Theory*, London: Routledge and Kegan Paul.

Obama, B. (2009) 'Obama's remarks on the economy,' *New York Times*, 14 April.

O'Brien, Y.-Y. J. C. (2007) 'Reserve requirement systems in OECD countries,' SSRN eLibrary.

Oda, S. H., K. Miura, K. Ueda and Y. Baba (2000) 'The application of cellular automata and agent models to network externalities in consumers' theory: a generalization of life game,' in W. A. Barnett, C. Chiarella, S. Keen, R. Marks and H. Schnabl (eds), *Commerce, Complexity and Evolution*, New York: Cambridge University Press.

O'Hara, M. (1995) *Market Microstructure Theory*, Cambridge: Blackwell.

Ormerod, P. (1997) *The Death of Economics*, 2nd edn, New York: John Wiley & Sons.

— (2001) *Butterfly Economics: A New General Theory of Social and Economic Behavior*, London: Basic Books.

— (2004) 'Neoclassical economic theory: a special and not a general case,' in E. Fullbrook (ed.), *A Guide to What's Wrong with Economics*, London: Anthem Press, pp. 41–6.

Ormerod, P. and A. Heineike (2009) 'Global recessions as a cascade phenomenon with interacting agents,' *Journal of Economic Interaction and Coordination*, 4(1): 15–26.

Ott, E. (1993) *Chaos in Dynamical Systems*, New York: Cambridge University Press.

Palley, T. I. (1996) *Post Keynesian Economics: Debt, Distribution and the Macro Economy*, London: Macmillan.

Patriarca, M., A. Chakraborti et al. (2004) 'Gibbs versus non-Gibbs distributions in money dynamics,' *Physica A: Statistical Mechanics and Its Applications*, 340(1–3): 334–9.

Paulson, H. M. (2010) *On the Brink: Inside the race to stop the collapse of the global financial system*, New York: Business Plus.

Perino, M. (2010) *The Hellhound of Wall Street: How Ferdinand Pecora's investigation of the Great Crash forever changed American finance*, New York: Penguin Press.

Peters, E. E. (1994) *Fractal Market Analysis*, New York: John Wiley & Sons.

— (1996) *Chaos and Order in the Capital Markets*, 2nd edn, New York: John Wiley & Sons.

Phillips, A. W. (1950) 'Mechanical models in economic dynamics,' *Economica*, 17(67): 283–305.

— (1954) 'Stabilisation policy in a closed economy,' *Economic Journal*, 64(254): 290–323.

— (1968) 'Models for the control of economic fluctuations,' in *Scientific Growth Systems, Mathematical Model Building in Economics and Industry*, London, Griffin, pp. 159–65.

Pierce, A. (2008) 'The Queen asks why no one saw the credit crunch coming,' *Daily Telegraph*, London.

Pigou, A. C. (1922) 'Empty economic boxes – a reply,' *Economic Journal*, 36: 459–65.

— (1927) 'The law of diminishing and increasing cost,' *Economic Journal*, 41: 188–97.

— (1928) 'An analysis of supply,' *Economic Journal*, 42: 238–57.

Poincaré, H. (1956 [1905]) 'Principles of mathematical physics,' *Scientific Monthly*, 82(4): 165–75.

Prescott, E. C. (1999) 'Some observations on the Great Depression,' *Federal Reserve Bank of Minneapolis Quarterly Review*, 23(1): 25–31.

Rassuli, A. and K. M. Rassuli (1988) 'The realism of Post Keynesian economics: a marketing perspective,' *Journal of Post Keynesian Economics*, 10: 455–73.

Renfro, C. G. (2009) *Building and Using a Small Macroeconometric Model: Klein Model I as an Example*, a MODLER Workbook, Philadelphia, PA: MODLER Information Technologies Press.

Ricardo, D. (1817) *On the Principles of Political Economy and Taxation*, Indianapolis, IN: Library of Economics and Liberty, www.econlib.org/library/Ricardo/ricP.html.

Robbins, L. (1928) 'The representative firm,' *Economic Journal*, 42: 387–404.

— (1952 [1932]) *An Essay on the Nature and Significance of Economic Science*, 2nd edn, London: Macmillan.

Robertson, D. H. (1924) 'Those empty boxes,' *Economic Journal*, 34: 16–31.

— (1930) 'The trees of the forest,' *Economic Journal*, 44: 80–9.

Robinson, J. (1971a) 'Continuity and the "rate of return,"' *Economic Journal*, 81(321): 120–2.

— (1971b) 'The existence of aggregate production functions: comment,' *Econometrica*, 39(2): 405.

— (1972) 'The second crisis of economic theory,' *American Economic Review*, 62(2): 1–10.

— (1975) 'The unimportance of reswitching,' *Quarterly Journal of Economics*, 89(1): 32–9.

— (1981) *What Are the Questions?: And other essays*, Armonk, NY: M. E. Sharpe.

Roosevelt, F. D. (1933) First Inaugural Address of Franklin D. Roosevelt, Washington, DC.

Rosdolsky, R. (1977) *The Making of Marx's Capital*, London: Pluto Press.

Rosser, J. B. (1999) 'On the complexities of complex economic dynamics,' *Journal of Economic Perspectives*, 13(4): 169–92.

Roth, T. P. (1989) *The Present State of Consumer Theory*, Lanham, MD: University Press of America.

Rothbard, M. (1970) *Power and the Market*, Kansas City: Sheed Andrews and McMeel Inc..

— (1972 [1963]) *America's Great Depression*, Kansas City: Sheed & Ward.

Rotheim, R. J. (1999) 'Post Keynesian economics and realist philosophy,' *Journal of Post Keynesian Economics*, 22: 71–103.

Salvadori, N. and I. Steedman (1988) 'No reswitching? No switching!' *Cambridge Journal of Economics*, 12: 481–6.

Samuelson, P. A. (1938a) 'A note on the pure theory of consumer's behaviour,' *Economica*, 5(17): 61–71.

— (1938b) 'A note on the pure theory of consumer's behaviour: an addendum,' *Economica*, 5(19): 353–4.

— (1948) *Foundations of Economic Analysis*, Cambridge, MA: Harvard University Press.

— (1956) 'Social indifference curves,' *Quarterly Journal of Economics*, 70(1): 1–22.

— (1966) 'A summing up,' *Quarterly Journal of Economics*, 80(4): 568–83.

Samuelson, P. A. and W. D. Nordhaus (2010) *Microeconomics*, New York: McGraw-Hill Irwin.

— (1991) 'A personal view on crises and economic cycles,' in M. Feldstein (ed.), *The Risk of Economic Crisis. A National Bureau of Economic Research Conference Report*, Chicago, IL, and London: University of Chicago Press, pp. 167–70.

— (1998) 'Report card on Sraffa at 100,' *European Journal of the History of Economic Thought*, 5: 458–67.

Sargan, J. D. (1958) 'The instability of the Leontief dynamic model,' *Econometrica*, 26: 381–92.

Sargent, T. J. and N. Wallace (1976) 'Rational expectations and the theory of economic policy,' *Journal of Monetary Economics*, 2(2): 169–83.

Sato, K. (1979) 'A note on capital and output aggregation in a general equilibrium model of production,' *Econometrica*, 47: 1559–68.

Sawyer, M. C. (ed.) (1988) *Post-Keynesian Economics*, Aldershot: Edward Elgar.

Say, J. B. (1967 [1821]) *Letters to Mr Malthus on several subjects of political economy and on the cause of the stagnation of commerce to which is added a Catechism of Political Economy or familiar conversations on the manner in which wealth is produced, distributed and consumed in society*, New York: Augustus M. Kelly.

Schumpeter, J. A. (1934) *The Theory of Economic Development: An inquiry into profits, capital, credit, interest and the business cycle*, Cambridge, MA: Harvard University Press.

Schwartz, J. H. (2000) *Sudden Origins: Fossils, Genes, and the Emergence of Species*, New York: John Wiley & Sons.

Sciabarra, C. (1995) *Marx, Hayek and Utopia*, New York: State University of New York Press.

Sent, E. M. (1997) 'Sargent versus Simon: bounded rationality unbound,' *Cambridge Journal of Economics*, 21: 323–8.

Seppecher, P. (2010) 'Dysfonctionnement bancaire, bulle du crédit et instabilité macroéconomique dans une économie monétaire dynamique et complexe' [Dysfunctional banking system, credit bubble and macroeconomic instability in a complex, dynamic, monetary economy – with English summary], *Revue Economique*, 61(3): 441–9.

Shafer, W. and H. Sonnenschein (1982) 'Market demand and excess demand functions,' in K. J. Arrow and M. D. Intriligator (eds), *Handbook of Mathematical Economics*, vol. II, Amsterdam: Elsevier.

Shafer, W. J. (1977) 'Revealed preference and aggregation,' *Econometrica*, 45: 1173–82.

Shaikh, A. (1982) 'Neo-Ricardian economics: a wealth of algebra, a poverty of theory,' *Review of Radical Political Economics*, 14: 67–83.

Sharpe, W. F. (1964) 'Capital asset prices: a theory of market equilibrium under conditions of risk,' *Journal of Finance*, 19(3): 425–42.

— (1970) *Portfolio Theory and Capital Markets*, New York: McGraw-Hill.

Shepherd, W. G. (1984) '"Contestability" vs. competition,' *American Economic Review*, 74: 572–87.

Shove, G. F. (1930) 'The representative firm and increasing returns,' *Economic Journal*, 44: 93–116.

Silvestre, J. (1993) 'The market-power foundations of macroeconomic policy,' *Journal of Economic Literature*, 31(1): 105–41.

Simon, H. A. (1996) *The Sciences of the Artificial*, Cambridge, MA: MIT Press.

Sippel, R. (1997) 'An experiment on the pure theory of consumer's behaviour,' *Economic Journal*, 107(444): 1431–44.

Smith, A. (1838 [1776]) *An Inquiry into the Nature and Causes of the Wealth of Nations*, Edinburgh: Adam and Charles Black.

Solow, R. M. (1956) 'A contribution to the theory of economic growth,' *Quarterly Journal of Economics*, 70(1): 65–94.

— (2001) 'From neoclassical growth theory to new classical macroeconomics,' in J. H. Drèze (ed.), *Advances in Macroeconomic Theory*, New York: Palgrave.

— (2003) 'Dumb and dumber in macroeconomics,' *Festschrift for Joe Stiglitz*, New York: Columbia University.

— (2007) 'The last 50 years in growth theory and the next 10,' *Oxford Review of Economic Policy*, 23(1): 3–14.

Sonnenschein, H. (1972) 'Market excess demand functions,' *Econometrica*, 40(3): 549–63.

— (1973a) 'Do Walras' identity and continuity characterize the class of community excess demand functions,' *Journal of Economic Theory*, 6: 345–54.

— (1973b) 'The utility hypothesis and demand theory,' *Western Economic Journal*, 11: 404–10.

Sornette, D. (2003) *Why Stock Markets Crash: Critical events in complex financial systems*, Princeton, NJ: Princeton University Press.

— (2011) 'Financial Crisis Observatory,' www.er.ethz.ch/fco.

Sraffa, P. (1926) 'The laws of returns under competitive conditions,' *Economic Journal*, 36(144): 535–50.

— (1930) 'The trees of the forest – a criticism,' *Economic Journal*, 44: 89–92.

— (1960) *The Production of Commodities by Means of Commodities: Prelude to a critique of economic theory*, Cambridge: Cambridge University Press.

Steedman, I. (1977) *Marx after Sraffa*, London: NLB.

— (1992) 'Questions for Kaleckians,' *Review of Political Economy*, 4: 125–51.

Stevens, G. (2008) 'Interesting times,' *Reserve Bank of Australia Bulletin*, December, pp. 7–12.

Stigler, G. J. (1957) 'Perfect competition, historically contemplated,' *Journal of Political Economy*, 65(1): 1–17.

Stiglitz, J. (1993) 'Post Walrasian and post Marxian economics,' *Journal of Economic Perspectives*, 7 (1): 109–14.

— (1998) 'The confidence game: how Washington worsened Asia's crash,' *New Republic Online*, 9 September.

— (2000) 'What I learned at the world economic crisis,' *New Republic*, 17–24 April, pp. 56–60.

Strange, S. (1997) *Casino Capitalism*, Manchester: Manchester University Press.

Swan, T. W. (2002) 'Economic growth,' *Economic Record*, 78(243): 375–80.

Sweezy, P. M. (1942) *The Theory of Capitalist Development*, New York: Oxford University Press.

Taleb, N. (2007) *The Black Swan: The Impact of the Highly Improbable*, New York: Random House.

Taslim, F. and A. Chowdhury (1995) *Macroeconomic Analysis for Australian Students*, Sydney: Edward Elgar.

Taylor, J. B. (1993) 'Discretion versus policy rules in practice,' *Carnegie-Rochester Conference Series on Public Policy*, 39: 195–214.

— (2007) 'The explanatory power of monetary policy rules,' *Business Economics*, 42(4): 8–15.

Tisdell, C. (1995) 'Evolutionary economics and research and development,' in S. Dowrick (ed.), *Economic Approaches to Innovation*, Aldershot: Edward Elgar.

Valentine, T., G. Ford et al. (2011) *Fundamentals of Financial Markets and Institutions in Australia*, Sydney: Pearson Australia.

Varian, H. R. (1984) *Microeconomic Analysis*, New York: W. W. Norton.

— (1992) *Microeconomic Analysis*, new edn, New York: W. W. Norton.

Veblen, T. (1898) 'Why is economics not an evolutionary science?' *Quarterly Journal of Economics*, 12(4): 373–97.

— (1899) 'The preconceptions of economic science,' *Quarterly Journal of Economics*, 13: 121–50.

— (1909) 'The limitations of marginal utility,' *Journal of Political Economy*, 17: 620–36.

— (1990 [1919]) 'The place of science in modern civilization,' in W. J. Samuels (ed.), *The Place of Science in Modern Civilization*, New Brunswick, NJ: Transaction Publishers.

Von Kurt, F. (1945) 'The discovery of incommensurability by Hippasus of Metapontum,' *Annals of Mathematics*, 46(2): 242–64.

Von Neumann, J. and O. Morgenstern (1953) *Theory of Games and Economic Behavior*, Princeton, NJ: Princeton University Press.

Walras, L. (1954 [1874]) *Elements of Pure Economics*, London: George Allen & Unwin.

Walters, B. and D. Young (1997) 'On the coherence of Post Keynesian economics,' *Scottish Journal of Political Economy*, 44: 329–49.

Whaples, R. (1995) 'Changes in attitudes among college economics students about the fairness of the market,' *Journal of Economic Education*, 26: 308–13.

Wilber, C. K. (1996) 'Ethics and economics,' in C. J. Whalen (ed.), *Political Economy for the 21st century*, Armonk, NY: M. E. Sharpe.

Wilde, L. (1989) *Marx and Contradiction*, Aldershot: Avebury.

Witt, U. (ed.) (1992) *Explaining Process and Change: Approaches to Evolutionary Economics*, Ann Arbor: University of Michigan Press.

Woodford, M. (2010) 'Simple analytics of the Government Expenditure Multiplier,' NBER Working Paper Series, Cambridge, MA: National Bureau of Economic Research.

Yao, X. and P. Darwen (2000) 'Genetic algorithms and evolutionary games,' in W. A. Barnett, C. Chiarella, S. Keen, R. Marks and H. Schnabl (eds), *Commerce, Complexity and Evolution*, New York: Cambridge University Press.

Yezer, A. M., R. S. Goldfarb and P. J. Poppen (1996) 'Does studying economics discourage cooperation? Watch what we do, not what we say or how we play,' *Journal of Economic Perspectives*, 10(1): 177–86.

INDEX

STATES AND DEVELOPMENT IN THE ASIAN PACIFIC RIM

edited by

Richard P. Appelbaum

and

Jeffrey Henderson

SAGE PUBLICATIONS
International Educational and Professional Publisher
Newbury Park   London   New Delhi

For information address:

SAGE Publications, Inc.
2455 Teller Road
Newbury Park, California 91320

SAGE Publications Ltd.
6 Bonhill Street
London EC2A 4PU
United Kingdom

SAGE Publications India Pvt. Ltd.
M-32 Market
Greater Kailash I
New Delhi 110 048 India

Printed in the United States of America

Library of Congress Cataloging-in-Publication Data

Main entry under title:

States and development in the Asian Pacific rim / edited by Richard P.
  Appelbaum, Jeffrey Henderson.
       p.   cm.
  Includes bibliographical references and index.
  ISBN 0-8039-4034-3 (cl).—ISBN 0-8039-4035-1 (pb)
    1. East Asia—Economic conditions.   2. East Asia—Economic policy.
  3. Industry and state—East Asia.   4. East Asia—Industries.
  I. Appelbaum, Richard P.   II. Henderson, J. W. (Jeffrey William),
  1947-
  HC460.5.S73   1992
  338.95—dc20   92-1150

92 93 94 95 10 9 8 7 6 5 4 3 2

Sage Production Editor: Astrid Virding

Contents

Acknowledgments

This book grew out of the papers presented at a conference held at the University of California, Santa Barbara, on March 22-25, 1990. We would like to thank the University of California Pacific Rim Program, the National Center for Geographic Information and Analysis (NCGIA), the UCSB College of Letters and Sciences, and Environmental Systems Research Institute (ESRI) for their generosity in providing funding for the conference. We would also like to acknowledge the tireless help of Cliff Kono, conference coordinator, as well as the staff of NCGIA in making the detailed arrangements required to host a conference bringing together scholars from four continents. Our thanks also go to the helpful staff at Sage Publications, particularly Marie-Louise Penchoen, Astrid Virding, and Megan McCue. Finally, a special note of appreciation for Michael Goodchild, Director of NCGIA, for realizing the importance of this research to geographers, and providing ongoing support for the several research efforts that have grown out of the original conference.

1

Situating the State in the
East Asian Development Process

JEFFREY HENDERSON

RICHARD P. APPELBAUM

The post-World War II economic transformation of East Asia has proven perplexing to development analysts influenced by the African and Latin American experiences. From Paul Baran to Andre Gunder Frank, from Samir Amin to Arghiri Emmanuel, we were led to believe that the possibilities for development in peripheral countries were severely circumscribed by the requirements of the capitalist world economic system.[1] The structures and dynamics of the world economy, controlled as they were from its centers—particularly the United States—locked peripheral societies into an unyielding downward spiral of exploitation and poverty. Under such circumstances it seemed that only one choice was available for Third World societies, and that in Frank's words was between "underdevelopment or revolution" (Frank, 1969a).

Given that revolution was conceived of in socialist terms, there appeared by the mid-1970s to be a number of successful candidates to serve as models of relatively egalitarian development: Cuba, China, Tanzania, and even North Korea appeared to vindicate socialism as the only genuine route to development in the Third World. In all of these countries gross national product (GNP) had expanded, agricultural and industrial productivity had increased, living standards had been improved, and abject poverty seemingly eradicated. When one compared the socialist colossus of China with India, its nearest capitalist equivalent in the Third World, the benefits of socialism seemed incontrovertible. At a minimum, China had fed, housed, rendered literate, and massively improved the health of its population; India, in much the same time frame, had not. On the left, with the exception of Trotskyist critiques of Third World socialism (cf. Harris, 1978, on China), problems of authoritarian rule, of internal repression, of personality cults—of Stalinism—were either not fully understood, or were justified as being no worse than their capitalist counterparts in Brazil, Argentina, or Chile; in Indonesia, the Philippines, or South Korea.

As early as the late 1960s, however, an alternative conception of the possibilities of Third World development under capitalism had begun to emerge. Constructed as it was in contradistinction to the "vulgar" dependency theories of Frank and others, and initially associated with the work of Brazilian sociologist Fernando Cardoso and his collaborators (e.g., Cardoso & Faletto, 1979), this conception began to forge the intellectual tools necessary to grasp the possibility of "dependent development." The argument of the "second wave" *dependistas* was that Third World societies (or at least Latin American ones) were not merely products determined by the structures of unequal exchange within the world economy, but that their present and future possibilities in part were of their own making. Specifically, under certain circumstances, Third World societies were able to achieve sufficient autonomy within the world system to be able to harness the dynamics of global capitalism for their own development purposes. While the economic and political relations of dependence remained a fact of life, and thus set the parameters or external limits to what any Third World society could achieve, some form of genuine development was still a possibility. Central to this possibility was the action of the national state, and in Peter Evans's work (1979), the nature of the triadic alliance that could be forged, at particular historical moments, between the state and indigenous and transnational capital.

The dependent development theorists were reinforced from another front—the American world-systems theorists, centered around Immanuel Wallerstein and the State University of New York's Braudel Center. In Wallerstein's (1979) view, it was possible for certain peripheral societies to break partially from the bonds of dependence and move to an intermediate position within the world economy—termed by Wallerstein the *semiperiphery*—where their economies extracted surplus from the periphery while at the same time yielding surplus to the core. Wallerstein's (1978) analysis emphasized the role of the national state in carving out a space for indigenous economic and political actors to play a role in both the global economy, and in the international state system. At the same time, however, Wallerstein failed to appreciate the restructuring of transnational capital such that some semiperipheral areas might actually become "way-stations" for corporate decision-making and control (Henderson, 1986).

If dependent development and world-systems theorists argued that some degree of development was indeed possible under global capitalism, other theorists sought to demonstrate that capitalism was in fact a precondition to such development. In Britain, Bill Warren and his associates (see Schiffer, 1981; Warren, 1980) extended Marx's analysis of capitalism as a progressive force to the Third World. In Warren's view, by revolutionizing the forces of production, breaking the stranglehold of feudalism, and bringing a working class onto the social and political stage, capitalism created the preconditions for genuine development in the Third World. Mobilizing a wealth of data on economic growth rates, GNP per capita, income distribution and the like, Warren sought to demonstrate that the most economically developed Third World societies were precisely those that were most penetrated by global capitalist relations. Many of Warren's showcase examples were from the East Asian region.

It was, in fact, the case of East Asia that forced a major rethinking of the relationship between global capitalism and Third World economic development. By the mid 1970s, it was clear that a number of East Asian societies were undergoing a process of "late industrialization" (Amsden, 1989). Beginning with Japan in the 1950s, Hong Kong in the 1960s, Taiwan, South Korea, and Singapore in the 1970s and 1980s, and possibly Malaysia today, East Asia seemed to outsiders to have come from nowhere to challenge successfully, and in some cases defeat, the traditional might of U.S. and Western European industrial capitalism. What was more, they seemed to some to have done so by successfully mobilizing the sheer power of the market.

That economies should not only grow, but grow at the spectacular double-digit rates of these East Asian cases, came as no surprise to those with a near-religious belief in the capacities of the "free market". Since the work of Jacob Viner (1953) and the British economists Peter Bauer and Basil Yamey (1957), those imbued with the neoclassical paradigm had been convinced that the blockages to development that existed in the Third World were largely self-imposed. They were alleged to be the result of distortions in markets for labor, capital, natural resources, and technology that arose from the endogenous cultural forms and social practices in many parts of the Third

World (Rostow, 1961), but especially from the meddling (and usually corruption) of the national state. That Japan and subsequently other East Asian countries had deliberately connected themselves to world markets and seemingly applied free market principles through to their logical conclusion, was seen as a vindication of the tenets of neoclassical economics and a defeat for those from Raul Prebisch onward who had argued for autarkic development strategies based upon import-substitution industrialization.[2] That the success of the East Asian economies might well signal the death knell of any socialist route to the modern world was a point to be hammered home by U.S. sociologist Peter Berger in his influential book, *The Capitalist Revolution* (1986).

The concluding part of this chapter, as well as those that follow it, will question the simplistic assumption that the East Asian "miracle" is indeed a vindication of free market capitalism. That notwithstanding, it remains true that for the theoretical traditions reviewed above, the experience of Japan, South Korea, Hong Kong, Taiwan, and Singapore has proven to be something of an enigma. Alice Amsden, for instance, has shown how difficult it is to try to explain Taiwanese development from within a dependency framework (Amsden, 1979), while Andre Gunder Frank (1982) has responded to the problem by simply denying that any genuine development has taken place. Similarly, while some attention has been paid by world-systems analysts to the historical antecedents of development in the region (see in particular Moulder, 1977, on Japan), little of it appears to have been focused on contemporary industrialization (but see So, 1986, on Hong Kong). Additionally, Henderson (1989) has pointed out the deficiencies of a world-system related thesis, that of the "new international division of labor" (Frobel, Heinrichs, & Kreye, 1980), for an analysis of high technology forms of industrialization in the region. Finally, Amsden (1990) has questioned the utility of Alain Lipietz's otherwise stimulating "global fordist" version of regulation theory (Lipietz, 1987) for an analysis of South Korean industrialization.

It seems then that we have not yet reached the point where some general theory of East Asian late industrialization can be advanced; for the moment, all we can do is to provide pointers in that direction. In what follows we offer one pointer by trying to "situate" the state, in a preliminary fashion, in relation to other potential candidates for the determination of East Asian development. The other chapters in this book develop "the case for the state" in detail, with regard to particular facets of state action in Japan, the "four tigers" (South Korea, Taiwan, Hong Kong, and Singapore), and in Malaysia, the society with the greatest recent potential for late industrialization.

Determinants of Development

In this section we assess the relative significance of five factors that have been advanced by a variety of scholars to explain East Asian economic transformation. These factors include the particular historical circumstances out of which their transformation emerged; the role of foreign capital; the importance of free markets; the significance of neo-Confucian cultural forms; and repressive labor systems that ensured supplies of cheap labor. The sixth factor, the role of state policy and influence, is dealt with in a subsequent section.

Historical Legacies

Is not the present after all in large measure the prisoner of a past that obstinately survives, and the past with its rules, its differences and its similarities, the indispensable key to any serious understanding of the present?

—(Braudel, 1984, p. 20)

Extrapolating from Braudel we can argue that history so infuses the present and sets the parameters for the emergence of the future that any social science that does not place it at the heart of its explanatory system is doomed to deliver woefully inadequate accounts of whatever phenomenon happens to be under scrutiny. Not withstanding the fact that this is precisely one of the central epistemological problems of much which passes for economic science in the contemporary world, history is one of the factors that has been utilized quite heavily in explanations of East Asian economic transformation. History in this sense has been used both in terms of the uniqueness of the national and collective pasts of East Asian societies but particularly in the form of historical conjunctures that have allowed structural space for the emergence of transformative dynamics.

There are five legacies of history that are seen to be of significance. The first concerns the circumstances surrounding the emergence of Japan as an industrializing society in the decades between the Meiji Restoration of 1867-1868 and the First World War. This includes Japan's emergence as an imperial power from the turn of the century and the significance of its incorporation of Taiwan and Korea into its colonial domain. The second concerns the impact of British colonialism in the region. The third relates to the geopolitical conjuncture in the East Asian region from 1945 to the early

1970s. The fourth, partially overlapping with the third, concerns the impact of the expansion of world trade associated with the "long boom" in North America and Western Europe from the late 1940s until the early 1970s. Finally, the reverberations of economic crisis in many of the core economies is regarded as having had important implications for development prospects, particularly amongst the second generation late industrializers (those other than Japan) in the region.

Japanese Industrialization and Colonialism. The "Japanese experience" has been the primary concern of the vast majority of scholars who have studied economic expansion in the region. The reasons for this are obvious given that Japan was the first—and still the only—non-Western economy to make it into the "big league." Its route to the modern world has been significant not only in itself, however, but also because it has constituted the prototype on which other East Asia economies—South Korea and Taiwan in particular—have based their development strategies. In this section we briefly mention some of the key elements that seem to have influenced Japan's own industrialization, before moving on to examine the significance of its imperial expansion for other societies in the region.

Frances Moulder, in her comparative study of Japan and China (1977), argues that contrasting experiences of Western imperialism largely explain the differential economic trajectories of these societies in the nineteenth and early twentieth centuries. Whereas China was absorbed into the expanding capitalist world economy, Japan was not, permitting Japan sufficient flexibility to adopt a relatively autarkic development strategy. As a result, while Japan was able to absorb Western ideas and technology, it was not subject to the economic, social, and political dependencies and exploitation that so often fell to societies touched by Western imperialism. While Moulder goes on to deal with the evolution of the state form, and with its "peculiar" relation with business, it seems clear that she places the weight of explanation on the legacy of the past and particularly the way in which external constraints on imperial expansion provided development opportunities for Japan that were denied other non-Western societies.

Michio Morishima (1982), in his concern to ground Japanese economic success in the articulation of Western technology with the Japanese "ethos," focuses more on the internal evolution of social structures and cultural forms. While his work is a major contribution to the analysis of the relation of a Confucian-based culture to economic expansion, he is at pains to show that Confucian ethics were adapted and transformed over time under the historical conditions that were unique to Japanese culture and society. While he places more emphasis than Moulder on internal historical dynamics, his analysis also emphasizes the conjuncture of Japanese historical isolation from the West with the technological and institutional fruits of contact when it did occur in the late nineteenth and early twentieth centuries. It should be said, in addition, that Morishima also emphasizes the significance of the state-business relation, but for him this arises out of, and in explanatory terms remains secondary to, Japan's unique history and culture.

The significance of imperialism also carries weight in explanations of economic development in Korea and Taiwan. In these cases, however, we are dealing not with Western imperialism, nor with the relative "hands-off" variety of that, which was the Japanese experience. Rather we are dealing with the absorption of both territories into the Japanese empire during the first half of the current century.

The thrust of the Japanese state into Taiwan in 1895 and Korea in 1910 came in the context of Japan's first wave of industrialization. Japan's initial material basis for imperial expansion was its drive to secure sufficient supplies of rice and other agricultural commodities that the rapidly industrializing and urbanizing society could no longer provide domestically. The Japanese were able to enhance agricultural productivity greatly in Korea and Taiwan by removing the absentee landlords and transforming their agricultural systems into smallholder cultivation (S. P. S. Ho, 1978). Additionally, with rising real wages and growing militarization at home in the 1930s, Japanese companies—encouraged by the state—began to invest in manufacturing facilities, particularly in food processing, textiles, wood pulp and paper, fertilizers, aluminum and copper refining, and shipbuilding. The social consequences of these developments were, first, the elimination of the feudal landlord class that has so bedeviled strategies for modernization in other developing societies, and second, the beginnings of the creation of an industrial working class (Amsden, 1979; Cumings, 1987; Gold, 1986). Furthermore, and particularly in the context of Korea, industry emerged in a highly centralized fashion, controlled as it was by six Japanese *zaibatsu* (Amsden, 1989, pp. 31-35). It appears that these firms provided the organizational model for the *chaebol* that have so come to dominate the South Korean economy in more recent years.

There are two other bequests by the Japanese to Taiwan and Korea that seem to have been of significance. First, in order to facilitate imperial control and export (to Japan) of agricultural produce and manufactured commodities, considerable investment went into such infrastructure as roads, railroads, and ports. Secondly, the military nature of Japanese colonial administration ensured the transmission of a military hierarchy with its attendant disciplinary codes and ethos to the colonial societies (Amsden, 1979, 1985; Cumings, 1987), laying the foundations for both a relatively efficient bureaucracy and for the authoritarian state forms that emerged during the Chiang regime in Taiwan and the Rhee and Park regimes in South Korea and that persist, though in a cosmetically democratic form, to the present day.

British Colonialism. The relation of the historical legacies to economic transformation in Hong Kong and Singapore have received less scholarly attention, probably because their historical antecedents are less tangible than those of South Korea and Taiwan. British colonialism in both Hong Kong and Singapore was much more"disinterested" than was its Japanese equivalent. These, after all, were viewed as insignificant backwaters of the British empire, rather than as "jewels in the crown" in the way that South Korea and Taiwan were for the Japanese. Hong Kong and Singapore were entrepôts and naval stations; not the sort of places to be developed for productive purposes.

This is not to say, however, that the legacy of British colonialism is unimportant in explaining development in these two city-states. The British did provide (and in Hong Kong continue to provide) efficient and relatively liberal bureaucratic and legal systems, which remain—particularly in the case of Singapore—probably the least corrupt in the entire region. Furthermore, by being nurtured as key regional nodes for intra-empire trade, both territories benefitted from extensive pre-existing networks of trading houses and specialized services as they began to develop their export-oriented industrialization strategies in the 1950s (Hong Kong) and 1960s (Singapore). It is probably fair to say, however, that in most regards the legacy of Japanese colonialism in Taiwan and South Korea proved to be more significant for subsequent economic development in those two countries than British colonialism did for the two city-states.

In Malaya, the economic requirements of the British Empire boosted tin and established rubber and palm oil production, the latter two remaining central to the Malaysian economy (Jomo, 1990). With the emergence of new industries came the demand for new labor supplies. The preservation of neo-feudal constraints on Malay peasant labor created the need to draw on migrant labor, hence the origins of the Chinese and Indian communities that now make up about 35% and 10% respectively of the Malaysian population. With the economic legacies of colonialism have come racial legacies as well. Superimposed as they have been on class divisions (Jomo, 1986), racial issues have provided a continuing source of potential and actual instability (as in the riots of 1969), and hence of particular legitimation problems not confronted by most of the other states in the region. "Tradition and previous generations", Marx wrote, "lie like a nightmare on the minds of the living". That this is probably nowhere more true in East Asia than in Malaysia, is a real problem of history that has conditioned that society's development. It may yet be a legacy that derails its future prospects. But it is also a legacy that presents an opportunity of greater global significance than the East Asian newly industrializing countries (NICs). Unlike them, Malaysia is relatively sectorially balanced: it has a vibrant agricultural sector. Also unlike them, it is racially diverse, and it has a democratic state both in form, and generally speaking in content. If Malaysia is successful in its late industrializer strategy, it will, therefore, be a much more apt model for Third World societies than the East Asian NICs could ever be. It would also call into question the notion that there is a necessary connection between late industrialization and authoritarian, non-democratic states.

East Asian Geopolitics. For all but one of the countries dealt with in this book, Malaysia, the geopolitics of the Cold War proved to be an important factor in industrialization. The economies of Japan, Taiwan, and South Korea —and the militaries of the latter two countries—were deliberately built with U.S. aid and technology transfer as bulwarks against communism. Additionally, Japanese industry benefited from the increased demands for steel, military equipment, and uniforms that emerged during the Korean War (1950-1953). Manufacturing in South Korea, Taiwan and particularly in Hong Kong also benefited from the U.S. war in Vietnam (early 1960s to the mid-1970s).

The formation of the Peoples' Republic of China in 1949, and its subsequent involvement in the Korean War, resulted in U.S. and U.N. trade embargoes that all but destroyed Hong Kong's entrepôt function. This, together with an influx of refugees from China, led to massive unemployment (Lin & Ho, 1980, p. 5). Serious social conflict was averted largely because of the growth of a relatively advanced textile and garment industry, based on refugee capital from Shanghai utilizing state-of-the-art technology. Drawing on the pre-existing trading networks referred to above, textile and garment production quickly became the basis for Hong Kong's emergence as East Asia's second industrial power (So, 1986; Wong, 1988; see also Henderson, 1989, pp. 77-80).

Singapore's emergence as a "late industrializer" also arose from regional geopolitics—the confluence of economic, racial and political stresses that had begun with British involvement in the Malayan peninsula during the latter half of the nineteenth century and reached its zenith following the creation of the Federation of Malaysia in 1957. The Chinese, who were numerically dominant in Singapore and economically dominant throughout the Federation, found themselves in conflict with the Malay majority, who held political (but not economic) power. Once Singapore was cut adrift from the Federation in 1965, the rapid development of a high productivity, high wage economy became essential to Singapore's legitimacy and indeed survival (Castells et al., 1990, part 2).

World Trade Expansion. With few exceptions (see, for example, the essays in Deyo, 1987), most analysts of East Asian development have overlooked the fact that the initial industrialization of Japan and the NICs coincided with an unprecedented expansion in world trade, particularly in the markets for manufactured commodities. Without such an historical coincidence, it is highly doubtful that Hong Kong and Singapore could have achieved their double-digit growth rates, or that South Korea and Taiwan could have made the switch from import-substituting to the export-oriented industrialization strategies, in the late 1950s and early 1960s. The sustained "long boom" in the cores of the world economy provided a "window of opportunity" that did not exist before and has not existed since. Without such an expansion in world trade, it is debatable whether there would have been any room for newcomers. The corollary of this, of course, is that the constraints on world trade over the past 10 to 20 years, which have resulted in deepening crisis tendencies within the global economy, may have helped ensure that there will be no more late industrializers (such as Malaysia).

Economic Crisis in the Core. The final set of historical circumstances partially accounting for the economic success of the East Asian NICs can be found in the economic downturns experienced by the industrial nations during the post-1970 period. As Frobel et al. (1980), Bluestone and Harrison (1982), and others have argued, growing trade union bargaining power in the 1950s and 1960s had contributed to a "wage drift" in industrial nations (particularly the United States) that cut into surpluses and damaged profit margins. This profit squeeze was reinforced by the general economic slowdown as well as recessions that further hurt industries in the core economies. In response, many firms—particularly in textiles, garments and electronics—began to locate overseas the more labor-intensive parts of the production process in order to take advantage of the large supplies of cheap, unorganized, and largely female labor that existed on the peripheries of the world economy (Frobel et al., 1980). A number of the East and Southeast Asian countries were among the initial preferred locations for investment in assembly plants. While these developments undoubtedly boosted the flow of foreign manufacturing capital into East Asia (with the exception of Japan), it is important to bear in mind that, with the exceptions of Singapore and Malaysia, foreign investment has not been a dominant feature of capital formation or firm ownership in the manufacturing sectors of the countries under discussion in this volume (see immediately below). Furthermore, direct foreign investment does not in itself ensure genuine economic development, as the dependency theorists, for instance, have clearly demonstrated.

The Role of Foreign Capital

In discussing the relation of foreign investment to economic development in East Asia, it is necessary to distinguish between foreign assistance (primarily by the U.S. government) through the early 1960s, and the foreign direct investment (FDI) and technology transfers on the part of corporations that has occurred since that time.

For South Korea and Taiwan—seen by the United States as East Asian bulwarks in the war against communism—U.S. foreign aid was extremely high prior to the mid-1960s. (Conversely, foreign aid to Hong Kong, Singapore, and Malaysia was negligible during this period.) Between 1953 and 1962, for example, U.S. aid financed 70% of total South Korean imports and 80% of total fixed capital formation; in Taiwan during the same period, U.S. aid financed 85% of the current account deficit and was responsible for 38% of gross domestic capital formation (Haggard & Cheng, 1987, p. 87). This was in addition to $6 billion in military aid to South Korea and $5.6 billion to Taiwan through 1979 (CIA data quoted by Haggard and Cheng, 1987, p. 87). U.S. foreign aid thus played a key role in the initial "take-offs" of South Korea and Taiwan; arguably, only the most corrupt of political economies could fail to develop in the face of such massive amounts of governmental assistance.

Much scholarship, particularly in the dependency tradition, has laid great emphasis on the relation between FDI and Third World industrialization (e.g., Frobel et al., 1980). While there has been much truth to this in Latin America, with the exceptions of Singapore and Malaysia, the significance of FDI to development in Japan, South Korea, Taiwan and Hong Kong has been limited. In terms of exports by value, the share of foreign-invested firms in recent years has been about 18% in South Korea, 15% in Taiwan, and only about 12% in Hong Kong (Henderson, 1989). In the cases of Singapore and

Malaysia, the proportions are about 70% and 45% respectively (Mirza, 1986).

While investment by overseas Chinese has been significant to some of the economies in question (Taiwan, Hong Kong, and Malaysia; see Haggard & Cheng, 1987; Redding, 1990), the acquisition of foreign technologies has been more important. For example, the early development of the Japanese semiconductor industry (in the 1950s) would have been inconceivable without the ability to acquire the technology from U.S. companies under licensing arrangements (Okimoto, Sugano, & Weinstein, 1984). Much the same applies to the development of the semiconductor and consumer electronics industries of South Korea and Taiwan, though in these cases the technology has been acquired largely through "strategic alliances" with U.S. and Japanese companies (Henderson, 1989). Alice Amsden in her work on South Korea (1989) argues that the key to late industrialization has been the ability to learn and adapt technologies and labor processes developed elsewhere. While "industrialization through learning" has indeed been central, the point remains that if it were not for the willingness of foreign corporations to transfer their technology in various ways, the "learning process" would have been more difficult and much slower than was in fact the case.

For many of the East Asian economies, therefore, substantial FDI was not necessary for development; moreover, where it did occur, it was not by itself sufficient. FDI is ultimately significant for economic transformation only when it stimulates local firm production linkages and/or when it results, over time, in shifts to higher value-added forms of production within the subsidiaries of the transnational corporations themselves. While the latter partly explains the successes of Singapore and Malaysia (Henderson, 1989), in other parts of the Third World neither significant linkages nor shifts to higher value-added production have resulted from FDI (cf. Sklair, 1989 on Mexico).

The Question of Free Markets

The free market explanation of East Asian development has probably carried more weight than any other. Indeed, among professional economists, it is difficult to think of any contribution that does not locate "unfettered enterprise" at the core of its explanatory scheme. Interestingly and perhaps surprisingly this is as true for economists indigenous to the region as it is for outside commentators. For instance, one of the region's leading economists, Edward Chen, argues that in the cases of Japan, South Korea, Taiwan, Hong Kong, and Singapore, "state intervention is largely absent. What the state provided is simply a suitable environment for the entrepreneurs to perform their function" (Chen, 1979, p. 41).

According to neoclassical economic reasoning, the East Asian economies (including Japan) have been successful because their governments have sought to maximize efficiencies putatively resulting from market-based resource allocation (Balassa, 1981). These governments, it is argued, have either never intervened in "normal" market allocation functions or if they have, they progressively "liberalized" their economies prior to the initial periods of rapid economic growth associated with export-oriented industrialization. Either way, state-induced market distortions have been kept to a minimum, and as a consequence markets have worked more efficiently than in other developing societies. Additionally, as Wade suggests (1990, pp. 23-24), there has been a secondary theme within the neoclassical literature that has recognized a modicum of state intervention. Here it is argued that at the aggregate level, East Asian governments have successfully balanced domestic market protection with export promotion policies. The overall effect then, has been the neutralization of one set of state-induced market distortions by a second set.

Michael Porter's (1990a, 1990b) influential comparative work on the determinants of economic success among nations, for example, advocates a limited degree of state intervention within a neoclassical framework stressing unfettered market competition as the key. According to Porter, "government's proper role is as a catalyst and challenger; it is to encourage—or even push—companies to raise their aspirations and move to higher levels of competitive performance" (1990a, p. 88). Governments should let wages rise according to the market for labor, permit exchange rates to fluctuate according to market conditions, enforce strict safety and environmental standards in order to assure the highest quality products, sharply limit direct cooperation among industry rivals, eliminate such barriers to competition as state monopolies or fixed prices, enforce strong domestic antitrust policies, and reject all forms of managed trade. Governments should also encourage the creation of a highly skilled, specialized work force, and in general promote goals that lead to "sustained investment in human skills, in innovation, and in physical assets" (Porter, 1990a, p. 88).

Porter partly attributes South Korea's rapid ascent in the world economy to the South Korean government's substantial investments in education and infrastructure, its aggressive export promotion policies (such as providing export insurance and tax credits), and its fostering of a national consensus on the importance of international competitive success. He notes that the South

Korean government has largely limited its intervention in capital markets to channeling heavily subsidized loans to globally competitive industries, and actively pursing technology transfer. While it has (unwisely, in Porter's view) engaged in some protectionism (as well as labor repression, which Porter does not discuss), any adverse effects of such interventions have been offset by intense domestic rivalry and competition.

Despite his professed concern with state policies, Porter tends to deal with the state as a relatively minor player who is best counseled to step out of the way, rather than as central to the dynamic of corporate success and economic transformation. This weakness is particularly noticeable in his chapter on South Korea, where he makes no mention of Alice Amsden's (1989) seminal work on the role of the state in South Korean industrialization. This omission is particularly striking since Amsden and Porter, both colleagues at Harvard Business School, were working on their projects at about the same time.

It is no coincidence that the principal counterweight to neoclassical arguments about the supposed pivotal role of free markets in East Asia has come from those who argue, in effect, that there are varieties of free market economies and that for some of them "free" is very much a relative term. While East Asian economies may indeed have quite small public sectors, and while their domestic economies may be intensely competitive, this does not mean that the role of the state with regard to economic transformation has been minimal. On the contrary, as we will argue in the conclusion of this chapter, late industrialization—and Japan and the East Asian NICs are so far the best examples—demands a decisive role for the state in setting and implementing national goals for economic growth.

In recent years the neoclassical orthodoxy has been successfully challenged in a steady stream of publications. Beginning with Chalmers Johnson's (1982) classic account of role of the Ministry of International Trade and Industry (MITI) in Japan's post-war industrialization, this literature includes Amsden's contributions on South Korea (1990) and Taiwan (1985), Gold's (1986) research on Taiwan, Luedde-Neurath's (1988) work on South Korea, and the chapters by Cumings (1987), Johnson (1987), and Koo (1987) on Northeast East Asia in general in Deyo (1987). Of particular note, however, is Robert Wade's (1990) "governed market theory" of East Asian development. Taking both the "free market" and the more sophisticated "simulated free market" versions of neoclassical theory, he systematically matches them to the empirical realities of economic transformation in the region and finds that they are severely wanting. For Northeast Asia at any rate, it is now simply impossible to argue that free markets have been the primary determinants of economic growth.

Hong Kong and Singapore, however, seem to have followed free market policies to a far greater degree than South Korea, Taiwan, or Japan. Unlike those countries, the two city-states have avoided protectionist policies, sectorially based export promotion, controlled credit, or, in general, controls on business. But as the work of Castells et al. (1990), Schiffer (1991), and Lim (1983) have shown, by means of public housing and other welfare expenditures, they have massively influenced both the price and reproduction of labor power. In the case of Hong Kong, state monopoly of land ownership has been used as a crucial budgetary tool, while in Singapore enforced savings via compulsory employer and employee contributions to the Central Provident Fund have played a similar role.

Collectively this new scholarship on the East Asian economies shows that, if anything, their development has been state-led. Indeed one analyst, speaking of South Korea, has gone as far as to suggest that its success has been "just as much a triumph of state capitalism as . . . . the achievements of the first Five Year Plans in the Soviet Union or the People's Republic of China" (Harris, 1987, p. 145). As the chapters in this volume show, to one degree or another these NICs have been led by "developmental states" that sought to secure legitimacy through active pursuit of economic growth policies. Continually to fail to recognize this fact is to persist with the fantasies of pure ideology.[3]

Culture and Development

For 1960s "modernization theory" (Rostow, 1961), traditional cultures were viewed as a barrier to economic development. Extended families, attitudes toward work, hereditary rather than meritocratic systems of advancement, and fatalistic value systems were alleged to be endogenous barriers to transformation and growth in the Third World. Underdevelopment was not the result of exploitative transnational corporations, unfavorable terms of trade, the global state system, or the legacies of colonialism—rather, it was due to the cultural failings of the people themselves. Although modernization theory was subjected to decisive critiques from the dependency theorists and others, it continued to survive in U.S. academic circles (for example, in the pages of *Economic Development and Cultural Change*), as well as within such interstate agencies as the World Bank.

In recent years the relationship of culture to development has taken on new credence through what we might term "neo-modernization" theory (e.g., Berger, 1986; Berger & Hsiao, 1988; Redding, 1990; Wong, 1986). Whereas modernization theory originally saw non-Western cultural forms and social practices as barriers to development in the Third World, the new scholarship argues that in at least one non-Western culture, an East Asian variant is capable of fostering the types of behavior necessary for rapid economic growth. It is suggested that their common Confucian heritage accounts for the developmental success of Japan and the East Asian NICs.

In essence the neomodernization literature suggests that the tenets of Confucianism, which are at the heart of traditional social practices in Chinese societies, Japan, and South Korea, have in recent decades come to constitute the basis of a new economic culture. This neo-Confucian economic culture, at least in the context of capitalist economic systems, has played a role akin to that of Protestantism during the initial rise of capitalism in Western Europe.

The elements of Confucianism that are seen as particularly important to this new economic culture are: filial respect and respect for one's elders and superiors; a high value placed on education; a commitment to meritocratic forms of personal advancement; a capacity for hard work; and an ascetic commitment to deferred gratification. In the neo-Confucian economic culture these elements have been transmuted into deferential attitudes toward managerial authority (resulting in greatly reduced labor relations problems); high rates of personal and corporate savings; a commitment to the firm as a collectivity; and a willingness to forego leisure in favor of long hours of committed work.

Neomodernization theorists do not ignore other determinants of East Asian development. As we have already mentioned, free markets tend to be regarded as a central context for the successful formation and operation of the economic culture, and by implication, therefore, a "light handed" state on the economic tiller is generally seen as an important factor. In the more sophisticated versions of the argument (especially Berger, 1986), the specific historical contingencies discussed above are also seen as important. Even so, however, it is the impact of a Confucian value system that is accorded primacy—an argument that always threatens to give way to racist claims. In the case of Berger's (1986, p. 166) statement that "it is inherently implausible to believe that Singapore would be what it is today if it were populated, not by a majority of ethnic Chinese, but by Brazilians or Bengalis—or, for that matter, by a majority of ethnic Malays," it appears as a peculiar form of inverted racism.

The principal problem with most neomodernization culturalist arguments lies not with their monocausality (Berger is an exception here) nor their tendency to degenerate into racial explanations, but rather in their failure to consider the concrete historical and institutional dynamics of the specific societies themselves. They have problems, for example, in explaining the Japanese "Confucian" stress on loyalty as against the Chinese "Confucian" stress on benevolence (Morishima, 1982); in explaining why there is so much diversity in the business systems of Confucian-based societies—in the nature of the firm, in organizational authority, or in state-business relations (Whitley, 1990, 1991); or, perhaps most significantly, in accounting for the far higher levels of internal political opposition and mobilization currently found in South Korea than any of the other "Confucian" NICs.

The thrust of our argument here is not to reject culture as an important source of "East Asian exceptionalism." Rather, we argue that one cannot understand the significance of culture outside of its relation with other structural elements of specific societies. Far more empirical work is required to identify the importance of culture in particular institutional contexts at particular historical moments.

Repressive Labor Systems

The presence of vast reserves of cheap, unorganized, and disciplined labor in East Asia has been widely used to account for both the region's "economic miracle" and for the corresponding decline in manufacturing and employment in the United States and Western Europe. The argument, developed most forcefully perhaps in Frobel et al.'s (1980) "new international division of labor" thesis, holds that one of the legacies of imperialism was the availability of large supplies of unskilled and underemployed labor on the peripheries of the world economy. The East Asian states, undemocratic, authoritarian, and in some cases (Taiwan and South Korea) militarized, frequently dealt repressively with internal opposition. Antilabor legislation, often banning oppositional trade union activity, meant that sweatshop conditions, long illegal in the core economies, could flourish in the periphery. This, in turn, provided the East Asian NICs, and later Malaysia and Thailand, with a major competitive advantage over the United States and Western Europe, particularly in industries that employed a largely female (and hence presumably culturally more submissive) work force (Heyzer, 1986). As a result, key industries—notably textiles, garments, and electronics—relocated their production operations in the periphery.

While there is clearly merit to the "new international division of labor" thesis, it overstates the importance of cheap labor in accounting for the developmental success of East Asia. First, there are many other parts of the Third World that have large supplies of cheap, unorganized, and frequently repressed labor, that have not experienced genuine development even when they have been the recipients of core-country plants. U.S. garment manufacturers—not to mention manufacturers from Hong Kong and South Korea—now operate factories in Mexico, the Caribbean, and the Indian subcontinent, yet these regions are hardly developing at double-digit rates.

Second, as Deyo (1989) convincingly demonstrates, the empirical record does not support the "docile labor" argument. All of the societies discussed in this volume have experienced major working class mobilizations in the past, and South Korea today remains a major "deviant" case, where internal opposition is widespread despite often violent state repression. In recent years both South Korea and Taiwan have witnessed considerable worker mobilization and the formation of new independent trade unions (Asia Monitor Resource Center, 1988; S. Y. Ho, 1990).

Finally, however important cheap labor may be in the early stages of late industrialization, the East Asian countries prosper today because they have upgraded their manufacturing to produce higher value-added, globally competitive goods. By investing in education, human skills, and technology, these NICs have succeeded in increasing productivity and real wages. Their comparative advantage no longer lies in their ability to deliver cheap, unskilled, and easily replicated labor, but rather in offering highly skilled engineers and technicians (albeit at wage rates far below those of their counterparts in the United States, Europe, or Japan; see Henderson, 1989).

In summary, then, we can say that while the availability of cheap labor was an important factor (among many others) in the early phases of East Asian industrialization, its significance for the more recent phases of industrialization has diminished as labor processes have become increasingly capital-intensive.

Situating the State

Nearly a quarter of a century ago Ralph Dahrendorf drew a distinction between two types of rationality that had begun to infuse industrial society. Market rationality, Dahrendorf (1968, p. 219) suggested, was based on the assumption that "a smoothly functioning market is in fact to the greatest advantage of the greatest number"; and it required a "politically passive . . . hands-off attitude in matters of legislation and decision-making." Plan rationality, in contrast, "has as its dominant feature precisely the setting of substantive social norms. Planners determine in advance who does what and who gets what" (Dahrendorf, 1968, p. 219). Dahrendorf regarded Western capitalist political economies as the closest empirical approximation to the former, and state socialist societies to the latter.

Dahrendorf's distinctions were developed at a time when liberal European intellectuals still harbored a residue of optimism about soviet-type societies, and when the industrializing societies of Asia, with the partial exception of Japan, were but a blur on the consciousness of most Western scholars. He can thus perhaps be forgiven for not adequately appreciating the inequities— or perhaps irrationalities—that in fact result from the "pure types" of both forms of political economy.

Chalmers Johnson (1982, pp. 18-26), building on Dahrendorf's distinction, has proposed that the concept of plan rationality is more appropriate to an understanding of Japan and other East Asian political economies than it is as a characterization of state socialist societies. He suggests encompassing the latter under a third distinction: *plan ideological*. We suggest completing this logical schema with a fourth distinction that addresses the Reaganite-Thatcherite "new right" economic policies currently in vogue in many parts of the world, including former state socialist societies such as Poland: *market ideological* political economies, according to which public policy is oriented above all toward assuring free market operations. Like plan ideological political economies, market ideological regimes arise from ideological dogma: in the case of the former, the wisdom and benevolence of state managers in a command economy; in the case of the latter, the wisdom and benevolence of an invisible hand in a supposedly unfettered market. In neither case do the requisite conditions in fact exist; in both cases, they are reified by intellectual traditions that remain impervious to disconfirming evidence.

Following the leads of Dahrendorf and Johnson, we refine the definition of market rational political economies to include the regulatory function of the state, which is viewed in such political economies as providing a framework wherein investment, production, and distributional decisions (which remain the preserve of business) can operate in a relatively efficient manner. In a parallel fashion, plan rational political economies are those in which state regulation is supplemented by state direction of the economy as a whole. Here national economic goals are identified, and the state operates with various degrees of influence or pressure to urge companies to act in accordance with these goals. The economy remains largely in private hands, and companies compete with one another under the watchful discipline of the market; yet the state also intervenes to achieve national goals where necessary. Should a sector be lacking what is deemed essential to economic growth, for example, the state will likely induce it, often through price supports, subsidies, and favorable credit arrangements. In Amsden's (1989, pp. 139-155)

felicitous phrase, the state will directly intervene to get "relative prices wrong," should this be believed necessary for national economic advance-ment. The simple and uncritical identification of corporate profits with national economic health—central to market ideological and market rational political economies—is thus broken.

While there are some similarities between plan rational and plan ideological political economies, especially in terms of the state's role in setting national economic goals, their differences are of greater significance. In plan ideological political economies the state owns and controls most if not all economic units. Resource allocations and investment decisions are a state rather than a corporate or market function, supposedly serving an overriding concern with equity in the distribution of wealth and income. Ideological dogma, rather than pragmatic analysis of consequences, dominates policy choices and applications.

These four constructs (market rational, plan rational, market ideological, and plan ideological) should be regarded as ideal types; actually existing political economies combine them in various historically contingent ways. Still, for any particular society, one will typically dominate, facilitating an overall characterization of its prevailing political economy. On the basis of these distinctions, therefore, we can now provisionally diagram the state-economy relations of the societies discussed in the present volume. For the sake of comparison, a number of other industrial and industrializing societies also are included.

Although the contents of Figure 1.1 should be regarded as no more than a first approximation, it does serve to indicate that many of the world's recently most successful political economies can be located in, or close to, the plan rational "quadrant". While it would go far beyond the scope of this chapter to try to justify this positioning for all of the cases so represented, a brief justification of some of the East Asian cases, at least in general terms, is in order.

The argument that the role of the state has been decisive in East Asian economic expansion—what Wade (1990) calls the "governed market" theory—does not rest on direct state ownership of key industries. Although this has been more significant than is often recognized (for example railways and earlier steel and banks in Japan; banks in South Korea; airlines, armaments, ship repairing in Singapore), it is rather the nature of the state-business partnership that has been important. While a corporatist state-business partnership is evident in other societies (such as the European social democracies), what is significant in East Asia, with the exception of Hong Kong, is that the

State & Business partnership

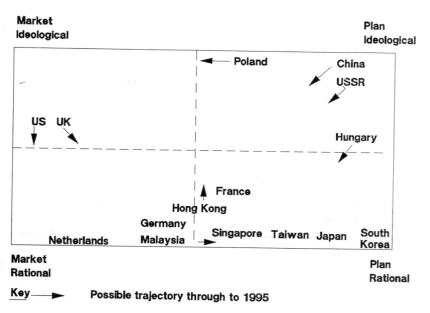

Figure 1.1. National Political Economies in 1991

state has been firmly in the driving seat. At particular historical moments, when the course of growth and development has required it, ministries and planning agencies in Japan and the NICs have engaged in the following forms of intervention: ~~State intervention Tactics~~

(1) They have "encouraged" or directed companies into higher value-added, higher wage and more technology-intensive forms of production. They have done this either by systems of constraints, such as controlling credit through the banking system (Japan, South Korea, Taiwan) and/or by rigging prices (Japan, South Korea, Taiwan, Singapore). In the Singaporean case, for instance, manual labor costs since 1978 have more than doubled as a consequence of government-induced increases in employer contributions to the Central Provident Fund (Castells et al., 1990, part 2).

(2) They have legislated to discourage short-term speculative domestic or overseas investment (Japan, South Korea, Taiwan) and thus indirectly have ensured its flow into manufacturing. An extreme example of such state-imposed discipline on investment practices is the South Korean law, dating from the early 1960s, which forbids the export of sums more than one million

U.S. dollars without government permission, on pain of penalties ranging from 10 years imprisonment to death (Amsden, 1990, p. 22).

(3) They have created industrial sectors that did not previously exist either through state companies or through the supply of credit and financial guarantees to private companies. Examples include steel, shipbuilding, transportation, petrochemicals, and semiconductors (Japan, South Korea, Taiwan, Singapore, Malaysia, in some though not all sectors in each case).

(4) They have invested heavily in the creation and refinement of new technologies, usually by setting up government research and development facilities and then transferring the results to private companies without transferring development costs (Japan, South Korea, Taiwan, Singapore).

(5) They have protected domestic markets, either across the board or (more recently) with regard to particular products (Japan, South Korea, Taiwan). For instance, the Taiwanese government still places restrictions on the import of many commodities that are directly competitive with domestic products, but has liberalized trade on those it does not seek to encourage directly, such as certain types of machine tools (Amsden, 1985; Wade, 1990).

(6) They have consistently monitored world markets in search of export opportunities, and in order to identify new types of demand that they may then encourage companies to meet (Japan, South Korea, Taiwan).

(7) They have sometimes used price controls to discourage domestic market exploitation in circumstances of near-monopolistic supply (South Korea), and have created cartels to contain the price of basic foodstuffs (Hong Kong) (Amsden, 1989, 1990; Schiffer, 1991).

(8) They have—in the case of Hong Kong—used state ownership of land as a budgetary mechanism to allow the delivery of a relatively extensive welfare system (by Asian standards), while maintaining low corporate and personal taxation and negligible foreign indebtedness (Castells et al., 1990, part 1; Schiffer, 1991).

(9) They have provided the world's largest public housing systems (in Singapore and Hong Kong), which have served to subsidize wages and legitimate centralized, autocratic—and in Hong Kong, colonial—political regimes (Castells et al., 1990; Schiffer, 1991).

(10) They have subjected companies receiving state-guaranteed credits to rigorous performance standards (including export performance), so as to minimize the possibility that subsidies will result in speculative, nonproductive investments or corruption (South Korea, Japan).

From this brief listing of the ways in which states in East Asia have intervened and directed or substantially influenced the course of economic transformation, it is clear that they have gone far beyond anything that could be encompassed within the neoclassical market ideological or even market rational frameworks. Furthermore, while it is difficult if not impossible, to disaggregate empirically the economic impact of state policy vis-à-vis the other possible determinants of economic growth (cf. Wade, 1990), the weight of circumstantial evidence suggests that state policy has been decisive.

Indeed, we would argue that while the role of the state in Japan and the East Asian NICs must be contextualized both culturally and historically, state policy and influence should now be accepted as the single most important determinant of the East Asian economic miracle. The chapters in this book, although following different theoretical logics, pursue this claim with regard to substantive issues and specific policies.

Notes

1. The principal contributions here are Baran (1957), Frank (1969b), Amin (1974), and Emmanuel (1972). Diana Hunt (1989, pp. 162-197) provides a particularly useful exposition and critique of their work.

2. Bauer and Yamey's (1957) work was an attempt to rebut that of Prebisch and the U.N. Economic Commission on Latin America (ECLA), which itself, at least in Prebisch's hands, had emerged from a critique to the neoclassic paradigm, both in theory and in terms of its policy derivatives and practical consequences (see Hunt, 1989, pp. 293-298).

3. Business economist Neil Kay (1984, pp. 187-188) has expressed the problems of neoclassical economics (including its analytic deficiencies) in more blunt terms: "mainstream economics has continued to be a fertile source of sterile theories . . . the individual intent on pursuing a career as an economist has to be bright enough to understand the abstract ramifications of neoclassical theory and dumb enough to have faith in them."

References

Amin, S. (1974). *Accumulation on a world scale.* New York: Monthly Review Press.

Amsden, A. H. (1979). Taiwan's economic history: A case of "etatisme" and a challenge to dependency theory. *Modern China, 5*(3), 341-379.

Amsden, A. H. (1985). The state and Taiwan's economic development. In P. Evans, D. Rueschemeyer, & T. Skocpol (Eds.), *Bringing the state back in* (pp. 78-106). New York: Cambridge University Press.

Amsden, A. H. (1989). *Asia's next giant: South Korea and late industrialization.* New York: Oxford University Press.

Amsden, A. H. (1990). Third World industrialization: "Global Fordism" or a new model? *New Left Review, 182,* 5-31.

Asia Monitor Resource Center. (1988). *Min-Ju No-Jo: South Korea's new trade unions.* Hong Kong: Asia Monitor Resource Center.

Balassa, B. (1981). *Newly industrializing countries in the world economy.* Elmsford, NY: Pergamon.

Baran, P. (1957). *The political economy of growth.* New York: Monthly Review Press.

Bauer, P. T., & Yamey, B. S. (1957). *The economics of under-developed countries.* London and Cambridge: James Nisbet and Cambridge University Press.

Berger, P. (1986). *The capitalist revolution: Fifty propositions about prosperity, equality and liberty.* New York: Basic Books.

Berger, P., & Hsiao, M. H. H. (Eds.). (1988). *In search of an East Asian development model.* New Brunswick, NJ: Transaction Books.

Bluestone, B., & Harrison, B. (1982). *The deindustrialization of America.* New York: Basic Books.

Braudel, F. (1984). *Civilisation and capitalism 15th-18th century. Volume III: The perspective of the world.* London: Fontana.

Cardoso, F., & Faletto, E. (1979). *Dependency and development in Latin America.* Berkeley: University of California Press.

Castells, M., Goh, L., & Kwok, R. Y. (1990). *The Shek Kip Mei syndrome: Economic development and public housing in Hong Kong and Singapore.* London: Pion.

Chen, E. K. Y. (1979). *Hyper-growth in Asian economies: A comparative study of Hong Kong, Japan, Korea, Singapore and Taiwan.* London: Macmillan.

Cumings, B. (1987). The origins and development of the Northeast Asian political economy: Industrial sectors, product cycles and political consequences. In F. C. Deyo (Ed.), *The political economy of the new Asian industrialism* (pp. 48-83). Ithaca, NY: Cornell University Press.

Dahrendorf, R. (1968). Market and plan: Two types of rationality. In R. Dahrendorf, *Essays in the theory of society* (pp. 215-231). London: Routledge & Kegan Paul.

Deyo, F. C. (Ed.). (1987). *The political economy of the new Asian industrialism.* Ithaca, NY: Cornell University Press.

Deyo, F. C. (1989). *Beneath the miracle: Labor subordination in the new Asian industrialism.* Berkeley: University of California Press.

Emmanuel, A. (1972). *Unequal exchange: A study in the imperialism of free trade.* London: New Left Books.

Evans, P. (1979). *Dependent development: The alliance of multinational, state and local capital in Brazil.* Princeton, NJ: Princeton University Press.

Frank, A. G. (1969a). *Latin America: Underdevelopment or revolution: Essays in the development of underdevelopment and the immediate enemy.* New York: Monthly Review Press.

Frank, A. G. (1969b). *Capitalism and underdevelopment in Latin America: Historical studies of Chile and Brazil.* New York: Monthly Review Press.

Frank, A. G. (1982, June 25). Asia's exclusive models. *Far Eastern Economic Review,* pp. 22-23.

Friedman, M., & Friedman, R. (1981). *Free to choose.* Harmondsworth, UK: Penguin.

Frobel, F., Heinrichs, J., & Kreye, O. (1980). *The new international division of labour.* Cambridge, UK: Cambridge University Press.

Gold, T. (1986). *State and society in the Taiwan miracle.* Armonk, NY: M. E. Sharpe.

Haggard, S., & Cheng, T. J. (1987). State and foreign capital in the East Asian NICs. In F. C. Deyo (Ed.), *The political economy of the new Asian industrialism* (pp. 84-135). Ithaca, NY: Cornell University Press.

Harris, N. (1978). *Mandate of heaven: Marx and Mao in modern China.* London: Quartet Books.

Harris, N. (1987). *The end of the Third World: Newly industrializing countries and the decline of an ideology.* Harmondsworth, UK: Penguin.

Henderson, J. (1986). The new international division of labour and urban development in the contemporary world system. In D. Drakakis-Smith (Ed.), *Urbanisation in the developing world* (pp. 63-81). London: Croom Helm.

Henderson, J. (1989). *The globalisation of high technology production: Society, space and semiconductors in the restructuring of the modern world.* London: Routledge.

Heyzer, N. (1986). *Working women in Southeast Asia.* Milton Keynes, UK: Open University Press.

Ho, S. P. S. (1978). *Economic development of Taiwan, 1869-1970.* New Haven, CT: Yale University Press.

Ho, S. Y. (1990). *Taiwan—After a long silence.* Hong Kong: Asia Monitor Resource Center.

Hunt, D. (1989). *Economic theories of development: An analysis of competing paradigms.* London: Harvester Wheatsheaf.

Johnson, C. (1982). *MITI and the Japanese miracle.* Stanford, CA: Stanford University Press.

Johnson, C. (1987). Political institutions and economic performance: The government-business relationship in Japan, South Korea and Taiwan. In F. C. Deyo (Ed.), *The political economy of the new Asian industrialism* (pp. 136-164). Ithaca, NY: Cornell University Press.

Jomo, K. S. (1986). *A question of class: Capital, the state and uneven development in Malaya.* Singapore: Oxford University Press.

Jomo, K. S. (1990). *Growth and structural change in the Malaysian economy.* London: Macmillan.

Kay, N. M. (1984). *The emergent firm: Knowledge, ignorance, and surprise in economic organization.* London: Macmillan.

Koo, H. (1987). The interplay of state, social class and world system in East Asian development: The cases of South Korea and Taiwan. In F. C. Deyo (Ed.), *The political economy of the new Asian industrialism* (pp. 165-181). Ithaca, NY: Cornell University Press.

Lim, L. Y. C. (1983). Singapore's success: The myth of the free market economy. *Asian Survey, 23*(6), 752-764.

Lin, T. B., & Ho, Y. P. (1980). *Export-oriented growth and industrial diversification in Hong Kong.* Hong Kong: Chinese University of Hong Kong, Economic Research Centre.

Lipietz, A. (1987). *Mirages and miracles: The crises of global Fordism.* London: Verso.

Luedde-Neurath, R. (1988). State intervention and export-oriented development in South Korea. In G. White (Ed.), *Developmental states in East Asia* (pp. 68-112). London: Macmillan.

Mirza, H. (1986). *Multinationals and the growth of the Singapore economy.* New York: St. Martin's.

Morishima, M. (1982). *Why has Japan "succeeded"?* Cambridge, UK: Cambridge University Press.

Moulder, F. (1977). *Japan, China and the modern world economy.* New York: Cambridge University Press.

Okimoto, D. I., Sugano, T., & Weinstein, F. B. (Eds.). (1984). *Competitive edge: The semiconductor industry in the U.S. and Japan.* Stanford, CA: Stanford University Press.

Porter, M. E. (1990a, March-April). The competitive advantage of nations. *Harvard Business Review,* pp. 73-93.

Porter, M. E. (1990b). *The competitive advantage of nations.* London: Macmillan.

Redding, S. G. (1990). *The spirit of Chinese capitalism.* Berlin: de Gruyter.

Rostow, W. W. (1961). *The stages of economic growth.* Cambridge, UK: Cambridge University Press.

Schiffer, J. (1981). The changing post-war pattern of development: The accumulated wisdom of Samir Amin. *World Development, 9*(6), 515-537.

Schiffer, J. (1991). State policy and economic growth: A note on the Hong Kong model. *International Journal of Urban and Regional Research, 15*(2), 180-196.

Sklair, L. (1985). Shenzhen: A Chinese development zone in global perspective. *Development and Change, 15*, 581-602.

Sklair, L. (1989). *Assembling for development: The maquila industry in Mexico and the United States.* Winchester, UK: Unwin Hyman.

Sklair, L. (1991). Problems of socialist development: The significance of Shenzhen special economic zone for China's open door development strategy. *International Journal of Urban and Regional Research, 15*(2), 197-215.

So, A. Y. (1986). The economic success of Hong Kong: Insights from a world-system perspective. *Sociological Perspectives, 29*(2), 241-258.

Viner, J. (1953). *International trade and economic development.* Oxford, UK: Clarendon Press.

Wade, R. (1990). *Governing the market: Economic theory and the role of government in East Asian industrialization.* Princeton, NJ: Princeton University Press.

Wallerstein, I. (1978). World-system analysis: Theoretical and interpretive issues. In B. B. Kaplan (Ed.), *Social change in the capitalist world economy* (pp. 219-235). Beverly Hills, CA: Sage.

Wallerstein, I. (1979). *The capitalist world economy.* Cambridge, UK: Cambridge University Press.

Warren, B. (1980). *Imperialism: Pioneer of capitalism.* London: Verso.

Whitley, R. D. (1990). East Asian enterprise structures and the comparative analysis of forms of business organisation. *Organisation Studies, 11*(1), 47-74.

Whitley, R. D. (1991). The social construction of business systems in East Asia. *Organisation Studies, 12*(1), 1-28.

Wong, S. L. (1986). Modernization and Chinese culture in Hong Kong. *The China Quarterly, 106*, 306-325.

Wong, S. L. (1988). *Emigrant entrepreneurs: Shanghai industrialists in Hong Kong.* Hong Kong: Oxford University Press.

PART I

THEORETICAL ISSUES

Having assessed the various determinants that have been advanced to explain economic transformations in East Asia in Chapter 1, we turn, in Part I, to three accounts of the relationship between state policy and economic development in the NICs of the region. These accounts focus on the complex and often contradictory interplay between economies that increasingly produce for a global market, and nationalistic states that seek legitimacy through active pursuit of economic growth.

In Chapter 2, Manuel Castells looks at the "Four Asian Tigers" (Hong Kong, Taiwan, Singapore, and South Korea) as examples of "developmental states" in which strong and often repressive states single-mindedly pursue development objectives. Contrary to their prevailing images, none of these countries can be regarded as bastions of free enterprise capitalism. A detailed examination of the four countries leads Castells to conclude that there are, in fact, marked differences in the developmental paths of each, as well as some common features.

The New International Division of Labor (NIDL) theory, for example, applies primarily to Singapore, where foreign firms overwhelmingly dominate; in Taiwan, on the other hand, foreign firms are a minority. While the South Korean economy is dominated by indigenous chaebols (conglomerates), Hong Kong's phenomenal growth was triggered by smaller local manufacturing firms. Nor did these economies develop through extensive specialization, as the NIDL theory would predict, but rather through flexible response to world economic conditions. In terms of social and labor policy, the welfare state played a more central role in Hong Kong and Singapore than it did in Korea and Taiwan. Despite oppressive labor regimes at various times in

27

Korea, Singapore, and Taiwan, labor docility has been a recent phenomenon: labor in all four began after World War II as volatile, and has subsequently been tamed. All four NICs ultimately developed through export-oriented industrialization, lacking—or having destroyed—a comprador bourgeoisie whose wealth was based in large landholdings. At the same time, all four fostered a highly educated labor force capable of being reskilled along the lines dictated by rapid industrialization. Inexpensive, efficient, and disciplined labor was therefore a common underlying factor in development. All four countries were able to adapt quickly to changes in the world economy through technical upgrading toward higher value-added production, with the state playing a crucial role in reorienting activities in this direction.

For Castells, the East Asian developmental state relied on economic development to forge a national identity. Economic development is not merely a goal, it is rather a crucial means for elite groups—through state action—to secure political legitimacy. In a country-by-country postwar historical review, Castells concludes that U.S. and British postwar security concerns—while entailing a degree of economic and political vassalage—at the same time provided a developmental space for the four countries. Freed of the need to spend vast sums of resources on defense, the internal elites were able to focus on growth, a path that was acceptable to both U.S. and British interests. In all four countries, increasingly educated workers proved to be a highly productive resource that could be exploited when the objectives of export-oriented industrialization (EOI) dictated repressive labor policies. Contrary to those theorists who explain the exploitation of labor in Asian countries as a direct consequence of an assumed Confucian passivity, Castells documents the repression and violence that often was invoked to keep wages down and workers compliant.

Castells demonstrates that with the partial exception of Hong Kong, the dominant classes were subordinated to the state or destroyed, while the working class was either repressed or incorporated directly into the development process. In this way, the respective states managed to acquire legitimacy by integrating their civil societies behind their development efforts. Yet this very success now seems threatened, as the emergence of powerful, independent capitalists and a growing, consumer-oriented middle class now challenge state power, laying the foundations for a new dialectic of development.

In Chapter 3, Nigel Harris seeks to dispel a number of myths concerning the relationship between state policy and economic development in South Korea, Taiwan, and Singapore. He questions the very notion that independent states exist in a world market. Rather, echoing the other writers in this volume, he argues that there is significant interpenetration of global capital and markets throughout the world. Yet at the same time, Harris argues, states cannot be ignored. There exists today a world political-economic order of competing states and companies, in which the former often contend along geographic and military (rather than economic) lines. While national rivalries and military adventurism at one time went hand-in-hand with economic development—economic growth providing the basis for military strength—this is no longer necessarily true.

With the end of colonialism, the Third World state elites were freed to pursue competitive economic strategies, whose favorable outcomes were partly assured by the rapid growth of global export markets between World War II and the early 1970s. Intense state rivalries thus provided a spur to EOI. Postwar reconstruction in South Korea, Taiwan, and Singapore in particular provided a powerful impulse for growth. The end of Japanese colonialism created a vacuum into which local developmental elites had relatively free play to pursue nationalist objectives through economic development. Capitalizing on an ideological climate that favored strong states, the elites in these countries instituted a variety of economic interventions, including controls over imports, exchange, credits, prices and wages; varying degrees of public ownership and investment; and often direct labor repression. As Castells earlier noted, what united these countries was a single-minded dedication to achieving nationalistic goals through EOI.

Harris—along with Castells—notes that paradoxically the very success of EOI now threatens to undermine the strong states that initially made it possible. Once free to do as they wished, the states in these countries now find themselves challenged by the powerful corporations they helped to spawn and nurture. As Gereffi demonstrates in Chapter 4, domestic and global capital interpenetrate in an export-based global economy, thereby weakening the power of the state. In Harris's apt phrase, the state is transformed "from the incubator of capitalism to one of its many and changing homes."

It would be premature to anticipate the demise of the developmental state, however. In a highly competitive global system, the state must successfully woo highly mobile global capital by assuring appropriate technology, flexible production, marketing opportunities, consumer access, skilled labor, and so forth. Furthermore, there may prove to be some significant barriers to continued economic growth in the NICs. A variety of historical conditions came together in the postwar period to provide the opening for EOI: increased labor productivity, the collapse of geographical barriers in the face of rapidly improving communication and transportation technology, changes in protectionism, the growth of markets in North America and Europe, and—most importantly—the existence of a virtually inexhaustible supply of initially cheap labor that would, through massive educational and training programs, become increasingly skilled. Contrary to Castells, in Harris's view, these conditions—not strong developmental states per se—account for developmental success in the NICs. In order to better understand the role of the state in economic development, it is necessary to understand the changing nature of capitalism in an export-based global economy. Gary Gereffi provides this analysis in Chapter 4, where he develops the concept of the "commodity chain" as the key production unit in the emerging global manufacturing system. Following Hopkins and Wallerstein, Gereffi defines *commodity chain* as the series of activities involved in commodity production and sales, ranging from raw material extraction to design and production, and ending with final marketing and sales. Gereffi argues that commodity chains are reshaping the geography of capitalism, creating new and distinct regional divisions of labor. By looking at production as a process that occurs over time and space, Gereffi alerts us to the fact that the principal profits need not occur at the manufacturing stage. On the contrary, he argues, profits are increasingly realized through design, marketing and retailing, while manufacturing (now largely done in the NICs) can be done with unskilled labor at low relatively costs (and with little surplus produced).

Within this framework, according to Gereffi, the newly industrializing countries are playing increasingly specialized roles in exporting manufactured goods to the developed nations. By comparing East Asia and Latin America, Gereffi is able to shed light on the degree to which these differing roles contribute to overall industrial development in the NICs of the two regions. Although economic development initially was based on such cheap-labor industries as textiles, clothing, and electronic assembly, increasingly the NICs are turning to higher value-added, high technology manufacturing as a way of remaining competitive and avoiding core country protectionism. Furthermore, while it is widely recognized that export-oriented industrialization (EOI) initially provided the key to developmental success in the NICs, Gereffi argues that in fact a combination of inward- and outwardlooking industrialization has actually occurred. In South Korea and Taiwan, for example, an initial reliance on EOI has been supplemented by a growing emphasis on import substitution, as these countries develop large and prosperous internal markets.

In a case study of the footwear industry, Gereffi argues that in the global division of labor, capitalists in core countries still dictate where much of the manufacturing will occur, in keeping with their own profit considerations. To remain competitive, the NICs must develop distinct "export niches," within which each country specializes in different types of footwear produced through distinct manufacturing systems. In Taiwan, for example, inexpensive men's leather footwear as well as cheap plastic or vinyl footwear is produced through networks of small firms, while in South Korea inexpensive leather footwear as well as athletic shoes are produced by large corporations. Yet as labor costs rise in the NICs, some footwear production is moving back to Mexico and the Caribbean, while the NICs are seeking to protect their market niches by further upgrading and specializing their footwear products.

Gereffi concludes his chapter by identifying the various roles that the NICs can play in the world economy—roles that range from different subcontracting and sourcing arrangements with core country corporations to the production, design, and marketing of their own manufactured goods. In each case, the more autonomy and control a country has, the closer it is moving to core economic activities. Gereffi calls for a new development theory for the 1990s, one that will take into account both local specialization and regional development in an increasingly integrated global economy.

2

Four Asian Tigers With a Dragon Head

A COMPARATIVE ANALYSIS OF THE
STATE, ECONOMY, AND SOCIETY
IN THE ASIAN PACIFIC RIM

MANUEL CASTELLS

The saga of economic development of the newly industrialized countries (NICs) in the Asian Pacific (South Korea, Taiwan, Hong Kong, and Singapore) in the last 25 years is now a well-known story.[1] But the understanding of the social processes that led to the dramatic improvement of overall economic conditions in these countries, albeit at the price of high social costs and political repression, remains obscured by the passion of ideological debate, although recent research contributions are setting a new, more promising course to find an adequate explanation for one of the most extraordinary experiences in the history of economic growth and structural change (see especially Deyo, 1987a). Indeed, the performance of these economies challenges the conventional wisdom of both dogmatic dependency analysis and neoclassical free market approaches in the field of development theory. Against the prevailing left-wing view, according to which sustained

AUTHOR'S NOTE: I wish to acknowledge the intellectual help provided by a number of colleagues and graduate students who educated me in whatever understanding I acquired of very complex, and for me very alien, social and historical realities. Among the literally dozens of scholars and social actors who agreed to share their time and knowledge with me, I want to name: Hsing You-tien, Hsia Chu-Joe, Kim Joo-Chul, Reginald Y. W. Kwok, Chua Beng-Huat, Lee Goh, Chin Pei-Hsiung, Jeff Henderson, Jonathan Schiffer, Miron Mushkat, and Victor Sit. Naturally, the analyses, statements, and opinions expressed in this text are my exclusive responsibility, and they should not be held accountable, directly or indirectly, for any such statements since I did not consult with them when writing this text.

33

economic development could not take place for dependent societies under the conditions of an integrated capitalist system, the four Asian "tigers" maintained the highest rate of GNP growth in the world over 25 years, and won substantial shares of the world market economy, entirely transforming in the process their economic structure and their social fabric. Furthermore, while exploitation and oppression were integral components of the development process (as was the case in the industrialization of Europe during the nineteenth century), economic growth was coupled with substantial improvement of basic living conditions for most of the population (as shown by health, education, and housing indicators), and with a less unequal income distribution in the society at large (although the trend toward improvement in income equality during the 1960s stabilized in the 1970s and deteriorated during the 1980s, it still shows a more equal distribution, according to the Gini Index, than the one existing in the early stages of the development process) (Barrett & Chin, 1987). To be sure, this process took place under extremely repressive political and ideological conditions, but such are also the conditions of most developing societies that remain, at the same time, unable to overcome the structural obstacles to economic development imposed upon them by their colonial or semicolonial heritage (Collier, 1979).

On the other hand, the economic success of the four Asian "tigers," while raising hope and a desire for emulation in a number of other industrializing countries, has fueled the ideological discourse of free market economists and politicians who try to find in the legendary reconstruction of the process of economic development in the Asian Pacific the lost paradise of "laissez faire" capitalism. And yet, any serious, unbiased observer of the Asian Pacific scene knows that systemic and comprehensive state intervention in the economy, as well as the state's strategic guidance of the performance of national and multinational companies located on the shores of its territory, has been a fundamental factor in creating the conditions for economic growth, as well as in ensuring the transition of the industrializing economies to each one of the different stages they were reaching in their evolving articulation to the world economy (Gereffi, 1989). Using the now classical concept proposed by Chalmers Johnson (1982) in his analysis of Japan's economic transformation, the "developmental state" lies at the core of the experience of the newly industrialized economies. There is widespread recognition of such fact for South Korea, Taiwan, and Singapore. On the basis of another stream of less well-known studies, including my own research, I will argue that such is also the case for Hong Kong.

But arguing that the state has been the driving force in the process of economic development of these countries raises more questions than it answers for development theory and for development policies. Because, given the widespread and generally inefficient state intervention in most of the Third World, we must reconstruct the complex web of relationships between the society, the state, and the economy in order to understand the historical structural sources of the specific mode of state intervention and the causes for the (always relative) success of such intervention in terms of the development outcome.

In the following sections I try to accomplish this task from within the framework of the historical-structural approach to development. The order of presentation begins with the most statist and ends with the least statist of the four economies in question.

Singapore: Multinational Corporations, the National State, and the Changing International Division of Labor[2]

In econometric terms, the analysis by Tsao Yuan (1988, pp. 17-65) on the sources of growth in Singapore for the 1965-1984 period shows the influx of capital as the main contributing factor, with labor input also being a positive factor, while total factor productivity had a negligible contribution, in a structure quite different from that demonstrated by Solow (1957) and the aggregate production function school for the advanced industrial economies.

Concerning labor, in 1966 Singapore had 9% unemployment with a 42.3% labor force participation rate. In 1983, the unemployment rate had gone down to 3%, with labor force participation of 63.8%, coming mainly from the massive incorporation of women into the labor force. A crucial factor was the substantial improvement in the education of the labor force, with mandatory English in the school system, and the expansion of vocational training.

But the critical factor was the massive flow of capital from two main sources: (a) Direct foreign investment that oscillated between 10% and 20% of gross domestic product (GDP) during the 1970s, and (b) an exceptional rate of growth of gross national savings that reached 42% of gross domestic product (GDP) in the mid-1980s, the highest savings rate in the world. For the overall period 1966-1985, gross national savings represented more than 74% of total gross domestic capital formation. Much of it was generated by the public sector (46%), mainly through the Central Provident Fund, a government controlled Social Security scheme designed to impose savings on the economy. However, only some of these savings were invested by the government, much of it in social and physical infrastructure, some in public corporations (more than 500 public companies), and in investments abroad to decrease the vulnerability of government revenues vis-à-vis the cycles of the Singapore economy. About one quarter of total government revenue was kept in a government development fund to stabilize the economy and allow for strategic government expenditures, actually providing the government with a substantial instrument to ensure monetary stability and to control inflation.

This left the responsibility of the dynamism of the economy to foreign direct investment. The Singapore government decided from the moment of its independence, in 1965, that its impoverished, tiny territory could only prosper by offering itself as an export platform to multinational corporations. In this sense, the origins of Singapore's growth fit well with the thesis of the new international division of labor as an expression of the process of productive decentralization from core to periphery in search of cheap, efficient labor, and political stability (Deyo, 1981). Still, it was the role of the Singapore government to provide the necessary incentives to attract foreign capital, and to reach out through the creation of an Economic Development Board that did strategic planning on the future directions of the international economy, and successfully sold Singapore to prospective investors through a network of offices across the world. Among the critical factors attracting a continuous flow of investment, initially in manufacturing, were: a favorable business environment including low labor costs, social peace (after the repression of independent trade unions in the early 1960s), an educated labor force, and lack of government environmental and industrial regulation; excellent industrial and communications infrastructure; an advantageous inflation differential; stable fiscal policy; and political stability (P. S. J. Chen, 1983).

In addition, the Singapore government was essential in making economic diversification possible and in upgrading the level of operations performed in Singapore, enhancing the value of the activities over time. Singapore shifted gradually from traditional services to manufacturing and to advanced services; from low-skill assembly manufacturing to advanced production processes, including R&D and wafer fabrication in electronics; and from an economy dominated by maritime trade and petroleum refining to a highly diversified economic structure, including machinery industries, electronics, transport equipment, producer services, and international finance. The government was also responsible for such upgrading by creating the necessary educational and technological infrastructure (including some of the best telecommunications and air transportation infrastructure in the world); by organizing the advanced services economy; and by upgrading labor through a series of bold measures, including a substantial increase in labor costs in 1979 to squeeze out companies looking for unskilled cheap labor, once the Singapore economy had overcome the survival stage of the 1960s. Efficient government management and political stability ensured through ruthless domination and social integration mechanisms gave the multinationals enough reasons to believe Singapore was the safest haven in a generally troubled world. Public housing of increasingly decent quality for 87% of the population, and heavily subsidized public health, public education, and mass transit, together with rapid economic growth, improved living conditions for the whole population and helped to calm the social, ethnic, and political unrest that had characterized Singapore in the 1950s and early 1960s. A sophisticated security apparatus took care of the few, generally middle class, political dissenters.

While the restructuring process of the early 1980s, to upgrade the technological and educational basis of the economy, plunged Singapore into its only recession (1985-1986), new measures aimed at liberalizing the economy and at articulating it more closely with the movements of the most dynamic sectors (in finance, advanced services, high technology manufacturing, and R&D) again propelled Singapore into the high growth path beginning in 1987 (rates of growth greater than 9% per annum). Coming from a devastated economy in the mid-1960s, forcibly cutoff from its natural Malaysian hinterland in 1965, and abandoned as entrepôt and military bases by the retreating British Empire in 1968, Singapore has established itself as a showcase of the new development process, building a national identity on the basis of multinational investment attracted and protected by a developmental city-state.

South Korea: The State Production of Korean Oligopolistic Capitalism, or, When Foreign Debt Becomes an Instrument for Development[3]

In the case of South Korea, although American intervention was fundamental in creating the basis for a modern economy in the 1948-1960 period (basically through land reform and by a massive influx of foreign aid that allowed the reconstruction and survival of the country after one of the bloodiest wars of modern history), the process of economic development is associated with the inception of the Park Chung Hee Regime, established by the military coup of May 1961, and institutionalized as the Third Republic by the rigged election of October 1963.

On the basis of military, financial, and political support from the United States—a support determined by the strategic interests of the Cold War against Communism in Asia, with the 38th Parallel in Korea playing the role of the Berlin Wall in Europe—the South Korean Military, and its political expression, the Democratic Republican Party, undertook the construction of a powerful South Korean economy as the foundation for its nationalist project. In the initial stages of the development process, the state assumed an entrepreneurial role via public corporations and government investments. Thus, in the 1963-1979 period, purchases by government and public enterprises represented an annual average of almost 38% of gross domestic capital formation. The Park Regime, however, heavily influenced by the Japanese model, aimed at creating a solid industrial structure based on large Korean companies organized in the form of conglomerates. To do so it established strong protectionist measures to preserve the domestic market, but given the narrowness of such a market for accumulation purposes, it privileged the expansion of export-oriented Korean manufacturing companies. By using the control of the banking system and of export and import licenses it deliberately pushed existing Korean companies to merge and constitute large conglomerates (the *chaebol*), similar to the Japanese *zaibatsu* but without financial independence. By 1977, 2.2% of Korean enterprises employed more than 500 workers each and together accounted for 44% of the labor force.

Through a series of 5-year economic plans established and implemented by the Economic Planning Board, the government also guided Korean companies toward the sectors considered strategic for the national economy, either in terms of creating self-sufficiency or in order to foster competitiveness in the international economy. Thus South Korea systematically walked the sectoral path of economic growth, investing sequentially in textiles, petrochemicals, shipbuilding, steel, electrical machinery, consumer electronics, and (in the 1980s) automobiles, personal computers, and microelectronics (with some spectacular successes in this field, including endogenous design capacity of 256K chips) (Lee, 1988). Often some of the strategic decisions were grossly misguided, leading to economic setbacks (Johnson, 1987). But the government was there to absorb the loses, reconvert the factories, and secure new loans (Lim & Yang, 1987).

As in the case of Singapore, but on a much larger scale, the critical role of government was to attract capital and to mobilize and control labor to make possible the formation and growth of the *chaebol* during the 1960s and 1970s. A critical share of capital was of foreign origin, but with a crucial difference from the Singapore experience. The nationalism of the Korean government rejected an excessive presence of foreign multinational corporations, fearful of their influence on the society and on the political fate of the Korean nation. Thus capital influx into South Korea mainly took the form of loans, guaranteed by the government under the sponsorship of the United States. Public loans (mainly from international institutions, such as the World Bank) were provided to the government to build the productive infrastructure. Private loans were channeled by the government to Korean companies, according to their compliance with the government's strategic plans. Foreign capital thus accounted for 30% of all gross domestic capital formation between 1962 and 1979, and thus the ratio of foreign debt to GNP rose to more than 26% in 1978, making South Korea one of the most endebted economies in the world by the early 1980s. Debt service as a proportion of exports was not excessive, however, and in fact declined from 19.4% in 1970 to 10.5% at the end of that decade. Indeed, the ratio of exports and imports to the GNP had jumped from 22.7% in 1963 to 72.7% in 1979. This well-known characteristic of the South Korean economy strongly indicates that endebtedness per se is not an obstacle to development: It is the proper use of the loans received that determines the outcome. Given U.S. military assistance to South Korea, the huge defense budget of the South Korean government did not need to have recourse to foreign lending for its financing, as was the case in several Latin American countries (particularly in Argentina), since the United States was paying the bill for this bulwark of anticommunism.

Only during the 1970s, when the foundations of the South Korean economy were established under the tight control of the *chaebol*, supported and guided by the state, did the government actively solicit direct foreign investment. But even then, strong restrictions were imposed on foreign companies: foreign equity holding was limited to a maximum of 50%, forcing them into joint ventures with Korean firms except in the Export Processing Zones isolated from the Korean market. Also, the government was very selective in allowing foreign investment, looking particularly for companies that could facilitate some technology transfer. Thus although Japanese companies invested in textiles, electrical machinery, and electronics, and American companies established a presence mainly in petroleum and chemicals, overall foreign direct investment remained quite limited, accounting in 1978 for only 19% of South Korean exports and for 16% of total manufacturing output.

While supporting and shaping the emergence of large Korean corporations aiming at the world market (and they indeed became major multinational players in the world economy during the 1980s), the South Korean developmental state organized the submissive incorporation of labor into the new industrial economy. Clearly, establishing the principle of producing first, redistributing later, Korean labor was, as in the other East Asian countries, a critical factor in Korean economic growth, being highly educated and generally hard working. However, the mode of incorporation of labor into the industrial structure was much more brutal and repressive in South Korea than in the other societies (Deyo, 1987b). Their concentration in large factories organized by means of quasi-military management favored the emergence of militant trade unionism, but autonomous workers' unions were forbidden, activism was severely repressed, and working conditions both at the factory and in terms of housing were kept at the minimum possible standards. Such repressive attitudes led to steady resistance among Korean workers, and has led to the formation of the most militant labor movement in East Asia, as the frequent and often violent strikes of the 1980s have shown. Keeping wages growing at a rate substantially lower than productivity and profits was a cornerstone of the government's economic policy.

Living conditions in general did improve, however, for the population at large as well as for industrial workers, because of the impressive performance of the economy under the impulse of export-led industrialization. But the benefits of growth were unevenly shared. For instance, during the critical period of the 1970s, between 1972 and 1979, government revenues increased at an stunning annual rate of 94.7%, the top 46 *chaebol* collected an annual increase in value-added of 22.8%, and real wages, while growing substantially by international standards, still trailed that performance, growing at an annual rate of 9.8%. Thus, while South Korea has a relatively equitable income distribution (better than the United States), mainly because of the phasing out of the landed class in the 1940s and 1950s, income distribution worsened during the 1970s, although living conditions improved for everybody (for instance, the share of the population below the poverty line went down from 41% in 1965 to 15% in 1975).

Finally, emphasis on science and technology and the upgrading of the quality of products and processes in Korean industry have been the obsession of all Korean governments since the mid-1960s, creating and staffing a series of specialized R&D institutes and linking them to industry under the guidance of the Ministry of Science and Technology. South Korea is probably the industrializing country that has most rapidly climbed the technology ladder in the new international division of labor (Ernst & O'Connor, 1990). For instance, between 1970 and 1986 Korea's engineering exports grew at an annual average rate of 39%, far exceeding the performance of Japan at 20% per year.

Thus behind the performance of "Asia's next economic giant," one that increased its share of the world's gross domestic production by growing by 345% between 1965 and 1986 (Federation of Korean Industries, 1987), lies the nationalist project of a developmental state that deliberately orchestrated the creation of major Korean multinational companies able to become influential players in the world economy on the basis of foreign lending, American military support, and ruthless exploitation of Korean labor.

Taiwan: The Rise of Flexible Capitalism Under the Guidance of an Inflexible State[4]

Even by the high standards of the Pacific Rim development experience, Taiwan is probably *the* success story, in terms of the combination of a sustained high rate of economic growth (annual average of 8.7% for 1953-1982, and of 6.9% for 1965-1986), increase in world share of GDP (multiplied by a factor of 3.63 in 1965-1986), increase in the share of world exports (that reached 2.08% in 1986, above all other NICs including South Korea), increase in the share of the world's manufacturing output (multiplied by a factor of 6.79 in 1965-1986 as compared to South Korea's growth factor of 3.59), and this within the context of relatively equal income distribution (Gini coefficients of .558 in 1953 to .303 in 1980, much better than the United States or the average of the EC, although the situation has deteriorated during the 1980s [Kuo, 1983]), substantial improvement of health, education, and living standards (Gold, 1986), and social stability (enforced by harsh police repression) for the period from 1950 to 1977.

At the core of Taiwanese economic growth lies the notion of flexible production, put into practice in Taiwan (Greenhalgh, 1988) before American academics discovered it on their Italian vacations. The flexibility concerns both the industrial structure itself, and the adaptability of the overall structure to the changing conditions of the world economy, under the guidance of an all-powerful state, supported and advised in the initial stages by U.S. Aid. In fact, throughout the historical process of development the logic of the model of economic growth changed quite dramatically, from import-substitution emphasis in the 1950s, to export-oriented industrialization in the 1960s (the take-off period), to what Thomas Gold (1986) calls "export-oriented import substitution" (that is, the deepening of the industrial base to feed exports of manufactured goods) during the 1970s and 1980s. In the 1980s, as Taiwan became an economic power in its own right, Taiwanese companies took on the world market, internationalizing their production and investments both in Asia (particularly in China) and in the OECD countries (particularly in the United States).

At each one of these four stages in the process we observe a different industrial structure that evolves and superposes on itself without major crises. But in all instances two features are critical for the understanding of the process; the Kuomintang (KMT) state is at the center of the structure and the structure itself is highly diversified, decentralized, and made up of networking relationships between firms, between firms and the state, and between firms and the world market through trading companies (mainly Japanese) and worldwide commercial intermediaries.

During the 1950s, the KMT state, with massive economic aid and military protection from the United States, undertook the reform of the economy after taking total control of the society through ruthless and bloody repression in the 1947-1950 period. An American-inspired land reform destroyed the land-owning class and created a large population of small farmers that, with state support, dramatically increased agricultural productivity. Agriculture was the original device for surplus accumulation, both in the form of transfer of capital and in terms of providing cheap food for the urban-industrial labor force. The government forced the farmers into unequal exchange with the industrial economy by controlling credit and fertilizers and organizing a barter system that exchanged agricultural inputs for rice. With the control of the banks (they were, and still are in the majority of cases, government owned) and control of import licenses, the government geared the Taiwanese economy toward import substitution industrialization, forming the beginning of a capitalist structure in a totally protected market. The government, with American aid, provided the necessary production and communications infrastructure and placed major emphasis on educating the labor force. To implement this strategy a series of government institutions, including four-year economic plans, were established.

Because of the exhaustion of the domestic market as potential demand to stimulate growth at the end of the 1950s, the state followed the advice (indeed, the instructions) of the U.S. agencies and embarked on an ambitious restructuring of the economy based on an outward orientation. In 1960, the 19-Point Program of Economic and Financial Reform liberalized controls on trade, stimulated exports, and designed a strategy to attract foreign investment. Taiwan was the first country to invent the notion of Export Processing Zones, and implemented one in Kaoshiung at the southwestern tip of the island. In 1964, General Instruments pioneered electronics assembly offshoring in Taiwan. Japanese *medium-sized* companies quickly moved to benefit from low wages, educated labor, and government support. Yet the nucleus of Taiwanese industrial structure was made up of a large number of local enterprises, set up with family savings and cooperative savings networks and supported by government bank credits, many of which were (and still are) located in the rural fringes of metropolitan areas, where family members work on the land and in the industrial shop at the same time. For instance, about half of the world's umbrellas come from a network of small companies, many of which are located in the semirural area near Tanyung, as I saw for myself during field work in the region. Thus the Taiwanese state attracted multinational investment as a way to generate capital and to obtain access to world markets. But foreign corporations were linked through subcontracting arrangements to a wide network of small firms that provided the substantial base of industrial production. In fact, with the exception of electronics, direct foreign investment does not represent a major component of the Taiwanese economy. For instance, in 1981 direct capital stock of foreign companies in Taiwan represented only 2% of the GNP, employment in foreign companies amounted to 4.8% of total employment, their output only 13.9% of total output, and their exports only 25.6% of total exports (Purcell, 1987, p. 81). A more important phenomenon in facilitating critical access to world markets was the intermediary role played by Japanese trading companies and by representatives of American large commercial chains looking for direct supplies from Taiwanese industrialists.

Thus the outward orientation of the economy did not imply control of the economy by the multinationals (as in Singapore), nor the formation of large Taiwanese conglomerates as the dominant force (although a number of major industrial groups did develop under the auspices of the state). Rather, it was enacted by a flexible combination of a decentralized network of Taiwanese firms acting as subcontractors for foreign manufacturers located in Taiwan (large American multinationals, medium-sized Japanese firms), and as suppliers of international commercial networks, either through Japanese trading companies or through representatives of large (mainly American) department stores. This is how "Made in Taiwan" merchandise ended up entering the whole realm of our everyday life: K-Mart acted as a KMT agent . . .

However, in spite of the importance of Taiwanese medium and small firms in the process of winning competitiveness through flexibility, I must insist on the fact that the state was the central actor in guiding and coordinating the whole process of industrialization, by setting up the needed infrastructure, attracting foreign capital, deciding the priorities for strategic investment, and imposing its conditions when necessary (for instance, the first attempt to initiate a Taiwanese automobile industry failed when the government refused to accept the conditions required by Toyota).

A critical factor in the growing productivity of the Taiwanese economy, as in the case of the other "tigers," was the high yield of labor through the combination of low wages, decent education, hard work, and social peace. Social control of labor in Taiwan was achieved first by establishing the precedent of unrestrained repression to any challenge to the state authority. But in addition to repression, a number of factors contributed decisively to diffuse conflict and to integrate workers into the industrial fabric. The state did provide a safety net in the form of subsidized health and education, but not housing, although housing cooperatives (helped by government banks) were a factor in delaying the housing crisis until it exploded in the 1980s in one of the most dramatic issues in today's Taiwanese society (Chin, 1988). But the most important factor contributing to social peace was the industrial structure itself, made up of thousands of small companies, many of which were based on family members and primary social networks, sometimes linked to part-time agricultural activity. In the multinational corporations, the bulk of the unskilled labor force, as in other Asian societies, were young women, who were subjected to the double patriarchalism of family and factory, thus effectively reducing them into subservience, since they actually came to see factory life as a space of relative freedom compared with life at home. While the situation is changing, with the formation of a conscious female working class, the gender structure of the work force was an important factor ensuring social peace during the critical moment of the industrial take-off.

In the 1970s and 1980s, to fight the threat of protectionism in the core markets and to counter the danger of political isolation after the entry of the People's Republic of China into the international community, the KMT state engaged in a process of upgrading and modernization of industry, particularly in high technology, including the creation of one of the most successful high technology parks in Asia, in Hsinchu, articulating the major government research institute in electronics, two leading technical universities, foreign firms, and Taiwanese companies, some of them spin-offs from the research institute. Taiwan has made rapid progress in electronics, particularly in personal computers and peripherals, and a number of Taiwanese firms have become major suppliers to electronics giants such as DEC or IBM

(Ernst & O'Connor, 1990). Other industrial sectors (in particular garments and textiles) have been pushed by the government to raise the quality of their goods in order to circumvent protectionism by going into higher value-added merchandise while not increasing the quotas calculated in volume terms.

In the 1980s Taiwan became such a mature, thriving economy that the Taiwanese industrial bourgeoisie developed a more assertive mood, increasingly breaking away from the state and trying to establish its own presence in the world, through its links with international capital. The most spectacular change refers to massive investment in China in open defiance of official KMT policy, very often using centuries-old village networks, which remain in place. Because of rising wages and increasing workers' organization in Taiwan, together with the tightening of quotas vis-à-vis Taiwanese-origin merchandise, the largest Taiwanese companies are offshoring production in China and other East and Southeast Asian countries (for instance, it is estimated that 40% of Taiwanese shoe manufacturing actually takes place in China [Hsing, 1990]) in a striking demonstration of the endogenous character of Taiwanese capitalism, finally reaching maturity at the very moment the KMT's ideology becomes irreversibly obsolete and the KMT state is losing its grip on the complex, industrial society it helped to create.

The Hong Kong Model Versus the Hong Kong Reality: Small Business in a World Economy and the Colonial Version of the Welfare State[5]

Hong Kong remains the historical reference for the free-market, free-trader, free-wheeler advocates of unrestrained capitalism whose ideology wrecked the American economy in the 1980s.[6] While the prominent role of the state in the hypergrowth economies of Japan, South Korea, Taiwan, and Singapore is too obvious to be denied, Hong Kong, with its early take-off during the 1950s and its apparently laissez faire brand of capitalism, reinforced by the Hong Kong government's stated policy of "positive non-intervention," incarnates the dreams of classical state-free capitalism and makes them into a model destined to survive the 1997 deadline for a society built "in a borrowed place, on borrowed time."

And yet, a careful analysis of the process of economic development of Hong Kong since the mid-1950s reveals a decisive role by the state in creating the conditions for economic growth, though in a more subtle, more indirect but not less important way than the intervention described in the case of the three other countries analyzed here (Leung et al., 1980; Schiffer, 1983; Youngson, 1982).

Let us first review certain facts. In the free-market paradise of Hong Kong, all land (with the exception of communal village land in the New Territories) is Crown Land, which the government has leased—not sold—over the years, in a land market entirely manipulated by government control to increase its revenue and subsidize its public housing projects as well as government-developed industrial estates and flatted factories.[7] Furthermore, during the critical years of economic take-off (1949-1980) while GDP grew by a factor of 13 (impressive in itself), real government expenditure grew by 26 times, and government expenditure in welfare (including housing, education, health, and social welfare) grew by an astounding amount of 72 times. Thus government expenditure as a proportion of GDP reached 20.3% in 1980. The government share of total capital formation grew during the 1960s and 1970s from 13.6% in 1966 to an all time high of 23.4% in 1983 before declining to about 16% during the mid-1980s (Ho, 1979; Youngson, 1982; also see statistical sources in Castells, Kwok, & Goh, 1990).

But more significant than the size of government expenditures or than the real extent of regulation (quite important, for instance, in the banking industry after a series of scandals threatened to wreck the financial markets during the early 1980s [Ghose, 1987]), is the strategic role played by government in making possible the specific mode of development that made Hong Kong into a nest of competitiveness in the thriving world economy of the 1960s. Thus we must briefly sketch the components of such a development process, to understand the crucial importance of indirect government intervention on the conditions of production and collective consumption that are at the source of the competitiveness of Hong Kong's business.

The classic econometric study by Edward K. Y. Chen (1979) on the sources of economic growth in Hong Kong for the period 1955-1974 shows that capital and labor inputs played a much greater role in Hong Kong than in the growth of advanced industrial economies. Also, he identifies export and international trade as the leading factors in explaining Hong Kong's growth. This interpretation is confirmed and expanded in the careful statistical analysis by Tsong-Biau Lin, Victor Mok, and Yin-Ping Ho (1980) on the close relationship between exports of manufacturing goods and economic growth, hardly a surprising finding but an observation full of meaning, particularly when the rise of Hong Kong as a financial and trade center in the 1980s tends to blur the original sources of the Territory's prosperity.

Their study also shows that exports have concentrated over time in the same few industries—textiles, garments, footwear, plastics, consumer electronics—in a different pattern than that observed in the other three countries. However, the expansion of exports is mainly due to what the authors call "changes due to differential commodity composition," that is, changes of product line and in the value of the products within the same industry. In this sense, what has been fundamental is the flexibility of Hong Kong manufacturers to adapt quickly and effectively to the demand of the world market within the same industries.

We still need to explain the competitiveness of these industries besides their ability to adapt to demand. Another econometric study by E. K. Y. Chen (1980) provides the clue: The critical explanatory variable in Hong Kong's growth equation is the differential between Hong Kong's relative prices and the level of income in the United States, the main market for Hong Kong's exports. The level of prices for manufactured goods in Hong Kong being mainly determined by wage levels in labor-intensive industries, it was the capacity of Hong Kong firms to keep wage increases well below the increase in U.S. income while still assuring an efficient, skilled, and motivated labor force that provided the ground-base for the expansion of manufactured exports, and thus for economic growth. Thus flexibility of manufacturing and competitive prices on the basis of low production costs are the main factors that explain Hong Kong's export success, which underlies Hong Kong's growth. But these "explanatory variables" are themselves the result of a specific industrial structure and of a given institutional environment that made possible the flexibility and competitiveness of the economy.

On the one hand, the flexibility is the result of an industrial structure characterized by small business; more than 90% of manufacturing firms in Hong Kong in 1981 employed less than 50 workers, and large enterprises (more than 100 workers) accounted for only 22.5% of manufacturing's contribution to GDP. Since 90% of manufactured goods are exported, we may assume that small businesses are similarly important in this area, although there are no data to show it directly. We do know that foreign manufacturers account for a small proportion of Hong Kong's manufacturing exports (10.9% in 1974, 13.6% in 1984). In fact the average size of manufacturing establishments in Hong Kong decreased over time: from an average of 52.5 workers per establishment in 1951 to 20 in 1981. The mystery is how these small firms were able to link up with the world market. Unlike in Taiwan, foreign trading companies were not important in Hong Kong. There were indeed the traditionally established British trading "hongs" (such as the legendary Jardine

Matheson or Swire groups), but their role in manufacturing exports was actually small. About 75% of exports, according to the study by Victor Sit (1982), were handled by local export/import firms. The great majority of these small firms were small businesses themselves: There were more than 14,000 such firms in Hong Kong in 1977. It was only in the 1980s that large department stores from the United States, Japan, and Western Europe established their own channels in Hong Kong to place orders with the local firms. Thus the basic industrial structure of Hong Kong consisted of networks of small firms, networking and subcontracting among themselves on an ad hoc basis, following the orders channeled by small firms specializing in export/import. Such a flexible structure, originating from the initial nucleus of Shanghainese textile entrepreneurs that immigrated after the Chinese revolution with little more than their know-how, became in fact the most adequate instrument for adapting to rapidly changing demand in a world market expanding at an increasing rate.

But how were these small businesses able to obtain information about the world market, to upgrade their production, to improve their machinery, to increase their productivity? The Hong Kong government played a significant though not decisive role in the matter. First, it organized the distribution of export quotas allowed under the MultiFibre Agreement among different companies in the textile industry, actually shaping the production networks under the guidance of the government's Industry Department. Second, it established (in the 1960s) a series of information and training centers, such as the Hong Kong Productivity Center, engaged in training programs and consulting and technology services, and the Hong Kong Trade Development Council, with offices around the world to promote exports and to disseminate information among Hong Kong's firms. Other services, such as the Hong Kong Credit Insurance Corporation, served to cover some of the risks incurred by exporters. In the late 1970s, when the need for restructuring and upgrading Hong Kong's economy became necessary to answer the challenge of protectionism in core markets, the government appointed a committee on Industrial Diversification that elaborated a strategic plan for Hong Kong's new stage of industrialization, a plan that was implemented by and large during the 1980s.

The fundamental contribution, however, of Hong Kong's government to the flexibility and competitiveness of small businesses was its widespread intervention in the realm of collective consumption, particularly through a huge public housing program that houses about 45% of the population in subsidized apartments whose initial appalling quality has considerably improved over time with the building of new towns and large housing estates. In addition, a comprehensive system of public education, public health, subsidized mass transit, social services, and subsidized foodstuffs, was put into place over the years, amounting to a major subsidy of indirect wages for the labor force. Schiffer (1983) calculated the impact of nonmarket forces on household blue-collar expenditures for 1973-1974: On average it amounted to a 50.2% subsidy for each household. In another study concerning only the public housing subsidy, Fu-Lai Yu and Si-Ming Li (1985) estimated a transfer-in-kind to the average public housing tenant equivalent to 70% of the household's income. Thus public housing and the special brand of welfare state that emerged in Hong Kong subsidized workers and allowed them to work long hours without putting too much pressure on their employers, most of them with little margin to afford salary increases. By shifting onto the government's shoulders the responsibility for the workers' well being, small businesses could concentrate on competitive pricing, shrinking and expanding their labor force according to the variations of demand.

Hong Kong's Colonial welfare state did perform two other important functions directly related to the competitiveness of the economy:

(a) It made possible industrial peace for a long period, a matter of some consequence given the historical tradition of social struggle (often overlooked) among the Hong Kong working class, an underlying current that surfaced with rampaging violence in the urban riots of 1956, 1966, and 1967 (Chan et al., 1986; Chesneaux, 1982; Endacott & Birch, 1978; Hong Kong Government, 1967).

(b) It created a safety net for low-risk entrepreneurialism that characterized the scene of small business in Hong Kong. In fact, small businesses in Hong Kong, as everywhere else, had a very high mortality rate (Sit, 1982), particularly in the presence of the black box of a distant world market. But most businesses were started by workers who bet their small savings and relied on family support and on the safety net of public housing and subsidized collective consumption to take their chance, withdrawing to their relatively secure position when their entrepreneurial attempt went wrong.

Thus social stability and subsidized collective consumption were critical for the moderation of direct wages, for stable industrial relations, and for the creation of a burgeoning nest of small and medium-sized entrepreneurs who were indeed the driving force of Hong Kong's development, but under social and institutional conditions quite different from those depicted by Milton Friedman in his novels about the economy.

Commonalities and Dissimilarities
in the Process of Economic Development
of Asia's Newly Industrialized Economies:
Are They Four Tigers or
One Dragon With Four Tiger Tails?

I have tried to reconstruct, as precisely as possible, the underlying specific logic of the process of economic development in the four countries under consideration. In my opinion, this is the necessary starting point for all attempts aimed at building a new theory of development. But to make progress on the path of theorizing we must now shift gears and reflect comparatively on the processes just described. The commonalities and dissimilarities in such processes should lead us to clues to understand the *social* sources of development in the new world economy.

Let us start with the *uncommon factors,* those that clearly differ in each case, and that therefore cannot be considered critical elements in the development process.

The most important dissimilarity is the industrial structure of each country. In particular, we should reject the "new international division of labor" thesis, according to which the new industrialization in the periphery is mainly the result of productive decentralization by multinational corporations from the core. They are fundamental for Singapore, but they played a secondary role in Taiwanese industrialization, and they are clearly minor players in South Korea and Hong Kong (although in Hong Kong international *financial* corporations became important during the 1980s). As we know, the industrial structure of Singapore is characterized by the direct connection between multinational corporations and the state; the South Korean economy is centered around the Korean *chaebol* nurtured and guided by the state; Taiwan blends into a flexible structure of large national firms, small and medium-sized businesses, and a significant but minority presence of foreign firms, either large (American) or medium (Japanese); and Hong Kong's economic growth, until the 1980s, was engineered by local manufacturing firms, most of them small and medium, supported by a benevolent colonial state that provided productive infrastructure and subsidized collective consumption. Thus there is no relationship between a given industrial structure and economic growth. They were all stunning success stories, but they reached similar rates of growth through seemingly different paths.

Nor is the sectoral specialization of the economies a common feature. It was not the concentration of industrial effort on textiles or on electronics that explains the competitiveness of these economies, since South Korea—and Taiwan to a lesser extent—gradually diversified their activities into a variety of sectors. Singapore started from the beginning on petroleum and electronics (mainly semiconductors), and Hong Kong basically deepened and upgraded its original specialization in textiles, garments, plastics, footwear, and consumer electronics. The one common feature is the adaptability and flexibility needed to deal with world market demands, but this was performed either by a simultaneous presence in various sectors, or by a succession of priority sectors (as in South Korea), or by upgrading the traditional sectors (as in Hong Kong). Economic competitiveness does not seem to result from "picking the winners" but from learning how to win.

The existence of a welfare state of sorts, through subsidized collective consumption, was a decisive element in the development of the city-states—Singapore and Hong Kong—but was clearly not so in South Korea (where the state did not take care of workers' needs and only the *chaebol* introduced some elements of social paternalism, such as company housing), nor in Taiwan where the state deliberately intended to improve the living conditions of the population and to lower income inequality, but it let the market provide the basic goods for the population, while it concentrated on providing education and ensuring that the economy would generate jobs and income.

Last but not least, the myth of social peace as a major component of the development process in East Asia does not stand up to research observations when data are gathered from historical records and direct interviewing of the social actors. Singapore became stable after massive repression and outlawing of the main trade union movement in the early 1960s. Taiwan was pacified after the 1947 massacre of an estimated 10,000 people resisting the imposition of the KMT state, and although it has been a politically conflictual society since at least the 1977 Chung Li riot, conflicts have not fundamentally endangered its economic dynamism. Hong Kong had for a long time a relatively high degree of unionized workers (Lethbridge, 1980) with the largest union federation controlled by Chinese communists; its "social peace" was repeatedly shattered by the riots of 1956, 1966, and 1967 (Miners, 1986; Lau, 1982), the last one being followed by several months of protests, including bombings. Since the late 1970s, powerful mobilizations at the community level have created the foundations of what is today an extremely active "democracy movement" that raises great concern both in Hong Kong and in Beijing. South Korea went from the 1960 student uprising that toppled Syngman Rhee to an endless succession of student demonstrations, workers struggles (most of them subdued and ignored), and citizen-workers insurrections, most notably the 1980 Kwangju uprising that was repressed at the price of more than 1,000 victims. Although South Korea's growth has recently been challenged by political instability, the occasional violent conflicts (actually triggering the process that ended the military dictatorship) as well as daily workers' resistance during the entire process of economic development, did not undermine the economic performance of the country (S. K. Kim, 1987; Park, 1990).

Thus while it is true that the search for social stability, and the partial achievement of such a goal, was a fundamental element in the development policy of the four countries, it was not a given of the society. Quite the opposite: All four countries started from potentially volatile social and political situations that had to be tamed, repressed, and later on controlled and prevented in order for the economy to work. Social stability was not a prerequisite but an always uncertain result of the process of economic growth in the Asian Pacific.

But we also find some *commonalities* in our observation. Without them, we could not even think about a recurrent pattern that would shed light on our understanding of the new historical processes of development.

The first common factor concerns the existence of an emergency situation in the society, as a result of major tensions and conflicts at the international level. It is obvious in the cases of South Korea and Taiwan. It should also be recalled that Hong Kong dramatically changed as a consequence of the Chinese revolution, losing most of its traditional role as entrepôt for China trade, thus being forced into manufacturing exports as a way to survive without being a burden on the Crown's budget. Indeed it was its role vis-à-vis China, together with its economic success that prevented Hong Kong from joining the decolonization process, since neither the United Kingdom nor China could accept its independence. That was also the case for Singapore, first prevented by British troops from being annexed by Indonesia, then expelled from the Federation of Malaysia and abandoned to its fate by Britain in 1965-1968, then saved politically and economically because of its support for the American effort in the Vietnam War. The critical element here, as compared for instance to the situation in Latin America, is that the United States perceived most of Asia as being clearly in danger of a general communist takeover (and in fact, there were enough elements to support such a perception). Therefore strategic considerations overshadowed all other calculations for U.S. policy in the region, which in fact gave much more freedom to maneuver to the local states in the running of their economies, although on the condition of remaining "vassal states" in terms of foreign policy and of repressing domestic communism (a condition to which they gladly agreed). If there is a fundamental common thread to the policies of the four countries (including Hong Kong) it is that, at the origin of their process of development we find *policies dictated by the politics of survival.* Another consequence of this context dominated by the Asian Cold War was the importance of American and British support for these governments and for their economies. As we know, American aid was the major element in the economies of South Korea and Taiwan during the 1950s. Although Hong Kong contributed to Britain more than the United Kingdom did to Hong Kong, some crucial functions like defense remained on British shoulders. Singapore did not receive much direct aid, and its economy could start only in the mid-1960s because of the profitable oil and ship repairing commerce with American forces in Vietnam.

A second major common factor is that *all four development processes were based on an outward orientation of the economy, and more specifically on their success in exporting manufactured goods.* Although for both South Korea and Taiwan import-substitution policies were extremely important at the onset of the process, particularly to set up an industrial base, they only prospered when they engaged in export-oriented manufacturing. In this sense, the explosion of world trade in the 1960s and the growing interdependence of the world economy form an indispensable background for understanding the success of the Asian tigers—which brings up the question of the historical replicability of such an exceptionally favorable situation.

A third common factor is the *absence of a rural landowning class,* nonexistent in Hong Kong and Singapore, and practically destroyed (or reconverted into an industrial bureaucracy) by the American-inspired land reforms of South Korea and Taiwan in the 1950s. It would appear that the existence of a powerful landowning class is indeed a major obstacle to the development of dynamic capitalism in the Third World, because when they convert themselves into "businesses" (as in Indonesia, for instance) they tend to confuse money making with capital accumulation, actually undermining the modernization efforts of the country and the improvement of its relative position in nontraditional exports (Yoshihara, 1988).

A fourth common, and critical, factor in the development of the four countries is the *availability of educated labor, able to reskill itself during the process of industrial upgrading, with high productivity at a level of wages very low for international standards. A fundamental factor for all the countries has been the ability to keep labor under control, in terms of work discipline and labor demands.* This goal has been achieved, by and large, through different means, but the success of labor policies cannot be equated with the existence of social peace, as already stated. Disciplined, efficient, cheap labor is a fundamental factor in the process of development of the

Asian NICs. But their discipline or effectiveness does not come from the supposedly submissive nature of Asian labor (plainly a racist statement) nor, in a more sophisticated vein, from Confucianism. Confucianism does explain the high value placed on education and therefore the high quality of labor once the state provides the minimum conditions for access to education. But Confucianism does not explain submissiveness, since in the Confucian philosophy authority must be legitimate and exercised in legitimate ways. Indeed, the long story of popular uprisings and social revolts in China, as well as the long tradition of a revolutionary working-class movement in Shanghai and Guangdong Province stands against the ill-informed statements of managerial ideology. In all cases labor discipline was imposed first by repression, as indicated in the specific analyses of each country. But in all cases there were also powerful elements of social integration that explain why an historically rebellious population ultimately accommodated to the exploitative conditions for most of the people for most of the period under study. Paramount among the integrative factors is the actual betterment of living conditions for workers. What was a low wage for an American or Japanese worker was a fortune for the new industrial labor force of extremely poor Asian countries. Furthermore, data show an improvement in income inequality during the first stage of the process and a dramatic improvement in real wage earnings overall. Besides, in the case of Hong Kong and Singapore a peculiar version of the welfare state, materially organized around public housing projects and new towns, did provide the privileged a channel both for the improvement of living conditions and for the establishment of social and political control by the state. In the case of Taiwan, the integration of rural and urban life and the vitality of primary social networks provided, at the same time, the social net to resist the shock of rapid industrialization and the mechanism of peer-group social control to discourage the highly risky enterprise of challenging the system. Thus through a combination of state repression, state integration, economic improvement, and social network protection and control, an increasingly educated labor force (many of whom were women) found it in their best interests to fulfill the expectations of a system that was as dynamic as it was ruthless. Only when the survival stage was passed did spontaneous social resistance start to take the shape of a labor movement dreaming of political alternatives, particularly in South Korea.

A fifth common factor in the Asian experience of rapid industrialization is the *ability of these economies to adapt to the changing conditions of the world economy, climbing the ladder of development through technological upgrading, market expansion, and economic diversification.* What is particularly remarkable (as in the case of Japan, which provided the role model for all the experiences with the possible exception of Hong Kong) is their understanding of the critical role played by R&D and high technology sectors in the new international economy (Ernst & O'Connor, 1990; Purcell, 1989). This emphasis on science and technology that mainly characterizes South Korea and Taiwan but is also present in the city-states, was decided and implemented by the state, but it was welcomed and adopted by industrial firms. Thus the four countries have in fact made their transition into the advanced productive structures of the informational economy, and while many activities remain rather primitive (as also happens in New York) it would be a fundamental mistake to consider their competitiveness to be based still on low-paid, low-skilled labor. It is the ability to shift from one level of development to another and from one form of incorporation into the world economy to a more competitive one, generating higher value, that was the clue for a cumulative process of development that led to endogenous economic growth, in contrast with the short-lived phases of economic growth followed by stagnation and crisis that was the experience of most of Latin America in the 1970s and 1980s (Fajnzylber, 1983).

Behind most of the critical factors found to be common to the four experiences appears what seems to be the most important of all commonalities: *the role of the state in the development process of each country.* The production of high-quality labor and its subsequent control, the strategic guidance through the hazardous seas of the world economy, the ability to lead the economy in periods of transition, the process of diversification, the creation of a science-and-technology base and its diffusion in the industrial system— these are all critical policies whose success determined the historical possibility of the overall process of development. And policies are, of course, the outcome of politics, enacted by the state. Thus in the various configurations of the industrial structure we have examined, the only invariant is the centrality or importance of the state. While the process of development gradually freed the economy and society from the tight control of the state, the historical origin and the main explanatory structural element in the generation of cumulative growth was the action of the state, as a number of empirical analyses presented here have shown. Thus to understand the secret of the new sources of economic development we must unveil the logic of the state. Behind the economic performance of the Asian tigers breathes the dragon of the developmental state.

The Historical Specificity
of the Developmental State in
the East Asian Newly Industrialized Countries

On the Concept of Developmental State

If the hypotheses presented in this text are plausible, understanding the development experience of the Asian NICs requires, first of all, a sociological and political analysis of the historical experience of the developmental state in these countries. Without such an analysis, the economists' efforts at replicating "the model" are doomed and likely to lead to ideologically driven economic policy, the worst possible recipe for developing societies.

In good methodology, the historical-structural approach I present in this analysis would at this point require a careful reconstruction of the socio-political process leading to the specific mode of state intervention in the economy of each of the four countries under consideration. However, I doubt the already too patient reader would tolerate such an exercise. Thus, I will try to summarize the main lines of the argument, while illustrating it, for each point of the presentation, with specific references to the social structure and political history of each country.

First, I need to define the precise meaning of *development state*. While I do not disagree with the main explicit or implicit notions of the developmental state in the social sciences literature (those of Chalmers Johnson, Peter Evans, or Frederic Deyo, for instance), I believe it would be clarifying to be unequivocal about my own use of the concept, as it emerges from the analysis of the East Asian experience (although, I think it can be extrapolated to other contexts).

A state is developmental when it establishes as its principle of legitimacy its ability to promote and sustain development, understanding by development the combination of steady high rates of economic growth and structural change in the productive system, both domestically and in its relationship to the international economy. This definition is misleading, however, unless we specify the meaning of *legitimacy* in a given historical context. Most political science theorists remain prisoner of an ethnocentric conception of legitimacy, related to the democratic state. Under such a conception, the state is legitimate when it establishes hegemony or consensus vis-à-vis the civil society. Yet, this particular form of legitimacy presupposes the acceptance by the state itself of its submission to the principle of representation of society as it is. But we know that states that have tried over history to break away from the existing order, did not recognize civil society-as-it-was as the source of their legitimacy. And yet, they were not pure apparatuses of naked power, as was the case with defensive military dictatorships in many historical instances. The clearest examples are revolutionary states, particularly those emerging from communist revolutions or national liberation movements. They never pretended to be legitimate in terms of the acquiescence of their subjects, but in terms of the historical project they embodied, as avant-gardes of the classes and nations that were not yet fully aware of their destiny and interests. The obvious and significant political and ideological differences between the communist and revolutionary states and the right-wing dictatorships of East Asia have, in my opinion, led to the overlooking of some fundamental similarities that go beyond formal resemblances to the heart of the logic of the state: the legitimacy principle holding together the apparatus, and structuring and organizing the codes and the principles for accessing power and for exercising it. In other words, the legitimacy principle may be exercised on behalf of the society (the democratic state) or on behalf of the societal project. When the state substitutes itself for society in the definition of societal goals, when such a societal project involves a fundamental transformation of the social order (regardless of our value judgment on the matter), I refer to it as the *revolutionary state*. When the societal project respects the broader parameters of social order (although not necessarily the specific social structure) but aims at a fundamental transformation of the economic order (regardless of the interests or desires of the civil society) I propose the hypothesis that we are in the presence of what we call the *developmental state*. The historical expression of such a societal project generally takes the form (and such was the case in most of the East Asian experience) of the building or rebuilding of national identity, affirming the national presence of a given society or a given culture in the world, although not necessarily coinciding with the territorial limits under the control of the developmental state (e.g., the Kuomintang state speaking on behalf of the "Republic of China," behind the safe refuge provided by the U.S. Seventh Fleet).

Thus ultimately for the developmental state, economic development is not a goal but a means.[8] To become competitive in the world economy, for all the Asian NICs, was first, their way of surviving, both as a state and as a society. Second, it also became their only way to assert their national interests in the world, that is, to break away from a dependency situation, even at the price of becoming unconditional military frontliners for the United States. In a deliberate parallel with Marx's theory of social classes, I propose the idea that the developmental state effects the transition of a political subject "in itself" to a political apparatus "for itself" by affirming the only legitimacy principle that did not seem to be threatening for the international powers overseeing its destiny: economic development. The basic logic of such a transition is nonetheless a fundamentally political logic, directly expressing a nationalist project, even if, in the same moment, the leaders of the new nation did personally benefit from their power, by ransacking the society and the economy as all nondemocratic states do.

The Rise of the Developmental State: From the Politics of Survival to the Process of Nation-Building

The general hypothesis I propose is that the East Asian developmental state, outside Japan, was born out of the need for survival, and then it grew on the basis of a nationalist project of self-affirmation of cultural/political identity in the world system.

Survival came first.

Singapore was a nonentity at the onset of its independence in 1965. An abandoned military outpost of the crumbled British Empire, a bankrupt entrepôt economy cut off from its ties with Indonesia, an integral part of Malaysia expelled from the Federation of Malaysia, and a multiethnic society subjected to the pressure of its Malay environment and torn by the internal violent ethnic and religious strife between the Chinese majority and the Muslim Malay and Hindu Tamil minorities. It could have easily become another Sri Lanka. The first concern of the People's Action Party (PAP) that led the anticolonial struggle against British domination was to hold Singapore together and to make it viable, while fighting off what was perceived as the menace of the guerrillas of the Malaysian Communist Party, led by Chinese and supported by the People's Republic of China (PRC).

South Korea had just survived an all-out assault from communist North Korea, and had barely escaped being caught in the middle of a nuclear war between MacArthur's imperial dreams and the quasi-victorious Chinese People's Liberation Army. In 1953 the country was in a shambles, the nation divided, and Syngman Rhee's First Republic was but a superstructure for America to build a strong defensive line (based on a new, modern Korean military) on the Northern Asian frontier in the relentless war against communism.

Taiwan was not Taiwan. It was an impoverished and terrorized island that had become the last bastion of the vanquished Kuomintang armies, kept in reserve by America as a potential threat and as a political standpoint against the rising power of the PRC. In fact, only the communist invasion of South Korea decided America on drawing the line in the Taiwan Straits, a decision that probably saved the KMT and allowed it to start living the ideological fantasy of reconstructing the Republic of China from Taiwan Province, a fantasy not shared by Chinese capitalists who migrated elsewhere.

Hong Kong was rapidly becoming an anachronism, after the Chinese Revolution and the embargo on China imposed by the United Nations on the occasion of the Korean War. With its entrepôt commerce with China downgraded to smuggling, it was on its way to being the last colony of a fading empire. Fundamental doubts about China's willingness to let it live outside Chinese control, as well as political fears that either the Labour Party or British public opinion would include the Territory in the next round of decolonization, kept Hong Kong wondering about its fate while wave after wave of Chinese immigrants/refugees were making the colony into their own trap, out of their escape either from revolution or misery.

The first reflex of the state apparatuses that later became developmental (the PAP state in Singapore, the Park Regime in South Korea, the KMT in Taiwan, and the colonial state in Hong Kong) was to ensure the physical, social, and institutional viability of the societies they came to be in charge of. In the process, they constructed and consolidated their own identity as political apparatuses.

However, according to the hypothesis I am proposing, *they shaped their states around the developmental principle of legitimacy on the basis of specific political projects that had, in each case, specific political subjects, all of which were created in rupture with the societies they were about to control.*

In Singapore (Chua, 1985) the PAP did lead the anticolonialist struggle, but it did so in the 1950s in close alliance with the left-wing movement (including the left-wing unions), and even with the communists, until the events of the early 1960s convinced the undisputed national leader, Lee Kwan Yew, that he had to repress the left (which he did ruthlessly) and to establish an autonomous political project aimed at transforming Singapore, out of necessity, from a colonial outpost into a modern nation. The PAP was in fact organized along Leninist lines, with tight mechanisms of social control and social mobilization, centralized forms of party power, and direct guidance of the economy through a well-paid, well-trained state technocracy. The social policies of the PAP, including public housing and community services, aimed at blending into one national culture the complex multiethnic structure of Singapore, while the emphasis on Confucianism and on Mandarin literacy among the Chinese deliberately sought to break up the subcultures organized around dialects and Chinese networks of various regional origins. Economic development was the means to achieve the goals of both making Singapore a viable nation and of affirming its presence in the world.

An even clearer case underlies the constitution of the developmental state in Taiwan (Gold, 1986). Once the KMT had to accept the reality of having lost China, it tried to convert Taiwan both into a platform for the mythical reconquest of the Mainland, and a showcase of what the reformed KMT could do for China and for the Chinese, after recognizing the disastrous economic management and the damage that their unrestrained corruption had done to their political control over China. A quasi-Leninist party, explicitly organized on the principles of democratic centralism, the KMT attempted to reform itself, made its adherence to Sun Yat-Sen's "three principles of the people" official ideology, and derived from it the emphasis on land reform, relative income equality, and providing for education of the population. The critical matter, however, was to assure the economic prosperity of the island, both to mobilize the population around the regime and to offer to the Chinese in the world at large an alternative project to Communist China. Indeed, the Chinese Open Door Policy of the 1980s was partly an answer to the impact of Taiwan's economic miracle, not only among the informed Chinese population, but among the Chinese leadership itself.

The origins of the Park Regime in South Korea can also be traced back to the emergence of a new political subject, breaking away both from the colonial order and from the corrupt, inefficient Rhee regime that had seen the remnants of the pro-Japanese bourgeoisie prosper through the state redistribution of American aid, while the country continued to suffer under the devastation of the war (Cole & Lyman, 1971; Lim, 1982). Although the 1961 coup actually toppled the short-lived civilian government of John Chang, its ideology and its practice were only partially linked to a law-and-order reflex. Its leaders were young nationalist military officers (Scalapino, n.d.) of a low rank, with the exception of Major General Park, who was in fact trained in Japan and who had served in the Japanese Army in Manchuria. The South Korean Military was an entirely new institution, whose organization and growth was obviously linked to the war. It grew from 100,000 in 1950 to 600,000 in 1961, making it one of the most numerous, well trained, and more professional armies in the world. Given the priority military interest of the United States in Korea, most of the effort of modernization and support was focused on the military. Thus the army's professional training and organizational capacity seems to have been quite above the rest of Korean society in the 1960s, with the exception of the small group of students and the intelligentsia. Thus in the presence of the disintegration of the state, economy, and society, the military officers who seized power in 1961-1963 seem to have been closer to the "Nasserite" brand of nationalist military regimes than to the mainstream Latin American tradition of pro-oligarchic military coups (Stepan, 1971). Lacking a social basis and feeling uncertain of the support of the United States toward the national projection of Korea beyond its limited military function, the Park Regime actually conceived, in explicit terms, the developmental strategy as an instrument of rebuilding the Korean nation and of winning shares of political autonomy.

But what about Hong Kong? How did the half-hearted, more subtle brand of Hong Kong's semidevelopmental state come into being? How could a colonial government identify itself with the destiny of the colony? If the traditional hongs and the new entrepreneurs cared only about their business, if the old British families dreamed about their retirement in Surrey, and the new Chinese industrialists about their green cards in Los Angeles, how could a political subject emerge in Hong Kong to make it into a thriving city-state projecting itself into the world economy?

Institutional power in Hong Kong during the entire development process was concentrated in the hands of the Colonial Governor, appointed by Westminster. Once appointed, however, the Governor was almost entirely autonomous in deciding domestic Hong Kong policies (Miners, 1986). More specifically, since 1957 the Hong Kong budget did not require formal approval from London. Thus the Colony was run by an autonomous state centered in the Governor and in a series of appointed Committees, headed by Secretaries also appointed by the Governor. This Executive Branch of government relied on the support of a number of legislative and advisory bodies made up of official and unofficial members, most of them also appointed by the government until the political reforms of the 1980s. These institutions are served by a numerous, well-trained, and extremely efficient government public service, numbering 166,000 civil servants in the 1980s. However, behind this formal structure of power, the political science study by Miron Mushkat (1982) and the historical-anthropological monograph by Henry Lethbridge (1970), as well as a number of other studies (Kwan & Chan, 1986) including my own field work, reveal an astounding, indeed fascinating power structure. The core of the Hong Kong power structure seems to be in the hands of what Miron Mushkat calls the "administrative class," a small, select group of civil servants who, until the 1970s, were recruited overwhelmingly in Britain by the Colonial Civil Service, generally out of the best British universities, and in general from Oxford and Cambridge. Between 1842 and 1941 there were only 85 "cadets" (as they were called until 1960) of the Hong Kong Colonial Civil Service. Even after the huge expansion of personnel in the 1970s, including massive recruitment of Chinese, there were only 398 "general grades administrative officers" in 1983 (Scott & Burns, 1984). It was this administrative class, with strong social and ideological cohesion and shared professional interests and cultural values, that seems to have controlled power within the Hong Kong state for most of the history of the Colony. They exercised this power while keeping in mind the interests of the business elite, but only to the extent that business would assure the economic prosperity of Hong Kong on which the power, income, prestige, and ultimately the ideological self-legitimation of the administrative class depended. Their interest in relationship to the future of Hong Kong was two-fold: to maintain the Colony in the midst of the turmoil of decolonization and the threatening anticolonial stands of the British Labour Party; and to show the world that the Colonial Service, on behalf of what was left of the tradition of the British Empire, was more able than any other political institution (in-cluding the new independent national states) to ensure the prosperity of the new Asian world, including to a large extent the well-being of its people, in a paternalistic attitude that could be considered typical of what history knows as "enlightened despotism." Although my ethnographic material on the mat-ter is too unsystematic to be conclusive, it did convince me that the dedica-tion and effectiveness of the elite colonial civil service of Hong Kong was tantamount to the last hurrah of the British Empire, building Hong Kong's prosperity as an ideological monument to their historical memory, along with the side-benefit of taking care of their retirement years.

Thus under different forms specific to each society, the developmental state in the Asian newly industrialized countries seems to have been the in-strument of a nation (or city) building (or rebuilding) process enacted by political subjects largely autonomous vis-à-vis their societies. However, it was only because such political subjects were able to both mobilize and con-trol their civil societies that they were able to implement their development strategy.

The State and Civil Society in the Restructuring of the Asian Pacific Region: How the Developmental State Succeeded in the Development Process

To identify the historical subjects of the development process in the Asian Pacific does not solve the fundamental issue of why they were able to suc-ceed, if by success we understand the achievement of their particular vision of economic development. Thus I will conclude this chapter by formulating some additional hypotheses about the factors that made possible such success. Fundamentally, they have to do with three series of questions: the relationship between developmental states and other states in the international system; the internal logic of developmental states; and the relationship between development states and their civil societies.

First, it is important to remember that the success of the East Asian developmental states cannot be explained without referring to the geopolitical context of their birth: the Asian Cold War and the unconditional, politically and militarily motivated support by the United States to these regimes. While we must reject the leftist oversimplification of seeing these states as "puppets of American imperialism" (in fact, they did show their strong autonomy as nation-building political subjects), it is equally important to recognize the historical specificity of their development process, including the crucial help they received in every aspect in the initial stages of their take-off process, both from the United States and, to a lesser extent, from Britain. I will propose the concept of "vassal states" for this particular political form. By *vassal state,* using the analogy of the feudal system, I understand a *state that is largely autonomous in the conduct of its policies, once it has abided by the specific contribution it has to make to its "sovereign state."* Thus these were not just "dependent states" in the precise sense in which dependent societies and dependent states are defined by the structural-historical theory of dependency. These are states with very limited autonomy in their contribution to the overall geopolitical system to which they belonged, in exchange for which they received protection along with a significant degree of autonomy in the conduct of their domestic affairs. I propose the notion that South Korea and Taiwan were—at least until the early 1970s in Taiwan and the early 1980s in South Korea—vassal states of America, while Hong Kong was all along a vassal state (rather than a classic colony) of the United Kingdom, and Singapore was a semivassal state of the United Kingdom during the 1960s and then of the United States until the early 1980s, including some curious linkages such as the training of its military by the Israelis. This "vassal" condition created a security umbrella, relieved much of the burden of the huge defense budget, and played a role in the critical initial stages in facilitating access to world markets (for Hong Kong to the Commonwealth markets; for Taiwan and South Korea to the U.S. market; for South Korea after its 1965 treaty with Japan to the Japanese market).

The second element explaining the success of the development strategy is *the construction of an efficient, technocratic state apparatus.* This has little to do with the traditional dichotomy between corrupt bureaucracies and clean bureaucracies. Corruption was widespread in South Korea, significant in Taiwan, much more limited (but present) in Hong Kong and Singapore. And yet the South Korean state or the KMT state were able to operate with a high level of efficiency, served by well-trained civil servants, and organized on flexible lines that changed according to the needs of each stage of development. In functional terms corruption is only an obstacle to efficiency when it prevents the apparatus from fulfilling its assigned performance. In the South Korean case, for instance, corruption was part of the pay-off for government officers and for the government party for running the country along policy lines that created huge benefits for the newly created Korean industrialists. Overall, these states were more technocratic than bureaucratic, since their apparatuses were set up to implement a strategic, historical project, and not only (but also) to reap the benefits of dictatorship.

Yet *the fundamental element in the ability of developmental states to fulfill their project was their political capacity to impose and internalize their logic on the civil societies.*

I have already objected to the Western racist myth of the submissive nature of Asian labor. While this relative submissiveness could apply (in Asia and elsewhere) to teenage women subjected to societal patriarchalism at the beginning of their life as workers (but not 10 years later), it certainly does not apply to the historical experience or to the cultural characteristics of Chinese or Korean workers. Thus the autonomy of the developmental states and their ability to implement their project with few concessions to the demands of civil society must be explained in empirical, historical terms, without referring to the metaphysics of Confucianism.

The first explanation is a simple one: *repression*. The Kuomintang executed between 10,000 and 20,000 people in establishing its hold on the island of Taiwan in 1947-1950, particularly in the Kaoshiung massacre of May 9, 1947, and went on for the next decades to establish a ruthless political control apparatus that arrested, tortured, and killed political dissenters from right or left, all being lumped under the communist label. The PAP in Singapore liquidated all serious political opposition in the 1961-1965 period, banning the main trade union and arresting the leaders of the opposition Barisan Socialists, which motivated the expulsion of the PAP from membership of the Socialist International. It later used the British Colonial Internal Security Act, allowing the government to detain with no charge for an indefinite period anyone suspected of "subversion." Hong Kong used British troops to quell the riots of 1956, 1966, and 1967, and kept a very large and efficient police force of more than 20,000 people, who did not hesitate to deport to China any dissident who became dangerous to the public order. And South

Korea, under the aegis of one of the most effective repressive apparatuses in the world, the Korean CIA, arrested, tortured, imprisoned, and killed dissidents, occasionally by the thousands, while forbidding all independent union activity and most independent political activity until the demise of the authoritarian regime in the 1980s.

Most Third World countries, however, practice the same repressive policies without much success in either containing protest or, even less, mobilizing their societies in their development path. Thus other factors must account for the organizational capacity demonstrated by the developmental states vis-à-vis their societies.

An important element is that *the dominant classes were either destroyed, disorganized, or made totally subordinate to the state, with the partial exception of Hong Kong.* Land reforms in Korea and Taiwan, and the absence of a noncolonial bourgeoisie in Singapore, actually destroyed the traditional oligarchy in these societies. What was left of the commercial-industrial bourgeoisie was made an appendix of the development strategy decided by the state. With no domestic base from which to accumulate, the role of the state as gatekeeper to the world economy made any local capitalist entirely dependent on bureaucratic licenses and government-sponsored credits. In Singapore, the multinationals quickly understood that the Lion City could be a tropical paradise for them only on the condition of not "messing up" with the government, and certainly of not giving orders in the way they used to do in Latin America or, closer to home, in Marcos's Philippines. In Hong Kong, as usual, a more complex pattern developed. The bourgeoisie, both traditional (the British Hongs) and newcomers (the Shanghainese industrialists), were co-opted via a number of government committees. The Chinese bourgeoisie was left to run its own business on the condition of reporting to the government and abiding by its instructions (Castells et al., 1990; see also King & Lee, 1981; Lethbridge, 1987; Scott, 1987). The Jockey Club socially "glued" the political and business elites together, but under the clear leadership of the arrogant, allpowerful "cadets." And a significant number of high-ranking government officials retired to become representatives of Hong Kong business associations, thus establishing an informal but effective channel of communication between government and business in a harmonious division of labor that was generally led by the government's enlightened technocracy.

As for the working class, the four states devised strategies of integration to complement repression and if possible to substitute for it in the long run. All four states counted on economic growth and the improvement of living standards, including access to education and health, to keep the workers content. In fact, the strategy was effective for most of the period. In spite of their exploitative working and living conditions, the rise of living standards in the four countries was the fastest in all of the world, including Japan. And, as we know, people judge according to the standard of their own experience, not in comparison to life in a Los Angeles suburb.

In addition, Taiwan practiced for some time a deliberate policy aimed at income redistribution, with substantially positive results. And both Singapore and Hong Kong created an Asian version of the British welfare state, centered around public housing and social services organized in new towns, that actually played a fundamental role in social integration and, in the case of Singapore, interethnic pacification. South Korea practiced a much harsher policy toward the working class and as a result it is now confronting one of the most militant labor movements in Asia. However, the extraordinary improvement of living conditions in general and the emergence of an affluent middle class allowed South Korea to maintain relatively stable industrial relations until the 1980s, paving the way for the creation of competitive advantage in the international markets.

Thus the developmental states were fully aware of the need to integrate their civil societies to the extent that such integration remained compatible with the economic conditions necessary to be competitive in the world economy. They were not just repressive dictatorships. Their project consisted of a two-edged plowshare that they did not hesitate to transform into a sword when required.

However, *the process of development they succeeded in implementing not only transformed the economy but completely changed the society.* A new, more assertive capitalist class, ready to take on the world, emerged in the 1980s, increasingly confident that they no longer needed a state of technocrats, racketeers, and political police. A new, consumer-oriented, educated, liberal middle class decided that life was all too good to be sacrificed for the historical project of an artificially invented nation. And a new, more conscious, better organized working class appeared ready to follow the same historical path that has been walked by any other working class in the history of industrialization: class struggle.

The success of the developmental states in East Asia ultimately leads to the demise of their apparatuses and to the fading of their messianic dreams. The societies they helped to engender through sweat and tears are indeed industrialized, modern societies. But their actual historical projects are being shaped by their citizens, now in the open ground of history making.

Notes

1. Detailed statistical and documentary references are not given for every figure or fact cited in this text, to avoid making it even more cumbersome. All citations must be considered "sources of sources" that could lead the reader to the appropriate empirical contrast of the hypotheses I suggest here. For a summary view of some statistical data on Asian NICs see: Dalhman, 1989, pp. 51-94; for an excellent analytical overview of the themes under discussion see White, 1988.

2. The analysis of Singapore relies on my own research in Singapore in 1987 and 1989, presented in Castells, 1988. A useful economic analysis of Singapore is in Krause, Koh Ai Tee, and Lee (Tsao) Yuan, 1987.

3. Useful sources for the analysis of the process of economic development in South Korea are Lim, 1982, a revised version of his excellent 1982 Harvard doctoral dissertation; and K.-D. Kim, 1987, particularly pp. 169-460. I also relied on a brief period of my own field work and interviewing in the fall of 1988.

4. The basic social analysis of Taiwanese development is in Gold, 1986. Another interesting source regarding our own interpretation of the process is Winckler and Greenhalgh, 1988. I also grounded this analysis in some field work and interviewing conducted in Taipei, Tanyung, and Kaoshiung in January 1989.

5. My analysis of Hong Kong is based on research I conducted at the University of Hong Kong in 1983 and 1987. For a presentation of my research findings and analyses see Castells, Goh, and Kwok, 1990.

6. Milton Friedman has been the main ideologue propagating the myth of the "Hong Kong Model," but his information relies on research conducted in Hong Kong by his disciple, Alvin Rabushka (see Rabushka, 1979).

7. In Hong Kong, people live, work, and produce goods "in the sky." Factories are organized vertically, in buildings reminiscent of blocks of apartments or "flats" (using the prevailing British English of the colony).

8. Japan's experience as a developmental state driven by a nationalist project fits, in my opinion, in the analysis presented here. See an important and often overlooked book on the political origins of the Japanese economic strategy by London School of Economics professor A. J. Allen (1979).

References

Allen, A. J. (1979). *The Japanese economy.* London: Macmillan.

Barrett, Richard, & Chin, Soomi. (1987). Export-oriented industrializing states in the capitalist world-system: Similarities and differences. In Frederic Deyo (Ed.), *The political economy of the new industrialism.* Ithaca, NY: Cornell University Press.

Castells, Manuel. (1988). *The developmental city state in an open world economy: The Singapore experience.* Berkeley: University of California, Berkeley Roundtable on the International Economy.

Castells, Manuel, Goh, Lee Kwok, & Reginald Y. W. (1990). *The Shek Kip Mei syndrome: Economic development and public housing in Hong Kong and Singapore.* London: Pion.

Chen, Edward K. Y. (1979). *Hypergrowth in Asian economies: A comparative analysis of Hong Kong, Japan, Korea, Singapore, and Taiwan.* London: Macmillan.

Chen, Edward K. Y. (1980). The economic setting. In David Lethbridge (Ed.), *The business environment of Hong Kong.* Hong Kong: Oxford University Press.

Chan, M. K., et al. (Eds.). (1986). *Dimensions of the Chinese and Hong Kong labor movement.* Hong Kong: Hong Kong Christian Industrial Committee.

Chin, Pei-Hsiung. (1988). *Housing policy and economic development in Taiwan.* Berkeley: University of California, Institute of Urban and Regional Development.

Chen, Peter S. J. (Ed.). (1983). *Singapore: Development policies and trends.* Singapore: Oxford University Press.

Chesneaux, Jean. (1982). *The Chinese labor movement: 1919-1927.* Stanford, CA: Stanford University Press.

Chua, Beng-Huat. (1985). Pragmatism and the People's Action Party in Singapore. *Southeast Asian Journal of Social Sciences, 13*(2).

Cole, David C., & Lyman, Princeton N. (1971). *Korean development: The interplay of politics and economics.* Cambridge, MA: Harvard University Press.

Collier, David (Ed.). (1979). *The new authoritarianism in Latin America.* Princeton, NJ: Princeton University Press.

Dalhman, Carl J. (1989). Structural trade and change in the East Asia newly industrial economies and emerging industrial economies. In Randall P. Purcell (Ed.), *The newly industrializing countries in the world economy* (pp. 51-94). Boulder, CO: Lynne Rienner.

Deyo, Frederic C. (Ed.) (1987a). *The political economy of the new industrialism.* Ithaca, NY: Cornell University Press.

Deyo, Frederic C. (1987b). State and labor: Modes of political exclusion in East Asian development. In Frederic C. Deyo (Ed.), *The political economy of the new Asian industrialism.* Ithaca, NY: Cornell University Press.

Deyo, Frederic C. (1981). *Dependent development and industrial order: An Asian case study.* New York: Praeger.

Endacott, G. B., & Birch, A. (1978). *Hong Kong eclipse.* Hong Kong: Oxford University Press.

Ernst, Dieter, & O'Connor, David C. (1990). *Technological capabilities, new technologies and newcomer industrialization: An agenda for the 1990's.* Paris: OECD Development Centre.

Fajnzylber, Fernando. (1983). *La industrializacion Truncada de America Latina.* Mexico: Nueva Imagen.

Federation of Korean Industries. (1987). *Korea's economic policies (1945-1985).* Seoul: Federation of Korean Industries.

Gereffi, Gary. (1989). Rethinking development theory: Insights from East Asia and Latin America. *Sociological Forum, 4*(4).

Ghose, T. K. (1987). *The banking system of Hong Kong.* Singapore: Butterworths.

Gold, Thomas B. (1986). *State and society in the Taiwan miracle.* Armonk, NY: M. E. Sharpe.

Greenhalgh, Susan. (1988). Families and networks in Taiwan's economic development. In Edwin A. Winckler & Susan Greenhalgh (Eds.), *Contending approaches to the political economy of Taiwan.* Armonk, NY: M. E. Sharpe.

Ho, H. C. Y. (1979). *The fiscal system of Hong Kong.* London: Croom Helm.

Hong Kong Government. (1967). *Kowloon disturbances, 1966: Report of Commission of Inquiry.* Hong Kong: Hong Kong Government.

Hsing, You-Tein. (1990). [Untitled.] Doctoral dissertation in progress. Berkeley: University of California, Department of City and Regional Planning.

Johnson, Chalmers. (1982). *MITI and the Japanese miracle.* Stanford, CA: Stanford University Press.

Johnson, Chalmers. (1987). Political institutions and economic performance: The government-business relationship in Japan, South Korea and Taiwan. In Frederic C. Deyo (Ed.), *The political economy of the new Asian industrialism.* Ithaca, NY: Cornell University Press.

Kim, Kyong-Dong. (Ed.). (1987). *Dependency issues in Korean development.* Seoul: Seoul National University Press.

Kim, Seung-Kuk. (1987). Class formation and labor process in Korea. In Kyong-Dong Kim (Ed.), *Dependency issues in Korean development.* Seoul: Seoul National University Press.

King, Ambrose Y. C., & Lee, Rance P. (Eds.). (1981). *Social life and development in Hong Kong.* Hong Kong: The Chinese University Press.

Krause, Lawrence B., Koh Ai Tee, & Lee (Tsao) Yuan. (1987). *The Singapore economy reconsidered.* Singapore: Institute of Southeast Asian Studies.

Kuo, Shirley W. Y. (1983). *The Taiwan economy in transition.* Boulder, CO: Westview.

Kwan, Alex Y. H., & Chan, David K. K. (Eds.). (1986). *Hong Kong society.* Hong Kong: Writers and Publishers Cooperative.

Lau, Siu-Kai. (1982). *Society and politics in Hong Kong.* Hong Kong: The Chinese University Press.

Lee, Chong Ouk. (1988). *Science and technology policy of Korea and cooperation with the United States.* Seoul: Korea Advanced Institute of Science and Technology, Center for Science and Technology Policy.

Lethbridge, Henry. (1970). Hong Kong cadets, 1862-1941. *Journal of the Hong Kong Branch of the Royal Asiatic Society,* 10, pp. 35-56.

Leung, Chi-Keung, Cushman, J. W., & Wang, Gungwu. (Ed.). (1980). *Hong Kong: Dilemmas of growth.* Hong Kong: University of Hong Kong, Centre for Asian Studies.

Lim, Hyun-Chin. (1982). *Dependent development in Korea: 1963-79.* Seoul: Seoul National University Press.

Lim, Hyun-Chin, & Yang, Jonghoe. (1987). The state, local capitalists, and multinationals: The changing nature of a triple alliance in Korea. In Kyong-Dong Kim (Ed.), *Dependency issues in Korean development* (pp. 347-359). Seoul: Seoul National University Press.

Lin, Tsong-Biau, Mok, Victor, & Ho, Yin-Ping. (1980). *Manufactured exports and employment in Hong Kong.* Hong Kong: The Chinese University Press.

Miners, N. J. (1986). *The government and politics of Hong Kong.* Hong Kong: Oxford University Press.

Mushkat, Miron. (1982). *The making of the Hong Kong administrative class.* Hong Kong: University of Hong Kong, Centre for Asian Studies.

Park, Young-Bum. (1990). *Public sector labor market and privatization in Korea* (Discussion Paper/25/1990). Geneva: International Institute for Labour Studies.

Purcell, Randall P. (Ed.). (1989). *The newly industrializing countries in the world economy.* Boulder and London: Lynne Rienner.

Rabushka, Alvin. (1979). *Hong Kong: A study in economic freedom.* Chicago: University of Chicago Press.

Scalapino, Robert A. (n.d.). Which route for Korea? *Asian Survey, 2*(7), 1-13.

Schiffer, Jonathan. (1983). *Anatomy of a laissez-faire government: The Hong Kong growth model reconsidered.* Hong Kong: University of Hong Kong, Centre for Urban Studies.

Scott, Ian. (1987). *Policymaking in a turbulent environment: The case of Hong Kong.* Unpublished report. Hong Kong: University of Hong Kong, Department of Political Science.

Scott, Ian, & Burns, John P. (Eds.). (1984). *The Hong Kong civil service.* Hong Kong: Oxford University Press.

Sit, Victor F. S. (1982). Dynamism in small industries: The case of Hong Kong. *Asian Survey, 22,* pp. 399-409.

Solow, Robert. (1957). Technical change and the aggregate production functions. *Review of Economics and Statistics, 39,* pp. 312-320.

Stepan, Alfred. (1971). *The military in politics.* Princeton, NJ: Princeton University Press.

Tsao, Yuan. (1986). Sources of growth accounting for the Singapore economy. In Lim Chong-Yah & Peter J. Lloyd (Eds.), *Singapore: Resources and growth.* Singapore: Oxford University Press.

White, Gordon. (Ed.). (1988). *Developmental states in East Asia.* New York: St. Martin's.

Winckler, Edwin A., & Greenhalgh, Susan. (Eds.). (1988). *Contending approaches to the political economy of Taiwan.* Amonk, NY: M. E. Sharpe.

Yoshihara, Kunio. (1988). *The rise of ersatz capitalism in southeast Asia.* Oxford, UK: Oxford University Press.

Youngson, A. J. (1982). *Hong Kong: Economic growth and policy.* Hong Kong: Oxford University Press.

Yu, Fu-Lai, & Li, Si-Ming. (1985). The welfare cost of Hong Kong's public housing program. *Urban Studies, 22,* pp. 133-140.

3

States, Economic Development, and the Asian Pacific Rim

NIGEL HARRIS

This chapter considers two questions. First, what has been the role of the State in the process of economic development, and does this conform to what happened in South Korea, Taiwan, and Singapore (Hong Kong is omitted, since this raises special issues outside the range of this chapter[1])? Second, how far was the development of the three economies a unique phenomenon?

States and Economic Development

The analysis of the relationship between economic activity and States is bedeviled by a number of fictions, the most extreme of which is the distinction between the domestic and the external. Once the polarity is assumed, then relating them becomes a problem; countries are "inserted" in the world, or the world "penetrates" the country, as if any countries had, in a serious sense, not been part of the world for much of recorded history.

Other assumptions can be no less debilitating. Take, for example, two. First, some observers politicize the world market, making it into an arena for the struggle of embattled national fiefdoms, each with a clearly demarcated territory, a peculiar people and a discrete segment of capital; then each of the terms, *society, economy,* and *culture,* have comfortably simple territorial perimeters, and *national* is the only feasible adjective to go with each concept. This is the tunnel vision from the vantage point (or better, slit trench) of each government. So far as the unity of government and capital is concerned, such a geopolitical vision was considerably more plausible between 1870 and the 1950s than either before or afterward, but even in its heyday, the perspective in effect denied a significant role to the most important source of change, world markets. All was decided in the chancelleries of the Great Powers.

On the other hand, some versions of Marxism reduce the political—of which the State is the preeminent institution—to an epiphenomenon, a cork—as it were—floating on the tides of economic activity (nowadays, a rare version) or of the domestic collision of classes. As a result of such a case, some leading Marxists at the time of the First World War assumed the integration of the European economy had rendered nationalism redundant, or, at most, restricted to the marginal issue of culture or language; they thus wildly underestimated the viability of nationalism in Europe and its material embodiment, the State. Without the idea of contradiction, such a view might suggest that world government would inevitably be the result of the integration of a world economy: politics was no more than a reflex of economics (Harris, 1990). A different error was to reduce the State to no more than the mouthpiece of a private capitalist class; indeed, public actions were seen as the means of identifying what the immediate interests of capital were, a proposition enshrining a methodology beyond empirical disproof (and one that excluded the possibility of the State making mistakes). Those, however, who shared the general approach but felt uncomfortable with the resulting tautology, were obliged then to embrace an addendum: on the "relative autonomy" of the State, or—in a cruder variant—"Bonapartism" (that is, the State is able temporarily to escape the control of the dominant classes by, in certain specific historical circumstances, playing one off against another). It should be noted in passing that whereas the first account subordinates all domestic conflict to the "external" struggle (it corresponds therefore to the viewpoint of the competitive State itself); in the second, there is often no external context at all; classes (or "fractions") struggle within national boundaries, and public action is primarily the reaction of capital to domestic issues.

The problems arise from a misspecification of the issues, a misspecification heightened by the changing nature of the world order. There are at least two systems operating in the world that are conceptually distinct although in practice continually interwoven and interacting: a system of competing companies (whether owned privately, by governments, or other agencies) that make and distribute a priced output of goods and services and, in sum, constitute a world economy; and a system of competing States, that administer clearly defined territories and populations and make up a world political order. There are—as is well known—quite different characteristics, functions, areas of primary operation, and powers associated with each set of agencies. States are defined by territory, by geography, companies in principle are not (although some may be); States have a monopoly within their territory of the use of physical power while companies rarely have more than security guards. The main source of finance of State power is expropriation, taxes. Companies engage directly in the process of production and distribution of goods, and so forth.

There are analogies. Firms can be bankrupted and liquidated; States can be destroyed. Companies can experience boardroom coups or takeovers, just as heads of States can be removed by coup and countries can be conquered. But they are only analogies and serve to underline the differences rather than the similarities, and particularly, the contrast between an institution characterized by the use of physical force and based upon the appropriation of value generated outside the public sector, and the financial power of an agency directly engaged in the generation of value.

The most important feature of States is that they compete with each other, and they do so, like companies, to secure their survival. Unlike companies, a crucial means to compete is precisely in the area of physical power. The primary task of States is to defend their national independence, and military competition is a key element in this. Of course, the more developed the world becomes, the greater the perceived dangers of rivalries to all States, so there are various attempts to cartelize the world order, establish stabilizing alliances, rules, fora for discussion, and so forth. The Concert of Europe was an early version of the attempt to establish a regulated order, and depended upon the Great Powers acting as self-appointed policemen to put down rebellions that threatened the State-system. However, the lack of an overarching power, a world government, mobilizing sufficient physical force to control all participants, undermines any simulation of national legal systems: if the issue at stake is sufficiently important, the strongest States can always defy international law. A Great Power, a participant with a particular interest, cannot be accepted for long as the embodiment of universal interests. Furthermore, today the cost of global policing is beyond even the richest powers and appears to be steadily increasing; the United States could only with difficulty sustain one Vietnam War—10 would have been impossible.

In the past, this continuing theme of military rivalry can be seen clearly. Indeed, competition in war-making capacity is itself an important element in the creation of the modern State, a point summarized in Charles Tilly's aphorism, "War made the State, and the State made war" (Tilly, 1975, p. 42). If war making or war preparation is in the foreground of the history of European governments, finding the means to pay for it is the obsession of much of the background. Late medieval rulers spent much of their time in desperate schemes and subterfuges to raise adequate funds to fight. It is this which so often led to administrative reforms, increasing centralization, the overriding of local liberties and extraordinary burdens of taxation—that in turn provided the source for the many rebellions that mark the path to the creation of the modern European State. It is also the source of the growing interest of monarchs—or their high officers—in economic questions and the growth of domestic capitalism. Capitalism owes much to the patronage of rulers searching for the revenues that would ensure the capacity to fight— rather than that patronage indicating the control of the State by capital. Of course, in a more general sense, the State's fundamental role in a world divided into competing States is to provide leadership for the whole ruling order (which includes the duty of *defining* what the national interest is, rather than simply reflecting interests defined elsewhere), and a private capitalist class may be part of that order; but this cannot simply be reduced to the interests of companies.

National economic development—as opposed to companies just making a profit—is invariably a by-product of the competition of States, not a spontaneous outgrowth of the operation of markets. Of course, the process may be more or less conscious. In the first case of industrialization historically, that of Britain, the role of the State and of warfare was crucial, but, one presumes, unconscious. During the 127 years between 1688 and 1815 when the key industrial transition was made, England (later Britain) was engaged in major wars for roughly 70 years. In the closing phases of this period during the Napoleonic Wars, there were 350,000 men under arms (1801), and half a million in 1811 (that is, equal to nearly 10% of the labor force), with many other hundreds of thousands engaged in keeping them supplied with arms, clothing, foodstuffs, and transport. For some 50 years (1780-1830), government consumption was larger than the value of exports, so that it appears that British economic development was, in the first phase, government, rather than export, led. By 1801, gross public expenditure may have been equal to over a quarter of total national expenditure (Deane, 1975, p. 91). Thus government and its military activities, the cost of systemic rivalries, raised and sustained output, transformed its structure (with disproportionate growth in the metallurgical and coal industries), and flattened the fluctuations that would have arisen from a market-led pattern of growth. The curtailment of imports from Europe added an element of import substitution stimulation that helped force an increase in the utilization of the factors of production. The process seems to have been based upon a familiar redistribution of income between classes: "the bulk of the increased indirect taxation necessitated by war seems to have been borne by consumers rather than producers, and the new direct taxes touched the mercantile and manufacturing classes relatively lightly" (Deane, 1975, p.97).

At the other end of the nineteenth century, Japan provided a striking parallel. Between 1874 and 1945, Japan was engaged in 10 major wars, two of them World Wars. From 1886, military spending was on average equal to 10% of the gross national product, and 12% in the three decades up to 1945. Initially, the country had very little modern military capacity, but by the 1920s Japan had become the third largest naval, and fifth largest military, power. Military demands were the source of both the giant subcontracting *zaibatsu* and the prodigious growth of the key industries: heavy and chemical, electrical equipment, and vehicles. Morishima (1982, pp. 96-97) concludes:

> This economic growth was certainly not achieved through using the mechanism of the free operation of the economy; it was the result of the government or the military, with their loyal following of capitalists, manipulating and influencing the economy in order to realize national aims . . . the price mechanism scarcely played an important role, and the questions of importance were how to raise capital to meet the government's demand and the nature of the demand generated from the enterprises at the receiving end of a government demand.

There are a sufficient number of other well documented examples of international rivalries impelling States to reorganize their domestic economies in the interests of military preparedness (Harris, 1986, p. 155 ff.) for it to seem a common theme. Of course, the conditions in which such rivalries take place are different, not only in terms of military technology (and the balance between imports and home produced equipment), the scale of required firepower, but also the organization of the domestic economy and labor force in order both to finance arms and to use them effectively. More refined measures of relative standing are derived, with much emphasis on comparative levels of labor productivity, education, and training, rather than simply firepower.

By the late nineteenth century, the emergence of a mass society in Western Europe and North America added a different dimension, for now the State was required to pursue its purposes in full public gaze and with some measure of popular participation—some accommodation to popular interests became the condition of effective policy; in turn, popular participation eased the two ancient restrictions on war-making capacity, the unwillingness of people either to pay taxes or to fight. Now, the concerns of the competitive

State increasingly went beyond the domain of the ruler or government to encompass the whole society. There was emerging a program of social transformation—from, for example, industrialization, mass education, and participation—required of an effective competitor.

The State system of the world and the rivalries of its leading powers set the terms of competition. Given the extraordinary inequality of States, the majority cannot match the most advanced levels of competition, but the largest make some attempt to do so, regardless of the per capita income of their countries (those developing countries that are said to possess nuclear weapons or the capacity to make them illustrate this). The majority of States, however, could not realistically defend themselves against the most powerful governments. They are not usually required to do so, only to defend their national independence against such things as local rivals or freebooters. The price of failure is the loss of independence or its radical qualification.

Governments in economically backward countries are thus today obliged by a competitive system to pursue economic development. Yet this itself imposes upon their societies new and extraordinary disciplines. Industrialization promotes an unprecedented degree of social and administrative centralization as well as new and quite frequently horrifying work disciplines, major social upheavals, moral revolutions, and so forth. For many of those in countries that recently attained national independence, it might seem the new disciplines are more onerous than those of being a colony: national liberation turned out to be only a means to force the liberated to compete. Indeed, it might appear that it was the State that was liberated, not the inhabitants.

The capacity to compete is powerfully influenced by the economic context. The output of each country is unique, so its relationship to world markets is highly specific, and therefore its capacity to earn the export revenues required to purchase vital imports, including defense equipment. The years after the Second World War were a sharp contrast to the interwar period in this respect. The possibilities of a growth of exports were much greater up to 1973 than either before the war or after 1973. The newly independent governments of this period were the unwitting beneficiaries of this generalized growth, able to claim that it was political independence itself that brought economic success rather than an unprecedented growth in world demand.

How does this relate to the development of South Korea, Taiwan, and Singapore? In essence, the military competition that drove the early developers to transform their domestic economies was, if anything, even more extreme for these three, particularly the first two (for Singapore, *Konfrontasi* was, however, of much importance, particularly after the break with Malaya and the evacuation of the British). The competition was much more severe than anything comparable in Latin America or Africa. In the case of Korea, it included extraordinary destruction from the cataclysm of a world war fought exclusively across its territory. In addition to this primary drive for survival, the State in both Korea and Taiwan was for a time peculiarly free of the social restrictions imposed by entrenched dominant classes. The entire ruling order of 1940 (except for part of the landed class) was Japanese and left when the Japanese empire collapsed. Given the third factor, the extraordinary growth in the world economy after 1950, if governments were able, by luck or design, to adopt nonobstructive policies, the prospects for high growth were most favorable. As we know, governments in South Korea, Taiwan, and Singapore went considerably further than this in promoting growth.

Rivalries promoted economic development in developing countries after the war. They had generated a no less sustained drive to *étatisme* in the industrialized countries in the 1930s. Two world wars and the Great Depression created a climate of opinion in which it was taken for granted that government power should supersede markets. The language of the war economy was bequeathed both to those who introduced protectionism after the interwar slump and to those who strove to develop backward countries after the Second World War. From the imperatives of Stalin's Soviet Union (where development, or "constructing socialism," coincided with preparation for war) to the milder corporatism of Britain in the 1930s, culminating in the period of Labour Government after 1945, there was a common theme of the control or supersession of market forces. Theorization about this supposedly new form of economy came much later; indeed, the Owl of Minerva (Galbraith, 1967; Shonfield, 1965) appeared in the mid-1960s when the counter-revolution was already beginning.

Thus the intellectual inheritance of the developing countries in the post-war period placed overwhelming emphasis on the role of the State. It is hardly surprising therefore that extreme forms of economic nationalism became almost universal among developing countries—import controls, over-valued exchange rates, large-scale public ownership and investment initiatives, directed investment with managed interest rates, prices and wages, and so forth. The program was embraced regardless of the political persuasion or external alliance of different governments—Chiang Kai-shek's Kuo Min Tang program of 1938 or Ngo Dinh Diem's aspirations in South Vietnam are hardly distinguishable from Nehru's brand of "social-ism." The program was impelled by the exigencies of external competition rather than domestic social priorities. South Korea, Taiwan, and to a lesser extent Singapore, were not particularly different in this respect. Their singularity lay not in their domestic arrangements or control of the national economic frontiers, but in their single-minded concentration on overseas markets for manufactured exports—at a time when, as will be suggested in the next section, a quite unanticipated and radical change in the structure of world demand was occurring.

However, success in the endeavor of building competitive capacity through economic development had a contradictory result. For where a domestic private sector was allowed to survive as a means to accelerate growth, the greater the success a government had in propelling development, the more it created a strong private capitalist class, ultimately capable of challenging the priorities of State policy where these collided with its interests. The public emergence of this conflict can be seen in the late 1970s in South Korea when the heavy industrial plans of General Park (more closely related to building a self-sufficient military power than the type of civil economy market imperatives might promote) were increasingly questioned, particularly when they seemed to be starving high exporting light industry of investment and driving the economy to crisis. Similar issues emerged around the same time in Taiwan (Harris, 1987). In Singapore, overwhelmingly dominated by foreign capital, the fantasies of Mr. Lee were of much less significance for a multinational capitalist class.

The change in the social weight of the business class at home is not the only implication. As the world economy becomes increasingly integrated, the mark of maturity of a national capitalist class is that world competition drives it to operate internationally, to merge increasingly with global capital. This is only feasible with the liberation of capital from all that mass of restrictions which national governments seek to impose in order to capture a larger share of any surplus (and to protect what was initially seen as their capital from foreign competition). National liberation freed the State; restructuring and liberalization now freed capital. A second range of issues between business and government in South Korea concerns such things as the type of controlled currency regime, rights to borrow abroad, or rights to import freely. We might hazard a guess that similar forces are at work in the managerial stratum of Eastern Europe and the former Soviet Union, a proto-capitalist class that might reasonably expect to inherit the newly privatized corporations; this might partly account for the speed of the transition.

Thus, paradoxically, national economic development that was impelled by the rivalries within the State system now produces a new component in the market system that in part contradicts the independence of the State. Governments become preoccupied with retaining a group of powerful companies within their borders and seeking to beg or bribe international companies to invest there in order to secure privileged access to the surpluses generated by world, rather than national, capital. The State moves from being the "executive committee of the (national) bourgeoisie" (if such a phrase was ever adequate) to a local authority for a world bourgeoisie, from the incubator of capitalism to one of its many and changing homes.

The role of the State, however, remains important for the economy, for world capital will locate in the country concerned only if the government can guarantee certain conditions of production of goods, the reproduction of labor of a certain quality and price, and of effective management. Competition by States in the economic field now shifts from geographically specific advantages (such as raw material endowments) to much less tangible elements. As DeAnne Julius recently put it,

> What is most important to competitive success is no longer a country's land or mineral endowment or even, in many cases, its labour costs. Rather it is a whole range of nongeographical factors: access to technology, flexible management techniques, marketing strategy, closeness to consumers, speed of response to changes in the marketplace etc. All these are firm-specific not territorially based. (Julius, 1990, p. 82)

How Unique Was the Economic Growth Process of the Gang of Four?

The type of public sectors and governments developed in the industrialized countries between 1930 and—say—1960, and that were constructed in the developing countries in the postwar period, were responses to systemic rivalries in a world where up to that time capital accumulation was founded upon a national basis (even if the national core was part of a wider empire). It was taken for granted that all capital was nationally identifiable and had a loyalty much as inhabitants were supposed to have. However, at different times in different sectors—for example, finance, capital movements, commodity trade—these assumptions began to change, particularly from the 1950s. Accumulation began to assume a primarily global form. Thus the conditions for effective macroeconomic policy were transformed. All the machinery constructed to protect a national economy became, if not redundant, positively obstructive in the task of increasing the power of any particular government in a world economy. It is this radical shift that has meant that almost all economies seem perpetually engaged in "restructuring," seeking to adjust national policy and structure to the new world economy, and transforming the public role to one of "facilitation" rather than implementation. From the continuing decontrol and privatization of the industrialized countries to the structural adjustment of much of the developing world to the momentous changes in Eastern Europe and the Soviet Union, all can be seen as continuing efforts to unwind the structures of the earlier period in order to reestablish the new conditions for sustained growth.

One of the first signs of the emergence of the new world economy in trading terms was the quite extraordinary growth of the Four Little Tigers of East and Southeast Asia. The most important case was Hong Kong simply because of the unusual openness of its economy which reacted to changes in world demand without public mediation through commodity or currency control. The growth of the four was faster and sustained over a longer period of time (despite fluctuations in the world economy) than other developing countries. But it was nonetheless part of a general change in the system, reflected to a greater or lesser degree in almost all developing countries. Indeed, the precipitation of quite rapid growth in the 1960s seems much cruder and simpler in purely economic terms than is often suggested. Where the structure of current output and pricing (including the exchange rate) were favorable, then it became possible to enter the learning process that, with luck and persistence, produced the goods to fit a particular niche in the world market for manufactured goods. In practice, initially few countries were socially and politically equipped to start, and it is here that the major obstacles to growth lie (and that the superiority of the Four Little Tigers was most clearly apparent). Furthermore, starting the process did not guarantee it could be continued: there were failures (Morawetz, 1982), particularly as world economic conditions became more unstable in the 1970s.

A key indication of a country's successful adjustment to the new structure of world demand was its capacity to export manufactured goods into the heartlands of the industrial world, in Europe and North America. No one in the development field in the 1950s had envisaged such an audacious possibility, and much ingenuity was devoted to explaining why it was impossible. Yet the change is clearly apparent. In an earlier analysis of the 27 developing countries exporting goods worth more than $1 billion in 1980 (Harris, 1986)—countries covering some 54% of the world's population—it could be seen that virtually all experienced a rate of growth of exports from 1960 well ahead of the increase in world trade. Some had rates of expansion that, for periods, were as dramatic as those in the Four Little Tigers. Furthermore, in all 27 countries, the increase in the export of manufactured goods was much faster than the growth of exports as a whole. Israel increased the share of manufactured goods in its exports between 1960 and 1980 from 62% to 82%; Yugoslavia from 38% to 73%; Portugal from 54% to 72%. Finally, in all cases, the skill intensity of manufactured exports increased (if we take as a surrogate of this, exports of machinery and transport equipment, which on average increased from 2% to 10% of the total, and for the nine leading countries, from 4% to 23%).

If we extend the period to include the 1980s when many developing countries experienced much greater obstacles to growth, the picture is the same, showing that the tendency is long term. Of the 77 countries with comparative data in the *World Development Report* (World Bank, 1990) (now including the countries of Eastern Europe), 12 had negative rates of growth but 22 had 4% or more annually (1980-1988), and this included some of the largest countries—China with 10.3%; Pakistan, 6.5%; Thailand, 6.0%; and India, 5.2%. In terms of exports, 22 had negative growth but 34 an annual growth of 4% or more; many cases here had extraordinary rates of growth in the 1980s—seven of them, more than 11% annually (Paraguay, 15.7%; Turkey, 15.3%; South Korea, 14.7%; Taiwan, 13.9%; China, 11.9%; Portugal, 11.6%; Thailand, 11.3%). Sixty-one of the 81 countries for which there are data increased the share of manufactured goods in their exports, and by now 50% or more of the exports of 21 countries are manufactured goods, although few rival the 91%-93% share of Taiwan, South Korea, or Hong Kong—the nearest are Portugal (81%), South Africa (80%), Haiti (74%), China (73%), India (73%), all well ahead of Singapore (at 55%) (World Bank, 1990).

What were the factors at stake in this remarkable expansion of manufactured exports by developing countries? There are some obvious features—the spread of education and infrastructure following decolonization and in conditions of relatively high growth. Health status has improved consistently in developing countries. The effects of these changes have been enhanced because they have been concentrated in particular localities (generally in and around the large cities). They make possible a narrowing of the gap in labor productivity in comparable plants in developed and developing countries. That was helped by specific industrial promotion programs and rising levels of domestic savings.

There were other factors that reduced the significance of geographical distance for selected commodities. Thus, the costs of transport and communications fell because of innovations in both equipment and fuel efficiency. As the costs of movement fell, the geographical perimeter of potential production sites extended.

Third are the changes in protectionism in the main markets, the developed countries. This has made for new patterns of territorial specialization and new comparative advantages making it impossible for firms in developed countries to compete in markets for labor-intensive manufactures.

Many of these factors, however, would have facilitated the redistribution of some manufacturing capacity but not caused it. For that we must assume not only general growth in the world system, but also a radical change in the world economy, in the geographical distribution of comparative advantages. A key element in this was the rapid exhaustion of labor supply in Europe in the 1950s, sending buyers beyond Europe in search of new sources of supply. Hong Kong, unlike the other three Little Tigers, was completely open to changes in external markets, and responded to this quite new demand, precipitating a process of remarkable self-transformation. The change is historically specific, since Hong Kong had always been an open economy but had not industrialized before. The other three of the Four then copied the process of export-led growth, but through deliberate State intervention (where the Japanese model became relevant, although Japanese growth at a comparable stage was not export-led).

The 1950s were crucial for this transition. It was then that rapid European growth transformed the demand for labor. The agricultural labor force was swiftly drawn into nonagricultural work. An increasing number of women were drawn out of the household into paid employment. Finally, immigrant workers became an increasingly important component of the labor force.

Thus as migrant workers moved one way, buyers of goods moved in the other in search of new supplies. Once begun, countries were able quite swiftly to upgrade the technical quality of their output, to develop.

By the 1970s, the process had become so advanced, it could scarcely be reversed. The industrial output of the more developed—let alone, the consumption level—depended upon imported manufactured goods. It is for this reason that the return of slump to the system in the 1970s did not produce a level of protectionism that, in the Great Depression of the interwar years, destroyed the world trading system.

The change in the structure of world demand does not explain why some countries rather than others were able to exploit the process so far as to transform their domestic economies. But that question has to presuppose the much larger factor of a fundamental change in the world economic order, beginning the creation of an integrated world manufacturing economy and a global capital. The role of the State in that context is radically changed.

Conclusions

With the benefit of hindsight, we can now see the period since 1930 as the heyday of State economic power. There was no clear date for the ending of this period—and it does not coincide with a reversal in the share of national incomes taken by the public sector. There were stages in the industrialized countries—in terms of finance, the convertibility of currencies, the emergence of offshore money markets, the floating of exchange rates, the different "Big Bangs" in different countries. Each step was pragmatic; that is, a response to specific short-term conjunctures rather than the implementation of a premeditated strategy. The same is true in developing countries, where pragmatic experiments in the promotion of manufactured exports as well as elements of liberalization have continued for long periods (and on occasions been reversed).

In the end, however, a new world economic order had been created. The old project of national economic development, creating a fully diversified independent national economy supplying the domestic market, had become both utopian and, for some, economically disastrous. Both the structures of public power and the corporatist social alliances that supposedly vindicated that power became redundant. World markets required increased specialization and so increased differentiation. The government still captained the boat, but with no power over wind and wave. It was less and less the leader, patron and manager of a discrete segment of world capital relating to an autonomous domestic market and controlled currency area. It was more the administrator of part of a world economy, a junction point for transactions that began and ended far beyond its authority. The key to public power lay not in access to domestic resources or capital, but in providing the right environment for external forces.

It was this new context that forced liberalization on most of the countries of the world. Three of the Four Little Tigers, South Korea, Taiwan, and Singapore, had conformed to the old prescription for national economic development and created a powerful directing State and a large public sector in a closely protected market (this last feature did not occur in Singapore). The State structures were defensive, to protect the country in a fiercely competitive State system. What was unusual in the postwar context was not this but that, by a series of accidents, they came to focus upon external markets for manufactured goods, thus directly connecting their economies to the most dynamic forces of growth in the world economy. It could not have been done without a fundamental change in world demand, a change which controverted most of the social science wisdom on the subject.

The ramifications of this change will be working themselves out long into the future—for the changes are not merely in the role of the State and its relationship to economic questions, nor in the geography of production. In a closed economy, the pricing of capital and labor, their relative scarcity, and the effect of this upon technology, optimal scales of production and the organization of work, are very different from what holds in a world economy. There is no scarcity of labor in the open economy, no necessity for labor saving innovations. Capital intensity, scales of concentration (of capital as well as in production units) and work patterns—between formal and informal—may all change radically as liberalization proceeds. Many cherished assumptions are being eroded, and many surprises are in store.

Note

1. Hong Kong's government administered no economically significant controls on external trade or currency movements, and this distinguishes it from almost all other governments. It was interventionist in certain respects (in land release and development, housing, etc.), but again, this was relatively small compared to another open economy, Singapore. Hong Kong reacts to world demand with very little public mediation, so it must be treated as a quite different case to the other three. This is discussed by me elsewhere (Harris, 1986).

References

Deane, Phyliss. (1975). War and industrialization. In J. M. Winter (Ed.), *War and economic development: Essays in memory of David Joslin*. London: Cambridge University Press.

Galbraith, J. K. (1967). *The new industrial state*. London: Hamish Hamilton.

Harris, Nigel. (1986). *The end of the Third World: Newly industrializing countries and the decline of an ideology*. London: Tauris.

Harris, Nigel. (1987). *Newly emergent bourgeoisies?* Working Paper, Hong Kong: University of Hong Kong, Centre for Urban Studies and Urban Planning. [To be republished in Harris, N. (in press). *Cities, class and trade: Economic and social change in the Third World*. London: Tauris.]

Harris, Nigel. (1990). *National liberation*. London: Tauris/Penguin.

Julius, DeAnne. (1990). *Global companies and public policy: The growing challenge of foreign direct investment*. London: Royal Institute of International Affairs/Pinter.

Morawetz, David. (1982). *Why the emperor's new clothes were not made in Colombia* (World Bank Staff Working Paper, 368). Washington, DC: World Bank.

Morishima, Michio. (1982). *Why has Japan "succeeded"? Western technology and the Japanese ethos*. Cambridge, UK: Cambridge University Press.

Shonfield, Andrew. (1965). *Modern capitalism: The changing balance of public and private power*. London: Royal Institute of International Affairs/Oxford University Press.

Tilly, Charles. (1975). Reflections on the history of European state-making. In Charles Tilly (Ed.), *The formation of nation states in western Europe*. Princeton, NJ: Princeton University Press.

World Bank. (1990). *The world development report 1990*. Washington, DC: World Bank.

4

New Realities of Industrial Development in East Asia and Latin America
GLOBAL, REGIONAL, AND NATIONAL TRENDS

GARY GEREFFI

Industrial capitalism on a world scale has undergone significant shifts during the past two decades. Industrialization today is the result of an integrated system of global production and trade, buttressed by new forms of investment and financing, promoted by specific government policies, and entailing distinctive patterns of spatial and social organization. The objective of this chapter will be to sketch some of these new trends at the global, regional, and national levels.

I will outline four central arguments. First, we are witnessing the emergence of a global manufacturing system that has different institutional foundations than in the past. Although government policies in core and peripheral nations have combined with new technologies to fuel this process, export networks are a significant new focal point in development studies.

Second, the concept of commodity chains offers an important analytical framework for understanding both productive and spatial interdependencies. Commodity chains permit us to engage in a rigorous analysis of industries that highlights the importance of productive networks and the social embeddedness of economic activities. The footwear industry will be used to exemplify this approach.

Third, distinct regional divisions of labor are reshaping the geographical anatomy of industrial capitalism. Though ultimately subordinate to the overall international division of labor, these regional configurations contain their own cores and peripheries with particular sets of unequal transactions, dependencies. and development possibilities. Illustrations of these trends will be drawn from the electronics and automobile sectors in East Asia and Latin America.

Fourth and finally, the newly industrialized countries (NICs) within these regional divisions of labor are playing specialized roles within the world economy. As we move from the dynamics of global production down to the specifics of region, community, and place (and back again) to explain the nature of these roles, it is necessary to introduce a complex set of intermediate variables that link the macro and micro levels of analysis. These include industrial organization, new process and product technologies, industrial and commercial subcontracting relationships, and social ties such as gender, ethnicity, kinship, and class.

A Global Manufacturing System

There have been striking changes in the structure and dynamics of the world economy during the past several decades. The growth in manufacturing since the 1950s has been fueled by an explosion of new products, new technologies, the removal of barriers to international trade, and the physical integration of world markets through improved transportation and communication networks. International trade has allowed nations to specialize in industry as distinct from other economic sectors, in different manufacturing branches, and increasingly even in different stages of production within a single industry. This situation has led to the emergence of a global manufacturing system in which production capacity is dispersed to an unprecedented number of developing as well as industrialized countries (see Harris, 1987; Gereffi, 1989a).

Trade and industrialization have reinforced each other. Between 1980 and 1986, the number of Third World countries (classified by the World Bank as low- and middle-income, excluding the high-income oil-exporting countries) that exported goods worth $1 billion or more increased from 27 to 49 (Harris, 1987, p. 93; World Bank, 1988, pp. 242-243). This expansion of Third World export capacity, particularly for manufactured goods, embraces such a diverse array of countries that it appears to be part of a general restructuring in the world economy.

The newly industrializing countries (NICs) from East Asia and Latin America are pivotal actors in the global manufacturing system. East Asian nations have clearly established themselves as the Third World's premier exporters. Hong Kong topped the list in 1988 with $63.2 billion in exports, followed closely by South Korea and Taiwan with export totals of just over $60 billion each. The People's Republic of China had $47.5 billion in exports and Singapore $39.2 billion. Brazil was the leading Latin American exporter at $33.7 billion, followed by Mexico with an export total of $20.7 billion. Several other Asian nations emerged as "near-NICs" by 1988 on the basis of their export performance: Malaysia, $20.8 billion in exports; Indonesia, $19.7 billion; and Thailand, $15.8 billion (see Table 4.1).

The rapidity of change in the Third World's export capacity is indicated by comparing these 1988 figures with those only three years earlier in 1985. East Asia's three "super-exporters"—Hong Kong, South Korea, and Taiwan—each doubled their official export totals between 1985 and 1988. The other Asian near-NICs also experienced major export gains during this period, with the exception of Indonesia whose exports rose only slightly (6%). Thailand's export total more than doubled (an increase of 123%), Singapore's and China's exports jumped by nearly 75% each, while Malaysia's rose by 36%. Brazil's exports increased by about one-third from 1985 to 1988, while Mexico experienced a slight export decline, explained in large part by the significant drop in the value of Mexico's oil sales abroad.

One explanation for this recent dramatic growth in exports, especially among the East Asian NICs, is the marked appreciation of their currencies vis-à-vis the U.S. dollar since the mid-1980s, which augmented the official value of their export totals in these years. The upward shift in the export capacity of these nations is far more than a statistical artifact, however, when one takes into account that nearly all the countries listed in Table 4.1, including Brazil and Mexico whose currencies were significantly devalued versus the dollar after 1985, had substantial export increments, especially of manufactured products. (Even though Mexico's overall exports declined slightly because of falling oil sales, its exports of manufactures nearly doubled from $5.9 billion to $11.4 billion between 1985 and 1988.)

This shift toward a prominent and growing role for manufactured exports in the NICs is readily apparent in Table 4.1. Manufactured products constituted more than 90% of total exports in Hong Kong, South Korea and Taiwan in both 1985 and 1988. While manufactures did not dominate the export profiles of any of the other NICs to this same extent, the seven remaining nations in Table 4.1 all showed remarkable gains in their manufactured exports between 1985 and 1988. Mexico, for example, doubled the manufacturing share in its export total from 27% in 1985 to 55% in 1988. Similarly, China's "manufactured exports expanded from 54% to 73% of its total

Table 4.1 Exports by the East Asian and Latin American NICs, 1985 and 1988

Country	Exports (US$ billions) 1985	1988	Exports/GDP (percentage) 1985	1988	Primary Commodities 1985	1988	Textiles and Clothing 1985	1988	Machinery and Transport Equipment 1985	1988	Other Manufactures 1985	1988
East Asian NICs												
Hong Kong	30.2	63.2	92[d]	108[b]	8	8	32	29	24	25	36	37
South Korea	30.3	60.7	35	35	9	7	23	22	36	39	32	32
Taiwan	30.7	60.4	52	57[b]	9[c]	8	18[c]	15	29[c]	34	44[c]	43
Singapore	22.8	39.2	131	164	41	26	4	5	32	47	22	23
Latin American NICs												
Brazil	25.6	33.7	14[d]	10	59[d]	52	3[d]	3	14[d]	18	24[d]	27
Mexico	21.9	20.7	12	12	73[d]	45	1[d]	2[b]	16[d]	33	11[d]	20
Other Asian Near-NICs												
People's Republic of China	27.3	47.5	10	13	46[d]	27	24[d]	24[b]	6[d]	4	24[d]	45
Malaysia	15.3	20.8	49	60	73[d]	55	3[d]	4	19[d]	26	5[d]	15
Indonesia	18.6	19.7	21	24	89[d]	71	2[d]	8	1[d]	1	8[d]	20
Thailand	7.1	15.8	19	27	65[d]	48	13[d]	17	7[d]	11	15[d]	24

Percentage Share of Exports[a]

SOURCE: World Bank (1987), pp. 220-223, 206-207; World Bank (1988), p. 244; World Bank (1990), pp. 182-183, 204-205, 208-209. The 1985 and 1987 export and gross domestic product figures for Taiwan are given in Council for Economic Planning and Development (1988), pp. 23, 208.

NOTES: a. Percentages may not add up to 100 due to rounding error.

b. 1987.

c. 1986.

d. 1984.

exports between 1985 and 1988, Thailand from 35% to 52%, Malaysia from 27% to 45%, and Indonesia from 11% to 29%.

Equally impressive are the figures which show the diversity of these manufactured exports. Hong Kong, South Korea, and Taiwan have retained a relatively strong base in two of the traditional industries that have been economic mainstays since the start of their export-led industrialization nearly three decades ago, textiles and clothing. What is surprising is the fact that machinery and transport equipment now is the leading export sector for three of the four East Asian NICs (the exception being Hong Kong), as well as for Mexico, Brazil, and Malaysia. The machinery and transport equipment sector comprises a set of capital- and technology-intensive industries that mark a definitive shift in emphasis from the labor-intensive exports of the past, despite the fact that some traditional products like clothing or footwear are still significant export items. Nontraditional textile/apparel exports now represent between three fifths and three fourths of all exports in the four East Asian NICs and around one half of total exports in the Latin American NICs. (The nontraditional label is an approximation based on the exclusion of textiles and clothing from the manufacturing total. There are some products within the "Other Manufactures" category, such as footwear, that ordinarily would be added to the traditional exports list.)

Finally, it should be pointed out that the NICs vary considerably in the degree of their external orientation. The East Asian nations are export-led economies in which exports in 1987-1988 accounted for 57% and 35% of gross domestic product (GDP) in Taiwan and South Korea, respectively, and for 108% and 164% of GDP in the entrepôt city-states of Hong Kong and Singapore (see Table 4.1). This compares with export/GDP ratios of only 10% to 12% in the much larger Latin American NICs, 13% in China, and about 25% in Indonesia and Thailand. Malaysia's export orientation was especially high at 60% of GDP. Thus, the East Asian NICs are far more dependent on external trade than their Latin American or other Asian counterparts (including Japan, which had an export/GDP ratio of only 9.3% in 1988).

In summary, the international division of labor has evolved beyond the old pattern by which developing nations exported primary commodities to the industrialized countries in exchange for manufactured goods. Today, developing countries like the East Asian NICs are among the world's most successful exporters of manufactures. Furthermore, the NICs have diversified from traditional labor-intensive exports, such as textiles, or those based on natural resources—such as plywood, leather, paper, and basic petrochemicals—to more complex capital- and skill-intensive exports like machinery, transport equipment, and computers.

While the diversification of the NICs exports toward nontraditional manufactured products is now a clear trend, less well recognized is the tendency of the NICs to develop higher levels of specialization in their export profiles. The global manufacturing system that has emerged in the last several decades and the related expansion in export activity by the NICs has led to increasingly complex product networks and an unprecedented degree of geographical specialization. The NICs within a given region, such as East Asia or Latin America, are becoming increasingly differentiated from one another as each nation is establishing specialized export niches within the world economy (see Gereffi, 1989a for illustrations of this trend). Export networks and export niches thus are becoming key units of analysis in the contemporary global manufacturing system.

National Development Strategies

National development strategies nonetheless have played an important role in shaping these new productive relationships in the world economy. Conventional economic wisdom has it that the NICs have followed one of two alternative development strategies: an inward-oriented path of import-substituting industrialization (ISI) pursued by relatively large, resource-rich economies in which industrial production is geared mainly to the needs of a sizable domestic market; and an outward-oriented approach (export-oriented industrialization, or EOI) adopted primarily by smaller, resource-poor nations that depend on global markets to stimulate the rapid growth of their manufactured exports. Whereas the Latin American NICs have been most closely associated with ISI. The East Asian NICs are considered as paradigmatic exemplars of the virtues of EOI.

This simplified view of the development trajectories of the Latin American and East Asian NICs, while useful up to a point, can be profoundly misleading, especially in terms of its policy implication that other Third World nations ought to attempt to emulate the successful economic experience of the East Asian NICs (for a fuller consideration of these issues, see Gereffi, 1989a and 1989b; Gereffi & Wyman, 1990). With regard to the relevance of national development strategies to the global manufacturing system described above, I want to highlight several major points.

First, it is a mistake to think of inward-oriented and outward-oriented development strategies as mutually exclusive alternatives. Each of the NICs in Latin America and East Asia has pursued a combination of both initial and advanced phases of ISI and different types of EOI in order to avoid the inherent limitations of an exclusive reliance on domestic or external markets. This mixed approach also facilitates the industrial diversification and upgrading that are required for these nations to remain competitive in the world economy (see Gereffi, 1989b; 1991). Rather than being mutually exclusive alternatives, the ISI and EOI development paths in fact have been complementary and interactive.

Second, the sharp divergence between inward-oriented and outward-oriented development strategies in the Latin American and East Asian NICs, respectively, in the 1960s, masks a significant convergence in their economic trajectories during the subsequent two decades. The countries in both regions established or expanded second-stage ISI industries to meet a variety of domestic development objectives and ultimately to enhance the flexibility of their export structures (this point is amply documented in Gereffi and Wyman, 1990). In the 1970s, South Korea and Taiwan launched major "Heavy and Chemical Industrialization" programs with a focus on steel, machinery, automobiles, shipbuilding, and petrochemicals. Singapore used its links with transnational corporations (TNCs) to push into capital-intensive sectors like oil refining, petrochemicals, telecommunications equipment, office and industrial machinery, and electronics in the 1970s. These shifts toward heavier industries in the East Asian NICs paralleled similar kinds of investments in the Latin American NICs a decade or two earlier. They also laid the groundwork for a far more diversified range of manufactured exports by the East Asian NICs in the 1980s.

The Latin American NICs moved toward a strategy of export diversification in the 1980s as well. In Mexico, sharp currency devaluations led to a spectacular increase of labor-intensive manufactured exports from the *maquiladora* ("bonded-processing") industries located along the U.S. border. In Brazil, the composition of industrial exports evolved toward more skill-intensive metalworking and machinery products initially developed for their domestic markets during the second stage of ISI, such as consumer durables, transport equipment, and capital goods. The automobile industry, for example, has emerged as one of the most dynamic export sectors for Mexico and Brazil in the 1980s. This industrial deepening along ISI lines in the Latin American and East Asian NICs contributed to a more diversified pattern of export growth in each region, illustrating the often unexpected synergy between inward-oriented and outward-oriented development strategies.

Third, EOI in the East Asian and Latin American NICs has been overwhelmingly centered on the U.S. market since the onset of their export-promotion efforts in the 1960s. Nonetheless, the degree of export reliance on the United States varied considerably among the NICs in the late 1980s. Mexico's dependence on the American market was the greatest in 1987, at 65%, followed by Taiwan at 44%; South Korea, 39%; Hong Kong and Brazil, around 28%; and Singapore, 25% (United Nations, 1989; Council for Economic Planning and Development, 1988, p. 222).

However, the willingness and ability of the United States to continue to fuel the NICs' export growth in the future is very doubtful. The United States had a world-record trade deficit of nearly $180 billion in 1987. With the exception of Germany, most of the other West European nations are running trade deficits as well. The political pressures for protectionism in the developed countries are well documented and likely to grow. How the NICs respond to this challenge rests to a large degree on their ability to diversify their export markets, both geographically and through product specialization.

Fourth, significant industrial upgrading has occurred in many of the EOI industries in the NICs, often in response to specific government policies. While the first significant wave of exports from the East Asian NICs in the late 1950s and the 1980s came from traditional, labor-intensive industries like textiles, apparel, and footwear that relied on low wages and an unskilled work force, there has been a very pronounced shift in the 1980s toward an upgraded, skill-intensive version of EOI. These new export industries include higher value-added items that employ sophisticated technology and require a more extensively developed, tightly integrated local industrial base. Products range from computers and semiconductors to numerically controlled machine tools, televisions, videocassette recorders, and sporting goods. This export dynamism in East Asia does not derive solely from introducing new products, but also from continuously upgrading traditional ones.

The Latin American NICs also have developed a sophisticated array of exports on the basis of their earlier import-substituting industries. American automobile companies are setting up world-class engine plants in Mexico, for example, partly to cope with Japanese competition (Shaiken & Herzenberg, 1987). Brazil too has developed state-of-the-art, technologically advanced, and increasingly export-oriented industries from an ISI base in fields like automobiles, computers, armaments. and assorted capital goods. Fifth, EOI industries in the NICs are spatially segregated from the older ISI industries, they have different kinds of labor forces, they attract alternative forms of capital investment, and they are promoted by distinctive government policies in the NICs and the core countries. In many of the NICs, governments want to move away from unskilled labor enclaves both because of rising labor costs and in order to create higher levels of domestic value-added. Core-country protectionism (tariffs, quotas, and voluntary export restraints) has had the perhaps unanticipated effect of encouraging industrial upgrading in the main exporting NICs. This often leads to import displacement as higher value-added NIC exports replace those lower on the value-added chain, rather than to effective import substitution favoring domestic producers in the core.

Sixth, the growing prominence of EOI industries in the NICs has created a qualitative shift in the international division of labor. Whereas the ISI industries established a pattern of national segmentation in which parallel national industries were set up to supply highly protected domestic markets, the turn to EOI has promoted a logic of transnational integration based on geographical specialization and global sourcing. Thus, national development strategies have helped to foster the emergence of a global manufacturing system.

Commodity Chains and the Footwear Industry

In the global manufacturing system of today, production of a single good commonly spans several countries, with each nation performing tasks in which it has a cost advantage. This is true for traditional manufactures, such as footwear and garments, as well as for modern products, like automobiles and computers. In order to analyze some of the implications of this worldwide division of labor for specific sets of countries like the East Asian and Latin American NICs, it is very helpful to utilize the concept of commodity chains.[1]

Commodity Chains

A *commodity chain,* as defined by Hopkins and Wallerstein (1986, p. 159), refers to "a network of labor and production processes whose end result is a finished commodity." One must follow two steps in building such a chain. First, to delineate the anatomy of the chain, one typically starts with the final production operation for a manufactured good and moves sequentially backward until one reaches the raw material inputs. The second step in constructing a commodity chain involves identifying four properties for each operation or node in the chain: (1) the commodity flows to and from the node, and those operations that occur immediately prior to and after it; (2) the relations of production (i.e., forms of the labor force) within the node;

(3) the dominant organization of production, including technology and the scale of the production unit; and (4) the geographic loci of the operation in question (Hopkins & Wallerstein, 1986, pp. 160-163).

The NICs are pivotal production sites in the commodity chains that cut across national boundaries and that help define core-periphery relations in the world system. However, the complexity of commodity chains for the kinds of export-oriented manufacturing industries that the NICs are predominant in today requires that the model proposed by Hopkins and Wallerstein be extended in several ways.

First, the dynamic growth of the NICs has revolved around their success in expanding their production and exports of a wide range of consumer products destined mainly for core-country markets. This means that it is extremely important to include forward as well as backward linkages from the production stage in the commodity chain. In the footwear industry, a full commodity chain encompasses the entire spectrum of activities in the world economy: the agro-extractive sector (cattle for leather, and crude oil as the basis for plastic and synthetic rubber inputs), the industrial sector (footwear manufacturing), and the service sector (the activities associated with the export, marketing, and retailing of shoes).

Second, the extension of commodity chains beyond production to include the flow of products to the final consumer market has important implications for where economic surplus is concentrated in a global industry. In the case of footwear, the comparative advantage of the NICs lies primarily in footwear production because of the relatively low labor costs in these non-core countries. A corollary of this fact, however, is that the main source of economic surplus within the footwear commodity chain generally is not at the production stage, but rather at the last stage of the chain where service activities predominate (i.e., the marketing and retailing of shoes). Product differentiation by means of heavily advertised brand names (e.g., Nike, Reebok, Florsheim) and the use of diverse retail outlets allows core-country firms, rather than those in the semiperiphery, to capture the lion's share of economic rents in this industry.

Third, an export-oriented industry like footwear provides a convenient baseline for measuring the relative success of countries as they compete with one another for shares of the world market. I will concentrate on footwear exports to the United States, which is the world's largest market for manufactured consumer exports from the NICs (Keesing, 1982). By mapping the changing shares of the major footwear exporters to the U.S. market during the past two decades, one gets a remarkably clear picture of competition not only among the East Asian and Latin American NICs, but also between these NICs and core-country exporters like Italy and Japan.

Figure 4.1 outlines a commodity chain for the global footwear industry. It is composed of four major segments: (1) raw material supply; (2) production; (3) exporting; and (4) marketing and retailing. In addition, the major footwear export niches in the U.S. market are included in order to illustrate the specialized nature of the competition that occurs among the major footwear exporters.

Patterns of Competition
Among the Footwear-Exporting NICs

The footwear industry is a very instructive case for exploring the mobility of the NICs in the contemporary world economy. Footwear has been the top export item from South Korea, Taiwan, and Brazil to the United States throughout most of the 1980s, and it is of growing importance to China. Although each of these countries has a very diversified profile of manufactured exports (see Table 4.1), it is notable that footwear continues to be a major export commodity, despite the fact that the export momentum of the NICs is shifting toward more sophisticated products such as automobiles, computers, color television sets, and videocassette recorders.

The United States is the largest footwear market in the world. During the past two decades, imports have steadily displaced local production within the American market. In 1968, imports accounted for 21.5% of all nonrubber footwear consumed in the United States; in 1979, one out of every two pairs of shoes purchased in the United States was imported; and by 1989, four out of every five pairs of shoes bought in the United States were made abroad (Footwear Industries of America [FIA], 1990).

The pattern of footwear exports to the American market shows several clear shifts. These can be seen in Table 4.2, which identifies the major sources of nonrubber footwear imports to the United States from 1968 to 1989. (Nonrubber footwear accounts for about 80% of all U.S. footwear imports.) In the late 1960s, the main footwear exporters to the American market were Italy, Spain, and Japan, This trio of nations accounted for three quarters of all U.S. footwear imports by value in 1968 (Gereffi & Korzeniewicz, 1990, table 1). Italy was the dominant exporter that year, with a market share of 41% by value and 34% by volume.

By the mid-1970s, however, the East Asian NICs were beginning to displace their European rivals, while Japanese imports had virtually disappeared from the American market. Taiwan led the way, followed by South

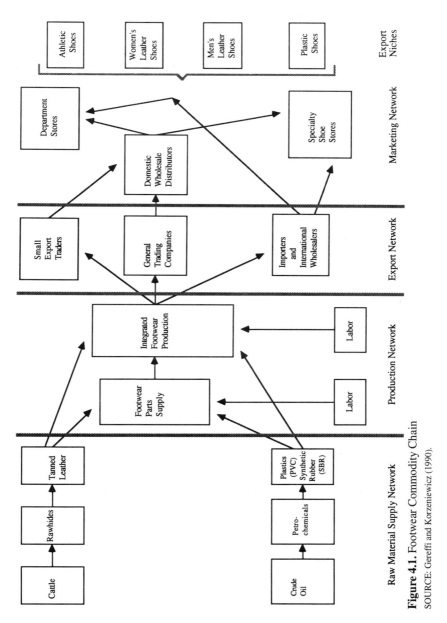

Figure 4.1. Footwear Commodity Chain

SOURCE: Gereffi and Korzeniewicz (1990).

Table 4.2 Major Sources of U.S. Nonrubber Footwear Imports, 1968-1989 (Millions of Pairs and Percentage Share of World Total)

	1968 Pairs	1968 %	1976 Pairs	1976 %	1981 Pairs	1981 %	1983 Pairs	1983 %	1985 Pairs	1985 %	1987 Pairs	1987 %	1989 Pairs	1989 %
Italy	59.0	33.7	47.2	12.7	50.1	13.3	56.3	9.7	74.7	8.8	47.7	5.1	41.7	4.8
Spain	14.2	8.1	38.7	10.5	18.9	5.0	26.7	4.6	55.5	6.6	28.2	2.9	22.6	2.6
Taiwan	15.3	8.7	155.7	42.1	118.5	31.6	243.4	41.8	372.5	44.2	427.0	45.5	262.1	30.5
South Korea	0.7	0.4	43.9	11.9	44.0	11.7	118.8	20.4	137.2	16.3	191.8	20.5	172.8	20.1
Brazil	a	0	26.7	7.2	43.0	11.5	64.4	11.1	113.2	13.4	108.2	11.6	112.8	13.1
China	a	0	0.8	0.2	7.1	1.9	7.2	1.2	20.8	2.5	47.3	5.1	143.5	16.7
All Other	86.1	49.1	57.0	15.4	94.0	25.0	65.1	11.2	68.8	8.2	87.5	9.3	104.9	12.2
World Total	175.3	100.0	370.0	100.0	375.6	100.0	581.9	100.0	842.7	100.0	937.7	100.0	860.4	100.0

SOURCE: U.S. Department of Commerce, Bureau of the Census, cited in Footwear Industries of America (1990).
NOTE: a. Less than 50,000 pairs.

Korea. In 1976, Taiwan exported 156 million pairs of nonrubber footwear to the United States, which represented 42% of total U.S. imports, more than triple the volume of Italy or South Korea, its closest competitors. The market position of the two East Asian NICs reached its zenith in 1987, when Taiwan and South Korea were supplying two thirds of U.S. nonrubber footwear imports (Table 4.2). Since the import share of the American footwear market has been more than 80% since 1985, this means that one out of every two pairs of shoes sold in the United States in 1987 was made in either Taiwan or South Korea.

In the early 1980s, Brazil emerged as a major shoe exporter to the United States, with China also entering the field in both rubber and nonrubber shoes by the end of the decade. In 1989, four nations—Taiwan, South Korea, China, and Brazil—accounted for more than 80% of all nonrubber footwear imports in the U.S. market (see Table 4.2).

This dramatic increase in the role of the East Asian and Latin American NICs in the American footwear market during the 1970s and 1980s is evidence of dynamic new sources of international competitiveness in this global industry. Mobility within the world-system is tied to a country's ability to upgrade its mix of core-peripheral economic activities. In order to advance in the world economy, countries typically strive to play a major role in those segments of commodity chains with the highest ratio of core to peripheral activities—that is, where the economic surplus is greatest.

The location of economic surplus in the footwear commodity chain is conditioned by four factors: labor, core and peripheral capital, the state, and economic organizations. First, footwear production is a relatively labor-intensive activity. Labor costs thus tend to drive the competitive strategies of footwear exporters, and are a major factor in explaining geographical shifts in the industry. Relatively inexpensive labor in the NICs is the key reason these nations acquired a significant cost advantage vis-à-vis core rivals like the United States and Italy. Since labor costs in the NICs (especially in East Asia) have been rising quite rapidly, however, these semiperipheral nations have had to select export niches which allow them to economize on labor and attain higher levels of value-added in the industry. This offers some measure of protection from cheap-labor footwear exporters like those in China, Mexico, and Thailand.

The connection between the cost of labor and its impact on the average value per pair of nonrubber shoes sold in the U.S. market can be seen in Table 4.3. For the three European nations (France, Italy, and Spain) and the United States, the relationship is quite direct: the higher the total hourly compensation (wages plus benefits) in the footwear industry in 1988, the higher

Table 4.3 Average Value per Pair of U.S. Imported Nonrubber Shoes and Overseas Wages in the Footwear Industry, 1988

Country	Average Value Per Pair of Nonrubber Shoes Imported into the United States (in U.S. dollars)	Total Hourly Compensation in the Footwear Industry (in U.S. dollars)
United States	16.75[a]	7.80[b]
France	31.19	11.08
Italy	18.55	9.77
Spain	15.48	5.52[c]
South Korea	10.83	1.71[b]
Brazil	8.42	0.65[d]
Taiwan	6.52	2.27[e]
Hong Kong	5.89	2.71
China	2.90	NA

SOURCE: Footwear Industries of America (1989, p. 4; 1990).
NOTES: a. Average factory price, cited in U.S. Department of Commerce (1990, pp. 36-46).
b. Nonrubber footwear.
c. Includes clothing and leather; 1987 data.
d. 1985 data.
e. Leather and leather products.
NA = Not available.

is the average value per pair of imported shoes. (This generalization also holds for the average factory price of domestically made shoes by U.S. manufacturers.) The linkage is less clear-cut for the NICs, however: Hong Kong and Taiwan have the highest levels of hourly compensation in the footwear industry ($2.71 and $2.27, respectively), followed by South Korea ($1.71) and Brazil ($0.65). Nonetheless, the average value per pair of imported shoes is greatest in South Korea ($10.83) and Brazil ($8.42), followed by Taiwan ($6.52), Hong Kong ($5.89), and China ($2.90). The most likely explanation for these discrepancies in the price/wage comparisons lies in the different export niches that each country occupies in the U.S. market, which will be discussed below, since these niches reflect diverse levels of value-added in the industry.

Second, the footwear industry requires a reconceptualization of the roles of core and peripheral capital in contemporary consumer-goods export industries in the world economy. The footwear industry is highly competitive at the international level, with little direct involvement by multinational corporations in the production and exporting of footwear. Local private capital, usually made up of small and medium-sized firms, is the principal actor in the footwear industry in the NICs.

Core capital does play a significant role, however, in the distribution and marketing stage of the footwear commodity chain. Unlike capital- and technology-intensive industries where multinational corporations frequently set up facilities for overseas production, core capital shapes the growth and evolution of the footwear industry in a more indirect way, mainly as a subcontractor and buyer of footwear made to the specifications of shoe companies and retail outlets in the United States.

The available information suggests that the most profitable segment of the footwear commodity chain is the distribution and marketing of shoes, rather than footwear production. The distributors' margins in the core countries are very large. In the United States, these margins averaged 50% in the mid-1970s, but were closer to 80% for imported goods. In Japan, "the price [of footwear] approximately doubles between the departure of the goods from the factory and their purchase by the consumer. The successive increases appear to be as follows: factory 55%, wholesaler 70%, and retailer 100%" (Organization for Economic Co-operation and Development, 1976, p. 39). A similar situation seems to prevail in Europe, where distribution costs amount to at least 100% of the manufacturers' price. The economic surplus that accrues to footwear distributors and retailers in core countries undoubtedly is much higher when production is done overseas rather than domestically.

Third, the state so far has maintained a relatively low profile in the footwear industry in both the semiperiphery and the core, contrary to the expectation in world-systems theory that semiperipheral states will play a leading role in upgrading the mix of core-peripheral economic activities. Within the semiperiphery, the state has no involvement in footwear production at all (in contrast to the prominence of state enterprises in heavy or strategic industries such as steel, oil, petrochemicals, and mining). The main impact of the state on manufactured exports from the NICs is in the area of exchange rate policies, export promotion schemes, and protection for domestic producers.

State policies in a core country like the United States are primarily important in terms of selectively restrictive trade measures such as tariffs, quotas, and other nontariff barriers that could impede footwear imports. In the footwear industry, for example, the United States established Orderly Marketing

Agreements (OMAs) with Taiwan and South Korea for a four-year period beginning in June 1977 (U.S. Department of Commerce, 1990, pp. 36-37). After the OMAs expired in 1981, imports from these two countries, which had declined during the OMA period, began to accelerate rapidly and by 1987 they had nearly quadrupled from their level of six years earlier (see Table 4.2).

Until recently, state policies in both the semiperiphery and the core have fostered a rapid expansion of footwear exports from the NICs. There is a growing perception, however, that the more or less open trading environment that has been supported by core states in the postwar world economy will become more closed. In particular, the favorable access to the U.S. consumer market on the part of East Asian manufacturers may be reduced as the geopolitical map of Asia is redrawn. An even more drastic scenario that has been mentioned is the possible emergence of regional trading blocs (Garten, 1989). This would fundamentally alter the role of the NICs in the world economy, and transform the structure of export-oriented industries like footwear.

Finally, the footwear industry demonstrates convincingly the importance of looking at economic organizations and other institutions within the NICs to explain their individual patterns of export success. Footwear firms in South Korea and Taiwan, for example, are quite different from one another in their organizational aspects, which reflects their distinct national industrial structures and social contexts. These contrasts help explain why these two nations have targeted diverse footwear export niches in the U.S. market, and why their future strategies in the industry are likely to vary.

In terms of size, the Taiwanese footwear industry is composed mainly of small firms, while the South Korean industry is dominated by very large companies. In Taiwan, the number of establishments with 500 workers or more comprised about 20% of value-added in the footwear sector in 1976; in South Korea, establishments of this size provided 90% of all footwear value-added (Levy, 1988). The relatively concentrated industrial structure in South Korea was enormously helpful in the mass-production of athletic footwear that followed the rapid boom in the demand for jogging shoes, and the entry of Nike into South Korea in 1976 and Reebok in the early 1980s. The Korean footwear sector has remained quite dependent on this one product (athletic footwear), however, which has shown cyclical patterns of growth. The smaller size of Taiwanese footwear producers, on the other hand, seems to have resulted in greater organizational flexibility that permits them to be responsive to design and fashion changes in core-country markets, and thus to respond more rapidly to shifting consumer preferences.

Export Niches in the U.S. Market

Export niches are segments or shares of world and national markets captured by firms of a single nationality within an industrial sector. The concept of export niches is a crucial analytical tool in understanding the trajectories of semiperipheral mobility. Export niches help explain how South Korea, Taiwan, Brazil, and China captured large shares of the American footwear market by specializing in products that were well suited to their raw material supply networks and domestic industrial capabilities.

The major export niches in the U.S. footwear market in 1989 are depicted in Table 4.4. (The term *export niche* is used because it helps to describe the distribution of exports by major footwear-producing nations, although from the vantage point of the United States these could also be called "import niches.") Men's leather footwear imports are quite widely distributed between Taiwan (19%), Brazil (16%), South Korea (14%), China (14%), and Italy (8%). A more pronounced division of labor emerges, however, when one looks at the average value of the men's leather footwear exported to the United States by each of these countries. The bulk of Italy's exports of men's leather shoes are in the most expensive "over $25" price category: Taiwan's and South Korea's men's leather footwear exports cluster in the $8 to $20 range; Brazil overlaps with the two East Asian NICs, but also has a large number of shoes whose average import value is $5 to $8; and China's exports are concentrated at the least expensive end of the price continuum, "not over $1.25" (FIA, 1989).

There are far higher levels of concentration by exporting countries in the other footwear niches identified in Table 4.4. Taiwan and China were the largest suppliers of vinyl or plastic footwear imports, with 49% and 31%, respectively, for men's shoes (not shown in the table); 68% and 24% for women's shoes; and 56% and 30% for juvenile footwear. South Korea accounted for nearly two thirds of the athletic leather footwear imported into the United States in 1989 and for almost one third of the juvenile leather shoes. The primary niche for Brazil was women's leather footwear (42% of total U.S. imports), while China was the largest exporter of rubber and fabric shoes (mainly sneakers) to the United States (50% of the total), followed by South Korea (18%) and Taiwan (11%).

In terms of the raw material supply networks highlighted in the global footwear commodity chain (see Figure 4.1), Italy, Spain, South Korea, and Brazil have all specialized in *leather* footwear, although the European producers have occupied the high-priced fashion shoe niches (especially Italy), South Korea an intermediate niche, and Brazil the lowest price ranges.

Table 4.4 Export Niches in the U.S. Footwear Market, 1989 (Thousands of Pairs and Percentage Share of Total World Imports)

Footwear Niches County	Men's Leather Pairs	%	Women's Leather Pairs	%	Women's Vinyl/Plastic Pairs	%	Juvenile Leather Pairs	%	Juvenile Vinyl/Plastic Pairs	%	Athletic Leather Pairs	%	Rubber/Fabric Pairs	%
Italy	5,014	7.7	25,630	11.5	1,685	1.1	5,770	12.9	298	0.4	1,061	0.7	NA	NA
Spain	3,620	5.6	14,115	6.4	335	0.2	2,670	6.0	286	0.4	104	0.1	NA	NA
Taiwan	12,196	18.8	24,529	11.1	103,998	67.5	5,746	12.8	38,471	56.4	27,417	17.2	20,619	10.9
South Korea	9,050	13.9	19,393	8.7	2,589	1.7	12,980	29.0	4,339	6.4	102,502	64.5	33,840	17.8
Brazil	10,419	16.1	92,388	41.6	609	0.4	7,148	16.0	628	0.9	1,117	0.7	NA	NA
China	8,859	13.6	22,170	10.0	37,656	24.5	4,408	9.9	20,766	30.4	8,736	5.5	95,252	50.1
All Other	15,764	24.3	23,864	10.7	7,152	4.6	5,991	13.4	3,463	5.1	17,919	11.3	40,345	21.2[a]
World Total	64,922	100.0	222,089	100.0	154,024	100.0	44,713	100.0	68,251	100.0	158,856	100.0	190,056	100.0
Export Niche Share[b]		[7.5]		[25.8]		[17.9]		[5.2]		[7.9]		[18.5]		c

SOURCE: U.S. Department of Commerce, Bureau of the Census, cited in Footwear Industries of America (1989).

NOTES: a. Mexico has 12.4% and Hong Kong 4.1% of U.S. rubber/fabric footwear imports.

b. The bracketed percentages represent the share of each niche in total U.S. nonrubber footwear imports. These six niches account for 82.8% of total U.S. nonrubber footwear imports of 860.4 million pairs in 1989.

c. This niche covers what is not included in the nonrubber footwear market.

NA = Not available.

Taiwan and China have been the primary suppliers of *plastic* and *vinyl* shoes, while China also has been the main producer of *rubber* and *fabric* footwear. Thus footwear-manufacturing nations are trying to consolidate and upgrade their international market positions within as well as between different categories of footwear that have diverse raw material starting points. In order to be competitive in these product clusters, a country has to have an assured and high quality source of raw material supply. This is particularly problematic for shoe producers relying on leather inputs (see Korzeniewicz, 1990).

The empirical evidence presented above helps piece together several interesting "stories" about global footwear production in the 1970s and 1980s. The East Asian and Latin American NICs succeeded in capturing important segments of the U.S. market, but they did so in different ways (Gereffi & Korzeniewicz, 1990). *South Korean producers* captured an extraordinarily dynamic market for athletic footwear at the time when the fitness boom hit a peak in the United States. South Korean shoemakers showed an amazing ability to dominate a niche that in a few years grew to comprise about 20% of the overall U.S. footwear import market. *Taiwanese producers* captured a rapidly growing market that was already in place, that of plastic and vinyl shoes, and competed most directly with American producers. Taiwanese firms seem to have been more effective than other shoemakers in diversifying their exports into various footwear sectors. *Brazilian producers* showed a capacity to capture a very large niche in their exports of women's leather footwear, in effect cutting Italy's share of this product market by more than one half during the 1970s and 1980s. This is an impressive record, even if part of this outcome reflects Brazilian producers filling niches that the Italian footwear firms abandoned by moving to higher-value shoes. Finally, *Chinese producers* have been the most recent major entrant into the U.S. footwear market. They have targeted the least expensive end of the footwear spectrum, with an emphasis on rubber shoes and women's and children's types of vinyl footwear.

The fierce competition that has thrown continuous waves of new entrants into the American footwear market shows no signs of abating, despite the fact that the American consumer is not buying as many shoes as before. The per capita consumption of footwear in the United States, which peaked in 1986 at 4.9 pairs, has fallen to about 4.4 pairs in 1990 (Fischer, 1990, p. 26). Although this decline in consumption has been matched by a decline in imports which fell from their record high of 941 million pairs in 1986 to 860 million pairs in 1989, import penetration during these years has remained stable at just over 80%.

The established East Asian and Latin American footwear exporters are in the process of upgrading their product offerings, just as the European shoe-makers did over a decade ago, in order to stay ahead of the competition from lower cost footwear-producing nations. Much of the low-cost production of women's and children's vinyl shoes has shifted from Taiwan to China, for example, as Taiwan has consciously upgraded its product mix to leather-type footwear. This is because manufacturers generally have been able to achieve higher profit margins on leather footwear compared with shoes made from other materials. As a result, the average value per pair of imported nonrubber shoes from South Korea, which emphasized leather athletic footwear since the late 1970s, was 66% higher than that of Taiwan in 1989 ($10.83 and $6.52, respectively) (see Table 4.3). However, South Korea also has been affected by competition from lower-cost countries. Thailand and Indonesia have quadrupled and doubled, respectively, their footwear exports to the United States from 1988 to 1989 as branded athletic footwear importers began to shift their sources of supply from South Korea to lower-cost facto-ries in these countries (U.S. Department of Commerce, 1990).

Finally, while the Pacific Rim is certainly unparalleled among U.S. foot-wear sources, there is another quietly growing source in what might be called the "Atlantic Rim." While Brazil manufactures almost 85% of the U.S. foot-wear imports from Latin America, its exports have stagnated at around 110 million pairs since 1984. Mexico, the Dominican Republic, and Colombia have begun to grab larger shares of the U.S. market during the past five years, although they have started from much smaller bases (Fischer, 1990). A good deal of this production is shoes and slippers made from precut footwear parts exported from the United States for final assembly abroad. The finished products are then re-exported to the United States under Section 807 of the U.S. Tariff Schedule, in which duties are then assessed only on the value-added content.

Whether the East Asian and Latin American NICs will get closer to the core countries, or whether any of them will actually enter the core, ultimately depends on their capacity for technological and institutional innovation, and their ability to adjust to the changing opportunities and constraints in the international political economy. What succeeded in the past is no guarantee for the future. The openness of the U.S. market has been a key factor in the rapid economic growth of all the export-oriented NICs, especially those in East Asia. Continued easy access to the American market is very much in doubt, given the staggering trade deficits that confront the world's leading core nation. For the NICs to ascend in the world economy, they will have to find new ways to move to the most profitable end of commodity chains. This requires a fundamental shift from manufacturing in the semiperiphery to marketing in the core, a daunting task indeed.

Differentiating the Roles
of the NICs in the World Economy

The foregoing analysis of the Latin American and East Asian NICs allows us to identify a differentiated set of roles that semiperipheral nations play in the world economy. From the perspective of world-systems theory, these roles reflect the mix of core-peripheral economic activities in the NICs, as well as the significance of core and peripheral capital in carrying out these development efforts. The roles are not mutually exclusive, and their importance for a given country or set of countries may undergo fairly dramatic shifts over time. These roles in the world economy are largely determined by domestic conditions, such as the pattern of economic, social, and political organization within the NICs, and thus are not simply a response to the "needs" of core capital.

This framework focuses on export production in the NICs, since this is the best indicator of a country's international competitive advantage. The NICs can be characterized in terms of at least five basic types of international economic roles: (1) the commodity-export role; (2) the commercial-subcontracting role; (3) the export-platform role; (4) the component-supplier role; and (5) the independent-exporter role.

The *commodity-export role* is of prime importance for the Latin American NICs, where natural resources account for two thirds or more of total exports, and also for Singapore, which processes and re-exports a large volume of petroleum-related products. Peripheral capital controls many of these natural-resource industries at the production stage in Latin America, with the petroleum and mining industries usually being run by state-owned enterprises. The agricultural and livestock industries often are owned by local capital, although foreign-owned food-processing companies still predominate in many of Latin America's most profitable lines of commercial agriculture. In Singapore, TNCs are the proprietors of most of the petroleum-related industries. These commodity exports are sent to a wide range of nations, with the main share going to core countries. The export and distribution networks are usually controlled by core capital.

The next three types of roles in the world economy refer to various kinds of international subcontracting arrangements (see Holmes, 1986). The first major distinction is between "commercial subcontracting" in which the finished goods output of the subcontracting firms is sold to either a wholesaler or a retailer, and "industrial subcontracting" in which parts production is carried out for use by other manufacturing firms. Furthermore, there are two major types of industrial subcontracting: "export platforms" with an emphasis on foreign-owned, labor-intensive assembly operations; and "component-parts supply" in capital- and technology-intensive industries in the periphery.

The *commercial-subcontracting role* refers to the production of finished consumer goods by locally owned firms, where the output is distributed and marketed by large chain retailers and their agents (Holmes, 1986, p. 85). This is one of the major niches filled by the East Asian NICs in the contemporary world economy. In 1980, three of the East Asian NICs (Hong Kong, Taiwan, and South Korea) accounted for 72% of all finished consumer goods exported by the Third World to OECD countries, other Asian countries supplied another 19%, while just 7% came from Latin America and the Caribbean. The United States was the leading market for these products, with 46% of the total (Keesing, 1983, pp. 338-339). In East Asia, peripheral capital controls the production stage of the finished-consumer-goods commodity chains (see Gereffi, 1990; Haggard & Cheng, 1987), while core capital tends to control the more profitable export, distribution, and retail marketing stages. While the international subcontracting of finished consumer goods is growing in Latin America, it tends to be subordinated to the export-platform and component-supplier forms of production.

The *export-platform role* corresponds to those nations that have foreign-owned, labor-intensive assembly of manufactured goods in export-processing zones. These zones offer special incentives to foreign capital, and tend to attract firms in a common set of industries: garments, footwear, and electronics. Virtually all of the East Asian and Latin American NICs have engaged in this form of labor-intensive production, although its significance tends to wane as wage rates rise and countries become more developed. In Taiwan and South Korea, export-processing zones have been on the decline during the past 10 to 15 years, largely because labor costs have been rapidly increasing. These nations have been trying to upgrade their mix of export activities by moving toward more skill- and technology-intensive products. The export-platform role in Asia is now being occupied by low-wage countries like China, the Philippines, Thailand, Indonesia, and Malaysia.

In Latin America, on the other hand, export-platform industries are on the upswing because the wage levels in most countries of the region are considerably below those of the East Asian NICs, and recent currency devaluations in the Latin American NICs make the price of their exports more competitive internationally. The export platforms in Latin America also have the advantage of geographical proximity to the most important core-country markets in comparison with Asian export platforms. Mexico's *maquiladora* industry, which was set up in 1965 as an integral part of Mexico's Northern Border Industrialization Program, is probably the largest and most dynamic of these export areas. The *maquiladora* industry doubled its foreign-exchange earnings from 1982 ($850 million) to 1987 ($1.6 billion). In the latter year, *maquila* exports were Mexico's second largest source of foreign exchange, surpassed only by crude oil exports (see Carrillo-Huerta & Urquidi, 1989). There are similar zones in Brazil, Colombia, Central America, and the Caribbean. Core capital controls the production, export, and marketing stages of the commodity chains for these consumer goods. The main contribution of peripheral nations is cheap labor.

The *component-supplier role* refers to the production of component parts in capital- and technology-intensive industries in the periphery, for export and usually final assembly in the core country. This type of international industrial subcontracting has at least two important subcategories: (1) "capacity" (or concurrent) subcontracting, in which the parent firm and the subcontractor engage in the fabrication of similar products in order to handle overflow or cyclical demand; and (2) "specialization" (or complementary) subcontracting, in which the parts produced by the subcontractor are not made in-house by the parent firm. Whereas "capacity subcontracting" involves a horizontal disintegration of production, "specialization subcontracting" is a vertical disintegration of production (see Holmes, 1986, p. 86).

Component supply has been a key niche for the Latin American NICs' manufactured exports during the past two decades. Brazil and Mexico have been important production sites for vertically integrated exports by TNCs to core-country markets, especially the United States, since the late 1960s. This is most notable in certain industries like motor vehicles, computers, and pharmaceuticals (see Newfarmer, 1985). American, European, and Japanese automotive TNCs, for example, have advanced manufacturing facilities in Mexico and Brazil for the production of engines, auto parts, and even completed vehicles for the U.S., and European markets.

This pattern is a striking contrast to the earlier version of Japanese automobile production, pioneered by Toyota, in which manufacturing efficiency seemed to require highly integrated production networks with factories clustered within a few miles of one another in a vast urban-industrial complex such as Toyota City (Hill, 1987). As countries like Mexico have developed their own networks of reliable parts suppliers in the automobile industry, facilitated in part by the investments of foreign auto manufacturers, and as protectionist barriers have made it more difficult for major exporting nations to penetrate core-country markets from centralized production sites, highly dispersed yet still coordinated production and export networks linking geographically distant nations have emerged for a wide variety of consumer goods (see Uchitelle, 1990, for a detailed discussion of these new trends in Mexico).

In Latin America, the manufacturing stage of the commodity chain in component-supplier production typically is owned and run by core capital, sometimes in conjunction with a local partner. The export, distribution, and marketing of the manufactured items are handled by the foreign firm. A major advantage of this production arrangement is that it is the one most likely to result in a significant transfer of technology from the core nations.

In East Asia there are two variants of the component-supplier role. The first is similar to the Latin American arrangement in which *foreign subsidiaries* manufacture parts or subunits in East Asia for products like television sets, radios, sporting goods, and consumer appliances that are assembled and marketed in the country of destination (most often, the United States). The firms that engage in this form of subcontracting can be considered to be "captive" companies that supply the bulk of their production (usually in excess of 75%) to their parent corporation.

The second variant of the component-supplier role in East Asia involves production of components by *local firms* for sale to diversified buyers on the world market. These "merchant" producers, in contrast to the captive companies mentioned above, sell virtually all of their output on the open market (see Henderson, 1989, p. 169, fn. 1). The importance of merchant producers is illustrated in the semiconductor industry. South Korean companies have focused almost exclusively on the mass production of powerful memory chips, the single largest segment of the semiconductor industry, which are sold as inputs to a wide range of domestic and international manufacturers of electronic equipment. Taiwan, on the other hand, has targeted the highest value-added segment of the semiconductor market: tailor-made "designer chips" that perform special tasks in toys, video games, and other machines. Taiwan now has 40 chip-design houses that specialize in finding export niches, and then develop products for them ("Sizzling Hot Chips," 1988). While the South Korean companies are engaging in a form of "capacity subcontracting," the Taiwanese producers of specialty semiconductor chips represent a third form of industrial subcontracting known as "supplier subcontracting." Here the subcontractor is "an independent supplier with full control over the development, design and fabrication of its product, but is willing to enter into a subcontracting arrangement to supply a dedicated or proprietary part to the parent [or purchasing] firm" (Holmes, 1986, p. 86). Taiwan, with its technological prowess, is acquiring the flexibility to move into the high value-added field of product innovation. However, without their own internationally recognized company brand names, a substantial advertising budget, and appropriate marketing and retail networks, Taiwan's ingenious producers will find it difficult to break free of the commercial-subcontracting role. South Korea probably has more potential to enter core-country markets successfully because its large, vertically integrated industrial conglomerates (*chaebols*) have the capital and technology to set up overseas production facilities and marketing networks. Thus South Korea's leading auto manufacturer, Hyundai Motor Company, has become one of the top importers into both Canada and the United States since the mid-1980s (see Gereffi, 1990).

The fifth role in this typology is the *independent-exporter role*. This refers to finished-goods export industries in which there is no subcontracting relationship between the manufacturer and the distributor or retailer of the product. These goods can range from construction materials (like cement, lumber, and standard chemicals) to a wide variety of food, clothing, and electronics items (such as beer, watches, jewelry, radios, etc.).

This typology of the different roles that the Latin American and East Asian NICs play in the world economy shows that the standard development literature has presented an oversimplified picture of the semiperiphery. The East Asian NICs have been most successful in the areas of commercial subcontracting and component supply, with secondary and declining importance given to the export-platform role emphasized in the "new international division of labor" literature. The Latin American NICs, on the other hand, have a different kind of relationship to the world economy. They are prominent in the commodity-export, export-platform, and component-supplier forms of production, but they lag far behind the East Asian NICs in the commercial-subcontracting type of manufactured exports.

Although each of these roles has certain advantages and disadvantages in terms of mobility in the world system, the prospects for the NICs can only be understood by looking at the interacting sets of roles in which these nations are enmeshed. If development theory is to be relevant for the 1990s, it will have to become flexible enough to incorporate both increased specialization at the commodity and geographical levels, along with new patterns of regional and global integration.

Note

1. This section is adapted, in part, from Gereffi and Korzeniewicz, 1990.

References

Carrillo-Huerta, Mario, & Urquidi, Victor L. (1989). *Trade deriving from the international division of production: Maquila and postmaquila in Mexico.* Unpublished manuscript, El Colegio de México, Mexico City.

Council for Economic Planning and Development (CEPD). (1988). *Taiwan statistical data book, 1988.* Taipei, Taiwan.

Fischer, John. (1990, August). Per capita consumption affects imports and domestic production. *American Shoemaking,* pp. 26-27.

Footwear Industries of America. (1989). Quarterly report, 4th quarter 1989. *Statistical Reporter.* Washington, DC: Footwear Industries of America.

Footwear Industries of America. (1990, February 27). *Nonrubber footwear industry in the United States: Fact sheet.* Washington, DC: Footwear Industries of America.

Garten, Jeffrey E. (1989). Trading blocs and the evolving world economy. *Current History, 88*(534), 15-56.

Gereffi, Gary. (1989a). Development strategies and the global factor. *Annals of the American Academy of Political and Social Science, 505,* pp. 92-104.

Gereffi, Gary. (1989b). Rethinking development theory: Insights from East Asia and Latin America. *Sociological Forum, 4*(4), pp. 505-533.

Gereffi, Gary. (1990). Big business and the state. In G. Gereffi & D. Wyman (Eds.), *Manufacturing miracles: Paths of industrialization in Latin America and East Asia.* Princeton, NJ: Princeton University Press.

Gereffi, Gary. (1991). International economics and domestic policies. In Neil J. Smelser & Alberto Martinelli (Eds.), *Economy and society: State of the art* (pp. 231-258). Newbury Park, CA: Sage.

Gereffi, Gary, & Korzeniewicz, Miguel. (1990). Commodity chains and footwear exports in the semiperiphery. In William Martin (Ed.), *Semiperipheral states in the world-economy* (pp. 45-68). Westport, CT: Greenwood Press.

Gereffi, Gary, & Wyman, Donald. (Eds.). (1990). *Manufacturing miracles: Paths of industrialization in Latin America and East Asia.* Princeton, NJ: Princeton University Press.

Haggard, Stephan, & Cheng, Tun-jen. (1987). State and foreign capital in the East Asian NICs. In Frederic C. Deyo (Ed.), *The political economy of the new Asian industrialism* (pp. 84-135). Ithaca, NY: Cornell University Press.

Harris, Nigel. (1987). *The end of the Third World.* New York: Penguin.

Henderson, Jeffrey. (1989). *The globalisation of high technology production: Society, space and semiconductors in the restructuring of the modern world.* London: Routledge.

Hill, Richard Child. (1987). Global factory and company town: The changing division of labor in the international automobile industry. In Jeffrey Henderson & Manuel Castells (Eds.), *Global restructuring and territorial development* (pp.18-37). Newbury Park, CA: Sage.

Holmes, John. (1986). The organization and locational structure of production subcontracting. In Allen J. Scott & Michael Storper (Eds.), *Production, work, and territory: The geographical anatomy of industrial capitalism* (pp. 80-106). Boston: Allen & Unwin.

Hopkins, Terence K., & Wallerstein, Immanuel. (1986). Commodity chains in the world-economy prior to 1800. *Review, 10*(1), 157-170.

Keesing, Donald. (1982). *Exporting manufactured consumer goods from developing to developed economies: Marketing by local firms and effects of developing country policies.* Mimeo. Washington, DC: World Bank.

Keesing, Donald. (1983). Linking up to distant markets: South to north exports of manufactured consumer goods. *American Economic Review, 73*, 338-342.

Korzeniewicz, Miguel. (1990). *The social foundations of international competitiveness: Footwear exports in Argentina and Brazil.* Unpublished doctoral dissertation, Duke University.

Levy, Brian. (1988). *Transaction costs, the size of firms, and industrial policy: Lessons from a comparative study of the footwear industry in Korea and Taiwan.* Research Memorandum Series. Williamstown, MA: Williams College.

Newfarmer, Richard. (Ed.). (1985). *Profits, progress and poverty: Case studies of international industries in Latin America.* Notre Dame, IN: University of Notre Dame Press.

Organization for Economic Co-operation and Development (OECD). (1976). *The footwear industry: Structure and governmental policies.* Paris: OECD.

Shaiken, Harley, with Stephen Herzenberg. (1987). *Automation and global production: Automobile engine production in Mexico, the United States, and Canada.* Monograph Series, 26. La Jolla: University of California, San Diego, Center for U.S.-Mexican Studies.

Sizzling hot chips: Asia is the source of the semiconductor industry's spectacular growth. (1988, August 18). *Far Eastern Economic Review,* pp. 80-86.

Uchitelle, Louis. (1990, September 25). Mexico's plan for industrial might. *The New York Times,* pp. C1-C2.

United Nations. (1989). *1987 International trade statistics yearbook, Vol. 1.* New York: United Nations.

United States Department of Commerce. (1990). Leather and leather products. *1990 U.S. Industrial Outlook.* Washington, DC: Bureau of the Census.

World Bank. (1987). *World development report 1987.* New York: Oxford University Press.

World Bank. (1988). *World development report 1988.* New York: Oxford University Press.

World Bank. (1990). *World development report 1990.* New York: Oxford University Press.

PART II

ECONOMIC POLICY

In Part II we examine further the interplay of state policy and economic development through four case studies—two of Korea, one of Malaysia, and one of Japan.

In Chapter 5, Hagen Koo and Eun Mee Kim focus on the relationship between state policy and capital accumulation in South Korea. The strong Korean state, Koo and Kim argue, has been largely autonomous from civil society, and therefore has been able to exert significant control over both domestic and foreign capital in the interests of spurring economic development. In examining the ways in which the Korean state helped to secure accumulation for the large *chaebols* (conglomerates), Koo and Kim look at differing policies during four phases of postwar Korean history: U.S. assisted import substitution during the 1950s; EOI based on cheap labor during the 1960s; "industrial deepening" in exports combined with import substitution in the 1970s; and the liberalization and globalization of the Korean economy during the past decade.

During the 1950s, the war-devastated Korean economy was highly dependent on U.S. military and economic assistance. Although the Rhee dictatorship was more concerned with U.S.-funded military buildup than with economic development, the preconditions for development were nonetheless established. Land reform virtually eliminated the landlord class, paving the way for a fairly open class structure. Japanese properties, and state owned enterprises and banks, were privatized and turned over to the Korean ruling elite, giving birth to today's Korean capitalist class. By the time a worker-student uprising toppled the Rhee regime in 1960, the economy was already beset by inflation, unemployment, and a decline in U.S. economic aid.

After a brief democratic interlude, Park Chung Hee's 1961 military coup launched a state-controlled "development decade" that he would oversee for twice that long. Elaborating on Castells and Harris, Koo and Kim's historical analysis shows that a primary objective of economic growth was to secure the legitimacy of Park's military regime (as well as fund it, in the face of declining U.S. military aid). This established a long-lasting alliance between capital and the military, an alliance that has left its stamp on the Korean economy. Koo and Kim argue that "guided capitalism" became the Park regime's "sacred mission." Given the historic weakness of civil society in Korea, the regime possessed the necessary autonomy to pursue its growth objectives. Through a series of five-year development plans, encouraged by foreign advisors from the International Monetary Fund (IMF) and the U.S. Agency for International Development, exports emerged as a key component of Korea's growth objectives. Export and currency policies were liberalized, and relations with Japan were normalized, partially opening the door to Japanese investment. Domestic private investment was steered toward the export sector by means of tight credit controls and artificially maintained below-market interest rates. Economic performance—as well as political connections (see Chon's detailed analysis in the next chapter)—dictated who received subsidized capital. Despite abuses (for example, land and credit speculation), these policies resulted in substantial private investment in both export and import substitution industries.

By the end of the 1960s, the limits of this approach had been reached. Firms found themselves increasingly in debt, resulting in an increasing number of bankruptcies; unemployment rose; and IMF-imposed austerity measures contributed to mounting student and worker unrest. Park responded to the impending crisis by issuing a series of emergency statutes that severely curtailed the right of labor to organize, strike, and even bargain. By 1972, he had declared himself lifetime president with unchecked powers. By a series of decrees he forgave a great deal of the accumulated private debt. The *chaebols* were protected from their creditors, providing a new foundation for growth at the expense of both finance capital and the thousands of middle class families involved in money lending. With the Heavy and Chemical and Industrialization Plan in 1973, Park also began to deemphasize the increasingly uncertain cheap labor approach to exports that Korea had pursued. Economic growth, achieved by investment in heavy industry, would secure domestic peace. The *chaebols* grew in strength, and substantial international investment flowed into Korea by the end of the decade. Exporting became the monopoly of a handful of government-licensed conglomerate giants who were able to finance their export activities through cheap government loans. By the end of the 1970s, rising debt, declining exports, and inflation threatened this economic success. An austerity response triggered labor unrest. As strikes spread across the country, Park was assassinated by the head of the Korean CIA in 1979. A broad alliance of workers, farmers, small business people, and the middle class—the *Min Jung* (People's) movement—mobilized support against the *chaebols* during the early 1980s. A 1979 military coup by Major General Chun Doo Hwan led to demonstrations and bloody repression. Lacking in legitimacy, the Chun government, as had its predecessor, sought legitimacy through economic expansion.

Economic growth was stabilized, limited welfare programs were introduced, and workers' wages were frozen. Although government economic policies were directed at promoting the growth of small and medium size firms, the *chaebols* have continued to grow in size and strength, fueled by growing exports and favorable international trade conditions. This economic success of the *chaebols* during the past decade has strengthened their position vis-à-vis the Korean state, while creating "new class forces"—the middle and working classes. As the strength of the *Min Jung* has increased along with the power of the *chaebols,* the relative autonomy of the developmental state has declined. Whether this will undermine development in the future remains to be seen.

In Chapter 6, Soohyun Chon extends the analysis of the relationship between politics and development in Korea, focusing specifically on the geographical origins of the developmental elite. She first shows that economic development in Korea has been uneven among the various regions of the country. Per capita income, for example, is highest in the southeastern provinces. There has been a significant redistribution in recent years in manufacturing employment from the Cholla provinces to rapidly growing provinces such as Kyonggi and Kyongsang. Historically, the Cholla provinces formed the seat of Korea's prosperous agricultural economy. But, with the shift to heavy industrial production described in the previous chapter, the economic fortunes of that region have declined relative to other areas of the country. Furthermore, while the Cholla provinces were at one time the rice bowl of Korea, urbanization has favored dry crops (fruit and vegetables) over rice production, resulting in geographical shifts that have been reinforced by investment in transportation and other infrastructure.

Industrial growth has occurred primarily in the northwest and southeast portions of the country. Textiles and precision machinery, two engines of Korea's rapid economic development, were found initially in Kyongsang and in the Seoul-Kyonggi provinces, although they have subsequently dispersed from these two provinces to adjacent areas. Chon explains the geographical concentration of specific industries as resulting from the logic of EOI pursued by the Park government. While government incentives encouraged exports, other policies promoted the import of intermediate products that could be used as inputs into the export-oriented industries. This simultaneous promotion of exports and imports required that industries locate themselves near ports as well as near sources of cheap labor. South Korea—like Hong Kong, Singapore, Taiwan, and Japan—is a relatively small country in which few areas are distant from the shoreline, an obvious advantage in a world where economic growth is dictated by the growth of external markets. According to Chon, "the geography of ports largely determines the location of industries" along the southeast and eastern coasts, with Pusan—the closest Korean port to Japan—emerging as the chief port. This geographical specialization was encouraged by railroads and express highways that linked Pusan with Seoul.

But economic and geographic factors are not the only explanations for the uneven geographical distribution of development in Korea. The internal politics of development amplified these patterns. Two out of the three presidents since Park have had geographic origins in the Kyongsang provinces. To legitimate his 1961 coup, Park sought to build a broad power base along classical Korean lines—"school, clan, and geographical affiliation." Park's close geographical ties with the north Kyongsang provinces reinforced the political power of a region that had historically been over-represented in prominent positions in government and industry. Chon shows that top-ranking officials as well as industrialists are disproportionately drawn from Seoul, with the Kyongsang provinces second. State development policies focused on particular favored industries rooted in the Kyongsang provinces—a pattern that was reinforced by intermarriage among the political, military, and economic elites.

Yet this pattern of geographical concentration may be undermined by the very success of Korean economic development. Because of skyrocketing real estate prices, the government now plans to disperse infrastructure and economic activities, with many of the new high technology industries to be located along the west coast. Such dispersal should also help to legitimate the Korean government, in the face of popular dissatisfaction over the geographical maldistribution of the fruits of economic development. Just as economic development now threatens the historical autonomy of a state that sought to legitimate itself through development (see Koo and Kim, Chapter 5), so it challenges the legitimacy of excessively spatially concentrated industrial development.

In Chapter 7, Paul Lubeck addresses the question of the "replicability" of the "East Asian model," focusing on the experience of Malaysia. Unlike the "four tigers," Malaysia has an ethnically heterogeneous social structure with a strong Muslim component, and is seeking export-driven industrialization a generation later—during a time of sluggish growth in the world economy when the competition for exports is fierce. To some degree, Malaysia fits the economic model of the developmental state: it has achieved impressive average annual growth rates of 7%-9%, relatively high per capita income, and has devoted a significant proportion of its economy to such export-oriented manufacturing as electronic components. At the same time, exports have been fueled by cheap labor, although in recent years labor shortages have encouraged illegal (although tolerated) immigration by as many as a million workers from Indonesia and other neighboring countries.

Malaysia's New Economic Policy (NEP)—instituted in 1971—was designed to incorporate the indigenous (Bumiputera) peoples—primarily Malays—into economic growth, promoting interethnic harmony through equalizing economic control among the Chinese, Malay, and other ethnic groups. Yet despite its seemingly impressive performance, Lubeck argues, the Malaysian economy masks structural weaknesses and deep ethnic divisions that distinguish it from the other East Asian NICs. Despite substantial government expenditure, globally competitive national industries have failed to develop; exporters are supplied by multinationals from Japan and other East Asian countries rather than indigenous firms. The key difficulty can be traced to ethnic separation between political and economic power: despite two decades of NEP, the Chinese continue to dominate business, while the Malays control the state, often acting as a comprador bourgeoisie in relationship to foreign capital while jealously seeking to control indigenous Chinese business growth.

Lubeck traces the historical roots of ethnic identities and cleavages to the ethnic division of labor imposed by British colonialism, which utilized "scientific" racial theories to allocate the "industrious" Chinese to business and trade activities, the "docile" Indians to rubber plantation labor, and the "indolent" but "courteous" Malays to farming (rice production). This stratification system reinforced pre-existing economic roles, contributing to a stereotyping that remains strong today.

Furthermore, unlike Japanese colonial policy in Korea and Taiwan—which destroyed the large landowning class, thereby paving the way for industrialization—the British supported the Malay feudal aristocracy, bringing it directly into colonial administration. As a result, Lubeck concludes, the bourgeoisie today remains weak relative to the rentier Malay administrative class, which—comfortably housed within the state bureaucracy—lacks both the temperament and history to function as a developmental state. It is this historical legacy that accounts for the "weak state technocratic impulse" whereby the Muslim aristocracy continues to wield enormous power, "blocking avenues of capitalist development for commoner Malays."

Why, after 20 years of NEP, have neither the Chinese nor the Malays overcome this historical legacy? Lubeck rejects cultural explanations that locate the explanation in the absence of a Confucian value system among the Muslim Malays, or a weakened Confucianism among the Chinese, many of whom also derive income as rentiers rather than industrialists. Rather, he argues, it is state industrial policy itself—which makes possible the amassing of fortunes without developing an indigenous industrial base—that is responsible. Lubeck argues that Islam is elsewhere associated with the rise of merchant capitalism, and that Muslim texts could well be reinterpreted to provide the basis for a highly equitable form of economic development, if political institutions favored such a reinterpretation. For the present, however, lacking "the confidence of the Chinese industrialists or a confident Malay class of industrialists," the country must continue to depend on foreign investment for its growth.

What does the future hold? Rapid demographic shifts favoring the Malay population, combined with growing income inequality, may exacerbate economic strains and undermine the NEP. While ethnic polarization is one possible outcome, a rethinking of the present arrangements is another. Some advisors are already calling for deep economic restructuring, promoting indigenous firms to support the export-oriented economy. There are strong pressures to encourage industrial development independent of ethnicity; whether these will prove sufficient to overcome the resistance of political elites remains to be seen. Until the Malaysian state fully commits itself to a broadly based development effort, however, it cannot be termed "developmental" along the lines of the other East Asian NICs.

In Chapter 8, Haruhiro Fukui offers some reflections on the role of the Japanese state that provide important insights into the nature of state-driven capitalism in the "four tigers." Fukui argues that Japanese capitalism is an "unorthodox and deviant" form, one that has muted class differences and emphasized national purpose and unity, a pattern that is repeated to varying degrees in the East Asian NICs.

Japanese capitalism has its roots in the strongly nationalistic and paternalistic Meiji Restoration of the mid-nineteenth century. The renegade samurai who led the revolt against the Tokugawa shogunate were determined to protect Japanese independence from Western colonialism. This they hoped to achieve through rapid industrialization and military power. The state sought to promote a high degree of domestic harmony and consensus, both through promotion of the emperor cult and the suppression of all opposition, particularly class-based politics: Marxist ideologies were banned, and socialist parties, leftist unions, and labor movements in general were ruthlessly suppressed. At the same time, industrial harmony was promoted through corporatist legislation that provided minimal protections for workers. These are all avenues that have been well-traveled in the East Asian NICs.

Furthermore, Fukui argues, systematic indoctrination of youth into the Shintoist emperor cult and Confucianist beliefs in state loyalty helped to promote national harmony and unity. Shinto became the state religion, and was self-consciously used to promote allegiance to the state; public pronouncements extolled the Confucian virtues of unity, family loyalty, and moral conduct. Mass public education inculcated these values, as children were taught to be "loyal, cooperative, and industrious, as well as literate and able workers in the service of the state." Nationalist values were guaranteed by strict state controls over curriculum and materials at the primary and secondary school levels, designed to assure appropriate "moral education." Youth groups and other organizations were formed with a similar intent.

In the industrial sector, unions were either incorporated into industry or destroyed. Thanks to literate, hard-driving, and nationalistic workers, manufacturing accounted for nearly one third of GDP by World War II, and annual growth rates exceeding 5% had already been achieved. Following the war growth continued and accelerated, despite (and perhaps because of) sweeping postwar reforms dictated by the armistice. These reforms banned ultranationalism and the emperor cult, democratized the educational system, assured freedom of assembly and speech, and guaranteed the right to organize and unionize. But these postwar changes did not seriously challenge the more moderate forms of nationalism, nor the Japanese psychological hostility to divisive ideologies. In fact, unionization, emancipation of women, and the opening up of the educational system all served to mute class-based ideologies. Undoubtedly, this is partly attributable to the emergence of a vast middle class (more than 90% of Japanese so identify), and partly through an educational system that stubbornly remains conservative, having successfully contained efforts by its often leftist teachers to introduce class-based materials into the classroom.

Perhaps nowhere is the defeat of class-based ideology more apparent than in the corporatist quality circle (QC) that is widely viewed as the hallmark of Japanese industry. Like many Japanese products, the QC is an American import that has thrived in Japanese factories, now reaching as much as 40% of the work force. They account in part for the high levels of productivity and quality in Japanese factories, as well as a leveling of all employees to common standards and commitments. This "groupism" actively promotes loyalty to the firm (and strongly discourages disloyalty as well)—loyalty reinforced by lifetime employment guarantees and seniority-based promotion and wage systems.

Despite its apparent success, Japanese capitalism—like that in the East Asian NICs—is presently undergoing significant changes. First, like capitalism elsewhere, it is becoming internationalized, as high labor costs, protectionism, and the appreciation of the yen have driven Japanese capital abroad. Of these three factors, protectionism is probably the decisive factor: growth in Japanese foreign investment has been especially rapid in North America and Europe, where hourly wage gains have been even more rapid than those in Japan. Capital flight has not led to unemployment, however; on the contrary, a severe labor scarcity exists in Japan, a problem addressed in part by a growing reliance on cheap immigrant labor. Whether Japanese firms on foreign soil can continue to retain their highly corporatist orientation is doubtful.

Second, lifetime employment and pay systems are experiencing difficulties. Always restricted to a minority of employees, the system depended on a much larger pool of part-time or temporary labor, typically women whose wages are slightly more than half those of their male counterparts. Japanese production also consists of elaborate networks of much smaller subcontractors who do not enjoy the same corporatist protections as are provided in the large industries. Even within the latter, however, lifetime security guarantees and seniority-based pay schemes have declined significantly recent years.

Third, despite continuing increases in real wages, the current real estate boom has threatened to undermine the consuming power of Japanese workers. Rampant real estate speculation has ballooned prices to a point where few workers can afford to buy apartments. High consumer prices—among the highest in the industrial world—also threaten to undermine workers' gains. Upsets in the July 1989 elections, where the long-dominant LDP suffered significant reversals, portend difficulties in the near future.

Fukui concludes that despite Japan's phenomenal success in creating one of the most rapidly growing and economically egalitarian industrial economies in the world, there are nonetheless problems below the surface that will likely change the nature of "Japanese-style capitalism" during the last decade of this century. We can add to this conclusion the observation that similar difficulties are likely to surface in the "four tigers" that are pursuing the Japanese model. As we have seen in Chapters 2, 3, 5, and 6, strong development states secured rapid growth through a variety of economic interventions, social policies, and labor controls, yet the extraordinary success of these policies now threatens to undermine the authority of state power. In Part III of this book, we turn directly to these issues, examining the social and labor policies that undergirded the East Asian development model.

5

The Developmental State and Capital Accumulation in South Korea

HAGEN KOO

EUN MEE KIM

By now there is no serious disagreement among scholars about an important role played by the state in the economic development of developing countries. The state is more than "brought back in." In fact, the statist perspective appears to be quickly establishing itself as a major paradigm in the development literature, spawning a large body of empirical work that seeks to explain economic development in the Third World, especially in East Asia, in terms of state intervention in the economy. At the center of these analyses is the developmental state—the state that intervenes in the economy in a positive way, in a "market-promoting" or "market-sustaining" way rather than in a "market-distorting" way.

A developmental state is most commonly defined by two characteristics: (1) its autonomy from societal forces—its economic bureaucracy can devise long-term economic policies without interference from private interests, and (2) its strength or capacity to implement economic policies effectively—the state can exercise a large measure of control over the behaviors of domestic and foreign capital (Haggard, 1990; Johnson, 1982, 1987; Wade, 1990). But as the concept becomes widely used in the development literature, the exact meaning of *developmental state* becomes increasingly vague and elusive. Not only do these concepts of state autonomy and strength involve variable empirical referents, but also the specific connections between these attributes of the state and development outcomes are unclear (Haggard & Moon,

1990; Moon, 1989). Furthermore, these concepts are often used in a somewhat tautological fashion, equating economic success to state strength post factum, or even measuring state strength by its presumed outcome.

It seems increasingly clear that in order for the statist perspective to move ahead, it must resist a temptation for reification and seek to develop theoretical specification based on grounded empirical analyses of the complex interactions among the state, market, and societal forces. The most critical void in the current literature on development is the lack of knowledge about the specific ways in which *political processes* circumscribe the nature and the behavior patterns of a developmental state.

The major aim of this chapter is to provide an analysis of the specific ways in which the South Korean developmental state has shaped the capital accumulation process in interactions with economic and political actors in the changing international and domestic economic environments. Several excellent studies of the South Korean political economy are available (Amsden, 1989; Cheng, 1991; Cole & Lyman, 1971; Haggard, 1990; Haggard & Moon, 1990; Jones & Sakong, 1980; S. K. Kim, 1987; Koo, 1987; Woo, 1990). The objective of this study is more specific, that is, to analyze the process of capital accumulation by focusing on the interactions between the state and capital. The analytic focus is on the process of capital accumulation rather than the general character of the South Korean political economy or the institutional character of the Korean developmental state. In this analysis, the developmental state is taken not simply as a *structure* but as a *process,* and not simply as an economic process but also as a political process. An important objective of the analysis is to examine *how* and for what specific *purposes* state managers use state organizations in the process of economic development. Thus we pay close attention to political processes as much as economic processes of development. By focusing our attention on the process of capital accumulation rather than economic growth, we can get closer to these dynamic processes of economic development.

Since its birth in 1948, South Korea has pursued four stages of economic development: (1) import-substitution industrialization (ISI) based on U.S. economic aid in the 1950s; (2) export-oriented industrialization (EOI) based on labor-intensive, light manufacturing in the 1960s; (3) industrial deepening along with export-oriented industrialization with selective use of ISI in the 1970s; and (4) liberalization and internationalization of the economy in the 1980s. Each stage is characterized by a particular kind of development strategy, state-economy relations, and development alliances. Thus our analysis follows through these four stages, attempting to isolate interesting patterns in the political economy of South Korean capital accumulation, with special attention to the dynamics of the state and the chaebol.[1]

The 1950s

After coming out of political and economic chaos in the postindependence period and the highly devastating Korean War (1950-1953), the South Korean economy more or less survived on the basis of U.S. economic and military aid in the 1950s. Between 1953 and 1961, the United States gave more than $4 billion in economic and military aid (Mason et al., 1980, p. 182). It was these foreign aids that determined not only the development strategy of the Rhee regime, but also the entire economic and social structures of Korea during the 1950s. Although this period is characterized by import-substitution industrialization, this was actually not a strategic choice of the state but was largely a response to the economic exigencies of the period. Preoccupied with domestic politics to maintain his ever decaying power, Rhee gave no systematic attention to economic development. Had there existed any strategic choice by Rhee, it was aid maximization, to squeeze as much economic and military aid possible from the United States by skillfully manipulating U.S. security interest in the peninsula (Cole & Lyman, 1971; Woo, 1990). The unrealistically overvalued exchange rates and other financial policies adopted during this period clearly reflected Rhee's primary interest in aid maximization.

While the economy drifted along with ISI, a few important economic changes took place during the Rhee period that were to have a serious impact on later development. The first was land reform, carried out in 1948-1950, which drastically changed the Korean class structure. There are many conflicting evaluations of this land reform. Many Korean scholars define it as a failure, because the reform measures passed by the landlord-dominated national assembly were far too moderate and because the implementation had been delayed so long that landlords had enough time to hide and sell their land. Nonetheless, the land reform achieved something only few nations in the world have done: the virtual elimination of the landlord class, and the creation of a relatively egalitarian class structure.

The second important change was the distribution of Japanese-owned properties (land, property, and production facilities) and privatization of state-owned enterprises and later state-owned banks. All these properties were distributed, at extremely low prices, to the individuals who had close political connections with the ruling elites. Practically, this was the origin of the modern-day Korean capitalist class. Having acquired these properties, many "political capitalists" further used their political connections to accumulate in well-protected import-substitution industries with privileged access to cheap U.S. dollars and aid materials (K. D. Kim, 1976). On his part, Rhee fostered these ties in order to squeeze maximum political funds, allowing widespread rent-seeking activities among leading businesspersons.

The downfall of the Rhee regime came in April 1960 with the uprising of the students, joined by workers and urban middle-class citizens, against the rigged presidential election. But even before this student revolution, the regime had been reaching its economic limits, caused by the exhaustion of ISI, the spiralling rates of inflation and unemployment, and most important, a drastic curtailment of U.S. economic aid.

After the fall of Rhee, the first democratic government was formed under the leadership of Chang Myon. Chang inherited the ill-managed economy with enormous economic problems, and he faced inordinate expectations for an immediate delivery of economic welfare and political democracy. Yet, comprised as it was of old opposition politicians with conservative class interests and no clear political or economic vision, the new regime was indecisive and slow in developing any coherent program to attack economic and social problems. The continuing economic difficulties combined with political instability invited a military coup on May 16, 1961. Korea's new economic era began with the emergence of the military regime.

The 1960s

Park Chung Hee, who led the coup and became a supreme ruler for the next two decades, distinguished himself from his two predecessors in terms of his strong commitment to economic development. He justified the coup in terms of the urgent need to "rescue the nation from the brink of starvation" as well as to defend it from the communist threats. A nation of wealth and power was not merely a political slogan but also his "dream," his firm conviction. No sooner had he captured the state power than he took bold steps to push the development plans.

A son of a poor farmer, with a strong anti-urban ideology, Park instantly relieved farmers of their private debts, guaranteed higher prices to farmers through subsidies, and created banks to allocate more funds to agricultural and small-to-medium businesses. More significantly, the junta arrested leading businesspersons on charges of "illicit wealth accumulation" during previous regimes, with full intention to punish them. Yet, very soon Park turned around completely, pardoning those arrested in exchange for economic cooperation. He asked them to participate in his ambitious industrialization projects as leading entrepreneurs, and subsequently allocated to them the bulk of foreign and domestic capital along with many other trade and tax privileges. This is the second time these large merchant capitalists (already called *chaebol* in the 1950s) escaped this accusation of "illicit wealth accumulation"; they had been convicted on the same charge during the Chang regime. This time, however, they not only escaped the crisis, but also found golden opportunities to prosper.

It was this narrow development alliance between the military regime and select large capitalists that eventually shaped the capital accumulation process during the period of export-oriented industrialization. Why did the Park regime forge this narrow developmental alliance rather than a broader "distributional alliance," as was the case in Taiwan, for example, that pursued a similar strategy of export-oriented industrialization? There are several reasons, but the most important was the urgent need of the military junta to establish its political legitimacy and consolidate its power. Park sought to achieve these goals by delivering impressive economic growth, and he believed that the quickest and the most reliable way to do this was by collaborating with the already proven group of large capitalists. This collaboration was also a convenient means to solve an immediate need of the military junta to raise a large sum of political funds to institutionalize its rule—the Democratic Republican Party and the Korean Central Intelligence Agency. Thus this "sword-won alliance" was the product of political exigencies and the existing class structure. The presence of a group of large capitalists with sizeable capital and organizational resources and entrepreneurial skills, a product of the previous period of accumulation, limited the choices of the new state elites—and thereby affected the capital accumulation process in the new stage. Once formed, this alliance had a lasting effect on the evolution of the Korean economy.

One of the most remarkable achievements of the Park leadership in the first years of its coming to power was the swift reorganization of the state structure into the so-called developmental state. He overhauled the bureaucracy, purging hundreds of corrupt and incompetent bureaucrats; he created the Economic Planning Board (EPB), a central economic decision-making agency with a large degree of autonomy from private interests and other agencies; and he restructured the financial system by nationalizing banks and bringing the central bank (The Bank of Korea) under the authority of the Ministry of Finance. Economic development was taken as the most important goal, a sacred mission, of the state, by which the power holders hoped to be judged by the people as to their right to rule. The regime's guiding economic philosophy was not really a free market economy, but a "guided capitalism."

Park's strong economic orientation, as he acknowledged himself, was shaped by his biographical background. But a more important reason is a structural one. As mentioned above, the 1950s was the period of enormous economic hardship and growing political instability arising from high unemployment and runaway inflation; it was also accompanied by widespread political discontent. As Cole and Lyman (1971) suggest, no one who came to power in the 1960s could ignore the huge popular demand for economic well-being. Park correctly perceived it and attempted to base his political legitimacy on economic performance.

State rulers' motivations and ideologies, however, explain only part of the emergence of a developmental state. A developmental state is a state that has a considerable amount of autonomy to adopt policies without interference from class interests and a capacity to implement these policies effectively. Fortunately, the Park regime inherited a state structure that had stood historically above the civil society, with an enormous amount of coercive capacity based on large police and military forces. The civil society, on the other hand, was weak and relatively undifferentiated, with no powerful class. In short, the historical conditions of state-society relations in Korea were amenable to the transformation of the Korean state into a developmental state. Given these structural preconditions, a critical variable that was required to transform a non-developmental state into a developmental one was the ideology, interest, and motivation of those who captured state power.

While restructuring the state structure, Park was anxious to move ahead with development plans. He ordered the technocrats to develop the first Five-Year Economic Development Plan, which they did by adapting an earlier plan adopted by the Chang Myon regime. The stated goal of the plan was to create a "self-reliant economy by terminating the previous aid-dependent and consumption-oriented structure." The plan selected 22 priority projects in such industries as electricity, fertilizer, oil-refining, synthetic fiber, and cement. Clearly, the policy priority was on import-substitution industries, not export industries. The government did stress the importance of promoting exports, not as a new development strategy but mainly to increase necessary foreign savings in order to improve the balance of payment situations. The transition to export-oriented industrialization occurred gradually in the following years mainly as a result of the strong advice by foreign advisers from the IMF and the U.S. AID mission, as well as the surprisingly positive market response to export promotion policies. The EOI strategy emerged as Korea's dominant development strategy around 1964, not as a conscious choice of the developmental state, but as a consequence of the unanticipated interactions of the world economy and domestic capital (Lim, 1985).

Between 1963 and 1965, the Park government carried out a set of major economic policy reforms, which included: (1) fiscal reform to promote government savings in 1963; (2) exchange rate and trade policy reforms to promote exports in 1964; and (3) an interest rate reform to promote domestic savings in 1965. These liberal policy reforms significantly reduced distortions in the market and stimulated export activities. Indeed, "getting the prices right" played a crucial role in this early transition to outward-oriented development strategy. In order to solve the capital shortage problem in Korea, the government adopted the Foreign Capital Inducement Law in 1966, while pushing through the enormously unpopular Normalization Treaty with Japan in 1965. This latter measure brought in a huge sum of reparation money ($500 million) from the Japanese government and opened the door to a large flow of Japanese private capital (Cole & Lyman, 1971; Mason et al., 1980).

The Park leadership took a cautious attitude toward foreign capital. It showed a preference toward public and commercial loans to foreign direct investment (Haggard & Cheng, 1987). Foreign loan capital provided the necessary foreign exchange without the involvement of management and control by the multinational corporations (MNCs). Foreign dominance in any form was lamented by the intellectual community as well as the public, due to the recent experience of Japanese colonialism and historical incidents of foreign invasion. Allowing MNCs to enter and operate in the Korean economy was interpreted as a first step toward economic and political domination by others. MNCs did not show interest in investing in Korea in the early 1960s. Korea was barely out of the ruins of the devastating Korean War, its GNP per capita was below $200, and it had very few natural resources.

In Korea, state strength has been enhanced by the inflow of foreign capital in the form of public as well as commercial loans.[2] The government distributed public loans to sectors it deemed important for its economic development plans. A large majority of foreign loans (approximately 90%) required government guarantees for payment and put the government in charge of distribution. But a more powerful mechanism of state control over the private sector was its control over domestic banks, which the military junta wrested from private ownership in the first months of coming to power. To a great extent, as Woo (1990) argues, the autonomy and capacity of the Korean developmental state resides in its control over the financial system.

The key feature of the Korean pattern of capital accumulation has been not really macro-economic policies ensuring the "right prices" but the specific manner by which the government has used its control over the allocation of domestic and foreign capital to mould the behaviors of private capital. Credit allocation has been clearly the most important tool of government control of business. Throughout the period of the Park government, domestic interest rates have been maintained artificially far below the real market prices; in fact, when adjusted to the inflation rates, they were negative in several years (see Table 5.1).[3] Foreign loans were even better. In the period between 1965 and 1970, the effective interest rates of dollar-denominated loans (nominal interest rate adjusted by changes in the foreign exchange rate) were between 5.6% and 7.1%, as compared with 25% to 30% for domestic bank loans (S. K. Kim, 1987, p. 123). Thus, obtaining bank loans itself constituted a major source of profits.

But access to these subsidized loans has been very selectively distributed. Bank credit allocation has been closely tied to the allocation of another key mechanism of capital accumulation, the investment licenses. Those who obtained major investment licenses received cheap loans through government-controlled banks; and those who were in a position to obtain a large loan were in an excellent position to obtain a new, profitable license. At the nexus of the two, there lies the most critical ingredient of Korean capital accumulation, that is, access to state power. Unlike the previous Rhee regime, the Park regime stressed economic performance as a major criterion of the allocation of both loans and investment opportunities (Amsden, 1989; Jones & Sakong, 1980). But there was no question that it was political connection, not just a firm's capability, that determined who could participate in profitable projects doled out by the government.

The vast majority of the projects specified in the First Five Year Economic Development Plan were monopolized by a group of the current *chaebols* that had been accused of illicit wealth accumulation. The decisions on the allocation of major investment licenses were personally made by Park himself (Institute of Korean Political Study, 1987; H. Lee, 1968). Park's main emphasis was consistently on the economies of scale and rapid economic growth that would result from it. His developmental orientation was clearly inclined toward the unbalanced, concentrated pattern of growth over which

Table 5.1 Interest Rates of Domestic Banks and the Curb Market, and Inflation Rates, 1961—1985 (%)

Year	Bank Lending Rates (A)[a]	Inflation (B)[b]	Real Interest Rate (A-B)	Curb Market Lending Rate
1961	17.5	14.0	3.5	N/A
1962	16.6	18.4	−1.8	N/A
1963	15.7	29.3	−13.6	52.6
1964	16.0	30.0	−14.0	61.8
1965	26.0	6.2	19.8	58.9
1966	26.0	14.5	11.5	58.7
1967	26.0	15.6	10.4	56.5
1968	25.2	16.1	9.1	56.0
1969	24.0	14.8	9.2	51.4
1970	24.0	15.6	8.4	50.2
1971	22.0	13.9	8.1	46.4
1972	15.5	16.1	−0.6	39.0
1973	15.5	13.4	2.1	33.2
1974	15.5	29.5	−14.0	40.6
1975	15.5	25.7	−10.2	47.9
1976	18.0	20.7	−2.7	40.5
1977	16.0	15.7	0.3	38.1
1978	19.0	21.9	−2.2	41.7
1979	19.0	21.2	−2.2	42.4
1980	20.0	25.6	−5.6	45.0
1981	17.0	15.9	1.1	35.3
1982	10.0	7.1	2.9	30.6
1983	10.0	3.0	7.0	25.8
1984	10.0	4.1	5.9	24.7
1985	10.0	3.6	6.1	N/A

SOURCES: Kim, S. K. (1987, p. 176); Bank of Korea (1972, p. 1221).
NOTES: a. At year end, one year maturity.
b. Change of GNP deflator.

the government exercised close supervision and guidance. The *chaebols* fitted in perfectly in this developmental orientation.

A major success of Park's developmental state in the 1960s was the transformation of merchant capital into industrial capital, thereby changing the accumulation process from a "zero-sum game" into a "positive-sum game" (Jones & Sakong, 1980). But this does not mean that profit making through rent-seeking activities was eliminated. To the contrary, a great deal of rent-seeking behavior existed in the 1960s and afterward, too. The most important source of such accumulation was real estate investment. Land investment was extremely profitable, not only because land prices increased much faster than inflation rates but also because real estate could be used as a collateral for bank loans. Large capital owners had access to secret information on new real estate development, and could reap handsome profits out of real estate investments.[4] Although no accurate information is available on the extent of land speculation among large business owners, it was serious enough to make the Park government enact regulations about the limit of land ownership by *chaebol* groups in the 1970s.

Another important source of rent-seeking is money lending in the underground money market. In the 1960s and through the first part of the 1970s, there existed a huge curb market in Korea. It was reported that in 1964, the estimated outstanding assets and liabilities in the informal financial market was almost double the commercial bank loans outstanding (S. K. Kim, 1987). Between 1964 and the end of 1969, the size of informal loans increased by 450% (Cole & Park, 1983, p. 126). The people who participated in the curb market as money lenders included professional money lenders and propertied middle-class people as well as business owners and top managers of the same industrial firms that were borrowing money from the curb market. Cole and Park reported, "[As of August 3, 1972] about 25 percent of the total informal debts (of all the business enterprises) were 'disguised informal loans', in that they were made by the owners, major stockholders, or executives of the borrowing firms" (Cole & Park, 1983, p. 127).

In sum, the large capitalists utilized a double-edged strategy of accumulation in the 1960s: one is productive investment in export and import-substitution industries, and the other is participation in speculative land investment and money lending in the curb market. For both types of investment, businesspersons depended heavily upon external finances. Given that interest rates of domestic and foreign loans were substantially lower than the unregulated market prices, those who obtained official loans had several easy avenues of making money. Productive investment was only one of them at this time.

Partly due to the investment structure, and partly due to the changes in world market conditions, the South Korean economy entered its first major crisis of export-oriented industrialization near the end of the 1960s. Of the two, changes in the world market conditions were more serious. At the end of the 1960s, the first principal payment was due on many commercial loans. At the same time, a continuous devaluation of the Korean currency raised Korean firms' costs of foreign debt servicing (the official rate of exchange increased from Korean won 272 to U.S. $1 in 1967, to 392 to 1 in 1972)

(Economic Planning Board, 1990). The debt service ratio as percentage of exports increased from 9.5% in 1968 to 13.7% in 1969, and to 19.4% in 1970 (World Bank, various years). Thus many firms had to turn to the curb market for their immediate cash flow needs. A large number of firms, small and large, which had overexpanded in the middle of the 1960s, went into bankruptcy. Business failures were especially serious among many foreign invested firms. It was reported that 45% of Japanese invested firms declared bankruptcy (D. Lee, 1984). Thus the government had to take over several dozens of "ill-managed companies" between 1969 and 1971, assuming the responsibilities to pay back their foreign debts.

What aggravated these financial and market troubles was increasing labor volatility toward the end of the 1960s. Also, as the labor market tightened with a substantial reduction of unemployment and underemployment in the latter half of the 1960s, wages increased fast, at an 8.8% annual rate of real wage increase between 1965 and 1969. The International Monetary Fund (IMF) forced the Park government to carry out stabilization measures, which aggravated the financial condition of firms that had already heavy debt burdens. In the political arena, Park's attempt to extend his tenure beyond the constitutional limit of two terms triggered strong opposition from students and the opposition party. Thus, after several years of smooth export-led growth, the Korean economy faced a major crisis.

The 1970s

Park took two drastic measures to address the growing economic and political crisis: He imposed severe restrictions on organized labor, while attacking financial capital. Both measures demonstrate both the strength and the "relative autonomy" of the Korean capitalist state very well. The state was willing and able to act against both labor and segments of capital, in the long-run interest of capitalists as a whole.

In 1969, Park proclaimed the Provisional Exceptional Law concerning labor unions and the settlement of labor disputes in foreign-invested firms. It imposed severe restrictions on labor organization, prohibiting strikes in foreign-invested firms. It was followed in 1971 by the proclamation of the state of emergency and the Law Concerning Special Measures for Safeguarding National Security, which suspended indefinitely the workers' right to collective bargaining and action. The culmination of all these authoritarian legislative actions was the installation of the Korean version of the bureaucratic-authoritarian regime, the *Yushin* regime, in October 1972. With this internal coup, Park closed all the political space and bestowed upon himself a lifetime presidency with unchecked executive power.

On the economic frontier, in order to rescue industrialists from serious debt problems, Park took a measure that would be difficult to conceive of in democratic capitalist societies. On August 2, 1972, Park announced the Presidential Emergency Decree for Economic Stability and Growth to become effective the next day (popularly called the "8-3 measure"). The decree included (1) the nullification of all the loan agreements between business firms and private money lenders as of August 3, 1972, replacing them with the requirement that borrowers would be given a three-year grace period, after which they would have to repay their informal loans over a five-year period at a substantially lowered interest rate; and (2) the replacement of a large amount of short-term loans (worth more than $500 million) by long-term loans at a lower interest rate payable over a five-year period after a three-year grace period. In addition, the government established a new industrial rationalization fund with some $125 million and lowered the overall bank interest rates (Bank of Korea, 1973).

Although this Emergency Decree was meant for capitalists in general, the results show that the largest *chaebols* were the main beneficiaries, while the small and medium-sized businesses were not helped substantially.[5] As a result, the emergency decree sought to rescue industrial capital from the private money lenders, even while threatening the sanctity of the private property system. The measure brought relief to business owners, providing new ground for dynamic growth in the 1970s. On the other hand, this bold attack on money capital hurt not only financial capitalists but also thousands of middle-class families who were involved in private money lending activities.[6]

These measures were preparatory steps toward a more ambitious project of Park's developmental state. In his New Year's address in January 1973, Park announced the Heavy and Chemical Industrialization Plan. The Plan was received with much reservation and criticism from both domestic and foreign capital. Nevertheless, the Park regime mobilized all the institutional and material resources at its disposal to push forward. The government selected six strategic industries: steel, electronics, petrochemicals, shipbuilding, machinery, and nonferrous metals. More than ever before, the Park government was willing to concentrate its resources in order to promote these target industries.

There were several reasons why the Park regime made this hasty move into heavy and chemical industrialization in the early 1970s. Both international economic conditions and internal political and economic factors influenced this decision. The international financial system became very unstable with the collapse of the Bretton Woods system in 1971. Economic nationalism began to rise, accompanied by increasing protectionism. As a result, continuous dependence on labor-intensive export industries seemed less promising, especially as domestic wages had been rising fast in this period. Another important factor was that Japan was moving into high-tech industries, and was willing to relinquish some of the labor-intensive sectors of heavy industries.

More important than these economic factors was the political environment of the period. In the early 1970s, significant changes took place in Far Eastern geopolitics. Nixon's visit to China and the ending of the "old" Cold War brought uncertainty to the Korean peninsula. The Nixon Doctrine stressed greater effort for self-defense among U.S. allies, and the Nixon administration made a partial withdrawal of U.S. military forces from South Korea in 1971. A former general, Park felt a great threat in all these changes and determined to strengthen Korea's military power domestically. His decision to promote steel and chemical industries was very much influenced by defense considerations.

But probably the most important factor was the changing domestic political situation. By the early 1970s, South Korea became a far more differentiated and politically active society than it had been in the early 1960s. Labor conflicts began to rise, student and political opposition movements intensified, the agricultural sector showed signs of disaffection, and the opposition party grew into a more formidable force under the leadership of a shrewd charismatic politician, Kim Dae Jung. Park was nonetheless intent on staying in power beyond the constitutional limit of two four-year terms. He changed the constitution and ran for the 1971 presidential election, in which he narrowly escaped defeat at the hands of Kim Dae Jung despite all the propaganda and alleged vote-buying by the regime. The installation of the *Yushin* system in October, 1972 was Park's response to these domestic political changes.

In short, the march to heavy and chemical industrialization was clearly a politically motivated plan to diffuse popular discontent and to mobilize people's energy for a new economic goal. This was justified in the name of building a prosperous nation that would be able to join the club of advanced industrial countries. Economically, this development strategy might have been a premature move but it proved to be a wise choice politically. In his January 1973 presidential press conference, Park made a promise to deliver a "$10 billion export, $1,000 GNP per capita, and my-car age" by the end of the decade. Once again, Park sought to buy political legitimacy with an economic delivery. And once again, recent Korean economic history suggests that political exigencies played a more important role in determining a development strategy than market factors.

The oil crisis in 1973, however, delayed the implementation of the heavy industrialization plan. Korea's oil import bill rose dramatically, and the growth rate of exports slowed down due to a low demand in the depressed world market. Foreign investment was very sluggish, and so was domestic investment in heavy industries. Many of the large-scale plants suffered from excess capacities and a poor financial situation, while many other projects that had not yet been undertaken were either canceled or postponed. As the world economy gradually overcame the first oil shock, and as the Middle East construction boom provided anew big investment opportunities, the South Korean economy began to bounce back after 1975. Exports increased noticeably, and the overseas construction business brought in a large amount of repatriated savings.

With this economic turnaround, the government and conglomerates resumed active investments in heavy and chemical industries. The *chaebols* were a critical element in implementing the government industrialization plan throughout the 1970s. The collusive relationships between the bureaucratic authoritarian state and big business deepened in this period. The *chaebols* were to deliver impressive economic performances and the state was to provide all the necessary conditions for capital accumulation.[7] During the 1970s, the *chaebols* were able to expand and entrench themselves as a formidable power bloc in the Korean political economy. Initially somewhat cautious and skeptical toward investment in heavy industries, the *chaebols* rushed in to obtain the state's investment licenses in these prime sectors of capital accumulation. Fierce competition for territorial expansion ensued amongst them.

International capital began to flow in large volume in the second half of the 1970s. As we can see in Table 5.2, the vast majority of international capital was composed of public and commercial loans; direct foreign investment constituted a very small portion. The MNC investments were restricted to a few limited areas.

In 1975, the state created a new organization, the General Trading Company (GTC), that had a tremendous impact on the Korean industrial structure. Modeled after the Japanese *Sogo-Shosha*, the government licensed a small number of large-scale GTCs to operate as the nation's export windows. By linking the trade-specialized organizations to small-sized manufacturing firms, both of them could specialize in their respective activities and at the same time improve their competitive positions in the world market. Thirteen *chaebols* were given GTC licenses (later three lost their licenses). These

Table 5.2 Inflow of Foreign Capital, 1959-1989[a](in $1,000)

Year	Total Foreign Capital	Loan			Direct Foreign Investment
		Total	Public	Commercial	
1959-1961	4,386 (100.0)[b]	4,386 (100.0)	4,386 (100.0)	0 (0.0)	0 (0.0)
1962-1965	138,276 (100.0)	118,775 (85.9)	52,836 (38.2)	65,939 (47.7)	19,501 (14.1)
1966-1970	1,757,232 (100.0)	1,692,772 (96.3)	549,396 (31.3)	1,143,376 (65.1)	64,460 (3.7)
1971-1975	4,998,780 (100.0)	4,510,598 (90.2)	2,027,250 (40.6)	2,483,348 (49.7)	488,182 (9.8)
1976-1980	12,280,637 (100.0)	11,748,708 (95.7)	4,774,606 (38.9)	6,974,102 (56.8)	531,929 (4.3)
1981-1985	11,371,912 (100.0)	10,635,083 (93.5)	7,499,026 (65.9)	3,136,057 (27.6)	736,829 (6.5)
1986-1989	11,192,059 (100.0)	8,383,000 (74.9)	3,357,000 (30.0)	5,026,000 (44.9)	2,809,059 (25.1)

SOURCE: Economic Planning Board, *Major statistics of Korean economy* [various years].
NOTES: a. The figures may not add up to 100.0% due to rounding
b. The figures in parentheses are percentages.

licenses were accompanied by an attractive package of trade, finance, and tax advantages, including a license to import raw materials, low-rate export financing, import financing for raw materials, and preferential treatment from the GTCs' overseas offices. An exporter who had valid evidence of an export order could borrow from the banks up to 90% of the dollar amount of the export at an interest rate far below the regular bank lending rate.[8] Thus the establishment of the GTC structure played an instrumental role for top-ranking *chaebol* firms to grow into an unchallengeable position in the economy.

The acquisition of ill-managed companies was another important source of the *chaebols'* accumulation. A major reorganization of these ill-managed companies did not take place until the early 1980s. But during the 1972-1979 period, 17 of them were sold to other private firms. Of these, 13 were purchased, at bargain prices and with additional financial and tax privileges, by the *chaebols* in the top-10 list. This acquisition allowed some *chaebols,* such as Daewoo, to make a strategic entry into key industries such as automobiles and shipbuilding, while Hyundai acquired Inchon Steel Co.

The developmental state of South Korea was at its peak in the second half of the 1970s. Industrial targeting was widely practiced, and the government was in tight control of the allocation of capital. In order to support strategic heavy and chemical industries, the government created the National Investment Fund in 1974. In the second half of the 1970s, somewhere between 53% and 63% of the total domestic loans were distributed as "policy loans" at a preferential rate. Approximately 70% of the policy loans went to the heavy and chemical industry sector. The majority of these loans were given to *chaebols,* since they were the ones who were assigned these strategic projects.

Thus the industrial deepening in the 1970s provided existing *chaebols* with golden opportunities to expand and strengthen their businesses. The 1970s was the period of empire building for the top 10 *chaebols*. Their accumulation strategy was mainly to diversify into many industries in order to strengthen their market positions in relation to the state. Growing big meant obtaining a stronger position to participate in the state's priority projects, and obtaining policy loans and other bank credits. Their dominance in the Korean economy grew tremendously in the 1970s (see Table 5.3).

In Korea, the *chaebols'* common strategy of territorial expansion was widely called the "octopus style" of accumulation, a strategy of stretching one's reach all around and swallowing up existing small-to-medium enterprises. The *chaebols'* horizontal and vertical integrations increased tremendously during the latter part of the 1970s. Between 1972 and 1979, the average number of firms owned by these 10 largest *chaebols* grew from 7.5 per *chaebol* in 1972 to 25.4 in 1979. And the number of different industries in which they operated increased from an average of 7.7 industries (by 2-digit industrial classification) in 1972 to 17.6 in 1979. In the same period, the 10 largest *chaebols* achieved a 47.7% compound average annual growth rate in terms of assets, while the annual average growth rate of the GNP (in real terms) was 10.2% (E. M. Kim, 1991). The figures in Table 5.4 show the tremendous growth of the top 10 *chaebols* in the 1970s.

The main source of this rapid growth of the *chaebols* was more or less the same as in the 1960s—the preferential allocation of subsidized loans. In general, *chaebol* firms relied more heavily on debts for investment. In the 1972-1979 period, 78.8% of the asset growth among the top 10 *chaebols* was financed by debt, compared to 59.7% for the average Korean firm.

Table 5.3 Dominance of the Top 50 Chaebols

Year	The Share of Top 10 Chaebols
	Sales in GNP
1974	15.1%
1977	26.0%
1980	48.1%
1984	67.4%
1987	68.8%

Year	The Share of Top 50 Chaebols		
	Shipment Shares	*Employment Shares*	*Value Added in GNP*
1977	35.0%	16.9%	13.4%*
1982	37.5%	16.0%	
1987	30.9%	14.5%	15.6%

SOURCES: Jones and Sakong (1980), p. 266; S. K. Kim (1987), p. 2; Lee and Lee (1990), p. 26; Management Efficiency Research Institute (1988), p. 29.
NOTE: * The figure is for the 46 largest chaebols' value added in GDP in 1975.

Table 5.4 The Growth of the Ten Largest Chaebols, 1971-1983

Rank[a]	Chaebol	Total Assets[b]		Average Annual Rate of Asset Growth (%)[c]		
		1971	*1983*	*1971-1980*	*1981-1983*	*1971-1983*
1.	Hyundai	158,261	4,469,342	38.0	19.2	32.1
2.	Samsung	415,978	3,371,603	18.4	35.4	19.1
3.	Daewoo	34,679	3,340,367	53.7	11.6	46.3
4.	Lucky-Gold Star	437,060	2,714,511	17.2	16.4	16.4
5.	Ssangyong	310,424	1,711,715	16.8	13.3	15.3
6.	Sun Kyong	40,049	1,477,873	36.7	0.6	35.1
7.	Han Jin	83,734	1,340,120	32.9	7.5	26.0
8.	Korea Explosives	256,424	1,173,064	11.7	37.0	13.5
9.	Dae Lim	64,522	943,307	31.8	5.7	25.1
10.	Kukje	153,489	896,205	19.3	8.8	15.8

SOURCE: Kim, E. M. (1973-1982); Maeil Kyungje Shinmun (1984; 1986).
NOTES: a. Ranking based on total assets in 1983.
b. Total assets in 1980 constant Korean thousand Won.
c. Average annual growth rate was calculated using 1980 constant prices.

Table 5.5 Debt and Debt Service, 1970-1987

Year	Total Long-Term Debt Disbursed and Outstanding[a]		Debt Service[b] as Percentage of	
	in $ million	% of GNP	GNP	Exports
1970	1,797	23.3	3.0	19.4
1980	16,274	28.8	4.9	12.2
1981	19,964	32.1	5.8	13.1
1982	20.061	28.3	5.2	13.1
1983	21,472	—	—	12.3
1984	29,990	37.0	6.6	15.8
1985	35,756	43.0	8.6	21.5
1986	34,304	36.1	10.8	24.4
1987	30,644	25.8	13.0	27.5

SOURCE: The World Bank, *World Development Report* (various years).
NOTES: a. Figures for 1970-1982 are based on public debt outstanding and disbursed.
b. Figures for 1984-1987 are based on total long-term debt service.

At the end of the 1970s, the South Korean economy faced several structural problems that originated from both external and internal sources. Externally, a recession in the world economy following the second oil shock in 1979 was a serious blow to the South Korean economy, which was by now very dependent on the world market. Korea's oil import bill doubled, while its exports slowed down due to decreasing demands and to the creeping protectionism in the advanced industrial economies. The current account deficit of Korea increased from US $1.1 billion in 1978 to $5.3 billion in 1980. By the early 1980s Korea's foreign debt had reached a dangerous level, and many foreign banks began to seriously question Korea's creditworthiness. The total long-term debt disbursed and outstanding increased from $2.0 billion in 1970 to $35.8 billion in 1985. Moreover, its share as percentage of GNP rose to 43.0% in 1985, almost double that of 23.3% in 1970 (see Table 5.5). Korea found it increasingly difficult to obtain long-term loans, thus relying more on short-term, high-interest loans.

Internally, the massive investment in heavy machinery and chemical industries resulted in severe overcapacity and a poor financial situation for many large firms. Chronic problems of high debt combined with export decline, especially in shipping and construction industries, pushed many firms toward insolvency. Throughout the 1970s, the inflation rate was generally high, but it was particularly high toward the end of the decade. The consumer price index rose by 28.7% in 1980 as compared to 14.5% in 1978. The business sector strongly complained that they were losing competitiveness in the export market due to a high rate of wage increase in the latter part of the 1970s.

The IMF pressured the Park government to undertake a stabilization program. In April 1979, the government adopted the Comprehensive Stabilization Plan, which was aimed at price stabilization and liberalization of the economy. The stabilization plan included a wage freeze, and the liberalization plan included cutting down on low-interest export loans to businesses and farm subsidies.

These economic problems and responses contributed to a rising level of labor unrest and protests by the urban poor. In 1979, a labor strike at a wig factory, the Y. H. Company, triggered a major political crisis when the striking women workers moved to the opposition party headquarters to continue their protest when they were forcefully evicted from their factory by the police. The opposition party's support of the workers and the violent police repression deepened the political crisis as angry protests and labor strikes spread across major industrial cities in the south. Faced with this crisis, the ruling group split internally, which eventually led to an abrupt ending of one chapter of Korean history. Park Chung Hee, the architect of the two decades of growth, was assassinated by the head of the Korean CIA on October 26, 1979.

During a short period of political liberalization following Park's death, a wave of labor unrest erupted across the country. Most labor conflicts were concerned with wage issues and layoffs, but a major focus of workers' struggles was to create independent labor unions and to destroy management-controlled (*oyong*) unions. Workers' resentment against the co-opted union leadership ran very deep, and their linkages with activist students and progressive church groups became closer and stronger in the latter part of the 1970s.

The 1980s

The turn of the 1980s saw the formation of a loosely formed "distributional alliance" under the banner of the *minjung* movement. *Minjung* (the people or the masses) is a broad alliance against the dominant governing coalition, the *chaebols,* and foreign capital. The rise of the *minjung* movement was a reaction to both the *Yushin* regime and the *chaebol*-dominated capital accumulation process. A strong sense of distributive injustice spread across diverse sectors of the population: factory workers, farmers, small-business persons, and white-collar workers. Although they did not belong to the same class, they were bound together by their common moral anger against the collusive relationships between the authoritarian state and the *chaebols.* The *minjung* movement grew as a reaction to the *Yushin* regime, and by the early 1980s it had become a potent political and social movement.

This short period of political liberalization and popular democratic aspirations was dashed, however, by a military coup in December 1979, led by Major General Chun Doo Hwan, then head of the Defense Security Command. The military junta declared martial law and arrested hundreds of dissident leaders. In May 1980, thousands of students and citizens of Kwangju revolted against the imposition of martial law and the arrest of Kim Dae Jung, the opposition leader who came from this region. But the military junta massacred some 200 people in its bloody repression of the rebellion. In February 1981, Chun elected himself to the presidency.

Coming to power without popular support, and with enormous economic troubles inherited from the previous regime, the Chun regime had to undertake bold economic restructuring. The pressure came from both international and domestic capital. International capital demanded that the Korean government open up its market for both foreign imports and foreign capital investment. The IMF and World Bank also kept up pressure on the new government to carry out a substantial stabilization program by freezing wages, reducing money supplies, and cutting government expenditures. The domestic sectors made conflicting demands. The business sector demanded that the government come to their rescue and save their ailing businesses, while the popular sectors demanded measures to control the growth of the *chaebols* and to increase distributive justice.

The military junta created a Standing Committee for Emergency National Security Measures on May 31, 1980, which implemented a few radical reforms. The general policy direction was to respond to both international and domestic pressures, especially to the former. The keystone of the new economic policies was *liberalization*: reduced government intervention in the economy, promotion of market mechanisms through enhanced competition, wider opening of the domestic market to foreign goods, and encouragement of direct foreign investment. Two rounds of liberalization measures were taken, in 1981 and 1982, which opened many new industries to foreign investors. In July 1984, important liberalization measures took place via the

Foreign Capital Inducement Law to attract more foreign direct investment. Instead of allowing only a few industries to be open for foreign direct investment (positive system), a negative system was adopted. This change increased the share of the manufacturing industries open to foreign direct investment to 92.5%. An automatic approval system was adopted as well to facilitate foreign investment (Economic Planning Board, 1986, pp. 31-33).

In the financial sector, the state privatized the ownership of city banks, although it did not relinquish its control over their personnel and key decision matters. The size of policy loans was reduced, and preferential interest rates applied to strategic industries were abolished. Similarly, large tax privileges that were previously given to target industries were reduced substantially as the system of designating target industries changed.[9] The government's priority was given to stable and balanced growth rather than to accelerated growth with which Park's economic planners had been so preoccupied. Chun modified Park's stabilization plan and implemented his new Comprehensive Plan for Stabilization and Structural Reorganization. The plan called for devaluation of the foreign exchange rate, reduction of domestic interest rates, and tightening of the money supply and government expenditure, as well as a curb on wage and dividend payments.

At the same time, responding to the demands of the "distributional coalition," to use Olson's terms (Olson, 1982), the regime promised that it would bring social welfare and distributive justice and would "purify" the corrupt political and business worlds. The usual five-year economic plan would now embrace social welfare goals, thus the 1982-1986 plan was labelled the Fifth Five-Year Economic and Social Development Plan.

While publicly stressing social welfare and broader distribution, however, the Chun regime took a harsher measure against labor than any previous regime. Hundreds of labor activists were arrested or fired, unions were restructured into enterprise-level unions, and collective action by new restrictive labor laws. Furthermore, workers' wages were frozen in the name of economic stabilization.

With regard to capital, the Chun regime was able to make a few changes. The most serious problem Chun faced was that of duplicate investment and excess capacity in the heavy and chemical industries. In August 20, 1980, the military junta issued the Investment Reorganization of the Heavy and Chemical Industries to reorganize the power plant equipment and automobile industries. Under the 8-20 measures, Daewoo was to integrate and monopolize the power plant equipment production sector by taking over Hyundai Heavy's and Hyundai International's investment, and Hyundai was to integrate the passenger automobile sector by merging with Daewoo Motors.

Kia Motors was to specialize in the production of special-purpose non-passenger cars. A similar measure followed in October to reorganize heavy electrical machinery, engine production, copper refining, and other industries. These measures were not fully implemented, in part because of the protests from the foreign joint-venture partners.[10]

In a similar move, the junta announced the "Measure to Rationalize Corporate Structure" on September 27, 1980. The Measure selected 26 *chaebols* and forced them to reorganize their group structure around specialized primary businesses. In order to accomplish this, the government urged them to relinquish their sideline businesses, sell non-business-related real estate, offer their stocks in the stock market, and improve their financial structures. The committee selected 135 firms (from the total of 631 firms owned by the 26 *chaebols*) as the "main line business firms," and ordered them to give up 166 firms by 1984. The government investigated all the real estate owned by the *chaebols* and their owner families, and told them to dispose of the majority of the land ownership.

The result was, however, far below the initial target. The *chaebols* gave up some of their firms but bought almost the same number of new firms. The 10 largest *chaebols* sold 18 member companies and merged 21 companies with their other member companies, but then purchased or created 38 new companies. The average number of firms owned by the top 10 *chaebols* remained practically the same between 1979 and 1985—24.3 and 24.2, respectively (Management Efficiency Research Institute, 1986). The *chaebols* were forced to sell their land in 1981 and 1982, but they purchased it back again as soon as the government and public campaign over the issue ended. They were also reluctant to go public; as of June 1984, only 24% of the firms owned by the 10 largest *chaebols* had gone public.

The government adopted the Fair Trade Act in April, 1981. The Fair Trade Committee was established in the EPB to monitor collusion and unfair behavior of firms, and an Assistant Deputy Prime Minister was appointed the director of the committee. The state selected the largest *chaebols* and put under close supervision their financial status and expansion through merger and acquisition. The government also monitored subcontracting practices between large and smaller firms in order to reduce abuses by the former. However, the fate of this Fair Trade Act was similar to previous measures to control the *chaebols;* the bark was much stronger than the bite.

At the same time, the Chun government adopted a few policies to promote small- and medium-sized firms. Banks were ordered to direct 40% to 50% of their total loans to small- and medium-sized firms. The government designated 110 product groups as off-limits to large firms, while allowing small and medium companies some collective monopolies in some designated areas. The government also concentrated its effort on selecting 5,000 "promising small and medium companies" for extra financial support and technical guidance. In spite of all these public gestures, the share of loans made to the small and medium enterprises actually declined from 45.2% in 1981 to 32.4% in 1985 (*Maeil Kyungie Shinmun,* September 5, 1985).

Thus despite much public fanfare, state actions taken against the *chaebol* firms in the early 1980s had no apparent effect in containing *chaebol* growth. The *chaebols* continued to achieve impressive growth in the 1980s. Between 1979 and 1985, the sales of the top 10 *chaebols* (top 10 in 1985) grew at an annual rate of 34.5%, and their assets grew 21.8% annually. As previously noted, however, the average number of member companies of the 10 largest *chaebols* remained constant. Their degree of diversification in terms of the 2-digit standard industrial classification showed a moderate increase from 16.7 in 1979 to 18.9 in 1985. These changes suggest that *chaebols* have entered a maturing stage in their evolution.

Since the mid-1980s, the *chaebols* have experienced rapid growth due to some favorable changes in the international economy. The popularly named "Three Low Period" has since 1986 allowed the *chaebols* to capitalize on lowered interest rates of major foreign banks, lowered exchange rate of the U.S. dollar against the Japanese yen, and the lower price of crude oil. The export business boomed for the *chaebols,* since the U.S. market found Japanese products to be increasingly unaffordable, and sought cheaper goods from Korea. This export boom allowed the *chaebols* to expand rapidly in the 1980s. It was very fortunate for Korean industry that the international economy turned upward at the same time the state was turning away from direct subsidies and other preferential treatment. Despite the changing policy environment, the success of the *chaebols* in exports significantly increased their leverage in dealing with the state and helped them become increasingly more self-reliant. The accumulation strategy of the *chaebols* also had to shift from relying on state guidance and support to the market mechanism. The *chaebols* became more active in striking deals with MNCs on their own without the supervision and mediation of the state, and have begun to establish subsidiaries abroad.

Conclusion

Several tentative conclusions can be drawn from this analysis of the political economy of capital accumulation in South Korea during the past three decades.

First, the strength of the state derived partly from the institutional inheritance from the past (such as a centralized bureaucracy, large police forces, and executive dominance) and partly from *statecraft,* that is, the ways in which state rulers use state instruments to enhance their power over civil society. Having inherited the same state institutions, Syngman Rhee and Park Chung Hee presided over states of quite different strength and autonomy. State strength also derives from both internal and external sources. The Rhee and Park regimes both used Korea's strategic geopolitical position skillfully to enhance its bargaining power with core nations considerably, while at the same time enhancing their own power inside the country.

Second, it is the character of a *regime* rather than a state structure that determines whether or not the state is developmental. There were no great differences in terms of state structure among the Rhee, Park, and Chun periods, but the specific manner in which the state intervened in the economy varied significantly among these three regimes. The most important element that determines the character of a regime, and consequently the ways in which state instruments are used, seems to be the manner and the social context in which state rulers came to power. Park came to power through a military coup in a social context that made heavy demands for economic welfare and in a historical period when economic development had a powerful ideological appeal. Park Chung Hee sought to establish his regime's political legitimacy on the basis of economic performance. The emergence of the Korean developmental state is intimately related to his quest for political legitimacy.

Third, the state's choice of a *developmental strategy* and major economic policies is not only determined by domestic and world market factors but also by *political* considerations. The Korean state's decision to make a hasty move into heavy and chemical industrialization in the early 1970s is a good example. It was not economic rationality but political rationality—a response to domestic politics and security threats—that propelled the Park regime to make such a move.

Fourth, the class character of the *development alliance* between the state and segments of capital shapes the dominant form of capital accumulation. Park Chung Hee forged a narrow development alliance with conglomerate capital (*chaebol*) in order to pursue rapid economic growth. This state-*chaebol* alliance facilitated a remarkably rapid rate of economic growth, but produced enormous capital concentration and a skewed distribution of wealth, engendering a wide sense of distributive injustice.

Fifth, the very success of development policies based on a narrow development coalition worked to undermine the unity of this coalition, by bringing into being *new class forces.* The expansion of the working class and the middle classes in Korea, the outcome of rapid export-led industrialization, led to the formation of the loosely organized "distributional coalition" under the banner of *minjung* (the people or the masses). The rise of the *minjung* movement in the 1980s strained the relationships between the Chun regime and the *chaebols,* as the state could no longer protect and favor this privileged segment of capital. But by the 1980s, the relative autonomy of the state vis-à-vis conglomerate capital declined considerably, and so did the ability to control the behavior of the *chaebols.* Consequently, the scope and effectiveness of the Korean developmental state diminished considerably.

Finally, a broader implication of the last two points is that the behavior pattern of a developmental state must be understood within the context of *class structure.* Until recently, the Korean state pursued an unbalanced, highly concentrated pattern of capital accumulation based on a narrow development alliance with the *chaebols,* largely because of the absence or weakness of "distributional alliances." The weakness of organized labor and other popular sectors allowed the capitalist state to adopt blatantly pro-capital and antilabor, or pro-growth and antidistributional policies. The effectiveness of the Korean state's development policies derived largely from the *consistency* of its policy implementation in favor of large capital. This consistency in the mode of state intervention in the economy has ensured "business confidence" and has promoted a favorable investment climate for both domestic and international capital. As the balance of class power changed, however, the state could not maintain a consistent approach, caught among pressures from big business, small business, labor, and farmers, resulting in a considerable weakening of the state's ability to manage the economy.

Notes

1. The *chaebol* is a large business conglomerate owned and managed by family members or relatives. Its main characteristics include large market share and wide range of businesses. Detailed analyses of *chaebol* organizations are available in E. M. Kim (1991); Steers et al. (1989); and Yoo & Lee (1987).

2. The first study that showed the positive impact of foreign capital on a less developed country was done by Jeff Frieden (1981). Frieden showed that loan capital, unlike foreign direct investment can strengthen and support state power in less developed countries. A similar argument is made by E. M. Kim (1989) and by Stallings (1991). Their studies showed that public loans strengthened state autonomy and capacity while foreign direct investment and some commercial loans undermined state autonomy.

3. In 10 of the 18 years of Park's regime (1961-1979), the rate of inflation was higher than the interest rate of domestic banks. In the years 1963, 1964, 1974, and 1975, the rate of inflation was greater than the interest rate of the banks with a difference of more than 10% (S. K. Kim, 1987, p. 176).

4. For example, Samsung Life Insurance Company of the Samsung *chaebol* bought land in Seochodong in Seoul between 1987 and the fall of 1989. The land was initially designated as a site for a public bus terminal. The plan to build the terminal was suddenly abandoned, however, and the lot was rezoned in December 1989 for commercial use. Therefore, the property value jumped and Samsung made a handsome profit. There are three possible explanations. One is that Samsung received information of the rezoning prior to the announcement, and another is that Samsung purchased the land and effectively lobbied the City for rezoning. Whichever the case may be, circumstantial evidence points to the influence and power of Samsung. The third and least plausible explanation is that Samsung was extremely lucky. Another incident was reported at the National Assembly meeting on April 16 and 17, 1990 by Lee Hae Chan of the Pyungmin-dang. According to this report, Hyundai, Samsung, and Keukdong Oil purchased land (200 thousand *pyung*) in the Choongnam Province. The problem was that the property was purchased at a cheap price before the land was approved for a land fill. The price of the land skyrocketed from $1.8-2.2 to $118-221 per *pyung* with the announcement. Therefore, the three *chaebols* made an enormous profit. Once again, no conclusive evidence was presented to prove that these *chaebols* had access to inside information. However, incidents such as this only fuel the suspicion that the *chaebols* do indeed have privileged access to critical information, and that they have real influence on the government. See Ham (1990) for more information.

5. The large *chaebols* were the largest borrowers of the curb market loans, thus becoming the main beneficiaries of the emergency relief measure. Furthermore, the results of the allocation of bank loans and the industrial rationalization fund showed that the *chaebols* were disproportionately favored. The fund and loans were targeted mainly for capital- and technology-intensive industries, which had large debts. The *chaebols* were predominant in such industries, and therefore became the largest recipient of the low-interest bank loans and funds. As a result, the *chaebols* came out once again as the winners.

6. Since banks' savings interest rates were unreasonably low, many middle-class families lent their money to business borrowers at that time. In 1971, the year preceding the emergency decree, the curb market lending rate was 46.4%, while that of the banks was only 22%. It is estimated that over $866 million worth of curb market loans were affected by this emergency measure, which was equivalent to 34% of the then outstanding domestic credit of the banking sector. See Bank of Korea (1972); Cole and Park (1983); and S. Lee (1985).

7. For example, the 10 largest *chaebols'* growth rate of total assets was more than 27% between 1971 and 1980. This rate is more than 2.5 times the rate of growth of the entire Korean economy (Economic Planning Board, 1990).

8. Between 1975 and 1979, the bank lending rates for each year were 15.5%, 18.0%, 16.0%, 19.0%, and 19.0%. On the other hand, the corresponding interest rates for export financing were 7.0%, 8.0%, 8.0%, 9.0%, and 9.0%. This shows that the interest rate for export loans was about half that of the domestic banks. See Economic Planning Board, *Major Statistics of Korean Economy* (various years).

9. During the drive for heavy and chemical industrialization in the 1970s, six target industries were chosen for heavy government support and protection under the government's careful planning. By the early 1980s with liberalization measures taking place, "targeting" took on a new meaning. Instead of being a long-term commitment of the government to allow for certain industries to grow under the auspices of the government, it became a short-term protection plan

for infant and declining industries. The changes, therefore, meant that becoming a target indus-try was no longer a guarantee for huge wind-fall profits, due to government subsidies, low-in-terest loans and tax cuts, and monopoly or oligopoly of the market. The selection of industries also changed from those that were deemed strategic and important by the government planners, to those requiring assistance due to market conditions. (Based on interviews with government officials in the Ministry of Commerce and Industry and the Economic Planning Board by Eun Mee Kim during the summer of 1988.)

10. For example, General Motors, which had been the joint-venture partner of Daewoo Motors, strongly opposed the 8-20 measure, forcing the government to back off from the initial plan.

References

Amsden, Alice H. (1989). *Asia's next giant: South Korea and late industrialization.* New York: Oxford University Press.

Bank of Korea. (1972). *Economic statistics yearbook.* Seoul: Bank of Korea.

Bank of Korea. (1973). *Full report on the president's decree of August 3, 1972.* Seoul: Bank of Korea.

Cheng, Tun-jen. (1991). Political regimes and development strategies: South Korea and Taiwan. In Gary Gereffi & Donald Wyman (Eds.), *Manufacturing miracles: Paths of industrialization in Latin America and East Asia.* Princeton, NJ: Princeton University Press.

Cole, David, & Lyman, Princeton. (1971). *Korean development: The interplay of politics and economics.* Cambridge, MA: Harvard University Press.

Cole, David C., & Park, Yung Chul. (1983). *Financial development in Korea, 1945-1978.* Cambridge, MA: Harvard University Press.

Economic Planning Board. (1986). *Analysis of economic policies of the 1980s.* Seoul: Economic Planning Board.

Economic Planning Board. (1990). *Major statistics of Korean economy.* Seoul: Economic Planning Board.

Frieden, Jeff. (1981). Third World indebted industrialization: International finance and state capitalism in Mexico, Brazil, Algeria, and South Korea. *International Organization, 35,* pp. 407-431.

Haggard, Stephen. (1990). *Pathways from the periphery: The politics of growth in the newly industrializing countries.* Ithaca, NY: Cornell University Press.

Haggard, Stephen, & Cheng, Tun-jen. (1987). State and foreign capital in East Asian NICs. In Frederic Deyo (Ed.), *The political economy of the new Asian industrialism.* Ithaca, NY: Cornell University Press.

Haggard, Stephen, & Moon, Chung-in. (1990). Institutions and economic policy: Theory and a Korean case study. *World Politics, 12,* pp. 210-237.

Ham, Young Jin. (1990, June). Speculative real estate investments by the chaebols [in Korean]. *Wolgan Chosun,* pp. 180-203.

Institute of Korean Political Study. (1987). *Park Chung Hee Sidae Kyungie Bihwa* [Economics behind stories during Park Chung Hee era]. Seoul: Tongkwang.

Johnson, Chalmers. (1982). *MITI and the Japanese miracle.* Stanford, CA: Stanford University Press.

Johnson, Chalmers, (1987). Political institutions and economic performance: The government-business relationship in Japan, South Korea, and Taiwan. In Frederic Deyo (Ed.), *The political economy of the new Asian industrialism* (pp. 136-164). Ithaca, NY: Cornell University Press.

Jones, Leroy, & Sakong, Il. (1980). *Government, business, and entrepreneurship in economic development: The Korean case.* Cambridge, MA: Harvard University Press.

Kim, Eun Mee. (1973-1982). Industrial organization and growth of the Korean *chaebol.* In *Korean company handbook.* Seoul: Korea Productivity Center.

Kim, Eun Mee. (1989). Foreign capital in Korea's economic development, 1960-1985. *Studies in Comparative International Development, 24,* pp. 24-45.

Kim, Eun Mee. (1991). The industrial organization and growth of the Korean chaebol: Integrating development and organizational theories. In Gary Hamilton (Ed.), *Business networks and economic development in East and Southeast Asia.* Hong Kong: Hong Kong University Press.

Kim, Kyong Dong. (1976, May). Political factors in the formation of the entrepreneurial elite in South Korea. *Asian Survey, XVI*(5), 465-477.

Kim, Seok Ki. (1987). *Business concentration and government policy: A study of the phenomenon of business groups in Korea, 1945-1985.* Unpublished D.B.A. dissertation, Harvard University.

Koo, Hagen. (1987). The interplay of state, social class, and world system in East Asian development: The cases of South Korea and Taiwan. In Frederic Deyo (Ed.), *The political economy of the new Asian industrialism* (pp.165-180). Ithaca, NY: Cornell University Press.

Lee, Dae Keun. (1984). The evolution of the loan-dependent economy [in Korean]. In Dae Keun Lee & Un Young Chung (Eds.), *Hankook Chabon Juuiron* [On Korean capitalism] (pp. 163-190). Seoul: Kkachi.

Lee, Hahn-been. (1968). *Korea: Time, change, and public administration.* Honolulu: University of Hawaii Press.

Lee, Kyu Uck, & Lee, Jae Hyung. (1990). *Gieob gyeolhab qwa gyeongjeryeog jibjung (Business groups and economic concentration). Seoul: Korea Development Institute.*

Lee, Sung Hyung. (1985). State, class and capital accumulation—Focusing on the 8.3 measure [in Korean]. In Jang Jip Choi (Ed.), *Hankook Chabon Chuuiwa Kookka* [Korean capitalism and the state] (pp. 229-286). Seoul: Hanul.

Lim, Hyun-Chin. (1985). *Dependent development in Korea 1963-1979.* Seoul: Seoul National University Press.

Maeil Kyungje Shinmun. (1984). *Maekyung: Annual corporation reports.* Seoul: Maeil Kyungje Shinmun.

Maeil Kyungje Shinmun. (1985). *Maekyung: Annual corporation reports.* Seoul: Maeil Kyongje Shinmun.

Maeil Kyungje Shinmun. (1986). *Maekyung: Annual corporation reports.* Seoul: Maeil Kyungje Shinmun.

Management Efficiency Research Institute. (1986). *Analysis of financial statements—Fifty major business groups in Korea.* Seoul: MERI.

Mason, Edward, et al. (1980). *The economic and social modernization of the Republic of Korea.* Cambridge, MA: Harvard University, Council on East Asian Studies.

Moon, Chung-in. (1989). Beyond statism: Rethinking the political economy of growth in South Korea [Special issue on East Asian development model, edited by Steve Chan & Cal Clark]. *International Studies Notes.*

Olson, Mancur. (1982). *The rise and decline of nations: Economic growth, stagflation, and social rigidities.* New Haven, CT: Yale University Press.

Stallings, Barbara. (1991). The role of foreign capital in economic development: A comparison of Latin America and East Asia. In Gary Gereffi & Donald Wyman (Eds.), *Manufacturing miracles: Paths of industrialization in Latin America and East Asia.* Princeton, NJ: Princeton University Press.

Steers, Richard, et al. (1987). *The chaebol.* New York: Harper & Row.

Wade, Robert. (1990). *Governing the market: Economic theory and the role of government in East Asian industrialization.* Princeton, NJ: Princeton University Press.

Woo, Jung-En. (1990). *Race to the swift: State and finance in Korean industrialization.* New York: Columbia University Press.

World Bank. *World development report.* (various years).

Yoo, Sangjin, & Lee, Sang M. (1987, Summer). Management style and practice of Korean chaebols. *California Management Review,* pp. 95-110.

6

Political Economy of Regional Development in Korea

SOOHYUN CHON

Since 1961, the Korean government has carefully planned and closely monitored the economic growth of the country. Through an intricate profit allocation system devised to promote export industries, the government was able to achieve impressive growth. As a result of Korea's successful economic growth in the past three decades, the living standard of the country's population has increased significantly. But the policy also had the effect of concentrating the benefits in the hands of a few large corporations and people from certain regions. While most of the industrial and urban activities are now concentrated in the Seoul and Pusan metropolitan areas, the central part of Korea—including the Chungchong provinces as well as the Cholla provinces in the southwest—lag behind in their economic development (Figure 6.1). This chapter is an attempt to explain how rapid economic growth and state intervention have affected spatial economic development. The author has sought to find explanations using:

(1) the economic structural transformations that favored regions with industrial bases;

(2) the relative agricultural income growth among different regions in Korea; and

(3) the political and elite power structure that consists of a majority of leaders from the southeast.

AUTHOR'S NOTE: The author would like to express sincere gratitude to Dr. Jin Yong Oh of the Sejong Institute and Professor Shin Haeng Lee of Yonsei University for their support, advice, and comments during the writing of this chapter. I would also like to thank Anneke Vonk for the maps.

Figure 6.1. Provinces of Korea

Table 6.1 Income Level by Regional Groupings (1983)

	Population (in Millions)	Per Capita Income (Percentage of National Average)
Central Provinces	5.9	80.1%
Southwestern Provinces	4.4	80.0%
Southeastern Provinces	10.4	112.0%

SOURCE: Ministry of Construction (1987).

The uneven distribution of economic growth is best illustrated by the skewed income distribution among these regions. A report by the Ministry of Construction provides income statistics that are not readily available from other sources (Ministry of Construction, 1987).[1] According to the report the "central provinces," including North and South Chungchong provinces as well as part of North Cholla province, had 5.9 million people comprising approximately 14.6% of the total population in 1983 (Table 6.1). The economies of the "central provinces" are under represented as their share of output amounted to only 12.3% of the total national output. Per capita income of the central region is about 80.1% of national per capita income as well.

The "southwestern provinces" include the entire South Cholla province and part of North Cholla province. This area contains 4.4 million people, about 10.7% of the total population of the country in 1983. The share of regional output of this area was 9.1% of the total national output of the country in 1983. The per capita income of this region also amounted to 80% of national per capita income in 1983. On the other hand, the "southeastern provinces," which include Pusan, Taegu, 13 cities, and 31 *kuns* (counties) in the southeast, had 26.7% of the total population of the country in 1983. Per capita income of this area was 112% of national per capita income in 1983.

The uneven distribution of economic development is not an anomaly that exists only in Korea, because factors of production are rarely distributed evenly. The regional disparity in Korea, especially between that of the Cholla provinces in the west and the Kyongsang provinces in the east, however, is an extreme case where political institutions and the economic structure has had a significant impact on redirecting resources and investment away from the Cholla provinces to the Kyongsang provinces. This has resulted in the Cholla's underdevelopment and the sense that Cholla's people have received a low share of the benefits from Korea's economic develop-

Table 6.2 Concentration Index of Industrial Output by Regions (1982)

	AP	*AS*
Cheju	0.08	0.04
Kangwon	0.19	0.06
Kyonggi	1.59	1.35
North Cholla	0.42	0.26
South Cholla	0.55	0.65
North Chungchong	0.57	0.26
South Chungchong	0.63	0.43
North Kyongsang	1.15	0.43
South Kyongsang	2.03	1.83
Inchon	2.52	40.63
Pusan	1.15	24.12
Seoul	0.74	23.73
Taegu	0.99	8.86

SOURCE: Korea Research Institute for Human Settlement (1985).

NOTE: $AP = \dfrac{\text{Regional Industrial Value Added / Total National Value Added}}{\text{Regional Population / Total National Population}}$

$AS = \dfrac{\text{Regional Industrial Output / Total National Industrial Output}}{\text{Area of Each Region / Area of South Korea}}$

ment. As illustrated in Table 6.2, for example, the share of the Chollas' manufacturing value-added falls far behind that of the Kyongsang provinces. This has led to deep resentment that divides these regions among different political parties.

The Cholla and Kyongsang provinces started out as the two most populous areas in the country comprising approximately 25% and 28% of the total population respectively in 1949. Today, the Kyongsang provinces have nearly 30% of Korea's population and the Cholla provinces approximately 12%. Such a drastic decrease in the proportion in the Cholla provinces is attributable to the lack of employment opportunities in manufacturing and hence of migration out of the area. For example, the share of manufacturing employment in the Chollas as a percentage of total Korean manufacturing employment has decreased from 13.1% in 1958 to 5.4% in 1983. The share of the Chollas' value-added has also decreased from 10.4% to 8.0% during the same period. Since the Korean economy has grown substantially during this period, the absolute total employment in manufacturing in Cholla has increased approximately three to four times in both North and South Cholla. However, this does not compare favorably with the more than 10-fold increase in employment in other economically vibrant provinces such as the Kyonggi and Kyongsang provinces. The Kyongsang provinces' share of manufacturing employment has increased from 28.6% to 41.0% between 1958 and 1983, and the share of value-added has increased from 35.2% to 40.2% during the same period. Table 6.2 presents a concentration index of industrial output by regions in 1982, as a measure of the degree of industrialization for each province. Here again, the prominence of Kyonggi and the Kyongsang provinces as industrial centers is apparent.

The Chollas experienced negative population growth between 1970 and 1985. North Cholla's population decreased from 2.4 million in 1970 to 2.2 million in 1985, while the population of South Cholla decreased from 4.0 million to 2.8 million during the same period. Out-migrants from the Chollas are found in large numbers in urban centers, living below the poverty level. In Seoul, people from North and South Cholla provinces comprise 28.3% of the total urban poor (M. H. Kim, 1988, p. 493). Since the Cholla's total population is approximately 12% of the total population of Korea, North and South Cholla provinces represent a disproportionately large share of urban poverty. Although it would be expected that recent immigrants would comprise a larger proportion of the underprivileged than the existing population as a whole, no statistics are available that permit this hypothesis to be tested. It would be of interest to compare recent urban immigrants from the Chollas versus other rural areas to find their share of the poor and to determine how quickly they assimilate into the middle class. Since there is a cultural bias against people from the Cholla provinces, one could expect that their assimilation into the middle class would be impeded (M. H. Kim, 1987).[2] The feeling of alienation both in their places of origin and of destination causes Cholla people to align themselves with a political party representing their own regional interests, the Peace and Democratic Party headed by Kim Dae Joong.

Table 6.3 Annual Growth Rate of Gross National Product

Year	Growth Rate (Percentage)	Year	Growth Rate (Percentage)
1955	5.4	1973	16.7
1958	5.2	1976	15.5
1961	4.8	1979	7.0
1962	3.1	1982	7.2
1964	8.6	1985	7.0
1967	7.8	1988	12.2
1970	7.9	—	—

SOURCE: Mason et al. (1980), p. 98; Korea Development Institute (1989), p. 27.

Structural Reasons for Underdevelopment in Cholla

Economic development, which encouraged fast industrialization with aggressive export promotion policies, had a significant impact on the structure of the Korean economy. As is always the case, economic development meant an increase in the importance of the industrial sector and a decrease in the relative importance of agriculture. Traditionally, the Cholla provinces were the most prosperous agricultural areas in Korea. The Far Eastern agricultural system, especially that of Korea and Japan, is characterized by a division of wet rice paddies and upland dry fields. Because rice is the major crop and has the highest productivity per unit land, the topography and availability of water largely determined the prosperity of an agricultural area. The Cholla provinces are endowed with fertile plains suitable for rice cultivation. They used to be the most wealthy agricultural areas in Korea and were known as the "Rice Bowl." It is not a coincidence that some of Korea's first modern entrepreneurial families, such as the Samyangsa Group, had its origins in fortunes built on Cholla agricultural wealth.[3]

Starting from 1961 when the military government of President Park Chung Hee came into power, Korea's economy started to grow at an accelerated rate due to the successful execution of the Five Year Economic Plans (Table 6.3). With fast economic growth, there emerged two trends that worked against the relative regional prosperity of the Cholla provinces compared to other areas. Rapid economic growth was accompanied by an increase in urban populations and their income. This was conducive to the production of high value dry-field crops such as fruits and vegetables. Consequently, North Chungchong, North Kyongsang, and Cheju Island, which used to be relatively poor agricultural sectors due to a high percentage of dry fields to total cultivable land, began to show fast growth in agricultural production. Between 1960 and 1974, North Chungchong province, North Kyongsang province, and Cheju Island experienced an average annual output growth rate of 6.2%, 4.7%, and 10.4% respectively (Ban, Moon, & Perkins, 1982, pp. 116-127). In contrast, areas such as South and North Cholla, as well as South Kyongsang, which are and have been major rice production areas, experienced decreases in their share of total agricultural output of the country. In North Cholla province, which has the highest percentage of paddy land, agricultural output grew by only an average of 1.7% per annum between 1960 and 1974. This compares unfavorably with the average annual agricultural output growth rate of 4.0% for the whole country during the same period.

As illustrated in Table 6.4, total agricultural output in monetary terms reveals that the differentials between the rate of growth in the rice growing regions and the predominantly dry-field regions are not as drastic as in the case of total output in tonnage. This is because rice's per unit land yield in monetary terms is as high as most commercial vegetables and fruits. It does show, however, that the agricultural output measured in monetary terms increased faster in regions with a higher percentage of dry fields. Again, areas with a high percentage of dry fields to total agricultural area, such as Cheju, North Kyongsang, and North Chungchong, show more than a 2.5 times increase in their farm output in monetary terms, while North Cholla and South Chungchong show the lowest increase.

Between the initiation of economic development by the military government in the early 1960s and early 1980s, most of the transportation network, especially highway construction, strengthened the existing Seoul-Pusan artery rather than building roads in poorly connected areas such as the Chollas. This pattern of infrastructure development put the Chollas at an even further disadvantage in commercial crop cultivation for major markets in urban centers (Ban et al., 1982, pp. 147-158; Keidel, 1979). Only recently in the 1980s, have four-lane highways connecting the capital city of South Cholla—Kwangju—to Seoul, Pusan, and Taegu been constructed.

Second, because the Cholla provinces were the most prominent agricultural regions at the outset of Korea's economic development, their relative

Table 6.4 Farm Output (Current Prices), 1960-1974 (Unit: Million 1970 Won)

	1960	*1965*	*1970*	*1974*	*Percentage Increase (1960-1974)*
Cheju	6,801	12,760	11,014	18,033	265
Kangwon	19,785	27,213	32,543	44,491	225
Kyonggi	52,313	62,621	92,849	118,487	226
North Cholla	47,810	73,440	82,585	103,246	216
South Cholla	65,220	104,274	116,570	149,688	230
North Chungchong	26,969	43,626	53,497	71,259	264
South Chungchong	52,703	75,880	89,725	113,870	216
North Kyongsang	67,305	120,398	130,806	169,835	252
South Kyongsang	54,374	107,637	106,353	124,481	229
Pusan	0	2,476	1,923	1,979	—
Seoul[a]	4,361	5,915	5,080	4,286	98

SOURCE: Keidel (1979), p. 211, Table B-17.
NOTE: a. Decrease in agricultural production around Seoul is an obvious case of speculation by landholders arount a fast growing urban center.

position against other provinces slipped when the share of industry and services in the Korean economy started to rise. Grouping investment sectors indicates that the industrial sector has received an increasingly larger share of total capital formation. While capital formation in the industrial sector increased from 42.8% in 1953-1955 to 57.5% in 1970-1972, the agricultural sector's capital formation decreased slightly from 9.6% to 9.0% during the same period (Kuznets, 1977, pp. 68-69). The gap continued to increase throughout the 1970s and 1980s. This might be due to the fact that estimating agricultural fixed capital formation can have a downward bias since the value of nonmonetized land improvements play a crucial role in agricultural output increases, but are relatively hard to measure. A large part of the investment channeled into improving agricultural capital—such as paddy or dry-field construction and maintenance—come from the labors of small-scale farmers. As a result, the investment is often left out of national account estimates. Nevertheless, agriculture's small investment share largely reflects the top priority given industrial development in the initial stages of the Five Year Economic Development Plans. With the decrease in relative importance of the agricultural sector in the economy, the Cholla provinces, which were predominantly agricultural regions, were adversely affected in their relative importance compared to other parts of the country.

Determinants of Industrial Locations

One glance at the distribution of different industries in Korea reveals that there is a heavy concentration in the northwest and southeast of the country. As the maps in Figure 6.2 and Figure 6.3 illustrate, most of the textile and precision machinery industries are located in the Kyongsang provinces and in the Seoul-Kyonggi area. Textiles are representative of light manufacturing, which played a major role at the initial stage of Korea's economic development. Even in 1983-1984, textiles comprised 21.6% of the country's total exports. Initially, textile industries were heavily concentrated in the Seoul and Pusan metropolitan areas comprising 40.0% of total textile employment in 1970. In 1984, the share of textile employment in these two metropolitan areas decreased to 27.0% as textile plants began to disperse to adjacent areas of Seoul and Pusan, such as Kyonggi and North Kyongsang provinces. In turn, the share of employment in textile industries in the Kyongsang provinces increased by 29.7% between 1970 and 1985, while Kyonggi province showed an increase of 42.0% during the same period. North Cholla province also experienced a 69.0% increase in its share of textile industry employment during the same period. This is partly because North Cholla started out with a small base comprising only 2.6% of total textile employment in 1970. By 1984, North Cholla's share was 4.4%. The share of the rest of the country, North Chungchong, South Chungchong, South Cholla, and Kangwon provinces decreased from 13.4% to 10.4% between 1970 and 1985. In the machinery, metals, and electronics industries that the government started to promote aggressively from 1973, concentration around Seoul and Pusan is even more pronounced. The Seoul and Pusan areas occupied 76.7% of the total employment in these industries in 1970. Precision industries also experienced dispersion of their locations to nearby provinces of Seoul and Pusan between 1970 and 1980. By 1984, Kyonggi province, excluding Seoul, occupied 38.6% of the total employment in precision machinery while North and South Kyongsang provinces, excluding Pusan, came to occupy 32.2%. Establishment of the Kumi and Changwon industrial complexes in North Kyongsang and South Kyongsang provinces respectively, accounts for the dispersion of these industries to the nearby provinces. In 1984, the Seoul-Kyonggi area and the Pusan-Kyongsang area had a total of more than 96.1% of the employment in precision machinery. On the other hand, the share of precision machinery manufacturing employment in North Chungchong, South Chungchong, North Cholla, South Cholla, and Kangwon provinces had remained the same—changing slightly from a meager 3.8% in 1970 to 3.6% in 1984. Similar patterns can be discerned in fabricated metal industries, electric machinery industries, and general machinery industries as illustrated in Table 6.5. Chemical industries are an exception, in that South Cholla's share is significant. This is because the second largest oil refinery and petrochemical complex in Korea is located in Yosu in the South Cholla province.

As much as the structural change of the Korean economy influenced differential regional growth levels, the existing geographical patterns of infrastructure and industry, along with the economic development policies of the Korean government, contributed to the concentration of industries in certain parts of Korea. At the initial stages of economic development, the military government of President Park Chung Hee decided that the route to fast economic growth would be fueled by an aggressive export-promotion policy. For Korea to secure foreign currency, which is needed to import such vital items as petroleum and food and to resolve chronic balance of payment deficit problems, it was necessary to promote export-oriented economic growth. Korea's limited market size is another factor that necessitated exports so that certain industries could achieve economies of scale.

Since the growth of exports depended on the enthusiastic cooperation of business with the government, the government devised various profit incentives to promote exports. Many benefits and incentives were given to export-oriented industries resulting in phenomenal economic growth. Such aggressive export-promotion policies and profit allocation schemes—more detailed examples of these profit allocation schemes to export industries are illustrated in the following section—given to export industries created a number of distortions in the structure of the Korean economy. Of the many impacts that these export-promotion policies had on the Korean economy, one of them was the profound imprint left on the country's industrial structure.

To achieve export goals, the Korean government became overly concerned about total export volume and hence geared its policies to reward

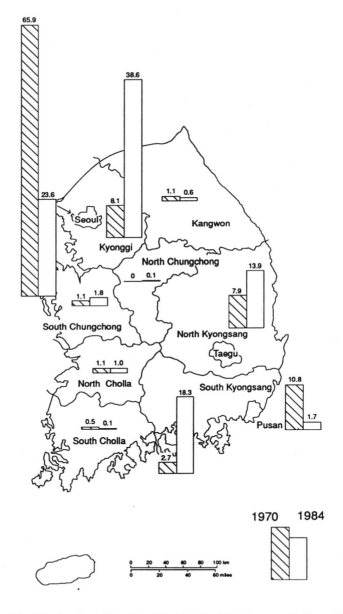

Figure 6.2. Distribution of Precision Machine Tool Employment in Korea (%)
SOURCE: Korea Educational Development Institute (1988, p. 353).

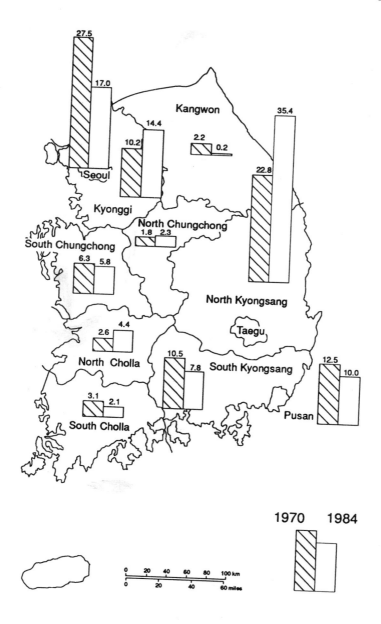

Figure 6.3. Distribution of Textile Employment in Korea (%)
SOURCE: Korea Educational Development Institute (1988,p. 348).

Table 6.5 Regional Distribution of Industrial Employment in Korea
(Unit: Percentage of Total National Employment)

| | Textiles | | Precision Machinery | |
	1970	1984	1970	1984
Kangwon	2.21	0.28	1.11	0.67
Kyonggi	10.20	14.45	8.12	38.61
North Cholla	2.66	4.45	1.12	1.07
South Cholla	3.19	2.17	0.57	0.14
North Chungchong	1.88	2.35	0.00	0.17
South Chungchong	6.34	5.83	1.16	1.88
North Kyongsang	22.88	35.49	7.91	13.95
South Kyongsang	10.54	7.80	2.72	18.31
Pusan	12.51	10.02	10.84	1.75
Seoul	27.55	17.05	65.90	23.67

| | Fabricated Metals | | Electric Machinery | |
	1970	1984	1970	1984
Kangwon	0.50	0.22	0.02	0.43
Kyonggi	10.05	28.71	17.40	36.32
North Cholla	3.46	1.00	0.25	0.64
South Cholla	2.99	0.90	6.65	0.43
North Chungchong	0.78	0.71	0.05	2.20
South Chungchong	3.06	2.15	0.67	1.23
North Kyongsang	15.12	8.49	2.06	5.29
South Kyongsang	2.23	17.27	1.31	15.27
Pusan	17.75	14.61	17.17	3.62
Seoul	43.77	25.87	54.37	29.29

| | General Machinery | |
	1970	1984
Kangwon	3.03	0.50
Kyonggi	9.00	25.47
North Cholla	1.69	0.37
South Cholla	4.93	1.66
North Chungchong	1.75	5.55
South Chungchong	7.43	2.32
North Kyongsang	13.53	11.05
South Kyongsang	13.24	22.13
Pusan	15.20	10.29
Seoul	29.69	20.65

SOURCE: Lee et al. (1988), pp. 348, 353.

businesses that had the highest volume of exports, instead of those with the highest value added. Therefore, exporters did not have much incentive to invest in the manufacturing of parts and intermediate products that required long-term investment in capital and technical resources. Instead, they reaped the benefits given to large exporters by importing parts and assembling products for export. This caused industry to rely heavily on imported inputs. As a result, Korea became import dependent as well as export dependent. While Korea's exports increased from $US 55 million in 1962 to $US 35 billion in 1986, imports increased from $US 442 million to $US 32 billion during the same period.[4]

This heavy dependency on both imports and exports necessitated that exporting industries locate near ports to have the advantage of low transportation costs. Often, the economic success of export-oriented market economies of the NICs' is credited to having highly skilled, low-wage labor that allowed them to build industries based on supplying labor-intensive products to world markets at competitive prices. Few scholars note their geographical advantage as relatively small countries with easy access to waterborne transportation. Hong Kong and Singapore are basically port cities. In Taiwan and Korea, and even in Japan, the most remote inland location is less than 100 miles from the coast. This geographical advantage has played an important role in allowing these newly industrialized countries to have an edge in transportation costs over other countries. This is especially true when one compares the NICs and Japan to geographically large countries such as the United States and Australia.

For Korea to compete with other NICs in the world market for labor-intensive low value products, it was essential to locate export industries near ports and along the major transportation arteries connected to ports. Because of the importance of access to waterborne transportation, the geography of ports largely determined the location of industries in Korea. In general, the east coast of Korea has favorable physical geography for deep seaports so that large ships can dock. Not only does the east coast have great water depth offshore, but also the tidal differences are a minimal 50 cm compared to tides of 1,000 cm on the west coast. For this reason, the major exporting ports are highly concentrated on the east and southeast coasts of Korea. On the west coast, Seoul's Inchon port is the only major cargo and container exporting port. On the southeast and east coasts, Mukho, Pohang, Ulsan, Masan, and Kwangyang are the exporting ports that handle the majority of cargo traffic. Pusan, located in the southeast corner of Korea and equipped with container as well as cargo handling facilities, is the prime port city of Korea, serving the entire nation.

Until very recently, the existing transportation network also played a important role because easy access to ports from inland was vital for export ing industries as well. This also explains the heavy concentration of indus tries along the Seoul-Pusan axis. Major railroad trunk lines built during the Japanese occupation to access resources in Manchuria connected Pusan to Shineuju via Seoul. The four-lane express highway constructed during the 1960s that served as the major transportation artery also linked Pusan to Seoul, inducing further development of the areas along the route.

There are other economic and geographical reasons as to why industrie are concentrated in the Seoul and Pusan areas. Seoul has always enjoyed the advantage of being the prime city, since it has been the country's capita since the Lee Dynasty (1392-1910). With nearly 25% of the country's tota population and 58% of total bank loans directed to industries concentrated in the city, it is only natural that business is attracted to Seoul. Access to skilled labor, infrastructure, and markets are only a few of the amenitie Seoul can offer.

There are also inherent locational advantages to Pusan compared to the southwestern part of Korea. During the Japanese occupation, Pusan had the advantage of being the major Korean port close to Japan. Thus, before Japan initiated massive heavy and chemical industrial development in North Korea as part of its industrialization efforts in Manchuria, Pusan served as the majo light manufacturing center of Korea. To maintain these light manufacturing activities, the colonial government established the basic infrastructure in thi area. Also, during the Korean War, as the only part of South Korea that wa not largely destroyed by the war and occupied by the communists, South Kyongsang province drew the majority of refugees. Consequently, there wa a massive transfer of wealth from the rest of the country to South Kyongsang province, especially to Pusan. From the combination of these two reasons the Kyongsang provinces emerged from the war with 24.4% of the total man ufacturing employment in the country. Following the war, the Kyongsang provinces received a large share of infrastructure investment through sof loans from international agencies such as the United Nations Korea Recon struction Agency (UNKRA). The Kyongsang provinces' share of total Ko rean reconstruction aid amounted to 17.3% of the total, second only to Seou which received 19.8% (M. H. Kim, 1987, pp. 32-33).

Having an export-oriented market economy heavily dependent upon im ports of raw materials and intermediate products dictates that industrial lo cations be concentrated near the ports or along major transportation arteries Because existing infrastructure and industry were concentrated in Seoul and Pusan at the initial stages of development, and because ports were easier to build on the east and southeast coasts of Korea, it was economical to locate new industries in these areas. Considering that much of the risk for new projects in developing countries comes from undertaking big infrastructure investments, it was an economically rational decision to take such locational factors into account. Thus, fast economic growth, with a heavy emphasis on nurturing industry and exports, found development along the Seoul-Pusan axis to be cost effective. This also allowed export industries to have the competitive advantages of cheap transportation costs and the agglomeration of activities. Such a policy might have been economically rational, but it brought about the uneven distribution of industrial development in Korea and political discontent in the regions that received a low share of the benefits from industrialization. Resolution of regional tension in the Chollas is becoming more urgent now that the new political alignment of Kim Young Sam and Kim Jong Pil with Roh Tae Woo may further alienate this area from the rest of the country.[5]

Geographical Affiliation of Political Power

If the existing economic structure and the existing infrastructure caused the concentration of industries in the Seoul-Kyonggi and Pusan-Kyongsang areas, the political power structure of the Korean government had the impact of exaggerating the locational advantages of these areas. Two of the three presidents since Park have geographical affiliations with the Kyongsang provinces. This has left a profound impact on the elite structure of the country and subsequent allocation of benefits to different parts of the country.

When President Park Chung Hee came to power in 1961 through a military coup, he needed to establish justification of his regime, since a coup is not a legitimate means of assuming a ruler's position. The interim government that Park toppled to grab power was established by the 1960 student revolt against the dictatorship of Syngman Rhee. Even though the interim government was extremely inefficient in dealing with the legacies and corruptions of the Rhee regime, it was symbolic in that it was the product of a successful democratic struggle against a decade-old dictatorship. Park's coup was a jolting event in which the democratization process of Korea regressed. In order to legitimize his rule, which signified regression to dictatorship and military rule, he had to build a broad power base with a large number of supporters.

With military rule, power is monopolized by the officers who participated in the coup and shared the risk. The officers who planned the coup with President Park were alumni of Taegu Sabum (Teacher's Vocational Training School of Taegu) and the Military Academy. Even though they held the most important positions in the government and government-owned corporations, the number of graduates from these schools was not large enough to draw upon as a power base. In a society where school, clan, and geographical affiliations are of crucial importance for social advancement, Park needed to establish his power base by connecting himself with other groups that could broaden his ties and help him establish his legitimacy. Park solved this problem by relying on his regional affiliation with the city of Taegu and the Kyongsang provinces.

The Taegu area of North Kyongsang traditionally had a strong core elite group dating back to the early part of the Lee Dynasty. As descendants and disciples of Yoo Sung Yong and Lee Toi Gey, who were prominent Confucian scholars and leaders of the *Namin* faction during the Lee Dynasty, these scholars held a tight informal network. Confucian schools (*Sawon*) located in Andong, Sangju, and Sunsan were the centers of their gatherings. Even though these groups of Confucian scholars had not held high ranking positions in the government since the latter part of the Lee Dynasty, they managed to maintain a close relationship through the modern period. During the Japanese occupation, their ties were strong enough that they could organize a relatively effective resistance against the colonial regime. Because the Taegu area used to be the center of education for both North and South Kyongsang provinces, these elites educated their children at Kyongbook High School in Taegu. The linkages drawn from these social and school connections were quite extensive and it was this geographical affiliation that Park could tap because he was born in Sunsan. By doing so he managed to establish ties with the elites of the most populous province of Korea, which now comprises approximately 30% of the total population.

The affiliation of a political leader with one region has many implications in the development of a country. Unusually large numbers of people from the Kyongsang provinces entered positions of influence throughout government and industry. They have consistently dominated high-level positions in the cabinet, politically appointed national assembly seats, and supreme court appointments. Statistics compiled by Kim Man Heum (M. H. Kim, 1987, pp. 22-23) shows that 32.0% of the high-level officials[6] from the Second Republic through the Fifth Republic have their family origins in the Kyongsang provinces.[7] A total of 14.6% and 13.0% of the high-level officials during this period were from the Chungchong provinces and Seoul respectively, while the Chollas produced 13.0% of the high-level officials. Examination of the chronological data indicates that the number of high-level officers from the Kyongsang provinces started to rise significantly during the Second Republic when the military government came into power, and reached its peak at 43.6% during the Fifth Republic. The Cholla provinces' share of high-level officers, on the other hand, steadily declined from 16.3% in the Second Republic to 9.6% in the Fifth Republic.

M. H. Kim standardized these figures by the population size of each province to determine whether any given province was producing a disproportionately large number of high-ranking officials. Regional affiliation in Korea is not determined by place of residence, but by the place of one's family origin. The population in each province does not necessarily reflect the number of people born in that province. The most reliable data on population by family origin was first compiled by the Japanese Colonial Government in 1943. Since then the population has been quite mobile within the country. Few statistics have been collected in classifying populations at the destination of migration by place of origin since then; therefore, the 1943 data is the best available source for determining the number of people by place of origin. The data have problems, however; for example, assumptions had to be made that the mortality and fertility rates of each province were uniform over half a century. Also it had to be assumed that there was no interregional migration of population within the country. Given these assumptions, certain demographic models can project population growth in a closed system given birth- and death rates by age and sex categories. Since the assumptions used by these models—such as mortality and fertility rates being uniform throughout the entire country in both urban and rural areas—are too unrealistic, thus the projections are rough estimates.

Using the base population data from 1943, the percentage of high-level officers from each province was divided by the percentage base population of each province.[8] The ratios reveal that Seoul still has the highest share ratio of 3.7 of top ranking officers from the Second Republic through the Fifth Republic. The Kyongsang provinces rank second to Seoul with a ratio of 1.5. Chungchong, Cholla, and Kangwon provinces have ratios of 1.4, 0.7, and 0.7, respectively. From this data, M. H. Kim concludes it is clear that a disproportionately large share of high ranking officers come from the Kyongsang and Seoul areas.

In some ways, the overrepresentation of the Seoul and Kyongsang provinces is not an anomaly in that these areas are economically more prosperous than other provinces. During the Fifth Republic, however, the Kyongsang provinces were overrepresented by 2.2 times their base population—a marked increase from their overrepresentation ratio of 1.5 in the Third and Fourth Republics.

Not only is there a quantitative difference in the number of high ranking officials from the Kyongsang and Cholla provinces, but there are also qualitative differences in the type of positions to which they are assigned. Since the Kwangju incident in 1980, no one from the Chollas has been appointed to security-related positions such as Minister of Justice, public procurator-general, or attorney general (Chun, 1988, p. 264). There was also a concerted effort to appoint at least one person from the Kyongsang provinces in either the public procurator-general's position or in the Minister of Justice position since the Fifth Republic (Chun, 1988, p. 266).

The overrepresentation of the Kyongsang provinces does not stop at high ranking government official positions. Of the 20 largest *chaebol* families in Korea, 9 of their founding fathers came from the Kyongsang provinces (W. W. Lee, 1988, p. 504). Of the top 5 *chaebols,*—if Kim Woo Joong of the Daewoo Group who was born in Taegu is considered to be from Kyongsang province—3 of the founding fathers are from these provinces. Considering that the top 5 *chaebols'* gross revenue equals 61% of the country's gross national product, the concentration of economic power in the Kyongsang provinces is remarkable indeed (Figure 6.4).

The concentration of economic power in the hands of a few *chaebols* resulted largely from the export-promotion policies at the initial stages of Korea's economic development. There are long lists of privileges that were granted to exporters to promote exports through the late 1970s. First, exporters have had literally unlimited access to imported inputs and have paid neither tariffs nor indirect taxes. Wastage allowances of imported intermediate products or raw materials were granted well over the amount required for export production.[9] Even though wastage allowances were later reduced to 10%, they provided exporters with handsome margins by producing goods for the domestic market. In a closed economy where consumer imports are a scarce resource, having access to them virtually guaranteed windfall profits for exporters.

Exporters, at the same time, were allowed preferential access to foreign loans. Between 1965 and 1970, for example, there was a large discrepancy between domestic and foreign interest rates. Korea had high inflation and high interest rates with an overvalued currency. The divergence between the domestic and foreign borrowing rates ranged from 4.4% to 18.0% during this period. For example, during 1966-1970, the foreign interest rate adjusted for foreign inflation averaged about 1.5% whereas the real cost of foreign borrowing faced by Korean borrowers was about –3.1% (Park, 1985,

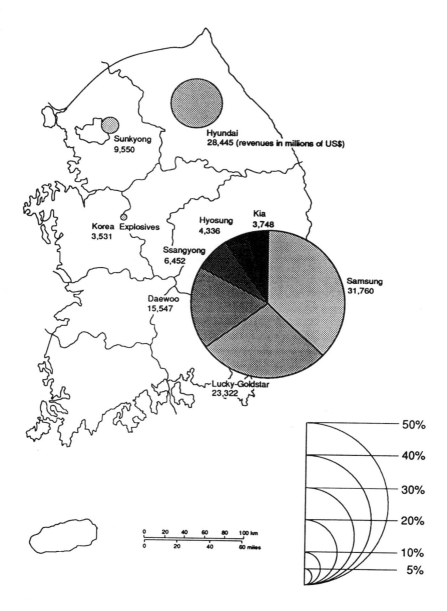

Figure 6.4. Origins of *Chaebols*: Share of Revenues in GNP
SOURCE: Bello and Rosenfeld (1990, p. 64).

pp. 11-12). When the real interest rate faced by borrowers is below market or negative, and an overvalued currency is maintained by government regulation, there is naturally a handsome arbitrage opportunity for those privileged people who have access to foreign loans. The fact that large Korean exporters were consistently able to take advantage of this arbitrage situation clearly indicates that Korea's financial markets were not efficient. Since borrowers expected a stable exchange rate resulting from government regulation, this expectation understated the true cost of borrowing as well, inducing Korean firms to borrow more than they would have done in an efficient financial market. One of the most often cited misallocations of financial resources due to this policy is the large capital investment in heavy and chemical industries that led to a serious economic downturn in the late 1970s.

The privileges mentioned above are only two of the many incentives and profit allocation systems that were given to exporters. With such support from the government, large trading houses grew into *chaebols.* In selecting who should be allowed the benefits among different business groups and exporters, the geographical affiliation, school connections, and kinship network played an important role. Even though it is beyond the scope of this study, the emergence of Lucky Gold Star and Samsung as the top ranking tycoons, and the relative decline of the indigenous capitalists such as Samyangsa Group and Kyongsung Textile Company is a good example of regional affiliations playing an important role.[10]

Intermarriages between the politically powerful families and *chaebols, chaebols* among themselves, and among the politically influential families are quite common. Relationships among the politicians, government officials, military, executives of government-owned corporations, and business elites are close as well (Hattori, 1987, pp. 346-362; Kang et al., 1991, pp. 80-81; W. W. Lee, 1988, pp. 504-505). It is through this network that a political power base was built and the interconnections between politics and business emerged. The fact that about 48% of business heads who previously held nonbusiness occupations came from a background in politics, government, national corporations, or the military is a clear indication that such a network connecting business to politics exists (Itoh, 1984, p. 162). Also, according to Itoh, of business elites who changed occupations, about 53% went into politics, government, national corporations, or the military during the same period.

A large number of military officers placed in high ranking positions in the government and corporations after discharge are from the Kyongsang provinces. The same is true for officials in high ranking positions in the government as well as the business elites mentioned above. The interrelationships among these groups of elites multiplies the impact of concentrated power in the hands of people from the Kyongsang provinces. This in turn induced excessive concentration of investment in industrial facilities and infrastructure in these regions compared to other parts of the country in the past, as was illustrated in Figures 6.2 and 6.3.

Korea did not have natural competitive advantages in heavy industry at the initial stages of its development; thus these industries had to be heavily subsidized in the beginning. The more an industry was supported by the government, the more likely it was that benefits were allocated to regions with political affiliations with the government. Since the allocation of privileged loans and foreign credits were more prominent in the more capital-intensive industries for the reasons explained above, the heavy and chemical industries are more concentrated in the Seoul-Kyonggi and Pusan-Kyongsang areas, while textile industries show relatively dispersed patterns of distribution throughout the country. The best example of this would be locating an electronics complex in Kumi, which used to be a little village not too far from Sunsan, President Park Chung Hee's hometown. The only mitigating factor for the Cholla provinces in heavy industry is that Korea's second largest oil refinery and petrochemical complex are located in Yosu. Recent construction of a large-scale modern steel mill at Kwangyang near Yosu is another exception. This explains the relatively high per capita value-added by the labor force for South Cholla province in 1983 amounting to approximately $US 2,500 in 1990 dollars, when the average per capita value-added from the whole country was $US 1,350 in the same year. It does not necessarily mean that these capital-intensive industries have effective backward linkages with the local economy. This is illustrated by the fact that the total value-added in petroleum and petrochemicals in South Cholla comprised 46.3% of total value-added in the province, when the number of employees in these industries was only 16.7% of total employment. (This does, however, represent a substantial improvement over 1960 when the petroleum and petrochemical sector provided 60.1% of the total value-added and 9.7% of total employment in the province.) There is, however, a limit to the labor absorptive capacity in heavy and chemical industries from the local economy.

The Future of Industrial Development Patterns in Korea

The economic development policies of the Korean government in the 1980s was characterized by a substantial reduction in government control over the economy. Concerted efforts are being made to allow free market mechanisms to take over and correct the distortions introduced by heavy government intervention in the past. Along with these changes in policies, the Korean government is trying to wean *chaebols* from the heavy support to which they are accustomed ("Tough times," Nov. 8). As a part of this policy, the government is attempting to disperse the geographical concentration of industrial development from the Seoul-Kyonggi and Pusan-Kyungsang regions to other parts of the country. This policy has a political motivation of wooing the Cholla provinces from developing increasingly hostile attitudes toward the government. Without having to address the responsibility of Kwangju directly, Roh is trying to appease the Cholla people and to differentiate himself from Chun Doo Hwan of the Fifth Republic by allowing them economic benefits.

There is an economic side to this change in policy that complements the change in the political climate. Korea's real estate prices have skyrocketed in recent years as a result of robust economic growth. When land prices are so high, certain industries that require extensive land, such as the chemical industry, are no longer profitable in Korea. Also due to concentrated development along the Seoul-Pusan arteries, most of the reasonably priced industrial land in these areas is fully utilized and there is little room for expansion.[11] Therefore, the Korean government is planning large-scale ports and infrastructure development along the southwest coast so that it can take advantage of the relatively cheap land prices for industrial development. For example, the land price in Kunsan, recently announced as an industrial complex on the west coast, is approximately $US 52,000 to $US 64,000 per acre at the 1990 exchange rate, while other industrial complexes located in Kyongsang and Kyonggi provinces have unit land price far exceeding $US 130,000 per acre (W. J. Kim, 1988, p. 424).

At the same time, of the $US 20 billion government budget allocated for national and regional development for the period of 1989 through 2001, approximately $US 12 billion will be assigned to the underdeveloped regions including Chungchong and the Cholla provinces (W. J. Kim, 1988, p. 427). Large-scale port construction plans are being drafted for west coast port cities such as Asan, Kunsan, and Namyang. According to the plan, the port capacity of Kunsan, for example, will be increased 40 times. This is quite a contrast to past infrastructure investment patterns where west coast port cities hardly received any investment at all. Express highways connecting port cities along the west coast from Inchon to Kwangyang on the south coast are being planned as well.

As a result of these policies, the spatial distribution of Korean industries is expected to be more evenly distributed in the future. Most of the new industries that will be located along the west coast of Korea will be capital and technology intensive, because the Korean economy already has passed the stage of relying on labor-intensive industries. Since the Chollas' industrial base is dominated by light manufacturing such as food processing, textiles, and clothing, creating a linkage between the existing industrial structure and new technology-intensive industries will largely determine the success of the government's efforts to bring an equal share of income to the Cholla provinces.

Making an effort to equalize the regional concentration of wealth would be one way of appeasing the general population that is becoming increasingly dissatisfied with slowing economic growth and widening income discrepancies. In the face of soaring labor costs, the Korean economy needs major restructuring away from labor-intensive industries to knowledge intensive industries in order to have a relative advantage in world trade. However, the technological level of Korean industry does not allow a smooth transition, for reasons that cannot be discussed in brief in the present chapter. Thus the economic growth perspective in Korea is not too optimistic in the short term. Since Koreans have become accustomed to fast growth in the past three decades, and they face an increasingly uneven wealth distribution as a result of soaring real estate prices and the recent stock market crash, they are starting to demand the rewards of economic growth. There is strong sentiment not to sacrifice for the benefit of economic growth any more. In such an event, the Korean government is faced with a decision whether to continue to aim for high economic growth or concentrate on an even distribution of wealth. Political pressure on the Roh government is the reason behind current development of the southwest of Korea.

Notes

1. Because the statistics published by the Ministry of Construction do not divide the regions along provincial boundaries, it is not possible to compare population and income statistics to provincial data from other sources. However, the Ministry of Construction data provide one of the few reliable regional income statistics able to shed light on the differential levels of regional development in Korea.

2. M. H. Kim (1987) provides various statistics that indicate there is a systematic bias against people from the Cholla provinces.

3. In terms of total agricultural product, the Chollas were prosperous regions comprising 29.4% of the total output of crops produced in the country in 1947 (Ban, Moon, & Perkins, 1982, p. 127). However, because of its high tenancy rate within the region, the poverty index of the Chollas was below the national average before land reform.

4. In 1986 Korea experienced a $US 3 billion overall trade surplus. However, the years between 1984 and 1989 were an anomaly in Korean trade in that Korea recorded trade surpluses for the first time in its history. This was largely due to the three lows—low interest rates, low oil prices, and a favorable exchange rate of the won in relation to the yen—rather than substantial changes in its economic and industrial structure. Before the mid 1980s, Korea was struggling with increasing current account deficits that had to be financed by snowballing foreign debt. The sheer size of debt, amounting to well over $US 40 billion in the mid 1980s, is a good indication of how Korea was still experiencing chronic current account deficits in spite of fast economic growth.

5. Prior to 1990, Korea had three opposition leaders: Kim Young Sam, Kim Dae Jung, and Kim Jong Pil. On January 2, 1990, Kim Young Sam and Kim Jong Pil formed a coalition party, the Democratic Liberal Party, by aligning themselves with Roh Tae Woo. Kim Young Sam has his power base in South Kyongsang around Pusan. Since Kim Jong Pil derives his support from the Chungchong provinces, and Roh Tae Woo draws his main support from North Kyongsang province, the result of this coalition was to alienate Kim Dae Jung whose support comes from the Cholla provinces.

6. According to M. H. Kim's definition, high-level officials are defined as ministers, under-secretaries, and directors at various ministries.

7. The First Republic is the government of Rhee Sueng Man. The Second, Third, and Fourth Republics were headed by Park Chung Hee. Chun Doo Whan was the founder of the Fifth Republic. Roh Tae Woo is the present president of the Sixth Republic.

8. These figures are calculated by dividing the percentage of high-level officers from each province by the percentage of the base population from that province. For example, 43.6% of high-level officers originated from Kyongsang province during the Fifth Republic. In 1985, Kyongsang province had 29.9% of the total population of Korea; 43.6 divided by 29.9 is approximately 1.5.

9. *Wastage allowance* is an accounting term that defines the difference between the volume of imports or production over export, thus allowing a percentage of imports or production to be sold to consumers domestically.

10. As mentioned earlier, Samyangsa Group originated from Gochang in South Cholla province. Kyongsong Textile is one of South Cholla's major industries along with Korea University and *Dong-A Ilbo,* Korea's best known daily newspaper.

11. Note that per unit land price is one variable that determines the rate of return on investment.

References

Ban, Sung Whan, Moon, Pal Yong, & Perkins, Dwight. (1982). *Rural development.* Cambridge, MA: Harvard University Press.

Bello, Walden, & Rosenfeld, Stephanie. (1990). *Dragons in distress: Asia's miracle economies in crisis.* San Francisco: Institute for Food and Development Policy.

Chun, Yool Woo. (1988, July). TK Sadan [TK Division]. *Shindonga,* pp. 254-267.

Hattori, Tamio. (1987, December). Formation of the Korean business elite during the era of rapid economic growth. *Development Economics,* pp. 346-362.

Itoh, Teichi. (1984). Formation of business elites in fast economic growth. *Kaihatsudozokukuno Bisinis Lidashipu* [Business leadership in a developing country]. Asia Kenkyusho [Institute of Developing Economies].

Kang, Chul Gyu, Choi, Joyng Pyo, & Chang, Ji Sang (1991). *Chaebol*. Seoul: Bibong Publications.

Keidel, Albert. (1979). *Korean regional farm product and income: 1910-1974*. Seoul: Korea Development Institute.

Kim, Man Heum. (1988, March). Insa Pyonjoong I Chiyok Kamjong Mandunda [Concentration of high ranking officials from Kyongsang Provinces in the government: Causes of regional confrontation]. *Shindonga,* pp. 486-499.

Kim, Man Heum. (1987). *Hankook Sahoe Chiyok Kamjong Yonku* [Study of regional conflict in Korean society]. Hyundai Sahoe Yonkuso [Hyundai Institute of Social Science Research].

Kim, Wha Joo. (1988, February). Hanbando Eu Saboon Eu Ili Bakuikoita [One fourth of Korean peninsula is changing]. *Wolgan Chosun,* pp. 427-437.

Korea Development Institute. (1989, Spring). *KDI quarterly economic outlook.*

Kuznets, Paul. (1977). *Economic growth and structure in the Republic of Korea.* New Haven, CT: Yale University Press.

Lee, Chan et al. (1988). *Korea: Geographical perspectives.* Seoul: Korea Educational Development Institute.

Lee, Woong Whan. (1988, March). Yongnam Chaebol Eu Inmaek [Human network of Yongnam Chaebols]. *Shindonga,* pp. 500-509.

Mason, Edward, et al. (1980). *The economic and social modernization of the Republic of Korea.* Cambridge, MA: Harvard University Press.

Ministry of Construction (ROK). (1987, December). *Chiyok Kyongjekwonbyol Chonghap Kaebal Keyhoek* [Plans for regional development]. Seoul: Ministry of Construction.

Park, Yungchul. (1985). *Foreign debt, balance of payment, and growth prospects: The case of the Republic of Korea, 1965-1988* (Studies on international monetary issues for the developing countries). [UNDP/UNCTAD Internal Report.]

Research Institute for Human Settlement (ROK). (1985). *Chiyok Charyo Pyonram (Sonamkown)* [Regional statistics (Southwest)].

"Tough times: Korea Goldstar faces a harsh new world under democracy." (1989, Nov. 8). *Wall Street Journal.*

7

Malaysian Industrialization, Ethnic Divisions, and the NIC Model

THE LIMITS TO REPLICATION

PAUL M. LUBECK

The Problem of Replication

Since the first industrial revolution, successful industrialization strategies have invited imitation and replication by economically backward states seeking rapid social and economic transformation. Gershenkron termed this the "demonstration effect," one of the few advantages possessed by late industrializers (Gershenkron, 1982). When applied to the question of states and economic development in the Asian-Pacific region, then the "demonstrated" economic success of the East Asian NICs—Korea, Taiwan, Singapore, and Hong Kong—has, indeed, stimulated much imitation and, inevitably, raises the question whether the policies and institutions responsible for the NIC's success are replicable or transferable, either wholly or partially, to the aspiring NICs of Southeast Asia—Malaysia, Thailand, the Philippines, and Indonesia. Paradoxically, during the 1980s, while Malaysian industrial planners consciously imitated NIC industrial policies, critics charge that they failed to replicate key political institutions or a strong class of indigenous industrialists that, of course, are the trademarks of the NIC model. Given the contradiction between intention and outcome, this chapter pursues the question: Can these aspiring NICs achieve rapid industrialization by replicating NIC industrial policies, even though they have radically different social structures, lack Confucian authority and cultural systems, and are attempting industrialization during a comparatively more sluggish, yet ruthlessly competitive, moment in the history of the international economy?

Appropriately, the Malaysian experience is ideal for evaluating the replicability of the model, for it has launched export-oriented industrialization (EOI), but retains a colonial-origin ethnic division of labor, whereby the Malays control the state apparatus and the Chinese dominate the capital accumulating private sector, a cleavage that undermines close business-state relations so essential to the successful NIC model. Also significant is the fact that all Asian NICs, with the partial exception of Singapore, are ethnically homogeneous societies, a feature that contrasts sharply with the ethnic diversity found in the aspiring NICs. The Malaysian experience forces scholars to consider several interrelated issues: whether the cohesive authority relations that articulate state and society in the NICs implicitly presume ethnic homogeneity; whether a long-standing ethnic division of labor poses an insurmountable obstacle to replicating the model; and, given the latter point, how aspiring NIC industrial strategists might overcome obstacles to industrialization presented by the ethnic division of labor. Let me first examine the achievements and failures of the Malaysian industrialization strategy, and then, in a later section, explore the structural origins of Malaysia's ethnic division of labor as well as the way ethnicity has been treated as an essentialist concept that, purportedly, explains Chinese and Malay investment patterns.

Lessons from the NIC Model

At first glance, Malaysia stands out from other "second tier NICS," not only for registering high rates of economic growth, but also for implementing its "Malaysia Incorporated" and "Look East" industrial policies in obvious imitation of Japan and the Asian NICs. Thus rhetorically, at the very least, Malaysia's industrial strategy is a variant of the East Asian model. What then are the essential features of this model? To be sure, there is variation among the East Asian NICs, arising from historical accidents and different political and social structures. Yet, all are "developmentalist" states, all strategies are administered by comparatively autonomous technocratic elites and all have succeeded by institutionalizing a close relationship between business leaders and state officials in the formation of a dynamic export-oriented regime of capital accumulation (Johnson, 1982). Besides constructing industrial infrastructure (harbors, communications, transportation, and industrial estates) and sponsoring intermediate industries (petroleum refining, steel, and fertilizer), so typical of "deep" import-substituting regimes, the NIC developmentalist state has wedded market rationality to state planning by constructing a "capitalist guided market economy" (White & Wade, 1988, p. 5). "Soft authoritarian" state intervention, to use Johnson's felicitous phase, seeks to augment market rationality, in the long term by reducing risks and uncertainty, as opposed to favoring market distorting interventions that create rent-seeking opportunities for officials and businessmen (Johnson, 1987, p. 141). "Market augmenting" does not, however, mean slavish obedience to free market principles. Not only is state ownership of intermediate and basic industries commonplace, but domestic markets are protected by tariff and nontariff barriers. Amsden convincingly demolishes neoclassical theoretical explanations of Korea's success by demonstrating that "getting relative prices 'wrong' " was, in fact "right." That is, she argues that by insisting on export quotas and other performance standards, Korea's price distortions enhanced growth, private investment, and efficiency over the long term. Firms that met state export quotas were allowed to sell in the domestic market at inflated prices, thus assuring profitability together with EOI (Amsden, 1989, pp. 144-145).

What really happens in practice? Developmentalist state planners constantly assess changing comparative advantages in the world economy in order to upgrade EOI targets that are allocated to domestic producers. While the mix of market-driven competition and market distorting interventions vary situationally according to plan targets, world market demand and productive capacity, that is, from toys to computers, a developmentalist state may provide cheap finance, fiscal incentives, monopoly rents, below-market cost inputs, technological parks, marketing services, or tariff protection in the domestic market. One recognizes, of course, significant variation in the forms of guidance offered by NIC stages in the literature, ranging from the *chaebol*-centered conglomerates nurtured by the corporativist Korean state to the family-centered firms favored by the Taiwanese state (Deyo, 1987; Hamilton & Biggart, 1988). Nonetheless, the essential characteristic of the NIC model rests upon the negotiated relationship between privately accumulating capitalist firms and target-setting state officials; a seminal relationship that links domestic and export-oriented strategies, so as to increase value-added, raise technical expertise, and maintain global competitiveness. Rhetoric aside, whatever slogans like "Look East" intend to communicate, Malaysian industrial policy must be judged by whether state and business elites do, in fact, institutionalize market augmenting policies and whether state subsidies create an innovative, competitive class of manufacturers or a protected, politically dependent class of rentier capitalists. Now let us first examine the case for Malaysia as a fledgling NIC state and then evaluate the critiques of this rosy interpretation.

The Case for "NICdom"

Supporters of the view that Malaysia has successfully entered the pantheon of "NICdom" argue forcefully that the economy has produced very impressive numbers (MIDA, 1990). Indeed, citing conventional statistical indicators, such as recent economic growth (7%-9%/annum), the weight of manufacturing in GDP (26%), the share of export-oriented to total manufactures (50%) and per capita income ($2,182), the financial press has declared Malaysia a NIC (MacFarquhar, 1980, p. 67; *Far Eastern Economic Review* [FEER], September 7, 1989, p. 96). It is the third largest producer of electronic components, after the United States and Japan, and the world's largest exporter of components that are assembled and tested by mostly American firms in export processing zones (EPZs). Recently, Japanese and NIC direct foreign investment (DFI) has mushroomed in other sectors, especially consumer electronics. Interestingly, explanations for the boom in DFI rest not on the exploitation of cheap labor as underdevelopment theorists like Frobel and Kreye argue, for the price of labor is lower in other ASEAN states (Frobel & Kreye, 1980). In fact, Malaysia suffers from a labor shortage, especially acute among skilled electronics workers. The demand for labor attracts an estimated 700,000 to 1 million illegal workers from the neighboring states of Indonesia, the Philippines, and Thailand to work in plantations and domestic service as well as manufacturing. Rather than cheap labor, Malaysia's DFI boom is driven by the interaction of Malaysia's comparative advantages and wide-ranging structural changes in the Pacific Rim economy: that is, by the appreciation of NIC and Japanese currencies, by new inventory and production systems (just-in-time, or JIT) that require local suppliers, by the loss of NIC access to the U.S. market under the tariff-free quotas of the General System of Preferences (GSP) and, relative to ASEAN rivals, by Malaysia's high standard of industrial infrastructure, political stability, civil service discipline, and human capital resources. Further, it can be argued that Malaysia's traditional raw material and commodity exports are efficiently produced and unusually diverse, that is, tin, rubber, palm products, lumber, cocoa, petroleum, and natural gas. Hence, they bolster EOI manufacturing by paying for the foreign exchange costs of importing capital goods and manufacturing inputs as well as by offering forward linkages to resource-based industries using rubber (gloves, tires), palm products (oleo-refining and cosmetics), wood (furniture), and petroleum and natural gas refining (fertilizers, plastics, and petrochemicals). Fortuitously, recent rises in petroleum prices encouraged Bank Negara to revise upward the estimated growth rate to more than 10% for 1990.

Finally, supporters argue that, like Taiwan and Korea, but unlike its ASEAN neighbors, Malaysia has achieved a comparatively equal distribution of income through the implementation of the New Economic Policy (NEP) in 1971 ("The New Economic Policy," 1989). The latter is a program of truly massive state intervention into Malaysia's economy and society, developed in response to ethnonationalist pressure from Malay capital and the shock from the racial riots of 1969 (Shamsul, 1986). To summarize a complex political and legal process, the NEP (1971) was designed:

(1) to eliminate absolute poverty especially among the Malay peasantry;
(2) to abolish the correlation between occupation and ethnicity through an "affirmative action" program requiring quotas for Malays in education, employment and government contracts; and
(3) to restructure the ownership of corporate equity holdings through state funding of Bumiputera (i.e., Malay and other indigenous peoples) "trust agencies" that purchases and holds equities for the Bumiputera community.

To achieve the last goal, the NEP authorized trust agencies to restructure corporate equity ownership among ethnic groups such that, by 1990, the equity share of Bumiputera would be increased from 1.9 to 30%, other Malaysians (Chinese and Indians) would be increased from 23.5% to 40% and foreigners reduced from 60.7% to 30% (Malaysia, 1973). Not unlike other indigenization of industry laws promulgated elsewhere (i.e., Mexico and Nigeria) during the 1970s, NEP represented a bold effort to increase Malaysian control at the expense of foreign equity holdings, to redistribute income to disadvantaged ethnic and class groups, and to abolish a colonial-origin ethnic division of labor, a cleavage that threatened to destroy Malaysia's multiracial democracy and prospects for economic development. Like all "affirmative action" programs, however, the NEP is neither market augmenting nor efficiency inducing in the short to medium term: instead, supporters argue that it has provided the social peace, analogous to social democracy's dampening of class tensions, that has created the institutional basis for economic growth and political stability since 1971. As an official at the Malaysian Industrial Development Authority (MIDA) bluntly stated in an interview: "The Chinese received political stability from the NEP. Racial turmoil attracts neither foreign nor local investment."

The Case for Structural Weakness

However impressive the Malaysian numbers on economic growth may appear when compared to most other second tier NICs, critics assert that the economy is suffering from deep structural weaknesses. From this perspective, massive state intervention into the economy since 1971 neither replicates the positive features of the NIC model, nor the autonomy of state economic planners, nor the articulated relationship between business and the state, nor, in structural terms, a deeper, innovative, and dynamic process of Malaysian, as opposed to foreign, capital accumulation. Instead of "NIC-dom," they see weaknesses, inefficiency, and enclaves. Impressive short-term growth rates, enclave EOI-manufacturing without linkages to the highly protected import-substitution sector, and dependence on raw material export-earnings confirm the existence of deep structural imbalances that require rationalization along market augmenting lines (Edwards, 1990; Jesudason, 1989; Jomo, 1990). Thus the impressive numbers are temporary and illusory, and certainly insufficient evidence for asserting Malaysia's NIC status. Critics stress that, rather than creating a "market augmenting" alliance between business and political elites, one that is committed to strengthening the technical and competitive position of Malaysian manufacturing capital, state industrial policy is riddled with contradictions, irrationalities, and outright corruption. As opposed to strengthening technocratic guidance toward planned goals, the political elite dominates decision making and undermines the comparatively weak technocracy's efforts to rationalize industrial policy. When compared to the high level of policy centralization found in the NIC states, the technocracy's authority is so fragmented among competing agencies (i.e., Malaysian Industrial Development Authority, Economic Planning Unit, State Economic Development Corporations, Ministry of Trade and Industry, HICOM, PETRONAS, etc.) that rational, market augmenting strategies are difficult to implement, even if the political elite consented. Equally important, the necessary consultation between state and business is neglected in favor of interethnic political bargains—money politics—that, though allegedly justified by the NEP, merely line the pockets of an unproductive rentier bourgeoisie who are beholden to a political patronage system that is legitimated by ethnic chauvinism and thus hostile to the discipline of market competition of any kind (Gomez, 1990, 1991).

Regarding income equality, while absolute poverty has probably been reduced to close to NEP targets, relative income inequality within the Malays and other ethnic groups has, in fact, increased significantly since the NEP. Critics, for example, cite the distribution of share ownership in ASN

(Amanah Saham Nasional), the unit trust share agency, which was allegedly created to broaden share ownership for all Malays. Like all the Bumiputera trust agencies, it lacks accountability to share holders. Moreover, less than a third of eligible Malays participate. Worse still from the point of view of inequality, "about three quarters of those participating have five hundred units [i.e., M$500] or less. At the other extreme, half of one percent of participants owns twenty-five thousand units or more" (Hirschman, 1989, p. 80). Furthermore, Hirschman cites Lim and Sieh's (Hirschman, 1989, p. 10) findings that one hundred or so families own almost half the capital in Malaysian corporations. Twenty years later income inequality has increased especially among the Malays, again in contrast to the NIC income profiles.

To be sure, sorting out this debate lies beyond the space limits of this chapter, but several points can be deduced with same certainty. Malaysia has achieved impressive growth figures in manufacturing and successfully emulated certain aspects of export-oriented manufacturing (EOI) in the EPZs. Unfortunately, the structure of production and the relationship between business and the state bear little relationship to either Taiwan or Korea, which are the appropriate comparative cases (MIDA/UNIDO, 1985). It is true that the older domestic manufacturing industries, that is, the ISI sector, are highly protected, dominated by transnational firms and, more significantly, possesses few linkages with the EOI sector: that is, they lack an organic, interactive relationship that would transform the productivity of both sectors as Amsden argues occurred in Korea (Amsden, 1989; see also Edwards, 1990). Despite the boom in direct foreign investment (DFI) in the EOI sector, value added is comparatively low; linkages to domestic suppliers are weak; and efficiency spin-offs that might raise productivity in the domestic ISI sector are absent. The rapidly expanding consumer electronics and appliance industries, to take a glaring example, use electronic chips and components, but there is no strong supplier linkage to Malaysia's components sector. Nor, for reasons discussed below, are Malaysian firms prominent in existing domestic linkages; rather, NIC and Japanese consumer electronics firms are bringing their own supplier firms. If the past record is predictive, any NIC state would certainly have planned to link these sectors and their domestic capitalists would have been assisted, coerced, and subsidized until they created productive linkages.

Curiously, despite the openness of the economy, Malaysia has created a model marked by an extraordinary degree of state intervention into the economy. Yet strong intervention has not performed effectively as a market augmenter, a guided capitalist, planner nor a technocratic prop for domestic

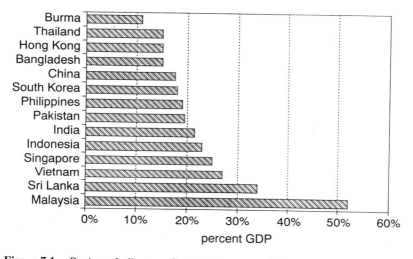

Figure 7.1.   Business Indicators: Central Governments' Expenditures as a Percentage of GDP

SOURCE: *Far Eastern Economic Review,* Hong Komng (1990, November 1, p. 75).

manufacturing capital. In practice, enormous sums have been poured into rural development schemes, heavy industries, Bumiputera loans and NEP trust agencies. Emulation of Korea's heavy industry program (i.e., HICOM) produced a nonfunctioning steel mill and a highly protected automobile, the Proton Saga, which is entirely dependent on Mitsubishi for inputs and management. Observe the astonishing size of Malaysia's central government expenditure relative to GDP presented in Figure 7.1. (Note that the expenditure of Malaysia's 13 states are not included or it would be even higher!) Undoubtedly, when state expenditure represents more than half of GDP, that is, almost three times that of centrally planned China, the propensity for patronage and rentier capitalism expands accordingly. At the same time, Figure 7.1 confirms that the financial resources are available to cover subsidies and set targets, even without foreign aid that was important in the NIC transitions. If a developmentalist state coalition emerged these resources could subsidize Malaysian capital with performance standards, improve efficiency and structural articulation between sectors, and/or enhance societal equity. The scale of these expenditures, together with detailed studies of political party holding companies, noncompetitive public sector contracting, abuses of loan schemes, and banking scandals, simply contradict the requirement that a NIC-developmentalist state be dirigiste, relatively autonomous and technocratic (FEER, November 1, 1990, p. 75; Gomez, 1990; Haggert & Cheng, 1987). Rhetorical claims of "Looking East" notwithstanding, the structure of Malaysia's manufacturing sector and state industrial policy bear only a distant relationship to the NIC states of Korea and Taiwan.

To respond to one of our original questions, it is now clear that the key relationship between technocratic state elites and Malaysian industrialists is aborted by the separation of economic and political power: The Malays control the state apparatus and the Chinese still, even after 20 years of the NEP, dominate the domestic commercial and manufacturing sector. Rather than aligning with the domestic bourgeoisie, the Malay-dominated state elite have, until now, aligned themselves with foreign capital in exchange for directorships, joint ventures, and other passive, essentially rentier rewards, garnered at the expense of Malaysian-controlled accumulation. Virtually all analysts stress that ethnic competition and cultural differences are the root causes of these structural weaknesses in the Malaysian economy. Jesudason, for example, concludes: "Because of Malay group resentment and envy of Chinese economic success, both aggravated by past Chinese exclusivity in their businesses, the Malay leaders strove to control Chinese business development" (Jesudason, 1989, p. 163). Although this descriptive analysis is true, and indeed suggests how difficult it is to replicate the NIC model in ethnically diverse societies elsewhere in Asia, it would be an error to accept, uncritically, an essentialist explanation that assumes that unchanging, primordial cultural differences are indelibly etched on Chinese and Malay personalities; or one that assumes that the numerically predominant Malays are incapable of altering their rentier mode of accumulation as industrialization deepens. How then does one resolve this conundrum?

First, a sufficient explanation of this cleavage requires a historical-structural explanation for the emergence of the ethnic division of labor from the onset of the colonial period. Second, inconsistencies contained within the dominant explanation—that is, the cultural theory of ethnicity that reproduces ethnic stereotypes recounting the backwardness of the Muslim Malays or the discipline of the Confucian Chinese—must be thoroughly demystified (or "deconstructed" to be more fashionable) in order to suggest routes to alternative futures for both groups. Finally, since no condition is permanent under a regime of rapid industrialization, the evidence suggesting a reconsideration of industrial policy by technocratic Malay elites should be factored into our evaluation.

Structural Origins of the
Ethnic Division of Labor

After reading Jesudason's (1989) description of ethnic competition, it might be easy to forget that our units of analysis, that is, the two ethnic groups now competing intensely with each other—Malay and Chinese—are rather recent social constructions of political solidarity in Malaysia. What were the structural forces that defined their present boundaries? Historically, like the German-speakers of nineteenth-century Central Europe, Malay-speaking groups in the Malay states shared many common cultural elements—language, customary law, and especially Islam—before the British unified the Malay states by gradually introducing "indirect rule." Earlier the Malay peoples in question not only recognized different political authorities, but these authorities were often located in Sumatra, Sulawesi, or Thailand. And, of course, competition, dynastic struggles, and war were common among rival Malay states (Andaya & Andaya, 1982). Hence, the territorial form and ethnonational boundary of Malays in contemporary Malaysia is a product of colonial rule and the political imagination of their community leaders (Anderson, 1983, p. 110).

Similarly the Chinese immigrants to Malaysia, though sharing a common *han* cultural identity, belonged to regionally distinct linguistic groups, which were not mutually intelligible. It is not surprising that the Chinese excluded each other from membership in dialect associations (*Pang*) that were formed by migrants initially attracted to the straits settlements by employment and trade, and later to the interior by the profits from the Chinese-organized tin mining industry. Yen describes the Chinese between 1800 and 1911 as "rig-idly divided" by economic competition and because, the leaders "did not foresee a homogenous Chinese society with one dialect, nor did they see the need for such a society" (Yen, 1986, p. 180). The dialect cleavages even "extended to the next world" through different burial grounds that were "intended to separate the spirits of the dead of one *Pang* from an other to whom the dialect would be unintelligible" (Yen, 1986, p. 179). Economic competition between Pangs was so fierce that it ignited a large scale riot in Penang in 1867, involving 35,000 people and lasting 10 days. Hence, history illustrates that the identities of Malaysia's competing ethnic groups are neither natural nor primordial, rather they were invented by leaders who constructed communities in the face of pressures from the world market and later by the constraints imposed by the ethnic division of labor under colonial rule. Is it not possible that new political identities will be constructed as products of rapid industrialization?

In Malaya, as elsewhere, British colonial policy relied on so-called scientific theories of race to organize the social division of labor. Officials assumed each racial and ethnic group possessed inherited predispositions toward performing needed roles in the colonial division of labor, be they martial arts, commerce, wage labor, efficient administration, or subsistence farming. In turn, these beliefs provided the necessary ideological rationalization of colonial Malaya's social order as well as the basis for profitability in the Imperial economic system: The Chinese organized labor and capital to export tin and dominated the intermediary trade between colonial merchant houses and consumers in the interior; the Indians were recruited to work on rubber plantations; and the Malay peasants were encouraged to produce padi rice for local consumption and prevented from planting rubber, a more lucrative crop reserved for plantations and commercial (Chinese) farmers. Alatas (1977) documents the ubiquity of these stereotypes in *The Myth of the Lazy Native,* where he shows how officials constructed a discourse on the docility of the Indians, the indolence and courtesy of the Malay, and the industry and competitiveness of the Chinese. Colonial policy, therefore, not only "consciously sought the ossification of Malay rural society" (Lim, 1984, p. 55), but created an ideology of racial and ethnic stereotypes that "inculcated feelings of superiority and inferiority among, and between, groups" (Abraham, 1983, p. 20). The origins of contemporary ethnic stereotypes lie in the colonial division of labor and in the official discourse on race. Sadly, the subjects still believe the myths and evaluate themselves and others accordingly. Let us examine how the structures of colonial rule inflated ethnic stereotypes and laid the foundation for a weak technocracy and a rentier bourgeoisie.

Structurally, Malaysia's ethnic cleavages emerged from colonial policies that buttressed the Muslim aristocracy on one hand, and crushed economic opportunities for the rural Malays from the commoner strata on the other hand. This is not to argue that the Chinese and Malay were matched equally in the ways of the modern, commercial economy prior to tin mining and British intervention, though a Malay trading class existed in the sixteenth century only to be destroyed by the advance of the Portuguese and Dutch empires. To be sure, originating as self-selected migrants from the highly commercialized regions of southern China, Chinese traders and workers were better positioned than the Malays to garner economic advantages from the colonial economy. Note that these are structural and organizational experiences not dependent solely on cultural values. Worse still for the majority of Malays, British colonial policy not only discouraged Malay rubber producers but introduced a land reservation policy (1913) that deliberately blocked Malay land sales to non-Malays, thus driving down land values by as much as 50% and reducing their creditworthiness (Lim, 1984). Hence, to institutionalize social stability under indirect rule, Malay education was thwarted; immigrants were recruited for clerical and technical positions; and Malay peasants were encouraged to plant low-value food crops without the technical agro-services that the British provided for the plantation sector and, for comparison with the NICs, that the Japanese provided for the peasantry of Taiwan and Korea. All of these policies heightened economic backwardness among the nonaristocratic Malays, thus preventing them from participating in the modern, urban, and commercial sector (Roff, 1967).

Aristocratic Allies
and Rentier Politics

The contrast with Japanese agrarian policy in colonial Taiwan and Korea underscores how indirect rule contributed to the economic backwardness of the Malay and the "rentier" economic orientation of the Malay political elite. However brutally administered in Taiwan and Korea, Japanese agrarian policy was economically progressive in that they expropriated large landlords, transformed the technology of agrarian production and rationalized landlord-tenant relations such that output increased dramatically so that it could be taxed accordingly (Amsden, 1985). Paternalistic indirect rule, informed by Western "orientalism," committed the British to supporting the ruling groups' right to administer customary law and the Islamic religion. Thus the British wedded the power of the colonial state to the decaying cultural authority of a backward feudal ruling class and, because of the organizational and technical superiority of the colonial state, actually strengthened the aristocracy's capacity to exploit their subjects through taxation, licenses, corruption and, above all, indirect control over land title transactions. As salaried officials who dominated recruitment to the civil service, the ruling groups had privileged access to state economic affairs like allocating mining concessions, the purchase of Malay-reserved land, and access to higher education. Talib's study of Trengganu documents the increasing economic insecurity of the peasantry at the same time as the "the new salaried class, by virtue of its political position and social connections, was able to maintain its continued interests in land even after the collapse of its former forms of domination" (Talib, 1984, p. 225).

Structurally, it is readily apparent that today's weak administrative state elite and the rentier bourgeoisie are the immediate progeny of indirect rule. The aristocrats became colonial civil servants; later they formed the leadership of United Malays National Organization (UMNO) as well as providing the first three prime ministers; and now they straddle the public and private spheres as company directors, trust managers, and heads of public corporations. It is for good reason they are labeled the "administocracy" (Jomo, 1986). Hence, the Malay bourgeoisie is weak, relative to the political-administrative class, in large part because "indirect rule" spawned a powerful rentier political class, one yet to be challenged and all too comfortably ensconced within the state. They remain the dominant class. Emerging from colonialism with all the titles and regalia of a nonproductive ruling class, it never felt the competitive pressure nor the financial necessity to pursue commercial and industrial capital accumulation. Initially, the latter role was allocated to the Chinese who formed an alliance with UNMO. Since the NEP, however, aspiring Malay capitalists must rely on the distribution of patronage from the political class whose control over state administration—from Kuala Lumpur to the remotest village—is crucial for obtaining access to wealth or capital (Shamsul, 1986). Even though the NEP expanded the economic power of the political class and opened its ranks to nonaristocrats like Finance Minister Daim bin Zainuddin, the pattern of rentier accumulation established during colonial-rule remains unchanged and, effectively, unchallenged. Interestingly, those among the Malay who became legitimate capitalists have tended to originate from "alien Malay" (Arabs, Indians, and Indonesians) who, though typically Muslim, could not follow the path of the administocracy (Jomo, 1986). This suggests that inherited structures of political domination, not the cultural attributes of the Muslim Malay, are responsible for the weak state technocratic impulse and indirectly for the ethnic division of labor that depended on bargaining among the ethnically based elites. Finally, to return to our comparison with Taiwan and Korea, whereas the American sponsored land reform in those countries abolished the political and cultural power of landlords as a class, essentially finishing what Japanese colonialism began, the contemporary Malaysian situation is just the opposite. The aristocracy retains juridical, political and economic power as a status group with large landholdings, great political influence on state government, and enormous informal influence in the countryside. Since the constitution defines Islam as the official state religion, cultural power is also retained: Each state's Islamic ruler is the enforcer of Islamic law over his Muslim subjects. All of which should be factored in when evaluating obstacles to replicating the NIC model in states like Malaysia.

Ethnic Essentialism or
State Industrial Policy?

If, as argued above, colonial structures were responsible for institutionalizing an ethnic division of labor, nurturing a rentier aristocratic cum administrative class, and blocking avenues of capitalist development for the commoner Malays, how can one explain the persistence of the ethnic division of labor since implementation of the NEP? To be sure, the NEP has thrust the Malay forward as managers, state administrators, professionals, merchants, and to some degree as industrialists. Yet, the problem of industrial linkages remains: Why have neither the Malays nor the Chinese entered manufacturing vigorously so as to develop the network of linkages necessary for the rapidly expanding manufacturing sector? It should be stressed that, while the Malay elite dominates the state apparatus and the coalition government, allied Chinese and Indian elites also share in the distribution of rentier patronage. And given the vast resources expended it is not surprising that the Malay-dominated state has created a Malay bourgeoisie, one largely limited to finance, property and construction, yet weak in manufacturing and generally dependent on state patronage. What, then, explains the weakness of Malay and, to a lesser degree, Chinese industrialists? Jesudason, writing sympathetically to the plight of Chinese business under the NEP, offers two "general reasons" for the failure of Malay businesses:

(1) the failure of Malays to develop the Weberian equivalent of a methodical rational approach to accumulation, and

(2) the very nature of state policies toward Malay business development. (Jesudason, 1989, p. 104)

Let us examine the assumptions and the implications of the first reason. Reference to the search for the "Weberian equivalent" of the Protestant ethic has an almost intoxicating appeal to cultural theorists such as MacFarquhar who hypothesize that a post-Confucian cultural orientation (i.e., family discipline, respect for authority, frugality, etc.) explains why East Asian capitalism has flourished (MacFarquhar, 1980). In his search for the essential culture of capitalism, Peter Berger notes with understandable irony that Weberians in the 1950s argued just the opposite: Confucianism was seen as an obstacle to capitalist development (Berger, 1986; Levy & Shih, 1949). Yet, even though he agrees that Weber was wrong about the potential of Asian capitalism, Berger remains convinced "that, as evidence continues to come in, this hypothesis will be supported" (Berger, 1988, p. 7). If a cultural ethos like Confucianism can be interpreted as an obstacle during one period and later as a "comparative advantage," then it is difficult to reconcile it as a viable independent variable. Instead, this anomaly suggests that any positive effect Confucianism may have on economic development is contingent on a third, probably structural factor, such as an organized-institutional framework or a particular class coalition.

Since all cultural traditions contain valuable moral lessons about honesty, discipline, and authority, often mutually quite contradictory, one supposes that anyone committed to a cultural explanation can, with some diligence, discover a tradition or verse from a sacred text to make the causal connection—from cultural value to observed behaviors—once a state achieves industrialization. Pursuing this line of reasoning, therefore, it is noteworthy that, despite their rich Confucian cultural endowment, Malaysian Chinese businesses have not performed their assigned role as the innovative, manufacturing capitalist as their Confucian counterparts have done elsewhere, or at very least not sufficiently to resolve Malaysia's manufacturing linkage problems. Furthermore, divisions between small-, medium-, and large-scale Chinese capital are significant. Because the major Chinese capitalists are allied with UNMO in a coalition government, they have shared in the same rentier forms of accumulation as the Malay (Gomez, 1991). Jesudason notes that they avoided long term risks by shifting investment away from productive manufacturing to "commercial property and residential housing"; thus "large firms were relatively unhurt by the NEP" (Jesudason, 1989, p. 163). Similarly, Yoshihara argues that the more disciplined Chinese capitalists became "contaminated" by the political networking and rent-seeking practiced by well-connected Malay political actors.

> This in turn affected the business ethics of Chinese capitalists. By working closely with Malay capitalist or Malay politicians, it became possible to make a large sum of money—an accomplishment that would take decades for the most successful Chinese capitalists before the NEP. (Yoshihara, 1988, p. 91)

Hence, Malaysia's structural weaknesses in indigenous manufacturing investment are not easily attributable to the essentialist ethnic attributes of either Malays or Chinese. Rather state industrial policy, or perhaps the lack of one, appears most significant.

Before discussing alternative strategies let us return to Jesudason's (1989) observation that Malays lack the Weberian equivalent of a disciplined, rational approach to accumulation, an obvious essentialist assertion about Malay culture. Writing on this same issue, Morishima argues in the Japanese case that Confucian ethics borrowed from China were reinterpreted in order to support the national goal of industrialization and political independence. Though starting from the same text, "as a result of different study and interpretation [it] produced in Japan a totally different national ethos" (Morishima, 1982, p. 3). A new interpretation combined with a new authority structure capable of institutionalizing new production norms, therefore, explains the success of industrialization in all of the Confucian societies: Japan, Taiwan, and Korea. Success, therefore, requires the combination of two changes: first, a reinterpretation of texts or values, and second, a new organizational structure of authority to institutionalize them. Organized power must exist before the reinterpreted texts may exert their influence.

Leaving aside the issue of organizational structure for a moment, it is readily apparent in the Malay case that any new interpretative framework encouraging methodical, rational accumulation in Weberian terms, that is, as an ethical orientation toward the world, is unlikely to arise solely from rural-origin Malay culture. Why not? Note first that the Malaysian constitution, which describes the special rights of the Malay, defines Malays as practicing Muslims. To reject Islam formally means risking forfeiture of those special rights. Demographically, Malays now constitute the largest urban ethnic group with the highest population growth rate whose rate of urbanization will surpass 50% in the early 1990s. Therefore, just as backward colonial structures created the prototypical rural Malay identity during the period of indirect rule, the rapid rates of urbanization and industrial participation are constructing the material basis for a new urban Malay identity. Not surprisingly, both the social discourse and social boundaries defining the modern urban Malay identity are framed in terms of Islamic texts and values, and not in terms of regionally based Malay equivalents. Hence, it is readily apparent that any reinterpretation of texts underlying a new authority orientation toward accumulation must come from a reinterpretation of the Islamic discourse on development and accumulation. Writing on the modern Islamic resurgence, Muzaffar concludes:

> More than language or any other facet of culture, Islam expresses Bumiputra, or more accurately, *Malay* identity in a manner that has no parallel. Islam touches the life of a Malay at a thousand points. (Muzaffar, 1987, pp. 24-25)

Space does not permit a detailed discussion of the numerous Islamic movements in Malaysia, but it is noteworthy that since independence the most significant opposition to the UNMO alliance has come from the PAS, the Islamic party; that the Islamic student movement's leader was co-opted by UMNO as education minister; and that, in response to the resurgence, the political administrative class has promoted some of the Islamic agenda. Furthermore, since the "reinterpretation" of texts for national development, cited as a prerequisite by Morishima (1982), is already a major intellectual industry among the world's Muslims, it is exceedingly likely that as inequality rises among Malays and the effects of the rentier system of accumulation are challenged, the Islamic discourse on development will be reinterpreted to construct a new authority structure; one designed to rationalize disciplined accumulation. Finally, just like his analysis of Confucianism and capitalism, numerous studies have shown the Weberian analysis of Islam to be false. Paradoxically, Islamization is, in fact, associated elsewhere with the rise of merchant capitalism, for example, Nigeria and in West Africa; and Islamic sects like the Mozabites and Tijaniyyis have reinterpreted Islamic texts so as to associate religiosity with success in the material world, personal frugality and the disciplined accumulation of capital (Abun-Nasr, 1965; Bordieu, 1962; Rodinson, 1978).

Thus it is textually possible for Islam to provide Morishima's reinterpretation of texts for potential Malay manufacturers. But even if this occurred, would it resolve the problems described by Jesudason (19889)? True, redefining *Malay* will not eliminate ethnic cleavages nor ethnic competition. Potentially for the Malays, it could "develop the Weberian equivalent of a methodical, rational approach to accumulation," and thus a sense of much needed confidence. Finally, instead of generating an orientation of clientelism and ethnic rent-seeking, it raises the potential for a cultural orientation toward industrial investment that is universalistic toward community members as well as consistent normatively toward others. And this would surely be a superior ethical orientation toward the material world than that of the present ethnic patronage system.

Regarding ethnic attributes, therefore, the evidence suggests that rentier and nonproductive forms of investment are very common among both the Chinese and the Malays. Ideally, while it is advantageous to possess a highly commercialized, historically deep, ethnic culture, emphasizing discipline, frugality, and reverence for education, culture alone is insufficient without an institutionalized authority relationship between state and business elites. Twenty years after the NEP, there is a new Malaysian dilemma. Armed by the sweeping authority of the NEP, as well as industry licensing laws like the Industrial Coordination Act, the political-administrative class has achieved hegemony over the Malaysian economy. Unlike the situation of 1970, this class now possesses enormous discretionary powers to approve or disapprove projects, to license intermediate industries, and to capitalize aspiring entrepreneurs, a combination that enables it to mediate most economic relations in Malaysia. What has been the result of the increased relative autonomy of the political-administrative class? On one hand, their policies have frightened away Chinese investments in productive manufacturing linkages, while, on the other hand, the hegemonic class has failed to create a disciplined class of industrialists from among their Malay clients in spite of truly staggering expenditures. Hence, without the confidence of the Chinese industrialists or a confident Malay class of industrialists, Malaysia is forced to rely on foreign investment to achieve those rosy numbers in its manufacturing sector, with all the attendant structural weaknesses.

Toward Structural Reform: The Search for Technocratic Guidance

Given the reality of structural weaknesses in the manufacturing sector, let us conclude by examining the potential for reform represented by the technocracy in the next decade. It is reasonable to assume that ethnic segmentation will remain part of the Malaysian social structure. And because of higher birthrates, the assimilation of Muslims into the Bumiputera, and higher outmigration rates for minorities, the proportion of Bumiputera will rise significantly, probably reaching two thirds of Malaysia's population in the 1990s. It follows that the Malays will continue to exercise control over the state and the economic technocracy. Given the assumption of Malay political dominance, what are the forces that might combine to rationalize state industrial policy in the direction of NIC-like market augmenting strategies, greater domestic investment in linkages, and higher value-added manufacturing?

The inexorable demographic shift toward the Malays coupled with rising income inequality raises the question of whether ethnically based redistribution policies at the core of the NEP can be sustained indefinitely. As the Malay political class becomes increasingly responsible for economic and investment policy and as the Malay rentier bourgeoisie becomes more visible within the economic elite, there will be proportionately less to redistribute to the Malay from others; and, at the level of communal party politics, there will be less plausibility in scapegoating the Chinese for Malaysia's economic problems and structural weaknesses. Recent electoral outcomes reflect these strains already. Ultimately, the lack of competitiveness and low rate of return from both state sponsored and subsidized Malay investments, aggravated by competitive pressures from the international economy, will force factions within the political elite to reform industrial policy. Whatever the outcome of this struggle, the Malay technocracy must play a powerful role in any reformulation.

One of the successes of the NEP has been the creation of a Malay technocratic, professional, and managerial class, one that is increasingly critical of the irrationality and failures imbedded in the present model of accumulation. Mindful of the reconsideration of NEP, which expires in 1991, Malay policymakers both within and outside the state have floated reform packages. Surprisingly, though often described as a think-tank for the Malay establishment, the Malaysian Institute of Economic Research (MIER) recently indicted the NEP for failing to alter the prevailing pattern of Bumiputera underrepresentation in the "commercial and industrial sector," for creating a "rentier entrepreneurial class" and for "the institutionalization of mediocrity" (Salih, 1988, pp. 2-3). Commenting on the future, MIER warned the Malay elite:

> The high degree of dependency created by government-supported programs and politicization of educational goals may also contribute to a closing of the Malay mind, and induce a heightened degree of ethnic polarization that will leave the young[er] generation confused and unprepared for the demands and competition of the twenty-first century. (Salih, 1988, p. 3)

Subsequently, a reformation of the NEP was proposed in a paper coauthored by the director of MIER and a colleague who is now an economic advisor to the Malaysian central bank. Again, they argue for greater competition, reduction in income inequality "regardless of race" and higher rates of "efficiency, innovation, technology and skills." Inattention to the latter, according to their analysis, "shows how much the problems of wastage, inefficient management and shortcomings in skill and manpower, and technological development need to be addressed in . . . the post-1990 economic policy" (Salih & Yusof, 1989, p. 23). Continuing, they dismiss the effort to create a Bumiputera commercial and industrial class by subsidy and patronage as a failure. Hence for these reasons, they argue against the current NEP policy of forced restructuring of corporate equities in Chinese firms (i.e., 30% Bumiputera), acknowledging that forced restructuring of Chinese and others has deterred investment and promoted rentier forms of accumulation (i.e., Ali Baba arrangements). Instead, they argue that fiscal incentives should be used to encourage Bumiputera equity sharing; that Bumiputera ownership of equity should not be a criteria for the establishment or expansion of an enterprise; that take-over actions by Bumiputera trust agencies be limited so that priority can be given to improving the efficiency and productivity of enterprises in which the trust agencies have an ownership stake (Salih & Yusof, 1989, p. 59). Overall, the thrust of their recommendations argue against state intervention on behalf of Malay rentiers and in favor of increasing productivity by forcing the Bumiputera managers, investors, and manufacturers to meet performance standards based upon efficiency. Undoubtedly, just as in other statist economies, there is an intense debate among Malays over the cost and benefit of the rentier model, the question remains whether the technocratic groups will prevail over the political elite that trades on redistribution of rent-seeking opportunities.

Finally, it should be noted that state technocrats charged with monitoring foreign investment and encouraging domestic linkages are also concerned with the irrationalities arising from current state industrial policy. Let us return to the problem of linkages in the booming electronics and electrical sector. Rasiah's work on the electronic components sector shows clearly that linkage and supplier firms have emerged in the Penang region mostly because of competition among international firms, support from the Penang Development Corporation and a ready supply of mostly Chinese small-scale industrialists (Rasiah, 1990). Modest linkage effects were achieved in spite of the relative indifference of the responsible Malaysian (federal) state agencies, largely because most are not Bumiputera owned and managed. Hence, the potential is there but the candidates are Chinese and Indian. If Salih and Yusof's recommendations about equity restructuring were followed, manufacturing linkages would increase immensely. It is important to note that many technocrats who were interviewed about such irrationalities were aware and voiced support of the reforms proposed by Salih and Yusof.

Finally, structural changes in the Pacific Rim economy have brought changes in foreign investment patterns especially in the booming electronics sector. Instead of originating solely from OECD states, much of the new investment arrives from the NICs, especially Taiwan, Singapore and Hong Kong. Taiwan was the largest foreign investor in 1989 and represented 42% of approved applications in the first nine months of 1990 (*The Star,* 1990). Part of Malaysia's attractiveness arises from Malaysia's Chinese-language schools that enable firms to recruit high quality managers and skilled labor. Since foreign firms that export are exempted from NEP equity restructuring regulations and since state planners must generate employment for the urbanizing Malays, foreign Chinese presence in Malaysia's industrial profile is increasing even in small- to medium-scale industries that supply the NIC firms. Hence, state policymakers have expressed concern during interviews that because NEP equity requirements and other regulations (i.e., ICA) discourage Malaysian Chinese from developing supplier firms but encourage foreign (often Chinese) firms to bring their own suppliers, the state is unintentionally *denationalizing* those very industries that could ameliorate the acknowledged structural weaknesses in the Malaysian manufacturing sector. These are some of the most blatant irrationalities that bedevil industrial policymakers. It is readily apparent that some members of the technocracy are debating policy reforms that would encourage linkage industries regardless of ethnicity. Whether they are capable of overcoming the resistance of political elites remains the pivotal question for industrial policy in the next decade.

References

Abraham, R. (1983). Racial and ethnic manipulation in colonial Malay. *Racial and Ethnic Studies, 6*(1).

Abun-Nasr, J. (1965). *The Tijaniyya.* London: Oxford University Press.

Alatas, S. (1977). *The myth of the lazy native.* London: Frank Cass.

Amsden, A. H. (1985). The state and Taiwan's economic development. In P. Evans, D. Rueschmeyer, & T. Skocpol (Eds.), *Bringing the state back in.* New York: Cambridge University Press.

Amsden, A. H. (1989). *Asia's next giant.* New York: Oxford University Press.

Andaya, B., & Andaya, L. (1982). *A history of Malaysia.* London: Macmillan

Anderson, Benedict. (1983). *Imagined communities: Reflections on the origins and spread of nationalism.* London: Verso.

Berger, P. (1986). *The capitalist revolution.* New York: Basic Books.

Berger, P. (1988). "An East Asian development model?" In P. Berger & Michael H. Hsin-Huang (Eds.), *In search of an East Asian development model.* New Brunswick, NJ: Transaction Books.

Bordieu, P. (1962). *The Algeriens.* Boston: Beacon Press.

Deyo, F. C. (Ed.). (1987). *The political economy of the new Asian industrialism.* Ithaca, NY: Cornell University Press.

Edquist, C., & Jacobsson, S. (1988). *Flexible automation: The global diffusion of new technology in the engineering industry.* New York: Blackwell.

Edwards, C. (1990). *Malaysian industrial policy in the 1990's.* Norwich, UK: University of East Anglia, School of Development Studies.

Far Eastern Economic Review. (various issues)

Frobel, F., & Kreye, O. (1980). *The new international division of labor.* Cambridge: Cambridge University Press.

Gershenkron, A. (1982). *Economic backwardness in historical perspective.* Cambridge, MA: Harvard University Press.

Gomez. T. (1990). *Politics in business: UMNO's corporate investments.* Petaling Jaya: Forum.

Gomez, T. (1991). *Money politics in the Barisan Nasional.* Petaling Jaya: Forum.

Gullick, John, & Gale, Bruce. (1986). *Malaysia: Its political and economic development.* Selangor, Malaysia: Pelanduk Publications.

Haggert, S., & Cheng, Tun-Jen. (1987). State and foreign capital in East Asian NICs. In F. Deyo (Ed.), *The political economy of the new Asian industrialism.* Ithaca, NY: Cornell University Press.

Hamilton, G., & Biggart, N. (1988). Market, culture and authority: A comparative analysis of management and organization in the Far East. *American Journal of Sociology, 94*(Suppl.), pp. 552-594.

Hing Ai Yun. (1984). Capitalist development, class and race. In S. Husein Ali (Ed.), *Ethnicity, class, and development.* Kuala Lumpur: University Malaysia, Persatuan Sains Social Malaysia.

Hirschman, C. (1989). Development and inequality in Malaysia. *Pacific Affairs, 62*(1), pp. 72-81.

Hoffman, Kurt. (1985). Microelectronics, international competition and development strategies. *World Development (special issue), 13*(3).

Horowitz, Donald. (1985). *Ethnic groups in conflict.* Berkeley: University of California Press.

Jesudason, J. (1989). *Ethnicity and the economy: The state, Chinese business, and multinationals in Malaysia.* Singapore: Oxford University Press.

Johnson, C. (1982). *MITI and the Japanese miracle.* Stanford, CA: Stanford University Press.

Johnson, C. (1987). Political institutions and economic performance: The government-business relationship in Japan, South Korea, and Taiwan. In F. Deyo (Ed.), *The political economy of the new Asian industrialism.* Ithaca, NY: Cornell University Press.

Jomo, K. (1986). *A question of class.* Singapore: Oxford University Press.

Jomo, K. (1990). *Growth and structural change in the Malaysian economy.* London: Macmillan.

Lim Teck Ghee. (1984, December). British colonial administration and the "ethnic division of labor" in Malaya. *Kajian Malaysia: Journal of Malaysian Studies, 3*(2).

Levy, M., & Shih, Kuo-Heng. (1949). *The rise of the modern Chinese business class.* New York: Institute of Pacific Relations.

Luedde-Neurath, Richard. (1984, April). State intervention and foreign direct investment in South Korea. *IDS Bulletin, 15*(2).

MacFarquhar, R. (1980, February 9). The post-Confucian challenge. *The Economist,* pp. 67-72.

Malaysia. (1973). *Mid-term review of the Second Malaysia Plan, 1971-1975.* Kuala Lumpur: The Government Printer.

MIDA. (1990). *Statistical information* (various). Kuala Lumpur: MIDA.

MIDA/UNIDO. (1985). Electronics and electrical industry. *Industrial master plan, Malaysia, 1986-1995. Vol. 2, part 8.* Kuala Lumpur: MIDA.

Morishima, M. (1982). *Why has Japan "succeeded"?* Cambridge, UK: Cambridge University Press.

Muzaffar, C. (1987). *Islamic resurgence in Malaysia.* Petaling Jaya: Penerbit Fajar Bakti.

Rasiah, Rajah. (1990). *The electronics industry in Malaysia: Implications for neo-classical and neo-Marxist theories.* Post Graduate Research Seminar Series (unpublished). Cambridge, UK: University of Cambridge, Faculty of Economics and Politics.

Rodinson, M. (1978). *Islam and capitalism.* Austin: University of Texas Press.

Roff, William. (1967). *The origins of Malay nationalism.* New Haven, CT: Yale University Press.

Salih, K. (1988). *The new economic policy after 1990* (Mier Discussion Papers, No. 21). Kuala Lumpur: MIER.

Salih, K., & Yusof, Z. (1989). Overview of the new economic policy and framework for the post-1990 economic policy. *Malaysian Management Review, 24*(2), 13-61.

Shamsul, A. (1986). *From British to Bumiputera rule.* Singapore: Oxford University Press.

The Star. (Kuala Lumpur). (1990, October 7).

Talib, S. (1984). *After its own image.* Singapore: Singapore University Press.

The new economic policy: Where now? (On equity and equitability.) (1989, August 1-15). *Malaysian Business.*

White, G. (Ed.). (1988). *Developmental states in Asia.* New York: St. Martin's.

White, G., & Wade, R. (1988). Developmental states and markets in East Asia. In G. White (Ed.), *Developmental states in East Asia.* New York: St. Martin's.

Yen, Ching-hwang. (1986). *A social history of the Chinese in Singapore and Malaya.* Singapore: Oxford University Press.

Yoshihara, K. (1988). *The rise of ersatz capitalism in South-east Asia.* Singapore: Oxford University Press.

8

The Japanese State and Economic Development
A PROFILE OF A NATIONALIST-PATERNALIST CAPITALIST STATE

HARUHIRO FUKUI

The main purpose of this chapter is to discuss selected aspects of the economic development of modern Japan in order to illustrate and highlight the role of the state as the designer and propagator, and private enterprise as the main beneficiary of an ideology conducive to rapid economic growth at certain developmental stages of a national economy. Like all other ideologies, this ideology is a complex of a number of dogmas, but nationalism and corporatism are the two that are most directly relevant to my explanation of the ideology's impacts on economic developments in modern Japan.

I shall first discuss the origins and evolution of the ideology in post-Tokugawa and pre-World War II Japan, then trace its transformation and impacts on the development of the postwar Japanese economy, and finally touch on recent political-economic changes and their implications for the future of Japanese capitalism in general and its ideological basis in particular. The discussion will demonstrate that capitalism has triumphed in modern Japan, in postwar Japan in particular. This, however, is an unorthodox and deviant species of capitalism that, unlike the orthodox capitalism defined and conceptualized by Marxists, rejects class interests as the legitimate, not to mention the sole, basis of social action and political organization. Its success therefore has more to tell us about the performance of a deviant and heretical variant of late-developer capitalism than about the performance of capitalism as such. My discussion will show that, if effectively inculcated in a literate and skilled work force and supported by an appropriate state and corporate institutions, an anticlass ideology that emphasizes national unity, corporate solidarity, and collective achievement serves the goal of rapid economic development very well.

The Pre-World War II Japanese State and Economic Development

Born in the mid-nineteenth century revolution known as the Meiji Restoration, modern Japan was founded as a state intensely nationalistic in its ideology and paternalistic in its view of domestic society and economy. It evolved during the next 70 years with remarkably little fundamental change either in its ideology or in its behavior. The nationalist/paternalist orientation of the state is owed both to the special circumstances of the revolution and to the special character of the leadership that dominated the post-Tokugawa state.

The special circumstances include both external and internal developments: that is, the growing threat to Japan's territorial integrity and political independence posed by advancing Western colonialism, the apparent inability of the Tokugawa shogunate to cope effectively with that threat, and the increasing disunity and conflict among the Japanese themselves (Saitō, 1981; Tanaka, 1976).[1] Gripped by a deepening sense of national crisis caused by these developments, bands of younger and lower-ranking samurai in outlying domains in southwestern Japan successfully revolted to build a new state in a mold reflecting their preoccupations and commitments. These preoccupations and commitments in turn reflected their underprivileged samurai backgrounds as well as the nature of the national crisis as perceived by them.

The majority of low-ranking samurai in Tokugawa Japan constituted a propertyless salaried class who performed mainly petty clerical duties in the service of either the Tokugawa shogunate or local domain (han) governments (Kimura, 1967, pp. 77-195; Omachi, 1970). They thus held a status distinct from and higher than those of farmers, artisans, and merchants. This status distinction was rigidly maintained until the end of the Tokugawa period even as a small but vigorous and thriving bourgeois class emerged in the major cities, notably Edo (later renamed Tokyo) and Osaka (Crawcour, 1965, pp. 17-44; Fujino, 1961, pp. 285-310, 459-492; Fukai, 1980, pp.148-194; Wakita, 1980, pp. 77-92). As the band of revolutionaries from the lower samurai ranks toppled the feudal regime and began to build a new state in the mid-nineteenth century amidst a national crisis, they were determined to ensure Japan's independence and integrity by rapid industrialization to build "a rich nation with a strong army" (*fukoku kyōhei*). Consistent, however, with the traditional distinction between the ruling samurai as managers and the ruled farmers, artisans, and merchants as producers, the new leaders of Meiji Japan attempted to achieve their goals by indirectly nurturing and managing, rather than directly running, new and old industries. During the first post-Tokugawa decade the new Meiji state set up and directly managed, at substantial financial losses in most cases, a number of mining and manufacturing operations, notably coal and silver mines, silk reeling and cotton spinning mills, shipyards, and cement factories (Asai, 1980, pp. 231-232; Smith, 1955). Most of them, however, were sold to a few select businessmen in the 1880s and, until the late 1930s, the state by and large limited its own role to indirectly nurturing private businesses in selected areas by tax breaks, subsidies, tariffs, and so forth.

Thus emerged a distinctively *nationalist/paternalist* state that was to survive the enormous changes in its internal and external environments in the next century, including a series of wars culminating in World War II. This was a state that would, by its very nature, promote domestic harmony, consensus, and unity, and suppress dissensus and conflict. It tried to ensure national unity, on the one hand, by the manipulation of the emperor cult—that is, the myth that the emperor was divine, and imperial rule eternal and inviolable—and, on the other, by ruthless suppression of ideas and ideologies that challenged the orthodoxy. Class theory in general and Marxist class theory in particular was especially offensive to the leaders of this state. Even more offensive and dangerous were actual industrial actions by workers and revolts by farmers inspired by such theory. The appearance of the first Japanese labor union in 1897 was met by the enactment of the Peace and Security Police Law in 1900, while a temporary resurgence of the labor movement in the wake of the Russo-Japanese War (1904-1905) was stalled by the brutal repression that followed the apprehension and prosecution in 1910-1911 of two dozen leaders of its radical wing on the charge of an assassination plot against the emperor (Tsujinaka, 1971). The anticlass and antilabor thrust of the Peace and Security Police Law was substantially sharpened in the Peace and Security Maintenance Law that replaced it in 1924. At the peak of the organized labor movement in pre-World War II Japan in the early 1930s, less than 8% of Japan's total industrial work force was unionized (Sheldon, 1987, p. 256).

Political parties espousing class theory were punished even more harshly. The Meiji state permitted the formation and activities of loyal political parties as early as the mid-1870s, that is, a decade and a half before the Constitution of the Japanese Empire was promulgated (1889), and a bicameral and partially elective parliament, the Imperial Diet, was instituted (1890). In fact, party government by loyal and conservative parties was accepted as the "normal" form of government by the turn of the century and remained so until the early 1930s, when it began to be increasingly overshadowed, but never totally replaced, by military government (Berger, 1988, pp. 97-153; Masumi, 1965-1980; Scalapino, 1967a). Parties espousing class theory, however, were an altogether different story. Japan's first left-wing party of a few hundred members, the Oriental Socialist Party, was banned within two months of its founding in 1882. Several socialist parties were nominally formed during the first two decades of the twentieth century, but each was banned within between two days and one year (Ōta, 1971; Yamakawa, 1979). The Japan Communist Party founded in 1922 met a particularly brutal response from the wary and nervous state: It was immediately declared illegal and thereafter subjected to constant police surveillance, harassment, and arrest and imprisonment of its leaders until its ranks, modest from the beginning, were virtually decimated by the mid-1930s (Koyama, 1967; Scalapino, 1967b).

At the same time, however, the Japanese government also followed, to a limited extent, precedents set by European, notably German, governments and attempted to bring about peace and harmony in industrial relations by providing a modicum of legal and economic protection for employees. The Factory Law enacted in 1911, for example, banned employment of children under the age of 12 and night work by women and minors and limited the workday to 12 hours (Mori, 1979, pp. 89-94, 126-134). The government also tolerated labor organizations, such as the Friendship Society (Yūaikai, 1912-1919), that showed willingness to cooperate with management, rather than advocating class ideology (Kobayashi, 1986, pp. 9-10; Suehiro, 1959, pp. 46-47). By the early 1920s, the Factory Law had been revised and several new laws enacted, with the blessing and assistance of the Home Ministry's newly created Bureau of Social Affairs, to provide better protection of employees' health and welfare (Ikeda, 1982, pp. 7-9, 23-30). By this time, corporatism had become a prominent feature of Japanese management's approach to docile and loyal labor, while, with the help of the state, it ruthlessly suppressed left-wing unions.

The leaders of the Meiji state were more circumspect from the beginning in responding to recurrent, and often violent, disputes between rural landlords and tenant farmers than in dealing with militant labor unions. During the Tokugawa period the ownership of land was a privilege reserved to the Tokugawa shogunate, the lords of the 300 or so feudal domains, and a small number of wealthy farmers (Fujino, 1961, pp. 333-400). The Meiji state, however, granted landownership to ordinary farmers in return for the payment of newly instituted land taxes and this led to the emergence of a substantial rural landlord class and its even more substantial but impoverished twin, a class of tenant cultivators. This bifurcation of the rural population in turn led to a series of often violent disputes between landlords and their tenants and, by the early 1920s, to the emergence of a militant national tenant organization. The government attempted, ultimately with considerable success, to defuse the rural conflicts and tension essentially by nurturing owner-cultivators ("middling farmers") with both modest material incentives—subsidies for irrigations works, expanded extension service, construction of agricultural schools, and so forth—and then controlling them through a network of government-sponsored rural organizations (Fujino, 1961; Tabata, 1981, pp. 15-27).

By far the most significant and successful means used by the prewar Japanese state to promote domestic harmony and national unity was, however, systematic indoctrination of the youth in a mixture of the Shintoist emperor cult and the Confucian ideology of loyalty to the state and its existing institutions. Shinto was originally just a variant of simple and primitive shamanistic animism common among rice farmers of monsoon Asia with its characteristic belief in ubiquitous spirits and ancestor worship. In late Tokugawa Japan, however, the animism was transformed, by a small group of nationalist scholars known as the Mito School, into an elaborate theology of a divine nation eternally ruled, or to be ruled, by a succession of emperors who descended directly from the Sun Goddess and who were themselves gods in human guise (Gotō, 1988, pp. 21, 32-40). This theology was further refined and exploited by the early nineteenth century nationalist revolutionaries, first, to bring down the Tokugawa shogunate and "restore" a 16-year-old boy emperor to his heaven-ordained rulership and, then, to unite and mobilize the entire nation in a frantic drive to build a "rich country with a strong army" (*fukoku kyōhei*) under the new government. Within a few years of the revolution, a number of new Shinto shrines were built around the country, all shrines in the nation were then systematically ranked, and Shinto rites regulated by law (Murakami, 1982, pp. 22-26). In short, Shinto became Japan's official state religion. Beginning in 1906, moreover, many of the 190,000 or so shrines scattered around the country were consolidated so that as a rule each and every village had one shrine. This "reform" paved the way for the use of Shinto parishes and parishioners as a tool to combat and quash the radical, and often Marxist-inspired, labor and peasant movements that arose in the wake of the Russo-Japanese War (Murakami, 1982, pp. 50-51).

Shinto in pre-Meiji Japan had evolved in close association with Confucianism, which was imported from China by the fifth century A.D., as well as with Buddhism, which reached Japan about a century later via China and Korea. It was, in fact, Confucianism rather than either Shinto or Buddhism that served as the "state religion" in Tokugawa Japan and the Confucian ideals of social order and harmony maintained by a moral and benevolent ruler and his loyal, disciplined, and industrious subjects that informed both the politics and society of the period (Imanaka, 1972). The Meiji government elevated Shinto above Confucianism—an obvious foreign import—as the new state religion, but it did not cease to exploit the core dogmas of Confucianism for exactly the same purposes as the Tokugawa shogunate had done, that is, to unite and mobilize the nation for tasks set by the state. The 1890 Imperial Rescript on Education thus referred to "loyalty to His Majesty and filial piety to parents" as the eternal "essence" of the Japanese polity (Imanaka, 1972, pp. 42-43; Togawa et al., 1987, pp. 4-5). Thereafter, Confucianism served as a "spiritual pillar" of the nation to help "maintain order in the state, in society, and within the family" and "nurture moral conduct" among the people, as an influential Confucianist organization recently declared (Togawa et al, 1987, pp. 18-19).

The new Shinto-derived state religion, reinforced by the core dogmas of Confucianism, was propagated in Meiji Japan not only by the newly built and embellished shrines and government-sponsored rites but, far more importantly, by a newly established system of public education. In one of their first and most important decisions, the leaders of the Meiji state undertook in 1872 to create a three-tiered system of public education composed of compulsory primary schools and voluntary middle and high schools and universities (Tamura, 1988, pp. 41-52). The enrollment of all children and their exposure to state-sanctioned standard textbooks was the central objective of the system from the beginning, an objective successfully achieved by the turn of the century, although the legally required enrollment period was initially four years and did not reach six years until 1907. By the first decade of the twentieth century, nearly all school-age children were enrolled, although no more than about three-quarters of them regularly attended classes.[2]

Shinto and Confucian dogmas played an important part in primary school textbooks from the beginning but became particularly salient after the 1910s. Children were taught to be loyal, cooperative, and industrious, as well as literate and able, workers in the service of the state. Only a small minority of these children went to one or another kind of secondary school, and an even smaller minority to high schools and universities.[3] The system as a whole emphasized a curious mixture of seemingly contradictory principles: Egalitarianism at the primary school level and elitism at the higher, especially the university, level. Emphasis on performance and achievement served as a sort of hinge between the two opposing principles.

The Meiji government's initial approach to public education was actually quite liberal and emphasized objectivity and universalism in the preparation of curricula. By the early 1880s, however, this initial approach was abandoned in favor of an explicitly and narrowly nationalistic policy with extensive use of Shinto and Confucian dogmas, as reflected in the series of Ministry of Education ordinances issued during the decade, particularly the 1886 decree on teachers colleges (Horimatsu, 1985, pp. 97-99, 114-115, 129-131; Kokumin kyōiku kenkyūjo, 1973, pp. 46-49, 59, 62, 71-73, 80-84; Kubo, 1979, pp. 10-11; Oe, 1974, pp. 42-48). Moral education, that is, inculcation of nationalist ideology was the task assigned mainly to primary and secondary schools and was administered mainly through ethics, Japanese language, Japanese history, and geography courses. After 1903, textbooks used in these four subject areas were screened and selected by the Ministry of Education, a practice extended to texts in mathematics and drawing in 1905 and sciences in 1910 (Horimatsu, 1985, pp. 150-151; Kubo, 1979, pp. 49-51). About half the hours (15 out of 28 hours per week for boys and 15 out of 30 for girls) spent in class by fifth and sixth graders was devoted to these subject areas, while about a third of the time spent in class by secondary school students was consumed by courses in those areas (Kubo, 1979, pp. 146-147, 154). A typical passage in a 1930 ethics text for upper primary school classes taught the pupils that "the easiest way to practice one's patriotism" was to "discipline oneself in daily life, help keep good order in one's family, and fully discharge one's responsibility on the job" (Murakami, 1982, p. 64). By comparison, both curricula and textbooks used at the postsecondary levels emphasized more specialized and technical subjects and were largely free of overtly ideological material (Kokumin kyōiku kenkyūjo, 1973, pp. 94-99).

Outside the formal education system, the increasingly strident and chauvinistic nationalist ideology was disseminated by a number of mass organizations, most sponsored directly or indirectly by the government. Youth associations were set up throughout the country in the 1910s, primarily to combat "alien," particularly, Marxist, ideologies in the wake of the Russo-Japanese War and effectively performed that function especially after they were brought under the centralized direction of a national headquarters in 1924 (Kokumin kyōiku kenkyūjo, 1983, p. 131; Waswo, 1988, pp. 572-576). More than 30 organizations were formed in the 1910s and 1920s for similar purposes, many with a membership running into several hundreds of thousands.

The private sector of the economy, especially its urban industrial part, took full advantage of both the work force thus nurtured and indoctrinated in state-controlled schools and the state-fostered ideological environment of the entire society. The dominant feature of that environment was nicely captured by Governor Murakami Yoshio of Ishikawa Prefecture in his 1904 speech at a prefectural trade school:

> Military warfare has its limits. Meanwhile, industry that lies at the base of national power rises or falls at each passing moment and the world situation compels all (nations) to participate in fierce competition (for industrial supremacy). . . . You must understand that war in peace time goes on constantly. In this kind of war, that is, struggle for survival, those who exploit scientific instruments to expand industry, produce goods at low costs, and thus absorb financial resources will nurture the strength of their own nation, enrich its resources, and thus emerge as winners, while those who fail to do so will gradually lose their financial resources and exhaust the strength of their nation . . . to end up as losers. For this reason, while we win a military war to guard our national security, protect our possessions, and expand our national influence, we must at the same time win the war in peace time so as to gain hegemony in East Asia, enrich our financial resources, and place ourselves in a position to lead [other nations in the region]. (Oe, 1974, pp. 159-160)

Labor unions were formed in the 1910s and thereafter, but they were all either effectively tamed by management and brought under its control or, if they insisted on fighting management, simply destroyed. Japan's first major labor federation that had evolved from the Friendship Society of the 1910s, the Japanese Confederation of Labor (*Nihon rodo sodomei*), embraced militant syndicalism for a short while in the early 1920s. It shifted its position to a moderate cooperationist line, however, following the 1923 Great Kanto Earthquake during which mass hysteria led to mob attacks—often with the acquiescence of or in collusion with local police—that proved fatal to a number of prominent Marxists as well as Koreans (Ikeda, 1982, p. 256). The 1925 Peace Preservation Law then banned all organizations denouncing either the principle of imperial sovereignty or that of private property (Murakami, 1982, pp. 55-56).

Harnessed to a massive amount of industrial machinery and technologies imported from abroad in great haste, the literate, hardworking, largely non-unionized, loyal, and achievement-oriented labor force drove the industrialization of the prewar Japanese economy. Agricultural labor that accounted for about three quarters of the total work force at the end of the Tokugawa period fell to about two-thirds by the turn of the century, less than one half by the early 1930s, and about 40% by the eve of World War II, while manufacturing output rose from 6% of the gross domestic product at the turn of the century to 30% by World War II (Patrick & Rosovsky, 1976, pp. 7-8). Meanwhile, the gross national product grew at an accelerating real annual rate of about 3.5% in the 1920s and more than 5% in the 1930s.

The economy that developed in pre-World War II Japan was clearly a market-based capitalist economy. It was, however, a capitalist economy nurtured in an ideological environment characterized by preoccupation with domestic harmony and unity and strong antipathy toward all divisive ideas and activities, especially Marxist theory of class warfare. It was also a remarkably successful economy that grew at a steadily accelerating rate to become one of the world's major industrial economies within a little more than half a century.

The Postwar Japanese State and Economic Development

If the success of the state-managed economy in pre-World War II Japan was remarkable, the performance of the postwar Japanese economy has been spectacular. To repeat a somewhat tired cliché, for the 40 years since 1950, it has maintained the highest, and by and large the most stable, average annual growth rate among the major industrial nations. Juxtaposed with its prewar counterpart, the postwar growth curve may give the impression that it has merely extended the prewar curve beyond 1950, with a roughly 10-year interval caused by the war and its immediate aftermath. Such an impression, however, is too simplistic, considering the magnitude of the postwar reforms implemented under the auspices of the Allied occupation authorities. These reforms reached and transformed virtually all important political, economic, and social institutions of the vanquished and occupied nation, from its constitution to business conglomerates (*zaibatsu*), rural landlordism, state Shinto, the status of women, and the educational system, not to mention the entire military establishment and police organizations.[4]

The prime targets of the sweeping reform program were virtually all of the institutions and practices that were responsible for the rapid industrialization and growth of the prewar Japanese economy. The emperor cult was condemned, as were all other forms of ultranationalist ideology, including Shinto and Confucian dogmas. School textbooks were purged of all affirmative references to "undemocratic" ideas and practices. In fact, long before the

Supreme Commander for the Allied Powers (SCAP) issued the first official decree on the subject of school textbooks, the Japanese government acted on its own to remove teaching materials likely to be targeted by SCAP sooner or later. As early as September 20, 1945, the Ministry of Education thus instructed all schools either to black out or treat with extreme care any part of textbooks in use, especially in Japanese language courses, that praised chauvinism or denigrated international peace and amity (Horimatsu, 1985, p. 253; Kubo, 1984, p.200). Most textbooks, especially those in ethics, contained so many potentially offensive passages that they were virtually soaked in the India ink used to black them out and became unusable. SCAP then followed the Japanese government's initiative by ordering suspension of all ethics, Japanese history, and geography textbooks in December and designating additional passages in Japanese language and mathematics textbooks to be blacked out (Horimatsu, 1985, p. 254; Kokumin kyōiku kenkyūjo, 1973, p. 203; Kubo, 1984, pp. 203-204).[5] These old textbooks were first mercilessly gutted and then replaced by brand new textbooks produced under the Ministry of Education's supervision in accordance with a set of strict SCAP guidelines aimed at thoroughly democratizing the entire Japanese educational system overnight.

Meanwhile, an extensive bill of rights guaranteed by the new Occupation-authored constitution to all Japanese citizens explicitly included the "[F]reedom of assembly and association as well as speech, press and all other forms of expression" (Constitution of Japan, Article 21). Left-wing political parties, including the Japan Communist Party, were now fully legal and free to espouse whatever political views they preferred, including Marxist class theory, as were labor unions to bargain collectively with management and any other kind of organizations to engage in any peaceful form of activity to advance the interests of their members. Moreover, most of these reforms, undoubtedly among the most thorough and radical of the kind ever undertaken in modern world history, were not only swiftly and effectively implemented but have since become integral and permanent components of the postwar Japanese polity and society.

The spectacular performance of the postwar Japanese economy has thus occurred despite the sweeping changes in both core institutions and ideology of the modern Japanese state. Any plausible explanation of the Japanese "miracle," then, must contend with the paradox between, on one hand, the real and profound impacts of the postwar reforms and, on the other, the apparent continuity and consistency in the pattern of the growth performance of the Japanese economy before and after those reforms. The following is a preliminary and obviously very incomplete attempt to formulate such an explanation.

As I have argued above, an outstanding feature of the core ideology of the prewar Japanese state was its commitment to building "a rich nation with a strong army" and another, and closely related feature was its preoccupation with national independence, integrity, and unity, and concomitant antipathy toward any ideas or activities that threatened to divide the nation, such as Marxist class theory. The basic ideological means to achieve these goals—for example, the emperor cult, Shinto and Confucian dogmas, and so forth—were designed and developed by the state and exploited by private industrialists and businessmen to train and tame their employees. The state attempted to accomplish its goals by, on one hand, indoctrinating youth with the correct ideology through the public education system and, on the other, indirectly managing and guiding the operations of economic and social groups in the private sector.

This strategy, however, failed to produce a totally loyal and dedicated work force and a great deal of physical coercion and repression had to be used against dissidents and rebels. This was particularly true in the period following the Russo-Japanese War, when class divisions sharpened in a postwar recession, peasant revolts spread, a series of industrial disputes erupted, strikes by copper miners and cotton mill women workers shook the nation, and Japan's first Marxist parties were formed (Ota, 1971, pp. 155-231). The government responded to the crisis with renewed emphasis on Shinto and Confucian teachings, as in a 1908 imperial rescript and in the 1910 revisions of school textbooks (Oe, 1974, p. 104).

The postwar reforms put an end to the state's sponsorship and instigation of the exclusivist and xenophobic nationalist ideology ("ultranationalism") as well as militarism. They also vastly expanded the sphere of private individual and collective activities free from state-imposed restrictions, as well as significantly strengthening egalitarianism in social and economic relations, especially in the education system. They did not, however, attempt to suppress, much less eliminate, either the more moderate form of nationalism—that is, the cultivation of national identity and the defense of national integrity and independence—or the psychological antipathy toward class theory and other divisive ideologies, as opposed to the legal proscription of them.[6] What actually happened, in large measure thanks to, rather than in spite of, the postwar democratic reforms, was in fact deeper penetration of society in general and the corporate world in particular by the anticlass ideology of consensus and cooperation. The promotion of the unionization of labor, land reform, emancipation of women, the democratization of the education system, and so forth, all contributed to the eclipse rather than the popularity of the ideology of class warfare, notably Marxism and its variants.

Like all interpretations of complex social phenomena, the validity of this conclusion cannot be directly proven. A number of well-documented developments in the past four decades, however, provide fairly strong, if not conclusive, circumstantial evidence. To cite only a few examples—the conservative Liberal Democrats, known for their consistent support of moderate nationalism and capitalism, have consistently received no less than about 42% of the valid ballots cast, representing about 30% of all eligible voters, in the House of Representatives general elections since 1955; by comparison, the Communists, known for their opposition to capitalism and suspect in their allegiance to nationalism, have never received more than about 10% of the ballots cast, representing about 7% of all eligible voters, in those elections (Curtis, 1988, appendix). Meanwhile, a series of annual public opinion polls administered by the Office of the Prime Minister since 1958 have shown that more than 70% of adult Japanese by the late 1950s, more than 85% by the mid-1960s, and more than 90% by the early 1970s identified themselves, albeit highly ambiguously and misleadingly, as "middle class" (*chūryū*).[7] The argument that this is a case of identification based on "false consciousness" may be correct but does not in any way detract from my point that the ideology of class warfare has been eclipsed by the ideology of national consensus and cooperation.

Another, and far more complex, example is found in the changing role of the education system and the teaching profession. The ideals of the Occupation-sponsored reform and democratization of the system were immortalized in a 1947 law, the Basic Law on Education. The law still remains in effect in its original form and its first article still declares that

> education aims at helping [children] to grow up as members of a peaceful state and society who love truth and justice, uphold the value of the individual, believe in hard work, take responsibility for one's action, display an abundant spirit of independence, and possess both physical and spiritual health. (Kyōiku kihon hō, 1985, article 1)

In a number of subtle ways, however, these lofty democratic ideals have been gradually whittled away over the years by a small but dedicated group of unreformed nationalists among conservative politicians and Ministry of Education bureaucrats with the support and encouragement of big business interests. The revisionist moves include, for example, the passage in 1954 of a pair of laws that made it illegal for school teachers either to make any "political" statement—such as criticizing a government, a political party or a policy—in class or to engage in off-campus political activities; a 1956 law that replaced the popular election of local education board members by their appointment by heads of local governments; and, beginning in 1957, the introduction of a uniform nationwide teacher evaluation system (Nakauchi et al., 1987). The revisionist assault was directed above all at the 600,000-member Japan Teachers Union—one of the largest and most explicitly Marxist of its kind in the world—that threatened to introduce class theory in classroom and thus subvert the core ideology of Japanese education that had already suffered a serious blow at the hands of the postwar Allied occupation.

For purposes of my argument, three aspects of the revisionist movement in the 1950s are particularly important. First, it was a response to a series of formal recommendations presented to the government by employer organizations, notably the Japan Federation of Employers' Associations (*Nihon keieisha dantai rengōkai* or *Nikkeiren*) that, among the major big business groups, concerned itself mainly with management-labor relations. These included, inter alia, a recommendation calling for a wholesale review of the postwar education system (1952) and another urging the promotion of scientific and technical education (1956) (Kokumin kyōiku kenkyūjo, 1973, pp. 256-258; Nakauchi, 1987, pp. 134-135). Second, the revisionist campaign succeeded in significantly limiting the influence of the left-wing Japan Teachers' Union, although not in killing the organization. Third, the campaign succeeded first in sanitizing primary and secondary school curricula against class ideology and then, in the 1960s, in strengthening science and technology curricula at the secondary and tertiary levels (Nakauchi, 1987, pp. 156-164).

The last example that points to the defeat of divisive class theory and the triumph of the ideology of unity and achievement is the spread of enterprise corporatism, a style of management-labor relations long advocated by the leadership of the national federation of private sector unions, the Confederation of Labor (*Dōmei*), and opposed by its public sector rival, the General Council of Japanese Trade Unions (*Sōhyō*). The so-called quality control (QC) circle is a representative product of this form of corporatism and its rapid spread since the 1960s is another indication of the resounding success of the anticlass ideology.

A QC circle is defined as a small group formed at any workplace by all employees who belong to that workplace and who engage, together and on a daily and continuous basis, in voluntary and self-governed activities aimed at improvement of both the quality of their products and management of their work through self-learning and mutual teaching.[8] The idea and methodology of scientific quality control (SQC) developed at a Bell Laboratory in the 1920s were known to a few Japanese statisticians before World War II, but these were introduced to Japanese businessmen and engineers in any significant way only during the postwar occupation by SCAP as a way to improve, primarily for military purposes, Japan's ramshackle and undependable telephone system (NHK shuzaihan, 1987, pp. 67-71, 110-113). The concept was widely popularized in the mid-1950s by the airing of special NHK (Japan Broadcasting Corporation) programs on the subject and QC circles began to appear in the early 1960s and spread "like wild fire" in the 1970s, especially in the automobile, steel, and electrical industries (Kuroda, 1988, p. 313). The national association launched in 1963 with an initial membership of about 200 circles had grown into an organization of nearly a quarter million affiliated circles with nearly 2 million members by 1986, while, according to one estimate, 7 to 10 times as many unaffiliated circles existed with a total membership approaching 10 million, or at least 40% of the total number (about 23 million) of Japanese employees.[9]

The Japanese QC circles as they have evolved over the past three decades are characterized by the wide use of and reliance on statistical data processing and analysis, development of a set of standard and fairly simple statistical measures accessible to employees at all educational levels, and participation by all employees at a given workplace (NHK shuzaihan, 1987, pp. 106-110). They have evolved as part of a wildly effective tool of the corporate strategy to improve the quality and competitiveness of products through employees' own "voluntary" efforts, that is, at minimum costs to management. As a 1969 *Nikkeiren* report pointed out, employers understood the value of "groupism as a distinctive feature of the Japanese national character" and of "the ZD [zero defect] movement and QC group activities . . . as devices effective in encouraging employees' voluntary commitment to work and in raising their morale" (*Nihon keieisha dantai rengōkai*, 1969, pp. 68-71).[10] Through the practice of self-learning and mutual teaching, a QC circle raises the standard of work performance by all employees, including the least able; under the group's collective pressure, all work overtime with nominal compensation, mavericks are brought into line, and recalcitrant dissidents—especially those who believe in class ideology—are forced either to change their ways or quit the job (Kuroda, 1988, pp. 313, 320; Watanabe, 1987, p. 193).[11]

Fervent advocates of enterprise corporatism, QC circles have inevitably competed with and, to an important extent, eroded the ranks of labor unions—themselves formed and operating within individual enterprises rather than entire industries or crafts. The percentage of unionized employees in the secondary and tertiary sectors fell from 28.0% in 1965 to 23.5% in

1985.[12] Moreover, many unions, particularly those at larger corporations, such as Toyota, now accept and cooperate with the ubiquitous QC groups (NHK shuzaihan, 1987, pp. 65-66).

The great success and popularity of enterprise corporatism in general and the QC circle movement in particular has been significantly helped by the so-called lifetime employment and seniority-based promotion and wage (i.e., pay-by-age) systems. These were introduced at management's initiative in prewar Japan primarily as means to recruit, train, and then keep scarce skilled workers, that is, essentially as tools of corporatist policy. In the early postwar period, unions demanded the preservation and expansion of both practices in the name of job security for and equality among all employees, and management went along (Kuroda, 1988, pp. 301-302; Tsuda, 1981, p. 29). Management, however, also used them as weapons to divide and rule labor. For one thing, issues of utmost concern to employees, such as job security, promotions, and wages, now became subjects to be discussed and settled strictly by management and employees of the given enterprise alone, and thus no business of outsiders; for another, within each enterprise some employees were granted lifetime job security and age-based promotion and wage increases, while others were not granted either. Even when the systems were at the peak of their popularity in the mid-1960s, they applied to no more than between 10% and one quarter of the total number of Japan's employees, depending on how broadly or narrowly one defines those terms (Tsuda, 1981, pp. 292-293).

At the beginning of the 1990s, QC circles continue to thrive in Japanese firms, whereas the nation's education system still runs the "reverse course" started in the early 1950s. In a number of important ways, however, Japan's nationalist/paternalist capitalism is undergoing a metamorphosis under the pressure of rapidly and dramatically changing domestic and international environments. In the process, some of its hallmarks mentioned above are being either tossed away outright or drastically modified so that Japan's political economy at the turn of the next century is bound to look quite different from what it has looked like in the past. Let me now turn to some of the major changes underway.

Japanese Capitalism at a Crossroad

First, Japanese capitalism is going through a rapid and traumatic process of internationalization. Capital began to move out of the country by the late 1950s and the outflow picked up considerably in the 1970s and, especially, the 1980s. Until the mid-1970s, Japanese foreign direct investments were concentrated mainly in the production and development of foodstuffs and industrial raw materials. Since then, however, two major considerations have driven Japanese investments abroad: (1) to reduce labor costs by relocating labor-intensive processing or assembling phases of the production of certain manufactures, such as watches, desk calculators, electric fans, and so forth, to nearby Newly Industrializing Countries (NICs) with still relatively cheap and abundant labor; and (2) to get around rising trade protectionism, especially increasingly stringent local content requirements, in the United States and Western Europe, by locally producing many of Japan's staple exports to those markets, such as automobiles, color televisions, semiconductors, and so forth (Toshida, 1989: 19-20, pp. 178-179).

Capital outflow from Japan increased dramatically in the 1980s, not so much because of rising labor costs in Japan as because of rising protectionism abroad and the sharp appreciation of the yen following the September 1985 Plaza Accord that started a successful concerted effort by the governments of the major industrial nations to drive up the value of the yen (and the West German mark) and drive down that of the U.S. dollar. Japanese direct investments abroad grew from about $4.7 billion in 1980 to $12.2 billion in 1985 and to $47.0 billion in 1988 (Keizai Koho Center, 1989, p. 56). The regional distribution of the invested funds significantly changed during this eight-year period: Asia's share, associated mainly with labor cost considerations, declined 25.3% to 11.7%, while North America's and Europe's, both associated mainly with market access considerations, rose, respectively, from 34.9% to 46.8% and from 12.3% to 19.1% (Fukiya, 1988, p. 55; Keizai Koho Center, 1989, p. 56).

That market access considerations were more important than labor cost considerations in Japanese investments in the United States and Europe becomes evident when one compares their wage growth rates. Over the period 1980-1988, real hourly wage rates in manufacturing industries grew considerably faster in the United States and the major West European economies than in Japan.[13] The differences may be explained largely by similar differences in the rates of change in the consumer price index: Japan's increased far more slowly than the other major economic nations'.[14] They were, however, also due to a substantial lag between the growth rate of real wages and that of labor productivity in Japan, that is, a consequence of a poor deal Japanese labor struck, whether willingly or unwillingly, in wage negotiations with management.[15] This lag in turn was due partly to the enormously successful campaign for corporatist control and mobilization of labor in general and activities of the host of QC circles in particular and, partly, to a relatively slack labor market. According to official statistics, Japan's unemployment rate has been consistently and significantly lower than that of the other major industrial nations, but it rose significantly following the 1985 Plaza Accord to reach about 3% by early 1987, a very high level by Japanese standards, while the ratio of job openings to job seekers fell as low as .61 (Keizai Koho Center, 1989, p. 72; Toshida, 1989, p. 74). More recently, however, the Japanese labor market has tightened considerably, with the unemployment rate falling to about 2.5% and the job openings per job seeker ratio rising to more than 1 by the summer of 1988; it continues to tighten as most Japanese industries and firms have seemingly adapted to the impacts of the strong yen.

The capital flight has therefore not resulted in a hollowing out of the Japanese economy in the sense of exporting jobs abroad and creating a serious unemployment problem at home. On the contrary, a shortage of labor, especially young and inexpensive labor, has become such a chronic and acute problem for many Japanese firms, especially for small businesses, despite the above-mentioned temporary slackening of the labor market in the mid-1980s, that a substantial and rapidly increasing number of foreign workers— as many as 200,000 in 1988, according to some estimates—are employed, legally or illegally, for the first time in Japan's history (*Ohara shakaimondai kenkyūjo*, 1989, p. 38). Along with foreign direct investments in Japan itself, which increased from less than $300 million in 1980 to nearly $2.6 billion in 1988 (Keizai Koho Center, 1989, p. 58), the growing presence of foreign workers in Japan brings internationalization home, so to speak.

The internationalization of the Japanese economy that thus proceeds both externally and internally is bound to have significant impacts on many of the ways of Japanese capitalism that I discussed in the preceding sections. It is highly doubtful, for example, that QC circles can be organized and run by foreign workers, whether in Japan or abroad, in the same way that they are organized and run by Japanese employees, even though hundreds of foreigners visit Japanese firms each year to see and learn about the organization and activities of these groups (NHK shuzaihan, 1987, pp. 85-86). Some 300 American firms had set up Japanese-style QC groups by the late 1980s, but only a few, such as Westinghouse of Pittsburgh, are reported to have made any significant impacts on the performance of the firms (NHK shuzaihan, 1987, pp. 91-95, 128-129). As I have argued, the success of Japanese QC circles owes a great deal to nationalist and corporatist ideologies derived largely from Shinto and Confucian dogmas. Absent such ideologies, and especially present an antithetical individualistic ideology, employees and their groups, whatever they are called, will behave differently from their Japanese counterparts.

Second, the lifetime employment and pay-by-age systems, both long regarded as shibboleths of Japanese-style management, are in trouble. As I have already suggested, neither system has ever applied to more than a small minority of Japanese employees in any case. In fact, the two systems could not have been simultaneously applied to the majority, not to mention all, employees in any but an imaginary enterprise with limitless resources; a typical real-world enterprise could not possibly afford to guarantee the majority of its employees "lifetime" job security—that is, employment up to a mandatory retirement age of 55 or 60 or 65—and, at the same time, promise them payment of wages that rise automatically and continuously each passing year as they grow older. The enterprise would be bankrupt in no time. The implementation of these systems therefore required the use of a large number of employees who would work without claim to their benefits, that is, "regular" employees excluded from the systems and "non-regular" employees hired on a part-time or temporary basis (NHK shuzaihan, 1987, pp. 303-304). Women employees accounted for an overwhelming majority of those in the first category and a large majority of the second, and were consequently paid grossly substandard wages. For example, women employed in the secondary and tertiary sectors in 1988 were paid per month on average slightly less than 55% of what men were paid (Rōdōdaijin kambō seisaku chōsabu, 1988b, pp. 132-133).[16] To cut down further on labor costs, many parts needed by larger manufacturers of complex products, such as automobiles and computers, were acquired from a large number of smaller firms serving as subcontractors.

The subcontracting system is critical to the successful operation of the lifetime employment and pay-by-age systems, and it is extremely complex. Just how complex can be seen in the case of the Yamaha Motors Company, a major motorbike manufacturer but not one of the biggest Japanese firms by any means: the company has 83 subcontractors (firms), one of which (the Sakura Industries that makes motorbike mufflers) alone has 70 subcontractors under its own wings, one of which has 40 subcontractors of its own, one of which has an unknown number of subcontractors of its own, and so on, so forth (NHK shuzaihan, 1987, pp. 173, 193-201). For a single motorbike manufacturer alone, then, between 2,000 and 3,000 (no dependable statistics exist) small firms, including a number of tiny family shops at the very bottom of the heap, make up an intricate and quasi-familial network. For Japan as a whole, two thirds of the 868,000 or so firms with no more than 300 employees serve as subcontractors for larger firms. Employees in the smaller contractor firms are paid considerably less than those in the parent firm or larger tractor firms (NHK shuzaihan, 1987, pp. 180, 182).[17]

With all these escape hatches carefully built into them, both the lifetime employment and pay-by-age systems have nonetheless substantially declined in popularity during the last decade, while reliance on nonregular workers and subcontracting has increased. Terms of employment, including both the lengths and types of service and the kinds and amounts of compensation, are determined increasingly on the basis of the type of job and the quality of performance. The mandatory retirement age for most employees has been raised from 55 to 60 by nearly 60% of firms with 30 or more employees and nearly 90% of those with 5,000 or more employees (*Ohara shakaimondai kenkyūjo*, 1989, pp. 114-115). In the meantime, however, commitment to lifetime job security has significantly declined.[18] Commitment to the pay-by-age system is even rarer these days.[19] One of the two representative hallmarks of Japanese-style management, the pay-by-age system, is thus nearly finished, while the other, the lifetime employment system, appears to be following the same fate.

Third, as far as the majority of Japanese citizens are concerned, Japanese-style capitalism has ceased to deliver as much as they have come to expect. While the Japanese economy was growing at a brisk pace in the 1950s and 1960s, the average real wage in the manufacturing industry steadily and substantially rose each passing year, until the 1973 oil crisis put an end to the period of double-digit growth rates. The average real wage has continued to rise even during the post-oil crisis period—except in 1980 when the mean real wage in the manufacturing sector registered a negative growth rate of −1.6%—but only at much lower rates (0.5%-3.1%) (*Ohara shakaimondai kenkyūjo*, 1989, p. 71; *Rōdōdaijin kambō seisaku chōsabu*, 1988a, pp. 14-15). The deceleration in the rise of wage rates in the mid-1970s gave rise to serious and widespread disaffection among some segments of the working class for the first time since the early 1950s. For the next decade, however, the disaffection was under control, until a sudden and frenetic surge in urban real estate prices hit the pocket books of urban white-collar and blue-collar workers in the late 1980s.

By the mid-1980s, urban real estate had become a prime object of investment for large and small corporations awash with idle funds accumulated during the years of slow but steady growth of the economy as a whole and booming export trade. In five short years from 1983 to 1988, the average prices of residential and commercial land rose, respectively, by 15% and 23% in the Nagoya metropolitan area, by 34% and 81% in the Osaka area, and 119% and 203% in the Tokyo area (Honma, 1988, pp. 37-40). In the last of these three major metropolitan areas of the country, the price of residential land shot up by nearly 70% in 1988 alone (*Asahi nenkan,* 1989, p. 694). This put even a tiny apartment in the metropolitan areas, especially Tokyo, far beyond the limits of the ordinary wage earner's purchasing power.

The disaffection among growing ranks of urban wage earners was further deepened by the discovery that, despite the impression one would get by simply comparing the CPI in different nations, the prices of most consumer goods, from foodstuffs to electronic gadgets, are actually much higher in Japan than in any other major industrial nation. The introduction of a new 3% across-the-board sales (consumption) tax in 1989, amidst a scandal involving many of the top LDP and government leaders, added fuel to the flame of popular anger and led to unprecedented electoral upsets that have shaken Japan's capitalist regime to its foundations. In the quadrennial Tokyo Metropolitan Assembly elections held in July 1989, the LDP lost 20 of the 63 seats it had won in the 1985 election, while the Japan Socialist Party (JSP) won 24 seats more than the 12 it had won in 1985; in the triennial House of Councillors (upper house) election held almost simultaneously, the LDP lost 33, while the JSP gained 24; and in the House of Representatives general election called in February 1990, the LDP lost 9, while the JSP gained 57 (Baerwald, 1989, 1990; *Asahi shimbun,* July 3 [evening ed.], 5, 25, 1989; *Yomiuri shimbun,* February 20, 1990).

The results of the most recent elections may have reflected the passing moods of a notoriously fickle electorate rather than a long-term trend. On the other hand, they may well have signaled a significant change underway in the political foundation of Japan's postwar political economy, a change that may sooner or later coalesce with the other changes already discussed to transform Japan's 120-year-old nationalist/paternalist capitalist state. Whether the Japanese state and capitalists prove resourceful enough to survive this gravest of the crises they have ever faced since the Meiji Restoration is yet to be seen.

Summary and Conclusions

Like all social phenomena, capitalism comes in different shapes and colors in different cultural and historical environs. I have argued that Japan's is one that is quite different from the classic model where economic rationality is the paramount criterion of worthy conduct and that it is, on the contrary, inspired and guided by an ideology, that is, irrationality. The main thrust of my thesis is undeniably Weberian, except that, in my argument, labor in pre-Meiji or post-Meiji Japan has never been quite a "calling" and an "end in itself" in Weber's or Martin Luther's sense, while a religion-inspired secular ideology (nationalism), rather than a religion itself (Protestantism), has driven the rise and expansion of Japan's late-developer capitalism (Weber, 1930, p. 62).[20] For that matter, my thesis has even closer affinity with Bellah's classic, *Tokugawa Religion* (Bellah, 1957).

I am also ready to admit that an important implication of my thesis is that what happens in political and social arenas, especially educational institutions, rather than what happens in economic arenas per se, is critical to the economic performance of a late-developing capitalist nation, if not that of any capitalist nation. One therefore looks very carefully at a government's political and social policies and society's responses to them, rather than at its economic policies, such as industrial policy or tax policy, in order to understand and explain the long-term pattern of a developing nation's economic performance. For the long-term performance of a developing capitalist economy, how many schools are built, who attends them, and what is taught there is more important than how many factories are built and what types of merchandise are produced.

Weberian as it may be, however, my thesis is not Hegelian; it recognizes the importance of objective material conditions, and class interests and relations based on such conditions. It also recognizes, if only implicitly, the importance of economic policies that affect those conditions. A critical point about modern Japan's economic policies, however, is that, like political and social policies, they have been aimed primarily at ensuring domestic peace and harmony and mobilizing voluntary and enthusiastic cooperation of the populace in the building of a rich nation, with a strong army before World War II and without one after the war.

The successful maintenance of domestic harmony and effective mobilization of popular cooperation have required, among other things, two conditions: the maintenance of a high and stable economic growth rate, and reasonably equal and fair distribution of the results of the economic growth. Statistics show that Japanese-style capitalism has, by and large, successfully met these two conditions. Not only has modern Japan's economy grown at a higher and more stable rate than any other major industrial economy, but the fruits of that growth have been distributed more equitably in postwar Japan, though not in prewar Japan, than in most other nations. A comparison of Gini coefficients based on the latest comparable statistics available show that in the late 1970s and early 1980s Japan had the most egalitarian overall income distribution among the major capitalist industrial economies.[21]

There have been, however, periods in modern Japanese history—for example, the post-Russo-Japanese War, post-World War I, and post-World War

II periods—when the growth rate fell and/or income (or wealth) inequalities rose so significantly that social harmony and cooperative public spirit were seriously undermined. These were periods of crisis for Japanese capitalism, to which it responded just as it was expected to do, that is, with a combination of improvised material and ideological palliatives. It is of great credit to the ingenuity and the shrewdness of leaders of the Japanese state and enterprise that this combination has usually worked in the past.

In the last decade of the twentieth century, however, it is far from certain that Japan's nationalist/paternalist capitalism may once again prove its genius and resiliency and successfully overcome the multiple and complex domestic and international pressures it faces. Even if it may survive the pressures, it will not remain intact. As I have pointed out, it is already being transformed in a number of significant ways. Japanese-style capitalism is thus unlikely to exist in the year 2000 in anything like its present shape and color.

Notes

1. Throughout this chapter, all Japanese personal names are given in the native order, that is, surname first, followed by given name.

2. By 1890, about half the school-age children were enrolled and the percentage figure rose to more than 80% by 1900, more than 95% by 1905, and more than 98% by 1910. See Horimatsu, 1985, pp. 140-141; Kokumin kyōiku kenkyūj, 1973, pp. 84, 88-89; Oe, 1974, pp. 40, 120.

3. The so-called multiple-track system of secondary and postsecondary education in prewar Japan was so complex, especially with regard to eligible ages, that it is difficult to estimate the ratios of students per appropriate groups of population. According to my own calculations, in 1935 secondary school, high school and college, and university students accounted, respectively, for no more than 4%, 1.5%, and 2% of the eligible populations, that is, those at the ages of, respectively, 12-17, 12-19, and 19-21. These estimates are based on data drawn from *Shōwa 16-nen Asahi nenkan,* 1940, pp. 90-91, 452-454; and Horimatsu, 1985, pp. 140-167. Others estimate that in the 1930s no more than about 1% of elementary school graduates could expect to enter any university, and no more than half as many of the seven imperial universities. See Passin, 1965, p. 104; Pempel, 1978, p. 34.

4. For detailed discussions of the wide-ranging reforms, see *Tokyo daigaku shakaikagaku kenkyūjo* (1974-1975). For an overview, see Fukui, 1988, pp. 155-184.

5. According to a survey conducted by SCAP's Civil Information and Education Section at the time, more than half (773 pp.) of the 1,502 pages of the twelve primary school Japanese language textbooks in use at the time contained language praising militarism, ultranationalism, Shinto dogmas and/or the emperor cult. See Kubo, 1984, p. 200.

6. Needless to say, at no time was encouragement of Marxism or any other anti-capitalist ideology part of the United States' policy for occupied Japan. See Iokibe, 1985, vol. 1, pp. 226-282; vol. 2, pp.227-259.

7. For a critical analysis of the significance and implications of this development, see Imada, 1989, pp. 149-164.

8. Quoted from the *QC Circle Charter* issued in 1970 by the national headquarters of QC circles, in *NHK shuzaihan,* 1987, pp. 26-27.

9. According to one recent survey, as many as 62% of enterprises had at least one QC circle and an additional 20% had similar employee groups, called either Zero Defect (ZD) or JK (for *jishu kanri* or self-management). The Toyota Motors Corporation alone had 6,500 separate circles in 1988, each with six members on average; and one was found in every workplace in the company's technical departments and 80% of its administrative departments. See NHK shuzaihan, 1987, pp. 32, 38, 75-76.

10. President Toyoda Shōichirō of Toyota Motors Corporation believes that improving employees' "motivation" is a far more important function of a QC circle than teaching statistical data processing methods. See NHK shuzaihan, 1987, p. 62.

11. See George Fields's similar comments in NHK shuzaihan, 1987, pp. 14-15.

12. During the same period, the left-wing *Sohyo's* membership fell from 11.7% to 8.3% and the corporatist *Domei's* from 4.5% to 4.0% of the total work force in the two sectors, or by 3.4 and 0.5 percentage points respectively. See Rōdōdaijin kambō seisaku chōsabu, 1988a, pp. 29, 189, 191.

13. The growth rates of wages in the comparable nations were: 40.2%, or 5.0% per year, in the United States; 39.1%, or 4.9% per year, in West Germany; 70.4%, or 8.8% per year, in Great Britain; 44.5% in 1980-1987, or 6.3% per year, in France; and 26.0%, or 3.2% per year, in Japan. See Rōdōdaijin kambō seisaku chōsabu, 1990a, p. 224.

14. Japan's increased by only 16.2% in the eight years, as compared to West Germany's 22.4%, Great Britain's 59.9%, France's 71.8%, and the United States' 43.6%. See Rōdōdaijin kambō seisaku chōsabu, 1990a, p. 228.

15. Labor productivity in the manufacturing sector as a whole rose by as much as 20.1% even in the three years between 1985 and 1988, and by at least twice as much between 1980 and 1988. See Rōdōdaijin kambō seisaku chōsabu, 1990a, p. 164.

16. For a good Marxist analysis of women's status and role in the Japanese economy, see Steven, 1983, chapter 5.

17. The average employee in a small firm with between 10 and 99 employees was paid per month about three-quarters of what the average employee in a large firm with 1,000 or more employees. See Rōdōdaijin kambō seisaku chōsabu, 1988b, pp. 132-133.

18. A recent survey conducted by a committee of labor management experts for the Ministry of Labor found that about 60% of firms with 1,000 or more employees were still committed to lifetime employment for their regular employees, but the remaining 40% practiced a "half-lifetime" system. See *Ohara shakaimondai kenkyūjo,* 1989, p. 109; Rōdōdaijin kambō seisaku chōsabu, 1990b, p. 56.

19. According to a 1988 Ministry of Labor survey, only about 17% of firms with 30 or more employees still offered their regular employees automatic annual wage raises on the basis of seniority, while the remaining 83% paid their employees on the basis of either job and performance alone or a combination of seniority and performance. See Kuroda (1988, pp. 198-199), *Ohara shakaimondai kenkyūjo* (1989, p. 117).

20. If one could replace religion by nationalist ideology, however, I could have easily borrowed and used Weber's lines, such as: "It [labor] cannot be evoked by low wages or high ones alone, but can only be the product of a long and arduous process of education" or "The ability of mental concentration, as well as the absolutely essential feeling of obligation to one's job, are here (in certain workers) most often combined with strict economy . . . which enormously increase performance." Weber (1930, pp. 62-63).

21. According to my calculations based on World Bank data, the comparable Gini values are: Japan (1979) = 0.2700; U.S. (1980) = 0.3292; U.K. (1979) = 0.3148; West Germany (1978) = 0.2952; France (1975) = 0.3424; Sweden (1981) = 0.3060; and the Netherlands (1981) = 0.2596. The Netherlands alone among the 24 Organization for Economic Cooperation and Development (OECD) member states had a more egalitarian pattern of income distribution than Japan. Data from World Bank (1989, p. 222, table 30).

References

Asahi nenkan 1989-nen ban [Asahi yearbook, 1989 edition]. (1989). Tokyo: Asahi shimbunsha.

Asai, Yoshio. (1980). Sangyō kakumei [An industrial revolution]. In K. Takahashi, et al. (Eds.), *Nihon kindaishi yōsetsu* [A summary discussion of modern Japanese history]. Tokyo: Tokyo daigaku shuppankai.

Baerwald, Hans H. (1989, September). Japan's House of Councillors election: A mini-revolution? *Asian Survey,* pp. 833-841.

Baerwald, Hans H. (1990, June). Japan's 39th House of Representatives election: A case of mixed signals. *Asian Survey,* pp. 544-559.

Bellah, Robert N. (1957). *Tokugawa religion: The values of pre-industrial Japan.* New York: Free Press.

Berger, Gordon M. (1988). Politics and mobilization in Japan, 1931-1945. In Peter Duus (Ed.), *The Cambridge history of Japan. Vol 6: The twentieth century* (pp. 97-153). Cambridge, UK: Cambridge University Press.

Crawcour, E. Sydney. (1965).The Tokugawa heritage. In William W. Lockwood (Ed.), *The state and enterprise in Japan.* Princeton, NJ: Princeton University Press.

Curtis, Gerald L. (1988). *The Japanese way of politics.* New York: Columbia University Press.

Duus, Peter. (Ed.). (1988). The twentieth century (The Cambridge history of Japan, vol. 6). Cambridge: Cambridge University Press.

Fujino, Tamotsu. (1961). *Bakuhan taiseishi no kenkyū* [A study of the history of the shogunal-domainal regime]. Tokyo: Yoshikawa kōbunkan.

Fukai, Jinzō. (1980). Kinsei toshi no hattatsu [The development of cities in early modern Japan]. In Shirō Matsumoto & Tadao Yamada (Eds.), *Genroku-kyōho-ki no seiji to shakai* [Politics and society in the genroku-kyoho (1688-1735) period] (Kōza: Nihon kinseishi [Series on early modern Japanese history], vol. 4). Tokyo: Yūhikaku.

Fukiya, Kenji. (1988). 1979-nendai ikō no kokusai shūshi to taigai tōshi [The balance of international payments and foreign investments since the 1970s]. In Sengo nihon keizai kenkyūkai [Association for the study of the postwar Japanese economy] (Ed.), *Nihon keizai no bunsuirei [Watersheds in Japanese economic development]. Tokyo: Bunshindō.*

Fukui, Haruhiro. (1988). Postwar politics, 1945-1973. In Peter Duus (Ed.), *The Cambridge history of Japan. Vol 6: The twentieth century.* Cambridge, UK: Cambridge University Press.

Gotō, Sōichirō. (1988). *Tennōsei kokka no keisei to minshū* [The formation of the emperor-system state and the people]. Tokyo: Kōbunsha.

Honma, Yoshihito. (1988). *Tochi mondai sōtenken* [A comprehensive survey of the land problem]. Tokyo: Yūhikaku.

Horimatsu, Buichi. (Ed.). (1985). *Nihon kyōikushi* [A history of Japanese education]. Tokyo: Kokudosha.

Ikeda, Makoto. (1982). *Nihonteki kōporatizumu no seiritsu* [The formation of Japanese-style corporatism]. Kyoto: Keibunsha.

Imada, Takatoshi. (1989). Shakai kaisō to seiji [Social strata and politics]. In Inoguchi Takashi (Ed.), *Gendai seijigaku sōsho* [Contemporary political science series, vol. 7]. Tokyo: University of Tokyo Press.

Imanaka, Kanji. (1972). *Kinsei nihon seiji shisō no seiritsu* [The formation of political ideologies in early modern Japan]. Tokyo: Sōbunsha.

Iokibe, Makoto. (1985). *Beikoku no nihon senryō seisaku: Sengo nihon no sekkeizu* [The United States' occupation policy: The blue-print for postwar Japan]. 2 Vols. Tokyo: Chūōkoronsha.

Keizai Koho Center. (1989). *Japan: An international comparison 1990*. Tokyo: Keizai Koho Center.

Kimura, Motoi. (1967). *Kakyūbushi ron* [On the lower-ranked samurai]. Tokyo: Hanawa shobō.

Kobayashi, Tango. (1986). *Nihon rōdōkumiai undōshi* [A history of the Japanese labor union movement]. Tokyo: Aoki shoten.

Kokumin kyōiku kenkyūjo. (Ed.). (1973). *Kindai nihon kyōiku shōshi* [A short history of education in modern Japan]. Tokyo: Sōdo bunka.

Koyama, Hirotake. (1967). *Nihon marukusushugishi gaisetsu* [An overview of the history of Japanese Marxism]. Tokyo: Haga shoten.

Kubo, Yoshizō. (1979). *Tennōsei kokka no kyōiku seisaku: Sono keisei katei to sumitsuin* [The educational policy of an emperor-system state: The formative process and the Privy Council]. Tokyo: Keisō shobō.

Kubo, Yoshizō. (1984). *Tainichi senryō seisaku to sengo kyō iku kaikaku* [The occupation policy for Japan and the postwar education reform]. Tokyo: Sanseidō.

Kuroda, Ken'ichi. (1988). Kyōsōteki shokuba chitsujo to rōmu kanri [Competitive workplace order and labor management]. In Sengo nihon keizai kenkyūkai [Association for the study of the postwar Japanese economy] (Ed.), *Nihon keizai no bunsuirei* [Watersheds in Japanese economic development]. Tokyo: Bunshindō.

Kyōiku kihon hō [Basic Law of Education]. (1985). In *Iwanami roppō zensho: Shōwa 61-nenban* [Iwanami compendium of the six codes: 1986 edition]. Tokyo: Iwanami shoten: 487.

Masumi, Junnosuke. (1965-1980). *Nihon seitō shiron* [A historical study of Japanese political parties], 7 vols. Tokyo: Tokyo University Press.

Mori, Kiichi. (1979). *Nihon no kindaika to rōdōsha kaikyū* [The modernization of Japan and the working class]. Tokyo: Nihon hyōronsha.

Murakami, Shigeyoshi. (Ed.). (1982) *Kokka shintō to minshū shūkyō* [State Shinto and popular religions]. Tokyo: Yoshikawa kōbunkan.

Nakauchi, Toshio, et al. (1987). *Nihon kyōiku no sengoshi* [The history of postwar Japanese education]. Tokyo: Sanseidō.

NHK shuzaihan [The Japan Broadcasting Corporation reporters' team). (1987). *Nihon kaibō 2: keizai taikoku no gensen: QC undō wa naze nihon de seikō shita ka* [An anatomy of Japan, vol. 2: Sources of an economic superpower: Why the QC movement has succeeded in Japan]. Tokyo: Nihon hōsō shuppan kyōkai.

Nihon keieisha dantai rengōkai [Japan federation of employers' associations]. (1969). *Nōryokushugi kanri: Sono riron to jissai* [Performance- and ability-based management: Theory and practice]. Tokyo: Nihon keieisha dantai rengōkai.

Oe, Shinobu. (1974). *Kokumin kyōiku to guntai: Nihon gunkokushugi kyōiku seisaku no seiritsu to tenkai* [Public education and the army: The creation and development of militarist education in Japan]. Tokyo: Shin nihon shuppansha.

Ohara shakaimondai kenkyūjo [Ohara Institute of Social Research]. (Ed.). (1989). *Nihon rōdō nenkan* [Japan labor yearbook], vol. 59. Tokyo: Rōdō jumposha.

Omachi, Masami. (1970). *Sōmō no keifu: Meiji ishin no teiryū* [The lineage of grassroots samurai: An undercurrent of the Meiji restoration]. Tokyo: San'ichi shobō.

Ota, Masao. (1971). *Meiji shakaishugi seitōshi* [A history of socialist parties in the Meiji period]. Tokyo: Minerva shobō.

Passin, Herbert. (1965). *Society and education in Japan*. New York: Columbia University Teachers College.

Patrick, Hugh, & Rosovsky, Henry. (1976). Japan's economic performance: An overview. In Hugh Patrick & Henry Rosovsky (Eds.), *Asia's new giant: How the Japanese economy works*. Washington, DC: Brookings Institution.

Pempel, T. J. (1978). *Patterns of Japanese policymaking: Experiences from higher education*. Boulder, CO: Westview.

Rōdōdaijin kambō seisaku chōsabu [Ministry of Labor Secretariat, Policy Planning and Research Department]. (Ed.). (1988a). *Rōdō tōkei yōran 1988-nenban* [Handbook of labor statistics, 1988 edition]. Tokyo Okurashō insatsukyoku.

Rōdōdaijin kambō seisaku chōsabu [Ministry of Labor Secretariat, Policy Planning and Research Department]. (Ed.). (1988b). *Dai-41-kai rōdō tokei nempō* [The 41st Year Book of Labor Statistics]. Tokyo: Rōdō hōrei kyōkai.

Rōdōdaijin kambō seisaku chōsabu [Ministry of Labor Secretariat, Policy Planning and Research Department]. (Ed.). (1990a). *Rōdō tōkei yōran 1990-nenban* [Handbook of labor statistics, 1990 edition]. Tokyo: Okurashō insatsukyoku.

Rōdōdaijin kambō seisaku chōsabu [Ministry of Labor Secretariat, Policy Planning and Research Department]. (Ed.). (1990b). *Rōdō tōkei nempō* [Yearbook of labor statistics]. Tokyo: Rōdō hōrei kyōkai.

Saitō, Nobuaki. (1981). *Meiji ishin kakumei* [The Meiji restoration revolution]. Tokyo: Sairyūsha.

Scalapino, Robert A. (1967a). *Democracy and the party movement in prewar Japan: The failure of the first attempt*. Berkeley and Los Angeles: University of California Press.

Scalapino, Robert A. (1967b). *The Japanese communist movement, 1920-1966*. Berkeley and Los Angeles: University of California Press.

Sheldon, Garon. (1987). *The state and labor in modern Japan*. Berkeley: University of California Press.

Shōwa 16-nen Asahi nenkan [1941 Asahi yearbook]. (1940). Tokyo: Asahi shimbunsha.

Smith, Thomas C. (1955). *Political change and industrial development in Japan: Government enterprise, 1868-1889*. Stanford, CA: Stanford University Press.

Steven, Rob. (1983). *Classes in contemporary Japan*. Cambridge, UK: Cambridge University Press.

Suehiro, Gentarō. (1959). *Nihon rōdōkumiai undōshi* [A history of the Japanese labor union movement]. Tokyo: Kyōdō tsūshinsha.

Tabata, Terumi. (1981). *Nihon no nōson fukushi* [Rural welfare in Japan]. Tokyo: Keisō shobō.

Tamura, Eiichirō. (1988). *Nihon no kyōiku to nashonarizumu* [Japanese education and nationalism]. Tokyo: Akashi shoten.

Tanaka, Akira. (1976). *Meiji ishin* [The Meiji restoration] (Nihon no rekishi [Japanese history], vol. 24). Tokyo: Shigakukan.

Togawa, Yoshio, et al. (1987). *Jukyōshi* [A history of Confucianism] (Sekai shūkyōshi sōsho [World religions series], vol. 10). Tokyo: Yamakawa shuppansha.

Tokyo daigaku shakaikagaku kenkyujo. (Ed.). (1974-1975). *Sengo kaikaku* [The postwar reforms], 8 vols. Tokyo: Tokyo daigaku shuppankai.

Toshida, Seiichi. (Ed.). (1989). *Nihon keizai no nagare wo yomu* [Reading currents in the Japanese economy]. Tokyo: Tōyō keizai shimpōsha.

Tsuda, Shinchō. (1981, July). Nihonteki keieiron no kiso shikaku [The basic perspective for a Japanese theory of management]. *Keizai hyōron*, (July).

Tsujinaka, Isao. (1971). *Meiji no rōdō undō* [Labor movements in the Meiji period]. Tokyo: Kinokuniya.

Wakita, Osamu. (1980). Kinsei toshi no seiritsu [The formation of early modern cities]. In Kōtarō Takahashi, et al. (Eds.), *Nihon kindaishi yōsetsu* [A summary discussion of modern Japanese history]. Tokyo: Tokyo daigaku shuppankai.

Waswo, Ann. (1988). The transformation of rural society, 1900-1950. In Peter Duus (Ed.), *The Cambridge history of Japan. Vol 6: The twentieth century* (pp. 97-153). Cambridge, UK: Cambridge University Press.

Watanabe, Osamu. (1987). Gendai nihon shakai no ken'iteki kōzō to kokka [The authority structure of contemporary Japanese society and the state]. In Isamu Fujita (Ed.), *Ken'iteki chitsujo to kokka* [Authority structure and the state]. Tokyo: Tokyo daigaku shuppankai.

Weber, Max. (1930). *The protestant ethic and the spirit of capitalism* (Talcott Parsons, trans.). New York: Scribner.

World Bank. (1989). *World development report 1989*. New York: Oxford University Press.

Yamakawa, Hitoshi. (1979). *Shakaishugi undō shōshi* [A short history of the socialist movement]. Tokyo: Shakaishugi kyōkai shuppankyoku.

PART III

SOCIAL POLICY

In this concluding section of the book, we examine in greater detail the central importance of state interventions in the production and reproduction of labor. The three chapters examine the ways in which the East Asian states actively promoted the exploitation of cheap female labor to foster economic development, along with other social and labor policies intended to keep labor inexpensive and relatively quiescent during the early years of industrialization, when development depended on the exportation of cheap commodities.

In Chapter 9, Lucie Cheng and Ping-Chun Hsiung document the central role played by female labor in the recent growth of the Taiwanese economy (this theme is taken up in a comparative context in the following chapter by Salaff). They argue that patriarchy and capitalism have reinforced one another to promote economic development. In Taiwan (as elsewhere in the world), women are shown to bear the "double burden" of providing labor in the larger economy as well as at home: Taiwan's economic success results in large part from "the specific use of women's labor as chief wage workers, unwaged family workers, and unpaid service providers." Yet while women provided the cheap labor that underpinned Taiwan's EOI, they have not reaped the fruits of their efforts.

Women now comprise more than one third of the work force in Taiwan, with labor force participation rates approaching 50%. The most rapid growth in female labor occurred during the explosion of EOI during the late 1960s and early 1970s. Yet despite the presence of substantial numbers of women in the work force, female labor force participation is highly volatile, reflecting ebbs and flows in the world economy, the local business cycle, and family situation. In Taiwan women enter the work force at an early age, withdraw when they get married and have children, and then reenter in their late thirties, as child-rearing responsibilities diminish. They also tend to retire from the work force earlier than men—around age 55—often to care for elderly males in their homes. When they do work, women are paid less than men, a fact that is trumpeted by the Taiwanese government to court foreign investment (the presumed docility of female workers is another frequently cited selling point). In industries such as agriculture, mining, manufacturing, construction, and commerce, there has been a progressive erosion of female earnings relative to male earnings since the early 1970s.

As Cheng and Hsiung demonstrate, the exploitation of women has been particularly severe in the sex industry, a major source of foreign exchange. Prostitution and open sex are used to lure millions of tourists—from the United States, Japan, and elsewhere—to the brothels, massage parlors, bath houses, and even barber shops of Taiwan. Government-distributed tourist booklets frequently contain advertisements touting the sexual attractiveness of Taiwanese women. It is estimated that as many as a third of a million women are involved in the sex industry at the present time.

Women provide an important source of unpaid domestic labor, a pattern that is actively pursued through state policy and reinforced by the traditional Chinese emphasis on women's roles in maintaining harmony and educating children. The amount of work that even middle-class Taiwanese women do at home is substantial. Homemaking duties frequently combine with unpaid or poorly paid labor intended to supplement factory output for the export sector. While homework is not uncommon in industrial nations, Taiwan is one of the few countries actively to pursue such cheap labor through state policies. Cheng and Hsiung discuss at length two examples of this "capitalist patriarchal state of Taiwan": the "living-room factories" and the "Mother's Workshops," both originating in the 1968 community development program. Under the former program, the Taiwanese government provides special incentives for families to purchase sewing machines and learn sewing skills for homework. This simultaneously increases the supply of cheap female labor while reducing its cost, since expenditures do not have to be made on facilities, energy, dormitories, or management. Nor are women who work at home provided with health insurance, minimum wage guarantees, or similar protections. The living-room factories are supported by the Mother's Workshops, which attempt to "educate" women into being good mothers and productive workers at home. Women are trained in community beautification, safety, vocational skills, sanitation, health, nutrition, culture, leisure, and even interior decoration. Government-sponsored workshops also train mothers in family virtues: etiquette, womanly comportment, the promotion of harmony in the family, the proper use of make-up, and—importantly—the skills necessary to be effective workers in living-room factories.

Women work long and hard in Taiwan; in Cheng and Hsiung's view, they are the untold story of that country's phenomenal economic growth. They provide a flexible work force that is secure, unprotected, and cheap. Without this form of patriarchal domination, Cheng and Hsiung conclude, Taiwanese capitalism would not have proven so successful.

In Chapter 10, Janet Salaff further examines the critical role played by women in the economic development of Hong Kong, Singapore, and Taiwan. She first examines the threefold nature of the Chinese family. It is patrilineal and patrilocal, a form that privileges the bond between the family and the son, while requiring the daughter to establish ties with her husband's family at the expense of her own. The family also functions as an economic unit, pooling the labor of the married daughters. Finally, Chinese mothers have close bonds with their children, creating a "uterine family" that assures an economic contribution by daughters despite their exclusion from the patriliny.

During the postwar period large families (reflected in growing dependency ratios) forced unmarried sons and daughters into the work force. Girls in particular, having already experienced the household division of labor, were readily absorbed into the larger economy; as adolescents they first serve as unpaid household laborers in "putting-out" systems (as Cheng and Hsiung document), moving into outside factory work as they grow older. During the early days of industrialization, unmarried daughters were expected to work, often delaying marriage so that the sons could continue their educations. The girls' wages contributed to household income, viewed as a form of compensation for the costs of their upbringing. In return, the daughters received a modest increase in disposable income, along with the satisfaction that derived from contributing to the family in a culture where such contribution is highly valued. Salaff finds that daughters contribute as much as three quarters of family income, rendering their labor a significant source of the household's living standard.

A large proportion of newly married couples initially live with the husband's parents, at least until the birth of their children removes the mother from the work force, creating an economic burden on the parents' household. The ability of a newly married woman to work depends on her level of education, the wage she can earn outside the household, and her ability to shift her homemaking responsibilities to unmarried sisters. Since women's wages are typically extremely low, most married women drop out of the work force while they are raising children. In recent years, however—as wages and women's educational attainment have increased—there is some evidence that women are remaining more active in the work force. Once women become mothers-in-law and grandmothers, they often reenter the work force, this time realizing a fair degree of economic independence.

Salaff concludes that family cycle, demographics, and the external economy interact to produce the labor patterns associated with EOI in the East Asian NICs. While the role of female labor was key to early development, in today's maturing economies an increasing number of women are demanding (and receiving) education and higher wages. As a result, growing numbers of women—including those who are married—are choosing to work outside the home. This will undoubtedly have a profound effect on family structure and economic development in the coming years.

In the final chapter, Frederic Deyo undertakes a broad comparative review of the various forms of social policy that have been used by the East Asian states to secure legitimacy. He argues that under EOI, economic policies typically drive social policies. Four different forms of social policy are examined: economic development itself, which, Deyo argues, has significant welfare implications as employment and wages rise; direct social welfare expenditures on health, housing, education, transportation, food, and various forms of public assistance; incomes policies, which influence wages and benefits; and income security programs, through pension programs, unemployment compensation, disability and health insurance, and other forms of social security. All four forms of social policy have been effectively utilized to promote economic development goals.

Economic development, as others in this volume have shown, was explicitly intended to secure legitimacy by reducing unemployment and boosting incomes—a strategy pursued with varying degrees of success in all four countries. By promoting development through the export of labor-intensive manufactured goods, labor surpluses typically turned into shortages within two decades; this, in turn, has resulted in a shift toward higher value-added manufacturing.

Unlike development strategies, direct expenditures on social welfare differ considerably across the four NICs. The provision of housing, health care, and subsidized foodstuffs helped to ease the upward pressure on wages, particularly in Hong Kong and Singapore, which provided vast public housing estates for workers. Public housing, Deyo argues, has been provided not in response to workers' demands, but rather as an instrument of development itself, sharply reducing the cost of labor and hence cheapening the cost of exports. In general, Deyo finds the percentage of government expenditures on the social wage to be highest in the two higher-urbanized city-states, with Hong Kong currently outspending Singapore even after the latter's more sizeable defense expenditures are subtracted from the base. Taiwan also spends more than Korea on social welfare, both per capita and relative to GDP. During the 1980s, all four countries increased social spending relative to other government outlays, a result that doubtless reflects some "maturing" of their developmental economies. Presently, if one looks only at social expenditures, South Korea and Singapore spend the highest percentage (roughly 63%) on education of the four NICs, with Hong Kong spending the lowest (34%); Taiwan spends the highest percentage on social security and welfare (41%); Singapore and Hong Kong spend the highest percentage on health (18%); while Hong Kong spends the highest percentage on housing and community service (36%, Singapore having completed its vast public housing programs by the early 1980s).

Incomes policies have changed considerably in recent years in the four countries. During the early phases of EOI, when cheap labor was the key to growth, strict controls over labor were the norm; the need to keep wages down—to assure international competitiveness—often led to a high degree of repression. In recent years, the turn away from cheap export manufacturing—necessitated by growing labor shortages, themselves the result of developmental success—has led to growing expenditures on the human capital formation, particularly education and health. As wage restraint becomes less compatible with economic growth, controls have been eased. There are, however, significant historical differences between the four NICs. South Korea, which emphasized heavy industry requiring large labor concentrations, until recently exerted the most repressive controls over its work force; South Korea's history of pitched battles and bloody repression is well known. While Taiwan also depended on cheap labor for its early developmental success, its form of economic organization (small, interlinked, family-based firms rather than large factories) did not so readily admit of labor repression, a pattern reinforced by historically paternalistic employer-employee relations. In Singapore, early (1960s) leftist leanings of the since-dominant People's Action Party assured the widespread provision of the national pension scheme (Central Provident Fund), public housing, and national health care. Since that time, labor has been fully incorporated and controlled, permitting repressive wage policies during the 1970s and human capital formation subsequently. Hong Kong combines the family-firm structure of Taiwan with larger factory employment; the steady influx of immigrants from mainland China, however, has helped to assure a relatively abundant (and docile) work force fearful of deportation.

Policies aimed at providing income security have varied across the NICs. In South Korea, social insurance guarantees have been primarily directed toward public sector workers, the military, and school teachers. In general, protections have tended to be privately financed and contributory in nature. Taiwan has a similar profile, although with somewhat broader state guarantees than South Korea. Singapore's Central Provident Fund—which was established prior to industrialization—provides a strong social insurance program, while Hong Kong guarantees such protections only to civil service workers.

In recent years, economic restructuring in all four NICs has led to a shift toward higher value-added production, entailing new investments in human capital formation. The highly interventionist governments of South Korea and Singapore have, not surprisingly, devoted more resources to education and training than have those of Taiwan and Hong Kong. More paternalistic labor relations have also helped to assure stability in Taiwan and Singapore. In South Korea, which has continued to emphasize heavy industry, a highly proletarianized work force has become increasingly militant, demanding (and, in the past few years, receiving) significant wage increases, a national pension plan, and national health insurance.

Taiwan has similarly experienced a liberalization of labor policies, although the economy continues to be characterized by small, paternalistic firms and weak labor. The government of Singapore—like that of South Korea—has played a key role in economic restructuring, primarily in the direction of greater corporatism in the form of house unions and the privatization of some social, educational, and welfare programs. Restructuring—even including the encouragement of higher-wage, higher value-added production—remains in the service of economic development. Finally, Hong Kong has experienced no major shifts in social policy, with continuing flows of immigrants assuring a pool of low-wage, largely female workers for export industries.

Deyo concludes that East Asian development has emphasized the "effective utilization of human resources." While the strength of the developmental state varies across the four countries (with Singapore and South Korea at one pole, Hong Kong at the other, and Taiwan occupying an intermediate position), in all four cases social policy has been subordinate to (and in support of) state developmental objectives. Social policies, in general, have increased labor productivity, provided education and training, and—in various ways—helped to control and/or subsidize wages. The state has thus in various ways played a key role in assuring rapid economic growth.

9

Women, Export-Oriented Growth, and the State
THE CASE OF TAIWAN

LUCIE CHENG

PING-CHUN HSIUNG

During the last decade, three areas of scholarship have developed independently of each other: development studies, feminist studies, and studies of the role of the state. Not until recently has there been some cross fertilization among the three areas (Charlton, Everett, & Staudt, 1989). This chapter, drawing on the insights of these fields, is an effort to contribute to the ongoing discussion of the relationship between economic development and the system of male domination. We argue that as patriarchy and capitalism have penetrated the family, enterprises, and the state they have promoted the exploitation of women as low-waged and nonwaged income-generating workers, and as nonwaged domestic workers responsible for the reproduction of labor and for care of the elderly. The twin ideologies that dominate state and society actively promote "the double burden" as an acceptable and even aspired-to woman's role in the service of national development. This role, in turn, is a necessary, although not a sufficient contributor to the nation's economic advancement in a competitive world system. We will ground our discussion on the period of rapid economic growth in Taiwan from the mid-1960s to the late-1970s and will include more recent data when relevant.

Among the many factors that have been identified as responsible for Taiwan's economic "miracle," perhaps the least controversial is the availability of an elastic and cheap labor supply. Several scholars have pointed out that women are an especially important component of this labor (Bian,

1985; Chou, 1989; Diamond, 1979; Gallin, 1984a, 1984b; Koo, 1987; Kung 1983; P. K.-C. Liu, 1984; Y.-L. Liu, 1985; Tsay, 1985). Despite their contributions to the economic growth of Taiwan, women as a group have not benefitted equally in comparison to men. Women are still underrepresented in the upper echelons of occupations (Y.-L. Liu 1985, p. 40), and their average wage continues to be a fraction of their male counterparts' (Bian, 1985 pp. 270-271; P.K.-C. Liu, 1984, p. 96). How is this gender difference maintained and reproduced? Research has focused on gender-specific socialization patterns, the influence of cultural traditions, and discriminatory practices of employers. We attempt to integrate these discussions by examining the role of the state vis-à-vis women and development. We will show how, under the "economy in command" orientation and with the support of a male-dominated civil society, the state manages to ensure the availability of an elastic and cheap female labor force by perpetuating and institutionalizing a patriarchal, capitalist ideology. The advancement of Taiwan's position in the world system is dependent on the specific use of women's labor as cheap wage workers, unwaged family workers, and unpaid service providers.

Women's Labor and Economic Development in Taiwan

Discussions of women's labor and economic development have largely concentrated on female labor force participation and employment. Taiwan is justifiably proud of its record on the quantity and quality of its female work force. In 1951, shortly after the Guomindang (GMD, the Nationalist Party) government relocated to the Islands, the male labor force participation rate was 90.0% and the rate for females was 42.1%. Both rates decreased until 1966 when male participation dropped to 81.4% and female to a low of 32.6%. The reasons for these decreases are not entirely clear. Based on age-specific data by sex, P. K.-C. Liu and Hwang (1987) attribute them to rising levels of education, a low economic growth rate, compulsory military service, high fertility rate, and statistical artifacts due to a change in reporting definition. In any case, the early trend of decline for female labor force participation is generally seen as benign or even to some extent "positive," a result related more to improvement of the quality of labor and intensified childbearing and not so much to traditional gender discrimination. This conclusion masks the fact that negative effects of demographic factors on women's labor force participation are not natural, but are socially produced.

There is no doubt that the expansion of educational opportunities for women has had many beneficial results. Among these has been an improvement in the quality of female labor force. Unfortunately, more education for women may not mean more gender equality. As Greenhalgh (1985) observes, up to a point the relationship between women's education and the decrease in their labor force participation reflects increased gender inequality. Young women were given the opportunity to finish junior high and high schools before entering the labor force to help their brothers gain more education. The increase in education for women in Taiwan has not increased women's status vis-à-vis men. Instead, it has resulted in higher returns to their families from their exploitation. Parents tended to increase investment in their daughters' education just enough to enable the child to gain a well-paid job.

The negative relationship between fertility and labor force participation observed by P. K.-C. Liu and Hwang (1987) is more a social construct than a physical inevitability. For example, the requirement that women leave the labor force for an extended period to assume responsibility for child care is a "social" rather than a "biological" one. By tying rewards exclusively to individual productivity while ignoring societal needs, what appear to be gender-neutral capitalist employment practices actually punish women.

Elasticity in Women's Labor Force Participation

Most discussions of gender and labor force participation in Taiwan begin with 1966 when the impact of economic restructuring was first reflected in the labor market. From that year on, women's labor force participation rate, despite its zigzag pattern, has shown an upward trend. By 1987, 3.1 million or 38.1% of the total labor force, were women (Directorate-General of Budget, 1989, p. 5). In comparison to 1966, when 32.6% of all females 15 years and older were in the labor force, the percentage for 1987 is 46.5. Three characteristics of women's labor force participation support the argument that women are especially important to Taiwan's economic growth: the timing of the increase, its long-term growth pattern, and women's low wage level.

The sharpest rise in women's labor force participation occurred between 1966 and 1973, the period marked by labor-intensive, export-oriented industrialization. During that period, as Table 9.1 shows, the female labor force participation rate rose from 32.6% to 41.5%, while male rates remained relatively stable with some decline. This trend reflects a change in the economic policy of Taiwan which in turn is conditioned by the transformation of the international division of labor.

Massive restructuring of capitalism in the mid-1960s created an opportunity for peripheral and semiperipheral countries to seek advancement in the world system. Taiwan was able to mobilize its resources to take advantage of this opportunity. Adequate foreign investment and domestic accumulation, enough state autonomy from both the constraints of world economy and powerful domestic interest groups, political stability, and access to markets provided the conditions for Taiwan to develop a viable economic policy based on export (Crane, 1982; Evans & Pang, 1989; Winckler and Greenhalgh, 1988. The pursuit of labor-intensive, export-oriented development required a particular kind of labor force, one relatively large in number, flexible in flow, and inexpensive in price. Female labor, for reasons that we will discuss later, fits these requirements especially well. The ready supply of female labor has reduced labor costs and increased Taiwan's competitiveness in the world market (Bian, 1985; Gallin, 1990). In addition, the use of female labor helps to ease the impact of inflation in core countries such as the United States (Mies, 1986). The elasticity of female labor relative to male labor is indicated by the greater fluctuation in women's participation rates over time. In contrast with male rates, female rates are more sensitive to changes in the world economy (Chiang & Ku, 1985, pp. 8-9). The rise and decline of female rates corresponds to business cycles in Taiwan (Chou, 1989, pp. 437-438).

Table 9.1 shows the difference in annual growth rates of male and female labor force participation. While male rates hover between 1.3 in 1980 and 4.9 in 1974, female rates not only have a much wider range, but also show a much wider zigzag pattern. The growth of women in the labor force peaked in 1973, when the rate reached 16%. This increase is due to labor-intensive industrialization. The growth rate, however, dropped to 0.3% in 1974 and reached a negative of −0.8% in 1975 when Taiwan's economy was severely affected by the oil crisis. Afterward, it took almost a decade for women's participation rate to reach the same average level of growth as before the economic recession. A comparison of the unemployment rates between women and men shows similarly greater elasticity for women (Table 9.1). There are more frequent fluctuations in women's rates and the difference between each change is generally larger.

Table 9.1 Labor Force Participation and Unemployment by Gender, Taiwan, 1965-1987

| | LFP Rate[a] | | Growth Rate[b] | | Unemployment Rate | |
	Male	Female	Male	Female	Male	Female
1965	82.6	33.1	2.1	0.8	2.3	5.9
1966	81.4	32.6	2.1	2.0	2.3	4.9
1967	80.9	33.7	3.0	7.5	1.8	3.5
1968	80.2	34.4	2.8	5.9	1.6	2.0
1969	79.2	35.4	2.9	7.0	1.6	2.6
1970	78.9	35.5	3.9	4.2	1.5	2.2
1971	78.4	35.4	3.5	3.7	1.5	2.1
1972	77.0	37.1	2.2	8.9	1.2	2.1
1973	77.1	41.5	3.4	16.0	1.1	1.7
1974	78.2	40.2	4.9	0.3	1.3	2.0
1975	77.6	38.6	2.7	–0.8	2.1	3.1
1976	77.1	37.6	2.7	0.8	1.6	2.1
1977	77.8	39.3	4.2	8.1	1.7	2.0
1978	78.0	39.2	4.5	3.2	1.6	1.9
1979	77.9	39.2	2.5	3.4	1.2	1.5
1980	77.1	39.3	1.3	3.0	1.1	1.5
1981	76.8	38.8	2.2	1.7	1.2	1.6
1982	76.5	39.3	2.3	4.1	2.3	2.3
1983	76.4	42.1	1.8	9.6	2.7	2.7
1984	76.1	43.3	2.0	5.2	2.4	2.5
1985	75.5	43.5	1.7	2.8	2.9	2.9
1986	75.2	45.5	2.0	7.1	2.8	2.5
1987	75.2	46.5	2.2	4.4	2.0	2.0

SOURCE: Directorate-General (1988), pp. 52-53.
NOTES: a. Percentage of LFP
. Increases in number of workers in labor market

Table 9.2 Labor Force Participation Rate by Age and Gender, Selected Years

| | 1966 | | 1974 | | 1983 | |
	Male	Female	Male	Female	Male	Female
15-19	54.6	54.7	49.9	52.4	76.4	39.2
20-24	84.0	46.6	78.7	54.3	36.2	60.9
25-29	97.3	28.9	96.6	36.7	75.9	46.5
30-34	98.1	28.7	98.8	37.8	95.3	46.9
35-39	98.3	33.2	98.8	53.5	98.1	48.9
40-44	96.9	30.6	98.5	47.9	98.1	48.0
45-49	95.1	27.4	96.1	41.4	96.1	52.9
50-54	89.1	20.0	89.0	32.6	89.8	35.0
55-59	71.4	11.7	82.8	19.4	79.7	26.8
60-64	46.2	6.0	52.7	7.0	60.2	15.6
65+	17.2	1.5	11.8	1.0	15.4	2.7

SOURCE: Tsay (1985), p. 303.

Women's employment is not only more susceptible to the business cycle, it is also more affected by individual and family life-cycle events. Age, marital status, and number of children play a more significant role in determining women's than men's labor force participation. Women tend to withdraw from the marketplace between age 25 to 34; that is, after the worker's marriage and the birth of her first child. They reenter the labor market after 35 as their family responsibilities lighten. A great majority leave the labor market entirely after 55 years of age, perhaps to care for the elderly members of the family. Males, on the other hand, stay in the job market until they reach retirement age (Table 9.2).

The differential impact of marital status is more obvious when we compare female and male rates in Table 9.3. While gender makes a difference in labor force participation, the difference is the smallest for single persons. For

Table 9.3 Percentage of LFP for Male and Female by Marital Status and Age, Taiwan, 1984

Age	Male			Female		
	Single	*Married*	*Divorced/ Widowed*	*Single*	*Married*	*Divorced/ Widowed*
15-19	30.2	90.8	—	33.4	30.7	100.0
20-24	70.5	97.3	100.0	76.8	34.1	91.3
25-34	91.2	98.9	94.7	86.1	41.8	71.5
35-44	89.0	98.4	96.2	76.0	50.0	63.2
45-54	83.3	94.6	90.3	61.5	39.5	43.3
55-64	50.3	75.4	56.7	42.6	21.8	20.5
65+	10.4	18.0	8.5	32.4	4.3	1.7

SOURCE: Liu (1985), p. 25.

those who are married, male rates are more than double those of female's for all age groups. The presence of children under six years of age greatly reduces the likelihood of married women's labor force participation (Y.-L. Liu, 1985, pp. 76-77). When employment and promotion rules are developed with male workers in mind, women are disadvantaged because of interruptions caused by domestic responsibilities. Women's more frequent and early exits from the labor market for reproductive and caring purposes perpetuate their exploitation as cheap labor.

Women's Labor as Cheap Labor

Just how cheap has women's labor been in Taiwan? We will examine both the difference between male and female wages, and women's wages alone. The Taiwan government has publicized the cheap wages and docility of its labor force to attract foreign investment. A number of scholars have emphasized low wage and lack of benefits as characteristic of female labor (Cumings, 1987; Deyo, 1989; Kung, 1983). In fact, many would argue that these features are the raison d'être of female employment in capitalism. As

Table 9.4 Gender Distribution by Industry, Taiwan, Selected Years

| | 1966 | | 1970 | | 1980 | | 1988 | |
	M	F	M	F	M	F	M	F
Agriculture, etc.	42.6	46.0	35.1	40.6	20.2	18.1	15.2	10.6
Mining	2.0	0.4	2.7	0.8	0.9	0.3	0.5	0.2
Manufacturing	17.2	17.5	19.7	21.9	29.3	39.9	31.7	39.0
Utilities	1.0	0.2	1.0	0.3	0.6	0.1	0.6	0.1
Construction	4.8	0.6	7.0	0.7	11.7	2.0	10.6	1.9
Commerce	11.4	13.7	14.0	16.1	15.0	17.9	17.7	22.5
Transportation, etc.	5.9	1.7	7.0	1.9	7.7	2.3	7.3	2.1
Finance	15.2	19.9	13.6	17.8	2.0	2.5	2.9	3.8
Services	—	—	—	—	12.8	16.8	13.7	19.9
N	2,702	945	3,121	1,425	4,357	2,191	4,946	2,986

SOURCE: 1966, 1970, 1980: P. K.-C. Liu & Hwang (1987), p. 100. 1988: Directorate-General (1988), pp. 8-9.
NOTE: Numbers (N) are in thousands, for age 15 and older.

Tables 9.4 and 9.5 show, after two decades of development, women workers are still concentrated in the most labor-intensive industries where wages are typically low (see Table 9.4), as well as at the lower end of the occupational ladder of all industries (see Table 9.5).

As in other countries, women's wages in Taiwan are only a fraction of their male counterparts. In fact, the gap between male and female earnings not only has persisted but, in some occupations and industries, has widened over the past two decades (P. K.-C. Liu, 1984, pp. 95-98; P. K.-C. Liu & Hwang, 1987; Y.-L. Liu, 1985, pp. 56-66). Table 9.6 shows that in five out of nine industries there has been a deterioration of women's wages relative to men's during the past decade. The gains in wage equality observed in the 1970s had mostly eroded by the 1980s. Using 1980 data, P. K.-C. Liu (1984) found that the wage differentials cannot be explained by human capital variables.

Table 9.5 Occupational Distribution by Gender, Taiwan, Selected Years

		1970 M	1970 F	1980 M	1980 F	1984 M	1984 F	1988[e] M	1988[e] F
Professional &	(a)	0.3	—	0.3	—	0.3	—		
Technical Workers	(b)	2.6	0.6	2.4	0.6	2.8	0.8		
	(c)	9.4	12.0	11.0	14.5	10.9	14.3		
	(d)	22.8	23.8	26.9	33.1	26.2	32.6	6.2	7.8
Administative &	(a)	0.1	—	—	—	—	—		
Managerial Workers	(b)	9.3	1.0	2.6	0.1	2.5	0.2		
	(c)	5.3	1.6	1.1	0.2	1.1	0.2		
	(d)	6.8	2.0	1.8	0.3	1.6	0.2	1.3	0.2
Clerical Workers	(a)	0.5	0.3	0.6	0.5	0.5	0.8		
	(b)	6.3	8.3	14.6	13.6	14.4	14.5		
	(c)	13.0	12.8	15.6	26.9	15.3	26.4		
	(d)	19.7	14.7	21.4	21.4	20.1	22.4	11.5	20.3
Traders	(a)	0.1	—	—	—	—	—		
	(b)	4.7	4.5	3.1	0.9	3.0	0.8		
	(c)	32.8	38.5	30.7	30.2	31.7	30.3		
	(d)	0.9	1.2	0.7	1.1	1.0	1.1	14.4	15.1
Service Workers	(a)	—	—	0.1	0.3	—	0.2		
	(b)	1.6	1.6	2.4	1.1	2.1	1.1		
	(c)	11.8	21.8	14.6	20.3	15.3	22.3		
	(d)	22.3	39.7	22.6	27.6	23.4	30.5	7.3	11.8
Agricultural &	(a)	98.0	99.5	98.4	99.0	98.4	98.7		
Related Workers	(b)	1.0	0.6	—	—	—	—		
	(c)	0.6	—	0.1	—	0.1	—		
	(d)	0.7	—	0.2	—	0.3	—	15.1	10.6
Production,	(a)	1.1	0.2	0.6	0.3	0.6	0.2		
Transportation, &	(b)	74.5	83.3	74.9	93.6	75.2	82.6		
Related Workers	(c)	27.2	13.2	26.9	7.8	25.6	6.4		
	(d)	26.8	18.6	26.4	16.5	27.4	13.2	44.1	34.2

SOURCE: P. K.-C. Liu & Hwang (1987), pp. 140-141; Directorate-General (1988).
NOTES: a. Agriculture
b. Manufacturing
c. Service
d. Commerce
e. All Industries

Table 9.6 Proportion of Average Monthly Female Wage to Male Wage by Industry, Taiwan

	1973	1978	1984	1988
Agriculture	—	56.8	51.9	55.0
Mining	37.2	65.8	53.6	55.2
Manufacture	54.4[a]	61.0	61.1	57.6
Utilities	68.5[a]	75.1	74.0	81.6
Construction	65.4	75.8	68.0	71.9
Commerce	—	72.6	68.0	68.4
Transport	71.7	71.2	75.0	76.7
Financial Services	—	59.2	68.0	65.1
Social and Personal	71.3	72.7	75.7	72.8

SOURCE: 1973: Directorate-General (1974), p. 682; 1978 and 1984: Y.-L. Liu (1985), pp. 61-62; 1988: Directorate-General (1988), pp. 90-91.
NOTE: a. For manufacturing and utilities, the percentages are calculated from data for 1972.

Gender discrimination is widely recognized in Taiwan, although not widely condemned. A study of employment advertisements in newspapers reveal that males are preferred for higher-paying jobs, while for lower-paying jobs ads often stipulate that "only females may apply" (*Funu Xinzhi*, 59, 1987, p. 8). The state, on the one hand proclaims that men and women are equal, but on the other condones gender discrimination in its own employment practice (Zheng & Bo, 1987). Women are excluded from participating in civil service examinations for certain prestigious government jobs, such as high level jobs in the customs department, the diplomatic services, international journalism, and the labor department. For some civil service jobs, the number of women can not exceed a certain quota. For example, in 1985, the civil service examination for consular personnel was slated to admit 50 persons, but the public was informed that no more than 7 would be women (Zheng & Bo, 1987, p. 8). When confronted with these and other discriminatory practices, government officials often respond by saying that it is better for women and for society if women concentrate on what they do best.

Table 9.7 Percentage Distribution of Women and Men as Unpaid Family Workers, Selected Industries, 1966-1986

		Agriculture		*Manufacturing*		*Commerce*		*Services*	
		M	F	M	F	M	F	M	F
1966	(a)	28.7	74.9	4.4	12.1	8.3	41.6	2.0	7.2
	(b)	48.8	51.2	48.6	51.4	31.9	68.1	34.9	65.1
1971	(a)	23.0	78.9	2.8	9.7	8.2	43.2	2.0	5.7
	(b)	38.4	61.6	32.3	67.7	27.0	73.0	36.5	63.5
1976	(a)	20.9	71.4	2.5	4.7	6.6	36.3	1.3	4.6
	(b)	38.0	62.0	44.6	55.4	26.5	73.5	34.2	65.8
1981	(a)	16.1	65.8	2.4	4.6	6.2	36.3	1.4	5.2
	(b)	37.1	62.9	43.1	56.9	22.0	78.0	28.6	71.4
1986	(a)	16.5	67.3	1.9	5.3	6.6	36.3	1.4	5.8
	(b)	34.7	65.3	30.7	69.3	19.9	80.1	22.5	77.5

SOURCE: Chou (1989), pp. 450-457.
NOTES: a. Proportion of total male/female employed who are unpaid
b. Proportion of total unpaid workers who are male/female

For example, the Minister of Interior proclaimed publicly that women should take pride in freeing their husband from family worries and not be so concerned about whether or not they themselves can become department heads (*Funu Xinzhi,* 5, 1982, pp. 13-14). The labor force participation and employment rates overestimate the progress women have made in remunerative work since both include a large number of unpaid family workers, most of whom are female. As Table 9.7 indicates, although unpaid work done by males and females has declined, there has been an increase in the proportion of unpaid work done by females since 1966. In every industry, the proportion of unpaid female workers exceeds that of their male counterpart. Among unpaid family workers, women exceed men by a large margin. What labor can be cheaper than unpaid labor?

The expansion of women's paid and unpaid income-generating labor is directly tied to the state's export-oriented growth strategy. Fiscal and tax policies favoring firms willing to export (Directory, 1963, pp. 164-174; Yu, 1981) provided incentives for families to send their women to work or to respond to the state-sponsored "living-room factories" program to take advantage of family and neighborhood female labor. By linking domestic and paid work in the same space, women's labor was intensified and their work days lengthened. The increase in women's labor force participation and employment does not necessarily indicate an improvement in women's lives, nor does it indicate a rise in women's status. On the contrary, it may simply reflect an intensification of women's exploitation resulting from the addition of nondomestic employment with meager reward to the burden of domestic work. Women's increased employment is a requirement for the survival of capitalism; it is not to be confused with a victory in gender equality.

Women, the Sex Industry, and the State

An often ignored area of women's labor that has contributed significantly to capital accumulation in Taiwan is their sexual labor. Discussions on this topic are quite numerous, but most have focused on its morality and the physical exploitation of women, not on its economic role. Since the 1950s, Taiwan has been considered a haven for male tourists. In addition to registered brothels, commercial sexual services under various guises are widely available. These include barber shops, bath houses, massage parlors, bars, coffee houses, and restaurants, some of which are conveniently labelled by the government as *teding* or *tezhong yingye* or specialized businesses. Table 9.8 shows that while the number of brothels declined after peaking in 1967, the number of *Jiujia* or "restaurants with waitresses" more than doubled during the same period. Unfortunately, data on these specialized businesses are no longer published, although it is widely known where one can buy sexual services (*Funu Xinzhi,* 66, 1987, p. 10). Most recently, a new type of sex business has come into being that is graphically referred to as the "beef market."

Two conditions greatly facilitated the growth of the sex industry in Taiwan and other developing countries: American military presence and the United States' initiative to tie tourism to Third World development. One of the well-known but relatively unexplored consequences of the Korean War and the Vietnam War is the increase of the sex trade in Asia. Used as favorite R&R sites for American soldiers, cities in Taiwan, South Korea, Thailand, and other Southeast Asian countries became lucrative markets for the exploitation of women's sexual labor (Kim, 1987; Truong, 1990). The infrastructures developed for the sex industry continued to serve a burgeoning tourist trade after the wars ended.

Table 9.8 Number of Sexually Oriented Businesses in Taiwan, 1946-1973

	Hotel	Tea & Coffee Room	Restaurant w/Waitress	Cabaret	Brothel
1946	866	—	—	11	216
1947	969	—	—	—	—
1948	932	—	—	—	—
1949	902	—	—	—	—
1950	801	—	31	—	—
1951	842	346	56	—	—
1952	892	546	88	—	—
1953	961	786	86	—	—
1954	1,093	930	54	—	—
1955	1,137	930	52	—	—
1956	1,251	1,001	—	—	—
1957	1,326	984	—	—	249
1958	1,479	1,043	—	—	349
1959	1,576	1,030	—	3	424
1960	1,671	963	—	8	463
1961	1,782	1,002	—	11	476
1962	1,897	793	—	15	453
1963	2,014	825	—	17	412
1964	2,143	801	—	27	529
1965	2,272	859	—	32	509
1966	2,403	756	—	31	489
1967	2,949	765	76	46	636
1968	2,662	629	163	33	452
1969	2,802	596	449	25	384
1970	2,864	568	429	25	355
1971	2,916	511	372	25	337
1972	2,974	485	342	25	319
1973	2,997	451	407	25	311

SOURCE: Directorate-General (1974), pp. 188-189.

The development of Third World tourism is closely related to the global political economy (Truong, 1990). Truong argues that in order to save the heavy investment banks had made in aircraft industries in the 1950s, the U.S. government began to promote tourism as a development strategy for the

Third World, especially for Asian countries (Truong, 1990). Tourism was hailed as a peace-maintaining, harmony-producing industry. But the political and cultural functions of tourism were not enough to induce developing countries to spend millions of dollars to buy passenger airplanes, construct luxurious hotels and build other tourism infrastructure. After a concerted effort of the United States, tourist projects became eligible for financial and technical assistance from the international development programs of the World Bank, the United Nations, and other international agencies. It was the attraction of tourism as a way to gain foreign currency that prompted many Asian countries to use tourism as a development strategy.

The Taiwan government began to promote tourism in the mid-1950s, immediately following the conclusion of the Korean War. Since then, heated debates over its efficacy have periodically taken place in the Provincial Assembly and among the populace. Supporters of tourism combine economic, political, and cultural arguments. They point to its potential in earning foreign exchange, attracting foreign investment, and expanding foreign trade (Deng, 1975, p. 402). Politically, tourists are described as valuable messengers who can tell the world about the progress in Taiwan and therefore raise its international status. In addition, tourism can promote Chinese traditional culture (Zhou, 1966). Opponents, however, argue that the net economic advantage of tourism has not been demonstrated, and the negative social effects overshadow all the other advantages (Y. Li, 1987; Qu, 1984). Women's organizations and human rights activists have accused the government of colluding with sex traders by not enforcing existing laws or passing new legislation that would legalize prostitution rather than making invidious and useless distinctions between "public" or registered sexual laborers and "private" or underground ones (*Funu Xinzhi,* 1986-1987). Even supporters admit that due to the profit-seeking motives of some businesses, tourism has led to the burgeoning of the sex trade and has "affected the moral fiber of Taiwan" (Zhan, 1966, pp. 5-9). In fact, the government keeps the price of sexual labor low by prohibiting women in the "specialized businesses" to form unions on the grounds that their occupation "violate the good mores of society" (*Funu Xinzhi,* 69, 1988, p. 14).

Tourism is an "experience commodity" that necessitates the commoditization of personal services (Truong, 1990). Tourists are to be made feel welcome and "at home." Promotional campaigns endorsed by government agencies and tourist industries attempted to build a market by focussing on aspects of hospitality, such as female submissiveness, caring, and nurturing, as well as sexual temptation (Directory, 1963, pp. 178-180). Tourist booklets distributed at government handicraft stores and offices contain advertisements that magnify the sexual appeals of Taiwan women. Operators of sex package tours give detailed descriptions in words and pictures of the kinds of sexual services available and their costs to show that foreign visitors can enjoy uninhibited sex. A government publication, praising the achievement of Taiwan since its recovery from Japanese occupation, highlighted the "inexhaustible sources of pleasure" available (Deng, 1975, pp. 403-404).

To combat sexually transmitted diseases, which would threaten the tourist business as well as embarrass the government, a number of laws were promulgated to control prostitution and other sex trade. These laws take two general approaches: to make sexual contacts safe by requiring prostitutes to obtain and display health certificates, and to limit the number of specialized businesses by increasing the licensing fees and tax. Although neither approach has been successful, these laws did provide an official guide to relatively safe sex, and increased the revenue of the state. The link between women's sexual labor and foreign trade is a popular theme among well-known local writers (Huang, 1981). While we have no way to determine the specific dollar contribution of the sex industry to the economy, it is certain that it forms an important part of the tourist revenue. Tourism is included in economic discussions as an export, its revenue ranks fourth to sixth of all exports during the last two decades (Deng, 1975, p. 402). Table 9.9 shows the increase in tourist revenues from 1956 to 1973, the period of export-led growth.

As Table 9.9 also shows, the number of tourists has jumped from 15 thousand to more than 824 thousand during the same period. The increase is largely due to the influx of Japanese tourists. In 1957, Americans outnumbered all tourists with 70%; by 1973, American tourists comprised less than 20% while Japanese made up 72% of all tourists (Directorate-General, 1974, pp. 516-517). Japanese males are notorious as consumers of sexual tours, and their behavior has been the target of continuing demonstration by Japanese women as well as women in other Asian countries (*Funu Xinzhi,* 1987; Kim, 1987; Truong, 1990). When the International Lions Club met in Taipei, newspapers splashed pages of materials on where visitors can go to "buy spring." Taiwan women demonstrated with banners in Chinese, English, and Japanese languages: "Welcome to Taiwan for Friendship, but not for sex tours" (*Funu Xinzhi,* 62, 1987, p. 6).

Traditional ideology of self-sacrifice and submissiveness plays an important role in the sex trade, as girls "volunteer" or are forced by their real or adoptive parents to trade sexual labor for family survival or for the education of their male siblings (*Funu Xinzhi,* 47, 1986, pp. 2-3; X. Lu, 1986). While no official figures are available, women workers in the sex industry are

Table 9.9 Tourist Industry In Taiwan

	Total Number of Tourists	Growth Rate (%)	Total Revenue from Tourism (U.S.$)	Growth Rate (%)
1956	14,974	—	935,876	—
1957	18,159	21.3	1,134,938	21.3
1958	16,709	8.0	1,044,313	−8.0
1959	19,328	15.7	1,208,000	15.7
1960	23,636	22.3	1,477,251	22.3
1961	42,205	78.7	2,637,914	78.7
1962	52,304	23.9	3,269,000	23.9
1963	72,024	37.7	7,202,000	120.3
1964	95,481	32.6	10,345,000	43.6
1965	133,666	40.0	18,245,000	76.4
1966	182,948	36.9	30,353,000	66.4
1967	253,248	38.4	42,016,000	38.4
1968	301,770	19.2	53,271,000	26.8
1969	371,473	23.1	56,055,000	5.2
1970	472,452	26.9	81,720,000	45.8
1971	539,755	12.2	110,000,000	34.6
1972	580,033	7.5	128,707,000	17.0
1973	824,393	42.1	245,882,000	91.0
1974	819,821	−0.6	278,402,000	13.2
1975	853,140	4.1	359,358,000	29.1
1976	1,008,126	18.2	466,077,000	29.7
1977	1,110,182	10.1	527,492,000	13.2
1978	1,270,977	14.5	608,000,000	15.3
1979	1,340,382	5.5	919,000,000	51.2
1980	1,393,254	3.9	988,000,000	7.5
1981	1,409,465	1.2	1,080,000,000	9.3
1982	1,419,178	0.7	953,000,000	−11.7
1983	1,457,404	2.7	990,000,000	3.9
1984	1,516,138	4.0	1,066,000,000	7.7
1985	1,451,659	−4.3	963,000,000	−9.7
1986	1,610,385	10.9	1,333,000,000	38.4

SOURCE: Directorate-General (1987), p. 397.
Revenue income for 1956-1961 from Taiwan Shengzhengfu Xinwenchu (1965), pp. 18-32.

popularly estimated at more than 300,000 in 1989, including those brought from Southeast Asia and girls as young as 11 from local ethnic groups. Their customers include a large number of overseas Chinese and foreign visitors looking to satisfy their sexual appetite at an affordable price, and more importantly, with state protection. Women's sexual labor, like women's labor in other areas, is consciously exploited in Taiwan's strategy for national development. It functions as an exotic commodity for "tourist attraction and helps to fill airplane seats and hotel rooms. National accounts benefit from taxes on accommodation, food, drinks and services. Unlike their flesh, the contribution of prostitutes' labor to the process of accumulation remains invisible." (Truong, 1990, p. 128). The state condemns the women who are engaged in this trade and periodically arrests those who lack official certification, yet the state also encourages the continuation of exploitation by treating sexual labor as a tourist attraction.

Women's Unwaged Domestic Labor

National statistics do not reveal the necessary but monotonous, fragmented, and time-consuming domestic work that most women do without wage. Studies continue to show that men do not participate in household labor to any appreciable degree in most societies, including Taiwan (Y.-H. Lu, 1984; Miller & Garrison, 1982). Those who share this work with women do so selectively and reluctantly. Taiwan women, socialized to believe that domestic work is part and parcel of womanhood, may complain, but do not generally expect help from their menfolks.

What is the relationship between women's unwaged domestic labor and economic development? At the most basic level, women, as housewives and mothers, reproduce the labor force that creates growth. But women's unwaged domestic work is more than the physical reproduction of labor. Surveys indicate that housewives are the principal agents of domestic consumption. In Taipei, household expenditures in 59.4% of all families are managed by the wife, and another 14.7% by other women in the family (*Funu Xinzhi,* vol. 16, 1983, pp. 6-7). The model of the middle-class housewife in Taiwan involves a highly developed consumption style, which provides a market for ever-increasing commodities and services. It is no wonder that consumer education is almost exclusively directed toward females, and women are beginning to realize their potential in influencing the behavior of large corporations.

Through the maintenance of the family, women provide stability and emotional support to its members. Chinese tradition views women's role in maintaining harmony at home and in the neighborhood as critical to national development (Diamond, 1973; P. K.-C. Liu & Hwang, 1987). Both Taiwan and the People's Republic of China continue to promote this image through mass campaigns, education, and media indoctrination.

The heated debates in the 1970s in Europe and in the United States among scholars and politicians regarding "wages for housework" point to the economic value of this unpaid work (Kaluzynska, 1980). Unpaid domestic work became a public issue in Taiwan when *Funu Xinzhi,* the leading feminist magazine, reported in 1983 that the economic value of a housewife in middle-income families was about NT$35,500 a month, more than the salary of an associate professor in a university (*Funu Xinzhi,* vol. 16, 1983, p. 17). This estimate only includes cooking, laundering, cleaning, caring for the elderly, and tutoring children twice a week. Excluded are the economic value of household management and consumption-related labor typical of housewives such as shopping for food, clothing, and daily necessities. More recently, the magazine *Money (Qian)* calculates that depending on the number and ages of children, a middle-class wife has to earn a minimum of NT$18,620 to $36,620 per month to make her employment outside worthwhile (*Qian,* p. 162). The cost to the family of having the housewife employed outside for wages is staggering when we consider that the median monthly income of college-educated women is NT$17,146.

Various types of caring, such as child care, care for the elderly, and care for the infirm performed by women without pay reduce the cost of social welfare for the state. These savings have been especially significant for Taiwan since it has allocated a large percentage of its resources to security and defense. Women's unpaid domestic labor frees capital to be directed toward more productive investment as defined by the state.

It has been argued that the benefits of economic development will trickle down to women. However, the experience of advanced countries gives us little confidence in this prediction. Economic development has not reduced the burden of women's household labor as expected. A male-dominated state apparatus does not treat women's interest as a high priority. Machines and services considered by women to be most useful to alleviate their work load are not easily accessible in developing countries. When household mechanization occurs, it changes the way some housework is done, but does not greatly reduce the time spent in doing housework. The time that is reduced in an area of work often is taken up by other housework, or by a rise in housework standards.

Mechanization and commercialization of housework create opportunities for waged work for all women but produce different consequences for women of different classes. Working-class women will make the machines and provide the household services to allow middle-class women to seek better employment. Both classes of women are increasingly required to earn a wage to prevent the family from slipping from its standard of living. While middle-class women will gain some alleviation from their domestic responsibilities, working-class women who cannot afford to buy the machines or hire others to perform the services will continue to be burdened. Data from Taiwan indicate that among married female professional and managerial workers, more than 15% rely on servants for child care (Y.-H. Lu, 1984, p. 367).

Economic growth has created more leisure, but this leisure has not led men to share domestic work with women. In fact, it is women's unpaid domestic labor that creates leisure time for men. Studies have shown that employed men have more leisure time than both employed women and full-time housewives (Waring, 1988, p. 163). Men prefer to spend their leisure with other men. In the United States they drink, play cards, attend sports events, go camping or fishing, or watch TV. In Taiwan, men may engage in other activities, but it is doubtful that they will do housework.

The flexible nature of domestic labor is especially conducive to exploitation. Much housework does not have to be done in a specific amount of time because the standards are variable: high or low standards of cleanliness, ironed or unironed clothes, and so forth. Therefore, it does not prohibit women from taking on either unpaid family income-producing work, or waged labor. In other words, it allows women to be doubly burdened without appearing so. The blind acceptance of a patriarchal concept of labor defined by men and based on the characteristics of male labor prevents the recognition of a large portion of women's labor as labor.

Waged Work and Unwaged Work: The Continuity of Women's Work

Mies (1986) argues that we are accustomed to viewing women's work with concepts developed on the basis of men's work under capitalism. Most men work for a certain number of hours a day, away from home, and uninterrupted by household concerns. Men are paid regularly and their jobs are to a varying extent protected by the state. Women's work does not have the same characteristics. Women are primarily household workers, although an increasing number are engaged in income-generating activities. Many work in the informal economy, insecure and unprotected. Their work is continuous and with frequent interruptions, but the interruptions are an integral part of women's work. It is misleading to think of women's work with categories developed for the accounting of men's work. Thus feminist scholars have argued the need for a new concept of labor built upon the concrete labor of women (Beneria, 1982; Mies, 1986; Waring, 1988). Some case studies of the working lives of women in Taiwan's export economy may be helpful in this construction.

Women's daily work schedules are arranged around their familial responsibilities as wife, mother, and daughter-in-law.

1. May-cheng comes to paint glasses at the small factory around 8 in the morning after her husband leaves for work. Around 11, she goes back to her apartment, which is five doors down the alley, to prepare lunch for him. After her husband leaves for work around 1 o'clock, she comes back to work until 5:30 or 6 when she goes home to prepare for dinner. She continues to paint the glasses at home after dinner while she waits for water to do the family's laundry or other chores. She doesn't go to sleep until after midnight.

2. A-hsia and her sister-in-law share the responsibility of caring for their father-in-law. They each take care of him for 15 days per month. During the half month of A-hsia's turn, she gets up around 6 and prepares both breakfast and lunch for him before she comes to work because he insists on eating his noon meal at 11:45. A-hsia goes home at 12 o'clock to eat the leftovers. She comes back to the factory at 12:50 and goes home to cook around 5:10. After dinner, she comes back to work in the factory until 9.

3. This week is A-chou's turn to stay at home and look after her father-in-law who has been confined to bed for the last 10 years. She can only work in the factory from 1 to 3 when he takes his nap. She rushes into the factory, squats on the floor, and removes as many rubber bands from the drawers as she possibly can. During the whole time, the only word she utters is "good-bye" when she leaves.

Women often have to compromise their waged labor outside the family with their unwaged labor in the family business. When a man is thinking of getting married, he calculates how much he has to spend for the engagement party, bride price, and wedding, and how much of his investment will be recovered when his wife joins the labor force.

When I congratulated Lin, an owner of a factory who just got engaged, he talked about his bride-to-be: "I don't intend to get a decorating vase. I also don't need sex; if I want sex, I can get cheap sex on the street. I heard that she is very good at bookkeeping. People say that she is really thrifty and hardworking too. The other day, I ran into her in the market, she was riding a 125 cc motorcycle. You know, she is really physically very strong." When I asked him how much he had to spend in total, he said it will be about NT$400,000. "It is worth it. People think I have a pretty good deal, you know," Lin said.

It is quite understandable why many women quit their jobs in the factory after their marriage; the totality of their labor, for income and for reproduction, is required by the family as unwaged labor.

> Lu finished elementary school and didn't want to continue because she didn't think she could pass the unified entrance examination for junior high. She went to work in a garment factory in the Tan-zi Export Processing Zone for more than 10 years. Her marriage was arranged by her parents. She had to quit her job because the factory run by her husband's family needed her labor. She didn't get paid working in the family's factory. It was only last year when the family business slowed down that Lu start looking for jobs outside. Even after Lu found a job in the neighborhood, she still had to compensate for her missed unwaged labor in the family factory by coming up with a special work arrangement:

> Lu's schedule starts around 7 in the morning. She has to get ready for work by 7:15. Before leaving home for waged work, she first works in the family factory for 30 minutes. She and her two sisters-in-law take weekly turns to cook for workers in the family factory. Lu works for wages in Xin-liang, a hardware store, from 8 to 12 during the weeks when it is not her turn to cook lunch, and returns at 1 p.m. In other weeks she leaves Xin-liang at 11 and gets back at 12:30 instead of at 1 p.m. when other workers come back from their lunch. After she finishes work at the hardware store, she resumes work in the family factory again from 4:30 to 5:30. Lu is paid hourly by the hardware store because she does not work 40 hours every week.

The complex and overlapping work schedule reflects the integration of women's productive and reproductive roles and their waged and unwaged labor.

How is the continuing exploitation of women's labor in all its complexity maintained, and the resulting gender inequality perpetuated? What role does the state play?

The Capitalist Patriarchal State of Taiwan

Several scholars have argued that the GMD state of Taiwan has been and continues to be a patriarchal state (Diamond, 1975; Gallin, 1984a, 1984b). This is best seen through the activities of its Women's Department and a semiofficial organization, the Chinese Women's Anti-Aggression League. Both of these institutions advocate patriarchal values and sponsor programs and projects that are mere extensions of women's familial roles. Women are encouraged to participate in

> voluntary sewing of clothing for military personnel, collection and donation of cash, clothes, and foodstuffs for needy military dependents, the operation of 35 milk-bars for needy children, the maintenance of schools and orphanages for war orphans and the children of civil servants and military personnel, assistance to retired servicemen, collections of clothing for Vietnamese refugees, and aid for KMT (GMD) soldiers returned from Burma and Vietnam, and relief services to needy women and overseas Chinese girl students in Taiwan. (Diamond, 1975, p. 15)

Women's subordination in Taiwan is not simply a continuity of traditional values and culture. It is a product of patriarchal capitalism in which the interests of the capitalist, the state, and the international market are served (Gallin, 1984b; Gates, 1979). As Gates (1979) puts it, "the KMT has fostered patterns that are more than conservative, for it has not simply maintained or returned to tradition. Instead, it has encouraged certain tendencies through new political means and a changing economy to a higher level than they could possibly have reached in the past."

Through the mass media and educational system, the state plays an active role in encouraging "an ideological environment that relegates women to menial labor and household tasks." The result is a patriarchal capitalist system whereby women's unpaid domestic and underpaid public labor are appropriated "without altering cultural definitions of male and female roles or transforming the structure of male status and authority within the family." (Gallin, 1984a, p. 398). A study of elementary and middle school textbooks used in Taiwan shows that scientists, positive political leaders, and scholars are invariably males; and those caring for households are all females. Furthermore, the personal qualities associated with male characters are ambition, courage, persistence, wisdom, adventurousness, and so forth, whereas those associated with female characters are filial obedience, courtesy, and warm-heartedness (*Funu Xinzhi,* 1988).

Fostering Women's Double Burden: The Community Development Program

As pointed out earlier, the adoption of an export-oriented development strategy necessitates the availability of a flexible and cheap labor supply, and women have met that need extremely well. But women's employment is also feared as potentially threatening to men and to family stability. These two concerns are reflected in the state's Community Development Program that promotes the perpetuation of women's double burden. In 1968, the government designed a 10-year community development program that was later extended several times. The goal of this program is to "improve the people's material as well as spiritual lives" (Taiwan Shengzhengfu Shehuichu, 1987, p. 19). The program not only deals with problems in food, clothing, living, transportation, and leisure, but also proposes to enhance Chinese traditional moral values and social norms in the local community. Women are important in the Community Development Program both as a target group for special training and as essential implementers of the Program. Their participation has been crucial to the success of the Program.

Organizational Structure

There are Community Development Committees at the provincial, district/county, and town/village levels. The Governor, Mayor, Chief, and other officials serve as the chair of the Committee at each respective level to monitor and evaluate the Program. In addition, each community has a Community Council with 9 to 17 members, one of whom is designated as the Director. Members are theoretically elected by the heads of households in the community, and the Director is either elected by council members or handpicked by the district/county official. Until 1983, more than one fourth (26%) of the council members and another one-fourth (24.4%) of the Directors were designated by the state (Taiwan Shengzhengfu Yanjiu Kaohe Weiyuanhui, 1983, pp. 67-68).

The incorporation of the newly established Community Development Program into the preexisting bureaucratic system means that women have been excluded from the decision-making process at the governmental level. Furthermore, since council members are elected by the heads of households rather than by individual residents in the community, women have almost no chance of becoming members of the Council in their own community. The exclusion of women in decision making at the local level is all the more serious when the state increasingly penetrates into the life of the community.

The result of this organizational pattern is seen in a survey conducted in 1983 to evaluate the achievement of the Community Development Program. Of the total 1,810 Council members from 127 communities, less than seven percent (6.7%) were women (Taiwan Shengzhengfu Yanjiu Kaohe Weiyuanhui, 1983, p. 54). When residents who hold decision-making positions in community affairs were asked who they thought best suited to be the director of the Council Committee, less than one percent (0.9%) mentioned women in the neighborhood (Taiwan Shengzhengfu Yanjiu Kaohe Weiyuanhui, 1983, p. 131).

Program Contents

There are three substantive areas of the Community Development Program: basic engineering/construction projects, production and social welfare, and ethics and morale. Within each of these three major areas, programs or activities are designed and carried out in local communities. The *Keting gongchang* or "Living-Room Factory," and the *Mama jiaoshi* or "Mother's Workshop" programs are directly related to women. These two programs illustrate that the state ideology on women's role remains patriarchal in essence though its emphasis shifts as Taiwan's economy develops.

Living-Room Factories

The "living-room factory" program is also referred to as the family subsidiary employment program. It is designed to solve the labor shortage problem by mobilizing surplus labor in the community/family to engage in production. State officials reasoned that by introducing homework and similar forms of production into the local area, people's living standard will be improved while national productivity is increased, thus "community development and economic development will enhance each other." (Economic Construction Commission [EEC], 1978, p. 1).

After surveys conducted under state sponsorship found that there were many "idle women" in local communities, a proposal to establish "living-room factories" was developed (EEC, 1978, p. 2). The government provided special loans for families intending to purchase machines to do homework. Workshops were conducted to train housewives to apply themselves to productive work. Many "living-rooms" were converted into "factories," housewives became workers, and work became "housewifized."

One of the consequences, of course, has been that those families whose female members do homework in their living-rooms experienced an improvement in their living standards. However, a greater benefit can be claimed by others. Capitalists were relieved of a labor shortage because a new segment of the population was incorporated into the production line. This helped to ease the pressure for potential wage increase. Since many living-rooms were converted into "factories" and the workers worked at home, capitalists were able to avoid expenditures on factory facilities, energy, dormitories, and management. The incorporation of women into living-room factory work is capitalist patriarchal because those homeworkers were treated more as homemakers who were willing to work, rather than workers who worked at home. They were not provided with health insurance to which most factory workers were entitled. Nor were they protected by the minimum wage regulations, since they were paid on a piece-rate basis. The society as a whole was able to benefit from productivity increases, consumer price stabilization, and economic growth. The state boasts that the informal/subsidiary employment arrangement typical of living-room factories reduces potential conflict between capitalists and workers (EEC, 1978, p. 3).

The consequences of homework in industrial Europe and America are well-known (Daniels, 1989). What distinguishes the Taiwan case is the active promotion of homework by the state, and the institution of national programs such as the Mother's Workshops to ensure that women will not lose sight of their responsibilities as "good wives and fine mothers."

Mother's Workshops

Mama jiaoshi, or the Mother's Workshop Program, a companion of the "living-room factories," is a subarea within the project of ethics and morality enhancement. Many state officials have underlined the importance of the program in itself and for the success of the Community Development Program as a whole. In 1984 Zhao Shoubo, Director of the Department of Social Affairs of the Province, stated:

> Mama Jiaoshi is a sound idea and a wonderful institution. To educate a woman into a good mother is equal to educate the whole family well. If every family lives in comfort and happiness, the society will be peaceful and prosperous, united and harmonious. Ultimately, the whole country will be strong and well-off. Therefore, the Mother's Workshop Program has a great responsibility. (Zhao, 1984, p.27)

An editorial in the official journal *Shequ Fazhan* (Community Development) points out that, among the 77 programs and activities proposed by the government to achieve the goals of the Community Development Program, at least 39 cannot be accomplished without the Mother's Workshop Program.

> Programs on community beautification. environmental improvement, community safety, vocational and skills training, sanitation and health instruction, nutrition improvement, cultural and leisure activities, interior decoration,

neighborhood harmony, adult education and public service, and so forth, are within the scope of the Mama Jiaoshi. . . . Unless these are taught, learned, discussed, and absorbed by women through the Workshops, these programs forever remain only as slogans. (*Shequ Fazhan Jikan,* 28, 1984, p. 4).

The Mother's Workshop Program, according to its initiator, Governor Xie Dongmin who later became the Vice-President of the Republic of China (1989), is also designed to "alleviate societal uneasiness and disorder created by economic development . . . such as increases in divorce rate and adolescent crimes, negligence of the elderly, and widespread hedonism and prodigality." As a government document (Taiwan Shengzhengfu Gonggao, 8027, 1973) states,

> Chinese society is built upon the family and sustained by traditional virtue. And, the mother is the center of a family. Only competent and virtuous mothers can raise stable families. The prosperity of the society and the strength and growth of the country all depend upon people's morality, which is contingent upon stable families. Therefore, we conclude that promoting virtuous and responsible motherhood is the most crucial issue today.

The state claims that the most important aim of the Mother's Workshop Program is to "propagate government orders, promote developmental and educational programs in the local community, and celebrate national festivals. Taking care of mother's interest and need is only secondary" (Zhao, 1984, p. 24). In other words, various courses held in the local community in the name of Mother's Workshop are simply means through which the main objectives set by the state can be accomplished.

Numerous Mother's Workshops were conducted in local communities. Beginning in 1977, the state has sponsored regular training courses for supervisors and instructors of local Mother's Workshops. The state has also published a 10-volume set called *Mother's Readers* to guide these workshops. Written in simple Chinese language and heavily illustrated, these volumes are no more than 30 pages each. Their subjects include family planning, child care, prenatal care, infant care, food and nutrition, housecleaning, family finance management, family life management, and clothing selection, construction, and care (Taiwan Shengzhengfu Shehuichu, 1977a). Additional materials, such as "Supplementary Readings for the Mother's Workshop," were published periodically (Sili, 1985). By 1989, a total of 8,130 supervisors had been trained by the government and more than 160,000 copies of the Readers have been distributed.

Table 9.10 Number of Mother's Workshops Sponsored by County/City, 1987

Number of Workshop Classes per Community per Year	Number of County/City
1+	1
3	1
6	4
8	1
12+	2
24	1
Non-specified	11
Total Communities	21

SOURCE: Taiwansheng (1987), pp. 20-40.

The influence of the Program can also be shown by the number of Workshops held. By 1984, a total of 4,063 communities had implemented the Community Development Program in Taiwan. About 90% of them held Mother's Workshops in their communities in 1984 alone. One third of the counties/cities in the province (7 out of a total of 21) have a community sponsor rate of 90%. Among them, three counties/cities have Mother's Workshop in every local community (Zhao, 1984, p. 26).

In 1987, local officials and representatives from 21 counties/cities responsible for the Mother's Workshop Program gathered at a conference called by the Department of Social Affairs. Every county/city gave a summary report on what has been accomplished. Ten reported statistics on how many classes of Mother's Workshop were organized in the local community of their counties/cities. The number of classes sponsored by each local community varied widely, and ranged from once a year to twice per month (see Table 9.10).

In urban areas most participants are middle-class housewives (Zhao, 1986), although women from various class backgrounds have attended the Program as well (Taiwansheng 74-75, 1987). Especially in rural areas, the Mother's Workshop Program has played important educational roles, such as distributing information on family planning, infant care, and nutrition.

Workshops are usually held at community centers over the weekend, and are centered around four areas, ethics and morality, sanitation and public health, homework and productive skills, and leisure activity and social services. The ultimate goals of ethics and morality education are to get women in the community to "practice proper etiquettes, respect womanhood virtues, pay attention to motherhood, and increase harmony in the family" (Zhao, 1984, p. 25). Women are taught, for example, how to prepare nutritious food for the family, what the proper make-up is when attending social gatherings with their husbands, and how to take care of the elderly with chronic diseases. Training on productive skills is connected with the "Living-Room Factory" program. Courses on leisure activity planning and social services encourage women to organize themselves "to visit the aged, orphans, the handicapped, the mentally retarded, and military and poor families [in the local community]" (Zhao, 1984, p. 26). A person in charge of the training courses for supervisors of the Mother's Workshops Program once said, "in a modern society, women have to play at least four different roles: they have to be pretty women, lovely wives, responsible mothers, and successful professionals" (M.-X. Xie, 1985). An example of the content and attendance of these workshops is provided in Table 9.11 for Tainan County between 1985 and 1986.

As Table 9.11 shows, more than one thousand classes were conducted with more than ten thousand participants in Tainan County in 1985 and 1986. The figures do not distinguish frequent participants from one-time attendants. However, the table does show that the most frequently sponsored courses are recreationally oriented. Women have also actively participated in courses on make-up, family relationships, homemaking, and public health.

State officials have lamented that some Mother's Workshop Programs have focused too much on recreation. Vice-President Xie claimed that "mothers in the community become indulged in such activities [folk dancing]. They neglect their husband and overlook their children. As a result, more problems have been created in the family" (J. Li, 1985, p. 59). Another government official points out that:

> The purposes of the Mother's Workshop is to bring forth sweet and happy family, thereby a stable and harmonious society eventually. Courses on parenting and occupation skills are means to achieve these goals. The Mother's Workshop is not limited to skill training, such as cooking, flower arranging, or folk dancing. Some local communities have focussed on such trivial activities and lost sight of the main objectives of the program. (Zhao, 1984, pp. 24-27)

Several points can be made regarding the "Living-room Factory" and the Mother's Workshop programs. First, the ways women were incorporated in the programs reinforced their submissive and dependent status in the family and society. Women's waged work was based on its subsidiary and supple-

Table 9.11 Activities and Attendancy of Mother's Workshops, Tainan County, 1985-1986

Courses & Activities	Total Classes		Attendance		Average Attendance per Class	
	1985	1986	1985	1986	1985	1986
Family relations (Mother & Son, Spouses, Mother-in-law & Daughter-in-law)	100	35	1,342	976	13.4	27.6
Public health (Sanitation, Family Planning, Emergency Care)	90	57	1,402	1,004	15.6	17.6
Homemaking (Cooking, Flower Arrangement, Interior Decoration)	308	170	2,735	1,725	8.9	10.1
New Knowledge (Crime Prevention, Make-up, Social Skills)	84	79	1,628	1,234	19.4	15.6
Productive Skills (Bamboo Handcrafts, Embroidery, Knitting, and Toys, Ornaments, and Pin Making)	66	61	851	612	12.9	10.0
Recreational Activities (Camping, B-B-Q, Folkdancing)	707	659	3,522	4,126	5.0	6.3
Social Services (Visit Elderly, Poor, and Community Services)	68	79	536	350	7.9	4.4
Total	1,423	1,150	12,016	10,018		

SOURCE: Taiwansheng (1987), pp. 32-33.

mentary character, even though their income was essential to the family. Women were not treated as workers but as housewives in need of some pocket money. Female workers at a living-room factory were told by local officials to lie about their wages to visitors to hide the fact that they were

paid below the minimum (Personal communication). They were also subjected to all the hazards of chemical pollution, unstable income, and other
problems faced by workers in the informal economy. Second, women's roles
as mother and caretaker were reinforced by programs emphasizing their
"moral obligation" to the family, and to other people in need. Women were
asked to take up the "double burden" for the good of the whole society.
Third, the Community Development Program was a top-down program. It is
based on the male-dominated bureaucratic structure and ignores preexisting
social networks in the community, which are often centered around women.
The failure to take into account these local personal networks has excluded
women's participation in the decision-making process, and by that exclusion
has created many unnecessary difficulties for the success of the state-
sponsored programs.

Conclusion

The demand for flexible labor in the contemporary world system means
that women are especially courted. They are often said to prefer flexible
work because of their own desire to care for their families. Stable families,
harmonious neighborhoods, and orderly society can be achieved through the
fulfillment of motherhood. Working for wages is encouraged by the state as
long as it does not interfere with women's role as wives, mothers, and daugh-
ters-in-law. And the best way for society to induce women to do both is to
provide opportunities for flexible work. It is not flexible work that we object
to, but its evaluation. Flexible work is cheap, insecure, unprotected, and
taken for granted. Here a socially produced condition is taken as natural, and
perpetuated by the state, the society, and the family. The success of the export-oriented growth strategy of Taiwan is related to a system of male domination that provides incentives for firms and families that exploit women's
labor. Beyond economic strategies, the state controls and disciplines female
workers by perpetuating the "double burden" ideology through educational
institutions and state-sponsored community programs such as the "Living-
Room Factory."

References

Beneria, Lourdes. (Ed.). (1985). *Women and development: The sexual division of labor in rural societies.* Westport, CT: Praeger.

Bian, Yu-yuan. (1985). Funu laodong dui jingji fazhang zhi gongxian [The contribution of female labor to economic development—A case study of Taiwan]. In Population Studies Center (Ed.), *Funu zai Guojia Fazhan guochengzhong de Jiaose Yantaohui Lunwenji* [Proceedings of conference on the role of women in the national development process in Taiwan] (pp. 261-274). Taipei: National Taiwan University, Population Studies Center.

Charlton, Sue Ellen, Everett, Jana, & Staudt, Kathleen. (1989). *Women, the state and development.* Albany: SUNY.

Chiang, Lan-hung Nora, & Ku, Yenlin. (1985). *Past and current status of women in Taiwan.* Taipei: National Taiwan University, Population Studies Center.

Chou, Bi-ar. (1989). Industrialization and change in women's status: A reevaluation of some data from Taiwan. In Hsin-huang Michael Hsiao, Wei-yuan Cheng, & Hou-sheng Chan (Eds.), *Taiwan: A newly industrialized state* (pp. 423-461). Taipei: National Taiwan University, Department of Sociology.

Crane, George T. (1982). The Taiwanese ascent: System, state and movement in the world economy. In Edward Friedman (Ed.), *Ascent and decline in the world-system* (pp. 93-113). Beverly Hills: Sage.

Cumings, Bruce. (1987). The origins and development of the northeast Asian political economy: Industrial sectors, product cycles, and political consequences. In Frederic Deyo (Ed.), *The political economy of the new Asian industrialization* (pp. 44-83). Ithaca, NY: Cornell University Press.

Daniels, Cynthia R. (1989). Between home and factory: Homeworkers and the state. In Eileen Boris & Cynthia R. Daniels (Eds.), *Homework.* Urbana and Chicago: University of Illinois Press.

Deng, Wenyi. (1975). Sanshinianlai de Taiwan Guanguang Luyu Shiye [Tourist industries in the last thirty years in Taiwan]. In Taiwan Shengzhengfu Xinwenchu (Ed.), *Taiwan Guangfu Sanshinian* [Thirty years after Taiwan's recovery from Japanese occupation] (pp. 337-409). Taizhong: Author.

Deyo, Frederic C. (Ed.). (1987). *The political economy of the new Asian industrialization.* Ithaca, NY: Cornell University Press.

Deyo, Frederic C. (1989). *Beneath the miracle: Labor subordination in the new Asian industrialism.* Berkeley: University of California Press.

Diamond, Norma. (1973, September). The middle class family model in Taiwan: Woman's place is in the home. *Asian Survey, 13,* pp. 853-872.

Diamond, Norma. (1975). Women under Kuomintang rule: Variations of the feminine mystique. *Modern China, 1*(1), pp. 3-45.

Diamond, Norma. (1979). Women and industry in Taiwan. *Modern China, 5*(3), pp. 317-340.

Directorate-General of Budget, Accounting and Statistics, Republic of China. [Various years]. *Zhonghuaminguo Tongji Nianjian* [Statistical yearbook of the Republic of China]. Taipei: Author.

Directorate-General of Budget, Accounting and Statistics, Republic of China. (1974). *Zhonghuaminguo Tongji Tiyao* [Statistical abstract of the Republic of China]. Taipei: Author.

Directorate-General of Budget, Accounting and Statistics, Republic of China, and Council for Economic Planning and Development, Republic of China. (1989). *Taiwan Diqu Renli Yunyung Diaocha Baogao* [Report on the manpower utilization survey in Taiwan area]. Taipei: Author.

Directory of Taiwan. (1963). Taipei: The China News.

Economic Construction Commission. (1978). *Ruhe yi Shequ Fazhan Fangshi Tuixing Jiating Fuye zhi Yanjiu* [How to promote family subsidiary work through community development]. Taipei: Author.

Evans, Peter, & Pang, Chien-kuo. (1989). State structure and state policy: Implications of the Taiwanese case for newly industrializing countries. In Hsin-huang Michael Hsiao, Wei-yuan Cheng, & Hou-sheng Chan (Eds.), *Taiwan: A newly industrialized state* (pp. 3-30). Taipei: National Taiwan University, Department of Sociology.

Funu Xinzhi [Awakening]. (1982-1989). [Various Issues.] Taipei.

Funu Xinzhi. (Ed.). (1988). *Liangxing Pingdeng Jiaoyu Shouce* [Handbook on gender equal education]. Taipei.

Gallin, Rita S. (1984a). The entry of Chinese women into the rural labor force: A case study from Taiwan. *Signs, 9*(3), pp. 383-398.

Gallin, Rita S. (1984b). Women, family and the political economy of Taiwan. *Journal of Peasant Studies, 12*(1), pp. 76-92.

Gallin, Rita S. (1990). Women and the export industry in Taiwan: The muting of class consciousness. In Kathryn Ward (Ed.), *Women workers and global restructuring* (pp. 179-192). Ithaca, NY: Cornell University Press.

Gates, Hill. (1979). Dependency and the part-time proletariat in Taiwan. *Modern China, 5*(3), pp. 381-407.

Greenhalgh, Susan. (1985, June). Sexual stratification: The other side of "Growth with Equity" in East Asia. *Population and Development Review, 11,* pp. 265-314.

Hsiao, Hsin-huang Michael, Cheng, Wei-yuan, & Chan, Hou-sheng. (Eds.). (1989). *Taiwan: A newly industrialized state.* Taipei: National Taiwan University, Department of Sociology.

Huang, Chunming. (1981). *Shayunala Zaijian* [Sayonara goodbye]. Taipei: Yuanjing.

Jones, Gavin. (Ed.). (1984). *Women in the urban and industrial workforce, Southeast and East Asia.* Canberra: Australian National University.

Kaluzynska, Eva. (1980). Wiping the floor with theory: A survey of writings on housework. *Feminist Review, 6,* 27-54.

Kim, Elaine. (1987). Sex tourism in Asia: A reflection of political and economic inequality. In Eui-young Yu & Earl H. Phillips (Eds.), *Korean women in transition* (pp. 127-144). Los Angeles: California State University, Center for Korean-American and Korean Studies.

Koo, Hagen. (1987). The interplay of state, social class, and world system in East Asian development: The cases of South Korea and Taiwan. In Frederic Deyo (Ed.), *The political economy of the new Asian industrialization* (pp. 165-181). Ithaca, NY: Cornell University Press.

Kung, Lydia. (1983). *Factory women in Taiwan.* Ann Arbor: University of Michigan Press.

Li, Jianxing. (1985, December). Shequ Mamajiaoshi yu Shequ Jiaoyu [Community Mother's Workshops and community education]. *Shequ Fazhan Jikan, 29,* pp. 58-59.

Li, Yuanzhen. (1987, February). Chuji Wenti, Bubu Jiannan [Difficulties in facing the problems of young prostitutes]. *Funu Xinzhi, 57,* 1.

Liu, Paul K.-C. (1984). Trends in female labour force participation in Taiwan: The transition toward higher technology activities. In Gavin Jones (Ed.), *Women in the urban and industrial workforce, Southeast and East Asia* (pp. 75-99). Canberra: Australian National University.

Liu, Paul Ke-chih, & Hwang, Kuo-shu. (1987). *Relationships between changes in population, employment and economic structure in Taiwan.* Taipei: Academia Sinica.

Liu, Yu-lan. (1985). *Taiwan diqu funu renli yunyung huigu yu zhanwang* [Utilization of women's labor in Taiwan: Past and future]. Taipei: Meizhi Tushu Gongsi.

Lu, Xiulian. (1986). *Qing* [Affection]. Taipei: Dunli.

Lu, Yu-hsia. (1984). Women, work and the family in a developing society: Taiwan. In Gavin Jones (Ed.), *Women in the urban and industrial workforce, Southeast and East Asia* (pp. 339-367). Canberra: Australian National University.

Mies, Maria. (1986). *Patriarchy, accumulation on a world scale.* London: Zed Books.

Miller, Joanne, & Garrison, Howard H. (1982). Sex roles: The division of labor at home and in the workplace. *Annual Review of Sociology, 8,* pp. 237-262.

Population Studies Center. (1965). *Funu zai Guojia Fazhan guochengzhong de Jiaose Yantaohui Lunwenji* [Proceedings of conference on the role of women in the national development process in Taiwan]. Taipei: National Taiwan University, Population Studies Center.

Qian [Money]. (1990). 5, pp. 156-186. Taipei.

Qu, Haiyuan. (1984). Seqing yu Changji Wanti [Sex and the prostitution problem]. In Guoshu Yang & Qizheng Ye (Eds.), *Taiwan Shehui Wenti* [Social problems in Taiwan] (pp. 543-571). Taipei: Juliu.

Shequ Fazhan Jikan [Community Development Quarterly]. [Various issues.] Taipei: Zhonghuaminguo Shequ Fazhan Yanjiu Sunlian Zhongxin.

Sili Shijian Jiazheng Jingji Zhuanke Xuexiao. (1985). *Mama Jiaoshi Buchong Jiaocai* [Supplementary instructional materials for Mother's Workshops]. Taizhong: Taiwan Shengzhengfu.

Taiwan Shengzhengfu. (1973). *Gonggao* [Public document] No. 8027. Taizhong.

Taiwan Shengzhengfu Shehuichu. (1977a). *Mama Duben* [Mother's readers]. 10 vols. Taizhong: Author.

Taiwan Shengzhengfu Shehuichu. (1987). *Taiwansheng Shequ Fazhan Houxu Dierqi Wunian Jihua Gongzuo Shouce* [Handbook of the second five-year community development program of the provincial government]. Taipei: Author.

Taiwan Shengzhengfu Xinwenchu. (1965). *Taiwan Guangfu Ershinian* [Twenty years after Taiwan's recovery]. Taipei: Author.

Taiwan Shengzhenqfu Yanjiu Kaohe Weiywanhue. (1983). *Taiwansheng Shinianlai Shequ Fazhan Chengxiao zhi Pingjian ji Weilai Fazhan zhi Yanjiu* [Evaluation of the Ten-year Community Development Program in Taiwan and Its Future Direction]. Taipai: Taiwan Shengzhengfu Yanjiu Fazhan Kaohe Weiyuanhui.

Taiwansheng 74-75 Niandu Shequ Mamajiaoshi Fudao Renyuan Zuotanhui Zonghe Jishi [Proceedings of the 1985-86 community Mother's Workshop supervisors seminar]. (1987). Taipei: Author.

Truong, Thanh-Dam. (1990). *Sex, money and morality: Prostitution and tourism in southeast Asia.* London: Zed Books.

Tsay, Ching-lung. (1985). Xingbie chayi [Sex differentials in educational attainment and labor force development in Taiwan]. In Population Studies Center (Ed.), *Funu zai Guojia Fazhan guochengzhong de Jiaose Yantaohui Lunwenji* [Proceedings of Conference on the Role of Women in the National Development Process in Taiwan] (pp. 277-308). Taipei: National Taiwan University, Population Studies Center.

Waring, Marilyn. (1988). *If women counted: A new feminist economics.* San Francisco: Harper & Row.

Winckler, Edwin A., & Greenhalgh, Susan. (Eds.). (1988). *Contending approaches to the political economy of Taiwan.* Armonk, NY: M. E. Sharpe.

Xie, Meng-xiong. (1985, December). Shequ Mamjiaoshi yu Jiazheng jiaoyu [The community Mother's Workshop and homemaking education]. *Shequ Fazhan Jikan, 29,* pp. 60-61.

Yu, Zongxian. (1981). Duiwai Maoyi [Foreign trade]. In Chia-lin Cheng (Ed.), *Woguo Jingji de Fazhan* [Economic development of our country] (pp. 301-384). Taipei: Shijie Shuju.

Zhan, Chunjian. (1966). Dangqian Fazhan Guanguang Shiye de Tujing [Directions of tourism development]. In Huiyan Zhou (Ed.), *Guanguang Shiye Lunji* [Essays on tourism], vol. 1. pp. 4-16. Taipei: Zhongguo Wenhua Xueyuan.

Zhao, Shoubo. (1984, December). The current status and future prospective of Mother's Workshops in Taiwan. *Shequ Fazhan Jikan, 28,* pp. 24-27.

Zhao, Shoubo. (1986). Qianghua Mamajiaoshi de Gongneng [Strenthening the function of Mother's Workshops]. In *Taiwansheng Mamajiaoshi Fudao Renyuan Yanxihui Shouce* [Handbook for supervisors of the Mother's Workshops, 1986] (pp. 1-2). Taipei: Author.

Zheng Zhihui & Bo Qingrong. (1987, March). Zhengshi Zhiye Funu soshou de Jiuye Qishi [Looking seriously at the discrimination faced by working women]. *Funu Xinzhi 58,* pp. 1-9.

Zhou, Huiyan (Ed.). (1966). *Guanguang Shiye Lunji* [Essays on tourism] vol. 1. Taipei: Zhongguo Wenhua Xueyuan.

10

Women, the Family, and the State in Hong Kong, Taiwan, and Singapore

JANET W. SALAFF

Hong Kong, Singapore, and Taiwan have since the early 1970s entered the ranks of the newly industrialized countries (NICs) based on manufacturing for export, in which women play key roles. Their great transformations occurred when few scholars expected them to prosper, and many other Third World nations, in contrast, had suffered from a decline in their living standards (Bello & Rosenfeld, 1990; *World Bank Report,* various years). Instead of declining, the "three dragons" bargain sharply for investors and markets. How they accumulate and invest capital and supply labor fascinates many scholars. A number of studies compare the state infrastructures that encourage investment in export-oriented industries in these places (Deyo, 1987; Henderson, 1989; Huang, 1989). Fewer have looked at how the state powers its labor supply, my concern here (Ong, 1987; Ward, 1990; D. Wolf, 1989). The present chapter describes how the Pacific Rim NICs proletarianized its populace by requiring families to earn money in industries and fitting the labor force into these industries. I discuss how the state buttresses the household authority over its members, and why anybody's daughter will do.

This chapter analyzes the strong Chinese family, conduit for state policies that deal with the economy and the sexual domain. Particular social-historical forces compel families to use the new economic institutions to chart their course. To start with, these include demographic pressures and the newly created commodity economy. Within the framework of the new economic options, the family turns to a familiar means, control over its labor power, to accomplish its goals of survival and progress. In fact, the Chinese family has more than one goal. We will see how the family presses women to work at three stages of their life cycles to meet a number of family goals. For instance, these family demands on the individual reach their fruition in myriad small family industries (Hamilton & Biggart, 1988). I introduce the concept of *substitutability,* to help us understand how women's earnings can replace those of men in each of these three life cycle stages. Although Singapore contains more than one ethnic group, here I focus solely on the Chinese to describe more precisely how family members enter the labor force.[1] The data are drawn from the early 1970s through the early 1980s. This period takes us from the early labor-intensive industry through to changes in the industrial mix for a more skilled labor force. This decade-long time span shows the ways the proletariat was reproduced at a crucial time in the evolution of the new industrial countries on the Pacific Rim.

Family Strategies
Encouraging Women to Work

As the states set new economic directions, forcing people into the money economy and providing opportunities to work, families in the three countries respond to the need to earn cash and the means to do so. Unable to live off the land, or grow or make goods themselves, people must earn money to survive. They must buy food, clothing, furnishings, education, and housing. Few any longer live in squatter or rural *kampung* villages, pick durian, ramutan, or star fruit, raise chickens, or sprout beans. They must work and now they have the opportunity to work. Young family members are not just attracted by wage work opportunities, but are forced by necessity to work. In this way government actions have created a stock of labor power.

But more than exterior conditions draw women to work. Families exploit the environment to get cash, in accord with the ecology and within the bounds of social structure. The location and timing of the new work opportunities differed from early work opportunities. Industrial work is located within daily traveling distance from the home, but outside it, and demands continuous work for a long period every day of the week, in all seasons. An industrial worker can no longer work around the home at piecework, peddling, domestic labor, or child care. And so to send members out of the home for wage work in industry means they must be expendable to the household or they must find others to do the work they formerly did at home.

In the places under study, the majority of these workers were women. But different cohorts of women were drawn into factory work at different stages of the industrializing process. This has to do with both the demand for workers and their supply. How this is so will be seen in the following cases of workers from Hong Kong, Taiwan, and Singapore. I first look at unmarried Hong Kong and Taiwan factory women at the height of the export-oriented industrial strategies in the mid-1970s. I compare them to young Singapore Chinese married women from working- and middle-class backgrounds around 1980. I then discuss older Taiwanese working women working in the mid-1980s.[2]

Types of Family

In supplying labor to the industrial work force, the Chinese family chooses those it can free from home tasks. Who these members are varies by family life cycle. This is because the Chinese family is not a single unitary type. It is a set of constructs that press upon its members with different meanings. These meanings and the members' responsibilities and obligations under each of the three family regimes vary by their life-cycle stage and gender. And so the workers that the family supplies also vary by the life-cycle stage of the family. We distinguish three conceptual units. The stage of the family's life cycle determines which of these three family units is stressed.

The first of these units, the *patriliny,* is the family core, composed of men linked by descent and with equal rights to inherited property (A. Wolf & Huang, 1972). It is this family that comes into mind when we envision the large extended family of Chinese literature, with three or four generations under one roof, under the authority of the older patriarch. This family type is dominant in the three areas discussed here, even though few households actually contain several generations. It is not necessary for several generations to live under one roof for the patrilineal concept to hold weight. Few families in the two city-states inherited land, and Taiwanese landholdings are small. Immigrant families in Hong Kong, and to some extent Singapore, grew up without a full set of paternal kin. In Taiwan, refugees from China and urban migrants from the village might also leave their kin behind. High wartime mortality also meant a low probability of survival of grandparents and parents in the region. But even though an ideal form of patrilocal household cannot come into existence, the patriliny still remains a guideline for behavior. This demands that families bear sons for economic and religious reasons. In such a patrilineal family, ties of women to their kin cause potential loyalty conflicts, which the patriliny attempts to dilute. Daughters are expected to sever their ties with their parents on marriage, and more fully turn their loyalty and energy to their husband's line.

The second conceptual family unit, the domestic or economic family (*jia*), focuses on present-day economic survival, rather than line of inheritance. All members of the economic family contribute to the common budget and draw their expenses from this common purse. Since all workers support the family, this permits substitutability: The earnings of any worker can help the household. The family's drawing upon the labor of the children and women stems from the economic family concept. Even after marriage, ties to women's kin are tolerated and even may be encouraged if they contribute to the economic well-being of the household. For instance, a woman's mother can help watch her children so that she can work, although according to the patrilineal concept, married women should not turn to their natal family for help (Judd, 1989).

The third family unit is formed by the bonds of sentiment between women and their children. Since the mother lacks the same rights as her husband in the line, she compensates by building bonds of support with her children. Emotional exchanges underlie these bonds of support. Where the father is emotionally distant from his offspring, as is common in Chinese families, the mother can more easily build up these alliances. Margery Wolf calls the female-centered family the "uterine family." The willingness of daughters to contribute to the economic family, despite their exclusion from the patriliny, family inheritance, and family future, is ensured by the sentimental bonds of support built in this family unit (M. Wolf, 1972).

Demographic Pressures and the Family Life Cycle

The choice of which member the family would send into the labor force was also shaped by the demographic processes. Most crucial of these were the demographic outcomes of the previous years of high birthrates, universal marriages, and low death rates. The high post-World War II birthrates in the three areas, and good chances for survival, created sizable families. Hong Kong women aged 40 to 44 in 1971 averaged 4.3 live births.[3] Youths who were born from 1948 to 1960, and were in their teens through twenties in the

Table 10.1 Ratio of Wage Earners to Family Dependents, 1960 to 1974

Respondents	1960	1965	1970	1973	1974
Working Class					
A-li	1:8	3:7	3:7	4:6	4:6
I-ling	1:4	2:4	3:3	3:3	3:3
Mae-fun	1:7	3:5	4:3	4:3	3:3
Wai-gun	2:7	3:6	3:6	4:5	5:4
Upper Working Class					
Ming	1:6	1:7	3:5	3:5	3:5
Middle Class					
Ju-chen	1:9	2:7	3:7	4:6	3:6

mid-1970s, had many brothers and sisters. Comparable large families are found among Singapore and Taiwanese mothers of the same age cohort. These large families gave rise to problems in societies without social assistance. Demographic pressures combined with the impossibility of surviving outside the wage economy created a situation that was not experienced in the same form during earlier historical periods, when higher mortality limited surviving births.

Let us look at the dependency ratio—the burden on wage earners as measured by the ratio of wage earners to dependents. In the families of my Hong Kong study, there was usually only the father as the single earner. The earnings of one working-class man were not enough for s sizable family. Worse, often the father's contribution diminished—he became ill, died, took a second wive, or deserted the family. This problem, a result of World War II wartime turmoil, was found in all three societies. For example, two fifths of the fathers in the 100 Singapore couples I studied had passed away before their children had grown up. Their early demise left the household of many children without a breadwinner. But even households with an adult male wage earner faced hard times because of high dependency ratios and low working-class wages. In the families I studied in Hong Kong, the dependency ratios ranged from 1:4 to 1:9 when respondents were youngsters, ca. 1960 (Table 10.1). These demographic pressures led in additional workers, to add to or substitute for the earnings of the father/household head. The first to enter the wage force were unmarried daughters.

Working Daughters. The high dependency ratio made the need to earn money overwhelming. But the mothers in the families could not earn much. Hong Kong and Singapore mothers were burdened with many small children, labor-intensive household chores, and insufficient help at home, and they lacked education or industrial labor force experience. In Taiwan they had farm tasks to perform. So mothers rarely worked for a wage outside the home. The demographic situation that intensified the problem also suggested the means to resolve it—sending children out to work. As youngsters, girls and boys already helped run the household. This was partly because of sheer household size. Sheer size in an organization entails rules of interaction, structuring authority, obedience, and emotional intimacy (W. J. Goode, 1982). The more functions filled, the more call there is for a strict definition of roles by age, sex, generation, and lineage (Winch, 1963). The family at the stage we are studying here is sizable enough to require a number of rules, which are generally accepted.

In addition to sheer family size, the labor-intensive household economy draws young daughters into the household division of labor, and sets the stage for their later employment. First was early training of children to participate in family tasks. By age 5 most girls learned many necessary tasks, and by age 12 all hauled water, cooked, washed clothes. As they neared adolescence, the older girls did putting-out work (piecing together plastic flowers, transistors, pressing metal eyelets, beading). They did this as part of a family-wide project, carried out in the home, and they received no individual wage or recognition. This was most common in Hong Kong, the earliest entrant to the new world economic order. In Taiwan, young girls often had housekeeping tasks that were associated with agriculture. They fed pigs, nipped the ends off bean sprouts. Singapore girls similarly performed subsistence work, helped in a family hawker enterprise, or did domestic work in other households.

Sex roles marked different expectations. When the young women born in the post-World War II years were growing up, there was rarely enough money to send both sons and daughters to school. Based on the patrilineal construct, looking toward the future they would share with their sons, parents saw daughters as "goods upon which one loses." Daughters would leave the domestic family upon marriage, while boys were the future of the family. Thus, in the 1950s and 1960s, girls received less schooling than boys. Certain that they would work for only a few years until their marriage, with enough education to give them literacy but not enough for them to enter skilled jobs with a future, young women were a prime labor force for low-waged, export-oriented industries. Their brothers, however, were to be contributors to the domestic economy throughout their lives, albeit unevenly due to their own domestic economic burdens. If there was a sum of money available for only one or two of the children to study, the boys were chosen. It was hoped that they could repay the family at a higher rate of return. Thus young daughters became the natural substitutes for their brothers in the labor force.

With this bridge of hard work—performing household tasks and working in family putting-out projects—working-class Hong Kong daughters who matured in the early to late 1960s entered the paid labor force between ages 12 and 14. They were child labor in the accepted definition of the International Labour Organization. Apart from working at home on the farm, some Taiwan daughters who matured at this time worked as bar girls until a few years later when factory work became available. Singapore girls started to work later still when factories began to reach out for them. Middle-class families in all countries were more likely to delay the entry of their daughters to the work force until they completed some or all of high school. They went to work at around age 16.

The young woman who went to work after primary school entered the new low-waged manufacturing work just then opening up in the 1960s. She gave most or all of her income to the household. Thereupon, family living standards markedly improved, as seen through the family dependency ratio. Take as an example Wai-gun's family of nine—seven children and two working parents. The proportion of dependents in the household dropped from 78% to 67% with just one daughter's entry into the labor force alone (Table 10.1). A turning point came in the fortunes of this family when the older working daughter reached aged 23, and the next younger sibling joined her at work: two parents and two daughters supported the household that included five school-age children (for a dependency ratio of 4:5). Eventually, the dependency ratio even reversed, with more workers than nonworkers in the household. And this was a common occurrence.

Parents long looked forward to the transition from a consuming to an earning household. They tried to stretch out the period, within limits. The lengthening of the daughters' years of contribution to the domestic economy was accomplished not only by their early entry to the labor force. Parents might also postpone their daughters' exit through marriage. Hong Kong parents sought a full decade of daughters' income contribution, the number of years largely determined by the desire to ensure younger siblings' schooling at a higher level. If the daughter was herself a younger sibling, the length of time she needed to contribute her wages to the household economy was reduced. Even so, Hong Kong daughters, younger and older, sought to repay their parents for the costs of their upbringing. Kung's study of Taiwanese factory women similarly notes the daughters' desire to repay their parents for the their upbringing (Kung, 1983). Thus for the daughters, early work substitutes for early marriage.

Social class differences came into play. Middle-class daughters with the longest period of education entered the labor force at an older age. They then were expected to contribute to the family budget for a number of years, and as a result delayed marriage longer than working-class women. It was not only parents who sought to delay their offspring's marriages, of course. Filial daughters themselves postponed marriage until their family dependency ratio improved, and the household could do without their input. The 1980 census of Taiwan shows that marriage age is directly associated with educational level in Taiwan (*Extract Report,* 1982, p. 62). Among the reasons for this delay is undoubtedly the period of posteducational employment, much of which aids their natal families.

We introduced the concept of substitutability. The young woman worker abandons her household roles, in her parents' or husband's household, and she also gives up her education for paid wage labor. She works at slightly different factory jobs than her brothers or father, but it is wage work nonetheless. She is in fact substituting for the work of men.

Families reward daughters very little for their employment and their input to the household. But the young women do get something out of their input, which keeps them in the exchange. Part of what they get is material. They earn money they can use themselves when their household income takes a turn for the better. Sometimes they also obtain a greater decision-making role in the family. Part of what they get is moral. Knowing that their families truly need their material input, they feel satisfied they are meeting their filial obligations as daughters. Thus we can look at the exchange through the three types of family forms. The patriline requires women to support the family of the male line (first their parents, later their husbands after marriage). The economic family demands material input to the household economy. And the uterine family ties give emotional satisfaction to women that help out at home. Thus the exchange is neither entirely material nor moral. Nor is it of short-term duration.

Although their wages were low, the Hong Kong and Taiwanese working daughters interviewed lived at home, and they at first earned so little that they only paid for bus fare and basic expenses of their own. As they gained work experience, they contributed more to the family coffers. In low-income households, purchases varied by the dependency ratio, a product of the life cycle. When, as young unmarried daughters, women first entered the labor

Table 10.2 Occupational Profiles, Family Members and Income

Occupation of Several Respondent's Family Members	Household Income per Month[a]		Percentage Contribution of All Daughters to Household Income, 1973
	1963	1973	
Mae-fun			
Father ————	$85	$120	
Mother —			
Sister ———	25	80	
Mae-fun ———	25	80	42%
Brother ————		100	
(seven members in family)	$135	$380	
Wai-gun			
Father ————	$50	$80[b]	
Mother ——	30	60	
Wai-gun ———	20	80	52%
Sister ———		70	
(nine members in family)	$100	$290	
Suyin			
Father ————	$15[b]	$20[b]	
Mother ——	30	60	
Suyin ———	30	120	73%
Sister ———	30	100	
(eight membrs in family)	$105	$300	
Chin-yiu			
Father ————	$—[b]	$200	
Mother —			
Chin-yiu ————	30	160	66%
Sister ————	30	170	
Sister ———		70	
(seven members in family)	$60	$600	
I-ling			
Father ————	$—[b]	$200	
Mother ——	30	60	
I-ling ———	30	100	28%
(six members in family)	$60	$360	

NOTES: a. All dollars are given in U.S. dollars at the rate of $5 HK = $1 U.S.
b. Father contributing little due to unemployment, layoffs, illness, or residence elsewhere.
Never worked = —
Unskilled = ——
Semiskilled = ———
Skilled = ————
Low-paid clerk = —————
Well-paid clerk = ——————

force within the context of a high dependency ratio, their wages helped their families buy necessities—rent, and food for the entire family. Medical care was an optional, but costly item, and families improved their care when extra money became available. Working women's income enabled extended education for younger siblings past the years provided by their governments. Gradually, their input moved the household living standard from a bare survival level to even modest prosperity (Table 10.2). As the dependency ratio improves, daughters in working-class families help raise the family living standard through the better education of their younger brothers. But since everyone in the society chases more education, there is a spiraling of credentials, and youngsters must remain in school longer just to keep in the same place. Nevertheless, the ability to help with younger brothers' education is most feasible when daughters have been working for a decade. By this time, too, telephones, televisions, small semiautomatic washing machines, and other consumer goods add to the household comfort of the working class, made possible through the combined earnings of the employed children.

Middle-class working daughters also add their earnings to their natal families. Many help their parents launch a small business, such as hawking, or a small subcontracting firm. The high savings propensity of the Chinese in Hong Kong, Singapore, and Taiwan, and their willingness to risk investment in the local economy has been documented (Topley, 1969). Earnings of the children that add to the family budget boost the export-oriented manufacture economy. The extent to which children aid their parents in building a small fund of capital for investment is worthy of future study.

The material consequences of women's work were crucial, much more so than a widening of their proper sphere. Although working daughters obtained a meaningful outcome from their employment, their employment cannot entirely be seen as a transaction between their families and themselves as equal parties, in which they have power to work or not to work. Unmarried Hong Kong, Taiwan, and Singapore women have less power in their households than their parents. Nevertheless, working daughters widened their sphere of decision making as it affected their own lives. So long as they could put in a good-sized portion of their wages to their family budget, Hong Kong and Taiwanese daughters kept some for their own spending money. They could thereby join peer activities, dress better, and use their free time in ways they themselves decided. By entering the spreading consumer economy, they became enmeshed in the new capitalist system. But working daughters could not greatly expand their input into decision-making processes in their families in either setting, and their wages did not confer upon them power to realign their dependence on the family itself.

Opting out (becoming a "swinging single") was limited by the expectation that women remain at home until marriage, despite earning money. This expectation was based on the slim wages they received as "dependents." It was reinforced by slurs cast on women who leave home ("loose women"). In addition, the Hong Kong and Singapore states dominate the housing market, and allot public housing only to families in need. It is thus hard for most women earners to live alone or with other women. They cannot leave home. In Taiwan, working daughters from rural areas lived in the main in tightly supervised factory dormitories, and those who moved into private flats found it was too expensive to meet their obligations to their families. Those who could live at home and commute to work did so, to save money. Although work did not confer a period of accepted physical independence from the family, women who lived apart from their families had the greatest chance to choose recreational activities and friends of their own. Hong Kong and Taiwan daughters enjoyed this period of making friends, participating in the newly expanding consumer culture, and going on group dates. These opportunities were more accessible when the working daughters lived in factory dormitories, and less accessible when they lived at home (Kung, 1983).

Daughters' wage labor for the family meets expected behavior associated with that family life stage. Their subordination to the family construct is often harmonious. Remaining at home and aiding the household in fact occurs only for a certain limited period. Sometimes, however, these different concepts come into conflict. While people will attempt to minimize the conflict of expected behaviors, at times conflict cannot be avoided, and the result may be particularly painful. Conflict is often structural as well, as when the three sets of family concepts clash (W. H. Goode, 1960).

An example is the case of a young Hong Kong working daughter, Wai-gun, depicted in Tables 10.1 and 10.2 above. She had worked since she was 11, and had contributed her wage to the family budget since she was 12 years old, first as an electronics assembler, then as a higher-paid garment seamstress. In 1971, when I first met her, she was employed at Fairchild Semiconductor factory. She was one of three contributors, including her parents and herself, in a family of nine members. As eldest daughter, she was the only child that worked for wages. By 1974, however, two younger siblings entered the labor force; there were five wage-earners and four dependents. Wai-gun's place in the domestic economy was now less essential. She was allowed to use more of her money for recreation and hobbies. She was also preparing to marry. Her intended was an eldest son, whose father was a businessman in the Philippines, and who lived with his mother in Hong Kong. The couple planned to marry in the near future, and saved money for the event. Then, unfortunately, Wai-gun's father became critically ill and passed away, while her mother, whose health was never strong, also began to deteriorate. Soon she was unable to earn money, and in 1976 the family dependency ratio unexpectedly took a turn for the worse. The eldest son left school to go to work, while the second daughter left work to nurse her mother. Three children (Wai-gun, her third younger sister, and first younger brother) supported four younger children and their ill mother (dependency ratio of 3:5). Now Wai-gun could not withdraw her earnings from the household, and thus could not marry. At this time, her fiancé was under pressure by his father to further the family line. He was expected to marry and bear a son in the patrilineal tradition. Thus the two potential partners were enmeshed in different family constructs—Wai-gun in the domestic economy, her fiancé in the patrilineal construct. Their relationship broke up under conflicting family demands. He returned to Fujian province in China and found a village bride in an arranged marriage. She turned her energies again to the household needs of her family. In this case, the progress of the family cycle was sent off course by the unexpected turn of events. The energies of the daughters, ready to be freed, were again reined in and turned to their natal household.

In sum, the young girl who matures into adolescence and then early adulthood in the early industrialization era finds her work life determined by demographic pressures. The three types of family units form the bounds within which demography is defined. The long-term stress on males, the domestic economy that supports the household, and the bonds of affection between mother and daughter propel her to add to the household economy.

Working Mothers. Household structure and composition also shape postmarriage patterns of work for women. The patrilineal construct prevails. Patrilocal residence is common for young couples. Most Hong Kong youth studied planned to move in with one set of parents after marriage, preferably the husband's. In Singapore, patrilocal residence was also common. Three fifths of the young couples I studied in 1975 had once lived with kin, most with the husband's family. By the time one or two children were born, just under half of the Singapore families studied still lived with kin, and two fifths still lived with the husband's parents. In Taiwan, too, recent retrospective survey data find a sizable proportion had lived with their parents after marriage, again most with the husband's parents.

The eldest son marries first by custom, and brings his wife into the household of his parents. If she is still in the labor force, this creates an extremely favorable dependency ratio. But it cannot last. The couple usually has children soon after marriage. From a low dependency ratio in the parental household, once again there is an unfavorable dependency ratio. When the next son plans to marry, it is hard to put all couples under one roof in a high-rise flat. The first son and his wife and children typically move out, and the newlyweds take their place, improving the dependency ratio once again.

Some married women work and some do not, but there is a relation between the two. Married women with young children are not automatically able to continue working. They must negotiate their work status with the wider kin group. They have to find substitutes for their household and mothering roles in other women. Their negotiation reflects the bargaining power of women in the labor force. Those with the better women's jobs are usually best able to bargain to stay.

In the patrilocal household of newly married Singapore women in my study, there are several working-age women, the bride, the bride's mother-in-law, and her sisters-in-law. Which ones go out to work depends on their earning power. Given the low wages of most at the time, it was hardest for the working-class bride with only a modest education to remain in the labor force, since she could not earn much in the kinds of women's jobs that were available. Expected to turn her energies to her new household, she will be requested to quit her job and do the housework. She might, thereby, free her unmarried sisters-in-law for work. But married women with above-average education who work in the slightly better paying women's jobs, like electronics assembly, might continue to work so long as other women are willing to undertake the housework in their stead. Actually, few Singapore women in my study at the turn of the 1980s earned a wage that justified their leaving their homemaking burdens to others. After all, women are designated to take over men's homemaking burdens. They work for a wage lower than would be charged if men paid full market value for the services needed to support them (M. E. Barrett & McIntosh, 1982). Thus women's wages are set by the presumption that they depend on their families for support, and do not themselves support others. Women's wages are further depressed by the large number of women who compete for a narrow range of "women's" jobs.

My study, which tracked through 1981 women recruited to work before 1975, found that as soon as they have children, women find it difficult to work in the prevailing low-paid women's jobs. They simply do not earn enough to justify giving their homemaking burdens and obligations to others. This leads to the typical *n*-shaped female labor force pattern of the region of the time, with high rates of labor force participation, peaking in their twenties, but dropping after that. Only 18% of Singapore women with two children were still in the labor force in 1973; similarly 23% of currently married Taiwan women were economically active in 1980 (*Extract Report,* 1982, p. 120).

This, however, has been changing: as the educational levels for women rise, they lengthen their work experience; the wage rates for electronics assemblists are also rising, and so is the families' need for cash (Lin, 1989, p. 118). In Hong Kong, in 1986, the proportion of economically active women peaked at age 20 to 24 at 84%, and dropped to 34% at ages 35 to 39, rose slightly, then gradually declined to one quarter by age 55 to 59. In Singapore, in 1987, the female activity rate peaked at ages 20-24, when 80% of females are economically active, and the proportion dropped to 56% at ages 30-34, and down to 17% at age 55 to 59 (*Yearbook of Labour Statistics,* 1988, pp. 32, 37).

Under these conditions, especially those of the time of my study, when work was not common for women with children, a newly married woman's right to work is decided upon as part of a household-wide strategy. Here, too, the division of labor can depend on household size, where many people may be accommodated and many functions performed. The older generation sets the division of labor. Where there are several adults in the household, the elders can choose the women with the strongest wage-earning power to work. In order to go out to work, women must find others to do the household chores, child care, and other internal ministering of the household for them. In a large household there is considerable work to do. A large household with a strong dependency ratio, however, also has the potential for a division of labor in which young women can find backup services of others in their homes.

My Singapore research of the mid-1970s showed that the nature of factory demands for women was crucial in determining who would go to work and who would remain as backup workers in the home. Women with above-average education, some technical skills, and longer industrial work experience were the most eligible for better paying factory jobs, such as in multinational electronics firms. Thus although most women had worked prior to marriage, many had done traditional types of work on farms, in workshops, or small factories packing peanuts, making gold paper used to burn for the dead, or in soy sauce factories. Their labor force experience could not command a good wage earning job after marriage. Those married women who worked were among the better educated, the women with superior class backgrounds in my sample.

Women whose families were in great need, whose husbands were quite poor, might also work for a wage, but typically they could only get low-paid

Table 10.3 Comparison of the Residences of Full-Time Wage-Earning Wives and Homemakers, Singapore ca. 1975

| Form of Residence | Wives' Employment Status | | | | | |
| | Wage-Earners | | Homemakers | | Total | |
	%	(Number)	%	(Number)	%	(Number)
Stem or Extended	65		31		49	
Neolocal	35		69		51	
	100	(52)	100	(48)	100	(100)

Table 10.4 Interaction Patterns of Working Wives and Housewives, Phase 1, Singapore ca. 1975

| | Wives' Employment Status | | | |
| | Wage-Earners | | Homemakers | |
	%	(Number)	%	(Number)
Isolates	10		35	
Interactors	90		65	
	100	(52)	100	(48)

work. They were then subsidized by other women in the household, who responded to their great need. Alternatively, some of them might do nonindustrial work in the neighborhood, take in washing, wash floors part-time for neighborhood women. This underground economy work was not registered in labor force statistics.

That household support is key in aiding married women to work is seen in a comparison of full-time wage-earning women and homemakers in our study (Table 10.3). Women who lived in the same home with other kin (stem or extended households) were more likely to work than women who lived neolocally. In addition, however, a number of women carved out support systems that crossed household walls and drew upon several kin in a community area. These women are "interactors" (see Table 10.4).[4] Thus wage-earners invariably had kin-based support systems to help them out.

The example of a Singapore woman, Tan Giok Bee, a domestic servant in the mid-1970s, shows the high level of overall cooperation between family members that goes into married women's work. She received only four years of primary school, quit to care for her five younger siblings, until at age 17 she entered domestic service like her mother and her older sister. She worked six days a week for only S$180 a month for foreign families living in Singapore.[5] She left temporarily to care for each of her three newborn daughters. After the first birth she tried another line of work and spent a year making incense sticks, but found that she could not fit the fixed factory hours to her demanding regime of household tasks. One of her daughters was subject to epileptic seizures, and caring for this child imposed an added burden on her. "I prefer to work as an *amah* [domestic servant] because I don't have to keep strict hours on this job. Sometimes I can go home early or choose my own day off, when I have to take my daughter to the hospital on a working day. Her husband, Poh Wah, a tinsmith, also earned a poverty-line wage of S$250. The couple lived with their three daughters in a rented two-room HDB flat with elder Mother Tan. Tan Giok Bee's mother-in-law helped care for the children, but because the elderly woman was not well, Tan Giok Bee still had to do much of the housework, the errands, and services entailed in mothering. Tan Giok Bee gave mother-in-law a small sum of cash in exchange for the child-care help. A typical day's chronology of household care arrangements for Tan Giok Bee is given in Table 10.5. (Poh Wah was, we note, not part of these arrangements.)

Many working women who lived in small households found it necessary to engineer child care arrangements of this type. With the wider help, however limited, Tan Giok Bee was thus able to put in a full working day, but she could not manage to work at the higher paying factory jobs just then opening up. Her earnings were not enough to live on, and she "borrowed right and left" from her mother, who lived with two working sons and one daughter. Without the help of kin, Tan Giok Bee could not afford to work for the low wage she earned. In turn, she could support her mother-in-law at a modest level. Interviewed six years later, Tan Giok Bee told us that her mother-in-law had passed away. Tan Giok Bee's household burden even increased somewhat. Although her eldest children could care for themselves, the girls did not do the housework. Tan Giok Bee was pressed into a heavier double day than before, and she had to reduce her working hours to do so. Other women also enter and create complex interpersonal relationships, and may, if their husband's mother cannot help them, draw from relatives on both sides, which helps them to remain in the labor force after marriage. In turn, their work often gives employment and needed support to their kin.

Married Singapore women directed their wages toward their economic family. Poverty stricken married Singapore women who worked could help

Table 10.5 Chronology of Help for Domestic Servant Tan Giok Bee

In 1975

6:30	Tan Giok Bee rises to prepare breakfast for her three daughters (ages 8, 10, and 11).
7:00	Tan Giok Bee takes middle daughter to primary school, then continues to the neighborhood market to shop for the day's vegetables.
8:00	Tan Giok Bee does the day's laundry by hand.
9:00	Tan Giok Bee leaves home for her job.
9:00–12:30	Mother Tan cares for the two children at home, cooks and serves them lunch.
13:00	The younger and elder girls walk to primary school for the afternoon session.
14:30	Tan Giok Bee returns from work, takes a nap, and on alternative days prepares dinner for the family.
19:00	Tan Giok Bee's husband returns from work to eat dinner.
20:00	Poh Wah goes out for an evening of drinking with his co-workers.

Chronology of Help for Tan Giok Bee in 1981

6:30	Tan Giok Bee rises.
7:00	Tan Giok Bee markets for the day's vegetables.
7:30	Tan Giok Bee cooks breakfast and lunch for her three daughters (ages 14, 16, and 17)
7:30	The younger two girls leave for secondary school, and the eldest goes to work as a dental receptionist.
9:00	Tan Giok Bee leaves home for her job as a household servant.
2:00	Tan Giok Bee returns home and does the day's laundry by hand.
15:30	Tan Giok Bee takes a nap and then prepares dinner for the family.
19:00	Poh Wah returns from work to eat dinner.
20:00	Poh Wah sits in front of the color television for a quiet evening at home.

pay for tutors for their own children, to improve their performance on competitive state examinations. Even middle-class women saw their work as possible only if they could successfully field their family obligations to others. Women enjoyed an enlarged sphere of action due to having money of their own, but with their funds they bought clothes for their children, rounded out the family budget, and/or provided small sums to their mothers or other kin, which could not legitimately be drawn from their husband's or the wider household budget. They could join peer outings with workmates on special occasions, and purchase presents with their earnings. However, in virtually all cases studied, married women placed the major part of their earnings at the disposal of their family, usually their nuclear family. They obtained a widened sphere for their small nuclear unit within the patrilineal construct (Cohen, 1976).

Working Grandmothers. Women have a greater chance to come into their own when they become mothers-in-law and grandmothers. It is at this point that the dependency ratio improves once again, and from the older woman's perspective, she is the one to benefit. As they age, women may have a chance to take direct control over their expenditures. A 1984 survey of married couples in Taiwan, most of whom did not live with their parents, found that if both worked they spent on average $113US on their parents a month (this sum was 8% of their income). Twenty-six percent of the parents depended entirely and 36% depended partly on their adult children to live.[6] Although they can count on such a sum of money, many older women try to augment this sum with their own earnings.

The study I conducted on firms that include older women as blue-collar employees found these middle-aged Taiwan working women are typically married with grown and even married children. They fell into two groups. One group was protected and nurtured by their grown offspring. They have the freedom to spend money on themselves. As also shown in a Taiwan labor force survey that looked into the expenditure patterns of employees by age, the spending patterns of women in their late fifties differed greatly from their younger counterparts. They are finally able to use their earnings as "pocket money." This factory or service sector wage is often the first real sum of money they have ever fully controlled. They spend their earnings variously on renting video tapes, gambling, group outings and excursions, dinners, and *kala-okay* hi-fi sets for singing parties, and drinking. In one factory, one section is known plant wide for the leisure activities organized by a 55-year-old illiterate worker who has become an informal leader. Apart from investing in household furnishings for a new apartment, in the main she felt free to spend her earnings on her enjoyment, depending on her retired husband and employed son to maintain the household economy. Her daughter-in-law ran the household. Her co-workers stressed to me that this dowager was able to enjoy herself because she did not have a "double day." In my view, the strength of the filial tie was also crucial, which meant that her son and daughter-in-law were willing to support their mother, and permit her this modicum of freedom with her earnings.

Apart from those with a solid family, some are on their own because they have broken families, and must support themselves. These are divorcees, or women with nonearning husbands or sons. They suffer from their low wages, and their lack of a wider economic household and uterine family to provide them with old age security they had looked forward to. They cannot spend their money on leisure and instead barely make ends meet. It is quite possible that the current period is an unusual one, in which the youths are still willing to meet their obligations in line with the three types of family forms. Later cohorts, brought up in school systems and society that do not extol the elderly so much, and with fewer siblings with whom to share this care, may find the burden of the aged too heavy. Then the need for the state to come forth with a universal social insurance system will be unprecedented.[7]

State Strategies in Promoting
Export-Led Industrialization:
The Overall Picture

The Hong Kong, Taiwan, and Singapore states have developed export-oriented economies. They propelled the populace into the money economy, which required families to earn cash. The three states do not direct industry in the same ways. Huang (1989), who compared the states of Taiwan and Singapore, stressed how their similarities in relation to the society enabled them to chart the development policy.

In both Taiwan and Singapore, the state leaders have been able to make decisions quite independent of the major social forces and groups in their own societies. This relative autonomy of the state to its civil society makes possible the relatively smooth shift to development policy from import substitution to export promotion without much resistance from groups of vested interests. (Huang, 1989, p. 98)

We have also seen the lack of responsiveness of the Hong Kong colonial state to the society.

Taiwan and Hong Kong, where the state plays the smallest economic role, depend more closely on the Chinese family firm as its industrial arm than does Singapore. Nevertheless, in establishing their industrial frameworks, all three make use of the Chinese family and its controls over the individual. In all three countries, the family helps put into place an economy that draws on female wage labor. The labor they use depends on the women's family cycle position. In the early stages of industrialization, they mostly drew upon the inexpensive labor of unmarried women, to a lesser extent married women, and still fewer middle-aged and older women. As the labor force became experienced and wages rose, and full employment of unmarried women was reached, married women were kept on the job and recruited for new positions. Finally, middle-aged women may be hired, especially in firms that pay too little to attract younger better educated women, but where the older women are able to earn "women's wages" because they either are not needed in the home, or they urgently need their income to support themselves. In these ways there is an articulation of the family structure and its economy with the development program.

Notes

1. There are many differences in the family regimes of Malays and Indians, as reflected in surveys on their family economies and studies on why may work and how their money is used (Ong, 1987; D. Wolf, 1989). I cannot cover all these materials in the present chapter, but a truly comparative family study would be welcome.

2. These cases come from the following sources: my in-depth study of 28 unmarried working-and middle-class women in Hong Kong, research by Linda Gail Arrigo (1984) and Lydia Kung (1984) on Taiwan factory women of the same ages, my case histories of 100 Singapore women, and data on 220 employed Taiwan women. My Hong Kong, Singapore, and Taiwan studies employed purposive sampling to meet quotas. The ages of the Hong Kong women studied were 20 to 24 in 1973, after which I studied them over a several-year time period. The Singapore women were married, with at least one child, and aged 20 to 30 when interviewed in the mid-1970s; they were also studied over time, the mid-1970s and early 1980s; the Taiwan data covers women of all ages from 20 firms with different types of work experience.

Kung did a two-pronged study (1983-1984), an ethnography of a market town and neighboring agrarian communities, and participant observation in an electronics factory west of Taipei (the capital city). Most of her respondents were unmarried. Arrigo (1984) also studied an American electronics firm in depth, through participant observation, survey, and case study methods. Although Kung and Arrigo did not explicitly select their sample of women workers within a particular age bracket, the labor force participation pattern of Taiwan women at the time limited most workers to the same age group of those I studied in Hong Kong, that is, their late teens and early twenties. For further discussion of sampling and other findings, see the following studies (Arrigo, 1984; Kung, 1984; Salaff, 1981, 1988).

3. These data come from the Census; the mothers were the ages of the mothers of the young employed women I studied.

4. "Interactors" are couples whose wives or husbands visited the same kin two or more times a week. Typically, kin cared for their children during the week, which helped wives work. Some women or their husbands worked with kin. Many of the exchanges that occurred aimed to reduce the homemaking burdens of these young mothers. Thus women could often draw upon this support system and go out to work.

5. In Singapore dollars, at the approximate rate of S$2.25 = US $1.

6. A Survey by China Youth Corps, reported in *Free China Journal,* June 17, 1984. Sixty percent of the adult couples surveyed did not live with their parents, 30% did, and in 17% of the cases the parents lived with each of their sons in turn, a common Taiwan solution for spreading the burden of support among offspring.

7. The "Conference on Economic Development and Social Welfare in Taiwan," sponsored by the Academia Sinica, Economics Research Centre, held in January, 1987, in Taipei, stressed this issue.

References

Arrigo, Linda Gail. (1984). Taiwan electronics workers. In Mary Sheridan & Janet W. Salaff (Eds.), *Lives: Chinese working women* (pp. 123-145). Bloomington: Indiana University Press.

Barrett, Michele E., & McIntosh, Mary. (1982). *The anti-social family.* London: Verso.

Bello, Walden, & Rosenfeld, Stephanie. (1990). *Dragons in distress.* San Francisco: Institute for Food and Development Policy.

Cohen, Myron. (1976). *House united, house divided.* New York: Columbia University Press.

Deyo, Frederic C. (Ed.). (1987). *The political economy of the new Asian industrialism.* Ithaca, NY: Cornell University Press.

An extract report on the 1980 census of population and housing, Taiwan-Fukien area, Republic of China. (1982). Taipei: Census Office of the Executive Yuan, R.O.C., Director General of Budget, Accounting, and Statistics.

Goode, William H. (1960, August). A theory of role strain. *American Sociological Review, 25,* pp. 483-496.

Goode, William J. (1982). *The family.* Englewood Cliffs, NJ: Prentice-Hall.

Hamilton, Gary G., & Biggart, Nicole Woolsey. (1988). Market, culture, and authority: A comparative analysis of management and organization in the Far East. *American Journal of Sociology, 94* [Supplement], pp. S52-S94.

Henderson, Jeffrey. (1989). The political economy of technological transformation in Hong Kong. *Comparative Urban and Community Research, 2,* pp. 102-155.

Huang, Chi. (1989, April). The state and foreign investment: The cases of Taiwan and Singapore. *Comparative Political Studies, 22*(1), pp. 93-121.

Kung, Lydia. (1983). *Factory women in Taiwan.* Ann Arbor: University of Michigan Research Press.

Kung, Lydia. (1984). Taiwan garment workers. In Mary Sheridan & Janet W. Salaff (Eds.), *Lives: Chinese working women* (pp. 109-122). Bloomington: Indiana University Press.

Judd, Ellen R. (1989). Niangjia: Chinese women and their natal families. *Journal of Asian Studies, 48*(4), pp. 525-544.

Lin, Vivian. (1987). Women electronics workers in southeast Asia: The emergence of a working class. In Jeffrey Henderson & Manual Castells (Eds.), *Global restructuring and territorial development* (pp. 112-135). Newbury Park, CA: Sage.

Ong, Aihwa. (1987). *Spirits of resistance and capitalist discipline: Factory women in Malaysia.* Albany: SUNY.

Salaff, Janet W. (1981). *Working daughters of Hong Kong.* Cambridge, UK: Cambridge University Press.

Salaff, Janet W. (1988). *State and family in Singapore: Restructuring an industrial society.* Ithaca, NY: Cornell University Press.

Topley, Marjorie. (1969). The role of savings and wealth among Hong Kong Chinese. In I.C. Jarvie & Joseph Agassi (Eds.), *Hong Kong society: A society in transition* (pp. 167-227). London: Routledge and Kegan Paul.

Ward, Kathryn. (Ed.). (1990). *Women workers and global restructuring.* Ithaca, NY: ILR Press.

Winch, Robert F. (1963). *The modern family.* New York: Holt, Reinhart & Winston.

Wolf, Arthur, & Huang, Chieh-shan. (1972). *Marriage and adoption in China, 1845-1945.* Stanford, CA: Stanford University Press.

Wolf, Diane. (1989). *Gender, households, and rural industrialization: Factory daughters and their families in Java.* Unpublished manuscript.

Wolf, Margery. (1972). *Women and the family in rural Taiwan.* Stanford, CA: Stanford University Press.

World Bank Report. [Various years.] Washington, DC: World Bank.

Year book of labour statistics. [Various years.] Taipei: Executive Yuan, R.O.C.

11

The Political Economy of Social Policy Formation
EAST ASIA'S NEWLY
INDUSTRIALIZED COUNTRIES

FREDERIC C. DEYO

Sustained rapid industrial development in South Korea, Hong Kong, Singapore, and Taiwan, East Asia's Newly Industrializing countries (NICs), has spawned a sizeable literature seeking to explain this remarkable economic expansion. Especially prominent in this literature is an ongoing debate over the role of the state in economic change. While this debate has centered mainly on the relevance of state policy for economic growth and export expansion, relatively little attention has been accorded the related issue of the state's role in provision for social welfare. Given the close linkage between economic development policy and the welfare role of the state, one's perspective on the developmental role of the state is reflected in one's understanding of social policy.

This chapter examines social policy differences among the East Asian NICs. It assesses the relationship between social policy and economic development policy in these countries, showing that under a development strategy of human-resource-intensive export oriented industrialization (EOI), social and economic development goals are often compatible and closely linked. Indeed, it is argued that with a few such exceptions as Singapore's early postindependence experience and recent political change in South Korea, East Asian social policy has been driven primarily by the requirements and

AUTHOR'S NOTE: I am indebted to Manuel Castells, Paul Evans, Jeffrey Henderson, Su-Hoon Lee, Minjoo Oh, Janet Salaff, Michael Shafer, and Richard Stubbs for critical comments on an earlier draft of this chapter.

outcomes of economic development policy, unlike the situation in Latin America, where extrabureaucratic political pressures have played a more prominent role in shaping social policy.

It is shown that temporal change in social policy among the East Asian NICs is in part explained by evolutionary changes in economic strategy, while cross-national variation in social policy is closely related to corresponding differences in the developmental roles of states as well as in the nature of the employment systems through which the East Asian NICs have wedded domestic labor to the requirements of export-oriented industrialization.

Major Components of Social Policy

At the most general level, social policy refers here to state policies, practices, and institutions that directly influence the economic welfare and security of popular sector groups (farmers, workers, middle classes, etc.). Such policy may be understood by reference to four major components. First, social policy is embedded in economic development policy insofar as economic policy has intended welfare consequences or reflects implicit or explicit socioeconomic priorities. Indeed, politically unacceptable levels of unemployment in the late 1950s and early 1960s were an important stimulus to policy reforms that ushered in labor-intensive export manufacturing and the attendant achievement of near-full employment and rising wages by the 1970s.

Social policy relates secondly to direct government provision for social welfare, in part through public services and subsidies that benefit major social sectors. Subsidized health, public housing, education, child care, subsidized foodstuffs, public transportation, and welfare payments and public assistance programs fall into this category typically referred to as the "social wage."

Third, social policy includes incomes policy, that assemblage of measures that influence wages and benefits in both public and private sectors.

Finally, the state may influence income security through pension schemes, disability and health insurance, unemployment insurance, and other measures typically included in social security systems. These schemes may apply to government workers or they may be mandated for private sector firms. In the latter case, there may be substantial variation in the extent of state financing.

This chapter compares social development policy among the East Asian NICs, looking in turn at social policy embedded in development strategy, the social wage, incomes policy, and social security. Discussion concludes with an explanation for policy differences among these countries, focusing especially on the relationship between social policy on the one hand, and economic political imperatives on the other.

Social Priorities Embedded in East Asian Development Policy

At the very outset of East Asian policy reforms that ushered in the export-led industrialization strategy of the 1960s, it was recognized that political stability and legitimacy depended in large measure on reduction of high levels of unemployment and enhancement of wages and standard of living. Acceptance of the need to adopt a strategy to achieve these ends, coupled with an absence of significant nonlabor agricultural, mineral, or other economic resources, encouraged an emphasis on light, labor-intensive manufacturing that might generate quick gains in employment. The success of this policy is seen in rapid declines in unemployment in these countries, bringing about, in fact, growing labor shortages by the 1970s. Indeed, many observers have argued that given the massive provision of jobs and wage gains under a successful strategy of labor-intensive industrialization, social policy would have been extraneous and irrelevant to welfare gains, or worse, that "premature" welfare programs might have reduced the competitiveness of East Asia's export-oriented manufacturing, thus undercutting both economic growth and associated employment gains.

By the mid-1970s, a policy shift toward promotion of higher value-added manufacturing prompted greater investment in "human capital" along with new strategies to enhance labor force stability and productivity. This strategic shift was associated with increased emphasis on education and training and on enhanced workplace benefits. Additionally, increased production for domestic consumer and producer markets paralleled by growing wage pressures in a tightened labor market encouraged substantial and continuing wage gains. Thus, economic policy changes in the 1970s eventuated in important gains in worker welfare.

Social Wage

If the East Asian NICs have generally shared a common development strategy since the 1960s, they have diverged in their social security and

Table 11.1 Social Expenditures in the East Asian NICs

	Per Capita ($US)	As % of GDP		As % of Total Government Expenditures	
South Korea	1987: 148	1980: 4.6	1987: 5.0	1980: 26.6	1987: 29.1
Taiwan	1988: 301	1981: 5.9	1988: 6.0	1981: 27.7	1988: 30.5
Singapore	1987: 862	1980: 5.1	1987: 10.6	1980: 30.6	1987: 29.5
Hong Kong	1987: 652	1980: 8.1	1987: 7.8	1980: 50.2	1987: 53.1

SOURCE: United Nations (1988); Republic of China (1990).

welfare policies. Some indication of these differences may be gleaned from available data on public social welfare expenditures (for education, social welfare, health, housing, and community services). Table 11.1 compares social expenditure outlays among these countries.

In large measure, the marked differences in per capita social expenditure between South Korea and Taiwan on the one hand, and Singapore and Hong Kong on the other, reflect differences in degree of urbanization and in corresponding differences in the need for government provision of social services. In order to take this fundamental structural difference into account, subsequent discussion emphasizes separate comparisons between South Korea and Taiwan, and between Singapore and Hong Kong.

Unlike per capita data, which reflect absolute levels of social expenditures, social expenditure as a percentage of Gross Domestic Product (GDP) measures the extent of the social wage relative to the size of the national economy. Here we again note moderately lower expenditures in South Korea than in Taiwan throughout the 1980s. More interesting is the reversal between Singapore and Hong Kong. Whereas Hong Kong's social expenditures were higher than those in Singapore at the beginning of the decade, only a few years later, social outlays in Singapore exceeded those in Hong Kong.

A useful measure of government policy priorities is provided by social expenditures as a percentage of total governmental outlays. This percentage rose moderately in three of the four countries, thus indicating greater attention to social development. It is apparent here that social expenditures have comprised a far smaller proportion of total expenditures in Singapore than in Hong Kong. The difference between the two city-states is only in part ex-

Table 11.2 Categories of Social Expenditure as a Percentage of Total Social Expenditures

		Education	*Social Security and Welfare*	*Health*	*Housing and Community Service*
South Korea	1980	64.4	23.9	4.6	7.1
	1987	62.5	22.5	9.0	6.1
Taiwan	1981	42.2	46.5	5.8	5.5
	1988	47.2	40.9	5.3	6.6
Singapore	1980	47.8	4.4	22.7	25.1
	1987	49.0	4.4	12.2	34.5
Hong Kong	1980	30.6	8.8	15.0	45.6
	1987	34.4	11.5	18.2	35.9

SOURCE: United Nations (1988); Republic of China (1990).

plained by the greater defense outlays in Singapore. As a percentage of non-defense expenditures, social expenditures comprise 34.5% of the total in Singapore, versus 54.8% in Hong Kong.

A further examination of the relative emphasis given the various components of social expenditures permits a fuller understanding of these cross-national differences. Table 11.2 shows recent social expenditures broken down by functional category.

These data provide a starting point for developing a social policy "profile" for the East Asian NICs. Taiwan stands out here in its relatively lower outlays for education and health services, and its greater emphasis on social security and welfare than South Korea. Similarly, Singapore's lesser emphasis on social security and welfare, and greater stress on education, contrasts with Hong Kong's stronger commitment to welfare. It should be noted in this regard that Singapore's housing expenditure increased dramatically during 1986 and 1987, in the context of a major reconstruction project. Similarly, Singapore's low social welfare expenditures in part reflect comprehensive welfare programs for workers provided by trade unions closely allied with the ruling People's Action Party.

Incomes Policy

Abandonment of import-substitution strategies in favor of export-led development in the 1960s had a further important consequence for social welfare. The global competitiveness of East Asia's manufactured exports was based in part on cheap, productive labor. This consideration, along with a further determination to prevent early wage gains from restraining employment growth, implied a low-wage policy extending well into the 1970s. In Singapore and South Korea, wage restraint invoked direct wage controls and restrictive policies toward trade unions. Beginning in 1974, Singapore's National Wages Council (NWC) issued annual guidelines to be applied in wage negotiations. Until 1979, these guidelines held wage gains to levels below productivity increases. Beginning in 1968, the Singapore government singled out "Pioneer Industries" (labor-intensive export industries promoted by the government) as free from any obligation to negotiate pay levels above the minima recommended by the NWC. Similarly, South Korea's Economic Planning Board issued yearly wage recommendations that held wage gains to a fixed percentage of inflation and productivity gains. And in Taiwan, trade unions were generally prohibited from pressing for large wage increases.

On the other hand, growing labor shortages soon created strong upward pressure on wages. These wage gains, it should be noted, flowed less from political pressures, as in Latin America, than from labor market outcomes of successful development strategies themselves. Indeed, subsequent policy change was in part driven by rising wages as East Asian planners sought to encourage productivity gains through capital and technology deepening and skill development during the 1970s and 1980s, in order to maintain globally competitive labor costs. In the case of Singapore, this policy shift was reflected in a marked realignment in wage policy, as the ruling party sought to preempt this otherwise slow readjustment by actively promoting wage increases in the late 1970s in order to discourage further investment in low-skill, labor-intensive manufacturing.

Income Security

The relatively minimal early social expenditure of South Korea (see Table 11.1) and its emphasis on human capital formation through education rather than community welfare (see Table 11.2) reflect a single-minded commitment to rapid, state-induced industrialization at whatever social cost necessary. A major exception to this "production first" approach relates to provision, under the 1963 Social Security Act, of pension, medical, and other benefits for civil service, military, and private school teachers (Chang, 1985) (public school teachers receive coverage as members of the civil service). Indeed, a substantial portion of total government social insurance and welfare expenditures target this politically important category of workers. Beyond this protected segment of the workforce, social insurance provision has been uneven and minimal (Park, 1975).

In response to political pressure, a national pension insurance plan was enacted in 1973, but this was only implemented in 1988, in the context of powerful new political forces associated with the democratic reforms of the late 1980s. Financing is almost entirely contributory in nature, and coverage during the first phase of implementation extends to only 4.4 million workers. Similarly limited is coverage under the 1983 Industrial Injury Compensation Insurance Act, which provides medical coverage for work-related injuries. This and other worker welfare programs are contributory in nature, thus avoiding large government expenditures (Chang, 1985). In fact, over half of all social welfare expenditures are privately financed. In addition, given inadequate public enforcement and widespread employer violation of newly mandated social insurance requirements, nominal work force coverage greatly exaggerates actual coverage. South Korea, it should also be noted, has yet to ratify most ILO conventions relating to worker rights and welfare.

In Taiwan, as in South Korea, government workers enjoy broad, if shallow, social security benefits. Private sector social insurance policy centers on state-mandated employer provision against death, disability, severance, and retirement for workers (International Commercial Bank of China, 1983). Coverage under the Labor Insurance Act of 1958 (as subsequently amended) is almost entirely contributory in nature although the government does help finance social insurance for self-employed persons under a voluntary insurance program (Chan, 1985). Under the 1984 Labor Standards Law, pension and severance benefits are obligatory for employers. While employer refusal to implement provisions of the 1984 law somewhat reduces effective coverage (Lee, 1989), it is clear that state-mandated social insurance is more fully developed here than in South Korea. But it must also be recognized that such insurance is almost entirely enterprise based.

The Labor Insurance Act of 1979 established, for the first time, limited unemployment insurance, but this program was indefinitely suspended "because of low levels of unemployment," and, significantly, because it was felt it would lead to "welfare dependency" (Chan, 1985). Assistance to unemployed is largely confined to public assistance for the very poor.

Singapore is unique among the East Asian NICs in having developed a comprehensive national pension plan (the Central Provident Fund, or CPF) prior to the period of rapid EOI development. While there is no national unemployment insurance program, severance pay and worker compensation programs are required of employers. Indeed, many social insurance programs (e.g. medical insurance) have been shifted to companies themselves during recent years.

The colonial government of Hong Kong has established a comprehensive social insurance scheme, covering severance, illness, and retirement for civil service workers (Hong Kong Social Welfare Department, 1989). But unlike Singapore, Hong Kong lacks a public social insurance program despite growing pressure for establishment of a colony-wide provident fund (Chow, 1985). Under recent legislation enacted during the mid-1980s, employers are now required to provide severance benefits for workers who have been employed at least 10 years. As of 1985, only about 14% of all workers were covered by pension and severance schemes. Many employers have been known to fire workers just before their tenth year of employment in order to avoid this legal obligation. While Hong Kong has ratified many (49) ILO labor standards conventions (International Social Security Association, 1989), enforcement in this area is similarly deficient.

Social and Economic Development Policy: The Question of Compatibility

Beginning in the 1930s and 1940s, social development policy in Argentina, Brazil, Mexico, and elsewhere in Latin America has been powerfully driven by extra-bureaucratic political forces. In some instances, such policy was preemptive and anticipatory, as under Cardenas in Mexico. In other cases, it was in reaction to existing political opposition and pressure, as in Brazil in the early 1960s and Chile in the early 1970s. Often, where such opposition severely threatened economic growth and the interests of economic elites, it was met by repression (e.g. Argentina, 1976; Brazil, 1964; Chile, 1973) rather than by accommodative social policy reforms. In most cases, pursuit of a capital intensive, exclusionary, and inequality-generating development strategy (Evans, 1979) heightened the incompatibility between economic and social policy, thus generating powerful currents of political and class conflict.

East Asian industrialization, on the other hand, has been relatively more compatible with positive social policy, especially during the period of economic restructuring and in the areas of social wage and incomes policy. To the extent this is true, it would tend to explain the continuing expansion of social development expenditures (Table 11.1) and policies during recent years, despite a general absence of effective political pressure from popular sector groups.

East Asian export-oriented industrialization has from the very outset centered on the effective utilization of human resources. In particular, in the absence of significant mineral or agricultural resources, low-cost labor has defined the competitive edge of these small, crowded countries. Labor cost containment in turn has entailed some combination of the following elements: low wage and compensation levels, high productivity, and low levels of labor conflict. During most of the period of rapid industrialization, labor conflict has been minimal (Deyo, 1989). But the relative importance of compensation levels on the one hand, and productivity and skill on the other, was reversed during the 1970s.

During the early period of light-industry-based development, plentiful, low-wage labor provided the key to export expansion and economic growth. At this time, a clear incompatibility existed between some elements of social policy and economic policy. In particular, a repressive incomes policy and a reluctance to impose income security expenses on employers often required strict political controls over labor. On the other hand, expansionary social policy in other areas often supported, rather than undermined, industrial expansion (Salaff, 1988, p. 27). In particular, provision of housing, health, subsidized foodstuffs, and other elements of social wage acted as a wage subsidy by reducing the cost of living and thus reducing upward pressure on wages. It will be suggested below that the massive housing programs in Singapore and Hong Kong may be understood in this way.

The later shift to higher-value-added industry greatly enhanced the degree of compatibility between social and economic development policy. Such increased compatibility related especially to the need for higher levels of skill and productivity in the context of declining unemployment and concomitant upward wage pressures. Most obvious is the productivity benefit derived from "human capital investment" in education (especially vocational training) and health. Similarly, as industrial restructuring proceeded, incomes policy could be relaxed. And as work force stabilization and enterprise loyalty were increasingly sought by employers as a precondition for increased investment in worker training, mandated enterprise-level social security benefits became ever more supportive of continued industrial transformation.

The extent of compatibility varied as well by the nature of the employment systems through which domestic labor was wedded to international capital, technology, and markets. Where proletarian labor controls relied extensively on the power of labor markets to discipline workers, especially during early industrialization, an enhanced social wage and income security measures that might have sheltered workers from the discipline of labor markets were incompatible with economic expansion. On the other hand, where labor controls relied to a greater extent on employer paternalism, social wage and income security measures were more compatible with economic policy.

It is clear, too, that the nature and extent of state guidance and intervention in the development process conditions the extent to which simple compatibility between social and economic policy is reflected in actual enactment of social development measures. Developmental states, whose governments have attempted systematically to restructure their economies by directly influencing investment decisions in targeted industries, are prone systematically to implement development-enhancing social measures. Less interventionist states, where economic growth is encouraged through more indirect means, tend to exhibit a looser correspondence between economic and social policy. Thus may be understood the greater social policy priority accorded education than social welfare (Table 11.2) in the more developmental states of South Korea and Singapore than in Taiwan and Hong Kong during recent years of industrial restructuring. It should be noted, however, that large public housing expenditures in Hong Kong, and publicly financed and privately mandated social security and welfare in Taiwan, have also played important, if less direct, roles in economic development. I return to this point below.

Having argued that East Asian development has posed a less sharp polarity between social and economic development policy than elsewhere, it should be reiterated that such polarity has presented itself most clearly at various developmental junctures and for particular aspects of social policy. In addition, even where social and economic development priorities have not clashed, governments have often been reluctant to pursue proactive social policy measures in the absence of strong political pressures. In both these instances, social policy has been determined more by political forces than by developmental considerations. Thus, in order to understand social policy differences and trends in East Asia, it is necessary as well to take into account the power of popular sector groups and organizations to influence governmental policy. The remaining discussion provides a brief overview of the way in which these developmental, economic structural, and political factors have influenced East Asian social policy during the early period of light-industry-based export-oriented industrialization in the 1960s, as well as during the more recent period of economic restructuring. Because during the earlier period, social and economic development policy were relatively less compatible, political factors acquire special importance. Conversely, given the greater compatibility of social and economic priorities under restructuring, economic requirements become more salient during the 1970s. Finally, political developments in the 1980s, flowing in part from rapid economic and class transformation, have resulted in a renewed importance of political forces, especially in South Korea.

Early Light-Industry-Based Development

In South Korea, as elsewhere, labor-intensive export-oriented industrialization was adopted in part to generate rapid gains in employment and thus to garner working-class support for ruling groups. But during the early phase of EOI, the implementation of such a strategy entailed more specific elements of social policy that bore down heavily on working classes. Most important in this regard were a low-wage policy alongside minimal provision for social services or income security. At the outset of export-led development in the 1960s, high unemployment levels sufficed to maintain low wages. Subsequent upward wage pressures were contained by progressively tougher political controls over the late 1960s and 1970s.

The need for deep, repressive labor controls in South Korea followed in part from a development strategy that encouraged large-scale industry and proletarian employment systems. Lacking either Singapore's corporatist union structure or Taiwan's enterprise paternalism, proletarianized Korean workers were better positioned to form locally independent organizations and unions, despite higher level political controls at the federation level. As union pressure mounted during the 1970s, the government's only available response was one of repression. The vicious cycle of repression and protest that issued from this early pattern was eventually to contribute to the democratic opening of the mid-1980s. In the shorter term, however, repression sufficed to scuttle demands for greater provision for social welfare and social insurance, to hold wages down, and to confine social policy primarily to education and training. Such exclusionary policies buttressed the economic power of employers, who in most cases were able freely to evade even those few wage and benefit requirements the government did enact, and encouraged continued reliance on proletarian labor strategies.

If early EOI development in Taiwan relied as strongly on low wages as in South Korea, a low-wage policy relied to a far lesser degree on state repression. The key to understanding this difference is to be found in characteristics of industrial structure and employment systems.

Industrial development in Taiwan centered more than elsewhere on elaborate subcontracting networks among small and medium-sized family-based firms. These firms, embedded as they were in the rich associational life of local communities, provided workers with a modicum of security against economic deprivation albeit at very low wage levels. Enterprise paternalism, given further encouragement under national legislation mandating a number of employment benefits, greatly enhanced the power of employers. The resulting weakness of trade unions, further ensured by preemptive political controls imposed under martial law at the outset of KMT rule in Taiwan, resulted in extremely weak social pressure for a proactive social policy. The major exception to this pattern was substantial social provision for government employees, a potentially important political support group for the ruling party.

At the outset of self government in Singapore in 1959, the ruling PAP drew substantial political support from leftist trade unions. This early circumstance, unique among the East Asian NICs, partly explains the relatively early provision of a national pension scheme, public housing, and a national health care system as well as a continued professed public commitment to welfare socialism. It should also be noted, however, that the developmental advantages of some of these programs were clear at the outset. The CPF, for example, has comprised a major source of finance for many government projects.

The chosen mode of developmental intervention has also influenced Singapore's social policy. Far more than its counterparts elsewhere, the PAP has employed labor policy as a central element in its broader economic strategy. Of particular importance has been the utilization of a tightly controlled NTUC to encourage and monitor compliance with various government policies. It is likely that without the impetus for PAP corporatist inclusion of the unions provided by a powerful labor movement in the early 1960s, a far less proactive social policy would have emerged in Singapore. On the other hand, it is also clear that the substantial leverage provided the PAP by Singapore's preemptively controlled labor movement was an essential element in maintaining a highly effective policy of wage compression over a 10-year period up to the late 1970s. This wage depressing policy, along with a number of welfare programs self-financed by trade unions, largely compensated for substantial employer costs incurred by required CPF contributions.

While patriarchal and paternalistic employment systems among Hong Kong's many family firms provided a close structural and political parallel to Taiwan, the concomitant growth of large-scale factory employment defined an important departure from the Taiwanese pattern. Continuing inflows of mainland immigrants provided cheap, politically vulnerable labor for local and foreign employers who operated outside traditional social relationships of mutual obligation. In these factories, transitory employment of low-skilled persons, especially young women at very low wages, adequately fulfilled the requirements of cheap, manageable labor for export production. Workers in this factory sector, like their counterparts in Hong Kong's smaller family firms, presented little challenge to employers or to the colonial government to adopt social insurance or welfare protection for workers (Deyo, 1989; Henderson, 1989). This weakness of organized labor, along with a determination on the part of the government to intervene only minimally in the colonial economy, has encouraged a continuing reluctance to introduce private-sector social insurance legislation. A major exception to this more general pattern of political insulation from popular sector pressure is to be found in the widespread riots of 1966-1967 that prompted expanded government welfare and social security programs in the 1970s (Chow, 1985).

On the other hand, lack of substantial expenditure in such other areas as economic services and defense in this nondevelopmentalist colonial dependency means that social expenditures comprise a relatively large portion of total government expenditure (Table 11.1). Most important has been a sizeable outlay for public housing. While Hong Kong's vast housing program may in part be explained by continuing waves of immigrants from the mainland and a corresponding need to accommodate their housing needs, the political weakness of this group, alongside a more general political insulation of the colonial regime from popular sector groups, would seem to require a more persuasive account of so massive a public undertaking. One possibility is that public housing in fact comprises an exception to the more general pattern of developmental nonintervention. Castells (1984) and Salaff (1988) argue that public housing has provided an important indirect stimulus to industrialization. Such housing resulted first in the elimination of informal sector nonwage work in traditional local communities that were displaced by such housing, while at the same time forcing newly housed families, and especially women, to enter the work force for the first time to earn wages for rent and other necessities. Beyond this impetus to work force expansion, public housing also attracts and accommodates light industry complexes that draw their work force largely from the local population of housing residents. Such complexes provide employment for many women whose household duties would otherwise preclude travel to more distant work. Finally, subsidized public housing, along with price-depressing government controls over food imports from China, acts as a wage subsidy for employers by holding down the cost of living (Henderson, 1989; Schiffer, 1991). In these ways, proactive social policy has encouraged industrial development.

Economic Restructuring and
Divergent Social Policy

Growing labor shortages and increased wage pressure in the 1970s, alongside growing protectionism in core economies, posed well known threats to continued export expansion among the East Asian NICs. But if an earlier crisis of import substitution eventuated in a convergence on light-industry-based export manufacturing, the new crisis precipitated more divergent responses in economic policy, in the employment systems that were associated with those responses, and in the empowerment of popular sector groups. These divergencies, in turn, had varied consequences for social policy.

Shared by all four countries was a need to restructure into higher-value-added economic activities, whether in manufacturing or other sectors, in order to accommodate increased wage costs. Economic growth somewhat reduced this cost-based pressure through an enhanced domestic market for both consumer and producer goods. On the other hand, export markets remained critical for continued growth while import liberalization, in part the result of external political demands, added further pressure for increased productivity and efficiency.

Economic restructuring in manufacturing required substantial new investments not only in physical capital, but also in expanded and upgraded education and training programs. As noted earlier, the more interventionist governments in South Korea and Singapore have devoted a far larger portion of social expenditure to education than their less developmental counterparts in Taiwan and Hong Kong. Although not shown in Table 11.2, Singapore's expenditure priorities shifted dramatically from housing and community services to education during the 1980s. There, as in South Korea, substantial attention has been directed to the expansion of vocational and technical training, at secondary and tertiary levels and in separate training institutes, as an essential instrument of state efforts to promote industrial restructuring.

As important, restructuring encouraged the development, particularly in Taiwan and Singapore, of more paternalistic labor relations that might encourage greater work force stability, better morale, and heightened enterprise loyalty in order to enhance productivity and returns to investments in worker training.

South Korea's ruling party, under greater political threat than its counterparts elsewhere, continued its reliance on political repression to contain labor costs and heightened inflationary pressures during the late 1970s and early 1980s. It should be noted that this repressive response was more effective during earlier years when U.S. backing for anticommunist regimes was most assured, and became less effective during the late-1970s with the diminution of this external regime support. An alternative turn to enterprise paternalism would probably have been impossible to achieve in the context of extreme hostility and volatility in labor relations during this period.

In addition, restructuring policies emphasized, to a greater extent than elsewhere, automobile, shipbuilding, and other heavy industry. While in the short term, repression sufficed to keep production and labor costs down and to resist growing pressure for positive social policy, continued prolatarianization along with rapid growth in heavy industry encouraged increasing labor militancy culminating in the protracted strike wave of 1987-1988. Such heightened political pressure resulted in substantial wage increases, the launching of a national pension scheme, and extension of coverage under the medical insurance program to the entire national population.

Taiwan's enterprise paternalism was in fact well adapted to the requirements of restructuring, insofar as workers were already closely bound to the fate of their companies through a range of economic and noneconomic sanctions and obligations. A continuing liberalization in state development policy over the 1970s and 1980s (Li, 1989), and a corresponding dependence on the continued vitality of small firm entrepreneurship for growth, built on this strength in traditional employment systems. Indeed, earlier social insurance requirements mandated for local employers were further expanded during the 1970s, especially under the provisions of the 1984 Labor Standards Law, thus encouraging a further deepening of enterprise paternalism (Liu, 1988). As a consequence, direct government social programs retained their self-consciously "residual" character. The power of organized labor has remained negligible. Indeed, despite appeals for labor representation during deliberations on the introduction of the new Labor Standards Law, union officials failed to participate. By default, therefore, labor's interests were largely represented by the Ministry of Labor.

As in South Korea, the Singapore government has played a dynamic role in engineering economic restructuring. This greater role is reflected, as well, in social policy reforms. In Singapore, a number of new measures encouraged paternalism in employment relations. Large industry-wide unions were decentralized, and house unions were encouraged. Many social insurance programs were partially decentralized to firms. A portion of CPF contributions reverted to enterprise-level social funds, while educational and welfare programs, and, later, medical coverage, devolved to firms. In these ways, the PAP emulated Taiwanese efforts to enhance work force stability and enterprise loyalty. It should be noted that throughout this recent period of transition, expanded government commitment to social welfare has been driven primarily by the needs of evolving development policy, rather than by the pressures of political dissent. Even Singapore's dramatic break with an earlier low-wage policy in 1979 was based almost entirely on a perceived need to phase out low-skill, light industries in favor of higher value-added production.

While social insurance and welfare outlays increased somewhat in Hong Kong, there, too, social policy underwent no decisive shift over the 1970s and 1980s. High rates of immigration until well into the 1970s encouraged a continued reliance on low-wage, export manufacturing (e.g., textiles) in lieu of a shift toward higher value-added manufacturing. This, along with the impending reality of the colony's reversion to Chinese control and a continued commitment to economic liberalism, ensured an absence of government reconstructive intervention in the economy. With the exceptions of housing, land, and food policies, with their supportive links to industrial expansion, social outlays were minimal and largely custodial, rather than developmental. Hong Kong continues to lag far behind Singapore in educational expenditures. To the extent economic restructuring has been systematically encouraged, it has centered on renewed growth in financial and service activities associated with Hong Kong's traditional entrepôt role.

Conclusion

With the exceptions of Singapore in the early 1960s and South Korea in the late 1980s, East Asian social policy has been more strongly shaped by the developmental priorities of politically insulated states than by extra-bureaucratic political forces as in Latin America. Political autonomy, whether or not associated with developmental states, has in turn been variably rooted in social organizational and economic structural factors that have muted labor opposition, or, alternately, in political regimes that have either co-opted or repressed popular opposition movements.

But political autonomy has not resulted in an absence of proactive social policy. Indeed, in some instances East Asian social policy has been far more progressive than that in other developing countries. That state autonomy has not eventuated in dismal social policy records, particularly during recent years, is in part explained by the nature of development strategy. East Asian export-oriented industrialization has centered on the effective utilization of human resources. Under such circumstances, economic development has been energized by social policies that have enhanced labor productivity, encouraged enterprise training, and subsidized wages. To this extent, economic development and proactive social policy have been mutually supportive.

The systematic use of social policy to pursue economic development goals has been most pronounced where states have intervened most directly in the development process. While developmentally supportive social policy is clearly in evidence in Taiwan and Hong Kong, it has been largely indirect and sometimes ambiguous in its intended purpose. By contrast, the government role in education, wage determination, and other elements of social policy has been more explicitly and directly linked to economic growth in South Korea and Singapore.

References

Castells, Manuel. (1984). *Small business in a world economy: The Hong Kong model, myth and reality.* Paper delivered at the Seminar on The Urban Informal Sector in Center and Periphery. Baltimore, MD: Johns Hopkins University.

Chan, Gordon Hou-Sheng. (1985). Taiwan. In John Dixon & Hyung Shik Kim (Eds.), *Social welfare in Asia.* London: Croom Helm.

Chang, In-Hyub. (1985). Korea, South. In John Dixon & Hyung Shik Kim (Eds.), *Social welfare in Asia.* London: Croom Helm.

Chow, Nelson. (1985). Hong Kong. In John Dixon & Hyung Shik Kim (Eds.), *Social welfare in Asia.* London: Croom Helm.

Deyo, Frederic C. (1989). *Beneath the miracle: Labor subordination in the new Asian industrialism.* Berkeley: University of California Press.

Evans, Peter. (1979). *Dependent development: The alliance of multinational, state, and local capital in Brazil.* Princeton: Princeton University Press.

Henderson, Jeffrey. (1989). Labour and state policy in the technological development of the Hong Kong electronics industry. *Labor and Society,* 14. pp. 20-21.

Hong Kong Social Welfare Department. (1989, June). Changes in social security provisions in Hong Kong. *Asian News Sheet,* 19(2).

The International Commercial Bank of China, Republic of China. (1983, November-December). The social welfare system and social welfare expenditures of the Republic of China. *Economic Review,* pp. 6-14.

International Social Security Association. (1989, June). ILO in Asia and the Pacific: A review of events and activities in the field of social security. *Asian News Sheet, 19*(2).

Lee, Joseph S. (1989, April 25). Labor relations and the stages of economic development. *Industry of Free China, 71*(4).

Li, K. T. (1989). *The evolution of policy behind Taiwan's development success.* New Haven, CT: Yale University Press.

Liu, Paul K.-C. (1988, October-November). Employment, earnings, and export-led industrialization in Taiwan. *Industry of Free China, 70*(4-5).

Park, Chong Kee. (1975). *Social security in Korea: An approach to socio-economic develop-
    ment.* Seoul: Korea Development Institute.
Republic of China, Executive Yuan. (1989). *Statistical yearbook.*
Salaff, Janet. (1988). *State and family in Singapore: Restructuring an industrial society.* Ithaca,
    NY: Cornell University Press.
Schiffer, Jonathan. (1991). State policy and economic growth: A note on the Hong Kong model.
    International Journal of Urban and Regional Research, 15.
United Nations, Economic and Social Commission for Asia and the Pacific. (1988). *Statistical
    yearbook for Asia and the Pacific.* Bangkok, Thailand: Author.

Name Index

Subject Index

About the Contributors

Richard P. Appelbaum is Professor and Chair of the Sociology Department at the University of California at Santa Barbara, where he also directs the UCSB Center for Global Studies. He received his B.A. from Columbia University in 1964, and M.P.A. from the Woodrow Wilson School of Public and International Affairs at Princeton University in 1966. After serving as a technical consultant to the National Planning Office of Peru he returned to graduate school, receiving his Ph.D. in sociology from the University of Chicago in 1971. Dr. Appelbaum has conducted research and published extensively in the areas of social theory, urban sociology, the sociology of housing and homelessness, and—most recently—the geography of economic development. His most recent books include *Rethinking Rental Housing* (with John I. Gilderbloom; Temple University Press, 1988), and *Karl Marx* (Sage, 1988). He is a principal author of H.R. 1122 (101st Congress), "A Comprehensive National Housing Program for America," and has testified before Congress on the problems of homelessness. Dr. Appelbaum's work has received a chapter award from the American Planning Association, and the Douglas McGregor Award for excellence in behavioral science research. Most recently, he has received grants from the Haynes Foundation and the University of California Pacific Rim Program to undertake a comparative study of several industries that span Los Angeles, northern Mexico, Hong Kong, Taiwan, and South Korea.

Manuel Castells is Professor of Planning and of Sociology at the University of California at Berkeley. He has been a Visiting Professor at the University of Hong Kong, and a Senior Visiting Fellow at the National University of Singapore. He has also lectured at Taiwan National University and at Seoul National University.

He has published 15 books, including *The Economic Crisis and American Society* (1980), and *The Shek Kip Mei Syndrome, Economic Development and Public Housing in Hong Kong and Singapore* (1990).

Lucie Cheng is Professor of Sociology and Founding Director of the Center for Pacific Rim Studies at the University of California, Los Angeles. She writes on international migration, ethnic relations, and gender issues. Her publications include *Labor Immigration Under Capitalism* (with Edna Bonacich), and "Women and Class Analysis in the Chinese Land Revolution," among others.

Soohyun Chon is presently the Academic Coordinator at the Center for Korean Studies at the Institute of East Asian Studies and a lecturer in geography, both at the University of California, Berkeley. She obtained her Ph.D. in economic geography from the University of Michigan (1984) and an MBA in finance from the University of Chicago (1985). She is currently working on a book dealing with the Industrial Structure Comparison between Korea and Taiwan: Implications for Future Industrial Growth.

Frederic C. Deyo is Associate Professor of Sociology at State University of New York at Brockport. He has written extensively on East Asian industrialization and labor, and is author of *Beneath the Miracle: Labor Subordination in the New Asian Industrialism.*

Haruhiro Fukui is Professor of Political Science at the University of California, Santa Barbara, and specializes in Japanese domestic politics and foreign policy. He has recently been a Visiting Fellow at All Souls College, Oxford University, and a Visiting Professor at the International University of Japan. He recently co-edited *Japan and the World* (Macmillan, 1988) and *The Politics of Economic Change in Postwar Japan and West Germany* (Macmillan, in press).

Gary Gereffi is Associate Professor in the Sociology Department at Duke University. He is the author of *The Pharmaceutical Industry and Dependency in the Third World* (1983) and co-editor (with Donald Wyman) of *Manufacturing Miracles: Paths of Industrialization in Latin America and East Asia* (1990). His current research is on international subcontracting and export networks in the garment, footwear, automobile, and computer industries in East Asia, Latin America, and the Caribbean, and the United States.

Nigel Harris, an economist, is Professor of Development Planning in the University of London, and former director of the Development Planning Unit at University College, London. He is the author of numerous works on economic development, class structures, trade, and urbanization in developing countries. He is currently working on the fourth volume of a work seeking to analyze the national implications of an integrating world economy. The volumes are: *Of Bread and Guns: Crisis in the World Economy* (1983); *The End of the Third World* (1986); *National Liberation* (1991). The final volume will concern the world labor market.

Jeffrey Henderson was born and raised in northern England and studied sociology and politics at the Universities of Birmingham, of California at Santa Barbara, of Leeds, and of Warwick. Currently Senior Fellow in Sociology and Comparative Management at the Manchester Business School, University of Manchester, he was until recently Reader in Sociology and Urban Studies at the University of Hong Kong. He has taught previously at the University of Birmingham and has held Visiting Professorships at the Universities of New England and of California at Santa Cruz. Additionally, he has held Visiting Fellowships at the Universities of Lodz, of California at Berkeley, of Melbourne, of Glasgow, and of Warwick. He has researched and published in the areas of race relations, labor processes, urban theory, and public housing (for which he was a recipient of the Donald Robertson Memorial Prize in 1983). More recently he has been concerned with the dynamics of global restructuring and high technology industrialization. His current research is concerned with transnational corporations, local linkages, and state policy in East Asia and Central Europe. He is a Corresponding Editor of the *International Journal of Urban and Regional Research* and his most recent book was *The Globalization of High Technology Production* (Routledge, 1989).

Ping-Chun Hsiung was a doctoral student in the Department of Sociology at the University of California at Los Angeles. She completed her dissertation on class, gender, and the satellite factory system in Taiwan. She is Assistant Professor in the Department of Sociology at the University of Toronto, Scarborough College.

Eun Mee Kim is an Assistant Professor of Sociology at the University of Southern California. Kim has been conducting research on various aspects of economic and political development of South Korea. Kim's articles on foreign capital, investment patterns of U.S.- and Japan-based multinational corporations, *chaebol* (Korean large business conglomerates), and democratization have been published in *Studies in Comparative International Development, Asian Affairs,* and *Pacific Focus.* Kim is currently working on a book about the political economy of state and capital in Korean development.

Hagen Koo is Associate Professor of Sociology at the University of Hawaii. His research interest is in the political economy of East Asian development and class formation in South Korea. He is completing a book, tentatively titled *Work and Class in South Korean Industrialization.*

Paul M. Lubeck is Professor of Sociology and History at the University of California, Santa Cruz, where he teaches sociology, political economy, and development studies. He has published extensively on NICs, Islamic social movements, and capitalist development in Africa. His book, *Islam and Urban Labor in Northern Nigeria,* received the Herskovits Prize in 1987. Taking Malaysia as a case study, his current research explores the tension between industrial policy formation and globalization processes in multi-ethnic states.

Janet W. Salaff did her studies in Sociology at the University of California, Berkeley, with a specialty in Chinese studies. She came to the Department of Sociology, University of Toronto in 1970, and has been teaching in Toronto since. Professor Salaff has researched the changes of family life as industrialization has permeated Asia. Among her main books are: *Working Daughters of Hong Kong: Female Filial Piety or Power in the Family?; Lives: Chinese Working Women; State and Family in Singapore: Restructuring an Industrial Society.* She is currently completing a manuscript comparing Chinese farmers and Chinese cowboys and cowgirls in Inner Mongolia. Professor Salaff has lived in Hong Kong, Taiwan, Singapore, and China for periods of time.